Proceedings

1999 International Conference on Parallel Processing

Proceedings

1999 International Conference on Parallel Processing

21-24 September 1999
Aizu-Wakamatsu City, Japan

Sponsored by

The Information Processing Society of Japan (IPSJ)
The International Association for Computers and Communications (IACC)

In cooperation with

The University of Aizu, Japan
The Ohio State University, USA

Edited by

Dhabaleswar Panda
Norio Shiratori

IEEE
COMPUTER
SOCIETY

Los Alamitos, California
Washington • Brussels • Tokyo

IEEE Computer Society Order Number PR00350
ISBN 0-7695-0350-0
ISBN 0-7695-0352-7 (microfiche)
ISSN 0190-3918

Additional copies may be ordered from:

IEEE Computer Society
Customer Service Center
10662 Los Vaqueros Circle
P.O. Box 3014
Los Alamitos, CA 90720-1314
Tel: + 1-714-821-8380
Fax: + 1-714-821-4641
E-mail: cs.books@computer.org

IEEE Service Center
445 Hoes Lane
P.O. Box 1331
Piscataway, NJ 08855-1331
Tel: + 1-732-981-0060
Fax: + 1-732-981-9667
mis.custserv@computer.org

IEEE Computer Society
Asia/Pacific Office
Watanabe Building,
1-4-2 Minami-Aoyama
Minato-ku, Tokyo 107-0062 JAPAN
Tel: + 81-3-3408-3118
Fax: + 81-3-3408-3553
tokyo.ofc@computer.org

Editorial production by Danielle C. Martin

Cover art production by Alex Torres

Printed in the United States of America by Technical Communication Services

IEEE
COMPUTER
SOCIETY

Table of Contents

1999 International Conference on Parallel Processing (ICPP'99)

Keynote Address

Mobile Communication toward the 21st Century
Dr. Keiji Tachikawa, NTT Mobile Communication Network, Japan

Session A1: Network-Based Computing

Chair: Jose Duato, Universidad Politécnica de Valencia, Spain

Session B1: Instruction-Level Parallelism

Chair: Kiyoshi Oguri, NTT Corporation, Japan

Session C1: Graph Model for Networks

Chair: Qian-Ping Gu, University of Aizu, Japan

Session B3: Compiler Support

Chair: P. Sadayappan, Ohio State University, USA

Session C3: Parallel Applications

Chair: W.-S. Eric Chen, National Chung-Hsing University, Taiwan

Keynote Address

Session A4: Distributed Shared Memory (DSM)

Chair: Nian-Feng Tzeng, University of Southwestern Louisiana, USA

Session C5: Distributed Algorithms
Chair: Sandeep Gupta, Colorado State University, USA

Session A6: Multimedia Systems
Chair: Wu-Chi Feng, Ohio State University, USA

Session B6: Adaptive Communication & Groupware Systems
Chair: Ken-Ichi Okada, Keio University, Japan

Message from the General Co-Chairs

This is the 28th in a series of the International Conference on Parallel Processing (ICPP), which was launched in 1972. During the past 28 years the field of parallel processing has matured and expanded into many areas of computer and communications technologies. As we move into the 21st Century and enter the era of the World Wide Web (WWW), we expect that parallel processing will remain as an important field in computer science and engineering.

The University of Aizu is very pleased and honored to host ICPP'99, which is for the first time being held outside of the United States. The University itself is an international community, where more than half of its faculty come from outside of Japan. We hope you will enjoy your stay here and engage in cultural exchange.

As General Co-Chairs, our main responsibility is to coordinate various tasks carried out by other willing and talented volunteers. First of all, we would like to thank Dr. Iwao Toda, Honorary Chair and President of the Information Processing Society of Japan (IPSJ) for his encouragement and support. Thanks are also due to Profs. Yutaka Matsushita and Chuan-lin Wu, who serve as Co-Chairs of the International Advisory Committee. Special thanks go to Prof. D. K. Panda and Norio Shiratori, Program Co-Chairs, for doing an excellent job of selecting high-quality papers for presentation at the conferences. Special thanks also go to Prof. Makoto Takizawa, who serves as Workshop Co-Chair and helps organize 8 workshops. Last but not least, we should like to express our sincere appreciation to Prof. Tse-yun Feng, the founder of ICPP and Chair of the Steering Committee, for his constant support and encouragement.

Thanks are also due to Profs. Wen-Tsuen Chen, Ten H. Lai and Yoshimi Teshigawara for serving as Awards Co-Chairs; to Profs. Yoshitaka Shibata and Fusun Ozguner for serving as Publicity Co-Chairs; to Prof. Hiroaki Higaki and Thomas W. Page for serving as Publication Co-Chairs; and to Prof. Tsuyushi Ishikawa for serving as Local Arrangements Chair.

Finally, we would like to thank Dr. Keiji Tachikawa, Dr. David M. Rouse and Prof. Yutaka Matsushita for accepting our invitation to be the keynote speakers. We trust that you will enjoy and appreciate their keynote speeches, which are timely and important as we move into the new century.

For your advance information, ICPP'2000 will be held on August 21-24, 2000 in Toronto, Canada. We hope many of you will also participate in ICPP-2000.

Shoichi Noguchi
Ming T. Liu

Message from the Program Co-Chairs

Welcome to the 28th Annual International Conference on Parallel Processing (ICPP '99) being held at the University of Aizu, Japan! It is a great pleasure to have ICPP being held for the first time outside of the USA. As the conference moves around the world in future years, it promises to bring true international spirit to the conference.

The conference features three keynote presentations and 62 contributed papers. Eight workshops are also being held in conjunction with this conference and the workshop papers are published in a separate proceedings.

A total of 194 papers were submitted for the conference from around the world. After submission, each paper was assigned to one of the Vice Chairs. Each Vice Chair then assigned the paper to at least three referees and/or program committee members for review. A total of 539 reviews were collected with the help from 12 Vice Chairs, 85 program committee members, and an additional 230 reviewers. The program committee meeting was held on May 1, 1999 in Columbus. The evaluations from the reviewers together with the recommendations from the program committee members were used by the Vice Chairs to select 62 papers (an acceptance rate of only 31.95%) for the final program.

The 62 papers have been organized into 24 sessions. In addition, there will be three keynote talks. We are very grateful to our keynote speakers Dr. Keiji Tachikawa of NTT Mobile Communication Network, Japan, Dr. David M. Rouse of Lucent Technologies, USA, and Prof. Yutaka Matsushita of Keio University, Japan.

Many individuals have contributed to the success of the conference. We would like to thank all Vice Chairs, Program Committee Members, and Reviewers for their hard work during the review process to bring out a strong technical program for the conference in a timely fashion. We would like to thank all of the authors who submitted papers to the conference. Many thanks to Prof. Mike Liu (General Co-Chair), Prof. Makoto Takizawa (Workshop Co-Chair), Prof. Steve Lai (ICPP '98 Program Chair) and the Awards Co-Chairs (Prof. Wen-Tsuen Chen, Prof. Steve Lai, and Prof. Yoshimi Teshigawara) for their excellent help, guidance, support, and encouragement during many difficult phases of organizing this conference. We would also like to express our sincere thanks to five students at the Ohio State University (Mohammad Banikazemi, Darius Buntinas, Dr. Donglai Dai, Vijay Moorthy, and Amit Singhal) for their great assistance in handling the electronic submissions and the reviews, and extending considerable help during the Program Committee meeting held in Columbus.

We hope that you will enjoy the strong technical program of this conference!!

Dhabaleswar K. Panda
Norio Shiratori

Organization and Program Committees

Honorary Chair

Iwao Toda, *Fujitsu Labs, Japan*

General Co-Chairs

Shoichi Noguchi, *The University of Aizu, Japan*
Ming T. Liu, *The Ohio State University, USA*

International Advisory Committee Co-Chairs

Yutaka Matsushita, *Keio University, Japan*
C.L. Wu, *National Chiao Tung University, Taiwan*

Program Co-Chairs

Dhabaleswar K. Panda, *Ohio State University, USA*
Norio Shiratori, *Tohoku University, Japan*

Program Vice Chairs

Architectures

Jose Duato, *Universidad Politécnica de Valencia, Spain*

Compilers and Languages

David Padua, *University of Illinois, USA*

Algorithms and Applications

Oscar Ibarra, *University of California at Santa Barbara, USA*

Resource Management

Joel Saltz, *University of Maryland, USA*

Multimedia Systems

Toshitaka Tsuda, *Fujitsu Labs, Japan*

Real-Time Computing

Wu-Chun Feng, *Los Alamos National Lab and Purdue University, USA*

Network-Based Computing

Marc Snir, *IBM T.J. Watson Research Center, USA*

Networking and Protocols

Behcet Sarikaya, *University of Aizu, Japan*

Mobile Computing

Tadanori Mizuno, *Shizuoka University, Japan*

Adaptive Communications Systems

Jun Matsuda, *ATR, Japan*

Cooperative and Groupware Systems

Ken-ichi Okada, *Keio University, Japan*

Agent-Based Computing

Kenji Sugawara, *Chiba Institute of Technology, Japan*

Workshops Co-Chairs

Makoto Takizawa, *Tokyo Denki University, Japan*
Hisao Koizumi, *Tokyo Denki University, Japan*
Yuko Murayama, *Iwate Prefectural University, Japan*
Haruhisa Ichikawa, *NTT Software Labs, Japan*
Wu-Chi Feng, *Ohio State University, USA*
Stephan Olariu, *Old Dominion University, USA*
Hyunsoo Yoon, *KAIST, Korea*

Awards Co-Chairs

Wen-Tsuen Chen, *National Tsinghua University, Taiwan*
Ten H. Lai, *Ohio State University, USA*
Yoshimi Teshigawara, *Soka University, Japan*

Publicity Co-Chairs

Yoshitaka Shibata, *Iwate Prefectural University, Japan*
Fusun Ozguner, *Ohio State University, USA*

Publication Chairs

Hiroaki Higaki, *Tokyo Denki University, Japan*
Thomas W. Page, *Ohio State University, USA*

International Liaison Co-Chairs

Makoto Takizawa, *Tokyo Denki University, Japan*

Mike Papazoglou, *Tilburg University, The Netherlands*
Athman Bouguettaya, *QUT, Australia*
Mohammad S. Obaidat, *Monmouth University, USA*

Registration Co-Chairs

Masakazu Tamaki, *NTT Data, Japan*
Michiaki Katsumoto, *CRL, Japan*
Elizabeth O'Neill, *Ohio State University, USA*

Local Arrangements Chair

Tsuyoshi Ishikawa, *The University of Aizu, Japan*

Steering Committee Chair

Tse-yun Feng, *Penn State University, USA*

Program Committee Members

Ashok Agrawala, *University of Maryland, USA*
Kiyoharu Aizawa, *University of Tokyo, Japan*
Yuichi Bannai, Canon Information Media Lab, Japan
Michel Barbeau, *University of Aizu, Japan*
Ramon Beivide, *Universidad de Cantabria, Spain*
Riccardo Bettati, *Texas A&M University, USA*
John Bruno, *University of California at Santa Barbara, USA*
Walter Burkhard, *University of California at San Diego, USA*
W.-S. Eric Chen, *National Chung-Hsing University, Taiwan*
Go Bong Choi, *ETRI, Korea*
Alok Choudhary, *Northwestern University*
Flaviu Cristian, *University of California at San Diego, USA*
Chita Das, *Pennsylvania State University, USA*
Petre Dini, *Concordia University, Canada*
T. Ebrahim, Swiss Fed. *Institute of Technology, Switzerland*
Omer Egecioglu, *University of California at Santa Barbara, USA*
David Forslund, *Los Alamos National Lab, USA*
Ian Foster, *Argonne National Lab, USA*
Juergen Friedrich, *University of Bremen, Germany*
Dennis Gannon, *University of Indiana, USA*
A. Gerasoulis, *Rutgers University, USA*
Sandeep Gupta, *Colorado State University, USA*
Andrew Grimshaw, *University of Virginia, USA*
Thomas Gross, *Carnegie Mellon University & ETH Zurich, Switzerland*

Reviewers

Bulent Abali
Khaled Abdel-Ghaffar
Gagan Agrawal
Ashok Agrawala
Kiyoharu Aizawa
Ibraheem Al-Furaih
Carles Aliagas
Mark Allen
George Almasi
Khaled AlSabti
Srinivas Aluru
Kazuyuki Amano
Henrique Andrade
Pedro Artigas
Rafael Asenjo
Eduard Ayguade
Azad Azdmanesh
M. Cemil Azizoglu
David A. Bader
Yuichi Bannai
Michel Barbeau
Luiz Andre Barroso
Sujoy Basu
Ines Beier
Ramon Beivide
Mladen Berekovic
Riccardo Bettati
Michael D. Beynon
Angelos Bilas
Wim Bohm
Jacir Luiz Bordim
Bella Bose
Kiril Boyanov
Bradley Broom
Walt Burkhard
Hakki Candan Cankaya
Qiang Cao

Enrique V. Carrera
Calin Cascaval
Dhruva R. Chakrabarti
Chialin Chang
Chung-Yen Chang
Chung-Ho Chen
Gen-Huey Chen
Wen-Shyen Eric Chen
Jianer Chen
Tien-Fu Chen
Xiao Chen
Cheng-Ta Chiang
Go-Bong Choi
Gwan Choi
Alok Choudhary
Sung Woo Chung
Marcelo Cintra
Jesus Corbal
Flaviu Cristian
Chita R. Das
Sajal K. Das
Atakan Dogan
Jeff Draper
R. Dssouli
Jose Duato
Shantanu Dutt
Touradj Ebrahimi
Alessandro Fabbri
Renato Ferreira
David Forslund
Ian Foster
Cong Fu
Tomokatsu Fuseya
Shigeru Fujita
Akihiro Fujiwara
Dennis Gannon
Mark K. Gardner

Maria Jesus Garzaran
T.V.Geetha
Jonathan Geisler
Apostolos Gerasoulis
Donald W. Gillies
Sanjay Goil
Antonio Gonzalez
Angeles Gonzalez-Navarro
Jose Gonzalez
Madhusudhan
Govindaraju
Ananth Grama
Jose Angel Gregorio
Andrew Grimshaw
Jonathan Grudin
Nicolas Guil
Anshul Gupta
Manish Gupta
Rajiv Gupta
Sandeep Gupta
John Gustafson
Susanne Hambrusch
Eui-Hong Han
Hideki Hara
Fumio Hattori
Gerben Hekstra
Christian Hentschel
Hiroaki Higaki
Kei Hiraki
Ching-Tien Ho
James C. Hoe
W. Hoefferkamp
Jay Hoeflinger
JoAnne Holliday
Jeff Hollingsworth
Choong Seon Hong
Tang Hong
Bob Horst

Yarsun Hsu
Seung Ku Hwang
Adriana Iamnitchi
Maximilan Ibel
Liviu Iftode
Michiko Inoue
Toru Ishida
Susumu Ishihara
Takashi Itoh
Michael Iverson
David V. James
Jerry James
Zhen Jiang
Lijie Jin
Greg Johnson
Magnus Jonsson
Pramod G. Joisha
Mahesh V. Joshi
Alin Jula
David Kaeli
Yoshiaki Kakuda
Dong-In Kang
Yi Kang
Abhay Kanhere
Magnus Karlsson
Hironori Kasahara
Peter Keleher
Ram Kesavan
Carl Kesselman
Ashfaq A. Khokhar
Samir Khuller
Jong Kim
Jungjoon Kim
Keiji Kimura
Tetsuo Kinoshita
Matthew Knepley
Cetin K. Koc
Hartmut Koenig
Clyde P. Kruskal
Ajay Kshemkalyani

Jui-Yuan Ku
Mark B. Kulaczewski
K.R. Ananda Kumar
Tahsin Kurc
Jesus Labarta
T.H. Lai
Vinh Lam
Zhiling Lan
S. Y. Larin
Jesper Larsson
Alexey L. Lastovetsky
Shahram Latifi
Jaejin Lee
Craig A. Lee
Jenq-Kuen Lee
Chengzhi Li
Wei-keng Liao
David Lilja
Kwei-Jay Lin
R. Lin
Yuan Lin
Jane Liu
Virginia M. Lo
Pedro Lopez
Honghui Lu
Mi Lu
Paul Lukowicz
Pedro Marcuello
Jose F. Martinez
Kenneth Mackenzie
Jun Maeda
Phil May
Collin McCurdy
Kathryn S. McKinley
Rami Melhem
John Mellor-Crummey
Sam Midkiff
Jose Miguel-Alonso
Nihar Mahapatra
Prasant Mohapatra

Bongki Moon
Reagan Moore
Vijay Moorthy
Jose E. Moreira
Christine Morin
Todd C. Mowry
John Mylopoulos
Tarun Nakra
Shunichiro Nakamura
Juan J. Navarro
David Nicol
Jim Nilsson
Satoshi Nojima
Andreas G. Nowatzyk
Motoki Obata
Julio Antonio Carvallo De Ocho
Wataru Ogata
Ken-ichi Okada
Naonobu Okazaki
S. Olariu
Fumitaka Ono
Daniel Ortega
Fusun Ozguner
David Padua
Yunheung Paek
Paolo Palazzari
Yi Pan
Yannis Papaconstantinou
Marcin Paprzycki
Panos A. Patsouris
Yale Patt
Shietung Peng
Michael Peter
Fabrizio Petrini
Mike Petropoulos
Timothy Pinkston
Oscar Plata
Enrico Pontelli
J. L. Potter
Jean-Pierre Prost

Chunming Qiao

Zhiquan Frank Qiu

F.A. Rabhi

Sanguthevar Rajasekaran

Ramu Ramamurthy

Alex Ramirez

Julian Ramos-Cozar

Sanjay Ranka

A. L. Narasimha Reddy

Mirek Riedewald

David F. Robinson

Daniel L. Rosenband

Larry Rudolph

Silvius Rus

P. Sadayappan

Joel Saltz

Jesus Sanchez

Vicente Santonja

B. Sarikaya

Dan Scales

Kirk Schloegel

Loren Schwiebert

Markus Schwiegershausen

Aruna Seneviratne

Seung-Woo Seo

Harish Sethu

Kai Shen

Xiaowei Shen

Li Sheng

Ambuj Singh

Mukesh Singhal

Meera Sitharam

Rajeev Sivaram

Marc Snir

Yan Solihin

Zhexuan Song

Ioana Stanoi

Michael Steinbach

Bob Steinberg

R. Steinberg

Per Stenstrom

David Stern

Craig Stunkel

Y. J. Suh

Bronis R. de Supinski

Kapil Surlaker

Alan Sussman

Kaoru Takahashi

Hong Tang

Valerie Taylor

Oliver Theel

Sashisekharan Thiagarajan

Takao Tobita

Atsushi Togashi

C-K. Toh

Zhanye Tong

Joseph Torellas

Wei K Tsai

Yu-Chee Tseng

Toshitaka Tsuda

Masahiko Tsukamoto

Ryuhei Uehara

Manuel Ujaldon

Gary Ushakov

Anirudha S Vaidya

Fernando Vallejo

Todd Veldhuizen

Javier Vinuesa

Michael Wan

Dajin Wang

Yu-Chung Wang

Paul Ward

Jean-Paul Watson

Andrew L Wendelborn

Linda Wills

David Wong

Patrick H. Worley

Jie Wu

Volker Wulf

Jianxin Xiong

Sudha Yalamanchili

Bwolen Yang

Ming-Hour Yang

Tao Yang

Yuanyuan Yang

Byoung-Kee Yi

Hao Yu

Ki Hwan Yum

C. Zaharia

Emilio L. Zapata

Chengqi Zhang

J. Zhang

Lynn Zhang

Zili Zhang

Qing Zhao

Huican Zhu

Keynote Address

Mobile Communication toward the 21st Century

Dr. Keiji Tachikawa
NTT Mobile Communication Network, Japan

Session A1

Network-Based Computing

Chair: Jose Duato
Universidad Politécnica de Valencia, Spain

cJVM: a Single System Image of a JVM on a Cluster

Yariv Aridor   Michael Factor   Avi Teperman
IBM Research Laboratory in Haifa
Matam, Advanced Technology Center, Haifa 31905, ISRAEL
yariv|factor|teperman@il.ibm.com

Abstract

cJVM is a Java Virtual Machine (JVM) that provides a single system image of a traditional JVM while executing on a cluster. cJVM virtualizes the cluster, supporting any pure Java application without requiring any code modifications. By distributing the application's work among the cluster's nodes, cJVM aims to obtain improved scalability for Java Server Applications. cJVM uses a novel object model which distinguishes between an application's view of an object and its implementation (e.g., different objects of the same class may have different implementations). This allows us to exploit knowledge on the usage of individual objects to improve performance.

cJVM is work-in-progress. Our prototype runs on a cluster of IBM IntelliStations running Win/NT and are connected via a Myrinet switch. It provides a single system image to applications, distributing the application's threads and objects over the cluster. We have used cJVM to run without change a real Java application containing over 10Kloc and have achieved linear speedup for another application with a large number of independent threads. This paper discusses cJVM's architecture and implementation, showing how to provide a single system image of a traditional JVM on a cluster.

1. Introduction

What if we wanted to use a cluster to improve the performance of an existing multi-threaded Java application ? How would we distribute the application's work among the cluster's nodes? How would we ensure that application is oblivious to the fact that it is executing on a cluster?

The answers to these questions have two parts. By focusing on existing Java applications, we are constrained to solutions that look to the application like a conventional implementation of a Java Virtual Machine (JVM)[12]. Thus, the first part of the answer is that we must provide a a single system image (SSI) view of a cluster to a Java application.

In other words, even though the application will execute on the multiple, independent nodes composing the cluster, it will have the illusion that the cluster is a single computing resource [15].

The second part of the answer is that we must intelligently manage the application's threads and objects to achieve a performance benefit for a large class of real applications. This paper focuses on the first part of the answer, namely what is required to give a Java application a SSI view of a cluster; we are currently building on this work to address the second part of the answer.

There are three approaches to enabling a Java application to see a cluster as a single computing resource, as seen in figure 1. First, we could provide an implementation above the JVM, e.g., using third-party Java packages. Several others have taken this approach (e.g., [16, 7, 11, 2]); due to Java's introspection facilities [9], in this approach, the implementation's distributed nature cannot be completely hidden. In other words, the view of a single system image is incomplete. Second, we could build a JVM upon a cluster-enabled infrastructure, e.g., a distributed shared memory, as was done in [18, 13]. While such an approach is capable of presenting a single system image, it is inherently incapable of taking advantage of the semantics of Java in order to improve performance. Finally, we can provide an implementation of a JVM which is aware of the cluster, but which completely hides the cluster from the application. This is our approach. To the best of our knowledge, we are the first to implement this approach.

cJVM is a cluster-enabled implementation of a Java Virtual Machine. By working at the JVM level, we enable exploiting optimizations based upon Java's semantics. Examples of such optimizations include caching individual fields, migrating a Java thread between nodes to improve locality, analyzing the code to prove that certain accesses are always local, etc.

cJVM is work-in-progress. It currently distributes an application's threads and objects across the nodes of the cluster, providing correct semantics for any application written in pure Java.

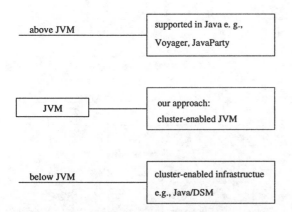

Figure 1. Three approaches to a cluster JVM

The major contributions we report upon in this work are:

1. an architecture providing a single system image of a JVM on a cluster.

2. a distributed memory model which supports cJVM.

3. a novel object model, which distinguishes between the application's view of an object's class and the implementation, enabling us to take advantage of knowledge of the usage of specific objects to improve performance.

4. a thread implementation which transparently supports distributed stacks.

The next section highlights the issues and difficulties in implementing a JVM on a cluster, defines a cluster and describes the type of applications which interest us. Section 3 highlights the essential ingredients of cJVM and Section 4 describes cJVM in detail. Section 5 summarizes the status of cJVM and section 6 describes related work. The final section summarizes our major contributions and describes future directions.

2. Background

2.1. Java Virtual machine

A Java Virtual Machine (JVM) is a platform-specific program that implements a well-defined, platform-independent virtual machine. There are currently implementations of JVMs for a range of platforms from embedded systems up to mainframes. This section presents only a brief overview of the JVM; for a complete specification see [12].

The basic memory model of a JVM consists of stacks and a heap. Each stack is a collection of stack frames, one for each method that was invoked and which did not yet return. Objects are allocated in a garbage collected heap.

To enable a JVM to execute a program, it internally maintains various "system" resources, including meta-data related to the program's classes, the program's instructions, and the constant pool.[1] A class's meta-data includes an object representing the class, the class's name, the class's superclass, information on the class's methods (kept in the method block structure), etc. Some of this meta-data is represented at run-time as normal Java objects allocated in the heap.

The program's instructions are represented by a set of bytecodes; all code belongs to a method which in turn belongs to a class. When executed, the bytecodes change the state of the stack and can create a mutative objects in the heap.

We divide the JVM bytecodes into three groups based upon the type of memory that they access; this division helps elucidate what is required to ensure correct semantics of the bytecode in a cluster. A large set of bytecodes only access system resources and the stack frame of the current method (e.g., load (store) to (from) a stack frame, control flow, arithmetic operations, etc.). It is relatively easy to ensure a single system image for these bytecodes as the code can be replicated and a stack frame is only accessed by a single thread. A smaller subset of the bytecodes access the constant pool. Most of these accesses are only on the first invocation, i.e., to resolve the bytecode's operand. Once resolved, the bytecode is rewritten to use a binary encoding of the previously symbolic information [12]. This group is also easy to handle as bytecode resolution is idempotent. The final group accesses the heap (e.g., to access a specific object's fields or static data). It is this group that is most interesting for a cluster JVM. If two nodes access the same object, they must see the same values, within the constraints of Java's memory consistency [3, 17].

The JVM is powered by an interpreter loop; on each iteration the next bytecode is executed. The interpreter loop can be viewed as a giant switch statement specifying a distinct action for each of the bytecodes.

The JVM is designed to support multiple concurrent threads; the Java language provides the programmer with convenient facilities to define threads. A programmer creates a new thread by creating an instance of a `java.lang.Thread` or one of its subclasses. The thread's behavior is defined either by implementing a method `run()` in a subclass of `java.lang.Thread` or by passing to the constructor an object that implements the `java.lang.Runnable` interface. On a uni-processor, parallelism between threads is obtained via time-slicing. On a multi-processor true parallelism is possible.

Java comes with a rich set of run-time core classes. Some of these classes, as well as application code, may use native methods implemented in a language other than Java.

---

[1] The constant pool is the Java equivalent to a symbol table.

These methods are used, in particular, to interface with the operating system. We do not focus on these native methods.

It is important to note that the JVM and Java are not identical; a JVM can support languages other than Java if they are translated to bytecodes. Our work puts the emphasis on the JVM, but is also trying to support classes that are part of the Java platform.

2.2. Clusters

Our focus is on dedicated compute clusters consisting of a collection of homogeneous (same operating system and architecture) machines connected by a fast (i.e., microseconds and not milliseconds latency) communications medium. Each cluster node is independent, having its own copy of the operating system. We assume that other than the interconnect, there are no physically shared resources between the cluster's nodes, i.e., there is no physically shared memory. For purposes of our prototype, we assume a logically shared file system, but this is not essential. Examples of such a cluster are a set of PCs connected by a switch or IBM's RS/6000 SP computer. While clusters are used for both scalability and high-availability, in this work we only look at scalability.

2.3. Java server applications

Our goal is to scale a particular class of Java applications. We call these applications: Java Server Applications (JSAs). These are second tier applications with the structure of a concurrent daemon that:

- Accepts a sequence of requests from clients.

- Typically accesses an external "database" in processing the request.

- Has some interactions (i.e., sharing) among requests.

In general terms, scalability for a JSA means increasing the number of client requests it can satisfy per unit time. Because we are interested in concurrent daemons, we assume that the application has been written to use Java threads. We are not trying to parallelize existing serial code.

3. cJVM approach

As stated in the introduction, our approach to virtualizing the cluster via a Java Virtual Machine is to cluster-enable an implementation of the JVM. Our prototype work started with Sun's reference implementation for the 1.2 JDK on Win/NT [5].

Figure 2 shows our basic approach. The upper half shows the threads and objects of a Java application as seen by programmer. This is a traditional JVM. The lower half shows

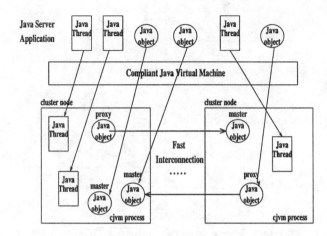

Figure 2. Cluster JVM

the objects and threads of the Java application distributed transparently (to the Java application) across the nodes of the cluster by the implementation of cJVM.

Each cluster node has a cJVM process. The collection of processes as a whole constitutes the JVM. Each cJVM process implements the Java interpreter loop while executing part of the application's Java threads and containing a portion of the Java objects defined by the application. To support distributed access to objects we use a master-proxy model. The node where an object is created has the *master* copy of the object; *proxies* are used on other nodes to access this object.

Two key challenges of cJVM towards a SSI are 1) giving the application the illusion that it is using a single monolithic heap and 2) hiding the distinction between master and proxy from the application. The first challenge is met by a new memory model based on a distributed heap. Objects are allocated in the local heaps of the cluster nodes, and are referenced locally by regular Java references. Upon passing an object as an argument to a remote operation, it is assigned a unique global identifier . This identifier is used to locate the corresponding proxy at the target node (see section 4). To help address the second challenge, we define a new object model. This model allows multiple implementations of a single method to coexist in a single class and allows selecting, according to the specific instance object, the precise code to execute for a given method.

When a node accesses a proxy, our basic approach is method shipping. The proxy, transparently to the application, redirects the flow of execution to the node where the object's master copy is located. This basic approach is enhanced with class and object specific caching and replication policies. An alternative to method shipping is thread migration; upon accessing a remote object, the execution of a thread is halted, its execution environment (e.g., program counter, stack) is serialized and moved to the host

6

containing the master copy of the object. It is an appropriate approach to use when remote accesses are infrequent and coarse-grained [1]. For such uses, the overhead of migration does not overwhelm the speedup gained by distributing the application's threads. However, the applications that we target for scaling, (see section 2.3) might have frequent remote accesses to shared objects and Java method invocations are often fine-grained computations.

Another alternative is object migration [10]. Whenever a thread accesses a remote object the object is brought to the node where the thread is executing. We did not choose its as our base approach since (1) we believe it is easier to extend method shipping with object-shipping-like function (e.g., caching) than the opposite and (2) it can be expensive and difficult to coordinate multiple threads that read and write fields of the same object without explicit synchronization (see [13] for a Java implementation that does this).

To enable a scalability gain, the application threads need to be distributed across the different cluster nodes. Unlike our base approach for objects, a new thread object is created at the best node as determined by a pluggable load balancing function. Further, our use of method shipping drives threads to become distributed entities. The new thread model is detailed in the next section.

To support method shipping and some additional functions, each cJVM process contains a set of server threads which receive and handle the corresponding requests. While a remote DMA approach [8], might be more efficient in some cases, e.g., accessing a primitive field of a remote object, it cannot handle other cases, e.g., locking a remote object. For reasons of simplicity of the implementation, we have, at this stage, a single implementation instead of an optimal implementation for each specific type of remote operation.

As described in section 2, there are a set of bytecodes which also access the heap. Since our memory model is based on a distributed heap, each of the bytecodes that accesses the heap must be modified to determine if the data it is accessing is located at the node where the bytecode is executed or if it is located at another node. In the later case, a remote access is required.

As mentioned, while there are several ways to take advantage of a cluster for a JVM, one rationale behind our approach of making a JVM cluster-aware is that we are able to take advantage of information obtained from knowledge of Java. One way to obtain this information is through code analysis. Since a Java application can dynamically construct and load a class, cJVM analyses the code of a method when a class is loaded, similar to the analysis performed by Java's bytecode verifier [12]. This analysis classifies methods based upon the way they access the heap. Based on this information we optimize cJVM execution. For example, we detect methods which do not access any object variables. We invoke these methods directly upon proxies, reducing the overhead of method shipping.

While our base approach for supporting objects in cJVM is a distributed heap with method shipping, for code we use replication. An application sees a class as an object, so we define a single master copy of a class. On any other node that uses the class, we create a proxy for that class, by a partial load (without invoking the class initialization method etc); this is a direct way to correctly build the internal data structures supporting the class and its code, e.g., constant pool, method blocks, etc. For any aspect that must be cluster-enabled, the node contacts the class's master object which loads the class in the same way a traditional JVM loads it.

There are a large number of additional changes we had to make to a traditional JVM to turn it into a cluster JVM. Among these are modifications to the JVM initialization such that only one node executes the application's main method (the entry-point of a Java program execution), changes to JVM termination and changes to numerous native methods. We do not further elaborate on these items.

4. cJVM architecture

This section focuses on the three of the more novel aspects of cJVM's architecture: the object model, the thread model and the memory model.

4.1. Object model

The object model of cJVM is composed of master objects and proxies. A master object is the object as defined by the programmer. A proxy is a surrogate for a remote object through which that object can be accessed. While a proxy is a fundamental concept used in systems supporting access to remote objects [7], we push the idea one step further. *Smart proxies* allow multiple proxy implementations for a given class while using the most efficient implementation on a per instance basis.

To motivate smart proxies, consider two different vector objects, both of which are accessed by multiple threads of an application:

- vector A is relatively small, accesses are bursty and at any point in time localized to a single thread, and accesses involve a mix of reads and writes.

- vector B is relatively large, accesses are sparse and not localized to a single thread, and accesses involve a mix of reads and writes.

It is clear that different proxy implementations for each of the two cases can improve performance. For vector A, it would be beneficial to use a caching proxy which employs exclusive caching. Vector B requires a simple proxy that directs all accesses to the master copy.

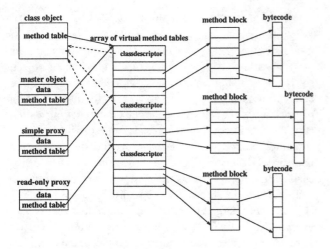

Figure 3. cJVM object model

There are two challenges applying smart proxies in the context of single system image:

1. preserving the application's illusion that is it executing on a single system, being unaware whether it is using a proxy or a master object.

2. designing efficient proxy implementations that do not violate Java's semantics.

The first challenge is met by (1) implementing proxy objects with the same internal representation (e.g., object header, method tables) as their master objects and (2) having all the proxy implementations coexist within a single class object. Specifically, the virtual method table of a class is logically extended into an array of virtual method tables, as seen in figure 3[2]. In addition to the original table of method code, each of the other tables (created when a class is loaded) refers to the code for a particular proxy implementation. Thus, every class has an array of at least two virtual tables: one for the original method code and one for the code of the most efficient proxy implementation. However, classes can maintain additional proxy implementations (see below). Upon creation of a master object or a proxy, the object points to the correct virtual table of its implementation which distinguishes it from other implementations; this distinction is only visible from within the implementation of cJVM. The application cannot distinguish between the masters and the proxies. It should be noted that cJVM architecture allows changing proxy implementations during run-time.

To help address the second challenge, we analyze every class during class loading and classify methods based upon the way they access the heap. We use this information to help choose the most efficient proxy implementation for each method. Examples of proxy implementations we have already implemented are:

simple proxy This is the default implementation which transfers all operations to the master.

read-only proxy This implementation applies the operation locally, based on the fact that it is guaranteed to access only fields which are never changed (e.g., fields that are only written in the constructor). The proxy maintains replicas of these fields.

proxy with locally invoked stateless methods We consider a method as stateless if it does not access fields of an object. While, it is semantically correct to apply any kind of method directly on a proxy,[3] there is a clear performance gain in doing so for stateless methods. In the general case, a method would have to remote access object fields, overwhelming any performance gained by invoking the method locally.

These are representatives of a large set of possible implementations whose logic can range from actions that are always beneficial to performance (e.g., replicating read-only fields and stateless methods) to actions whose worthiness depends upon run-time conditions (e.g., caching an object at the node where it is being used).

In addition to proxy implementations based on code analysis, we are currently designing proxy implementations that determine at run time, whether to apply methods locally or remotely based upon run-time conditions. In case a method accesses few objects which are all collocated with the master target object, then invoking the method remotely is probably most efficient. Otherwise, a local invocation might be more efficient than a remote one. If a method is applied several times; a special proxy can try both ways while measuring their execution times. Afterwards, it can choose the most efficient way for successive invocations of this method. Thus, we can construct proxies whose logic depends both upon profiling information and upon code analysis to exploit static and dynamic knowledge on specific objects and classes.

4.2. Thread model

To gain scalability on a cluster, objects and threads need to be distributed to (1) utilize less loaded nodes while dynamically balancing load and (2) improve locality to other objects they access. cJVM's thread model needs to support accessing an object whose master copy is on another node. Naturally, this is not supported by a traditional JVM so we need to extend the thread model in the context of cJVM. We discuss this model in detail through the rest of this section.

Thread creation. With method shipping, we need to distribute newly created threads in order to obtain scalability

---

[2]Patent pending.

[3]Since all bytecodes have been cluster-enabled.

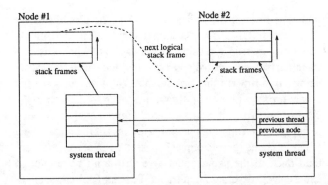

Figure 4. A distributed stack

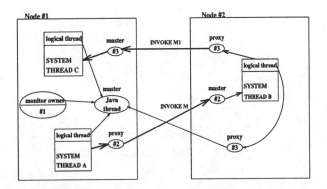

Figure 5. Using logical identifiers in cJVM

improvements. As described in section 2, the code to be executed by a Java thread is either specified by a subclass of the `java.lang.Thread` class or by a class implementing the `java.lang.Runnable` interface.

In both cases, we need to be able to create the instances of these classes remotely to allow distribution of the application's threads. In the first case, the thread itself will be distributed via a load balancing function while in the later case, the thread will be co-located (see below) with the instance of the class specifying its code, distributed via a load balancing function.

To support remote thread creation, we modified the semantics of the `new` opcode. Specifically, whenever a class is loaded it is marked as `Runnable` if it implements the `java.lang.Runnable` interface.[4] Upon execution of the `new` opcode, if the class is not marked as `Runnable`, cJVM follows the standard behavior of the JVM as described in [12]. Otherwise, the `new` opcode is rewritten into `remote_new` pseudo bytecode which is private to the implementation of cJVM. When executed, the pseudo bytecode uses a pluggable load-balancing routine to determines the *best* node in the cluster on which to create the new `Runnable`. Unless it is the current node, it sends that node a request to create the instance of the class, creates a local proxy for that instance and pushes the proxy's reference on the stack, as if the original `new` opcode was executed.

Upon subsequent executions, each of the rewritten bytecodes will directly and correctly apply either local or remote object creations. Such analysis and bytecode rewriting demonstrate the capabilities, at the level of JVM to apply implicit solutions for cluster-enabled functionality.

One case of thread creation which is not supported with this localized bytecode rewriting is co-locating a thread with a given `Runnable` object. For this case we apply heuristic techniques which are out of the scope of this paper.

Distributed stacks. Method shipping causes the stack of a Java thread to be distributed across multiple system threads

(handling the remote operations) at different nodes, as seen in figure 4. The thread model of a traditional JVM needs to be modified to maintain the application's illusion of a thread running all its code on one node. Specifically, that new model should guarantee that:

- The Java thread's stack can be traversed even though it is distributed (different stack segments are located at different nodes).[5]

- A consistent and correct value is returned by `Thread.currentThread()`, regardless of the node on which it was invoked.[6]

- The Java thread is identified as the owner of monitors obtained by any frame of the distributed stack, regardless of which system thread actually entered the monitor.

- A change in the state (i.e., running or suspended) of a system thread involved in method shipping (e.g., due to methods like stop()), must apply to all of the system threads involved.

To enable traversing a stack and changing the state of system threads along the chain, all the local segments of that stack are concatenated, as seen in figure 4. In addition, the implementation of those methods that change a thread's state and access stack frames are modified.

To help maintain thread identification, every Java thread is assigned a logical identifier, the global address of the thread object, which is passed with every remote operation.

cJVM uses this logical identifier to identify the owner of an object's monitor and to refer to the current thread. Figure 5 demonstrates how logical identifiers maintain the thread identity over multiple hosts. In this scenario, a system thread A, bound to a Java application thread, invokes

---

[4]The `java.lang.Thread` class also implements the `java.lang.Runnable` interface.

[5]The stack is accessed by methods like `printStackTrace()` and `countStackFrames()`.

[6]This method returns a reference to the thread object which invokes it.

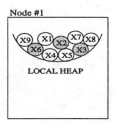 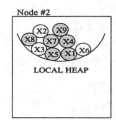

Figure 6. cJVM distributed heap

a method (M) upon proxy #2. Consequently, the method is shipped to node 2 and invoked upon the master object #2 by system thread B. During execution of the method, method (M1) is invoked upon proxy #3. Again, the method is shipped; it is applied by system thread C on node #1 where the master object #3 resides. With logical identifiers,

1. if `Thread.currentThread()` is invoked by system thread B it will return the reference to the proxy of the Java thread.

2. although two threads are involved, system thread C is able to enter the monitor of object #1 which is already held by system thread A, since A and C have the same logical identifiers.

4.3. Memory model

While the cJVM object model provides uniform access to proxies and master objects, a new memory model is required to (1) enable all proxies to locate and refer to the master object and (2) provide an application with an illusion of a single monolithic heap.

cJVM maintains a distributed heap built on top of the local heap implementations found in a traditional JVM. Figure 6 shows two cluster nodes with their local heaps. Masters are noted by empty ellipses while proxies are grayed out. New objects (both master objects and proxy objects) are allocated in the local heap , in the same way as in a traditional JVM. Each node independently manages its portion of the distributed heap.

When a reference to a local object is passed, for the first time, to a remote node, it becomes global and the remote node will create a proxy for the object in its local heap. The local address of the master object and the local address of the proxy have no relationship to one another. In order for the nodes to communicate about objects, objects used by more than one node are given *global addresses*.

A global address is an identifier of a global object which is unique over the cluster. It is generated the first time that object is passed as an argument to a remote operation.

In practice, every time an object is passed between two nodes in the cluster, we pass a two-tuple containing the

global address of the object (GAO) and the global address of its class (GAC). At the target node, these two global addresses are resolved using a local hash table that is used to translate between global addresses and local objects. While using a two-tuple of the form (GAO, GAC) we can construct a new proxy without additional messages to determine the class of the proxy, it incurs a slightly higher overhead due to locating and packaging the global address of the class object when the same remote object is passed as an argument more than once to the same node. We still don't have enough experience to evaluate that tradeoff in real applications.

5. Status

cJVM is implemented on a cluster of IBM Intellistation stations running Windows NT [5], connected via a Myrinet switch [6]. Communication is through MPI [4] which we use for portability, implemented over HPVM [14]. The prototype provides a single system image of a JVM to applications, distributing the application's threads and objects over the cluster. The prototype supports all of core classes with pure Java implementations and a portion of the core classes which include native methods in their implementation. The prototype is based upon Sun's Java 1.2 implementation for Win/NT [5]. We have used cJVM to run without change a Java application containing over 10Kloc as well as numerous smaller applications. For an internal embarrassingly parallel application, with only very limited interactions between the application's threads, cJVM achieves super-linear speedups on a small cluster. From this application, we learn that cJVM does not add significant overhead in those cases where interactions between the threads is not required.

6. Related work

Java on distributed machines has been extensively studied since Java was announced. From a programmer's point of view, tools and infrastructure supporting Java applications on a cluster range from completely explicit solutions to implicit solutions similar to cJVM.

Explicit approaches assume an architecture of multiple JVMs while handling remote objects and threads, following a master-proxy model. For example, with Voyager [7], programs are always mapped to specific network configurations defined in advance (e.g., every node runs a daemon with a specific port). With DO! [11], special framework classes are used to restructure the Java program, to cluster objects to improve object locality. With Java// [2], a remote object is created by a special utility method on a run time support class. JavaParty [16] supports implicit remote object creations. However, it requires the use of an explicit remote attribute to distinguish classes of remote objects. Moreover, in all cases, when applying Java's run-time introspection, the type of a proxy is different than the type of its master object. To summarize, unlike cJVM, none of these systems completely hide the underlying distribution model from the programmer.

In contrast with the aforementioned frameworks, Java/DSM [18] is an implicit approach, at the level of infrastructure. It is a modified JVM whose heap is implemented on top of a page shipping. Objects are allocated from the shared (DSM) region. Conceptually, Java/DSM supports SSI; its implementation, however, is incomplete. For example, it does not support thread migration and a thread's location is not transparent. In addition, it does not support wait() and notify() between threads on different processors, although it does support synchronized methods. Above all, unlike cJVM, a DSM technology does not take advantage of Java semantics to gain better performance; on the contrary, it can potentially cause false sharing that degrades performance.

Hyperion [13] is a JVM implementation on top of an object-based distributed shared memory; in some respects this is a hybrid implementation, containing both elements of a cluster-enabled JVM and a JVM on top of a cluster-enabled infrastructure. It has several features in common with cJVM, mainly, a distributed heap and implicit remote thread creation. However, it differs by using an object shipping model, in which a copy of a remote object is brought to the accessing node. The node uses this local cached copy which is written back to the server at Java synchronization points as required by the Java's memory semantics ([9],chapter 17). This homogeneous approach should be contrasted with cJVM's uses of smart proxies which allows each instance object to be cluster-enabled in the appropriate way for it.

7. Conclusions and future work

This paper presents an approach and implementation of a single system image for a JVM on cluster machines: cJVM. In its essence, there is an object model that separates between an application's view of an object (e.g. every object is a unique data structure) and its implementation (e.g. objects may have consistent replications). It enables the exploitation of knowledge on the usage of individual objects to improve performance (e.g., using object replica to increase object locality).

Having completed a prototype of cJVM that supports SSI, our next step is addressing the issues of defining and handling multiple kinds of implementations for objects applying caching and replications (i.e. (e.g., read only fields) towards gaining high performance for real Java server applications. Furthermore, we would like to use run-time profiling to detect behavior change in objects and switch proxies during run-time for better performance. Finally, while currently cJVM works only with the interpreter loop, we plan to integrate a JIT compiler after stabilizing the code of our current implementation.

8. Acknowledgments

We would like to thank Oded Cohn, Tamar Eilam, Zvi Harel, Hillel Kolodner, Assaf Schuster and Yoram Talmor for their input to cJVM. Special thanks to Alain Azagury who initiated this research activity.

References

[1] A. Barak and L. Ami. Mos: A multicomputer distributed operating system. *Software Practice and Experience*, 15(8), 1995.

[2] D. Caromel and J. Vayssiere. A Java framework for seamless sequential, multi-threaded, and distributed programming. In *ACM 1998 Workshop on Java for High-Performance Network Computing*. INRIA Sophia Antipolis, France, 1998.

[3] A. Gontmakher and A. Schuster. Characterizations for Java memory behavior. pages 682-687. Intl. Par. Proc. Symp. (1st Joint IPPS/SPDP), March 1998.

[4] http://www.mcs.anl.gov/mpi.

[5] http://www.microsoft.com.

[6] http://www.myri.com/.

[7] http://www.objectspace.com/voyager/.

[8] http://www.viarch.org/.

[9] B. J. J. Gosling and G. Steele. *The Java Language Specification*, chapter 17. Addison-Wesley, 1996.

[10] E. Jul, H. Levy, and N. Hutchinson. Fine-grained mobility in the emerald system. *ACM Transactions on Computer Systems*, 6(1):109–133, 1988.

[11] P. Launay and J. Pazat. A framework for parallel programming in Java. Technical Report 1154, IRISA, December 1997.

[12] T. Lindholm and F. Yellin. *The Java Virtual Machine Specification*. Addison-Wesley, 1997.

[13] M. MacBeth, K. McGuigan, and P. Hatcher. Executing Java threads in parallel in a distributed-memory environment. IBM Center for Advanced Studies Conference, Canada, NovemberDecember 1998.

[14] H. P. V. Machine. User Documentation, August 1997.

[15] G. Pfister. *In Search of Clusters: The Coming Battle in Lowly Parallel Computing*. Prentice-Hall, 1995.

[16] M. Philippsen and M. Zenger. Javaparty: Transparent remote objects in Java. *Concurrency: Practice and Experience*, 11(9):1125–1242, 1997.

[17] W. Pugh. Fixing the Java memory model. In *ACM Java Grande Conference*, pages 682-687, June 1999.

[18] A. Yu and W. Cox. Java/DSM a platform for heterogeneous computing. In *ACM 1997 Workshop on Java for Science and Engineering Computation,*, june 1997.

Push-Pull Messaging: A High-Performance Communication Mechanism for Commodity SMP Clusters[*]

Kwan-Po Wong and Cho-Li Wang
Department of Computer Science and Information Systems
The University of Hong Kong
Pokfulam, Hong Kong
kp.wong@graduate.hku.hk, clwang@csis.hku.hk

Abstract

Push-Pull Messaging is a novel messaging mechanism for high-speed interprocess communication in a cluster of symmetric multi-processors (SMP) machines. This messaging mechanism exploits the parallelism in SMP nodes by allowing the execution of communication stages of a messaging event on different processors to achieve maximum performance. Push-Pull Messaging facilitates further improvement on communication performance by employing three optimizing techniques in our design: (1) Cross-Space Zero Buffer provides a unified buffer management mechanism to achieve a copy-less communication for the data transfer among processes within a SMP node. (2) Address Translation Overhead Masking removes the address translation overhead from the critical path in the internode communication. (3) Push-and-Acknowledge Overlapping overlaps the push and acknowledge phases to hide the acknowledge latency. Overall, Push-Pull Messaging effectively utilizes the system resources and improves the communication speed. It has been implemented to support high-speed communication for connecting quad Pentium Pro SMPs with 100Mbit/s Fast Ethernet.

1. Introduction

A cluster refers to a group of whole computers that works cooperatively as a single system to provide fast and efficient computing services. As the cost of multiprocessor machines decreases, typically those small-scale SMPs with two to four processors, building a low-cost *Cluster Of Multi-Processors* (COMP) is a cost-effective solution to achieve high computing power.

Effective and efficient clustering requires high-speed communication between nodes. However, messaging in a cluster environment is non-trivial since the sender and receiver are usually not synchronized. The asynchronous nature of message passing leads to additional overheads in buffering, queuing/de-queuing, and synchronizing communication threads. Building COMPs brings new challenges in designing a high-performance communication system.

In recent years, several research works were conducted for developing COMPs. COMPaS developed by RWCP [11], Clumps by UC Berkeley [7], and FMP by Tsinghua University [9], are the most successful SMP-type COMPs. All these small-scale COMPs used Myrinet as the connection network. Thus, most implementations can achieve low point-to-point communication latency. The performance, however, mostly bounded by the co-processor performance, which was poorer than the performance of the processors in the SMP machines.

To further improve the communication speed in COMP, we can exploit the unrevealed power of SMP processors to handle messages. In a COMP, all processors in a SMP node can process different messages in parallel. However, they may have to share some common system resources, such as NICs and messaging buffers. Efficient messaging mechanism should minimize the locking effect and reduce the synchronization overhead while multiple user and kernel processes are accessing the shared resources, and intelligently use any idle or less loaded processor in the SMP node to handle the messages.

In this paper, we discuss *Push-Pull Messaging* and its optimizing techniques to achieve low latency and high bandwidth communication between processes in the COMP environment. The idea of *Push-Pull Messaging* is similar to the classical *three-phase protocol*. In three-phase protocol, the communication pattern guarantees buffers along the communication path are not overflowed, thus reducing the amount of retransmission overhead. The protocol, however, introduced a significant amount of overheads during the handshaking phase.

To adopt the good qualities in the protocol while avoiding the penalty in the handshaking phase, we introduce *Push-Pull Messaging*. The messaging process is

---

[*] The research was supported by Hong Kong Research Grants Council grant HKU 7030/97E, HKU 1998/99 Large Equipment grant, and HKU CRGC grant 10200544.

started by the send party. The send party transmits a message by first directly "pushing" a portion of the message to the receive party. The receive party starts the *pull* phase after the receive operation has been issued and the pushed message has arrived. The rest of the message is sent after an acknowledgement from the receive party is received by the send party.

This communication pattern likes the three-phase protocol guarantees buffers to be properly managed. Unlike the three-phase protocol, Push-Pull Messaging can reduce the handshaking delay for the short message transfers. In addition, the pattern makes it possible to apply various optimizing techniques to remove those unexpected overheads from the critical path.

We have implemented the Push-Pull Messaging on quad Pentium Pro SMPs, connected through 100Mbit/s Fast Ethernet. We have measured the single-trip latency of 34.9 μs, and the peak bandwidth of 12.1 MB/s for the internode communication. The single-trip latency between processes within the same SMP node can be as low as 7.5 μs, and the achievable bandwidth is 350.9 MB/s. We also developed an *early* and *late receiver* tests for examining the run-time performance of the proposed messaging mechanism. We found using Fast Ethernet is a low-cost solution to achieve high-speed communication, other than using expensive interfaces like Myrinet, ATM, or future network interface VIA [12].

For the rest of the paper, we first discuss a generic communication model for COMP in Section 2. In Section 3, we present the basic idea of Push-Pull Messaging. In Section 4, we discuss the proposed optimizing techniques. In Section 5, the performance results are shown. Analysis is presented for both internode and intranode cases. Finally, the conclusion is given in Section 6.

2. A generic communication model for SMP

The communication between a pair of COMP nodes can be viewed as a communication pipeline with various processing stages. A generic communication model with four pipelining stages is examined below and the related design issues are discussed.

Stage 1: Transmission thread invocation

User applications initiate the transmission by issuing a send operation in user space. Then, the data transmission thread will be invoked to format outgoing packets. The thread puts the packets to the outgoing first-in-first-out (FIFO) queue in the data dump of the network interface card (NIC). In a COMP, several processors may access the NIC simultaneously. To ensure the correctness of the invocation in the multiprocessor environment, the system has to restrict that only one user or kernel thread invokes the thread at a time. Efficient synchronization between concurrent processes in the

COMP node is crucial to the communication performance [5].

Stage 2: Data pumping

After the submission of packets, the NIC pumps packets to the physical network through the hardware on the NIC. The time spent in data pumping mainly depends on the hardware performance. For example, it can be affected by the performance of DMA engines in the host node and the NIC, and the network switch performance [8].

Stage 3: Reception handler invocation

The data arrives at the receive party and stores in a designated buffer in the NIC. *Interrupt* and *polling* are two main mechanisms to invoke the handler to serve the data arrival requests. For COMP nodes, there are two types of interrupt – *asymmetric* and *symmetric* interrupt. With asymmetric interrupt, requests are always delivered to one pre-assigned processor. With symmetric interrupt [4], requests can be delivered to different processors, where the selection of processors is governed by an arbitration scheme. On the other hand, polling is a light-weight approach to handle incoming packets. Polling routine watches the change of state variables and starts the handling routine if necessary. The frequency of polling determines the reliability of communication [3,6].

Stage 4: Reception processing

After invoking the reception handler, the handler processes packets immediately. Reception processing involves re-assembly of packets, copying between buffers, de-queuing buffer entries and pending requests, and synchronization between user and kernel threads. In a COMP node, there are multiple active user-level receiving threads. Without careful coordination between these communication threads and the reception handler in kernel space, high-speed communication is impossible.

3. Push-Pull Messaging

The basic idea of Push-Pull Messaging is based on the communication model discussed in Section 2. Figure 1 illustrates the communication architecture of Push-Pull Messaging.

As shown in the figure, each send or receive process has its application-allocated buffer, *source buffer* and *destination buffer* respectively, resided in the user space. Each process also shares three data structures with the kernel. The *send queue* stores the information of pending send operations. The *receive queue* stores the information of pending receive operations. The *buffer queue* and *pushed buffer* stores pending incoming packets where their destinations in memory are undetermined.

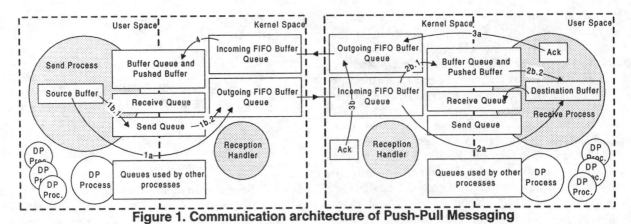
Figure 1. Communication architecture of Push-Pull Messaging

In Push-Pull Messaging, the send process first *pushes* a part of the message to the receive party as shown in arrow 1a. The *pushed message*, which contains BTP (Bytes-To-Push) bytes, is then handled by the reception handler in the receive party. The rest is registered in the send queue through arrow 1b.1. Depending on the timing of the receive operation performed by the receive process, the *pushed message* will be stored in the *pushed buffer* if the receive operation is not yet started as shown in arrow 2b.1. Otherwise, the message will be copied to the *destination buffer* as shown in arrow 2a by the registered information in the receive queue. Once the receive operation started, either the reception handler in the receive party or the receive process itself will *pull* the rest of the message from the send process.

The *pull* phase will be started by sending an *acknowledgement* (or "Ack" in the figure), which implicitly contains request information, through arrow 3a or arrow 3b. The reception handler in the send party processes the *acknowledgement*. If the request is granted, the send handler will *send* the requested part of the message in the send queue through arrow 1b.2 to the receive party. The reception handler in the receive party handles the message and directly copies the message to the destination buffer without buffering in the *pushed buffer* through arrow 2a using the registered information in the receive queue.

The important parameter BTP defines the number of bytes to be pushed by the sender at the beginning. This number is chosen based on the speed of the network and the memory system. The method to obtain this parameter is explained in Section 5.2.

Memory is a valuable resource for improving the communication performance. A pinned memory area is usually used as communication endpoint in either user or kernel spaces to improve the communication performance [1,2,11]. Although this approach could achieve low-latency communication by avoiding the delay in paging overheads, inefficient use of these pinned memory areas will limit the communication bandwidth when multiple communication channels are concurrently connected between SMP nodes. This leads to poor scalability in maintaining high-speed communication in COMP.

In Push-Pull Messaging, only a small buffer of BTP bytes is needed as the *pushed buffer*. Applications can dynamically change the size of the *pushed buffer* to adapt to the runtime environment.

4. Optimizing techniques

In this section, we discuss optimizing techniques to further improve the communication performance based on the Push-Pull Messaging mechanism.

4.1. Exploiting parallelism in COMP nodes

In a COMP node, *push* and *pull* phases can be carried out on different processors to produce maximum performance. After the *push* phase, the rest of the message will be transferred by the *pull* operation. As the *pull* phase is designed to make a direct transfer from the source buffer to the destination buffer without intermediate buffering, this phase can be handled by a lightly loaded processor. It is not necessary to be handled by the same processor as the one used in applications.

The selection of the processor depends on the reception handler invocation method. In all of our tests, we used *symmetric interrupt* mechanism in our optimized Push-Pull Messaging. This mechanism allows the pull phase to be executed on a least-loaded processor. Because of running the *pull* phase on another processor, the phase can be overlapped with the computation or communication events carrying on other processors. This overlapping can hide a portion of the communication latency in the internode test. The latency hiding mechanisms are discussed in Section 4.3 and 4.4.

In the *push* phase, we did not choose the lightly loaded processor to push data. This is because offloading the processing overhead to other processors could not exploit the temporal cache locality in the original processor. Contrarily, it may introduce a large number of cache misses. Instead of offloading, we execute the *push* phase on the processor same as the one serving the send process.

14

4.2. Cross-space zero buffer

Cross-Space Zero Buffer is a technique to improve the performance of data copying across different protected user and kernel spaces. In common message passing libraries, the syntax of the communication APIs is usually defined as follows.

send(*source_buffer_address*, *buffer_length*)
receive(*destination_buffer_address*, *buffer_length*)

The send operation accepts a virtual address of the source buffer and its length. Like the send operation, the receive operation requires the virtual address of the receive buffer and its length. Both buffers are allocated by applications in the process space. As process spaces are protected, direct communication cannot be carried out between two user processes. Typically, the communication is taken place through a *shared memory* facility provided by the kernel. Using shared memory approach, however, introduces an unavoidable memory copy operation. The unavoidable copy operation and implicit synchronization result in extra processing overheads, thus lengthening the communication latency and consuming more memory resources.

We attacked the problem by employing a *cross-space zero buffer* technique which realizes *one-copy* data transfer across process spaces, thus reducing the memory copy overheads. To realize the one-copy transfer across process spaces, physical addresses of source and destination buffers are needed. Although the virtual addresses of buffers are continuous, the corresponding physical addresses may be discontinued across pages. Since buffers may not reside in contiguous memory space, pairs of *physical address* and *length* need to be obtained before the actual data movement. The *physical address* points to the starting address of the multiple buffer pages. The *length* denotes the number of contiguous bytes at the corresponding address. Since this data structure only contains addresses and length values but not the actual messages, we call it *zero buffer*. By knowing the physical addresses of both buffers, data transfer from the source buffer to the destination buffer can be performed by a kernel thread. Therefore, one-copy data transfer across different process spaces could be achieved.

In Push-Pull Messaging, *zero buffers* are not only employed to improve the performance of intranode communication between user processes. The buffers are also implemented to allow direct transfer of data from the NIC designated buffer to the destination buffer in internode communication.

4.3. Address translation overhead masking

Address translation overhead masking is a technique to hide the address translation overhead in the internode communication. With the implemented *zero buffer*, the data transfer from the NIC buffer to the destination buffer on the same machine can be carried out directly by the kernel without the user process's involvement. However, Push-Pull Messaging needs to perform address translation before using *zero buffers*.

The address translation overhead grows linearly as the size of the message increases. Since the communication event requires relatively long latency time to complete than the address translation, we can schedule every network communication event in the *push* and *pull* phases before the address translation to mask the overhead.

However, not all translations can be safely scheduled. The translation of the pushed message needs to be done before initiating the first network transmission. To further hide this translation overhead, the operation of copying the pushed message to the NIC's outgoing buffer has to be performed in user space. This can be done by *direct thread invocation method*, which invokes the transmission thread in the NIC at the user level without using system calls. This method is achieved by mapping NIC control registers and buffers onto the user process space. Thus, the send process can directly trigger the NIC to start the send operation. Similar approaches can be found in DP [8], GAMMA [1] and U-Net [2].

Since all address translations can be safely scheduled, the translation overhead is removed from the critical path in communication. Figure 2 illustrates this masking technique. The address translation, which is shown as "Find out physical addresses", is delayed in the send and receive parties.

4.4. Push-and-acknowledge overlapping

Push-and-Acknowledge is an optimizing technique to hide the acknowledge latency in the internode case. Originally in Push-Pull Messaging, sending the acknowledge message is on the critical path. To further enhance the performance of Push-Pull Messaging, we overlap the push and acknowledge phases in order to hide the long acknowledge latency. This optimization is also shown in Figure 2.

The pushed BTP bytes, originally used in Push-Pull Messaging, are split into two parts. The *first-pushed message* of BTP(1) bytes, is pushed to the destination at the beginning. Transmission of the *second-pushed message* of BTP(2) bytes, is overlapped with the transmission of the acknowledge message. The latency of the acknowledge message is masked. This technique can also minimize the size of the *pushed buffer*, where only the larger values of BTP(1) and BTP(2) is used as the size of the buffer.

5. Performance results and analysis

The proposed Push-Pull Messaging was implemented and evaluated on two ALR Revolution 6X6 Intel MP1.4-

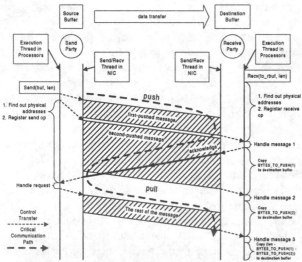

Figure 2. Overhead Masking and Push-and-Acknowledge Overlapping are used in Push-Pull Messaging.

complaint SMP computers. Each computer consisted of four Intel Pentium Pro 200 MHz processors with 256 Mbytes of main memory. Each Intel processor had 8-Kbyte L1 instruction cache and 8-Kbyte data cache. The size of the unified L2 cache is 512 Kbytes. The computers were connected by Fast Ethernet with the peak theoretical bandwidth of 100 Mbit/s. Each computer attached one D-Link Fast Ethernet 500TX card with Digital 21140 controller. Linux 2.1.90 was installed on each machine with symmetric interrupt enabled.

We evaluated the performance of intranode and internode communication. In each case, the single-trip latencies of the communication system with different values of the parameter BTP were measured. In all benchmark routines, source and destination buffers were page-aligned for steady performance. The benchmark routines used hardware time-stamp counters in the Intel processor, with resolution within 100 ns, to time the operations. Each test performed one thousand iterations. Among all timing results, the first and last 10% (in terms of execution time) were neglected. Only the middle 80% of the timings was used to calculate the average.

The round-trip latency test measured the ping-pong time of two communicating processes. The bandwidth test measured the time to send the specified number of bytes from one process to another process, plus the time for the receive process to send back a 4-bytes acknowledgement. The time measured was then subtracted by the single-trip latency time for a 4-byte message. Thus, the bandwidth was calculated as the number of bytes transferred in the test divided by the calculated time.

5.1. Intranode communication

Push-Pull Messaging with different BTP parameters was tested for intranode communication. The parameter varied from zero (Push-Zero) to the whole message length (Push-All). Push-Pull Messaging used 16 bytes as the BTP parameter. The single-trip latency is shown in Figure 3. In the intranode communication, when the size of the message was below 16 bytes, Push-Pull and Push-All Messaging performed equally well and both outperformed Push-Zero Messaging. In this case, both send and receive operations were equally "light". The receive operation could not complete the registration of the operation before the send operation started the actual data transfer. Therefore, Push-Pull and Push-All needed to utilize the *pushed buffer*. However, copying the message twice between the buffers only costs a small amount of overhead, as the message was so small. Push-Zero Messaging tried to avoid copying twice by synchronizing the send and receive parties. However, the synchronization resulted in a larger amount of overhead.

From 10 bytes to 3000 bytes, the receive operation could register the destination buffer information before the send operation started the actual data transfer. All mechanisms could proceed without using the *pushed buffer*, including Push-All for most of the cases. They all used *zero buffers* to minimize the transfer overhead. For messages shorter than 16 bytes, Push-Pull operated like Push-Zero. For messages larger than 16 bytes, Push-Pull returned to its standard operation. This change in communication pattern allowed Push-Pull to effectively reduce the number of memory copies in the *pull* phase. Push-Zero also synchronized the send and receive parties before transferring the message. This synchronization and the change in pattern allowed both messaging mechanisms utilizing their *zero buffers*. Therefore both messaging mechanisms outperformed Push-All. Around 4000 bytes, the latency of Push-All Messaging was abruptly increased but Push-Pull and Push-Zero kept increasing steadily. The cause of this sudden performance lost was the timing of the send and receive operations. Originally, the receive operation could register the destination buffer information before the actual data transfer. However, the address translation overhead grows with the message size. As the receive operation became

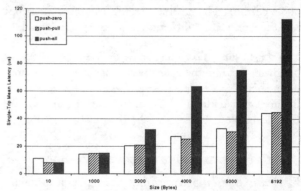

Figure 3. Intranode communication with the pushed buffer of size 12 Kbytes.

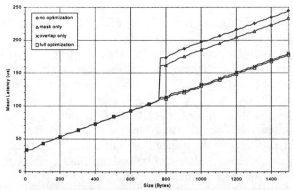

Figure 4. Performance measurement of the internode communication using three optimizing techniques.

"heavier", Push-All could not always proceed without using the *pushed buffer*. The registration could not be completed before the actual transfer in most of the times. Consequently, the transfer process utilized the *pushed buffer* and could not exploit the *zero buffer*. The average performance was further degraded around 3000 to 4000 bytes. Push-All performed poorer than Push-Pull and Push-Zero for most of the message sizes.

Zero buffer played an important role in minimizing the latency in all messaging mechanism. However, to practically exploit the mechanism, a proper communication pattern should be adopted. Since the communication pattern of Push-Pull and Push-All reinforced the execution order of the registration and data transfer phases, the performance of *zero buffer* could be exploited effectively. The *zero buffer* mechanism not only shortened the latency of the messaging, but it also improved the bandwidth of the communication since only one memory copy is needed. The measured peak bandwidth of Push-Pull is 350.9 Mbytes/s when sending around 4000 bytes, almost 66% of the theoretical 533-Mbyte bus bandwidth. The minimum latency for sending a 10-byte message is only 7.5 μs.

5.2. Internode communication

We carried out three latency tests to evaluate the effectiveness of Push-Pull Messaging in the internode communication. *Symmetric interrupt* was chosen as the reception handler invocation method in all tests.

We used 80 bytes and 680 bytes as the value of BTP(1) and BTP(2) respectively. These parameters were obtained independently by two separate tests.

The first test measured the latency by varying the value of BTP(2) but let BTP(1) be zero. This test only exploited the Push-and-Acknowledge Overlapping technique. As the value of BTP(2) increased, the latency of a longer second-pushed message could be hidden effectively. Thus, the remaining bytes of the message to be pushed could become shorter. Since the pulled

message was on the critical path in communication, the overall latency could be shortened as the value of BTP(2) increased. However, there was an upper limit on the BTP(2) value since the latency of the overlapped acknowledge phase was about the single-trip time of a short message. If the value of BTP(2) was too large, the overall latency would increase as the reception handler was unable to serve the second-pushed message and the pulled message in parallel. In this test, we obtained 680 bytes as the value of BTP(2).

In the second test, we fixed 680 bytes as the value of BTP(2) and varied the value of BTP(1). We then measured the overall latency. As the first-pushed message was on the critical path as shown in Figure 2, the latency grew with the value of BTP(1) when the BTP(1) value was larger than a threshold value. However, when the value was smaller than the threshold value, the latency would actually decrease. This reduction is caused by filling the time gap between serving the first and the second pushed message, which is illustrated as "Handle message 1" in Figure 2. As the time to handle the message was a little bit faster than the time to initiate the transmission of the second-pushed message, the receive party would have more time to process the first-pushed message. Therefore sending a longer first-pushed message would save some bandwidth, thus shortening the overall latency. In this test, we obtained 80 bytes as the value of BTP(1).

We compared the raw performance of Push-Pull Messaging with three optimized Push-Pull Messaging – Address Translation Overhead Masking (represented by [Δ]), Push-and-Request Overlapping (represented by [×]) and their combined version (represented by [□]) – as shown in Figure 4.

Before 760 bytes, all four messaging mechanisms behaved the same since the whole message was pushed to the receive party directly. After 760 bytes, the messaging mechanisms with Address Translation Overhead Masking and Push-and-Acknowledge Overlapping efficiently masked the overheads at both send and receive parties. Therefore, both techniques showed significant improvement over the non-optimized messaging mechanism. When we compared these two techniques, Push-and-Acknowledge Overlapping showed larger improvement. It is because the acknowledge latency, which is hidden by Push-and-Acknowledge Overlapping, is larger than the translation overhead saved in Address Translation Overhead Masking. In the figure, the full optimization showed the most promising solution, which integrated both orthogonal techniques.

5.3. Early and late receiver tests

In a cluster environment, the sender and receiver operate in an asynchronous manner. Extra blocking time happens when the receive party starts earlier than the send party; while overheads are always caused by the late start of the receive process. When we measured the latency of

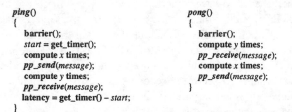

```
ping()                              pong()
{                                   {
    barrier();                          barrier();
    start = get_timer();                compute y times;
    compute x times;                    pp_receive(message);
    pp_send(message);                   compute x times;
    compute y times;                    pp_send(message);
    pp_receive(message);            }
    latency = get_timer() – start;
}
```

Figure 5. The redesigned ping-pong benchmark routine for testing early and late receivers

the internode communication, the ping-pong benchmark routine was redesigned to simulate a typical compute-then-communicate parallel program to examine the runtime performance of Push-Pull Messaging.

As shown in Figure 5, the *ping* and *pong* procedures compute before communicate. Before taking the measurement, we further synchronized both parties with a barrier operation, which was a simple ping-pong operation.

In the test, we varied both computations by inserting different number of NOP (No Operation) instructions. Two variations were tested. In the *early receiver* test (denoted by the word "early" in Figure 6 left), we forced the receive operation started before the send operation. The value of x and y were chosen to be 500,000 and 100,000 respectively.

The other one is called *late receiver* test (denoted by the word "late" in Figure 6 right). In this test, we forced the receive operation always started after the send operation. The value of x and y were chosen to be 100,000 and 300,000 in this test. In other words, we forced all messaging mechanisms utilizing the *pushed buffer*. The number of NOPs was pre-computed with the consideration of the barrier synchronization delay since the *ping* process always late about a single-trip latency time spent in waiting the implicit synchronization message from the *pong* process.

We carried out the tests for the three messaging mechanisms, namely Push-Zero, Push-Pull and Push-All, with full optimization. For the *early receiver* test, since the receive operation always finished before the send operation, the address of the destination buffer was known to the reception handler at the receive party before issuing the send operation. Therefore, the reception handlers in all three messaging mechanisms could copy the received data directly to the destination buffer using zero buffers without intermediate buffering. Thus, the size of the pushed buffer did not significantly affect the performance for all message lengths.

However, because of the difference in the communication pattern, Push-Pull and Push-All always outperformed Push-Zero. It is because the *push* phase in Push-Zero was not used to perform any useful data transfer. This phase was originally used to preserve the execution order of the registration of the pending receive operation and the pull communication. This ordering, however, was already reinforced due to the lightly loaded receiver and the heavily loaded sender. Therefore, the push phase in Push-Zero was wasting the communication bandwidth. Push-Zero was constantly slowed down.

Push-Pull outperformed Push-All in most cases in the early receiver test because the address translation overhead was effectively hidden. Push-All could not hide the overhead as the communication pattern did not allow doing so. The improvement of Push-Pull over Push-All, however, was not significant because the translation overhead was not large and the number of memory copies in both mechanisms was the same. During the *push* phase, Push-All could bypass the intermediate buffer as the receive operation was completed like Push-Pull. Therefore, the performance of Push-All was similar to the performance of Push-Pull.

For the late receiver test, as the computation on the receive party was on the critical measurement path, the computation contributed part of the latency. In this test, the transmission of the pushed messages, if any, were always pushed to the *pushed buffer*. Since the receive

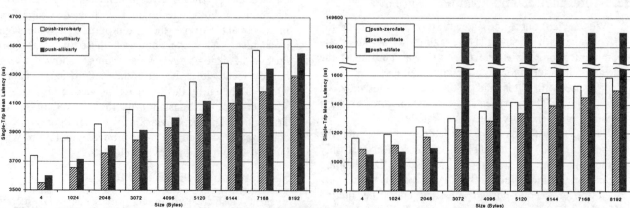

Figure 6. Performance comparison of Push-Pull Messaging for *early* and *late receive* tests with the pushed buffer 4 Kbytes.

operation was initiated so late, the reception handler in the receive party could not process the remaining part of the message without intermediate buffering in the *pushed buffer*. Therefore, the handler had to copy the message one more time before copying to the destination.

Before 3072 bytes, Push-All performed more satisfactory than Push-Pull and Push-Zero because whenever the receive operation was started, the *pushed buffer* contained the whole message. The message could then be copied directly to the destination buffer by the receive process. However in Push-Pull and Push-Zero, the receive operation always needed to initiate the transmission of an acknowledgement. Therefore, Push-Zero performed poorly for all message sizes whereas Push-Pull introduced long network latency time after around 800 bytes.

Although Push-All delivered messages faster than others did, the performance was degraded significantly after around 3000 bytes. This degradation showed that the *pushed buffer* in Push-All was overwhelmed by incoming packets. Most of the packets were lost during the communication. With the implemented go-back-n reliable protocol [10], Push-All could resume the transmission afterwards but it still could not outperform others. It took around 150 ms to transfer a 3072-byte message while Push-Zero took 1303.58 μs and Push-Pull even took only 1227.42 μs.

On the other hand, Push-Pull always outperformed Push-Zero in this late receiver test. The reason is that Push-Pull had sent BTP bytes to the receive party during the *push* phase. Therefore during the *pull* phase, shorter message was delivered.

Overall, the Push-Pull Messaging showed very steady performance in all cases as compared with Push-All and Push-Zero. Push-Pull Messaging could flexibly adapt to the cluster environment with different computation load and maximize the performance. The peak bandwidth could be as high as 12.1 Mbytes/s in fully optimized Push-Pull Messaging.

6. Conclusion

Building COMPs brings new challenges in designing a high-performance communication system. Our communication system is able to achieve very low-latency and high-bandwidth interprocess communication in the COMP environment. *Cross-Space Zero Buffer* mechanism efficiently eliminates all unnecessary memory copy operations in the intranode communication, where a peak bandwidth of 350.9 MB/s is achieved. *Address Translation Overhead Masking* hides the address translation overhead, around 12-13 μs for long messages, from the critical path in the internode communication. The *Push-and-Acknowledge Overlapping* can hide the acknowledge latency from the critical path. Among these optimizing techniques, *Push-and-Acknowledge*

Overlapping can reduce most of the overheads in the internode communication, while *Cross-Space Zero Buffer* can significantly improve the communication bandwidth in the intranode communication.

Currently, the bandwidth of Fast Ethernet is still low compared with the peripheral bus bandwidth. We believe the next important step is to design a more general mechanism to work with multiple network interfaces using multiple processors.

References

[1] G. Ciaccio. "Optimal Communication Performance on Fast Ethernet with GAMMA", *Proc. of International Workshop on Personal Computers based Networks Of Workstations 1998* (PC-NOW '98), Orlando, March 30/April 3, 1998.

[2] T. von Eicken, A. Basu, V. Buch and W. Vogels. "U-Net: A User-Level Network Interface for Parallel and Distributed Computing", *Proc. of the 15th ACM Symposium on Operating Systems Principles* (SOSP'95), December, 1995.

[3] B. Falsafi and D. A. Wood. "Scheduling Communication on an SMP Node Parallel Machine", *Proc. of the 3rd International Symposium on High-Performance Computer Architecture* (HPCA-3), 1997, pp. 128-138.

[4] "Intel Architecture Software Developer's Manual Volume 3: System Programming Guide", Intel Corporation.

[5] S. S. Lumetta and D. E. Culler. "Managing Concurrent Access for Shared Memory Active Messages", *Proc. of the 12th International Parallel Processing Symposium* (IPPS'98), 1998, pp. 272-278.

[6] B. H. Lim, P. Heidelberger, P. Pattnaik and M. Snir. "Message Proxies for Efficient, Protected Communication on SMP Clusters", *Proc. of the 3rd International Symposium on High-Performance Computer Architecture* (HPCA-3), 1997, pp. 116-127.

[7] S. S. Lumetta, A. M. Mainwaring and D. E. Culler. "Multi-Protocol Active Messages on a Cluster of SMP's", *Proc. of Supercomputing '97 High Performance Networking and Computing* (SC97), November, 1997.

[8] C. M. Lee, A. Tam, and C. L. Wang, "Directed Point: An Efficient Communication Subsystem for Cluster Computing", *Proc. of the 10th International Conference on Parallel and Distributed Computing and Systems* (IASTED '98), Las Vegas, 1998.

[9] J. Shen, J. Wang and W. Zheng. "A New Fast Message Passing Communication System for Multiprocessor Workstation Clusters", Tech. Rep., Dept. of Computer Science and Technology, Tsinghua Univ., China, 1998.

[10] A. S. Tanenbaum. "Computer Networks", 3rd Edition, Prentice-Hall International, Inc., 1996, pp. 207-213.

[11] Y. Tanaka, M. Matsua, M. Ando, K. Kubota and M. Sato. "COMPaS: A Pentium Pro PC-based SMP Cluster and its Experience", *Proc. of International Workshop on Personal Computers based Networks Of Workstations 1998* (PC-NOW '98), Orlando, March 30/April 3, 1998.

[12] "Virtual Interface Architecture Specification. Ver. 1.0", Compaq, Intel and Microsoft Corporations, 1997, http://www.giganet.com/.

Session B1

Instruction-Level Parallelism

Chair: Kiyoshi Oguri
NTT Corporation, Japan

Impact on Performance of Fused Multiply-Add Units in Aggressive VLIW Architectures

David López, Josep Llosa, Eduard Ayguadé and Mateo Valero
Department of Computer Architecture. Polytechnic University of Catalunya.
UPC-Campus Nord, Mòdul D6. Jordi Girona 1-3, 08034 Barcelona (Spain)
E-mail: { david | josepll | eduard | mateo }@ac.upc.es

Abstract

Loops are the main time consuming part of programs based on floating point computations. The performance of the loops is limited either by recurrences in the computation or by the resources offered by the architecture. Several general-purpose superscalar microprocessors have been implemented with multiply-add fused floating-point units, that reduces the latency of the combined operation and the number of resources used. This paper analyses the influence of these two factors in the instruction-level parallelism exploitable from loops executed on a broad set of future aggressive processor configurations. The estimation of implementation costs (area and cycle time) enables a fair comparison of these configurations in terms of final performance and implementation feasibility. The paper performs a technological projection for the next years in order to foresee the possible implementable alternatives. From this study we conclude that multiply-add fused units may have a deep impact in raising the performance of future processor architectures with a reasonable increase in cost.

1. Introduction

Current high-performance microprocessors rely on hardware and software techniques to exploit the inherent instruction-level parallelism (ILP) of the applications. These processors make use of deep pipelines in order to reduce the cycle time and wide instruction issue units to allow the simultaneous execution of several instructions per cycle.

Very Long Instruction Word (VLIW) architectures are oriented to exploit ILP. In a VLIW architecture, an instruction is composed of a number of operations that are issued simultaneously to the functional units (i.e. the scheduling is performed at compile time so the dispatch phase is very simple). Although there are few commercial general purpose VLIW processors, these architectures have been widely used in the DSP arena (as in the Texas Instruments 'C6701 [21] and Equator Map1000 [22]), they have been subject of research in the last years and will constitute the core of future designs [19].

The static nature of VLIW schedulings require good compilation techniques to effectively exploit the ILP available in real programs [5]. Software pipelining [10] is a compilation technique that extracts ILP for the innermost loops by overlapping the execution of several consecutive iterations. In a software pipelined loop, the number of cycles between the initiation of successive iterations (termed *Initiation Interval*) is bounded either by the recurrences in the dependence graph or by the resource constrains of the target architecture [4][23][24].

Several techniques have been proposed to increase the performance of loops bounded by the resource constrains. The loops performance can be augmented by increasing the number of functional units (replication technique), by exploiting data parallelism at the functional unit level (like in vector processors [27] or, in superscalar and VLIW processors, using the widening technique [13][14][20]), or by using functional units that can perform multiple operations as a monolithic operation (e.g. *fused multiply and add* FMA floating-point units perform a multiplication and a dependent addition as a single operation).

As the number of transistors on a single chip continues to grow, more hardware can be accommodated on a chip, so future designs will use these techniques to exploit ILP aggressively. Unfortunately, most of these techniques focus on increasing the performance of resource-bound loops. Consequently, the more aggressive become the architectures, more critical become the recurrences.

The FMA operation reduces the latency of the recurrences. Several current microprocessors implement this operation (like the IBM RS/6000 [7] and POWER2 [28], and the MIPS R8000 [6] and R10000 [30]). This paper studies the influence of fused multiply-add functional units (fusion technique) in future ILP aggressive architectures. We study the maximum ILP achievable using this technique, combined with other techniques that increase the performance of resource-bound loops. In order to perform a fair comparison of the different techniques, it is mandatory to evaluate the effect in the final performance of several factors: the influence of the compiler, the influence of the register file size, and the hardware cost in terms of chip area and cycle time.

The area cost defines those configurations that could be implemented in the next microprocessor generations, according to the predictions of the *Semiconductor Industry Association* [26]. For each generation we estimate the performance of a set of implementable configurations taking into account the number of cycles required to execute the programs and the cycle time. From this study we conclude that the fusion technique has a significant effect on the final performance of aggressive configurations. The technique has a good theoretical performance, but also reduces the register pressure, it gives more opportunities to the compiler to find an optimal scheduling, and also has good performance/cost efficiency.

All the evaluations have been performed for VLIW architectures and numerical programs. Our workbench is composed of 1180 loops that account for 78% of the execution time of the Perfect Club [2]. The loops have been obtained using the experimental tool Ictíneo [1] and software pipelined using *Hypernode Reduction Modulo Scheduling*

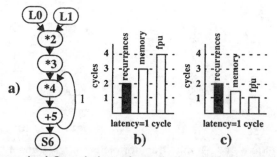

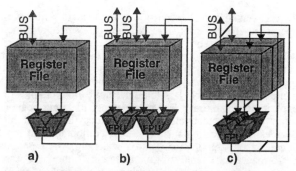

Figure 1: a) Sample loop dependence graph and limits for two processor configurations: b) 1 bus and 1 functional unit, c) 2 buses and 4 functional units.

Figure 2: Different processor configurations based on replication and widening: a) base configuration, b) replication and c) widening.

[17][18], a register pressure sensitive heuristic that achieves near optimal schedules. Register allocation has been performed using the wands-only strategy and the end-fit with adjacency ordering [25]. When a loop requires more than the available number of registers, spill code is added and the loop is rescheduled [15][16].

The organization of the paper is as follows: Section 2 describes the replication, widening and fusion techniques and illustrates, with an example, their performance limits. Section 3 describes the FPUs that implement the FMA operation and outlines its cost. Section 4 evaluates the performance of a set of processor configurations where the studied techniques are combined. First we perform an estimation of the theoretical ILP limits of the techniques, assuming perfect scheduling, a register file of infinite size and a perfect memory. Then we evaluate the effect of the scheduler and having a finite register file. Finally, we take the costs into account and study the performance/cost trade-offs of the techniques. Section 5 summarizes the main conclusions of this work.

2. Motivating example

In a software pipelined loop, the number of cycles between the initiation of successive iterations is named *Initiation Interval* (*II*). The *II* defines the maximum performance that can be obtained from the loop and is bounded either by resources constrains in the architecture (*ResMII*) or by cyclic dependence chains (recurrences) in the dependence graph (*RecMII*). Its lower bound is termed the *Minimum Initiation Interval* (*MII*) and is computed as *MII* = *max* (*ResMII*, *RecMII*).

In this section we use a sample loop (whose dependence graph is shown in Figure 1.a.) to show these bounds and possible alternatives to reduce them. In the Figure, nodes represent operations (memory accesses or arithmetic computations) and edges represent data dependences between pairs of nodes. There are 3 memory operations (loads L0 and L1, and store S6) and 4 arithmetic operations (products *2, *3, *4 and addition +5). All dependences are intra-loop dependences (i.e. occur between two operations performed in the same iteration and have distance 0) except for dependence (+5, *4) in which the result of +5 is used by *4 one iteration later (loop-carried dependence of distance 1). In this graph, there is a recurrence composed of edges (*4, +5) and (+5, *4) spawning over one iteration.

Figure 1.b illustrates the factors that contribute to *ResMII* and *RecMII*, assuming an architecture with a single memory unit and a single arithmetic unit (all of them fully pipelined and with a latency of one cycle):

• Resources. In this case, 3 cycles are required at least to execute the 3 memory operations in the memory access unit (bar labelled *memory*) and 4 cycles are required at least to execute the 4 arithmetical operations in the arithmetical unit (bar labelled *fpu*). Therefore, the arithmetic operations put higher constraints in the execution of the loop and limit the *ResMII* to 4.

• Recurrences. There is a single recurrence in the loop that may limit its execution. For the architecture being considered, 2 cycles are required to sequentially execute the operations within the recurrence, and therefore the *RecMII* is 2 (bar labelled *recurrences*).

For a given architecture, and depending on the values of *ResMII* and *RecMII*, loops can be classified into three groups: *balanced* (*ResMII* = *RecMII*), *resource-bound* (*ResMII* > *RecMII*) and *recurrence-bound* (*ResMII* < *RecMII*) loops. For example, our working example fits in the resource-bound cathegory limited by the arithmetic operations. Making the architecture more aggressive in terms of number of functional units can convert resource-bound loops into balanced or recurrence-bound loops. Also, reducing their latency can convert recurrence-bound loops into balanced or resource-bound loops. In the next subsections we analyse different architectural alternatives to improve each of these 2 factors.

2.1 Resource-bound loops

In order to increase the performance of resource-bound loops, the resources of the processor must be increased. In this section we analyse two alternatives to make the architecture more aggressive: resource *replication* and *widening*. On one side, resource replication consists on increasing the number of functional units available in the processor. On the other side, resource widening [13] consists on increasing the number of operations that each functional unit can simultaneously perform per cycle (i.e. functional units that operate with short vectors).

For example, Figure. 2.a shows a base configuration in which we have one bus and one floating-point functional unit (FPU). In this case, one memory and one arithmetical operation can be issued per cycle. Higher performance can be obtained by adding another bus and another FPU (replication technique, Figure 2.b); in this case, two independent memory accesses and two independent arithmetic operations can be issued per cycle. The same peak performance can also be obtained by duplicating the width of both, the bus and the FPU (widening technique, Figure 2.c); in this case, two memory and two arithmetical operations can also be issued per cycle. However, widening is less versatile than replication, because it requires the operations to be *compactable* (i.e. the same arithmetic operation has to be performed in consecutive iterations without data dependences between them, or access to consecutive memory locations in the case of memory operations). This analysis of compactability can be done at compile time [12][14]. Although replication enables the exploitation of more ILP than widening, its larger costs (in terms of area and cycle time) precludes the use of high degrees of replication in favour of a combination of small degrees of replication and widening. A detailed performance/cost analysis of different future processor configurations based on a combination of replication and widening can be found elsewhere [13].

The use of aggressive configurations (using replication and/or widening) for the processor core does not affect the performance of recurrence-bound loops and may covert balanced or compute-bound loops into recurrence-bound loops. In our working example, when the number of resources is increased (as shown in Figure 1.c), the bars due to memory and arithmetic operations are reduced. Notice that at this point the dominant bar is the one due to the recurrences, the performance will not improve even in an architecture with an unbounded number of resources.

Figure 3 shows, for our workbench, the percentage of time spent in recurrence, compute and memory bound loops for different processor configurations (executed on an HP 9000/735 workstation and compiled with the +O3 flag, which performs software pipelining among other optimizations). Each configuration xZ includes Z functional units and Z buses, with a latency of 4 cycles. For a configuration with 1 FPU and 1 bus (as the one shown in Figure 2.a) 61.8% of the total time is spent in compute-bound loops, 30.7% in memory-bound loops and only 7.5% in recurrence-bound loops. This indicates that the loops of our workbench are slightly compute-bound. Notice that the percentage of time spent in loops that become recurrence bound increases when the aggressiveness of the architecture increases. For configurations greater than x4, more than 50% of the total time is spent in recurrence-bound loops. As a consequence, techniques to improve the performance of this kind of loops are necessary in order to impact the final performance of aggressive architectures.

2.2 Recurrence-bound loops

In order to improve the performance of loops bounded by recurrences, the number of cycles needed to perform the operations in the recurrence has to be reduced. This reduction can be achieved either by reducing the latency of the functional units or by solving complex operations in the same amount of time. The later option has been included in the design of some current microprocessors with functional units that execute a multiply instruction and an associated

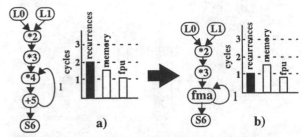

Figure 4: Graph transformation and impact in performance limits in an architecture with 2 buses and 4 FPU: a) without FMA and b) with FMA.

addition operations (FMA) as a single instruction. These functional units reduces both the number of cycles needed to execute the recurrence and the number of slots used to schedule these operations.

For example, the dependence graph in our working example has a recurrence composed of two nodes where a product is followed by an addition. Figure 4 shows how the graph is transformed when these two operations are fused in a single FMA operation, thus reducing the number of operations of the recurrence from 2 to 1, and reducing the recurrence limit to 1 cycle.

A static analysis of our workbench reveals that 591 out of the 1180 loops can make use of FMA functional units. For these loops, Figure 5 shows the percentage of time spent in loops that would benefit from having FMA operations for different xZ processor configurations. For each one:

- dotted line: it shows the percentage of time spent in compute-bound loops that would benefit from having FMA operations. Notice that in our base configuration, more than 60% of the time is spent in this kind of loops. As configurations become more aggressive, the number of compute-bound loops are reduced, becoming less than 1% in the largest configuration considered.
- dashed line: it shows the percentage of time spent in recurrence-bound loops that would benefit from having FMA operations (i.e. those in which this operation occurs in the most limiting recurrence). As configurations become more aggressive, the percentage of time spent in these loops increase.

The solid line summarizes both effects and represents the total percentage of time spent in loops that would benefit from having FMA operations. Notice that this kind of complex operations are dominant in numerical applications and may affect the performance when aggressive architectures are considered. In order to validate this thesis, this paper analyses the impact of FMA operations in the performance of future aggressive processor configurations based on a performance/cost evaluation where ILP, area and cycle time are taken into consideration.

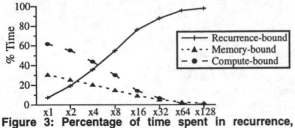

Figure 3: Percentage of time spent in recurrence, compute and memory bound loops for different processor configurations.

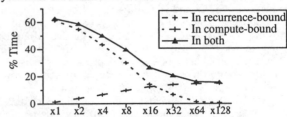

Figure 5: Percentage of time spent in loops than would benefit from implementing the FMA operation for different processor configurations.

3. Cost of Fused Multiply-and-Add FPUs

Some current microprocessors implement FPUs that execute the *fused multiply-and-add* operation (FMA) as a single instruction as $T = (A \times C) + B$. In these FPUs, the floating-point hardware is designed to accept up to three operands for executing FMA instructions, while other floating-point instructions requiring fewer than three operands may utilize the same hardware by forcing constants into the unused operands. In general, FPUs with FMA implementations use a multiply array to compute the AC product, followed by an adder to compute AC+B.

This operation has been implemented in the floating-point units of the IBM RS/6000 [7], IBM POWER2 [28], MIPS R8000 [6] and MIPS R10000 [30] microprocessors. In the MIPS R10000, the FMA operation has been implemented by chaining the multiplier FPU output with the adder FPU input requiring rounding and alignment between them. Therefore the MIPS R10000 requires 2 cycles to compute an add or a mul, and 4 cycles to compute a FMA operation providing no latency benefit. The only benefit is the reduction in instruction bandwidth and in the registers requirements (no register is required to store the intermediate result). On the contrary, processors like the IBM POWER2 implement the FMA operation integrating the multiplier and the adder without rounding and alignment in the middle. Therefore in the POWER2, the FMA operation has the same latency (two cycles) as the individual add or mul operations

Implementing the FMA functional unit in a microprocessor incurs several costs in terms of area and cycle time. With respect to the FPUs, the area required for the extra hardware needed to implement the FMA operation is practically negligible because the area of a general-purpose floating-point unit is mainly governed by the area of the multiplier [9]. The main additional cost is due to the associated register file. The overall size of a register file is determined mainly by the size of a register cell. The other components that are needed to access the register file typically represent less than 5% of the area required by the register cells [11].

The area of the register cell grows approximately as the square of the number of ports added because each port forces the cell to increase both the height and the width [8][11][12]. Implementing the FMA operation requires one additional read port for every FPU, so it results in an increase of the register file size. To illustrate this cost, Table 1 shows the area cost of one configuration (named A) with 2 buses and 2 FPUs. In this case, each bus requires 1 read and 1 write ports, and each FPU requires 2 read and 1 write ports. Assuming a register file of 32 registers, the register file cost results in $32.08 \times 10^6 \lambda^2$ (the details of this cost model can be found elsewhere [12]). If the FPUs implement the FMA operation, one more read port is required for each FPU (configuration B), resulting in a register file area of size 1.37 times greater. But a configuration with 2 FPUs that implement FMA can issue 2 multiplications and 2 additions per cycle, the same as a configuration with 4 FPUs (configuration C) but at a lower cost (the area of B is 46.7% of the area of C).

In addition, the register file access time can force the cycle time in a VLIW architecture, and the access time is governed by the number of registers, the width of the registers and the size of each register cell (which depends on the number of read and write ports). To calculate the impact of the number of ports in the access time, we use a model

Table 1: Area cost for several 32-RF configurations.

Configuration	Ports	Area of a memory cell	Total RF area (λ^2)
A) 2 bus + 2 fpu	6R+3W	$14664\ \lambda^2$	32.08×10^6
B) 2 bus + 2 FMA fpu	8R+3W	$21420\ \lambda^2$	43.87×10^6
C) 2 bus + 4 fpu	10R+6W	$45820\ \lambda^2$	93.84×10^6

[13] based on the CACTI model for cache memory [29]. Next we show the impact of the number of ports using the same configurations of the area cost example (A, B and C of Table 1). Configuration B has an access time 8% slower than configuration A, while the access time of configuration C (4 FPUs without FMA) is 42% slower than the access time of configuration A. To reduce the access time, the register file can be partitioned into several files, maintaining copies of all the data [3], but at the cost of increasing the total area cost. For example, configuration C has 10 read plus 6 write ports. This RF can be also implemented by two identical copies, where all functional units can write in both copies of the RF, but only 1 bus and 2 FPUs read each copy. In this case, 5 read plus 6 write ports are required for each copy. This implementation increases the register file area by 12.7%, but reduces the access time from 42% to 21% slower than A.

4. Performance evaluation

In this section we first show an evaluation of the performance limits that are expected from the use of replication, widening and fusion techniques. We first consider an ideal framework with a perfect scheduling and an infinite register file. Then we make real both aspects and analyse the influence of using a heuristic algorithm to do software pipelining and having a finite register file. Finally we consider implementation costs (area and cycle time) and draw a set of conclusions from a performance/cost conscious evaluation of the different implementation alternatives.

The processor configurations considered in this section are named using two different possibilities: XwY and xZ (where Z equals X times Y). Each one of these configurations has X bidirectional buses (to perform load/store operations) and twice the number of functional units[1]. The width of the resources is Y words. For instance, configuration 2w1 has 2 buses and 4 FPUs and all the resources have a width of 1 word, while configuration 1w2 has 1 bus and 2 FPUs, all of width 2 words. As the baseline configuration that we consider is *1w1*, both configurations can be also named *x2* because they can issue 2 times the number of operations of the baseline. The latencies are as follows: a store is served in 1 cycle; division and square root are not pipelined and require 19 and 27 cycles, respectively; the rest of the operations (load, add,...) are fully pipelined and require 4 cycles to be executed. We append F to those configurations in which FMA is implemented. The memory is ideal and all references always hit in the cache.

4.1 Maximum ILP achievable

First of all we analyse the performance of FMA under the following ideal situations: perfect scheduler (i.e. always achieves the *MII*) and unbounded number of registers (so there is no need to perform spill code).

1.Preliminary studies show that a relation of 2 FPUs for each bus is the most balanced configuration (see Figure 3). Also, we have based the cost calculations on the MIPS R10000, which can issue 2 floating point and 1 memory operation per cycle.

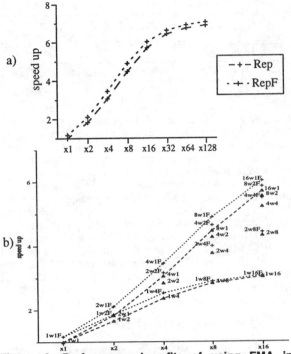

Figure 6: Performance benefits of using FMA in processor configurations based on a) replication and b) a combination of replication and widening.

Figure 6.a shows the additional performance benefits of using FMA for a set of processor configurations based on replication (*xZ* with *Zw1*). On one side, notice that the performance that is obtained does not scale with the peak performance of the architecture. This is due to the fact that aggressive configurations convert resource-bound loops into recurrence-bound loops; as a consequence, adding more resources does not contribute to a real increase in performance. On the other hand, notice that the difference between using FMA (dotted plot) or not using FMA (dashed plot) is practically a constant; this is due to the fact that the FMA operation produces benefits to recurrence-bound loops in very aggressive configurations (see Figure 5), maintaining an increase of performance similar to the obtained for compute-bound loops in configurations with a smaller degree of aggressiveness.

Figure 6.b shows the additional performance benefits of using FMA for a reduced set of processor configurations that apply combinations of both replication and widening. Notice that FMA can play an important role, specially in aggressive configurations where replication is used (for instance, configuration *1w8F* has a performance 2.1% better than *1w8*, while *8w1F* has a performance 9.4% better than *8w1*).

4.2 The effect of spill code on performance

The goal of the studied techniques is to increase the ILP of loops by reducing their Initiation Interval. Regretfully, reducing the *II* can increase the register requirements [15]. If the number of registers required to schedule a loop on an architecture exceeds the number of physical registers available, spill code must be introduced in order to free some registers [16]. However, spill code increases the memory traffic and can result in an increase of the *II*, with the associated performance degradation. We schedule the loops

using the HRMS heuristic [17][18], a register pressure sensitive heuristic that achieves near optimal schedules. Register allocation is performed using the wands-only strategy and the end-fit with adjacency ordering [25].

Figure 7 shows the performance for different processor configurations and sizes of the register file (*r-RF* configuration uses a register file of *r* registers, *Y* words wide). The baseline configuration considered is *1w1* with a *256-RF*. This configuration does not require spill code and therefore is equivalent to the baseline configuration in Figure 6. Notice that the configuration *8w1* does not include the *32-RF* bar; this is because this configuration can produce 24 results per cycle (8 memory and 16 FPU), and we consider a 4-cycle latency configuration. In this case, the register pressure is so high, that the scheduler fails to produce a valid schedule with the available registers. This situation becomes more critical in configurations with a factor higher than x8, and this is the reason why we do not present the results of these configurations with this latency model. Figure 7 shows the expected results: the performance grows with the aggressiveness of configurations, and the register file size has an important impact on the final performance. The FMA operations (white portion in each bar) improves the performance of all configurations but the increase is higher for those configurations with high register pressure.

Another important point can be observed in this Figure: there is a significative difference between the performance reported in this section, and the theoretical performance shown in section 4.1. For instance, there is an increase of the theoretical performance of 7.5% from configuration 8w1 to configuration 8w1F; when the loop is scheduled with a 64-register file, this difference grows up to 20.5%. This difference is due to other factors that have an important contribution on the final performance. In this point we are going to analyse these factors.

The total amount of cycles required to execute a loop in a given architecture can be divided into three components:
- the *MII*: this is the minimum number of cycles required to execute a loop; it depends on the characteristics of the loop itself and on the architecture.
- cycles due to spill code: these are the cycles due to the code introduced to fit the scheduling in the available number of registers.
- and cycles due to the scheduler heuristic: these are the cycles added by the scheduler when it fails in finding the optimal scheduling.

Figure 8 shows, for the same processor configurations, the distribution of cycles introduced by each of these components. Each plot is divided in 8 columns grouped in pairs representing the register file size (horizontal axis): the

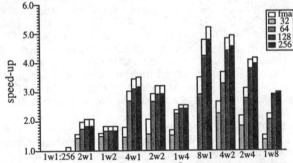

Figure 7: Performance of some processor configurations for several sizes of the register file. Baseline: configuration 1w1 with a 256-RF

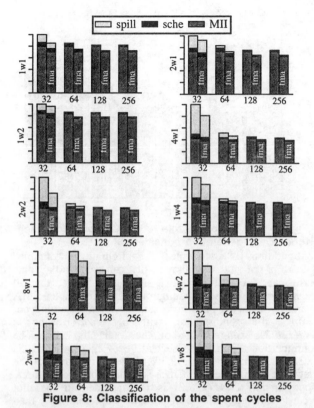

Figure 8: Classification of the spent cycles

right column in each pair represents an architecture with FMA and the left column an architecture without FMA. The use of FMA reduces the cycles required for all the factors previously defined:

- the dark gray part represents the minimum theoretical cycles, so it is independent of the register file size. Notice that using FMA reduces the MII because some operations have been fused (and there are less operations to be scheduled). For instance, the number of cycles is reduced in 10.7% when FMA is used in configuration *4w1*.

- the light gray part shows the spill code cycles. FMA reduces the register pressure of the loops because it does not require a register to store the intermediate result (e.g. the number of cycles due to spill code is reduced in 35.7% when FMA is used in configuration *4w1* with a 32-RF).

- the black part represents the scheduler cycles. The reduction of the number of operations to schedule (due to the reduction of operations in the loop and to the reduction in the spill code required) makes the graph less complex; therefore, the scheduler has more opportunities to find a schedule closer to the optimal. For example, the number of cycles added by the scheduler is reduced in 20.9% when FMA is used in configuration *4w1* with a 32-RF.

From the analysis of Figure 8, one can conclude that using FMA has an impact on the final performance greater than the performance that we can expect if we only take into account the theoretical analysis. For instance, configuration *4w1F* with a 32-RF has a performance 22.9% better than configuration *4w1*, while the difference in the theoretical analysis was 10.7%.

4.3 Performance/cost trade-offs

In this section we try to identify the role of replication, widening and FMA when their implementation is taken into consideration. Area and cycle time cost can easily offset any gain in ILP or even worse, make a configuration non implementable. The 1994 *Semiconductor Industry Association* (SIA) predictions [26] are used to define a set of future technology generations and their characteristics.

Table 2: SIA predictions in 1994

	1998	2001	2004	2007	2010
λ (μm)	0.25	0.18	0.13	0.10	0.07
Size (mm^2)	300	360	430	520	620
λ^2 per chip (x10^6)	4800	11111	25443	52000	126530
λ^2 / mm^2 (x10^6)	16	30.86	59.17	100	204.08

We study a broad set of architectures that implements the replication, widening and fusion techniques. In order to perform a realistic study, the register files of the configurations have been partitioned to reduce their access time (and therefore, the configurations cycle time). Configurations are labelled $XwY(Z:n)$ (i.e. X buses and $2*X$ FPUs, all of width Y, with a RF of Z registers of width Y, partitioned in n-blocks) or $XwYF(Z:n)$ (i.e. the same but the FPUs can implement the FMA operation).

The methodology used for this evaluation is as follows. First we calculate the cost of the tested configurations and decide which is implementable for each technology generation (we consider that a configuration is implementable for a technology generation if its FPUs area plus its register file area do not exceed 20% of the total chip area). Second, for each implementable configuration we calculate its cycle time, assuming that the cycle time is defined by the register file access time. Each FPU requires an amount of time to perform one operation; its latency in cycles depends on the processor cycle time. The cycle models we have used are listed in Table 3 and assume that the baseline configuration (*1w1*) uses the 4-cycles model.

Table 3: Cycle models.

cycle model	latency (in cycles)			
	store	+,*, load	div	sqrt
4-cycles	1	4	19	27
3-cycles	1	3	15	21
2-cycles	1	2	10	14
1-cycle	1	1	5	7

Other configurations will fit into the appropriate model depending on its relative (from the *1w1* configuration) cycle time. A configuration with a relative cycle time Tc belongs to the z-cycles model, where z= ⌈4/Tc⌉. Finally, we perform the scheduling to find the cycles required[1]. The cycles required to execute all the loops times the cycle time give us the final performance. In all cases, we use a fixed timing model based on technology parameters for λ=0.25. We have not attempted to factor-in reductions in cycle time due to future technology generations.

Before going into the final results, let us analyse the individual effects of some parameters on the configurations evaluated:

- Number of registers. Having large register files reduces the register pressure and the need of spill code. However, the increase in the cycle time may counteract this gain. For example, Figure 9.a shows the performance/cost ratio

1. The cycles required are calculated as the cycles per iteration (Initiation Interval) times the number of iterations performed in the original loop execution.

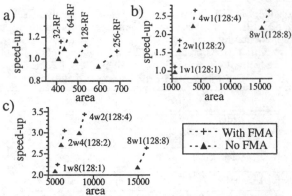

Figure 9: effect of a) increasing the RF size, b) replication and c) different ways to implement a configuration with the same peak performance. All figures compare FPUs with and without FMA.

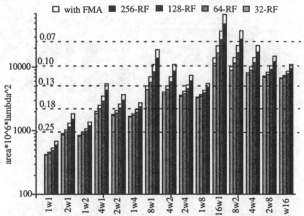

Figure 10: Implementable configurations for each tehcnology generation considered.

when we increase the number of registers available in the register file, for configuration 1w1. Notice that the performance for this configuration declines when we use a register file larger than 64. This configuration has negligible need for spill code when a 64-RF (or bigger) is available, so an increase of the registers file does not affect the cycles required, but increases the cycle time.

• Replication. Configurations based on replication report good increases in ILP. However, high degrees of replication can make the configuration unimplementable (they occupy more than 20% of the total chip area) or suffer a decrease in performance because a small increase in IPC (instructions per cycle) is counteracted with a high increase of the cycle time. For instance, Figure 9.b shows the performance/cost ratio when only replication is applied.

• Replication and widening. The same peak performance can be obtained by applying different degrees of replication and widening. Although replication is more versatile and reported higher ILP returns, cycle time puts configurations based on small degrees of widening in a better position, as shown in Figure 9.c for *x8* configurations.

• Fused Multiply-add. FMA returns good performance relative to its low implementation cost. The three plots in Figure 9 also shows the performance of the same configurations when FMA is included (the cross marks). For instance, configuration *8w1F(128:8)* performs 21.1% better than *8w1(128:8)*, with an increment of only 8.3% in the area. Also, configuration *2w4F(128:2)* has a performance 2% better than configuration *4w2(128:4)* and only has 72% of its area requirements.

Assuming the SIA predictions and our area cost models, Figure 10 shows the area cost for a broad range of processor configurations that include replication, widening and FMA with different sizes for the RF (notice that the vertical axis has logarithmic scale). Each horizontal line represents, each technology generation, the 20% in area devoted to implement this processor core and therefore defines the set of implementable configurations for this technology.

Figure 11 shows, for each technology, the five configurations that achieve the best performance. First of all, notice that none of the most aggressive configurations are in the top-five configurations due to their high cost: the configurations that offer best performance are the ones that combine small degrees of replication and widening. For each technology, we have also highlighted the "eligible"

configurations (black triangles). A configuration is "eligible" if there is not any configuration that can achieve the same performance, or better, with a small cost. Notice that all except for two "eligible" configurations implement the FMA operation in their FPUs. For example, for a technology of λ=0.13, the configuration with best performance is *2w4(128:2)*, using 18.7% of the total chip area. The configuration with the second best performance is *2w2F(64:2)* that achieves 99.3% of the performance of the first one, using only 8.18% of the total chip area. Configuration *2w4F(128:2)* is not included in the plot because it requires 20.6% of the total chip area (more than 20%) but offers a performance 12.5% greater than 2w4(128:2).

We can conclude that using FPUs that implement the FMA operation has some costs, but the benefits that offers

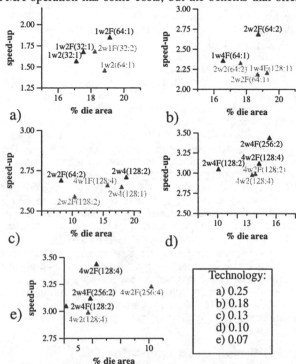

Figure 11: Top five configurations. The increment of the clock speed has not been taken into account

overcome these costs, so it is a good solution to increase the performance of aggressive configurations.

5. Conclusions

In order to exploit the inherent ILP of numerical applications, aggressive processors are required. More operations can be executed per cycle by either increasing the number of functional units (replication technique) or by increasing the number of data each functional unit can process per cycle (widening technique). However, the more aggressive the processor more critical become the recurrences. Fused multiply-add functional units increase the number of operations performed by cycle and improve performance in recurrence-bound loops that contain multiply-add chains in their critical recurrence.

In this paper we have evaluated the impact on performance and cost of FMA functional units in aggressive architectures. In particular we have evaluated the influence of FMA units in combination with the widening and replication techniques. The evaluations have been performed over a large number of software pipelined loops from the Perfect Club benchmarks assuming a VLIW architecture.

We have analysed the effects of FMA on resource-bound loops and on recurrence-bound loops. We have studied the ILP limits of each configuration in optimal conditions, showing that FMA units provide a significant advantage. This is because FMA units increase the peak number operations that can be performed per cycle and can reduce the latency of critical recurrences. When a limited number of registers is considered, the advantage of using FMA increases. This increment in performance is due to two reasons: the influence of spill code (the register requirements are reduced) and the influence of the scheduler (it has a simpler task since there are less operations to schedule).

Taking into account that using FMA units is more expensive in terms of area cost and cycle time, we have estimated the cost of the configurations considered. We compare the performance of the configurations that can be built for the next processor generations. The performance has been calculated using the register file cycle time. To perform a realistic comparison, the register file cycle time has been reduced using the partitioning technique and the FPUs latency has been adapted to the cycle time. From this study we conclude that, for a given technology, the best performance is obtained for configurations that use FMA units requiring less area.

Acknowledges

This work has been supported by the Ministry of Culture and Education of Spain under contract TIC 98-0511 and by CEPBA (European Center for Parallelism of Barcelona).

References

[1] E. Ayguadé, C. Barrado, A. González, J. Labarta, J. Llosa, D. López, S. Moreno, D. Padua, F. Reig, Q. Riera and M. Valero. "Ictíneo: A tool for Instruction-Level Parallelism Research". Tec. Rep. UPC-DAC-1996-61 U. Politècnica Catalunya. Dec 1996.
[2] M. Berry, D. Chen, P. Koss and D. Kuck. "The Perfect Club benchmarks: Effective performance evaluation of supercomputers". Tec. Rep. 827, CSRD-U. Illinois at Urbana-Champain, Nov. 1988.
[3] A. Capitanio, N. Dutt and A. Nicolau. "Partitioned register files for VLIWs: A preliminary analysis of tradeoffs". In Proc. MICRO-25, pp 292-300, Dec. 1992.
[4] J.C. Dehnert and R.A. Towle. "Compiling for Cydra 5". In Jour. Supercomputing, vol. 7 no. 1/2, pp 181-228, May 1993.
[5] W.-M. W. Hwu, S.A. Mahlke, W.Y. Chen, P.P. Chang, N.J. Warter, R.A. Bringmann, R.G. Ouellette, R.E. Hank, T. Kiyohara, G.E. Haab, J.G. Holm and D.M. Lavery. "The superblock: An effective technique for VLIW and superscalar compilation". In Jour. Supercomputing, vol. 7 no. 1/2, pp 229-248, May 1993.
[6] P.Y.T. Hsu. "Design of the TFP microprocessor". IEEE Micro, vol. 14 no. 2 pp 23-33. April 1994.
[7] IBM. Special issue on the RS/6000. IBM Jour. Res. and Develop. vol. 34 no. 1. January 1990.
[8] R. Jolly. "A 9-ns 1.4 gigabyte 17-ported CMOS register file". J. of Solid-State Circuits, vol. 25 no. 10 pp 1407-1412, Oct. 1991.
[9] R.M. Jessani and M. Putrino. "Comparison of single- and dual-pass multiply-add fused floating-point units". In IEEE Trans. on Computers, vol. 47 no. 9, pp 927-937, Sep. 1998.
[10] M. Lam. "Software pipelining: An effective scheduling technique for VLIW machines". In Proc. PLDI-88, pp. 318-328, June 1988.
[11] C. G. Lee. "Code Optimizers and Register Organizations for Vector Architectures". Ph.D. thesis U. C. Berkeley. May 1992.
[12] D. López, J. Llosa, M. Valero and E. Ayguadé. "Resource widening vs. replication: Limits and performance-cost trade-off". In Proc. ICS-12, pp 441-448. July 1998.
[13] D. López, J. Llosa, M. Valero and E. Ayguadé. "Widening Resources: A Cost-effective Technique for Aggressive ILP Architectures". In Proc. MICRO-31 pp 237-246. Nov.-Dec. 1998.
[14] D. López, M. Valero, J. Llosa and E. Ayguadé. "Increasing memory bandwidth with wide buses: Compiler, hardware and performance trade-off". In Proc. ICS-11, pp 12-19. July 1997.
[15] J. Llosa, E. Ayguadé and M. Valero. "Quantitative evaluation of register pressure on software pipelined loops". In Jour. of Parallel Programming, vol. 26 n. 2 pp. 121-142. 1998
[16] J. Llosa, M. Valero and E. Ayguadé. "Heuristics for Register-Constrained Software Pipelining". In Proc. MICRO-29, pp. 250-261, Dec. 1996.
[17] J. Llosa, M. Valero, E. Ayguadé and A. González. "Hypernode Reduction Modulo Scheduling". In Proc. MICRO-28, pp 350-360, Dec. 1995.
[18] J. Llosa, M. Valero, E. Ayguadé and A. González. "Modulo Scheduling with reduced register pressure". In IEEE Trans. on Computers, vol. 47 no. 6 pp 625-638, June 1998.
[19] Microprocessor Report vol 11, no. 14. Intel HP make EPIC disclosure. October 1997.
[20] Microprocessor Report vol 12, no. 6. AltiVec vectorizes PowerPC. May 1998.
[21] Microprocessor Report vol 12, no. 12. TI aims for floating-point DSP lead. September 1998.
[22] Microprocessor Report vol 12, no. 16. MAP1000 unfolds at Equator. December 1998.
[23] B.R. Rau. "Iterative modulo scheduling: An algorithm for software pipelining loops". In Proc. MICRO-27 pp.63-74, Nov. 1994.
[24] B.R. Rau and C.D. Glaeser. "Some scheduling techniques and an easily schedulable horizontal architecture for high performance scientific computing". In Proc. 14th Ann. Microprogramming Workshop, pp. 183-197, October 1981.
[25] B.R. Rau, M. Lee, P. Tirumalai, and P Schlansker. "Register allocation for software pipelined loops". In Proc. Progr. Lang. Des. and Impl. (PLDI-92), pp. 283-299, June 1992.
[26] Semiconductor Industry Assoc. The National Technology Roadmap for Semiconductors. SIA , San Jose, California 1994.
[27] T. Watanabe. "The NEC SX-3 supercomputer system". In CompCon91 pp. 303-308, 1991
[28] S.W.White and S. Dhawan. "POWER2: Next Generation of the RISC System/6000 family". IBM Jour. Res. Develop. Vol 38 no 5, pp 493-502. September 1994.
[29] S.J.E. Wilton and N.P. Jouppi. "CACTI: An enhanced cache access and cycle time model". IEEE Jour. of Solid-State Circuits, Vol. 31 no 5, pp 677-688, May 1996.
[30] K.C. Yeager. "The MIPS R10000 superscalar microprocessor". IEEE Micro v. 16 n. 2 pp. 28-40, March 1996.

Trace-Level Reuse

Antonio González[†], Jordi Tubella[†] and Carlos Molina[‡]

[†]Dpt. d'Arquitectura de Computadors
U. Politècnica de Catalunya, Barcelona, Spain
{antonio,jordit}@ac.upc.es

[‡]Dpt. d'Enginyeria Informàtica i Matemàtiques
U. Rovira i Virgili, Tarragona, Spain
cmolina@etse.urv.es

Abstract

Trace-level reuse is based on the observation that some traces (dynamic sequences of instructions) are frequently repeated during the execution of a program, and in many cases, the instructions that make up such traces have the same source operand values. The execution of such traces will obviously produce the same outcome and thus, their execution can be skipped if the processor records the outcome of previous executions. This paper presents an analysis of the performance potential of trace-level reuse and discusses a preliminary realistic implementation. Like instruction-level reuse, trace-level reuse can improve performance by decreasing resource contention and the latency of some instructions. However, we show that trace-level reuse is more effective than instruction-level reuse because the former can avoid fetching the instructions of reused traces. This has two important benefits: it reduces the fetch bandwidth requirements, and it increases the effective instruction window size since these instructions do not occupy window entries. Moreover, trace-level reuse can compute all at once the result of a chain of dependent instructions, which may allow the processor to avoid the serialization caused by data dependences and thus, to potentially exceed the dataflow limit.

1. Introduction

Data dependences[1] are one of the most important hurdles that limit the performance of current microprocessors. The amount of instruction-level parallelism (ILP) that processors may exploit is significantly limited by the serialization caused by data dependences. This limitation is more severe for integer codes, in which data dependences are more abundant. Some studies on the ILP limits of integer applications have revealed that some of them cannot achieve more than a few tens of instructions per cycle (IPC) in an ideal processor with the sole limitation of data dependences [16]. This suggests that techniques to avoid the serialization caused by data dependences are important to boost ILP, and they will be crucial for future wide-issue microprocessors.

Two techniques have been proposed so far to avoid the serial execution of data dependent instructions: *data value speculation* and *data value reuse*. This paper focuses on the latter technique. Data value reuse is a technique that exploits the fact that many dynamic instructions or dynamic

sequences of instructions (traces) are repeatedly executed, and most of these repetitions have the same inputs, and thus generate the same results. Data value reuse exploits this fact by buffering previous inputs and their corresponding outputs. When an instruction/trace is encountered again and its current inputs are found in that buffer, its execution can be avoided by getting the outputs from the buffer. This reduces the functional units utilization and, more importantly, reduces the time to compute the results, and thus, shortens the lengths of critical paths of the execution.

Techniques that try to reuse single instructions will be referred to as *instruction-level reuse*, whereas those techniques that handle dynamic sequences of instructions will be denoted by *trace-level reuse*. Data value reuse can be exploited through software or hardware mechanisms. In this work, we explore hardware techniques for trace-level reuse. Exploiting reuse at trace-level implies that a single reuse operation can skip the execution of a potentially large number of instructions. More importantly, these instructions do not need to be fetched and thus they do not consume fetch bandwidth. Finally, since these instructions are not placed in the reorder buffer[2], they do not occupy any slot of the instruction window and thus, the effective instruction window size is increased as a side effect. Particularly interesting is the fact that this technique may compute all at once the results of a chain of dependent instructions (e.g. in a single cycle), which allows the processor to exceed the dataflow limit that is inherent in the program.

In this paper, we first propose and approach to implement trace-level reuse on a superscalar processor. Then, we analyze the performance potential of such technique under different scenarios. We also compare the benefits that may be achieved by trace-level reuse with respect to instruction-level reuse. We show that trace-level reuse is more effective than instruction-level due to the reduction in fetch bandwidth and instruction window requirements outlined above. Moreover, trace-level reuse has lower overhead since a single reuse operation can avoid the execution of a long sequence of instructions.

The rest of this paper is organized as follows. Section 2 reviews the concept of data value reuse and the most relevant work. Section 3 describes a trace-level reuse mechanism. The performance of trace-level reuse and its comparison versus instruction-level reuse are analyzed in section 4. Finally, section 5 summarizes the main conclusions of this work.

---

1. In this paper, data dependences refer to true dependences (output and anti-dependences are not included).

2. As discussed below, some instructions are placed in the reorder buffer in order to provide precise exceptions, but in general they are much less than the number of instructions in the trace.

2. Related Work

The sources of instruction repetition are investigated in [13] and a study of the differences between value prediction and value reuse is presented in [14].

Data value reuse can be implemented by software or hardware. Software implementation is usually known as *memoization* or *tabulation* [2] [11]. Memoization is a code transformation technique that takes advantage of the redundant nature of computation by trading execution time for increased memory storage. The results of frequently executed sections of code (e.g. function calls, groups of statements with limited side effects) are stored in a table. Later invocations of these sections of code are preceded by a table lookup, and in case of hit, the execution of these sections of code is avoided.

A hardware implementation of data value reuse was proposed by Harbison for the Tree Machine [5]. The Tree Machine has a stack-oriented ISA and the main novelty of its architecture was that the hardware assumed a number of compiler's traditional optimizations, like common subexpression elimination and invariant removal. This is achieved by means of a *value cache*, which stores the results of dynamic sequences of code (called *phrases*). For each phrase, the value cache keeps its result as well as an identifier of its input variables. For the sake of simplicity, input variables are represented by a bit vector (called *dependence set*), such that multiple variables share the same codification. Every time that the value of a variable changes, all the value cache entries that may have this variable as an entry are invalidated.

Another hardware implementation of data value reuse is the *result cache* proposed by Richardson [10] [11]. The objective was to speed-up some long latency operations, like multiplications, divisions and square roots, by caching the results of recently executed operations. The result cache is indexed by hashing the source operand values, and for each pair of operands it contains the operation code and the corresponding result.

Result caching is further investigated by Oberman and Flynn [9]. They evaluate *division caches*, *square root caches* and *reciprocal caches*, which are similar to Richardson's result cache, but for just one type of operation: division, square root and reciprocal respectively. They also investigate a shared cache for reciprocals and square roots.

Sodani and Sohi propose the *reuse buffer* [12], which is a hardware implementation of data value reuse (or dynamic instruction reuse, as it is called in that paper). The reuse buffer is indexed by the instruction address. They propose three different reuse schemes. In the first scheme, for each instruction in the reuse buffer, it holds the source operand values and the result of the last execution of this instruction. In the second scheme, instead of the source operand values, the buffer holds the source operand names (architectural register identifiers). In the third scheme, in addition to the information of the second scheme, the buffer stores the identifiers of the producer instructions of the source operands. In this scheme, dependent instructions that are fetched simultaneously can be reused by chaining their individual reuses. However, the reuse of each individual instruction is still a sequential process since it must wait until the reuse of all previous instructions has been checked.

Jourdan *et al.* propose a renaming scheme that exploits the phenomenon of instruction-level reuse in order to reduce the register pressure. The basic idea is that several dynamic instructions that produce the same result share the same physical register [7].

Another application of data value reuse has been presented in [17]. Weinberg and Nagel describe a technique that reuses high-level language pointer-expressions with the aid of compiler inserted hints. Basically, once the input operand set of an expression matches a previously executed instance of the same expression, the result is obtained from a table instead of recomputing it.

Molina, González and Tubella presented a reused scheme referred to as *Redundant Computation Buffer* [8]. The underlying concept is the removal of redundant computations, and in particular, the run-time elimination of quasi-common subexpressions and quasi-invariants.

Finally, Huang and Lilja have recently proposed a scheme to reuse basic blocks [6]. Basic block reuse is a particular case of trace-level reuse in which traces are limited to basic blocks. Trace-level reuse is more general and can exploit reuse in larger sequences of instructions, such as subroutines, loops, etc.

3. Trace-Level Reuse

This section describes an approach to integrating a trace-level reuse scheme in a superscalar processor.

A trace refers to any dynamic sequence of instructions. The objective of trace-level reuse is to avoid the individual execution of the instructions in a trace. All changes in the processor state that would be produced by these instructions are done by applying again the changes that were produced in a past execution of the same trace, provided that both executions have the same inputs.

Reusing traces requires the processor to include some type of memory to store previous traces, an approach to decide which traces are worthwhile to be stored, a mechanism to identify when the forthcoming trace can be reused, and a final process to update the processor state if the trace is reusable. These issues are addressed below in more detail.

3.1. The Reuse Trace Memory

The reuse trace memory (RTM) is a memory that stores previous traces that are candidate to be reused. From the point of view of reuse, a trace is identified by its input and its output (see figure 1). The input of a trace is defined by: (i) the starting address, i.e. initial program counter (PC), and (ii) the set of register identifiers and memory locations that are live, and their contents before the trace is executed. A register/memory location is live if it is read before being written.

The output of a trace consists of: (i) the set of registers and memory locations that the trace writes and their contents after the trace is executed, and (ii) the address of the next instruction to be executed after the trace.

The RTM can be indexed by different schemes. For

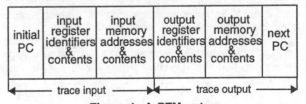

Figure 1: A RTM entry.

31

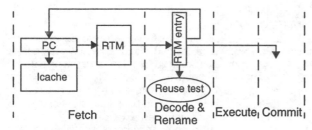

Figure 2: Reusing a trace.

instance, it can be indexed by PC (as considered in this paper), or by a hashing of the PC and the contents of a given register, etc.

3.2. Dynamic Trace Collection

The processor dynamically decides which traces of the dynamic stream are candidates to be reused. Different heuristics can be used to decide the starting and ending points of a trace. We will show later that a convenient criterion could be to start a new trace when a reusable instruction is encountered and to terminate the trace just before the first non reusable instruction is found. Another possibility that we also evaluate in this paper is to consider fixed-length traces which can be dynamically expanded once they are reused.

Note that traces may have a variable number of instructions. In fact, the instructions that make up a trace are not stored in the RTM. Obviously, there may be implementation parameters that limit the size of a trace such as the number of input and output values that can be stored in each RTM entry, but the number of instructions in a trace is not by itself a limitation.

3.3. Reuse Test and Processor State Update

At some points of the execution (e.g. at the fetch of the initial trace instruction, or whenever an input trace operand becomes ready) the processor checks whether the current trace can be reused. If this is the case, then the processor uses the information of the trace obtained from the RTM to update its state in the following way (see figure 2): (i) the PC is updated with the *next PC* field so that the fetch unit proceeds with the instructions that follow the trace. Instructions that belong to the trace do not need to be fetched; (ii) the output registers and output memory locations are updated with the values obtained from the RTM entry.

There are basically two approaches to identify whether a trace is reusable. One possibility is to read the current values of all input registers and memory locations and compare them with the values in any RTM entry associated to the current PC. Another possibility is to add to each RTM entry a valid bit. When a trace is stored its valid bit is set. For every register/memory write, all the RTM entries with a matching register/memory location in its input list are invalidated. The latter approach requires a much simpler reuse test (just checking the valid bit).

The final reuse process that updates the processor state can be implemented by inserting in the instruction window instructions that write the corresponding values in the trace output (registers and memory) locations. In this way, precise exceptions could be guaranteed in an out-of-order processor following the conventional mechanism.

4. The Performance Potential of Reuse at Instruction and Trace Levels

In this work, we are interested in studying the data value reuse phenomenon, understanding the differences between trace-level reuse and instruction-level reuse and investigating the performance potential of these techniques.

We focus on scenarios with a limited instruction window but infinite number of functional units. In this way, we do not consider the benefit of reducing functional unit contention, which due to the continuous increase in transistors per chip will have a low impact in future high-performance processors. Moreover, when the number of functional units is a bottleneck, increasing the number of functional units is more cost-effective than implementing a reuse scheme. We also consider the case of an infinite instruction window as an indication of the limits of the potential of these techniques.

For the infinite window scenario, the execution time is only limited by data dependences among instructions, both through register and memory. For the limited window scenario, the execution order inside each sequence of W instructions, W being the instruction window size, is only limited by data dependences, whereas any pair of instructions at a distance greater than W must be sequentially executed.

We compute the IPC for each different scenario as an extension of the approach proposed in [1]. The IPC for an infinite window machine is computed by analyzing the dynamic instruction stream. For each instruction, its completion time is determined as the maximum of the completion time of the producers of all its inputs plus its latency. The inputs of an instruction may be register or memory operands. Therefore, for each logical register and each memory location, the completion time of the latest instruction that has updated such storage location so far is kept in a table. The latency of the instructions has been borrowed from the latency of the Alpha 21164 instructions [3]. Once all the dynamic instruction stream has been processed, the IPC is computed as the quotient between the number of dynamic instructions and the maximum completion time of any instruction.

The process of computing the IPC for the limited instruction window scenario is an extension of the unlimited window approach. The extension consists of computing the graduation time of each instruction as the maximum completion time of any previous instruction, including itself. Then, the completion time of a given instruction is computed as the maximum among the completion time of all the producers of its inputs and the graduation time of the instruction W locations above in the trace, plus the latency of the instruction. Note that only the graduation time of the latest W instructions must be tracked.

For the performance analysis of data value reuse, we first consider a reuse engine with infinite tables to keep history of previous instructions/traces and we analyze the effect of different reuse latencies. The reuse latency corresponds to the time that a reuse operation takes. It usually involves a table lookup and some comparisons. In the last part of this section, we measure the amount of trace-level reusability when finite reuse tables are considered. In this case, different reuse trace memory sizes and dynamic trace collection heuristics are considered. The reuse test is based on an associative search of the traces that start at the same PC.

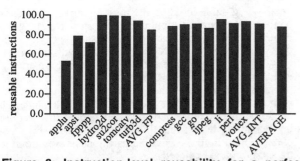

Figure 3: Instruction-level reusability for a perfect engine.

4.1. Benchmarks

The benchmark programs are a subset of the SPEC95 benchmark suite, composed of both integer and FP codes: *compress, gcc, go, ijpeg, li, perl* and *vortex* from the integer suite, and *applu, apsi, fpppp, hydro2d, su2cor, tomcatv* and *turb3d* from the FP suite.

The programs have been compiled with the DEC C and Fortran compilers with full optimization ("-non_shared -O5 -tune ev5 -migrate -ifo" for C codes and "-non_shared -O5 -tune ev5" for Fortran codes). Each program is run using the reference input for 50 millions of instructions after skipping the first 25 millions. The study of the maximum degree of reusability requires to store a huge amount of data, which prevents from analyzing the whole program execution. In this way, the results give a flavor of the overall behavior of the SPEC95 suite.

The compiled programs have been instrumented with the Atom tool [15] and their dynamic trace has been processed in order to obtain the IPC for each configuration. Results are shown for individual programs, and in some cases we show the average for integer programs, FP programs or the whole set of benchmarks. Average speed-ups have been computed through harmonic means and average percentages have been determined through arithmetic means.

4.2. Limits of Instruction-Level Reusability

This section is focused on measuring the potential of data value reuse at instruction-level. Hence, we consider here the maximum instruction-level reuse that can be exploited.

For each static instruction, all the different input values of its previous executed instances are stored in a table. For a given dynamic instruction, if its current inputs are the same as in a previous execution, the instruction is reusable. The percentage of reusable instructions will be referred to as the *instruction-level reusability* of a program. Note that the reusability of a program takes into account any kind of instructions, including memory accesses.

We can observe in figure 3 that instruction-level reusability is very high. For most programs it is higher than 90% of all dynamic instructions and on average it is 88%. The reusability ranges from 53% to 99%, *applu* and *hydro2d* being the programs with the lowest and highest reusability respectively. We can also observe that there are not high differences between integer and FP codes (91% and 85% of instruction-level reusability respectively). We can conclude that instruction-level reuse is abundant in all types of programs.

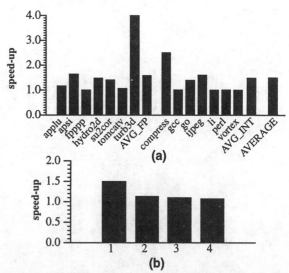

Figure 4: Speed-up of instruction-level reuse for an infinite instruction window and: (a) a 1-cycle reuse latency, (b) a reuse latency varying from 1 to 4

4.3. Performance Improvement of Instruction-Level Reuse

The ultimate figure in which we are interested is the effect of instruction-level reuse on execution time. For this scenario, the IPC is computed by extending the mechanism described for an unlimited or limited window configuration respectively. The completion time of a non-reusable instruction is computed in the same way as in the base machine, whereas the completion time of a reusable instruction is computed as the maximum of the completion time of all the producers of its inputs (an instruction cannot be reused until all its inputs are available) plus a *reuse latency*. In any case, if the completion time of a reused instruction is higher than the completion time of the normal execution of that instruction, the latter will be chosen. This is equivalent to assuming that an oracle determines the best approach for each instruction.

Figure 4.a shows the speed-up provided by instruction-level reuse when the reuse latency is assumed to be 1 cycle. Note that the speed-ups are very dependent on the particular benchmark. On average, it is around 1.50, and it is slightly higher for FP than for integer programs. However, there are some programs that can significantly benefit from instruction-level reuse, such as *turb3d* and *compress*, which show a speed-up of 4.00 and 2.50 respectively. On the other hand there are also programs that hardly benefit from instruction-level reuse, such as *fpppp* and *gcc*. In general, this performance result may look low if one takes into account the very high percentage of reusable instructions (figure 3).

Figure 4.b shows the effect of the reuse latency on performance, for a latency varying from 1 to 4 cycles per reuse (only averages are shown). Note that the benefits of instruction-level reuse significantly decrease when more than a 1-cycle latency is assumed. This indicates that the instructions that are in the critical path are usually low-latency instructions, and thus, the latency reduction achieved by instruction reuse is effective only if the reuse latency is very low. For a configuration with a limited number of functional units the benefits will be a bit higher due to the reduction in

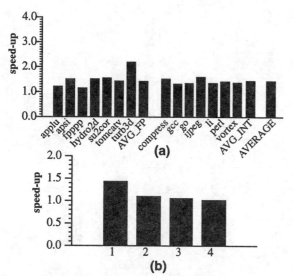

Figure 5: Speed-up of instruction-level reuse for a 256-entry instruction window and: (a) a 1-cycle reuse latency, (b) a reuse latency varying from 1 to 4 cycles.

functional unit contention. However, as pointed out above, adding functional units is a more cost-effective approach to reduce contention than including a reuse scheme since the latter solution is significantly more complex.

Instruction-level reuse in the case of a limited instruction window (256 entries) behaves almost in the same way as in the case of an unlimited instruction window. This is shown in figure 5.a that shows the speed-up for a 1-cycle reuse latency. On average the speed-up is 1.43, with minor difference between integer and FP codes (1.44 and 1.42 respectively). Differences among individual programs are smaller than those observed for an infinite window. The benefits for those programs that had the highest speed-ups for an unlimited instruction window (*turb3d* and *compress*) are now reduced. Finally, in figure 5.b it is shown that the benefits of instruction-level reuse when the reuse latency is greater than 1 cycle is also significantly reduced, like in the infinite window configuration (see figure 4.b).

To summarize, the benefits of instruction-level reuse are moderate for a 1-cycle reuse latency and very low for higher latencies, in spite of the fact that the percentage of reusable instructions is very high. The reason for this is that instruction reuse cannot be exploited until the source operands are ready and thus, the reuse of a chain of dependent instructions is still a sequential process.

4.4. Limits of Trace-Level Reusability

Reuse of traces is an attractive technique since a single reuse operation may skip the execution of a potentially long sequence of dynamic instructions, even if they are dependent among them. To evaluate the performance limits of this technique we should compute the maximum reuse that can be attained for any possible partition of the dynamic instruction stream into traces. Since there is not any constraint about the contents of each trace, the different ways to partition a dynamic instruction stream into traces are practically unlimited, which prevents an exhaustive exploration of all of them.

Given that each reuse operation has an associated

latency (e.g. table lookup), the most effective schemes will be those that reuse maximum length traces. That is, given a dynamic instruction stream that corresponds to the execution of a program, we are interested in identifying a set of reusable traces such that: a) the total number of instructions included in those traces is maximum and b) the number of traces is minimum. In other words, if a trace is reusable, it is more effective to reuse the whole trace in a single reuse operation than to reuse parts of it separately. However, finding maximum length reusable traces would be still a complex problem if all the possible partitions of a program into traces should be explored.

We can however prove that if we consider just those traces that are formed by all maximum-length dynamic sequences of reusable instructions, we have an upper-bound of the reusability that can be exploited by maximum-length traces (condition (a) above) and a lower bound of the number of traces required to exploit it (condition (b) above). This is supported by the theorems below. The performance provided by assuming that such traces are reusable will provide an upper-bound of the performance limits of trace reuse.

Theorem 1. Let T be a trace composed of the sequence of dynamic instructions $<i_1, i_2, ..., i_n>$. If T is reusable, then i_k is reusable for every $k \in [1,n]$.

Proof. Refer to the enclosed appendix in page 8.

Theorem 2. Let T be a trace composed of the sequence of dynamic instructions $<i_1, i_2, ..., i_n>$. If i_k is reusable for every $k \in [1,n]$, then T is not necessarily reusable.

Proof. Refer to the enclosed appendix in page 8.

Theorem 1 implies that the number of instructions whose execution can be avoided by any trace reuse scheme is limited by the amount of individual instructions that are reusable. Thus, we can compute an upper-bound of the benefits of trace-level reuse by assuming that the amount of trace-level reusability is equal to the amount of instruction-level reusability, and the overhead of trace-level reuse is given by grouping reusable instructions into the minimum number of traces (i.e. assuming maximum-length traces). Theorem 2 states that this approach results in an upper-bound that may not be reached.

4.5. Performance Improvement of Trace-Level Reuse

The process to compute the IPC for this scenario is the following. The completion time of every instruction that do not belong to a reusable trace is computed in the same way as in the base machine. For a reusable trace, the completion time of all instructions that produce an output is computed as the maximum of the completion time of all the producers of its inputs plus the *reuse latency*. Moreover, two ways to consider the reuse latency have been analyzed. In one of them, the reuse latency is assumed to be a constant time per reuse operation. In the other, the reuse latency is assumed to be proportional to the number of inputs plus the number of outputs of the trace. Note that the former is more appropriate when the reuse test just requires to check a valid bit, whereas the latter models the fact that reusing a trace requires the processor to read all its inputs and check that they are the same as in a previous execution. In any case, if the completion time of an instruction in a reusable trace is higher than the completion time of the normal execution of that instruction, the latter will be chosen.

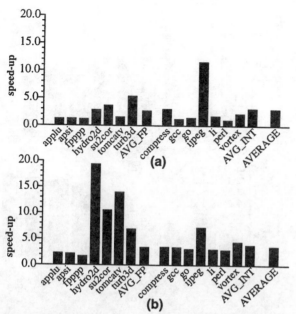

(a)

(b)

Figure 6: Speed-up of trace-level reuse when considering a 1-cycle reuse latency for a) an infinite instruction window, b) a 256-entry instruction window.

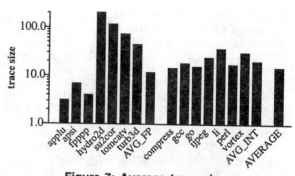

Figure 7: Average trace size.

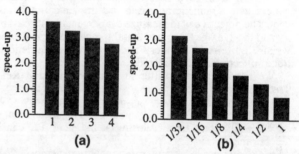

(a)

(b)

Figure 8: Speed-up of trace-level reuse for a 256-entry instruction window and a reuse latency that a) varies from 1 to 4 cycles, b) is proportional to the number of inputs plus outputs of the trace.

Performance figures of trace-level reuse are shown in figure 6. Figure 6.a corresponds to an infinite window scenario while figure 6.b is associated to a 256-entry instruction window. In both cases, a 1-cycle reuse latency has been considered. First of all, note that the average speed-up is much higher than the obtained for instruction-level reuse.

For the infinite window scenario, speed-up has increased from 1.43 to 3.03. The highest benefit is experienced by *ijpeg* (11.57). Nonetheless, there are also programs with a negligible speed-up in this scenario (*perl* with 1.01).

The difference between trace-level and instruction-level reuse is even higher for the limited window scenario. In this case, trace-level reuse may provide a very important additional advantage: it may avoid fetching instructions in reused traces and may increase the effective instruction window. If a trace is determined to be reusable (using any of the approaches described in section 3.3), the whole trace can be reused without fetching nor executing the remaining instructions of the trace. As a consequence, the speed-up of trace-level reuse for a limited instruction window is even higher than for an unlimited window (3.63 vs. 3.03), whereas for instruction-level reuse we observed the opposite trend.

It is also interesting to observe figure 7, which shows the average trace size, and correlate it with figure 6.b. Note that in general, larger traces imply higher speed-ups, which can be attributed to their higher potential to artificially increase the effective instruction window size. Integer programs have a quite uniform trace size, ranging from 14.5 to 36.7 instructions, and they also exhibit a quite homogeneous speed-up. On the other hand, some FP programs have very short traces, such as *applu*, *apsi* and *fpppp*, and they exhibit very low speed-up, whereas the others have large traces (up to 203 instructions for *hydro2d*) and they also have higher speed-ups.

It is also remarkable the fact that trace-level reuse, unlike instruction-level reuse, provides significant speed-ups even if the reuse latency is higher than 1. This is shown in figure 8.a, where it can be observed that the average speed-up for a reuse latency ranging from 1 to 4 cycles is not much degraded.

Note that a trace is reused provided that all input values are the same as in a previous execution. Therefore, a trace reuse operation may imply a check of as many values as inputs the trace has. Moreover, as a consequence of a trace reuse, all the output values of the trace must be updated. Hence, it may be more realistic to assume that the reuse latency is proportional to the number of input and output values. That is, it is equal to a constant K multiplied by the number of input/output values. K is the inverse of the read/write bandwidth of the reuse engine; for instance, $K=1/16$ implies that the reuse engine can read or write 16 values per cycle. Under this scenario, the speed-up of trace-level reuse is shown in figure 8.b, where the X axis represents different values of K. It can be observed that the speed-up of value reuse is still high, although it is significantly affected by the reuse latency. Note that it is reasonable to assume that future microprocessors may have the capability to perform around 16 reads+writes per cycle, including register and memory values. In fact, current microprocessors such as the Alpha 21264 [4] can perform 14 reads+writes per cycle (8 register reads, 4 register writes and 2 memory references). Thus, looking at the bar corresponding to $K=1/16$ in figure 8.b, we can conclude that a speed-up around 2.7 is reasonable to be expected from trace-level reuse. This also suggests that even the slowest approach to checking reusability that is based on comparing all inputs (see section 3.3) can significantly improve performance.

On average, we have measured that the number of input values per trace is 6.5 (2.7 register values and 3.8 memory values), and the number of output values is 5.0 (3.3 register values and 1.7 memory values). Since the average number of instructions per trace is 15.0, this means that each reused instruction requires 0.43 reads and 0.33 writes, which is significantly lower than the number of reads and writes required by the execution of an instruction. We can thus conclude that trace-level reuse also provides a significant reduction in the data bandwidth requirements, and thereby it can reduce the pressure on the memory and register file ports.

4.6. Trace-Level Reusability with Finite Tables

In the previous section we have demonstrated the high potential of trace-level reuse. In the final part of this work we evaluate a realistic approach that implements this concept. The objective is to measure the percentage of reusability and the average trace size that this technique can provide when a finite reuse memory and a particular heuristic for trace collection are considered.

We have evaluated different capacities for the Reuse Trace Memory (RTM):
- 512 entries: A 4-way set-associative memory (5-bit index) with 4 entries per initial PC. This means that up to 4 different traces starting at the same PC can be stored.
- 4K entries: A 4-way set-associative memory (7-bit index) with 8 entries per initial PC.
- 32K entries: A 8-way set-associative memory (8-bit index) with 16 entries per initial PC.
- 256K entries: A 8-way set-associative memory (11-bit index) with 16 entries per initial PC.

In all cases, the memory is indexed by the least-significant bits of the PC register. Replacement policy is LRU, that is, the older trace with the same PC that has been reused is the one that is being replaced when a new trace is collected. For each trace, the number of inputs and outputs have been limited to 8 registers and 4 memory values.

Three different heuristics for dynamic trace collection have been considered:
- ILR NE: A trace consists of a sequence of dynamic instructions that are reusable at instruction-level. In this case, a different reuse memory used for testing instruction-level reusability is also needed. This memory has as many entries as the RTM.
- ILR EXP: The same as before with the difference that traces can be dynamically expanded when two consecutive traces are reused or instructions following a reused trace become reusable.
- I(n) EXP: A trace is formed by a fixed number of n instructions. When a trace is reused, it is expanded with n new instructions.

The reuse test is performed for every fetch operation. When a trace beginning at a given PC contains the same values in its input locations as the current ones, the trace is reusable. Figure 9 shows the percentage of reusable instructions and the average trace size for each scheme. First, we can observe that dynamic trace expansion is an important issue to increase the granularity of reusable traces while the total amount of reusability remains almost constant (see heuristics ILR NE and ILR EXP). Note also that heuristic I(n) outperforms ILR, that is, a policy to collect traces should consider any kind of instructions rather than those reusable at instruction level.

Another important figure is the relation between the

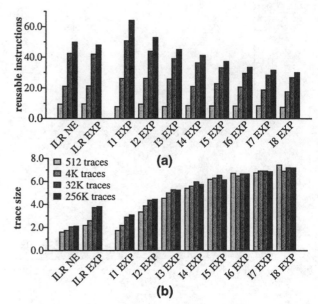

Figure 9: Trace-level reusability with a realistic implementation. a) Percentage of reusable instructions. b) Average trace size.

RTM size and the achieved reusability. For instance, a 4K-entry RTM can reuse 25% of the dynamic instructions with an average trace size of 6 instructions. The percentage of reused instructions significantly grows with the RTM capacity. Finally, note the trade-off between percentage of reused instructions and trace size. Increasing the trace size reduces the number of reused instructions. However, to achieve a given degree of reuse, the reuse overhead is reduced when the trace size increases.

5. Conclusions

We have presented a trace-level reuse mechanism and analyzed its performance. We have shown that trace-level reuse can reuse a lower percentage of instructions than instruction-level reuse. However, the former is more effective because of several reasons: a) it reduces the fetch bandwidth requirement by avoiding fetching instructions of reused traces; b) it increases the effective instruction window size by avoiding storing instructions of reused traces in the instruction window; c) it has a lower overhead since it requires a lower number of operations per reused instruction.

For a 256-entry instruction window and infinite history tables, trace-level reuse provides a speed-up of 3.6 in average, which ranges from 1.7 to 19.4 for individual programs, when the reuse latency is 1 cycle. Similar results are obtained when the reuse latency is considered proportional to the number of inputs and outputs of a trace.

Finally, we have evaluated the impact of a limited-capacity history table. For instance, for a 4K-entry Reuse Trace Memory we have observed that the percentage of reusability is around 25% of all dynamic instructions while the average trace size is around 6 instructions. For a 256K-entry Reuse Trace Memory, around 60% of instructions can be reused.

Acknowledgements

This work has been supported by grants CICYT TIC 511/98 and ESPRIT 24942. The research described in this paper has been developed using the resources of the European Center for Parallelism of Barcelona (CEPBA).

References

[1]   T.M. Austin and G.S. Sohi, "Dynamic Dependence Analysis of Ordinary Programs", in *Proc. of Int. Symp. on Computer Architecture*, pp. 342-351, 1992

[2]   H. Abelson and G.J. Sussman, *Structure and Interpretation of Computer Programs*, McGraw Hill, New York, 1985

[3]   Digital Equipment Corporation, *Alpha 21164 Microprocessor. Hardware Reference Manual.* 1995

[4]   L. Gwennap, "Digital 21264 Sets New Standard", *Microprocessor Report*, vol. 10, no. 14, Oct. 1996.

[5]   S.H. Harbison, "An Architectural Alternative to Optimizing Compilers", in *Proc. of Int. Conf. on Architectural Support for Programming Languages and Operating Systems*, 1982

[6]   J. Huang and D. Lilja, "Exploiting Basic Block Value Locality with Block Reuse", in *Proc. of 5th. Int. Symp. on High-Performance Computer Architecture*, 1999

[7]   S. Jourdan, R. Ronen, M. Kekerman, B. Shormar and A. Yoaz, "A Novel Renaming Scheme to Exploit Value Temporal Locality through Physical Register Reuse and Unification" in *Proc. of 31st. Ann. Int. Symp. on Microarchitecture*, 1998

[8]   C. Molina, A. González and J. Tubella, "Dynamic Removal of Redundant Computations" in *Proc. of the ACM Int. Conf. on Supercomputing*, Rhodes (Greece), June 1999

[9]   S.F. Oberman and M.J. Flynn, "On Division and Reciprocal Caches", Technical Report CSL-TR-95-666, Stanford University, 1995

[10]   S. E. Richardson, "Exploiting Trivial and Redundant Computations", in *Proc. of Symp. on Computer Arithmetic*, pp. 220-227, 1993

[11]   S. E. Richardson, "Caching Function Results: Faster Arithmetic by Avoiding Unnecessary Computation", Technical Report SMLI TR-92-1, Sun Microsystems Laboratories, 1992

[12]   A. Sodani and G.S. Sohi, "Dynamic Instruction Reuse", in *Proc. of Int. Symp. on Computer Architecture*, 1997

[13]   A. Sodani and G.S. Sohi, "An Empirical Analysis of Instruction Repetition" in *Proc. of Int. Conf. on Architectural Support for Programming Languages and Operating Systems*, 1998

[14]   A. Sodani and G.S. Sohi, "Understanding the Differences Between Value Prediction and Instruction Reuse", in *Proc. of 31st. Ann. Int. Symp. on Microarchitecture*, 1998

[15]   A. Srivastava and A. Eustace, "ATOM: A system for building customized program analysis tools" , in *Proc of the 1994 Conf. on Programming Languages Design and Implementation*, 1994.

[16]   D.W. Wall, "Limits of Instruction-Level Parallelism", Technical Report WRL 93/6, Digital Western Research Laboratory, 1993.

[17]   N. Weinberg and D. Nagle, "Dynamic Elimination of Pointer-Expressions", in *Proc. Int. Conf. on Parallel Architectures and Compilation Techniques*, pp. 142-147, 1998.

A. Appendix

In this appendix we present the proof of theorems 1 and 2. In fact, we will prove a more general formulation of theorem 1 and 2, in which, a trace is considered to be a sequence of consecutive traces of a smaller size. Theorem 1 and 2 are the particular case in which the size of every smaller trace is one instruction.

Definitions. An *input* of a trace T is a register, condition code or memory location that is read and has not been written before in such trace. An *output* of a trace T is a register, condition code or memory location that is written in such trace. Let $IL(T)$ be the sequence of *input* storage locations of trace T. Notice that $IL(T)$ is a sequence and not a set. The order of the sequence is given by the order in which the inputs are read. Let $OL(T)$ be the sequence of *output* storage locations of trace T. The order of the sequence is given by the order in which the outputs are written. Let $IV(T)$ be the sequence of *input* values of trace T, in the order in which they are read. Let $OV(T)$ be the sequence of *output* values of trace T, in the order in which they are written.

If A and B are two sequences, we will say that $A \subseteq B$ if A is a subsequence of B. Moreover, $A \cup B$ will refer to any sequence that is composed of the elements of A and B, no matter the order of the elements. Different dynamic instances of the same trace will be denoted by using the same symbol to refer to the trace, with a superscript that corresponds to the dynamic execution order. Notice that different instances of the same trace will always have the same input/output registers but may have different input/output memory locations.

If a trace T is reusable, it must happen that $IL(T^i) = IL(T^j)$ and $IV(T^i) = IV(T^j)$ for some $j < i$. This obviously implies that $OL(T^i) = OL(T^j)$ and $OV(T^i) = OV(T^j)$. That is, if the inputs are the same and have the same value, then the outputs will also be the same and will have the same values.

Theorem 3 (generalization of theorem 1). Let T be a trace composed of a sequence of traces $<t_1, t_2, ..., t_n>$. If T is reusable, then t_k is reusable for every $k \in [1,n]$.

Proof. If T^i is reusable, then $IL(T^i) = IL(T^j)$ and $IV(T^i) = IV(T^j)$ for some $j < i$. Notice that $IL(t_1^i) \subseteq IL(T^i) = IL(T^j)$, which implies that $IL(t_1^i) = IL(t_1^j)$ and $IV(t_1^i) = IV(t_1^j)$. Therefore, $OL(t_1^i) = OL(t_1^j)$ and $OV(t_1^i) = OV(t_1^j)$. Thus, t_1 is reusable.

Notice that $IL(t_2^i) \subseteq IL(T^i) \cup OL(t_1^i) = IL(T^j) \cup OL(t_1^j)$. Since $IL(t_2^i) \subseteq IL(T^j) \cup OL(t_1^j)$ and $OV(t_1^i) = OV(t_1^j)$, we have that $IL(t_2^i) = IL(t_2^j)$ and $IV(t_2^i) = IV(t_2^j)$. Thus, t_2 is reusable, that is, $OL(t_2^i) = OL(t_2^j)$ and $OV(t_2^i) = OV(t_2^j)$.

In general, we can prove that t_{k+1} is reusable provided that t_i is reusable for any $i=1..k$. Notice that $IL(t_{k+1}^i) \subseteq IL(T^i) \cup OL(t_k^i) \cup OL(t_{k-1}^i) \cup ... \cup OL(t_1^i) = IL(T^j) \cup OL(t_k^j) \cup OL(t_{k-1}^j) \cup ... \cup OL(t_1^j)$. Thus, $IL(t_{k+1}^i) = IL(t_{k+1}^j)$ and $IV(t_{k+1}^i) = IV(t_{k+1}^j)$, which means that t_{k+1} is reusable.

Theorem 4 (generalization of theorem 2). Let T be a trace composed of the sequence of traces $<t_1, t_2, ..., t_n>$. If t_k is reusable for every $k \in [1,n]$, then T is not necessarily reusable.

Proof. If $t_1^i, t_2^i, ..., t_n^i$ are reusable, then each of them have their inputs equal to those of some previous execution. That is, $IV(t_1^i) = IV(t_1^{j1})$, $IV(t_2^i) = IV(t_2^{j2})$, ..., $IV(t_n^i) = IV(t_n^{jn})$, but $j1, j2, ..., jn$ may be different. Therefore, $IV(T^i) \subseteq IV(t_1^i) \cup IV(t_2^i) \cup ... \cup IV(t_n^i) = IV(t_1^{j1}) \cup IV(t_2^{j2}) \cup ... \cup IV(t_n^{jn})$, but $IV(T^i)$ may be different from $IV(T^j)$ for every $j < i$, and thus, T^i may be non-reusable.

Session C1

Graph Model for Networks

Chair: Qian-Ping Gu
University of Aizu, Japan

Correction Networks*

Marcin Kik [†]   Mirosław Kutyłowski [‡†]   Marek Piotrów [†]

[†]*Institute of Computer Science, Wrocław University, Poland*
[‡]*Department of Mathematics and Computer Science, Poznań University, Poland*
{*kik,mirekk,mpi*} @*tcs.uni.wroc.pl*

Abstract

We consider the problem of sorting sequences obtained from a sorted sequence of n keys by changing the values of at most k keys at some unknown positions. Since even for $k = 1$ a lower bound $\Omega(\log n)$ on the number of parallel comparison steps applies, any comparator network solving this problem cannot be asymptotically faster than the AKS sorting network. We design a comparator network which sorts the sequences considered for a large range of k's, has a simple architecture *and achieves a runtime $c \cdot \log n$, for a* small constant c. *We present such networks of depth $4 \log n + O(\log^2 k \log \log n)$ with a small constant hidden behind the big "Oh". In particular, for $k = o(2^{\sqrt{\log n / \log \log n}})$ the networks are of depth $4 \log n + o(\log n)$.*

1. Introduction

Sorting is one of the most fundamental problems considered in computer science. Despite research lasting over decades, substantial improvements are still reported. Due to new application areas, such as packet handling in communication networks, it is necessary to design methods designed for specific practical settings. Particularly interesting are methods falling into category of parallel processing, especially those to be performed by hardware.

We consider the problem of sorting strings of n keys obtained from sorted strings by changing at most k keys at unknown positions – we call such sequences *k-disturbed*. Thus we would like to reorder some dynamic data which is kept in a sorted string, but may be changed at random. This is a typical situation in many application areas. Since there is no satisfactory dynamic solution, a typical approach is to reorder the data completely after some period of time.

If the changes are made explicitly and the keys are stored in a data structure such as dictionary, there are many methods to cope with this problem, even in a parallel setting. We may delete a key that has been changed and reinsert it into the dictionary (for a starting point for an overview see [3]). These methods, however, fall into a category of "software" solutions.

In this paper we consider algorithms working on comparator networks. This is a simple setting that can be easily implemented in VLSI circuits. Since the lower bound $\log n$[1] applies even for $k = 1$, we are interested in solutions that are of depth $O(\log n)$ for small constants hidden by the big "Oh". Theoretically, we can sort n keys in time $O(\log n)$ [1], however the constants hidden behind the big "Oh" are so large that the method of choice for a practical use are Batcher networks [2] of depth $\Omega(\log^2 n)$. For 1-disturbed strings, Schimmler and Starke [11] present an elegant network of depth $2 \log n - 1$. For higher values of k, we may pipeline their networks, but this yields solutions of depth higher than the depth of the networks we propose.

Some widely known sorting networks have certain features that makes them relatively efficient in sorting k-disturbed strings. For instance, the Shearsort algorithm [10] designed for mesh architecture can be adopted to handle this case: the sorting time is reduced to $O((\sqrt{n} + k) \log k)$ from $O(\sqrt{n} \log n)$. Other promising direction of research in this area is to make use of periodic networks, especially of a small period (see [5] for fast sorting networks of a constant period). Since the steps of the algorithm repeat periodically, there is a chance that these networks may perform well in a dynamic systems, where some number of keys are changed at every moment.

Some related issues are considered for sorting on faulty comparator networks. A common strategy in this case is to consider a sorting network combined with some correcting network that puts misplaced items into the right places (these misplacements result from the faults in the network). However, the sorting and correcting parts cannot be separated, since we do not know where the faults occur – in particular, they may take place in the "correcting part" of the network. In this context, Piotrów [8] presented a depth-

---

*partially supported by Komitet Badań Nauk., grant 8 T11C 032 15

[1]In this paper all the logarithms are taken base 2.

optimal, k-fault tolerant correction network that corrects k items in time $O(\log n + k)$ (see also [7]).

In this paper we improve the result of Schimmler and Starke [11]. For different ranges of k, we give two constructions, each of depth $O(\log n + \log^2 k \log\log n)$:

Theorem 1.1 *Let n and k be arbitrary positive integers such that $k \leq n$. Then there is an explicit construction of a comparator network of depth $4\log n + O(\log^2 k \log\log n)$ that sorts any k-disturbed input sequence.*

Note for $k = o\left(2\sqrt{\log n / \log\log n}\right)$, the depth of the network is $4\log n + o(\log n)$.

2. Preliminaries

A comparator network may be described as a set of registers $V = \{R_1, \ldots, R_n\}$, where each register may hold exactly one key. The input is stored in the registers, the ith input key in register R_i. The output is the sequence of keys stored in the registers $R_1, \ldots, R_n$. The registers are connected by comparators. A comparator (R_i, R_j) between registers R_i and R_j, $i < j$, compares the keys stored currently in R_i and R_j, moves the bigger key to R_j and the smaller one into R_i (thus, we consider only *standard* networks, another variant would be to move the bigger key into the register with the smaller index). In a comparator network, the comparators are grouped into *layers* so that within one layer no register is an endpoint of more than one comparator. The layers of the network are applied consecutively; the number of layers, called *depth* of the network, describes parallel sorting time. Usually, we represent a comparator network by listing its layers: $(L_1, L_2, \ldots, L_d)$. Often we precede this list by the number of registers and the network depth, that is, an n-register network of depth d is denoted by $(n, d, (L_1, L_2, \ldots, L_d))$. If s denotes a sequence stored in registers $R_1, \ldots, R_n$ immediately before applying layer L, then $L(s)$ denotes the string stored in the registers after applying L.

By a 0-1-sequence we mean a sequence consisting of zeroes and ones. We may confine ourselves to 0-1-sequences, since the well known 0-1 Principle [6] can be easily re-proved for k-disturbed sequences:

Lemma 2.1 *A comparator network N sorts all k-disturbed sequences if and only if N sorts all k-disturbed 0-1-sequences.*

Let us note another simple property:

Lemma 2.2 *For any k-disturbed 0-1-sequence s of length n consisting of x zeroes and $n - x$ ones:*

- *there are at most k ones on positions 1 through x, and*

- *there are at most k zeroes on positions $x + 1$ through n.*

Let s be a 0-1 sequence of length n and x zeroes given as the input of the comparator network. We call the first x registers a *zero area*, and the remaining registers a *one area*. We call all the ones that are out of the one area and all the zeroes that out of the zero area *displaced* elements. Note that Lemma 2.2 says that any k-disturbed 0-1-sequence has at most k displaced ones and at most k displaced zeroes.

3. Auxiliary networks

In this section we present some basic constructions used in the rest of the paper.

Networks I_n^1 and I_n^0 For any $n = 2^m$, it is easy to construct a network I_n^1 of depth $2m - 1$ that sorts any 0-1 sequence obtained from some sorted 0-1 sequence by replacing one 0 by a 1. Its definition is recursive: $I_2^1 = (2, 1, (\{(R_1, R_2)\}))$. For $n = 2^m$, $m \geq 1$, if $I_n^1 = (n, 2m - 1, (L_1, L_2, \ldots, L_{2m-1}))$, then we $I_{2n}^1 = (2n, 2m + 1, (L_1', L_2', \ldots, L_{2m+1}'))$ where:

- $L_1' = \{(R_{2i}, R_{2i+1}) \mid 1 \leq i \leq n - 1\}$,

- $L_{2m+1}' = \{(R_{2i-1}, R_{2i}) \mid 1 \leq i \leq n\}$,

- $L_t' = \{(R_{2i-1}, R_{2j-1}) \mid (R_i, R_j) \in L_{t-1}\}$ for $t \in [2, 2m]$

So for $2 \leq j \leq 2m$, all comparators in the layers L_j' are incident to odd numbered registers only and the network I_{2n}^1 without the first and the last layers and even registers is isomorphic to I_n^1. So, by a simple induction we get:

Lemma 3.1 *Let $k \leq n$. Let w be a 0-1 input sequence such that on the first k positions there is exactly one 1. Then network I_n^1 applied to w outputs a sequence with no 1 on positions 1 through $k - 1$.*

Lemma 3.1 shows that I_n^1 sorts an input obtained by changing a zero into a one in a sorted 0-1 sequence. Let I_n^0 be a network dual to I_n^1, i.e. $I_n^0 = (n, 2m - 1, (L_1', \ldots, L_{2m-1}'))$ with $L_t' = \{(R_i, R_j) \mid (R_{n-j+1}, R_{n-i+1}) \in L_t\}$, where L_t denotes layer t of I_n^1.

The above simple construction is a basis of a (quite tricky) network S_n of Schimmler and Starke [11]. The network S_n is a standard comparator network of depth $2\lceil \log n \rceil - 1$ that sorts any 0-1 sequence containing one displaced one and one displaced zero (so it replaces I_n^0 and I_n^1 but needs no more layers than any of them).

Bucketing S_n Given a network $M = (n, d, L)$, we define the *k-merge version of M* as the network $M_k' = (kn, c_k d, L')$, where c_k is the depth of the Batcher merging network [2, 6] for two sequences of length k, each register R_i from M is

41

replaced in M_k' by a group of k registers $R_{(i-1)k+1}, \ldots, R_{ik}$, called *bucket* i of M_k', and each comparator (i,j) from the layer L_t of M is replaced by the Batcher merging network for buckets i and j.

For $n, k \in \mathbb{N}$, we define the network $S_{n,k} = (nk, d_k + c_k(2\lceil \log n \rceil - 1), L)$ (where d_k is depth of the Batcher sorting network for k elements) as follows:

- The first d_k layers of $S_{n,k}$ sort each of its buckets of size k using Batcher's algorithm.

- The remaining layers form the k-merge version of S_n

Theorem 3.1 $S_{n,k}$ *sorts any k-disturbed sequence of length nk.*

Theorem 3.1 seems to follow directly from the correcting properties of S_n. The idea is that each bucket contains enough place to store all displaced ones (zeroes), so they cannot block themselves while going to the final destinations. This seems to be a correct argument, but there is a gap in it. The problem is that in $S_{n,k}$ the displaced elements need not to follow the same routes between the buckets as between the registers in S_n. May be, they make some shortcuts. This seems to make no harm (and even accelerate sorting). In general this intuition is wrong. Perhaps the most spectacular known case of this phenomenon is two-dimensional Bubble Sort on a mesh. Its runtime reduces dramatically, if we remove certain comparators [9, 5].

Proof of Theorem 3.1. Let $a = (a_1, \ldots, a_{nk})$ be a k-disturbed 0-1 sequence with x zeroes. Let $a' = (a_1', \ldots, a_{nk}')$ be a sequence obtained after sorting the buckets within the first d_k layers of $S_{n,k}$. Let $x' = \lceil x/k \rceil$. Thus bucket x' is the last one that intersects the zero area.

For $1 \le v \le y < w \le n$, let $\gamma_{v,w,y}$ denote a sequence obtained from the sorted 0-1 sequence with exactly y zeroes by changing a zero on position v into a one and a one on position w into a zero. Let $d_{v,w,y}$ denote the minimal d such that after applying the first d layers of S_n on input $\gamma_{v,w,y}$ we get a sorted sequence. Note that layer d is the only layer within which the displaced zero is compared with the displaced one.

We consider all displaced zeroes in a' in buckets $x' + 1, \ldots, n$. We show that $S_{n,k}$ gets rid of displaced zeroes in these buckets. In the same way, we may show that $S_{n,k}$ gets rid of displaced ones in buckets $1, \ldots, x' - 1$. Since $S_{n,k}$ outputs bucket x' in a sorted state, it follows that the whole output is sorted.

Let m be the number of (displaced) zeroes in buckets $x' + 1, \ldots, n$ in a' and let W denote the set of their positions. Let l denote the number of ones in buckets 1 through x' in a' and let V be the set of their positions (some of these ones are displaced, those from bucket x' are not necessarily displaced). Obviously, $m \le l$ and $m \le k$. For each $j \in W$, we choose an $i \in V$ using the following inductive procedure:

- $V_0 = V$ and $W_0 = W$.

- For each t, $1 \le t \le m$, we choose as (i_t, j_t) a pair $(v, w) \in V_{t-1} \times W_{t-1}$ that minimizes $d_{\lceil v/k \rceil, \lceil w/k \rceil, x'}$.

- $V_t = V_{t-1} \setminus \{i_t\}$ and $W_t = W_{t-1} \setminus \{j_t\}$.

The idea is the following. A displaced zero terminates to be displaced at the moment when the bucket containing it is merged with a bucket with an index at most x' and containing a one. In fact, if the second bucket contains less ones than there are zeroes in the first bucket, then some of the zeroes remain displaced in the first bucket. Our definition fixes for each displaced zero a one that may cause the zero to finish its status of an displaced element.

Let $\gamma_{v,w,y,t}$ denote the sequence obtained after applying the first t layers of S_n on input $\gamma_{v,w,y}$. For $1 \le i \le n$ and $0 \le t \le 2\lceil \log n \rceil - 1$, let $p_{i,t}$ denote the number of sequences among $\gamma_{\lceil i_1/k \rceil, \lceil j_1/k \rceil, x', t}, \ldots, \gamma_{\lceil i_m/k \rceil, \lceil j_m/k \rceil, x', t}$ that contain ones at position i. Let $p_{i,t}'$ denote the number of ones in bucket i after applying the first $d_k + t \cdot c_k$ layers of $S_{n,k}$ to input a. We prove the following technical lemma (the reader may skip the proof at the first reading, since its ideas are not used in the main construction):

Lemma 3.2 (a) *If $1 \le i \le x'$, then $p_{i,t} \le p_{i,t}'$.*
That is, the number of ones in the bucket i at moment t is at least $p_{i,t}$.

(b) *If $x' < i \le n$, then $m - p_{i,t} \ge k - p_{i,t}'$.*
That is, the number of zeroes in the bucket i at moment t is at most $m - p_{i,t}$.

Note that by Lemma 3.2(b), for $x' < i \le n$, the output of $S_{n,k}$ contains at most $m - p_{i,2\lceil \log n \rceil - 1}$ zeroes, i.e. no zero, in bucket i. As already noticed, this implies Theorem 3.1.
Proof of Lemma 3.2. The proof is by induction on t. The case $t = 0$ follows from the definitions. Let $t > 0$. For each register R_i of S_n, $1 \le i \le n$, there are three possibilities:

1. there is no comparator incident to R_i in layer t of S_n.

2. there is an comparator (R_j, R_i) in layer t of S_n.

3. there is an comparator (R_i, R_j) in layer t of S_n.

In the first case, we have $p_{i,t} = p_{i,t-1}$ and $p_{i,t}' = p_{i,t-1}'$, so (a) and (b) follow from the induction hypothesis.

Part (a): $\quad 1 \le i \le x'$

In the second case, $p_{i,t} = p_{i,t-1} + p_{j,t-1}$ and, as always, $p_{i,t} \le m \le k$. In $S_{n,k}$ there is a network merging buckets j and i in the corresponding layers. Thus $p_{i,t}' = \min\{k, p_{i,t-1}' + p_{j,t-1}'\}$. Combining this with the induction hypothesis we get $p_{i,t} \le p_{i,t}'$.

In the third case, there are two sub-cases: either $j \leq x'$ or $j > x'$. If $j \leq x'$, then $p_{i,t} = 0$ and hence $p_{i,t} \leq p'_{i,t}$. The reason is that a one in each of the sequences $\gamma_{\lceil i_q/k \rceil, \lceil j_q/k \rceil, x', t-1}$ can freely move to any position j, $i < j \leq x'$.

The sub-case $j > x'$ is more tedious. We claim that $p_{i,t} \leq \max\{0, p_{i,t-1} - (m - p_{j,t-1})\}$. Indeed, if $\gamma_{\lceil i_r/k \rceil, \lceil j_r/k \rceil, x', t-1}$ contains a displaced one at position i and a displaced zero at position j, then $\gamma_{\lceil i_r/k \rceil, \lceil j_r/k \rceil, x', t}$ contains a zero at position i. Therefore it contributes to decrease of p_i. So if $p_{i,t} > \max\{0, p_{i,t-1} - (m - p_{j,t-1})\}$, then there are two different pairs (i_r, j_r) and $(i_{r'}, j_{r'})$ such that $\gamma_{\lceil i_r/k \rceil, \lceil j_r/k \rceil, x', t}$ contains a displaced one at position i and $\gamma_{\lceil i_{r'}/k \rceil, \lceil j_{r'}/k \rceil, x', t}$ contains a displaced zero at position j. Then of course, $d_{\lceil i_r/k \rceil, \lceil j_r/k \rceil, x'} > t$ and $d_{\lceil i_{r'}/k \rceil, \lceil j_{r'}/k \rceil, x'} > t$, since we have detected displaced elements after step t. On the other hand, $d_{\lceil i_r/k \rceil, \lceil j_{r'}/k \rceil, x'} \leq t$, since in the worst case the displaced zero and displaced one meet at layer t. So we should have chosen a pair $(i_r, j_{r'})$ instead of the first of (i_r, j_r) and $(i_{r'}, j_{r'})$. Contradiction, so we have proved our claim. On the other hand, $p'_{i,t} = \max\{0, p'_{i,t-1} - (k - p'_{j,t-1})\}$. By the induction hypothesis, $p_{i,t-1} \leq p'_{i,t-1}$ and $(m - p_{j,t-1}) \geq (k - p'_{j,t-1})$. Combining this all we get $p_{i,t} \leq p'_{i,t}$.

Part (b): $\quad x' + 1 \leq i \leq n$

In the second case, we distinguish two sub-cases: either $j > x'$ or $j \leq x'$. In the first sub-case $k - p'_{i,t} = 0$, since the total number of zeroes in buckets j and i is not greater than m, $m \leq k$, and the corresponding merging sub-network moves all the zeroes to bucket j. Hence (b) holds.

Now let $j \leq x'$. Note that $m - p_{i,t} \geq (m - p_{i,t-1}) - p_{j,t-1}$, since in at most $p_{j,t-1}$ cases $\gamma_{\lceil i_r/k \rceil, \lceil j_r/k \rceil, x', t-1}$ contains a one on position j. Thus, for at most $p_{j,t-1}$ cases a zero at position i is exchanged with a one at step t. On the other hand, $k - p'_{i,t} = \max\{0, (k - p'_{i,t-1}) - p'_{j,t-1}\}$. By the induction hypothesis, $k - p'_{i,t-1} \leq m - p_{i,t-1}$ and $p_{j,t-1} \leq p'_{j,t-1}$. Hence $k - p'_{i,t} \leq m - p_{i,t}$.

In the third case $m - p_{i,t} = (m - p_{i,t-1}) + (m - p_{j,t-1})$ and $k - p'_{i,t} = \min\{k, (k - p'_{i,t-1}) + (k - p'_{j,t-1})\}$. So the claim follows by the induction hypothesis.

∎ (Lemma 3.2 and Theorem 3.1)

4. Construction of network $N_{n,k}$

In this section we describe a construction of correction network $N_{n,k} = (n, D, (L_1, \ldots, L_D))$ sorting k-disturbed sequences of length n where $3 \leq k \leq \frac{1}{2} n^{\frac{1}{3+\log\log n}}$.

We assume that the input for $N_{n,k}$ is a k-disturbed 0-1-sequence. Let x be the number of zeroes in this sequence.

First we arrange n registers in the matrix $n_1 \times n_2$ (i.e. with n_1 rows and n_2 columns) in the row-major order. The values n_1, n_2 will be specified later. The rows are numbered 1 through n_1 starting at the top of the matrix and the

columns are numbered 1 through n_2 starting at the leftmost column. Note that the rows $1, \ldots, x' - 1$, where $x' = \lceil x/n_2 \rceil$, are contained in the zero area and the rows $x' + 1, \ldots, n_1$ are contained in the one area. The row x' may intersect both areas.

The network consists of five groups of layers performing computations called below *phases*. The crucial part of the computation is Phase 4.

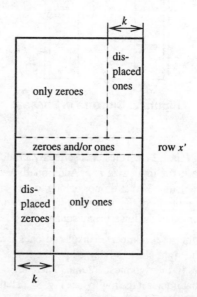

Figure 1. The situation after Phase 1

4.1. Phase 1

For each row we apply network $S_{n_2/k,k}$. For the case of a k-disturbed sequence, this suffices to sort each row. Note that after applying Phase 1 we have the following configuration (see Fig. 1): In the rows $1, \ldots, x' - 1$ all the (displaced) ones are in the k rightmost columns, and in the rows $x' + 1, \ldots, n_1$ all the (displaced) zeroes are in the k leftmost columns, and each row of the matrix is sorted.

4.2. Phase 2

The aim of Phase 2 is to move the displaced zeroes that are below the row $x' + 1$ to the leftmost column and the displaced ones that are above the row $x' - 1$ to the rightmost column.

We partition the sub-matrix of k rightmost (respectively. leftmost) columns into the squares of size $k \times k$. For each right (respectively, left) square, except the lowest one, the subset consisting of the first $k - 1$ columns of the square and the last column of next lower square (respectively first column of the the square and the $k - 1$ last columns of the next lower square) is called a *cluster* (see Fig. 2).

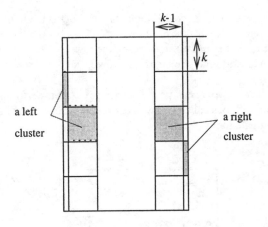

Figure 2. Clusters in Phase 2

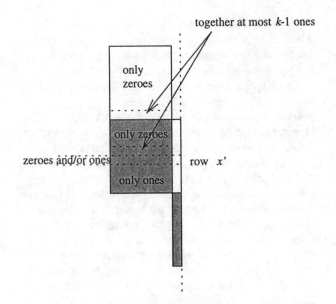

Figure 3. Clusters intersected by row x'

During Phase 2 each cluster is sorted by a Batcher's sorting network for input size k^2. Additionally, we sort the parts of the squares that do not belong to any cluster: the last $k-1$ columns of the uppermost left square and the first $k-1$ columns of the lowest right square.

Since the total number of displaced ones is at most k, each of the right clusters lying above the row x' will have all its ones in the rightmost column. There are at most two clusters that intersect the row x' (see Fig. 3), call them *upper* and *lower* cluster for a moment. Consider the first $k-1$ columns of these two clusters after sorting them. This area contains at most $k-1$ displaced ones. (It follows from the fact that at least one displaced one must be in the rightmost column after the first two phases.) All those $k-1$ ones are placed in the the last row of the left $k-1$ columns of the upper cluster and in the last row of the lower cluster that is in the zero area.

4.3. Phase 3

This phase ensures that all displaced ones above row x' are in the rightmost column, except may be some displaced ones in row $x'-1$. Analogous actions are taken for zeroes. As we have seen, after Phase 2 this property might not be fulfilled in the clusters crossing the row x', which we have called lower and upper cluster.

For each (except the lowest one) of the right squares, for $1 \leq l \leq k-1$, we apply network I_k^1 on the sequence of the lth register from the last row of the square followed by the $k-1$ uppermost registers from column $k-l$ column of the next (lower) square (see Fig.4). It is easy to see that in this way all misplaced ones from the upper cluster will be moved to row $x'-1$ or lower.

4.4. Phase 4

This phase is the core of the construction. Its purpose is to move all displaced ones from the rightmost column to rows x', $x'-1$ and $x'-2$ (and simultaneously, the displaced zeroes from the leftmost column to rows x', $x'+1$, $x'+2$). The first idea could be to apply network $S_{n_1/k,k}$ inside the rightmost (and the leftmost) column. However, this would yield runtime approximately $\log k \cdot (\log n_1 + \log n_2) = \log k \log n$ for Phases 1 and 4. We may perform much better using the fact that in the middle of the matrix of registers are no displaced ones in rows $x'-2$ and higher. This leaves an empty room for constructing "channels" through which displaced ones may fall down.

The basic element of the construction is the network $I_{n_1}^1$. However, we apply this network for an input containing many displaced ones, and these ones may block each other on their way to the proper positions. We allude this problem by providing "second opportunities" for the blocked ones. Each time when blocking may occur, we split $I_{n_1}^1$ into two copies. The additional copy works on a column that has obtained no displaced one so far. At the moment of splitting, the displaced ones blocked by another displaced ones from the "old copy" are allowed to fall into the "new copy" into the same position that they aimed for in the "old copy". Since there are still no displaced ones in the "new copy", no blocking occurs. Thus for an individual displaced one, its route down is just the same as in $I_{n_1}^1$. The only difference is that from time to time a falling one has to change the column.

Now we describe in detail how to implement this idea.

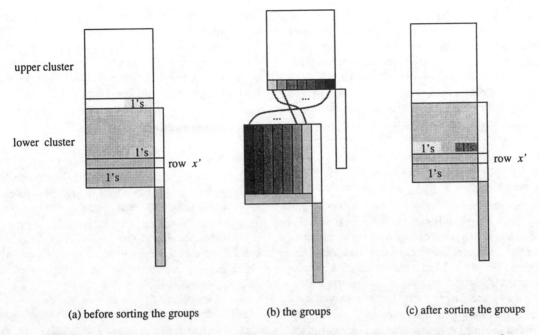

upper cluster		

(a) before sorting the groups   (b) the groups   (c) after sorting the groups

Figure 4. Groups of registers in two neighboring clusters sorted during Phase 3

For $d = 1, 2, \ldots$ we define a tree T_d with edges labeled by positive integers. T_0 contains only the root and no edges. For $d \geq 0$, tree T_{d+1} consists of two trees T'_d where T'_d denotes T_d with all edge labels increased by one. The root of the second T'_d is the root of T_{d+1}. The root of the first T'_d is connected through an edge labeled 1 with the root of T_d and is the leftmost child of the root.

Note that a node of T_d may be incident to many edges with different labels. For instance, the root is incident to edges with labels $1, 2, \ldots, d$. The following property is easy to check by induction.

Lemma 4.1 *If a node x of T_d is connected with its parent with an edge with label r, then the edges connecting x with its children have labels $r+1, r+2, \ldots, d$.*

Let T^t_d denote the subtree of T_d consisting of the vertices at distance at most t from the root. Let α^t_d denote the number of vertices in T^t_d and $\alpha = \alpha^{\lceil \log k \rceil}_{2 \cdot \lceil \log n \rceil - 1}$. Now we fix the parameters n_1, n_2 so that $n_2 = 2 \cdot \alpha$ (and of course $n = n_1 \cdot n_2$).

In order to describe Phase 4, we label the columns of the matrix of registers by the nodes of a graph G that consists of two disjoint copies of tree $T^{\lceil \log k \rceil}_{2 \cdot \lceil \log n \rceil - 1}$ called respectively the *right* and the *left* tree. The right tree is used to move down the displaced ones while the left tree takes care of the displaced zeroes. The $n_2/2$ columns from the left half of the matrix are labeled by the nodes of the left tree. The leftmost column corresponds to the root of the left tree. Symmetrically, the $n_2/2$ columns from the right half of the matrix

are labeled by the nodes of the right tree and the rightmost column is labeled by the root of the right tree.

Now we describe the next $4 \lceil \log n_1 \rceil - 2$ layers of the network. Let d denote the number of layers of the first three phases. For $1 \leq l \leq 2 \cdot \lceil \log n_1 \rceil - 1$, the layers L_{d+2l-1} and L_{d+2l} in the right half of the matrix of registers are defined as follows:

- Let C be a column from the right tree labeled either by the root of the tree or by a node connected with its parent in G through an edge with a label less than l, we insert comparators corresponding to the lth layer of $I^1_{n_1}$. If this level contains a comparator between registers r_1 and r_2, then there is a comparator between the registers r_1 and r_2 of C in layer L_{d+2l-1}.

- Let C' be a child of C in G connected to C by an edge of label l. Layer L_{d+2l} contains comparators connecting columns C and C': if layer l of $I^1_{n_1}$ contains a comparator between registers r_1 and r_2, then there is a comparator between register r_1 of C and register r_2 of C'.

In the left half, the construction is symmetric. The main property is that if layer l of $I^1_{n_1}$ contains comparator between registers r_1 and r_2, then for each column C from the right tree with a child C' connected by an edge of label l, there are two comparators incident to register r_1 of C in the layers L_{d+2l-1} and L_{d+2l}. The first of these comparators has its lower endpoint at register r_2 of column C. The second one has its lower endpoint at register r_2 of column C'. The idea

45

is that if a displaced one from register r_1 of C is blocked by another displaced one from register r_2 of C in the layer L_{d+2l-1}, then in the layer L_{d+2l} the blocked one has a second chance of reaching row r_2. The second chance is given by switching to the column C'. Note that the column C' does not contain any displaced ones (above the row $x' - 1$) until the layer L_{d+2l} is applied. This follows from the fact that T is a tree. Therefore the one from the register r_1 of C cannot be blocked by a displaced one (above the row $x' - 1$) in the layer L_{d+2l}.

Note that if we had labeled the columns by the nodes of $T_{2\lceil \log n \rceil - 1}$ instead of $T = T_{2\lceil \log n \rceil - 1}^{\lceil \log k \rceil}$, then it would follow that every displaced one falls down as in $I_{n_1}^1$ without being blocked by another displaced ones. Indeed, each time a displaced one is blocked by another displaced one in the same column, on the next level the blocked one is sent into another column to the row it aimed for in the original column. The depth of the tree would be sufficient to perform all levels of $I_{n_1}^1$: if a displaced one arrives at a column with a label being a leaf of the tree, then the execution of $I_{n_1}^1$ is over. The problem is that the number of columns of $T_{2\lceil \log n \rceil - 1}$ is too large.

In our construction, we label the columns only by the nodes of $T_{2\lceil \log n \rceil - 1}$ of depth at most $\lceil \log k \rceil$. The reason is that in fact we do not need "second chances" for the displaced ones arriving at the columns labeled by the nodes of depth $\lceil \log k \rceil$. We shall see that in such columns at most one displaced one may arrive during Phase 4. Note that if columns C and C' are connected by an edge with label l, then only at layer L_{d+2l} some displaced ones may enter C'. For each such one there is a one left in C that caused blocking. By a simple induction we get the following lemma:

Lemma 4.2 *For $0 \leq m \leq \lceil \log k \rceil$, if column C is labeled by a node of T at level m, then there are at most $k/2^m$ (displaced) ones above the row $x' - 1$ in column C during Phase 4. In particular, any column labeled by a node of T at level $\lceil \log k \rceil$ may contain at most one 1 above row $x' - 1$.*

We see that after Phase 4 no displaced one is above row $x' - 2$. So they are all in the rows x', $x' - 1$ and $x' - 2$. A similar property is obtained for displaced zeroes: they are in the rows x', $x' + 1$, $x' + 2$.

4.5. Phase 5

After Phase 4, above row $x' - 2$ there are only zeroes, below row $x' + 2$ there are only ones, and perhaps there is a dirty area with zeroes and ones in rows $x' - 2$ through $x' + 2$. The rows $x' - 2, \ldots, x' + 2$ form a k'-disturbed sequence, $k' \leq k$.

First we partition the rows into groups of 4 consecutive rows and in each group apply network $S_{4n_2/k, k}$. Since for each such a group the input of $S_{4n_2/k, k}$ is at most k-disturbed, the result will be a sorted sequence. However, since the "dirty" rows $x' - 2, \ldots, x' + 2$ may be inside two groups, we need to merge sorted sequences. First we merge sequences in groups $2i - 1$ and $2i$, for $i = 1, 2, \ldots$, and then merge sequences in groups $2i$ and $2i + 1$ for $i = 1, 2, \ldots$.

5. Runtime analysis

We start with an estimation of the depth of $S_{n,k}$. This network uses nk registers. One can easily observe that we can apply the same construction for a number of registers which is not divisible by k. Indeed, let $SS_{m,k}$ denote the network $S_{\lceil m/k \rceil, k}$ with deleted registers $R_{m+1}, R_{m+2}, \ldots, R_{k \cdot \lceil m/k \rceil}$ and comparators pointing to them. Obviously, $SS_{m,k}$ sorts any k-disturbed input sequence of m items, because it emulates $S_{\lceil m/k \rceil, k}$ provided that we input $+\infty$ to registers $R_{m+1}, \ldots, R_{k \cdot \lceil m/k \rceil}$.

Recall that $\text{depth}(S_{n,k}) = d_k + c_k \cdot (2\lceil \log n \rceil - 1)$, where $c_k = 1 + \lceil \log k \rceil$ is the depth of Batcher's merging network applied to two sorted sequences of length k and $d_k = c_k \cdot \frac{\lceil \log k \rceil}{2}$ is the depth of Batcher's sorting network for k inputs. Putting these things together, we get

$$\begin{aligned} \text{depth}(SS_{n,k}) &= c_k \left(\tfrac{1}{2} \lceil \log k \rceil + 2 \log \lceil \tfrac{n}{k} \rceil + 1 \right) \\ &\leq 2 \log n \left(1 + \lceil \log k \rceil \right) - \tfrac{3}{2} \log^2 k + 2 \log k + 7 \quad (1) \end{aligned}$$

Now we are ready to estimate the depth of $N_{n,k}$. Let D_i, $1 \leq i \leq 5$, denotes the depth of the network constructed in Phase i. Then

$$\begin{aligned} D_1 &= \text{depth}(SS_{n_2, k}) = c_k \left(\tfrac{1}{2} \lceil \log k \rceil + 2 \log \lceil \tfrac{n_2}{k} \rceil + 1 \right), \\ D_2 &= d_{k^2} = c_{k^2} \cdot \tfrac{\lceil \log(k^2) \rceil}{2} \leq \lceil \log k \rceil \cdot (1 + 2 \lceil \log k \rceil), \\ D_3 &= \text{depth}(I_k^0) = 2\lceil \log k \rceil - 1, \\ D_4 &= 2 \cdot \text{depth}(S_{n_1}) = 4\lceil \log(\tfrac{n}{n_2}) \rceil - 2 \\ &\leq 4 \log n - 4 \log n_2 + 2, \\ D_5 &= \text{depth}(SS_{4n_2, k}) + 2c_{4n_2} \\ &= c_k \left(\tfrac{1}{2} \lceil \log k \rceil + 2 \log \lceil \tfrac{4n_2}{k} \rceil + 1 \right) + 2\lceil \log n_2 \rceil + 6. \end{aligned}$$

After a few transformations, we get

$$\begin{aligned} D_1 + D_5 &\leq (1 + \lceil \log k \rceil)(\lceil \log k \rceil + 4 \log n_2 - 4 \log k + 8) \\ &\quad + 2 \lceil \log n_2 \rceil + 6, \\ D_2 + D_3 &\leq 2\lceil \log k \rceil^2 + 3\lceil \log k \rceil - 1. \end{aligned}$$

Finally,

$$\text{depth}(N_{n,k}) \leq 4 \log n + 4 \log n_2 (\lceil \log k \rceil + \tfrac{1}{2}) + O(1) \quad (2)$$

The only thing which is left to do is an estimation of n_2 — the number of columns in the register matrix of $N_{n,k}$. We

46

have defined n_2 as $2 \cdot \alpha_{2\lceil \log n \rceil - 1}^{\lceil \log k \rceil}$, the number of vertices of depth at most $\lceil \log k \rceil$ in the labeled binomial tree $T_{2\lceil \log n \rceil - 1}$. It is well known that there are exactly $\binom{m}{i}$ nodes at depth i in a binomial tree T_m. Thus

$$n_2 = 2 \cdot \sum_{i=0}^{\lceil \log k \rceil} \binom{2\lceil \log n \rceil - 1}{i} \qquad (3)$$

Lemma 5.1 *If $n \geq 256$ and $3 \leq k \leq \frac{1}{2} n^{\frac{1}{3 + \log \log n}}$, then $\log n_2 \leq \lceil \log k \rceil (\log \log n + 2)$ and $n_2 \leq n/k$.*

Proof. By an easy induction one can prove that $\sum_{i=0}^{j-1} \binom{m}{i} \leq \binom{m}{j}$ for $m \geq 2$ and $j \leq \frac{m+1}{3}$. In our case

$$\lceil \log k \rceil \leq \left\lceil \frac{\log n}{3 + \log \log n} \right\rceil \leq \frac{2}{3} \lceil \log n \rceil \leq \frac{(2\lceil \log n \rceil - 1) + 1}{3}.$$

Therefore, we can apply the inequality to the sum (3) without the last term and obtain $n_2 \leq 4 \binom{2\lceil \log n \rceil - 1}{\lceil \log k \rceil}$. Applying Stirling formula, $\binom{m}{j} \leq \frac{1}{\sqrt{2\pi j}} \left(\frac{me}{j}\right)^j$, and taking logarithm of both sides we get

$$
\begin{aligned}
\log n_2 \quad &\leq \quad \left(\frac{3}{2} - \frac{1}{2}\log(\pi \lceil \log k \rceil)\right) \\
&+ \lceil \log k \rceil \left(\log \log n + \log \frac{e(2 + 1/\log n)}{\lceil \log k \rceil}\right)
\end{aligned}
$$

Since $\lceil \log k \rceil \geq 2$ and $\log n \geq 8$, the expression in the first parentheses is bounded by 0.2 and $\log \frac{e(2 + 1/\log n)}{\lceil \log k \rceil} \leq 1.6$. The first part of the lemma follows. The second one is a simple consequence of the first part and the upper bound on k: $\lceil \log k \rceil \leq 1 + \log k \leq \frac{\log n}{3 + \log \log n}$ and $\log n_2 \leq \lceil \log k \rceil (\log \log n + 3) - \log k \leq \log \frac{n}{k}$. ∎

Lemma 5.1 shows that the construction in Section 4 is correct: the required number of columns does not exceed the total number of registers and there are at least k rows.

Proof Theorem 1.1. If $n \leq 256$ or $k \leq 2$, the Batcher sorting network or pipelined networks S_n of Schimmler and Starke do the job and have depth $4 \log n + O(1)$. Thus we will use networks constructed in this paper only if $n \geq 256$ and $k > 2$. The network $N_{n,k}$ is used if $k \leq \frac{1}{2} n^{\frac{1}{3 + \log \log n}}$ and $SS_{n,k}$ otherwise. In both cases, the depth of the selected network is bounded by $4 \log n + O(\log^2 k \log \log n)$. To prove this in the case of $N_{n,k}$ one should apply the equation $\log n_2 = O(\log k \log \log n)$ from Lemma 5.1 in (2):

$$
\begin{aligned}
\text{depth}(N_{n,k}) \quad &= \quad 4 \log n + O(\log n_2 \log k) \\
&= \quad 4 \log n + O(\log^2 k \log \log n).
\end{aligned}
$$

In the case of $SS_{n,k}$, $k > \frac{1}{2} n^{\frac{1}{3 + \log \log n}}$ and then $\log n \leq (\log k + 1)(3 + \log \log n) = O(\log k \log \log n)$. So by (1):

$$\text{depth}(SS_{n,k}) = O(\log n \log k) = O(\log^2 k \log \log n). \quad ∎$$

6. Conclusions

Our methods work for moderately large values of k. However, further research is necessary for applications where the value of n is small (in this case the small "oh" terms in the expression for the depth of the network play a substantial role and prevent immediate practical applications).

Another very interesting and important area of research would be to apply techniques of correcting disturbed sequences for the case of sorting sets of keys with dynamically changing values.

References

[1] M. Ajtai, J. Komlós and E. Szemerédi: Sorting in $c \log n$ parallel steps. *Combinatorica* **3** (1983) 1–19.

[2] K. E. Batcher: Sorting networks and their applications, in *AFIPS Conf. Proc. 32*,1968, 307–314.

[3] M. Dietzfelbinger, F. Meyer auf der Heide: An optimal parallel dictionary, *Information and Computation* **102.2** (1993) 196-217.

[4] Marcin Kik, Correction Network, *manuscript*, Wrocław University, 1997.

[5] M. Kutyłowski, K. Loryś, B. Oesterdiekhoff, and R. Wanka: Fast and feasible periodic sorting networks of constant depth, in *Proc. 35th IEEE FOCS*, 1994, 369-380.

[6] D. E. Knuth: *The Art of Computer Programming*, Vol. 3: *Sorting and Searching* (Addison-Wesley, 1973).

[7] T. Leighton, Yuan Ma, and C. G. Plaxton: Breaking the $\Theta(n \log^2 n)$ Barrier for Sorting with Faults, *JCSS* **54.2** (1997) 265–304.

[8] M. Piotrów: Depth Optimal Sorting Networks Resistant to k Passive Faults, in *Proc. 7th ACM-SIAM SODA*, 1996, 242–251.

[9] S. A. Savari: Average case analysis of five two-dimensional bubble sorting algorithms, in *Proc. 5th ACM Symposium on Parallel Algorithms and Architectures*, 1993, 336–345.

[10] I. D. Scherson, S. Sen, and A. Shamir, Shear-sort: A true two-dimensional sorting technique for VLSI networks, in *Proc. IEEE ICPP*, 1986, 903–908.

[11] M. Schimmler and C. Starke, A Correction Network for N-Sorters, *SIAM J. Comput.* **6.6** (1989) 1179–1187.

The Index-Permutation Graph Model for Hierarchical Interconnection Networks

Chi-Hsiang Yeh and Behrooz Parhami
Department of Electrical and Computer Engineering,
University of California,
Santa Barbara, CA 93106-9560, USA

Abstract

In this paper, we present the index-permutation (IP) graph model, and apply it to the systematic development of efficient hierarchical networks. We derive several classes of interconnection networks based on IP graphs to achieve desired properties; the results compare favorably with popular interconnection networks, as measured by topological (e.g., node degree and diameter) and algorithmic properties, and are particularly efficient in view of their sparse inter-module communication patterns. In particular, the diameters of suitably-constructed super-IP graphs, a subclass of IP graphs, are optimal within a factor of $1 + o(1)$, given their node degrees. The IP graph model can also be used as a common platform that unifies the architectures and algorithms for a vast variety of interconnection networks.

1 Introduction

In [4] Akers and Krishnamurthy presented a group-theoretic model called the *Cayley graph model* for designing, analyzing, and improving symmetric interconnection networks. Many subclasses of Cayley graphs are strongly hierarchical and have small diameters and node degrees. In particular, k-ary n-cubes, cube-connected cycles (CCC) [21, 22], and hypercubes are some well-known examples of Cayley graphs [3, 4]. In [4], Akers and Krishnamurthy showed that Cayley graphs are vertex-symmetric and that most vertex-symmetric graphs can be represented as Cayley graphs; it has also been shown that every vertex-symmetric graph can be represented as a *Cayley coset graph*. Both the Cayley graph model and the Cayley coset graph model have been used to derive a wide variety of interesting networks for parallel processing and have since received considerable attention [4, 5, 9, 14, 17, 19, 20, 29, 30]. In particular, the star graph [3] is a well-known Cayley graph that has a number of desirable properties, such as degree, diameter, and average distance smaller than those of a similar-size hypercube, symmetry, strong embedding capability, and fault tolerance properties.

In this paper, we present the *index-permutation (IP) graph model* for the systematic development of communication-efficient interconnection networks. In contrast to Cayley coset graphs [4, 17], which can represent any vertex-symmetric graph, we show that *any graph* has an IP graph automorphism. We focus on a subclass of IP graphs, called *super-IP graphs*, that use identical copies of a small network as their basic modules. Based on the notion of super-IP graphs, we present several efficient networks that can have node degree and/or diameter smaller than those of a similar-size star graph or hypercube and have strong embedding capability. We use the notion of IP graphs to derive symmetric and regular variants of super-IP graphs, called *symmetric super-IP graphs*. Our designs, based on super-IP graphs and symmetric super-IP graphs, compare favorably with other popular parallel architectures, as measured by topological (e.g., node degree and diameter) and algorithmic properties. In particular, the diameter of a suitably constructed (symmetric) super-IP graph can be optimal within a factor of $1 + o(1)$ from a universal lower bound, given its node degree. Moreover, the required data movements when performing many important algorithms on (symmetric) super-IP graphs are largely confined within basic modules, leading to small network delay when the delay associated with transporting a message through an on-module (e.g., on-chip or on-board) link is small. We define the *inter-cluster degree* as the maximum of the average-per-node off-module (or inter-cluster) links over all modules (or clusters), and the *inter-cluster diameter* as the maximum number of off-module (or inter-cluster) transmissions required for routing between two nodes. We compare the DD-cost (the product of degree and diameter [7]), ID-cost (the product of inter-cluster degree and diameter), and the II-cost (the product of inter-cluster degree and inter-cluster diameter) for super-IP graphs and several popular networks and show that super-IP graphs outperform other networks significantly under these figures of merit.

Due to the impact of inter-processor communication mechanism on the scalability and performance of parallel computers, numerous interconnection topologies have been proposed and intensely studied, forming a "sea of interconnection networks." Among them, certain classes of hierarchical networks, including hierarchical cubic networks (HCN) [15], hierarchical folded-hypercube networks (HFN) [13], hierarchical hypercube networks (HHN) [34], recursively connected complete (RCC) networks [16], and hierarchical shuffle-exchange (HSE) networks [10], have been shown to possess various appealing properties and are gaining considerable attention. Although these networks were proposed and studied independently and their structures may not resemble each other at first glance, we show in this paper and in [28, 33] that these networks and many other interconnection networks, including shuffle-exchange networks [21], hierarchical swap networks (HSN) [24, 25, 26] cyclic-shift networks [27, 32], super-flip networks, and CCC, belong to the class of super-IP graphs or symmetric super-IP graphs and share many properties and algorithms in common. Therefore, the IP graph model, a natural extension of the Cayley graph model [4], not only provide new insight to the design of novel communication-efficient networks, but also serves as a framework that ties together a vast variety of previously proposed interconnection topologies. Suitably constructed super-IP graphs can emulate a corresponding higher-degree network, such as a hypercube, with asymptotically optimal slowdown under various communication models. A variety of important network topologies can also be embedded in super-IP graphs with constant dilation. More details can be found in [28, 33].

The remainder of this paper is organized as follows. In Section 2, we present the index-permutation (IP) graph model. In Section 3, we discuss several efficient subclasses of super-IP graphs and their symmetric variants. In Section 4, we present routing algorithms for super-IP graphs and derive diameters of (symmetric) super-IP graphs. In Section 5, we consider implementation issues and compare the hardware and communication efficiency of several networks. Section 6 concludes the paper.

2 The Index-Permutation Graph Model

In this section, we introduce a mathematical game called the *ball-arrangement game (BAG)*. We then relate the game to the index-permutation graph model in an attempt to provide some intuition and to help in visualizing the model.

In the ball-arrangement game, we are given k balls, each stamped with a number. Different balls may be assigned the same or different numbers. The goal of the game is to rearrange the balls so that the numbers on the balls appear in a desired order. At each step the player can take an arbitrary action from a set of d permissible moves, each being a particular permutation of the balls. The set of permissible moves remains the same throughout the game, independent of the current configuration of the balls. There are $N \leq k!$ possible configurations of the balls (i.e., states) when playing the game, where N depends on the set of permissible moves and how balls are stamped with numbers initially. If we view each of the states as a network node and a permissible move leading from one state to another as a directed link connecting the nodes corresponding to those two states, then a network with N nodes results, where each node has d outgoing links. In other words, the network can be obtained by drawing the state transition graph for the corresponding ball-arrangement game with specified movements. One can then relate playing a ball-arrangement game to routing in the corresponding network, where the initial and final states correspond to the source and destination nodes and the movements performed to solve the game correspond to the links along the routing path. Since the in-/out-degree of the derived network is upper bounded by the number d of permissible movements and the diameter is the maximum number of steps required to solve the game, we generally prefer to select a small number of permissible moves that allow us to solve the game in a small (or optimal) number of steps for

any initial and final states.

Recall that a Cayley graph is defined by a set of generators for a finite group, where the vertices correspond to the elements of the group and the edges correspond to the action of the generators [4, 8]. In the model proposed in [4], any element in the group is a permutation of a set of distinct symbols and generators are also permutations. For example, the label of a node in a 6-dimensional star graph (i.e., an element in the finite group) can be represented as $X = x_1x_2x_3x_4x_5x_6 = 123654$, and the generators of the 6-star are

$$\pi_1 = 213456 = (1,2), \quad \pi_2 = 321456 = (1,3),$$

$$\pi_3 = (1,4), \quad \pi_4 = (1,5), \quad \text{and} \quad \pi_5 = (1,6),$$

where a *cycle representation* (i,j) represents a permutation that interchanges symbols at positions i and j [3, 4]. Then the actions of generators lead to the following neighbors for node X:

$$X\pi_1 = \pi_1(X) = \pi_1(x_1x_2x_3x_4x_5x_6) = x_2x_1x_3x_4x_5x_6 = 213654,$$

$$X\pi_2 = \pi_2(X) = \pi_2(x_1x_2x_3x_4x_5x_6) = x_3x_2x_1x_4x_5x_6 = 321654,$$

$$X\pi_3 = 623154, \quad X\pi_4 = 523614, \quad \text{and} \quad X\pi_5 = 423651.$$

Applying the same set of generators to these 5 neighbors generates 20 new neighbors. If we continue this process at least 7 times, we will obtain 720 distinct labels (including node X), which form the set of vertices in a 6-star (that is, all the elements in the corresponding finite group). We can see that any given Cayley graph corresponds to a certain ball-arrangement game, where each symbol corresponds to a ball that has a distinct number and the set of generators correspond to the set of permissible moves.

Just as a ball-arrangement game with distinct ball numbers can be used to derive a corresponding Cayley graph, an *arbitrary* ball-arrangement game can be used to derive a corresponding network, called an *index-permutation (IP) graph*, where each ball corresponds to a symbol and the set of permissible movements correspond a set of generators. In the definition of an index-permutation graph, there may be several identical symbols in the label of a node. Therefore, the index-permutation graph model can be viewed as an extension of the Cayley graph model where the restriction of "distinct" symbols for elements in the definition of a Cayley graph has been relaxed. More precisely, an IP graph is defined by a set of generators and a *seed element*, where a generator is a permutation, the edges correspond to the action of the generators, and the vertices correspond to the elements obtained by applying generators on the seed element or a generated element. For example, the label of the *seed node* in a certain IP graph might be represented as $Y = y_1y_2y_3y_4y_5y_6 = 123321$, and the generators of the IP graph can be permutations

$$\pi_1 = (1,2), \quad \pi_2 = (1,3), \quad \text{and} \quad \pi_6 = 456123.$$

Then the actions of generators lead to the following 3 neighbors for node Y:

$$Y\pi_1 = \pi_1(Y) = \pi_1(y_1y_2y_3y_4y_5y_6) = y_2y_1y_3y_4y_5y_6 = 213321,$$

$Y\pi_2 = \pi_2(Y) = \pi_2(y_1y_2y_3y_4y_5y_6) = y_3y_2y_1y_4y_5y_6 = 321321,$

$Y\pi_6 = \pi_6(Y) = \pi_6(y_1y_2y_3y_4y_5y_6) = y_4y_5y_6y_1y_2y_3 = 321123.$

Repeatedly applying the 3 generators to generated nodes will result in 36 distinct nodes for this IP graph example. We will show that this simple extension is quite powerful and leads to novel and useful classes of parallel architectures.

In what follows we represent a few well-known networks using the IP graph model to make the idea clearer. HCN(n,n) [15] without diameter links can be viewed as an IP graph with the generator

$$T_{2,2n} = (2n+1)(2n+2)(2n+3)\cdots(4n)123\cdots(2n)$$

plus the n generators for an n-cube (that is, the generators with cycle representations $(1,2)$, $(3,4)$, $(5,6),...,(2n-3,2n-2)$, and $(2n-1,2n)$) applied on the seed element

$$12\ 34\ 56\ \cdots\ (2n-1)(2n)\ 12\ 34\ 56\ \cdots\ (2n-1)(2n).$$

Note that, in contrast to distinct symbols in Cayley graphs, both halves of the seed element for the HCN use the same sequence of symbols. Consider HCN(n,n) with $n=2$. By applying the three generators

$$T_{2,4} = 5678\ 1234,\ (1,2),\ \text{and}\ (3,4)$$

on the seed 12 34 12 34, we first obtain three generated nodes 1234 1234, 21 341234, and 12 43 1234, respectively. Note that, in this example, the first generated node is the seed itself. Also note that the space between symbols is used only to better visualize the action of a generator or the applied action on a label. If we continue applying the generators on the derived nodes for another 4 iterations, we will finally obtain all the 16 nodes in an HCN(2,2) (Fig. 1a). Note that using the label of any of the 16 nodes as the initial seed will eventually generate exactly the same graph. We can also use other types of labels for the seed to obtain a graph with exactly the same connectivity, even though the labels of network nodes will be different. For example, if we use 12 12 12 12 as the seed, we obtain a graph with the same connectivity (see Fig. 1a). For the original description of the construction of HCNs, we refer the reader to [15].

As another example, an n-dimensional de Bruijn graph, one of the densest known graphs, can be defined by generators

$$L_{1,2} = 34\ 56\ 78\cdots(2n-1)(2n)\ 12$$

$$\bar{L}_{1,2} = 34\ 56\ 78\cdots(2n-1)(2n)\ 21$$

applied to the $2n$-symbol seed 12 12 12$\cdots$12.

In [4], Akers and Krishnamurthy showed that Cayley graphs are vertex-symmetric and that most vertex-symmetric graphs can be represented as Cayley graphs; it was also shown that every vertex-symmetric graph can be represented as a *Cayley coset graph*. The analog of the preceding results for IP graph is given in the following theorem [28, 33]:

Theorem 2.1 *Any graph has an IP graph automorphism.*

In what follows, we will focus on super-IP graphs, IP graphs that use *super-generators*, which are a special class of permutations that interchange two or several sequences of symbols of equal-length. As an example, the generator $T_{2,2n}$ for an HCN(n,n) without diameter links is a super-generator that interchanges 2 sequences of $2n$ symbols.

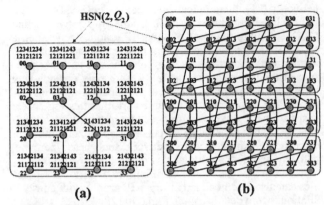

Figure 1. Structures of HSN(l,Q_2), $l = 2,3$, represented with radix-4 node labels. (a) Structure and ranking of an HSN($2,Q_2$) = HCN(2,2) without diameter links. (b) an HSN($3,Q_2$).

3 (Symmetric) Super-IP Graphs

In this section, we show how to derive communication-efficient networks based on super-IP graphs.

3.1 Definition of Super-IP Graphs

In this subsection, we give the definitions of super-IP graphs and introduce some related terminology.

Super-IP graphs are derived from ball-arrangement games with l (initially identical) boxes, each having m balls in it. The permissible moves in the game can be any permutation of the balls within the leftmost box or any permutation of the boxes (without reordering the balls within them). In other words, a super-IP graph is a special class of IP graphs where the seed label consists of l identical groups (boxes) of m symbols (balls) and the generators of the IP graph can either permute the m symbols (the m balls) within the leftmost group (box) or permute the m-symbol groups (m-ball boxes) without changing the order of symbols (balls) within any of the groups (boxes). We call each of the m-symbol groups in the label a *super-symbol*. The generators that permute the symbols within the leftmost super-symbol are called *nucleus generators* and the generators that permute super-symbols are called *super-generators*. For example, with the seed label 123 123, the permutation 321 456, which permutes 123 123 to become 321 123, defines a nucleus generator, whereas the permutation 456 123, permuting 321 123 to 123 321, corresponds to a super-generator. For each of the super-symbols, there must exist a sequence of super-generators that can bring it to the leftmost position. The small IP graph whose seed label is a super-symbol of the seed label of a super-IP graph and whose generator set consists of all the nucleus generators of the super-IP graph is called the *nucleus graph* of the super-IP graph. Since the nucleus determines the nucleus generators and the seed of the super-IP graph, a super-IP graph can be completely specified by its super-generators and its nucleus.

If we place each of the nuclei of a super-IP graph

within the same module, then its inter-cluster degree, upper bounded by the number of off-module links per node in the super-IP graph, is no larger than the number of its super-generators, leading to the following theorem.

Theorem 3.1 *The degree of an IP graph is no larger than the number of its generators, and its inter-cluster degree is no larger than the number of its super-generators.*

In this paper, l always signifies the number of super-symbols in the label of a node in a super-IP graph, m always signifies the number of symbols in a super-symbol, and N represents the number of nodes in a network. The size of super-IP graphs is given in the following theorem [28, 33].

Theorem 3.2 *The size of a super-IP graph is $N = M_N^l$, where M_N is the number of nodes in the nucleus graph.*

3.2 Transposition Super-Generators

In this subsection we introduce several communication-efficient networks based on a special class of generators called *transposition super-generators*, each of which exchanges a pair of super symbols. The transposition super-generator that swaps the first and the ith m-symbol groups (super-symbols of length m) will be denoted by $T_{i,m}$.

An l-level *hierarchical swap network* (also called *hierarchical swapped network*) [24, 25, 26], HSN(l, G), is a super-IP graph that has the seed $\underbrace{S_1 S_1 \cdots S_1}_{l}$, the generators for the nucleus G, and the transposition super-generators $T_{2,m} = (1,2)_m$, $T_{3,m} = (1,3)_m$, $T_{4,m} = (1,4)_m, \ldots, T_{l,m} = (1,l)_m$, where S_1 is the label of a (seed) node in the nucleus G and $(1,i)_m$ represents the permutation that interchanges the first super-symbol and the ith super-symbol. The subscript m in $(i,j)_m$ denotes the fact that super-symbols of length m at positions i and j are interchanged. In other words,

$$T_{2,m}(Y) = T_{2,m}(Y_1Y_2Y_3Y_4Y_5Y_6\cdots Y_l) = Y_2Y_1Y_3Y_4Y_5Y_6\cdots Y_l,$$

$$T_{3,m}(Y) = T_{3,m}(Y_1Y_2Y_3Y_4Y_5Y_6\cdots Y_l) = Y_3Y_2Y_1Y_4Y_5Y_6\cdots Y_l,$$

$$T_{4,m}(Y) = T_{4,m}(Y_1Y_2Y_3Y_4Y_5Y_6\cdots Y_l) = Y_4Y_2Y_3Y_1Y_5Y_6\cdots Y_l,$$

where Y_i is a super-symbol, $i = 1,2,3,\ldots,l$. An example of HSN$(3, Q_2)$ is shown in Fig. 1b, where Q_2 is a 2-cube. We can see that an HCN(n,n) without diameter links is equivalent to the special case HSN$(2, Q_n)$. As shown in [26, 33], an HSN can embed corresponding homogeneous product networks such as hypercubes or k-ary n-cubes, with dilation 3. Efficient VLSI layout for HSNs can be found is [31].

3.3 Cyclic-Shift Super-Generators

Cyclic-shift networks (CN) (also called *cyclic networks*) [27, 28] form a special case of super-IP graphs that use super-generators which can perform "cyclic shifts" over the super-symbols. Some subclasses of cyclic-shift networks have fixed node degree and small diameter.

A basic-CN(l, G) (also called ring-CN(l, G)) is defined by nucleus G and super-generators $L_{1,m} =$

$(1 \leftarrow)_m$ and $R_{1,m} = L_{-1,m} = (1 \rightarrow)_m$, where the super-generator $L_{i,m} = (i \leftarrow)_m$ changes the node label $X = X_1X_2\cdots X_l$ into

$$L_{i,m}(X) = X_{i+1}X_{i+2}\cdots X_l\, X_1X_2X_3\cdots X_i$$

and the generator $R_{i,m} = (i \rightarrow)_m$ changes X into

$$R_{i,m}(X) = X_{l-i+1}X_{l-i+2}\cdots X_l X_1X_2X_3\cdots X_{l-i}.$$

3.4 IP Graphs Based on Flip Super-Generators

Another example for the design of super-IP graphs is to use *flip super-generators* $F_{i,m}$, where the super-generator $F_{i,m}$ flips the first i super-symbols, $i = 2,3,\ldots,l$ for an IP graph with l super-symbols in a node label. For example,

$$F_{2,m}(X_1X_2X_3X_4) = X_2X_1X_3X_4,\ F_{3,m}(X_1X_2X_3X_4) = X_3X_2X_1X_4.$$

A super-IP graph with l flip super-generators and nucleus G is called a *super-flip network based on G*. Note that super-flip networks can emulate cyclic-shift networks efficiently since flip super-generators can emulate transposition and cyclic-shift super-generators efficiently, while the latter cannot emulate the former as efficiently. More details can be found in [33].

3.5 Symmetric Super-IP Graph

A *symmetric super-IP graph* is a special type of IP graph whose generator set consists of nucleus generators and super-generators and whose seed label consists of distinct symbols. Since symmetric super-IP graphs form a subclass of Cayley graphs [4], they are vertex-symmetric and regular. In this subsection, we develop a simple and systematic method, based on symmetric super-IP graphs, to obtain symmetric and regular variants of IP graphs.

Recall that an HSN(l, G) can be defined by the transposition super-generators $T_{2,m} = (1,2)_m$, $T_{3,m} = (1,3)_m$, $T_{4,m} = (1,4)_m, \ldots, T_{l,m} = (1,l)_m$, the generators for the nucleus G, and the seed $\underbrace{S_1 S_1 \cdots S_1}_{l}$, where $S_1 = 123\cdots m$ for some nuclei G. If we replace the original seed with a new seed $S_1S_2S_3\cdots S_l$, where $S_i = (i-1)m+1, (i-1)m+2, (i-1)m+3,\ldots,im$, the resultant graph, called a *symmetric HSN(l, G)*, becomes a symmetric super-IP graph which is vertex-symmetric and regular. The seed labels of many HSNs whose nuclei use other type of seed labels can also be transformed into labels that have no repeated symbols, leading to corresponding symmetric HSNs. Since a symmetric HSN(l, G) uses the same generator set and the same nucleus graph as those of an HSN(l, G), we can expect that they share some properties and algorithms. If we assign color i to the super-symbol containing symbol im, then there are $l!$ possible orders of colors for the labels of nodes in a symmetric HSN(l, G). As a result, a symmetric HSN(l, G) has $l!M_N^l$ nodes, $l!$ times more than that of an HSN(l, G), where M_N is the number of nodes in the nucleus G.

A similar strategy can be applied to other super-IP graphs. If we can replace the seed node of a CN(l, G) with the seed $S_1S_2S_3\cdots S_l$, the resultant graph becomes a symmetric super-IP graph, called a symmetric $CN(l, G)$, which is vertex-symmetric and regular. A symmetric $CN(l, G)$ has lM_N^l nodes since there are l different orders for the colors of super-symbols. Note that these properties are common to all cyclic-shift networks, including ring-CNs, complete-CNs [27, 28], and their intermediate variants.

Similarly, this strategy can be applied to virtually any IP graph, such as an HCN, HFN, RCC, shuffle-exchange network, de Bruijn graph, HSE, or super-flip network, to obtain its symmetric and regular Cayley-graph counterpart. Note that even though the derived Cayley graphs have size and connectivity that are different from the original networks, they still share some properties and algorithms in common due to the similarity in their generator sets.

4   Routing and Network Diameter

Recall that the routing algorithms on Cayley graphs and, in particular, star graphs, can be viewed as "sorting" the symbols in the label associated with the source node until that of the destination node is obtained. Routing within any IP graph can also be performed in a similar manner.

Theorem 4.1 *Let t be the minimum number of applications of the super-generators of a super-IP graph in order for each super-symbol to appear at the leftmost position at least once. Then the diameter of the super-IP graph is $lD_G + t$, where l is the number of super-symbols in a node label and D_G is the diameter of the nucleus of the super-IP graph.*

Proof: In what follows we present a routing algorithm for the super-IP graph by sorting the label of the source node to the label of the destination node. Choose a particular t-step rearrangement of the l super-symbols such that each super-symbol is brought to the leftmost position at least once. Let d_i be the final position of the super-symbol initially in position i. We first use the nucleus generators of the super-IP graph to sort the leftmost super-symbol to that of the d_1-th super-symbol of the destination node address. We then use the above t steps to bring each of the super-symbols of a node label to the leftmost position at least once. When the super-symbol initially in position i is brought to the leftmost position for the first time, we use the nucleus generators of the super-IP graph to sort the current leftmost super-symbol to that of the d_i-th super-symbol of the destination node address.

Since the diameter of the nucleus graph is D_G, the time required for the nucleus generators to sort a super-symbol is no more than D_G. Therefore, routing in the super-IP graph can be performed in no more than $lD_G + t$ time.

Let A' and B' be the addresses of two nodes that have distance D_G within the same nucleus G. Routing from node $A = \underbrace{A'A'\cdots A'}_{l}$ to node $B = \underbrace{B'B'\cdots B'}_{l}$ requires at least $lD_G + t$ steps since each of the l super-symbols with value A' has to be sorted to the state with value B', and the super-symbols have to be brought to the leftmost position so that they can be sorted. This completes the proof. □

It can be seen that the parameter t in Theorem 4.1 is at least $l - 1$ for any super-IP graph and is equal to $l - 1$ for all

the super-IP graphs introduced in Section 3. This, combined with Theorems 4.1 and 3.2, leads to the following corollary.

Corollary 4.2 *The diameter of an N-node HSN, RHSN, RCC, cyclic-shift network, directed cyclic-shift network, or super-flip network is*

$$(D_G + 1)\log_{M_N} N - 1,$$

where M_N is the number of nodes in the nucleus graph and D_G is the diameter of the nucleus graph.

The proofs and examples for the following theorems can be found in [33].

Theorem 4.3 *Let t_S be the minimum number of applications of the super-generators of a symmetric super-IP graph in order for each super-symbol to appear at the leftmost position at least once and for the super-symbols to be eventually arranged to any possible order. Then the diameter of the symmetric super-IP graph is $lD_G + t_S$, where l is the number of super-symbols in a node label and D_G is the diameter of the nucleus of the super-IP graph.*

Theorem 4.4 *The diameter of an HSN, cyclic-shift network, directed cyclic-shift network, super-flip network, RCC, RHSN, or any of their symmetric super-IP graph variants is asymptotically optimal within a factor of $1 + o(1)$ from its lower bound (given its node degree) if the diameter of the nucleus graph is asymptotically optimal within a factor of $1 + o(1)$ from its lower bound and $d_S = d_N^{1+o(1)}$, where d_S is the number of super-generators, d_N is the number of nucleus-generators, and D_G and d_N are not constant. The diameter of any of these networks is asymptotically optimal within a constant from its lower bound if the diameter of the nucleus graph is asymptotically optimal within a constant from its lower bound and $\log_2 d_S = O(\log d_N)$.*

To obtain (symmetric) super-IP graphs with optimal diameters, we can use networks such as a generalized hypercube [7] of proper size and dimension as the nucleus.

5   Comparison of Several Networks

In this section, we look into several implementation and performance issues, including the assignment of processors to chips (or modules), pin limitations, bandwidth of on-chip and off-chip links, and the number of off-module transmissions required for routing.

5.1   Comparison of DD-Cost

Although diameter and average distance may be less important for networks using wormhole routing under light traffic, they are crucial for network performance under heavy load. The maximum possible throughput of a network is inversely proportional to these parameters for any switching technique. Figure 2 shows a rough comparison of some of the interconnection networks discussed so far and certain other popular networks on the basis of the product of node degree and network diameter (which is regarded as

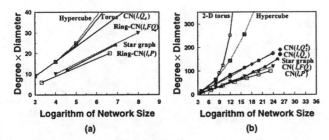

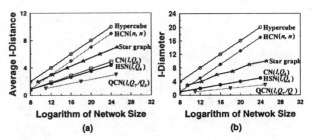

Figure 2. Comparison of DD-cost, the product of node degree and network diameter, for several interconnection networks, where P is the Petersen graph, and FQ_4 is a 4-dimensional folded hypercube.

Figure 3. Comparison of the (a) average inter-cluster distance and (b) inter-cluster diameter for several networks, assuming that at most 24 processors are available per cluster (module). Quotient-CN$(l, Q_7/Q_3)$, abbreviated QCN$(l, Q_7/Q_3)$ here, is obtained by merging each 3-cube in CN(l, Q_7) into a node. HCN(n, n) in the above figures are HSN$(2, Q_n)$ = HCN(n, n) without diameter links.

a suitable composite figure of merit [7] and is called *DD-cost* in this paper). When the sum of the capacities of all the links of a node is fixed (i.e., unit node capacity) and packet-switching is used (or wormhole/cut-through routing is used but messages are very short), the latency of a network with light traffic is approximately proportional to its DD-cost. From Fig. 2, we can see that cyclic-shift networks have DD-cost that is comparable to that of the star graph, and outperform other popular topologies significantly under this criterion, especially when the network size is large. In [2, 11], it has been shown that low-dimensional k-ary n-cubes perform better than high-dimensional ones under the constraint of constant bisection bandwidth. In [1], Abraham and Padmanabhan examined network performance under pin-out constraints and showed that higher-dimensional networks performed better. Generally speaking, low-dimensional k-ary n-cubes outperform super-IP graphs under the constant bisection-bandwidth constraint; while super-IP graphs outperform k-ary n-cubes and hypercubes under constant pin-out constraint. Detailed comparisons based on such considerations are outside the scope of this paper.

5.2 I-Diameter and Average I-Distance

In present computing environments, processors are expensive and memory is relatively cheap. Therefore, an optimization question is: "how large should the memory be to utilize the processor(s) efficiently?" The utilization of processors in parallel computers is not as efficient as that in a single-processor computer for general-purpose applications, so that the latter achieves better performance per dollar. In future computing environments, however, the roles might be reversed, so that memory is expensive and processors are relatively cheap. Therefore, the question might become: "how many processors are appropriate to utilize the memory efficiently?" As pointed out by Dally [12] and researchers working on processor in memory (PIM) or computing in RAM [18, 23], multiple processors per chip, integrated with memory banks, can increase memory-processor bandwidth considerably and improve the utilization of memory significantly. Moreover, with the rapid advances in VLSI technologies, the number of transistors and the number of processors that can be put onto a chip are expected to continue their exponential growths. Therefore, single-chip multiprocessors are expected to achieve better performance per dol-

lar even for general-purpose applications and may become a mainstream in the future computing market. Another trend in the synthesis of multicomputers is to use off-the-shelf PC or workstation boards (or processor chips) as building modules.

In either case, a parallel computer is built from several chips on a board and multiple such boards in a card-cage. Modules at each level of the packaging hierarchy have their respective characteristics in terms of the number of pins, maximum capacity, bisection bandwidth, maximum wire length, and channel bandwidth [6]. In what follows, we consider the case where several nodes (processors, routers, and associated memory banks) of a network are implemented on a single chip, or more generally, a single module (e.g., chip, board, wafer, or multi-chip module (MCM)). Since transmissions over off-chip (or off-module) links are more expensive than transmissions over on-chip (or on-module) links, it is generally preferred to reduce the number of off-chip (or off-module) transmissions for a routing task. Figure 3a compares the *average inter-cluster distance (average I-distance)* (also called *average inter-module distance*), the average number of inter-cluster or off-module (e.g., off-chip or off-board) transmissions required for routing between two nodes, in several interconnection networks, assuming that at most 24 nodes can be placed within a module, if the parallel system is to execute a random routing problem with uniformly distributed sources and destinations. Figure 3b compares the *inter-cluster diameter (I-diameter)* (also called *inter-module diameter*), the maximum number of inter-cluster (off-module) transmissions for routing between two nodes, in several interconnection networks. It can be shown that the maximum throughput of a network is inversely proportional to its average inter-cluster distance when the off-module links are uniformly utilized and the off-module bandwidth is the communication bottleneck.

5.3 Comparison of Inter-cluster Degree

We define the *inter-cluster degree (I-degree)* (or *inter-module degree*) as the maximum of the average-per-node inter-cluster (off-module) links over all clusters (modules). Since the number of available off-module pins per node is one of the major constraints limiting the performance and

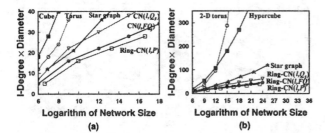

Figure 4. Comparison of ID-cost, the product of inter-cluster degree and diameter, for several interconnection networks, assuming that no more than 10 nodes can be placed in a cluster (module).

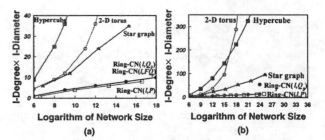

Figure 5. Comparison of II-cost, the product of inter-cluster degree and inter-cluster diameter, for several interconnection networks, assuming that no more than 10 nodes can be placed in a cluster (module).

the number of processors that can be put on the module, it is desirable to minimize the *inter-cluster degree* when assigning network nodes to basic building modules. Also, to eliminate the "number of parts" problem, it is preferred that the building chips be identical or of only a few types. To satisfy the above criteria, we can place each of the nuclei of a super-IP graph within the same module when partitioning the network. Then the maximum number of off-module links per node in an l-level ring-cyclic network is equal to 1 when $l = 2$ and 2 when $l \geq 3$; the corresponding numbers for an l-level HSN, complete-CN [27, 28], or super-flip network are 1,2,3,4, respectively, when $l = 2,3,4,5$. As a comparison, the maximum numbers of off-module links per node in an n-dimensional hypercube and star graph are $n - 3$ (or $n - 4$) and $n - 2$ (or $n - 3$), when a 3(or 4)-cube or a 3(or 4)-star is placed within the same module, where $n = \log_2 N$ for an N-node hypercube and $n = O(\log N / \log \log N)$ for an N-node star graph. For example, a node in a 17-cube has 14 (or 13) off-module links and a node in a 8-star has 6 (or 5) off-module links.

If we assume *unit node off-module capacity*, where the average off-module bandwidth per node (i.e., the sum of the bandwidth of all off-module links per node) is the same for parallel architectures based on different networks, then an off-module link of a super-IP graph has bandwidth considerably larger than that of a hypercube or star graph. The maximum number of off-module links per node in a de Bruijn graph is equal to 4 when assigning nodes with the same most significant bits into the same module, so the bandwidth of an off-module link of a ring-cyclic network or an HSN(l, Q_4) (or complete-CN(l, Q_4)) of practical size is also better than that of a de Bruijn graph using such a partitioning. Note that when wormhole or cut-through routing is used and messages are long, the delay of a network with light traffic is approximately proportional to its inter-cluster degree.

5.4 Comparison of ID-Cost and II-Cost

We define the *ID-cost* of a network as the product of its inter-cluster degree and its diameter. The inter-cluster degree is usually (approximately) equal to the number of off-module links per node, which is the case for the networks considered in Figs. 2,3, and 4, except for 2-D tori. When the sum of the capacities of all the off-module links of an M-node module is cM, where c is a constant (i.e., the sum of the capacities of all the off-module links of a node is fixed for

networks considered in Fig. 4, except for 2-D tori), the delay of a packet-switched network with light traffic is proportional to its ID-cost. The delay of a network using wormhole or cut-through routing is also approximately proportional to its ID-cost when the traffic is light and the messages are short. From Fig. 4, it can be seen that cyclic-shift networks have ID-cost that is considerably smaller than those of other popular topologies, for small- to large-scale networks.

In the preceding arguments, we have assumed that the speeds of all links, including on-module and off-module links, are the same and the traffic is approximately balanced over all network links. However, on-chip links are significantly shorter than off-chip links and do not need extra delay to drive off-chip pins, they can be driven at a considerably higher clock rate. Moreover, since the cost for an on-chip connection is much smaller than that of an off-chip connection, the channel width of an on-chip link can be increased, if required, without significantly increasing the hardware cost. When transmissions over on-module links are considerably faster than over off-module links, the delay of a packet-switched network with light traffic is approximately proportional to its *II-cost*, defined as the product of its inter-cluster degree and inter-cluster diameter. Moreover, when the traffic is heavy and the utilization of off-module links is higher than that of on-module links, the delay of a packet-switched network is also approximately proportional to its II-cost even when all links in the network have the same speed, since the average waiting time required for a packet to be transmitted over an off-module link is considerably larger than that required for an on-module link. From Fig. 5, we can see that cyclic-shift networks have II-cost that is considerably smaller than those of other popular topologies, for small- to large-scale networks, even when module size is limited to 8 or 10 nodes. When the module size is larger than 10 nodes, the superiority of super-IP graphs over other network topologies is even more pronounced.

6 Conclusion

In this paper, we have presented an extension of Cayley graphs, called the IP graph model, for the development of communication-efficient interconnection networks. We presented several interconnection networks based on super-IP and symmetric super-IP graphs that have certain desirable properties. The diameters and inter-cluster diameters of suitably constructed (symmetric) super-IP graphs are asymptotically optimal within a small constant factor from their respective lower bounds. IP graphs provide flexibility in the design of parallel architectures in view of the possibility of selecting several parameters, nuclei, super-generators, seed labels, and/or the nodes to be merged, an appropriate combination of which can mitigate performance bottlenecks and balance system resources. In particular, a dense nucleus graph reduces the diameter and average distance, a strong set of super-generators enhances the embedding capability, a seed label consisting of distinct symbols generates a symmetric and regular network, a quotient variant [28, 33] minimizes the required off-module data transmissions, and their combined effect determines the algorithmic properties of the resulting network.

References

[1] Abraham, S. and K. Padmanabhan, "Performance of multicomputer networks under pin-out constraints," *J. Parallel Distrib. Comput.*, Vol. 12, no. 3, Jul. 1991, pp. 237-248.

[2] Agarwal, A., "Limits on interconnection network performance," *IEEE Trans. Parallel Distrib. Sys.*, Vol. 2, no. 4, Oct. 1991, pp. 398-412.

[3] Akers, S.B., D. Harel, and B. Krishnamurthy, "The star graph: an attractive alternative to the n-cube," *Proc. Int'l Conf. Parallel Processing*, 1987, pp. 393-400.

[4] Akers, S.B. and B. Krishnamurthy, "A group-theoretic model for symmetric interconnection networks," *IEEE Trans. Comput.*, Vol. 38, Apr. 1989, pp. 555-565.

[5] Akl, S.G., *Parallel Computation: Models and Methods*, Prentice Hall, Englewood Cliffs, NJ, 1997.

[6] Basak D. and D.K. Panda, "Designing clustered multiprocessor systems under packaging and technological advancements," *IEEE Trans. Parallel Distrib. Sys.*, vol. 7, no. 9, Sep. 1996, pp. 962-978.

[7] Bhuyan, L.N. and D.P. Agrawal, "Generalized hypercube and hyperbus structures for a computer network," *IEEE Trans. Comput.*, vol. 33, no. 4, Apr. 1984, pp. 323-333.

[8] Biggs, N., *Algebraic Graph Theory*, 2nd edition, Cambridge, Cambridge University Press, 1993.

[9] Corbett, P.F., "Rotator graphs: an efficient topology for point-to-point multiprocessor networks," *IEEE Trans. Parallel Distrib. Sys.*, vol. 3, no. 5, pp. 622-626, Sep. 1992.

[10] Cypher, R. and J.L.C. Sanz, "Hierarchical shuffle-exchange and de Bruijn networks," *Proc. IEEE Symp. Parallel and Distributed Processing*, 1992, pp. 491-496.

[11] Dally, W.J., "Performance analysis of k-ary n-cube interconnection networks," *IEEE Trans. Comput.*, Vol. 39, no. 6, Jun. 1990, pp. 775-785.

[12] Dally, W.J. and S. Lacy, "VLSI architecture: past, present, and future," *Proc. Advanced Research in VLSI Conf.*, 1999, to appear.

[13] Duh, D., G. Chen, and J. Fang, "Algorithms and properties of a new two-level network with folded hypercubes as basic modules," *IEEE Trans. Parallel Distrib. Sys.*, vol. 6, no. 7, Jul. 1995, pp. 714-723.

[14] Fragopoulou, P. and S.G. Akl, "Edge-disjoint spanning trees on the star network with applications to fault tolerance," *IEEE Trans. Computers*, vol. 45, no. 2, Feb. 1996, pp. 174-185.

[15] Ghose, K. and R. Desai, "Hierarchical cubic networks," *IEEE Trans. Parallel Distrib. Sys.*, vol. 6, no. 4, Apr. 1995, pp. 427-435.

[16] Hamdi, M., "A class of recursive interconnection networks: architectural characteristics and hardware cost," *IEEE Trans. Circuits and Sys.–I: Fundamental Theory and Applications*, vol. 41, no. 12, Dec. 1994, pp. 805-816.

[17] Huang, J.-P., S. Lakshmivarahan, and S.K. Dhall, "Analysis of interconnection networks based on simple Cayley coset graphs," *Proc. IEEE Symp. Parallel and Distributed Processing*, 1993, pp. 150-157.

[18] Kogge, P.M., "EXECUBE – a new architecture for scalable MPPs," *Proc. Int'l Conf. Parallel Processing*, vol. I, 1994, pp. 77-84.

[19] Lakshmivarahan, S., J.-S. Jwo, and S.K. Dhall, "Symmetry in interconnection networks based on Cayley graphs of permutation groups: a survey," *Parallel Computing*, Vol. 19, no. 4, Apr. 1993, pp. 361-407.

[20] Latifi, S., M.M. Azevedo, and N. Bagherzadeh, "The star connected cycles: a fixed-degree network for parallel processing," *Proc. Int'l Conf. Parallel Processing*, vol. I, 1993, pp. 91-95.

[21] Leighton, F.T., *Introduction to Parallel Algorithms and Architectures: Arrays, Trees, Hypercubes*, Morgan-Kaufman, San Mateo, CA, 1992.

[22] Preparata, F.P. and J.E. Vuillemin, "The cube-connected cycles: a versatile network for parallel computation," *Communications of the ACM*, vol. 24, no. 5, May 1981, pp. 300-309.

[23] Sterling, T., P. Messina, and P. Smith, *Enabling Technologies for Petaflops Computing*, MIT Press., 1995.

[24] Yeh, C.-H. and B. Parhami, "Parallel algorithms on three-level hierarchical cubic networks," *Proc. High Performance Computing Symp.*, Mar. 1996, pp. 226-231.

[25] Yeh, C.-H. and B. Parhami, "Hierarchical swapped networks: efficient low-degree alternatives to hypercubes and generalized hypercubes," *Proc. Int'l Symp. Parallel Architectures, Algorithms, and Networks*, 1996, pp. 90-96.

[26] Yeh, C.-H. and B. Parhami, "Recursive hierarchical swapped networks: versatile interconnection architectures for highly parallel systems," *Proc. IEEE Symp. Parallel and Distributed Processing*, Oct. 1996, pp. 453-460.

[27] Yeh, C.-H. and B. Parhami, "Cyclic networks – a family of versatile fixed-degree interconnection architectures," *Proc. Int'l Parallel Processing Symp.*, Apr. 1997, 739-743.

[28] Yeh, C.-H., "Efficient low-degree interconnection networks for parallel processing: topologies, algorithms, VLSI layouts, and fault tolerance," Ph.D. dissertation, Dept. Electrical & Computer Engineering, Univ. of California, Santa Barbara, Mar. 1998.

[29] Yeh, C.-H. and E.A. Varvarigos, "Macro-star networks: efficient low-degree alternatives to star graphs," *IEEE Trans. Parallel Distrib. Sys.*, vol. 9, no. 10, Oct. 1998, pp. 987-1003.

[30] Yeh, C.-H. and E.A. Varvarigos, "Parallel algorithms on the rotation-exchange network – a trivalent variant of the star graph," *Proc. Symp. Frontiers of Massively Parallel Computation*, Feb. 1999, pp. 302-309.

[31] Yeh, C.-H., B. Parhami, and E.A. Varvarigos, "The recursive grid layout scheme for VLSI layout of hierarchical networks," *Proc. Merged Int'l Parallel Processing Symp. & Symp. Parallel and Distributed Processing*, Apr. 1999, pp. 441-445.

[32] Yeh, C.-H. and B. Parhami, "Routing and embeddings in cyclic Petersen networks: an efficient extension of the Petersen graph," *Proc. Int'l Conf. Parallel Processing*, Sep. 1999, to appear.

[33] Yeh, C.-H. and B. Parhami, "A unified model for hierarchical networks based on an extension of Cayley graphs," *IEEE Trans. Parallel Distrib. Sys.*, to appear.

[34] Yun, S.-K. and K.H. Park, "Hierarchical hypercube networks (HHN) for massively parallel computers," *J. Parallel Distrib. Comput.*, vol. 37, no. 2, Sep. 1996, pp. 194-199.

Session A2

Routing & Deadlock

Chair: Wu-Chun Feng
Los Alamos National Lab and Purdue University,
USA

Adaptive Bubble Router: a Design to Improve Performance in Torus Networks[*]

V. Puente, R. Beivide, J.A. Gregorio, J.M. Prellezo, J. Duato[*], and C. Izu[**]

Universidad de Cantabria
39005 Santander, Spain
{vpuente,mon,jagm,prellezo}@atc.unican.es

[*] Universidad P. de Valencia
46071 Valencia, Spain
jduato@gap.upv.es

[**] University of Adelaide
SA 5005 Australia
cruz@cs.adelaide.edu.au

Abstract

A router design for torus networks that significantly reduces message latency over traditional wormhole routers is presented in this paper. This new router implements virtual cut-through switching and fully-adaptive minimal routing. Packet deadlock is avoided by providing escape ways governed by Bubble flow control, a mechanism that guarantees enough free buffer space in the network to allow continuous packet movement.

Both deterministic and adaptive Bubble routers have been designed in VLSI using VHDL synthesis tools. Adopting a fair quantitative comparison, we demonstrate that Bubble routers exhibit a reduction in base latency values over 40% with respect to the corresponding wormhole routers, without any penalty in network throughput. With much lower VLSI costs than adaptive wormhole routers, the adaptive Bubble router is even faster than deterministic wormhole routers based on virtual channels.

Keywords: Interconnection subsystem, parallel computers, hardware routers, performance evaluation, VLSI design, simulation.

1 Introduction

Multiprocessor performance has considerably increased during the last decade. On the one hand, distributed shared-memory multiprocessors (DSMs) are becoming widespread (SGI Origin 2000 [16], Cray T3E [20]). On the other hand, nowadays message-passing multicomputers constitute the frontier of computing power (ASCI Project [15]). As processor computing power increases, communication performance should increase accordingly in order to adequately balance the system.

Interconnection networks have also significantly evolved, reducing message latency and increasing throughput. Most of these improvements come from architectural advances. A significant architectural advance has been the use of pipelined switching techniques. In particular, wormhole switching considerably reduces message latency by routing a message as soon as its header arrives at a router [7]. Data follow immediately after the header. This strategy splits messages into small units of information, or flits [6], performing flow control at the flit level. As a consequence of this unique feature, flit buffers can be very small, leading to compact and fast routers [4]. These benefits led to the implementation of wormhole switching in most commercial routers [2, 13, 19].

Moreover, this pipelined message transmission makes latency less sensitive to the distance in the network provided that messages are long enough, facilitating the search for optimal topologies. Several researchers recommended the use of low-dimensional direct networks in the k-ary n-cube class [1, 8]. As a result, the use of bidimensional or three-dimensional meshes and tori or limited-degree hypercubes is common in multicomputers and DSMs.

However, wormhole switching has also some disadvantages. A main one is that messages block in place when the link requested by the header is busy. So, data flits span over multiple routers, leading to significant link contention. Contention can be reduced by multiplexing physical bandwidth among several messages. This can be achieved by using separate buffers, or virtual channels [9], associated with each physical link. Virtual channels have also been proposed to avoid message deadlock [7]. Another way to reduce the negative effects of link contention consists of using adaptive routing, allowing packets to follow alternative paths. Fully adaptive routing also requires virtual channels to avoid deadlock in k-ary n-cube wormhole networks [10]. Finally, link contention can also be mitigated implementing buffers large enough to store full messages. For example, the Cray T3E router uses these three techniques: the virtual channel buffers have capacity for 12 and 22 flits, thus being able to store one and two messages, respectively. Moreover, adaptive virtual channels are added to the oblivious ones, only accepting a new message if there are enough empty flit buffers to store the whole message [19].

Other routers such as the Intel Cavallino [2], the SGI SPIDER [13] also employ a few virtual channels per phys-

[*]This work is supported in part by TIC98-1162-C02-01

ical link with the latter implementing fully adaptive routing as well. Both features improve throughput significantly [9, 10], and may reduce the execution time for bandwidth-limited parallel applications. However, virtual channels and adaptive routing have been shown to increment router delay [4], thus increasing the execution time of latency-sensitive parallel applications. For those applications, it has been suggested that routers should implement neither virtual channels nor adaptive routing [23]. Therefore, including virtual channels and adaptive routing in a wormhole router is a design tradeoff.

In this paper a new virtual cut-through (VCT) router is proposed. We show that router delay can be reduced with respect to a wormhole (WH) router while keeping the same functionality. We have considered a context similar to the one for the Cray T3E router, i.e., torus topology and short messages, developing complete router designs for WH and VCT switching. Both deterministic and fully adaptive minimal routing have been explored.

The contributions of this paper are: 1) a simple and efficient strategy to implement fully adaptive VCT routers, 2) a quantitative evaluation of deterministic and adaptive routers for wormhole and virtual cut-through flow control, showing that VCT router delay can be kept smaller than that of an oblivious WH router, and 3) an evaluation of 2-D and 3-D tori router networks under different traffic patterns, showing that VCT routers considerably outperform their WH counterparts.

The rest of this paper is organized as follows. Section 2 will present the framework and motivation for this research. An informal and intuitive description of our adaptive routing proposal will be presented in Section 3, followed by a description of the Bubble router architecture. Section 3 will also provide VLSI cost values for the proposed router as well as other router alternatives. A quantitative comparison of all routers will be presented in Section 4. Finally, Section 5 will summarize the findings of this work.

2   Motivation and Related Work

When comparing among routers he benefits of the faster ones are visible across all applications, whatever will be their network load, in a consistent fashion. In particular, for cc-NUMA machines, network latency at low load is critical because many applications use the network resources within this operational zone.

Base latency strongly depends on router complexity; any increment in router complexity implies either a decrement in the router clock frequency or an increment in the number of router pipeline stages. So, we should aim at designing simpler and faster routers with few or no virtual channels and simple routing algorithms. However, if we simplify router design, how do we reduce the contention that typically arises when executing very demanding parallel applications?

A way to reduce congestion without requiring virtual channels consists of using virtual cut-through switching [14]. This switching technique requires buffers with capacity for one or more packets, thus removing blocked packets from the network. However, buffer requirements prevented the widespread use of VCT in multiprocessor interconnection networks. As mentioned before, recent wormhole-based routers already incorporate large buffers to deal with contention. Thus, the main difference, between VCT and WH routers is the size of their flow control unit. VCT performs flow control at the packet level instead of at the smaller data units employed in WH routers. Moreover, DSMs only require the transmission of very short messages (10 flits at most in the Cray T3E [19]) so buffer requirements can be kept reasonably low. This scenario is also similar for cc-NUMA machines.

Our goal is to design a fast VCT router which will provide lower latency than current wormhole routers at any working load. A number of reasons support this purpose. To start with, VCT flow control is simpler than WH and therefore faster when implemented. Secondly, if we consider the traffic properties under VCT flow control, we could simplify deadlock avoidance as shown in [3], reducing the required number of virtual channels under deterministic routing from two down to one. We will take this approach, which increases router speed as well. To make our router competitive at medium and high loads, adaptivity should be achieved with minimal implementation cost. The simplest fully adaptive wormhole router [11] implies the addition of one or more virtual channels to an existing deadlock-free network. Similarly, we could add one queue (virtual channel) to the deadlock-free proposal cited above, thus obtaining adaptivity at the minimum possible cost.

With respect to other related work, most of the research effort in the last decade has focused on improving wormholed-based routers by means of different routing and deadlock avoidance/recovery strategies. Little has been done, though, for virtual cut-through networks. To the best of our knowledge, few proposals, apart from our own, have considered $VCT's$ impact on network behavior ([18] [5] [17] among others): the more close to our proposal are the Chaos router [18], which implements non-minimal adaptive routing, and the minimal adaptive routing proposed by Cypher and Gravano [5].

3   The Bubble Router

In this section we propose a minimal fully adaptive routing algorithm for k-ary n-cube networks using virtual cut-through switching. After an informal description of this algorithm, we describe the VLSI design of the Bubble router, discussing low level issues.

3.1 Adaptive Routing Algorithm for Torus Networks

We will present our adaptive routing algorithm informally. A formal description and subsequent proofs have been developed but they have been omitted in this paper for the sake of simplicity.

Consider a full-duplex torus network; each link can be viewed as two unidirectional links in opposite directions. Each unidirectional link has two FIFO queues associated to its input edge. These queues will be referred to as the *adaptive* and the *escape* queue, respectively. Bidirectional routers can be simply obtained by duplicating links and queues for the opposite directions as well as increasing the crossbar size. Routers for n-dimensional torus can also be easily obtained by extending the basic router resources, i.e., links with their associated queues and crossbar size. Each of the input queues is conceptually identical to a virtual channel in a wormhole-based router. As we assume VCT switching, each queue must be able to store at least one packet: thus, we measure the capacity of a queue in terms of packet units.

Our adaptive algorithm is based on combining two strategies: dimension-order routing (DOR) with Bubble flow control in the escape queues [3], and fully adaptive minimal routing in the adaptive queues [12]. Packets can move from an adaptive queue to an escape queue or viceversa, fulfilling the rules described below. If both queues are available, preference is given to the adaptive one. Packets using a escape queue can freely use, if available, an adaptive queue at the next router. The resulting routing algorithm is minimal fully adaptive and reduces hardware requirements with respect to previous proposals. As a result, router delay is considerably reduced, as it will be shown in the next subsection.

Packets travelling through escape queues use DOR paths and are regulated by Bubble flow control. Bubble flow control works as follows. Consider the set of unidirectional links along a given direction in a dimension of a n-dimensional torus network. Those links form a unidirectional ring as can be seen in Figure 1. Considering only the escape queues, packets (shaded units at each queue) are allowed to progress (shaded arrows) to another queue along the ring if there is an empty packet unit at that queue, that is, there is enough buffer space to store the whole packet. Note that this is the basic requirement of virtual cut-through switching. Thus, no additional constraints are imposed at this point. However, packet injection into the ring is only allowed if after injection there is at least one empty packet unit in the set of queues for the whole ring corresponding to the dimension (and direction) requested by the incoming packet. That is the key to avoid deadlock in any ring because the empty packet unit acts as a *bubble* which allows continuous packet movement along the ring. Although a number of solutions to provide a bubble exist, in our final implementation, before allowing a new packet injection in

a ring at an arbitrary node, we check for the existence of two free packet units in the escape queue at that node corresponding to the requested ring (*Bubble Condition*).

Similarly, when a packet attempts to change to the next dimension, it will be granted access to the escape queue if there are at least two empty packet units in the requested ring. Thus, moving to another dimension is treated as a packet injection.

In short, Bubble flow control avoids deadlock inside rings. Additionally, it is well known that DOR avoids deadlock involving several dimensions because they are crossed in order and there are no cyclic dependencies between buffer resources [7]. Therefore, the whole set of network escape queues is deadlock-free.

Packets travelling through adaptive queues can use any minimal path and are regulated by virtual cut-through flow control. Packets can use adaptive queues without any constraint provided that there is enough space for one packet. This applies to any packet, independently of where it comes from. Bubble flow control will only be applied if the next selected queue is an escape one. When both the adaptive and escape queue of a profitable channel are available, priority is given to the adaptive one. This selection policy provides a high routing flexibility, allowing packets to follow any minimal path available in the network.

The adaptive routing algorithm described above is also deadlock-free. As indicated in [12], adding queues to a deadlock-free routing algorithm cannot induce any deadlock, regardless of how packets are routed in the additional queues. The only constraint is that the routing algorithm should not consider the queue currently storing the packet when computing the set of routing options. This constraint is met by our routing algorithm because a packet can be routed on both escape and adaptive queues at any router, regardless of the queue storing it. Taking into account that DOR with Bubble flow control is deadlock-free, it follows that the whole routing algorithm is also deadlock-free.

When all the adaptive queues are full, as in Figure 2.(a), the network behaves as if only escape queues existed, as shown in Figure 2.(b). From the point of view of the escape queues, this state is identical to that depicted in Figure 1. It is clear from Figure 2 that escape queues are used by the packets stored in adaptive queues, avoiding any deadlock situation in the network with only two queues per physical link.

A VCT network which applies only Bubble flow control may lead to starvation. This problem arises in deterministic routing because packets advancing along a given unidimensional ring have a higher priority than those that are trying to enter that ring. For example, in Figure 3, packets going from router A to router D have a higher priority than packets trying to be injected at router B. Thus, if traffic between A and D is not stopped, a packet can be indefinitely waiting to enter at B. However, starvation cannot occur for the adaptive Bubble algorithm because the access to the adaptive queues is not restricted. This means that

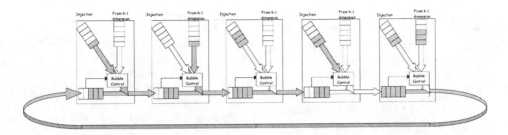

Figure 1. Deadlock avoidance in a ring by using Bubble flow control.

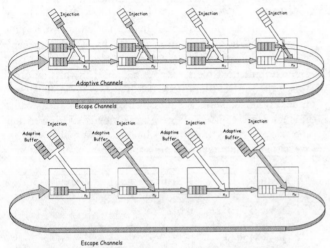

Figure 2. Representation of adaptive and escape queues when all adaptive ones are busy and equivalent network.

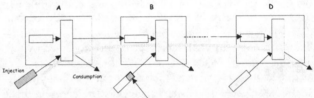

Figure 3. Example of starvation in deterministic Bubble flow control. It is avoided in our proposal.

3.2.1 Basic Router Blocks

The main blocks of the proposed router architecture are shown in Figure 4. There is an escape queue and an adaptive queue for each physical link. They behave as described in the previous section. Both of them are implemented as FIFO queues with an additional *synchronization* module to support the asynchronous communication between routers.

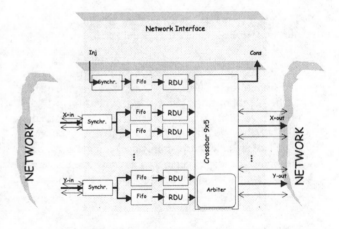

Figure 4. Router organization for a 2-D torus.

packets in transit have the same probability to acquire the adaptive queue as incoming packets. In the previous example, the packet to be injected at B will succeed entering next node's adaptive queue. Even if that queue is temporarily full, a packet unit will eventually become free because the network is deadlock-free.

3.2 Bubble Router Design

In order to validate our proposal, a router for bidirectional n-dimensional torus networks has been designed. In particular, this router has been specified using the hardware description language VHDL. Internal router components are clocked synchronously but communications with neighbor routers are asynchronous in order to avoid clock skew problems.

This section describes the design of the Bubble router, highlighting the differences with respect to other design alternatives.

Input queues and output ports are connected through a crossbar. A round-robin policy has been chosen to select among packets contending for the same output link. Moreover, taking into account that link multiplexing is performed on a packet-by-packet basis, a virtual channel controller is not required at the crossbar output. This reduces the latency of packets crossing the router. Besides, it is not necessary to send acknowledgment signals for every transmitted phit, and therefore, communication is less sensitive to wire delays.

Physical data links (and phits) in the current implementation are 9 bits wide, 8 bits for data and 1 bit for indicating the packet tail. Packets are 16 phits long, including the n-phit header which represents the destination address as a tuple of n offsets, i.e., the x and y offsets in a 2D torus.

The *routing decision unit* (RDU) associated to each input queue selects the output port taking into account the information in the packet header, the available local output ports and the status of the neighbor's queues. This status is known through external signals which are processed by the crossbar arbiter. If the selected output port and queue are available, the RDU updates the header phits so that the offset in the selected dimension is decremented, and sent first. This decrement operation is carried out simultaneously for x and y offsets, and in parallel with the crossbar arbitration. However, only one of the modified offsets will be forwarded as the first phit according to the selected output.

In order to keep the arbiter complexity low, potential output ports are requested in a cyclic sequential manner, one port per cycle until one of them is selected. Although this strategy may seem to decrease throughput, our experiments showed no noticeable degradation [22].

Queues are requested to the crossbar arbiter in the following order:

1. The adaptive queue of the neighbor along the incoming dimension, if the first offset is not zero.

2. The adaptive queue of the neighbor along the other dimension, if the second offset is not zero.

3. The escape queue of the neighbor along the first dimension, if the x offset is not zero or the escape queue of the neighbor along the second dimension if the x offset is zero. Before requesting an escape queue, the RDU verifies the Bubble condition. To do so, it checks that there are at least two empty packet units at the current router's escape queue. To guarantee the existence of one free packet unit it needs to ask for two; the latter may be acquired during that cycle by a transit packet.

Therefore, the routing decision in an empty network will take one cycle except for the $x - to - y$ turn and the delivery to the consumption channel. Both cases need two cycles as they examine both header phits. Finally, it is worth mentioning that the operations carried out by the routing decision unit depend on packet destination but they do not depend on the queue storing the packet. Thus, the RDU is identical for both adaptive and escape queues.

3.2.2   Time and Area of the Current Design

We have designed the entire Bubble router using the *Synopsys v1997.08* synthesis tool. Then, we mapped our design into 0.7 μm (two metal layers) technology from ATMEL/ES2 foundry under typical working conditions with standard cells from *Es2 Synopsys design kit V5.2*. Although the obtained results for area and time are estimated by *Synopsys* in a pessimistic way, they provide us with values very close to the physical domain.

Table 1 shows both delay and area for each one of the router blocks. As the design is pipelined, the block in the critical path with highest delay determines the maximum clock frequency of the device. In this particular case it is the crossbar, due to its arbitration complexity, which imposes a cycle time of 5.65 ns. For the queue blocks we have considered three possible sizes: 32, 64, and 128 phits, in order to see the impact that queue depth has on its management time. For this design, 128 phits is the optimal value because it is the largest queue whose access time is still lower than the selected cycle time. Nevertheless, as we will see below, we actually use queues 64 phits long.

Module	Critical Path (ns)	Area(mm^2)
Sync.	3.53	0.51($\times$5)
Queue (32 phits)	5.19	0.41
Queue (64 phits)	*5.22*	*0.59($\times$9)*
Queue (128 phits)	5.25	0.94
Routing Dec. Unit	5.64	0.80($\times$9)
Crossbar & Arbiter	5.65	3.70($\times$1)
Total (64 phits)	5.65	18.76

Table 1. Characteristics of the router modules under typical conditions.

These results lead to the number of clock cycles represented in Figure 5. Crossbar and FIFO stages consume one cycle each. One or two cycles are spent in the routing decision unit depending on the direction followed by the packet (turns and consumption are penalized with an additional cycle). Finally, because of its asynchronous behavior, the synchronization module spends a variable amount of time (1 cycle on average).

3.3   Design of Alternative Router Organizations

Once the new router has been designed, the next step is to assess its performance for specific networks. However, it is not enough to obtain absolute performance figures for our router. We also need to compare it with other proposals using the same design methodology.

To achieve this goal, three additional routers have been designed for the same topology. Their organizations represent standard solutions for routers to be included into toroidal networks.

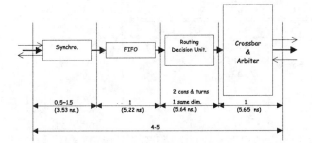

Figure 5. Delay in clock cycles for each module in the Bubble router pipeline.

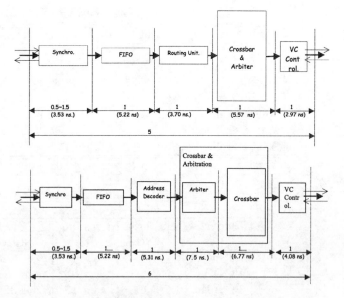

Figure 6. Pipeline structures for VC DOR and VC Adaptive routers.

A fully adaptive wormhole router that uses Duato's routing algorithm [11] for avoiding message deadlock has been designed . It requires at least three virtual channels per link. The crossbar size is 13×13 for a two-dimensional router. As in the router for the Cray T3E, wormhole switching is used but the maximum message length is limited. By doing so, the restriction on the use of adaptive channels can be eliminated, and therefore, the presence in the same queue of flits belonging to different messages is allowed. Although other alternatives for flow control have been tested, this is the one that offers the best results.

Additionally, in order to measure the cost of adaptivity, two routers using deterministic routing (DOR) have been designed. The first one, based on [6], uses wormhole switching and two virtual channels to avoid deadlock. We have not used more advanced algorithms for handling virtual channels, like the one proposed in [11], because it increases the router complexity and diminishes the main advantage of deterministic routers: low latency. The second deterministic router is based on the Bubble algorithm [3], with only one set of queues which follows the same flow control strategy as the escape queues described in Section 3.1.

The pipelined structures for wormhole routers are shown in Figure 6. The results for area and cycle time for each of these three designs, obtained from the hardware synthesis tools, are shown in Table 2. Note that the building blocks differ in each implementation as it was described in each original proposal but we apply the same VLSI design style. Additionally, due to the long arbitration delay in the adaptive wormhole router, the crossbar and arbiter stage has been split into two stages. To fairly compare among designs, we assume a total buffer capacity for the set of queues attached to each input channel of 128 flits for WH routers and 128 phits for VCT routers. It can be seen in Table 2 that this buffer capacity penalizes the clock cycle value for the Bubble DOR implementation. The small difference in time between the crossbar and arbiter units of both wormhole VC DOR and Bubble adaptive routers (Table 1)is due to the later having to control channel multiplexing.

4 Quantitative Router Evaluation

In this section, we compare the Bubble router performance with those of the alternative routers. First, we will compare router delay and its impact on network base latency based on the time analysis presented above. Then, we will analyze router behavior inside specific networks.

4.1 Evaluation of VLSI Router Cost

Table 3 summarizes, for all the routers, the required silicon area and time delays presented in the previous section. It is clear that methods based on Bubble flow control are, at least, a realistic alternative to the classical wormhole solutions based on virtual channels.

In our designs, the circuit's critical path is the arbiter plus crossbar unit except for the VC adaptive router in which the arbiter and the crossbar are decoupled, being the arbiter the stage that dictates the cycle time. This time is strongly related to the number of virtual channels that can request a given output port. Therefore, the cycle time for our *adaptive* Bubble router is similar to that of the *deterministic* wormhole router. Traditional wormhole routers require a virtual channel controller in order to provide link multiplexing at the flit-level. Bubble-based routers eliminate one pipeline stage per node because, as mentioned above, they do not require a virtual channel controller at each output port. This reduces silicon area for the adaptive Bubble router which uses only 56% of the required area for the adaptive wormhole counterpart. Besides, a shorter pipeline also reduces the hop time.

	Bubble DOR (*VCT*)		VC. DOR (*WH*)		VC. Adaptive (*WH*)	
Module	Time(*ns.*)	Area(mm^2)	Time(*ns.*)	Area(mm^2)	Time(*ns.*)	Area(mm^2)
Sync.	3.53	0.51($\times 5$)	3.53	0.51($\times 5$)	3.53	0.51($\times 5$)
Standard Queue	**5.25**	0.94($\times 4$)	5.22	1.18($\times 4$)	5.22	1.51($\times 4$)
Injection Queue	**5.25**	0.94($\times 1$)	5.25	0.94($\times 1$)	5.25	0.94($\times 1$)
Crossbar & Arbiter	4.31	2.15($\times 1$)	**5.57**	6.30($\times 1$)	6.77,**7.50**	7.86($\times 1$)
Routing Unit	3.58	0.13($\times 5$)	3.70	0.06($\times 9$)	–	–
Address decoder	–	–	–	–	5.31	0.86($\times 13$)
VC Controller	–	–	2.97	0.17($\times 4$)	4.08	1.20($\times 4$)
Total	5.25	10.05	5.57	15.73	7.5	33.37

Table 2. Characteristics of alternative router designs for 2-D tori.

Router	Clock Cycles	Crossbar Size	Queue Sizes	Cycle time (*ns.*)	Area (mm^2)	Hop Time (*ns.*)
Bubble DOR	4	5×5	128	5.25	10.05	21.0
VC DOR	5	9×9	64 + 64	5.57	15.73	27.85
VC Adap.	6	13×13	64 + 32 + 32	7.5	33.37	45
Bubble Adap	*4-5*	*9 × 5*	*64 + 64*	*5.65*	*18.76*	*25.43*

Table 3. Characteristics of router designs for 2-D tori.

Although a hardware design of a Bubble 3-D router has not yet been completed, preliminary results have been obtained by designing in VLSI the most critical parts of the routers. The additional costs are basically due to the increment in the number of inputs and outputs links. Thus, a 3-D router increases its pin-count by a factor of 7/5 with respect to a 2-D counterpart; obviously, this produces an increment in both silicon area and clock cycle.

Taking into account the bottlenecks found in 2-D routers, we encountered that the most critical component was the crossbar arbiter, and therefore, we paid more attention to the crossbar unit. In fact, we have developed VHDL instances of each one of the necessary crossbars for the four 3-D routers under analysis. Table 4 shows preliminary results.

Router	Clock cycles	Crossbar size	Crossbar critical path	Router cycle time
Bub. DOR	4	7×7	4.92	5.25
VC DOR	5	13×13	5.79	5.79
VC Adap	6	19×19	8.71	8.71
Bub. Adap	5	13×7	6.28	6.28

Table 4. Main characteristics of 3-D torus routers.

4.2 Network Analysis

Besides comparing stand-alone routers, we should compare their behavior when used to build specific networks. Although the physical implementation of the whole network would be the best way to assess its performance, accurate results can also be obtained by employing simulation tools.

Simulations have been performed at low level, using *Vhdlsim* and *Leapfrog*, VHDL simulators from *Synopsys* and *Cadence* respectively. In this way, every part of the router is accessible and can be monitored. However, this method has the drawback of requiring long simulation time. For instance, the average time for simulating 20000 clock cycles of an 8×8 2-D torus is about 10 hours running *Vhdlsim* and 2.5 hours for *Leapfrog* in the same conditions on an UltraSparc2 with 128 Mbytes.

With the aim of reducing the design cycle, an object oriented simulator has been written in C++. This simulator, called *SICOSYS (SImulator for COmmunication SYStem)* [21], has a remarkable feature: low-level characteristics of each router have been incorporated into the code, including the component delays obtained by using VLSI tools. This approach guarantees the delivery of accurate results which are very close to those obtained through VHDL simulation (discrepancies in latency less than 4%).

The results presented below have been obtained using *SICOSYS* and applying the component delays presented in section 3. The results correspond to 16-ary 2-cube networks under two different message destination patterns: random and specific permutations. In the first case, all the nodes have the same probability of becoming the destination for a given message. Two message length distributions were considered for this pattern: only short messages (16 phits[1]) and a mix of short and long messages in order to simulate bimodal traffic (16 phits and 160 phits[2], respectively). The latter resembles the traffic generated in DSM multiprocessors in which short messages correspond to requests (or invalidation primitives for cc-NUMA), and long messages correspond to cache lines.

For the specific permutation experiments, three traffic patterns were taken into account: matrix transpose, bit reversal, and perfect-shuffle. All three cases are frequently used in numerical applications, such as in ADI methods to solve differential equation systems and in FFT algorithms, among others. In all the experiments, the traffic generation rate is uniform and randomly distributed over time.

4.2.1 Network Latency at Zero Load

Base latency depends on the router complexity. Therefore, adaptive routers tend to exhibit lower performance in low load situations. In our proposal this drawback has been minimized in two ways: limiting the number of queues per link to only two, and implementing a sequential arbiter to manage the requests for the router output links.

Table 5 shows the base latency for all the router designs and traffic patterns considered. The corresponding values have been obtained when the load applied to the network was around 0.05% of the bisection bandwidth.

Router	Rand	Bimo	Mtra	BitR	PerfS
Bub. DOR	276.5	358.2	284.2	282.2	279.7
VC DOR	338.6	424.6	348.5	346.2	342.8
VC Adap.	515.4	652.2	543.7	539.5	518.5
Bub. Adap	303.8	406.6	318.8	316.3	306.1

Table 5. Base latency (ns).

As we have previously mentioned, our main goal is to reduce the latency values in the most frequently used scenarios of network operation because many parallel applications for DSM machines are latency-limited, thus benefiting from reductions in message latency [23]. As expected, the deterministic Bubble router, which has the lower through delay, exhibits the lowest network base latency. Even when adaptivity is supported, the adaptive Bubble router exhibits latency values better than those obtained by deterministic wormhole routers. On the contrary, supporting fully adaptive routing in a wormhole-based router comes at a high cost: an increment of more than 50% in base latency.

4.2.2 Maximum Sustained Throughput

In spite of message latency being the main figure of merit in order to reduce the execution time of most parallel applications, another metric like the maximum throughput is frequently used to measure the performance of a specific interconnection network. Determining the saturation point of the network is nearly impossible in our context because this value strongly depends on the simulation conditions such as the random generation of values and the seeds election. Notwithstanding, the maximum value of the accepted traffic can give an idea of the network behavior in congestion conditions. These values expressed in structural terms (phits accepted per network cycle) and technological terms (phits accepted per nanosecond) can be seen in Table 6 for the different traffic patterns and routers. In all cases, the Bubble adaptive router achieves the largest throughput when measured in phits/ns.

4.2.3 Network Latency and Throughput at Variable Load

To complete this quantitative comparison, we need to consider network behavior under different message patterns and variable network loads. To justify the additional cost of adaptivity, we need to evaluate both deterministic and adaptive routers at medium to high workloads.

For space restriction only can show in Figure 7 the plots for the average message latency and throughput for 256-node 2-D torus versus applied load which is expressed only in phits per nanosecond for matrix transpose traffic. It should be noted that latency values include injection buffer delays. Injection delays must be taken into account in order to produce reliable results because they depend not only on the traffic load but also on the traffic pattern.

These results clearly show the superior behavior of both Bubble-based routers over wormhole-based counterparts in torus networks. The differences in latency values observed for zero load are maintained along the workable load range. For loads close to network saturation, all routers exhibit latency values which are even up to five times greater than the original base latency. This values can be prohibitively large for most parallel applications.

Obviously, for random traffic (see Table 6) the Bubble DOR router outperforms its adaptive counterpart but only by a small amount. It should be noted, though, that the adaptive Bubble router shows a behavior similar or even better than the VC DOR router, and clearly outperforms the VC adaptive one. However, a random destination traffic with a bimodal length distribution is more susceptible to congestion and benefits from adaptivity.

As it can be seen in Tables 5, the adaptive Bubble router reduces latency for medium to high loads. Furthermore, the adaptive Bubble router considerably improves network throughput when non-uniform traffic is being considered, consequently expanding the range of network load that can be efficiently handled. This is interesting for bandwidth-limited parallel applications which are expected to generate workloads close to the saturation region. The VC adaptive router achieves slightly higher throughputs in structural terms (see Table 6) for most permutation patterns but this

---

[1]In wormhole routers 1 phit = 1 flit

[2]in VCT routers the long messages are fragmented in 10 smalls packets

Traffic	Random		Bimodal		M. Transpose		P.Shuffle		Bit Reversal	
Router	Phits/cycle	Phits/ns	Phits/cycle	Phits/ns	Phits/cycle	Phits/ns	Phits/cycle	Phits/ns	Phits/cycle	Phits/ns
Bub. DOR	88.35	16.83	68.86	13.12	28.67	5.46	32.13	6.12	24.32	4.63
VC DOR	75.14	13.49	52.55	9.97	30.10	5.40	27.14	4.87	28.08	4.50
VC Adap	98.68	13.15	91.90	12.50	60.41	8.05	48.38	6.42	85.25	11.37
Bub. Adap	94.84	16.79	83.32	14.74	54.78	9.70	43.78	7.49	74.24	13.14

Table 6. Maximum achievable throughput for 2-D networks for the four routers under various traffic patterns.

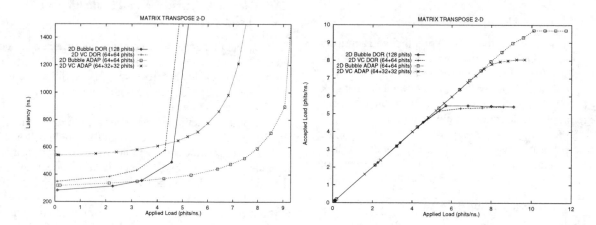

Figure 7. Latency and Throughput for a 256-node 2-D Torus under Matrix Transpose Traffic.

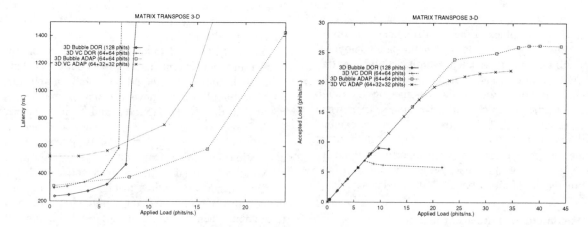

Figure 8. Latency and Throughput for a 512-node 3-D Torus under Matrix Transpose Traffic.

66

gain disappear if the cycle time is taken in account.

We have evaluated the four routers in a 3-D torus topology, which is the case for the Cray T3E router. As indicated above, these simulations use delay values from preliminary VLSI designs, and further optimization is in progress. Figure 8 shows the results on a 512-node 3-D torus with matrix transpose traffic. Although the adaptive Bubble router exhibits 10% higher base latency than the deterministic wormhole router, it is still a very competitive alternative, specially for non-uniform workloads for which it exhibits lower latency than the adaptive wormhole router (in the order of 40%) and higher throughput.

5 Conclusions

We have presented in this paper a simple mechanism to implement fully adaptive virtual cut-through routers, based on Bubble flow control. This flow control technique guarantees continuous message movement through any ring in the network by preserving at least one empty packet unit in the ring's queues. The queues that apply this deadlock avoidance strategy are used as escape ways for messages. Thus, DOR routing in the escape queues can be combined with additional queues using any other adaptive routing algorithm. Consequently, the Bubble router employs deadlock-free fully adaptive minimal routing for torus networks of any number of dimensions.

The obtained results demonstrate noticeable performance gains for the proposed router with respect to routers based on wormhole flow control and virtual channels. Our Bubble router design can be implemented with lower costs, in silicon area and delay, than those for wormhole routers based on virtual channels. The delay per hop in the Bubble routers is lower than those exhibited by both deterministic and adaptive wormhole routers. This translates into better network performance at most loads. Despite being a fully adaptive router, the latency exhibited by the adaptive Bubble router is similar to, or in most cases, lower than that of the deterministic wormhole router. Besides, it clearly outperforms the adaptive wormhole router. For instance, under random traffic we obtain gains in base latency of 41% and 37% for 16-ary 2-cube and 8-ary 3-cube networks, respectively, using only 57% of the required silicon area for an adaptive wormhole router.

In summary, the adaptive Bubble router is a feasible alternative to existing commercial routers based on virtual channels and wormhole switching, such as SGI Spider, Cray T3E, and Intel Cavallino routers.

References

[1] A. Agarwal, "Limits on interconnection network performance," *IEEE Transactions on Parallel and Distributed Systems*, vol. 2, no. 4, pp. 398–412, October 1991.

[2] J. Carbonaro and F. Verhoorn, "Cavallino: The teraflops router and NIC," *Proceedings of Hot Interconnects Symposium IV*, August 1996.

[3] C. Carrión, R. Beivide, J.A. Gregorio and F. Vallejo, "A flow control mechanism to avoid message deadlock in k-ary n-cube networks," *Fourth International Conference on High Performance Computing*, pp. 322-329, India, December,1997.

[4] A.A. Chien, "A cost and speed model for k-ary n-cube wormhole routers," *Proceedings of Hot Interconnects'93*, Palo Alto, California, August 1993.

[5] R. Cypher and L. Gravano. "Storage-efficient deadlock-free packet routing algorithms for torus networks", *IEEE Trans. on Computers*, vol. C-43, no. 12, pp. 1376-1385, 1994.

[6] W. J. Dally and C. L. Seitz, "The torus routing chip," *Journal of Distributed Computing*, vol. 1, no. 3, pp. 187–196, October 1986.

[7] W.J. Dally and C.L. Seitz, "Deadlock-free message routing in multiprocessor interconnection networks," *IEEE Trans. on Computers*, vol. C-36, no. 5, pp. 547-553, 1987.

[8] W. J. Dally, "Performance analysis of k-ary n-cube interconnection networks," *IEEE Transactions on Computers*, vol. C–39, no. 6, pp. 775–785, June 1990.

[9] W.J. Dally, "Virtual-Channel Flow Control," *IEEE Trans. on Parallel and Distributed Systems*, vol. 3, no. 2, pp. 194-205, March 1992.

[10] J. Duato,"A new theory of deadlock-free adaptive routing in wormhole networks." *IEEE Trans. on Parallel and Distributed Systems*, vol.4, no.12, pp.1320-1331, December 1993.

[11] J. Duato and P. Lopez,"Performance of adaptive routing algorithms k-ary n-cubes" *Proceedings of the Workshop on Parallel Computing Routing and Communications*, May 1994.

[12] J. Duato,"A necessary and sufficient condition for deadlock-free outing in cut-through and store-and-forward networks". *IEEE Trans. on Parallel and Distributed Systems*, vol.7, no.8, pp.841-854, August 1996.

[13] M. Galles, "Scalable pipelined interconnect for distributed endpoint routing: The SPIDER chip," *Proceedings of Hot Interconnects Symposium IV*, pp. 141-146, August 1996.

[14] P. Kermani and L. Kleinrock, "Virtual cut-through: a new computer communication switching technique,"*Computer Networks*, vol. 3, pp. 267-286, 1979.

[15] A. R. Larzelere II, "Creating simulation capabilities," *IEEE Computational Science & Engineering*, pp.27-35, January-March 1998.

[16] J. Laudon and D. Lenoski, "The SGI Origin: A cc-NUMA highly scalable server," *International Symposium on Computer Architecture*, pp. 241-251, June 1997.

[17] A. G. Nowatzyk and M. C. Browne and E. J. Kelly and M. Parkin "S-Connect: from NetWorks of Workstations to Supercomputer Performance," *International Symposium on Computer Architecture*, pp. 71-82, June 1995.

[18] K. Bolding, M. Fulgham, and L. Snyder, "The Case of Chaotic Adaptive Routing", *IEEE Trans. on Computers*, vol. 46, no. 13, pp. 1281-1292, December 1997.

[19] S.L.Scott and G. Thorson, "The Cray T3E network: Adaptive routing in a high performance 3-D torus", *Hot Interconnects Symposium IV*, pp. 147-155, August 1996.

[20] S.L.Scott, "Synchronization and Communication in the T3E Multiprocessor", Proc. ASPLOS VII, Cambridge, MA, October 1996

[21] J.M. Prellezo, V. Puente, J.A. Gregorio and R. Beivide, "SICOSYS: an interconnection network simulator for parallel computers," Universidad de Cantabria Technical Report TR-ATC2-UC98, June 1998.

[22] V. Puente, J.A. Gregorio, C. Izu, R. Beivide and F. Vallejo "Low-level Router Design and its Impact on Supercomputer System Performance", *International Conference on Supercomputing*, June 1999.

[23] A.S. Vaidya, A. Sivasubramaniam and C.R. Das, "Performance benefits of virtual channels and adaptive routing: An application-driven study," *International Conference on Supercomputing*, pp. 140-147, July, 1997

Deadlock Avoidance for Switches based on Wormhole Networks

Olav Lysne
Department of Informatics
University of Oslo
Norway
E-mail: olav.lysne@ifi.uio.no

Abstract

We consider the use of wormhole routed networks as internal interconnects of switches. The interconnection of two wormhole networks that are free from deadlocks does not necessarily produce a deadlock free network. This is problematic when wormhole networks are used as switch-internal fabrics, because it severely restricts the possibilities for coupling the switches together. This paper presents a theory that can be effectively used to control this phenomenon caused by aggregated dependencies. We show that all aggregated dependencies can be removed from wormhole networks by careful inclusion of a limited number of virtual channels.

1: Introduction

Since the seminal work of Kermani and Kleinrock on *virtual cut through* [14] and later Dally and Seitz on *wormhole routing* [4, 5] we have seen an ever increasing body of research on these routing techniques. They are now the predominant paradigms in multicomputer interconnection. For a survey of interconnection networks we refer to [7].

In recent years we have also seen that wormhole routing has been taken up in new application areas like high speed local and system area networks [1, 13]. Another emerging area is the use of wormhole routing networks as the internal fabric of switches [19, 17, 20], and there are several developments underways based on this idea [15, 11, 12]. The work reported in this paper concerns the utilization of wormhole routed networks within switches.

The problem we attack is that when two or more deadlock free interconnection networks are coupled together, the result may not be deadlock free. This problem becomes acute for the application of interconnection networks within switches, because it puts restrictions on the ways the switches can be coupled together. This is illustrated in figure 1, where we see a configuration of two switches to the left. This configuration uses the up-most link for packets traveling between the switches from left to right, and the down-most link for traffic in the other direction, and is clearly deadlock free. In the middle we see a simple interconnection network that is deadlock free for the minimal routing strategy. To the right, however, we see that if the switches in the configuration to the left have the interconnect network in the middle as their fabric, the result is a well known deadlocking configuration: a 2-ary 2-cube that routes clockwise.

In [17] and [20] a design for wormhole switches for high-speed LANs is discussed. The papers identify the problem we address, and they distinguish between *inter*-switch deadlock and *intra*-switch deadlocks respectively. The actual control and avoidance of inter-switch deadlocks is, however, not covered in the papers.

The reason why the configuration to the left in figure 1 appears to be deadlock free is that there are no cyclic dependencies between the channels (buffers) stemming from the routing strategy. The interconnect network we use as the fabric inside the switches, however, creates *aggregated dependencies* from $a4$ to $a3$ and from $b1$ to $b2$, and thereby closes the cycle of dependencies. In this paper we develop a method for avoiding aggregated dependencies created by switching fabrics based on wormhole networks. Thereafter we use this method to remove the potential for aggregated dependencies from some well known topologies.

2: Preliminaries

By the term *switch* we shall denote a unit that has a set of *ports*. Each port will from our point of view consist of one *input buffer*, receiving data from the outside world and one *output buffer* receiving data from the internal structure of the switch.

We shall only consider switches whose *switching fabric* (internal structure) consists of a wormhole routed network, and we shall refer to this network as the *worm-*

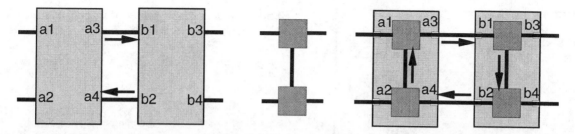

Figure 1. To the left we see a simple topology of two switches that are interconnected into a deadlock free configuration, and in the middle we see a network of routing nodes that is deadlock free as well. To the right, however, we see that the configuration to the left deadlocks when the network in the middle is used as the fabric of the switch.

hole fabric. Furthermore we shall use the term *routing node* to denote the internal routers of the switching fabric. The task of the fabric is solely to transport data packets from input buffers to output buffers according to a predefined switching table. Our model of a switch is depicted in figure 2.

We suppose that the switches may be cascaded with other switches. A network of switches together with an inter-switch routing function is called a *configuration*.

We say that there is a *basic dependency* from input buffer I to output buffer O in a switch if the switch is part of a configuration where there might stream data from I to O. An *aggregated dependency* from I to O is informally defined as the cases where the switch does *not* stream data from I to O, but where I might be blocked as a result of O being blocked.

We put no restrictions on the properties of the wormhole fabric. In particular it may be routed adaptively and the physical channels may be split up into several virtual channels (see [5] for an introduction to virtual channels).

There exist many different ways to define routing functions, and some of them have been categorized in [8]. In this paper we assume that the wormhole fabrics of the switches are routed using a variant of the *Vertex Dependent* method. This means that the physical output channel chosen for a packet is a function of the current routing node and the destination output-buffer of the packet only. However we allow for the choice of *virtual* channel within the physical channel to be done on the basis of the source input buffer of the packet as well. All results in this paper assumes our variant of the vertex dependent method in the wormhole fabric.

3: Aggregated dependencies

Our aim is to be able to control the set of aggregated dependencies in a switch. We start our approach by introducing a set of notions that form the building blocks of basic and aggregated dependencies. First of all we need the concept of *dependency graph*. Whenever a packet holds one channel within a wormhole routed network and at the same time requests another, we say that there is a *dependency* from the former channel to the latter. This concept induces a directed graph where the channels are the vertices and the dependencies are arcs. It is well known that a wormhole network is deadlock free if the channel dependency graph is acyclic [5]. Clearly the notion of dependency graphs applies both to configurations of wormhole switches and to the wormhole fabrics inside the switches. For obvious reasons we shall only consider deadlock free wormhole fabrics, thus we shall also use the notion *dependency DAG*[1] of a fabric. More rigid definitions of dependency graphs and elaborations on deadlock control in wormhole networks can be found in e.g. [5, 6, 8].

Definition 1 *If a wormhole fabric is located in a configuration where it will need to stream packets from input buffer I to output buffer O, we say that its stream from I to O is enabled. If the configuration never requires the fabric to send packets from I to O, we say that the stream is not enabled.*

The notion of enabled streams captures the idea that a switch in a configuration will have a routing table that restricts the way packets stream through the switch. In e.g. dimension order routing there will be no enabled streams from input buffers coming in on a lower dimension to output buffers going out on a higher dimension.

---

[1]DAG stands for Directed Acyclic Graph

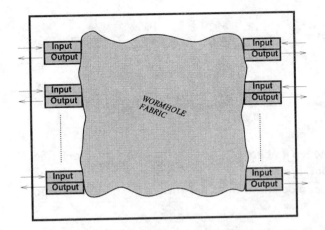

Figure 2. Our model of the switch.

Consider the configuration to the right in figure 1 again. Examples of enabled streams in the rightmost switch are from $b3$ to $b2$ and from $b1$ to $b4$. There is, however, no enabled stream from $b1$ to $b2$.

Definition 2 *The* enabled dependency DAG *of a wormhole fabric in a given configuration is the subgraph of the dependency DAG that stems from enabled streams.*

Informally the enabled dependency DAG of a fabric indicates what channels in it may be blocked in a given configuration, when some output buffer stops accepting packets from the fabric.

Definition 3 *There is a* basic dependency *from input buffer I to output buffer O in a wormhole fabric if the stream from I to O is enabled.*

There is an aggregated dependency *from I to O in a wormhole fabric if there is not a basic dependency, and there is a path from the channel leaving I to the channel going into O in the enabled dependency DAG of the fabric.*

In figure 1 there are aggregated dependencies from $a4$ to $a3$, and from $b1$ to $b2$.

In standard reasoning on deadlocks we are used to regarding basic dependencies only. When the fabric of the switch is a network of wormhole routing nodes, aggregated dependencies must be taken into account as well.

Assume a wormhole switch with a wormhole fabric. If there is an aggregated dependency from I to O across the switch we say that this dependency *induces* a dependency from the input link connected to I to the output link connected to O.

Theorem 1 *A configuration of wormhole switches with wormhole fabrics is deadlock free if its channel dependency graph extended with channel dependencies induced by the aggregated dependencies in the switches is free from cycles.*

Sketch of proof: Let us consider only the global structure of routing nodes, and disregard the facts that they are grouped together in switches and that there are extra buffers on the channels where the switches are interconnected. If the channel dependency graph of this structure is free from cycles, then the entire configuration is deadlock free. Our obligation is therefore to prove that if the premise of the theorem is true then the channel dependency graph of the global structure is cycle free.

Observe first that the dependencies in the channel dependency graph of the global structure are exactly the dependencies in the enabled dependency DAGs of all of its routing fabrics. This means that there is a path in the global dependency graph that passes through a wormhole fabric from buffer I to buffer O if and only if there is a basic or an aggregated dependency from I to O. But then any cycle in the global channel dependency graph will induce a cycle in the basic and aggregated dependencies as well, and vice versa, thus the theorem follows.

Theorem 2 *A configuration of store and forward, or virtual cut-through switches with wormhole fabrics is deadlock free if its buffer dependency graph extended with the aggregated dependencies in the switches is cycle free.*

The second theorem is easily proven in the same manner by building on the fact that deadlock in store and forward networks implies cycles in the buffer dependency graph [16, 9, 10].

4: Avoiding aggregated dependencies

Concerning the control of aggregated dependencies there are two approaches that spring to mind. The first is to put restrictions to the way the switches should be interconnected. However, such restrictions do easily become both complex and severe thus we believe that they should be avoided as far as possible.

The other approach is to construct the fabric such that aggregated dependencies do not occur. Consider the rightmost switch in the configuration to the right in figure 1 again. Assume that we divide the internal channel between the two routing nodes in the fabric of this switch into two virtual channels, and let packets coming from $b1$ use one, and packets coming from $b3$ use the other. This will break the aggregated dependency from $b1$ to $b2$, because the enabled stream from $b1$ to $b4$ no longer shares buffer resources with the enabled stream from $b3$ to $b2$. In this section we shall develop a method for avoiding aggregated dependencies by careful inclusion of virtual channels.

Definition 4 *A switch with a wormhole fabric is* free *from aggregated dependencies* if there is no possible set of enabled streams through the switch that induces aggregated dependencies from any input buffer to any output buffer.

Definition 5 *To each channel in a wormhole fabric we assign the set* $\{I_1O_1, I_2O_2, \ldots, I_nO_n\}$ *where each* I_iO_i *in the expression denotes that a stream (enabled or not) from* I_i *to* O_i *uses this channel. We call this the* user set *of the channel.*

Definition 6 *A channel in a wormhole fabric is* source unique *if all the streams in its user set have the same source input buffer. It is* destination unique *if all of its streams have the same destination output buffer.*

In the sequel we shall use the terms *source* and *destination* meaning the buffers local to the switch that marks the start and end point respectively of a stream crossing a wormhole fabric.

Definition 7 *A wormhole fabric is* resource unique *if*

1. *all of its channels are either source unique or destination unique, and*

2. *all streams through the fabric, enabled or not, follow paths that can be divided in two parts, where the first path only contains source unique channels, and the second only contains destination unique channels.*

We shall return to examples of resource unique networks later in the paper.

Theorem 3 *A resource unique wormhole fabric is free from aggregated dependencies.*

Before we prove the theorem itself we establish the following lemma:

Lemma 1 *Let c be a non source unique (and thus destination unique) channel in a resource unique wormhole fabric. Furthermore let O be the (only) output buffer represented in the user set of c. Then O is the only output buffer reachable from c by following paths in the dependency DAG of the wormhole fabric.*

Proof: The proof is by contradiction. Assume that there is a path from c to $O' \neq O$ in the dependency DAG. If we follow this path we will at some point reach the last channel that is destination unique with O represented in its user set. Let us call this channel c_L.

Since c_L is destination unique, all dependencies from c_L must be induced by streams with O as destination, thus any channel reachable from c_L by one dependency must also carry streams destined for O. Furthermore, since the fabric is resource unique, all these channels must also be destination unique. This means that c_L is not the last channel in the path that is destination unique and carrying traffic destined for O and we have contradiction. $\square$

Now we can prove theorem 3:

Proof: The proof is by contradiction and is illustrated in figure 3.

Assume that we have a resource unique wormhole fabric. Furthermore assume that there exists a set of enabled streams through the fabric that would induce an aggregated dependency from I to O_I. Then there is at least one path in the enabled dependency DAG of the wormhole fabric leading from I to O_I. Let us follow one such path.

Since the dependency from I to O_I is aggregated, there is no enabled stream going all the way from I to O_I. Therefore at some point we reach the last virtual channel used by enabled streams from I. Let c be this last virtual channel, and assume that the stream starting in I that uses this channel ends in O.

Since c is on a path in the DAG leading to O_I, there is another enabled stream, say from I' to O', that uses c and continues in the direction of O_I. Thus c is used by two streams; from I to O and from I' to O'.

Now $I \neq I'$ because c is the last channel that carries enabled streams starting from I. That means that c is not source unique. Furthermore, lemma 1 implies that O is the only output buffer we can reach by following the DAG from c. This means that this path in the DAG can never reach O_I and we have contradiction. $\square$

At this point our method for generating a wormhole fabric that is free from aggregated dependencies should be clear:

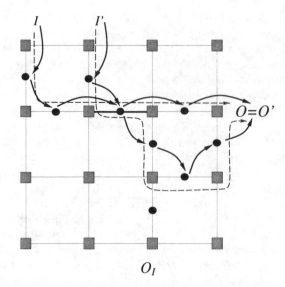

Figure 3. This is an illustration of the proof of theorem 3. The dashed lines represent the possible paths of the enabled streams, and the relevant parts of the enabled dependency DAG of the fabric is drawn in. The channel c is indicated with a more solid line than the other channels. The case we have illustrated is with deterministic routing (only one possible path per enabled stream) and no virtual channels, but the theorem and the proof is valid for adaptive routing and with virtual channels as well.

1. Start with a topology and a routing function.
2. Divide the physical channels in the topology in two disjoint sets A and B, such that no packet will pass through a channel in set A after it has passed a channel in set B.
3. Divide each physical channel into virtual channels such that the user set of a virtual channel from A has identical sources, and the user set of the channels from B has identical destinations.

Observe that after having applied this method, the routing algorithm of the fabric may need to choose between virtual channels on the basis of the source of the packet as well as the destination.

In the next section we shall apply our method to some relevant topologies.

5: A study of relevant topologies

5.1: Meshes

Meshes might not be ideally suited for intra switch routing because the external ports are not all at the edge of the network. Still we start with meshes with dimension order routing since that is the most common configuration in the literature of wormhole routing.

In figure 4 we have depicted the user sets of two physical channels in four by four meshes, and we assume that the routing is by dimension order, vertical first. We apply our method in the following way: let channels in the vertical direction be source unique, and the channels in the horisontal direction be destination unique.

The following result should be clear from figure 4:

In a mesh of radix K with dimension order routing it suffices with at most $K - 1$ virtual channels for each physical channel in order for the network to be free from aggregated dependencies.

Note that for all bidirectional links (consisting of two physical channels) in the mesh, the sum of the virtual channels needed in both directions is K.

5.2: Clos-networks

Clos is a class of multistage networks that was first described in [2]. It was initially intended for telephone switching, but it has later been advocated as internal structure of e.g. ATM switches due to its low blocking probability [3].

A classic clos-network consists of three stages, and each stage consists of a set of routing nodes. There is

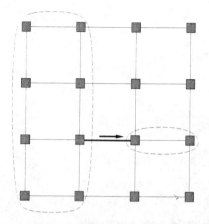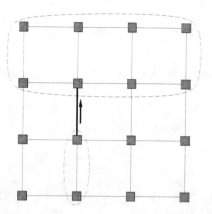

Figure 4. The user sets of two physical channels in a mesh with dimension order routing. The user set of the links in question consists of all pairs of sources (input buffers) and destinations (output buffers) where the sources come from one marked area and the destinations from the other marked area.

full connectivity between the stages, such that there is a bidirectional link from each routing node in stage n to each routing node in stage $n + 1$. A study of how the clos scheme scales to any number of ports even with fixed size routers can be found in [18].

We assume a shortest path routing strategy that is fully adaptive into the center stage, and deterministic from there. An example of a clos with four routing nodes in each stage is depicted in figure 5. Here the user sets of the two different classes of channels are also illustrated: The user set of a channel going into the center stage contains streams starting at input buffers connected to one particular routing node and ending in output buffers connected to any other routing node. Channels leaving the center stage have user sets containing streams whose output buffers are all connected to the same routing node, and where the input buffers are connected to any of the other routing nodes.

When using our method we let the channels going into the center stage be source unique, and the channels leaving the center stage be destination unique. From figure 5 we easily reach the following conclusion:

In a three stage clos network with fully adaptive routing into the center stage, the number of virtual channels needed for freedom from aggregated dependencies equals the number of input (or output) buffers connected to each end stage routing node.

In the network in figure 5 it thus suffices with four virtual channels per physical channel.

6: Conclusion

We have presented a theory for controlling the aggregated dependencies of a wormhole routed network. Such control is particularly important when wormhole networks are used as the fabric of switches.

The method we propose is based on careful inclusion of virtual channels, and we have through examples demonstrated that the number of virtual channels needed is quite reasonable for several relevant topologies and routing functions.

In this paper we have only investigated the possibility of avoiding all possible aggregated dependencies. It appears that our method can be improved, at least theoretically, by only braking the aggregated dependencies where necessary. This would, however, imply complex reasoning on configurations including the internal structure of the switches. Our contribution is a switch design that allows the user of the switches to reason on deadlocks assuming that the switches have full crossbars internally.

Our approach removes aggregated dependencies by introducing virtual channels. Another possibility is to circumvent such dependencies by introducing end to end protocols across the fabric. This approach has to some extent been followed in [12].

It is our belief that this method can be used in other settings as well. One major problem faced by researchers is that reasoning on deadlock freedom has to be done globally. Therefore distributed algorithms for routing around faulty regions for instance have been complex and restricted to few topologies. By regarding the aggregated dependencies induced by a rerouting in

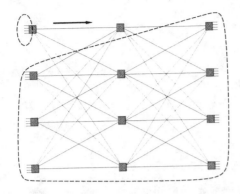 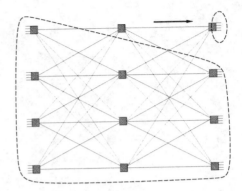

Figure 5. The user sets of two physical channels in a clos network.

a restricted area, reasoning can be done locally. This gives possibilities for more general methods for fault tolerance as well as dynamic reconfiguration.

Acknowledgements: Thanks are due to José Duato for valuable comments on an early version of this paper.

References

[1] N. J. Boden, D. Cohen, R. E. Felderman, A. E. Kulawik, C. L. Seitz, J. N. Seizovic, and Wen-King Su. Myrinet – a gigabit-per-second local-area network. IEEE MICRO, 1995.

[2] C. Clos. A study of non-blocking switching networks. *Bell Syst. Tech. J.*, 32:406–424, 1953.

[3] P. Coppo, M. D'Ambrosio, and R. Melen. Optimal cost/performance design of ATM switches. *IEEE/ACM Transactions on Networking*, 1(5):566–575, 1993.

[4] W. J. Dally and C. L. Seitz. The torus routing chip. *Distributed Computing*, 1:187–196, 1986.

[5] W. J. Dally and C. L. Seitz. Deadlock-free message routing in multiprocessor interconnection networks. *IEEE Transactions on Computers*, C-36(5):547–553, 1987.

[6] J. Duato. A necessary and sufficient condition for deadlock-free adaptive routing in wormhole networks. *IEEE Transactions on Parallel and Distributed Systems*, 6(10):1055–1067, 1995.

[7] J. Duato, S. Yalamanchili, and L. Ni. *Interconnection Networks an engineering approach*. IEEE Computer Society, 1997.

[8] E. Fleury and P. Fraigniaud. A general theory for deadlock avoidance in wormhole-routed networks. *IEEE Transactions on Parallel and Distributed Systems*, 9(7):626–638, 1998.

[9] D. Gelernter. A DAG-based algorithm for prevention of store-and-forward deadlock in packet networks. *IEEE Transactions on Computers*, C-30:709–715, October 1981.

[10] K. D. Günther. Prevention of deadlocks in packet-switched data transport systems. *IEEE Transactions on Communications*, COM-29:512–524, April 1981.

[11] B. Halfen and G. Horn. SCI to HIC bridge based on the LC2 and RCube chips. In *Scalable Coherent Interface: Technology and Applications, Proceedings of SCI Europe '98 (Hosted by EMMSEC 98)*, pages 123–130. Cheshire Henbury, 1998.

[12] G. Horn, I. Theiss, O.Lysne, and T. Skeie. Switched SCI systems. In *Scalable Coherent Interface: Technology and Applications, Proceedings of SCI Europe '98 (Hosted by EMMSEC 98)*, pages 13–24. Cheshire Henbury, 1998.

[13] R. W. Horst. Tnet: A reliable system area network. *IEEE Micro*, 15(1):37–45, 1995.

[14] P. Kermani and L. Kleinrock. Virtual cut-through: A new computer communication switching technique. *Computer Networks*, 3:267–286, 1979.

[15] Lockheed Martin. SCI switch specification sheet, 1998.

[16] P. M. Merlin and P. J. Schweitzer. Deadlock avoidance in store-and-forward networks – I: Store-and-forward deadlock. *IEEE Transactions on Communications*, COM-28:345–354, March 1980.

[17] L. M. Ni, Wenjian Qiao, and Mingyao Yang. Switches and switch interconnects. In *Proceedings of the Fourth International Conference Massively Parallel Processing Using Optical Interconnections*, pages 122–129, 1997.

[18] T. Skeie, O. Lysne, and G. Horn. Scalable non-blocking networks with fixed size routers. In *Proceedings of the International Conference on Parallel and Distributed Processing Techniques and Applications (PDPTA'97)*, pages 1308–1314, 1997.

[19] V. Vuppala and L. M. Ni. Design of a scalable IP router. In *Hot Interconnects V*, 1997.

[20] M Yang and L. M. Ni. Design of scalable and multicast capable cut-through switches for high-speed lans. In *Proceedings of the 1997 International Conference on Parallel Processing*, 1997.

Characterization of Deadlocks in Irregular Networks[*]

Sugath Warnakulasuriya

WorkPlace Systems
36 West Colorado Boulevard, Suite 206
Pasadena, California 91105
sugath@workplace-systems.com

Timothy Mark Pinkston

SMART Interconnects Group
University of Southern California
Los Angeles, CA 90089-2562
tpink@charity.usc.edu

Abstract

This paper characterizes how various network parameters influence message blocking and deadlocks in irregular networks. Information on blocking behavior is provided that is useful in making design trade-offs between restricting routing freedom and allowing the possibility for deadlocks to form in irregular networks. This work also identifies ways in which a network's susceptibility to deadlock can be reduced and provides guidelines for designing irregular networks which maximize routing flexibility and resource utilization. Finally, a new empirical evaluation methodology for classifying irregular topologies and relating network behavior to various classes of network topologies is introduced.

1 Introduction

The recent emergence of powerful workstations and high-performance off-the-shelf network switches has made it possible to use networks of workstations (NOWs) as low-cost alternatives to custom-built multiprocessors. NOWs connect small groups of processors to a network of switching elements which can form irregular topologies, thus accommodating the wiring flexibility and incremental expansion requirements of Local Area Network (LAN) settings. Examples of commercially available switches for use in these types of networks include Autonet [1], Myrinet [2], ServerNet [3], SGI Spider [4], and the Intel Cavallino router [5]. In designing NOWs, one of the primary goals is to provide high message throughput while maintaining low message latency by efficiently utilizing network re-

sources. However, the irregularity of the interconnection patterns in NOWs make this a challenging task.

A number of important techniques have been developed in recent years to accomplish efficient message routing in regular networks for multicomputers, including cut-through switching, virtual channels and adaptive routing [6]. All three of these techniques have migrated into high performance switches intended for implementing NOWs. In implementing these techniques, the critical issue of deadlock behavior must be addressed. Deadlocks in routing can occur when messages block waiting for channel resources while holding onto other channel resources. Cyclic dependencies formed by groups of such blocked messages can lead to the indefinite postponement of messaging activities and, if allowed to persist, can bring the entire system to a halt. Routing approaches for addressing deadlock can be based either on *avoiding* deadlock or on *recovering* from deadlock.

Deadlock avoidance techniques proposed for irregular networks range from those that impose partial ordering of channel resources in order to altogether prevent resource dependency cycles [1, 7] to those that provide some adaptivity along with a set of escape resources [8]. Very few unrestricted deadlock recovery routing schemes have been proposed for irregular networks [9]. The primary distinction between deadlock avoidance and deadlock recovery approaches is the decision made in trading off routing freedom and deadlock formation. The circumstances under which either deadlock avoidance or deadlock recovery routing is preferable depend both on the frequency with which deadlocks occur and on the degradative effects of correlated message blocking behavior which can lead to deadlock. Therefore, designing an optimal approach to handling deadlock requires thorough understanding of the relationship between network design parameters, deadlock, and other harmful correlated message

---

[*]This research was supported in part by an NSF Career Award, grant ECS-9624251, and an NSF grant, CCR-9812137.

blocking phenomena. Previous approaches for handling deadlock in irregular networks have been proposed without the benefit of this important insight.

In this paper, network design parameters which significantly influence deadlock formation are identified and their effects on message blocking and deadlock are empirically evaluated through simulation for a class of irregular networks representing an "average" case. This increases our understanding of the nature and likelihood of deadlocks and provides insight into the implications of deadlock forming phenomena on network and routing algorithm design. The next section provides background on the type of message blocking and deadlock phenomena that can occur in irregular interconnection networks. Section 3 presents the evaluation approach and empirical results. Section 4 discusses the results. Section 5 presents related work, and, finally, conclusions are presented in Section 6.

2 Message Blocking and Deadlocks in Irregular Networks

2.1 Depicting Deadlocks

A model of consumer-resource interaction developed in previous work [10] uses channel wait-for graphs (CWGs) to represent resource allocations and requests existing within the network at a given point in time. The model supports various switching techniques including wormhole, buffered wormhole, and virtual cut-through as well as various policies for buffer usage, including atomic and non-atomic buffer allocation [11]. In this work, CWGs are used in a similar fashion for describing deadlocks, correlated message blocking, and for detecting and characterizing deadlocks in irregular networks.

Figure 1 illustrates a CWG depicting resource allocations and requests existing at a certain point in time in an irregular network. The source and destination of message m_i are labeled s_i and d_i in the network graph, and vertices vc_i in the CWG represent channels (physical or virtual). Solid and dashed arcs between vertices represent the dependencies between resources caused by messages acquiring and requesting them. The resource model represented by this CWG correspond to the "OR request model" of consumer-resource interaction [12]. It has been established for distributed systems in general [13] and interconnection networks in particular [10] that, for the OR request model, a wait-for graph containing a knot contains a deadlock. Each instance of a knot formed within the corresponding CWG of a network is considered a unique deadlock

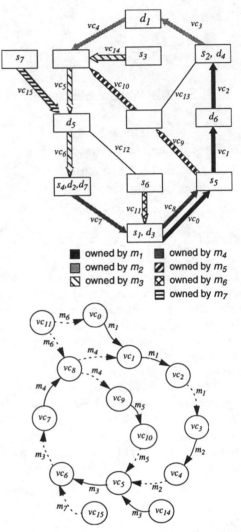

Figure 1: (a) A "multi-cycle deadlock" consisting of messages $m_1 \ldots m_5$ formed under minimal adaptive routing in an irregular network. (b) The set of vertices $\{vc_1 \ldots vc_{10}\}$ forms a knot in the CWG.

event. Hence, the terms knot and deadlock are used interchangeably.

Previous work [14, 15] further establishes that deadlocks can be characterized by three attributes: *deadlock set*, *resource set*, and *knot cycle density*. The deadlock set is the set of messages which own the virtual channels involved in the knot and represents the expanse of the deadlock in terms of the messages involved. The resource set is the set of all virtual channels owned by members of the deadlock set and represents the expanse of the deadlock in terms of the resources involved. The knot cycle density represents the number of unique cycles within a knot. It is a useful attribute for representing the complexity in cor-

76

related resource dependency required for deadlock to form.

2.2 Reducing the Probability of Deadlock

A key factor which influences the probability of deadlock formation in irregular interconnection networks is *routing freedom*. Routing freedom corresponds to the number of routing options available to a message being routed at a given node within the network. It can be increased by adding physical channels, implementing multiple virtual channels per physical channel, and/or increasing the adaptivity of the routing algorithm. The total number of physical channels can be increased by adding them either arbitrarily in a random fashion (i.e., within minimum and maximum node degree constraints) or uniformly in a regular fashion. The former does not necessarily increase routing options for all packets in the network, whereas the latter does. Increasing the number of virtual channels increases routing options for all packets along each physical channel. Increasing the routing adaptivity increases flexibility in the use of physical and virtual channel resources by packets However, the amount of adaptivity provided by a routing algorithm for packets is location dependent due to the uneven distribution of physical channels in irregular network topologies. The work in [16], which characterizes irregular topologies based on clustering, is useful in identifying such network "blocking points" which can instigate deadlock.

As routing freedom is increased, the probability that messages block in the network decreases. More importantly, the degree of correlation required among blocked messages to form a knot increases substantially although the number of cycles that can form when messages block also increases (i.e., at network saturation). Given enough routing freedom, this correlation requirement offsets the opposing effect on deadlock probability caused by the increase in the number of resource dependency cycles. For instance, networks with little-to-no routing freedom have a one-to-one correspondence between cycles and deadlocks, i.e., single-cycle deadlocks form. However, networks with greater routing freedom can offset the opposing effects from cyclic blocking of messages as a large number of cycles can exist without the formation of deadlock, i.e., cyclic non-deadlocks form. This effect of routing freedom is substantiated empirically in the next section by quantifying the influence of various network design parameters on deadlock forming phenomena for a class of irregular networks.

3 Empirical Study of Deadlocks in Irregular Networks

3.1 Evaluation Methodology

The approach used for precisely detecting deadlocks is based on the theoretical framework described in [10]. A deadlock detection algorithm implemented in *IRFlexSim*[1] is used to identify knots within the CWG of an ongoing network simulation. It correctly distinguishes between congestion and deadlocks, precisely detecting and characterizing all deadlocks occuring during simulation. A number of topological analysis tools are also used to narrow the scope of networks evaluated to specific classes of irregular networks. This allows for more meaningful results to be obtained.

3.1.1 Classification of Irregular Topologies

A new approach which classifies irregular network topologies based on relevant network attibutes is used that strongly associates empirical results to certain classes of irregular topologies. In this approach, network configurations specify the number of router switches, physical links, and minimum/maximum switch degree constraints. Six network attributes (summarized in Table 1) are used to reflect the quality of an interconnection pattern. Topologies which represent the average case for a given network configuration are evaluated.

In order to select topologies which represent the average case for their respective network configurations, hundreds of connected topologies of each network configuration listed in Table 1 were randomly generated. All topologies were then analyzed to determine their values for each of the six attributes. Only those network topologies which met the narrow criterion that each of its attributes fall within ±5% of its respective mean value were selected to represent the respective "normal" cases of each network configuration.

Shown in Table 1 are the average as well as minimum and maximum values of the attributes for the randomly generated topologies of the network configurations evaluated. This table also indicates the percentage of topologies within each network configuration which met the selection criterion mentioned above. The evaluation of these topologies is intended to demonstrate the average deadlock and message blocking behavior of each network configuration. This

---

[1] *IRFlexSim* is a flit-level simulator for irregular networks which is based on the *FlexSim* regular network simulators previously developed by the *SMART* Interconnects Group at USC.

Network Configuration Identifier	Average Number of Routing Options at each Node.	Average Number of Alternate Minimal Paths per Node Pair	Average Diameter	Average Inter-Node Distance	Inter-Cluster Bandwidth Index [16]	Inter-Cluster Link-Cost Index [16]	Percent of Topologies with all attributes within +/- 5% of mean.
64:64	1.00	1.00	10.00	5.45	0.1034	0.9548	
	1.01	**1.03**	**12.90**	**6.06**	**0.2761**	**1.1359**	**3.0%**
	1.02	1.30	17.00	7.66	0.4545	1.2930	
64:128	1.37	1.64	5.00	3.01	0.0079	0.6532	
	1.46	**1.91**	**6.29**	**3.12**	**0.1087**	**0.9768**	**3.2%**
	1.55	2.24	9.00	3.34	0.3763	1.2931	
64:256	2.16	2.68	4.00	2.20	0.0159	0.7871	
	2.25	**2.92**	**4.01**	**2.25**	**0.0811**	**1.0217**	**1.0%**
	2.36	3.23	5.00	2.31	0.2075	1.2617	
64:512	2.76	3.23	3.00	1.79	0.0492	0.8625	
	2.98	**3.54**	**3.00**	**1.80**	**0.0871**	**1.0046**	**1.0%**
	3.12	3.85	3.00	1.82	0.1797	1.1304	

Table 1: Summary of minimum, maximum, and mean (in bold) values for selected attributes of randomly generated topologies of each configuration. The Network Configuration Identifier gives the the number of switches followed by the number of links.

approach not only allows observing message blocking and deadlock for the particular class of networks examined in this study, but also provides a basis for studying other classes of topologies by varying one or more of the normalized attributes.

3.1.2 Simulation Parameters

The default network configuration assumed consists of 64 switches, 128 physical channels, a minimum switch degree of 1 and a maximum switch degree of 8 (not counting the locally connected processors). For all network configurations used, each switch is connected locally to four processors (bristling factor of 4) using independent physical injection/delivery channels. Only one virtual channel per physical channel is assumed unless mentioned otherwise. Networks of other configurations containing different numbers of physical channels, and/or switch connectivity are used to evaluate the effects of various parameters on deadlock. For example, in evaluating the effect of physical channels on deadlock behavior, networks with 64 switches and 64, 128, 256, 384, and 512 physical channels are assumed. The minimum switch degree is always set to one physical channel. The maximum switch degree allowed for switch connectivity is always set to twice the average switch degree. This assumption on switch degree differs from previous evaluation approaches [8, 9] which require all switches to have uniform switch de-

gree, thereby eliminating much of the irregularity of randomly generated topologies.

All simulations are run for normalized loads up to full network bisection capacity or until the network saturates with respect to the number of resource dependency cycles, whichever occurs first. In most cases, this saturation load exceeds the loads at which network performance (latency and throughput) saturates. The performance saturation points are denoted in the figures by vertical lines. The saturation loads represent the worst case scenarios for the network as attempts to inject additional traffic into the network does not yield additional throughput or other performance gains. However, in many cases, deadlocks do not begin to form until the network is deeply saturated. Therefore, simulations are performed using loads well into deep saturation in order to properly observe and characterize deadlock behavior. Each simulation is run for a duration of 200,000 simulation cycles beyond steady state. For those experiments in which no deadlock initially formed, simulations are further extended for an additional duration of 200,000 cycles to provide greater opportunity for deadlock to occur.

During simulation, the deadlock detection algorithm is invoked every 100 cycles. If deadlock is detected, it is immediately "broken" by removing a single randomly selected message in the deadlock set from the network in a flit-by-flit manner so as to emulate a recovery procedure similar to that described in [17]. Deadlock frequency is measured in relative terms by the normalized number of deadlocks—which is the ratio of the number of deadlocks to the number of messages delivered. Deadlock complexity is measured in terms of the size of the deadlock sets, resource sets, and knot cycle density. Measurements such as the total number of resource dependency cycles formed and the number and percentage of blocked messages are also used to measure message blocking as well as to estimate the likelihood of deadlock.

Other default parameters used for simulation include 32 flit messages, 8 flit buffers, wormhole switching, atomic buffer allocation, and a random channel selection policy. Uniform traffic patterns are used for most simulations. Additionally, non-uniform "hotspot" traffic which emulates client-server behavior found in LAN type settings is also used. For adaptive deadlock recovery routing, a minimal *true fully adaptive routing (TFAR)* algorithm is used which allows unrestricted use of any available virtual channel along any profitable path [18]. For non-adaptive deadlock recovery routing, an algorithm which allows the use of any virtual channel along a single minimal path

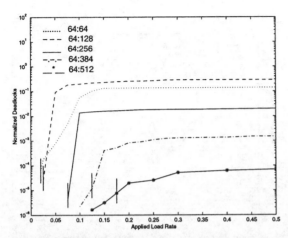

Figure 2: Normalized number of deadlocks versus load rate for 64:64, 64:128, 64:256, 64:384, and 64:512 networks using *Static* routing.

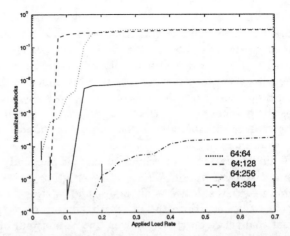

Figure 3: Number of normalized deadlocks versus load rate for for 64:64, 64:128, 64:256, and 64:384 network configurations using *TFAR*.

between any node pair is used (*Static*). This singular path allowed between a given node pair is predetermined and does not change during simulation. Given that no other routing restrictions are enforced, deadlocks are possible in both *Static* and *TFAR*.

3.2 Impact of Routing Freedom

The impact that routing freedom has on deadlock formation is evaluated by varying the amount of physical channels, routing adaptivity, and virtual channels in the simulated networks.

3.2.1 Effect of Arbitrarily Adding Physical Channels and Routing Non-adaptively

The effect on deadlock probability of arbitrarily adding physical channels to an irregular network which uses static (non-adaptive) routing is evaluated by varying the number of bidirectional physical channels randomly added, following the minimum/maximum node degree constraints discussed in the previous section. All other network parameters are set to default values. Figure 2 plots the normalized number of deadlocks versus load rate for the 64:64, 64:128, 64:256, 64:384, and 64:512 networks. Both the absolute number of deadlocks (not shown) and normalized deadlocks initially increase as the number of physical channels increase to a point, then, subsequently, decrease as the number of physical channels is further increased.

As static routing supplies each message with only a single routing option at each intermediate node, each resource dependency cycle formed constitutes a dead-

lock. Formation of such single-cycle deadlocks requires that there be cycles within the physical topology along which these deadlocks could form. A connected network topology with n nodes and n links such as the 64:64 network can contain, at most, a single topological cycle—all deadlocks must form in one of the two directions along this topological cycle. Therefore, the number of deadlocks which can form within the 64:64 network is constrained by the availability of topological cycles along which resource dependency cycles can form. The relatively large number of deadlocks which occur in the 64:64 network despite this limitation suggests that the resolution of most deadlocks is quickly followed by the formation of another deadlock along the same topological cycle.

These results indicate that increasing the number of physical channels arbitrarily placed yields only a moderate reduction in message blocking and deadlocks when using static routing, even when substantial numbers of channels are added. This is due to static routing's inability to exploit the increased channel resources and the random placement of additional channels. Although the total number of physical channels are increased, the number and severity of "blocking points" in the network are not necessarily decreased. Thus, routing freedom largely remains unaffected.

3.2.2 Effect of Arbitrarily Adding Physical Channels and Routing Adaptively

To examine the effects of better utilizing available physical channel resources, minimal *TFAR* is used in irregular networks with varying numbers of additional arbitrarily placed bidirectional channels. All other network parameters are set to default values. Figure 3 plots the number of normalized deadlocks versus load rate for the 64:64, 64:128, 64:256, and 64:384 networks. Very few cycles or deadlocks occurred for the 64:512 network, so this network is not included in the figures. These figures indicate that deadlocks increase as the number physical channels is increased initially, but reduce substantially as the number of channels is further increased.

Unlike static routing which always supplies only a single routing option, *TFAR* allows routing over all minimal paths between all nodes and is, therefore, able to better utilize the increased number of physical channel resources. However, the results indicate that the increased routing freedom gained by arbitrarily adding physical channel resources from 64 to 128 is insufficient to overcome the increased opportunities for deadlocks posed by the greater number of topological cycles. Nevertheless, as routing freedom is further increased by arbitrarily adding physical channels beyond 128, the resulting decrease in message blocking helps to reduce deadlock frequency.

Despite the higher average number of routing options made available at each node as physical channels are increased, a relatively high number of deadlocks (mostly single-cycle) appear in all but the 64:512 network. The predominance of single-cycle deadlocks in all network configurations indicate that most deadlocks form when messages exhaust adaptivity and/or reach the boundaries of "clusters" where only a single physical channel option remains along the chosen minimal path. Results indicate that for all of the networks evaluated, 92 to 99% of the messages block waiting for only a single channel option at saturation.

Finally, the results indicate that a large number of additional, randomly connected physical channels (i.e., a channel-to-switch ratio of 8:1) is needed to significantly reduce deadlock frequency. Although adaptive routing increases routing freedom to some extent, the number and severity of "blocking points" in the network are not significantly decreased by the addition of randomly placed channels. Hence, the main deadlock-reducing benefit comes from adaptive routing.

3.2.3 Effect of Uniformly Adding Channel Resources and Routing Adaptively

The effects on deadlock probability of uniformly adding channel resources are evaluated by considering routing which allows *unrestricted use* of 1, 2, 3, and 4 virtual channels along non-adaptive predetermined paths (*Static*1, *Static*2, *Static*3 and *Static*4) as

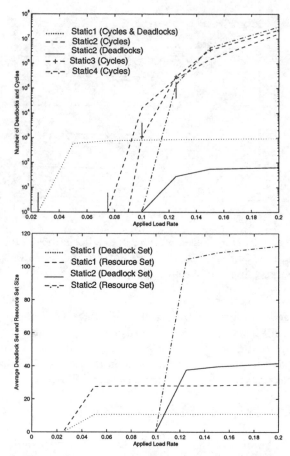

Figure 4: (a) Number of deadlocks and cycles versus load rate and (b) average deadlock and resource set sizes versus load rate for *Static* routing with 1, 2, 3, and 4 VCs per physical channel in 64:128 networks.

well as along minimal *TFAR* paths (*TFAR1*, *TFAR2*, *TFAR3*, and *TFAR4*). All other network parameters are set to default values.

Figure 4a plots the absolute number of deadlocks (not normalized) and cycles versus load rate for *Static*1, *Static*2, *Static*3 and *Static*4. As *no deadlocks occurred for Static routing with 3 or 4 virtual channels*, only cycles are shown for these networks. *Static*1 is inherently limited to only single-cycle deadlocks when deadlocks form, therefore a single curve represents both cycles and deadlocks for this network. For each node pair, static routing allows the use of only those virtual channels which belong to physical channels along a single predetermined path. The increase in the degree of message correlation required for deadlock as caused by increasing routing freedom using 2 virtual channels eliminates most deadlocks. Further increasing routing freedom using 3 and 4 virtual channels eliminates virtually all deadlocks.

Figure 4b plots the average deadlock set and resource set sizes for the deadlocks formed in *Static*1 and *Static*2. The average deadlock set size for *Static*2 is roughly three to four times larger than for *Static*1. Correspondingly, the average resource set size for *Static*2 is also three to four times larger than for *Static*1. *Static*1 leads to single-cycle deadlocks only while *Static*2 leads to multi-cycle deadlocks with knot densities as large as 6,000 cycles. These deadlock characteristics indicate that when routing freedom is increased, the fewer deadlocks that form are much larger and more complex due to the higher degree of correlation among messages required for deadlock to form.

In contrast to Static, minimal TFAR can use all virtual channels along all profitable paths which lead to a destination, thus yielding much greater routing freedom. Figure 5a plots the number of deadlocks and cycles versus load rate and Figure 5b plots the percent of messages blocked versus load rate for *TFAR1*, *TFAR2*, *TFAR3*, and *TFAR4*. These figures also include information regarding *Static*1, *Static*2, *Static*3, and *Static*4 for reference. As *no deadlocks occurred for TFAR routing with 2, 3, or 4 virtual channels*, only cycle information is shown for these networks.

As with regular networks [15], combining adaptive routing with multiple virtual channels has a drastic effect on reducing deadlocks. Results also indicate that adaptive routing, when used with only a single virtual channel, does not provide enough routing freedom to offset the opposing effects of blocked messages and resource dependency cycles. However, when using two virtual channels, the increased routing freedom in adaptive routing increases the degree of correlation required for deadlock so as to eliminate those deadlocks suffered in static routing with 2 virtual channels.

Results indicate that *TFAR2*, *TFAR3*, and *TFAR4* as well as *Static*2, *Static*3, and *Static*4 lead to a large number of cyclic non-deadlocks immediately following saturation. As shown in Figure 5a, the number of cycles begin to grow rapidly at the point where a large number of messages begin to block. This is shown in Figure 5b which plots congestion (percentage of messages in the network that are blocked) for all of the networks evaluated. This indicates that the addition of each virtual channel reduces congestion and allows higher loads to be applied before a large number of cyclic non-deadlocks form. It also indicates the congestion reducing benefits of using any given number of virtual channels in an unrestricted, true fully adaptive manner. The sharp growth in cycles observed in the figure is due to the combined effects of a large number of messages which block at saturation and the

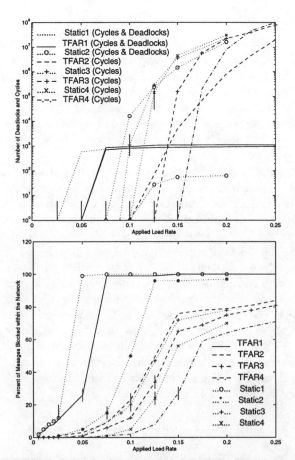

Figure 5: (a) Number of deadlocks and cycles versus load rate and (b) percent of messages blocked in the network versus load rate in 64-node 128-link networks using *Static* and *TFAR* with 1, 2, 3, and 4 VCs.

increased routing freedom of virtual channels which allow each message to wait on a larger number of channel resources. In the absence of deadlock for these networks, the large number of cycles indicate the formation of large cyclic non-deadlocks.

In lieu of virtual channels, a similar significant reduction in deadlock frequency can also be achieved by uniformly adding physical channels in a regular redundant fashion. When used unrestrictedly, redundant physical channels provide the same routing freedom as virtual channels while allowing greater performance as no channel multiplexing is required. This approach can straightforwardly be implemented by utilizing unused switch ports and implementing multiple physical channel links between switch pairs. In this case, the size (number of ports) of each switch would have to be sufficiently large so as not to limit the scalability of the network.

3.2.4 Effect of Non-Uniform Traffic

In addition to uniform traffic, a non-uniform traffic pattern which emulates client-server interaction found in LAN settings is also used. In this traffic pattern, 10% to 20% of the nodes in the network with the highest node degree were identified as being servers. All other network nodes were assumed to be clients. A disproportionate amount of traffic generated by all nodes were sent to the nearest server.

Almost all of the experiments performed using this non-uniform traffic pattern resulted in nearly identical deadlock frequencies and characteristics as those found using uniform traffic. One notable exception was for TFAR with two virtual channels. None of the 64:128 networks with TFAR and 2 VCs led to any deadlock when using uniform traffic. However, a small number of deadlocks (1 for every 750,000 messages delivered) were found for some cases of 64:128 networks under client-server traffic. An examination of these deadlocks reveals that they were caused by a high rate of messages exchanged between a small number of server nodes which were close to each other in proximity. The use of a third virtual channel eliminates these deadlocks.

3.3 Impact of Non-Atomic Allocation

Trends in implementation technology make the use of large channel buffers feasible in irregular network switches. In many instances, the relatively large physical distances between network nodes in NOW settings require the use of large buffers for efficient flow control. However, large buffers cannot be efficiently utilized under assumptions of atomic buffer allocation. Also, the heterogeneous nature of traffic in NOWs containing messages of many different sizes make the efficient use of large buffers even more critical. Allowing messages to share channel buffers (non-atomic buffer allocation) can greatly increase the utilization of channel resources. However, it can also reduce the routing freedom of messages which block before arriving at the heads of shared queues.

To examine the effects of non-atomic buffer allocation on deadlock behavior, minimal *TFAR* is used with two virtual channels and a fixed message length of 16 flits in 64:128 networks with channel buffer depths of 16, 32, 48, and 64 flits (NAT 16:16, NAT 16:32, NAT 16:48, and NAT 16:64). All other network parameters are set to default values. A network which uses atomic buffer allocation with 16 flit messages and 16 flit channel buffers (AT 16:16) is also evaluated for comparison. (Note that larger buffer configurations for the

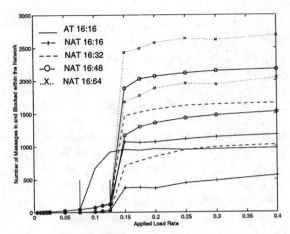

Figure 6: Messages in the network and messages blocked before reaching the head of a queue vs. load rate for 64:128 networks with 2 VCs and buffer depths of 16, 32, 48, and 64 flits using wormhole routing with non-atomic buffer allocation. *TFAR* with uniform traffic and a message length of 16 flits is assumed.

atomic buffer allocation network (i.e., AT 16:64) have the same behavior as only one message is allowed in each VC queue at any one time.)

No deadlocks appeared for any of the irregular networks for loads well into saturation. Thus, Figure 6 shows message blocking behavior: the number of messages in the network (upper curve)—which, at saturation, nearly all become blocked—and the number of messages blocked prior to reaching the head of a VC queue (lower curve). The NAT 16:16 network is able to support nearly 200% more messages than the AT 16:16 network at their respective saturation points and approximately 20% more messages in deep saturation. As compared to atomic buffer allocation, non-atomic buffer allocation improves the load at which the network saturates by about 66%. Results also indicate that although the use of larger buffers (as opposed to smaller buffers) with non-atomic allocation allows more messages to be in the network, it does not significantly improve the throughput saturation load of the network, which is approximately .125 for all buffer sizes.

The percentage of messages which block at the heads of queues for the non-atomic networks decreases as the buffer size increases, but a significant percentage (25-40% in deep saturation) remains regardless of buffer size. These messages wait for multiple channels resources when blocked, thus preserving routing freedom. The routing freedom of these messages serves to decrease the probability of deadlock due to the high degree of correlation required for deadlock to form.

The absence of deadlock, especially of the single-cycle variety, indicates that each resource dependency cycle contains at least one message which has reached the head of its queue, as formally proved in [11].

The effects of non-atomic buffer allocation for virtual cut-through routing is also examined (but not plotted) using 64:128 networks with a fixed message length of 16 flits, channel buffer depths of 32 and 64 flits, and two virtual channels. As with the non-atomic wormhole networks, no deadlocks occurred for the virtual cut-through networks with two virtual channels. The overall message blocking behavior is seen to be similar to that of the non-atomic wormhole networks.

Apparently, non-atomic buffer allocation in wormhole switching offers similar inter-message compaction within buffers as does virtual cut-through switching while not significantly affecting the degree of correlation in message blocking required for deadlock, even though messages commit earlier to virtual channels as compared to atomic buffer allocation. As mentioned previously, at least one message in each resource dependency cycle reaches the head of its queue, thus preserving the freedom to adaptively choose among multiple channel resources.

4 Discussion

The uneven distribution of channels in irregular networks limits the routing freedom of messages at various points in the network. Blocking points make congestion and deadlock more likely in irregular networks than in regular networks as less correlated resource dependencies are needed for deadlock to form. Arbitrarily adding channel resources only moderately alleviates congestion and reduces deadlock frequency. For more effective results, channel resources should be added at points in the network where the irregular topology creates blocking points. This serves to increase routing freedom at the points in the network where it is lowest, thus increasing the degree of correlation in resource dependency needed for deadlock to form.

The use of virtual channels is a step in this direction. With this technique, channel resources are increased uniformly across the network, including at the blocking points of a network. Those messages which block waiting for a single physical channel benefit from having multiple (virtual) channel resources from which to choose, assuming unrestricted routing *within* physical channels. The benefits of this technique in increasing the resource correlation required for deadlock

to form is amplified when unrestricted routing is allowed *across* physical channels. Results indicate that uniformly increasing the number of channel resources between switches by a factor of two is much more effective at reducing deadlock frequency than arbitrarily increasing the number of channel resources between switches by a factor of four. Thus, it can be concluded that *how* channels (physical or virtual) are added to reduce deadlock frequency is more important than *how many* channels are added.

Furthermore, improving resource utilization by allowing the sharing of channel buffers for both wormhole and virtual cut-through switching yields some benefits in reducing congestion, as seen by the higher saturation load rate. However, this technique does not increase routing freedom, which is key to reducing the probability of deadlock. Therefore, non-atomic buffer allocation should be used in conjunction with other techniques, such as virtual or redundant physical channels and adaptive routing, to gain maximum benefit.

5 Related Work

The work in [19] models the probability of deadlock in operating systems. However, no such work has been performed for deadlock in interconnection networks. Original studies which measured deadlock frequency in interconnection networks did so using crude approximations based on network congestion and message blocking via time-outs as the primary means for detecting deadlocks [18, 20, 21]. Subsequent work [14, 15] has improved upon this by not only precisely measuring actual deadlock, but by relating key network parameters to their influence on deadlock for regular interconnection networks. That work is extended here to characterize deadlocks for irregular networks.

Previous work based on the use of a relatively small sample of randomly generated topologies implicitly assumes that all irregular networks of a particular size behavior similarly regardless of their interconnection patterns [8, 9]. In addition, these studies limit their investigation to only those irregular topologies which have uniform switch degree, thus restricting the applicability of their results. In contrast, this work quantitatively classifies topologies so as to relate results to the crucial properties of the interconnection patterns of a topology. Also, this study includes topologies which have non-uniform switch degree, an important characteristic which contributes significantly to the irregularity of a topology.

6 Conclusions and Future Work

This work characterizes the effects of various network parameters on the frequency of blocked messages, resource dependency cycles and deadlock. The interrelationships between routing freedom, blocked messages, correlated resource dependencies and deadlock formation have been empirically quantified for a class of irregular interconnection networks.

It has been shown that as routing freedom is uniformly increased, i.e., through the unrestricted use of multiple virtual channels, the complexity in the correlation of resource dependencies required for deadlock substantially increases so as to virtually eliminate the occurance of deadlock. However, non-uniform increase in routing freedom, i.e., through the addition of physical channels arbitrarily, may accentuate "blocking points" in the network instead of relieving them, thus having little-to-no effect on increasing the complexity in correlation of resource dependency required for deadlock. It is safe to conclude that correlated message blocking and deadlock in irregular networks can be highly improbable when sufficient routing freedom is properly provided by the network and fully exploited by the routing algorithm. Unstricted routing on irregular networks with two or more virtual channels or, alternatively, redundant (uniformly added) physical channels is seen to virtually eliminate the occurance of deadlock.

Research which builds on the results of this study can be explored in future work. This includes empirical analysis using hybrid bursty traffic loads generated by real applications, evaluation of other classes of irregular topologies, development of an improved method of classifying irregular topologies, and investigation of efficient techniques for injection limitation, deadlock detection and resolution required for practical implementation of deadlock recovery routing.

References

[1] M.D. Schroeder et al., "Autonet: A high-speed, self-configuring local area network using point to point links", Technical Report SRC research report 59, DEC, April 1990.

[2] N.J. Boden, D. Cohen, R.E. Felderman, A.E. Kulawik, C.L Seitz, J. Seizovic, W. Su, "Myrinet - A gigabit per second local area network", *IEEE Micro*, pp. 29-36, February 1995.

[3] D. Garcia and W. Watson, "ServerNet II", In *Proceedings of the 2nd PCRCW*, page 109, Springer-Verlag, June 1997.

[4] M. Galles, "Spider: A High Speed Network Interconnect", *IEEE Micro*, pp. 34-39, February 1997.

[5] J. Carbonaro and F. Verhoorn, "Cavallino: The Teraflops Router and NIC", In *Proceedings of Hot Interconnects IV*, pp. 157-160, August 1996.

[6] J. Duato, S. Yalamanchili, and L. Ni, "Interconnection Networks: An Engineering Approach". IEEE Computer Society Press, 1997.

[7] Wenjian Qiao and Lionel M. Ni, "Adaptive Routing in Irregular Networks Using Cut-Through Switches". In *Proceedings of 1996 International Conference on Parallel Processing*, 1996.

[8] F. Silla, M.P. Malumbres, A. Robles, P. Lopez, J. Duato, "Efficient Adaptive Routing in Networks of Workstations with Irregular Topology", In *Proceedings of CANCP*, 1997.

[9] F. Silla, A. Robles, and J. Duato, "Improving Performance of Networks of Workstations by using Disha Concurrent", In *Proceedings of the Fourth International Conference on High-Performance Computing*, pp. 80-87, December 1997.

[10] Sugath Warnakulasuriya and Timothy Mark Pinkston, "A Formal Model of Message Blocking and Deadlock Resolution in Interconnection Networks", To appear in *IEEE Transactions on Parallel and Distributed Systems*.

[11] Jose Duato and Timothy M. Pinkston, "A General Theory for Deadlock-Free Adaptive Routing", Submitted to *IEEE Transactions on Computers*, October 1998.

[12] Edgar Knapp, "Deadlock Detection in Distributed Databases", *ACM Computer Surveys*, 19(4):303-328, December 1987.

[13] R. C. Holt, "Some Deadlock Properties of Computer Systems", *ACM Computer Surveys*, vol. 4, no. 3, pp. 179-196, September 1972.

[14] Timothy Mark Pinkston and Sugath Warnakulasuriya, "On Deadlocks in Interconnection Networks", In *Proceedings of the 24th International Symposium on Computer Architecture*, pp. 38-49, June 1997.

[15] Timothy Mark Pinkston and Sugath Warnakulasuriya, "Characterization of Deadlocks in *k*-ary *n*-cube Networks", To appear in *IEEE Transactions on Parallel and Distributed Systems*.

[16] Wai Hong Ho and Timothy Mark Pinkston. "A Clustering Approach in Characterizing Interconnection Networks". In *Proceedings of the 5th International Conference on High Performance Computing*, pp. 277-284, Chennai India, December 1998.

[17] J.M. Martinez, P. Lopez, J. Duato, and T.M. Pinkston, "Software-Based Deadlock Recovery Technique for True Fully Adaptive Routing in Wormhole Networks", In *Proceedings of the 1997 International Conference on Parallel Processing*, August, 1997.

[18] Timothy Mark Pinkston, "Flexible and Efficient Routing Based on Progressive Deadlock Recovery", in *IEEE Transactions on Computers*, Vol. 48, No. 7, July 1999.

[19] C. A. Ellis, "Probabilistic Models of Computer Deadlock", Report CU-CS-041-74, Department of Computer Science, University of Colorado, Boulder, CO, April 1974.

[20] J. Kim, Z. Liu, and A. Chien, "Compressionless Routing: A Framework for Adaptive and Fault-tolerant Routing". In *IEEE Transactions on Parallel and Distributed Systems*, vo. 8, no. 3, pp. 229-244, March 1997.

[21] Anjan K.V. and Timothy M. Pinkston, "An Efficient, Fully Adaptive Deadlock Recovery Scheme: Disha", In *Proceedings of the 22nd International Symposium on Computer Architecture*, pp. 201-210, June 1995.

Session B2

Compiler Optimizations

Chair: Satoshi Okawa
University of Aizu, Japan

Access Descriptor based Locality Analysis
for Distributed-Shared Memory Multiprocessors

Angeles G. Navarro, Rafael Asenjo, Emilio L. Zapata
Dept. de Arquitectura de Computadores
Univ. de Málaga
{angeles,asenjo,ezapata}@ac.uma.es

David Padua
Dept. of Computer Science
Univ. of Illinois at Urbana-Champaign
padua@uiuc.edu

Abstract

Most of today's multiprocessors have a Distributed-Shared Memory (DSM) organization, which enables scalability while retaining the convenience of the shared-memory programming paradigm. Data locality is crucial for performance in DSM machines, due to the difference in access times between local and remote memories. In this paper, we present a compile-time representation that captures the memory locality exhibited by a program in the form of a graph known as Locality-Communication Graph (*LCG*). *In the LCG, each node represents a DO loop nest which can have at most one level of parallelism. Not all loops need to be represented within a node and, therefore, the LCG may contain cycles. Our representation works whether the loops represented by the nodes are perfectly nested or not, and the subscript expressions and loop limits can be affine or non-affine expressions of the loop indices. The LCG provides essential information that a parallelizing compiler can use to automatically choose a good iteration/data distribution and to schedule the communication operations required during program execution.*

1. Introduction

In this paper, we discuss a new compiler internal representation of locality in *Distributed-Shared Memory* (*DSM*) multiprocessors. We assume that the program contains a collection of DO loop nests (henceforth called *loop nests* for simplicity) where at most one level of parallelism is exploited in each nest. IF statements, WHILE loops, DO loops and other constructs control the execution of the loop nests. Because access time to remote memories is usually much higher than to local memories, data locality enhancement is clearly a key issue for performance. By locality enhancement we mean selecting an efficient data distribution in which, whenever possible, the data are placed in the lo-

cal memories of the processors needing them. We reported earlier some experimental results that clearly show the significant impact of locality analysis on the efficiency of automatic parallelization [10]. Although, there have been several research projects on locality enhancement for DSMs, as discussed below, there is still room for much improvement and, for that reason, we decided to initiate this study, the first results of which are reported in this paper.

As part of this project, we have developed techniques to schedule parallel iterations and distribute the shared arrays across the local memories to minimize the parallel execution overhead resulting from load unbalance and communications. When remote accesses are unavoidable, our techniques can identify them to estimate execution costs and generate communication primitives. Our techniques are based on the *Linear Memory Access Descriptor* (*LMAD*) introduced in [9] which can be accurately computed in relatively complex situations, such as array reshaping resulting from subroutine calls and non-affine expressions in subindex expressions and loop bounds. One advantage of LMADs is that they can be computed inter-procedurally by applying essentially the same approach used to compute their values intra-procedurally.

Our technique uses a *Locality-Communication Graph* (*LCG*) that reflects the locality and communication patterns of a parallel program. The program is divided into *phases*, each being a DO loop nest with at most one parallel loop. These loop nests do not have to be perfectly nested. The *LCG* contains a directed, connected graph for each array in the program. Each node in these graphs corresponds to a phase accessing the array represented by the graph. Notice that these phases do not have to include outermost DO loops. That is, the phases could be inside one or more DO loops. The nodes are connected according to the program control flow. The connected graphs are not necessarily trees because not all loops are part of a phase. The *LCG* supports all the functions of our technique, including program optimization and automatic generation of communication operations.

There are a variety of approaches to automatically solve the iteration/data distribution problem [4], [5], [3], [6], [1]. However, as mentioned above, we believe that they suffer limitations that should be resolved, if possible. With these approaches, the array dimensions must be static and known at compile time, and array reshaping, therefore, is not addressed. In addition, these approaches require that the loops be perfectly nested and that the subscript expressions and loop limits be affine expressions of the loop indices. Furthermore, they do not satisfactorily solve the BLOCK-CYCLIC distribution and do not consider the *reverse distribution* case. In contrast, as mentioned above, our techniques can handle array reshaping and, as a result, can be directly applied inter-procedurally. Our techniques can handle non-affine access functions and can compute BLOCK-CYCLIC distributions, the most general type of distributions among those commonly used today. And our approach covers the reverse distribution as well.

The organization of the paper is as follows. In Section 2, we describe the main concepts in our model: the *array reference descriptor*, the *phase descriptor*, and some operations to simplify their representation. Section 3 introduces *iteration descriptors*, which describes the memory region accessed by a parallel loop iteration. In Section 4, we address the locality analysis (*intra-phase and inter-phase localities*) that generates the annotated LCG to reflect the memory locality that can be exploited in the code. In addition, we present two applications of the LCG. Due to space limitations, we have omitted formal proofs, but the theorems and statements are quite simple and we expect that the reader will have no difficulty believing their correctness.

2. Array reference descriptor and phase descriptor

To generate descriptors of memory access patterns we assume that loops have been normalized and that all arrays have been converted into one-dimensional arrays as traditionally done by conventional compilers.

The *array reference descriptor* (ARD) of the s-th reference to array X in phase F_k is defined as: $\mathcal{A}_s^k(X, \vec{i}_k) = \left(\vec{\alpha}_s, \vec{\delta}_s, \vec{\lambda}_s, \tau_s \right)$. Here, $\vec{i}_k$ is the vector of indices of the loop nest F_k. There is one (and only one) element in ARD vectors $\vec{\alpha}_s$, $\vec{\delta}_s$, and $\vec{\lambda}_s$ for each loop index from the nest. Let us assume that the subscript expression of the sth reference to X is ϕ_s. Element j of $\vec{\delta}_s$ contains the absolute value of the *stride* of ϕ_s for $i_k(j)$, the jth loop index in loop nest F_k. This stride is the difference between the values ϕ_s obtained by evaluating it at two consecutive values of $i_k(j)$. The jth element of $\vec{\lambda}_s$ is 1 if the jth stride is positive and -1 otherwise. The jth element of $\vec{\alpha}_s$ is the difference between the values of ϕ_s with $i_k(j)$ evaluated at the limits of the jth

loop divided by the jth element of the stride. The value of vector $\vec{\alpha}_s$ multiplied element-by-element by the stride is the *span* defined in [9].

For example, consider the two references to X shown in Figure 1 containing a loop nest of TFFT2 from the NASA benchmarks. The $P = 2^p$ and $Q = 2^q$ input parameters are constant. Initially, we do not take into account the different kinds of accesses (read/write). Therefore, for this loop nest, there are two non-affine subscript expressions: $\phi_1 = (2 \cdot P \cdot I + 2^{L-1} \cdot J + K)$ and $\phi_2 = (2 \cdot P \cdot I + 2^{L-1} \cdot J + K + P/2)$. In addition, in this example, the upper bound of J loop and the upper bound of the K loop are non-affine expressions dependent on the L index. The ARDs for the two X references are shown in Figure 2.

1. F_3: **doall** $I = 0$ **to** $Q - 1$
2.   **do** $L = 1$ **to** p
3.   **do** $J = 0$ **to** $P \cdot 2^{-L} - 1$
4.   **do** $K = 0$ **to** $2^{L-1} - 1$
5. $\ldots X(2 \cdot P \cdot I + 2^{L-1} \cdot J + K) \ldots$
6. $\ldots X(2 \cdot P \cdot I + 2^{L-1} \cdot J + K + P/2) \ldots$
7. $\vdots$
8.   **enddo**
9.   **enddo**
10.   **enddo**
11.   **enddo**

Figure 1. X in phase F_3 of TFFT2

The ARD $\mathcal{A}_1^3(X, \vec{i}_3)$ from Figure 2 contains three vectors and one scalar: $\vec{\alpha}_1 = (Q, (P-2) \cdot 2^{-L} + 1, P \cdot 2^{-L}, 2^{L-1})$ containing the span divided by the stride for each loop index. The vector $\vec{\delta} = (2 \cdot P, J \cdot 2^{L-1}, 2^{L-1}, 1)$ contains the *stride* for each loop index of ϕ_1. The vector $\vec{\lambda} = (1, 1, 1, 1)$ contains the stride signs. Finally, $\tau_1 = 0$ is the *offset* of the ϕ_1 access function with respect to the basis position in the X array (which is 0).

Once we have obtained the ARDs for array X in a phase, say F_k, a *phase descriptor* (PD) representing all the elements of X accessed by a phase can be computed. The general form of a phase descriptor is $\mathcal{P}^k(X, i) = \bigcup_{j=1:m} \mathcal{A}_j^k(X, \vec{i}_k) = \mathcal{A}_1^k(X, \vec{i}_k) \cup \mathcal{A}_2^k(X, \vec{i}_k) \cup \ldots \mathcal{A}_m^k(X, \vec{i}_k)$. This PD has the form $\vec{\mathcal{P}}^k(X, \vec{i}_k) = \left(A, \vec{\delta}, \Lambda, \vec{\tau} \right)$ and represents m ≥ 1 of the occurrences of X within the phase. A, and Λ are matrices of dimension m $\times$ n which represent the spans divided by strides, and the stride signs, respectively. The vector $\vec{\delta}$ represents the vector of all possible strides for all levels of nesting and all occurrences of X. The value n is the dimension of vector $\vec{\delta}$. Each row of the matrices represents the $\vec{\alpha}$ and $\vec{\lambda}$ vectors, respectively, for each occurrence of X represented by $\mathcal{A}_j^k$. The vector $\vec{\tau}$ contains the offset for each occurrence. In the rest of the paper, for the sake of simplicity, we will assume that all the strides have a positive sign so that we can avoid the matrix Λ. For the code example in Figure 1, the resultant

87

$$\mathcal{A}_1^3(X, \vec{\imath}_3) = \left[(Q, \quad (P-2)\cdot 2^{-L}+1, \quad P\cdot 2^{-L}, \quad 2^{L-1}), \begin{pmatrix} 2\cdot P \\ J\cdot 2^{L-1} \\ 2^{L-1} \\ 1 \end{pmatrix}, (1, \quad 1, \quad 1, \quad 1), 0 \right]$$

$$\mathcal{A}_2^3(X, \vec{\imath}_3) = \left[(Q, \quad (P-2)\cdot 2^{-L}+1, \quad P\cdot 2^{-L}, \quad 2^{L-1}), \begin{pmatrix} 2\cdot P \\ J\cdot 2^{L-1} \\ 2^{L-1} \\ 1 \end{pmatrix}, (1, \quad 1, \quad 1, \quad 1), P/2 \right]$$

Figure 2. ARDs for X in phase F_3 of TFFT2

PD for the array X is shown in Figure 3(a). In the PD for an array X, the stride vector $\vec{\delta}$ contains some strides associated with the parallel loop and some other strides associated with the sequential ones. Recall that each phase contains at most one parallel loop. For example, in Figure 3(a) the first component of stride vector $\delta_1 = 2\cdot P$ is associated with the **doall** loop. The remaining components of the stride vector, which are associated with the sequential loops, appear in loop order: ($\delta_2 = J\cdot 2^{L-1}; \delta_3 = 2^{L-1}; \delta_4 = 1$).

2.1. Phase descriptor transformations

A PD can be simplified by applying transformations such as *stride coalescing* and *access descriptor union*. As mentioned above, a program is represented here by a collection of control flow graphs, one for each array in the program. The nodes of these graphs correspond to DO loop nests containing accesses to the array associated with the control flow graph. The access representation of array X can be further improved by avoiding the redundancies that may arise between PDs corresponding to different phases. In order to accomplish this task, we also need to carry out other simplification operations: *descriptors homogenization* and *offset adjustment* operations. All these operations are briefly described next. Detailed descriptions can be found in [7].

An element of the stride vector $\vec{\delta}$ may be safely deleted when it is a multiple of another and the *span* corresponding to the former is greater than the span of the latter. Our goal in the *stride coalescing* operation is to reduce the number of indices involved in the PD. Given a PD for an array X, $\mathcal{P}^k(X, \vec{\imath}_k) = \left(A, \vec{\delta}, \vec{\tau} \right)$, the *stride coalescing* operation removes *redundant stride* columns [7] from $\vec{\delta}$ and the corresponding columns from matrix A without losing the access information. The basis of the stride coalescing operation was introduced in [9].

An important case arises when the access functions are non-linear and/or the loop bounds are non-constant: the PDs are non-constant. This means that either some coefficients α_{ij} from matrix A or some δ_j from $\vec{\delta}$ are a function of the index loop variables. For example, consider the loop nest descriptor in Figure 3(a), which is expressed in terms of the loop indices L and J. The element δ_3 is a multiple of element δ_4. Therefore, we can remove δ_3 and the third

column of A. However, this implies updating the fourth column of A. Figure 3(b) shows the new phase descriptor that results from the application of coalescing. In this PD, element δ_2 is again redundant with respect to δ_4. By applying the coalescing algorithm again, we get the final PD, which is shown in Figure 3(c).

In some cases, it may be possible to find for two ARDs a PD representation containing a single $\mathcal{A}_j^k$ term due to misalignments in the access functions. For example, this is the case when two ARDs describe the same access pattern but one of the regions they represent is shifted relative to the other (we say two ARDs have the same access pattern when they have a *similar* [7] size vector, $\vec{\alpha}$, and the same stride vector, $\vec{\delta}$). The ARDs of these access functions can be aggregated in such a way that they can be represented as a single row within a PD. This single row represents the union of the two ARDs. This is the goal of the access descriptor union operation. For example, applying access descriptors union to $\mathcal{A}_1^3(X, \vec{\imath}_3)$ and $\mathcal{A}_2^3(X, \vec{\imath}_3)$ ARDs from Figure 3(c) produces the PD shown in Figure 3(d).

There are several cases in which two PDs describe the same access pattern, but one of the regions is shifted with respect to the other. Since we are interested in the whole region of an array X accessed with the same access patterns, we can aggregate both PDs into one which represents the union of such regions. In order to do this, we apply a union operation similar to the one described above for ARDs. Both PDs are replaced by the result of the union operation. This is the *descriptor homogenization* operation.

The goal of the *offset adjustment* operation is to express the region accessed for each PD with respect to τ_{min}, which is the base position for array X. If the PD of F_k does not contain the minimum offset, we rewrite the smaller offset of that nest (τ_1^k) in terms of τ_{min}. For this, we define the *adjust distance* operation, R^k, as $R^k = \left\lfloor \frac{\tau_1^k - \tau_{min}}{\delta_1^k} \right\rfloor$.

3. Iteration descriptor

Consider a loop nest with a single parallel loop. To describe the elements of array X accessed by one iteration, say i, of the parallel loop in phase F_k, we use the *iteration descriptor* (ID) whose general form is $\mathcal{I}^k(X, i) = \bigcup_{j=1:m} \mathcal{I}_j^k(X, i) = \mathcal{I}_1^k(X, i) \cup \mathcal{I}_2^k(X, i) \cup \ldots \mathcal{I}_m^k(X, i)$,

$$\vec{\mathcal{P}}^3(X,\vec{i}_3) = \left[\begin{pmatrix} Q & (P-2)\cdot 2^{-L}+1 & P\cdot 2^{-L} & 2^{L-1} \\ Q & (P-2)\cdot 2^{-L}+1 & P\cdot 2^{-L} & 2^{L-1} \end{pmatrix}, \begin{pmatrix} 2\cdot P \\ J\cdot 2^{L-1} \\ 2^{L-1} \\ 1 \end{pmatrix}, \begin{pmatrix} 0 \\ P/2 \end{pmatrix} \right] \qquad \vec{\mathcal{P}}^3(X,\vec{i}_3) = \left[\begin{pmatrix} Q & P/2 \\ Q & P/2 \end{pmatrix}, \begin{pmatrix} 2\cdot P \\ 1 \end{pmatrix}, \begin{pmatrix} 0 \\ P/2 \end{pmatrix} \right]$$

(a)

(c)

$$\vec{\mathcal{P}}^3(X,\vec{i}_3) = \left[\begin{pmatrix} Q & (P-2)\cdot 2^{-L}+1 & P/2 \\ Q & (P-2)\cdot 2^{-L}+1 & P/2 \end{pmatrix}, \begin{pmatrix} 2\cdot P \\ P/2 - 2^{L-1} \\ 1 \end{pmatrix}, \begin{pmatrix} 0 \\ P/2 \end{pmatrix} \right] \qquad \vec{\mathcal{P}}^3(X,\vec{i}_3) = \left[\begin{pmatrix} Q & P \end{pmatrix}, \begin{pmatrix} 2\cdot P \\ 1 \end{pmatrix}, (0) \right]$$

(b)

(d)

Figure 3. (a) PD of X in F_3; (b) after removing δ_3; (c) after removing δ_2; (d) after the access descriptor union

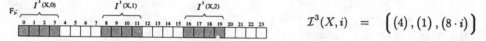

$$\mathcal{I}^3(X,i) = \left((4),(1),(8\cdot i) \right)$$

Figure 4. IDs for X associated with parallel iterations i=0, i=1 and i=2 of F_3

where $\mathcal{I}^k(X,i) = \left(B,\vec{\delta}_B,\vec{\tau}_B(i),\vec{\Delta} \right)$. The ID represents a super-set of all elements of array X accessed in such a parallel iteration. A simple way to compute an ID is to manipulate the corresponding PD as follows: B is computed from A by removing the sizes associated with the parallel loop; $\vec{\delta}_B$ represents the stride associated with the sequential loops, and $\vec{\tau}_B(i)$ is the extended offset vector. $\vec{\tau}_B(i)$ contains, for $j = 1:m$, $\tau_B(j,i) = \tau_j + i\cdot\delta_P(j)$, where $\delta_P(j)$ is the stride associated with the parallel loop of the jth occurrence. $\tau_B(j,i)$ points to the first memory position of the sub-region accessed by the $\phi_j(\vec{i}_k)$ access function in the i-th iteration of the parallel loop. $\vec{\Delta}$ is originally a null vector that will be computed next. Figure 4 (with $\vec{\Delta}$ omitted) shows a graphic representation of the IDs associated with each iteration of the parallel loop of F_3 for the array X of the TFFT2 example of Figure 2 when $Q = 3$ and $P = 4$. The shaded memory positions of X represent the data sub-regions described by each $\mathcal{I}^3(X,i)$. The $\vec{\Delta}$ component of each ID term can be used to take advantage of *storage symmetry*. It is used to represent as a single term several $\mathcal{I}_j^k(X,i)$ terms from the original form of the ID. For each type of storage symmetry we define a *distance*: a) *Shifted storage*: With a shifted storage distance, two array sub-regions with the same access pattern but shifted can be represented by a single ID term. In this situation, we define the *shifted storage distance*, Δ_d; b) *Reverse storage*: this represents two array sub-regions that are accessed with a reverse access pattern (this means that one access function is increasing and the other is decreasing with respect to the parallel loop index). In this case, we define the *reverse storage distance* Δ_r; c) *Overlapping storage*: this represents two array sub-regions which are partially overlapped. In this case, we calculate the *overlapping distance*, Δ_s. In Figure 5, we show some examples of storage symmetry and their corresponding IDs and distances. The three kinds of storage symmetry we have just defined are not exclusive to

each other, and they can appear at the same phase descriptor.

4. Memory access locality analysis

In developing our analysis and transformation algorithms, we have assumed: i) The total number of processors, H, to be involved in the execution of the program is known at compile time; and ii) The iterations of each parallel loops are statically distributed between the H processors involved in the execution of the code following a BLOCK-CYCLIC pattern.

The first part of the algorithm is to identify when it is possible to distribute iterations and data in such a way that all accesses to an array X are to local memory. We call this part of the algorithm *memory access locality analysis*. Obviously, is not always possible to find a static iteration/data distribution such that all accesses required by a given processor are local. In such cases, a remote access (communication) to the memory of the processor owning the required data is necessary. Actually, the communication operation is implemented in our model via a *put* [2] operation. This operation is an example of what is known as single-sided communication primitives. In our approach, the data distribution may change dynamically from phase to phase. In fact, with our locality analysis framework, it is possible to identify sets of consecutive phases that cover the same data sub-region of an array X for a number of parallel iterations scheduled on each phase. For this set of phases, we can select a static data distribution for X such that all accesses to this array are going to be local.

In this Section, we analyze the conditions that must hold to ensure the memory access locality for each phase (*intra-phase locality*) and between phases (*inter-phase locality*). The goal of this analysis is to compute the LCG. We assign an attribute to each node of the LCG identifying the type

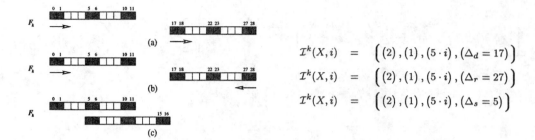

$$\mathcal{I}^k(X,i) = \Big((2), (1), (5 \cdot i), (\Delta_d = 17) \Big)$$

$$\mathcal{I}^k(X,i) = \Big((2), (1), (5 \cdot i), (\Delta_r = 27) \Big)$$

$$\mathcal{I}^k(X,i) = \Big((2), (1), (5 \cdot i), (\Delta_s = 5) \Big)$$

Figure 5. (a) Shifted st. $\Delta_d = 17$; (b) Reverse st. $\Delta_r = 27$; (c) Overlapping st. $\Delta_s = 5$

of memory access for that array in the corresponding phase. When the memory access for an array X in a phase is write only, the associated node in the X graph is marked with the attribute W; when the memory access is read only, the attribute is R; and, finally, for read and write accesses, the attribute is R/W. A special case arises when array X is privatizable in a phase (we restrict the definition of privatizable array given in [10] because we consider the value of X is not lived after the execution of F_k): the corresponding node is marked with attribute P. Figure 6 shows the LCG for a fragment of our motivating TFFT2 example. This LCF comprises two graphs: one for array X and one for array Y. Each graph contains 8 nodes (phases). As noted earlier, the nodes are labeled with an access attribute: W, R, P, and R/W. On each graph, the edges connecting nodes are also annotated with additional labels: L, which means that is possible to exploit memory access locality between the connected nodes, and C, which means that it is not possible to assure memory access locality. This C label stands for "communication", because the lack of memory access locality implies non-local accesses or, in other words, the necessity of communication between processors. In these cases, the communication operations will be placed just after the execution of the source connected phase and before the execution of the drain connected phase. The locality labels, L and C, will be determined at the end of the locality analysis.

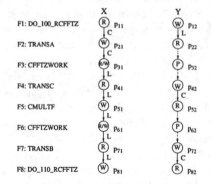

Figure 6. LCG for a TFFT2 code section

4.1. Intra-phase locality

Let $\mathcal{I}^k(X,i)$ be the ID for array X in the i-th parallel iteration of phase F_k. Let us assume that this i-th iteration is scheduled in the processor PE. We say that all *accesses to X are local* to processor PE if the region described by $\mathcal{I}^k(X,i)$ belongs to processor PE. From here, we propose an intuitive idea.

Theorem 1. Let us suppose that the i-th parallel iteration of phase F_k is scheduled in processor PE. The sufficient condition to ensure that all accesses to array X in phase F_k are local to processor PE (**intra-phase locality**) is that this processor local memory holds $\mathcal{I}^k(X,i)$ and a) X is privatizable, or b) X is non-privatizable and there is not overlapping storage for array X in phase F_k, or c) X is non-privatizable, there is overlapping storage for X in F_k and accesses to array X in that phase are only reads. □

Theorem 1 sets three different situations:

a) Array X is privatizable. If the local memory of each processor contains a copy of the region of the privatizable array X accessed in the corresponding parallel iteration (which is described in $\mathcal{I}^k(X,i)$), we can guarantee that all accesses to X in the phase F_k are local, as we show in Figure 7(a) for array Y. *Array replication* is a particular case of this situation.

b) Array X is non-privatizable and there is not overlapping storage for array X in phase F_k ($\nexists \Delta_s$). In this case, when the local memory of processor PE (which executes the i-th parallel iteration of phase F_k) contains the region described in $\mathcal{I}^k(X,i)$, all the access functions in this phase only generate local accesses to the memory of processor PE, as we see in Figure 7(b) for array Y.

c) Array X is non-privatizable and there is overlapping storage for X in F_k ($\exists \Delta_s$), then $\mathcal{I}^k(X,i)$ contains overlap sub-regions that are replicated in other processor memories. This is shown in Figure 7(c). In this case, when accesses are reads only, it is not necessary to update the replicated sub-regions (overlap sub-regions). Therefore, no communications will be necessary, and all accesses will be local to the memory of processor PE.

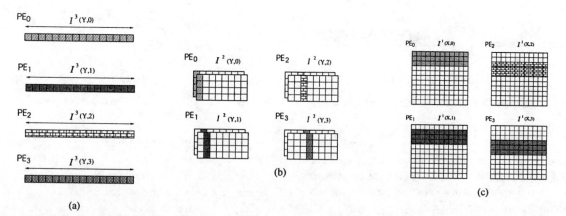

Figure 7. (a) Y is priv.; (b) Y is non-priv. and non-overlap.; (c) X is non-priv., overlap. and is only-read

Theorem 1 can be extended for a collection of parallel iterations. Then, for each parallel iteration scheduled in a processor the corresponding ID must be allocated in the processor local memory.

4.2. Inter-phase locality

Once we have established the intra-phase locality condition in a phase (which implies there will be no communication operations in the execution of that phase), the next step is to extend the locality analysis and to determine when two phases F_k and F_g $(k < g)$ access the same local region of X, so as to avoid communication operations between the execution of these phases (*inter-phase locality*).

There are two concepts that help us to relate the sub-region accessed by a number of parallel iterations to those parallel iterations: the *upper limit* and the *memory gap* [7]. The upper limit of array X for a parallel iteration i, $\mathcal{UL}(\mathcal{I}^k(X,i))$, represents the farthest memory position of the sub-region described by the ID of X in the i-th iteration of the parallel loop of phase F_k. In general, the upper limit of array X for a chunk of p parallel iterations, starting in the iteration i, $\mathcal{UL}(\mathcal{I}^k(X,i),p)$, represents the farthest memory position of all the sub-regions described by the IDs of X from the ith to the $(i+p-1)$th iterations of the parallel loop. There may be phases in the program in which the sequential loops do not access all the memory positions between two consecutive parallel iterations. In other words, there could be memory gaps between the farthest memory position of the sub-region associated with the ID of the i-th parallel iteration and the lower memory position of the next sub-region (associated with the ID of the $(i+1)$-th parallel iteration). To cover these cases, we define the memory gap, h^k, of array X in phase F_k. Figure 8 shows the upper limit of each ID for the parallel iterations $i=0$, $i=1$ and $i=2$ of F_3 and the memory gap for the array X in the TFFT2 example of Figure 4.

Let $\mathcal{I}^k(X,i)$ and $\mathcal{I}^g(X,i')$ be the IDs of X for i and i'

parallel iterations in phases F_k and F_g $(g > k)$. Let h^k and h^g be the memory gap of X in each of these phases. We define the **balanced locality condition** for array X as:

$$\mathcal{UL}(\mathcal{I}^k(X,i),p_k) + h^k = \mathcal{UL}(\mathcal{I}^g(X,i'),p_g) + h^g \tag{1}$$

$$1 \le p_k \le \left\lceil \frac{u_{k1}+1}{H} \right\rceil \tag{2}$$

$$1 \le p_g \le \left\lceil \frac{u_{g1}+1}{H} \right\rceil \tag{3}$$

where u_{k1} and u_{g1} represent the upper bounds of the parallel loops in phases F_k and F_g. $0 \le i + p_k - 1 \le u_{k1}$ and $0 \le i' + p_g - 1 \le u_{g1}$. Equation 1 determines the number of consecutive parallel iterations (p_k, p_g) that needs to be scheduled in each phase in order to ensure that the sub-region they describe is the same. Therefore, if these iterations are scheduled in processor PE, the accesses to this region are local when the region is stored in the PE local memory. That is, in processor $PE = 0$ will be scheduled $i = 0 : p_k - 1$ of F_k and $i' = 0 : p_g - 1$ of F_g; In $PE = 1$ will be scheduled $i = p_k : 2 \cdot p_k - 1$ of F_k and $i' = p_g : 2 \cdot p_g - 1$ of F_g, and so on following a CYCLIC(p_k) and CYCLIC(p_g) (BLOCK-CYCLIC) scheduling of the parallel iterations. Equations 2 and 3 limit the maximum number of parallel iterations that can be scheduled in a processor for phases F_k and F_g, thereby taking care of the load balance. By solving the system of Equations 1-3, we get the unknowns p_k and p_g, which give us the size of the chunk in the BLOCK-CYCLIC distributions as we describe in [7].

Theorem 2. To ensure that all accesses to array X in phases F_k and F_g are carried out without communication operations between the execution of these phases (**inter-phase locality**) one of these conditions suffices: 1) X is non-privatizable in phases F_k and F_g, and the intra-phase locality condition is fulfilled in phase F_k, and the balanced locality condition holds; 2) X is privatizable in phase F_k (F_g), and the intra-phase locality condition is fulfilled in phase F_g (F_k); 3) X is privatizable in phases F_k and F_g. $\square$

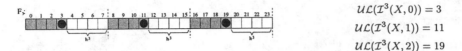

$$\mathcal{UL}(\mathcal{I}^3(X,0)) = 3$$
$$\mathcal{UL}(\mathcal{I}^3(X,1)) = 11$$
$$\mathcal{UL}(\mathcal{I}^3(X,2)) = 19$$

Figure 8. Symbol ● represents the upper limit of each $\mathcal{I}^3(\mathbf{X},\mathbf{i})$; $\mathbf{h}^1 = 4$ is the memory gap

Theorem 2 is based on Theorem 1 which establishes the conditions to avoid communications within a phase. Three situations may arise when we analyze the transition between the intra-phase locality condition in phase F_k and the intra-phase locality condition in phase F_g:

1. Array X is non-privatizable in phases F_k and F_g, and the intra-phase locality condition is fulfilled in phase F_k. There will be communication operations for array X between the execution of these phases if the balanced locality condition does not hold. For example, the balanced locality condition for array X in phases F_2 and F_3 of TFFT2 is expressed as:

$$p_2 + 2 \cdot Q \cdot P - P = 2 \cdot P \cdot p_3 \quad (4)$$

$$1 \le p_2 \le \left\lceil \frac{P}{H} \right\rceil \quad (5)$$

$$1 \le p_3 \le \left\lceil \frac{Q}{H} \right\rceil \quad (6)$$

The integer solution that verifies Equation 4 is $p_2 = P$, $p_3 = Q$. However, this solution does not verify Equations 5 and 6. This fact points out that all accesses to X in phases F_2 and F_3 are local if the processor PE executes all iterations of phases F_2 and F_3. That is, F_2 and F_3 would be executed sequentially, and the local memory of PE should store the whole array to avoid communication operations. Actually, this means that there will be communication operations if we do not take into account the sequential execution possibility.

On the contrary, let us analyze the balanced locality condition for non-privatizable array X in phases F_3 and F_4 of TFFT2, which is in Figure 9(c). In this case, we get $\left\lceil \frac{Q}{H} \right\rceil$ integer solutions, which verifies the balanced locality condition. Suppose that we select as a solution for the balanced locality condition $p_3 = p_4 = 1$. Figure 9(a)(b) shows the IDs associated with $p_3 = p_4 = 1$ for processor $PE = 0$. We can see that the covered data region is the same in the two phases and that the intra-phase locality condition is fulfilled in phase F_g for $p_g = 1$. As a result, all accesses to X in F_3 and F_4 are local.

2. Array X is privatizable in phase F_k (F_g). By definition the value of X in F_g (F_k) does not depend on the value of X in phase F_k (F_g). In these cases, the intra-phase locality condition (Theorem 1) holds in the phase where array X is privatizable. For the other phase, if the intra-phase locality condition is fulfilled, we are assured that, in F_k and F_g, all accesses to X are local and that they do not generate

any communication operations. Here, we say that phases F_k and F_g are *un-coupled*.

3. Array X is privatizable in phases F_k and F_g. Again, these two phases are un-coupled.

Table 1. Classification of labels for edges in a LCG

$F_k - F_g$	Overl. ($\exists \, \Delta_s$)		Non overl. ($\nexists \, \Delta_s$)	
	Bal. loc.	Non-bal. loc.	Bal. loc.	Non-bal. loc.
$R - R$	L	C	L	C
$R - W$	L	C	L	C
$R - R/W$	L	C	L	C
$R - P$	D	D	D	D
$W - R$	C	C	L	C
$W - W$	C	C	L	C
$W - R/W$	C	C	L	C
$W - P$	C	C	D	D
$R/W - R$	L	C	L	C
$R/W - W$	L	C	L	C
$R/W - R/W$	L	C	L	C
$R/W - P$	D	D	D	D
$P - W$	D	D	D	D
$P - R/W$	D	D	D	D
$P - P$	D	D	D	D

Table 1 summarizes all possible cases in a LCG when Theorem 2 is applied. In the first column of the table, we show all the possible attribute combinations between the two nodes for which we are analyzing the inter-phase locality. Bear in mind that by using memory access locality analysis we aim to find out how to label the edges in the LCG. We have divided the table columns into two major parts to show whether there is parallel iteration overlapping in phase F_k ($\exists \, \Delta_s$). Each major column, is sub-divided into two additional ones, to show whether there is verification of the balanced locality condition in phases F_k and F_g. By applying Theorem 2, the edges will be labeled with C if there are communication operations between the execution of the two connected phases, or with L if it is possible to avoid communications by exploiting locality (i.e., Theorem 2 holds). In Table 1, for the labels set to L we assume that the intra-phase locality condition of phase F_k holds. We use the label D to annotate those edges that bind two un-coupled phases. For example, to build the LCG of TFFT2, shown in Figure 6, we just needed to apply the 4-th and 5-th columns of Table 1 because there is not overlapping storage in any phase (i.e., $\nexists \, \Delta_s$). For array Y, phases (F_2, F_3), (F_3, F_4) and (F_5, F_6), (F_6, F_7), are un-coupled; thus, the corresponding edges (the dashed edges in Figure 6) are first

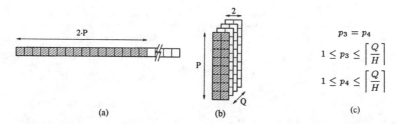

Figure 9. (a) $\mathcal{I}^3(\mathbf{X}, 0)$ is shaded; (b) $\mathcal{I}^4(\mathbf{X}, 0)$ is shaded; (c) the balanced locality condition

marked with D, and later removed.

4.3. Locality analysis applications

Once the LCG has been built, we can use it for at least two applications: (a) implementing an *integer programming model* to find out the iteration/data distribution that minimizes the parallel execution overhead; and (b) generating the communication routines between the phases that have been marked with label C.

a) The set of nodes of a LCG that are connected consecutively with L edges covers a common data sub-region of array X; we call this a *chain* of nodes. There can be more than one chain for an array, and each column of the LCG has at least one chain. In the LCG, the chains of array X are separated by C edges. The nodes of the chains define the constraints of our integer programming model. Those nodes $(k - g)$ of the LCG connected with C represent a redistribution (*Global communications*) or an updating of overlapped subregions (*Frontier communications*), which are the communication patterns that our approach can handle. These nodes take part in the definition of the objective function (where $C^{kg}(X, p_k)$ is the communications cost function) because communications are one of the overhead sources. The other overhead source is the accumulation of the parallel load unbalance assigned to processors in each phase (where $D^k(X, p_k)$ is the load unbalance cost function). Due to space limitations, we leave the full description in [8], where we present and validate by measurements the cost functions. Table 2 illustrates all the constraints for the LCG of the TFFT2 code example (Figure 6). The objective function that models the parallel overhead is shown in Equation 7, where X_j represents one of the two arrays of the program.

$$o.f. = Min \left\{ \sum_{j=1:2} \sum_{k=1:8} D^k(X_j, p_k) + C^{kg}(X_j, p_k) \right\} \quad (7)$$

The solution to this problem allows us to find p_k. As a reminder, this is the size of the chunk of parallel iterations scheduled in each node (phase), following a CYCLIC(p_k) scheme. Once the iteration distribution of a node has been selected, we can compute the data distribution for each array of that node. To do this, the data distribution function

must hold the intra-phase locality requirements imposed by the IDs associated with the chunks of parallel iterations scheduled in each processor. However, it is possible to find a global data distribution for all the nodes of the chain such that all the accesses to X in any of the connected nodes of the chain are in the local memory of the processors. The reason is that all nodes belonging to the same chain cover the same data region of array X (inter-phase locality). Thus, the data allocation procedure of array X only takes place before the first node of the chain. Therefore, for each array X in the LCG, after the execution of the last phase of a chain, and before the execution of the first phase of the next chain, a data allocation procedure (redistribution) must re-allocate the data of X. We describe this procedure in [8].

b) In [8] we also outline, how to automatically generate the communication routines for array X when there is a C edge connecting two nodes in a LCG. In the communications routines generation we take into account two communications patterns: the Frontier Communications and the Global Communications. In addition, message aggregation is performed in our approach.

Some experiments were conducted in [10] and [7] to probe the effectiveness of the iteration/data distributions and communication generation obtained with our approach for a set of six real codes. The parallelization procedure is as follows. First, the Polaris parallelizer marked the parallel loops of each code. Then, the LCG of each code was built, and the integer programming problem of each code was derived. Here we used GAMS to obtain the iteration/data distributions of each phase; the solutions of the integer programming problems were obtained in few seconds in a R1000. Finally, those distributions were hand-coded for each program, including the communications generation when necessary. These parallel codes were executed in a Cray T3D. We achieved parallel efficiencies of over 70% in the Cray for 64 processors.

5. Conclusions

We have shown a compile-time representation that handles array reshaping, non-affine access functions and non-perfectly nested loops, that is suitable for general inter-

Table 2. Constraints for TFFT2 code

	X	Y
Locality const.	$p_{31} = p_{41}$ $P \cdot p_{41} = Q \cdot p_{51} \qquad p_{51} = p_{61}$ $p_{61} = p_{71} \qquad 2 \cdot Q \cdot p_{71} = p_{81}$	$p_{12} = Q \cdot p_{22}$ $P \cdot p_{32} = Q \cdot p_{52}$ $2 \cdot Q \cdot p_{62} = p_{82}$
Load bal. const.	$1 \leq p_{11}, p_{81} \leq \left\lceil \dfrac{P \cdot Q}{H} \right\rceil \quad 1 \leq p_{31}, p_{41} \leq \left\lceil \dfrac{Q}{H} \right\rceil$ $1 \leq p_{21}, p_{51}, p_{61}, p_{71} \leq \left\lceil \dfrac{P}{H} \right\rceil$	$1 \leq p_{12}, p_{82} \leq \left\lceil \dfrac{P \cdot Q}{H} \right\rceil \quad 1 \leq p_{32}, p_{42} \leq \left\lceil \dfrac{Q}{H} \right\rceil$ $1 \leq p_{22}, p_{52}, p_{62}, p_{72} \leq \left\lceil \dfrac{P}{H} \right\rceil$
Storage const.	$p_{81} \cdot H \quad \leq \quad \Delta_d^{81} = P \cdot Q$ $p_{81} \cdot H \quad \leq \quad \dfrac{\Delta_r^{81}(1)}{2} = \dfrac{P \cdot Q}{2}$ $p_{81} \cdot H \quad \leq \quad \dfrac{\Delta_r^{81}(2)}{2} = \dfrac{2 \cdot P \cdot Q}{2}$	$p_{12} \cdot H \quad \leq \quad \Delta_d^{12} = P \cdot Q$ $Q \cdot p_{22} \cdot H \quad \leq \quad \Delta_d^{22} = P \cdot Q$ $p_{82} \cdot H \quad \leq \quad \Delta_d^{82} = P \cdot Q$ $p_{82} \cdot H \quad \leq \quad \dfrac{\Delta_r^{82}(1)}{2} = \dfrac{P \cdot Q}{2}$ $p_{82} \cdot H \quad \leq \quad \dfrac{\Delta_r^{82}(2)}{2} = \dfrac{2 \cdot P \cdot Q}{2}$
Affinity const.	$p_{11} = p_{12} \quad p_{21} = p_{22} \quad p_{31} = p_{32} \quad p_{41} = p_{42}$ $p_{51} = p_{52} \quad p_{61} = p_{62} \quad p_{71} = p_{72} \quad p_{81} = p_{82}$	

procedural analysis. Using this representation, we build the LCG graph to capture the memory locality exhibited by a program (intra-phase locality and inter-phase locality). The LCG graph summarizes the phases of the program for which all accesses can be local or communication operations are required. This graph is a powerful tool that can be easily handled by the compiler in later optimization stages: iteration partition, data distribution, array replication, and communication scheduling. The framework comprising these last steps is presented in [7], where an integer programming problem results in the iterations/data distributions (including array replication) that minimize the number of remote accesses while keeping a good load balance for all the parallel loops in the code. Experimental results support the effectiveness of the data distributions and the control of communication operations derived with our approach for the set of tested programs.

References

[1] J. Anderson and M. Lam. Global optimizations for parallelism and locality on scalable parallel machines. In *Proceedings of SIGPLAN'93 Conference on Programming Language Design and Implementation (PLDI)*, Alburquerque, New Mexico, June 1993.

[2] R. Barriuso and A. Knies. SHMEM user's guide for Fortran. Cray Research Inc., August 1994. Revision 2.2.

[3] D. Bau, I. Kodukula, V. Kotlyar, K. Pingali, and Stodghill. Solving alignment using elementary linear algebra. In K. P. et al., editor, *Proceedings of LCPC'94*, number 892 in LNCS. Springer Verlag, Ithaca, N.Y., August 1994.

[4] S. Chatterjee, J. Gilbert, and R. Schreiber. The alignment-distribution graph. In U. Banerjee, editor, *Proceedings of LCPC'93*, number 768 in LNCS. Springer Verlag, Portland, OR., August 1993.

[5] C. Huang and P. Sadayappan. Communication-free hyperplane partitioning of nested loops. *J. Parallel and Distributed Computing*, 19:90–102, 1993.

[6] K. Kennedy and U. Kremer. Automatic data layout for high performance Fortran. In *Supercomputing'95*, San Diego, CA, December 1995.

[7] A. G. Navarro and E. Zapata. An automatic iteration/data distribution method based on access descriptors for DSM multiprocessors. Technical report, Department of Computer Architecture, University of Málaga, 1999.

[8] A. G. Navarro and E. L. Zapata. An automatic iteration/data distribution method based on access descriptors for DSMM. In *Twelfth International Workshop on Languages and Compilers for Parallel Computing (LCPC'99)*, The University of California, San Diego, La Jolla, CA USA, August 4–6 1999.

[9] Y. Paek, J. Hoeflinger, and D. Padua. Simplification of array access patterns for compiler optimizations. In *Proceedings of the SIGPLAN Conference on Programming Language Design and Implementation*, June 1994.

[10] Y. Paek, A. Navarro, E. Zapata, and D. Padua. Parallelization of Benchmarks for scalable shared memory machines. In *IEEE Int'l. Conf. on Parallel Architectures and Compilation Techniques (PACT'98)*, pages 401–408, Paris, France, October 12–18 1998.

A Framework for Interprocedural Locality Optimization Using Both Loop and Data Layout Transformations

Mahmut Kandemir*   Alok Choudhary*   J. Ramanujam†   Prithviraj Banerjee*

Abstract

There has been much work recently on improving the locality performance of loop nests in scientific programs through the use of loop as well as data layout optimizations. However, little attention has been paid to the problem of optimizing locality in whole programs, particularly in the presence of procedures. Current techniques do not propagate layout optimizations across procedures boundaries; this is critical for realistic scientific codes, since the cost of explicitly transforming memory layouts across procedure boundaries might be very high. In this paper we present a locality optimization framework that uses both loop and data transformations to improve cache locality program-wide. Our framework propagates layout (or locality) constraints as a system of equalities across procedures and involves two traversals in the call graph representation of the program. Preliminary experimental results obtained on an R10000 based system demonstrate the power of the framework.

1 Introduction

A key challenge in achieving high levels of performance on modern computer systems is the reduction of the time spent stalled waiting for data from memory as much as possible. Several architectural advances in memory hierarchy design has led to systems with multiple levels of memory hierarchy. Exploiting the memory hierarchy has become the most important problem in realizing the performance potential of modern machines. In the area of scientific computation, efforts have been aimed at the development of portable library routines such as LAPACK [3] in order to alleviate the difficulty if exploiting the memory hierarchy. Nevertheless, getting good performance remains difficult and we believe that this task is best left to optimizing compilers.

There has been much work on cache locality optimization techniques for loop nests. One group of these optimizations aim to reorder the iterations of a loop to improve both temporal and spatial locality; these include unimodular [31] and non-unimodular [25] linear loop (iteration space) transformations, loop distribution [27], fusion [27], and tiling [32, 31, 6, 22, 23]. These are limited by dependence constraints and are not readily applicable to imperfectly nested loops [8]. A second group consists of transformations that modify the memory storage order [8, 29, 30, 24, 17] of multidimensional arrays, referred to as *data transformations*. These are not constrained by dependences and are applicable to imperfect nests but have no effect on temporal locality; in addition, the effect of changing the memory layout of an array is program-wide. This has led to the use of combined loop and data transformations [29, 21, 18, 19].

Except for a few papers [10, 30], the impact of data reorganization necessitated at procedure boundaries has not received much attention. This is unfortunate, since practical codes contain procedure calls and the cost of data reorganization is very high. In this paper we present a locality optimization framework that uses both loop and data transformations to improve cache locality program-wide. Our framework propagates layout (or locality) constraints as a system of equalities across procedures and involves two traversals in the call graph representation of the program. We also show how to handle the cases where the callers of the same procedure demand conflicting memory layouts for the same array. Preliminary experimental results obtained on an R10000 based system demonstrate the power of the framework.

The rest of this paper is organized as follows. In Section 2 we present an outline of our approach along with details on the intra-procedural optimization framework. Section 3 describes in detail our solution—the bottom-up and the top top-down traversal techniques—to the inter-procedural locality optimization problem. In Section 4 we report performance results obtained on an SGI Origin 2000 distributed-shared-memory multi-processor. In Section 5 we review related work on compiler-based locality optimizations. In Section 6 we present our conclusions which are followed by a brief outline of on-going work.

2 Our Approach

Our approach performs two traversals on the *call graph* representation of the program. A call graph $G_c = (V_c, E_c)$ is a multi-graph where each node $p_i \in V_c$ represents a procedure and there is an edge $e \in E_c$ between p_i and p_j if p_i calls p_j [2]. In such a graph the leaves represent the procedures that do not contain any calls. If desired, the edges can be annotated by suitable information related to call sites such as the actual parameters passed to the procedure, the line number where the call occurs and so on.

Before the first traversal, we run an intra-procedural locality optimization algorithm on each leaf node. The details of this algorithm are explained in Section 2.1. In the first traversal, called *bottom-up*, we start with the leaves and process each node in the call graph if and only if all the nodes it calls have been processed. After all the callee nodes for a given caller have been processed, we propagate a system of equalities (called the layout or locality constraints) to the caller. The caller adds this system to its own local set of equalities (obtained using the intra-procedural locality optimization algorithm) and propagates the resulting system to its callers and so on. This bottom-up traversal is discussed in greater detail in Section 3.1. When we reach the root (the main program), we have all the locality constraints of the program. We solve these constraints at root and determine the layouts of the (global and local) arrays accessed by the root. The next step is the top-down traversal; in this traversal, each caller propagates down the layouts determined so far to its callees. The algorithm terminates when all the leaf nodes have been processed. The details of the top-down traversal are given in Section 3.2. Note that in this paper we assume that either array re-shaping does not occur or when it occurs it is possible to undo its effect using de-linearization [26].

2.1 Intra-procedural Locality Optimization Algorithm

This subsection presents our intra-procedural *static* locality optimization algorithm. While it resembles the previous approaches in

*CPDC, Department of Electrical and Computer Engineering, Northwestern University, Evanston, IL 60208. e-mail: {mtk,choudhar,banerjee}@ece.nwu.edu

†Department of Electrical and Computer Engineering, Louisiana State University, Baton Rouge, LA 70803. e-mail: jxr@ee.lsu.edu

spirit [18, 19], it has the advantage of looking at the big picture before starting to solve the problem; if desired, the previous approaches can also be represented in our framework. The algorithm determines static memory layouts in the sense that there is a single memory layout for each array throughout the entire procedure being analyzed.

2.1.1 Background

An n-deep loop nest with loop indices $i_1, i_2, ..., i_n$ in the program is represented by an integer polyhedron bounded by the loop limits. Each point in this polyhedron is represented by a vector $(i'_1, i'_2, ..., i'_n)^T$ and corresponds to an execution of the loop body when $i_k = i'_k$ for all $1 \leq k \leq n$; $\bar{I} = (i_1, i_2, ..., i_n)^T$ is called the *iteration vector*, where i_1 is the outermost loop index and i_n is the innermost loop index. Similarly the memory storage of an m-dimensional array can also be viewed as a (rectilinear) polyhedron. The extents of the array determine the bounds of the polyhedron and each point (array element) can be indexed using a column vector $(j_1, j_2, ..., j_m)^T$.

We assume that the array subscript expressions and loop bounds are affine functions of enclosing loop indices and loop-invariant constants; that is, we are assuming an affine loop nest. Under this assumption, in an n-deep loop nest, each reference to an m-dimensional array can be modeled by an *access matrix* $\mathcal{L}$ of size $m \times n$ and an m-dimensional *offset vector* $\bar{o}$ [25, 31, 33], i.e., modeled as $\mathcal{L}\bar{I} + \bar{o}$, where $\bar{I}$ is the iteration vector. In this paper $\mathcal{L}_{uij}$ ($\bar{o}_{uij}$) denotes the jth reference matrix (offset vector) for array U in nest i.

For such a loop nest, we consider an iteration space transformation [31, 25, 33] that can be represented by integer $n \times n$ non-singular square transformation matrix T. Such an invertible loop transformation matrix realizes the following transformation $\mathcal{L}\bar{I} + \bar{o} \rightarrow \mathcal{L}T^{-1}\bar{I}' + \bar{o}$, where $\bar{I}' = T\bar{I}$ is the new iteration vector (after the transformation). Similarly, for a m-dimensional array, an $m \times m$ non-singular data transformation matrix M has the following effect [24, 29, 17]: $\mathcal{L}\bar{I} + \bar{o} \rightarrow M\mathcal{L}\bar{I} + M\bar{o}$.

Consequently, applying *both* loop and data transformations to a reference represented by $\mathcal{L}$ and $\bar{o}$ gives us the following transformation: $\mathcal{L}\bar{I} + \bar{o} \rightarrow M\mathcal{L}T^{-1}\bar{I}' + M\bar{o}$. Since we are not interested in shift-type (alignment-like) data transformations in this paper, we only focus on the transformed access matrix $M\mathcal{L}T^{-1}$. Most of the previous approaches to loop and data transformations can be cast as problems of determining either or both of the matrices T and M (with some legality conditions) such that $M\mathcal{L}T^{-1}$ will have some desired form for a given objective such as optimizing locality [31] or maximizing parallelism [33]. An iteration space transformation matrix T is legal if it preserves all data dependences in the original loop nest [33]. Also, the data transformation matrix M should be applied to all the references to the array in question and and to all its aliases [7]. In this paper we use T_i to denote the loop transformation matrix for the nest i; we use M_u to refer to the data transformation matrix for the array U in a given procedure.

An element is said to be *reused* if it is accessed by more than once in a loop nest. There are two types of reuses: *temporal* and *spatial*. [31, 25]. Temporal reuse occurs when two references (not necessarily distinct) access the same memory location; and spatial reuse arises between two references that access nearby memory locations (e.g., elements mapped on the same cache line) [33]. In this paper, we focus primarily on self-reuses (i.e., reuses originating from individual references [31]); we do not discuss the extension to handle group-reuses.

It is important to note that the most important reuses (whether temporal or spatial) are the ones exhibited by the *innermost* loop. If the innermost loop exhibits temporal reuse for a reference (e.g., the reference $U(i)$ in a loop nest where i is *not* innermost), then the element accessed by that reference can be kept in a register through-

out the execution of the innermost loop. Similarly, spatial reuse is most beneficial when it occurs in the innermost loop (as in $U(i, j)$ assuming U is column-major and i is innermost); because, in that case it *may* enable unit-stride accesses to consecutive locations in memory.

2.1.2 Problem Definition for Intra-procedural Optimization

Let $\mathcal{U}$ be the set of arrays accessed in a procedure P and $N_1, ..., N_l$ are the nests in the said procedure. We want to determine a M_u for each $U \in \mathcal{U}$ and a T_i for each N_i ($1 \leq i \leq l$) such that the overall cache locality of the procedure P will be improved. We also insist that T_i should observe the data dependences in N_i and each M_u ($U \in \mathcal{U}$) should be applied taking legality considerations [7] into account.

2.1.3 Approach

Our approach to the intra-procedural locality optimization problem is based on forming a set of locality constraints (equalities) and solving them using a heuristic so that the solution of the constraints will produce loop and data transformation matrices that collectively achieve the desired cache locality. We are mainly interested in exploiting temporal and spatial locality in the *innermost* loops where they are most useful, although our approach can be extended and/or integrated with tiling to exploit locality in higher loop levels. Assuming that the array layouts are *column-major*, in order to have a good locality in the *innermost* loop

$$M_u \mathcal{L}_{uij} \bar{q}_i = (\times, 0, ..., 0, 0)^T$$

should hold for all $1 \leq i \leq l$, $U \in \mathcal{U}$, and $1 \leq j \leq s_{ui}$, where s_{ui} is the number of references to the array U in the nest N_i. In this formulation, which we call a *layout* or *locality constraint*, $\bar{q}_i$ is the last column of T_i^{-1}, the inverse of the loop transformation matrix for the nest N_i. For the rest of the paper we use $\bar{c}$ instead of $(\times, 0, ..., 0, 0)^T$ for clarity. Notice that if $\times = 0$ we have temporal reuse in the innermost loop; if $\times \neq 0$ and $\times < $ *cache-line-size*, we have spatial reuse in the innermost loop. As an example, consider the procedure P shown in Figure 1(a). For this procedure we have the following set of layout (or locality) constraints:

$$\{M_u \mathcal{L}_{u11} \bar{q}_1 = \bar{c} \quad\quad M_v \mathcal{L}_{v11} \bar{q}_1 = \bar{c}$$
$$M_u \mathcal{L}_{u21} \bar{q}_2 = \bar{c} \quad\quad M_w \mathcal{L}_{w21} \bar{q}_2 = \bar{c}\},$$

where $\mathcal{L}_{u11} = \begin{pmatrix} 1 & 0 \\ 0 & 1 \end{pmatrix}$, $\mathcal{L}_{v11} = \begin{pmatrix} 0 & 1 \\ 1 & 0 \end{pmatrix}$,

$\mathcal{L}_{u21} = \begin{pmatrix} 1 & 0 & 1 \\ 0 & 0 & 1 \end{pmatrix}$, and $\mathcal{L}_{w21} = \begin{pmatrix} 0 & 0 & 1 \\ 0 & 1 & 0 \end{pmatrix}$.

This set of equalities is represented as a bipartite graph $G = (V_l, V_a, E)$, called the *locality* (or *layout*) *constraint graph* (LCG), as shown in Figure 1(b). In a locality constrained graph G, V_l is the set of loop nests in the procedure and V_a is the set of arrays (global or local) accessed by the procedure. There is an edge $e \in E$ between a $v_a \in V_a$ and $v_l \in V_l$ if and only if the array represented by v_a is accessed in the nest represented by v_l.

Notice that such a set of equations can be solved in a number of ways and this fact will be used later in the paper to handle different cases. For our current example, six alternative solutions are shown in Figure 1(c). The numbers associated with arrows indicate the processing order; the arrows with the same number can be processed in any order. For example, on the upper-leftmost solution, we first apply a loop transformation to the first nest (we start with the vertex marked *1*). This loop transformation, in turn, allows us to determine the layouts of U and V (step 1). Next, using the layout of array U, we determine an appropriate loop transformation for the second nest (step 2). In the last step (step 3), using the new loop order of the second nest we find an appropriate memory layout for the array W. Of course, different solutions have different qualities and some solutions can cause potential conflicts. Consider the solution given on the lower-rightmost. We first transform layouts of V and W for locality, which in turn determine appropriate transformations for the first and second nests. However, since both these nests access the same array U, in determining its layout we *may* have a conflict; that is, the two nests may require *different* layouts for the same array. Notice that this is a potential conflict, not a certain one as it may happen such that the two nests agree on the same layout. It is also interesting to see how the previous approaches to procedure-wide locality optimization problem map on the locality constrained graph. As an example, the solution proposed in [18] first orders the loop nests according to a cost criterion. It then optimizes the layouts of the arrays accessed by the most-costly nest. Afterwards using the layouts found so far it optimizes the next most-costly nest and so on. Assuming that the nest *1* in our example is costlier than the nest *2*, this solution corresponds to the one shown on the upper-leftmost of Figure 1(c). If, on the other hand, the nest *2* is the most-costly, the solution is the one shown on the lower-leftmost of Figure 1(c).

In general, in order to solve the problem, we can adopt the following *graph-theoretical* solution strategy on the LCG.[1] First, we convert each edge in the locality constraint graph to a bidirectional arc (arrow) so that the end points can be visited in either order. Then we run a *maximum-branching algorithm*[2] on the resulting graph and determine all the nodes that can be covered in a conflict-free manner. For the example LCG shown in Figure 1, the upper-leftmost figure given in Figure 1(c) depicts one possible solution obtained using maximum-branching. As another example, consider the locality constraint graph shown in Figure 2(a). After the edges have been converted to arrows (Figure 2(b)), the maximum-branching algorithm generates the solution shown in Figure 2(c) (assume again that the numbers on arrows denote the processing order); note that optimal solution here is not unique. In this solution, only two edges shown in Figure 2(d) (corresponding to two locality constraints) are left unsatisfied. Of course, whether these two unsatisfied constraints will really cause any conflict or not depends on actual access matrices. As a convention, we put the directions of these unsatisfied edges from nest nodes to array nodes. To sum up, in this example, two references can go unoptimized. Figure 2(e) shows the complete solution. We refer to this complete solution as a *maximum-branching solution*.

In case we have some edges whose directions have already been selected (decided), we have a *restricted* LCG, or RLCG for short. In that case, the solution is in general imposed by these selected edges (corresponding to the locality constraints that have already been solved so far). Consider Figure 2(a) again, this time assuming that the layout of U and the loop transformations for the nests *2* and *4* have already been determined; i.e., we have a fixed arrow going from node U to node *2* and another arrow from U to *4*. The problem now is to find a maximum branching solution such that when combined with the arrows between U and *2* and between U and *4* will lead to *minimum* number of conflicts. Such a solution is shown in Figure 2(f). As another example, let us assume that the edge between nodes W and *2* has already been selected. A maximum-branching solution in that case is given in Figure 2(g). Figures 2(h) and (i), on the other hand, depict, respectively, the

unsatisfied constraints for the solutions shown in Figures 2(f) and (g). And finally, Figure 2(j) gives the final solution for Figure 2(f).

3 Inter-procedural Locality Optimization

3.1 Bottom-up Traversal

In bottom-up traversal, we take a slightly different approach from what was described above. In the leaf nodes, we collect all locality constraints, but we do not attempt to solve them immediately. Instead, for each procedure R which calls procedure P, the locality constraints are propagated from P to R. Notice that we need to propagate only the constraints on global variables and formal parameters. Of course, the latter should be *re-written* in terms of actual parameters passed to P (Recall that we do *not* allow array re-shaping). As an example, consider the code fragment shown in Figure 3(a). After the procedure P (the callee) has been processed, we have the following locality constrains:

$$\{M_u \mathcal{L}_{u11} \bar{q}_1 = \bar{c} \qquad M_x \mathcal{L}_{x11} \bar{q}_1 = \bar{c}$$
$$M_y \mathcal{L}_{y11} \bar{q}_1 = \bar{c} \qquad M_z \mathcal{L}_{z11} \bar{q}_1 = \bar{c}\},$$

where $\bar{q}_1$ is the last columns of the inverse of the loop transformation matrix for the nest in P. Notice that the first constraint is on the global array variable U and the last constraint is on the local array variable Z. The second and the third constraints, on the other hand, are on the formal parameters X and Y. When we process the caller R, the second and the third constraints are *re-written* in terms of the actual parameters V and W passed to the callee P whereas the first constraint is propagated as it is. There is no need to propagate the last constraint as Z is a local variable. Thus, the total constraints in R are as follows:

$$\{M_u \mathcal{L}_{u11} \bar{q}_1 = \bar{c}; M_v \mathcal{L}_{v11} \bar{q}_1 = \bar{c}; M_w \mathcal{L}_{w11} \bar{q}_1 = \bar{c}; \text{ and}$$
$$M_u \mathcal{L}_{u21} \bar{q}_2 = \bar{c}; M_v \mathcal{L}_{v21} \bar{q}_2 = \bar{c}; M_w \mathcal{L}_{w21} \bar{q}_2 = \bar{c}\},$$

where $\bar{q}_2$ is the last columns of the inverse of the loop transformation matrix for the nest in R. The last three constraints are the local constraints to R. As can be seen, the call statement in R is treated as a program construct (e.g., a loop nest) that somehow generates the first three constraints. Note that our propagation technique is also able to handle the cases where *aliasing* between the formal parameters occur. For example, consider the program fragment shown in Figure 3(b). Notice that in procedure P we have two constraints $\{M_x \mathcal{L}_{x11} \bar{q}_1 = \bar{c}; \quad M_y \mathcal{L}_{y11} \bar{q}_1 = \bar{c}; \}$, where $\bar{q}_1$ is the last columns of the inverse of the loop transformation matrix for the nest in P. This system, if considered alone, can assume many (equivalently optimized) solutions. (e.g., we can apply an identity loop transformation and select row-major layout for X and column-major layout for Y or alternatively we can apply loop interchange and select column-major layout for X and row-major layout for Y). However, after the propagation of these constraints (and re-writing), we have a 'more constrained' set: $\{M_v \mathcal{L}_{v11} \bar{q}_1 = \bar{c}; \quad M_v \mathcal{L}_{v12} \bar{q}_1 = \bar{c}; \}$, where

$$\mathcal{L}_{v11} = \mathcal{L}_{x11} = \begin{pmatrix} 1 & 0 \\ 0 & 1 \end{pmatrix} \text{ and } \mathcal{L}_{v12} = \mathcal{L}_{y11} = \begin{pmatrix} 0 & 1 \\ 1 & 0 \end{pmatrix}.$$

The solution now is to *skew* [31] the loop nest and assign diagonal layout for U; that is, we select

$$M_v = \begin{pmatrix} 1 & 0 \\ 1 & 1 \end{pmatrix} \text{ and } T = \begin{pmatrix} 1 & 1 \\ 0 & -1 \end{pmatrix}.$$

We continue to propagate the constraints from children (callees) to parents (callers) until we reach the root (the main program). As we move up the call graph, the locality constraints from callee procedures are propagated to the caller procedures. The static locality

---

[1] Dion, Randriamaro, and Robert [12] uses a similar graph-based strategy for the automatic data alignment problem.

[2] An *arborescence* is defined as a *tree* in which no two arcs are directed into the same node. A *branching* is defined as a *forest* in which each tree is an arborescence. Now associate a unit *weight* to each arc. A *maximum-branching* of a graph is any branching of the same graph with the largest possible weight [28]. Notice that within our problem domain this corresponds to satisfying as many locality constraints as possible.

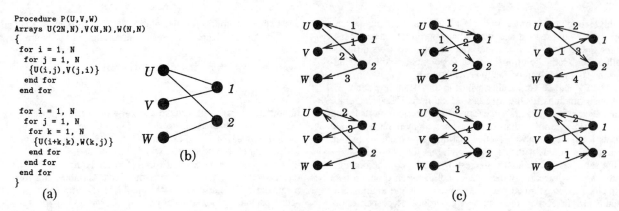

```
Procedure P(U,V,W)
Arrays U(2N,N),V(N,N),W(N,N)
{
  for i = 1, N
    for j = 1, N
      {U(i,j),V(j,i)}
    end for
  end for

  for i = 1, N
    for j = 1, N
      for k = 1, N
        {U(i+k,k),W(k,j)}
      end for
    end for
  end for
}
      (a)
```

(b)

(c)

Figure 1: (a) A procedure that contains two nests (Arrays U, V, and W are formal parameters). (b) Locality constraint graph. (c) Example solution strategies.

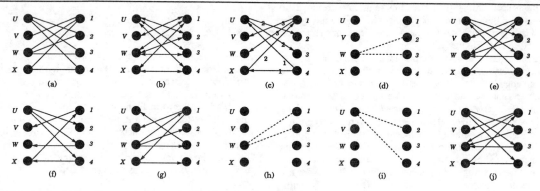

Figure 2: (a) An example locality constraint graph. (b) After the edges have been converted to bidirectional arcs (arrows). (c) A maximum-branching solution. (d) Unsatisfied edges (constraints). (e) A complete (maximum-branching) solution. (f) The solution starting from the vertex U. (g) The solution starting from the vertex W. (h) The unsatisfied edges for the solution shown in (f). (i) The unsatisfied edges for the solution shown in (g). (j) Complete solution for (f).

optimization algorithm is then run on the caller procedures. Afterwards the relevant locality constraints are passed up the call graph to their callers and so on.

When we reach the root, we have all the necessary locality constraints. In the root node, we construct a *global layout (locality) constraint graph* (GLCG) and attempt to solve these locality constraints using the graph theoretical approach discussed earlier. Notice that this GLCG has all the arrays accessible from the root node and all the nests in the root. It can also have some nests belonging to the other procedures which also reference the arrays accessed by the root. When the system has finally been solved, we have (1) the loop transformation matrices for (some of) the nests in the program and (2) the data transformation matrices for the global and local arrays accessible from the root. For example, consider again the code given in Figure 3(a). Figures 4(a) and (b) show the LCGs for the procedures P and R, respectively, when they are considered separately. Figure 4(c), on the other hand, illustrates the GLCG after all locality constraints have been gathered in the root R. Note also that the nest in P (numbered *1*) also appears in this GLCG. A maximum-branching solution is for this GLCG depicted in Figure 4(d). Using our convention, Figure 4(e) gives the complete solution. Notice that this solution determines all memory layouts as well as the loop transformations for the two nests in the program.

3.2 Top-down Traversal

In this traversal, the layouts found so far are propagated from caller procedures to callee procedures. In receiving the layouts, a callee procedure computes the loop transformation matrices for the nests it contains (if they have not been determined so far) as well as the memory layouts of its *local* arrays. In the example shown in Figure 3(a), the callee procedure P takes the layouts of U, V, and W from its caller, R. The layouts of V, and W automatically determine the layouts of X and Y, respectively. Then using these layouts, the algorithm determines the layout of the local array Z.

In terms of our graph-theoretical solution, we represent the constraints inherited from a parent as a RLCG. This RLCG contains the nodes corresponding to all the arrays accessed by the procedure being analyzed, its nests as well as (some of) the nests accessed by other procedures below this procedure in the call graph. The problem now is to find a maximum-branching solution on this RLCG. Returning to the example code shown in Figure 3(a), after the root procedure (R) has been processed, the locality constraints solved are transferred to P as an RLCG as shown in Figure 4(f). The complete maximum-branching solution for the procedure P is shown in Figure 4(g). The only thing performed when working in the RLCG of P was to determine the layout for Z, considering the loop transformation already found for the nest it contains.

Notice that not all the nests in the program have to appear in the GLCG built for the root procedure. For example, consider a program with two procedures, R (main) and P (callee). Assume

```
Arrays U(N,2N)
Procedure R(V,W)
Arrays V(2N,N),W(N,N)
{
 for i = 1, N
  for j = 1, N
   {U(i,j),W(j,i),V(i+j,i)}
  end for
 end for
 ...
 call P(V,W)
 ...
}

Procedure P(X,Y)
Arrays X(2N,N),Y(N,N)
{
 Arrays Z(N,N)
 for i = 1, N
  for j = 1, N
   for k = 1, N
    {X(i+k,k),Y(k,j)
     Z(i,j),U(i,j+k)}
   end for
  end for
 end for
}
        (a)


Procedure R(V)
Arrays V(N,N)
{
 ...
 call P(V,V)
 ...
}

Procedure P(X,Y)
Arrays X(N,N),Y(N,N)
{
 for i = 1, N
  for j = 1, N
   {X(i,j),Y(j,i)}
  end for
 end for
}
      (b)
```

```
Procedure main(U_1,U_2,U_3,U_4)
Arrays U_1(N,N),U_2(N,N),
       U_3(N,N),U_4(N,N)
{
 call P_1(U_1,U_2)
 for i = 1, N
  for j = 1, N
   {U_1(j,i),U_2(i,j),
    U_3(i,j),U_4(j,i)}
  end for
 end for
 call P_2(U_2,U_3)
}

Procedure P_1(V_1,V_2)
Arrays V_1(N,N),V_2(N,N)
{
 Arrays V_3(N,N)
 for i = 1, N
  for j = 1, N
   {V_1(i,j),V_2(j,i),V_3(i,j)}
  end for
 end for
 call P_3(V_1,V_3)
}

Procedure P_2(W_2,W_3)
Arrays W_2(N,N),W_3(N,N)
{
 Arrays W_1(N,N)
 for i = 1, N
  for j = 1, N
   {W_1(j,i),W_2(i,j),W_3(i,j)}
  end for
 end for
 call P_3(W_1,W_2)
}

Procedure P_3(X,Y)
Arrays X(N,N),Y(N,N)
{
 Arrays Z(N,N)
 for i = 1, N
  for j = 1, N
   {X(i,j),Y(j,i),Z(j,i)}
  end for
 end for
}
      (c)
```

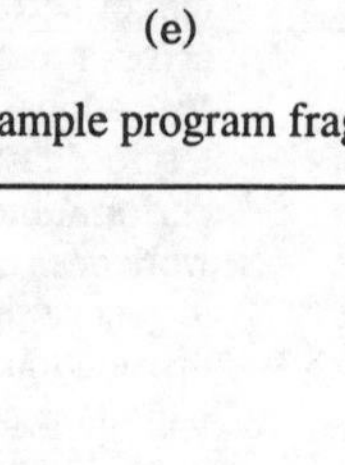

```
Procedure main(U_1,U_2,U_3,U_4)
Arrays U_1(N,N),U_2(N,N),
       U_3(N,N),U_4(N,N)
{
 call P_1(U_1,U_2)
 for j = 1, N
  for i = 1, N
   {U_1(i,i),U_2(i,j),
    U_3(i,j),U_4(i,i)}
  end for
 end for
 call P_2(U_2,U_3)
}

Procedure P_1(V_1,V_2)
Arrays V_1(N,N),V_2(N,N)
{
 Arrays V_3(N,N)
 for i = 1, N
  for j = 1, N
   {V_1(j,i),V_2(j,i),V_3(j,i)}
  end for
 end for
 call P_3copy2(V_1,V_3)
}

Procedure P_2(W_2,W_3)
Arrays W_2(N,N),W_3(N,N)
{
 Arrays W_1(N,N)
 for j = 1, N
  for i = 1, N
   {W_1(i,j),W_2(i,j),W_3(i,j)}
  end for
 end for
 call P_3copy1(W_1,W_2)
}

Procedure P_3copy1(X,Ycopy1)
Arrays X(N,N),Ycopy1(N,N)
{
 Arrays Zcopy1(N,N)
 for i = 1, N
  for j = 1, N
   {X(j,i),Ycopy1(j,i),Zcopy1(j,i)}
  end for
 end for
}

Procedure P_3copy2(X,Y)
Arrays X(N,N),Ycopy2(N,N)
{
 Arrays Zcopy2(N,N)
 for j = 1, N
  for i = 1, N
   {X(j,i),Ycopy2(i,j),Zcopy2(i,j)}
  end for
 end for
}
      (d)
```

(e)

Figure 3: (a-d) Example program fragments. (e) Call graph for (c).

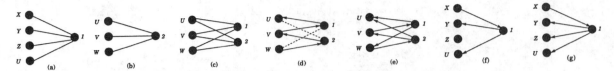

Figure 4: The locality constraint graphs and solutions for the program shown in Figure 3(a).

that R contains a single nest (nest 1) that accesses three arrays U, V, and W. Assume further that R calls P passing V and W as parameters which, respectively, map to X and Y in P. Suppose that the procedure P contains four nests; the first one (nest 2) accesses X, Y, and Z; the second one (nest 3) accesses Z and L; and finally, the third one (nest 4) accesses L and K. Figures 5(a) and (b) show the LCGs for R and P, respectively. Figure 5(c), on the other hand, illustrates the GLCG obtained after the bottom-up traversal. A complete solution to this GLCG is shown in Figure 5(d). Notice that this solution satisfies all the constraints but one. Finally, Figure 5(e) shows a maximum-branching solution on the RLCG for the procedure P. In this graph, the node 2 inherits a constraint from the solution given in Figure 5(d). This constraint corresponds to the edge between X and 2. The rest of the solution in Figure 5(e) builts upon this constraint, and determine all the remaning layouts (of L, Z, and K) as well as the loop transformations for the nests 3 and 4.

In case there are multiple paths from different callers to the same callee procedure, there is a possibility that the different callers may impose conflicting layouts for the same array in the callee. In this case, our approach uses *selective cloning* [11]. Selective cloning is a goal-directed approach that selectively decides which procedures to clone and how many different instances to create. Figure 3(c) shows an example program with its call graph given in Figure 3(e). Figure 3(d) shows the transformed code where the procedure P_3 is cloned. The first and the third nests are transformed using loop interchange [33] whereas the second nest is left unmodified. For the fourth nest, on the other hand, two copies have been created with different loop orders.

4 Experiments

In order to validate the approach presented in this paper, we conducted experiments with four common scientific programs that contain procedure calls: three programs from SPECfp92 benchmark and an alternate direction integral (ADI) code. For each code, we used three different versions: `Base` is the code with most classical locality optimizations (used in commercial compilers) except tiling and loop unrolling turned off. `Intra_r` is an optimized version using the intra-procedural optimization method described in Section 2.1. However, the arrays are *re-mapped* explicitly at procedure boundaries. Note that most of the published papers on data layout optimizations do not take this explicit array re-mapping costs into account. Our performance numbers reported below, however, indicate that these costs can easily outweigh any gains made by transforming array layouts for enhancing cache locality. Finally, `Opt_inter` is the version obtained using the approach described in this paper.

The experiments are performed on an SGI Origin 2000 architecture. Each node of the Origin contains two R10000 CPUs which run at a clock rate of 195 MHz. Each processor has an instruction cache of 32 Kbytes and a Level-1 (L1) data cache of 32 Kbytes as well as a 4 Mbyte secondary (L2) unified instruction/data cache. The node board is configured with 4 Gbytes of main memory. The R10000 CPUs operate on data that are resident in their caches. When programs use the caches effectively, the access time to mem-

ory is unimportant because the great majority of accesses are satisfied from the caches. The processors can also prefetch data that are not in cache. Independent work can be carried out while these data move from memory to cache, thus hiding the access time.

The intra-procedural optimization strategy based on maximum-branching described in Section 2.1 is currently being implemented on top of Parafrase-2. The bottom-up and top-down traversals, however, are performed by hand for the time being. For all three versions the transformed codes are compiled using the native optimizing compiler with the following optimization flags: `-n32 -mips4 -Ofast=ip27 -OPT:IEEE_arithmetic=3 -LNO:blocking=off -LNO:outer_unroll=1`.

The results are shown in Table 1 for the single-processor and eight-processor cases; we report Cache Line Reuses as well as MFLOPS rates (measured by using an outer timing loop). The L1 Cache Line Reuse is the number of times, on the average, that a primary data cache line is reused after it has been moved into the cache. It is calculated as 'graduated loads' plus 'graduated stores' minus 'primary data cache misses', all divided by 'primary data cache misses'. The L2 Cache Line Reuse is defined similarly for the L2 Cache. All these values have been collected through the hardware counters of the R10000. These cache line reuse values show that `Opt_inter` is more successful than the other two versions in exploiting cache locality.

The MFLOPS results show that propagating array layouts across procedures is very critical in fully exploiting the advantage of memory layout optimizations. This is true for both the single and eight processor cases. It should be noted that there is only a marginal difference in the MFLOPS rates between `Base` and `Intra_r`. Actually, in the ADI code using eight processors, the performance of `Intra_r` is even worse than that of `Base`. Good performance results are obtained only with the codes optimized using the approach described in this paper.

5 Related Work

The area of locality optimization has received much attention. Several researchers have proposed the use of loop restructuring techniques to improve locality in a loop nest [1, 31, 25, 27, 32, 33, 6, 23]. Recently, some research groups have advocated the use of memory layout transformations for multi-dimensional arrays [24, 29, 21, 17]. In addition, there have been proposed techniques aimed at exploiting the benfits of loo as well data transformations by combining the two [8, 4, 21, 18, 29].

Very few papers have addressed the problem of inter-procedural optimization of locality. Cierniak and Li [10] address the problem of performing data layout transformations that are propagated across procedure boundaries. But they do not consider loop transformations at all. Our work also relates to recent work on interprocedural data distribution [5]. Anderson [5] was the first to perform inter-procedural analysis to derive data distributions. Her work does not address cache locality explicitly; rather, it is intended to reduce the inter-processor communication incurred due to data distribution. In addition, her work on inter-procedural data distribution does not consider general linear loop and data transformations. It is important to note that the work presented in this paper is

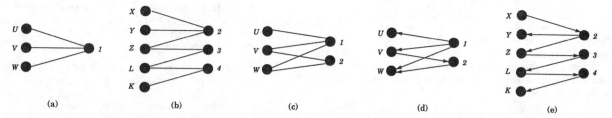

Figure 5: An example scenario which contains a main procedure whose LCG is shown in (a) and a callee whose LCG is shown in (b). (c) gives the GLCG and (d) shows a complete maximum-branching solution. (e) shows a solution for the RLCG for the callee.

closest in spirit to Anderson's work [5]. Our solution mechanism (using maximum branching) and the type of constraints we handle are different from hers, though.

6 Conclusions and Future Work

While a large number of recent papers have addressed the use of loop and data layout optimizations aimed at improving locality, very few have addressed such locality optimizations that work in whole program with procedure calls. If data layout decisions are not propagated across procedures, then either expensive data layout re-mapping is needed or one has to settle for the resulting poor performance. In this paper we present a locality optimization framework that uses both loop and data transformations to improve cache locality program-wide. Our framework propagates layout (or locality) constraints as a system of equalities across procedures and involves two traversals in the call graph representation of the program. We also show how to handle the cases where the callers of the same procedure demand conflicting memory layouts for the same array. Preliminary experimental results obtained on a R10000 based system demonstrate the power of the framework.

At this point, our approach does not consider array re-shaping. We are working on including array re-shaping in our framework. We note that the problem of inter-procedural data and loop transformations and the problem of inter-procedural data distribution are closely related in the case of multiprocessors. We are working on extending our framework to include the effects of parallelism and false sharing on the locality characteristics of whole programs with procedure calls.

Acknowledgments   The work of M. Kandemir and A. Choudhary were supported in part by NSF Young Investigator Award CCR-9357840, NSF grant CCR-9509143 and Air Force Materials Command under contract F30602-97-C-0026. P. Banerjee was supported in part by DARPA under contract F30602-98-2-0144 and by NSF grant CCR-9526325. J. Ramanujam was supported in part by NSF Young Investigator Award CCR-9457768.

References

[1] W. Abu-Sufah. *Improving the Performance of Virtual Memory Computers*, Ph.D. thesis, University of Illinois at Urbana-Champaign, November 1978.

[2] A. V. Aho, R. Sethi, and J. Ullman. *Compilers: Principles, Techniques, and Tools.* Addison-Wesley, 1986.

[3] E. Anderson, Z. Bai, C. Bischof, J. Demmel, J. Dongarra, J. Du Croz, A. Greenbaum, S. Hammarling, A. McKenney, S. Ostrouchov, and D. Sonensen, editors. *LAPACK Users' Guide*, SIAM, 1995.

[4] J. Anderson, S. Amarasinghe, and M. Lam. Data and computation transformations for multiprocessors. In *Proc. 5th ACM SIGPLAN Symp. Principles & Practice of Parallel Programming (PPoPP'95)*, pp. 166–178, July 1995.

[5] J. Anderson. *Automatic Computation and Data Decomposition for Multiprocessors*. Ph.D. dissertation, Stanford University, March 1997.

[6] L. Carter, J. Ferrante, S. Hummel, B. Alpern, and K. Gatlin. Hierarchical tiling: A methodology for high performance. *UCSD Tech Report CS 96-508*, November 1996.

[7] R. Chandra, D. Chen, R. Cox, D. Maydan, N. Nedeljkovic, and J. Anderson. Data-distribution support on distributed-shared memory multiprocessors. *Proc. SIGPLAN Conf. Programming Language Design & Implementation (PLDI'97)*, pp. 334–345, 1997.

[8] M. Cierniak and W. Li. Unifying data and control transformations for distributed shared memory machines. *Proc. SIGPLAN Conf. Programming Language Design & Implementation (PLDI'95)*, pp. 205–217, June 1995.

[9] M. Cierniak and W. Li. Recovering logical structures of data. In *Languages and Compilers for Parallel Computing*, C. Huang et al. (Eds.) Lecture Notes in Computer Science, Vol. 1033, Springer-Verlag, 1996.

[10] M. Cierniak and W. Li. Inter-procedural array re-mapping. In *Proc. the International Conference on Parallel Architectures and Compilation Techniques (PACT '97)*, Nov 1997.

[11] K. Cooper, M. W. Hall, and K. Kennedy. A methodology for procedure cloning. *Computer Languages*, 19(2), April 1993.

[12] M. Dion, C. Randriamaro, and Y. Robert. Compiling affine nested loops: how to optimize the residual communications after the alignment phase. *Journal of Parallel and Distributed Computing (JPDC)*, 38(2):176–187, 1996.

[13] M. W. Hall. *Managing Interprocedural Optimization*. PhD thesis, Rice University, Houston, TX, May 1991.

[14] M. W. Hall and K. Kennedy. Efficient call graph analysis. *ACM Letters on Programming Languages and Systems*, 1(3), September 1992.

[15] M. W. Hall, J. M. Mellor-Crummey, A. Carle, and R. Rodriguez. FIAT: A framework for interprocedural analysis and transformation. In *Proceedings of the Sixth Annual Workshop on Languages and Compilers for Parallel Computing*, 1993.

[16] M.W. Hall, S.P. Amarasinghe, B.R. Murphy, S. Liao, and M.S. Lam. Detecting coarse-grain parallelism using an interprocedural parallelizing compiler. In *Proceedings of Supercomputing '95*, December 1995.

Table 1: Performance results on an SGI Origin 2000 multiprocessor. (The data sizes: Btrix, the parameters JD, KD, LD, and MD are set to 100. Vpenta, size parameter is set to 850. Cholsky, size parameter is set to 800. ADI, 1040 × 1040 × 3 arrays. All these are in double precision elements).

(a) Btrix

1 proc

	Base	Intra_r	Opt_inter
L1 Cache Line Reuse	7.75	7.48	8.38
L2 Cache Line Reuse	27.15	31.29	39.86
MFLOPS	29.09	33.62	90.71

8 procs

	Base	Intra_r	Opt_inter
L1 Cache Line Reuse	16.89	11.43	18.11
L2 Cache Line Reuse	26.01	26.93	44.03
MFLOPS	158.16	164.12	660.16

(b) Vpenta

1 proc

	Base	Intra_r	Opt_inter
L1 Cache Line Reuse	3.34	3.40	4.52
L2 Cache Line Reuse	14.18	17.01	21.33
MFLOPS	44.01	55.04	71.82

8 procs

	Base	Intra_r	Opt_inter
L1 Cache Line Reuse	4.51	4.39	4.97
L2 Cache Line Reuse	13.82	15.13	24.79
MFLOPS	240.19	264.82	434.17

(c) Cholsky

1 proc

	Base	Intra_r	Opt_inter
L1 Cache Line Reuse	2.20	2.40	4.88
L2 Cache Line Reuse	11.06	12.13	20.51
MFLOPS	25.80	26.04	60.90

8 procs

	Base	Intra_r	Opt_inter
L1 Cache Line Reuse	2.11	2.39	4.82
L2 Cache Line Reuse	12.82	13.13	23.00
MFLOPS	128.62	134.82	383.10

(d) ADI

1 proc

	Base	Intra_r	Opt_inter
L1 Cache Line Reuse	2.73	2.86	3.56
L2 Cache Line Reuse	174.78	180.04	242.67
MFLOPS	93.45	98.65	139.00

8 procs

	Base	Intra_r	Opt_inter
L1 Cache Line Reuse	4.04	4.32	4.62
L2 Cache Line Reuse	109.00	104.55	201.73
MFLOPS	515.74	513.48	780.69

[17] M. Kandemir, A. Choudhary, N. Shenoy, P. Banerjee, and J. Ramanujam. A hyperplane based approach for optimizing spatial locality in loop nests. In *Proc. ACM International Conference on Supercomputing (ICS'98)*, pp. 69–76, July 1998.

[18] M. Kandemir, A. Choudhary, J. Ramanujam, and P. Banerjee. A matrix-based approach to the global locality optimization problem. In *Proc. 1998 Intl. Conf. Parallel Architectures & Compilation Techniques (PACT'98)*, October 1998.

[19] M. Kandemir, A. Choudhary, J. Ramanujam, and P. Banerjee. Improving locality using loop and data transformations in an integrated approach. In *Proc. MICRO-31*, December 1998.

[20] M. Kandemir, A. Choudhary, J. Ramanujam, and P. Banerjee. A graph based framework to detect optimal memory layouts for improving data locality. In *Proc. IPPS 99*, April 1999.

[21] M. Kandemir, J. Ramanujam, and A. Choudhary. A compiler algorithm for optimizing locality in loop nests. In *Proc. 11th ACM International Conference on Supercomputing (ICS'97)*, pp. 269–276, July 1997.

[22] I. Kodukula, N. Ahmed, and K. Pingali. Data-centric multilevel blocking. In *Proc. Programming Language Design and Implementation (PLDI'97)*, June 1997.

[23] M. Lam, E. Rothberg, and M. Wolf. The cache performance and optimizations of blocked algorithms. In *Proc. the 4th International Conference on Architectural Support for Programming Languages and Operating Systems (ASPLOS'91)*.

[24] S.-T. Leung and J. Zahorjan. Optimizing data locality by array restructuring. Technical Report TR 95-09-01, Dept. Computer Science and Engineering, University of Washington, 1995.

[25] W. Li. *Compiling for NUMA Parallel Machines*. Ph.D. Thesis, Cornell University, Ithaca, NY, 1993.

[26] V. Maslov. Delinearization: an efficient way to break multiloop dependence equations. In *Proc. SIGPLAN Conf. Programming Language Design & Implementation*, pp. 152–161, June 1992.

[27] K. McKinley, S. Carr, and C. Tseng. Improving data locality with loop transformations. *ACM Transactions on Programming Languages & Systems*, 18(4):424–453, July 1996.

[28] E. Minieka. *Optimization Algorithms for Networks and Graphs*, Marcel Dekker, Inc., 1978.

[29] M. O'Boyle and P. Knijnenburg. Non-singular data transformations: definition, validity, applications. In *Proc. 6th Workshop on Compilers for Parallel Computers (CPC'96)*, pp. 287–297, 1996.

[30] M. O'Boyle and P. Knijnenburg. Integrating loop and data transformations for global optimisation. In *Proc. International Conference on Parallel Architectures and Compilation Techniques (PACT'98)*, October 14–17, 1998.

[31] M. Wolf and M. Lam. A data locality optimizing algorithm. In *Proc. SIGPLAN Conf. Programming Language Design & Implementation (PLDI'91)*, pp. 30–44, June 1991.

[32] M. Wolfe. More iteration space tiling. In *Proc. Supercomputing'89*, pp. 655–664, November 1989.

[33] M. Wolfe. *High Performance Compilers for Parallel Computing*, Addison-Wesley, 1996.

Compiler Optimizations for Parallel Sparse Programs with Array Intrinsics of Fortran 90*

Rong–Guey Chang[†]   Tyng–Ruey Chuang[‡]   Jenq Kuen Lee[†]

[†]Department of Computer Science
National Tsing Hua University
Hsinchu 300, Taiwan

rgchang@puma.cs.nthu.edu.tw
jklee@cs.nthu.edu.tw

[‡]Institute of Information Science
Academia Sinica
Taipei 115, Taiwan

trc@iis.sinica.edu.tw

Abstract

In our recent work, we have been working on providing parallel sparse supports for array intrinsics of Fortran 90. Our supporting library uses a two-level design. In the low-level routines, it requires the input sparse matrices to be specified with compression/distribution schemes for array functions. In the high-level representations, sparse array functions are overloaded with Fortran 90 array intrinsic interfaces so that programmers need not concern about low-level details. This raises a very interesting optimization problem in the strategies to transform high-level representations to low-level routines by automatic selections and supplies of distribution and compression schemes for sparse arrays. In this paper, we propose solutions to this optimization problem. The optimization problem is shown to be NP-hard. We develop a heuristic algorithm based on annotated program graphs, and the algorithm is shown to be practical. Experimental results on an IBM SP-2 show that the selection algorithms are effective in improving the performances of application programs that use sparse data sets.

1 Introduction

The usage of array intrinsic functions in Fortran 90 provide a rich source of parallelism. In our recent work, we have been working on providing parallel sparse supports for array intrinsics of Fortran 90 [6, 4]. Our supporting library uses a two-level design. In the low-level routines, it requires the input sparse matrices to be specified with compression/distribution schemes for array functions. In the high-level representations, sparse array functions are overloaded with Fortran 90 array intrinsic interfaces so that programmers need not concern about low-level details.

The use of two-level design in our library raises a very interesting optimization problem. What are the strategies to transform the high-level representations to

low-level routines? In this paper, we address compiler issues in transforming the high-level representations to low-level routines by automatic selections of distribution and compression schemes for sparse arrays. Previously, research work were carried out to perform automatic data alignments and distributions mainly for dense arrays [12, 5, 13, 15]. There has been lacking research efforts to investigate the issues of automatic selection of distribution and compression schemes for sparse data sets on distributed memory environments. Our work is distinguished from previous research work on data alignments and distribution for dense arrays [5, 12, 13, 15], and from previous work on sparse array optimization [2] on four key elements. First, in our work, the selections of distributions schemes for sparse arrays are mainly based on the sparsity structures of arrays [6], while in previous work the selections of distributions schemes for dense arrays are mainly based on the index domains of arrays. Second, we need to select the compression schemes for sparse arrays, while there is no such need in the dense cases. The compression schemes being considered are Compressed Row Storage (CRS), Compressed Column Storage (CCS), and dense representations. In addition, in our library, we extend conventional two-dimensional compression schemes (such as CRS and CCS) into higher-dimensional arrays. As we are interested in providing compiler solutions for Fortran 90 programs, the compression schemes need to be applicable to higher-dimensional sparse arrays [4]. Third, our selection algorithms not only need to work with element-wise array expressions, but also with array intrinsics in Fortran 90 as well. These array intrinsic operations include CSHIFT, EOSHIFT, MATMUL, MERGE, PACK, SUM, RESHAPE, SPREAD, TRANSPOSE, UNPACK, and section moves [1]. Many array intrinsics prefer specific representations of their input sparse arrays (in terms of distribution and compression schemes) for efficiency reason. We have incorporated such characteristics in our heuristic algorithm. Finally, we also perform experiments to actually compare the performance of different representation selections on sparse programs in distributed memory machines.

Since finding the optimal selections is NP-hard, we have developed a cost model and proposed a heuristic algorithm that is based on the cost model and the annotated pro-

*This research is supported, in part, by National Science Council of Taiwan under contracts NSC 87-2213-E-007-083, NSC 88-2213-001-007, and NSC 89-2213-001-005.

```
integer, parameter :: row = 1000
real, dimension(row,2*row-1) :: A
real, dimension(row) :: x, b
integer, dimension(2*row-1) :: shift

b = sum(A*eoshift(spread(x, dim=2, &
    ncopies=2*row-1), dim=1, &
    shift=arth(-row+1, 1, 2*row-1)), dim=2)
```

Figure 1: Code Fragments of Bandmul.

gram graph. The heuristic is shown to be practical. It proceeds in two phases. In the first phase, we first coarsen the program graph into a simpler form. Then a tree-pruning algorithm, based on (local) optimal selections at each tree level, is used on the coarse graph for compression scheme selection. In the second phase, the distribution scheme is again selected based on the annotated program graph and the tree-pruning algorithm. Experimental results show that our selection algorithms are effective in selecting proper compression and distribution schemes to improve the performance of application programs with sparse data sets. The experiments are perform on an IBM SP-2, with the support of our parallel sparse library for Fortran 90 array intrinsics.

The remainder of the paper is organized as follows. Section 2 gives a motivating example for this work. Section 3 describes the cost model and formulate the optimal solution of the problem. In Section 4, the heuristic algorithm is presented. Experimental results are then given in Section 5. Section 6 discussed related work, and Section 7 concludes this paper.

2 A Motivating Example

Consider the code segment shown in Figure 1. This code segment represents the multiplication of a banded matrix and a vector. In other words, it calculates $b = Ax$, where A is a skewed representation of a banded matrix and x a vector [16, page 1019 and 1338]. This code uses Fortran 90 array intrinsics eoshift, spread, and a reduction function sum. as well as the built-in (elemental) element-wise multiplication operator, *.

Our libraries are built for sparse versions of array intrinsics in Fortran 90, and for both sequential and parallel environments [4]. Below we show the banded multiplication code fragments written with high-level sparse array intrinsics.

```
integer, parameter :: row = 1000
type(sparse2d_real) :: A
type(sparse1d_real) :: x, b
integer, dimension(2*row-1) :: shift

call bound(A, row, 2*row-1)
call bound(x, row)
call bound(b, row)

b = sum(A*eoshift(spread(x, dim=2, &
    ncopies=2*row-1), dim=1, &
    shift=arth(-row+1, 1, 2*row-1)), dim=2)
```

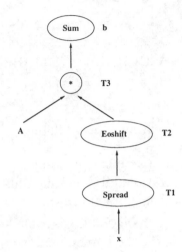

Figure 2: Expression tree with array intrinsic functions in Bandmul.

array	compressed scheme	distribution scheme
x	$1d$	(Block)
T1	CRS	(*,Block)
T2	CCS	(*,Block)
T3	CRS	(*,Block)
A	CRS	(*,Block)
b	$1d$	(Block)

Table 1: Assignment that needs two extra compression conversions

Figure 2 shows the expression tree for the banded multiplication code fragments. T1, T2, and T3, are temporary arrays generated in the parse tree. In the case that the distribution and compression schemes of source and target arrays are already specified by programmers, we will still need to figure out the proper compression schemes and distribution mechanisms for arrays such as T1, T2, and T3, as they are temporary arrays and will never be assigned distribution and compression schemes by programmers. Two different assignments of compression schemes to arrays in the banded multiplication routine are shown in Table 1 and 2, respectively. They will be used to illustrate the effects of compression scheme selections. The compression schemes being considered are CRS and CCS; the distribution being considered are (Block, *), (*, Block), and (Block, Block) partitions. Let us simplify this example by ignoring the distribution schemes for the moment, and focus on the compression schemes. We say the assignments in Table 1 is not as good as those in Table 2, as Table 1 contains two cases of non-conforming compression assignments in array operations. When an array operation is operated on arrays with non-conforming compression, we need to either convert one array from one compression scheme to the another, or to spend more time in access array elements.

In the first assignment, A is compressed by CRS. In addition, T1 is in CRS form. The first compression con-

array	compressed scheme	distribution scheme
x	$1d$	(Block)
T1	CCS	(Block,*)
T2	CCS	(Block,*)
T3	CCS	(Block,*)
A	CCS	(Block,*)
b	$1d$	(Block)

Table 2: Assignment with less compression conversions.

version cost is needed, as T1 needs to be shifted along the column direction. After the conversion and the shift operation, the result is assigned to T2 in the form of CCS. We now need to perform an element-wise array multiplication operation on A and T2. However, A is compressed by CRS, and T2 is compressed by CCS; hence we need the second compression conversion cost. The second assignment is a better than the first assignment because it does not need these two conversions. In the next two sections, we will give a cost model and propose a heuristic algorithm for the selection of both the compression and distribution schemes of sparse arrays.

3 Cost Model

We now introduce the cost model for selecting the compression and distribution schemes for sparse programs with array intrinsics. Our cost model consists of three components. They are computation cost, communication cost, and compression conversion costs. In the parallel environment, the computation cost for sparse programs is related to the numbers of non-zero elements in the arrays, and to whether the workload is balanced among the processors. In addition, we will need to minimize the communication cost and compression conversion cost.

3.1 Sparsity Inference

In the selection process, the sparsity information can be given by programmers, by profiling, or by probabilistic inference schemes [6]. In our work, we assume that the sparsity of source arrays can be profiled to obtain initial information. The sparsity for the rest of the arrays (including temporary arrays) resulting from sparse array intrinsics can be estimated with a probability inference scheme. The scheme is described briefly as follows. For a sparse array A, we use $S[A] = \alpha$ to denote that a scalar of A is non-zero with probability (at most) α. Using this notation, we can estimate the non-zero ratios of the target arrays after the contents of input arrays of intrinsic operations are sampled. Due to space limitation, we only give an example to show how to estimate non-zero ratios of target arrays by using our probability inference scheme. In case that $G = merge(T, F, M)$. The elements of the target array G comes from T if the corresponding logical element in M is a true value, otherwise it comes from F. T and F in `merge` are of the same type, and M must be of type logical. Thus, function merge needs to scan all non-zero elements of these three arrays, and the corresponding computational complexity is proportional to the total number of non-zero elements in the three ar-

rays. Furthermore, the non-zero ratio of target array G is estimated as $S[G] = S[T]S[M] + S[F](1 - S[M])$.

The sparsity estimations of target arrays for other array intrinsics are similarly formulated. Once sparsity of all arrays are estimated, we can estimate the communication cost for sparse programs with given distribution schemes, by assuming uniform distributions of non-zero elements in the arrays, or by the given sparsity structures of the arrays.

3.2 Optimal Solution

We formulate the optimal solution of the selection problem based on the program graph, $G = (V, E)$. Assume that there are n node in V, and $V = \{v_1, v_2, \cdots, v_n\}$. Let Ω represent the set of all possible compression schemes, and D represent the set of all possible distribution schemes. Our goal is to find a compression scheme assignment τ, and a distribution assignment δ to each node that minimize the total cost.

That is,

$$\tau : V \to \Omega$$

$$\delta : V \to D.$$

In addition, we define a function $\phi(u)$ for the total cost of the subtree rooted at node u, with the given assignments τ and δ. For each internal node v, we also define a function θ which computes the cost of executing the array expression associated with node v, as well as the cost for accessing all immediate child nodes of v (i.e., argument arrays needed for v), with the supplied compression and distribution schemes τ and δ. For example, suppose there the k immediate child nodes for v are $v_1, v_2, \ldots, v_k$. The cost function θ is evaluated by $\theta(< v, \tau(v), \delta(v) >, << v_1, \tau(v_1), \delta(v_1) >, \cdots, < v_k, \tau(v_k), \delta(v_k) >>)$.

For a given node v, and its k immediate child nodes $v_1, v_2, \ldots, v_k$, the cost for node v is then

$$\phi(v) = (\Sigma_{i=1}^{k} \phi(v_i)) + \theta(< v, \tau(v), \delta(v) >, << v_1, \tau(v_1),$$

$$\delta(v_1) >, \cdots, < v_k, \tau(v_k), \delta(v_k) >>).$$

Our goal is to find τ (compression assignment) and δ (distribution assignment) that minimizes the total cost. It is formulates as

$$Minimize : \phi(root).$$

We will use $MinCost$ to represent the minimum cost obtained from $Minimize : \phi(root)$. In fact, finding the optimal compression schemes and distribution schemes (including alignment and distribution) is NP-hard, as this is a special case of the dense array problem which is known to be NP-complete. In the extreme cases, all arrays in the program can be dense arrays. Then the best compression schemes for the arrays will the dense representations (without any compression), and the best alignment and distribution schemes will be the same as those from the alignment and distribution problem for the dense arrays. We then have the following theorem.

Theorem 1 Calculating $MinCost$ is NP-hard.

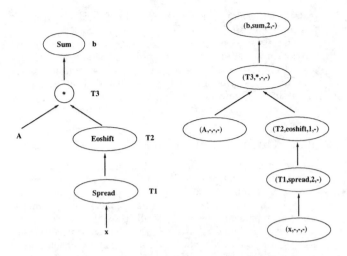

Figure 3: The expression tree and the annotated graph for the banded multiplication example.

1. $\Psi_p(u)$ is the set of parents of u.

2. $\Psi_s(u)$ is the set of children of u.

3. $\Psi_{ne}(u)$ represents the set of neighboring nodes of u. That is, $\Psi_{ne}(u) = \{v \in V \mid e(u,v) \in E\}$ and $\Psi_{ne}(u) = \Psi_p(u) \cup \Psi_s(u)$.

Following the above definitions, and considering the annotated graph in Figure 3, we have node $(b, sum, 2, -)$ as the root, $\Psi_p((T_3, *, -, -)) = \{(b, sum, 2, -)\}$, $\Psi_s((T_3, *, -, -)) = \{(A, -, -, -), (T_2, eoshift, 1, -)\}$, and $\Psi_{ne}((T_3, *, -, -)) = \{(b, sum, 2, -), (A, -, -, -), (T_2, eoshift, 1, -)\}$.

4.2 Heuristic Algorithm

In this section, we present a heuristic algorithm to automatically select compression and distribution schemes for arrays of sparse programs with array intrinsics in Fortran 90. Our heuristic algorithm is designed with a two-phase scheme. In the first phase, we try to select the compression schemes for arrays based on the conversion cost and sparsity of arrays. In the second phase, we try to select the distribution schemes for sparse arrays of Fortran 90 programs based on the communication set and sparsity of arrays.

Figure 4 first shows the key idea of our algorithm in the first phase to select the compression schemes. There are four major steps in our algorithm. First, we try to construct the annotated graph described earlier in Section 4.1 for a given sparse program. We then reduce the graph into a smaller (coarse) graph by merging some of the neighboring nodes, together. The nodes reduced into one node are those nodes having compression or dimension schemes conforming to each other. Among Fortran 90 array intrinsics, operators such as eoshift, cshift, reduction (sum and product), and so on have preference with compression schemes. Step 2 of Figure 4 gives three rules for merging nodes into one compound node. First, The node with the form $u = ([A_1, \cdots, A_n], op_1, -, \lambda_1)$ will matched with the node $v = ([B_1, \cdots, B_m], op_2, dim, \lambda_2) \in \Psi_p(u)$ as the compound node $(([B_1, \cdots, B_m, A_1, \cdots, A_n], op_2, dim, -)$. Second, a node $u = ([A_1, \cdots, A_n], op_1, -, \lambda_1)$ can be matched with the node $v = ([B_1, \cdots, B_m], op_2, dim_2, \lambda_2)$ into the compound node $(([B_1, \cdots, B_m, A_1, \cdots, A_n], op_2, dim_2, -)$ if $v \in \Psi_p(u)$ and $dim_1 = dim_2$. Finally, although spread operation specifies dimension, it can still be merged with other operators. The process in coarsening the graph can be done repeatedly until no more merging can be done according to the three rules in our algorithm.

Figure 6 shows the coarsening process for the graph with banded multiplication example shown earlier. G_{c_1} is the graph after initial iteration reductions. Array A, $T2$, and $T3$ are merged into a compound node, as the operators with both array A and $T3$ do not prefer the compression dimensions. These three arrays are merged into one compound node by Rule 1. Similarly, array $T1$ and x are merged into one compound node again by Rule 1. G_{c_2} in the LHS of the figure is the graph after next iteration phase. The merging is done according to Rule 3. In addition, G_{c_2} is the final reduced graph (we normally use the representation G_{c_f} for the final graph), as reduction and eoshift operations specify two different dimensions in this case. Note that we also use underscore to specify the leading array (boundary array) in each compound node. Array $T3$ and b are the leading (boundary) arrays for each

Proof:

Proof: The automatic alignment and distribution problem for dense arrays is shown to be NP-complete [13, 17]. As the dense problem is a special case of the sparse problem formulated above, and can be reduced to the sparse problem by a many-to-one reduction, it follows that calculating $MinCost$ is NP-hard.

Q.E.D.

4 Selection Algorithms for Distribution and Compression Schemes

In this section, we will first describe the annotated graph we use in our optimization algorithms, then describe our heuristic algorithm.

4.1 Annotated Graph

For a sparse program, we can construct an annotated graph, $G = (V, E)$, according to the expression tree of a program. Each node of the annotated graph contains four items. Suppose v is a node. Then in the graph, node v will have the form (A, op, dim, λ), where A is the target array of the node, op is the corresponding array operation in the node, dim is the specified or preferred dimension for the array operation op in the node, and λ the distribution scheme assigned to array A in the node. In addition, the symbol "-" will be used if op, dim, or λ is not specified. For example, Figure 3 shows the annotated graph for the program fragment of the banded multiplication example shown earlier in Figure 1. Initially, the distribution schemes of all arrays are unknown. The symbol "-" is used as the distribution schemes. In addition, spread is done along the second dimension, eoshift is done along the first dimension, and the reduction operator (sum) along the second dimension. All of the dimension information are annotated with the nodes in the graph.

Below we give auxiliary definitions that are needed in describing our heuristic algorithms.

Definition 1 Let $G = (V, E)$ be a annotated program graph. For any node $u \in V$, we have the following auxiliary definitions:

Input: $G = (V, E)$
Output: The compression schemes for all arrays in G
Begin_Of_Algorithm

    Step 1: To construct the annotated graph G' from the input graph

    Step 2: To reduce the annotated graph to a coarse graph for compression scheme selections as follows.

        Loop until the graph is reduced to the smallest graph possible

            Nodes in the graph is merged following the direction from leave nodes to root node if one of the three cases met.

            Rule 1: The node with the form $u = ([A_1, \cdots, A_n], op_1, -, \lambda_1)$ will be merged with

                $v = ([B_1, \cdots, B_m], op_2, dim, \lambda_2) \in \Psi_p(u)$ into the compound node $(([B_1, \cdots, B_m, A_1, \cdots, A_n], op_2, dim, -)$.

            Rule 2: A node $u = ([A_1, \cdots, A_n], op_1, dim_1, \lambda_1)$ in a reduce graph can be matched with the node

                $v = ([B_1, \cdots, B_m], op_2, dim_2, \lambda_2)$ as the compound node $(([B_1, \cdots, B_m, A_1, \cdots, A_n], op_2, dim_2, -)$

                if $v \in \Psi_p(u)$ and $dim_1 = dim_2$.

            Rule 3: The *spread* can be matched with other operation.

        end loop-do

    Step 3: To assign compression schemes to the internal node of each node in the final reduced graph.

        a) The internal nodes of one compound in the final reduced graph will be assigned
        the same compression scheme.

        b) We keep the best k compression assignments and their conversion cost for the internal
        node assignment of each compound node.

    Step 4: We will then assign the compression schemes to the leader (or the boundary node) of each compound node
    in the final reduced graph.

        a) The selection is basically based on tree-pruning for the exhaustive solutions on the coarse graph.

        b) Initially, we go from leave nodes, and select the best compression schemes
        for each leave node (we still keep the best k solutions for each node).

        c) Loop until all the nodes are assigned including the root node.

            We go to the next level nodes (parent nodes) of the last assigned nodes,
            and select the best compression schemes for each node (we still keep the best k solutions for each node).

        end loop-do

End_Of_Algorithm

Figure 4: Compression Scheme Selection Algorithm

Input: $G = (V, E)$
Output: The distribution schemes for all arrays in G
Begin_Of_Algorithm

    Step 1: To construct the annotated graph G' from the input graph

    Step 2: To use the sparsity inference scheme to obtain the sparsity information for arrays of the graph.

    Step 3: We will then assign the distribution schemes to each node.

        a) The selection is basically based on tree-pruning for the exhaustive solutions on annotated graphs.

        b) Initially, we go from leave nodes, and select the best distribution schemes
        for each leave node (we still keep the best k solutions for each node).

        c) Loop until all the nodes are assigned including the root node.

            We go to the next level nodes (parent nodes) of the last assigned nodes,
            and select the best distribution schemes for each node (we still keep the best k solutions for each node).

        d) To deal with with sharing nodes.

            In our mechanism, if a compression scheme of a sharing node is pruned to be removed
            from the possible solutions, we will notify all the nodes and paths using that node for sharing to
            prune that particular solution from the solution set.

        end loop-do

End_Of_Algorithm

Figure 5: Distribution Scheme Selection Algorithm

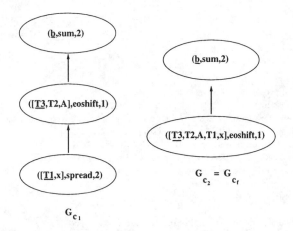

Figure 6: Reduced graphs of the banded multiplication example for compression selections

compound node. The rest of the arrays in each compound node is called internal arrays.

We now focus the third step of the compression selection algorithm shown in Figure 4. In this step, we try to assign the same compression scheme to the internal arrays of each compound node. Since a compound node has the preference in dimensions, we can assign the compression schemes to those arrays. In our example in Figure 6, we will assign CCS (compressed along the first dimension) to array $T2$, A, and $T1$, as the first dimension is specified here. In general, our heuristic will keep the best k assignments for the internal arrays of each compound node. For the higher-dimensional cases, the specification of dimensions in each compound node might still only specifies the compression information for one of our 2-d basis. For other 2-d basis, we will try to keep k plausible solutions for the global tree-pruning to decide the best solution in the next phase.

Finally, we try to assign the compression schemes to the leading array (boundary array) of each compound node globally for the reduced graph. Our approach is a tree-pruning algorithm based on the exhaustive and optimal solution with our cost model on the reduced graph. Initially, we go from leave nodes, and select the best compression schemes for each leave node (we still keep the best k solutions for each node). We then go to the next level nodes. The process is repeatedly until all the nodes are assigned including the root node. In the selection process, we always keep the best k solutions so far rooted by each node. In addition, we also need to take care the case with sharing nodes. In our mechanism, if a compression scheme of a sharing node is pruned to be removed from the possible solutions, we will notify all the nodes and paths using that node for sharing to prune that particular solution. We now assign the compression schemes for the boundary arrays ($T3$) of the compound node for the banded multiplication example in Figure 6. In this case, either CCS or CRS can be chosen, as both of them require one conversion cost.

Next, we present a heuristic algorithm to automatically select distribution schemes for arrays of sparse programs with array intrinsics in Fortran 90. Our selection algorithm is implemented based on annotated graphs by con-

sidering the communication cost and sparsity of arrays. Figure 5 gives the key idea of our distribution selection algorithm.

First, we try to construct the annotated graph described earlier in Section 4.1 for given sparse programs. Second, we use the sparsity inference scheme described earlier in Section 3 to obtain the sparsity information for all arrays. Finally, we try to assign the distribution schemes to the array of each node in the graph. Our approach is a tree-pruning algorithm based on the exhaustive and optimal solution with our cost model. Initially, we go from leave nodes, and select the best distribution schemes for each leave node (we still keep the best k solutions for each node). We then go to the next level nodes. The process is repeatedly until all the nodes are assigned including the root node. In the selection process, we always keep the best k solutions so far rooted by each node. In addition, we also need to deal with sharing nodes. In our mechanism, if a distribution scheme of a sharing node is pruned to be removed from the possible solutions, we will notify all the nodes and paths using that node for sharing to prune that particular solution from possible choices. We again use the banded multiplication example shown earlier in Figure 3 to illustrate the idea of distribution selections.

5 Experimental Results

In this section, we illustrate the performance effects for numerical routines and application programs with or without our selection algorithms. Our experiments are done on IBM SP-2 with the support of our parallel sparse array intrinsics of Fortran 90. In our software library, we provide parallel sparse supports for array intrinsics of Fortran 90. In our experiments we will run programs in our high-level representation, but the compression schemes and distribution schemes are assigned according to our cost model and heuristic selection algorithms.

In our first example, we report performance results of sparse codes for banded matrix multiplication (banmul) described earlier in Figure 1. The banmul code segment is taken from [16, page 1019 and 1338]. The base version is the preliminary softwares we reported the performances earlier when a quick implementation just built-up[4], and the assignments are listed in Table 3 for references. The optimization version using the compression and distribution assignments chosen in our heuristic algorithm is the one listed in Table 2 of Section 2.

Table 4 gives the performance results for these two different assignments. The optimized version with the help of our selection algorithm significantly out-performs the base version. The time is measured in seconds. In the experiment, the test matrix A has a nonzero ratio of 0.0005, and the test vector x has a nonzero ratio 0.1. In addition, we also show the performance of the code fragments running on sequential Fortran 90 without any compression schemes. The optimized compressed version on 8 processors is running 56 times faster than the dense sequential code executed on native Fortran 90 compiler on IBM SP-2.

Our second experiment is with the cgsolver code segment translated from the MATLAB code in [7, page 354, Fig. 8]. In cgsolver, we replace the dense-matrix/dense-vector multiplication ($Ap = MATMUL(A,p)$) to a sparse-matrix/dense-vector version (A is sparse while p and Ap dense). The test matrix A is a 16384 × 16384 sparse matrix with non-zero ratio of 0.0003. It is translated from 128 × 128 unstructured grid applications. This

array	compressed scheme	distribution scheme
x	$1d$	(Block)
T1	CRS	(*,Block)
T2	CCS	(Block,*)
T3	CRS	(*,Block)
A	CRS	(*,Block)
b	$1d$	(Block)

Table 3: Base assignments for sparse arrays in banded multiplication example.

no. of proc.	F90 dense code	base version	optimized version
1	1.48	0.66	0.159
2	-	0.38	0.081
4	-	0.22	0.044
8	-	0.14	0.026

Table 4: Performance results of banded multiplication example.

is the part of our joint effort with the work [14]. Again we show the performance differences with a good and poor selection assignments. Table 5 shows the performance for the optimized version with our selection algorithm, and a suite with poor selections. The time is measured in seconds, and for six iterations of sparse conjugate gradient methods. The optimized version is with CRS compression and (*,Block) distribution. The poor selection uses CCS compression scheme and (Block,*) distribution scheme for array A. The optimized version is 1.74 times faster than the one with poor selection on 8 processors. This again shows the importance of a good selection scheme.

Finally, we conduct experiments to demonstrate the performances of the sparse intrinsics beyond two dimensions. Our system extends two-dimensional compression schemes into higher dimensional arrays. We evaluate the system with a 3D group-by operations related to OLAP (on-line analytical processing). The group-by operator computes aggregations over all possible subsets of the specified dimensions. In this experiment, group-by operator is applied by performing a sequence of sum functions operated on sparse arrays ABC, AB, AC, BC, A, B, and C. We also have ABC with a nonzero ratio of

no. of proc.	a Suite with poor assignments	optimized version
1	0.453	0.430
2	0.259	0.235
4	0.169	0.134
8	0.160	0.092

Table 5: Performance results of cgsolver.

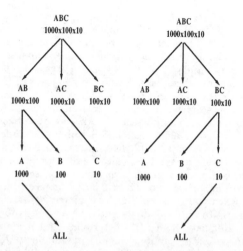

Figure 7: Two different ways to calculate the group-by operation according to the lattice.

no. of proc.	LHS Tree of Lattice	RHS Tree of Lattice
1	0.317	0.271
2	0.171	0.146
4	0.118	0.093
8	0.095	0.071

Table 6: Performance results of 3d group-by.

0.01. In group-by operation of OLAP, the relationships among these sparse arrays can be represented as a a lattice [9]. These are mainly dealing with large scale sparse data sets. Our work can help the group-by operator for parallel sparse computations for the following ways. First, original Fortran 90 dense array intrinsics in the code can be replaced with the corresponding sparse routines from our library. Second, our selection algorithm can be used to select the compression and distribution schemes for the algorithm. Finally, due to the natural functionalities of group-by and OLAP to be represented as a lattice, if our compiler can recognize the computation to be a group-by operation, we can actually re-arrange the computation as well as the compression and distribution scheme for the group-by operation.

Figure 7 shows two possible ways to achieve group-by operation for the same functionality. According to our cost model, the RHS one is better than the LHS one, due to smaller number of computations as well as communications. The RHS selection is the best one according to our cost model. Table 6 show the performance results for these two assignments. Our selected suite is 1.33 times faster than the original code fragments with sparse intrinsics on 8-node IBM SP-2.

6 Related Work

Previous research work[6, 18, 19] considered the distribution and compressed schemes related to one dimension and two dimension arrays. The work in [19] pioneered the research directions to annotate sparse notations and distributions for HPF-style languages. In our recent work [4], we built an extension applicable to higher-dimensional arrays. The approach to deal with higher-dimensional arrays is to employ 1-d and 2-d sparse arrays as the bases and compose them for higher-dimension arrays. The work with Fortran 77 syntax in [2] addressed the sparse compiler issues on shared memory environments.

In the past, many research work were done to perform automatic data alignments and distributions on dense arrays. Knobe et al. [12] first investigated the relationships among arrays for a data parallel program to construct a preference graph. They then proposed a heuristic algorithm for selections based on preference graphs. Li and Chen [13] considered axis alignment by developing a heuristic to reduce it to weighted bipartite graph matching. Kennedy et al. [11] determine data layouts automatically on distributed memory environments by using 0-1 integer programming [3]. Gupta et al. [8] extend the work of Li and Chen by presenting a framework based on weighted graphs. Kandemir et al. [10] present a framework that can automatically determine data layouts with respect to loop transformations. Their work can find optimal data layouts for all arrays at compiler time. Chatterjee, Gilbert, Schreiber, and Teng [5] presents a framework for the automatic determination of array alignments. They developed a heuristic algorithm to solve axis, stride, and offset alignment on their computation directed acyclic graphs. Philippsen [15] presented a heuristic algorithm for automatic alignment of array data and processes at compiler time. The work is also based on preference graphs.

7 Conclusion

In our recent work, we have been working on providing parallel sparse supports for array intrinsics of Fortran 90. Our library uses a two-level design. In the low-level routines, it requires the input sparse matrix to be specified with compression/distribution schemes for each function. In the high-level representation, sparse array functions are overloaded for array intrinsic interfaces so that programmers need not concern about the low-level details. This raises a very interesting optimization problem in the strategies to transform high-level representations to low-level routines by automatic selections and supplies of distribution and compression schemes for sparse arrays. In this paper, we propose solutions to address this optimization issue that transform the high-level representations to low-level routines by automatic selections and supplies of distribution and compression schemes for sparse data sets. Experimental results show that our selection algorithms are consistent with our cost model, and effective in selecting the proper compression and distribution schemes to improve performances of application programs with sparse data sets.

References

[1] Jeanne C. Adams, Walter S. Brainerd, Jeanne T. Martin, Brain T. Smith, and Jerrold L. Wagener. *Fortran 90 Handbook*. Intertext Publications/McGraw-Hill Inc., 1992.

[2] Aart J. C. Bik and Harry A. G. Wijshoff. Automatic data structure selection and transformation for sparse matrix computations. *IEEE Transactions on Parallel and Distributed Systems*, 7(2):109–126, February 1996.

[3] R. Bixby, K. Kennedy, and U. Kremer. Automatic data layout using 0-1 integer programming. Technical Report CRPC-TR93349-S, Rice University, 1993.

[4] Rong–Guey Chang, Tyng–Ruey Chuang, and Jenq Kuen Lee. Efficient support of parallel sparse computation for array intrinsic functions of Fortran 90. In *12th ACM International Conference on Supercomputing*, pp. 49–56. Melbourne, Australia, July 1998.

[5] S. Chatterjee, J. Gilbert, R. Schreiber, and S. H. Teng. Automatic array alignment in data-parallel programs. In *20th ACM Symposium on Principles of Programming Languages*, pp. 16-28. 1993.

[6] Tyng–Ruey Chuang, Rong–Guey Chang, and Jenq Kuen Lee. Sampling and analytical techniques for data distribution of parallel sparse computation. In *Eighth SIAM Conference on Parallel Processing for Scientific Computing*, March 1997.

[7] J. R. Gilbert, C. Moler, and R. Schreiber. Sparse matrices in MATLAB: Design and implementation. *SIAM Journal on Matrix Analysis and Applications*, 13(1):333—356, January 1992.

[8] M. Gupta and P. Banerjee. PARADIGM: A compiler for automatic data distribution on multicomputers. In *ACM International Conference on Supercomputing*. July 1993.

[9] V. Harinarayan, A. Rajaraman, and J. D. Ullman. *Implementing data cubes efficiently*. In *Proceedings of SIGMOD '96*.

[10] M. Kandemir, A. Choudhary, N. Shenoy, and P. Banerjee, and J. Ramanujam. A linear algebra framework for automatic determination of optimal data layouts. *IEEE Transaction on Parallel and Distributed Systems*, 10(2):115–135, February 1999.

[11] K. Kennedy and U. Kremer. Automatic data layout for distribution-memory machines. *ACM Transaction on Parallel Lnguages and Systems*, 20(4):869–916, July 1998.

[12] K. Knobe, J. D. Lukas, and G. L. Steele. Data optimization: Allocation of arrays to reduce communication on SIMD machines. *Journal of Parallel and Distributed Computing*, 8(2):102-118, 1990.

[13] J. Li and M. Chen. The data alignment phase in compiling programs for distributed-memory machines. *Journal of Parallel and Distributed Computing*, 13:213-221, October 1991.

[14] C. M. Lin, Yue-Chee Chuang, Jenq Kuen Lee, K. L. Wu, C. A. Lin. Parallelizing pressure correction method on unstructured grid. In *Parallel CFD '98*.

[15] Michael Philippsen. Automatic alignment of array data and process to reduce communication time on DMPPs. In *Proceedings of the Fifth ACM SIGPLAN Symposium on Principles & Practice of Parallel Programming*, pp. 112–122, July 1995.

[16] William H. Press, Saul A. Teukolsky, William T. Vetterling, and Brian P. Flannery. *Numerical Recipes in Fortran 90: The Art of Parallel Scientific Computing*. Cambridge University Press, 1996.

[17] T. J. Sheffler, R. Schreiber, J. R. Gilbert, and S. Chatterjee. Aligning parallel arrays to reduce communication. In *Proceedings of Frontiers '95*, pp. 324–331, February 1995.

[18] M. Ujaldon, S. D. Sharma, J. Saltz, and E. L. Zapata. Run–time techniques for parallelizing sparse matrix problems. In Afonso Ferreira and José Rolim, editors, *Parallel Algorithms for Irregularly Structured Problems: 2nd International Workshop*, pages 43–57. Lyon, France, September 1995. Lecture Notes in Computer Science, Volume 980, Springer–Verlag.

[19] Manuel Ujaldon, Emilio Zapata, Barbara M. Chapman, and Hans P. Zima. New data–parallel language features for sparse matrix computations. In *Proceedings of the 9th International Conference Parallel Processing Symposium*, pp. 742–749, April 1995.

Session C2

Parallel Algorithms

Chair: Oscar Ibarra
University of California at Santa Barbara, USA

A Parallel Optimal Branch-and-Bound Algorithm for MIN-Based Multiprocessors[*]

Myung K. Yang

Dept. of Electrical and Computer Engineering
University of Ulsan
PO Box 18, Ulsan, 680-749, Korea
mkyang@uou.ulsan.ac.kr

Chita R. Das

Dept. of Computer Science and Engineering
The Pennsylvania State University
University Park, PA 16802
das@cse.psu.edu

Abstract

In this paper, a parallel Optimal Best-First search Branch-and-Bound(B&B) algorithm(obs) is proposed and evaluated for MIN-based multiprocessor systems. The proposed algorithm decomposes a problem into a number of subproblems and each subproblem is processed on a small group of processors. A performance analysis is conducted to estimate the speed-up of the proposed parallel B&B algorithm. It considers both the computation and communication times to evaluate the realistic performance. Simulation data are given along with analysis results for model validation. It is shown that the proposed algorithm performs better than other reported schemes with its various advantageous features such as: less subproblem evaluations, proper load balancing, and limited scope of remote communication through the network.

1. Introduction

Branch-and-Bound(B&B) algorithm is a well known technique to solve various combinatorial search problems[1-3]. It has been classified into four different categories according to the selection rule: Breadth-First search[1], Depth-First search[1], Best-First search[3-4], and Random search[5].

The Best-First search is the most attractive in terms of time complexity. Wah, et al.[3-4] have proposed a parallel Global Best-First search B&B algorithm(*gbs*; It is called Global since only one global active subproblem list(*AS* list) is maintained in the entire system. This centralizes the control of subproblem selection to the host processor.) and have simulated its performance on a special architecture called MANIP. The speed-up reported here is optimistic since it does not count in the interprocessor communication.

A decomposition approach moderates the critical impact of remote communication of parallel algorithms. Karp and Zhang[6] have presented a parallel Decomposite Best-First search B&B algorithm(*dbs*) with randomized load balance strategies for a distributed memory environment. Kumar and Rao[7-8] have proposed a parallel Decomposite Depth-First search B&B algorithm(*dds*). Load balancing is accentuated to increase the processor utilization. This, however, may not be very elegant when the remote communication is expensive. A parallel Decomposite Random search B&B algorithm(*drs*) has been analyzed by Janakiram, et al[5]. The number of evaluated nodes in this analysis shows large discrepancy with the simulation results as the problem size increases.

Quinn[9] has analyzed the execution time of loosely synchronous and asynchronous parallel B&B algorithms on a hypercube multicomputer. The active subproblem list(*AS* list) of the search space is centralized for the loosely synchronous algorithm as for the *gbs*. The asynchronous algorithm maintains multiple *AS* lists that are updated after every branching operation to achieve load balance. Mohan[10] has examined two types of parallel Best-First search techniques to solve Traveling Salesman problems on a Cm*. The first approach is a synchronous algorithm that is similar to the *gbs* and the second approach is a decomposition algorithm. It is shown that the decomposition scheme provides better performance compare to the synchronous approach.

A parallel Decomposite Best-First search B&B algorithm(*dbs*) has been proposed for a class of multiprocessors that uses multistage interconnection network(MIN) as the communication medium[11]. The speed-up of the algorithm is derived including communication time and compared with other parallel algorithms. It is shown that the *dbs* performs better than other reported schemes as the number of processors increases when the communication overhead is taken into consideration.

---

[*] This research is supported by the Institute of Information Technology Assessment.

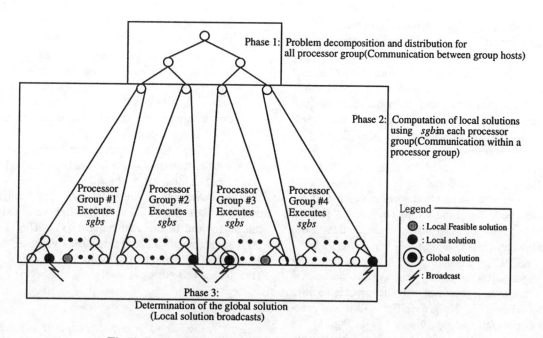

Phase 1: Problem decomposition and distribution for all processor group(Communication between group hosts)

Phase 2: Computation of local solutions using *sgbs* in each processor group(Communication within a processor group)

Processor Group #1 Executes *sgbs*

Processor Group #2 Executes *sgbs*

Processor Group #3 Executes *sgbs*

Processor Group #4 Executes *sgbs*

Legend

⬤ : Local Feasible solution

● : Local solution

◉ : Global solution

⚡ : Broadcast

Phase 3: Determination of the global solution (Local solution broadcasts)

Fig. 1. Parallel Optimal Best-First search B&B Algorithm($G = 4$)

An interesting phenomenon is observed from the speed-up comparison between *gbs* and *dbs*. The *gbs* is preferable when the number of processors is limited. This is due to fewer node evaluations with perfect load balance and acceptable communication overhead. On the other hand, the *dbs* shows better performance with a large MIN-based system environment. This speed-up observation motivates the design of a new algorithm, called the parallel Optimal Best-First search B&B algorithm(*obs*). The main concept of the *obs* is to decompose a given problem into G subproblems where G denotes the number of processor groups in a system. Each subproblem is assigned to a processor group that consists of a small number of processors. A processor group executes the parallel sub-Global Best-First search to computes the local solution of assigned subproblem. The processor groups broadcast their local solutions to determine the global solution. This broadcast provides not only the comparison function of G local solutions but also the side effect of load balancing among the processor groups.

A performance analysis is conducted to estimate the speed-up of the proposed algorithm. Both the computation and communication times are considered to evaluate the realistic performance of the algorithm. The simulation of algorithm on a MIN-based system is carried out to validate the proposed analysis model. It is also shown that the proposed Optimal Best-First search B&B algorithm performs better than other reported schemes.

This paper is organized as follows. In section 2, the new algorithm, named parallel Optimal Best-First search B&B algorithm(*obs*), is described. Speed-up analysis as well as the subproblem nodes evaluation time and communication time of the proposed algorithm are presented in section 3. In section 4, comparison of various parallel Best-First search B&B algorithms is discussed. The last section summarizes the research efforts.

2. The Proposed Parallel B&B Algorithm

The proposed parallel Optimal Best-First search B&B algorithm(*obs*) has three distinct phases:

1). Problem decomposition and distribution for all processor group.
2). Computation of local solutions using the parallel sub-Global Best-First search B&B algorithm(*sgbs*) in each processor group.
3). Determination of the global solution(*GS*).

Before the algorithm is applied, all processors in a system are clustered into G groups. Each processor group includes P processors. Thus $N = P \times G$, where N is the number of processors in the system. The first phase works until the original problem is decomposed into G subproblems. Then, each processor group executes the parallel sub-Global Best-First search B&B algorithm(*sgbs*) for finding a local solution(*LS*) of the assigned subproblem in the second phase. Finally, all the G local solutions are compared via *LS* broadcast to find the global solution in the third phase. Each group maintains two solution variables, one is for *LS* and the other is for global feasible solution(*GFS*). These variables are initialized in the beginning of the second phase. The first group that completes processing of the assigned subproblem broadcasts its *LS* to other groups and this value becomes the first *GFS* for all groups. A busy group uses this new *GFS* to update its local *AS* list[1] if necessary, and keeps working to complete the computation. Thus, the *LS* broadcast provides the side effect of load balancing among the processor groups with reasonable amount of extra remote communication. When the next *LS* is obtained, the corresponding group broadcasts it if the value is better than the current *GFS*. Otherwise, the group host broadcasts a local task-end signal. This process continues until *G* groups complete the computation and the global feasible solution is updated by congruence. Finally, the group whose *LS* and *GFS* match sends the data set to the system host processor.

Fig. 1 presents an example of the algorithm behaviors and the major communication activities of the corresponding phases. It is assumed that the processors in a system are clustered by four groups(*G* = 4) and the problem space is decomposed into binary tree in Fig. 1. The first phase divides a given problem into four subproblems. Only group host processors are involved in the first phase. Here, *G* subproblems are generated and distributed via intergroup communications.

Each processor group executes *sgbs* to solve an allocated subproblem in the second phase. A local group *AS* list is maintained in each group. These distributed *AS* lists not only limit the remote communication boundary but also provide the load balancing among the processors in a group. The second phase spends most processing time of the *obs*. The intragroup data transfers to maintain the local *AS* list are major communication activities in the second phase.

The third phase determines the global solution by comparing the *LS*s. A group host processor broadcasts either its own *LS* or the local task-end signal. This broadcast provides both the comparison function of *LS*s and the load balancing effect among the processor groups.

3. Performance Evaluation

The analytical model is developed under the following assumptions that are derived from the general properties of Best-First search B&B algorithm to solve the minimization problems, such as Traveling salesman and Vertex covering problems, etc.

1). The problem is decomposed into a balanced *a*-ary

---

[1] Note that this can reduce the work load of the busy groups since the *AS* lists of the corresponding groups can be shortened using this new *GFS*.

tree of depth *D*.

2). The value difference between a parent and its child subproblem node is defined as a link value(x_l). The link value is an independent and identically distributed positive random integer for the minimization problems. It lies in the range x_b(smallest link value) and x_c(largest link value). The x_b and x_c values are problem dependent.

3). If any subproblem node value in the given tree is smaller than the *final solution*, then this node as well as its children are evaluated.

These assumptions are valid and have been used by previous researchers[3]. The integer link value assumption can be relaxed to use real numbers[11]. The value of a child subproblem(v_c) can be decided by adding its parent node value(v_p) and the link value(x_l), i.e. $v_c = v_p + x_l$. Therefore, a node value at level *d*, v_d, is given as

$$v_d = v_{root} + \sum_{i=1}^{d} x_i , \tag{1}$$

where x_i is the link value between depth (*i* - 1) and *i*. Note that $v_{d=1}$ is equally distributed in the range of ($v_{root} + x_b$) and ($v_{root} + x_c$) for depth 1. The distribution of v_d shows normal distribution within the range of ($v_{root} + x_b \times d$) and ($v_{root} + x_c \times d$) as the tree depth *d* increases.

It is also assumed that the number of processors in the system is *N*. The processors are clustered into *G* groups and each group includes *P* processors. The analyses are provided here for an *a*-ary tree of depth *D*, where $\log_a G$ and $\log_a P$ are integers. The local host memory is assumed large enough to handle the search operation of the allocated subtree.

3. 1. Subproblem nodes evaluation time

The subproblem nodes evaluation time, *TE*(*D*, *a*, *N*), is defined as the computation time to solve the subproblems. It is required for the early two phases of the algorithm. The first phase uses the *step-by-step spread* technique[11] that takes $\Upsilon(= \log_a G)$ iterations and, for each iteration, one subproblem node is evaluated in the corresponding local host processor(s). Thus the node evaluation time for the phase 1, *TE*(*D*, *a*, *N*)$_{phase 1}$, is calculated as

$$TE(D, a, N)_{phase1} = \Upsilon \times t_e, \tag{2}$$

where t_e represents the time to solve one subproblem node by a processor.

In the second phase, each processor group executes the parallel sub-Global Best-First search B&B algorithm(*sgbs*) to solve the assigned *a*-ary subtree of depth *D**, where *D** = (*D* - Υ). The expected number of evaluated subproblem nodes in a processor for the phase 2, $E(D^*, a, P)_{phase2}$, can be obtained as

$$E(D^*, a, P)_{phase2} = max\{ E(D^*, a, 1)/P,$$
$$\varpi + 1 + a \times (D^* - \varpi)\}, \qquad (3)$$

where $\varpi = \log_a P$. $E(D^*, a, 1)$ denotes the number of evaluated subproblem nodes for an a-ary subtree of depth D^* using the serial Best-First search B&B algorithm. It is given in [11]. The first term of max in equation (3) shows linear speed-up of $sgbs$ in terms of the number of evaluated subproblems[3]. The second term in max presents the minimum number of evaluated subproblems to be solved in a processor. Decomposition and distribution of the assigned subroot problem using the *step-by-step spread* technique needs evaluation of ϖ nodes in the corresponding processors. Then each processor evaluates $(1 + a \times (D^* - \varpi))$ subproblem nodes until the first local feasible solution is found. If this first feasible solution bounds the further process, the algorithm is terminated with evaluating a minimum number of subproblem nodes.

The time required for the phase 2, $TE(D^*, a, P)_{phase2}$, is calculated using $E(D^*, a, P)_{phase2}$ as

$$TE(D^*, a, P)_{phase2} = max\{ E(D^*, a, 1)/P,$$
$$\varpi + 1 + a \times (D^* - \varpi)\} \times t_e. \quad (4)$$

Total subproblem nodes evaluation time of obs, $TE(D, a, N)_{obs}$, can be written as

$$TE(D, a, N)_{obs} = TE(D, a, N)_{phase1} + TE(D^*, a, P)_{phase2}. \quad (5)$$

3. 2. Communication time

Communication requirements of the proposed obs are classified into three categories according to the corresponding phase of algorithm behavior. These are

1). Subproblem distribution using the *step-by-step spread* technique.
2). Communication for the execution of the parallel sub-Global Best-First search B&B algorithm($sgbs$).
3). Local group solution broadcast for finding the final global solution.

The first phase requires Υ iterations and each iteration has $s(= \lceil \log_2 a \rceil)$ steps. Here, in the jth step of each iteration $\lambda[j](= \lfloor \lambda[j-1]/2 \rfloor)$ subproblem data sets are transferred through the network, where $\lambda[0] = a$ and $\lambda[s] = 1$. Thus, the communication time for phase 1, $TC(D, a, N)_{phase1}$, can be calculated as

$$TC(D, a, N)_{phase1} = \Upsilon \times \sum_{j=1}^{s} \lambda[j] \times \sigma \times t_{rb}, \qquad (6)$$

where σ is the number of memory blocks for a data set and

t_{rb} is a remote block transfer time.

The communication activities in the second phase are for the execution of the $sgbs$ in each processor group. Each processor group executes the $sgbs$ on an assigned a-ary subtree of depth $D^*(= D - \Upsilon)$. Again, we classify the communication activities for the execution of the $sgbs$ into two stages: (i) subproblem decomposition and distribution, and (ii) local group AS list maintenance.

The subproblem decomposition and distribution in stage (i) of the second phase is a continuing process of the first phase. Here, a subproblem allocated in the local host processor after the first phase is partitioned until P processors in a group are assigned. This requires $\varpi(= \log_a P)$ iterations and each iteration has $s(= \lceil \log_2 a \rceil)$ steps. Thus, communication time required for stage (i) of phase 2, $TC(D^*, a, P)_{phase2.i}$, can be written as

$$TC(D^*, a, P)_{phase2.i} = \varpi \times \sum_{j=1}^{s} \lambda[j] \times \sigma \times t_{rb}. \qquad (7)$$

Each local host processor maintains a group AS list in stage (ii) of the second phase. Communication activities required for the group AS list maintenance are *Prune test, Aggregation, Cutoff, Selection, Insertion, Distribution*[11]. While prune test, cutoff, selection, and insertion are processed by local access within a corresponding local host processor, aggregation and distribution require interprocessor remote traffics through the network. These two activities take major portion of the communication time for the execution of $sgbs$.

3. 2. 1. Communication time for aggregation

Aggregation of all newly expanded subproblems from each local processor to local host processor within a group is executed to select the best P subproblems for the next expansion and to update the group AS list. Total number of aggregated subproblem nodes using $sgbs$ on an a-ary subtree of depth D^*, $AGGR[D^*, a, P]$, is calculated recursively as

$$AGGR[D^*, a, P] = a \times P$$
$$+ \sum_{d=\varpi+2}^{D^*-1} \theta_{d-1} \times \sum_{y=v_{d-1}(min)}^{v_{parent}(lim)} \left(P\{v_{d-1}=y\} \times \sum_{j=1}^{a} [\binom{a}{j} m^j (1-m)^{a-j} \times j] \right)$$
$$+ \theta_{D^*-1} \times \sum_{y=v_{D^*-1}(min)}^{v_{parent}(lim)} \left(P\{v_{D^*-1} = y\} \times \sum_{j=1}^{a} [\binom{a}{j} m^j (1-m)^{a-j}] \right)$$
$$+ AGGR[D^*-1, a, P], \qquad (8)$$

where $D^*>\varpi(= \log_a P)$, $\theta_{d-1} = (a^{\varpi+1} - P) \times a^{d-2-\varpi}$, $v_{parent}(lim)$ $= \lfloor \Phi_{D^*} - x_b \rfloor$, $m = \dfrac{\min\{\Phi_{D^*} - y - x_b + 1, x_c - x_b + 1\}}{x_c - x_b + 1}$, and $AGGR[\varpi + 1, a, P] = a^{\varpi} = P$. v_{d-1} is the value of a parent node which is in subdepth $(d-1)$, and Φ_{D^*} is the local solu-

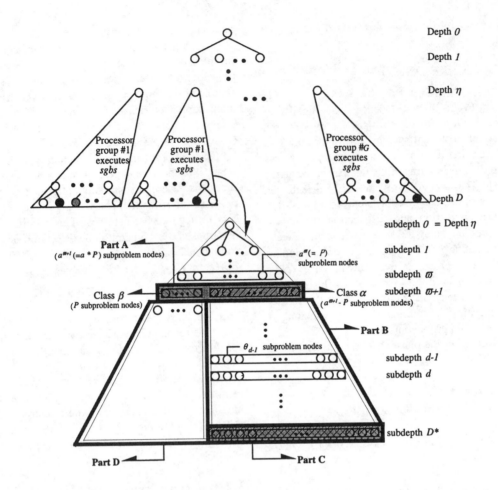

Fig. 2. Decomposition of an a-ary subproblem search space to analyze the communication time

tion for an a-ary subtree of depth D^*. Derivation of Φ_{D^*} is given in [11]. $v_{parent}(lim)$ is the maximum value of a parent node so that its child node can survive from the prune test iff the corresponding link value is minimum, x_b. If subtree depth D^* is equal to ($\varpi + 1$), each processor solves a leaf nodes(local *feas*) after finishing the operation of stage (i) of phase 2. These a leaf nodes are compared and the node with the smallest value in each processor is sent to the local host to find the local solution. Thus the total number of aggregated nodes for the search tree of depth ($\varpi + 1$), $AGGR[\varpi + 1, a, P]$, is P, i.e. one node from each processor in a group.

Equation (8) can be explained better using Fig. 2 where the search space is divided into four parts. Part A in Fig. 2 consists of the first aggregated ($a \times P$) subproblem nodes. These nodes are compared and grouped into two classes α and β according to their node values ($\varepsilon_0, \varepsilon_1, \dots, \varepsilon_{a \times P-1}$) such that subproblem nodes in class α have values (ε_P, $\varepsilon_{P+1}, \dots, \varepsilon_{a \times P-1}$) and those in class β have values (ε_0, $\varepsilon_1, \dots, \varepsilon_{P-1}$), and $min\{\alpha\} \geq max\{\beta\}$. The subproblems who-

se subroots are grouped in class α constitute part B and part C. The second add term of equation (8) presents the number of aggregated nodes in part B of Fig. 2. For each depth d in part B, from depth ($\varpi + 2$) to depth ($D^* - 1$), there are θ_{d-1} parent nodes. $P\{v_{d-1} = y\}$ shows the probability that a parent node at depth ($d - 1$) has the value y, where $v_{d-1}(min) \leq y \leq v_{parent}(lim)$. If any parent node at depth ($d - 1$) has value y, its child nodes at depth d are expanded and are tested for pruning. If j out of a child node values are still smaller than the solution(Φ_{D^*}), those j nodes are sent to the local host for the selection of next decomposition candidates. Finally m denotes the probability that a link value is in the range of x_b and $min\{\Phi_{D^*} - y, x_c\}$. This implies that the child node survives from prune test when a parent node value is y. Unlike part B, part C of Fig. 2 consists of leaf nodes only at subdepth D^*. The node expansion strategy used here is the same as in part B. However, in part C, even though the multiple child nodes survive from the prune test, only the smallest feasible solution in each processor is sent to the local host. Thus the number of aggregated nodes in part C can be calculated as in the third term of equation (8). The number of aggregated nodes in part D can be written recursively as $AGGR[D* - 1, a, P]$.

Let us suppose the $AGGR[D*, a, P]$ subproblem nodes are equally generated from the processors in a group, i.e. each processor generates $AGGR[D*, a, P]/P$ nodes to be sent to the local host. The *step-by-step shrink* technique is applied for the conflict free aggregation. It is similar to a reverse procedure of the *step-by-step spread* technique. Suppose each processor has one data set which will be sent to the local host. One *step-by-step shrink* operation is required to aggregate those data sets into the local host, and it consists of $\xi (= \lceil \log_2 P \rceil)$ steps. In the jth step, a sending processor has at most 2^{j-1} data sets to transfer. There are $(P - 2^{\xi-1})$ data sets to be transferred by a sending processor in the last step. Therefore, the communication time for aggregation, T_{aggr}, can be calculated as

$$T_{aggr} = \frac{AGGR[D*, a, P]}{P} \times \left(\sum_{j=1}^{\xi-1} 2^{j-1} + (P - 2^{\xi-1}) \right) \times \sigma \times t_{rb} \quad (9)$$

where $\xi = \lceil \log_2 P \rceil$. σ and t_{rb} are given in equation (6).

3. 2. 2. Communication time for distribution

Once the newly expanded subproblem nodes are aggregated at the local host, P or less than P nodes, depending on the number of previous aggregated nodes and the number of subproblems in AS list, are selected and distributed for the next expansion. The total number of distributed nodes, $DIST[D*, a, P]$, can be written as

$$DIST[D*, a, P] = P$$
$$+ \sum_{d=\varpi+1}^{D*-1} \theta_{d-1} \times \sum_{y=v_{d-1}(min)}^{v_{parent}(lim)} \left(P\{v_{d-1}=y\} \times \sum_{j=1}^{a} [\binom{a}{j} m^j (1-m)^{a-j} \times j] \right)$$
$$+ DIST[D*-1, a, P], \quad (10)$$

where $D* > \varpi$, and $DIST[\varpi +1, a, P] = 0$. θ_{d-1}, $v_{parent}(lim)$, $v_{d-1}(min)$, and m are defined in equation (8). No more distribution is required when subtree depth $D*$ is equal to ($\varpi + 1$) because all subproblem nodes are evaluated when the first aggregation is executed. Total number of distributed nodes analysis is similar to that of aggregated nodes analysis. $(a \times P)$ nodes are gathered from part A of Fig. 2. P nodes in class β are distributed for the next expansion and other nodes in class α are stored in the group AS list for future examination. The number of distributed nodes in part B and in class α of part A is calculated in the second term of equation (10). No node is distributed from the leaf in part C. The third term of equation (10) is a recursive expression for the part D of Fig. 2. Thus the communication time for subproblem distribution, T_{dist}, is written as

$$T_{dist} = \frac{DIST[D*, a, P]}{P} \times \sum_{j=1}^{\xi} 2^{\xi-j} \times \sigma \times t_{rb} \quad (11)$$

Unlike the original *step-by-step spread* technique in the first phase where subproblems are generated at each iteration, all subproblems to be distributed are available at the local host in the second phase. Suppose the local host has P data sets which will be distributed. The *step-by-step spread* operation needs $\xi (= \lceil \log_2 P \rceil)$ steps. In the jth step, $2^{\xi-j}$ data sets are transferred.

3. 2. 3. Other communication time

All other communication activities in stage (*ii*) of the second phase such as prune test, insertion, cutoff, and selection are accomplished by local communication assuming that the local host memory is large enough to manage the group AS list. Communication time for these local activities can be approximated as the communication time required to solve the problem with a single processor, $TC(D*, a, 1)_{sb\&b}$, which is given in [11]. The communication time in the phase 2, $TC(D*, a, P)_{phase2}$, is obtained as

$$TC(D*, a, P)_{phase2} = \varpi \times \sum_{j=1}^{s} \lambda[j] \times \sigma \times t_{rb}$$
$$+ T_{aggr} + T_{dist} + TC(D*, a, 1)_{sb\&b} \quad (12)$$

The communication activities in the third phase consist of three different types of remote data transfers. These are *local group solution broadcast, local group task-end message broadcast, and global solution data set transfer*. All these communications, except the *global solution data set transfer*, need one word remote write access which takes t_{rw}. Each local host processor executes either *local group solution broadcast* or *local group task-end message broadcast* in phase 3. The time taken for these are $G \times t_{rw}$. For the *global solution data set transfer*, a remote block transfer time, $\rho \times t_{rb}$, is required. The communication time for the third phase, $TC(D, a, N)_{phase3}$, is thus calculated as

$$TC(D, a, N)_{phase3} = G \times t_{rw} + \rho \times t_{rb} \quad (13)$$

Total communication delay for *obs* operation, $TC(D, a, N)_{obs}$, is obtained by adding all communication time of the three phases obtained in equations (6), (12), and (13). It is

$$TC(D, a, N)_{obs} = \Upsilon \times \sum_{j=1}^{s} \lambda[j] \times \sigma \times t_{rb}$$
$$+ \varpi \times \sum_{j=1}^{s} \lambda[j] \times \sigma \times t_{rb} + T_{aggr} + T_{dist} + TC(D*, a, 1)_{sb\&b}$$
$$+ G \times t_{rw} + \rho \times t_{rb} \quad (14)$$

where $\lambda[0] = a$, and $\lambda[s] = 1$. Total time required to execute the *obs* on an a-ary tree of depth D by N processors, $T(D, a, N)_{obs}$, is obtained from equations (5) and (14) as

$$T(D, a, N)_{obs} = TE(D, a, N)_{obs} + TC(D, a, N)_{obs} \quad (15)$$

Table I. Execution time of the *obs* on a binary tree

$x_b = 1, x_c = 10, D = 15, P = 4, \sigma = 1.0, t_e = 500\mu sec, t_{lr} = 0.53\mu sec, t_{lw} = 0.39\mu sec, t_{rb} = 72\mu sec, t_{rw} = 4\mu sec.$

No. of Processors	Avg. No. of evaluated nodes		Communication time(μsec)		Total execution time($msec$)	
	simulation	analysis	simulation	analysis	simulation	analysis
1	1375.14	1359.29	2192.5	2063.8	689.762	681.709
2	666.77	679.64	46341.2	42752.1	379.726	382.572
4	329.40	339.82	69902.4	64598.0	234.602	234.508
8	229.73	237.38	48322.9	45020.7	163.188	163.711
16	161.85	169.82	34361.5	32208.8	115.287	117.119
32	114.47	119.16	24237.2	22566.6	81.471	82.147
64	81.70	86.31	16965.9	16270.1	57.816	59.425

The speed-up of the *obs*, $S(N)_{obs}$, is then

$$S(N)_{obs} = \frac{T(D, a, 1)_{sb\&b}}{T(D, a, N)_{obs}} \qquad (16)$$

where $T(D, a, 1)_{sb\&b}$ is the time taken by a single processor to complete the serial Best-First search on an *a*-ary tree of depth *D*. This is derived in [11].

Table I shows the comparisons of analytical and simulation results for various parameters of the *obs* algorithm on a binary tree of depth 15. Each processor group consists of 4 processors. The t_{lr}, t_{lw}, t_{rw}, and t_{rb} values used here are from the Butterfly GP1000[12]. Simulation results are given along with analytical result for model validation. We have compared these results for variable problem sizes. For a given problem size, 1500 different problems are simulated and the average value of each parameter is used for comparison with the analytical results. It has been observed that the analytical results match nicely with the simulation results for all cases as in Table I.

4. Comparison

Three parallel Best-First search B&B algorithms: *gbs*, *dbs*, and the newly proposed *obs* are examined. A performance comparison of these algorithms is conducted on the Butterfly configuration. Fig. 3 depicts the speed-up of these algorithms. We have applied the conflict free mapping schemes to all algorithms for the fairness.

The *gbs* maintains only one global *AS* list in the host processor. The global *AS* list provides the advantages of less subproblem nodes evaluation with its superior load balance. However, two types of frequent remote accesses, aggregation and distribution, are inevitable. Because of these frequent remote traffics, the *gbs* provides poor performance as the number of processors increases. It has been shown before that the *gbs* can provide linear speed-up when communication overhead is not considered. Some-

times there happens to be an acceleration anomaly where the speed-up is better than linear[13]. The speed-up, however, reduces significantly in a realistic environment due to the communication overhead.

In the decomposition approach, there are *N* local *AS* lists: one for each processor. It takes the advantage of less interprocessor communication overhead using these distributed *AS* lists. Thus the *dbs* provides better speed-up than the *gbs* on a large system due to the negligible remote communication. However, the *dbs* suffers redundant subproblem nodes evaluation due to the limited interprocessor communications that cause the load unbalance among the processors.

The proposed parallel Optimal Best-First search B&B algorithm(*obs*) takes advantages of both *gbs* and *dbs*. By grouping a small number of processors, which execute parallel sub-Global Best-First search on a decomposed subproblem, it takes the benefits of *gbs*: less number of node evaluation and excellent load balancing within a processor group. The *obs* also inherits the merit of *dbs* by partitioning a search space and maintaining multiple distributed local *AS* lists. Fig. 3 shows that the *obs* outperforms the other two parallel Best-First search B&B algorithms for all possible system sizes.

5. Conclusions

A new parallel Optimal Best-First search B&B algorithm(*obs*) along with its performance evaluation on a MIN-based multiprocessor has been presented. The proposed algorithm combines the advantages of both *gbs* and *dbs*. It decomposes the original problem into smaller subproblems and each subproblem is solved using a small group of processors that executes the parallel sub-Global Best-First search B&B algorithm(*sgbs*). Each group manages its own *AS* list and maintains load balance among

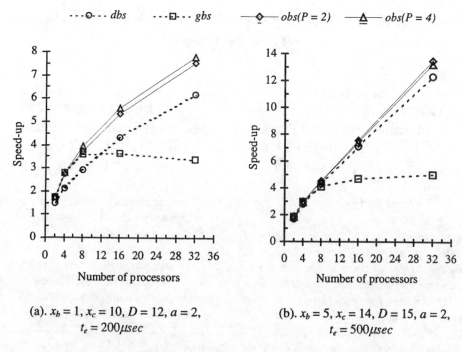

(a). $x_b = 1$, $x_c = 10$, $D = 12$, $a = 2$, $t_e = 200\mu sec$

(b). $x_b = 5$, $x_c = 14$, $D = 15$, $a = 2$, $t_e = 500\mu sec$

Fig. 3. Speed-up comparison of the parallel Best-First search B&B algorithms

intragroup processors. Timing analyses and speed-up calculation of the *obs* are derived. These analyses include the communication time for predicting a more realistic performance. Speed-up comparison of various parallel Best-First search B&B algorithms shows that the proposed *obs* performs better than other schemes with its various advantageous features such as: less number of node evaluations, good degree of load balancing, and tolerable communication overhead.

References

[1] E. L. Lawler and D. W. Wood, "Branch-and-Bound methods: A survey", *Oper. Res.*, Vol. 14, pp. 699-719, 1966.

[2] M. J Quinn, "Parallel Computing, Theory and Practice", McGraw Hill, 1994.

[3] B. W. Wah and C. F. Yu, "Stochastic Modeling of Branch-and-Bound Algorithms with Best-First Search", *IEEE Trans. on Software Eng.*, Vol. SE-11, No. 9, pp. 922-934, Sep. 1985.

[4] B. W. Wah and Y. W. Eva Ma, "MANIP - A Multicomputer Architecture for solving Combinatorial Extremum-Search Problems", *IEEE Trans. on Computers*, Vol. C-33, No. 5, pp. 377-390, May 1984.

[5] V. K. Janakiram, D. P. Agrawal, and R. Mehrotra, "A Randomized Parallel Branch-and-Bound Algorithm", *Proc.*

Intl. Conf. on Parallel Processing, pp. 69-75, Aug. 1988.

[6] R. M. Karp and Y. Zhang, "A Randomized Parallel Branch-and-Bound Procedure", *Proc. of the ACM Symposium on Theory of Computing*, pp. 290-300, May, 1988.

[7] V. N. Rao and V. Kumar, "Parallel Depth-First Search on Multiprocessors Part I: Implementation, and Part II: Analysis", *Intl. Journal of Parallel Programming*, Vol. 16, No. 6, 1987.

[8] V. Kumar and V. N. Rao, "Parallel Depth-First Search Ring Architecture", *Proc. Intl. Conf. on Parallel Processing*, pp. 128-132, Aug. 1988.

[9] M. J. Quinn, "Analysis and Implementation of Branch-and-Bound Algorithms on a Hypercube Multicomputer", *IEEE Trans. On Computers*, Vol. 39, No. 3, pp. 384-387, Mar. 1990.

[10] J. Mohan, "Experience with Two parallel Programs Solving the Traveling Saleaman Problem", *Proc. Intl. Conf. On Parallel Processing*, pp. 191-193, Aug. 1983.

[11] M. K. Yang and C. R. Das, "Evaluation of a Parallel Branch-and-Bound Algorithm on a Class of Multiprocessors", *IEEE Trans. on Parallel and Distributed Systems*, Vol. 5, No. 1, pp. 74- 86, Jan. 1994.

[12] -,"Butterfly GP1000 - Overview", *BBN Advanced Computer Inc.*, Nov. 1988.

[13] T. -H. Lai and S. Sahni, "Anomalies of Parallel Branch-and-Bound Algorithms", *Comm. Of the ACM*, pp. 594-602, June 1984.

A Strictly-Optimal Strategy to Access Multi-Dimensional Data on Parallel Disk Systems *

Sajal K. Das
Department of Computer Science
University of North Texas
Denton, TX 76203-1366
E-mail: das@cs.unt.edu

M. Cristina Pinotti
Ist. Elab. Infor.
National Council of Research
Pisa, ITALY
E-mail: pinotti@iei.pi.cnr.it

Abstract

The disk allocation problem addresses the issue of how to distribute large files among several disks so as to maximize the concurrent disk accesses in response to partial match queries. In the past this problem has been studied for binary as well as for p-ary cartesian product files. In this paper, we propose a strictly-optimal disk allocation strategy for non-uniform cartesian product files for every partial match query. Our strategy is based on a large and flexible class of maximum distance separable (MDS) codes, namely the redundant residue codes. A new family of residue codes, called the redundant non-pairwise prime residue codes, is also introduced.

Keywords   : Partial match queries, non-uniform cartesian product files, optimal disk allocation, parallel disk systems, pairwise prime residue codes, redundant non-pairwise prime residue codes.

1 Introduction

The demand for efficient retrieval methods in large databases has increased significantly in the recent years. Important practical applications such as spatial databases, airline reservation systems, cartography, and Web accesses require voluminous amount of data (often of the order of terabytes) which are too large to store on a single secondary storage device like a disk. Moreover, distributing files on to multiple disks that are accessible concurrently allows us to retrieve data in parallel, thus reducing the retrieval time.

1.1 Cartesian Product Files

This paper deals with the disk allocation problem of non-uniform cartesian product files. An *n-attribute file* is a set of *n*-tuples, called *records*. Assuming that the

---

*This work is partially supported by Texas Advanced Technology Program grant TATP-003594031, Texas Advanced Research Program TARP-003594013 and Collaborazione IEI e Provincia Autonoma Trento.

*i*th attribute ranges in the interval D_i, for $1 \le i \le n$, a record is an element of the space $D_1 \times D_2 \times \ldots \times D_n$, and a file is a subset of this space. A file is stored on a disk by partitioning the records into *buckets* (or *pages*), containing mutually disjoint sets of records. In order to distribute the records over the buckets such that the load on each bucket is balanced, each interval D_i is divided into m_i disjoint sets. Each bucket is denoted by a string of integers $< x_1, x_2, \ldots, x_n >$ where $x_i \in [0, 1, \ldots, m_i - 1]$ and $1 \le i \le n$. From now on, we will refer to m_i as the *domain* of the *i*th attribute. In this paper, we will deal with an *n*-attribute file at the bucket level, and a file will be viewed as a subset of the *n*-tuples space $m_1 \times m_2 \times \ldots m_n$.

A *p-ary cartesian product file* is a file in which the domains m_i, for $1 \le i \le n$, assume identical value p, that is, $m_1 = m_2 = \ldots = m_n = p$. A *binary cartesian product file* is a special case for $p = 2$.

A *non-uniform cartesian product file* is a file in which the domains m_i assume different values, that is $m_i \ne m_j$, for $1 \le i < j \le n$. Selecting different ranges for the domains m_i of the attributes can be very useful when the original intervals D_i are quite different from each other.

Clearly, a non-uniform and a *p*-ary cartesian product file consist of, respectively, $M = \Pi_{i=1}^{n} m_i$ and $M = p^n$ buckets.

1.2 Disk Allocation Problem

An *m-disk allocation strategy* distributes the buckets of a cartesian product file on to m disks. A *partial match query*, q, is defined as an *n*-tuple $q = < q_1, \ldots, q_n >$, where q_i is either a value from the domain m_i of the *i*th attribute (i.e., q_i is specified) or is unspecified. A bucket *qualifies* for a partial match query q if its associated string coincides with q on the specified attributes.

For any given query q, the *query response set* of q is the set of buckets that qualify for q. The size $N(q)$ of the query response set is $N(q) = \Pi_{j=1}^{k} m_{i_j}$ if $q_{i_1}, q_{i_2}, \ldots, q_{i_k}$ are the unspecified attributes of q. The *response time* $R(q)$ of a query q is defined as $R(q) = \max\{N_1(q), N_2(q), \ldots, N_m(q)\}$, where $N_i(q)$

is the number of qualifying buckets for q on disk i where $1 \le i \le m$. Clearly, $N(q) = \sum_{i=1}^{m} N_i(q)$. Hence, the best possible response time is obtained distributing the $N(q)$ qualifying buckets on different disks as evenly as possible and performing the disk retrievals concurrently.

Thus, given an m-disk system, a disk allocation strategy is termed *strictly-optimal for a query q* [5, 1], if its response time for q is $\left\lceil \frac{N(q)}{m} \right\rceil$, while it is called *strictly-optimal* if, *for every query q*, its response time is $\left\lceil \frac{N(q)}{m} \right\rceil$.

1.3 Previous Results

In some of the earlier work related to disk allocation buckets were assigned to an m-disk system with the help of a (pseudo)random number generator, with $1/m$ as the probability of assigning a bucket to a particular disk. This method has no constraints either on the number of disks or the cardinality of the domains of the attributes. Subsequently, more sophisticated strategies have been proposed for binary and p-ary cartesian product files most of which exhibit a better performance than this simple method.

Foe example, Du and Sobolewski [4] proposed the *Disk Modulo* allocation method which, assuming an m-disk system, $d_0, \ldots, d_{m-1}$, assigns the bucket $< x_1, \ldots, x_n >$ to the disk unit d_j such that $j = (\sum_{i=1}^{n} x_i) \bmod m$. Such a method is *strictly-optimal* for the following cases: (i) partial match queries with only one unspecified attribute; (ii) partial match queries with at least one unspecified attribute j whose domain m_j satisfies $m_j \bmod m = 0$; (iii) all possible partial match queries when $m_i \bmod m = 0$ or $m_i = 1$ for all $1 \le i \le n$; and (iv) all possible partial match queries when $m = 2, 3$.

The idea of [4] to find an (ad hoc) hash function, to be applied to the bucket strings was followed by Kim and Pramanik [6] who proposed the *Field Exclusive-Or* allocation method. Given an m-disk system and letting [+] denote the bitwise exclusive-or, a bucket $< x_1, \ldots, x_n >$ is allocated to the device $[([+]_{i=1}^{n} x_i) \bmod m]$. This approach is shown to be strictly-optimal for any partial match query (i) with two unspecified attributes; or (ii) with more than two unspecified attributes if there exists at least one unspecified field whose range is larger than m.

Faloutsos and Metaxas [5] discussed a heuristic for the disk allocation method based on linear binary error-correcting codes and this method applies to binary cartesian product files with n-attributes. The intuitive idea is to group the buckets for each disk in such way that the associated binary strings form a linear $d - 1$-error-detecting binary code. The construction guarantees that

buckets whose associated strings differ in less than d digits will be allocated to different disks. Therefore, partial match queries with less than d unspecified attributes exhibit a constant response time using a 2^d-disk system. Although this allocation method is strictly-optimal, in general, for arbitrary values of n and d, there may exist no codes with such properties, and hence no disk allocation method.

Abdel-Ghaffar and El Abbadi [1] extended the results of [5] to p-ary cartesian product files, where $p > 2$, and they prove the equivalence between the strictly-optimal allocation methods and *maximum distance separable* (MDS) codes. Then, based on the *Reed-Solomon Codes* which gives a large family of p-ary MDS codes, they proposed strictly-optimal allocation methods for declustering p-ary cartesian product files with at most $p - 1$ attributes among m disks, where m is a power of p. A limitation of this approach is that there exists only a few MDS codes for the general case of p-ary cartesian product files with n ($\ge p$) attributes. (A complete table of the known MDS codes can be found in [8].) However, among the existing solutions to the disk allocation problem, the approach based on codes achieves a better performance, especially for partial match queries with a large number of unspecified attributes.

1.4 Motivations and Our Contributions

In this paper we propose a disk allocation strategy for non-uniform cartesian product files. The main contribution is to draw attention to a very large and flexible class of semi-linear MDS codes, called the *redundant residue codes*, that apply to the disk allocation problem for *non-uniform* cartesian product file leading to a strictly-optimal disk allocation strategy for arbitrary queries. Let us first elaborate on the motivation behind our work.

Today's technology offers systems with a very large number of disks. Therefore, it is practically feasible to use the redundant MDS residue codes, although they may require more disks than the p-ary MDS codes.

Non-uniform cartesian product files are also more realistic. In fact, having non-uniform ranges for attribute domains may help in obtaining (optimal) buckets as argued below. Consider a 3-attribute file (the attributes assume only integer values) such that the first attribute ranges in $D_1 = [1..1000]$, the second in $D_2 = [1..21]$, and the third in $D_3 = [1..9]$. Also suppose that there are at most $1000 \times 21 \times 9$ records (one for each attribute value) in the file, and a disk page (or bucket) contains 100 records.

Now let us examine the scenario when a p-ary cartesian product file is used. For $p = 4$, we obtain very large buckets, each containing $250 \times 6 \times 3$ records, which do not fit in one disk page. The choice $p = 20$ will imply at most $50 \times 2 \times 1$ records in each bucket. Although a bucket perfectly fits in a page, yet the file is mapped into 20^3 buckets, most of them being empty.

On the other hand, if we use a non-uniform file system with different partitions, we will have a better solution. For example, consider $m_1 = 20$, $m_2 = 11$ and $m_3 = 9$. Then each bucket has at most $(1000/20) \times (\lceil 21/11 \rceil) \times (\lceil 9/9 \rceil) = 50 \times 2 \times 1 = 100$ records, and we consider $20 \times 11 \times 9 = 1980$ buckets.

Furthermore, as will be clear later, for $p = 20$, a strictly-optimal disk allocation method, which is based on the Reed Solomon Codes and leads to a constant response time for every partial match query, will require $20^2 = 400$ disks in the system. Whereas, using the proposed non-uniform partitions, a strictly-optimal disk allocation strategy, based on pairwise prime residue codes, also yielding a constant response time for every query, requires only $20 \times 11 = 220$ disks.

The paper is organized as follows. Section 2 gives a general overview of relevant properties of codes. The residue codes are reviewed in Sections 3 and the new class of redundant non-pairwise prime residue codes is presented in Section 4. The disk allocation strategy is proposed in Section 5.

2 Code Terminology and Maximum Distance Separable Codes

Given a set of n positive integer *radices*, denoted as $m_1, m_2, \ldots, m_n$, let $S = m_1 \times m_2 \times \ldots m_n$ be the space of all the $M = \Pi_{i=1}^{n} m_i$ n-tuples such that, for every choice of the n digits, $a_1, a_2, \ldots, a_k, a_{k+1}, \ldots, a_n$ where $a_i \in [0, 1, \ldots, m_i - 1]$, there is a unique n-tuple $X = \; < x_1, x_2, \ldots, x_n > \in S$ satisfying $x_1 = a_1, x_2 = a_2, \ldots, x_n = a_n$.

A *code* C of radices $m_1, m_2, \ldots, m_n$, is a subset of n-tuples of S. Each n-tuple of C is called a *codeword*. Let the *size* of C be its cardinality.

A *linear* code is closed under the addition and subtraction operations. That is, a code C is linear if, given two codewords $x = x_1, x_2, \ldots, x_n$ and $y = y_1, y_2, \ldots, y_n$ of C, both $x + y = (x_1 + y_1) \bmod m_1, (x_2 + y_2) \bmod m_2, \ldots, (x_n + y_n) \bmod m_n$ and $x - y = (x_1 - y_1) \bmod m_1, (x_2 - y_2) \bmod m_2, \ldots, (x_n - y_n) \bmod m_n$ are also codewords of C. A *semi-linear* code is a code which is linear under certain conditions.

The *Hamming weight* of a codeword is defined as the number of its nonzero components. The *Hamming distance* between two codewords is the number of digits in which they differ. The *minimum distance* of the code C is defined as the minimum Hamming distance between all pairs of distinct codewords in C. The minimum distance d of the linear code C is the weight of the codeword (other than the all-zero) of minimum Hamming weight.

Let $C = [n, \gamma, d]$ denote a linear code of length n, having size γ and minimum distance d.

A set of k positions $\{i_1, i_2, \ldots, i_k\}$ is said to be an *information set* of the code C if for every choice of all the k digits $a_{i_1}, a_{i_2}, \ldots a_{i_k}$, where $a_{i_j} \in [0, m_{i_j})$, there is a unique codeword $< x_1, x_2, \ldots, x_n >$ such that $x_{i_1} = a_{i_1}, x_{i_2} = a_{i_2}, \ldots, x_{i_k} = a_{i_k}$. In other words, a code has an information set of size k if there are k positions that assume all their possible values over the set of all the codewords of C. A code with an information set is called a *systematic* code. The size of a systematic code is given by $\gamma = \Pi_{j=1}^{k} m_{i_j}$.

Given a set of n radices $m_1, \ldots, m_n$ and an integer γ, the main problem in coding theory is to determine the maximum value d such that there exists a code $C = [n, \gamma, d]$. Namely, a code of minimum distance d is able to detect at least all non-zero error n-tuples with weight at most $d - 1$, and also corrects all error n-tuples of weight $\leq \lfloor (d-1)/2 \rfloor$.

In this context, the following result is crucial [8].

Singleton bound : Given a linear code C of radices $m_1, m_2, \ldots, m_n$ and of size γ such that $\max \left\{ \Pi_{i=1}^{k} m_{j_i} \right\} \geq \gamma > \max \left\{ \Pi_{i=1}^{k-1} m_{j_i} \right\}$, the minimum distance d of such a code C yields $d \leq n - k + 1$.

A code C whose minimum distance satisfies the equality of the Singleton bound, i.e., $d = n - k + 1$, is said to be a *maximum distance separable* (MDS) code.

It can be shown that: (i) a code is an MDS code if and only if any k digits represent γ different n-tuples, and (ii) every MDS code is a systematic code.

3 Residue Codes

Consider a set of n *pairwise primes*, $m_1, m_2, \ldots, m_k, m_{k+1}, \ldots, m_n$, called *moduli*, and the associated space $S = m_1 \times m_2 \times \ldots \times m_n$ of $M = \Pi_{i=1}^{n} m_i$ n-tuples. Let the *residue representation* of an integer X in the *Residue Number System* (RNS) of pairwise prime radices $m_1, \ldots, m_n$ be defined as the n-tuple $< x_1, x_2, \ldots, x_n >$ such that $x_i \equiv X \bmod m_i$. Then, applying the Chinese Remainder Theorem [2], each n-tuple of the vector space S can be uniquely associated with the residue representations of an integer $X \in [0, M)$.

For an arbitrary value of k, $1 \leq k \leq n$, the *redundant pairwise prime residue code* (or simply, *residue code*),

C, is the subset of S consisting of the residue representations of the integers in $[0, M_I - 1]$ where $M_I = \Pi_{i=1}^k m_i$. We note the following.

- Each codeword of C has length n and C has size M_I;
- Given two codewords X and Y of C, the codewords $X + Y$ and $X - Y$ belongs to C if $X + Y < M_I$ and $X - Y > 0$, respectively. By this property the redundant residue codes are termed *semi-linear* codes [7]. Under these restrictions, all the properties of the linear codes also hold for the semi-linear codes.
- The moduli $m_1, \ldots, m_k$, are necessary and sufficient to represent the integers in $[0, M_I - 1]$. These moduli are called *non-redundant*. The remaining $n - k$ moduli form the set of *redundant* moduli. By this terminology, the code C is said to be associated with a *redundant residue number system*.
- Let $M_I = \Pi_{i=1}^k m_i$ and $M_R = \Pi_{i=k+1}^n m_i$ be, respectively, the product of the non-redundant and redundant moduli of the RNS of radices $m_1, \ldots, m_n$. Given a systematic residue code C consisting of the residue representations of all the integers in $[0, M_I)$, the minimum distance of the code C is d if and only if, for $1 \le j_i \le n$,

$$\max \left\{ \Pi_{i=1}^d m_{j_i} \right\} > M_R \ge \max \left\{ \Pi_{i=1}^{d-1} m_{j_i} \right\}.$$

A sufficient condition to construct an MDS residue code is given below.

Fact 1 *[2, 7] Let us consider the radices $m_1, \ldots, m_n$ sorted in the increasing order such that $m_1 < m_2 < \ldots < m_n$. A residue code C is an MDS code of minimum distance d, for $1 \le d \le n - 1$, if $m_{n-d+2}, \ldots, m_n$ are its redundant moduli.*

The following proposition will be crucial in our new solution to the disk allocation problem.

Proposition 1 *Given an RNS of radices $m_1, \ldots, m_n$, and the residue code $C = [n, M_I, d]$ whose codewords correspond to the residue representations of the integers in $[0, M_I)$, where $M_I = \Pi_{i=1}^k m_i$, let C_j be the code consisting of the residue representations in S corresponding to the integers in the range $[jM_I, (j+1)M_I - 1]$, for $0 \le j \le \frac{M}{M_I} - 1$. Then, $C_0 = C, C_1, \ldots, C_{\frac{M}{M_I}-1}$ form a partition of S.*

Moreover, for each pair X_1, X_2 of codewords in C_j, $d(X_1, X_2) = d(X', X'')$, where X', X'' are two codewords of C such that $X_1 = X' + jM_I$ and $X_2 = X'' + jM_I$. Therefore,

Corollary 1 *For $0 \le j \le \frac{M}{M_I} - 1$, the jth partition is given by $C_j = [n, M_I, d]$.*

3.1 Non-Pairwise Prime Residue Codes

Let us now consider a set of n non-pairwise primes radices (or, moduli) $m_1, m_2, \ldots, m_k, m_{k+1}, \ldots, m_n$. Let $P = \Pi_{i=1}^n m_i$ and $M = \text{l.c.m.}(m_1, m_2, \ldots, m_n)$ be, respectively, the product and the least common multiple of these moduli.

Again, let the n-dimensional space $S = m_1 \times m_2 \times \ldots \times m_n$ be the set of P n-tuples $< x_1, \ldots, x_n >$ where $x_i \in [0, m_i)$. Unlike the case for pairwise prime radices, some n-tuples of S do not correspond to the residue representation of any integer in the associated RNS. Indeed, while S consists of P strings, only the integers in $[0, M)$ have a residue representation in the RNS associated with the moduli $m_1, m_2, \ldots, m_n$, according to a general form of the Chinese Remainder Theorem [9]. Precisely, let $d_{ij} = \text{g.c.d}(m_i, m_j)$ be the greatest common divisor of the moduli m_i and m_j. Then, only those n-tuples which satisfy the congruences

$$x_i \equiv x_j \mod d_{ij}, \text{ for } 1 \le i, j \le n \qquad (1)$$

are *valid* representations in such an RNS.

The M valid residue representations, that is the residue representations of the integers in $[0, M)$, form a subset of S and they define, in a very natural way, a *non-pairwise prime residue code*. For such codes, the only way to compute their minimum distance is to generate the code itself. Since we need to know explicitly the code distance, we introduce next a new family of residue codes with non-pairwise prime radices.

4 Redundant Non-Pairwise Prime Residue Codes

Definition 1 *Let $m_1, m_2, \ldots, m_n$ be the non-pairwise prime radices of the residue number system (RNS), and let the first k moduli be the* non-redundant *radices while the remaining $n - k$ moduli are the* redundant *radices. The redundant non-pairwise prime residue code, C, associated with such an RNS consists of $\Lambda = \text{l.c.m}(m_1, m_2, \ldots m_k)$ number of n-tuples, $< x_1, \ldots, x_n >$, such that $x_i \equiv X \mod m_i$ and $X \in [0, \Lambda)$.*

Let $\wp$ and τ denote, respectively, the l.c.m. of the redundant moduli and the product of all the moduli. Moreover, let μ and ν be, respectively, the l.c.m. of $d - 1$ and d radices of the RNS; and let $\overline{\mu}$ (resp., $\overline{\nu}$) be the l.c.m. of the $n - d + 1$ (resp., $n - d$) radices not belonging to μ (resp., ν).

Theorem 1 *Given the radices $m_1, \ldots, m_n$ and the non-redundant moduli $m_1, \ldots, m_k$, the code C consisting of the residue representations of $\Lambda =$*

l.c.m.$(m_1, m_2, \ldots m_k)$ *integers has the minimum distance d if and only if the following relation holds:*

$$max\left(\frac{\nu}{\gcd(\nu, \overline{\nu})}\right) > \frac{\wp}{\gcd(\Lambda, \wp)} \geq max\left(\frac{\mu}{\gcd(\mu, \overline{\mu})}\right). \tag{2}$$

By the Singleton bound, an MDS code satisfies $d = n - k + 1$. Thus we have:

Corollary 2 *A simple way to construct an MDS code* $C = [n, \Lambda, n - k + 1]$ *is as follows:*

- *choose k on-redundant moduli* $m_1, \ldots, m_k$ *such that* $\Lambda = l.c.m(m_1, \ldots, m_k)$ *and* $\Lambda > \frac{\Pi_{i=1}^{k} m_i}{min m_j}$, *for* $1 \leq j \leq k$;

- *choose* $n - k$ *redundant moduli* $m_{k+1}, \ldots, m_n$ *in such a way that*

  - $\wp = l.c.m(m_{k+1}, \ldots, m_n)$ *and* $\wp > \frac{\Pi_{i=k+1}^{n} m_i}{min m_j}$, *for* $1 \leq j \leq k$; *and*

  - $g.c.d.(\Lambda, \wp) = 1$.

The following two propositions will be useful in the rest of the paper.

Proposition 2 *Given a set of n non-pairwise prime radices* $m_1, \ldots, m_k, m_{k+1}, \ldots, m_n$ *such that* $m_1, \ldots, m_k$ *and* $m_{k+1}, \ldots, m_n$ *are, respectively, the redundant and the non-redundant moduli, let* $C = [n, \Lambda, d]$ *be the redundant non-pairwise prime code associated with these radices. Recalling that* τ *and* Λ *denote the least common multiple, respectively, of all the radices and of the non-redundant moduli, all the integers in* $[0, \tau - 1]$ *can be partitioned into* $\frac{\tau}{\Lambda}$ *codes, each having the same size and the same distance as* C. *Precisely, for* $0 \leq j \leq \frac{\tau}{\Lambda} - 1$, *the partition is* $C_j = [n, \Lambda, d]$ *where* $C_0 = C$.

The remaining non-valid n-tuples of the space S associated with the radices $m_1, \ldots, m_n$ do not correspond to any residue integer representations. In order to partition them let us introduce three new operations: sum, difference, and multiple-sum.

The *sum U* of two n-tuples $t = < t_1, \ldots, t_n >$ and $w = < w_1, \ldots, w_n >$ is defined as the n-tuple $U = t + w = < u_1, \ldots u_n >$ such that $u_i = (t_i + w_i) \bmod m_i$. Similarly, the difference V of t and w is given as $U = t - w = < u_1, \ldots u_n >$ such that $u_i = (t_i - w_i) \bmod m_i$. Finally, for a given an n-tuple $t \in S$, the multiple-sum of a set C of n-tuples is defined as the subset $C[t] = \{X + t | X \in C\}$, obtained by summing t over all the n-tuples of C.

Proposition 3 *Let* $T = \{t_0, t_1, \ldots, t_{\frac{P}{\tau}-1}\}$ *be a set of* $\frac{P}{\tau}$ n-tuples such that

- t_0 *is the all-zero codeword;*

- *for every pair* $t_i, t_j \in T$, $t_i - t_j \notin C$ *or* $t_j - t_i \notin C$.

From the code $C = [n, \Lambda, d]$, *we construct the subsets* C_j *consisting of the residue representations of the integers in the interval* $[j\Lambda, (j+1)\Lambda - 1]$ *where* $0 \leq j \leq \tau/\Lambda - 1$. *Then the space* S *can be partitioned into* $\frac{P}{\Lambda}$ *subsets* $C_j[t_i] = t_j + C_j$, *for* $0 \leq j \leq \tau/\Lambda - 1$ *and* $0 \leq i \leq P/\tau - 1$. *Each subset can be interpreted as a code and, in particular,* $C_j[t_i] = [n, \Lambda, d]$. *Note that* $C_j[t_0] = C_j$, *for* $0 \leq j \leq \tau/\Lambda - 1$.

4.1 An Illustrative Example

Consider the redundant residue number system (RNS) associated with the non-pairwise prime radices, $m_1 = 3, m_2 = 6, m_3 = 5$. Let m_1, m_2 be the non-redundant moduli while m_3 be the redundant one. According to our definitions, $P = 90, \tau = 30$, and $\Lambda = 6$. In words, the space S consists of $3 \times 6 \times 5$ number of 3-tuples, but the RNS's associated with the moduli m_1, m_2, m_3 and m_1, m_2, can represent the integers in $[0, 29]$ and $[0, 5]$, respectively. Let the code $C = [3, 6, 2]$ consist of the residue representations of the integers in $[0, 5]$ in the RNS of radices $m_1 = 3, m_2 = 6, m_3 = 5$. That is, $C = \{< 0, 0, 0 >, < 1, 1, 1 >, < 2, 2, 2 >, < 0, 3, 3 >, < 1, 4, 4 >, < 2, 5, 0 >\}$.

From Proposition 2, the valid residue representations are partitioned into $\frac{90}{6} = 15$ codes. Precisely, code $C_j[0, 0, 0]$ corresponds to the residue representations of the integers in the range $[6j, 6(j+1)-1]$, for $0 \leq j \leq 4$. In particular,
$C_1 = \{< 0, 0, 1 >, < 1, 1, 2 >, < 2, 2, 3 >, < 0, 3, 4 >, < 1, 4, 0 >, < 2, 5, 1 >\}$,
$C_2 = \{< 0, 0, 2 >, < 1, 1, 3 >, < 2, 2, 4 >, < 0, 3, 0 >, < 1, 4, 1 >, < 2, 5, 2 >\}$,
$C_3 = \{< 0, 0, 3 >, < 1, 1, 4 >, < 2, 2, 0 >, < 0, 3, 1 >, < 1, 4, 2 >, < 2, 5, 3 >\}$, and
$C_4 = \{< 0, 0, 4 >, < 1, 1, 0 >, < 2, 2, 1 >, < 0, 3, 2 >, < 1, 4, 3 >, < 2, 5, 4 >\}$.

Now let $T = \{t_0 = < 0, 0, 0 >, t_1 = < 1, 0, 3 >, t_2 = < 2, 3, 0 >\}$ which verifies the conditions in Proposition 3. Namely, any of the following 3-tuple, $t_1, t_2, t_1 - t_2 = < 2, 3, 3 >$ and $t_2 - t_1 = < 1, 3, 2 >$, does not belong to C.

Hence, the codes $C_j[1, 0, 3] = \{< 1, 0, 3 > + C_j[0, 0, 0]\}$ and $C_j[2, 3, 0] = \{< 2, 3, 0 > + C_j[0, 0, 0]\}$, where $0 \leq j \leq 4$, partition the remaining n-tuples of S.

124

5 A Disk Allocation Strategy Based on Codes

Let us now consider the problem of allocating an n-attribute non-uniform cartesian product file F to multiple disks.

Throughout this section, m_i will denote the domain of the i-th attribute of F. Let a bucket of F be characterized by a string $< x_1, x_2, \ldots, x_n >$ of length n, where $x_i \in [0, m_i - 1]$, and let the strings of F form the n-tuple space $S = m_1 \times m_2 \times \ldots m_n$ of size $M = \Pi_{i=1}^n m_i$.

To distribute the M buckets of the file F into a multiple disk system, we partition the space S according to a given code C, called the *seed code*, associated with the RNS of radices $m_1, m_2, \ldots, m_n$, as outlined in the procedure below.

Procedure Decluster $(F, C = [n, z, d],$ $D = M/z)$

- Based on the seed code C, partition S into $\frac{M}{z}$ code-partitions, according to

  - Proposition 1, if the domains of the attributes of F are pairwise prime,

  - Proposition 3, if the domains of the attributes of F are non-pairwise prime;

- assign each code-partition to a distinct disk. Altogether D disks are required.

Theorem 2 *Applied to a file F the Decluster procedure based on a seed code $C = [n, z, d]$, every partial match query q with at most $d - 1$ unspecified attributes yields a constant response time.*

If the domains of the attributes of the file F are pairwise prime, the following result holds.

Theorem 3 *Let $m_1, \ldots, m_n$ be n pairwise prime moduli, sorted in the increasing order. Let M_I and M_R be the product of the leftmost $n - d + 1$ and rightmost $d - 1$ moduli, respectively. If we are given a file F whose ith attribute ranges in m_i and also given the MDS residue code $C = [n, M_I, d]$ as the seed code, then assuming an M_R-disk system, the disk allocation strategy obtained by applying the Decluster procedure to the file F is strictly-optimal for every partial match query q.*

Proof. For the query with at most $d - 1$ unspecified attributes, the result follows immediately from Theorem 2.

For the general case, let q be an arbitrary query whose attributes $q_{i_1}, \ldots, q_{i_u}$ are unspecified, and the remaining $n - u$ attributes are $q_{i_{u+1}} = a_{i_{u+1}}, q_{i_{u+2}} = a_{i_{u+2}}, \ldots q_{i_n} = a_{i_n}$.

By the Chinese Remainder Theorem, the $(n - u)$-tuple $a_{i_{u+1}}, a_{i_{u+2}}, \ldots, a_{i_n}$ corresponds, in the residue number systems of radices $m_{i_{u+1}}, m_{i_{u+2}}, \ldots, m_{i_n}$, to the residue representation of an integer X in the range $[0, M_s = \Pi_{j=u+1}^n m_{i_j})$.

Considered the residue number system associated with the radices $m_1, \ldots, m_n$, the n-tuples, associated with the buckets qualifying for q, correspond to the residue representations of the integers $X + kM_s$, with $0 \leq k < \frac{M}{M_s}$. In fact, for any two integers $X + k_1 M_s$ and $X + k_2 M_s$, with $0 \leq k_1, k_2 < \frac{M}{M_s}$, it holds $(X + k_1 M_s) \bmod m_{i_j} = (X + k_2 M_s) \bmod m_{i_j} = X \bmod m_{i_j}$, for $u + 1 \leq j \leq n$ because $M_s \bmod m_{i_j} = 0$.

Recalling that, by Proposition 1, the code C_j associated to the jth disk, with $0 \leq j \leq M_R - 1$, consists of the residue representations of the integers $[jM_I, (j+1)M_I)$, the buckets whose strings correspond to the integers $X + kM_s$, with $jM_I \leq X + kM_s \leq (j + 1)M_I - 1$ belong to the jth disk. Hence, at most $\left\lceil \frac{M_I}{M_s} \right\rceil$ buckets qualify for q in each disk, that is the strategy has $\left\lceil \frac{M_I}{M_s} \right\rceil$ response time.

Now, to prove that the disk allocation strategy is strictly-optimal, observed that $N(q)$ is the product of the domains of the d unspecified attributes, we have:

$$\left\lceil \frac{M_I}{M_s} \right\rceil = \left\lceil \frac{M}{M_s M_R} \right\rceil = \left\lceil \frac{\frac{M}{M_s}}{M_R} \right\rceil = \left\lceil \frac{N(q)}{M_R} \right\rceil.$$

Since an MDS residue code of minimum distance d can be obtained for every value of d, for $1 \leq d \leq n$, it holds:

Corollary 3 *Let $m_1, \ldots, m_n$ be n pairwise prime moduli, sorted in increasing order. For $1 \leq d \leq n$, using $M_R = \Pi_{i=n-d+2}^n (m_i)$ disks, there exists a strictly-optimal disk allocation strategy for every query q.*

Therefore, whatever is the number D of disks available, we can apply the Decluster procedure perhaps using a subset of the available disks. In fact, let $m_1, \ldots, m_n$ be the n pairwise prime domains, sorted in increasing order, of the attributes of a file F. Let D, with $\Pi_{i=n-d+1}^n (m_i) < D \leq \Pi_{i=n-d+2}^n (m_i)$, be the number of disks available. Then, utilizing $\Pi_{i=n-d+2}^n (m_i)$ disks, a strictly-optimal disk allocation method is obtained immediately applying the Decluster procedure based on the MDS residue seed code $C = [n, \Pi_{i=1}^{n-d+1} m_i, d]$ consisting of the residue representation of the integers in $[0, \Pi_{i=1}^{n-d+1} m_i - 1]$.

Before proceeding further, let us define a disk allocation strategy as β-*strict optimal* if β is the ratio $\left\lceil \frac{R(q)}{R^*(q)} \right\rceil$ of the response time $R(q)$ and the response time of the strictly-optimal disk allocation strategy in a D-disk system, that is, $R^*(d) = \lceil \frac{N(q)}{D} \rceil$. In other words, a β-strict optimal disk allocation strategy is at most β times slower than a strictly-optimal disk allocation strategy.

Corollary 4 *Given a D-disk system, and given an n-attribute file F, whose ith attribute ranges in m_i, with $m_1, \ldots, m_n$ be pairwise prime, sorted in the increasing order, let $\Pi_{i=n-d+1}^{n}(m_i) < D \leq \Pi_{i=n-d+2}^{n}(m_i)$. The disk allocation strategy on $\Pi_{i=n-d+2}^{n}(m_i)$ disks, obtained by applying the Decluster procedure, based on the MDS residue seed code $C = [n, \Pi_{i=n-d+2}^{n}(m_i), d]$, is $\left\lceil \frac{D}{\Pi_{i=n-d+2}^{n}(m_i)} \right\rceil$-strict optimal.*

Proof. Immediately, since $\left\lceil \frac{N(q)}{M_R} \right\rceil = \left\lceil \frac{N(q)D}{M_R D} \right\rceil \leq \left\lceil \frac{D}{M_R} \right\rceil \left\lceil \frac{N(q)}{D} \right\rceil$.

Finally, for files with attributes whose domains non-pairwise prime, we derive the following result.

Theorem 4 *Let $m_1, \ldots, m_n$ be n non-pairwise prime moduli, sorted in the increasing order, and $P = \Pi_{i=1}^{n} m_i$. Given a file F whose ith attribute ranges in m_i, given the MDS redundant residue code $C = [n, \Lambda, d]$ as the seed code, and assume a $\frac{P}{\Lambda}$-disk system. Applying the Decluster procedure, for each query q with at most $d - 1$ unspecified attributes at most 1 bucket is returned from each disk. Moreover, each query q with s specified attributes, $q_{i_1}, \ldots, q_{i_s}$, has at most $\left\lceil \frac{\Lambda}{M_s} \right\rceil$ response time, with $M_s = l.c.m.\Pi_{j=1}^{s} m_{i_j}$. Such a disk allocation strategy is $\left\lceil \frac{\Pi_{j=1}^{s} m_{i_j}}{l.c.m.\Pi_{j=1}^{s} m_{i_j}} \right\rceil$- strict optimal.*

5.1 Capturing Dynamic Scenario

Let us see how the coding theory approach can work when either the number of available disks or the number of the attributes of the file to be distributed change dynamically. The *relocation* process is a measure of the buckets redistribution required by the dynamic solution. Moreover, if each moved bucket can be delivered during the relocation process only to a subset of the disks in the entire system, we say that the relocation process preserves *locality*.

For simplicity, in what follows we only consider the case of pairwise prime attribute domains. Given an n-attribute file F whose ith attribute ranges in m_i, with $m_1 < m_2 < \ldots < m_n$, let the MDS redundant residue code $C = [n, M_I = \Pi_{i=1}^{n-d+1} m_i, d]$ be the seed code used to initially distribute F on $M_R = \Pi_{i=n-d+2}^{n} m_i$ disks.

Let us first concentrate on the case that the number of the available disks changes from M_R to $M_R m_{n-d+1}$. F can be declustered according to the seed code $C^+ = [n, \frac{M_I}{m_{n-d+1}}, d+1]$ which assignes less buckets to each disks. Now, according to Proposition 1, the buckets whose associated strings correspond to the residue representations of the integers in $[j\frac{M_I}{m_{n-d+1}}, (j+1)\frac{M_I}{m_{n-d+1}} - 1]$ will be assigned to the jth disk, with $0 \leq j \leq M_R m_{n-d+1} - 1$. Since initially the buckets whose associated strings correspond to the residue representations of the integers in $[jM_I, (j+1)M_I - 1]$ were assigned to the same disk j, with $0 \leq j \leq M_I - 1$, it means that each initial code is separated among m_{n-d+1} disks. In other words, each disk d_r, with $0 \leq r \leq M_R - 1$, initially in the disk-system, is replaced by the $d_{rm_{n-d+1}+j}$ disks, with $0 \leq j \leq m_{n-d+1} - 1$, on which the buckets initially in d_r are spreaded out. Hence, the relocation process preserves the bucket locality. It is noteworthy that the disk allocation remains strictly-optimal for the new set of disks. Moreover, in the new system, since the code distance increases from d to $d + 1$, the partial match queries with d unspecified attributes will return exactly one bucket from each disk. In other words, all the capabilities of the larger disk system are exploited.

Viceversa, if the number of disks available will reduce from M_R to $\frac{M_R}{m_{n-d+2}}$, the new seed code $C^- = [n, M_I m_{n-d+2}, d - 1]$ will be used to decluster the file F. The buckets distribution changes in the opposite way than the previous case. That is, the buckets distribute in m_{n-d+2} consecutive disks in the initial disk system are now collapsed in a single disk of the new disk system. Again, the disk allocation remains strictly-optimal although only the partial math queries with up to $d - 2$ will now exhibit constant response time.

In summary, if the number of available disks changes, some buckets must be relocated. Fortunately, the relocation involves only adjacent disks and can be organized efficiently and in parallel for all the disks initially in the system. However, as a drawback, note that the number of the disks must increase or decrease by a multiplicative factor. We cannot just add or subtract few disks.

Let us then concentrate on the case that the number of the attributes of the file F changes, while the number of the available disks remains the same. This is the case when we need to make search according to a new attribute of F or a previously used attribute is become obsolete.

Suppose first that the n-attribute file F must be searched according to a new file attribute, m_{n+1} Looking at the file with major detail, each bucket $a_1, \ldots, a_n$ will be decomposed into m_{n+1} buckets $a_1, \ldots, a_n, x_{n+1}$ with x_{n+1} assuming all values in the range $0, \ldots, m_{n+1} - 1$. So, the number of buckets increases from $M = \Pi_{i=1}^{n} m_i$ up to $M' = M m_{n+1}$. Since the number of disks is unchanged, we must assign more buckets to each disk. Thus, assumed $C = [n, M_I, d]$ be the seed code F was distributed according to, the new code will be $C^\dagger = [n+1, M_I m_{n+1}, t]$, with $t \leq d$.

In order to describe the relocation process, observe that, given the residue representation of the integer X, with $0 \leq X \leq M_I$, $a_1, \ldots, a_n$, the residue representations $a_1, \ldots, a_n, x_{n+1}$, with $0 \leq x_{n+1} \leq m_{n+1} - 1$, correspond to the integers $X + kM$, with $M = \Pi_{i=1}^{n} m_i$ and $0 \leq k \leq m_{n+1} - 1$. Therefore, according to Proposition 1, a disk allocation method based on the seed code $C^\dagger$ requires that the buckets originated by each single bucket are redistributed among the entire disk system. In this case, no locality property can be claimed for the relocation process. Moreover, the response time is optimal, but it is longer according to the new code distance t.

Finally, reading backward the solution for the case that the number of attributes of F increase, we got a solution for the case that the number of the attributes of F decrease that starts with a code $C^\dagger$ and obtains a new code C. Hence, even in this case the relocation process involves all the disk system.

6 Conclusion

In this paper, we have discussed the disk allocation problem for non-uniform cartesian product files. Based on a large and flexible class of maximum distance separable codes, the residue codes, we have derived strictly-optimal allocation methods for every query q for the case of attribute domains which are pairwise prime. Strictly optimal allocation methods can be derived almost independent of the number of disks available. A new family of residue codes, called the *redundant non-pairwise prime residue codes*, have been introduced to deal with files whose attributes have non-pairwise prime domains.

References

[1] K.A.S. Abdel-Ghaffar, A. El Abbadi, "Optimal Disk Allocation for Partial Match Queries", *ACM Trans. on Database Systems*, Vol. 18, No.1, March 1993, pp. 132-156.

[2] F. Barsi, P. Maestrini, "Error Correcting Properties of Redundant Residue Number Systems", *IEEE Trans. on Computers*, Vol. 22 , 1973, pp.307-315.

[3] F. Barsi, P. Maestrini, "Error Codes in Residue Number Systems with Non-Pairwise-Prime Moduli", *Information and Control*, Vol. 46, No. 1, July 1980, pp. 16-25.

[4] H.C. Du, J.S. Sobolewski, "Disk Allocation for Cartesian Product Files" *ACM Trans. on Database Systems*, Vol. 7, No. 1, March 1982, pp. 82-101.

[5] C. Faloutsos, D. Metaxas, "Disk Allocation Methods using Error Correcting Codes", *IEEE Trans. on Computers*, Vol. 40, No. 8, August 1991, pp. 907-913.

[6] M.H. Kim, S. Pramanik, "Optimal File Distribution for Partial Match retrieval" in *Proceedings of the ACM-SIGMOD Int'l Conference on Management of Data*, Chicago, 1988, pp. 173-182.

[7] H. Khrisna, K. Lin and J. Sun, "A Coding Theory Approach to Error Control in Redundant Residue Number Systems – Part I: Theory and Single Correction", *IEEE Trans. on Circuits and Systems, II*, Vol. 39, No. 1, January 1992, pp. 8-17.

[8] F. J. MacWilliams and N. J. A. Sloane, *The Theory of Error-Correcting Codes, Parts I and II*, North-Holland, New York, 1977.

[9] O. Ore, "The General Chinese Remainder Theorem", *Amer. Math. Monthly*, 1952, pp. 365-370.

An Offline Algorithm for Dimension-Bound Analysis

Paul A.S. Ward
Shoshin Distributed Systems Group
Department of Computer Science
University of Waterloo
pasward@styx.uwaterloo.ca

Abstract

The vector-clock size necessary to characterize causality in a distributed computation is bounded by the dimension of the partial order induced by that computation. In an arbitrary distributed computation the dimension can be as large as the width, which in turn can be as large as the number of processes in the computation. Most vector clock algorithms, and all online ones, simply use a vector of size equal to the number of processes. In practice the dimension may be much smaller. It is the purpose of this paper to provide empirical evidence that the dimension of various distributed computations is often substantially smaller than the number of processes. We have found that typical distributed computations, with as many as 300 processes, have dimension less than 10. To achieve this quantification we developed various theorems and algorithms which we also describe.

1 Motivation

An important problem in distributed systems is monitoring and debugging distributed computations. This problem is hard because events in the computation can be concurrent. The events form a partial order, not a total one. While displaying this partial order can be a useful debugging aid, for any non-trivial computation it is not possible to display the whole partial order. As a result, distributed debugging systems such as POET [13] need to provide much more than just a drawing. It is necessary to intelligently scroll around the display [20], search for interesting patterns [10], compute differences between subsequent executions of a computation [8], detect race conditions [23], determine appropriate abstractions to provide higher level views [12], and so on. To perform these operations it is frequently necessary to determine event precedence. That is, given two events, it is necessary to be able to efficiently determine if they are ordered or if they are concurrent.

Event precedence may be determined in several ways, depending on how the partial order is represented. If the partial order is stored as a directed acyclic graph, then precedence determination is a constant time operation. This is because the partial order is transitively closed and so there is an edge between any two events that are ordered. However, the space consumption for this method is unacceptably high. If, on the other hand, the transitive reduction of the partial order is used, much less space is needed. Unfortunately, this requires a (potentially quite slow) search operation on the graph to determine precedence. To compensate for this deficiency a vector clock [3, 15] is associated with each event. If the processes in which the events occur are known, then it is possible to determine precedence with vector clocks in constant time.

The size of a vector clock necessary to capture causality is bounded by the dimension of the partial order induced by the computation. Charron-Bost [2] has shown that the dimension can be as large as the width, and all online vector clocks developed to date require a vector with size equal to the number of processes (which forms an upper bound on the width). Since we need to associate such a vector clock with every event in the computation, we are substantially constrained in the number of processes that we can observe. In POET we have found that due to this limitation we can handle at most a few-hundred processes.

The Charron-Bost proof, while true, relies on a very specific distributed computation. It was our belief, and this paper provides empirical evidence to support it, that this computation, or variations on it, simply does not occur in practice, and that those computations that do occur in practice tend to have a much lower dimension than the number of processes involved. In this paper we provide an algorithm for estimating the dimension of the partial order induced by a distributed computation. While we do not yet have a bound on the quality of the algorithm, the results we present show that the dimension of typical computations is substantially smaller than the number of processes involved in the computation. It is therefore possible to use a much

128

smaller vector clock than is used at present for any offline analysis. We are still working on developing an online vector clock whose size is bounded by dimension, not by the number of processes.

In the remainder of this paper we will specify first the formal model of distributed computation and why this leads to a problem with vector-clock size. In Section 3 we will describe the theorems and algorithms we developed to determine the dimension bound of distributed computations. We then discuss the results we achieved from this after executing the algorithms over several computations in various parallel, concurrent and distributed environments. Finally we indicate what work remains to be completed to achieve online vector clocks whose size is dimension-bounded

2 Background

We use the standard model of distributed systems, initially defined by Lamport [14]: a distributed system is a system comprising multiple sequential processes communicating via message passing. Each sequential process consists of three types of events, send, receive and unary, totally ordered within the process. A *distributed computation* is the partial order formed by the "happened before" relation over the union of all of the events across all of the processes. We will refer to the set of all events with E, the set of events within a given process by E_i (where i uniquely identifies the process) and an individual event by e_i^j (where i identifies the process and j identifies the event's position within the process). Then the Lamport "happened before" relation ($\rightarrow \subseteq E \times E$) is defined as the smallest transitive relation satisfying

1. $e_i^j \rightarrow e_i^l$ if $j < l$

2. $e_i^j \rightarrow e_k^l$ if e_i^j is a send event and e_k^l is the corresponding receive event

Events are concurrent if they are not in the "happened before" relation.

$$e_i^j \parallel e_k^l \iff e_i^j \not\rightarrow e_k^l \wedge e_k^l \not\rightarrow e_i^j \qquad (1)$$

Each event in the computation has an associated vector clock for event precedence determination. Since we are working in a debugging context, the vector clock is not a part of the computation. Rather, it is computed separately by the debugging agent. We must now describe some partial-order terminology in order to explain why these vectors are of size equal to the number of processes in the computation.

2.1 Partial-order terminology

The following terminology is due to Trotter [21]. A *strict partial-order* (or partially-ordered set, or poset) is a pair

(X, P) where X is a finite set[1] and P is an irreflexive,[2] antisymmetric and transitive binary relation on X. A *subposet*, $(Y, P|_Y)$, is a poset whose set Y is a subset of X, and whose relation $P|_Y$ is the restriction of P to the subset. An *antichain* is any completely unordered poset. The *width* of a poset is the longest antichain contained in that poset. In the context of a distributed computation, the width must be less than or equal to the number of processes.

An *extension*, (X, Q), of a partial order (X, Q) is any partial order that satisfies

$$(x, y) \in P \Rightarrow (x, y) \in Q$$

If Q is a total order, then the extension is called a *linear extension*. If (Y, R) is an extension of the subposet $(Y, P|_Y)$ of (X, P), then (Y, R) is said to be a *subextension* of (X, P). A *realizer* of a partial order is any set of linear extensions whose intersection forms the partial order. The *dimension* of a partial order is the cardinality of the smallest possible realizer.

Finally, we say that "y is an *immediate predecessor* of z" or "z is an *immediate successor* of y" if y precedes z and there is no intermediate element in the partial order between y and z.

$$y <: z \iff y \rightarrow z \wedge (\not\exists_w y \rightarrow w \wedge w \rightarrow z) \qquad (2)$$

2.2 The vector-clock size problem

There are two reasons why vector clocks have size equal to the number of processes in the distributed computation. The first reason is algorithm availability. The best online algorithms for vector clocks are typically Fidge/Mattern variants [3, 15], which require a vector of size equal to the number of processes. While there is an alternate, the Ore timestamp (to be discussed in Section 2.3), whose size is bounded by the dimension of the partial order, it is an offline technique.

The second reason is more theoretical. To capture precedence in a partial order it is necessary to have a vector (or equivalent) of size equal to the dimension of that partial order [16]. Further, the dimension of a partial order can be as large as the width [21]. Crown S_n^0 is the standard example of such a partial order, and is shown in Figure 1(a). By shifting each B_i element of this partial order we create the distributed computation shown in Figure 1(b). While this computation does not violate our model of distributed

---

[1] Since we are modeling distributed computations, all of the sets will be finite.

[2] If P is reflexive, it is a *partial order* rather than a *strict partial order*. The difference is not an important point in our context. The "happened before" relation, as defined by Lamport [14], is irreflexive, and so we use strict partial orders.

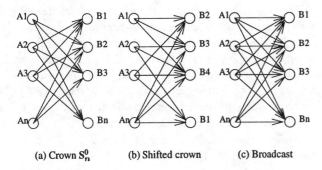

(a) Crown S_n^0 (b) Shifted crown   (c) Broadcast

Figure 1. Crown and broadcast partial orders

computation, it is unusual in that it requires both multicast send operations and corresponding multi-receive operations. While both of these operations do have real systems counterparts, it is important to emphasize that neither is necessary. Charron-Bost's study [2] relies only on point-to-point computation, though the sample computation produced is, in essence, the same as that of the Figure 1(b). Both correspond to all processes sending a message to all other processes, with the exception of their left neighbour.

The limitation of the Charron-Bost proof is precisely in the nature of what the crown S_n^0 distributed computation represents. In practical terms, this is not a realistic distributed computation. In addition, the more likely computation, in which each process broadcasts a message to all other processes (shown in Figure 1(c)), has dimension 2. It is therefore the objective of this paper to determine a bound on the dimension of actual distributed computations, rather than theoretical ones that are doubtful to ever occur in practice. This bound would represent a more accurate requirement for the size of timestamps necessary to capture causality.

Before we describe how we compute the dimension bound, and what our results are for typical distributed computations, we wish to justify that there are in practice alternate timestamps that are more compact than Fidge/Mattern vector clocks. We will also discuss work related to our own.

2.3 Ore timestamps

There is an alternate timestamp to the Fidge/Mattern vector clock, whose size is bounded by the dimension, not the width, of the partial order. This is the Ore timestamp [16]. Given a realizer for partial order (X, P), the timestamp associated with each $x \in X$ is simply the vector of its position in the various linear extensions that form the realizer. It is then straightforward to see that causality between two events, x and y, can be determined by comparing the various elements in the vectors of the two events. If they are all less, then precedence is established. If some are less and

some are greater then concurrency is established. While this timestamp is offline, and it is beyond the scope of this paper to correct this deficiency, it does indicate that timestamps whose size is bounded by the dimension, not the width, of the partial order are not only possible in theory but exist in practice.

2.4 Related work

Before proceeding to describe how we computed dimension bounds, we will briefly describe some of the work related to our own. There are essentially two categories of related work. The first group is those who are developing systems for visualizing parallel and distributed systems in a process-time fashion. Such work includes GOLD [17], ParaGraph [9] and our own system, POET [13]. Other than our own, these systems tend to use vector-clocks or variants within the computation, rather than have the information sent to a central server which computes the vector-timestamps for visualization purposes. These systems tend to take the approach of just using what is presently available, and not being concerned with substantial scalability. The GOLD system uses dependency vectors, developed by Fowler and Zwaenepoel [5], which will be size $O(n)$ by the time they are attached to individual events. ParaGraph has the ability to provide space-time diagrams, but there is no attempt to determine causality. It is merely a visualization based on, possibly badly synchronized, local clocks. It is up to the user to trace the dependencies. Indeed, the authors acknowledge that the size would not scale well beyond 128 processes, as the display becomes too cluttered. POET uses standard Fidge/Mattern timestamps, and so it too requires vectors of size equal to the number of processes.

The second group is those who are trying to reduce the vector-clock size, but in the context of maintaining vector-clocks by the processes involved in the computation. There are three main algorithms in this area. The first technique, due to Singhal and Kshemkalyani [18], sends a differential vector of what has changed since the last communication to the receiving process. It requires two additional vectors of size n at each process to recover the timestamp information. The second method, due to Fowler and Zwaenepoel [5], is to maintain only direct dependency vectors. That is, only the scalar time at the local process is transmitted to a receiver. A graph search is needed to go from this information to full precedence information. The third algorithm, due to Jard and Jourdan [11], creates a pseudo-direct relation that is stronger than direct dependency. The basic problem with all of these techniques is that they do not apply in the debugging or monitoring context. In the context of maintaining vector time in a distributed computation, they all succeed, to one degree or another, in reducing the message-size overhead required. In our context, we must maintain vectors for all events at all times. What is relevant is not, therefore, the message-size overhead, as we send no messages but rather compute the vectors separately from the computation. What is relevant is the amount of information necessary to determine precedence.

Finally, there are no performance results that we are aware of concerning the actual behaviour of the various systems of the first group or algorithms of the second group in the context of large numbers of processes. In this respect, our paper is unique.

3 Bounding the dimension

In this section we will describe the algorithms we have developed to compute the dimension of the partial order. This is done in a two-phase process. We first compute the critical pairs of the partial order, and then we create a set of extensions that reverses those pairs. We will first describe the formal justification for this approach, and then describe the two phases. Finally we will provide some analysis of the algorithm.

Computing the exact dimension of a partial order is known to be NP-hard for any partial order of dimension greater than two [22]. We therefore approached the problem by attempting to simply bound the dimension. For our purposes, an order of magnitude difference between the dimension bound and the number of processes would be sufficient to justify proceeding. It was then necessary to develop an algorithm to achieve a reasonable bound in a reasonable amount of time. Rather than take the direct approach of generating linear extensions and then determining if they formed a realizer we chose an indirect route based on the concept of *critical pairs*.

Definition 1 (critical pair) (x, y) *is a critical pair of partial order* (X, P) *if* $x \parallel y$ *and* $(X, P \cup \{(x, y)\})$ *is a partial order.*

An equivalent definition is $(x, y) \in CP$ if and only if

$$x \parallel y \wedge \forall_{z \in X} z \to x \Rightarrow z \to y \wedge y \to z \Rightarrow x \to z$$

where CP is the set of all critical pairs of the partial order (X, P). The significance of critical pairs, as regards dimension, is in the following theorem [21].

Theorem 1 *The dimension of a partial order is equal to the least number of subextensions of that partial order required to reverse all of its critical pairs.*

A critical pair (x, y) is said to be reversed by a set of subextensions if one of the subextensions in the set contains $y \to x$. In simpler terms, it is sufficient to simply reverse the critical pair events. Specifically, all events that are not part of a critical pair may be ignored. Further, not every

subextension need contain all critical pairs. Note also, that it is not necessary for the subextensions to be linear. They merely have to reverse the critical pairs.

The approach we have then taken to the problem of bounding the dimension is to first compute all of the critical pairs of the partial order (a polynomial-time problem) and then create extensions that reverse these critical pairs (an NP-hard problem).

3.1 Computing critical pairs

While it is possible to use the given definition of critical pairs to compute the set of all critical pairs, any such algorithm would likely be very inefficient. To achieve reasonable performance in the computation it is necessary to develop an association of critical pairs with the relations that hold for the partial order. To this end, we define the sets leastConcurrent(e) and greatestConcurrent(e).

Definition 2 (leastConcurrent(e)) *The set of events that are* leastConcurrent *to an event* e *are those events that are concurrent with* e *and which have no predecessor which is also concurrent with* e.

In formal terms, leastConcurrent(e) is the set:

$$\left\{ e_l \mid e_l \| e \wedge \left(\not\exists_{e'_l} \ e'_l \| e \wedge e'_l \to e_l \right) \right\} \tag{3}$$

Likewise the set greatestConcurrent(e) is:

$$\left\{ e_g \mid e_g \| e \wedge \left(\not\exists_{e'_g} \ e'_g \| e \wedge e_g \to e'_g \right) \right\} \tag{4}$$

This then leads to the following theorem.

Theorem 2 (x, y) *form a critical pair if and only if*

$$x \in \text{leastConcurrent}(y) \wedge y \in \text{greatestConcurrent}(x)$$

This theorem enabled the development of the following algorithm.

```
1:∀_y y ∈ Events in Computation {
2:    l_C ← leastConcurrent(y)
3:    ∀_x x ∈ l_C {
4:        g_C ← greatestConcurrent(x)
5:        if (y ∈ g_C) {
6:            (x, y) is a critical pair
7:        }
8:    }
9: }
```

Some comments should be made about this algorithm. First, it is not obvious from the above why we perform the computation in what appears to be the reverse order. That is, we take each event as a possible second element of a critical pair, rather than a first element. The reason has to do with the relative cheapness with which we can compute the leastConcurrent set versus the comparative expense of computing the greatestConcurrent set. We implemented our algorithm as a client to the POET server. As such we have access to Fidge/Mattern timestamps for each event. An important property of these timestamps is that they give the set of events that are the greatest predecessors in each process to the event for which they form the timestamp. What this means is that we can efficiently compute the leastConcurrent set of an event as follows.

```
 1: leastConcurrent(e) {
 2:    l_C ← timestamp(e) + 1
 3:    ∀_x x ∈ l_C {
 4:       if (x ∦ e) {
 5:          l_C ← l_C - x
 6:       }
 7:    }
 8:    ∀_x x ∈ l_C {
 9:       ∀_y y ∈ l_C {
10:          if (x → y) {
11:             l_C ← l_C - y
12:          }
12:       }
13:    }
14:    return l_C
15: }
```

In words, to compute leastConcurrent(e) we start with the timestamp of e, which represents those events that are the greatest predecessors to e in their respective processes. We advance this timestamp by one; that is, we increment each element of the timestamp. This now represents a set of events that are either concurrent or successors to e. We refer to this set as the set of potentially least concurrent events of e. We remove from this set any event that is not concurrent with the event e and any event that is preceded by some other event within the set. This leaves those events that are leastConcurrent(e). This computation costs $O(w^2)$ where w is the width of the partial order (that is, the number of processes in the computation). The reason is that the number of iterations of the outer and inner loops of the nested loop is equal to the cardinality of the lC set, which can be as large as the width.

The greatestConcurrent(e) set is more expensive to calculate. To compute it we start with the greatest predecessors (*i.e.* the Fidge/Mattern timestamp) of e. We iterate along each process' set of events until we reach the event immediately prior to a successor event to e, or we come to the last event in that process. This yields the potentially greatest concurrent set. We then remove all events in this set that are not concurrent with e or that precede any other events in the set. This leaves the greatestConcurrent(e)

set. The cost of this operation can be quite substantial, since we must compare with an arbitrary number of successors to the greatest predecessors of e. This motivated the discovery of the following theorem.

Theorem 3 *If two events, x and y, are concurrent then either $y \in$ greatestConcurrent(x) or x precedes some immediate successor of y.*

Since we will not compute greatestConcurrent(x) until we know that $x \in$ leastConcurrent(y) we know that $x \parallel y$. What this means in practice is that we do not compute the greatestConcurrent(x) set at all, but rather simply check whether x is a predecessor of all immediate successors of y. If it is, then (x, y) form a critical pair. Thus the algorithms becomes:

```
 1: ∀_y y ∈ Events in Computation {
 2:    l_C ← leastConcurrent(y)
 3:    ∀_x x ∈ l_C {
 4:       l_S ← {s | y <: s}
 5:       if (∀_s s ∈ l_S ⇒ x → s) {
 6:          (x, y) is a critical pair
 7:       }
 8:    }
 9: }
```

Since we only support point-to-point communication, the set of events that are immediate successors to an event has cardinality less than 3. This means that the cost to compute the critical pairs is $O(w^2)$ per event or $O(w^2 n)$, where n is the total number of events, for the whole distributed computation.

3.2 Reversing critical pairs

Building the minimum number of extensions that reverses the critical pairs of a partial order is NP-hard for dimension greater than two [22]. Instead we propose a reasonably efficient algorithm that will not give an optimal solution, but will provide an upper bound on the minimum number of extensions necessary (that is, the dimension). Insofar as the dimension-bound we compute is small, it is a satisfactory tradeoff. To achieve this we developed a two-step algorithm. First we select the desired extension in which we will reverse the current critical pair and then we insert it into that extension.

In accordance with Theorem 1, it is sufficient to develop subextensions that reverse the critical pairs of the partial order. We do not have to insert all critical pairs in all subextensions. We merely have to find one subextension that will reverse the critical pair. Each subextension then is composed of some reversed critical pair events and nothing else. Note that this approach would not be sufficient for generating Ore

132

timestamps. It is insufficient as each subextension contains just a subset of the events of the partial order, not all of the events. Further, Ore timestamps require that the extensions are linear. Note also that using subextensions, rather than extensions, has implications on how we can insert critical pairs into the subextension.

To understand the algorithm we must define what it means to insert a critical pair into an subextension. It means that we can add the events of the critical pair such that they are reversed, and that it violates neither the partial order, nor the additional constraints that the reversal requires. It may also be the case, if the insertion algorithm is not optimal, that a subextension rejects the critical pair even though it did not violate these conditions, but rather violated some aspect of the structure in which the subextension was kept.

It is, perhaps, helpful to consider a simple example. Suppose we have a partial order consisting solely of two concurrent events, a and b. It has critical pairs (a, b) and (b, a). Once (a, b) has been inserted into a subextension, that subextension must reflect the constraint $b \rightarrow a$. As such (b, a) cannot be inserted into that subextension, since it would require the subextension to reflect $a \rightarrow b$.

We say that a subextension *accepts* a critical pair if the critical pair may be inserted into that subextension. A subextension *rejects* a critical pair if it does not accept it. Since a subextension may reject a critical pair, insertion into a subextension may fail. Therefore the first step of the algorithm must have a strategy for selecting an alternate subextension in which to place the critical pair. We can now describe the specific algorithms used for the two steps.

The algorithm we use for the extension-selection step is a simple greedy one. We insert the current critical-pair events into the first extension that will accept it. In the event that all current extensions reject the critical pair, we create a new extension, containing no events, that must, by definition, accept the critical pair. The critical pair is inserted into the new extension. Thus, the first step algorithm is:

```
1: insert(x,y) {
2:    for (i = 0; i < numberExtensions; ++i) {
3:       if (insert(extension[i], x, y)) {
4:          return
5:       }
6:    }
7:    create(extension[numberExtensions])
8:    insert(extension[numberExtensions], x, y)
9:    ++numberExtensions
10:   return;
11: }
```

3.2.1 Subextension insertion

For the second step of the algorithm, we had to define a method for inserting critical pairs into an subextension. The initial algorithm that we developed was a greedy one that worked on the principle "place the event before the first event it *must* precede." While this approach produces some promising results, it also produces some spectacularly bad ones.

We therefore decided to develop an optimal solution to this second step. We maintain a directed acyclic graph for each subextension. To add a critical pair we add the two events in turn and then determine if the graph is still acyclic. If it is acyclic we have accepted and inserted the critical pair. If it is not, we reject the critical pair, and remove the evidence of the addition. This method proved to be acceptable, as we can see in Section 4.

The data structure for a given node of the DAG representing event e maintains the following information: the vector timestamp of e, the sets $\{\lambda \mid (\lambda, e) \in \mathrm{CP}_S\}$ and $\{\rho \mid (e, \rho) \in \mathrm{CP}_S\}$ (where $\mathrm{CP}_S \subseteq \mathrm{CP}$ is the subset of the critical pairs that this subextension S has reversed), and a set of pointers to some of the successors to e in the DAG. The actual successors pointed to will depend on the order in which events are inserted. It is not typically the minimum set of successors needed, but neither is it the full transitive closure.

We now define event precedence between two DAG events as follows.

$$x \prec_S y \Longleftrightarrow x \rightarrow y \vee (y, x) \in \mathrm{CP}_S$$

where CP_S is the set of critical pairs that are reversed by subextension S, as defined above. Event x precedes y in subextension S if and only if x precedes y in the partial order or (y, x) is a critical pair that is reversed by this subextension. Note that if events a and b are in a subextension S and (a, b) form a critical pair this does not necessarily imply that $(a, b) \in \mathrm{CP}_S$. The pair (a, b) is only in CP_S if the subextension S has accepted, that is reversed, it. A simple example of this case is if the subextension S already contains the critical pair (b, a).

A second significant aspect of this definition is that it does not capture transitivity. Thus if z is an immediate successor to x and both are concurrent to y, with (x, y) forming a critical pair, then $y \prec x$ and $x \prec z$ but $y \not\prec z$. Appropriate transitivity can only be captured by traversing the DAG.

We designate a special node *root* with the property that $\forall_x root \prec_S x$. The root node enables us to enter the DAG at a single point, rather than potentially multiple concurrent points.

The insertion algorithm is then as follows. We traverse the DAG in a depth-first search order, starting at the root, comparing the event being inserted with the current node.

We determine if the event equals, succeeds, precedes or is concurrent with the current node. Only one of these must be the case, and if more than one has occurred, we abort the insertion. It has failed. If the event precedes or equals the current node, then it must not succeed or equal any successors to the current node. We therefore set a mustNotSucceedOrEqual variable to this effect. If this variable has been set before, and the event succeeds or equals the current node, we will abort the insertion.

If the event succeeds the current node, then we may have to add successor pointers to the event from the current node. We have to add a successor pointer from the current node to the event if it precedes any of the successors to the current node, or if it is concurrent with all of the successors. In the former case we will also add a pointer from the event to the successor node that it precedes, and remove the pointer from the current node to the successor node, since there is a path through the event.

We repeat these operations for the successor nodes of the current node, in depth-first order. The mustNotSucceedOrEqual variable is stored and recovered from the depth-first search stack.

To traverse the DAG there is a "mark" integer associated with each node. Before each traversal we increment the mark value in the root. As we visit a node, we set the value of the mark at that node to the value of the mark at the root. We only visit a node if the mark is less than the root mark value. Since we simply use an integer for this mark, if we ever reach about half-a-billion critical pairs this value will wrap. This defect can be easily fixed when the need arises.

To enable us to undo any changes we make, before we make any change we create a copy of the DAG node. We only do this if we do not yet have a copy. After successful insertion of both events of the critical pair, we traverse the DAG completely to commit the changes. That is, we traverse the DAG and delete the copy at any node that has one. If the insertion of the events is unsuccessful, we traverse the DAG and abort the changes. That is, we traverse the DAG and, wherever there was a copy made we restore that copy over the existing node.

3.3 Algorithm analysis

We now turn to studying the quality of the algorithm. There are two aspects to this. We wish to study the efficiency of the algorithm and we would like to know how tight the dimension-bounds are that it produces, given that the algorithm does not produce the optimal bound.

We have already seen that the computation cost to determine the critical pairs is $O(w^2)$ per event. The cost of reversing a critical pair is in the worst case equal to the cost of attempting to insert it into all of the extensions. We presume that each extension in turn rejects the insertion. If the

dimension bound produced is d then there will be d such attempts. The cost of each insertion attempt is, again in the worst case, $O(bn)$ where n is the total number of events and b is the branching factor of the extension DAG, since each successor must be explicitly compared with the event being inserted and all nodes in the DAG must be examined. Thus, the total cost of the algorithm is $O(bdw^2n^2)$. This bound is probably not tight, and we already know of ways in which we could reduce the algorithm complexity, though this was not our prime concern.

The quality of the dimension-bound produced is something that we are currently investigating. We know that the bound we produce will never exceed w, as to do so would require more than w mutually conflicting critical pairs. This would imply that the dimension could exceed the width, which we have already seen is not possible. We also know that the algorithm will never give a bound that is less than the dimension of the computation. In this respect it is conservative. Given this fact, and since the dimension bound produced tends to be in single digits, the algorithm is in general producing an answer that is within a factor of 5 of the actual dimension (it is trivial to determine that all of the computations have a dimension of at least 2).

The only step in the algorithm that is not optimal (from a dimension-bound perspective) is the subextension selection step. We have therefore experimented with varying the ordering in which subextensions are selected. There are several variations we have considered, which largely fall into two camps: random selection and deterministic selection. The random selection techniques includes a random selection for every attempt and randomly selecting the first attempt and then deterministically choosing the remaining selections. The deterministic approaches consider generating the critical pairs in different orders (in particular, generating them in a linearization of the partial order, selecting processes in different orders, and generating the pairs ordered by the first event in the pair rather than the second). Thus far these variations have made little difference to the results that are generated. This suggests at least some degree of robustness in the algorithm. Our current objective is to attempt to determine the quality of the dimension-bound analytically.

4 Results and observations

We have executed our dimension-bound algorithm over several dozen distributed computations covering over half-a-dozen different parallel, concurrent and distributed environments and a range of 3 to 300 processes. The environment types are the Open Software Foundation Distributed Computing Environment [4], the μC++ shared memory concurrent programming language [1], the Hermes distributed programming language [19], the Parallel Virtual

Number of Processes	Number of Events	Number of Critical Pairs	Dimension Bound
5	45	12	3
19	90	27	2
20	121	61	4
40	249	124	3
42	291	164	3
42	467	183	4
44	297	237	4
70	499	443	5
72	501	496	6
110	833	1490	9
112	817	1378	8
114	928	1738	7
115	902	1402	8
159	1560	3579	10

Table 1. Dimension bounds for OSF DCE

Number of Processes	Number of Events	Number of Critical Pairs	Dimension Bound
7	15	38	2
59	2687	2360	4
66	3252	3044	4
66	2612	2032	3
95	49791	6622	3
96	3272	5906	4
109	7426	10019	6
110	4028	8439	6
112	7928	6969	3
112	35266	6675	4
120	30048	7999	3
178	9826	18464	6

Table 2. Dimension bounds for Java

Number of Processes	Number of Events	Number of Critical Pairs	Dimension Bound
12	360	156	2
12	1750	853	5

Table 3. Dimension bounds for μC++

Number of Processes	Number of Events	Number of Critical Pairs	Dimension Bound
125	1888	1323	5
127	1944	1429	5
267	4164	4403	7
297	14086	21401	6

Table 4. Dimension bounds for Hermes

which illustrates the increase in Fidge/Mattern vector-clock size as the number of processes increases.

In addition to testing with distributed computations, we created a series of broadcast patterns and crown S_n^0 patterns. The result from our program for the crown S_n^0 patterns was a dimension bound of n. For the broadcast patterns the bound was 3, irrespective of the number of processes involved in the broadcast. Both of these dimension bounds are optimal. However, it should not be inferred that the algorithm is in general producing optimal results. All we can deduce from the current data is that the dimension bounds achieved for a reasonable number and variety of distributed computations is substantially better than the assumed default value of the number of processes involved.

5 Further work

There are several areas in which we are actively working. We have developed an online algorithm for dimension-bound analysis, which we hope will lead us to an online variant of the Ore timestamp. This will not render this offline algorithm obsolete. The offline algorithm is far more useful for checking robustness assumptions under different orderings of the critical pairs (recall that this is the only aspect of the algorithm that is not optimal in terms of computing the dimension). We are also actively attempting to discover the analytical quality of the bounds produced by this algorithm.

Machine [6] and the Java programming language [7]. The raw results are shown in Tables 1 through 5.

The quick summary is that the dimension bound that we discovered over this range of computations and environments was always 10 or less. For computations of process count greater than 20 there is a minimum of an order of magnitude difference between the dimension and the number of processes. When the number of processes is greater than 100, it is usually a factor of 15 or greater. To help visualize what these results imply, we created a graph, shown in Figure 2, which plots dimension as a function of the number of processes. The two graphs shown are the same, but with differing scales. The horizontal axis is the number of processes while the vertical axis is the dimension bound. We also plot two additional lines. First we show the "dimension = 10" line, as all results were less than or equal to that value. Second, we show the "dimension = width" line,

Number of Processes	Number of Events	Number of Critical Pairs	Dimension Bound
16	138	270	3
64	1338	4782	5
128	2682	17759	5

Table 5. Dimension bounds for PVM

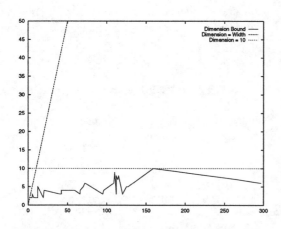

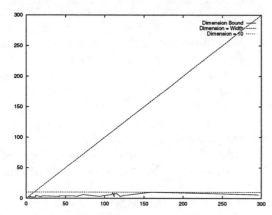

Figure 2. Dimension bound as a function of number of processes

Acknowledgment

The author would like to thank IBM for supporting this work and David Taylor for many useful discussions.

References

[1] P. A. Buhr, G. Ditchfield, R. A. Stroobosscher, B. M. Younger, and C. R. Zarnke. μC++: Concurrency in the Object-Oriented Language C++. *Software — Practice and Experience*, 22(2):137–172, Feb. 1992.

[2] B. Charron-Bost. Concerning the Size of Logical Clocks in Distributed Systems. *Information Processing Letters*, 39:11–16, July 1991.

[3] C. Fidge. Fundamentals of Distributed Systems Observation. Technical Report 93-15, Software Verification Research Centre, Department of Computer Science, The University of Queensland, St. Lucia, QLD 4072, Australia, November 1993.

[4] O. S. Foundation. *Introduction to OSF DCE*. Prentice-Hall, Englewood Cliffs, New Jersey, 1993.

[5] J. Fowler and W. Zwaenepoel. Causal Distributed Breakpoints. In *Proceedings of the 10th IEEE International Conference on Distributed Computing Systems*, pages 134–141. IEEE Computer Society Press, 1990.

[6] A. Geist, A. Begulin, J. Dongarra, W. Jiang, R. Manchek, and V. Sunderam. *PVM: Parallel Virtual Machine*. MIT Press, Cambridge, Massachusetts, 1994.

[7] J. Gosling, B. Joy, and G. Steele. *The Java Language Specification*. Addison-Wesley, 1996.

[8] J. Z. Han. Automatic Comparison of Execution Histories in the Debugging of Distributed Applications. Master's thesis, University of Waterloo, Waterloo, Ontario, 1998.

[9] M. T. Heath and J. A. Etheridge. Visualizing the Performance of Parallel Programs. *IEEE Software*, pages 29–39, September 1991.

[10] C. E. Jaekl. Event-Predicate Detection in the Debugging of Distributed Applications. Master's thesis, University of Waterloo, Waterloo, Ontario, 1997.

[11] C. Jard and G.-V. Jourdan. Dependency Tracking and Filtering. Technical Report 851, IRISA, Beaulieu, France, August 1994.

[12] T. Kunz. *Abstract Behaviour of Distributed Executions with Applications to Visualization*. PhD thesis, Technische Hochschule Darmstadt, Darmstadt, Germany, 1994.

[13] T. Kunz, J. P. Black, D. J. Taylor, and T. Basten. POET: Target-System Independent Visualisations of Complex Distributed-Application Executions. *The Computer Journal*, 40(8):499–512, 1997.

[14] L. Lamport. Time, Clocks and the Ordering of Events in Distributed Systems. *Communications of the ACM*, 21(7):558–565, 1978.

[15] F. Mattern. Virtual Time and Global States of Distributed Systems. In M. C. et al., editor, *Proceedings of the International Workshop on Parallel and Distributed Algorithms*, pages 215–226, Chateau de Bonas, France, December 1988. Elsevier Science Publishers B. V. (North Holland).

[16] O. Ore. *Theory of Graphs*, volume 38. Amer. Math. Soc. Colloq. Publ., Providence, R.I., 1962.

[17] J. L. Sharnowski and B. H. C. Cheng. A Visualization-based Environment for Top-down Debugging of Parallel Programs. In *Proceedings of the 9th International Parallel Processing Symposium*, pages 640–645. IEEE Computer Society Press, 1995.

[18] M. Singhal and A. Kshemkalyani. An Efficient Implementation of Vector Clocks. *Information Processing Letters*, 43:47–52, August 1992.

[19] R. E. Strom et al. *Hermes: A Language for Distributed Computing*. Prentice-Hall, Englewood Cliffs, New Jersey, 1991.

[20] D. J. Taylor. Scrolling Displays of Partially Ordered Execution Histories. In preparation.

[21] W. T. Trotter. *Combinatorics and Partially Ordered Sets: Dimension Theory*. Johns Hopkins University Press, Baltimore, MD, 1992.

[22] M. Yannakakis. The Complexity of the Partial Order Dimension Problem. *SIAM Journal on Algebraic and Discrete Methods*, 3(3):351–358, September 1982.

[23] Y. M. Yong. Replay and Distributed Breakpoints in an OSF DCE Environment. Master's thesis, University of Waterloo, Waterloo, Ontario, 1995.

Session A3

Architectural Support & Performance Evaluation

Chair: Timothy M. Pinkston
University of Southern California, USA

Pre-allocating control bandwidth in an optical interconnection network. *

C. Salisbury † and R. Melhem

Department of Computer Science
University of Pittsburgh

Abstract

To fully exploit the performance of optics in parallel processor interconnection networks, the connections must be entirely optical. This requires the use of circuit switching. Techniques such as time division multiplexing *(TDM) can be used to provide a large number of circuits without the need for program directed control operations. We describe two protocols for dynamically establishing circuits in an interconnection network. We show how TDM can be used to multiplex communication for data and control purposes together in a single optical network. We explore the ability of the protocols and TDM to exploit locality in the communication pattern to improve performance.*

Keywords: *optical networking, time division multiplexing, network control, communication protocols, parallel processing, locality.*

1 Introduction

Future high performance computing needs may be met through the use of clusters of networked computers. Optical technology may be needed to provide the high bandwidth, low latency communication required for these systems. To avoid opto-electronic signal conversions, buffering, and electronic processing delays, the connections through the network should be entirely optical. Such connections are managed through the use of circuit switching techniques.

Circuit switched interconnection architectures often use preallocation techniques for circuit establishment, as those described in [1, 6]. Alternatively, dynamic protocols have been developed to establish circuits in response to the changing needs of parallel and distributed applications. Many dynamic control techniques are based on the use of a broadcast bus, which can be implemented optically using a passive star [5, 8]. However, to interconnect a large number of processors requires the use of a more scalable network architecture. Typically, the architectures which have been proposed are either controlled using packet switching, or do not provide complete all-optical connectivity. Scalable architectures do not provide a broadcast channel for control, and cannot use the dynamic control protocols developed for bus-based architectures [7]. Dynamic control protocols for a multistage interconection network (MIN) have been described in [2, 9]. These approaches rely on the use of a separate electronic network to handle the control protocol.

Alternatively, control information and data flow can be provided through a single physical network. One technique for sharing network resources is *time division multiplexing* (TDM) [4, 12]. Using special hardware, a set of circuits is provided by placing the network in a desired state during an assigned time slice long enough to transmit a data packet. The number of netowrk states which are assigned a time slice is called the *multiplexing degree*. A global clock is needed to synchronize the time slices at all processors. A dynamic control protocol that uses TDM to transmit both data and control information over a single network is described for a partitioned optical passive star (POPS) network in [3].

TDM can be used in both optical and electronic networks. It may improve performance when timeslicing a set of network states is more efficient than executing a control protocol to establish new circuits. The concepts of *locality of reference* and *working set* can be applied to the communication patterns of parallel programs, and will affect the performance of a network multiplexed with TDM. The application of dynamic control techniques to the communication patterns found in interprocessor interconnection networks is described in detail in [10].

In the remainder of this paper, we will focus on techniques for dynamic, distributed control where TDM is used to provide circuits for both control and data communication over a single physical network. In Section 2 we introduce three schemes which preallocate different amounts of network bandwidth for control purposes. In Section 3, we

---

*This work is supported in part by NSF award MIP-9633729 to the University of Pittsburgh

†Current address: Mathematics and Computer Science Division, Argonne National Laboratory, Argonne Illinois

138

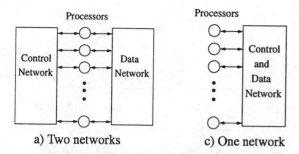

a) Two networks   c) One network

Figure 1. Distributed network control

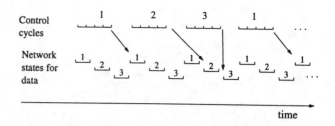

Figure 2. Round robin use of control cycles to build network states. ($K = 3$, $n = 4$)

describe two general approaches to dynamic allocation of network resources based on the use of a control cycle. We examine the performance of these techniques in Section 4, and show how locality of reference can be exploited to improve performance. Our conclusions are in Section 5.

2 Distributed control with TDM

In a circuit switched network, the processing of control messages must take place outside the switching fabric. With a centralized technique, requests are gathered over a control network and a network controller determines the state that will be established in the data network.

Figure 1(a) depicts distributed control with a dedicated control network. Processors exchange control information over the control network. A distributed algorithm is used to allocate network resources for circuits in the data network. Distributed approaches involve multiple steps of communication and processing. Since processors do not have global knowledge, decisions are based on local information and may not be optimal.

The states for control can be multiplexed together with the states for data in a single network using TDM. This is pictured in Figure 1(b). A portion of the bandwidth is allocated for control communication, reducing the bandwidth available for data communication. The allocation also affects the latency of control operations and the rate at which they can be performed.

We consider distributed control techniques where requests are processed in a batch to resolve contention and allocate network resources. The control protocol is executed in a *control cycle* of n steps. Each step has a communication phase to gather or exchange requests, and may be followed by a control information processing phase. The communication pattern is predetermined by the distributed control algorithm, so that each step has an associated network state. The use of a control cycle for processing requests might be appropriate for networks which have globally shared resources. For example, when each processor has a single receiver, the receiver is shared globally. Network architectures could include multi-stage interconnection networks

(MINs), optical passive stars, and crossbars.

A straight-forward way of managing a set of multiplexed data states is to build them in a round-robin manner. The relationship between control cycles and network states for data communication is pictured in Figure 2. The steps of a control cycle are shown as being continuous, although this is not necessary. Each control cycle builds a single network state for data communication. These network states can be implemented using time slots in the data network. Circuits are established in the assigned time slot until the data state is rebuilt by a subsequent control cycle.

2.1 An example of distributed control

A dynamic control technique must describe both the pattern of control communication and the method for allocating network resources in response to requests for circuits. Both of these are network specific. To investigate the performance of dynamic control, we developed techniques for controlling a banyan interconnection network for parallel processing systems. A banyan architecture was selected because it is scalable and can be constructed from simple 2×2 optical switches. Unlike a crossbar architecture, all paths through a banyan network pass through the same number of switches. Thus, optical power loss is the same along all paths.

A banyan network interconnecting $N = 2^n$ processors is built with n stages of 2×2 crossbar switches. Each stage has $N/2$ switches. A banyan network provides a unique path between any pair of attached nodes. An example of a banyan network is shown in Figure 3.

As an example of distributed control, we summarize below the control algorithm for a banyan network that was described in detail in [11]. Each step of the control cycle resolves contention for one stage of switches at a time, proceeding from stage 0. Thus, a control cycle requires $\log N$ steps to create a new network state.

Each processor requests a connection by building a control message describing the states of network switches required to form the circuit. The states required to connect processor 0 with processor 5 are shown in Figure 3 ('-' in-

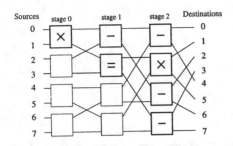

Figure 3. A "reverse cube" banyan network.

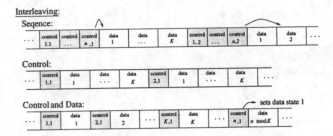

Figure 4. Interleaving data and control.

Interleaving	Max. nr. of packets	Control bandwidth
Sequence	K	$1/(\frac{K}{n}b+1)$
Control	nK	$1/(Kb+1)$
Control and Data	n	$1/(b+1)$

Table 1. Interleaving characteristics.

dicates "don't care"). Since a message from a processor can pass through any of $N-1$ switches, the protocol uses a control message of $\mathbf{O}(N)$ bits.

Each switch in the network can be associated with a subset of processors that could require the switch as part of a circuit. At step i of the control cycle, processors whose addresses differ only in bit position i exchange control information. With this single exchange, each processor obtains information about all possible contention for switches accessible at stage i.

Each processor then resolves contention for network switches by pseudo-randomly selecting one request as the winner, and discarding the losing request. The results are retained for setting the network state. A new control message is then built which combines the requirements of all winning requests, and the procedure is repeated for the next stage of switches. After n steps, a complete network state has been built. Each processor can compare its request to the final state to determine if its request was successful and data can be transmitted in the associated time slot. Requests that fail must be resubmitted into a later control cycle.

2.2 Multiplexing control and data together

The n networks states for control communication must be provided in a predetermined sequence. We assume the K states for data communication are also provided in a sequence. The states in each sequence may or may not be provided in contiguous time slots. We call the use of contiguous slots for both control and data sequences *sequence interleaving*. When data states are not contiguous, every data state must be followed by a control state. We call this *data interleaving*. Similarly, *control interleaving* occurs when control states are not contiguous, and every control state is followed by a data state.

The resulting interleaved sequences are shown in Figure 4. Data interleaving by itself is not shown because it is meaningful only when $K=1$, and its result is identical to that of sequence interleaving. In the figure, states for control are labeled with the step number within the control cycle and the number of the data state that will be affected. An arrow extending from the nth control state points to the

data slot affected by that control cycle.

The duration of a time slot for data communication may differ from the duration of a slot for control communication. The durations are based on the size of a data packet and a control message. Since the resource allocation algorithm must execute between the end of one control communication and the start of the next, the duration of a control slot may need to be extended to provide this time. Alternatively, control interleaving can be used to overlap control processing with data transmission. Let the length of a control time slot be 1 time unit, and the length of a data time slot be b units.

Many performance characteristics of the network can be computed directly from the number and duration of network states for data and control, and the manner in which they are interleaved. These include, for example, the minimum latency to build a network state, the percent of network bandwidth allocated for control, and the number of packets that can be sent over a circuit before the data state will be rebuilt. The latter two values are shown in Table 1. Selection of the interleaving technique represents a tradeoff between the competing needs for network control and data transmission.

3 Dynamic Control Protocols

We consider communication functions to be split between the application program and the processor's interface to the network.

- The program requests the network interface to obtain a circuit to the desired destination. This may be done by a specific network call, or implicit in a SEND.

- The interface constructs a control message and pro-

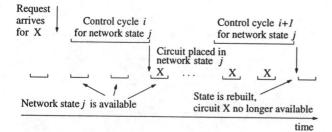

Figure 5. RFE operation.

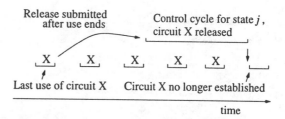

Figure 6. Releasing paths with RER.

cesses the request through a control cycle. The control protocol is executed by the interface hardware.

- If the request is granted, messages sent by the application will be transmitted by the interface in the appropriate time slot.

- If the request is denied, the interface can notify the application or it can automatically process it through a subsequent control cycle.

We next describe two classes of dynamic protocol, distinguished by their approach to the reservation of network resources. We then present enhancements that exploit communication locality.

3.1 Reservation with Fixed Expiration

One approach to establishing circuits is to reserve network resources for a fixed duration of time, *e.g.* a fixed number of time slots. We call this protocol Reservation with Fixed Expiration (RFE). When a round-robin scheme is used to manage multiple network states, the time at which each state is rebuilt can be easily computed. At the beginning of each control cycle, all resources are unassigned. The operation of RFE is depicted in Figure 5.

For example, a 2×2 switch is a resource in a banyan network. When allocated during control cycle processing, it changes from an undefined state to either the "straight" or "cross" state. After the entire network state is built, circuits are established by setting the switches in the required position in the appropriate time slot.

There are three consequences of beginning each control cycle with resources in an undefined state. First, a request may be submitted into any control cycle. Second, circuits which are needed longer than provided by the fixed expiration time must be rerequested, even when the communication requirements of the program are not changing. Third, the circuits provided in a network state are determined in a single control cycle. The number of circuits provided reflects the effectiveness of a single execution of the distributed algorithm.

When processing a rerequest for an established circuit, contention could cause the request to fail and disrupt the use of the circuit. This could be a problem if timing constraints or bandwidth guarantees are violated. The next protocol does not have this problem.

3.2 Reservation with Explicit Release

The Reservation with Explicit Release (RER) protocol reserves circuits for as long as they are needed. Network resources remain allocated until they are explicitly released by all processors using them. With this approach, control messages are processed as updates to an existing network state. Control cycle processing rejects all requests that would alter the state of reserved network resources. RER can therefore be used to support a higher level protocol that guarantees bandwidth or timing.

With RER, each circuit must be processed through two control cycles: one to reserve the circuit and one to release it. A control message that releases network resources is not subject to contention and always completes successfully. Circuit release is shown in Figure 6. A release control message may be submitted after the last use of a circuit, and network resources are made available for the next control cycle for that state.

Circuit reservation and release

Both circuit reservation and release can be controlled directly by the application. This would allow a circuit to be requested prior to the availability of data in order to overlap control latency with other program activities. However, it is possible for a processor to require a circuit which cannot be accommodated in any of the K multiplexed network states. This represents a potential deadlock situation.

An alternative is to allow the network interface to control circuit establishment and release. A request for a circuit can be generated at the time of a SEND. Similarly, circuits can be released by the interface immediately after the message has been transmitted. This ensures that once a circuit is reserved, the message can be sent, the circuit will be released, and network resources will become available again. Automatic generation of release messages therefore avoids deadlock and provides complete flexibility in the choice of multiplexing degree.

Network state selection

With RER, a request for a circuit will be unsuccessful if it requires a change in the state of a reserved resource. Processing such a request is unproductive. This can be avoided if the processor retains the network state information developed at the end of each control cycle, and only submits requests which do not require reserved resources to change state. In Section 4, we will show that this restriction can have a significant impact on performance.

In some cases, it may be possible to insert a newly required circuit into any of several network states. In these cases, it may be possible to request the circuit in a state that optimizes performance. For example, the selected state may be the one containing the maximum number of switches already used for other circuits. This may increase the average number of circuits in a network state. Alternatively, a processor may select the state which will be updated the earliest. The optimization algorithm may exploit knowledge of the communication pattern and network topology. For some situations, good optimization algorithms may not be known. However, RER provides the potential for these network optimizations, while RFE does not.

Unlike RFE, the RER protocol allows circuits to be placed into a network state by multiple control cycles. When messages are long enough to reserve circuits over several control cycles, the additional cycles provide opportunities for processors to request circuits that are compatable with the circuits already established. These additional cycles can increase the number of circuits provided in each state, thereby improving performance.

3.3 Protocol enhancements for locality

The basic function of the two protocols cannot exploit repetitive patterns of requests, *i.e.* communication locality, to improve performance. To add this capability, we allow resources which are not reserved to remain in the physical state used during the most recent reservation. Thus, the network state may continue to provide a circuit even after its reservation has expired. Requests for new circuits are compared by the interface to the circuits currently provided by the network. If the circuit is found, data transmission may begin immediately and can safely continue until the network state containing the circuit is rebuilt. This technique should reduce the latency for satisfying some requests by eliminating the need for a control operation.

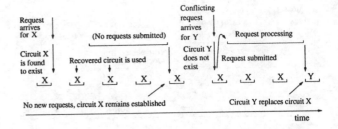

Figure 7. Path recovery in RFE.

Recovery in RFE

We call locality recognition for RFE path *recovery*. A processor looks for a requested circuit in the network state where the circuit was last established. If it still exists, it can be used immediately and can continue to be used until the state is rebuilt without the circuit. Checking only a single state is consistent with keeping the complexity of the RFE protocol to a minimum. The use of recovery is shown in Figure 7.

Discovery in RER

Since an RER request may need to be compared to every network state to find a time slot which can accommodate the new circuit, it is natural to search all network states for the previous existance of a requested circuit. We call this capability path *discovery*. If the entire message can be transmitted before the network state can be changed, it is not necessary to reserve the circuit. If not, a request must be submitted in the appropriate control cycle. It is possible to give priority to these discovered paths during contention resolution, at the cost of increased implementation complexity.

Discovery can be extended further to reduce the use of control cycles by continuing to transmit over the discovered path until either the message is sent or a request from another processor changes the state of a network component in the path. In this latter case, a control cycle is required to reserve the circuit. The advantage is that if the message can be transmitted without reserving network resources, the processing of a release is no longer required. We call this the *don't request* option of discovery. This can provide significant performance gains in parallel processing workloads with repetitive communication patterns, as will be shown in the next section.

4 Performance

The performance of TDM was simulated with the interleaving schemes of Section 2.2 and parallel processing applications using a banyan network.

4.1 Simulation environment

The simulator is written in CSIM and consists of processor components that execute an application script and a network component that simulates the protocol. The application script has a looping structure and specifies a sequence of messages to be generated in each loop iteration and the number of times the loop is to be executed.

While performance was simulated for three communication patterns, space considerations limit our discussion here to only one pattern. The pattern simulates a parallel program in which each processor executes a single loop. In each loop iteration, each processor sends a message to four different destinations. The destinations are chosen randomly at the start of the simulation, and do not change for the duration of the run. The result is a communication pattern with a randomly generated working set. All messages were non-blocking, and processors synchronize at the completion of each loop iteration. Computation and synchronization delays are assumed to overlap communication.

Simulations were also run with a shuffle pattern that could be analyzed manually and a random pattern that did not have a working set. A discussion of these results can be found in [10].

Two message lengths were used. Short messages consisted of a single packet. Long messages were of variable length, with the number of packets taken from a uniform distribution between 25 and 35. Each processor sends 12,000 packets during the simulation.

RER simulations were made using automatic generation of "release" control messages after each data message was sent. In addition, the *don't request* option was used. The length of a control time slot was chosen to be equal to the time required to transmit a control message and did not provide time for control processing. A parallel system of $N = 64$ processors was used, communicating through a reverse cube banyan interconnection network. The network data transfer rate was 1 Gigabit per second, and packet size was set at 50 bytes. Throughput was used as the key measure of network performance. This is reported as the percent of network bandwidth actually used to transmit data.

4.2 Random working set workload

We investigated performance with a range of multiplexing degrees from one to a value sufficient to contain the entire working set. Figures 8 and 9 show the results for the base protocols using short messages. Since the circuit requirements change after every message is sent, the base protocols perform best with a large amount of control bandwidth. For RFE, performance mirrors the allocation of bandwidth for control. RER performs worse than RFE due to release processing.

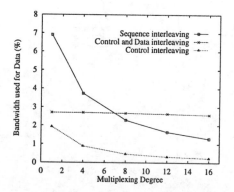

Figure 8. Short messages, RFE base cases.

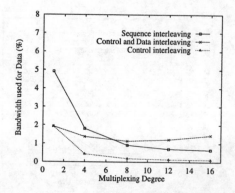

Figure 9. Short messages, RER base cases.

Figures 10 and 11 show the performance with locality recognition. The dramatic improvement at a multiplexing degree of 12 suggests that this degree is capable of containing the entire working set. RFE performance at this degree is still related to the amount of control bandwidth. It requires more control activity to place the working set into 12 network states than it does to place the working set into 16 network states. As the multiplexing degree increases, interleaving to provide additional data bandwidth performs better. The effectiveness of the protocol determines where this transition occurs.

For two interleaving techniques, RER outperforms RFE because it is more effective at grouping requests into non-conflicting subsets. The key reason for this is that the requests submitted into a control cycle for RER do not conflict with the set of circuits currently in the state. Thus, the requests are correlated and the probability of contention between them is less than would be expected from a random set of requests. This increases the portion of requests which can be satisfied during contention resolution. Over many control cycles, the result can be a significant performance improvement even with a multiplexing degree of one, and even when the communication pattern does not have a working set [10].

RER performs poorly with control and data interleaving

143

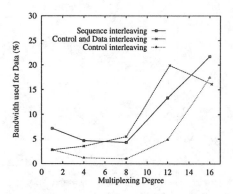

Figure 10. Short messages, RFE with locality.

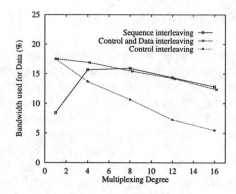

Figure 12. Long messages, RFE base cases.

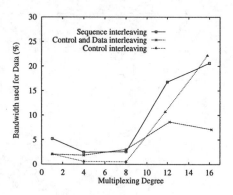

Figure 11. Short messages, RER with locality.

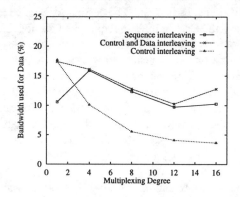

Figure 13. Long messages, RER base cases.

and a large degree of multiplexing. A timing analysis reveals that a circuit will be requested when control latency is less than the delay for circuit discovery. Performance is subsequently degraded by release processing.

With locality recognition, the results from individual simulation runs were highly variable when multiplexing at or above the optimal degree. At the minimum, performance slightly exceeded the base protocols. At best, performance approached the maximum attainable network utilization. (This maximum can be estimated from the number of packets to be sent and the number of time slots provided for data.)

From studies of the shuffle workload, we found two sources for this variation in performance. First, there can be multiple ways for circuit expiration and control cycle processing to synchronize into a repetitive pattern. Different patterns produce different values of steady state performance. Second, the random nature of the contention resolution algorithm causes the time to reach this synchronization to vary.

Figures 12 and 13 show the throughput of the base cases with long messages. For both protocols, the best performance is obtained with a multiplexing degree of one. Sequence interleaving performs poorly at this multiplexing de-

gree because it provides less than half the data bandwidth of the other techniques. As the multiplexing degree increases, performance decreases. This is because the latency for changing a network state increases, resulting in unused time slots after the last packet of every message has been transmitted.

Figures 14 and 15 show the effect of locality recognition. RFE performance is relatively insensitive to the multiplexing degree. As with short messages, RER is able to identify the working set with a multiplexing degree of 12.

5 Conclusions

We have described two general classes of dynamic control protocols for circuit-switched networks, based on the use of a control cycle. The RFE protocol provides circuits for a fixed amount of time by automatically releasing network resources. The RER protocol allows circuits to remain as long as needed, at the cost of additional implementation complexity. RER is suited to applications that require guaranteed bandwidth. Both protocols can exploit communication locality of reference to increase their performance.

We investigated protocol performance for a looping parallel application in a banyan network. We found that multiplexing improves performance when the protocol has suffi-

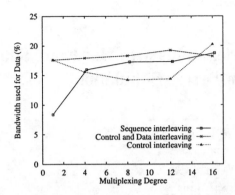

Figure 14. Long messages, RFE with locality.

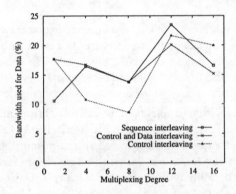

Figure 15. Long messages, RER with locality.

cient power to identify the communication working set and the multiplexing degree is sufficient to contain it. RER is more powerful than RFE since it reduces contention between requests for new circuits. In some cases, this may allow the control bandwidth allocation to be reduced.

Without locality recognition, best performance is often achieved using control operations to change the circuits provided by a single network state. Locality recognition provides a mechanism for identifying the communication working set of a parallel program and placing it into a set of states. When the number of states is sufficient, the capabilities of multiplexing hardare can be exploited to improve communication performance.

References

[1] S. Araki et al. Experimental free-space optical network for massively parallel computers. *Applied Optics*, 35(8):1269–81, March 1996.

[2] R. D. Chamberlain, M. A. Franklin, R. R. Krchnavek, and B. H. Baysal. Design of an optically-interconnected multiprocessor. In *Proceedings of MP-POI '98*, pages 114–122. IEEE Comp. Soc. Press, Los Alamitos, California, June 1998.

[3] D. M. Chiarulli, S. P. Levitan, R. G. Melhem, J. P. Teza, and G. Gravenstreter. Partitioned optical passive star (POPS) multiprocessor interconnection networks with distributed control. *Journal of Lightwave Technology*, 14(7):1601–1612, July 1996.

[4] I. Chlamtac and A. Ganz. Channel allocation protocols in frequency-time controlled high speed networks. *IEEE Trans. on Communications*, 36(4):430–440, April 1988.

[5] P. Dowd. Random access protocols for high-speed interprocessor communications based on an optical passive star topology. *IEEE Journal of Lightwave Technology*, 9(6):799–808, 1991.

[6] P. Dowd, K. Bogineni, K. Aly, and J. Perreault. Hierarchical scalable photonic architectures for high-performance processor interconnection. *IEEE Transactions on Computers*, 42(9):1105–1120, September 1993.

[7] G. Liu, K. Lee, and H. Jordan. TDM hypercube and TWDM mesh optical interconnections. In *GLOBECOM '94: Proceedings of the IEEE Global Telecommunication Conference*, pages 1953–1957, Piscataway, NJ, 1994. IEEE.

[8] B. Mukherjee. WDM-based local lightwave networks part I: Single-hop systems. *IEEE Network*, 6(3):12–27, May 1992.

[9] C. Qiao and R. Melhem. Reconfiguration with time division multiplexing MINs for multiprocessor communications. *IEEE Transactions on Parallel and Distributed Systems*, 5(4):337–352, 1994.

[10] C. Salisbury. *Online Control of Multiplexed, Circuit-switched, Optical Interconnection Networks*. PhD thesis, University of Pittsburgh, December 1998.

[11] C. Salisbury and R. Melhem. Distributed, dynamic control of circuit-switched banyan networks. In *Proceedings of IPPS/SPDP '98*, pages 156–161. IEEE Comp. Soc. Press, Los Alamitos, California, March 1998.

[12] R. Thompson. The dilated slipped banyan switching network architecture for use in an all optical local area network. *IEEE Journal of Lightwave Technology*, 9(12):1780–1787, December 1991.

Performance Evaluation of Networks of Workstations with Hardware Shared Memory Model Using Execution-Driven Simulation*

J. Flich, M. P. Malumbres, P. López and J. Duato

Dpto. Informática de Sistemas y Computadores

Universidad Politécnica de Valencia

Camino de Vera, 14, 46071–Valencia, Spain

E-mail: {jflich,mperez,plopez,jduato}@gap.upv.es

Abstract

Networks of workstations (NOWs) are becoming increasingly popular as a cost-effective alternative to parallel computers. Typically, these networks connect processors using irregular topologies, providing the wiring flexibility, scalability, and incremental expansion capability required in this environment. Similar to the evolution of parallel computers, NOWs are also evolving from distributed memory to shared memory programming model. However, physical distances between processors are longer in NOWs than in tightly-coupled distributed shared-memory multiprocessors (DSMs), leading to higher message latency and lower network bandwidth. Therefore, the network may be a bottleneck when executing some parallel applications in a NOW supporting a shared-memory programming paradigm.

In this paper we analyze whether the interconnection network is able to efficiently handle the traffic generated in a NOW with the shared memory model. In particular, we are interested in analyzing the influence of the routing mechanism in the performance of the system. We evaluate the behavior of a NOW with irregular topology by means of an execution-driven simulator using SPLASH-2 applications as the input load. The results show that the routing algorithm can considerably reduce the total execution time of applications. In particular, routing adaptivity can reduce the total execution time by 58 % in some applications. These results confirm the behavior observed in previous works using synthetic traffic loads.

1 Introduction

Research in parallel computers has focused on multicomputers and multiprocessors during the last decades. These machines provide high computing power by arranging tens or hundreds of processors that work in a coordinated way in order to solve a given task. The communication needed to coordinate and synchronize these processors is carried out through the interconnection network.

Large-scale parallel computers evolved from multicomputers (iPSC/1, iPSC/2, nCUBE-2, nCUBE-3, TMC CM-5, Intel Paragon) to distributed shared-memory multiprocessors (DSM), either with cache coherence (SGI Origin 2000) or without cache coherence (Cray T3D, Cray T3E). The higher architectural complexity required to provide a single memory address space is worth its cost. It provides a simpler programming model in which communication is achieved by accessing shared memory locations, and synchronization is performed by using barriers. Additionally, sequential applications that require a large amount of memory to be executed efficiently can be directly ported to DSMs. In general, this is not possible in a multicomputer because each processor has a relatively small local memory.

However, due to the increasing computation power of microprocessors and the high cost of parallel computers, networks of workstations (NOWs) are currently being considered as a cost-effective alternative for small-scale parallel computing. Although NOWs do not provide the computing capacity available in multicomputers and multiprocessors, they meet the needs of a great variety of parallel computing problems at a lower cost. Moreover, the nature of NOWs allows an incremental expansion of the system.

Nevertheless, most commercial interconnects for NOWs only provide support for message-passing. These networks consist of a network interface card that is plugged into the I/O bus of each workstation, and one or more switches interconnecting the interface cards through point-to-point links [3]. In general, the bandwidth provided by currently available interface cards and switches is high enough for the requirements of message-passing applications. However, the performance of some parallel applications is limited by

*This work was supported by the Spanish CICYT under Grant TIC97–0897–C04–01 and by Generalitat Valenciana under Grant GV98-15-50

146

message latency.

Similarly to the evolution of parallel computers, NOWs are also evolving from distributed memory to shared memory. Most approaches implement the shared memory model in software [1, 28]. However, a few commercial interface cards support the shared-memory programming model. This is the case for the SCI-PCI adapter from Dolphin [6]. This card does not support cache coherence in hardware because memory traffic cannot be seen from the I/O bus. Also, interface cards are reaching the limits of I/O buses.[1] In order to provide a higher bandwidth and lower latency, some researchers have started to develop interface cards that are plugged directly into the memory bus providing support for shared-memory [18], also implementing a cache-coherence protocol.

2 Motivation

A decade ago, the invention of wormhole switching led to very fast interconnection networks [2]. As a consequence, the interconnection network was no longer the bottleneck in a multicomputer. However, DSMs require faster interconnection networks than multicomputers because messages are shorter (a typical message consists of a cache line and some control information) and much more frequent [15]. While the interconnection network is not the bottleneck yet, some researchers reported that a lower latency and a higher network bandwidth may significantly reduce the execution time of several parallel applications [29, 4, 27]. As processor clock frequency is increasing at a faster rate than network bandwidth, the interconnection network may become a bottleneck within the next years [8].

The situation is more critical for NOWs supporting a single memory address space. Physical distance between processors is higher in NOWs than in DSMs, leading to higher latency (due to the propagation delay) and lower bandwidth (due to the use of narrower links).[2] Additionally, the use of irregular topologies makes routing and deadlock handling much more complex. Existing routing algorithms are either deterministic [3] or provide some degree of adaptivity [20, 19, 26]. Some of them lead to a frequent use of non-minimal paths and an unbalanced use of physical links. As a consequence channel utilization is low, reducing the effective network bandwidth even more. Therefore, we can expect the network to be a bottleneck when executing some parallel applications on a NOW supporting a shared-memory programming paradigm. Then, it is important to

analyze the behavior of parallel applications on these machines.

In this paper, we analyze whether the interconnection network in a NOW is able to handle the traffic generated by the execution of some parallel applications. In particular, we evaluate different routing algorithms on NOWs with irregular topology, using the total execution time as the main performance parameter. These results will provide a more precise idea of the impact of routing algorithms on application performance than previous results based on trace-driven simulations [27]. As applications, we have selected a subset of the SPLASH-2 suite [30]: FFT, Radix, Barnes, and LU. The execution of these applications is simulated on a DSM test-bed with a hardware supported cache-coherence protocol. This environment allows the execution of a parallel program on the simulated machine, using a given cache-coherence protocol that generates coherence commands and memory traffic to a detailed interconnection network simulator subsystem. The main goal of this study is to determine whether the routing schemes affect the total execution time of an application, in order to evaluate their impact on the network design. We show that the use of adaptive routing helps to significantly reduce the execution time of these applications.

The rest of this paper is organized as follows. In Section 3, NOWs are introduced, describing several techniques to improve performance. Section 4 presents the test-bed used in the evaluation. In Section 5, the performance of different routing algorithms is evaluated using SPLASH-2 applications. Finally, in Section 6 some conclusions are drawn.

3 Networks of Workstations

NOWs are usually arranged as switch-based networks with an irregular interconnection pattern. Some of the switch ports are attached to processing elements, while the rest of the ports are connected to other switches to provide connectivity between processors, or left open. Generally, links connecting switches are bidirectional full-duplex.

Most of the NOWs proposed up to now implement wormhole switching [3, 14]. Since this is the most commonly used switching technique, we will restrict ourselves to wormhole switching in this paper.

Routing in irregular networks is more complex than in regular ones, due to the irregularity and unpredictability of the network topology at design time. Two approaches can be used: source routing and distributed routing. In source routing, when a processor generates a message it looks up in a routing table that provides the path towards the destination processor and stores that information in the message header. Thus, the path followed by a given message is fixed at the source node. This approach is used in Myrinet networks [3]. On the other hand, in distributed routing each switch has a

---

[1]For example, link bandwidth in Myrinet is 160 Mbytes/s. ServerNet II [11] and ChaosLAN [17] provide links with 1 Gigabit/s peak bandwidth. However, a 32-bit PCI bus running at 33 MHz only achieves a peak bandwidth of 133 Mbytes/s.

[2]For example, Cray T3E, Cray T3D, and SGI SPIDER routers [23, 22, 10] use 14, 16, and 20 data wires per link, respectively. ServerNet II [11] and Myrinet [3] use serial and 8-bit links, respectively.

routing table. When a message has to be routed at some switch, the routing algorithm looks up in the associated table, obtaining the output link to be used. Therefore each switch computes only the next link to be used, leading to more routing flexibility. In both cases, before the network is ready to deliver messages, some network configuration algorithm must be executed in order to fill the routing tables with the suitable information. This information depends on the routing algorithm. Several distributed deadlock-free routing schemes have been proposed for irregular networks, like the up*/down* routing scheme [20], the Eulerian-trail routing algorithm [19] or the adaptive routing scheme proposed in [26, 24].

We will restrict the scope of this paper to distributed routing, analyzing the behavior of NOWs with up*/down* and adaptive routing. To make the paper self-contained, we will summarize these routing schemes in the following sections.

3.1 Up*/Down* Routing

Up*/down* is a distributed deadlock-free routing algorithm that provides partially adaptive routing in irregular networks. In order to fill the routing tables, a breadth-first spanning tree (BFS) on the graph of the network is computed first using a distributed algorithm. Routing is based on a direction assignment to all the links in the network. In particular, the "up" end of each link is defined as: (1) the end whose switch is closer to the root in the spanning tree; (2) the end whose switch has the lower ID, if both ends are at switches at the same tree level. The result of this assignment is that each cycle in the network has at least one link in the "up" direction and one link in the "down" direction. To avoid deadlocks, this routing scheme uses the following up*/down* rule: a message cannot traverse a link in the "up" direction after having traversed a link in the "down" direction.

When a message arrives at a switch, the routing algorithm is computed by accessing the routing table. The address of the table entry is obtained by concatenating the input port number with the address of the destination node stored in the message header. If there are several suitable outgoing ports, one of them is selected.

Up*/down* routing is not always able to provide a minimal path between every pair of nodes due to the restriction imposed by the up*/down* rule. As the network size increases, this effect becomes more important.

3.2 Adaptive Routing

We will summarize the design methodology for adaptive routing algorithms on irregular networks proposed in [24, 26]. This methodology starts from a deadlock-free

routing algorithm, splitting all the physical channels in the network into two virtual channels. We will refer to them as the *original* and *new* channels, respectively. Next, the routing algorithm is extended so that new channels are freely used with the only restriction that they must forward messages closer to their destination, and original channels are used in the same way as in the original routing function. Additionally, when a message is injected into the network, it can only leave the source switch through new channels, since they provide a higher degree of adaptivity and, usually, a shorter path. Also, when a message arrives at an intermediate switch, it first tries to reserve a new channel. If all the suitable outgoing new channels are busy, then an original channel belonging to a minimal path is selected. If none of the original channels provides a minimal path to the destination, then one of the original channels that provide the shortest path will be used. To ensure that the new routing function is deadlock-free, once a message reserves an original channel, it can no longer reserve a new one [24, 26]. This message will be routed through original channels until it arrives at the destination switch.

The minimal adaptive algorithm [24, 26] is an application of this design methodology to the up*/down* routing algorithm. This routing algorithm provides fully adaptive minimal routing between all pairs of nodes until messages are forced to move to original channels. When a message starts using original channels, it provides the same adaptivity as the up*/down* routing algorithm.

4 EDINET: An Execution-Driven Simulator to Evaluate Interconnection Networks

The EDINET (Execution Driven Interconnection NETwork) simulator [9] allows executing a shared-memory application on a simulated DSM or NOW system. It is composed of two simulators. The first one is Limes [16], an execution-driven simulator that allows parallel program execution and models the memory subsystem. The second one is the interconnection network simulator that we have already used in several evaluation studies [24, 7]. The memory simulator part of Limes simulates the memory subsystem sending requests to the interconnection network simulator in order to simulate the transmission of messages.

4.1 Processor and Memory Model

The processor model has been chosen based on modern processor designs [13]. We assumed at each node a 480 MHz single-issue microprocessor with a perfect instruction cache and a 128 KB 2-way set associative data cache with a line size of 64 bytes. The memory bus was assumed to be 8 bytes wide. On a memory block access, the first word of the block was assumed to be returned in 16 processor cycles;

the successive words follow in a pipelined fashion, one per clock cycle. The machine used a full-mapped directory with an invalidation-based cache coherence protocol [5] implemented in hardware. The network interface has two separated queues to process incoming and outgoing requests. To avoid coherence protocol deadlocks we have implemented the approach proposed in [5]. In this approach when an input buffer is full, requests are rejected with a NACK command. Later, the source will send again the request after a random delay.

We have used a sequential memory consistency model. In this model, there is at most one outstanding request per processor. Therefore, a data miss stalls the processor until the data is returned. So, there is a bounded number of messages traversing the network at the same time. We have used this model because it is the simplest to implement and the easiest to program. Other memory consistency models may help in improving performance by increasing processor utilization [12]. So, with more flexible consistency models more traffic may be generated, and thus, processors may issue more requests to the network.

4.2 Network Model

The network is composed of a set of switches. Network topology is completely irregular and was generated randomly, taking into account three restrictions. First, we assumed that there are exactly 4 nodes (processors) connected to each switch. Second, all the switches in the network have the same size. We assumed that each switch has 8 ports (so, there are 4 ports available to connect to other switches). Finally, two neighboring switches are connected by a single link.

Each switch has a routing control unit that selects the output channel for a message as a function of its destination node, the input port number, and the output channel status. Table look-up routing is used. Up*/down* and adaptive routing (see section 3) may be used. Routing delay is assumed to be three processor clock cycles[3]. The routing control unit can only process one message header at a time. It is assigned to waiting messages in a demand-slotted round-robin fashion. When a message gets the routing control unit, but it cannot be routed because all the alternative output channels are busy, it must wait in the input buffer until its next turn. A crossbar inside the switch allows multiple messages traversing it simultaneously without interference. It is configured by the routing control unit each time a successful routing is made. The time needed to transfer a flit across the crossbar is assumed to be 3 processor clock

cycles. Considering that wires in NOWs are usually long, and assuming a Myrinet link bandwidth of 160 MB/s and maximum wire length of 10m, physical channel propagation delay is assumed to be equal to 36 processor clock cycles. Transmission of data across channels is pipelined [21], assuming that a new flit can be injected into the physical channel every 3 processor clock cycles. Flits are one byte wide. Physical links are one flit wide.

As physical channels may be split into several virtual channels, the "stop and go" flow control protocol [3] is used to efficiently use the available link bandwidth. In this protocol, the receiving switch transmits a stop (go) control flit when its input buffer fills over (empties below) 66% (40%) of its capacity. Considering that there can be up to 12 flits on the wire and assuming a one-cycle delay to decode control flits, input buffer size must be equal to 75 flits. Output buffer size has been fixed to 4 flits.

Table 1. Applications and the input sizes used.

Application	Problem Sizes
LU	16×16 to 512×512 doubles, 8×8 blocks
Radix	256K, 512K, and 1M keys, 1K radix, max 1M
FFT	2^{12} to 2^{18} complex data points
Barnes	1024, 2048, and 4096 particles

4.3 Network Load

We injected into the network the traffic generated by the execution of several parallel benchmarks. In particular, we used a subset of the SPLASH-2 suite (FFT, LU, Radix, and Barnes) [30]. These are challenging computational applications. Table 1 lists the actual problem sizes used for the applications.

5 Performance Evaluation

In this section, we evaluate the impact of using different routing algorithms on total execution time and network behavior, using the execution-driven test-bed introduced above. In particular, the up*/down* (UD) and minimal adaptive (MA-2VC) routing algorithms are compared. As MA-2VC algorithm requires two virtual channels per physical channel, in order to make a fair comparison, we have also evaluated the up*/down* routing algorithm with two virtual channels (UD-2VC). Also, we have included an ideal network model called PNET (Perfect NETwork). In this model, messages cross the interconnection network without contention using minimal paths. Message latency is

---

[3]We assume that the router clock runs at 160MHz, as in current Myrinet switches. This clock frequency is three times slower than processor clock frequency. Routing takes one router clock cycle, that is, three processor clock cycles. In what follows, all the references to clock cycles will refer to processor clock cycles.

assumed to be equal to the base latency, that is, the propagation delay along the shortest path from source to destination.

We have evaluated a system with 64 nodes. Taking into account that there are 4 processors connected to each switch, the network has 16 switches.

The main performance measure is the total execution time of the applications. Also, other measures like average message latency and average network throughput have been considered. In particular, we obtained the average message latency and average throughput during program execution at regular intervals. In all simulations the applications finished correctly and the application results were the expected ones.

5.1 Simulation Results

Figure 1 shows the total execution time of the applications for the routing algorithms analyzed.

In the FFT kernel (Figure 1-a), the MA-2VC routing algorithm reduces the total execution time by 38 % for the lowest problem size and by 53 % for the highest problem size with respect to the UD. When comparing with UD-2VC, MA-2VC reduces total execution time by 25 % for the lowest problem size and by 36 % for the highest problem size. These results show that the key to improve performance is not only adding virtual channels but using them in a more flexible way, as the MA-2VC does. This adaptive routing algorithm allows messages to follow alternative paths instead of blocking, waiting for channels to become free. Additionally, it balances link utilization, improving throughput (as we will see later) and providing a higher effective network bandwidth.

On the other hand, PNET reduces execution time from 42 % for the lowest problem size to 43 % for the highest problem size with respect to the MA-2VC. Although results obtained by MA-2VC are still far from the ones obtained by the PNET model, the relative difference remains constant for all the complexity points evaluated. Comparing with UD, PNET outperforms UD by 64 % for the lowest problem size and by 73 % for the highest problem size.

In the LU, Radix, and Barnes applications (Figures 1-b, 1-c, and 1-d) results are qualitatively similar. The MA-2VC outperforms both the UD and UD-2VC in terms of application execution time. The largest improvements are achieved for the highest problem size and are equal to 38 % (LU), 58 % (Radix), and 46 % (Barnes) when comparing MA-2VC with UD, and equal to 19 % (LU), 40 % (Radix), and 30 % (Barnes) when comparing MA-2VC with UD-2VC. As can be seen, adaptivity and virtual channels are very useful in all the cases.

Adaptive routing helps in reducing application execution time. However, it is important to characterize the network traffic requirements of the applications. Network through-put and latency indicate how loaded the network is.

Figure 2 shows the average latency measured as the elapsed time from message generation at the source node to message delivery at the destination node for the applications considered. Again, as expected, average message latency is reduced when using MA-2VC routing algorithm.

Figure 3 shows the average network throughput (measured in flits/cycle/switch) achieved by each application for every routing algorithm analyzed. As can be expected, network throughput increases when application complexity increases. The exceptions are Radix and Barnes, in which network throughput is almost constant for all the sizes of the data set we analyzed. In all the cases, the use of MA-2VC routing strongly increases network throughput with respect to UD routing. The explanation is very simple. The amount of generated messages is almost the same, regardless of the routing algorithm. As we have seen, MA-2VC reduces total execution time by allowing the use of shorter and alternative paths to forward messages toward their destinations. As a consequence, the ratio between the number of flits transferred and the elapsed time increases.

On the other hand, maximum throughput never exceeds 0.2 flits/cycle/switch. In [26], it was shown that network throughput could be as high as 0.08, 0.15, and 0.25 flits/cycle/switch using UD, UD-2VC, and MA-2VC routing algorithms, respectively, for a uniform distribution of message destinations and a similar network topology. As a consequence, the network is not saturated, on average. But there may exist hidden hot spots that saturate the network.

The analysis of traffic rate and average latency during the execution of the application allows us to analyze application behavior more precisely. Moreover, we are interested in analyzing how good adaptivity is in the presence of hot spots. We have gathered statistics for 1000 points at regular intervals during all the simulation. For the sake of brevity, results are only shown for the FFT and Radix applications and for the largest data set analyzed (2^{18} points in FFT and $1M$ keys in Radix). Figures 4 and 5 show the average traffic rate and average latency during the sampling intervals, for both applications considered.

As can be seen, in the FFT application the three curves for throughput and latency have almost the same shape, with three phases of high traffic rate separated by synchronization points, in which traffic rate is very low. The main differences are quantitative. The MA-2VC routing algorithm achieves the highest throughput and the lowest latency in all the sampled intervals. Notice that peak latencies are reduced from more than 2000 cycles in the UD to 600 cycles in the MA-2VC. However, only in the intervals with high traffic rate the increased flexibility offered by the adaptive routing algorithm makes a difference. These intervals are shorter when a higher degree of adaptivity is used in the routing algorithm. As expected, the case for the MA-2VC is

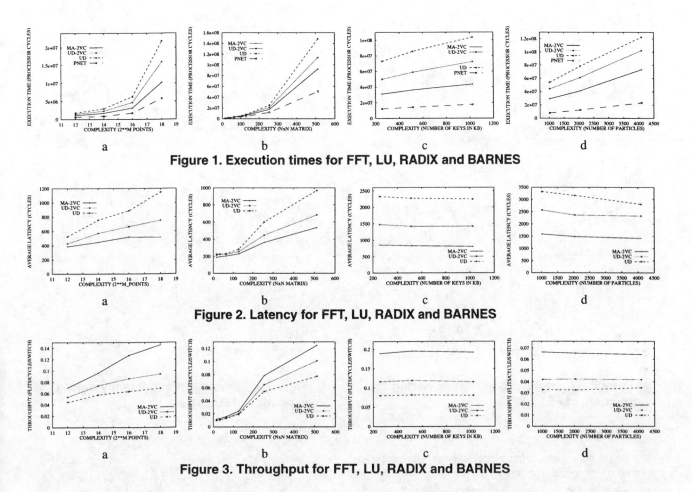

Figure 1. Execution times for FFT, LU, RADIX and BARNES

Figure 2. Latency for FFT, LU, RADIX and BARNES

Figure 3. Throughput for FFT, LU, RADIX and BARNES

the shortest one. On the other hand, intervals with low traffic rate are almost identical regardless of the routing scheme used. A similar behavior is obtained for the Radix application.

We can also see with the Radix application that the network reaches throughput values up to 0.4 flits/cycle/switch, which are higher than the maximum throughput achievable with a uniform distribution. At first glance, these points seem to be saturation points. However, this is not the case. Figure 6 shows the average distance traveled by messages for each time interval with the UD routing algorithm. We can observe that in the high traffic points the average distance decreases, indicating that the traffic pattern is changing to a highly local traffic pattern. On the other hand, we can see that the average distance decreases to less than one, indicating that many messages do not leave the source switch. Thus, the RADIX application does not saturate the interconnection network at these points. However, taking into account that we are using a sequential consistency memory model, the interconnection network could saturate with a more aggressive memory model.

In summary, routing algorithm has a great impact on ap-

plication execution time in a NOW with a hardware shared memory model. The running applications generate a very specific traffic pattern. This traffic is handled in a different way depending on the routing algorithm implemented within the interconnection network. With minimal adaptive routing, messages cross the interconnection network through minimal paths, leading to reduced latencies. In addition, adaptive routing also allows the use of alternative paths, achieving a more balanced use of resources and increasing network throughput. As a consequence, applications finish earlier.

6 Conclusions

In this paper we analyzed the influence of routing algorithm on the performance of a NOW with a hardware shared memory model using the traffic generated by some real applications. This analysis has been performed by simulating the behavior of networks with irregular topology, using an execution-driven environment. Several SPLASH-2 applications (Barnes-Hut, FFT, Radix, and LU) were used on a distributed shared-memory multiprocessor (DSM) simula-

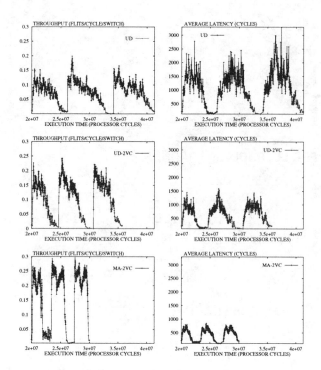

Figure 4. Throughput and latency during the execution of FFT

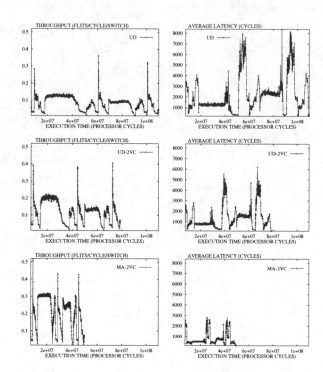

Figure 5. Throughput and latency during the execution of RADIX

tor with 64 processors, a hardware cache-coherence protocol and a network consisting of 16 switches (4 nodes per switch). The execution time of these applications was the main performance measure.

We conclude that the routing algorithm plays a key role in the design of interconnection networks for NOWs using a hardware shared memory model. In particular, when using a sequential consistency model (there are a maximum of p requests per time unit in a system with p processors), the interconnection network reaches high traffic loads in some critical phases of program execution. Hence, efforts must be done in routing algorithm design. These efforts must be oriented toward adding more adaptivity to current routing algorithms like up*/down*. The low latencies and high throughput achieved by more adaptive routing schemes noticeably decrease the overall execution time of the considered applications. Reduction time ranges from 38 % in the worst case to 58 % in the best case. Thus, virtual channels and minimal routing are the key to achieve a significant performance improvement in NOWs systems with a hardware shared memory model.

References

[1] C. Amza, A.L. Cox, S. Dwarkadas, P. Keleher, H. Lu, R. Rajamony, W. Yu, and W. Zwaenepoel, "TreadMarks: Shared

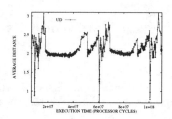

Figure 6. Average distance traveled by messages for RADIX with UD

Memory Computing on Networks of Workstations," in *IEEE Computer*, Vol. 29, No. 2, pp. 18-28, February 1996.

[2] W. C. Athas and C. L. Seitz, "Multicomputers: Message-passing concurrent computers," in *IEEE Computer*, vol. 21, no. 8, pp. 9–24, August 1988.

[3] N. J. Boden, D. Cohen, R. E. Felderman, A. E. Kulawik, C. L. Seitz, J. Seizovic and W. Su, "Myrinet - A gigabit per second local area network," in *IEEE Micro*, pp. 29–36, February 1995.

[4] G. T. Byrd and M. J. Flynn, "Evaluation of communication mechanisms in invalidate-based shared memory multiprocessors," in *Proceedings of the 1997 Parallel Computer Routing and Communication Workshop*, June 1997.

[5] D. E. Culler and J. P. Singh, *Parallel computer architecture : a hardware-software approach*, Morgan Kaufmann, 1999.

[6] Dolphin, *The Dolphin SCI Interconnect*. Dolphin Interconnect Solutions, `http://www.dolphinics.no`.

[7] J. Duato and P. López, "Performance evaluation of adaptive routing algorithms for k-ary n-cubes," in *Parallel Computer Routing and Communication*, K. Bolding and L. Snyder (ed.), Springer-Verlag, 1994.

[8] J. Duato, S. Yalamanchili and L. M. Ni, *Interconnection Networks: An Engineering Approach*. IEEE Computer Society Press, 1997.

[9] J. Flich, P. López, M.P. Malumbres and J. Duato, "EDINET: An Execution Driven Interconnection Network Simulator for DSM Systems," in *Lecture Notes in Computer Science 1469*, Springer-Verlag, September 1998.

[10] M. Galles, "Spider: A high speed network interconnect," in *IEEE Micro*, vol. 17, no. 1, pp. 34–39, January-February 1997.

[11] D. Garcia, "Servernet II," in *1997 Parallel Computer Routing and Communication Workshop*, June 1997.

[12] K. Gharachorloo, A. Gupta and J. Hennessy. "Performance Evaluation of Memory Consistency Models for Shared-Memory Multiprocessors," in *Technical Report CSL-TR-90-456*, Computer Systems Laboratory, Stanford University.

[13] J. L. Hennessy and D. Patterson. *Computer Architecture: A Quantitative Approach*, Second Edition, Morgan Kaufmann, 1996.

[14] R. Horst, "ServerNet deadlock avoidance and fractahedral topologies," in *Proc. of the Int. Parallel Processing Symp.*, April 1996.

[15] D. Lenoski, et al., "The Stanford DASH multiprocessor," *IEEE Computer*, vol. 25, no. 3, pp. 63–79, March 1992.

[16] D. Magdic, "Limes: A Multiprocessor Simulation Environment," *TCCA Newsletter*, pp 68-71, March 1997.

[17] N. R. McKenzie, K. Bolding, C. Ebeling and L. Snyder, "ChaosLAN: Design and Implementation of a Gigabit LAN Using Chaotic Routing," *1997 Parallel Computing Routing and Communication Workshop*, pp. 211–223. June 1997.

[18] A. G. Nowatzyk, et al., "S-Connect: From networks of workstations to supercomputer performance," in *Proceedings of the 22nd International Symposium on Computer Architecture*, pp. 71–82, June 1995.

[19] W. Qiao and L. M. Ni, "Adaptive routing in irregular networks using cut-through switches," in *Proceedings of the 1996 International Conference on Parallel Processing*, August 1996.

[20] M. D. Schroeder et al., "Autonet: A high-speed, self-configuring local area network using point-to-point links," in *Technical Report SRC research report 59*, DEC, April 1990.

[21] S. L. Scott and J. R. Goodman, "The Impact of Pipelined Channels on k-ary n-Cube Networks," in *IEEE Transactions on Parallel and Distributed Systems*, vol. 5, no. 1, pp. 2–16, January 1994.

[22] S. L. Scott and G. Thorson, "Optimized routing in the Cray T3D," in *Proceedings of the Workshop on Parallel Computer Routing and Communication*, pp. 281–294, May 1994.

[23] S. L. Scott and G. Thorson, "The Cray T3E networks: adaptive routing in a high performance 3D torus," in *Proceedings of Hot Interconnects IV*, August 1996.

[24] F. Silla, M. P. Malumbres, A. Robles, P. López and J. Duato, "Efficient Adaptive Routing in Networks of Workstations with Irregular Topology," in *Workshop on Communications and Architectural Support for Network-based Parallel Computing*, February 1997.

[25] F. Silla and J. Duato, "On the Use of Virtual Channels in Networks of Workstations with Irregular Topology," in *1997 Parallel Computer Routing and Communication Workshop*, June 1997.

[26] F. Silla and J. Duato, "Improving the Efficiency of Adaptive Routing in Networks with Irregular Topology," in *1997 Int. Conference on High Performance Computing*, December 1997.

[27] F. Silla, M.P. Malumbres, J.Duato, D. Dai, and D.K. Panda, "Impact of Adaptivity on the Behavior of Networks of Workstations under Bursty Traffic," in *Proceedings of the 1998 International Confence on Parallel Processing. IEEE Computer Society*, August 1998.

[28] Speight and J.K. Bennett, "Brazos: A third generation DSM system," in *Proceedings of the 1997 USENIX Windows/NT Workshop*, August, 1997.

[29] A. S. Vaidya, A. Sivasubramaniam, and C. R. Das, "Performance benefits of Virtual Channels and Adaptive Routing: An Application Driven Study," in *International Conference on Supercomputing*, 1997

[30] S. C. Woo et al., "The SPLASH-2 Programs: Characterization and Methodological Considerations," in *Int. Symp. on Computer Architecture*, 1995.

Performance and Architectural Features of Segmented Multiple Bus System

Jungjoon Kim
Access Network Lab.
Korea Telecom, Korea
jungkim@kt.co.kr

Ahmed El-Amawy
Dept. of Elec. & Computer Eng.
Louisiana State University, U.S.A.
amawy@sol.ee.lsu.edu

Abstract

The paper introduces a new class of bus-based systems called the Segmented Multiple Bus System (SMBS). The SMBS overcomes the architectural limitations of bus-based shared memory systems while maintaining their advantages in terms of high degree of fault tolerance, ease of expansion and ease of programming. In addition SMBS's are scalable; unlike conventional MBS's. Another interesting feature of the SMBS is that it supports wormhole routing which is traditionally used in direct network topologies. Using approximate Mean Value Analysis, we evaluate performance in terms of processing efficiency and request response time. We show good scalability for the SMBS. The approach we adopt in developing the models is comprehensive in the sense that the models incorporate features of both direct and indirect networks. This makes our performance models easily adaptable to several other network topologies.

1. Introduction

Wide variety of interconnection networks have been proposed for multiprocessor systems[1]. They can be classified into crossbar networks[2], single bus and multiple bus systems[3,4], multistage interconnection networks[1,5] and direct (static) networks[6]. In a direct network architecture, each node has a point-to-point connection to a set of neighboring nodes. Because nodes do not physically share memory, they must communicate by passing messages over the interconnection network. Direct networks scale well and allow the exploitation of communication locality. A major constraint with direct networks is their static topologies; once a machine is built it cannot be changed. Some recent distributed shared memory designs use low dimensional direct networks.

To the contrary, indirect networks such as the crossbar switch and multistage interconnection networks do not integrate processors and switches. Consequently, communication between two processors in an indirect network (as well as in multiple bus systems) is achieved through a shared memory. The crossbar switch network[2] gives full connectivity such that all permutations between

processors and shared memory modules are possible. However, this network is unsuitable for systems with a large number of processors. Multistage interconnection networks[1,5] allow a rich subset of one-to-one simultaneous connections between processors and memory modules. The disadvantage of multistage interconnection networks is that they are not easily scalable and are subject to high communication latency. A major common disadvantage of the crossbar switch and multistage interconnection networks is that they are not inherently fault tolerant.

A multiple bus interconnection network[3,4] is a good alternative. It provides high degree of fault tolerance, cost effectiveness, ease of broadcasting and ease of expansion. Usually a bus-based system suffers from severe problems unique to the bus itself, although it has the natural advantages of a bus. Bus loading is a major problem. Therefore, the bus itself becomes a major limitation to system scalability. In some cases, taking advantage of the locality of communication and/or locality of memory reference present in most applications can help in reducing the inter-node distance[14]. However, a conventional MBS cannot take advantage of such locality because a bus is a mutually exclusive resource to which all processors are connected.

In this paper, we introduce and investigate a new bus-based system called the *Segmented Multiple Bus System* (SMBS in short) which is targeted at overcoming the above mentioned drawbacks of bus-based shared memory systems. The SMBS is targeted at exploiting reference locality, scalability and versatility, features that are not found in any of the existing bus-based systems.

To avoid bus loading problems in bus-based systems it is essential to allow only a certain small number of connections to a bus. Segmenting a large bus system into a number of smaller ones can be an attractive option. A large multiple bus system could be segmented into smaller partitions, which we call *segments*. If these segments can be connected somehow such that bus loading effects are avoided, this makes it possible to overcome most problems associated with traditional bus-based systems. Each segment is in effect a multiple bus system whose size is chosen so as to avoid bus loading problems. The short bus results in removing bus loading problems and permits maintaining a fast bus cycle.

The SMBS supports wormhole routing[7] which is mostly used in direct network topologies. Together, both segmentation and wormhole routing could make the system largely scalable even though it is a bus-based system. This is a major hypothesis underlying the work we report here. The rest of this paper is organized as follows. Section 2 discusses architectural features of the SMBS such as its interconnection structure and arbitration mechanism. In Section 3, we overview a performance model of the SMBS with single flit buffers. When buffer capacity is unlimited, wormhole routing is equivalent to an optimized virtual cut-through scheme[9]. In Section 4 we examine the impact of memory reference locality on the mean response time and scalability. We also address the issue of how performance changes by varying system configurations and workloads. Section 5 summarizes the research reported in this paper and presents ideas for future research.

2. Segmented Multiple Bus Systems

In this section, the architecture of the SMBS along with its distinguishing features are introduced. Architectural features of the SMBS such as its interconnection and arbitration mechanism are described.

2.1. Interconnection

The SMBS may be classified as a general purpose asynchronous MIMD machine with shared memory. The SMBS consists of N processors and M shared memory modules which are evenly divided into g identical segments numbered from 0 to $g-1$. Each segment is thus a relatively small multiple bus system that is composed of $n = N/g$ processors, $m = M/g$ memory modules, and b segment buses. Here we shall refer to a bus in a segment as a *segment bus*. The segment bus is bidirectional. Figure1 illustrates the interconnection of the SMBS, where each segment is assumed to have a full bus connection.

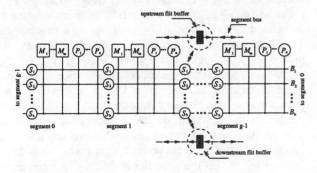

Figure 1. Segmented multiple bus system

In the SMBS we will use wormhole routing. At both ends of a segment bus we utilize *segment switches*. The segment switch is unidirectional and is a switching device with its own flit buffer. Although the segment bus is bidirectional, the bus behaves as a unidirectional bus when it is involved in an inter-segment access in which a memory request (or a reply) may be transferred to a neighboring segment through a unidirectional segment switch. The segment switch supports wormhole switching and has intelligence so that it could handle memory requests across segments. The segment switch checks the destination address of a memory request (or reply) and forwards the request (or reply) to the appropriate memory module (or processor). Aside from routing functions, segment switches also serve the function of isolating (or buffering) adjacent segments. Thus, in SMBS's, bus loading is not an issue if segments are not too large. In each segment, the switches are divided into two groups of equal size but opposite direction . We call the flit buffers in the first group of segment switches *upstream flit buffers* and the flit buffers in the second group *downstream flit buffers*, based on the direction of flow they support.

We define *a local memory module* as a memory module directly accessible by a segment switch to which the memory module is connected by a segment bus. Other memory modules are referred to as *non-local* with respect to the given segment switch. From a processor's point of view, memory modules connected by the segment bus that the processor is connected to, are called *local* and the other memory modules are referred to as *non-local*. The *bus cycle* is also considered the *flit time*. It is equal to the time needed to take a flit from one switch to the next over a segment bus or to a local memory module. Passing flits between two adjacent segment switches uses a handshaking protocol similar to the one described in[10]. A dedicated single-bit Request/Acknowledge line is associated with two adjacent segment switches. A flit is moved to the adjacent flit buffer only if it is empty.

To reserve bus bandwidth, only those buses that have a non-empty flit buffer at the sending side and an empty flit buffer at the receiving end may participate in the bus assignment process in any given cycle. Each memory module has an input buffer and an output buffer. This makes it possible for memory modules to serve requests continuously without having to wait to transmit the response packet back to the requesting processor before serving other requests. When a memory request is issued by a processor, the request will traverse segment switches if the requested memory module is non-local or will be sent directly to the memory module if the module is local. To make such determination, each segment switch should "listen" to the segment bus. However, this may cause the segment switch to suffer the unnecessary overhead of decoding every request. In order to resolve this problem, we assume that the request has one extra bit which indicates whether it is an intra-segment (local) request or an inter-segment (non-local) request. This eliminates unnecessary buffering of the request at a segment switch. The connection topology of the system could be a linear connection of g segments or a ring with end-around connections.

2.2. Arbitration Mechanism

We assume that all memory modules are single-port memories, so that at most one access can be made to a module at a time. The SMBS is a cascaded connection of g identical segments. Each segment is similar to a conventional multiple bus system except that these segments are connected via a set of segment switches. A memory request from a processor may be directed toward a local memory module or it may be transferred to a neighboring segment through a segment switch. The former is called *an intra-segment access* and the latter is called *an inter-segment access*. In the case of an inter-segment access, the packet for a memory request traverses (possibly several) segment switches and is eventually sent to the target memory module. A response packet from the memory module takes a return path which could be different from the forward path. We assume that a transient packet at a segment switch has priority over other packets in bus assignment. This is intended to reduce network contention.

Instead of using a central arbitration system, which would hamper the scalability goal for the SMBS, we employ a distributed arbitration mechanism. Each segment has an identical arbitration system and arbitration in each segment is independent of those in other segments. Hence, we can consider arbitration within a segment only. Resources within a segment consist of n processors, m shared memory modules, b segment buses, and a total of $2b$ segment switches which are located on the boundary of the segment. Notice that there are b segment switches on each side of the segment ($2b$ total) but only half of those can access segment buses and memory modules in the segment. For simplicity, we assume that the number of buses in a segment is even. The segment buses are divided into two groups: *an upper half bus group* and *a lower half bus group*. Each bus group is associated with a bus arbiter. The upper bus group (lower bus group) consists of the first half (second half) of segment buses which are bidirectional. The segment switches which are unidirectional are also divided into two groups of equal size but opposite direction.

Two sources of conflict exist, which are the same as those in a conventional MBS. First, more than one request can be made to the same memory module. Second, available buses may not be enough to accommodate all the requests. As in a conventional MBS, the arbitration scheme in a segment employs a processor selection function and a bus assignment function. These two functions can be implemented partially in parallel, like those in an MBS, as we explain next. In each segment, a two-phase arbitration scheme is employed to resolve the conflicts mentioned above. In the first phase, a segment bus is assigned to a segment switch if a request exists at the switch. The request could be caused by a transient packet or a terminating one. In the second phase, both processor selection and bus assignment are needed. In the case of an intra-segment access, these two functions can be implemented in parallel as would be the case in an MBS. Processor selection is needed when simultaneous multiple requests for a shared memory module occur. In this phase at most b outstanding requests from segment switches (selected in the first phase) and at most n requests from local processors can coexist. Contention for a given memory module is solved by using an $(n+b)$-user 1-server arbiter. Thus, a total of m such arbiters is performed per segment. If the arbiter selects a request from a segment switch that passed the first phase, the request is immediately assigned to the memory module. If the selected memory request is from a processor, that request must obtain the final grant from a bus arbiter in the same way as in the parallel arbitration of the MBS[11].

Together with memory module arbitration, bus assignment for free buses is employed in the second phase. Each segment has two $(2m+n)$-user $b/2$-server arbiters for bus assignment: one for the upper bus group and one for the lower bus group. Each such arbiter assigns at most $b/2$ buses by selecting requests from $2m+n$ request inputs. Among the $2m$ requests, up to m requests could come from memory response packets and up to m requests could come from outstanding memory requests selected by the memory arbiters. Notice that in each segment, there may be $(2m+n)$ different request inputs for bus assignment: n for inter-segment accesses by processors, m for requests from memory output queues for reply packets, and m for outstanding memory requests from intra-segment accesses. However, notice that the maximum number of requests that could actually participate in the bus assignment part of the second phase is $(m+n)$ because the n inter-segment accesses from processors and the m outstanding memory requests from intra-segment accesses must originate at the same set of n processors. The bus assignment process is designed so as to immediately assign a bus (if available) to a memory module with a response packet or to a processor requesting an inter-segment access. If a bus is assigned to an outstanding memory request, however, this bus assignment, together with the output of the corresponding $(n+b)$-user 1-server type memory arbiter, is used to produce the final grant. Thus, arbitration for an intra-segment access is done in parallel as in the traditional MBS. The complete arbitration system that each segment of the SMBS needs to have is built with m arbiters of the $(n+b)$-user 1-server type and two arbiters of the $(2m+n)$-user $b/2$-server type.

3. Overview of Performance Analysis Model

This section overviews a performance analysis model for studying SMBS's with single flit buffers employed at each segment switch. Detailed development of the model can be found in[12].

3.1. Assumptions and Performance Issues

Two types of messages are generated in the shared memory SMBS: a request and a reply. A request message represents a memory *read* or a memory *write* request. A reply message is either an *acknowledgment* message or a *data* reply message. For simplicity, each message is assumed to be a single packet of a constant size, although our analysis can be extended to the case of different request and reply sizes. The read and write requests are assumed to be treated equally in the sense that a processor will remain idle after submitting a request until it receives either data for a read request or an acknowledgment for a write request. Thus, the total number of packets in the system at any time is constant and is equal to the number of processors in the system. Hence, the entire system behaves like a closed queueing network. The model we develop is general enough so as to allow analysis of patterns. Memory requests within a segment are assumed to be uniformly distributed. However, at the segment level, references are assumed to be distributed arbitrarily. Each memory module is assumed to have an input buffer and an output buffer so that the memory module may serve requests continuously without having to wait to transmit reply packets back to their requesting processors. The sizes of the memory input and output buffers are assumed unbounded. A reply packet is assumed to be immediately consumed as soon as it arrives at the requesting processor. The service centers of the model represent the processors, memory modules and segment switches (together with their associated segment buses) of the SMBS. We make the following additional assumptions:

1. Each processor generates request packets with exponential distribution of inter-request interval with a mean of τ_p.

2. Read and write accesses in a memory module require the same service interval and take a constant time, τ_m.

3. A transient packet has priority over other packets for bus assignment. This assumption is based on the expectation that quickly delivered packets will reduce contention for network resources.

4. Arbitration time is included in a bus cycle time and a

fair selection policy is utilized in each arbitration phase.

5. Bus service time is deterministic and is equal to a bus cycle time which is also equal to the flit time.

6. The queueing discipline at each memory queue is first-come first-served (FCFS). In the case when requests arrive simultaneously, these requests are served in random order.

As we discussed earlier, the SMBS supports wormhole routing. A segment switch begins forwarding a packet as soon as the header flit is received, provided that the flit buffer in the next segment switch can accept that flit and the next segment bus is available. Thus, the flits of a packet are transmitted from one segment switch to the next in a pipelined fashion and may occupy several segment switches and their associated segment buses along the path from source to destination. Only the header flit contains routing information. If the header flit is blocked because the flit buffer in the next segment switch along the path is full or the associated segment bus is occupied by another packet, all the trailing flits of the blocked packet are blocked in place. Therefore, the segment switches and segment buses occupied by the flits are also blocked. If more than one flit can be buffered at a flit buffer, flits behind the header flit can catch-up at the flit buffer until the available buffer space is filled. At this point, they become blocked and can continue only after the header flit is unblocked. In the case that a header flit arrives at a target memory module, the remaining flits will always catch-up with it at the target memory module. We assume this method of routing throughout the paper.

When flit buffer capacity is unlimited, the wormhole routing scheme is equivalent to an optimized form of virtual cut-through switching. In virtual cut-through switching, if the header flit is blocked at a switch, the entire packet has to be buffered before the packet is forwarded. However, under the condition of unlimited flit buffer capacity, wormhole routing allows a partially received packet to be forwarded as soon as the header flit can advance.

We use *Approximate Mean Value Analysis*[8,13]. This technique has been shown to provide efficient and accurate solutions for non-separable models[8,15,16]. Model input parameters are summarized as follow. The SMBS consists of g identical segments numbered from 0 to g-1. Each segment is composed of n processors, m memory modules and b segment buses. The length of a packet is L. Each packet consists of t flits and each flit has length L_f. W_B denotes the segment bus bandwidth. A request generated by a processor in segment s (i.e., a class s request packet) directed to a memory module in segment d will have probability P_{sd}. The subscript sd in P_{sd} signifies a request of class s directed to a target memory module in segment d (in the forward path). Similarly, the subscript ds

in P_{ds} will signify a reply to a class s request directed to the requesting processor in segment s from the target memory module in segment d (in the return path).

We evaluate several parameters such as response time, processing efficiency, scalability of the SMBS under various configurations (various system sizes, flit buffer sizes and connection topologies) and under different workloads (varying memory request rates and uniform or non-uniform memory reference patterns).

3.2. Overview of the Model

Consider a request of class s for a memory module located in segment d. A processor will generate a request packet of class s traveling in its forward path from s to d and will receive a reply packet of the same class from the targeted memory module in segment d. The mean residence time experienced by the request in its forward trip to the target memory and that experienced by the reply in the return trip is dependent on the request's class. Hence, the mean response time of a request from a processor in segment s (a class s request) is

$$R[s] = R_{proc}[s] + R_{network}[s] + R_{mem}[s] \quad s = 0,...,g-1.$$

$R[s]$ is the sum of the mean residence times (queueing and service) for a class s request packet in the processor $R_{proc}[s]$, in the network $R_{network}[s]$ and in the memory module $R_{mem}[s]$. In short, we call $R[s]$ the mean response time of a class s request. The overall mean response time is given by

$$R = \frac{1}{g} \sum_{s=0}^{g-1} R[s].$$

$R_{proc}[s]$ denotes the mean residence time that the header flit of a class s packet experiences at the head of a processor output queue. This includes the mean waiting time for a segment bus plus the time for transferring the header flit to the first segment switch (in the case of an inter-segment access) or the time for transferring the header flit on a segment bus to a local target memory module (in the case of an intra-segment access).

The residence time in the network is the weighted sum of the mean residence times in the forward path (for a request packet) and in the return path (for a reply). Thus,

$$R_{network}[s] = \sum_{d=0}^{g-1} P_{sd} (R_{sd,network} + R_{ds,network})$$

$$s = 0,...,g-1,$$

where $\sum_{d=0}^{g-1} P_{sd} = 1$. $R_{sd,network}$ denotes the average residence time in the network of a class s request packet from the first segment switch on the forward path to the target memory in segment d. $R_{ds,network}$ denotes the average residence time in the network of a class s reply packet from the first segment switch in the return path to the

processor that originated the request. The residence time at a segment switch consists of the mean delay spent in the flit buffer waiting for a segment bus and the time for transferring the header flit to the next switch (for intermediate segment switches) or to the target memory module (for the final segment switch in the forward path) or to the original requesting processor (for the final segment switch in the return path).

The residence time in the network includes the catch-up times which occur both in the forward and return paths. The catch-up time in the forward path is defined as the mean delay until all the remaining flits reach the destination after the header flit arrives at the target memory module. The catch-up time in the return path is defined as the mean delay until all the remaining flits reach the processor after the header flit returns to the requesting processor. In the case of an intra-segment access, the residence time in the network is the sum of the catch-up times in the forward and return paths because a packet does not traverse any segment switches.

The residence time in a memory module is given by

$$R_{mem}[s] = \sum_{d=0}^{g-1} P_{sd} (R_{d|s,mem_{in}} + R_{d|s,mem_{out}})$$

$$s = 0,...,g-1.$$

$R_{d|s,mem_{in}}$ is the sum of the average delay that a class s request packet experiences in the input queue of the target memory module (in segment d) and the memory service time, τ_m. $R_{d|s,mem_{out}}$ consists of two parts. For an inter-segment access, it includes the mean queueing delay of a class s reply packet in the memory output queue, the mean waiting time for a segment bus at the head of the memory output queue and the time for transferring the header flit to the first segment switch in the return path. For an intra-segment access, it consists of the mean queueing delay at the memory output queue, the segment bus waiting time at the head of the memory output queue and the time for transferring the reply header flit back to its local processor.

We will also utilize another performance metric known as *processing efficiency* to evaluate SMBS's. Processing efficiency is defined as the fraction of time a processor is busy. If a processor generates request messages with the mean interval, τ_p, then the mean processor utilization of class s, $\rho_{proc}[s]$, can be expressed as

$$\rho_{proc}[s] = \frac{\tau_p}{\tau_p + R[s]} \quad s = 0,...,g-1,$$

where $R[s]$ is the mean response time of a class s request. Notice that the above expression does not distinguish among processors in the same class (segment) which is consistent with our model.

4. Numerical Results and Discussion

The flit time of $\frac{L_f}{W_B}$ will be used as our basic timing unit and normalized as one unit of time. Considering a 32-bit wide segment bus and the fact that message length (packet length) is expected to be about 100 bits on average in a shared memory multiprocessor[17], we assume basic packet length to be three flits ($t=3$). However, to study the effect of number of flits per packet, the number of flits per packet will be varied from 3 to 5. The mean time of the request interval, τ_p, is varied from 30 to 200 time units.

Values of τ_p higher than 200 show very little performance improvement. For values of $\tau_p \leq 30$ time units, some segment buses, most likely in middle segments, are nearly saturated particularly in experiments dealing with a baseline system with finite flit buffers. For such low values of memory request intervals, our model does not show a reasonable evaluation functionality. However, through extensive simulations, the given range for τ_p is shown to be reasonable enough to study the performance of our model. The mean memory service time, τ_m, is set to 4 units of time.

We used event-driven simulations to verify the correctness of our analytical models. The simulator implemented wormhole routing and bus assignment priority of a transient packet exactly. The chosen 95% confidence interval was observed to be within 10% of the mean. Simulation estimates were derived by using the method of batch means. To deal with the start-up transient of the simulation, we truncated the first 10% of memory requests. Simulation results verified the correctness of our analytical models[12].

To examine how SMBS's scale with increasing system size, we evaluated processing efficiency of the systems with single flit buffers under uniform memory reference as a function of the number of segments for different request rates ($1/\tau_p$). Figure 2 shows that the performance is poor as processing efficiency decreases rapidly with increasing number of segments (system size) at moderate request rates ($1/\tau_p \geq 0.02$). We observe that the low processing efficiency is primarily due to the increase in bus contention as request rate increases, as we can easily imagine particularly since buffer size is finite.

In an SMBS with finite flit buffers, bus contention tends to contribute to blocking to a greater extent. When contention is an issue, the pipelining property contributes greatly to low system performance, along with the finite size of flit buffers. Hence, the effect of bus contention in the SMBS expected to be more profound because processors must share segment buses with memory modules as well as with segment switches. The effect of

bus contention on performance in bus-based systems could be as significant as distance related latency in direct networks. Hence, a plausible way for reducing the probability of contention is to increase flit buffer size. To study how performance changes with different flit buffer size, we examined the two extreme cases that set bounds on the performance of systems: namely systems with single flit buffers and systems with infinite flit buffers. We also studied the behavior of systems with packet-sized flit buffers based on event-driven simulations, along with the two extreme cases.

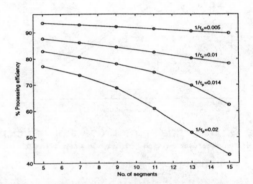

Figure 2. Processing efficiency of single flit buffer model under uniform memory reference: $n=10$, $m=10$, $b=10$, $\tau_m = 4$ and $t=3$

Figure 3 shows the behavior of processing efficiency, with different flit buffer sizes. There is no significant performance change among different flit buffer size cases when request rates are low ($1/\tau_p < 0.015$). As the request rate becomes higher, the performance gap between the infinite flit buffer and finite flit buffer cases becomes progressively larger. However, the performance gap between the single flit buffer and packet-sized flit buffer cases is relatively small for different request rates. The performance degradation of the finite flit buffer case as request rate increases is largely attributed to increased blocking caused by the finite buffering spaces. Thus, we conclude that the performance of the SMBS with finite flit buffers deteriorates by contention rather than by network distance. In an SMBS, increasing flit buffer size reduces the probability of contention and provides performance improvement. Furthermore, this property allows the cut-through advantage of wormhole routing to be fully exploited.

The results presented thus far assume a uniform memory reference model. We next examine the impact of memory reference locality on performance. Applications exhibiting memory reference locality can take advantage of architectural features of the SMBS to realize performance gains. An application with high locality is expected to reduce bandwidth demands on the system. This in turn could cause the contention effect to be reduced significantly. Figure4 shows processing efficiency of a single flit buffer model as a function of the number of segments for varying memory reference localities. Processing efficiency improves substantially with increasing locality because locality reduces bus contention as well as average network distance.

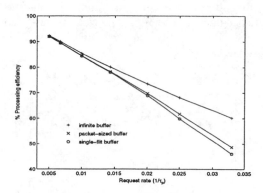

Figure 3. Comparison of processing efficiency with different flit buffer sizes: *n*=10, *m*=10, *b*=10, *g*=9, τ_m = 4 and *t*=3

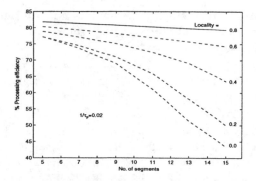

Figure 4. Effect of memory reference locality for single flit buffer model: *n*=10, *m*=10, *b*=10, τ_m = 4, $1/\tau_p$ = 0.02 and *t*=3

The number of flits per packet, *t*, is another factor that can affect system performance. In direct networks, when there is no contention and packet length is relatively large, network latency is almost insensitive to network distance. Contrary to direct networks, the SMBS is more susceptible to network contention because it is a bus-based system. Hence, the SMBS favors a small number of flits per packet because the small number of flits reduces the possibility of blocked packets occupying simultaneously several network resources. Figure5 shows performance degradation with increasing number of flits per packet. As request rates become high, performance deterioration is severe as we might expect. Figure 6 shows mean response time comparison, for the single flit buffer case, with varying number of segment buses per segment. We can

explain the abrupt change by stating that shortage of segment buses increases bus contention which in turn increases blocking. Increased blocking further increases contention. This cycle of negative effects stimulates the abrupt performance degradation. Therefore, we can point out, at least, the fact that the performance of an SMBS is very sensitive to the effect of bus contention.

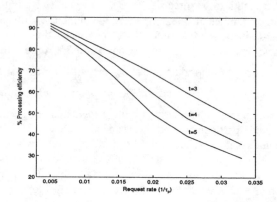

Figure 5. Processing efficiency with varying flit numbers per packet: *n*=10, *m*=10, *b*=10, *g*=9 and τ_m = 4

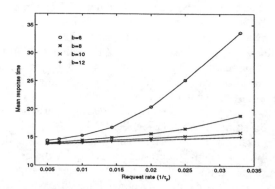

Figure 6. Mean response time of single flit buffer case with varying segment buses per segment: *n*=10, *m*=10, *g*=5, τ_m = 4 and *t*=3

5. Conclusion

In the SMBS, the bus loading problem associated with traditional multiple bus systems is not an issue if segments are not too large, although each segment is a full connection multiple bus system. We have employed a distributed parallel arbitration mechanism. Each segment has an arbitration system that is identical in all other segments and arbitration in each segment is independent of those in other segments. Hence, the arbitration delay in the SMBS (although it is relatively large) is dependent not on system size but on the size of a segment; i.e., arbitration delay is not a function of the number of segments in the system. This is another attractive feature of the SMBS.

We have made some observations. While performance in low dimensional direct networks is generally network distance limited, performance in an SMBS with finite flit buffers is likely to be bus contention limited. If the number of flits per packet is relatively large, the negative effects of long network distance in low dimensional direct networks are minimized. Contrary to direct networks, the SMBS is likely to be adversely affected by an increased number of flits per packet since it would lead to high levels of bus contention.

There are still several issues open for future research. It would be worthwhile to develop an analytical performance model for the SMBS with any finite-sized flit buffers that help in determining the flit buffer size required to match the performance of an infinite flit buffer case to within a certain percentage. The approach in this work can possibly be applied to several other network topologies which are classified as direct and/or indirect networks. For instance, if the shared memory in an SMBS is distributed to the processors (becomes local to processors), the model would be easily applicable to the resulting message passing environment.

Reference

[1] T. Y. Feng, "A Survey of Interconnection Networks," *IEEE Comput. Mag.*, Vol.14, No.12, December 1981, pp. 12-27.

[2] W. A. Wulf and C. G. Bell, "C.mmp - A Multi-Mini-Processor," *Proc. Fall Joint Comput. Conf.*, AFIPS, December 1972, pp. 756-777.

[3] T. Lang, M. Valero, and I. Alegre, "Bandwidth of Crossbar and Multiple-Bus Connections for Multiprocessors," *IEEE Trans. Comput.*, Vol. C-31, No.12, December 1982, pp. 1227-1234.

[4] T. N. Nudge, J. P. Hayes, and D. C. Winsor, "Multiple Bus Architectures," *IEEE Comput.*, June 1987, pp. 42-48.

[5] H. J. Siegel, *Interconnection Networks for Large Scale Parallel Processing: Theory and Case Studies*, Lexington Books, Lexington, MA, 1984.

[6] H. Sullivab and T. R. Bashkow, "A Large Scale, Homogeneous, Fully Distributed Parallel Machine," *ACM Proc. 4th Annual Int. Symp. Comput. Architecture, IEEE*, March 1977, pp. 105-124.

[7] W. J. Dally and C. L. Seitz, "The Torus Routing Chip," *Distributed Comput.*, Vol.1, No.3, 1986, pp. 187-196.

[8] E. D. Lazowska, J. Zahorja, G. S. Grahm, and K. C. Sevcik, *Quantitative System Performance - Computer System Analysis using Queueing Network Models*, Englewood Cliffs, NJ: Prentice-Hall, 1984.

[9] P. Kermani and L. Kleinrock, "Virtual Cut-Through: A New Computer Communication Switching Technique," *Comput. Network*, Vol.3, May 1987, pp. 547-553.

[10] W. J. Dally and P. Song, "Design of a Self-Timed VLSI Multicomputer Communication Controller," *Proc. Int'l Conf. Computer Design, IEEE*, Los Alamitos, CA, 1987, pp. 230-234.

[11] E. Lugue, D. Rexachs, J. Sorribes and A. Ripoll, "A Modular Arbitration System for Multiple Buses Multiprocessors," *Microcomputers, usage and design*, Euromicro 1985, pp. 579-585.

[12] Jungjoon Kim, "Performance and Analysis of Segmented Multiple Bus Systems," Ph.D.'s Dissertation, Electrical and Computer Eng. Dept., Louisiana State University, August 1997.

[13] J. R. Jackson, "Jobshop-Like Queueing Systems," *Management Science*, Vol.10, No.1, October 1963, pp. 131-142.

[14] K. L. Johnson, "The Impact of Communication Locality on Large-Scale Multiprocessor Performance," *ACM Proc. 19th Annual Int. Symp. Comput. Architecture*, May 1992, pp. 392-402.

[15] V. S. Adve and M. K. Vernon, "Performance Analysis of Mesh Interconnection Networks with Deterministic Routing," *IEEE Trans. Parallel and Distributed Systems*, Vol.5, No.3, March 1994, pp. 225-246.

[16] D. L. Willick and D. L. Eager, "An Analytical Model of Multistage Interconnection Networks," *Proc. ACM SIGMETRICS Conf. on Measurement Modeling Comput. Syst.*, May 1990, pp. 192-202.

[17] D. Chaiken, C. Field, K. Kurihara, and A. Agarwal, "Directory-Based Cache Coherence in Large-Scale Multiprocessors," *IEEE Comput. Mag.*, Vol.23, June 1990, pp. 41-58

Session B3

Compiler Support

Chair: P. Sadayappan
Ohio State University, USA

Compiler Optimizations for I/O-Intensive Computations

Mahmut Kandemir*   Alok Choudhary*   J. Ramanujam[†]

Abstract

This paper describes transformation techniques for out-of-core programs (i.e., those that deal with very large quantities of data) based on exploiting locality using a combination of loop and data transformations. Writing efficient out-of-core program is an arduous task. As a result, compiler optimizations directed at improving I/O performance are becoming increasingly important. We describe how a compiler can improve the performance of the code by determining appropriate file layouts for out-of-core arrays and finding suitable loop transformations. In addition to optimizing a single loop nest, our solution can handle a sequence of loop nests. We also show how to generate code when the file layouts are optimized. Experimental results obtained on an Intel Paragon distributed-memory message-passing multiprocessor demonstrate marked improvements in performance due to the optimizations described in this paper.

1 Introduction

As the speed of the disk subsystem is increasing at a much slower rate than the processor, interconnection network and memory subsystem speeds, any scalable parallel computer system running I/O-intensive applications must rely on some sort of software technology to optimize disk accesses. This is especially true for out-of-core parallel applications where a significant amount of time is spent in waiting for disk access. We believe that the time spent on disk subsystem can be reduced through at least two complementary techniques:

- reducing the number of data transfers between the disk subsystem and main memory, and

- reducing the volume of data transferred between the disk subsystem and main memory.

A user may accomplish these objectives by investing substantial effort trying to understand the peculiarities of the I/O subsystem, studying carefully the file access pattern, and modifying the programs to make them more I/O-conscious. This poses a severe problem in that user intervention based on low-level I/O decisions makes the program less portable. It appears to us that it is possible and in some cases necessary to leave the task of managing I/O to an optimizing compiler for the following reasons. First, current optimizing compilers are quite successful in restructuring the data access patterns of in-core computations (i.e., computations that do not use disk subsystem frequently) such that better cache and memory locality can be achieved. It is reasonable to expect that the same compiler technology can be used (at least partly) in optimizing the performance of the main memory-disk subsystem hierarchy as well. Second, although currently almost each scalable parallel machine has its own parallel file system that comes with a suite of commands to handle I/O, the standardization of I/O interface is underway. In fact, MPI-I/O [8] is a result of such an effort. We believe that an optimizing compiler can easily generate I/O code using such a standard interface much like most compilers for message-passing parallel architectures use MPI to generate communication code.

This paper presents a compiler approach for optimizing I/O accesses in regular scientific codes. Our approach is oriented towards minimizing the number as well as the volume of the data transfers between disk and main memory. It achieves this indirectly by reducing the number of I/O calls made from within the applications. Our experiments show that such an approach can lead to huge savings in disk access times.

The rest of this paper is organized as follows. Section 2 briefly discusses several approaches to locality optimization and summarizes the relevant work on data locality and out-of-core computations. Section 3 introduces our technique which is based on modifying both the loop access pattern and the file layouts and shows through an example how an input program can be transformed to out-of-core code. This technique is a direct extension of an approach originally designed for improving cache locality. We present the algorithm as well as the additional I/O related issues. Section 4 presents performance results on the Intel Paragon at Caltech. Section 5 concludes the paper with a summary and brief outline of the work-in-progress.

2 Related Work

Abu-Sufah et al. [1] were among the first to derive compiler transformations for out-of-core computations. They proposed optimizations to enhance the locality of programs in a virtual memory environment. Our approach is different from theirs in that we rely on explicit I/O rather than leaving the job to the virtual memory management system.

Compilation of out-of-core codes using explicit I/O has been the main focus of several studies [6, 5, 4, 19]. Brezany et al. [6] developed a run-time system called VIPIOS which can be used by an out-of-core compiler. Bordawekar et al. [5, 4] focused on stencil computations which can be re-ordered freely due to lack of flow dependences. They present several algorithms to optimize communication and to indirectly improve the I/O performance of the parallel out-of-core applications. Paleczny et al. [19] incorporate out-of-core compilation techniques into the Fortran D compiler. The main philosophy behind their approach is to choreograph I/O from disks along with the corresponding computation.

These previous techniques were all based on re-ordering the computation rather than on the re-organization of the data in files. In contrast, we show that locality can be significantly improved using a combined approach which includes both loop (iteration space) and data (file layout) transformations. This framework is potentially more powerful than any existing linear transformation technique as it can manipulate both loop and data spaces, and can apply non-singular linear transformations to both spaces. Due to the nature of the domain we are dealing with, our approach includes loop tiling as well.

Cormen and Colvin [9] introduce ViC* (Virtual C*), a preprocessor that transforms a C* program which uses out-of-core data structures into a program with appropriate library calls from ViC* library that read/write data from/to disks. We believe that data layout optimizations are complementary to computation re-ordering optimizations, and there are some programs that can benefit from a combined approach [7].

---

*CPDC, Department of Electrical and Computer Engineering, Northwestern University, Evanston, IL 60208. e-mail: {mtk,choudhar}@ece.nwu.edu

[†] Department of Electrical and Computer Engineering, Louisiana State University, Baton Rouge, LA 70803. e-mail: jxr@ee.lsu.edu

2.1 Data Locality Optimizations

Several techniques exist for optimizing data locality in loop nests. In general, these techniques can be divided into three categories: (a) Techniques based on loop transformations alone; (b) Techniques based on data transformations alone; and (c) Techniques based on combined loop and data transformations.

Techniques Based on Loop Transformations

These approaches attempt to improve locality characteristics of programs by modifying the iteration space traversal order. The extent of this modification maybe an important factor in determining the locality behavior of the program. The work in this category can be grouped into two sub-categories described below:

Non-singular Linear Loop Transformations: These transformations can be expressed using square non-singular matrices, called loop transformation matrices. A loop transformation should observe all data dependences [24] in the program. Apart from this, some approaches also require the loop transformation matrix to be of a specific form. The most widely used form is the permutation matrix [24]. This matrix contains only a single 1 in each row and each column; the remaining entries are all zero. Using this transformation matrix, an optimizing compiler can interchange the order of two loops in a loop nest in an attempt to improve spatial and/or temporal locality. A more comprehensive group includes unimodular transformation matrices. A unimodular matrix is an integer matrix with a determinant ±1. An important characteristic of a unimodular transformation is that it preserves the volume of the iteration space. Li [16] and Ramanujam [20] show how to generate code when a loop nest is transformed using a general non-singular transformation matrix. In principle, the more general the loop transformation matrix is, the more loop nests can be handled with it and also the more difficult to generate code.

Iteration Space Tiling: In its general form tiling decomposes each loop in a loop nest into two loops [24, 23]. The outer loop is called the *tile loop* whereas the inner loop is referred to as the *element loop*. Then the tile loops are hoisted into upper levels in the nest whereas the element loops are positioned inside. Typically, the trip count (number of iterations) for the element loops is chosen such that the amount of data accessed for an execution of all the iterations of the element loops fit in the fastest level of the memory hierarchy. Tiling can be used as a complementary solution along with linear loop transformations. A suggested approach is first to use linear loop transformations to optimize locality and then use tiling to further improve it [17]. Wolf and Lam [23] use unimodular loop transformations and then apply tiling to the loops which carry reuse. Li [16] present a framework where general square loop transformation matrices are used. He also illustrates how to generate the optimized code automatically. McKinley at al. [17] present a locality optimization algorithm which uses loop permutation, distribution, and fusion. None of these approaches [23, 16, 17] consider layout optimizations. Since a loop transformation may not be able to exploit locality for all the arrays referenced in the nest, it may result in sub-optimal performance.

Techniques Based on Data Transformations

These techniques focus on modifying layouts of multi-dimensional arrays rather than modifying the loop access patterns. As before, the extent of this modification is the main factor which distinguishes between different approaches. The most important category is dimension re-ordering (or dimension re-indexing). This consists of dimension-wise layout transformations (e.g., converting layout of

a two-dimensional array from column-major to row-major). In this category, the layout of a multi-dimensional array is seen as a nested traversal of its dimensions in a pre-determined order. Fortunately, these types of transformations can handle a large set of access patterns found in scientific applications. The second category consists of general data transformations that can be expressed by square non-singular transformation matrices. Using these transformations, an optimizing compiler can convert, for example, a column-major layout to a diagonal layout, if doing so improves spatial locality. An important difference between this and dimension re-ordering is that the former may cause some increase in the amount of the space allocated to the array. The last category in data transformations are blocked layouts. Anderson et al. [2] show that blocked layouts can be useful in optimizing locality for distributed-shared-memory multiprocessors.

Recently researchers have investigated the use of data transformations. Kandemir et al. [12], O'Boyle and Knijnenburg [18], and Leung and J. Zahorjan [15] use general data transformations to improve spatial locality. In [12], the explicit layout representations are used whereas in [18] the primary focus is on how to generate the optimized code given a data transformation matrix. Leung and Zahorjan [15] concentrate more on minimizing extra space consumption when array layouts are modified. The main limitation of data transformations is that they cannot optimize temporal locality directly, and a layout transformation impacts all the nests that access the array in question.

Techniques Based on Combined Loop and Data Transformations

These techniques apply both loop and data transformations for optimizing locality. Both transformations may be of different extents. In principle, the most general transformations are non-singular loop and data transformations. The work on integrated loop and data transformations is relatively new. Cierniak and Li [7] use both loop and data transformations for optimizing locality. Their loop transformation matrices can contain only 1s and 0s, and their data transformations are dimension re-ordering. Kandemir et al. [11] also use dimension re-ordering for array layout transformations. However, their loop transformations use general non-singular matrices and cover a larger search space than the approach given in [7]. In [13] Kandemir et al. proposed an integrated optimization approach that uses general non-linear loop and data transformations for optimizing data locality. In this paper we use that algorithm for optimizing out-of-core computations.

3 Our Approach

In this section we present a compiler-directed approach that employs both loop and data transformations. Our loop and data transformation matrices are non-singular square matrices. To the best of our knowledge, this is the most general framework that uses *linear* transformations for optimizing locality in I/O-intensive codes. Another important characteristic of our approach is that we optimize locality globally, i.e., for several loop nests simultaneously.

Our objective is to optimize the I/O accesses of out-of-core applications through compiler analysis. Since the data sizes in these applications may exceed the size of main memory, data should be divided into chunks called *data tiles*, and the program should operate on one chunk (from each array) at a time that is brought from disk into memory. When the operation on this chunk is complete, the chunk should be stored back on disk (if it is modified). In such applications, the primary issue is to exploit the main memory–disk subsystem hierarchy rather than cache–main memory hierarchy; that is, a data tile brought into memory should be reused as much as possible. Also the number of I/O calls required to bring the said data tile into memory should be minimized. Note that the latter problem is peculiar to I/O-intensive codes.

Notice that the necessity of working with data tiles implies that loop tiling should be used. Thus, tiling, which is an optional optimization for in-core computations, is a "must" for out-of-core programs. Given a series of loop nests that access (possibly different) subsets of out-of-core arrays declared in the program, our optimization strategy proceeds as follows:

(1) Transform the program into a sequence of independent loop nests using loop fusion, distribution, and code sinking.

(2) Build an *interference graph* and identify the *connected components*. The interference graph is a bipartite graph (V_n, V_a, E) where V_n is the set of loop nests, V_a is the set of arrays, and E is the set of edges between loop nodes and array nodes. There is an edge $e \in E$ between $v_a \in V_a$ and $v_n \in V_n$ if and only if v_n references v_a.

(3) For each connected component:

    (3.a) Order the loop nests according to a *cost* criterion using profile information.

    (3.b) Optimize the most costly nest using only data transformations and then tile this nest.

    (3.c) For each of the remaining nests in the connected component (according to their order):

        (3.c.a) Optimize the nest using loop and data transformations taking the file layouts found so far into account and then tile the nest.

        (3.c.b) Propagate the file layouts found so far to the remaining nests.

A few points need to be noted. First, our method of tiling a nest for out-of-core computations is different from the traditional tiling used to exploit cache locality. We will discuss this issue in detail later on in this paper. Second, the loop transformations found should preserve the data dependences in the program. We ensure this by using Bik and Wijshoff's completion technique [3]. Third, a data transformation in its most general form can increase the space requirements of the original array. This is because of the requirement in conventional languages that arrays have a rectilinear shape. While in in-core programs this extra space may not be an issue, in out-of-core computations, this may not be the case. Later on in the paper we also discuss how we alleviate this problem to some extent.

Figure 1 illustrates using an example how Steps (1) and (2) of the optimization strategy works. The original program on the left part of the figure consists of a sequence of two imperfectly nested loop nests. Within the loop nests are the names of the arrays accessed separated by commas. All arrays are assumed to be out-of-core and reside in files on disk(s). As a first step, the compiler transforms these loop nests to a sequence of perfectly nested loops using a combination of loop fusion, loop distribution, and code sinking [24]. In this example, we assume that this can be achieved using loop fusion for the first imperfectly nested loop nest and using loop distribution for the second. In the next step, the compiler builds an interference graph, and runs a connected component algorithm on it. The two connected components shown in the figure correspond to two program fragments which access disjoint sets of arrays. The first fragment accesses arrays U, V, and W whereas the second one accesses arrays X and Y. Since connected components do not have a common array, the rest of the approach can operate on a single connected component at a time.

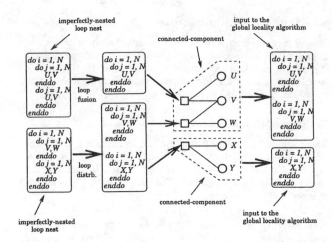

Figure 1: Example application of file locality optimization algorithm.

3.1 Motivation

In this subsection we illustrate through an example why a combined approach to locality is required. Consider the following program fragment assuming that the arrays are out-of-core and the default file layout is *column-major* for all arrays. For example, this fragment may correspond to the first connected component in Figure 1.

$$
\begin{aligned}
&do\ i = 1, N \\
&\quad do\ j = 1, N \\
&\quad\quad U(i,j) = V(j,i) + 1.0 \\
&\quad end\ do \\
&end\ do
\end{aligned}
$$

$$
\begin{aligned}
&do\ i = 1, N \\
&\quad do\ j = 1, N \\
&\quad\quad V(i,j) = W(j,i) + 2.0 \\
&\quad end\ do \\
&end\ do
\end{aligned}
$$

An approach based on linear loop transformations alone (e.g., [16], [17]) cannot optimize spatial locality for both arrays in the first nest as there are spatial reuses in orthogonal directions. The same is true for the second nest also. Therefore, two out of four references will go unoptimized. An approach based on linear data transformations alone, on the other hand, (e.g., [12], [18]) can select row-major layout for U and column-major layout for W. Since there are conflicting layout requirements for array V, one of the references will be unoptimized. The approach discussed in this paper proceeds as follows. Assuming that the first nest is costlier than the second, it first focuses on this nest and (using data transformations) selects row-major layout for U and column-major layout for V. Then it moves to the second nest. Since the layout for V has already been determined, it takes this into account and interchanges the loops so that the locality for array V will be good assuming column-major layout. This new loop order imposes array accesses along the rows of array W; consequently, our approach selects row-major layout for this array. To sum up, using a combination of loop and data transformations we are able to optimize locality for all the references in this program fragment.

3.2 Technical Details

3.2.1 Hyperplanes and array layouts

Our approach uses a simple linear algebra concept called a *hyperplane*. We focus on programs where array subscript expressions

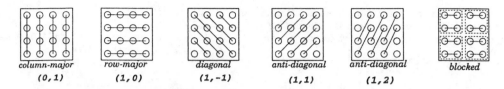

Figure 2: Example file layouts and their hyperplane vectors.

and loop bounds are affine functions of the enclosing loop indices and symbolic (loop-invariant) constants. In such a program, a reference to an m–dimensional array appearing in a k–dimensional loop nest can be represented by an access (or reference) matrix $\mathcal{L}$ of size $m \times k$ and an offset vector $\bar{o}$ of size m [23]. For example, the reference $V(j, i)$ in the first nest of the example fragment shown earlier can be represented by $\mathcal{L}\bar{I} + \bar{o}$, where

$$\mathcal{L} = \begin{pmatrix} 0 & 1 \\ 1 & 0 \end{pmatrix}, \bar{I} = \begin{pmatrix} i \\ j \end{pmatrix}, \text{ and } \bar{o} = \begin{pmatrix} 0 \\ 0 \end{pmatrix}.$$

In an m-dimensional data space, a *hyperplane* can be defined as a set of tuples

$$\{(a_1, a_2, ..., a_m) \mid g_1 a_1 + g_2 a_2 + ... + g_m a_m = c\}$$

where $g_1, g_2, ..., g_m$ (at least one which is nonzero) are rational numbers called *hyperplane coefficients* and c is a rational number called hyperplane constant [21]. We use a row vector $g^T = (g_1, g_2, ..., g_n)$ to denote a hyperplane family (for different values of c).

To keep the discussion simple, we focus on two dimensional arrays; the results presented in this paper extend to higher dimensional arrays as well. In a two-dimensional data space, the hyperplanes are denoted by row vectors of the form (g_1, g_2). In that case, we can think of a hyperplane family as parallel lines for a fixed coefficient set (that is, the (g_1, g_2) vector) and different values of c. An important property of the hyperplanes is that two data points (array elements) (a, b) and (c, d) lie along the same hyperplane if $(g_1, g_2) \begin{pmatrix} a \\ b \end{pmatrix} = (g_1, g_2) \begin{pmatrix} c \\ d \end{pmatrix}$. For example, a hyperplane such as $(0, 1)$ indicates that two elements belong to the same hyperplane as long as they have the same value for the column index (i.e., the second dimension); the value for the row index does not matter.

It is important to note that a hyperplane family can be used to partially define the file layout of an out-of-core array. In the case of a two-dimensional array, the vector $(0, 1)$ is sufficient to indicate that the elements in a column of the array (i.e., the elements in a hyperplane with a specific c value) will be stored consecutively in file and will have *spatial locality*. The relative order of these columns in file is not as important provided that array size is large enough compared to the memory size which almost always holds true in out-of-core computations. In other words, the vector $(0, 1)$ can be used for representing column-major file layout. A few possible file layouts and their associated hyperplane vectors for two-dimensional arrays are shown in Figure 2. The last layout given is an example of blocked layouts where each dashed square constitutes a block. Our method currently does not handle blocked layouts, although as it is it can be used for determining optimal storage of blocks in file with respect to each other. It should be emphasized that these file layouts are only a handful of the set of all possible layouts, and there are many other hyperplanes which can define file layouts in two-dimensional space. For example, $(7, 4)$ also defines a hyperplane family and a file layout such that two array elements (a, b) and (c, d) lie along a same hyperplane (i.e., have spatial locality) if $7a + 4b = 7c + 4d$.

3.2.2 Loop transformations

Nest-level optimizations transform a loop nest to increase data locality. Essentially, the objective is to obtain either temporal locality or stride-one access of the arrays which is important. To understand the effect of a loop transformation let us represent a loop nest of depth k which consists of loops $i_1, i_2, \cdots, i_k$ as a polyhedron defined by the loop limits. We use a k-dimensional vector $\bar{I} = (\imath_1, \imath_2, \cdots, \imath_k)$ called the iteration vector to denote the execution of the body of this loop nest with $i_1 = \imath_1, i_2 = \imath_2, \cdots, i_k = \imath_k$.

Recall that we assume that the array subscript expressions and loop bounds are affine functions of enclosing loop indices and loop-index-independent variables. The class of iteration space transformations we are interested in can be represented using linear non-singular transformation matrices. For a loop nest of depth k, the iteration space transformation matrix T is of size $k \times k$. Such a transformation maps each iteration vector $\bar{I}$ of the original loop nest to an iteration $\bar{I}' = T\bar{I}$ of the transformed loop nest. Therefore, after the transformation, the new subscript function is $\mathcal{L}T^{-1}\bar{I}' + \bar{o}$. The problem investigated in papers such as [23] and [16] is to select a suitable T such that the locality of the reference is improved and all the data dependencies in the original nest are preserved. For example, in a loop nest of depth 2, loop interchange is represented by a *unimodular* transformation matrix

$$T = \begin{pmatrix} 0 & 1 \\ 1 & 0 \end{pmatrix}.$$

3.2.3 Combining loop and data layout transformations

The following claim gives us an important relation between a loop transformation, the file layout, and the access matrix in order for a given reference to have spatial locality in the innermost loop (see [13] for the proof).

Claim 1 *Consider a reference $\mathcal{L}\bar{I} + \bar{o}$ to a 2-dimensional array in a loop nest of depth k where $\mathcal{L} = \begin{pmatrix} a_{11} & a_{12} & \cdots & a_{1k} \\ a_{21} & a_{22} & \cdots & a_{2k} \end{pmatrix}$ and let $Q = \begin{pmatrix} q_{11} & q_{12} & \cdots & q_{1k} \\ q_{21} & q_{22} & \cdots & q_{2k} \\ \vdots & \vdots & \ddots & \vdots \\ q_{k1} & q_{k2} & \cdots & q_{kk} \end{pmatrix}$ be the inverse of the loop transformation matrix. In order to have spatial locality in the innermost loop, this array should have a file layout represented by hyperplane (g_1, g_2) such that $(g_1, g_2)\mathcal{L}(q_{1k}, q_{2k}, \cdots, q_{kk})^T = 0$.* □

Since both (g_1, g_2) and $(q_{1k}, q_{2k}, \cdots, q_{kk})^T$ are unknown, this formulation is non-linear. However, if either of them is known, the other can easily be found. If we know the last column of Q,

$$(g_1, g_2) \in Ker\left\{\mathcal{L}(q_{1k}, q_{2k}, \cdots, q_{kk})^T\right\}. \quad (1)$$

Similarly, if we know (g_1, g_2), then

$$(q_{1k}, q_{2k}, \cdots, q_{kk})^T \in Ker\left\{(g_1, g_2)\mathcal{L}\right\}. \quad (2)$$

167

Usually *Ker* sets may contain multiple vectors in which case we choose the one such that the gcd of its elements is minimum. Returning to the example given at the beginning of Section 3.1, we find the access matrices for nest 1 are $\mathcal{L}_U = \begin{pmatrix} 1 & 0 \\ 0 & 1 \end{pmatrix}$, and $\mathcal{L}_{V_1} = \begin{pmatrix} 0 & 1 \\ 1 & 0 \end{pmatrix}$; and for nest 2 are $\mathcal{L}_{V_2} = \begin{pmatrix} 1 & 0 \\ 0 & 1 \end{pmatrix}$, and $\mathcal{L}_W = \begin{pmatrix} 0 & 1 \\ 1 & 0 \end{pmatrix}$. As mentioned earlier, for the first nest we apply only data transformations; that is, $(q_{12}, q_{22})^T = (0,1)$ (Q is identity matrix). Using Relation (1) given above, for array U,

$$(g_1, g_2) \in Ker \left\{ \mathcal{L}_U \begin{pmatrix} 0 \\ 1 \end{pmatrix} \right\} \Longrightarrow (g_1, g_2) \in Ker \left\{ \begin{pmatrix} 0 \\ 1 \end{pmatrix} \right\}.$$

A particular solution is $(g_1, g_2) = (1,0)$; i.e., array U should be stored row-major. For V,

$$(g_1, g_2) \in Ker \left\{ \mathcal{L}_{V_1} \begin{pmatrix} 0 \\ 1 \end{pmatrix} \right\} \Longrightarrow (g_1, g_2) \in Ker \left\{ \begin{pmatrix} 1 \\ 0 \end{pmatrix} \right\}.$$

Selecting $(g_1, g_2) = (0,1)$ results in column-major layout for array V.

Having fixed the layouts for these two arrays, we proceed with the second nest, assuming again that Q is the inverse of the loop transformation matrix for this nest. First, using Relation (2), we find the loop transformation which satisfies the reference to array V in this nest:

$$(q_{12}, q_{22})^T \in Ker \{(0,1)\mathcal{L}_{V_2}\} \Longrightarrow (q_{12}, q_{22})^T \in Ker \{(0,1)\}$$

A particular solution is $(q_{12}, q_{22})^T = (1,0)^T$, which in turn can be completed (using the approach in [3]) as $Q = \begin{pmatrix} 0 & 1 \\ 1 & 0 \end{pmatrix}$. Notice that this matrix corresponds to loop interchange [24]. The only remaining task is to determine the optimal file layout for array W. By taking into account the last column of Q and using Relation (1) once more,

$$(g_1, g_2) \in Ker \left\{ \mathcal{L}_W \begin{pmatrix} 1 \\ 0 \end{pmatrix} \right\} \Longrightarrow (g_1, g_2) \in Ker \left\{ \begin{pmatrix} 0 \\ 1 \end{pmatrix} \right\}$$

which means that array W should have a row-major file layout. The resulting program is as follows.

```
do u = 1, N
  do v = 1, N
    U(u,v) = V(v,u) + 1.0
  end do
end do

do u = 1, N
  do v = 1, N
    V(v,u) = W(u,v) + 2.0
  end do
end do
```

3.3 Tiling of Out-of-Core Arrays

As mentioned earlier in the paper, tiling is mandatory for out-of-core computations. Several transformations [24, 23] may need to be performed prior to tiling to ensure its legality. In our running example no such a transformation is necessary. A traditional tiling approach can derive the following code. Here B is the *tile size* and all the loops are tiled with this tile size. The loops UT and VT are the tile loops whereas the loops u' and v' are the element loops. Notice that tile loops are placed in the outer positions in each nest.

```
do UT = 1, N, B
  do VT = 1, N, B
    < read data tiles for arrays U and V from files >
    do u' = UT, min(UT+B,N)
      do v' = VT, min(VT+B,N)
        U(u',v') = V(v',u') + 1.0
      end do
    end do
    < write data tile for array U to its file >
  end do
end do

do UT = 1, N, B
  do VT = 1, N, B
    < read data tiles for arrays V and W from files >
    do u' = UT, min(UT+B,N)
      do v' = VT, min(VT+B,N)
        V(v',u') = W(u',v') + 2.0
      end do
    end do
    < write data tile for array W to its file >
  end do
end do
```

Although such a tiling strategy allows data reuse for the data tiles in memory, its I/O performance might be unexpectedly poor. The reason for this can be seen when we consider the tile access pattern shown in Figure 3(a). In this figure each circle corresponds to an array element and the arrows connecting the circles indicates file layouts (horizontal arrows for row-major and vertical arrows for column-major). The top two arrays are U and V in the first nest and the bottom two arrays are V and W in the second nest. Assuming that we have a main memory size of 32 elements (for illustration purposes), we can allocate this memory evenly across the arrays in a nest. Traditional tiling causes the tile access pattern shown in Figure 3(a). Let us focus on array V in the first nest. In order to read a 4×4 data tile from the file we need to issue 4 I/O calls. Notice that the alternative of reading the entire array and sieving out the unwanted array elements may not be applicable in out-of-core computations. For array V, we are able to read 4 elements per I/O call. The same situation also occurs with other array accesses.

Now consider the tile access pattern shown in Figure 3(b). Focusing on array V in the first nest, we see that in order to read 16 elements from the file we need to issue only 2 I/O calls (assuming that in a single I/O call *at most* 8 elements can be read or written). Notice that in both cases (Figure 3(a) and Figure 3(b)) we are using the *same amount* of in-core memory. This small example shows that by being a bit more careful about how to read the array elements from file into memory (i.e., how to tile the loop nests) we might be able to save a number of I/O calls.

The important point is to see that we can achieve this optimized tile access pattern by *not* tiling the innermost loop. This is in contrast with the traditional tiling strategy in which the innermost loop in the nest is almost always tiled (as long as it is legal to do so). Unfortunately, tiling the innermost loop in out-of-core computations (where disk accesses are very costly) can lead to excessive number of I/O calls as this loop (after linear transformations) exhibits spatial locality. Therefore, as a rule after applying the loop and data transformations to improve locality, tiling should be applied to all but the innermost loop in the nest. The tiled program corresponding to the access pattern shown in Figure 3(b) is as follows.

```
do UT = 1, N, B
  < read data tiles for arrays U and V from files >
  do u' = UT, min(UT+B,N)
    do v' = 1, N
      U(u',v') = V(v',u') + 1.0
    end do
```

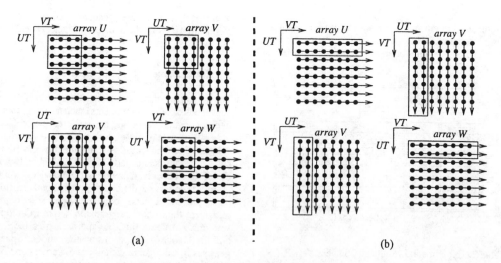

(a)   (b)

Figure 3: Different tile access patterns.

```
      end do
   < write data tile for array U to its file >
   end do

do UT = 1, N, B
   < read data tiles for arrays V and W from files >
   do u' = UT, min(UT+B,N)
      do v' = 1, N
         V(v',u') = W(u',v') + 2.0
      end do
   end do
   < write data tile for array W to its file >
end do
```

3.4 Reducing the Extra Storage Requirements

When data transformations other than dimension re-indexing are applied, there might be an increase in the size of the array in question. The reason is that in conventional languages such as Fortran and C the arrays need be declared as rectilinear.

Consider the access matrix $\begin{pmatrix} a & b \\ c & 0 \end{pmatrix}$ for an array U after the locality has been optimized and the transformed loop indices are u and v from outermost. Assume that $a, b, c > 0$ and $a \geq c$. Further assume that $1 \leq u \leq N'$ and $1 \leq v \leq M'$. Thus, the transformed reference $U(au + bv, cu)$ is good from the locality point of view assuming column-major layout. However considering the bounds for u and v the array region accessed by this reference consists of $(N' + M' - 1)(a + b) \times (N' - 1)c$ elements. The transformed array should be declared as $U[a + b : aN' + bM', c : (N' - 1)c]$.

Consider now applying a data transformation represented by the transformation matrix $\begin{pmatrix} 1 & -1 \\ 0 & 1 \end{pmatrix}$ to this access matrix. The new access matrix is $\begin{pmatrix} 1 & -1 \\ 0 & 1 \end{pmatrix} \begin{pmatrix} a & b \\ c & 0 \end{pmatrix} = \begin{pmatrix} a-c & b \\ c & 0 \end{pmatrix}$. Now this array needs to be declared as $U[a - c + b : (a - c)N' + bM', c : (N' - 1)c]$ covering a region of $(a - c + b)(N' + M' - 1) \times (N' - 1)c$ elements. Depending on the actual values for a and c we may obtain a huge amount of reduction in the layout requirements. If $a < c$ then we can use the following data transformation matrix: $\begin{pmatrix} -1 & 1 \\ 0 & 1 \end{pmatrix}$.

The data transformation matrix chosen should have two important properties. First, it should not distort the good locality obtained by the previous data transformations. In our example, the 0 element in the access matrix should stay as 0. Second, it should result in a reduction in the size requirements. Although not unique nor the best, the transformation matrix given above has the desired properties. The determination of the data transformation which minimizes the space requirements is an issue that we will re-visit in the future.

4 Experimental Results

In this section we present experimental results obtained on the Intel Paragon at Caltech. Paragon uses a parallel file system called PFS which stripes files across 64 I/O nodes with 64KB stripe units. In the experiments we applied the following methodology. We took ten codes from several benchmarks and math libraries. The salient features of these codes are shown in Table 1. Then we parallelized these codes for execution on the Paragon such that the inter-processor communication is eliminated. This allowed us to focus solely on the I/O performance of the codes and the scalability of the I/O subsystem. After this parallelization and data allocation, we generated five different out-of-core versions of each code using the PASSION runtime library [22]:

- `col`: fixed column-major file layout for every out-of-core array
- `row`: fixed row-major file layout for every out-of-core array
- `l-opt`: loop-optimized version: no file layout transformations
- `d-opt`: file layout-optimized version: no loop transformations
- `c-opt`: integrated loop and file layout transformations
- `h-opt`: hand optimized version using blocking and interleaving

The `col` and `row` are the original (unoptimized) programs. For the `l-opt` version, we used the best of the resulting codes generated by [16], [17], [23]. For the `d-opt` version, we used the best of the resulting codes generated by [18], [15], and [12]. `c-opt` (compiler optimized) version is the one obtained using the approach discussed in this paper. In obtaining `h-opt` we used chunking and interleaving in order to further reduce the number of I/O calls. For all the versions except `c-opt` all the loops carrying some form of reuse are tiled. For the `c-opt` version we used the tiling strategy explained in Section 3.3.

For each code we set the memory size allocated for the computation to 1/128th of the sum of the sizes of the out-of-core arrays

169

Table 1: Programs used in our experiments. The `iter` column for each code shows the number of iterations of the outermost timing loop. The `arrays` gives the number and the dimensionality of the arrays accessed by the code.

program	source	iter	arrays
mat	-	2	three 2-D
mxm	Spec92	3	three 2-D
adi	Livermore	5	three 1-D, three 3-D
vpenta	Spec92	3	seven 2-D, two 3-D
btrix	Spec92	2	twenty-five 1-D, four 4-D
emit	Spec92	2	ten 1-D, three 3-D
syr2k	BLAS	2	three 2-D
htribk	Eispack	3	five 2-D
gfunp	Hompack	3	one 1-D, five 2-D
trans	Nwchem	3	two 2-D

Table 2: Experimental results on 16 nodes.

program	col	row	l-opt	d-opt	c-opt	h-opt
mat	257.20	93.3	65.1	56.8	60.8	54.3
mxm	220.01	181.5	100.0	112.6	79.8	67.0
adi	144.12	134.9	22.8	46.5	22.8	22.8
vpenta	135.00	47.1	100.0	47.1	47.1	29.9
btrix	91.45	66.6	100.0	61.3	61.3	42.3
emit	88.64	176.5	100.0	100.0	100.0	100.0
syr2k	215.34	86.3	52.0	77.4	52.0	47.6
htribk	248.61	110.8	127.2	81.1	81.1	72.6
gfunp	86.05	128.4	73.3	68.0	46.9	34.0
trans	181.90	100.0	100.0	48.2	48.2	48.2
average:		112.5	84.0	69.9	60.0	51.9

accessed in the code. Each dimension of each array used in the computation is set to 4,096 double precision elements. However, some array dimensions with very small hard-coded dimension sizes were not modified as modifying them correctly would necessitate full understanding of the program in question.

Table 2 shows the results on 16 processors. For each data set, the `col` column gives the total execution time in *seconds*. The other columns, on the other hand, give the respective execution times as a fraction of that of `col`. As an example, the execution time of `c-opt` version of `gfunp.4` is 46.9 percent of that of `col`. From these results we infer the following. First, the classical locality optimization schemes based on loop transformations alone may not work well for out-of-core computations. On average `l-opt` brings only a 16% improvement over `col`. The approaches based on data transformations perform much better. Our integrated approach explained in this paper, however, results in a 40% reduction in the execution times with respect to `col`. Using a hand optimized version (`h-opt`) brings an additional 8% reduction over `c-opt`, which encourages us to incorporate array chunking and interleaving into our technique.

Table 3, on the other hand, shows the speedups obtained by different versions for processor sizes of 16, 32, 64, and 128 using all 64 I/O nodes. It should be stressed that in obtaining these speedups we used the single node result of the respective versions. For example, the speedup for the `c-opt` version of `emit.3` was computed for $p \in 16, 32, 64, 128$ as

$$\frac{\text{Execution Time of the c-opt version of emit.3 on 1 node}}{\text{Execution Time of the c-opt version of emit.3 on p nodes}}$$

Since the execution times of the parallelized codes on single nodes may not be as good as the best sequential version, these results are higher than we expected. Also, since the codes were parallelized

such that there is no interprocessor communication, the scalability was limited only by the number of I/O nodes and the I/O subsystem bandwidth.

5 Conclusions

The increasing disparity between the speeds of disk subsystems and the speeds of other components (such as processors, memories, and interconnection networks) has rendered the problem of improving the performance of out-of-core programs (i.e., programs that access very large amounts of disk-resident data) very important and difficult. Programmers usually have to embed code for staging in and out of data between memory and I/O devices explicitly in the program. Often this results in non-portable and error-prone code. This paper presents a technique that an optimizing compiler can use to transform the in-core programs to derive I/O-efficient out-of-core versions. In doing this, the approach uses loop (iteration space) and file layout (data space) transformations. Specifically, this paper uses linear algebra techniques to derive good file layouts along with the accompanying loop transformations. Preliminary results show that our technique substantially reduces the time spent in performing I/O. Currently we are working on extending our approach across procedure boundaries. We are also working on the problem of determining optimal file layouts using techniques from integer linear programming.

Acknowledgments Mahmut Kandemir and Alok Choudhary are supported in part by NSF Young Investigator Award CCR-9357840 and NSF CCR-9509143. J. Ramanujam is supported in part by an NSF Young Investigator Award CCR-9457768.

References

[1] W. Abu-Sufah, D. Kuck, and D. Lawrie. On the performance enhancement of paging systems through program analysis & transformations, *IEEE Trans. Comp.*, C-30(5):341–355, 1981.

[2] J. Anderson, S. Amarasinghe, and M. Lam. Data and computation transformations for multiprocessors. In *Proc. 5th ACM SIGPLAN Symp. Prin. & Prac. Par. Prog.*, July 1995.

[3] A. Bik, and H. Wijshoff. On a completion method for unimodular matrices. Technical Report 94–14, Dept. of Computer Science, Leiden University, 1994.

[4] R. Bordawekar, A. Choudhary, K. Kennedy, C. Koelbel, and M. Paleczny. A model and compilation strategy for out-of-core data-parallel programs. In *Proc. SIGPLAN Symp. Prin. & Prac. Par. Pro.*, July 1995.

[5] R. Bordawekar, A. Choudhary, and J. Ramanujam. Automatic optimization of communication in out-of-core stencil codes. In *Proc. 10th ACM Int. Conf. Supercomp.*, pp. 366–373, 1996.

[6] P. Brezany, T. Muck, and E. Schikuta. Language, compiler and parallel database support for I/O intensive applications, In *Proc. High Performance Computing & Networking*, 1995.

[7] M. Cierniak, and W. Li. Unifying data and control transformations for distributed shared memory machines. Technical Report 542, CS Dept., University of Rochester, November 1994.

[8] P. Corbett, D. Feitelson, S. Fineberg, Y. Hsu, B. Nitzberg, J. Prost, M. Snir, B. Traversat, and P. Wong. Overview of the MPI-IO parallel I/O interface, *Proc. 3rd Workshop I/O in Par. & Dist. Sys.*, Apr. 1995.

Table 3: Results on scalability of different versions.

program	version	number of processors			
		16	32	64	128
mat.2	col	10.9	20.6	34.8	64.3
	row	11.0	20.9	35.6	66.0
	l-opt	13.9	27.6	53.8	100.4
	d-opt	14.5	28.1	55.0	104.2
	c-opt	14.0	27.7	54.8	102.7
	h-opt	15.2	30.9	60.9	115.6
mxm.2	col	11.1	21.2	37.6	70.0
	row	8.2	15.4	30.0	52.6
	l-opt	11.1	21.2	37.6	70.0
	d-opt	9.7	17.0	32.1	56.4
	c-opt	13.7	24.8	56.4	106.6
	h-opt	13.7	24.8	56.1	107.2
adi.2	col	12.0	22.2	51.2	70.9
	row	6.89	10.9	18.6	31.4
	l-opt	15.3	28.2	61.4	107.5
	d-opt	13.8	24.0	55.5	74.9
	c-opt	15.3	28.2	61.4	107.5
	h-opt	15.3	28.2	61.4	107.5
vpenta.6	col	10.0	24.2	51.3	78.9
	row	14.5	28.0	60.9	109.8
	l-opt	10.0	24.2	51.3	78.9
	d-opt	14.5	28.0	60.9	109.8
	c-opt	14.5	28.0	60.9	109.8
	h-opt	14.7	29.0	62.4	108.2
btrix.4	col	10.0	18.1	27.0	42.7
	row	12.9	23.9	45.8	87.1
	l-opt	10.0	18.1	27.0	42.7
	d-opt	13.9	25.1	46.2	98.1
	c-opt	13.9	25.1	46.2	98.1
	h-opt	13.1	24.6	44.3	93.1

program	version	number of processors			
		16	32	64	128
emit.3	col	12.7	23.1	45.0	89.9
	row	6.8	11.0	18.5	33.9
	l-opt	12.7	23.1	45.0	89.9
	d-opt	12.7	23.1	45.0	89.9
	c-opt	12.7	23.1	45.0	89.9
	h-opt	12.7	32.1	45.0	89.9
syr2k.2	col	10.3	20.0	36.5	71.5
	row	11.7	22.0	38.9	78.0
	l-opt	13.8	26.8	51.0	95.1
	d-opt	12.5	24.1	45.6	87.4
	c-opt	13.8	26.8	51.0	95.1
	h-opt	14.1	26.0	51.0	95.3
htribk.2	col	11.7	20.3	37.7	76.6
	row	9.5	16.9	30.0	55.4
	l-opt	8.8	15.0	24.3	44.0
	d-opt	11.9	21.5	37.9	76.9
	c-opt	11.9	21.5	37.9	76.9
	h-opt	12.1	21.6	40.1	76.9
gfunp.4	col	10.9	20.4	38.4	70.8
	row	9.5	17.0	32.6	60.6
	l-opt	8.1	15.7	28.2	52.2
	d-opt	14.0	25.0	56.0	102.3
	c-opt	14.0	25.0	56.0	102.3
	h-opt	14.5	24.7	57.0	105.7
trans.2	col	13.0	22.7	31.6	67.7
	row	13.0	22.7	31.6	67.7
	l-opt	13.0	22.7	31.6	67.7
	d-opt	15.4	30.9	60.2	113.0
	c-opt	15.4	30.9	60.2	113.0
	h-opt	15.4	30.9	60.2	113.0

[9] T. H. Cormen, and A. Colvin. ViC*: A preprocessor for virtual-memory C*. Dartmouth College Computer Science Technical Report PCS-TR94-243, November 1994.

[10] M. Kandemir, R. Bordawekar, and A. Choudhary. Data access reorganizations in compiling out-of-core data parallel programs on distributed memory machines. In *Proc. IPPS 97*, pp. 559–564, April 1997.

[11] M. Kandemir, J. Ramanujam, and A. Choudhary. A compiler algorithm for optimizing locality in loop nests. In Proc. *11th ACM Int. Conf. Supercomp.*, pp. 269-278, July 1997.

[12] M. Kandemir, A. Choudhary, N. Shenoy, P. Banerjee, and J. Ramanujam. A hyperplane based approach for optimizing spatial locality in loop nests. In *Proc. 1998 ACM Int. Conf. Supercomp.*, July 1998.

[13] M. Kandemir, A. Choudhary, J. Ramanujam, and P. Banerjee. A matrix-based approach to the global locality optimization problem. In *Proc. PACT'98*, October 1998.

[14] M. Kandemir, M. Kandaswamy, and A.Choudhary. Global I/O optimizations for out-of-core computations. In *Proc. High-Performance Computing Conference (HiPC)*, 1997.

[15] S. Leung, and J. Zahorjan. Optimizing data locality by array restructuring. Technical Report, CSE Dept., University of Washington, TR 95-09-01, Sep. 1995.

[16] W. Li. Compiling for NUMA parallel machines. Ph.D. dissertation, Cornell University, 1993.

[17] K. McKinley, S. Carr, and C.W. Tseng. Improving data locality with loop transformations. *ACM Transactions on Programming Languages and Systems,* 1996.

[18] M. O'Boyle, and P. Knijnenburg. Non-singular data transformations: Definition, validity, applications. In *Proc. 6th Workshop on Compilers for Par. Comp.*, pp. 287–297, 1996.

[19] M. Paleczny, K. Kennedy, and C. Koelbel. Compiler support for out-of-core arrays on parallel machines. CRPC Technical Report 94509-S, Rice University, Dec. 1994.

[20] J. Ramanujam. Non-unimodular transformations of nested loops. In *Proc. Supercomputing 92*, pp. 214–223, 1992.

[21] J. Ramanujam, and P. Sadayappan. Compile-time techniques for data distribution in distributed memory machines. *IEEE Trans. Par. & Dist. Sys.*, 2(4):472–482, Oct. 1991.

[22] R. Thakur, A. Choudhary, R. Bordawekar, S. More, and S. Kuditipudi. PASSION: Optimized I/O for parallel applications, *IEEE Computer*, (29)6:70–78, June 1996.

[23] M. Wolf, and M. Lam. A data locality optimizing algorithm. In *Proc. ACM SIGPLAN 91 Conf. Prog. Lang. Des. & Impl.*, pp. 30–44, June 1991.

[24] M. Wolfe. *High Performance Compilers for Parallel Computing*, Addison-Wesley, 1996.

Exploiting Multiple Levels of Parallelism in OpenMP: A Case Study

Eduard Ayguadé, Xavier Martorell, Jesús Labarta,
Marc Gonzàlez and Nacho Navarro

European Center for Parallelism of Barcelona, Computer Architecture Department (UPC),
cr. Jordi Girona 1-3, Mòdul D6, 08034 - Barcelona, Spain

Abstract

Most current shared–memory parallel programming environments are based on thread packages that allow the exploitation of a single level of parallelism. These thread packages do not enable the spawning of new parallelism from a previously activated parallel region. Current initiatives (like OpenMP) include in their definition the exploitation of multiple levels of parallelism through the nesting of parallel constructs. This paper analyzes the requirements towards an efficient multi–level parallelization and reports some conclusions gathered from the experience in the parallelization of two benchmark applications. The underlying system is based on: i) an OpenMP compiler which accepts some extensions to the original definition and ii) a user-level threads library that supports the exploitation of both fine-grain and multi–level parallelism.

1. Introduction

Parallel processing is being accepted by the computer industry as the path to increase the computational power of low–end workstations and even personal computers. Parallel architectures, ranging from multiprocessor workstations (with 2 to 4 processors) to medium scale shared–memory systems (up to 64 processors) are becoming more and more affordable and common. However, making these parallel machines truly usable requires easy–to–understand and portable programming models that allow the exploitation of parallelism out of applications written in standard high–level languages. They usually offer new mechanisms or extensions to the language to express the available parallelism of the application.

These extensions are usually offered by means of high–level directives and language constructs (the effort done within the OpenMP initiative [13] or the HPF High Performance Fortran Forum [9]) or by a set of services offered by a user–level thread package. Pro-

gramming models in the first group offer a loosely synchronous programming model in which parallel jobs can be executed fully in parallel and synchronize at global points (by means of barriers or critical sections). Services included in most user–level thread packages allow a more general exploitation of parallelism (either at subroutine call level and at loop level) but at the expenses of higher programming effort.

Most current systems (compilers and run–time threads support) are based upon the exploitation of a single level of parallelism around loops (for example, the current version of the SGI MP library, the SUIF compiler infrastructure [6] or the MOERAE portable thread–based interface for the Polaris compiler [8]). Exploiting a single level of parallelism means that there is a single thread (master) that produces work for other processors (slaves). Once parallelism is activated, new opportunities for parallel work creation are ignored by the execution environment. Exploiting this parallelism may incur in low performance returns as one increases the number of processors to run the application.

Multi–level parallelism enables the generation of work from different simultaneously executing threads. Once parallelism is activated, new opportunities for parallel work creation result in the generation of work for all or a restricted set of processors. We believe that multi–level parallelization will play an important role in new scalable programming and execution models. Nested parallelism may provide further opportunities for work distribution, both around loops and sections; however, new issues may arise in order to attain high performance. OpenMP [13], jointly defined by a group of major computer hardware and software vendors, includes in its definition the exploitation of multi–level parallelism through the nesting of parallel constructs.

Previous work on supporting multi–level parallelism focused on providing some kind of coordination support to allow the interaction of a set of program modules in the framework of data parallel programs for distributed memory architectures. Some of them combine the use of two programming models and interfaces. For example, [3] proposes a library–based approach that provides a set of functions for coupling multiple HPF tasks to form task–parallel computations. Other alternatives [2, 5, 16] proposed a small set of Fortran directives to integrate task and data parallelism parallelism also in an HPF framework.

The Illinois–Intel Multithreading library [4] targets shared–memory systems. It also supports multiple levels of general (unstructured) parallelism. Application tasks are inserted into work queues before execution, allowing several task descriptions to be active at the same time. Kuck and Associates, Inc. has made proposals to OpenMP to support multi-level parallelism through the WorkQueue mechanism [10], in which work can be created dynamically, even recursively, and put into queues. Within the WorkQueue model, nested queuing permits a hierarchy of queues to arise, mirroring recursion and linked data structures. These proposals offer multiple levels of parallelism but do not support the logical clustering of processors in the multilevel structure, which may lead to better work distribution and data locality exploitation.

The approach presented in this paper takes Fortran applications fully annotated with directives to be parallelized by the compiler targeted to shared–memory architectures. Some extensions have been included in the OpenMP definition to enable an efficient exploitation of multiple levels of parallelism in numerical applications. Although the compiler may identify additional parallelism in the application through data and control dependence analysis, this aspect is out of scope for this paper. From the analysis of the program, the compiler generates an intermediate representation of the parallel application taking the form of a *Hierarchical Task Graph* (HTG [15]). The HTG representation captures parallelism information at different levels of granularity. An efficient user–level threads library allows the compiler to map the parallelism structure of the application into a Fortran code with calls to the services offered by the library.

The rest of the paper is organized as follows: Section 2 briefly describes the applications used along the paper as a case study. Section 3 presents the OpenMP programming model used in our environment and the thread–level support currently provided by run–time libraries. Section 4 presents some extensions proposed towards a more flexible and efficient multi–level parallelization and the thread–level support that is required. Section 5 analyzes the multi–level parallelization for both applications (running on top of an SGI Origin2000 platform). Finally, Section 6 concludes the paper.

2. Two SPEC95FP applications

In this paper two different applications have been selected from the SPEC95 benchmark set: Hydro2D, which computes the movement of galactical jets using Navier Stokes' equations for a variable number of points in the space; and Turb3D, which simulates isotropic homogeneous turbulences in a cube with periodic boundary conditions.

2.1. Hydro2D

Hydro2D works primarily with four different two-dimensional matrices (RO, EN, GR and GZ) of 402x160 elements. The main work of the application is done in function *advnce*, called directly from a timestep loop. This loop is repeated 200 times when the reference input is used. Each call to this function performs two steps over these four matrices.

In the first step, these matrices are used to calculate three sets of new matrices. The latter ones are combined, producing four intermediate matrices, onto which the *fct* is computed. The results of the four *fct* are the new versions of matrices RO, EN, GR and GZ, which are then used to perform the second step. The structure of the second step is very similar to that of the first one, calculating the final values for the matrices.

The central part in Figure 1 shows the parallelism structure for one of the two steps in function *advnce*. First of all, the computation of the three sets of matrices from the primary matrices can be done in parallel (nodes 2, 3 and 4). The functions involved in these computations are *corix*, *stagx1* and *stagx2*, where *x* stands for *f* or *g*, depending on the step. They contain both section and loop–level parallelism inside, as shown in the right part of Figure 1. After that, functions *trans1* and *trans2* are invoked (nodes 5 and 6),

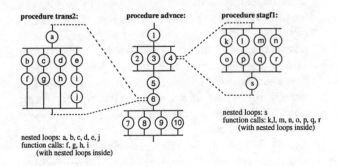

Figure 1. Parallelism structure for the SPEC95 Hydro2D application.

with the parallelism structure shown in the left part Figure 1. Again, they contain parallelism at the level of sections and loops. The computation of the four *fct* that follows *trans2* (nodes 7–10) can also be performed in parallel. Each *fct* contains function calls and nested loops with loop–level parallelism inside.

The application structure and data used in each node of the task graph enables the definition of processor groups. Each of the four sections that appear in different parts of the application is devoted to the computation of one of the above mentioned matrices. If one ensures that the same processors are always used for the execution of related sections, locality exploitation will be improved. This is the purpose of the extensions to OpenMP that we present in Section 4.

For this application, current parallelizing compilers, like PFA for the SGI Origin 2000 architecture [17] or SUIF [6] only detect the loop–level parallelism described above. In particular, the performance reported in the SPEC CFP95 summaries [18] for this program (using PFA) shows an speed–up of 3.93 and 4.28 for 8 and 16 processors[1], respectively.

2.2. Turb3D

The structure of the main loop in the application is shown in the left part of Figure 2: it consists of an iterative loop that alternates a series of Fourier–to–physical space and physical–to–Fourier space FFTs over six three–dimensional arrays (U, V, W, OX, OY and OZ of size 66x64x64) with the computation of a non-linear term on the physical space in between, and a time stepping phase before the end of each iteration. Each node is a loop or nested loop that iterates over one or several dimensions of the above mentioned arrays.

For instance, nodes 1, 7, 13, 20 and 26 perform different parts of the computation over matrix U. From the point of view of parallelization, nodes 7 and 26 may be parallelized in the loops that access the second dimension of array U while nodes 13 and 20 in the loops that access the third dimension of the same array. Node 1 can be parallelized in any of the loops that access the three different dimensions. These computations for each array can run completely in parallel. However, nodes 19 and 32 update some of the previously computed arrays with contributions from the rest of the arrays; for instance, node 19 updates arrays OX, OY and OZ with contributions from U, V, W, OX, OY and OZ. Deeper in the hierarchy of tasks (and through and intricate set of procedure invocations), nodes 7–

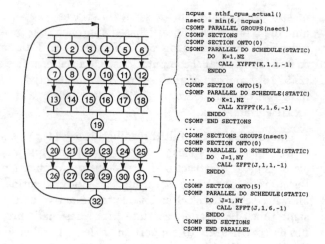

Figure 2. Parallelism structure for the SPEC95 Turb3D application.

18 and 20–31 contain calls to direct and reverse two–dimensional FFTs.

The application presents multiple levels of parallelism. On the one side, the application offers parallelism at the level of sections that perform the same computation over 6 different arrays. On the other side, each section reveals two nested levels of loop parallelism (through several procedure invocations) and other nodes reveal loop–level parallelism. Some compilers, like PFA only detect the innermost level of parallel loops; this parallelization strategy does not report any speed–up, even for a small number of processors. In particular, the performance reported in the SPEC CFP95 summaries shows an slow–down of 0.8 and 0.75 for 8 and 16 processors[1], respectively. Other compilers, like SUIF are able to detect the outermost level of parallel loops; as we will report at the end of the next section, this parallelization strategy performs much better than the previous one.

3. OpenMP and thread–level support

The programming model used in this paper is based on OpenMP [13], the application program interface proposed to offer a programming model for portable parallel programming across shared memory architectures from different vendors. Fortran directives are translated by a compiler to code (based on a highly optimized thread interface) directly injected into the high–level Fortran code.

OpenMP offers a set of parallel, work–sharing and synchronization constructs to specify the parallelism structure of the application. It allows the definition of multi–level parallelism through the nesting of PARALLEL constructs. However, most current execu-

---

[1]These speed–ups are for a SGI Origin2000 system with R10k processors at 250 MHz, 4 Mb of secondary cache and 2 or 4 Gb of main memory, respectively.

tion environments serialize inner parallel constructs because the supporting threads implementation does not support nested parallelism. For instance, the current implementation of the SGI MP library provides a very efficient mechanism based on a unique work descriptor, located at a fixed memory location, from where all processors determine the work to be executed. The descriptor contains, among other information, the pointer to the procedure that encapsulates the work to be done. This descriptor cannot be reused until all processors finish the work assigned.

In OpenMP, the static iteration scheduling policies specified in the parallel DO work–sharing directive do not assume any specific assignment of chunks of iterations to processors. In general, chunks are assigned to processors following their lexicographical order, starting from the chunk that contains the lower bound of the iteration space which is assigned to the first processor in the group of processors involved in the parallel execution. This assignment is a consequence of the unique work descriptor mechanism used to generate work. The descriptor contains the lower and upper bounds and step of the whole iteration space; each thread determines from its own thread identifier the chunk or chunks of iterations that has to execute. Similarly, in the SECTIONS work–sharing construct, the assignment of code segments parceled out by each SECTION directive is not predefined by the OpenMP model. However, its usual conversion to a parallel loop that conditionally branches to each part also establishes a default lexicographical order.

In order to conclude this section, we summarize the performance results for both applications when a single level of loop parallelism is exploited; Section 5 performs the complete evaluation for several parallelization strategies. In order to generate these results, we have generated an OpenMP version of the parallelization strategies proposed by the SUIF compiler, as included in the SUIF–SPEC95 distribution [18]. The strategy corresponds to the parallelization of the outermost loops. Figure 3 shows the speed–up obtained for this parallelization. Notice that in both cases this parallelization provides a relatively good performance up to a certain number of processors (between 16 and 32). Since the parallelization efficiency decreases as the number of processors is increased (diminishing returns are obtained as the number of processors is increased), one may argue if using a small degree of task parallelism (if exists) together with the loop parallelism above would contribute to get higher returns when the number of processors is increased.

4. Efficient multi–level parallelization

In this section we describe the set of extensions to the OpenMP programming model oriented towards the definition of processor groups. In addition to that, we will also analyze the functionalities needed at the thread–level library.

4.1 Extensions to OpenMP

A group of processors is defined by a 'master' thread and a number of 'slave' threads. The definition of groups may be originated in any parallel construct. Once defined, work–sharing constructs inside the parallel construct will assign work to the master threads (instead of assigning the work to all the threads available). The slave threads will cooperate with the master in the exploitation of any additional parallelism inside these work–sharing constructs.

The extensions proposed allow the definition of the groups (i.e. the number of master threads and the number of slave threads assigned to each master). Once defined, other extensions allow the particular assignment of work to the groups. This allows the user to control the allocation of work and may result in a more efficient exploitation of multi–level parallelism; the appropriate assignment of work to groups may improve data locality and reduce load unbalance.

4.1.1 GROUPS clause

The GROUPS clause can be applied to any parallel construct. It establishes the groups of processors that will execute any work–sharing construct inside and nested parallel constructs:

```
C$OMP PARALLEL [DO|SECTIONS] [GROUPS(gdef[,gdef])]
...
C$OMP END PARALLEL [DO|SECTIONS]
```

where each group definer gdef has the following form:

```
[name:]ncpus
```

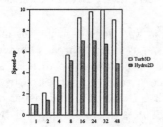

Figure 3. Speed–up for the loop parallelization in Hydro2D and Turb3D.

The name attribute is optional and is used to identify the group. The ncpus attribute is used to determine, from the number of currently available processors, the number of processors that will be assigned to the group. By default, groups are numbered from 0 to an upper value; this upper value is the number of groups defined within the clause GROUPS minus one.

A shortcut is available to specify the simplest group definition: GROUPS(number). In this case, the user specifies the definition of number groups, each one receiving the same number of processors.

For instance, assume that the following definition of groups is provided in a PARALLEL construct: GROUPS(a:2,b:3,one:1,two:2). In this case, four groups are set. Processors 0–1 would constitute the first group (a), processors 2–4 would constitute the second group (b), processor 5 would constitute the third group (one) and processors 6–7 would constitute the fourth group (two).

If the number of processors available at the time of reaching the parallel construct is different than the sum of processors specified in the clause, the numbers specified are considered as proportions; the runtime system has to be able to distribute (in the more fair way and with minimum overhead) the total number of processors according to these proportions.

4.1.2 ONTO clause

The default assignment of iterations in a DO work-sharing construct or individual sections in a SECTIONS work-sharing construct to processors can be changed by using the ONTO clause.

```
C$OMP DO [ONTO(expr)]
```

When this clause is used, expr specifies the group of processors that will execute a particular chunk of iterations (in fact, only the master of each group will execute the work). If the expression contains the loop control variable, then the chunk number (numbered starting at 0) is used to perform the computation; otherwise, all chunks are assigned to the same processor. In all group computations, a 'modulo the number of active groups' operation is applied. If not specified, the default clause is ONTO(i), being i the loop control variable of the parallel loop.

For example, assume the previous definition of groups and the following ONTO clause:

```
C$OMP DO SCHEDULE(STATIC,4) ONTO(2*i)
        do i = 1, 1000
            ...
        enddo
C$OMP END DO
```

In this case, only groups a and one will receive work from this work-sharing construct. In particular, the master of the first group (processor 0) will execute iterations 1:4,9:12, ... and the master of the third group (processor 5) will execute iterations 5:8,13:16, ...

For example, for the same definition of groups, an ONTO(2*k) clause would specify that the master processor of the group 2*k (modulo the number of active groups) would execute all the iterations of the loop.

For the SECTIONS work-sharing contruct, the ONTO(expr) clause is attached to each SECTION directive to specify the group that would execute each section. Each expression expr can be different and is used to compute the group that will execute the statements parceled out by the corresponding SECTION directive. If the ONTO clause is not specified the compiler will assume an assignment following the lexicographical order of the sections.

For instance, when defining a SECTIONS work-sharing construct with four SECTION inside, the programmer could specify that following clauses: ONTO(a) in the first section, ONTO(one) in the second section, ONTO(b) in the third section and ONTO(two) in the fourth section. In this case, processors 0, 5, 2 and 6 would execute the code parceled out by the sections, respectively.

For example, the right part of Figure 2 shows how these clauses are used to specify the multi-level parallelization strategy and processor groups described in Section 2 for the Turb3D application. Notice that the user is defining nsect groups in the outer parallel construct. This value is computed as the minimum between 6 and the number of currently available processors (returned by a service of the threads library). The master of each group will execute one of the sections, according to the number provided in the ONTO clause. Each master will encounter the inner loop-level parallel construct and spawn work for the processors available in his team (for instance ncpus divided by nsect, as indicated by the threads library through a specific call).

4.2. Supportive user-level threads library

In this section we briefly describe the main services required from the user-level threads library. Although the library has been defined to directly support the execution of the parallelism expressed by means of a *Hierarchical Task Graph* [15], this paper only focuses on the functionalities needed to support the OpenMP programming model.

Each parallel construct expressed inside the application is transformed in such a way that the original code is encapsulated in a function. In its place, the compiler inserts the specific code to generate the parallelism. Generating parallelism consists on building the description of the work to be executed and calling the user-level threads library to supply work to the participating processors.

The threads package has been designed to provide different mechanisms to spawn parallelism. Depending on the hierarchy level in which the application is running, the requirements for creating work are different. When spawning the deepest (fine grain) level of parallelism, the application only creates a work descriptor and supplies it to the participating processors. The mechanism is implemented as efficiently as the one provided by most current systems [11]. However, the design allows processors spawning parallelism to generate more than one descriptor and supply them to the slaves before they terminate with previous parallelism, thus supporting multiple levels of parallelism.

When the application knows that it is spawning coarse grain parallelism, not at the deepest level, it can pay the cost of supporting nested parallelism. Higher levels of parallelism, containing other parallel regions, are generated using a more costly interface that provides threads (called nanothreads) with a stack [12]. Owning a stack is necessary for the higher levels of parallelism to spawn an inner level, because the stack is used to maintain the context of the higher levels, along with the data structures needed for joining the parallelism, while executing the inner one. In addition, nanothreads have been designed so that the compiler can specify precedence relations among them.

An important aspect of the library design is the support for processor groups. This requires extra functionalities to set the current groups definition (used when clause GROUPS is found in a PARALLEL construct) and to get to actual groups composition (used to decide the subset of processors receiving work in each work sharing construct). All this information is maintained by the library in order to allow orphaned directives.

Processors waiting for work search first for work descriptors and then for nanothreads. Each entity is managed in a specific way: nanothreads are enqueued in ready queues; work descriptors are supplied to lists using a more efficient mechanism. Two different structures co-exist for holding these entities: global (accessed by all the processors) and local (per processor). They enable the compiler to decide, for each work-sharing construct, if locality or load balancing are the issues that need to be considered in its parallel execution. Local structures are needed to allow the execution model based on processor groups.

5. Experimental evaluation

This section evaluates the performance obtained for the two applications described in Section 2. The experimental framework includes the following components: i) an OpenMP compiler [1] developed on top of Parafrase–2 [14]; ii) the user–level threads library NthLib [12] developed on top of Quick–Threads [7]; iii) and a Silicon Graphics Origin2000 system with 64 R10k processors, running at 250 MHz with 4 Mb of secondary cache each. For all compilations we use the native f77 compiler with flags set to -64 -Ofast=ip27 -LNO:prefetch_ahead=1:auto_dist=on.

5.1. Hydro2D benchmark

Two different versions of this benchmark have been executed using the reference input file, as provided by the SPEC definition. The sequential execution time is 154.7 seconds. The first one implements a single level parallelization strategy around loops. Figure 4 shows the speed–up obtained when this parallelization strategy is executed on top of NthLib, using up to 64 processors. Notice that the performance grows up to 16 processors and then declines. This is due to the fact that the parallelism available in the loops is not enough for such large number of processors.

The second parallel version implements the multi-level parallelization described in Section 2. In particular, one of the levels of parallelism has been intentionally omitted because it introduces an important loss of locality: nodes 2–4 in Figure 1 are executed sequentially. In addition to that, we define 4 processor groups. For instance, a group of processors is responsible for the execution of nodes b, f, k, o and 7; loop–level parallelism inside these nodes is executed only by the set of processors assigned to the group. All the processors collaborate in the execution of nodes where a single level of parallelism is available (like nodes a, 1, and s). Notice that this parallelization strategy returns better performance than the loop–level strategy when more than 16 processors are used, reaching a maximum speed–up of 9.1 with 48 processors.

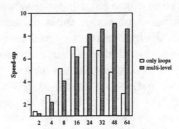

Figure 4. Speed–up for the Hydro2D program.

Figure 5 shows the behavior of the parallelization strategies in terms of secondary cache misses, which in a NUMA architecture may require access to remote memory, and external invalidations that occur per processor, as reported by the *perfex* tool. Notice that in general, the numbers for the multi–level strategy are higher that for the loop–level strategy. This is due to the data movement that happens when flowing from parts of the application where groups of processors concentrate in some nodes of the task graph to parts of the application where all processors collaborate in the execution of the same loops. This justifies the low speed–up reported for the multi–level strategy when less than 16 processors are used. When more than 16 processors are used, the additional overhead of the data movement is counteracted by the gain produced by a better distribution of work among groups of processors. Using more than 48 processors produces a decrease of the speed-up because of the poor distribution of work among processors within each group.

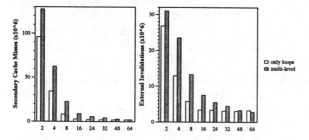

Figure 5. Average number of secondary cache misses and external invalidations (per processor) in Hydro2D.

5.2. Turb3D benchmark

For this application, the following parallelization strategies have been analyzed. The first one is the proposed by the automatic parallelizer PFA for the SGI Origin2000 architecture. In this case, the compiler suggests the parallelization of the innermost loops in the routines that compute the two–dimensional FFT; this parallelization will be referred in the rest of this section as 'inner'. The second parallelization analyzed is the one suggested by the SUIF compiler, consisting on the parallelization of the outer loops that compute 2D FFTs over different planes of three–dimensional matrices; this parallelization strategy will be referred as 'outer'. Finally, the third and fourth strategies studied are multi–level parallelizations where we parallelize the section–level parallelism described in section 2 and either the inner or the outer loops mentioned above; these two strategies will be named 'mlv–inner' and 'mlv–outer'.

We have conducted a set of experiments in order to analyze the behavior of the different parallelization strategies and number of processors. For the multi–level parallelizations, we first try to assign as many processors as possible to the outermost level (sections level) and the rest of processors to the innermost one; in this case, groups of processors concentrate on the execution of each individual section. Figure 6 summarizes the performance results.

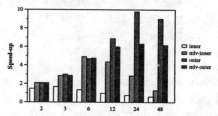

Figure 6. Speed–up for the Turb3D program.

First of all, notice that the 'inner' parallelization strategy fails for this application and that increasing the number of processors to exploit this level of parallelism actually results in a reduction of parallel performance. This is due to the small size of the two–dimensional FFTs (64x64) that are computed at the innermost level. Second, the 'mlv–inner' parallelization performs better than the 'inner' parallelization. The performance for this strategy increases when using up to six processors; this corresponds to exploiting a single level of parallelism: sections for nodes 1–18 and 20–31, and loops for nodes 19 and 32. When more than 6 processors are used (i.e. when processors are allocated to the execution of the innermost FFTs in nodes 1–18 and 20–31), the performance drops.

For this application, the 'outer' parallelization always outperforms the 'mlv–outer' parallelization. This is due to the additional data movement among processors that occur in the multi–level parallelization. This data movement can be observed in the amount of secondary cache misses and external invalidations that each processor suffers:

- The 'outer' strategy parallelizes the loops that traverse the second dimension of the arrays in nodes 1–12 and 26–32; for the rest of nodes, the loops that traverse the third dimension are parallelized. This means that, at each iteration of the outer loop, two transpositions of the six arrays occur.

- With up to six processors, in the 'mlv–outer' parallelization there is no data movement during the execution of any sequence of nodes that use the same array (for example nodes 1, 7 an 13). However, the averaging nodes (19 and 32) imply high data movement.

- When more than six processors are used in the 'mlv–outer' strategy, the additional transpositions within each group of processors introduce additional overhead.

Figure 7 shows the number of secondary cache misses and external invalidations that occur in the application per processor, as reported by the *perfex* tool. Notice that in general, the number of external invalidations for the 'mlv–outer' strategy are higher that for the 'outer' strategy. Also, when more than 6 processors are used in the application, the number of secondary cache misses of the 'mlv–outer' strategy is higher than 'outer'; this corresponds to the point where the performance of the 'mlv–outer' strategy saturates in Figure 6

In order to analyze the influence of the averaging computations in the 'mlv–outer' parallelization, we have generated a synthetic benchmark from the original SPEC application so that nodes 19 and 32 are executed at each iteration, once every 2, 5, 10, 25 or 50 iterations, or never executed. In this case we are reducing the data movement overhead due to them. Figures 8 and 9 show the speed–up and number of secondary cache misses and external invalidations, respectively, for different values of the `NAVG` variable. Notice that for this application, it would be enough to keep data locality inside the groups during two consecutive iterations to have a higher speed–up in the 'mlv–outer' parallelization. In particular, notice that in the 'never' situation the number of secondary cache misses and invalidations is always smaller in the 'mlv–outer' version than in the 'outer' version. In the 'NAVG=2' situation, this is also true when using less than 24 processors; otherwise, the 'outer' version outperforms 'mlv–outer'.

Summary

In the Hydro2D benchmark, multi–level parallelism boosts the performance of the parallel execution; the comparison with the traditional loop–level parallelism gives a 30% improvement on 32 processors. Although

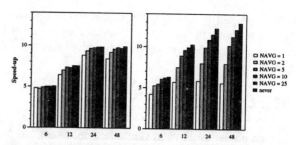

Figure 8. Speed–up for the synthetic Turb3D program for the 'outer' (left) and 'mlv–outer' (right) strategies.

the memory behavior is worse, the better work distribution that is achieved in the multi-level version raises the performance.

In the Turb3D benchmark the multi–level strategy does not improve the performance. We have generated a synthetic version in order to analyze the influence of having parts in the application that benefit from multiple levels of parallelism and parts that only have one level of loop parallelism. For instance, for 12 processors, the classical outer–level loop parallelizations reports an speedup of 6.41 while a multi–level parallelization obtains 5.68 when the degree of interaction is high (each iteration of the outer loop). When this degree of interaction decreases, the multi–level parallelization starts to outperform the classical one. When the interaction is performed half the number of times in the original program, the performance increases by 6%; when this degree of interaction is reduced to a minimum, the performance increases up to 36%.

Grouping of processors has also been proposed as an extension in the context of OpenMP. In this case we have proposed a clause in the directive to specify these groups. If no groups are specified, any additional parallelism that is created inside an active parallel region involves all the processors allocated to the application. For this application, the behavior of a 'mlv–outer'

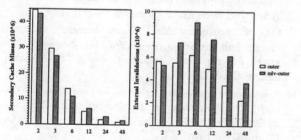

Figure 7. Average number of secondary cache misses and external invalidations (per processor) for the 'outer' and 'mlv–outer' parallelizations in Turb3D.

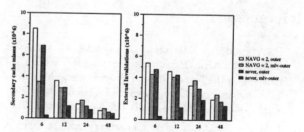

Figure 9. Average number of secondary cache misses and external invalidations (per processor) for the synthetic Turb3D program for the 'outer' (left) and 'mlv–outer' (right) strategies.

strategy without grouping is very close to the behavior of the 'outer' one; in this case, the outer level is created but then all processors are involved in the execution of the inner level.

6. Conclusions

In this paper we have presented some extensions to the current definition of OpenMP oriented towards the definition of processor groups when multiple levels of parallelism exist in the application. Most current compilers and run–time systems only support the exploitation of single–level parallelism around loops. In order to exploit multiple levels of parallelism, several programming models are combined (e.g. message passing and OpenMP). We believe that a single programming paradigm should be used and should provide similar performance. The paper also discuses the requirements and functionalities needed in the threads library.

The experimental evaluation shows that multi–level parallelism may play its role in increasing performance. We have analyzed a set of parallelization strategies for two SPEC95FP applications. The purpose of the evaluation has been to figure out situations in which multiple levels of parallelism are worth to be exploited. The two applications suffer from frequent patterns of interaction between parts of the application where multiple or single levels of parallelism exist. Although this does not benefit the exploitation of the multiple levels of parallelism, the results are encouraging and show some of the key factors that need to be addressed.

Acknowledgments

This research has been supported by the Ministry of Education of Spain under contracts TIC98-511 and TIC97-1445CE, the ESPRIT project 21907 NANOS (www.ac.upc.es/nanos) and the CEPBA (European Center for Parallelism of Barcelona).

References

[1] E. Ayguadé, X. Martorell, J. Labarta, M. Gonzalez and J.I. Navarro. Exploiting Parallelism Through Directives on the Nano-Threads Programming Model. In *10th Workshop on Languages and Compilers for Parallel Computing*, Minneapolis (USA), August 1997.

[2] I. Foster, B. Avalani, A. Choudhary and M. Xu. A Compilation System that Integrates High Performance Fortran and Fortran M. In *Scalable High Performance Computing Conference*, Knoxville (TN), May 1994.

[3] I. Foster, D.R. Kohr, R. Krishnaiyer and A. Choudhary. Double Standards: Bringing Task Parallelism to HPF Via the Message Passing Interface. In *Supercomputing'96*, November 1996.

[4] M. Girkar, M. R. Haghighat, P. Grey, H. Saito, N. Stavrakos and C.D. Polychronopoulos. Illinois-Intel Multithreading Library: Multithreading Support for Intel Architecture–based Multiprocessor Systems. *Intel Technology Journal*, Q1 issue, February 1998.

[5] T. Gross, D. O'Halloran and J. Subhlok. Task Parallelism in a High Performance Fortran Framework. *IEEE Parallel and Distributed Technology*, 2(3), Fall 1994.

[6] M. W. Hall, J. M. Anderson, S. P. Amarasinghe, B. R. Murphy, S.-W. Liao, E. Bugnion and M. S. Lam. Maximizing Multiprocessor Performance with the SUIF Compiler. *IEEE Computer*, December 1996.

[7] D. Keppel. Tools and Techniques for Building Fast Portable Threads Packages. Tech. Rep. UWCSE 93-05-06, Univ. of Washington, 1993.

[8] S.W. Kim, M. Voss, and R. Eigenmann. MOERAE: Portable Interface between a Parallelizing Compiler and Shared-Memory Multiprocessor Architectures. Tech. Rep. Purdue Univ. ECE-HPCLab-98210.

[9] C.H. Koelbel, D.B. Loveman, R.S. Schreiber, G.L. Steele and M.E. Zosel. The High Performance Fortran Handbook. *Scientific Programming*, 1994.

[10] Kuck and Associates, Inc. WorkQueue Parallelism Model. http://www.kai.com, Fall 1998.

[11] X. Martorell, E. Ayguadé, J.I. Navarro, J. Corbalán, M. González and J. Labarta. Thread Fork/join Techniques for Multi–level Parallelism Exploitation in NUMA Multiprocessors. In *13th Int. Conference on Supercomputing*, Rhodes (Greece), 1999.

[12] X. Martorell, J. Labarta, J.I. Navarro, and E. Ayguadé. A library implementation of the nano-threads programming model. In *Euro-Par'96*, 1996.

[13] OpenMP Organization. Fortran Language Specification, v. 1.0, www.openmp.org, October 1997.

[14] C.D. Polychronopoulos, M. Girkar, M.R. Haghighat, C.L. Lee, B. Leung, and D. Schouten. Parafrase-2: An environment for parallelizing, partitioning, and scheduling programs on multiprocessors. *International Journal of High Speed Computing*, 1(1), 1989.

[15] C.D. Polychronopoulos. Nano-threads: Compiler driven multithreading. In *4th Int. Workshop on Compilers for Parallel Computing*, Delft (The Netherlands), December 1993.

[16] S. Ramaswamy. Simultaneous Exploitation of Task and Data Parallelism in Regular Scientific Computations. PhD Thesis. University of Illinois at Urbana–Champaign, 1996.

[17] Silicon Graphics Computer Systems SGI. *MIPSpro Fortran 77 Programmer's Guide*, 1996.

[18] SPEC Organization. *The Standard Performance Evaluation Corporation*, www.spec.org.

Compiler Support for Data Forwarding
in Scalable Shared-Memory Multiprocessors[1]

David Koufaty[2] and Josep Torrellas

Department of Computer Science
University of Illinois at Urbana-Champaign, IL 61801
dkoufaty@ichips.intel.com   torrella@cs.uiuc.edu
http://iacoma.cs.uiuc.edu

Abstract

As the difference in speed between processor and memory system continues to increase, it is becoming crucial to develop and refine techniques that enhance the effectiveness of cache hierarchies. One promising technique in the context of scalable shared-memory multiprocessors is data forwarding. Forwarding hides the latency of communication-induced misses by having producer processors send data to the caches of potential consumer processors in advance. Forwarding can hide the latency effectively, has low instruction overhead, and uses few machine resources.

This paper presents a complete implementation of a data forwarding pass in an industrial-strength parallelizing compiler. Complete Fortran applications are analyzed for dependences and, based on the analysis, automatically annotated with forwarding directives. We propose a forwarding framework that includes 4 new instructions: *write-forward*, *write-broadcast*, *write-update*, and *write-through*. New microarchitectural support is proposed. In our analysis, we assume that the assignment of loop iterations to processors is known. We perform simulations of multiprocessors with different cache, memory, machine sharing, and process migration parameters. We conclude that data forwarding delivers large speedups (six 32-processor applications ran an average of 40% faster), gets close to the upper bound in performance, and needs compiler support of only medium complexity.

1 Introduction

As increases in processor speed continue to outstrip increases in memory speed, it becomes crucial to develop and refine techniques that enhance the effectiveness of memory hierarchies. An important reason why memory hierarchies are sometimes not very effective in multiprocessors is the intrinsic interprocessor communication required by parallel applications. To cope with this communication, popularly known as data sharing, researchers have proposed techniques that overlap the communication latency with processor computation. Perhaps the most well-studied of these techniques is data prefetching. Work by many researchers has shown that prefetching is highly effective [5, 15, 19].

Another way of hiding communication latency is for producer processors to forward the data to the caches of the potential consumer processors in advance. This technique is known as data forwarding [1, 12, 17, 18, 20]. Data forwarding is appealing for three reasons. The first one is that the producer can forward the data as soon as it generates it, therefore maximizing the chances of hiding the communication latency. Secondly, if we forward when the data is produced, we only need to generate the address of the data once, possibly saving instructions over prefetching. Finally, forwarding minimizes the use of network and directory resources by reducing the number of transactions needed to transfer the data over prefetching.

Of course, data forwarding has shortcomings. Unlike prefetching, forwarding is only effective for communication-induced cache misses. In addition, the compiler and hardware support for forwarding may be more complicated.

Because of all these issues, Poulsen and Yew [17], Koufaty et al [12], Ramachandran et al [18], Abdel-Shafi et al [1], and Sivasubramaniam [20] among others have examined data forwarding. The work of all these researchers is largely based on analysis of traces of applications that have been instrumented with forward statements. These researchers uniformly conclude that forwarding can deliver large benefits. In addition, Ohara also showed good performance gains in a hardware-only approach [16].

The contribution of this paper is a complete, fully-automated implementation of a data forwarding pass in the Polaris parallelizing compiler [4]. Only with a complete implementation we can get a true picture of forwarding. We also propose a new framework with four flavors of forwarding and new microarchitectural support. Our analysis assumes that we know the assignment of loop iterations to processors.

Techniques similar to ours have been applied to compilers for message-passing multiprocessors [3, 10, 23]. Besides the obvious differences in the required hardware support, the key difference with our approach is that we do not use the *owner-computes* paradigm to insert the required communication. In the owner-computes paradigm, a processor owns the data allocated in its memory and is required to send the current copy of the data. In our approach, the last processor to write the data sends it to potential consumers. Additionally, our approach addresses the tradeoff between compiler analysis complexity and performance differently because we are not concerned with maintaining program correctness – the underlying cache coherence protocol guarantees it.

Other researchers have proposed similar techniques for page-based, software DSMs. Dwarkadas et al [7] proposed the insertion of primitives to inform the run-time system of data access patterns. Although part of their analysis is similar to ours, their approach is intended for the large overheads of software DSM communication, uses a page-sized grain, and makes the run-time system responsible for sending the data from producers to consumers.

In the second part of this paper, we evaluate data forwarding under many simulated scenarios, including favorable and unfavorable values of cache size, memory size, machine sharing, and process migration parameters. We conclude that fully-automated data forwarding delivers large speedups (six 32-processor applications ran an average of 40% faster), gets

---

[1]This work was supported in part by the National Science Foundation under grants NSF Young Investigator Award MIP-9457436, ASC-9612099, and MIP-9619351, DARPA Contract DABT63-95-C-0097, NASA Contract NAG-1-613, and gifts from Intel and IBM.
[2]Now at Performance Microprocessors Division, Intel Corporation.

close to the upper bound in performance, and needs compiler support of only medium complexity. Due to space constrains, we do not discuss results on the integration of prefetching with forwarding, which gets an extra 15% increase in performance [13].

This paper is organized as follows: Section 2 presents the architectural support required; Section 3 presents the compiler algorithm; Section 4 discusses the evaluation environment; and Section 5 presents the evaluation.

2 Architecture

Building on past work, we use a type of forwarding that is embedded in the directory-based cache coherence protocol of a scalable shared-memory multiprocessor. This implies that, when a processor forwards a datum, it updates its cache and sends the corresponding memory line to the caches of the predicted consumer processors via the directory. The message goes through the directory to avoid protocol races [12]. The directory also sends invalidations to the caches of the non-consumer processors that have a copy of the line.

In the most favorable case, when the consumer processor reads the datum, it finds it in its cache and a miss is avoided. There are, however, three less favorable cases: the consumer processor requests the data before the forward reaches its cache, the forwarded data is displaced from the consumer cache before being used, and the forwarded data displaces useful data from the consumer cache. In practice, the first case cannot occur in our applications because a producer and a consumer access are always separated by a synchronization. However, forwarding can slow down synchronization because a release cannot complete until all pending transactions, including forwards, are completed. Overall, therefore, forwarding can speed up applications by removing coherence misses and cold misses on data that have been written by other processors. However, forwarding can slow down applications by adding extra instructions, inducing extra traffic and misses, and slowing down synchronization.

In this section, we describe the architectural support for this type of forwarding: the primitives (Section 2.1), the base (Section 2.2) and advanced (Section 2.3) microarchitecture support, and the application to physical processors (Section 2.4).

2.1 Forwarding Primitives

The insight that we gained from doing a complete compiler implementation suggested the use of a four-primitive forwarding framework.

Write-Forward. The producer processor updates its cache, the memory, and the cache of a single consumer processor specified as part of the primitive. At the same time, all other processors that shared the updated line are invalidated. We do not support multicast to a subset of processors because it was found that most producer writes have only one consumer [12].

Write-Broadcast. The producer processor updates its cache, the memory, and the caches of all processors. This primitive should be used when all the processors will consume the data.

Write-Update. The producer processor updates its cache, the memory, and the caches of all the processors that, as indicated in the directory, currently share the line. This primitive should be used when there is a strong indication that the consumers are the past sharers.

Write-Through. The producer processor updates its cache

and the memory, while invalidating all processors that currently cache the updated line. Although this primitive does not eliminate any coherence misses, it reduces the latency of the next consumer read to the line because the memory has an up-to-date copy. This primitive should be used when the others are not suitable.

2.2 Base Microarchitecture

To support these primitives in a directory-based scalable shared-memory multiprocessor with multi-word cache lines we need four new assembly instructions and some modest changes to the cache coherence protocol, write buffers, and caches. Specifically, each of the primitives can be implemented with a different assembly instruction that is inserted in lieu of the producer write instruction. These forwarding instructions behave like an ordinary write with respect to the memory consistency model. Since, in this paper, we consider a release-consistent memory system, the forwarding instructions do not stall the processor. Like ordinary writes, forwarding instructions can only be performed after all previous acquires are performed, and must be performed before any subsequent release is allowed to perform. These forwarding instructions take as argument the address of the data to forward. In addition, the write-forward instruction takes as an implicit argument a register with the ID of the single consumer processor.

The protocol changes are as follows. Consider the write-forward instruction. If the write-forward hits a line that is dirty in the producer's cache, the line is marked shared and the whole line is forwarded. If, instead, the write-forward hits a shared line or misses in the producer's cache, only the updated word is forwarded to the directory-memory. If the access missed in the producer's cache, the directory-memory returns the complete line to the producer processor. In all cases, the producer, the directory and the memory are updated, the updated line is sent to the consumer processor, and the producer and the consumer processors are marked as sharers in the directory. The consumer processor will allocate the forwarded line in its cache in the same way that it accommodates any requested line. If, however, it has to evict a dirty line and the write back buffer is full, the forwarded line is not allocated to avoid a potential deadlock. Finally, all the other processors that currently have the line are sent invalidations and are removed from the sharer list in the directory. When all these changes are completed, an acknowledgment message is sent to the producer processor. At that point, the producer processor removes the write-forward's entry from its write buffer. The only other protocol change needed to support the other primitives is that the directory needs to know the type of forwarding primitive and send the appropriate combination of invalidations and updates.

The support in the write buffer is that it needs to be deeper. This is because it needs to keep an entry for each pending forward. Finally, the second level caches need to be designed to accept cache lines that were not requested and may not even be there, namely the forwarded lines. Note that we push the data to the second-level caches only. The updates are not propagated into the first-level cache unless the line is already there, for fear of displacing good data.

2.3 Advanced Microarchitecture

Based on our experiments, we also add the following extra hardware to make forwarding work better.

Forward Delay & Local Combining. Often, a producer forwards different words of the same cache line to the same consumer in a short interval of time. This may occur, for example, when the producer walks down an array of data (Figure 1-(a)). If we combine these forwarding messages into one in a coalescing write buffer, we will reduce the utilization of the directory, network, and caches. More crucially, we will reduce the number of write buffer entries used and, therefore, the chances that the processor stalls due to write-buffer overflow.

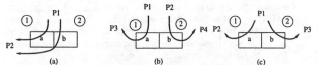

Figure 1: Combining forwards. In the figure, arrows represent forwards, and the encircled numbers are the order of the operations.

To enable this optimization, when a forward is deposited into the write buffer, it is not launched into the network immediately. Instead, it is delayed for a certain *delay* period. If, during that period, another forward of any word of the same line to the same consumer is deposited in the buffer, the two are combined. Then, the combined forward waits again for a *delay* period before being launched. This is similar to the approach used by Glasco et al [8] for update-based coherence protocols. If the other forward is to a different consumer, the forwards cannot be combined and the second forward will be completed after the first one. In practice, a single delay value might not deliver the best performance for all applications. We select a delay that maximizes the average performance gain.

Directory Combining. Another common pattern is what we call *Consumer False Sharing*. This occurs when two consumer processors are forwarded different parts of a cache line. The forwarded data can come from different producers (Figure 1-(b)) or from a single producer (Figure 1-(c)). The problem is that the second forward may invalidate the line in the cache of the first consumer processor before the latter has consumed it.

To solve this problem, we need to detect, in the directory, a stream of forwards of the same line to different consumers. Then, we need to ensure that these forwards do not invalidate the current sharers but, instead, update them. This can be easily done by adding a U bit (for update) to each directory entry. When a forward reaches a directory entry, if U is zero, it sets it. Otherwise, the forward is accessing the same line as a previous forward. Therefore, the forward is part of a stream of forwards as indicated before and, instead of invalidating all processors other that the consumer one, the directory will update all current sharers too. This will eliminate any misses resulting from consumer false sharing. The U bit will remain set as long as the accesses to that directory entry are initiated by any of the four forwarding primitives. Once a regular read or write reaches the directory entry, the U bit is reset. This is because such an access is often an indication that the clean producer-consumer behavior is over.

Memory Forwarding. For some applications, the second level cache may be too small and many of the forwards may be displaced before they are used. Worse yet, the forwards may displace the current working set of the application. Hence, we consider the effect of pushing the data to the processor's memory module only. This is possible in COMA machines, where memory modules are organized as caches. Of course, the forward propagates to the caches if they cache the line.

No Home-Processor Updating. In our protocol description, the memory in the home node gets a copy of the forwarded data every time that a line is forwarded. This will help reduce latencies in cases of consumer misprediction or displacement from the consumer's memory hierarchy. How-

ever, in COMA machines, we have the option of not leaving a copy of the forwarded line in the home memory. Not leaving a copy there may avoid the displacement of useful data.

2.4 Forwarding to Physical Processors

The identity of the consumer processor in a write-forward instruction is a *logical* processor number between 0 and the number of threads in the parallel application minus one. This logical processor number needs to be translated at run-time into the number of the physical processor executing the consumer thread. The translation needs to be totally hidden from the application. It can be done either in the producer node or in the node that owns the directory entry for the forwarded data. This is because, in a forwarding transaction, the data is first delivered to the directory before being sent to the consumer processor. In this discussion, however, we focus on the case where the directory performs the translation.

Figure 2 shows the microarchitecture required: a register in each processor called the *forwarding program identifier (fpid)* register. The *fpid* register can only be set in supervisor mode. It holds a unique number assigned by the operating system to each parallel program that uses data forwarding. This number is the same for all the processes in the same program. The *fpid* register is saved and restored by the operating system during context switches. The number in the *fpid* register is automatically appended to each forwarding message issued by a processor.

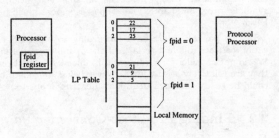

Figure 2: Per-node support needed to apply forwarding to physical processors.

The operating system keeps a software data structure called the logical-to-physical (*LP*) processor translation table. A copy of this table exists in the memory of each node so that the protocol processor in each node can perform a fast local lookup. The table contains a subtable for each possible value of the *fpid*. Each subtable records the mapping of logical to physical processors for a particular program (Figure 2). The operating system modifies the *LP* table on program creation and termination, and on process creation, *migration*, and termination. In a CC-NUMA machine, the copies of this table must be kept consistent by the operating system; in a COMA machine, the hardware keeps all the copies up to date.

When a directory receives a write-forward message, the protocol processor uses the *fpid* in the message and the logical consumer processor number in the message to index its *LP* table. The number retrieved from the table is the ID of the physical processor to forward the data to. This approach transparently solves the problem of mapping logical to physical processors. It can handle process migration and programs with more or fewer processes than physical processors. In the remainder of this paper, all references to processors refer to logical processors.

3 Compiler Algorithm

To insert the forwarding primitives automatically in realistic codes, we have added a pass to the *Polaris* parallelizing compiler [4]. Our pass has two phases. The first one identifies write-read pairs that have a producer-consumer relationship. For each of these pairs, the second phase chooses and inserts in the code the best forwarding primitive. In the following, we describe Polaris, the two phases, and then briefly compare our algorithm to message-passing systems.

3.1 The Polaris Parallelizing Compiler

Polaris is a parallelizing compiler developed at the University of Illinois. It takes a Fortran 77 program as input and generates a transformed Fortran program annotated with directives. These directives specify the parallelism in the code and are used to run the code efficiently on a parallel computer. Examples of directives are DOALL, SHARED, PRIVATE, FIRSTVALUE, and RANGEWRITTEN. DOALL means that the loop is parallel. In each loop, SHARED and PRIVATE identify shared and private data respectively, while RANGEWRITTEN and FIRSTVALUE identify the data being written and read respectively.

The model of parallelism in Polaris is loop-based. A program consists of a sequence of parallel and serial sections, and processors synchronize after each section. Polaris includes advanced algorithms that perform array privatization, data dependence testing, induction variable recognition, and symbolic program analysis. These passes expose much parallelism.

In this paper, we use data forwarding to hide communication *between* different serial sections or fully-parallel loops. We do not consider forwarding within *doacross* loops because they are relatively less frequent. Nevertheless, our algorithms could be easily extended to support doacross loops too.

3.2 Finding Producer-Consumer Pairs

The first phase of our forwarding pass identifies the pairs of statements that produce and consume the same datum. In our analysis, we focus only on accesses to arrays because scalars have little weight in the codes considered. In addition, since it has been suggested that it is necessary to analyze the codes interprocedurally [12], and Polaris lacks good interprocedural analysis, we inline the programs. The steps in this phase are as follows:

1. Building the Data Flow Graph. We first build a data structure called the data flow graph (DFG). Each node in the DFG corresponds to a serial or a parallel section of the program. Consecutive serial statements get merged into one serial section. Each edge in the graph corresponds to the flow between one section and another. Figure 3 shows the DFG for a code segment from SPEC95's *tomcatv*.

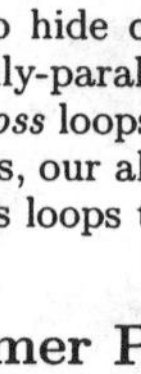

Figure 3: A code segment and its data flow graph.

2. Array Sections Written and Read. We now apply a Polaris pass that returns the array sections that are read and those that are written in each DFG node. The array sections that are read appear in the FIRSTVALUE directive, while those that are written appear in the RANGEWRITTEN one. For example, the code in Figure 3 now becomes that in Figure 4. The array sections are specified with the lower bound, upper bound, and stride of the accesses. For instance, RANGEWRITTEN rx(a:b:c, d) means that the dth column of array rx is written with stride c from row a to row b. Note that, while the figure shows the directives for the parallel loops only, serial sections also have them.

```
        DO j = 1, n-3, 1
           DOALL i = 2, n-1, 1
CSRD$ FIRSTVALUE ...
CSRD$ RANGEWRITTEN rx(2:n-1:1, n-j-1), ...
              rx(i, n-j-1) = ...
           ENDDO
        ENDDO

        DOALL j = 2, n-1, 1
CSRD$ FIRSTVALUE rx(2:n-1:1, 2:n-1:1), ...
CSRD$ RANGEWRITTEN ...
           DO i = 2, n-1, 1
              ... = rx(i, j) ...
           ENDDO
        ENDDO
```

Figure 4: Annotations with the sections read and written.

In this step, the effectiveness of array section analysis in Polaris is of vital importance. The analysis is enhanced with new techniques to handle conditionally defined and used variables and to analyze the symbolic expressions in the array sections. These techniques use the gated single assignment form of a program to perform conditional data flow analysis and demand-driven symbolic analysis [22].

3. Data flow Analysis. This step uses standard data flow algorithms to compute the set of definitions that reach each node in our DFG. For each node, we intersect the reaching definitions with the array sections that the node uses (as given in the FIRSTVALUE for the node). If such an intersection is not empty, we have found some potential producer-consumer pairs. Each pair is composed of a write and a read reference in the source code that produce and consume a given array section respectively. In our example, a pair is composed of reference "rx(i, n-j-1) =" and reference "= rx(i,j)".

3.3 Instruction Selection

For each producer-consumer pair that we identify, the second phase of our pass selects and inserts the best forwarding primitive. In our analysis, we assume that serial sections are always executed by the same processor, namely logical processor 0. Our algorithm proceeds as follows.

1. Write-forward to processor 0. If the producer write is in a parallel section and the consumer read in a serial section, we use write-forward to processor 0.

2. Write-broadcast. If, instead, the consumer read is in a parallel section, we examine its index expression ("i, j" in Figure 4). If the expression is independent of the consumer loop's index variable ("j" in Figure 4), then all processors will read the same data. In that case, we use write-broadcast in the producer point.

3. Write-forward. If the index expression in the consumer read depends on the index variable of the consumer loop, it is possible that different processors read different data. In that case, we try to use write-forward. We want to determine the consumer processor for each iteration of the producer loop.

We proceed in two steps. First, we try to determine, for each iteration in the producer loop, what iteration in the consumer loop consumes its data. This is done by solving the equation:

Index expression in the consumer read = Index expression in the producer write

If the equation is beyond the capabilities of our compiler, as explained in Section 3.3.1, we give up on write-forward. The second step is to determine, for each iteration in the consumer loop, what processor executes it. This is possible only if we know the schedule of the consumer loop. With these two steps, we can determine the consumer processor for each iteration in the producer loop and, therefore, can generate the forward expression. Section 3.3.1 gives an example of the complete process.

4. Write-update. If we could not use write-forward, we try to use write-update. We use it when the compiler finds a repeated consumer pattern: a serial loop enclosing a producer and a consumer loop, such that the index expression in the consumer read is independent of the index variable of the enclosing serial loop. In this case, the same processor consumes the same array location across iterations of the serial loop. If, in addition, the index expression in the producer write is also independent of the serial loop's index variable, the update messages flow between the same pair of producer-consumer processors in every iteration of the serial loop. Otherwise, this scheme may effectively degenerate into a situation close to broadcasting.

5. Write-through. Finally, if none of the previous conditions is satisfied, we use write-through to write the data to memory immediately. This will reduce the penalty of the next consumer read.

In our analysis, we introduce an optimization to reduce unnecessary forwarding overhead. Since we know the schedule of producer and consumer loops, if a processor is producing data for only itself to consume, we cancel the producer-consumer pair.

Overall, we can compare our primitives in terms of compiler support complexity and instruction overhead. For write-forward, the compiler needs to determine the consumer identity. This is harder than to determine that all processors consume (write-broadcast) or that there is data reuse (write-update). Write-through needs no extra compiler support. Regarding instruction overhead, only write-forward involves adding extra instructions.

3.3.1 Generating the ID of the Consumer Processor

A hard part of the algorithm is to determine the ID of the consumer processor in the write-forward primitive. We now show how to do it for the example in Figure 4. In the example, the consumer read induces parallel accesses along the second dimension of array rx. Consequently, in the first step of our algorithm, we build an equation based on the index expressions in the second dimension of array rx for the producer and consumer accesses. If we denote the indices in the producer and consumer loops as j^p and j^c respectively, the producer and consumer iterations that access the same array entry are related by:

$$j^c = n - j^p - 1 \tag{1}$$

We need to express the index of the consumer loop as a function of the index of the producer loop. In the case of Equation 1, this is already done. The equation says that iteration j^p in the producer loop produces data consumed by iteration $n - j^p - 1$ in the consumer loop. In general, however,

to get to this point, we need to perform several transformations. In our analysis, we give up on write-forwarding if the transformations are too complicated. Specifically, we only handle the cases where the left side of Equation 1 is a linear function of the consumer loop index, with the linear coefficient and the independent term being invariant expressions (a function of constant and loop-invariant variables). This analysis is performed on all the dimensions of the shared array that are dependent on the consumer loop index. If the equations do not all have the same solution, then we give up on write-forward.

The second step is to determine, for each iteration in the consumer loop, what processor executes it. This is possible only if we know the schedule of the consumer loop. How we proceed depends on the type of schedule used. There are several policies, including round-robin, chunk, and block scheduling [11]. For each type of scheduling, the appropriate mapping function is used. To simplify our discussion, let us use block scheduling. In that case, given a loop with N iterations, P processors, and with an index normalized to start at l and to have a step of 1, the pid of the processor executing iteration i is

$$pid(i) = \left\lfloor \frac{i - l}{\left\lceil \frac{N}{P} \right\rceil} \right\rfloor$$

In the example, the number of iterations in the consumer DOALL is $n - 2$, the index starts at 2 and the step is 1. Therefore, the scheduling function $pid(j^c)$ is:

$$pid(j^c) = \left\lfloor \frac{j^c - 2}{\lceil (n-2)/P \rceil} \right\rfloor \tag{2}$$

From Equations 1 and 2, the data produced in iteration j^p of the producer loop is consumed by processor

$$\left\lfloor \frac{n - j^p - 3}{\lceil (n-2)/P \rceil} \right\rfloor \tag{3}$$

Therefore, in Figure 3, we replace the regular write to rx(i, n-j-1) by a write-forward whose target processor is given by Equation 3. We indicate this by adding the FORWARD directive to the source code. Figure 5 shows the resulting code. The floor function is not needed in integer division, while the ceiling of (n-2)/P is (n-3)/P+1 with integer division. Since the forwarding expression is loop invariant with respect to the innermost loop, we can move the code that evaluates the expression out of the innermost loop.

```
        DO  j = 1, n-3, 1
          DOALL i = 2, n-1, 1
CSRD$       FORWARD (n-j-3)/((n-3)/P+1)
            rx(i, n-j-1) = ...
          ENDDO
        ENDDO

        DOALL j = 2, n-1, 1
          DO i = 2, n-1, 1
            ... = rx(i, j) ...
          ENDDO
        ENDDO
```

Figure 5: Code after adding forwarding.

In general, depending on the producer and consumer loop bounds, we may be forwarding data that no processor will consume. If, after examining the loop bounds, we conclude that this is happening, we can do two things to avoid unnecessary forwards. We can either enclose the write-forward in a conditional statement or, alternatively, we can split or peel the producer loop to separate the forwarding from the non-forwarding sections of the code.

3.3.2 Merging of Forwarding Primitives

Before generating the final code, the compiler must handle the case where an access belongs to several producer-consumer pairs. Figure 6-(a) shows the two possible cases. A consumer read that belongs to several producer-consumer pairs poses no problem: each producer write is handled separately. However, a producer write that belongs to several producer-consumer pairs may cause a problem: the separate analysis of each producer-consumer pair may lead to different forwarding primitives for the write.

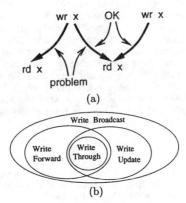

Figure 6: Merging of forwarding primitives.

When this occurs, we select the most appropriate primitive based on the hierarchy of Figure 6-(b). In the figure, the primitives are represented as sets. If one set includes a second one, the first primitive is preferred over the second one in case of conflict. For example, the write-through set is included in all sets, which means that any other primitive is preferred over write-through. The reason is that the action of a write-through, namely, updating memory, is also performed by all the other primitives. As another example, the write-broadcast is preferred over any other primitive. This is because its action, namely updating memory and all caches, includes the actions performed by the other primitives.

When we have a write-forward and either another write-forward with different target processor or a write-update, we choose one of the two based on which one is more likely to be useful. To determine the most useful one, we assign frequency weights to the different edges of the DFG graph (Section 3.2). The weights are assigned using the 90/50 rule, which assumes that backward branches are taken 90% of the time and forward branches 50%. We then select the primitive assigned to the highest-weighted edge. In the future, we plan to add more complex static or dynamic profiling information. Note that the type of dynamic profiling needed would be limited to the frequency of transitions between sections, not the taken frequency of all branches. Overall, however, even if we mispredict, the cost will only be a miss satisfied by the home memory. The reason is that all primitives update memory.

3.4 Comparison to Message-Passing

Most compilers for message-passing multiprocessors are based on the *owner-computes* rule [3, 10, 23]. In the owner-computes paradigm, a processor owns the fraction of the data that is allocated in its local memory. Each processor executes the operations that write to data it owns. The operands of these operations, if they are not owned by the processor, are sent-in by the owners using messages.

One difference between compiler support for forwarding and

for message-passing is in the algorithm used to compute the places where communication is needed. In a message-passing compiler, communication is needed in a statement if, given the program data distribution, a processor does not own the data it needs. Regardless of when or where the data was last written, the owner processor has to send the current copy of the data. In forwarding, instead, communication is given by the data flow in the program. We identify places where the data is written and read, and use data flow techniques and loop scheduling information to determine when data needs to be transferred.

A second difference is that forwarding addresses the tradeoff between compiler analysis complexity and performance differently. The reason is that forwarding does not need to maintain the correctness of the program; the underlying cache coherence protocol guarantees it.

4 Simulation Environment

To evaluate our compiler algorithm, we use TangoLite [9] execution-driven simulations of applications parallelized by Polaris and annotated by our forwarding pass. The architecture model that we simulate is a scalable Flat COMA multiprocessor [21] with 32 processors cycling at 300 MHz under the release consistency model. Each processor has a two-level cache hierarchy. The first-level cache is direct-mapped, has a size of 16 Kbytes, and has a line size of 32 bytes. The second-level cache is 4-way set-associative, varies in size from 32 to 512 Kbytes depending on the application, and has a line size of 32 bytes. We justify the choice of these small cache sizes in the next few paragraphs. The write buffer between the caches and between the second-level cache and memory has a depth of 20 entries and a width of a cache line. The attraction memory in each node is 4-way set-associative and has a line size of 32 bytes. Peak memory bandwidth is approximately 400 MBytes/sec. The network is a 2D mesh topology. Table 1 shows the latencies for a round trip from the processor to different levels of the memory hierarchy without contention.

Level	Latency (Cycles)
First-level cache	1
Second-level cache	10
Local attraction memory (AM)	70
Remote AM (Data in home memory)	≈ 400
Remote AM (Data in third node)	≈ 600

Table 1: Latencies of contention-free round-trip accesses to different levels of the memory hierarchy.

The ratio of the application's total data size to the total memory in the machine is called the memory pressure. In our experiments, we perform two sets of experiments, namely one with a low memory pressure (40%), and one with a higher one (60%). Cache coherence is maintained using a DASH-like [14] directory-based protocol. The protocol is extended with the new data forwarding transactions described in Section 2. All transactions are modeled in detail. We model a simple protocol processor per node to handle the coherence transactions. It has an occupancy of 30 cycles and a latency of 20 cycles per transaction.

To drive the simulations, we use six Polaris-parallelized Fortran applications from a wide variety of sources to cover as many cases as possible (Table 2). The applications are *emit* and *gmtry* from the NAS benchmark set [2], *swim* and *tomcatv* from SPEC95, *fft* from the CMU suite [6], and *lu*, a custom-developed LU factorization. For the SPEC95 applications, we

Name	Small L2			Large L2			
	Cache (Kbytes)	Miss Rate (%)	Conflict Misses (%)	Cache (Kbytes)	Miss Rate (%)	Conflict Misses (%)	Speedup for 32 Proc.
emit	32	3.7	39	128	2.3	5	5.0
fft	64	6.3	61	256	5.4	54	3.9
gmtry	32	1.6	48	128	1.0	6	14.1
lu	32	2.2	10	256	1.3	2	12.9
swim	64	4.1	94	512	1.2	60	16.8
tomcatv	64	4.5	46	512	2.6	6	12.3

Table 2: Applications studied.

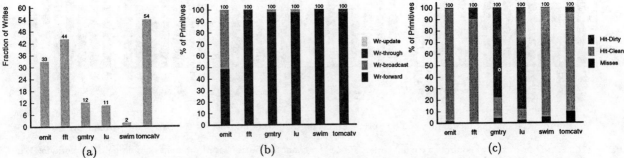

Figure 7: Some dynamic characteristics of forwarding.

use the test data set. For the applications considered, the test and the reference data sets differ only in the number of iterations executed, not in the data set size. Consequently, the results of our experiments are largely the same for both data sets. As explained in Section 3.2, Polaris limitations forced us to use inlined programs. For this reason, we did not evaluate the other SPEC95 applications: their code size is so large that the compiler fails to inline them. Finally, we schedule the loops in the applications statically using block scheduling. This is a good schedule because, in these applications, loops tend to be load-balanced and there is substantial reuse of data across same-numbered blocks in different loops.

We use relatively small caches in the simulations for two reasons. First, because we run small applications, their working sets tend to be small, making larger caches unnecessary. Second, large caches will tend to underestimate any cache pollution caused by forwarding, so it is interesting to look at smaller cache sizes. For the second-level caches, we use two different sizes: one that is large enough to hold the working set of the application and one that is not. These two cache sizes are shown in Table 2. For a given application, we find these sizes by measuring the miss rate as we vary the size of the cache [11]. The table also shows, for each data cache, the miss rate and the fraction of the misses that are caused by conflicts. Finally, the table shows the speedup of these compiler-parallelized applications for 32 processors and the architecture with large L2 caches. All the data in the table corresponds to the low memory pressure.

5 Experimental Results

We evaluate forwarding under several environments. First, we consider an environment with the large L2 caches and the low memory pressure, where the application runs alone in the machine, and there is no process migration. This environment we call baseline. Then, we consider environments where these conditions change. In our discussion, we provide an upper bound for the performance of any data forwarding algorithm that forwards to second-level caches. In this upper bound, called *Ideal*, all L1-missing reads that consume data produced by another processor, including those not identified by our compiler pass, magically find the data requested in the second-

level cache.

5.1 Characterizing Forwarding

To understand the effectiveness of forwarding, we examine three dynamic parameters, namely the fraction of writes that are replaced by forwarding primitives, the type of forwarding primitive used, and the state of the line to be forwarded in the producer cache. The fraction of writes that are replaced by a forwarding primitive is shown in Figure 7-(a). In the figure, we include all the writes in the application. As we can see, this fraction varies from 2% to 54%. However, we find no correlation between this number and the speedup of an application due to forwarding.

Figure 7-(b) shows the type of forwarding primitives used. In all applications except one, the large majority of uses are for write-forwards. Only a few write-broadcasts are used. The exception is *emit*, where all processors often consume the same data. Finally, there are a few write-throughs, and practically no write-updates at all. This data shows that restricting the analysis for write-forwards to linear functions (Section 3.3.1) is not a serious limitation in our applications: in only a few cases we have to give up on write-forwarding and fall back to write-through.

Finally, Figure 7-(c) shows the state of the line to be forwarded in the producer cache. In all the applications, the miss rate of these accesses is very small. However, while in most applications, the line to be forwarded is usually in state clean, in *gmtry* and *lu*, the line is usually in state dirty. If the line is dirty, a plain write would be carried out locally and, unlike a forwarding primitive, not use the write buffer. Consequently, we can expect that, in *gmtry* and *lu*, forwarding will put more pressure on the write buffers.

5.2 Baseline Environment

Figure 8 shows the execution time of each application under the baseline environment. *Base* is the no-forwarding architecture. *Fwd* is *Base* plus forwarding. *Fwd-L* is *Fwd* plus local forward combining with a delay of 100 cycles. This delay delivers the best average performance gain for our applica-

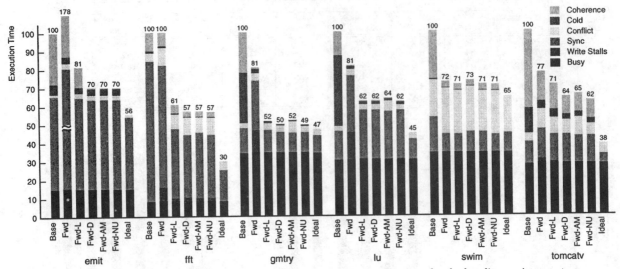

Figure 8: Impact of forwarding and its optimizations on the execution time for the baseline environment.

tions [11]. *Fwd-D* is *Fwd-L* plus directory combining. *Fwd-AM* is *Fwd-D* except that the forwarded data is left in the attraction memories instead of being pushed to the second-level caches. *Fwd-NU* is *Fwd-D* except that the home node does not get a copy of the line being forwarded. Finally, *Ideal* is the upper bound on the performance of data forwarding discussed above.

In all applications, the bars are normalized to *Base*, and divided into 6 categories: stall time due to coherence (*Coherence*), cold (*Cold*), and conflict (*Conflict*) misses, synchronization time (*Sync*), stall time due to write buffer overflow (*Write Stalls*) and useful busy time (*Busy*). Forwarding targets directly the *Coherence* time plus, in our applications, all the *Cold* time because all cold reads access data initialized by another processor.

The figure shows that *Fwd* reduces the execution time of four applications by only a modest 20-30%. In addition, *fft* does not change and *emit* runs significantly slower. These disappointing results are despite the fact that the *Coherence* and *Cold* times often decrease significantly and that the instruction overhead of forwarding only induces a negligible 1% increase in the *Busy* time of the applications. There are three reasons for the poor results. The first one is that *Fwd* induces some write stall time. This is especially noticeable in *gmtry* and *lu*, the two applications that, as indicated in Section 5.1, put more extra pressure on the write buffer.

The second reason is that *Sync* increases in many applications. What causes this is that the processors that stall because of write buffer overflow force the faster processors to wait longer in barriers. In addition, if many forwards are issued right before a lock release, the latter is likely to get delayed.

The third reason for the poor results is that forwarding fails to eliminate much of the *Coherence* time in applications like *emit* and *tomcatv*. In *emit*, the problem is consumer false sharing (Section 2.3), while in *tomcatv*, the problem is that some data is consumed by a subset of processors. Since we do not have multicast, we use write-forwarding to a single processor.

We now apply the forwarding optimizations. Local forward combining (*Fwd-L*) eliminates nearly all the write stalls. As a result, the synchronization time also decreases. In addition, combining also generally decreases the usage of network and directory. As a result, *Coherence*, *Conflict*, *Cold*, and synchronization time tend to decrease in all applications. The applications now run 33% faster than *Base* on average. In [11], we

examine the impact of different combining delay periods. We conclude that the best design point is about 100 cycles.

If we add combining in the directory (*Fwd-D*), we eliminate consumer false sharing. This type of pattern is present in *emit* and, to a lesser extent, in *tomcatv*. As a result, *emit* and *tomcatv* run 14% and 10% faster respectively. Although aside from these two applications the changes are minimal, we recommend this optimization because it is cheap. Finally, the last two optimizations (*Fwd-AM* and *Fwd-NU*) have only a marginal impact. *Fwd-NU* is slightly better than the rest. Overall, with *Fwd-NU*, the applications run an average of 40% faster than in *Base*. The average application speedup with 32 processors has changed from 11 in *Base* (Table 2) to 18.

Even after all our optimizations are applied, there still remains some *Coherence* time, most notably in *tomcatv*. In addition, there is still some room for improvement to get close to the *Ideal* scenario, which is about 50% faster than *Base*. The major limitations of our scheme are the failure to completely eliminate the clustering of forwards before releases and the lack of a multicast forward primitive (*tomcatv*). A lesser problem is the inability to use write-forwards with non-linear expressions.

5.3 Varying Cache Size and Memory Pressure

Figure 9 presents the results of the previous experiments with the small L2 caches listed in Table 2. While conflict misses accounted for 22% of the misses in the large caches, they now account for 50%. As a result, *Conflict* time is relatively more important. Additionally, forwarding sometimes increases the amount of *Conflict* time. However, the impact of the different forwarding optimizations follows similar trends as in Figure 8. Furthermore, since *Conflict* does not account for most of the execution time of the applications, the absolute impact of forwarding does not change much: *Fwd-NU* and *Ideal* speed up the applications by an average of 35% and 50%, respectively.

We also repeat the experiments with the baseline environment with the higher memory pressure of 60%, as discussed in Section 4. The result is an increase in the relative contribution of the *Conflict* time in the applications due to memory conflicts. We omit the results here, however, because the impact of the different forwarding optimizations follows similar trends as in Figure 8. *Fwd-NU* speeds up the applications by an average of 30%, while *Ideal* does it by 50% [11].

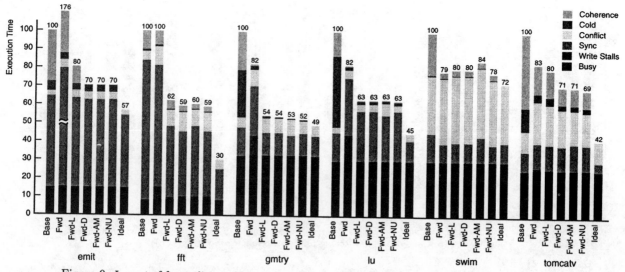

Figure 9: Impact of forwarding and its optimizations on the execution time for the baseline environment with small L2 caches.

5.4 Context Switching and Process Migration

Finally, we estimate the impact of forwarding when an application time-shares the machine with other applications and when the processes of the application migrate between processors. To model time-sharing without migration, we assume that, when a process is preempted, all its cache state is lost. This includes lines that are present in its cache and lines that are being forwarded to the process. We assume, however, that the attraction memory is large enough to maintain the state. Process migration is worse in that the preempted process can reuse neither the state in its caches nor the state in its attraction memory. Note, however, that the hardware described in Section 2.4 ensures the delivery of forwards across process migration.

For these experiments, we simulate the baseline architecture of Section 5.2 and add periodic state invalidations. To emulate context switching (*BaseSwi*), we invalidate the caches every 10 ms. To emulate context switching with process migration (*BaseMig*), we invalidate the caches and reschedule the process on a different node every 10 ms. We repeat these experiments under *Fwd-NU* forwarding, additionally canceling in-flight forwards when the context switches occur. These environments are called *Fwd-NUSwi* and *Fwd-NUMig*. Notice that this model mimics a gang-scheduled system. We choose a small time quantum of 10 ms to compensate for the small caches that we use. This means that, on average, each application suffers 15 context switches during its execution.

Figure 10-(a) shows the execution time of *BaseSwi* and *Fwd-NUSwi*, while Figure 10-(b) does it for *BaseMig* and *Fwd-NUMig*. In the figures, the execution times are normalized to *BaseSwi* and *BaseMig* respectively. Note that, in the environments with process migration (*BaseMig* and *Fwd-NUMig*), the *Cold* time is larger than before. The reason is that, when a process gets rescheduled after a migration, first-time misses on data that it already accessed before the migration should be counted as *Cold* misses. Forwarding, of course, can eliminate these *Cold* misses too.

From the figures, we see that, in both environments, forwarding is still able to speed up the applications significantly. The periodic loss of state affects both the forwarding and the non-forwarding environments, making the relative impact of forwarding only slightly worse than in the baseline environment of Section 5.2. While, in that environment, applications

were sped up by an average of 40%, under context switching they are sped up by an average of 36%, and under context switching plus process migration by an average of 31%. More discussion can be found in [11].

5.5 Limitations of the Algorithm

In the previous sections, we have shown that the forwarding primitives speed up applications by an average of 40%. However, in several applications, the *Ideal* execution time is much smaller than what we can do with forwarding. Some reasons for this difference are that our forwarding techniques suffer from the clustering of forwards before releases and the lack of multicast.

There are, however, some other things that we can do in our compiler algorithm to improve the performance of our data forwarding. First, the computation of array sections that are read and written could be improved and integrated seamlessly with our pass. Much of the information collected by this pass, including the source statement, is lost. Second, data flow analysis produced many uninteresting pairs due to small or overlapping sections being propagated. This can also be improved. Finally, the lack of interprocedural analysis forced us to inline programs. Interprocedural analysis techniques need to be modified and added.

6 Concluding Remarks

The main contribution of this paper has been the complete implementation of a data forwarding pass in the Polaris parallelizing compiler. Our new framework includes four primitives, namely *write-forward*, *write-broadcast*, *write-update*, and *write-through*, and new microarchitectural support. We evaluated forwarding with simulations for different cache size, memory size, machine sharing, and process migration parameters. We concluded that forwarding delivers large speedups: six 32-processor applications ran an average of 40% faster. In addition, forwarding gets close to the upper bound in performance, and needs compiler support of only medium complexity. To extract the remaining performance, it is necessary to improve on two areas: preventing the clustering of forwards before lock releases, and supporting some form of multicast.

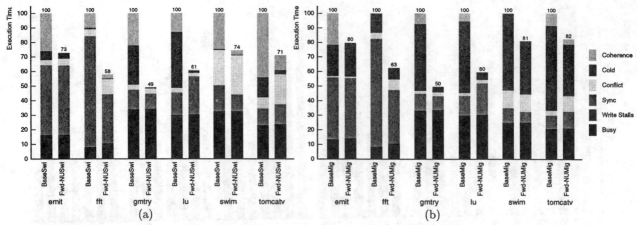

Figure 10: Estimating the impact of forwarding on the execution time of the baseline environment with context switching (Chart (a)), and context switching plus process migration (Chart (b)).

References

[1] H. Abdel-Shafi, J. Hall, S. V. Adve, and V. Adve. An Evaluation of Fine-Grain Producer-Initiated Communication in Cache-Coherent Multiprocessors. In *Proceedings of the Third International Conference on High-Performance Computer Architecture*, February 1997.

[2] D. H. Bailey and J. T. Barton. The NAS Kernel Benchmark Program. Technical report, Numerial Aerodynamic Simulations Systems Division, NASA Ames Research Center, June 1986.

[3] P. Banerjee, J. A. Chandy, M. Gupta, J.G. Holm, A. Lain, D. J. Palermo, S. Ramaswamy, and E. Su. The PARADIGM Compiler for Distributed-Memory Message Passing Multiprocessors. In *Proceedings of the First International Workshop on Parallel Processing*, pages 322–330, December 1994.

[4] W. Blume, R. Doallo, R. Eigenmann, J. Grout, J. Hoeflinger, T. Lawrence, J. Lee, D. Padua, Y. Paek, B. Pottenger, L. Rauchwerger, and P. Tu. Parallel Programming with Polaris. *IEEE Computer*, 29(12):78–82, December 1996.

[5] T. F. Chen and J. L. Baer. A Performance Study of Software and Hardware Data Prefetching Schemes. In *Proceedings of the 21st Annual International Symposium on Computer Architecture*, pages 223–232, April 1994.

[6] P. Dinda, T. Gross, D. O'Hallaron, E. Segall, J. Stichnoth, J. Subhlok, J. Webb, and B. Yang. The CMU Task Parallel Program Suite. Technical Report CMU-CS-94-131, Carnegie-Mellon University, March 1994.

[7] S. Dwarkadas, A. L. Cox, and W. Zwaenepoel. An Integrated Compile-Time/Run-Time Software Distributed Shared Memory System. In *Proceedings of the 7th International Conference on Architectural Support for Programming Languages and Operating Systems*, pages 186–197, October 1996.

[8] D. Glasco, B. Delagi, and M. Flynn. Update-Based Cache Coherence Protocols for Scalable Shared-Memory Multiprocessors. In *Proceedings of the 27st Annual Hawaii International Conference of System Sciences*, pages 543–545, January 1994.

[9] S. Goldschmidt. Simulation of Multiprocessors: Accuracy and Performance. Ph.D. Thesis, Stanford University, June 1993.

[10] S. Hiranandani, K. Kennedy, and C. Tseng. Compiling Fortran D for MIMD Distributed Memory Machines. *Communications of the ACM*, 35(8):66–80, August 1992.

[11] D. Koufaty. *Hiding Communication-Induced Misses: Data Forwarding and Prefetching*. PhD thesis, Department of Computer Science, University of Illinois at Urbana Champaign, October 1997.

[12] D. Koufaty, X. Chen, D. Poulsen, and J. Torrellas. Data Forwarding in Scalable Shared-Memory Multiprocessors. *IEEE Trans. on Parallel and Distributed Systems*, 7(12):1250–1264, December 1996.

[13] D. Koufaty and J. Torrellas. Comparing Data Forwarding and Prefetching for Communication-Induced Misses in Shared-Memory MPs. In *Proceedings of the International Conference on Supercomputing*, pages 53–60, July 1998.

[14] D. Lenoski, J. Laudon, K. Gharachorloo, W. Weber, A. Gupta, J. Hennessy, M. Horowitz, and M. S. Lam. The Stanford Dash Multiprocessor. *IEEE Computer*, pages 63–79, March 1992.

[15] T. C. Mowry. Tolerating Latency Through Software-Controlled Data Prefetching. Ph.D. Thesis, Stanford University, March 1994.

[16] M. Ohara. Producer-Oriented versus Consumer-Oriented Prefetching: A Comparison and Analysis of Parallel Application Programs. Technical Report CSL-TR-96-695, Computer Systems Laboratory, Stanford University, June 1996.

[17] D. K. Poulsen and P.-C. Yew. Data Prefetching and Data Forwarding in Shared Memory Multiprocessors. In *Proceedings of the 1994 International Conference on Parallel Processing*, volume II, pages 276–280, August 1994.

[18] U. Ramachandran, G. Shah, A. Sivasubramaniam, A. Sigla, and I. Yanasak. Architectural Mechanisms for Explicit Communication in Shared Memory Multiprocessors. In *Proceedings of Supercomputing 1995*, December 1995.

[19] V. Santhanam, E. Gornish, and W.-C. Hsu. Data Prefetching on the HP PA-8000. In *Proceedings of the 24th Annual International Symposium on Computer Architecture*, pages 264–273, June 1997.

[20] A. Sivasubramaniam. Reducing the Communication Overhead of Dynamic Applications on Shared Memory Multiprocessors. In *Proceedings of the 3rd International Symposium on High-Performance Computer Architecture*, pages 194–203, February 1997.

[21] P. Stenstrom, T. Joe, and A. Gupta. Comparative Performance Evaluation of Cache-Coherent NUMA and COMA Architectures. In *Proceedings of the 19th Annual International Symposium on Computer Architecture*, pages 80–91, May 1992.

[22] P. Tu. *Automatic Array Privatization and Demand-Driven Symbolic Analysis*. PhD thesis, Department of Computer Science, University of Illinois at Urbana Champaign, May 1995.

[23] H. P. Zima and B. M. Chapman. Compiling for Distributed-Memory Systems. *Proceedings of the IEEE*, 81(2):264–287, February 1993.

Session C3
Parallel Applications

Chair: W.-S. Eric Chen
National Chung-Hsing University, Taiwan

Parallel Algorithms for the Tree Bisector Problem and Applications

Biing-Feng Wang[1], Shan-Chyun Ku[1], Keng-Hua Shi[1], Ting-Kai Hung[1], and Pei-Sen Liu[1]

[1]*Department of Computer Science, National Tsing Hua University*
Hsinchu, Taiwan 30043, Republic of China
[1]*Institute for Information Industry, Taipei, Taiwan, Republic of China*

Abstract

An edge is a bisector of a simple path if it contains the middle point of the path. In this paper, efficient parallel algorithms are proposed on the EREW PRAM for the single-source and all-pairs tree bisector problems. Two $O(\log n)$ time single-source algorithms are proposed. One uses $O(n)$ work and the other uses $O(n\log n)$ work. The one using $O(n)$ work is more efficient but only applicable to unweighted trees. One all-pairs parallel algorithm is proposed. It requires $O(\log n)$ time using $O(n^2)$ work.

1. Introduction

An edge is a *bisector* of a simple path if it contains the middle point of the path. In case the middle point is located at a vertex, both of the two edges connecting the vertex are bisectors. Let $T=(V, E)$ be a tree. Given a *source vertex* $s \in V$, the *single-source tree bisector problem* is to find for every vertex $v \in V$ a bisector of the simple path from s to v. The *all-pairs tree bisector problem* is to find for every pair of vertices u, $v \in V$ a bisector of the simple path from u to v.

It was showed in [11] that in the sequential case solving the single-source tree bisector problem of a weighted tree has a time lower bound $\Omega(n\log n)$. Assuming that T is unweighted, Becker and Perl [1] proposed an $O(n)$ time sequential algorithm for the single-source tree bisector problem. As we will show in section 2, their algorithm can be easily extended to weighted trees. The extended algorithm requires $O(n\log n)$ time. According to the $\Omega(n\log n)$ lower bound, the extended algorithm is optimal.

In this paper, parallel algorithms are proposed on the EREW PRAM for the single-source and all-pairs tree bisector problems. Two $O(\log n)$ time single-source algorithms are proposed. One uses $O(n)$ work (time-processor product) and the other uses $O(n\log n)$ work. The one using $O(n)$ work is more efficient but only applicable to unweighted trees. One all-pairs parallel algorithm is proposed. It requires $O(\log n)$ time using $O(n^2)$ work. All the proposed algorithms are cost-optimal.

The problem of optimally locating a service facility in a network has been of considerable interest for more than twenty years. Recently, parallel algorithms on the EREW PRAM have been proposed for many location problems on trees [5, 6, 8, 9]. Besides being of theoretical interest, efficient algorithms for the single-source and all-pairs tree bisector problems have practical applications to several facility location problems on trees. We will elaborate on the details in section 6 of this paper.

The rest of this paper is organized as follows. In the next section, we give necessary notation and preliminaries. Then, in sections 3 and 4, respectively, parallel single-source algorithms are proposed for unweighted trees and weighted trees. In section 5, a parallel all-pairs algorithm is proposed. In section 6, applications of our bisector algorithms are given. Finally, in section 7, we conclude this paper with some remarks.

2. Notation and preliminaries

Let $T=(V, E)$ be a free tree with vertex set $V=\{1, 2, ..., n\}$. Each edge $e \in E$ has an arbitrary non-negative length $w(e)$. If $w(e)=1$ for every edge $e \in E$ then T is *unweighted*, otherwise T is *weighted*. For each pair of vertices u, $v \in V$, let $path(u, v)$ be the unique path from u to v and let $d(u, v)$ be its length. The above notation and definitions will be used throughout this paper.

Assuming that T is unweighted, Becker and Perl [1] showed that the single-source tree bisector problem can be solved in $O(n)$ sequential time as follows. Let s be the given source. First, T is oriented into a rooted tree with root s. Then, we perform a depth-first traversal on T. During the traversal, the path from s to the current vertex is maintained in an array P such that each $P[i]$, $i \geq 1$, stores the i-th vertex on the path. And, while visiting a vertex v, a bisector of $path(s, v)$ is computed as $(P[\lfloor l/2 \rfloor], P[\lfloor l/2 \rfloor+1])$, where l is the depth of v. Becker and Perl's algorithm can be easily extended to weighted trees as follows. During the depth-first traversal, we additionally maintain an array H such that each $H[i]$, $i \geq 1$, stores the depth of $P[i]$. While visiting a vertex v, a bisector of $path(s, v)$ is determined in $O(\log n)$ time by performing a binary search for $l/2$ on H. The extended algorithm requires $O(n\log n)$ time, which is optimal according to the lower bound in [11].

3. Single-source: unweighted Trees

Let $s \in V$ be given as the source. Throughout this section, we assume that T is unweighted.

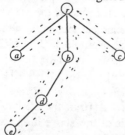

Figure 1. An Euler tour of a rooted tree.

We begin by defining an Euler tour of a rooted tree. An *Euler tour* of a rooted tree is a directed path starting and ending at the root and traversing each tree edge forward and backward exactly once [4]. For example, an Euler tour of the rooted tree depicted in Figure 1 is

$$r \to a \to r \to b \to d \to e \to d \to b \to r \to c \to r.$$

An Euler tour of a rooted tree stores the information about all subtrees of the tree. In general, given an Euler tour of a rooted tree, the subtree rooted at a non-leaf vertex v of the tree corresponds to the sub-path enclosed by the first and the last occurrences of v in the Euler tour. In case v is not the root of the tree, the edge before the first occurrence of v is a downward edge from its parent and the edge after the last occurrence of v is an upward edge to its parent. If a vertex is a leaf of the tree, it occurs in the Euler tour exactly once. There are $2 \times (n-1)$ edges contained in an Euler tour of a rooted tree of n vertices. Thus, there are $2n-1$ vertices on an Euler tour of a rooted tree of n vertices.

For easy discussion, in the remainder of this section, we assume that T is a rooted tree with root s. Let U be an array storing an Euler tour of T such that each $U[i]$, $1 \le i \le 2n-1$, stores the i-th vertex on the tour. In the sequential case, the array U can be obtained in $O(n)$ time by simply applying a depth-first search on T and recording the sequence of visited vertices. Using the Euler-tour technique [4] and an optimal list ranking algorithm [4], U can be constructed in $O(\log n)$ time using $O(n)$ work on the EREW PRAM.

For each $v \in V$, let $depth(v)$ be the length of the path from s to v. The following lemma shows that an Euler tour of T is very helpful to our problem.

Lemma 1: For each element $U[i] \ne s$, $1 \le i \le 2n-1$, if an element $U[j]$, $1 \le j < i$, is the nearest element to the left of $U[i]$ satisfying $depth(U[j]) < depth(U[i])/2$, then the edge $(U[j], U[j+1])$ is a bisector of $path(s, U[i])$.

Lemma 1 is applicable to both weighted and unweighted trees. Due to the limitation of pages, its proof is omitted here.

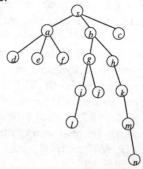

(a) An unweighted rooted tree T.

i	1	2	3	4	5	6	7	8	9	10
$U[i]$	s	a	d	a	e	a	f	a	s	b
$depth(U[i])$	0	1	2	1	2	1	2	1	0	1

11	12	13	14	15	16	17	18	19	20
g	i	l	i	g	j	g	b	h	k
2	3	4	3	2	3	2	1	2	3

21	22	23	24	25	26	27	28	29
m	n	m	k	h	b	s	c	s
4	5	4	3	2	1	0	1	0

(b) An array U storing an Euler tour of T.
Figure 2. An illustrative example.

As an illustrative example of Lemma 1, let T and U be given as the unweighted tree and the array showed in Figure 2. Consider the vertex m. There are two occurrences of m in U, which are $U[21]$ and $U[23]$, respectively. The depth of m is 4. Within the array U, $U[18]$ is the nearest element to the left of $U[21]$ and $U[23]$ that has depth smaller than $depth(m)/2$. Thus, by Lemma 1, the edge $(U[18], U[19])$ $(=(b, h))$ is a bisector of $path(s, m)$.

For convenience, we define a problem, called the 1/2-left-match problem, as follows. Given an array A of m non-negative numbers, the *1/2-left-match problem* is to find for every element $A[i]$, $1 \le i \le m$, the nearest element to its left that is smaller than $A[i]/2$, whenever it exists. The element found for each $A[i]$ is called the *1/2-left-match* of $A[i]$. According to Lemma 1, solving the tree bisectors problem can resort to an algorithm that solves the 1/2-left-match problem. Such an idea is described formally in the following algorithm.

193

Algorithm 1. Single-Source Tree Bisector Problem

Input: A tree $T=(V, E)$ and a vertex $s \in V$.

Output: An array *Bisector*, in which *Bisector*[v], $v \in V$ and $v \neq s$, stores a bisector of *path*(s, v).

Step 1: Orient T into a rooted tree with root s.

Step 2: For each vertex $v \in V$, compute *depth*(v).

Step 3: Construct an array U such that each $U[i]$, $1 \leq i \leq 2n-1$, stores the i-th vertex on an Euler tour of T.

Step 4: Compute an array M such that each $M[i]$, $1 \leq i \leq 2n-1$, stores the nearest element to the left of $U[i]$ that has depth smaller than *depth*($U[i]$)/2 resorting to an algorithm that solves the 1/2-left-match problem.

Step 5: For each i, $1 \leq i \leq 2n-1$ and $U[i] \neq s$, if $U[i]$ is the first occurrence of the vertex stored in it, set *Bisector*[$U[i]$]=($U[j]$, $U[j+1]$), where $U[j]$ is the element stored in $M[i]$.

The correctness of the above algorithm is not difficult to check. Its time complexity and detailed implementation are described as follows. Using the Euler-tour technique [4], Steps 1 and 2 can be done in $O(\log n)$ time using $O(n)$ work. Using tree contraction [4], the Euler-tour technique, and Cole and Vishkin's optimal list ranking algorithm [4], Step 3 can be implemented in $O(\log n)$ time using $O(n)$ work. Step 4 is the most critical step, its implementation will be discussed later. Each vertex $v \in V$ may occur several times in U. Thus, to avoid write-conflicts in Step 5, we set *Bisector*[$U[i]$]=($U[j]$, $U[j+1]$) only for every $U[i]$ storing the first occurrence of a vertex. To determine whether an element $U[i]$ stores the first occurrence of a vertex is equivalent to determine whether $U[i-1]$ is the parent of $U[i]$ (or to determine whether ($U[i-1]$, $U[i]$) is a downward edge). Thus, Step 5 can be performed in $O(1)$ time using $O(n)$ work. Consequently, except Step 4, all steps in Algorithm 1 require $O(\log n)$ time on the EREW PRAM using $O(n)$ work.

Let A be an array such that each $A[i]$, $1 \leq i \leq 2n-1$, stores *depth*($U[i]$). In the remainder of this section, we present an algorithm on the EREW PRAM for finding the 1/2-left-match of every element in A. The presented algorithm requires $O(\log n)$ time using $O(n)$ work. Applying it, Step 4 of Algorithm 1 can be implemented in the same time using the same work.

Since T is unweighted, all elements of A are integers smaller than n and any two consecutive elements of A only differ by 1. Thus, we can obtain the following lemma trivially.

Lemma 2: Let A be an array storing the depths of the vertices on an Euler tour of an unweighted rooted tree of n vertices. For each i, $1 \leq i \leq 2n-1$ and $A[i] \neq 0$, the 1/2-left-match of $A[i]$ is the nearest element to its left that has value $\lceil A[i]/2 \rceil - 1$.

For each k, $0 \leq k \leq n-1$, let $A^{(k)}$ denote the sequence obtained from A by extracting all elements with $A[i]=k$.

Lemma 3: Let $A^{(k)}=(A[x_1], A[x_2], ..., A[x_s])$ and $A^{(k')}=(A[y_1], A[y_2], ..., A[y_t])$, where $1 \leq k \leq n-1$ and $k'=\lceil k/2 \rceil - 1$. For each i, $1 \leq i \leq s$, the 1/2-left-match of $A[x_i]$ is $A[y_q]$ if q is the largest integer such that $y_q < x_i$.

Consider the example in Figure 2 again. Let $k=4$ and $k'=1$. We have $A^{(k)}=(A[13], A[21], A[23])$ and $A^{(k')}=(A[2], A[4], A[6], A[8], A[10], A[18], A[26], A[28])$. The index of $A[13]$ is between those of $A[10]$ and $A[18]$. Thus, by Lemma 3, $A[10]$ is the 1/2-left-match of $A[13]$.

On the basis of the above discussion, an algorithm for finding the 1/2-left-match of each $A[i]$, $1 \leq i \leq 2n-1$, is proposed as follows.

Algorithm 2. Computing 1/2-Left-Matches: unweighted trees

Input: An array A, in which each $A[i]$, $1 \leq i \leq 2n-1$, stores the depth of the i-th vertex on an Euler tour of an unweighted rooted tree T.

Output: An array M, in which $M[i]$, $1 \leq i \leq 2n-1$ and $A[i] \neq 0$, stores the 1/2-left-match of $A[i]$.

Step 1: For each k, $0 \leq k \leq n-1$, compute $A^{(k)}$ as the sequence of $A[i]$'s with $A[i]=k$.

Step 2: For each k, $1 \leq k \leq n-1$, compute the 1/2-left-match of every element in $A^{(k)}$ by performing the following sub-steps.

2.1: Let $k'=\lceil k/2 \rceil - 1$. Assume $A^{(k)}=(A[x_1], A[x_2], ..., A[x_s])$ and $A^{(k')}=(A[y_1], A[y_2], ..., A[y_t])$. Merge $(A[x_1], A[x_2], ..., A[x_s])$ and $(A[y_1], A[y_2], ..., A[y_t])$ into a sorted sequence $B^{(k)}$ according to the indices x_i and y_i.

2.2: For each q, $1 \leq q \leq t$, duplicate the element $A[y_q]$ such that every $A[x_i]$, $1 \leq i \leq s$ and $y_q < x_i < y_{q+1}$, obtains one copy of $A[y_q]$. (Assume that $A[y_{t+1}]=\infty$.)

2.3: For each i, $1 \leq i \leq s$, set $M[x_i]$ as the copy of $A[y_q]$ that $A[x_i]$ obtained in the last sub-step.

The correctness of Algorithm 2 is ensured by Lemma 3. The running time is analyzed as follows. To obtain $A^{(k)}$'s, we sort the elements of A according to their values in a stable way. Since T is unweighted, in the sequential case Step 1 can be done in $O(n)$ time using counting sort. To the author's knowledge, so far no cost-optimal $O(\log n)$ time algorithm for sorting n integers has been developed. Currently, the best $O(\log n)$ time parallel algorithms use $O(n\log n)$ work [4]. Fortunately, since A is defined by an Euler tour of an unweighted tree, our work is simpler than the problem of sorting an arbitrary sequence of n integers. We can apply the following elegant result, which is due to Diks and Rytter, to our work.

Lemma 4 [3]: Let $I=(i_1, i_2, ..., i_n)$ be a sequence of n integers such that $|i_k-i_{k+1}| \leq c$, where $1 \leq k < n$ and c is a constant. The sequence I can be sorted in a stable way in $O(\log n)$ time on the EREW PRAM using $O(n)$ work.

We can apply Diks and Rytter's result to obtain all $A^{(k)}$'s in $O(\log n)$ time using $O(n)$ work. The problem of merging two increasing sequences can be solved in logarithmic time using linear work on the EREW PRAM [4]. Thus, sub-step 2.1 requires $O(\log n)$ time using $O(n)$ work. Sub-step 2.2 is implemented as follows. For simplicity, assume that $y_{t+1}=\infty$. Let $A[y_q]$, $1 \leq q \leq t$, be an element in $A^{(k)}$. After sub-step 2.1, the elements $A[x_i]$'s with $y_q < x_i < y_{q+1}$ are stored in a consecutive portion of $B^{(k)}$, which is between the locations of $A[y_q]$ and $A[y_{q+1}]$. Thus, using the doubling technique or the balanced binary tree method [4], $A[y_q]$ can be duplicated such that every element $A[x_i]$ with $y_q < x_i < y_{q+1}$ obtains one copy of it. The duplication takes $O(\log n)$ time using $O(n)$ work. Sub-step 2.3 takes $O(1)$ time using $O(n)$ work. Therefore, Algorithm 2 performs in $O(\log n)$ time using $O(n)$ work.

Theorem 1: The single-source tree bisector problem of an unweighted tree can be solved in $O(\log n)$ time using $O(n)$ work on the EREW PRAM.

4. Single-source: weighted trees

As we had mentioned, Lemma 1 holds for weighted trees. Thus, Algorithm 1 is also applicable to weighted trees. In the last section, the implementation of Step 4 was based upon the assumption that T is unweighted, but those of all the other steps were not. Therefore, to show that the single-source tree bisector problem of a weighted tree can be solved in $O(\log n)$ time using $O(n \log n)$ work, we only need to show that while T is weighted, Step 4 can be implemented in $O(\log n)$ time using $O(n \log n)$ work.

Let A be an array of m non-negative numbers. In the remainder of this section, we propose an algorithm for finding the 1/2-left-match of each element in A, whenever it exists. Without loss of generality, assume that m is an exact power of 2.

For convenience, we describe our algorithm on the segment tree of A, which is defined as follows. The *segment tree* [7] of A is a complete binary tree of m leaves such that the i-th leaf, from the left, representing the element $A[i]$ and each internal node v representing the subarray defined by the leaves of the subtree rooted at v. It consists of $\log m + 1$ levels. The levels are numbered 0 to $\log m$, from top to down. Denote the subarray represented by the j-th node at level l as $A_{(l,j)}$, $0 \leq l \leq \log m$ and $1 \leq j \leq 2^l$, and the k-th element in it as $A_{(l,j)}[k]$,

$1 \leq k \leq m/2^l$. By definition, $A_{(l,j)}[k]$ is correspondent to $A[(j-1) \times m/2^l+k]$.

For each i, $1 \leq i \leq m-1$, we define a set R_i as follows. Let $\{u_1, u_2, ..., u_q\}$ be the set of nodes in the segment tree of A that are on the path from the root to the leaf representing $A[i+1]$ and are right children of their parents. The set R_i is defined as the set of subarrays represented by the left siblings of $u_1, u_2, ..., $ and u_q. For example, consider the segment tree depicted in Figure 3. In this example, we have $R_{11}=\{A_{(1,1)}, A_{(3,5)}, A_{(4,11)}\}$ and $R_{14}=\{A_{(1,1)}, A_{(2,3)}, A_{(3,7)}\}$.

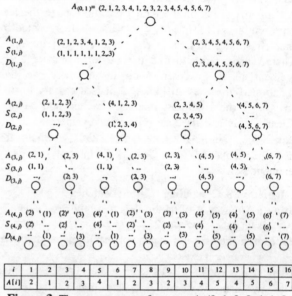

Figure 3. The segment tree of an array $A=(2, 1, 2, 3, 4, 1, 2, 3, 2, 3, 4, 5, 4, 5, 6, 7)$.

A *partition* of a sequence is a set of subsequences obtained by splitting it. From the construction of a segment tree, we can obtain the following lemma easily.

Lemma 5: For each i, $1 \leq i \leq m-1$, R_i is a partition of $(A[1], A[2], ..., A[i])$.

Our strategy for computing 1/2-left-matches is as follows. Let $A[i]$, $1 \leq i \leq m$, be an element in A. We compute the 1/2-left-match of $A[i]$ in two steps. First, we find in every $A_{(l,j)}$ of R_{i-1} the rightmost element smaller than $A[i]/2$, whenever it exists. The elements found are called *candidates*. Then, we compute the 1/2-left-match of $A[i]$ as the rightmost one among the candidates.

The correctness of our strategy is trivially ensured by the property that R_{i-1} is a partition of $(A[1], A[2], ..., A[i-1])$. To implement our strategy for finding 1/2-left-matches efficiently, we compute two arrays $S_{(l,j)}$ and $D_{(l,j)}$ for each subarray $A_{(l,j)}$, $1 \leq l \leq \log m$ and $1 \leq j \leq 2^l$. The array $S_{(l,j)}$ stores the suffix minima of $A_{(l,j)}$. The *suffix minima* of a sequence $(x_1, x_2, ..., x_q)$ is defined as the sequence

$(y_1, y_2, ..., y_q)$, where y_i is the minimum of $x_i, x_{i+1}, ... x_q$. The array $D_{(l,j)}$ stores the sorted sequence of the elements in $A_{(l,j)}$. As an illustrative example, see the segment tree in Figure 3. Above each node (l, j) of the segment tree, we show the content of $S_{(l,j)}$ if j is odd and the content of $D_{(l,j)}$ if j is even. In the figure, we do not show the contents of $S_{(l,j)}$ with even j and $D_{(l,j)}$ with odd j. Because, they are unnecessary to the algorithm we shall propose.

The reason for the computation of $S_{(l,j)}$ and $D_{(l,j)}$ is as follows. Let x and y be a pair of two sibling nodes in the segment tree of A. Let $A_{(l,2a-1)}$ and $A_{(l,2a)}$, respectively, be the subarrays represented by x and y. For each element $A[i]$ in $A_{(l,2a)}$, y is on the path from the root to the leaf representing $A[i]$. Thus, $A_{(l,2a-1)}$, which is represented by the left sibling of y, is in R_{i-1} for every $A[i]$ in $A_{(l,2a)}$. Therefore, in order to find the 1/2-left-match of every element in $A_{(l,2a)}$ based upon the strategy we had mentioned, for every $A[i]$ of $A_{(l,2a)}$ it is necessary to find in $A_{(l,2a-1)}$ the rightmost element smaller than $A[i]/2$. Clearly, this can be done efficiently by merging $D_{(l,2a)}$ and $2 \times S_{(l,2a-1)}$ in a stable way, where $2 \times S_{(l,2a-1)}$ denotes the sequence obtained from $S_{(l,2a-1)}$ by multiplying every element by 2.

Algorithm 3. Computing 1/2-Left-Matches

Input: An array A of m non-negative numbers, where m is an exact power of 2.

Output: The 1/2-left-match of each element in A, whenever it exists.

Step 1: For each $A_{(l,j)}$, $1 \le l \le \log m$ and $1 \le j \le 2^l$, compute two arrays $S_{(l,j)}$ and $D_{(l,j)}$ such that $S_{(l,j)}$ stores the suffix minima of $A_{(l,j)}$ and $D_{(l,j)}$ stores the sorted sequence of the elements in $A_{(l,j)}$.

Step 2: For each pair of $(l, 2a-1)$ and $(l, 2a)$, $1 \le l \le \log m$ and $1 \le a \le 2^{l-1}$, by merging $D_{(l,2a)}$ and $2 \times S_{(l,2a-1)}$, we obtain an array $Q_{(l,2a)}$ in which $Q_{(l,2a)}[k]$, $1 \le k \le m/2^l$, stores the rightmost element in $A_{(l,2a-1)}$ that is smaller than $A_{(l,2a)}[k]/2$. In case $A_{(l,2a-1)}$ does not contain elements smaller than $A_{(l,2a)}[k]/2$, $Q_{(l,2a)}[k]$ stores -1.

Step 3: For each i, $1 \le i \le m$, perform the following sub-steps to compute the 1/2-left-match of $A[i]$.

3.1: Compute the set $Candidate_i = \{Q_{(l,2a)}[k] \mid A_{(l,2a-1)}$ is in R_{i-1}, $A_{(l,2a)}[k]$ is correspondent to $A[i]$, $Q_{(l,2a)}[k] \ne -1$, $1 \le l \le \log m$, $1 \le a \le 2^{l-1}\}$.

3.2: Compute the 1/2-left-match of $A[i]$ by determining the rightmost element in $Candidate_i$.

It is not difficult to check that Algorithm 3 takes $O(\log n)$ time using $O(n)$ work.

Theorem 2: Let A be an array of m non-negative numbers. We can find for every element $A[i]$ the nearest element smaller than $A[i]/2$ to its left in $O(\log m)$ time on the EREW PRAM using $O(m \log m)$ work.

Theorem 3: The single-source tree bisector problem of a weighted tree can be solved in $O(\log n)$ time using $O(n \log n)$ work on the EREW PRAM.

5. All-pairs

For each $v \in V$, define $C(v)$ as the sequence storing the vertices of V in increasing order of their distances from v. One step of our all-pairs algorithm is to compute $C(v)$ for every vertex $v \in V$. The computation is complicated. We describe it first in subsection 5.1. Our all-pairs algorithm is then proposed in subsection 5.2.

5.1 Computing $C(v)$

Let $r \in V$ be an arbitrary vertex. For easy discussion, throughout this subsection, we assume that T is a rooted tree with root r. For each $v \in V$, let $p(v)$ be the parent of v, T_v be the subtree rooted at v, and $size(v)$ be the number of vertices in T_v.

Using Cole's parallel merge sort, we can compute $C(v)$ for a vertex $v \in V$ in $O(\log n)$ time. If sorting is applied for every vertex $v \in V$, the total work will be $O(n^2 \log n)$. To reduce the work, in the following, we give some properties showing that in some cases $C(v)$ can be computed more efficiently.

Lemma 6: Let x and y be two vertices in T such that $x = p(y)$. Using $C(x)$, we can compute $C(y)$ in $O(\log n)$ time using $O(n)$ work.

Proof: Let X be the subtree of T attached to y through the edge (x, y). The vertices of X appear in $C(x)$ and $C(y)$ in the same order. Also, the vertices of T_y appear in $C(x)$ and $C(y)$ in the same order. Thus, using $C(x)$ we can compute $C(y)$ as follows. First, by extracting vertices of X from $C(x)$ we obtain the sequence A storing vertices v of X in increasing order of $d(v, y)$. Then, by extracting vertices of T_y from $C(x)$ we obtain the sequence B storing vertices v of T_y in increasing order of $d(v, y)$. Finally, $C(y)$ is computed by merging the vertices in A and B according to their distances to y. Q.E.D.

Using Lemma 6, we can compute $C(v)$ for every vertex $v \in V$ in $O(n^2)$ work as follows. First, we compute $C(r)$ for the root vertex r by sorting and set $K = \{r\}$. Then, we repeatedly perform the following until $K = V$: select a vertex $y \in V-K$ that is adjacent to a vertex in K, compute $C(y)$, and then put y into K. The work of such a computation is optimal. However, it is purely sequential. To speedup the computation, we need more properties.

Lemma 7: Let x be a vertex in T such that the number of vertices in T_x is $O(n/\log n)$. Let y be a descendant of x. Using $C(x)$, we can compute $C(y)$ in $O(\log n)$ time using $O(n)$ work.

Proof: Let Z be the subtree of T attached to x through the edge $(p(x), x)$. The computation of $C(y)$ is as follows. First, using sorting we compute A as the sequence storing the vertices v of T_x in increasing order of $d(v, y)$. Since $|T_x|=O(n/\log n)$, this step requires $O(\log n)$ time using $O(n)$ work. Then, by extracting vertices of Z from $C(x)$ we obtain the sequence B storing vertices v of Z in increasing order of $d(v, y)$. Finally, we obtain $C(y)$ by merging A and B.   Q.E.D.

Lemma 8: Let x and z be two vertices in T such that x is an ancestor of z. Let y be a vertex on $path(x, z)$. Using $C(x)$ and $C(z)$ we can compute $C(y)$ in $O(\log n)$ time using $O(n)$ work.

Proof: Let X be the subtree of T attached to y through the edge $(p(y), y)$. The computation of $C(y)$ is as follows. First, by extracting vertices of X from $C(z)$ we obtain the sequence A storing the vertices v of X in increasing order of $d(v, y)$. Then, by extracting vertices of T_y from $C(x)$ we obtain the sequence B storing the vertices v of T_y in increasing order of $d(v, y)$. Finally, we obtain $C(y)$ by merging A and B.   Q.E.D.

Our strategy for computing $C(v)$ for every vertex $v \in V$ is as follows. First, we compute a subset $F \subset V$ of size $O(n/\log n)$. Each element in F is called a *firelighter*. For each *firelighter* $f \in F$, we compute $C(f)$ by sorting. Then, using $C(f)$ of the firelighters, we compute $C(v)$ of the other vertices $v \in V-F$ by algorithms in the proofs of Lemmas 6, 7, and 8.

The set of firelighters is computed as $F=\{r\} \cup \{v|\ v \in V, size(v) \geq \log n, size(s) < \log n$ for every child s of $v\}$. According to the computation of F, it is not difficult to prove the following two lemmas.

Lemma 9: $|F|=O(n/\log n)$.

Lemma 10: For each vertex $v \in V-F$, either $size(v) < \log n$, or $size(v) \geq \log n$ and v has a descendant in F.

Algorithm 4. Computing $C(v)$

Input: A tree $T=(V, E)$.

Output: $C(v)$ of every vertex $v \in V$, which stores all vertices u of V in increasing order of $d(u, v)$.

Step 1: Select an arbitrary vertex $r \in V$ and orient T into a rooted tree with root r.

Step 2: Compute $F=\{r\} \cup \{v|\ v \in V, size(v) \geq \log n, size(s) < \log n$ for every child s of $v\}$,
$G=\{g\ |\ g \in V-F, g$ has a descendant in $F\}$,
$H=\{v\ |\ v \in V, size(v) < \log n, size(p(v)) \geq \log n\}$, and
$I=\{v\ |\ v \in V, size(v) < \log n, size(p(v)) < \log n\}$.

Step 3: For each vertex $f \in F$, compute $C(f)$ by sorting.

Step 4: For each $g \in G$, compute $C(g)$ using $C(r)$ and $C(f)$, where f is a descended of g in F.

Step 5: For each $h \in H$, compute $C(h)$ using $C(p(h))$.

Step 6: For each $v \in I$, find its lowest ancestor a in $F \cup G \cup H$ and then compute $C(v)$ using $C(a)$.

Applying tree-contraction, the Euler-tour technique, and Lemmas 6-10 to Algorithm 4, we obtain the following theorem.

Theorem 4: Let $T=(V, E)$ be a tree. Computing $C(v)$ for every vertex $v \in V$ can be done in $O(\log n)$ time using $O(n^2)$ work on the EREW PRAM, where $C(v)$ is the sequence storing all vertices of V in increasing order of their distances from v.

5.2 An all-pairs algorithm

Consider an edge $e=(x, y) \in E$. Let X_e be the subtree attached to y through e and A_e be the sequence storing the vertices u of X_e in increasing order of $d(u, x)$. Similarly, let Y_e be the subtree attached to x through e and B_e be the sequence storing the vertices v of Y_e in increasing order of $d(v, y)$. Let u be a vertex in A_e. Clearly, for every vertex $v \neq u$ in T, e is a bisector of $path(u, v)$ if and only if v is in Y_e and $d(u, x)-w(e) \leq d(v, y) \leq d(u, x)+w(e)$. The sequence A_e stores the vertices u of X_e in increasing order of $d(u, x)$. The sequence B_e stores the vertices v of Y_e in increasing order of $d(v, y)$. Thus, using A_e and B_e we can efficiently determine for every vertex $u \in X_e$, the set of vertices $v \in Y_e$ satisfying $d(u, x)-w(e) \leq d(v, y) \leq d(u, x)+w(e)$ by merging.

Algorithm 5. All-Pairs Tree Bisector Problem

Input: A tree $T=(V, E)$.

Output: A two-dimensional array *Bisector*, in which *Bisector*[u, v], where $u, v \in V$, stores a bisector of $path(u, v)$.

Step 1: For each vertex $v \in V$, compute $C(v)$ as the sequence storing the vertices u of V in increasing order of $d(u, v)$.

Step 2: For each edge $e=(x, y) \in E$, perform the following sub-steps.

2.1: Get a copy of $C(x)$.

2.2: Obtain A_e from $C(x)$ by extracting vertices of X_e, and obtain B_e from $C(x)$ by extracting vertices of Y_e.

2.3: For each vertex u in A_e, compute two values $first_u$ and $last_u$, where $first_u$ and $last_u$, respectively, are the numbers of vertices v in B_e with $d(v, y)<d(u, x)-w(e)$ and $d(v, y) \leq d(u, x)+w(e)$.

2.4: For each vertex u in A_e, set *Bisector*[u, v]$=e$ for every $v \in \{B_e[first_u+1], B_e[first_u+2], ..., B_e[last_u]\}$.

By Theorem 4, Step 1 requires $O(\log n)$ time using $O(n^2)$ work. Sub-steps 2.1, 2.2, and 2.3 can be implemented in $O(\log n)$ time using $O(n^2)$ work. For each edge $e \in E$, the number of $path(u, v)$, $u, v \in V$, having bisector e is $\sum_{u \text{ in } A_e}(last_u - first_u)$. Different edge e has

different value of $\sum_{u \text{ in } A_e}(last_u - first_u)$. However, since

each $path(u, v)$ has at most two bisectors, we have

$\sum_{e \in E}\sum_{u \text{ in } A_e}(last_u - first_u) = O(n^2)$. Therefore, after allocating

$last_u$-$first_u$ processors to each vertex u in A_e, sub-step 2.4

can be done $O(1)$ time using $O(\sum_{e \in E}\sum_{u \text{ in } A_e}(last_u - first_u)) =$

$O(n^2)$ work. The allocation can be done efficiently in $O(\log n)$ time using $O(n^2)$ work by performing an optimal prefix sums algorithm. Therefore, in total Step 2 requires $O(\log n)$ time using $O(n^2)$ work.

Theorem 5: The all-pairs tree bisector problem of a weighted tree can be solved in $O(\log n)$ time using $O(n^2)$ work on the EREW PRAM.

6. Applications

Consider the following problem in a tree-shaped multimedia network $T=(V, E)$. Assume that there is a service facility, such as a video server or a multimedia file server, located at a vertex p of T and we are going to select another vertex of T to set up a new one. To obtain a good quality of service (QoS), we wish to reduce the total distance from every vertex to the facility nearer to it. (Equivalently, we wish to reduce the average distance from a vertex to the facility nearer to it.) For easy description, we call the best vertex of T for setting up the new facility the *step-up medium of T with respect to the vertex p*. The problem of finding the step-up medium of a tree is practical. In the following, we show that it can be solved efficiently using our single-source tree bisector algorithms.

For a vertex $v \in V$ and a subgraph S of T, we denote $dist(v, S)$ as the distance from v to the vertex nearest to it in S. For two subgraphs Q and S of T, let $Sum_Q(S)$ as the total distance from every vertex of Q to the vertex nearest to it in S. By definition, $Sum_Q(S)$ is equal to $\sum_{v \in Q}dist(v, S)$, and our problem is to find the vertex $v \in V$ minimizing $Sum_T(\{p, v\})$.

For each edge $(v, u) \in E$, denote n_u^v and s_u^v, respectively, as the number of vertices in the subtree X and the value of $Sum_X(v)$, where X denotes the subtree of T hanged on v through the edge (v, u). Note that for two

adjacent vertices v, $u \in V$, n_u^v and s_u^v are different from n_v^u and s_v^u.

For easy discussion, assume that T is rooted at p. Consider a vertex v in T. Let $b_v=(x, y)$ be a bisector of $path(p, v)$. Assume that x is the parent of y. Let X be the subtree of T hanged on y through the edge b_v. Let Y be the subtree of T hanged on x through the edge b_v. Between the two vertices p and v, every vertex of X is closer to p, but every vertex of Y is closer to v. Therefore, if we select v to set up the new facility, we have $Sum_T(\{p, v\})=Sum_X(p)+Sum_Y(v)$. The values of $Sum_X(p)$ and $Sum_Y(v)$ can be computed as follows. For each vertex a in Y, we have $dist(a, p)=dist(a, x)+dist(x, p)$. Thus, $Sum_Y(p) = Sum_Y(x) + dist(x, p) \times$ (the number of vertices in Y). Therefore, we have $Sum_X(p) = Sum_T(p) - Sum_Y(p) =$

$Sum_T(p) - (s_y^x + depth(x) \times n_y^x)$. Similarly, we have

$Sum_Y(v) = Sum_T(v) - (s_x^y + (depth(v) - depth(y)) \times n_x^y)$. Therefore, once a bisector $b_v=(x, y)$ of $path(p, v)$ is computed, the value of $Sum_T(\{p, v\})$ can be immediately determined using the values of $Sum_T(p)$, $Sum_T(v)$,

$depth(x)$, $depth(v)$, $depth(y)$, s_y^x, n_y^x, s_x^y, and n_x^y.

Algorithm 6. The Step-Up Medium Problem
Input: A tree $T=(V, E)$ and a vertex $p \in V$.
Output: The step-up medium of T with respect to the vertex p.

Step 1: For each edge $(v, u) \in E$, compute n_u^v and s_u^v.

Step 2: Orient T into a rooted tree with root p.

Step 3: For each vertex $v \in V$, compute $Sum_T(v)$ and $depth(v)$.

Step 4: For each vertex $v \in V$, perform the following sub-steps.

  4.1: Find a bisector edge $b_v=(x, y)$ of $path(p, v)$. Assume that x is the parent of y.

  4.2: Compute $Sum_T(\{p, v\})$ as $Sum_T(p) - (s_y^x + depth(x)$

  $\times n_y^x) + Sum_T(v) - (s_x^y + (depth(v)-depth(y)) \times n_x^y)$.

Step 5: Find the step-up medium of T by determining the vertex $v \in V$ minimizing $Sum_T(\{p, v\})$.

Using tree contraction, it is not difficult to compute the values of n_u^v, s_u^v, $Sum_T(v)$, and $depth(v)$ for every vertex $v \in V$ in $O(\log n)$ time using $O(n)$ work. Thus, applying our single-source tree bisector algorithms to sub-step 4.1, we obtain the following result.

Theorem 6: Finding the step-up medium of a tree with respect to a vertex can be done in $O(\log n)$ time using $O(n\log n)$ work. In case T is unweighted, the work can be further reduced to $O(n)$.

The second location problem to be discussed is called the *p*-point core problem, which was defined by Becker and Perl [1]. Let T be a tree and p be a vertex of T. The *p-point core problem* is to find a path L not containing p in T that minimizes $Sum_T(\{p\}\cup\{L\})$. Like Algorithm 6, Becker and Perl's solution in [1] to the *p*-point core problem mainly depends on finding a bisector edge of $path(p, v)$ for every $v\in V$. Readers may refer to [1] for the details. Using our single-source tree bisector algorithms, we can implement Becker and Perl's algorithm to obtain the following theorem.

Theorem 7: Given a tree T and a vertex p in T, finding the *p*-point core of T can be done in $O(\log n)$ time using $O(n\log n)$ work. In case T is unweighted, the work can be further reduced to $O(n)$.

Recently, Wang et al. defined and studied a new location problem on a weighted tree in [10], which is called the *k*-tree core of bounded diameter problem. The problem arises in a distributed database system. The first step of their algorithm is to find for every pair of vertices u and v in the tree the middle point of the path from u to v. Clearly, the step is equivalent to solve the all-pairs tree bisector problem. Wang et al.'s implementation of this step requires $O(\log n)$ time using $O(n^3)$ work on the EREW PRAM. Using our all-pair algorithm, we can reduce the work of their first step to $O(n^2)$.

In the following, we give another location problem to which our all-pairs algorithm applies. Let $T=(V, E)$ be a tree and $P\subset V$ be a subset of vertices. Assume that there is a facility located at every vertex $p\in P$. Our problem is to find the vertex $v\in V$ minimizing $Sum_T(P\cup\{v\})$ in order to set up a new facility. The vertex v minimizing $Sum_T(P\cup\{v\})$ is the *step-up medium of T with respect to the set P*. With some efforts, we can obtain the following result using our all-pairs tree bisector algorithm.

Theorem 8: Finding the step-up medium of a tree with respect to a set of vertices can be done in $O(\log n)$ time using $O(n^2)$ work.

7. Concluding remarks

The $\Omega(n\log n)$ lower bound in [11] may not hold if the tree under consideration is one in which every edge has an integer length bounded by n^c, where c is a constant. Therefore, it is intuitive to expect that solving the single-source tree bisector problem for a tree in which every edge has an integer length is simpler than solving the problem for a general weighted tree.

Let T be a tree in which every edge has an integer length bounded by a constant. We can solve the single-source tree bisector problem of T as follows. First, we obtain an unweighted tree T' by introducing additional vertices into T such that every edge having length $l>1$ is split into l edges of unit length. Then, we solve the single-source tree bisector problem of T by solving the same problem of T'. Since T' has $O(n)$ vertices, the above computation takes $O(\log n)$ time using $O(n)$ work. Thus, solving the single-source tree bisector problem of a tree in which every edge has an integer length bounded by a constant can be done more efficiently than a general weighted tree. However, at this writing, the authors do not know whether or not solving the problem for a tree in which every edge has an integer length bounded by n^c, where c is a constant, can be done more efficiently. This problem requires further studies.

References

[1] R. I. Becker and Y. Perl, "Finding the two-core of a tree," *Discrete Applied Mathematics*, vol. 11, no. 2, pp.103-113, 1985.

[2] T. H. Cormen, C. E. Leiserson, and R. L. Rivest, *Introduction to Algorithms*, the MIT Press, 1994.

[3] K. Diks and W. Rytter, "On optimal parallel computations for sequences of brackets," *Theoretical Computer Science*, vol. 87, pp. 251-262, 1991.

[4] J. Jaja, *An Introduction to Parallel Algorithms*, Addison Wesley, 1992.

[5] S. Peng and W.-T. Lo, "A simple optimal algorithm for a core of a tree," *Journal of Parallel and Distributed Computing*, vol. 20, pp. 388-392, 1994.

[6] S. Peng and W.-T. Lo, "Efficient algorithms for finding a core of a tree with a specified length," *Journal of Algorithms*, vol. 20, pp. 445-458, 1996.

[7] F. P. Preparata and M. I. Shamos, *Computational Geometry: An Introduction*, Springer-Verlag, 1985.

[8] B.-F. Wang, "Finding a *k*-tree core and a *k*-tree center of a tree network in parallel," *IEEE Transactions on Parallel and Distributed Systems*, vol. 9, no. 2, pp. 186-191, 1998.

[9] B.-F. Wang, "Efficient parallel algorithms for optimally locating a path and a tree of a specified length in a weighted tree network," *Journal of Algorithms*, accepted.

[10] B.-F. Wang, S. Peng, and W.-K. Shih, "Finding a *k*-tree core of bounded diameter in a tree network," manuscript.

[11] B.-F. Wang, S.-C. Ku, and K.-H. Shi, "Cost-optimal parallel algorithms for the tree bisector problem and applications," manuscript.

Acknowledgements. This research is supported under the Notional Science Council of the Republic of China under grant NSC-87-2213-E-007-066.

Efficient Compositing Methods for the Sort-Last-Sparse Parallel Volume Rendering System on Distributed Memory Multicomputers

Don-Lin Yang, Jen-Chih Yu, and Yeh-Ching Chung[1]

Department of Information Engineering
Feng Chia University, Taichung, Taiwan 407
TEL: 886-4-451-7250x3700
FAX: 886-4-451-6101
E-mail: {dlyang, jcyu, ychung}@fcu.edu.tw

Abstract

In the sort-last-sparse parallel volume rendering system on distributed memory multicomputers, as the number of processors increases, in the rendering phase, we can get a good speedup because each processor renders images locally without communicating with other processors. However, in the compositing phase, a processor has to exchange local images with other processors. When the number of processors is over a threshold, the image compositing time becomes a bottleneck. In this paper, we proposed three compositing methods, the binary-swap with bounding rectangle method, the binary-swap with run-length encoding and static load-balancing method, and the binary-swap with bounding rectangle and run-length encoding method, to efficiently reduce the compositing time in the sort-last-sparse parallel volume rendering system on distributed memory multicomputers. The proposed methods were implemented on an SP2 parallel machine along with the binary-swap compositing method. The experimental results show that the binary-swap with bounding rectangle and run-length encoding method has the best performance among the four methods.

1. Introduction

Volume visualization is a well-known methodology for exploring the inner structure and complex behavior of three-dimensional volumetric objects. Existing volume visualization algorithms are commonly divided into two categories, surface rendering and (direct) volume rendering. Surface rendering extracts a given volume data to form a contour surface with a constant-field value and renders the contour surface geometrically. Volume rendering projects the entire volume data semi-transparently onto a two-dimensional image without the aid of intermediate geometrical representations. It is important for users to interactively explore the volume data in real time. However, both surface rendering and volume rendering of a large volume data are still time consuming and are difficult to realize the interactive rendering rate on a single processor.

To achieve the goal of interactive volume visualization, parallel rendering is very useful for this aim. Molnar *et al.* [12] classified parallel rendering into three categories, sort-first, sort-middle, and sort-last. Among them, the sort-last is the most common used scheme in parallel rendering. There are three phases, the partitioning phase, the rendering phase, and the compositing phase, in a sort-last parallel volume rendering system as shown in Figure 1. In the partitioning phase, a processor partitions entire volume data into several subvolume data and distributes these subvolume data to other processors. In the rendering phase, each processor uses some volume rendering or surface rendering algorithms to render the assigned subvolume data into a 2D subimage. In the compositing phase, some compositing algorithms are used to composite the subimages of processors into a full image. The image is then displayed on screen or is saved as an image file.

A number of parallel volume rendering algorithms for the sort-last class have been proposed in the literature. Most of algorithms are implemented on MIMD/SIMD distributed memory multiprocessor systems. In the rendering phase, there are several volume visualization algorithms can be used. The March cube algorithm [10] was used for surface rendering. The ray tracing [9], the shear-warp [7], and the splatting [15] algorithms were

---

[1] The corresponding author

proposed for volume rendering. In the compositing phase, the implementations of the image compositing can be divided into two categories, full-frame merging and sparse merging [12]. In the full-frame merging implementation, processors exchange full 2D subimage frames without considering the contents of the frames. The full-frame merging is very regular and easy to be implemented in software and hardware. But it is not efficient if the contents of 2D subimage frames are sparse. On the other hand, in the sparse merging implementation, processors exchange non-blank pixels of 2D subimage frames. This implementation is more complicated than the full-frame merging implementation. However, it can reduce the communication and the computation overheads in the compositing phase when the 2D subimage frames are sparse.

From Figure 1, in the rendering phase, we can see that each processor renders its local subvolume data without communicating with other processors. A linear speedup can be expected as the number of processors increases. However, because of exchanging subimages with other processors in the image compositing phase, a speedup is restricted to a threshold as the number of processors increases. This indicates that the compositing phase is a bottleneck in a sort-last parallel volume rendering system when the number of processors is over a threshold.

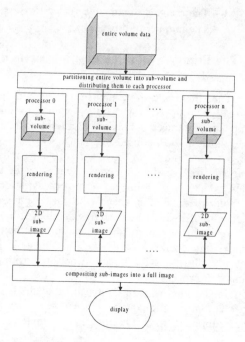

Figure 1. Three phases in a sort-last parallel volume rendering system.

In this paper, we proposed three compositing methods to efficiently reduce the image compositing time

in the sort-last-sparse parallel volume rendering system on distributed memory multicomputers. They are the binary-swap with bounding rectangle (BSBR) method, the binary-swap with run-length encoding and static load-balancing (BSLC) method, and the binary-swap with bounding rectangle and run-length encoding (BSBRC) method. The terms sort-last-sparse and sort-last sparse merging are used interchangeably in this paper. The proposed methods were implemented on an SP2 parallel machine along with the binary-swap compositing method [11]. The experimental results show that the BSBRC method has the best performance among the four methods.

The rest of the paper is organized as follows. The related work of parallel compositing methods will be given in Section 2. In Section 3, the proposed methods will be described and analyzed in details. In Section 4, the experimental results of the proposed methods will be presented.

2. Related Work

Many parallel volume rendering algorithms in the sort-last class have been proposed for distributed memory multiprocessor systems. In the image compositing phase, the compositing methods can be divided into two cases, buffered case and sequenced case [14]. In the buffered case, each processor is responsible for handling a fixed portion of the image. Each processor allocates a buffer and receives pixels in the same fixed portion of the image from other processors once. After compositing pixels in the buffer, each processor generates the final image of the portion it handles. In the buffered case, each processor needs to send and receive $n - 1$ messages at the same time. Hsu [4] and Neumann [14] used the buffered case method to composite subimages into a final image. In the sequenced case, such as tiling approach [6], parallel pipeline [8], binary-tree [1], and binary-swap [11], each processor receives a message from one processor and composites received pixels immediately in each compositing stage. Each processor repeats the same step in each compositing stage until it generates the portion of the final image. Since our methods are based on the binary-swap compositing method, we will describe it in details in Section 3.1.

The compositing methods described above can be applied to the sort-last-sparse or the sort-last-full implementations. Some methods for the sort-last-sparse parallel volume rendering system have been proposed in the literature [1, 2, 8, 11]. In the following, we briefly describe them.

Ahrens and Painter [1] proposed a compression-based image compositing algorithm. They used a lossless compression technique, run-length encoding [3], to compress non-blank pixels. They applied this scheme to the binary-tree compositing method for parallel surface rendering. Because of the surface rendering, a pixel value is represented using red, blue, green, depth, and count fields. The algorithm initially uses the first pixel as the base pixel and compares it with next pixel. Iterating through the pixels of the image by column or row, the algorithm compares the base pixel with the current pixel. If the values of red, blue, green, and depth of the two pixels are equal, the value of the count field in base pixel is increased by one. Otherwise the base pixel is the encoded pixel. The base pixel value is then set to the current pixel value and the value of its count field is set to 1. In the compression phase, the time complexity of the algorithm is $O(n)$, where n is the number of pixels of the input image. In a compositing compressed images phase, two images are input and one result image is output. There are two cases in this phase. One case is that one input image contains a *run* (an encoded pixel) and the other does not. In this case, an output pixel's value is extracted from the run and the count field in the run is decreased by 1. The other case is that both two input images contain runs. The runs of pixels can be composited together. The length of runs to be composited is equal to the smaller count value of the two runs. The value of the count field of one run with larger count value is set to its count value subtracts the count value of the other run. The comparison continues until there has no more runs. In the compositing phase, the time complexity of the algorithm is $O(n)$ for the worst case and is $O(1)$ for the best case.

Lee [8] proposed a direct pixel forwarding method and applied it to the parallel pipeline compositing algorithm for the sort-last-sparse polygon rendering. In the direct pixel forwarding method, an explicit information is used to locate non-blank pixel positions in a subimage. For each non-blank pixel, its value is represented by red, blue, green, depth, and the x and y coordinates of the pixel. In the compositing phase, each processor only composites non-blank pixels and stores result pixels in correct positions according to the x and y coordinates of pixels. Cox and Hanrahan [2] also applied this scheme to a distributed snooping algorithm for polygon rendering.

Molnar *et al.* [12] indicated that the sort-last sparse merging methods are load unbalanced if a processor sends more non-blank pixels than other processors. To solve the load imbalance problem, one can assign each processor an interleaved array of non-blank pixels such that each processor sends almost equal number of pixels to other processors. Lee [8] applied this scheme to the parallel pipeline compositing algorithm with direct pixel forwarding.

To avoid sending blank pixels and some overheads of non-blank pixels, the bounding rectangle [3] is a good choice. Iterating through the pixels in an input image, the bounding rectangle scheme records the coordinates of the upper-left and the lower-right corners of the bounding rectangle. In the compositing phase, each processor only handles pixels in the bounding rectangle. Lee [8] applied the bounding rectangle scheme to the parallel pipeline compositing algorithm. Ma *et al.* [11] also used a bounding rectangle to cover all non-blank pixels at each compositing stage.

3. The Proposed Compositing Methods

In this section, we first describe the binary-swap (BS) compositing method proposed by Ma *et al.* [11]. Then we describe the proposed compositing methods, the binary-swap with bounding rectangle (BSBR) method, the binary-swap with run-length encoding and static load-balancing (BSLC) method, and the binary-swap with bounding rectangle and run-length encoding (BSBRC) method, in details.

A summary of the notations used in this paper is listed below.

- $T_{comp}(L)$ – The computation time of method L.
- $T_{comm}(L)$ – The communication time of method L.
- T_s – The start-up time of a communication channel.
- T_c – The data transmission time per byte.
- T_o – The computation time of "over" operation per pixel.
- A – The image size in pixels, $A^{1/2} \times A^{1/2}$.
- P – The number of processors.

3.1 The Binary-Swap Compositing Method

The binary-swap compositing method [11] was originally proposed for parallel volume rendering to composite ray-traced subimages to a full image. The key idea is that, at each compositing stage, two processors are paired. One processor in a pair exchanges half of its subimage (the sending subimage) with that of the other. After exchanging subimages, each processor composites the half image that it keeps (the local subimage) with received half image (the receiving subimage) by using the *over* operation. Continuing the pairing, exchanging, and compositing operations until the final image is produced. Figure 2 illustrates the binary-swap compositing method using four processors.

In the binary-swap compositing method, it requires $\log P$ communication steps. When the compositing of local subimage to a full image is completed, the total number of pixels transmitted is $P \times \sum_{k=1}^{\log P} \dfrac{A}{2^k}$ and each pixel consists of intensity and opacity. Each pixel is represented by 16 bytes. Therefore, for each processor, the local computation time and the communication time in the binary-swap compositing method are

$$T_{comp}(BS) = \sum_{k=1}^{\log P}\left(T_o \times \frac{A}{2^k}\right) \qquad (1)$$

and

$$T_{comm}(BS) = \sum_{k=1}^{\log P}\left(T_s + \left(16 \cdot \frac{A}{2^k}\right) \times T_c\right), \qquad (2)$$

respectively.

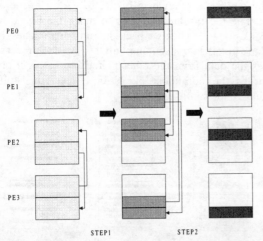

Figure 2. The binary-swap compositing method using four processors.

3.2 The Binary-Swap with Bounding Rectangle (BSBR) Method

Ma *et al.* [11] used a bounding rectangle to cover all nonblank pixels at each compositing stage. Each processor only binary-swaps pixels within this bounding rectangle. When applying the bounding rectangle scheme to the binary-swap compositing method, termed BSBR, we have two cases. We show these two cases in Figure 3. In the first case as shown in Figure 3(a), for each processor pair, PE and PE', PE needs to send (receive) pixels to (from) PE' if the sending subimage (the receiving subimage) contains a portion of bounding rectangle. The portion of bounding rectangle sent (received) to (from) PE' is called the sending (receiving) bounding rectangle of PE. The portion of bounding rectangle retains in PE is called the local bounding rectangle of PE. For the second case as shown in Figure 3(b), for each processor pair, PE and PE', PE need not send (receive) pixels to (from) PE' if the sending subimage (the receiving subimage) contains no portion of bounding rectangle. In order to obtain the bounding rectangle information, processor in each pair has to exchange its bounding rectangle information in each compositing stage.

The advantage of the BSBR method is that it can quickly find an approximate number of non-blank pixels

with less additional fields to record these pixels' positions. In the BSBR method, it takes $O(A)$ time to search the sending bounding rectangle and local bounding rectangle in the first compositing stage. In the later compositing stages, each processor generates a new local bounding rectangle by comparing the local bounding rectangle and the receiving bounding rectangle information. The time complexity is $O(1)$ in comparing bounding rectangle. The disadvantage of the BSBR method is that it sends not only non-blank pixels but also blank pixels within the sending bounding rectangle. As the non-blank pixels' density of a sending bounding rectangle is dense, the BSBR method performs well. Conversely, it performs poorly as the non-blank pixels' density of a bounding rectangle is sparse.

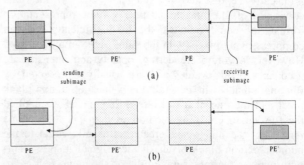

Figure 3. Two cases for the BSBR method. (a) The first case. (b) The second case.

The BSBR method is implemented as follows. We use four short integers to represent the upper-left and the lower-right coordinates of the bounding rectangle. First, each processor finds the boundary of the sending bounding rectangle and packs pixels in the sending bounding rectangle into a sending buffer. Then, for each PE in a processor pair, it sends the sending buffer to PE' and receives the receiving bounding rectangle from PE'. If the receiving bounding rectangle contains no pixels, the pixel compositing is completed in this compositing stage. Otherwise, it composites the pixels in the receiving bounding rectangle with pixels in the local bounding rectangle. The compositing time of the BSBR method is $O(RECV_i^k)$ for the ith processor at the kth compositing stage, where $RECV_i^k$ is the number of pixel in a receiving bounding rectangle. The local computation time and the communication time for the BSBR method are

$$T_{comp}(BSBR) = T_{bound} + \max_{i=0}^{P-1}\left\{\sum_{k=1}^{\log P}\left(T_o \times RECV_i^k\right)\right\} \qquad (3)$$

and

$$T_{comm}(BSBR) = \max_{i=0}^{P-1}\left\{\sum_{k=1}^{\log P}\left(T_s + \left(8 + 16 \cdot RECV_i^k\right) \times T_c\right)\right\}, \qquad (4)$$

respectively, where T_{bound} is the computation time for finding a sending bounding rectangle and local bounding rectangle in the first compositing stage.

3.3 The Binary-Swap with Run-Length Encoding and Static Load-Balancing (BSLC) Method

The run-length encoding is better than explicit x and y coordinates by using less position information to record non-blank pixels. In [1], they used the values of pixels to do encoding. It is a good scheme for surface rendering, but not efficient for volume rendering due to an additional field is used to record a count of the same pixel's value. In surface rendering or polygon rendering, a pixel's value is usually represented by integer. Due to the data coherence of 2D images and pixel's value representation format, the count field can be used efficiently. It can compress many pixels with the same value into one pixel. However, in volume rendering, opacity and intensity are used as a pixel's values and are usually represented by floating points. In general, the values of a non-blank pixel and the one next to it are different. If we applied the run-length encoding method used in [1] for volume rendering, the image size created is usually equal to the number of non-blank pixels of the original image. This will increase the message size due to the count field. To avoid this case, we use the background/foreground value of a pixel (blank/non-blank) instead of the value of a pixel to do encoding.

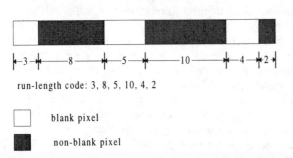

run-length code: 3, 8, 5, 10, 4, 2

☐ blank pixel

■ non-blank pixel

Figure 4. The case of run-length encoding by using the background/foreground values of pixels.

Figure 4 shows the case of run-length encoding by using the background/foreground values of pixels. In the run-length encoding, non-blank pixels transmitting and pixels compositing may not be balanced because of uneven non-blank pixels distribution. They can be more balanced by using some static load-balancing methods. An interleaved array distribution is a good choice for balancing compositing load without significant processor overheads. Figure 5 shows the load-balancing scheme of an interleaved array distribution in the binary-swap compositing method.

In the BSLC method, the rule of dada exchange is the same as the binary-swap compositing method. The different is that we send the interleaved array of a subimage instead of the half array of a subimage. In the run-length encoding, iterating through the pixels of the image using an interleaved method, the algorithm checks a pixel's value (opacity or intensity) whether it is equal to zero or nonzero, i.e., the pixel is blank or non-blank. The algorithm records the numbers of the continuous blank and non-blank pixels as shown in Figure 4. After encoding, we generate the run-length codes to index the blank and non-blank pixels. Then we pack the run-length codes and non-blank pixels into a sending buffer. As one processor receives the data from the other paired processor, it only composites the non-blank pixels in a receiving buffer according to the run-length codes.

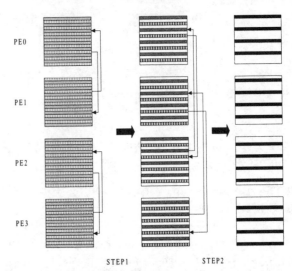

Figure 5. An interleaved array distribution scheme in the binary-swap compositing method.

The time complexity of a run-length encoding phase in the BSLC method is $O(\frac{A}{2^k})$ at the kth compositing stage. The size of run-length codes depends on an image. As the image contains almost continuous blank and non-blank pixels, it generates fewer codes than blank and non-blank pixels in discrete distribution. In the worst case, i.e., the blank and non-blank pixels are appeared in turn, the size of run-length codes is equal to the scheme of explicit x and y coordinates. The compositing time in the BSLC method is $O(LOPA_i^k)$ for the ith processor at the kth compositing stage, where $LOPA_i^k$ is the number of non-blank pixels in a receiving subimage. The local computation time and the communication time in the BSLC method are

$$T_{comp}(BSLC) = \underset{i=0}{\overset{P-1}{MAX}} \left\{ \sum_{k=1}^{\log P} \left(T_{encode} \times \frac{A}{2^k} + T_o \times LOPA_i^k \right) \right\} \quad (5)$$

and

$$T_{comn}(BSLC) = \underset{i=0}{\overset{P-1}{MAX}} \left\{ \sum_{k=1}^{\log P} \left(T_s + \left(2 \cdot CODE_i^k + 16 \cdot LOPA_i^k \right) \times T_c \right) \right\}, \quad (6)$$

respectively, where T_{encode} is the computation time of run-length encoding per pixel, and $CODE_i^k$ is the size of run-length codes. Each element of run-length codes is represented by two bytes.

3.4 The Binary-Swap with Bounding Rectangle and Run-Length Encoding (BSBRC) Method

The disadvantage of the BSLC method is that it has to iterate through all the pixels of a sending subimage whether the pixels are blank or non-blank. The disadvantage of the BSBR method is that as the bounding rectangle is sparse, a processor sends too many blank pixels to the paired processor. By combining the bounding rectangle and the run-length encoding, the disadvantages of the BSBR method and the BSLC method can be avoided. We call this method BSBRC. In the BSBRC method, a processor not only reduces the computing time by the bounding rectangle but also sends fewer data to the paired processor by run-length encoding. In the BSLC method or the method proposed by Ahrens *et al.* [1], it has to iterate through all pixels in the sending subimage in the run-length encoding phase. The BSBRC method only iterates through the pixels in the sending bounding rectangle of the subimage. In the run-length encoding phase, processors process the pixels within the sending bounding rectangle. It reduces encoding time and generates fewer run-length codes. In the compositing phase, processors composite the non-blank pixels instead of all pixels in the receiving subimage according to the run-length encoding. It reduces compositing time and sends fewer data since the number of the run-length codes and the non-blank pixels is less than the number of pixels of an image. The BSBRC algorithm is given as follows.

Algorithm BSBRC(P) {
  1. For all PEs do in parallel
  2. /* Find the bounding rectangle */
  3. For all pixels in the subimage do
  4.   Find the boundary of the local bounding rectangle to cover all non-blank pixels;
  5. For $k = 1$ to $\log P$ do {
  6.   Use the centerline of the subimage to divide the local bounding rectangle into the new local bounding rectangle and the sending bounding rectangle;

  7.   For all pixels in the boundary of the sending bounding rectangle do
  8.   Use the run-length encoding to generate the codes to index the non-blank pixels and pack non-blank pixels into a temporary buffer;
  9.   Pack the sending bounding rectangle information into the sending buffer;
  10. If sending bounding rectangle is not empty {
  11.   Pack the run-length codes into the sending buffer;
  12.   Pack the pixels in a temporary buffer into the sending buffer;
       }
  13. Send the sending buffer to the paired PE';
  14. Receive the receiving buffer from the paired PE';
  15. Unpack the receiving bounding rectangle information from the receiving buffer;
  16. If the receiving bounding rectangle is not empty {
  17.   Unpack the run-length codes from the receiving buffer;
  18.   Unpack the pixels from the receiving buffer into a compositing buffer;
  19.   For each pixel in a compositing buffer do
  20.   Composite the pixel with the corresponding pixel in the local subimage according to the run-length codes
       }
  21. Calculate the new local bounding rectangle by combining the local bounding rectangle with the receiving bounding rectangle;

  }
} *end_of_BSBRC*

The local computation time and the communication time for the BSBRC method are

$$T_{comp}(BSBRC) = T_{bound} + \underset{i=0}{\overset{P-1}{MAX}} \left\{ \sum_{k=1}^{\log P} \left(T_{encode} \times SEND_i^k + T_o \times BOPA_i^k \right) \right\} \quad (7)$$

and

$$T_{comn}(BSBRC) = \underset{i=0}{\overset{P-1}{MAX}} \left\{ \sum_{k=1}^{\log P} \left(T_s + \left(8 + 2 \cdot CODE_i^k + 16 \cdot BOPA_i^k \right) \times T_c \right) \right\}, \quad (8)$$

respectively, where $SEND_i^k$ is the number of pixels in a sending bounding rectangle for the ith processor at the kth compositing stage, and $BOPA_i^k$ is the number of non-blank pixels in a receiving subimage.

4. Performance Study and Experimental Results

To evaluation the performance of the proposed methods, we have implemented these methods on an SP2 parallel machine [5] along with the binary-swap (BS) compositing method. The SP2 parallel machine is located in the National Center of High performance Computing (NCHC) in Taiwan. This super-scalar architecture uses a CPU model of IBM RISC System/6000 POWER2 with a clock rate of 66.7 MHz. There are 80 IBM POWER2 nodes in the system and each node has a 128KB 1st-level data cache, a 32KB 1st-level instruction cache, and 128MB of memory space. Each node is connected to a low-latency, high-bandwidth interconnection network called the High Performance Switch (HPS).

The proposed methods were written in C language with MPI [13] message passing library. The test samples are *Engine_low* (256 × 256 × 110), *Engine_high* (256 × 256 × 110), *Head* (256 × 256 × 113), and *Cube* (256 × 256 × 110). The images of the test samples are shown in Figure 6. In the rendering phase, for each test sample, a ray tracing algorithm is used to generate 8-bit graylevel images on 384 × 384 pixels and 768 × 768 pixels. To evaluate the performance of the proposed methods, we run the test samples on 2, 4, 8, 16, 32, and 64 processors.

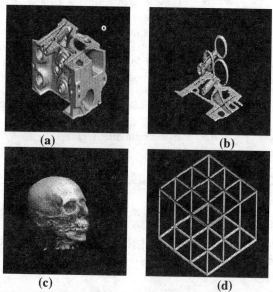

(a) (b)

(c) (d)

Figure 6. The images of the test samples. (a) *Engine_low,* **(b)** *Engine_high,* **(c)** *Head,* **(d)** *Cube.*

We use the maximum received message sizes to evaluate the performance of the proposed methods. For each processor, it calculates the message sizes it received at all compositing stages by $m_i = \sum_{k=1}^{\log P} \left(R_i^k \right)$, where R_i^k is the received message size by bytes for the ith processor at the kth compositing stage. The maximum received message size, M_{max}, among processors is defined as $M_{max} = \underset{i=0}{\overset{P-1}{MAX}} \left(m_i \right)$. From Equations (2), (4), (6), and (8), in general, we have that

$$M_{max}^{BS} \geq M_{max}^{BSBR} \geq M_{max}^{BSBRC} \geq M_{max}^{BSLC} \qquad (9)$$

where M_{max}^{BS}, M_{max}^{BSBR}, M_{max}^{BSBRC}, and M_{max}^{BSLC} are M_{max} in the BS, BSBR, BSBRC, and BSLC methods, respectively.

Figures 7 and 8 show the compositing time of the proposed methods for *Engine_low* and *Head*. These two test samples are denser than the other two. In these cases, $T_{comp}(BSBRC)$ is larger than $T_{comp}(BSBR)$ when the number of processors is greater than 8. In Figure 7, $T_{total}(BSBRC)$ is less than $T_{total}(BSBR)$ because the difference between $T_{comm}(BSBRC)$ and $T_{comm}(BSBR)$ is larger than that between $T_{comp}(BSBRC)$ and $T_{comp}(BSBR)$. However, in Figure 8, $T_{total}(BSBRC)$ is larger than $T_{total}(BSBR)$ in some cases where the number of processors are 8, 16, and 32. Though $T_{comm}(BSLC)$ is the smallest among the four methods, $T_{total}(BSLC)$ is larger than $T_{total}(BSBR)$ and $T_{total}(BSBRC)$ in denser cases due to $T_{comp}(BSLC)$.

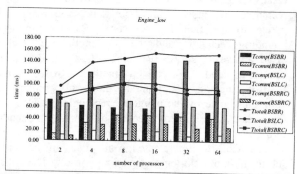

Figure 7. The compositing time of the BSBR, BSLC, and BSBRC methods for *Engine_low***.**

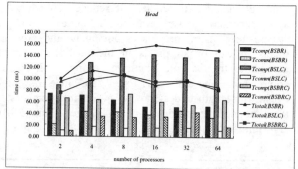

Figure 8. The compositing time of the BSBR, BSLC, and BSBRC methods for *Head***.**

Figures 9 and 10 show the compositing time of the proposed methods for *Engine_high* and *Cube*. In the sparser cases, $T_{comp}(BSBRC)$ is larger than $T_{comp}(BSBR)$ when the number of processors is greater than 32. The BSBRC method performs better than other methods, especially as the bounding rectangle of a subimage is large, but is much sparser, such as *Cube*. In Figure 10, $T_{total}(BSBRC)$ is much less than $T_{total}(BSBR)$ in all test cases.

$T_{total}(BSLC)$ is less than $T_{total}(BSBR)$ when the number of processors is less than 8.

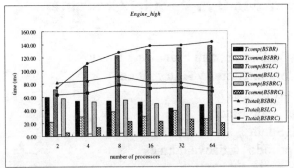

Figure 9. The compositing time of the BSBR, BSLC, and BSBRC methods for *Engine_high*.

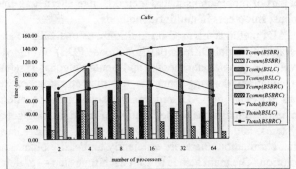

Figure 10. The compositing time of the BSBR, BSLC, and BSBRC methods for *Cube*.

5. Conclusions

In this paper we have presented three compositing methods, the binary-swap with bounding rectangle (BSBR) method, the binary-swap with run-length encoding and static load-balancing (BSLC) method, and the binary-swap with bounding rectangle and run-length encoding (BSBRC) method, for the sort-last-sparse parallel volume rendering system. We have implemented these three methods along with the binary-swap method on an SP2 parallel machine and demonstrated the performance improvements of the proposed methods. From the experimental results, in general, we have $T_{total}(BSBRC) < T_{total}(BSBR) < T_{total}(BSLC) < T_{total}(BS)$.

References

[1] J. Ahrens and J. Painter, "Efficient Sort-Last Rendering Using Compression-Based Image Compositing," *Proc. 2nd Eurographics Workshop on Parallel Graphics & Visualization*, 1998.

[2] M. Cox and P. Hanrahan, "Pixel Merging for Object-Parallel Rendering: a Distributed Snooping Algorithm," *Proc. 1993 Parallel Rendering Symp.*, pp. 49-56, New York, 1993.

[3] J. D. Foley, A. van Dam, S. K. Feiner and J. F. Hughes, "*Computer Graphics: Principles and Practice Second Edition in C*," Mass.: Addison-Wesley, 1990.

[4] W. M. Hsu, "Segmented Ray Casting for Data Parallel Volume Rendering," *Proc. 1993 Parallel Rendering Symp.*, pp. 7-14, San Jose, Oct. 1993.

[5] IBM, IBM AIX Parallel Environment, Paralllel Programming Subroutune Reference.

[6] G. Johnson and J. Genetti, " Volume Rendering of Large Datasets on the Cray T3D," *In 1996 Spring Proceedings (Cray User Group)*, pp. 155-159, 1996.

[7] P. Lacroute, "Analysis of a Parallel Volume Rendering System Based on the Shear-Warp Factorization," *IEEE Computer Graphics and Application*, vol. 2, no. 3, pp. 218-231, 1996.

[8] T. Y. Lee, C.S. Raghavendra, and J.B. Nicholas, "Image Composition Schemes for Sort-Last Polygon Rendering on 2D Mesh Multicomputers," *IEEE Transactions on Visualization and Computer Graphics*, vol. 2, no. 3, pp. 202-217, Sep. 1996.

[9] M. Levoy, "Efficient Ray Tracing of Volume Data," *ACM Transactions on Graphics*, vol. 9, no. 3, pp. 245-261, July 1990.

[10] W. E. Lorensen and H.E. Cline, "Marching Cubes: A High Resolution 3D Surface Construction Algorithm," *Computer Graphics*, vol. 21, no. 4, pp. 163-169, July 1987.

[11] K. L. Ma, J. Painter, C. Hansen, and M. Krogh, "Parallel Volume Rendering Using Binary-Swap Compositing," *IEEE Computer Graphics and Application*, vol. 14, no. 4, pp. 59-67, July 1994.

[12] S. Molnar, M. Cox, D. Ellsworth, and H. Fuchs, "A Sorting Classification of Parallel Rendering," *IEEE Computer Graphics and Application*, vol. 14, no. 4, pp. 23-32, July 1994.

[13] MPI Fourm, MPI: A Message-Passing Interface Standard, May 1994.

[14] U. Neumann, " Volume Reconstruction and Parallel Rendering Algorithms: A Comparative Analysis," PhD dissertation, Dept. of Computer Science, Univ. of North Carolina at Chapel Hill, 1993.

[15] L. A. Westover, " SPLATTING: A Parallel, Feed-Forward Volume Rendering Algorithm," PhD dissertation, Dept. of Computer Science, Univ. of North Carolina at Chapel Hill, July 1991.

Solution of Alternating-Line Processes on Modern Parallel Computers

David Espadas, Manuel Prieto, Ignacio M. Llorente, and Francisco Tirado
Departamento de Arquitectura de Computadores y Automática
Facultad de Ciencias Físicas
Universidad Complutense de Madrid
28040 Madrid, Spain
{despadas, mpmatias, llorente, ptirado}@dacya.ucm.es

Abstract

The aim of this paper is the study of different methods for the solution of alternating-line problems, taking into account the evolution of architectural parameters on modern parallel computers, i.e. processors, memory hierarchy, and interconnection network performance. Three different kinds of solvers are studied: The Pipelined Gaussian Elimination scheme, the Matrix Transposition scheme, and the new one which is presented in this paper: the Mapping Transposition *scheme, whose performance clearly betters, in many cases, that obtained by all the other methods, due to its better fitting to the characteristics of modern parallel computers. The experimental results have been obtained on a Cray T3E and on an SGI Origin 2000, up to 512 and 32 processors, respectively.*

1 Introduction

Over the last few years, the evolution of parallel computers can be characterised by three defining factors: The continuous increasing of processors performance, the even faster increasing performance of interconnection networks, and the slower improvements on memory technologies. These three facts lead us to the point where it is of critical importance to take proper advantage of what the hierarchical memory structure offers to the developer of scientific codes [23, 18], by making appropriate decisions on what algorithms are more profitable in terms, not only of the number of operations —this would be a too mathematical point of view, denying the special characteristics of the target architecture—, but also in terms of their suitability to the characteristics of modern parallel computers [12].

Alternating-line processes are widely applied in scientific computing: they appear as iterative solvers, like ADI (Alternating Direction Implicit) discretization methods, or as part of more sophisticated methods, like alternating-line robust smoothers in multigrid methods.

ADI methods are used on multidimensional elliptic and parabolic Partial Differential Equations (PDE) in order to avoid the problematic hepta- and penta-diagonal systems of equations deriving from the full discretizations of 2D and 3D PDE [6]. ADI reduces the solution of equations in higher dimensions to the solution of multiple tridiagonal systems, and so fast sequential algorithms, such as Gaussian elimination, therefore efficiently and easily obtain the solution. The main idea is to split each time step —or iteration sweep in the elliptic case— into a number of phases to compute each coordinate separately. For example, the solution of an elliptic PDE on the 2D structured grid shown in figure 1, by a full finite difference or volume discretization method implies the solution of a penta-diagonal system with N^2 equations. ADI discretization implies the solution of N systems of N equations twice: first, lines parallel to the X-axis and, second, lines parallel to the Y-axis.

Another example of an alternating-line process is the smoothing of high frequency components of the error on anisotropic PDEs. Classical multigrid algorithms based on point-wise smoothers do not exhibit good convergence rates when solving anisotropic discrete operators. In these cases, robustness can be achieved using alternating-line relaxation —dumped Jacobi or zebra Gauss-Seidel— combined with standard coarsening [10].

When trying to implement an alternating-line process —for example, ADI— in parallel, three possibilities are available. First, parallelise the algorithm itself [13, 11, 1, 8, 21, 17, 4]. Second, pipeline the resolution of many systems of equations at a time —Pipelined Gaussian Elimination— [7, 15, 14]. Or, finally, moving the data, and using a sequential solver —Matrix Transposition and Mapping Transposition—.

This paper is organised as follows. In section 2 we treat the effect of data locality on the effective bandwidth of message passing. The Pipelined Gaussian Elimination (PGE)

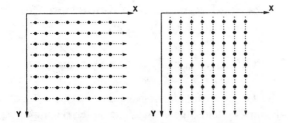

Figure 1. For each line along the x and y axis there is a tridiagonal system to solve

scheme for the solution along the partitioned directions of alternating-line processes is presented in section 3, along with the discussion about the existence of an optimal pipe size. Also the blocking of the Y-sweep in order to improve the PGE data locality (B-PGE) is studied in this point. In section 4, the Matrix Transposition (MT) approach is introduced, discussing its main drawbacks, which will take us straight to section 5, in which the Mapping Transposition (MappT) is explained and compared to PGE, B-PGE, and MT. Also in this section, the experimental results on the solvers' efficiency are presented up to 32 processors, since we think that this is the machine size that can be considered as average. In point 6 the performance of these algorithms on bigger machines —a Cray T3E with up to 512 processors— is studied, to show the effect of architectural parameters on the suitability of the algorithms. The paper ends with some conclusions on the subject, discussing the benefits of both B-PGE and MappT, and their most appropriate ranges of application

2 Effect of Data Locality on Message Passing

2.1 The Cray T3E Message Passing Performance

The T3E-900 system used in this study has 40 DEC Alpha 21164 (DEC Alpha EV5) running at 450 MHz processors. The EV5 contains no board-level cache, but the Alpha 21164 has two levels of caching on-chip: 8 KByte first-level instructions and data caches, and a unified, 3-way associative, 96-KByte write-back second-level cache.

The local memory is distributed across eight banks, and its bandwidth is enhanced by a set of hardware stream buffers that improve the bandwidth of small-strided memory access patterns and instruction fetching. Each node augments the memory interface of the processor with 640 (512 user and 128 system) external registers (E-registers). All remote communication and synchronisation is done between these registers and memory. Using E-registers as a vector memory port can hide the latency of remote memory access. They also provide efficient support for non-unit-stride

memory access.

Data does not cross the processor bus; it flows from memory into E-registers and out to memory again in the receiving processor. E-registers enhance performance when no locality is available by allowing the on-chip caches to be bypassed. However, if the data to be loaded were in the data cache, then accessing that data via E-registers would be sub-optimal because the cache-backmap would first have to flush the data from data cache to memory [19, 2, 12].

The processors are connected via a 3D-torus network. Its links provide a raw bandwidth of 600 MB/s in each direction with an inter-processor data payload communication bandwidth of 480 MB/s. However, as we have studied in a previous research [12], the effective one-way bandwidth using MPI is smaller due to overhead associated with buffering and with deadlock detection. The maximum achievable bandwidth for large messages is only around half of the peak (315 MB/s). Moreover, we obtained almost the same asymptotic bandwidth for all the processor pairs, and so no difference was found in this case between close and distant processors [16].

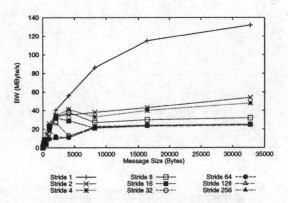

Figure 2. Cray T3E message passing performance using non-contiguous data

Figure 2 shows the impact of the spatial data locality. We use also the echo test with only two processors, but we modify the data locality by means of different strides between successive elements of the message. The *stride* is the number of double precision data between successive elements of the message, so stride-1 represents contiguous data. Due to memory constraints the larger message does not allow to obtain the asymptotic bandwidth for the stride-1 case, but these measures are significant anyway.

2.2 SGI Origin 2000 Message Passing Performance

We repeated these tests in a SGI Origin 2000. The Origin is a distributed shared-memory system with an hypercube network in which each processing node contains two processors, a portion of the shared memory, a directory for cache coherence, and interfaces to I/O devices and other system nodes. The system used in this study has the MIPS R10000 running at 250 MHz. Each processor has 32 KByte two-way set-associative primary instruction and data cache and a combined two-way set-associative secondary instruction and data cache of 4-MByte. One important difference between this system and the T3E is that it caches remote data, while the T3E does not. Two processors are mounted on a node card together with a local part of the memory and a HUB chip, that connects the node card to the other node cards and the I/O facilities of the system. The raw bandwidth of the connections on the node card is 780 MBytes/sec. However, the two processors have to share this bandwidth when accessing data from memory [3, 9, 22, 20]

It is interesting to note that the measured bandwidth decreases when the message sizes are larger than the second level cache —buffer copies above 4 MB do not fit into the secondary cache—. The current MPI implementation might be at the base of this effect [22].

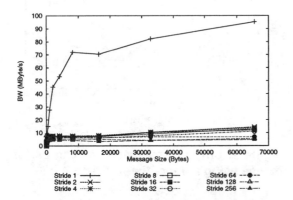

Figure 3. SGI Origin 2000 message passing performance using non-contiguous data

Figure 3 shows the impact of the spatial data locality; the legend below is referred to the stride, as explained before. For non-contiguous data, the reduction in the effective bandwidth is even greater than in the T3E case. For 64 KByte messages, stride-1 bandwidth is around 6.7 times better than stride-2. This difference grows with the stride, being 20.7 times for stride-256. The memory interface of the Origin is cache-line based, making references to single data more inefficient than in the Cray T3E.

3 Pipelined Gaussian Elimination for an Alternating-line Problem

3.1 PGE on a Set of Equation Systems

The Gaussian Elimination method for the solution of tridiagonal systems, the optimal one on serial computers, is divided into two stages: forward elimination and backward substitution. On the forward elimination, starting from the upper equation, the lower secondary diagonal is zeroed by means of linear combinations with the upper row. On the backward substitution, independent solutions are found by zeroing the upper secondary diagonal [6].

The Pipelined Gaussian Elimination method sequences the solution of several systems of equations among processors, so that each one remains busy almost all the time, except during the idleness phase due to the arrival of the first packet of data from the preceding processor. This delay increases with what we will call *pipe size*, i.e. the number of systems computed on each pipeline, needed before the next processor can start working on its calculation. In figure 4 a graphical representation of the computation and communication patterns over the global domain is shown [5]. Note that pipelining is used in both forward and backward sweeps.

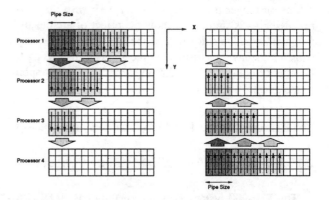

Figure 4. The pipelined gaussian elimination scheme, for 4 processors and a pipe size of 4. Blocks computed concurrently are equally shadowed

Although this algorithm has been widely studied, even developing theoretical models in order to establish the obtainable efficiencies, and discussing the optimal election of parameters, like the pipe size [15, 14], these models do not take into account the influence that the cache memory has on the performance, so not considering the high importance that data locality has on modern parallel computers [12]. Trying to fill this gap between models and reality, our work presents experimental results and its discussion rather than trying to build a model.

From this point of view, the parameter that strongly determines the performance of this scheme is the pipe size, because it defines the trade-off between communications — the bigger the pipe, the longer the message, and so the less important the message overhead— and pipelining delay — the smaller the pipe, the faster the pipe filling, but the more important the message overhead—. Moreover, the partitioning of the local domain, as it is shown in the next point, will also influence the decision about the pipe size.

3.2 PGE on an ADI process

There are two possible one-dimensional domain decompositions for the 2D problem —an (Y,X) C-coded matrix—, which are identified as X and Y decompositions, each one determining the data structure of the boundaries that will be interchanged between the processors. In the Y-partition, the artificial frontier is a set of contiguous-in-memory data —in Fortran this would be the X partition—, while in the X-partitioning, the data belonging to the interchangeable boundaries are strided, i.e. each element is a fixed number of elements distant in memory from the previous and following elements of the frontier [5].

In figure 5, the difference between choosing the optimal block or the worse one is shown for both target machines and different numbers of processors. This difference is higher for the case of Y decomposition, i.e. for the case of calculations without spatial locality been pipelined [5].

These results show that there exists a range of optimal block sizes for the PGE scheme, and that the solver's performance is strongly dependent of this election. From now on, for every result concerning PGE, the optimal block size will be used.

3.3 Blocking of the Y-Sweep

So far, the local Y-sweeps have been done straight in one step, but this produces very low data locality, as long as cache lines are aligned along rows, not along columns. The importance of this lack of locality is shown in figure 6 for the Cray machine. This can be improved by means of the *blocking* of this Y-sweep, i.e. calculating along every column on a certain number of rows. So, we have to adjust another parameter of the algorithm, the *block* size, to take the maximum advantage from this. In all the following results, the optimal block size has been used for this kind of schemes —those labeled *PGE-Block* in the figures—. Of course, the blocking strategy will be also used for the sequential solver.

On the T3E, as will be shown in figure 9, the Y-partitioned blocked-PGE is the most efficient one on the Cray T3E, although the X one remains being the best on the

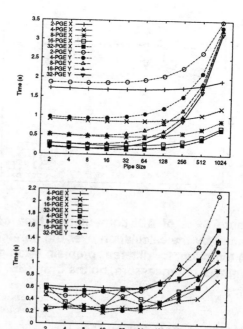

Figure 5. Execution time of ADI for the 1024×1024 on the Cray T3E (*up*) and 2048×2048 on the SGI Origin 2000 (*down*) problem, for both possible decompositions, different numbers of processors, and varying the pipe size

Origin 2000 —figure 10—, because the big second level of cache on the SGI machine (4 MBytes) takes much more advantage of locality even if blocking is not directly used, so blocking is much less effective.

This change to which is the best decomposition on the T3E is due to the fact that, once the Y-sweep is blocked, the calculation time for both decompositions is almost the same —as long as a similar amount of locality is found on both X and Y sweeps—, and so it is the communications time the one that makes the difference between one decomposition and the other. On the Y decomposition, both boundaries, and the messages to be interchanged between processors, are contiguous, but on the X-sweep, these messages are non-contiguous in memory, and so they suffer from the loss of effective bandwidth that was noted in section 2 (figures 2 and 3). This illustrates the importance of considering locality at the time of making domain decomposition decisions.

Despite all these considerations, the high efficiency obtained with B-PGE clearly makes it a very profitable one, but some alternative approaches can be explored, as it will be done in the forthcoming sections.

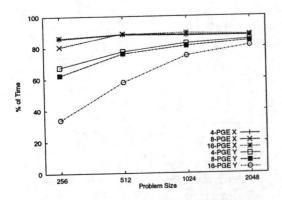

Figure 6. % of ADI computation time consumed by the calculation over the non-local (Y) direction, for different problem sizes and numbers of processors, on the Cray T3E

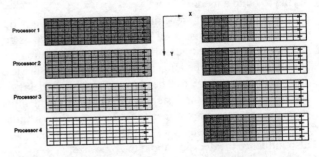

Figure 7. Matrix transposition scheme. On the Y-sweep, the blocks are internally transposed prior to the calculation, not only moved

4 Matrix Transposition (MT)

In the previous section calculations have only been done on data sets that remained fixed during the calculations, but we will now study an absolutely different approach to the problem, that is: moving the data, so modifying the local data sets, rather than parallelising the algorithm itself, or applying the pipelining approach. This method has been not very well rated in the literature [4] for reasons that can be easily understood —the poor performance typically obtainable from the matrix transposition algorithm, due to its high communications to calculations ratio—. This being true, as will be shown in the next points, it is the starting point that will lead us to the introduction of a slightly modified algorithm whose performance, maybe surprisingly compares, and in some cases betters, the one achieved by the blocked PGE.

As with the PGE, one of both sweeps is always totally sequential, either X or Y depending on the domain decomposition done, and it is on the other sweep where we need the parallel solution. Once the sequential sweep is done, we now completely transpose the global matrix, which is actually distributed among the processors, by means of an *All-to-all* communications scheme, and a following inner transposition of the blocks. After this transposition, we only have to repeat the sequential sweep over the new local domain, to have the final solution matrix (transposed, of course). Figure 7 shows a graphical representation of this. The sequential sweep will always be the X one, as long as the calculations are aligned along cache lines. The use of MPI, its derived datatypes and collective communications (`MPI_Type_vector` and `MPI_Alltoall` function), allow the easy implementation of this algorithm.

Figures 9 and 10 show that MT method is inefficient

compared to the B-PGE schemes —or even compared to the non-blocked PGE on the Origin—. Moreover, for big problems on the T3E, the difference between MT and B-PGE increases up to a factor of two, since the B-PGE approach takes advantage of the blocking strategy, more often finding data in cache than for a smaller problem, while MT has to transpose bigger matrices, worsening the effect that the lack of locality has on it. On the Origin 2000, the complete interchanging of data sets that the transposition implies is very expensive in terms of communication resources, as long as each pair of processors on this machine are sharing memory and network interface, producing a much higher rate of network contention that the same process does on the T3E, whose processors have direct access to the interconnection network —it is because of this high communication costs that both MT and Mapping Transposition methods will yield bad results on this machine—.

5 The Mapping Transposition Scheme (MappT)

So far, matrix transposition has been presented and its drawbacks exposed and discussed, and we now introduce an alternative approach to the problem, which will be called *Mapping Transposition*. The main problem with complete transposition of the matrix —apart from the high network traffic, inherent to this scheme, and responsible of its poor performance on the Origin 2000— is that it is very difficult to produce a certain degree of locality on the process, so making it extremely slow compared to the pipelined approach, especially when the PGE locality has been improved by means of blocking of the algorithm, as was shown in previous points. However, one algorithm is now being presented in order to take advantage of the benefits of the transposition scheme —i.e. leaving much of the work to the communications system, and not having the problem of the pipe filling delay—, without having to completely transpose the whole matrix, and trying to find as much locality on the calculations as the blocked PGE. This is the Mapping Transposition scheme.

The key idea is using two different local domains for the X and Y sweep, in such a way that results, after the same collective operation to that in the pure transposition, in the same data distribution that would have been obtained if we had taken the processor's grid and transposed it over the global data array —hence the name *Mapping Transposition*—. Figure 8 graphically shows this scheme.

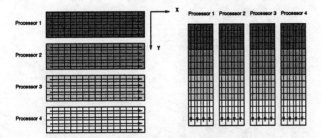

Figure 8. Mapping transposition scheme

This algorithm, although it takes more memory than the PGE, performs better on the T3E than all the previous ones, as can be seen in figure 9, for all problem sizes and number of processors considered —although in the Origin 2000 it works almost as badly as the Matrix Transposition scheme itself—. The only drawback one could find would possibly be the amount of extra memory needed for undertaking the mapping transposition but, this being true, is also true that the algorithm itself is easier to code than the PGE and that, as long as the interconnection networks keep on improving their performance faster than the computing elements —processors and memories—, relative performance of the Mapping Transposition with respect to PGE will increase, as MappT relies on communications more than PGE does.

Experimental results for all the previously described solvers, on both target machines, and for different problem sizes and number of processors, are shown in figures 9 and 10. Efficiencies with respect to the best sequential solver are shown —Blocked Gaussian Elimination scheme—; thus, these data are inverse proportional to execution time results.

6 Influence of Architectural Parameters on Algorithm Tuning and Election. Scalability of the Algorithms

At this point, influence of the architectural parameters on the election of the optimal algorithm and its tuning will be considered, i.e. when ported to bigger machines than the ones where all previous measures have been done, will the Mapping Transposition scheme still be the most efficient one, to what extent, and why?. First, some considerations must be made about the following data, because, if

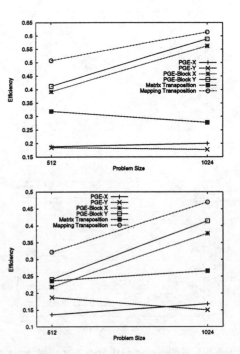

Figure 9. Efficiency of the parallel solvers, on the Cray T3E for 16 (*up*) and 32 (*down*) processors.

we only wanted to measure efficiency with respect to the sequential problem, we would not be being very realistic about the practical uses of the algorithms, that is, if one is able to use up to, say, 512 processors, why restrict the maximum problem size to the maximum one for the sequential problem?. In other words, the scalability of the above algorithms must be considered, making comparisons on execution time, not on efficiency with respect to the sequential problem, for problems whose sizes scale with the number of processors.

First, the inverse of the execution times is presented in figure 11 for the 4096×4096 and 8192×8192 problems — 16 and 64 times bigger than the maximum biggest problem used before—, showing how, for a fixed problem, algorithm performance scales with the number of processors. We use this data instead of execution times because they are proportional to the efficiency for a given problem, and moreover, it is not possible to obtain sequential results for this problem sizes, due to unavoidable memory limitations. From now on, the PGE solutions will be disregarded and only the pipeline-like B-PGE displayed, as long as B-PGE has proved to be better in all cases and, anyway, is almost the same algorithm.

In figure 12 the inverse of calculation time is also presented for different numbers of processors, but now for the biggest size possible of the local domain, that is,

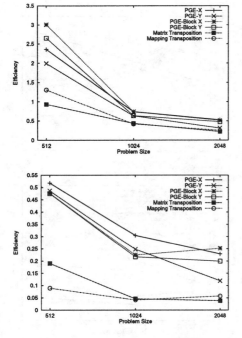

Figure 10. Efficiency of the parallel solvers, on the SGI Origin 2000 for 16 (*up*) and 32 (*down*).

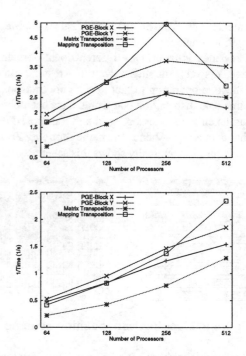

Figure 11. Inverse of calculation time, for the 4096×4096 (*up*) and 8192×8192 (*down*) ADI problem, for both B-PGE schemes, MT, and Mapping Transposition, varying the number of processors, for a Cray T3E

1024×1024, by scaling the global problem accordingly. This keeps the computational load constant, but measures the pure effect of scaling the problem, which mostly influences communications, and not calculations.

As can be concluded from figure 11, the minimum execution time is obtained for the MappT algorithm, but it is not the most efficient one for all number of processors. In fact, as a general case, one could be tempted to say that it is the Y-decomposed B-PGE that in most of cases, yields higher performance. This is true, but it is also true that the Mapping Transposition performance is always comparable to the Y-decomposed B-PGE, it is much easier to code, and, as was suggested in section 5, is presumed to improve its behavior relative to PGE in the future. For all these reasons, we consider that Mapping Transposition should be considered as a very profitable alternative for the solution of alternating-line processes on modern parallel computers.

7 Conclusions and Future Work

In this work, different methods for the solution of alternating-line processes on parallel computers have been studied, finally introducing a worthy one, the Mapping Transposition scheme, that, with very little modification of the well known and efficient Gauss algorithm, achieves

high performances compared to the highly efficient Blocked Pipelined Gaussian Elimination on the Cray T3E. The interconnection network bandwidth in the Cray machine is much higher than in the SGI Origin 2000, and this explains why on the SGI machine the algorithm does not perform as fine. The key idea of the Mapping Transposition is obtaining as much data locality as possible and leaving an important part of the work to the communications system. These conclusions have been verified by experimental results on a SGI Origin 2000 with up to 32 processors, and on a Cray T3E with up to 512 processors, which allowed us to measure the scalability of the studied algorithms and their behaviour on big machines, and see that the Matrix Transposition scheme behaves very well, obtaining the highest efficiency of all the methods, for a fixed problem size. Mapping Transposition is also easier to code —making it very profitable in terms of performance/cost ratio—, and is expected by the authors to improve its behaviour with the increasing performance of interconnection networks, which is the real bottleneck for this algorithm.

As future work, comparison with other well-known resolution methods —Wang's specially— will be done in order to put the efficiencies obtained into a correct perspective. Also, a more detailed analysis of results will be done, to

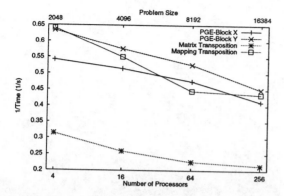

Figure 12. Inverse of calculation time of the ADI problem, for the biggest local domain size (1024×1024), for all solvers for a Cray T3E, varying the number of processors. The global problem size scales accordingly

understand why the Mapping Transposition is the most efficient one in absolute terms, and its relation to the local domain size, which is probably the key to the correct election of the algorithm.

Acknowledgements

This work has been supported by the Spanish research grants TIC 96-1071 and TIC IN96-0510, and the Human Mobility Network CHRX-CT94-0459. We would like to thank CIEMAT, the Department of Computer Architecture at the University of Málaga, and the CSC (Supercomputing Center at Complutense University), for providing access to the parallel computers that have been used in this research.

References

[1] J. C. Aguí and J. Jiménez. A binary tree implementation of a distributed tridiagonal solver. *Parallel Computing*, 21:667–686, 1995.

[2] E. Anderson, J. Brooks, C. Grassl, and S. Scott. Performance of the CRAY T3E multiprocessor. In *Proceedings of Supercomputing '97*. ACM - IEEE, November 1997.

[3] D. E. Culler, J. P. Singh, and A. Gupta. *Parallel Computer Architecture. A Hardware/Software Approach*. Morgan Kaufmann Publishers, 1999.

[4] C. C. Douglas, S. Malhotra, and M. H. Schultz. 'transpose free' alternating direction smoothers for serial and parallel multigrid methods. At http://www.mgnet.org, 1997.

[5] D. Espadas, M. Prieto, I. M. Llorente, and F. Tirado. Parallel resolution of alternating-line processes by means of pipelining techniques. In *Proceedings of the 7th. Euromicro Workshop on Parallel and Distributed Processing*, pages 289–296. IEEE Computer Society Press, February 1999.

[6] G. Golub and J. M. Ortega. *Scientific Computing. An Introduction with Parallel Computing*. Academic Press, 1993.

[7] F. F. Hatay, D. C. Jespersen, G. P. Guruswamy, Y. M. Rizk, C. Byun, and K. Gee. A multi-level parallelization concept for high-fidelity multiblock solvers. In *Proceedings of Supercomputing'97*. ACM - IEEE, November 1997.

[8] A. Krechel, H.-J. Plum, and K. Stüben. Parallelization and vectorization aspects of the solution of tridiagonal linear systems. *Parallel Computing*, 14:31–49, 1990.

[9] J. Laudon and D. Lenoski. The SGI Origin: A ccNUMA highly scalable server. In *Proceedings of the International Symposium on Computer Architecture (ISCA '97)*, June 1997.

[10] I. M. Llorente and D. Melson. Robust multigrid smoothers for three dimensional elliptic equations with strong anisotropies. Technical Report 37, ICASE - NASA, 1998.

[11] J. López, O. Plata, F. Argüello, and E. L. Zapata. Unified framework for the parallelization of divide and conquer based tridiagonal systems. *Parallel Computing*, 23:667–686, 1997.

[12] M. P. Matias, I. M. Llorente, and F. Tirado. Partitioning regular domains on modern parallel computers. In J. M. L. M. Palma, J. Dongarra, and V. Hernandez, editors, *Proceedings of the 3rd. International Meeting on Vector and Parallel Processing (VECPAR '98)*, pages 305–318, 1999.

[13] N. Mattor, T. J. Williams, and D. W. Hewett. Algorithm for solving tridiagonal matrix problems in parallel. *Parallel Computing*, 21:1769–1782, 1995.

[14] A. Povitsky. Parallel directionally split solver based on reformulation of pipelined thomas algorithm. Technical Report 45, ICASE - NASA, 1998.

[15] A. Povitsky. Parallelization of the pipelined thomas algorithm. Technical Report 48, ICASE - NASA, 1998.

[16] M. Prieto, D. Espadas, I. Martin, and F. Tirado. Message passing evaluation and analysis on Cray T3E and SGI Origin 2000 systems. In *Proceedings of the 4th. Euro-Par Conference (Euro-Par '99)*. Springer-Verlag in Lecture Notes in Computer Science Series, August 1999. To be published.

[17] F. Reale. A tridiagonal solver for massively parallel computer systems. *Parallel Computing*, 16:361–368, 1990.

[18] A. Saulsbury, F. Pong, and A. Nowatzyk. Missing the memory wall: The case for processor/memory integration. In *Proceedings of the International Symposium on Computer Architecture (ISCA '96)*, May 1996.

[19] S. L. Scott. Synchronization and communication in the T3E multiprocessor. In *Proceedings of the ASPLOS VII*, October 1996.

[20] SGI Inc. Origin servers. Technical report, SGI, April 1997.

[21] X.-H. Sun and S. Moitra. A fast parallel tridiagonal algorithm for a class of CFD applications. Technical Report 3585, NASA, August 1996.

[22] H. J. Wassermann, O. M. Lubeck, and F. Bassetti. Performance evaluation of the SGI Origin 2000: A memory-centric characterization of LANL ASCI applications. In *Proceedings of Supercomputing '97*. ACM-IEEE, November 1997.

[23] W. A. Wulf and S. A. McKee. Hitting the memory wall: Implications of the obvious. *Computer Architecture News*, March 1995.

Keynote Address

Convergence of Voice Networks and Packet Networks

Dr. David M. Rouse
Lucent Technologies, USA

Session A4

Distributed Shared Memory (DSM)

Chair: Nian-Feng Tzeng
University of Southwestern Louisiana, USA

Dynamic Adaptation of Sharing Granularity in DSM Systems

Ayal Itzkovitz*
Department of Computer Science, CIMS
New York University
ayali@cs.nyu.edu

Nitzan Niv   Assaf Schuster
Computer Science Department
Technion – Israel Institute of Technology
{nitzann,assaf}@cs.technion.ac.il

Abstract

The tradeoff between false sharing elimination and aggregation in Distributed Shared Memory (DSM) systems has a major effect on their performance. Some studies in this area show that fine grain access is advantageous, while others advocate the use of large coherency units. One way to resolve the tradeoff is to dynamically adapt the granularity to the application memory access pattern.

In this paper we propose a novel technique for implementing multiple sharing granularities over page based DSMs. We present protocols for efficient switching between small and large sharing units during runtime. We show that applications may benefit from adapting the memory sharing to the memory access pattern, using both coarse grain sharing and fine grain sharing interchangeably in different stages of the computation. Our experiments show a substantial improvement in the performance using adapted granularity level over using a fixed granularity level.

1 Introduction

Software DSM systems combine the ease of shared memory programming with the low cost of message passing architectures. Their performance, however, is strongly affected by the memory sharing granularity. The basic implementation method relies on the page protection mechanisms handled by the virtual memory manager, which imposes a sharing unit equal to the size of the virtual memory page [12]. In many cases, the page size is much larger than the optimal sharing unit, and the result is false sharing: due to the mismatch between the data allocation unit and the data sharing unit, two unrelated data items that happen to reside on the same page are treated as if they were shared. False sharing can cause the DSM to send redundant messages, as well as redundant data in messages which carry truly shared data.

---

*Much of this work was done while the author was with the Computer Science Department at the Technion, Israel.

The ill effects of false sharing can be reduced using a relaxed memory consistency protocol [4, 6, 10, 18] or prefetching strategies [9, 11]. However, the price for using these methods is a change in the memory semantics which creates a difficulty for the programmer. In addition, relaxed consistency protocols introduce substantial additional overhead [19].

Fine-grain access has been proposed [15, 16] to overcome the false sharing problem, but its implementation usually involves code instrumentation and is limited to certain machine architectures. Recently [7] the MULTIVIEW technique used the multiple mapping capabilities of the operating system to allow fine-grain access to shared data.

However, in many cases a fixed granularity setting seems insufficient. Several recent studies deal with the tradeoff between false sharing elimination and aggregation [1, 13, 23]. On one hand, fine granularity can eliminate false sharing and fragmentation, and reduce unnecessary network traffic. On the other hand, coarse granularity reduces the number of page faults and other expensive consistency protocol operations. Therefore, in addition to setting the granularity level per application [7, 14], performance can be improved by setting different granularity levels in different stages of the execution [13].

In this paper we present ADAPTABLEVIEW, a novel technique for providing multiple sharing granularities in page-based DSMs. ADAPTABLEVIEW extends MULTIVIEW by providing application controlled, multiple sharing granularities during a single execution. We present the mechanism and the protocol for switching between different granularity levels efficiently during runtime, so that the size of the sharing unit is adapted to the memory access pattern of the application.

We implemented ADAPTABLEVIEW on the MILLIPAGE system and tested it on three benchmark applications. Our results show a performance improvement of up to 80% when applications use multiple granularities provided by ADAPTABLEVIEW, compared to running the application with the best fixed granularity.

The rest of this paper is organized as follows. The rest of

220

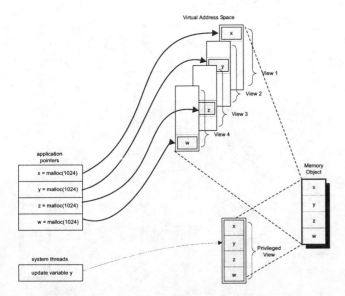

Figure 1. The basic memory layout of MULTI-VIEW

this section describes MULTIVIEW. In Section 2 we explain how MULTIVIEW can be extended to support multiple sharing granularities, and describe implementation of ADAPTABLEVIEW on the MILLIPAGE DSM system. We describe optimizations to the ADAPTABLEVIEW implementation in Section 3. We provide performance evaluation of ADAPTABLEVIEW in Section 4, describe related work in Section 5, and conclude in Section 6.

1.1 Background

The data sharing granularity of page-based DSMs is the size of a memory page, which is usually a few KB. This sharing unit is considered much larger than the effective sharing of applications. In systems which implement MULTIVIEW [7], the single, shared memory space, called *memory object*, is mapped to several regions of virtual addresses, called *views*. A memory element in the memory object can be accessed via any of the views using the virtual memory mapping mechanisms. MULTIVIEW allows the DSM to manipulate each memory element (*minipage*) through a dedicated virtual memory page which belongs to one of the views. The protection for a minipage is controlled by manipulating the protection of the associated virtual memory page.

Figure 1 depicts a sample memory layout of a general DSM system that uses MULTIVIEW. Shared variables x, y, z and w, are allocated on the same page, but false sharing is prevented by associating each variable with a separate view, so each variable resides in its own minipage.

2 ADAPTABLEVIEW: Providing Multiple Sharing Granularities

Consider a program which is composed of phases. In certain phases processors read relatively large sections of memory, or write to memory regions which are not accessed by the other processors. In other phases each processor updates a portion of the variables whose placement in memory is interleaved with that of variables accessed by other processors. We will refer to the first phase type as a *coarse phase* and to the second as a *fine phase*.

A programmer who uses MULTIVIEW can allocate each data element in a separate minipage to avoid false sharing. Clearly, this is best suited to the memory access pattern of a fine phase. However, accessing a large memory region in a subsequent coarse phase will cause many faults which must be handled by the DSM. Performance may be improved for the coarse phase by coarser grain sharing, which will allocate several data elements in the same minipage.

We propose to adapt the granularity of the sharing units to that of the memory access pattern. The proposed method, ADAPTABLEVIEW, is an extension of MULTIVIEW.

2.1 Providing Multiple Memory Granularities

Using MULTIVIEW, a page containing k data elements may be mapped onto a set of k views, creating k distinct, non-overlapping and independent minipages. Such memory allocation scheme is said to use a *sharing level* of k.

In order to support l different sharing levels $k_1, k_2, \ldots, k_l$ (assuming $k_1 > k_2 > \ldots > k_l$), we allocate a total of $\sum k_i$ views. Each set of k_i views is used to split the page into k_i minipages and provide a sharing level of k_i.

The memory used by each variable is now overlapped by l views. Therefore, each variable is effectively associated with l distinct minipages of different sizes, each providing a different sharing level. All the minipages associated with the same variable are just different means to access its data, which is contained in the single memory object. Maintaining a consistent protection setting among overlapping minipages produces the desired behavior: Accessing variables through minipages with the finest granularity (sharing level k_1) provides fine-grain sharing, while accessing variables through coarser views (e.g., sharing level k_l) provides coarse-grain sharing.

Figure 2 shows the memory mapping involved in supporting multiple sharing levels 4, 2 and 1, using ADAPTABLEVIEW. When a fine phase is due, the system accesses all variables using the set of views that give sharing level 4 (views 1-4). When a coarse phase is about to start, all further accesses will use a single view which gives sharing level 1 (view 7). If variable z was only accessible for reading in a certain host during the fine phase, then when the coarser phase is about to start, the corresponding mini-page containing z should not have permission higher than `ReadOnly`, unless the protocol makes sure this is not violating the memory consistency (e.g., by invalidating other copies of z if the consistency is sequential).

In general, a certain phase might be coarse for one set of variables, while being fine for a different set of variables. ADAPTABLEVIEW can be used to change the sharing granularity of each set of variables independently, simply by associating them with minipages of different sizes.

Selecting the appropriate sharing granularity for a given set of variables at a certain execution phase can be done by the DSM system, according to some smart analysis [3, 17]. In the remainder of this article selecting the sharing level is enforced by programmer's hints, requiring only minimal changes to the application code.

The programmer informs the DSM what are the granularities expected for each variable. During allocation, the shared memory region that contains the variable is mapped to several views. A minipage that contains the variable is created for each granularity, so every variable is associated with a set of pointers, one for each minipage that contains it. A single pointer is selected for each phase in the application.

We assume that all the threads of an application use the same sharing granularity for a specific variable at every point in time. Therefore, granularity changes should be done at global synchronization points. Our implementation uses the existing barriers in the application code to signal a possible change in granularity. The programmer identifies for the DSM the set of variables that should have a new sharing granularity after the barrier, and the new sharing level. In response, the DSM hands the application a set of pointers to these variables according to the requested granularity.

2.2 Switching Granularities

We implemented ADAPTABLEVIEW on the MILLIPAGE DSM system. MILLIPAGE [7] is a software implementation of a sequentially-consistent DSM that uses MULTIVIEW.

MILLIPAGE uses *managers* (sometimes called *home nodes*) to store minipages' global state such as placement and protection. The manager keeps the information for the minipages of *the finest granularity*. The availability of a coarse minipage is inferred from the availability of its composing fine minipages.

Most of the modifications required in order to implement ADAPTABLEVIEW on MILLIPAGE are related to the phase transitions. Switching granularities involves setting the protection of the target views and exchanging data between the hosts (when switching to a coarse granularity). For efficiency, we defer these actions until the minipages are actually accessed for the first time after a granularity switch

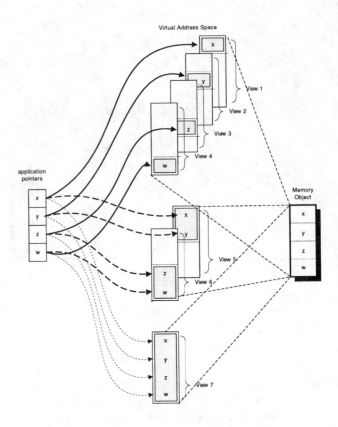

Figure 2. ADAPTABLEVIEW: The memory mapping used to support three different sharing granularities for a single execution

(see subsection 3.1). When this happens, a page fault occurs, and a minipage request is sent to the respective manager. The behavior of MILLIPAGE following such a request depends on the granularity of the minipage.

2.2.1 Switching from a Fine Phase to a Coarse Phase

When moving from a fine phase to a coarser phase, a coarse minipage may be fragmented (i.e., different sections of it may reside in different hosts). Therefore, before a coarse page can be used, the data of its composing fine minipages may need to be gathered from the hosts in which they reside, and assembled together.

The manager initiates the process of gathering and assembling the minipage according to the global state (data availability) of the minipage. The manager may find out that the requesting host already holds all the data, so there is no need to collect it, and only the protection should be changed. In this case, the requester is informed that it may change the protection and resume execution. The manager may discover that all the minipage's data resides at a single, remote host. In this case, the manager forwards the request to this remote host, which processes the request as if the minipage was already assembled (resulting in a single data transfer and a single protection change). In the general case, no host has all the fine minipages, so the fragments that are not available on the requester must be brought in from their remote locations. The manager forwards requests to all the hosts which contain these fragments, and these hosts send back the data to the requester. Communication overhead is reduced by batching requests and replies, so that only a single message is sent to each host. Once all the data arrives at the requester, the coarse minipage is assembled, and its protection is set according to the request type.

2.2.2 Switching from a Coarse Phase to a Fine Phase

During the service of each request for a coarse minipage, the manager updates the availability information for the fine minipages that it contains. On the other hand, local protection changes for the fine minipages are not performed during a coarse phase. When a fine minipage is accessed for the first time after the switch to a finer granularity, a page request is sent to the manager. The manager directs the request to a host that has the requested data, and the requester changes the protection when it receives the data.

2.2.3 Operation during a fixed granularity phase

After the initial assembly of a minipage at the granularity switch, the protocol for processing minipage requests is similar to the one used in a fixed granularity. The application accesses the shared memory using a pointer that references the appropriate minipage containing the variable. The beginning address and the size of this minipage determine the address range from which data is transferred and to which protection changes may apply, according to the memory consistency. When the manager receives a request for a coarse minipage it updates the copyset for each of the finest minipages which compose it.

3 Optimizing the Granularity Switch

In this section we present the ideas used to eliminate potential sources of inefficiency during the granularity switch.

3.1 Lazy Granularity Switch

During the phase transition data is collected and the minipages' protection is set in the target views according to their global state. Performing these tasks for all the minipages requires costly communication, and it is not necessary for minipages that will not be accessed in the coming phase.

We avoid this penalty by adopting a lazy approach. During the granularity switch, the protection of all the target views is set to NoAccess, and the data is not collected. This makes the granularity switch very efficient, as setting the protection of a large region of memory using a single operating system call is much faster than setting it page by page. If and when a minipage is accessed a fault occurs, and the fault handler gathers the minipage in a consistent fashion.

There is no need to set the protection of the minipages in old granularity (i.e., the protection of the respective views), since the application does not access them at all in the new phase. The minipages' consistency is preserved in the new granularity, since their protection is first set to NoAccess and then modified by each host according to their new state, but only when all the data is available.

3.2 The Protection Cache Table

As shown in subsection 3.1, the access permissions of a minipage may be set to NoAccess, even though the data it contains is up to date. For instance, during a coarse granularity phase we do not want to waste time on updating the protection of fine minipages, but after switching to a finer granularity, we would like to utilize the data that remains on each host from the previous coarse phase.

The communication overhead of memory faults caused by our lazy approach (i.e., the minipage's data is available locally, but it has a NoAccess protection) can be avoided by keeping on every host the access permission that is allowed for each minipage by the consistency policy in a *Protection Cache Table* (PCT).

When a page fault occurs, the DSM checks in the PCT if the requested access to the minipage is allowed. If this is the case (a PCT *hit*) the protection is changed locally, without any communication. Otherwise (a PCT *miss*) the DSM invokes the remote protocol which brings in the minipage.

The PCT is further utilized by setting the protection of a consecutive range of minipages (with a single operating system call) at the first access to any of them. This usage of spatial locality avoids page faults for these minipages.

The PCT is updated in an analogous way to the update of the memory protection in a DSM, and the PCT updates for a minipage can be piggybacked on the messages sent when processing a request for it.

4 Performance Evaluation

In this section we analyze the performance implications of using ADAPTABLEVIEW in the MILLIPAGE DSM system. Our testbed environment consists of a network of eight

Pentium II 300Mhz uniprocessor machines with 128MB of RAM, running Windows NT Workstation 4.0 SP3. The cluster is interconnected by a switched Myrinet [2] LAN. We report our performance measurements on three versions of the MILLIPAGE system: MILLI-MV is the original system (without ADAPTABLEVIEW), that provides fixed-granularity (tailored to the data elements using MULTI-VIEW), MILLI-ADAPT is the modified system which supports lazy ADAPTABLEVIEW (without the PCT optimization), and MILLI-ADAPT-PCT is the modified system which supports lazy ADAPTABLEVIEW with the additional PCT optimization.

4.1 ADAPTABLEVIEW Overheads - Basic Operations

Table 1 summarizes the times of basic operations on MILLI-MV, MILLI-ADAPT and MILLI-ADAPT-PCT. The time spent preparing the new granularity (i.e., invalidating memory and setting pointers) is negligible (1%) compared to the barrier waiting time.

In fine granularity, the overhead incurred by ADAPTABLEVIEW for read and write operations due to the granularity switch activity is small (no more than 9% for reads and 15% for writes). Reading a coarse minipage in MILLI-ADAPT is more expensive than in MILLI-MV when performed immediately after a fine phase, because it might require the data fragments of the minipage to be collected from several hosts. On the other hand, writing a coarse minipage in MILLI-ADAPT is cheaper, because multiple invalidations are not required, and some of the data may already exist at the requester and need not be transferred.

Remote reads and writes are about 10% more expensive in MILLI-ADAPT-PCT than in MILLI-ADAPT, but their number is significantly lower, since each local handling of a single PCT hit replaces hundreds of remote minipage requests caused by false faults (memory faults that occur even though the local data is up to date).

For both read and write faults, the overheads are not affected by the size of the fine-grain minipages and the number of processors.

4.2 Applications

Most of the applications commonly used as DSM benchmarks [22] have a regular access pattern. Thus, good performance is achieved when the sharing granularity is fixed (possibly varying for different variables) [7]. Our target applications are characterized by irregular access pattern in different phases of execution, that reveals itself in the prefered sharing granularity, so these applications perform poorly when the granularity is fixed. We created two applications that imitate a kernel of an N-Body application

with a predictable sharing pattern. In addition, we chose to experiment with the Barnes application from the SPLASH suite, that performs poorly on DSM systems.

NBodyW imitates kernels of N-body applications. The main data structure is a large array of *bodies*, each of which is an array of chars. The application iterates over a loop which is composed of the following three phases:
read all: Each of the P processes reads the entire array.
update mine: Each process reads and writes $1/P$ of the bodies. The bodies of all of the processors are perfectly interleaved in memory.
sequential update: A single process updates the entire array.
Only the second phase involves false sharing. In the first phase there are no updates, and in the third phase there is no concurrent work. Therefore, the first and last phases are thought of as *coarse* and the second phase is *fine*.

We ran NBodyW for 4096 bodies with 256 bytes in each body. We tested two granularity levels: a fine granularity, where each minipage contains a single body, and a coarse granularity level of 1, where each minipage is effectively a page of the operating system containing 16 bodies. In MILLI-ADAPT and MILLI-ADAPT-PCT we modified the application code to use the coarse granularity for the first and third phases and the fine granularity for the second phase.

NBody is similar to NBodyW, except that it contains only the first two phases. All the processors read all the bodies and select the bodies they will modify exclusively. After a synchronization point, each process updates its selected set of bodies. The coarse phase is solely used here for defragmenting the data and fetching it to all the processors as fast as possible.

Barnes is a simulation of the interaction of a system of bodies in three dimensional space over a number of time steps, using the Barnes-Hut hierarchical N-body method. The computational domain is represented as an octree, of which the leaves contain information on the bodies. The size of a body structure is 104 bytes. There are 16K bodies. During each time step, there is a *fine-grain* phase when the bodies are read and updated by all the processes, and a *coarse-grain* phase when the entire body array is read by all the processes. Minimal code changes were required to allow Barnes to use ADAPTABLEVIEW.

Figure 3 shows the execution times of the three applications for fixed granularities on the eight-host cluster. It seems that Barnes gets the best execution times for the finest granularity (minipage=one body) and for granularity of eight (minipage=eight bodies=832 bytes). In contrast, NBody and NBodyW get the best execution times when the granularity is coarsest (minipage=4KB).

Table 1. Cost of basic operations (in μs) on each system

Operation	MILLI-MV	MILLI-ADAPT	MILLI-ADAPT-PCT
fine gran. read	565	615	652
fine gran. write	1287	1498	1778
coarse gran. read	731	1778	1971
coarse gran. write	1074	705	829
PCT hit	-	-	244
gran. switch	-	14909	
barrier	896978		

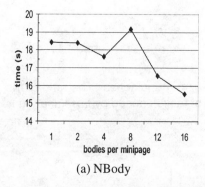

(a) NBody

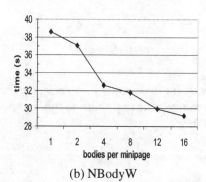

(b) NBodyW

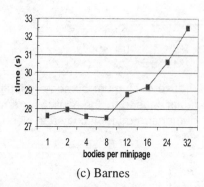

(c) Barnes

Figure 3. Execution times for fixed granularities on eight hosts

4.3 Performance Analysis

In order to study the performance implications of ADAPTABLEVIEW we compare the behavior of our benchmark applications on MILLI-ADAPT, MILLI-ADAPT-PCT and MILLI-MV.

4.3.1 Fault Reduction

The opposite effects of false sharing and memory chunking are clear from Figure 4, which presents the number of access faults in each of the granularity levels. The number of page faults is usually smaller in coarse granularity than in fine granularity due to the aggregation. On the other hand, most of the faults in the coarse granularity are caused by false sharing. ADAPTABLEVIEW gives the benefits of both aggregation and false sharing elimination: In MILLI-ADAPT-PCT, the number of faults is lower by a factor of 3-5 compared to MILLI-MV that uses fine granularity, and it is 2-3 times better than MILLI-MV that uses coarse granularity.

The number of processors affects the memory access pattern and the performance in the different sharing levels. Since each process writes approximately $1/P$ of the shared memory in the shared phases, the number of write faults (for each process) decreases as the number of processors increases. However, false sharing in the coarse granular-

ity phases causes additional faults and offsets this trend in the number of write faults. For read faults, increasing the number of processors implies that more data must be read from other hosts during the non-shared phases. Therefore, as the number of processors increases, the number of read faults increases in fine granularity, but due to aggregation the number of read faults remains the same in the coarse and adaptive granularities. Consequently, in adaptive granularity the total number of page faults clearly drops as the number of processors increases; none of the fixed granularities exhibit this trend.

4.3.2 Speedups

Figure 5 shows the speedups achieved on MILLIPAGE with ADAPTABLEVIEW, when running the benchmarks on 1 to 8 processors. For comparison, we also show the performance with a fixed, fine granularity and with a fixed coarse granularity. Clearly, ADAPTABLEVIEW achieves superior results (up to 80% improvement) over any fixed granularity. Moreover, with the fixed granularities we got slowdowns in Barnes. Only when using ADAPTABLEVIEW we were able to achieve speedups, and these are increasing with the number of hosts. Our results here, using sequential consistency, are comparable to the state-of-the-art results reported for relaxed consistency DSM systems (e.g., [18]).

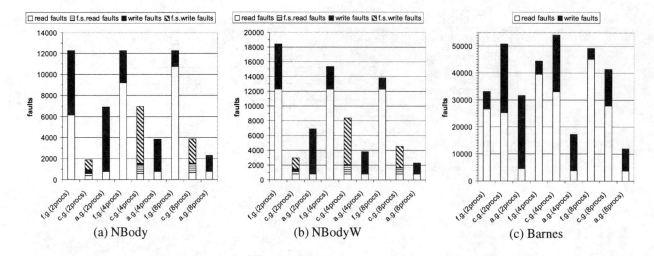

Figure 4. Number of memory faults using fine, coarse and adaptive sharing granularities. The ratio of the faults caused by the application's memory access pattern to the number of faults caused by false sharing is demonstrated for Nbody and NbodyW

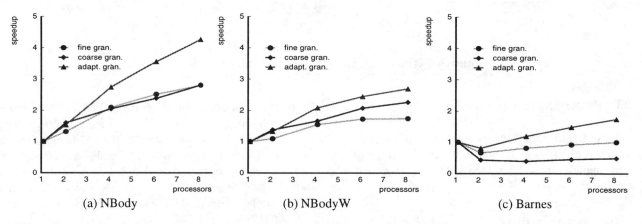

Figure 5. Speedups (relative to a sequential run) of adaptive granularity compared to two fixed granularities (fine and coarse). Adaptive granularity outperforms both fixed granularities

5 Related Work

Several researchers have investigated the effects of the sharing granularity on the performance of DSM systems, and concluded that changing the sharing granularity dynamically improves the performance of many applications. Others [5, 8, 21] have investigated multiple sharing granularities and data layout optimization as the solutions to false sharing in the context of multiprocessor caches.

Amza et al. [1] suggest increasing the consistency unit in a page-based DSM to a multiple of the virtual memory page size, unless the page faults behavior reveals an increase in false sharing. They conclude that the performance gained by dynamic aggregation approaches the one obtained with the best static consistency unit size. Park and Saavedra

[13] present Adaptive Granularity that integrates two protocols: for small data sets, the granularity is fixed to that of a cache line, and for large array data, the granularity varies depending on the sharing behavior of applications at runtime, grouping together adjacent data blocks with the same owner. The protocol of Yeung et al. [23], targeted at clusters of Scalable SMPs, uses a fine grain sharing unit (cache line) within an SMP, and a coarse grain sharing unit (memory page) between SMPs. The two layer DSM design integrates hardware DSM (within an SMP) and software DSM (between SMPs), and provides release consistency shared memory. Tamir and Janakiraman [20] propose a hierarchical coherency management for shared virtual memory computers: page level management is used for non-shared (private) memory pages, and block level management is used

for shared memory pages. Pages change state dynamically between private and shared status.

Our work allows the application to determine the fine granularity sharing unit for each set of data elements, and permits several granularity levels to be defined without any hardware support. ADAPTABLEVIEW is used in DSM with sequential consistency while keeping the protocol simple. Prefetching mechanisms like the ones suggested in [11] and [9] may be used to guide the granularity switch, instead of using program annotations.

6 Conclusions

In this paper we presented ADAPTABLEVIEW, a mechanism which can be used by DSM systems to dynamically adapt the memory sharing granularity to the changing memory access demands of the applications. ADAPTABLEVIEW enables refinement of the consistency unit when false sharing causes contention between processes, and it enables large consistency units to be used when the number of page faults becomes the performance bottleneck. ADAPTABLE-VIEW makes it possible to strike the best balance between these opposing considerations for each phase in the application and for each set of variables. Therefore, for a large domain of applications, the performance achieved when using this method is much better than the performance achieved when using any fixed granularity.

7 Acknowledgments

We are grateful to the anonymous referees, whose comments helped us improve the paper.

References

[1] C. Amza, A. L. Cox, K. Ramajamni, and W. Zwaenepoel. Tradeoffs between false sharing and aggregation in software distributed shared memory. In *Proc. of the Sixth ACM SIGPLAN Symp. on Principles and Practice of Parallel Programming (PPOPP'97)*, pages 90–99, June 1997.

[2] N. J. Boden, D. Cohen, R. E. Felderman, A. E. Kulawik, C. L. Seitz, J. N. Seizovic, and Wen-King Su. Myrinet: A gigabit-per-second Local Area Network. *IEEE Micro*, 15(1):29–36, February 1995.

[3] B. Buck and P. Keleher. Locality and performance of page- and object-based dsms. In *Proc. of the First Merged Symp. IPPS/SPDP 1998)*, pages 687–693, March 1998.

[4] J. B. Carter. Design of the munin distributed shared memory system. *Journal of Parallel and Distributed Computing*, 29(2):219–227, September 1995.

[5] C. Dubnicki and T. LeBlanc. Adjustable block size coherent caches. In *Proc. of the 19th Annual Int'l Symp. on Computer Architecture (ISCA'92)*, pages 170–180, May 1992.

[6] L. Iftode, J. P. Singh, and K. Li. Scope consistency: A bridge between release consistency and entry consistency. In *Proc. of the 8th ACM Annual Symp. on Parallel Algorithms and Architectures (SPAA'96)*, pages 277–287, June 1996.

[7] A. Itzkovitz and A. Schuster. MultiView and Millipage — Fine-Grain Sharing in Page-Based DSMs. In *Proc. of the 3rd Symp. on Operating Systems Design and Implementation (OSDI'99)*, pages 215–228, New Orleans, February 1999.

[8] T.E. Jeremiassen and S.J. Eggers. Reducing false sharing on shared memory multiprocessors. In *Proc. of the Fifth ACM SIGPLAN Symp. on Principles and Practice of Parallel Programming (PPOPP'95)*, pages 179–188, 1995.

[9] M. Karlsson and P. Stenstrom. Effectiveness of dynamic prefetching in multiple-writer distributed virtual shared memory systems. *Journal of Parallel and Distributed Computing*, 43(2):79–93, June 1997.

[10] P. Keleher, A. L. Cox, and W. Zwaenepoel. Lazy release consistency for software distributed shared memory. In *Proc. of the 19th Annual Int'l Symp. on Computer Architecture (ISCA'92)*, pages 13–21, May 1992.

[11] A. I-C. Lai and C-L. Lei. Data prefetching for distributed shared memory systems. In *Proc. of the 29th Hawaii Int'l Conf. on System Sciences (HICSS29)*, volume I, pages 102–110, January 1996.

[12] K. Li. Ivy: A shared virtual memory system for parallel computing. In *Proc. of the 1988 Int'l Conf. on Parallel Processing (ICPP'88)*, volume II, pages 94–101, August 1988.

[13] D. Park and R. H. Saavedra. Adaptive granularity: Transparent integration of fine- and coarse-grain communication. In *Proc. of the 1996 Conf. on Parallel Architectures and Compilation Techniques*, pages 260–268, October 1996.

[14] D. J. Scales and K. Gharachorloo. Performance of the shasta distributed shared memory protocol. Technical Report WRL-TR-97/2, Digital Western Research Laboratory, February 1997.

[15] D. J. Scales, K. Gharachorloo, and C. A. Thekkath. Shasta: A low overhead, software-only approach for supporting fine-grain shared memory. In *Proc. of the 7th Symp. on Architectural Support for Programming Languages and Operating Systems (ASPLOSVII)*, pages 174–185, October 1996.

[16] I. Schoinas, B. Falsafi, A. R. Lebeck, S. K. Reinhardt, J. R. Larus, and D. A. Wood. Fine-Grain Access Control for Distributed Shared Memory. In *Proc. of the 6th Symp. on Architectural Support for Programming Languages and Operating Systems (ASPLOSVI)*, pages 297–306, October 1994.

[17] A. Schuster and L. Shalev. Using Remote Access Histories for Thread Scheduling in Distributed Shared Memory Systems. In *12th Intl. Symp. on Distributed Computing*, pages 347–362, Andros, September 1998.

[18] W. E. Speight. *Efficient Runtime Support for Cluster-Based Distributed Shared Memory Multiprocessors*. PhD thesis, Department of Electrical and Computer Engineering, Rice University, July 1997.

[19] M. Swanson, L. Stroller, and J. B. Carter. Making distributed shared memory simple, yet efficient. In *Proc. of the 3rd Int'l Workshop on High-Level Parallel Programming Models and Supportive Environments (HIPS'98)*, pages 2–13, March 1998.

[20] Y. Tamir and G. Janakiraman. Hierarchical coherency management for shared virtual memory multicomputers. *Journal of Parallel and Distributed Computing*, 15(4):408–419, August 1992.

[21] J. Torrellas, M.S. Lam, and J.L. Hennessy. False sharing and spatial locality in multiprocessor caches. *IEEE Transactions on Computers*, 43(6):651–663, 1994.

[22] S.C. Woo, M. Ohara, E. Torrie, J.P. Singh, and A. Gupta. The SPLASH-2 Programs: Characterization and Methodological Considerations. In *Proc. of the 22nd Annual Int'l Symp. on Computer Architecture (ISCA'95)*, June 1995.

[23] D. Yeung, J. Kubiatowicz, and A. Agarwal. MGS: A mutigrain Shared Memory System. In *Proc. of the 23rd Annual Int'l Symp. on Computer Architecture (ISCA'96)*, May 1996.

Evaluating the Impact of the Programming Model on the Performance and Complexity of Software DSM Systems *

Cristiana B. Seidel[†‡], Ricardo Bianchini[†], and Claudio L. Amorim[†]

[†]COPPE Systems Engineering
Federal University of Rio de Janeiro, Brazil

[‡]Dept. of Systems Engineering
State University of Rio de Janeiro, Brazil

{seidel,ricardo,amorim}@cos.ufrj.br

Abstract

In this paper we evaluate the impact of the programming model on the performance and complexity of Entry Consistency-based software distributed shared-memory systems (software DSMs). We study three novel software DSMs that can all take advantage of lock-style primitives but impose different variations of the shared-memory programming model. The first variation is a plain shared-memory model based on barriers and mutual exclusion locks, where the association between shared data and lock variables is determined transparently by the system. The second model dictates that all accesses to shared data must be delimited by lock/unlock-type primitives (with or without mutual exclusion), even though the lock-data association is still performed transparently. The third model requires that all shared data accesses be delimited by lock/unlock-type primitives and the association between locks and data is specified explicitly by the programmer. A comparison of our software DSMs shows that increasing the model complexity simplifies the systems substantially. Our results also show that the second model can perform significantly worse than the first model, while the third model improves performance by 25% and 27% on average compared to the first and second models, respectively. We conclude that increasing the burden on the programmer is not necessarily a good option for software DSMs; only the most elaborate model we study achieves performance that justifies its programming complexity.

1 Introduction

The programming model has great potential to affect the performance and complexity of parallel computing systems, as can be observed comparing the message passing and shared memory programming models (e.g. [10]): message passing requires the programmer to orchestrate all communication between processes, but usually achieves very good performance and can be implemented with relatively simple software and hardware; shared memory, on the other hand, allows the programmer to abstract from the details of communication, but frequently leads to inferior performance and requires great software and/or hardware sophistication.

Researchers in the parallel programming community sometimes

extrapolate this reasoning to the several variations of the shared memory programming model, such as those of CRL [8] and Midway [2], assuming that more elaborate variations of the shared-memory programming model always lead to better performance and simpler systems. However, whether this intuitive extrapolation is always valid has never been proven to date. Even more importantly, the impact of these variations has never been quantified.

In this paper we evaluate the impact of the programming model on the performance and complexity of software distributed shared-memory systems (software DSMs) based on the Entry Consistency (EC) model [2]. We accomplish this by studying a family of novel software DSMs, where each system imposes a different variation of the shared-memory programming model. Our software DSMs are identical (even in terms of their actual codes), except for the optimizations that their particular programming models allow. The systems exploit the Lock Acquirer Prediction (LAP) [14] technique, which predicts the next acquirer of a lock at the time of the release based on the previous history of lock transfers, so that the acquirer can be updated sometimes even before requesting ownership of the lock. Thus, in our software DSMs a processor entering a lock/unlock-delimited section will likely have already received the data associated with the section.

The extent to which lock-style primitives is used in applications has a direct impact on whether the advantages of EC and LAP can be exploited to the fullest. Thus, we investigate a range of possible models where lock-style primitives are used with varying degrees of intensity. More specifically, the simplest model we study is that of the Affinity Entry Consistency system (AEC) [14], which is a plain shared-memory programming model based on barriers and mutual exclusion locks, where the association between shared data and lock variables is determined transparently by the system. Programming under the AEC-light system is a little more complicated than under AEC, in that all accesses to shared data must be delimited by lock/unlock-type primitives (with or without mutual exclusion), even though the lock-data association is still performed transparently by the system. The most restrictive programming model we study is that of the AEC-bind system, where all shared data accesses must be delimited by lock/unlock-type primitives and the association between locks and data is specified explicitly by the programmer. Note that going from AEC to AEC-bind we are also lowering the level of abstraction presented to programmers slightly.

---

*This research was supported by Brazilian FINEP/MCT and CNPq.

The implementation of our three software DSMs shows that increasing the complexity of the programming model indeed simplifies the systems, sometimes significantly. As a rough illustration of the complexity differences, we compared the number of lines of code involved in each system. This comparison shows that AEC-light involves 13% fewer lines than AEC, while AEC-bind involves 42 and 34% fewer lines than AEC and AEC-light, respectively.

Our detailed study of six parallel applications running under our software DSMs on an 8-node SP2 multicomputer shows that: (a) AEC-light does not achieve better performance than AEC for three applications, while gains are pretty small for the other three applications; and (b) AEC-bind improves performance by 25% and 27% on average compared to AEC and AEC-light, respectively. These results not only quantify the performance and complexity effects of different programming models, but also demonstrate that increasing the programming model complexity does not always lead to performance improvements.

To the best of our knowledge, this paper is the first evaluation of the performance and system complexity implications of different variations of the shared-memory programming model. The paper that comes closest to addressing this issue is by Adve *et al.* [1], where systems based on Lazy Release Consistency (LRC) and EC (with explicit lock-data bindings) are compared. However, their paper focuses on a comparison of consistency models and on their possible implementations. Our work takes a totally different approach and compares various programming models implemented for systems that are all based on the same consistency model.[1]

Based on our study of software DSMs based on EC and LAP, we conclude that increasing the burden on the programmer is not necessarily the best option for software DSMs; only the most complex model we study achieves performance that justifies its programming complexity. Further work is required to determine exactly what the ideal programming model is for each type of DSM system.

The remainder of this paper is organized as follows. The next section describes our novel software DSMs concentrating on the details of their programming models. Section 3 presents our methodology and application workload. In section 4 we present the results of our most important experiments. We relate our work to previous research in section 5. Finally, in section 6, we present our conclusions and proposals for future work.

2 The AEC* Family of DSM Systems

In this section we describe our family of novel software DSMs: AEC, AEC-light, and AEC-bind. Our software DSMs are identical (even in terms of their actual codes), except for the optimizations allowed by their particular programming models. Due to space limitations, we concentrate our descriptions on the programming model imposed by the different systems; the actual coherence actions taken by each system are only overviewed.

---

[1] We claim that all our systems are based on the EC model, even though some researchers consider systems that transparently associate locks and data to be based on Scope Consistency (ScC) [7]. We belong to the group of researchers that prefer the more abstract definition of EC, under which the specific way the lock-data association is accomplished is an implementation issue that is independent of the consistency model. Thus, we regard ScC as an implementation of EC, rather than a new consistency model.

2.1 The AEC System

An initial version of AEC was proposed and evaluated in simulation in [14]. The current version of the system has been optimized in several ways as a result of our greater experience with the system and the specific characteristics of our target computing platforms.

2.1.1 Programming Model

Just like under other systems based on relaxed consistency models (e.g. Munin [3] and TreadMarks [9]), applications under the AEC programming model must be synchronized with system-supplied primitives such as lock/unlock and barrier. However, not all programs that execute correctly under other relaxed consistency models are guaranteed to execute correctly under EC, the consistency model of all systems in the AEC* family. To run correctly under EC the application must satisfy the following conditions [7]: (a) lock-protected modifications to shared data are not expected to be visible at processor p before at least one of the locks that protect the data is acquired by p; and (b) shared data modifications not protected by locks are not expected to be visible before the next barrier. Although program modifications are sometimes necessary to ensure correctness, these modifications are as simple as extending critical sections in the vast majority of cases.

Just like in other systems based on EC (e.g. Midway [2]), in AEC a processor entering a critical section only receives information about the data associated with the section. This association between lock variables and the data they protect is done transparently to the programmer by AEC however, like in the Scope Consistency (ScC) [7] and Brazos [15] systems. Thus, we can say that AEC imposes the simplest possible programming model for EC.

A very simple (and inefficient) program written under the AEC programming model can be found in figure 1. The variable declarations and the initialization code are not included for simplicity.

```
main()
{
    Aec_barrier(b); /* Init phase */
    if (Aec_proc_id == 0)
        for (i = 0; i < max; i++)
            shared_array[i] = 0;
    Aec_barrier(b); /* Computation phase */
    Aec_lock(s);
    for (i = 0; i < max; i++)
        shared_array[i] += Aec_proc_id;
    Aec_unlock(s);
    Aec_barrier(b); /* Output phase */
    for (i = 0; i < max; i++)
        printf(" %d", shared_array[i]);
}
```

Figure 1: Simple Example of the AEC Programming Model.

2.1.2 Overview of the Protocol

AEC is a page-based software DSM system that allows multiple concurrent writers per page to alleviate false sharing problems and utilizes the twinning and diffing mechanism to detect the actual modifications made by a processor to a page. Each lock has a different manager, which is responsible for keeping track of the lock acquisition order information for the lock.

The basic idea behind the AEC system is to give a different treatment to shared data modified inside and outside critical sections. Shared data modified inside critical sections can take advantage of the LAP technique and are kept coherent via a (highly selective) update protocol. At each lock release point, the lock holder generates the diffs isolating the modifications made inside the critical section and sends them to the processor that was predicted as the next acquirer of the lock. The generation of these diffs is done in a way that the releasing processor can merge the new modifications with older ones received from previous holders of the same lock. When the lock releaser makes a correct prediction, the protocol overlaps the communication and coherence overheads of the releaser with useful computation on the acquirer. In case of an incorrect prediction, the overlapped updates are wasted and the acquirer has to invalidate all pages ever modified inside the critical section protected by the lock. On the first access fault inside the critical section, the processor then requests all the diffs from the last holder of the lock.

Shared data modified outside of critical sections cannot use the LAP technique, so they are kept coherent via an invalidate protocol. More specifically, diffs of barrier-protected data are generated eagerly, at the time of a lock acquire or a barrier arrival, and propagated to other processors only on page faults. The idea here is to have processors exchange notices of their page modifications (aka write-notices) and information about the locks they held during each barrier operation. Since shared data protected by locks and barriers are treated differently, there are two types of write-notices: write-notices-in (for modifications made inside critical sections) and write-notices-out (for modifications made outside critical sections). On a page fault, a processor collects the diffs corresponding to write-notices-out from all processors that have written to the page and collects diffs corresponding to write-notices-in only from the last holder of the lock.

2.2 The AEC-light System

The design and code of the AEC-light system are based on those of the AEC system. In fact, AEC-light is almost a simplified version of AEC. However, the two systems differ in terms of the programming models they impose as explained in the following subsection.

2.2.1 Programming Model

The programming model of the AEC-light system shares some of the characteristics of the AEC model: applications must also be synchronized with system-supplied primitives and the association between lock variables and shared data is also done transparently by the system. However, under the AEC-light programming model, *all* shared data accesses must be performed in sections of code that are delimited by lock/unlock primitives; barriers are only used for synchronization, they do not involve coherence actions. In addition, the programmer must make sure that each shared data structure is always accessed within sections delimited by the same lock.

Applications can be written to conform to the AEC-light programming model simply using mutual exclusion lock and unlock primitives. However, this would cause tremendous performance

degradation, since mutual exclusion would be enforced even when no processor could possibly write the data within the critical sections. To avoid this type of degradation, AEC-light defines two additional pairs of lock-style primitives: *lock-reader/unlock-reader* and *lock-alone/unlock-alone*. The lock-reader/unlock-reader primitives can be used to delimit sections of code within which processors will only read the shared data. The lock-alone/unlock-alone primitives can be used to delimit sections of code within which a single processor accesses the shared data and this access may involve writing the data. Lock-reader and lock-alone primitives do not enforce mutual exclusion. When there is a possibility by processors may access the data concurrently for reading and writing, the standard mutual exclusion lock/unlock primitives must be utilized. From now on we will refer to the set of lock-style primitives introduced with AEC-light as lock* primitives.

The same program of the previous subsection now written under the AEC-light programming model can be found in figure 2. Note that the code of the first and third phases of execution now include lock* operations.

```
main()
{
    Aec_barrier(b); /* Init phase */
    if (Aec_proc_id == 0) {
        Aec_lock_alone(s);        /* AEC-light */
        for (i = 0; i < max; i++)
            shared_array[i] = 0;
        Aec_unlock_alone(s);   /* AEC-light */
    }
    Aec_barrier(b); /* Computation phase */
    Aec_lock(s);
    for (i = 0; i < max; i++)
        shared_array[i] += Aec_proc_id;
    Aec_unlock(s);
    Aec_barrier(b); /* Output phase */
    Aec_lock_reader(s);           /* AEC-light */
    for (i = 0; i < max; i++)
        printf(" %d", shared_array[i]);
    Aec_unlock_reader(s);         /* AEC-light */
}
```

Figure 2: Example of Figure 1 Under AEC-light.

Even though the AEC-light programming model may at first seem unreasonably expensive to implement, recall that its use of additional lock-style primitives allows AEC-light to exploit LAP more extensively than AEC. In addition, as explained in the next subsection and confirmed in section 4, the AEC-light programming model allows the system to combine messages more frequently than AEC.

2.2.2 Overview of the Protocol

Just like AEC, AEC-light is page-based and allows for multiple concurrent writers per page, using the twinning and diffing mechanism to detect the modifications made by each processor. AEC-light uses the same implementation as AEC for lock/unlock primitives. In addition, given the more extensive use of lock* primitives imposed by the AEC-light programming model, LAP can be used even more aggressively than in AEC. In fact, given that multiple processors may hold lock-readers at the same time, the operation of the LAP technique for the data protected by these locks resembles that of producer-consumer update strategies found in systems such as ADSM [11]. Lock-alone/unlock-alone primitives isolate the modifications made inside the sections they define from other modifications, just like lock/unlock primitives.

Despite the similarities between the systems, the coherence protocol of AEC-light is much simpler than that of AEC, as a result of the more elaborate programming model the former system imposes. This simplicity comes from the fact that data requests in AEC-light only take place during lock-reader or lock-alone operations and on access faults within sections of code delimited by lock/unlock primitives. On a lock-reader or lock-alone operation, all the shared data associated with the lock variable are fetched from the previous lock holder, if LAP incorrectly predicted the current lock holder. This combined transfer of multiple diffs is in sharp contrast with faults that must be taken on the first access to each invalid page protected by a barrier in AEC, where the faulting processor may have to communicate with several processors in order to service the fault. In effect, AEC-light trades-off some protocol overhead (involved in lock-reader/unlock-reader and lock-alone/unlock-alone primitives) for lower data access overheads than in AEC.

In terms of the implementation, AEC-light is a much simpler version of the AEC code. The greater simplicity of the AEC-light system allowed us to simplify the AEC code that implements barrier and to eliminate all the AEC code related to access faults that occur outside of critical sections. In addition, write-notices-out were eliminated. Obviously, the code implementing the lock-reader/unlock-reader and lock-alone/unlock-alone sets of primitives was included in the AEC-light implementation. A comparison of the number of lines of code dedicated to access faults, locks, and barriers (the three most important modules of any software DSM system) provides a rough illustration of how much simpler than AEC AEC-light is. AEC-light involves 51 and 38% fewer lines of code than AEC for the implementation of faults and barriers, respectively, and has 15% more lines of code than AEC for the implementation of locks. Taking all three modules into account, AEC-light reduces the code by 18%. Overall, AEC-light has 13% fewer lines of code than AEC.

2.3 The AEC-bind System

The design and code of the AEC-bind system are based on those of the AEC-light system. However, the two systems differ in terms of the programming models they impose as explained in the following subsection.

2.3.1 Programming Model

Under the programming model of the AEC-bind system, applications must be synchronized with system-supplied primitives and all shared data accesses must be performed within lock*-delimited sections of code, just like under the AEC-light programming model. However, the association between lock variables and shared data must be explicitly provided by the programmer, using a bind primitive. This primitive effectively defines the regions of the address space that should be associated with each lock variable.

The same program of the previous subsections now written under the AEC-bind programming model can be found in figure 3. Note that the only difference between this code and that of figure 2 is the Aec_bind call before the first barrier.

```
main()
{
    Aec_bind(s, shared_array,
        max*sizeof(int));       /* AEC_bind */
    Aec_barrier(b); /* Init phase */
    if (Aec_proc_id == 0) {
        Aec_lock_alone(s);
        for (i = 0; i < max; i++)
            shared_array[i] = 0;
        Aec_unlock_alone(s);
    }
    Aec_barrier(b); /* Computation phase */
    Aec_lock(s);
    for (i = 0; i < max; i++)
        shared_array[i] += Aec_proc_id;
    Aec_unlock(s);
    Aec_barrier(b); /* Output phase */
    Aec_lock_reader(s);
    for (i = 0; i < max; i++)
        printf(" %d", shared_array[i]);
    Aec_unlock_reader(s);
}
```

Figure 3: Example of Figure 1 Under AEC-bind.

2.3.2 Overview of the Protocol

Given the programming model imposed by AEC-bind, it is now much more natural to use the regions [12, 8] defined by the programmer as the coherence units, instead of the page. In addition, regions obviate the need for supporting multiple concurrent writers, as false sharing disappears. Nevertheless, the LAP technique can still be useful, but the regions themselves replace the diffs as the structures transferred between consecutive holders of locks.

Despite the similarities between the AEC-bind and AEC-light systems, the coherence protocol of the former system is much simpler than that of the latter, as a result of its more elaborate programming model. This simplicity comes from two characteristics of AEC-bind: (a) the system does not involve twin creation and diff generation and application operations; and (b) since all access faults are eliminated, data requests only take place during lock* operations for which LAP did not correctly predict the current lock holder.

AEC-bind does not even try to determine the exact modifications made to each region, assuming that a certain region has been written simply by the use of lock or lock-alone primitives on the synchronization variable associated with the region. Even though AEC-bind is not a multiple-writer protocol, it is important to justify transferring whole regions, instead of detecting the exact modifications made to regions and only transferring the modifications. We believe that this characteristic of AEC-bind should rarely cause performance problems for two reasons: (a) When applications define critical sections to protect large data structures, these structures are usually completely re-written every time they are touched because, otherwise, the application would be excessively serialized. When the data structures are completely re-written, they must be sent as

Appl	Problem Size	Synchro
IS	$N = 2^{23}, B_{max} = 2^{15}, 10$ iters	locks + barriers
MigFreq	128×128	locks + barriers
MigDepth	128×128	locks + barriers
SOR	2000×1000, 100 iters	barriers
FFT	$64 \times 64 \times 16$, 100 iters	barriers
Water	512 mol, 10 iters	locks + barriers

Table 1: Application Characteristics.

a whole anyway; and (b) When applications define critical sections to protect small data structures, the inclusion of a few extra bytes in each message generates negligible overhead.

Again, a comparison of the number of lines of code dedicated to access faults, locks, and barriers provides a rough illustration of how much simpler than AEC-light AEC-bind is. AEC-bind completely eliminates the code for access faults, and involves 48 and 35% fewer lines of code than AEC-light for the implementation of locks and barriers, respectively. Taking all three modules into account, AEC-bind shortens the code by 51%. Overall, AEC-bind involves 34 and 42% fewer lines of code than AEC-light and AEC, respectively.

3 Methodology and Workload

Our experimental environment consists of a completely dedicated IBM SP2 with eight 66MHz Power2 processors. The nodes are connected by a 40 MBytes/s Omega switch. All our software DSMs communicate using the UDP protocol.

Our applications follow the SPMD model. We report results for six parallel scientific applications. Four of them are from the TreadMarks distribution: 3D-FFT, Integer Sort (IS), SOR, and Water. The other two applications are seismic migration programs [6], MigFreq and MigDepth, from the Brazilian oil company, Petrobras. In table 1 we show the applications' problem sizes and synchronization styles.

IS, originally defined in the NAS suite, ranks an array of N integer keys in the range [0, Bmax]. SOR performs successive over-relaxation on a grid of doubles for several iterations. FFT, also originally defined in the NAS suite [4], solves a partial differential equation using forward and inverse FFT's. Water, originally from the SPLASH suite [16], simulates the dynamics of water molecules. MigFreq performs 2D post-stack seismic migration using the $\omega - x$ algorithm. The program generates a 2D seismic section from a 2D array of seismic input data. Parallelization is done by assigning a block of frequencies to each processor. Parallel execution lasts for a single phase of execution, where each processor migrates a block of frequencies without the need for communication with other processors. MigDepth solves the same problem as MigFreq, but uses depth partitioning rather than frequency partitioning to create parallel work. In this approach, each processor extrapolates the seismic section at a particular set of depths. Processor communication takes place because migrating for a certain depth depends on the previous depth. The computation flows like a pipeline where all shared data accesses are executed within critical sections. MigDepth achieves a higher degree of parallelism at the expense of much higher communication than in MigFreq.

None of the applications in our workload required modifica-

tions to run correctly under the AEC programming model. For the AEC-light and AEC-bind programming models however, the applications were modified to include lock/unlock-reader, lock/unlock-alone, and bind operations as appropriate. These modifications are listed below.

IS. To satisfy the restrictions imposed by the AEC-light model, we inserted lock-alone/unlock-alone operations in the shared array initialization phase and lock-reader/unlock-reader operations in the beginning of the third phase. To comply with the AEC-bind programming model, we included the explicit binding between the shared array and the only synchronization variable in IS.

MigFreq. MigFreq required minor modifications to run correctly under the AEC-light model. We inserted lock-alone/unlock-alone operations in its initialization phase and included lock/unlock operations to protect the computations of seismic sections. In this application there is one lock variable per processor, so to comply with the AEC-bind model, we associated each lock with the seismic section the corresponding processor is responsible for.

MigDepth. To satisfy the restrictions imposed by the AEC-light model, only one modification to the MigDepth application was required: the inclusion of a single pair of lock-alone/unlock-alone operations in the initialization phase. To comply with the AEC-bind model, each lock variable was explicitly bound to a block of frequencies.

SOR. To satisfy the AEC-light restrictions, we created a different lock synchronization variable for each boundary row of the two matrices involved in the computation. We inserted lock-reader/unlock-reader operations when a matrix is being read, and lock-alone/unlock-alone operations when a matrix is being written. The explicit association that is necessary under the AEC-bind model is trivial: each boundary row of the matrices is associated with one of the synchronization variables.

FFT. To comply with the AEC-light model, we introduced an array of locks $L : nprocs \times nprocs$, where each lock L_{ij} protects the S_k subarray (where $k = i * nprocs + j$) of the 3D array used as input. In the first phase of this application, the FFTs are performed within lock-alone/unlock-alone pairs of operations. Each processor acquires one row of the L array. In the following phase, the array transpose is also executed within lock-alone/unlock-alone pairs of operations, but the locks are acquired in a different order. Each processor acquires a column of the L lock array, as it is going to work with distinct array slices. To obey the AEC-bind model, we included the explicit association between each lock variable and its corresponding subarray. The subarrays, however, are not allocated contiguously in memory. Thus, several binding operations are necessary for each lock variable.

Water. The AEC-light programming model required lock-alone/unlock-alone operations to be inserted in the initialization phase of this application. In the intra-molecule phase, lock-alone/unlock-alone operations were included when updating each molecule. In the inter-molecule phase, we inserted lock-reader/unlock-reader operations to read the movement values of molecules that are updated by other processors. In the fourth phase of Water, lock-alone/unlock-alone operations were included to compute correct molecule attributes and boundary conditions. To satisfy the AEC-bind model, we inserted the explicit association between each water molecule and its lock variable.

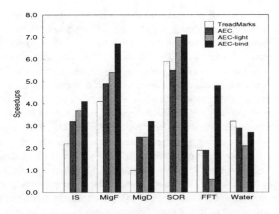

Figure 4: Application Speedups.

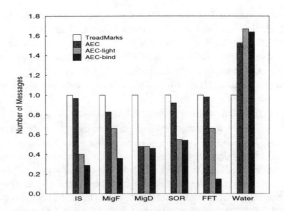

Figure 5: Number of Messages Transferred.

4 Experimental Results

We start this section by comparing the performance of our systems against that of TreadMarks, which is an efficient and well-known software DSM system. This comparison is simply intended to put our results in perspective, since we are more interested in comparing the different programming models of our EC-based software DSMs. Thus, we follow our initial results with a detailed analysis of the performance of our applications under the AEC* family of systems.

4.1 Speedup Performance

Figure 4 shows the speedup of our applications running on our 8-node SP2 under TreadMarks, AEC, AEC-light, and AEC-bind. The speedups are relative to the uniprocessor execution time of the parallel applications. The figure shows that the speedup achieved by our software DSMs exceeds that of TreadMarks in the majority of cases, demonstrating that our systems are indeed very efficient.

The applications in our suite exhibit different overall behaviors. For IS and MigFreq, the speedups achieved by our systems increase with an increase in programming model complexity. For IS, the speedup gains of our systems with respect to TreadMarks are 38, 60, and 82% for AEC, AEC-light, and AEC-bind, respectively. These same gains for MigFreq are 18, 32, and 62%. For MigDepth, AEC-light performs only as well as AEC; both systems achieve a speedup that is 143% higher than that of TreadMarks for this application. AEC-bind, in contrast, produces even better performance, achieving a speedup that is 200% higher than that of TreadMarks for MigDepth. For SOR, AEC exhibits slightly lower speedup than TreadMarks, while both AEC-light and AEC-bind achieve speedups that are about 20% higher than that of TreadMarks.

FFT and Water are interesting applications. For FFT, TreadMarks and AEC exhibit the same speedup, but the results for AEC-light and AEC-bind are widely different. AEC-light exhibits tremendous performance degradation, leading to a speedup that is lower than 1 on 8 processors. In sharp contrast with this result, AEC-bind achieves speedup that is 158% higher than that of TreadMarks. Water is an example application for which none of our systems performs better than TreadMarks; the speedups of AEC, AEC-light, and AEC-bind are 12, 31, and 15% lower, respectively. As we will show later, this Water result is a consequence of a specific characteristic of this ap-

plication. A slightly improved version of Water achieves about the same speedup (4.2) under TreadMarks, AEC, and AEC-bind, and slightly lower speedup (3.8) under AEC-light.

Overall, a comparison between TreadMarks and AEC results shows that our system performs better for 3 applications (IS, MigFreq, and MigDepth), while it performs as well or slightly worse than TreadMarks for the other 3 applications. These performance differences are a consequence of the characteristics of these two systems, since TreadMarks and AEC lead to the same programming model for the applications in our suite. Nevertheless, a comparison between the systems in the AEC* family does illustrate the performance effect of different programming models. Comparing AEC and AEC-light results, we find that the more elaborate programming model of AEC-light only leads to significantly higher speedup for one application (SOR), while for two others (FFT and Water) this model degrades performance substantially.

The advantages of increasing programming model complexity only become obvious when comparing AEC-light and AEC-bind results. AEC-bind achieves better performance than AEC-light for all applications and performance differences are often quite significant. Comparing our extremes in terms of programming model complexity, AEC and AEC-bind, we find that our most complex model indeed provides performance gains in all cases, except for the Water application, for which the two systems perform comparably.

4.2 Communication Traffic

Figure 5 presents the number of messages transferred by each of our applications under the systems we study. All bars are normalized to the TreadMarks results.

This figure shows that our systems entail fewer messages than TreadMarks for all applications except Water, which is a very good result given that TreadMarks is already optimized for avoiding message transfers whenever possible. The number of bytes transferred (not shown here due to space limitations) roughly follows the number of messages results except for FFT under AEC-light. The reason for these results is that our systems save a large number of request messages by using the LAP technique and by combining data transfers. More specifically, AEC reduces the communication with respect to TreadMarks because it avoids access faults inside critical sections when LAP is successful and transfers all diffs associated with a lock in response to a single request when LAP is not successful. AEC-light extends the use of lock-style primitives to all shared data accesses and, thus, can use LAP and message combining to save even further on communication. Similarly, AEC-bind saves communication by transferring programmer-defined regions during lock operations.

FFT and Water behave differently than other applications. For FFT, AEC-light transfers about 7 times more bytes than the other systems, as a result of a poor association between lock variables and shared data. For Water, our systems transfer more messages and bytes than TreadMarks. This results from a particular aspect of Water: requesting data on a lock* section basis leads to a larger number of request messages than under TreadMarks. In the following section, we detail the behavior of each of our applications and systems, including the problems with FFT and Water.

These communication results suggest that in most cases our systems should compare even more favorably against TreadMarks on more modern machines, where the gap between computation and communication speeds is somewhat wider than in our IBM SP2 platform. These results also indicate that the speedup of our systems should compare favorably against those of other software DSMs. We are currently running experiments on larger configurations of our IBM SP2 to confirm this intuition.

4.3   Detailed Analysis

Figures 6 and 7 present the execution time of each of our applications running under the AEC, AEC-light, and AEC-bind systems. The execution times are normalized to the AEC results. From bottom to top, each bar is broken down into: useful computation time (busy), which includes cache and TLB miss overheads; lock synchronization time (lock), which includes the time spent on all lock/unlock-style primitives; barrier synchronization time (barrier); data access fault overhead (data); and the IPC overhead (ipc), which accounts for the time spent servicing requests coming from remote processors. Note that data overheads are not present in AEC-bind numbers because this system does not involve access faults.

Protecting all shared data accesses with lock* operations under AEC-light reduces the **IS** execution time by 14% with respect to AEC. These reductions are mainly a result of reduced data access overheads during the second and third phases of execution. In the second phase, processors access the whole shared data structure inside of mutual exclusion sections. Under AEC, each processor takes an access fault inside of its critical section and needs to communicates with the previous lock holder (when LAP makes a wrong prediction) and with processor 0, which initialized the data structure during the first phase. Under AEC-light, a processor also takes an access fault inside the critical section when LAP makes a wrong prediction, but only has to communicate with the previous lock holder to receive the combined modifications made by that processor and by processor 0. (Recall that under AEC-light and AEC-bind processor 0 initializes the shared data within a lock-alone/unlock-alone section.) This data access overhead reduction effectively reduces the length of the critical sections and has a direct impact on the overhead of the following barrier, since the lock serialization is reduced.

In the third phase of the execution of IS, processors access the whole shared data structure outside of critical sections under the AEC programming model. Thus, a processor takes several access faults to fetch the data structure; one for every invalid page it touches. Under the AEC-light model, these accesses are performed within lock-reader/unlock-reader sections and, thus, the access faults are replaced by a single request to transfer of all diffs associated with the lock variable. As a result, data access overheads are not completely eliminated under AEC-light; part of this overhead is indeed eliminated but another part appears as lock overhead.

Explicitly binding locks and data (and consequently using regions as coherence units) under AEC-bind improved performance with respect to AEC-light by 12% for IS. These reductions result mainly from the total elimination of diff-related overheads (twin creation, diff generation and application), which reflects itself directly on the overhead of lock-style synchronizations.

The AEC-light programming model improves performance for **MigFreq** by 11% with respect to AEC. Again, these reductions are mainly a result of reduced data access overheads. During the parallel phase of MigFreq, a processor accesses the main shared data structure inside and outside of mutual exclusion sections under the AEC programming model. Under the AEC-light model, the latter type of accesses is performed within lock-reader/unlock-reader sections, while the data initialization is performed by processor 0 within a lock-alone/unlock-alone section. In the same way as for IS, AEC-light improves data access overheads by combining data transfers and by restricting requests for data to a single processor (the previous lock holder).

The AEC-bind programming model improved performance with respect to AEC-light by 18% for MigFreq. Again, these reductions come from the elimination of diff-related overheads and the consequent improvement of the lock synchronization, which in turn improves the barrier overhead in this application.

As expected, **MigDepth** performs the same under AEC and AEC-light, since this application protects all its shared data accesses with mutual exclusion locks during the parallel part of the execution and these locks are treated in the same way by both systems. On the other hand, explicitly binding data to locks allows AEC-bind an execution time reduction of 19% with respect to AEC and AEC-light. Again, the elimination of diff-related overheads is the main reason for the improved performance of AEC-bind.

Accessing all shared data within lock*-delimited sections under the AEC-light model improves the performance of **SOR** by 22% with respect to AEC. This performance gain comes from reductions in data access and barrier synchronization overheads. Data access overheads are reduced mainly because LAP is very successful for this application and it is used more aggressively under AEC-light than AEC. Barrier overheads are reduced because of better load balancing under AEC-light. The explicit lock-data association required by the AEC-bind model does not lead to better performance than already achieved by AEC-light. The reason for this is two fold: (a) AEC-light dynamically associates exactly the right data (the boundaries of each matrix) to their corresponding locks; and (b) the diff-related overhead is small compared to the total SOR execution time.

FFT exhibits terrible performance under AEC-light. This results from a mismatch between the way lock-readers and lock-alones are acquired and the dynamic association between locks and data. More specifically, the problem here is that these locks are acquired by

234

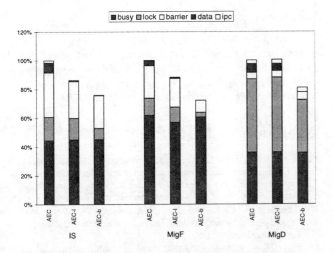

Figure 6: Execution Time of AEC, AEC-light, and AEC-bind.

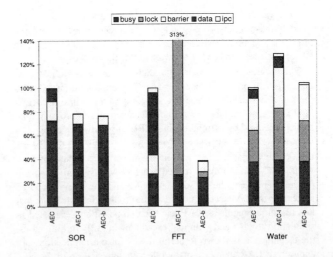

Figure 7: Execution Time of AEC, AEC-light, and AEC-bind.

processors in a nested manner in FFT, forcing the system to assign the data accessed inside the nest to all locks currently held by a processor. As a result, locks carry much more data than actually needed and generate an immense increase in data traffic, degrading all aspects of the execution of FFT under AEC-light.

The explicit association between locks and data under AEC-bind prevents this type of problem from ever happening to this system. The AEC-bind execution time for FFT is 61% lower than that of AEC. This reduction comes from a lock-related overhead that is 91% lower than the data access overhead of AEC. This significant performance improvement is a result of associating non-contiguous regions (subarrays of the matrix) to locks. In AEC, fetching a whole subcube takes several pages faults.

AEC-light also exhibits worse performance than AEC for **Water**; the performance difference between the systems is 29% for this application. This performance degradation is due to the fact that the time spent fetching data during lock-reader and lock-alone operations in AEC-light is twice the data access overhead for faults occurring outside of critical sections in AEC. The problem here is that, due to the specific pattern of accesses to Water molecules, a single page fault in AEC involves fetching the modifications made to all 12 molecules that are allocated on the page. On the other hand, AEC-light executes several lock* operations (one per molecule) to fetch the same amount of data, even if all these requests for data are to be sent to the same processor. This granularity problem is not solved by explicitly assigning data to locks under the AEC-bind system, but the elimination of diff-related overheads does improve performance due to the large number of lock* operations involved in this application. Overall, AEC-bind performs 19% better than AEC-light and only slightly worse than AEC.

The granularity of lock* operations in Water need not be fine, however. In fact, if Water had been written with AEC-light or AEC-bind in mind, the granularity of these operations would naturally be coarser. To evaluate the effect of this granularity, we implemented a coarser version of Water, where each lock delimits the access to 8 molecules. Our experiments show that this version of Water performs better than the original application under all systems. In addition, AEC-light and AEC-bind perform significantly better with

respect to AEC for the new Water code. More specifically, AEC-light performs only 8% worse than AEC, while AEC-bind executes 3% faster than AEC and 10% faster than AEC-light.

Taking all applications into account, our execution time results show that AEC-light does not achieve better performance than AEC for three applications, while gains are pretty small for the other three applications. In addition, our results show that AEC-bind improves performance by 25% and 27% on average compared to AEC and AEC-light, respectively.

5 Related Work

This paper presents the first evaluation of the performance and system complexity implications of different variations of the shared-memory programming model. However, a few papers and systems addressed related issues.

The work by Adve *et al.* [1] focuses on a comparison of consistency models (LRC and EC with explicit lock-data bindings) and on their possible implementations. Their performance results show that neither LRC nor EC consistently outperform the other. Even though a comparison between LRC and EC is not the main point of our paper, we did compare the performance of an EC-based system with explicit lock-data bindings (AEC-bind) against that of an LRC-based system (TreadMarks) to put our results in perspective. In this comparison we confirmed the observations made by Adve *et al.* qualitatively. However, in terms of actual performance, AEC-bind compared more favorably against TreadMarks than any EC-based system studied in [1]. Essentially, there are four reasons for this: (1) AEC-bind exploits the LAP technique; (2) AEC-bind require neither write trapping nor write collection; (3) our lock-alone/unlock-alone primitives allow us to avoid synchronization; and (4) none of the applications in our study requires any more synchronization (such as extended critical sections) under EC than under the LRC model.

The paper on application-specific shared-memory protocols [5] is also related to our research in the sense that the performance of applications under a plain shared-memory programming model was compared against that of applications enhanced with programmer directives specifying the best protocol to use at each point. However, we believe that it is unlikely that most programmers will be able to apply these sophisticated and low-level directives effectively; the programming models we consider are much simpler and concentrate all sophistication inside the software DSMs themselves.

The programming models required by our systems are instances of previously proposed models. The AEC programming model is the same as that of the ScC and Brazos systems, while the AEC-light and AEC-bind models include characteristics of programming models required by systems such as CRL and Midway.

In terms of overall protocol structure, AEC and AEC-light are most closely related to Brazos and the all software version of ScC, while AEC-bind is directly related to the Midway system. The main difference between the our software DSMs and previously proposed systems is the LAP technique and all the protocol infrastructure that this technique requires. LAP has been proposed and evaluated in simulation in [14] and with real executions in [13]. In both cases, the technique was shown to perform well for our applications. In addition to LAP, there are many other implementation differences between previous systems and ours. In contrast with Brazos, our systems do not support multithreading and avoid relying on multi-cast communication. In contrast with ScC, our systems transfer data directly between lock holders, instead of staging the data through home nodes. In contrast with Midway, AEC-bind does not implement any write trapping or collection, transferring whole regions.

6   Conclusions

In this paper we studied the impact of different variations of the shared-memory programming model on the performance and complexity of software distributed shared-memory systems. To accomplish this we utilized a family of systems that exploit Entry Consistency and the Lock Acquirer Prediction technique and, thus, can exploit lock-style primitives to improve performance. Starting from a system that imposes a plain shared-memory programming model for Entry Consistency, we showed that delimiting all shared data accesses with lock-style primitives and explicitly binding locks to the data they protect reduce the complexity of system implementations.

We also showed that the programming model has direct effect on the performance of our systems, but this effect is somewhat different than one would expect. Having the programmer delimit all shared data accesses with lock-style primitives does not always lead to performance improvements, as exemplified by the FFT and Water applications, even though the Lock Acquirer Prediction technique can be used aggressively and most data transfers can be combined under this programming model. Nevertheless, explicitly binding locks to the data they protect does improve performance consistently.

Thus, it seems that the best choice of programming model depends on how quickly the underlying system must be designed and implemented and on how experienced application programmers are. Systems that are harder to code applications for are easier to design and implement and, depending on the specific characteristics of the programming model, achieve better overall performance. The problem is defining exactly what these specific characteristics are. This paper quantified the performance and complexity impact of three programming models for a particular class of systems. Further work is required to determine exactly what the ideal programming model is for each type of shared-memory system.

Acknowledgements

We would like to thank Leonidas Kontothanassis and Liviu Iftode for comments that helped improve this paper significantly. We would also like to thank Luis R. Monnerat and Petrobras for the seismic migration applications we use in this study. We also acknowledge the support of Sergio Guedes from NCE/UFRJ.

References

[1] S. Adve, A. Cox, S. Dwarkadas, R. Rajamony, and W. Zwaenepoel. A Comparison of Entry Consistency and Lazy Release Consistency Implementations. In *Proceedings of the 2nd IEEE Symposium on High-Performance Computer Architecture*, pages 26–37, February 1996.

[2] B.N. Bershad, M.J. Zekauskas, and W.A. Sawdon. The Midway Distributed Shared Memory System. In *Proceedings of the '93 CompCon Conference*, February 1993.

[3] J.B. Carter, J.K. Bennett, and W. Zwaenepoel. Implementation and Performance of Munin. In *Proceedings of the 13th ACM Symposium on Operating Systems Principles*, pages 152–164, October 1991.

[4] D. Bailey et al. The NAS Parallel Benchmarks. Technical Report RNR-94-007, NASA Ames Research Center, March 1994.

[5] B. Falsafi *et al.* Application-Specific Protocols for User-Level Shared Memory. In *Proceedings of Supercomputing '94*, November 1994.

[6] P. Figueiredo. Exploitation of Parallelism in Seismic Migration. Master's thesis, University of Illinois at Urbana-Champaign, April 1995.

[7] L. Iftode, J.P. Singh, and K. Li. Scope Consistency: A Bridge Between Release Consistency and Entry Consistency. *Theory of Computing Systems*, 31:451–473, 1998.

[8] K. L. Johnson, M. F. Kaashoek, and D. A. Wallach. CRL: High-Performance All-Software Distributed Shared Memory. In *Proceedings of the 15th ACM Symposium on Operating Systems Principles*, pages 213–228, December 1995.

[9] P. Keleher, S. Dwarkadas, A.L. Cox, and W. Zwaenepoel. TreadMarks: Distributed Shared Memory on Standard Workstations and Operating Systems. In *Proceedings of the 1994 Winter Usenix Conference*, pages 115–131, January 1994.

[10] H. Lu, S. Dwarkadas, A. L. Cox, and W. Zwaenepoel. Message-Passing vs. Distributed Shared Memory on Networks of Workstations. In *Proceedings of Supercomputing'95*, December 1995.

[11] L. R. Monnerat and R. Bianchini. Efficiently Adapting to Sharing Patterns in Software DSMs. In *Proceedings of the 4th IEEE Symposium on High-Performance Computer Architecture*, pages 289–299, February 1998.

[12] H. S. Sandhu, B. Gamsa, and S. Zhou. The Shared Region Approach to Software Cache Coherence on Multiprocessors. In *Proceedings of the 4th Symposium on Principles and Practice of Parallel Programming*, pages 229–238, July 1993.

[13] C. B. Seidel. *The Lock Acquirer Prediction Technique and its Use in Distributed Shared-Memory Systems*. PhD thesis, COPPE Systems Engineering, Federal University of Rio de Janeiro, September 1998. In Portuguese.

[14] C. B. Seidel, R. Bianchini, and C. L. Amorim. The Affinity Entry Consistency Protocol. In *Proceedings of the 1997 International Conference on Parallel Processing*, pages 65–78, August 1997.

[15] W. E. Speight and J. K. Bennett. Brazos: A Third Generation DSM System. In *Proceedings of the 1997 USENIX Windows/NT Workshop*, pages 95–106, August 1997.

[16] S. Woo, M. Ohara, E. Torrie, J. Singh, and A. Gupta. The SPLASH2 Programs: Characterization and Methodological Considerations. In *Proceedings of the 22nd Annual International Symposium on Computer Architecture*, May 1995.

Session B4

Commercial Workload

Chair: Jose Angel Gregorio
University of Cantabria, Spain

Optimization of Instruction Fetch for Decision Support Workloads[*]

Alex Ramirez, Josep Ll. Larriba-Pey,
Carlos Navarro, Xavi Serrano, Mateo Valero
Universitat Politecnica de Catalunya
Jordi Girona 1–3, D6
08034 Barcelona (Spain)
{aramirez,larri,cnavarro,mateo}@ac.upc.es

Josep Torrellas
3314 Digital Computer Laboratory
1304 West Springfield Avenue
Urbana, IL 61801 (USA)
torrella@cs.uiuc.edu

Abstract

Instruction fetch bandwidth is feared to be a major limiting factor to the performance of future wide-issue aggressive superscalars.

In this paper, we focus on Database applications running Decision Support workloads. We characterize the locality patterns of ia database kernel and find frequently executed paths. Using this information, we propose an algorithm to lay out the basic blocks for improved I-fetch.

Our results show a miss reduction of 60-98% for realistic I-cache sizes and a doubling of the number of instructions executed between taken branches. As a consequence, we increase the fetch bandwith provided by an aggressive sequential fetch unit from 5.8 for the original code to 10.6 using our proposed layout. Our software scheme combines well with hardware schemes like a Trace Cache providing up to 12.1 instruction per cycle, suggesting that commercial workloads may be amenable to the aggressive I-fetch of future superscalars.

1 Introduction

Future wide-issue superscalars are expected to demand a high instruction bandwidth to satisfy their execution requirements. This will put pressure on the fetch unit and has raised concerns that instruction fetch bandwidth may be a major limiting factor to the performance of aggressive processors. Consequently, it is crucial to develop techniques to increase the number of useful instructions per cycle provided to the processor.

The number of useful instructions per cycle provided by the fetch unit is broadly determined by three factors: the branch prediction accuracy, the cache hit rate and the number of instructions provided by the fetch unit for each access. Clearly, many things can go wrong. Branch mispredictions cause the fetch engine to provide wrong-path instructions to the processor. Instruction cache misses stall the fetch engine, interrupting the supply of instructions to the processor. Finally, the execution of non-contiguous basic blocks prevents the fetch unit from providing a full width of instructions.

Much work has been done in the past to address these problems. Branch effects have been addressed with techniques to improve the branch prediction accuracy [10] and to predict multiple branches per cycle [20, 24]. Instruction cache misses have been addressed with software and hardware techniques. Software solutions include code reordering based on procedure placement [7, 6] or basic block mapping, either procedure oriented [16] or using a global scope [8, 21]. Hardware solutions include set associative caches, hardware prefetching, victim caches and other techniques. Finally, the number of instructions provided by the fetch unit each cycle can also be improved with software or hardware techniques. Software solutions include trace scheduling [4], and superblock scheduling [9]. Hardware solutions include branch address caches [24], collapsing buffers [2] and trace caches [5, 19].

While all these techniques have vastly improved the performance of superscalar I-fetch units, they have been largely focused and evaluated on engineering workloads. Unfortunately, there is growing evidence that popular commercial workloads provide a more challenging environment to aggressive instruction fetching.

Indeed, recent studies of database workload performance on current processors have given useful insight [1, 12, 14, 15, 18, 23]. These studies show that commercial work-

[*]This reserach has been supported by CICYT grant TIC-0511-98 (all UPC authors), the Generalitat de Catalunya grants ACI 97-26 (Josep Ll. Larriba-Pey and Josep Torrellas) and 1998FI-003060-26 (Alex Ramirez), the Commission for Cultural, Educational and Scientific Exchange between the United States of America and Spain (Josep Ll. Larriba-Pey, Josep Torrellas and Mateo Valero), the Spanish Ministry of Education grant PN98 43443683-1 (Carlos Navarro), NSF grant MIP-9619351 (Josep Torrellas), and CEPBA.

loads do not behave like other scientific and engineering codes. They execute fewer loops and have many procedure calls. This leads to large instruction footprints. The analysis, however, is not detailed enough to understand how to optimize them for improved I-fetch engine performance.

The work in this paper focuses on this issue. We proceed in three steps. First, we characterize the locality patterns of database kernel code and find frequently executed paths. The database kernel used is PostgreSQL [13]. Our data shows that there is significant locality and that the execution patterns are quite deterministic.

Second, we use this information to propose an algorithm to reorder the layout of the basic blocks in the database kernel for improved I-fetch. Finally, we evaluate our scheme via simulations. Our results show a miss reduction of 60-98% for realistic instruction cache sizes and a doubling of the number of instructions executed between taken branches to over 22. As a consequence, a 16 instruction wide sequential fetch unit using a perfect branch predictor increases the fetch bandwidth from 5.6 to 10.6 instructions per cycle when using our proposed code layout.

The software scheme that we propose combines well with hardware schemes like a Trace Cache. The fetch bandwith for a 256 entry Trace Cache improves from 8.6 to 12.1 when combined with our software approach. This suggests that commercial workloads may be amenable to the aggressive instruction fetch of future superscalars.

This paper is structured as follows. In Section 2, we give a detailed account of the internals of a database management system and compare PostgreSQL to it. In Section 4, we analyze the locality and determinism of the database execution. In Section 5, we describe the basic block reordering method that we propose. In Section 6 we give details on related work. In Section 7 we evaluate the performance of our method and compare it to other hardware and software techniques. Finally, in Section 8 we conclude and present guidelines for future work.

2 Database Management Systems

Database Management Systems are organized in different software modules. Those modules correspond to different functionalities to run queries, maintain the Database tables or use statistics on the Database data among others. Our interest focuses on those modules that take charge of running relational queries which are the most time consuming part of a RDBMS.

In order to run a relational query, it is necessary to perform a number of steps as shown in Figure 1. The query is specified by the user in a declarative language that determines what the user wants to know about the Database data. Nowadays, the Structured Query Language (SQL) is the standard declarative language for relational Databases [3].

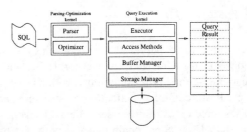

Figure 1. Steps required for the execution of an SQL query and all the RDBMS modules involved.

The SQL query is translated into an execution plan that will be processed by the Query Execution kernel. The query execution plan has the form of a tree, with nodes representing the different operations.

The task of the Parsing-optimization kernel is to check the grammatical correctness of the SQL expression and to generate the best execution plan for the given query in a specific computer and Database. While the importance of the Parsing-optimization module is paramount to generate a plan that executes fastest on a specific computer, the time employed to run it can be considered small compared to the total time spent in executing the query.

2.1 The Query Execution Kernel of a RDBMS

The Executor of a RDBMS (Figure 1) contains the routines that implement basic operations like Sequential Scan, Index Scan, Nested-Loop Join, Hash Join, Merge Join, Sort, Aggregate and Group. It also contains the routines that schedule the execution of those basic operations as described by the execution plan.

Just below the Executor, are the lower modules of the DBMS, the Access Methods, the Buffer Manager and the Storage Manager. This modular structure hides the different semantic data levels from the Executor. Now, we describe those semantic data levels and the communication data structures for the lower modules of the DBMS.

The tables of a Database are stored as files following a given logic structure. The Storage Manager is responsible for both managing those files and accessing them to provide file blocks to the Buffer Manager.

The Buffer Manager is responsible for managing the blocks stored in memory similarly to the way the OS Virtual Memory Manager does. The Buffer Manager provides memory blocks to the Access Methods Module.

The Access Methods of a RDBMS provide tuples to the Executor module. Depending on the organization of each table, the Access Methods will traverse the required index structures and plain database tables stored in the blocks managed by the Buffer Manager. Each DBMS will implement different Access Methods for its own index and database table structures.

2.2 PostgreSQL

PostgreSQL is a public domain, client/server database developed at the University of California-Berkeley, very popular among the Linux community, with a large number of users. PostgreSQL has a client/server structure and compromises three types of processes; clients, backends and a postmaster. Each client communicates with one backend that is created by the postmaster the first time the client queries the database. The postmaster is also in charge of the initialization of the database.

The structure of the server backend of PostgreSQL corresponds to that of a general DBMS that we explained before, shown in Figure 1.

The execution of a query in PostgreSQL is performed in a pipelined fashion. This means that each operation passes the result tuples to the parent operation in the execution plan as soon as they are generated, instead of processing their whole input and generating the full result set. This explains the lack of loops and the long code sequences found in the PostgreSQL and other DBMS kernels [15].

2.3 DSS Workloads and TPC-D

In this paper we use the Transaction Processing Performance Council benchmark for Decision Support Systems (TPC-D) [22] as a workload for our experiments. DSS workloads imply large data sets and complex, read-only queries that access a significant portion of this data.

TPC-D has been described in the recent literature on the topic [1, 23] and for this reason we do not give a detailed account of it. At a glance, the TPC-D benchmark defines a database consisting of 8 tables, and a set of 17 read-only queries and 2 update queries. It is worth noting that the TPC-D benchmark is just a data set and the queries on this data; it is not an executable. The tables in the database are generated randomly, and their size is determined by a Scale Factor. The benchmark specification defines the database scale factor of 1 corresponding to a 1GB database. There are no restrictions regarding the indices that can be used for the database.

3 Database Setup

We set up the Alpha version of the Postgres 6.3.2 database on Digital Unix v4.0 compiled with the $-O3$ optimization flags and the cc compiler. A TPC-D database is generated with a scale factor of 0.1 (100MB of data). With the generated data we build two separate databases, one having Btree indices and the other having Hash indices. Both databases have unique indices on all tables for the primary key attributes (those attributes that identify a tuple) and multiple

entry indices for the foreign key attributes (those attributes which reference tuples on other tables).

4 Analysis of the Instruction Reference Patterns

Next, we examine the instruction reference patterns of the database focusing on locality issues by counting the number of times each basic block is executed, and recording all basic block transitions.

We select our Training set based on the importance of the Qualify and Scan operations, and the large number of misses attributed to the Access Methods and Buffer Manager modules [17].

The Training set used to obtain the profile information consists of executing queries 3, 4, 5, 6 and 9 on the Btree indexed database only. This set also includes queries with and without an extensive use of the Aggregate, Group and Sort operations, because they need all their children's results to be executed, which stops the normal pipelined execution of queries in the PostgreSQL database, and implies the storage of large temporary results. Furthermore, these operations store and access the temporary data without going through the Access Methods, which makes them somehow unique.

4.1 Reference locality

The data in Table 1 illustrates an important characteristic of the database code. Only 12.7% of the static instructions were referenced for an execution of the Training set, which means that the database contains large sections of code which are rarely accessed.

	Total	Executed	Percent
Procedures	6.813	1.340	19.7%
Basic blocks	127.426	15.415	12.1%
Instructions	593.884	75.183	12.7%

Table 1. Total number of static program elements, and the fracion of them that are actually used.

Figure 2 plots the percentage of the dynamic basic block references captured by a given number of static basic blocks. We observe that the 1000 most popular basic blocks (0.7% of the total count) accumulate 90% of the dynamic references, and that 2500 blocks gather as much as 99%.

This large concentration of the basic block references implies a large potential for exploiting locality. To further explore temporal locality, we counted the number of instructions that were executed between two consecutive invocations of a basic block.

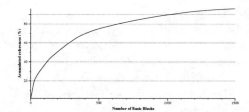

Figure 2. Percentage of total basic block references for a number of basic blocks.

If we consider the subset of the most popular basic blocks which concentrate 75% of the dynamic basic block references, we observe that they have a probability of 33% of being re-executed in less than 250 instructions, and as much as 19% of being referenced twice in less than 100 instructions.

4.2 Execution determinism

Next, we study how deterministic are the sequences of executed basic blocks.

We classify basic blocks in one of four kinds attending at how they affect the program flow. Fall-through basic blocks do not end with a branch instruction, so execution always continues on the next basic block. Branch basic blocks end with a conditional or unconditional branch. Subroutine call basic blocks end with a subroutine invocation or indirect jump, and may have many successors. Return basic blocks have many possible successors, as a subroutine may be referenced from several places.

BB Type	Static	Dynamic	Predictable
Fall-through	24.4%	22.4%	100%
Branch	42.4%	50.2%	59%
Subroutine call	8%	13.7%	100%
Subroutine return	25.2%	13.7%	100%

Table 2. Percentage of basic blocks executed by type, both static and dynamic. Percentage of the dynamic number that behaves in a fixed way.

Most basic block transitions have a very high, or very low probability of being executed. Looking at the numbers in Table 2, fall-through basic blocks, subroutine calls and returns compromise 50% of the dynamic basic blocks, and these usually have a fixed target. Also, 59% of the branch basic blocks (30% of the total basic blocks) tend to behave in a fixed way, either always taken or always not taken. Overall, 80% of the basic block transitions are predictable, which means that the executed sequences of basic blocks are fairly deterministic.

We have shown that there is a large concentration of references in a small set of very popular basic blocks and that there is substantial temporal locality to be exploited, as the most popular blocks are referenced every few instructions. Also, the execution paths are quite deterministic, allowing us to exploit spatial locality by mapping basic blocks executed sequentially in consecutive memory locations. This allows us to build basic block traces at compile time, arranging them carefully in memory to avoid conflict misses.

5 Method description

Instrumenting the database and running the Training set, we obtained a directed control flow graph with weighted edges.

To improve the fetch bandwidth, we build our basic block sequences placing in consecutive memory positions those basic blocks executed sequentially, maximizing the number of instructions executed between taken branches.

Also, to reduce the instruction cache miss rate, we will map the most frequently executed code sequences in a reserved area of the cache and other popular sequences close to other equally popular ones, reducing interference among them.

5.1 Seed selection

We first tried an automatic seed selection (*auto* selection). The list of seeds contains the entry points of all functions, in decreasing order of popularity. This selection tries to expose the maximum temporal locality, building first the sequences for the most popular functions.

The second seed selection (*ops* selection) was based on our knowledge of the database structure. We limited the list of seeds to the entry points of the Executor operations. This seed selection will obtain longer sequences than the first one, as most functions will be included halfway through the main sequence, as they are referenced by it. However, some important basic blocks may be left out, as they will be unreachable from the selected seeds, or some intermediate basic block will not pass the Exec or Branch thresholds.

Also, the sequences built this way will have lower temporal locality as they include less frequently referenced basic blocks surrounding the most popular ones.

5.2 Sequence building

Using the weighted graph obtained running the training set, and starting from the selected seeds, we implement a greedy algorithm to build our basic block traces targeting an increase in the code sequentiality. Given a basic block, the algorithm follows the most frequently executed path out of it. This implies visiting a subroutine called by the basic block, or following the control transfer with the highest probability of being used. All the other valid transitions from the basic block are noted for future examination.

For this algorithm we use two parameters called *Exec Threshold*, and *Branch Threshold*. The trace building algorithm stops when all the successor basic blocks have been visited or have a weight lower than the Exec Threshold, or all the outgoing arcs have a branch probability less than the Branch Threshold. In that case, we start again from the next acceptable transition, as we noted before, building secondary execution paths for the same seed. Once all basic blocks reachable from the given seed have been included in the main or secondary sequences, we proceed to the next seed.

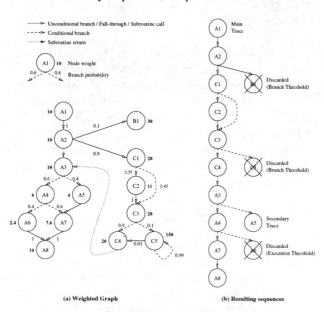

Figure 3. Trace building example.

Figure 3.a shows an example of the weighted graph and Figure 3.b shows the resulting sequences. We use an ExecThresh of 4 and a BranchThresh of 0.4. Starting from seed $A1$ and following the most likely outgoing edge from each basic block we build the sequence $A1 \rightarrow A8$ (Figure 3.b). The transitions to $B1$ and $C5$ are discarded due to the Branch Threshold. We noted that the transition from $A3$ to $A5$ is a valid transition, so we start a secondary trace with $A5$, but all its successors have been already visited, so the sequence ends there. We do not start a secondary trace from $A6$ because it has a weight lower than the Exec Threshold.

5.3 Sequence Mapping

Figure 4 shows the sequence mapping scheme. We define a logical array of caches, equal in size and address alignment to the physical cache. The sequences found in the first pass of the algorithm described in Section 5.2 are mapped from the start of the logical cache array. Then, we place the rest of the sequences in order, one pass at a time, keeping the area used by the sequences in the first pass free of code in all logical caches. This way, the first sequences

will not be replaced from the cache by any other code, and so will be free of interference. We call this area the Conflict Free Area (CFA), and derives directly form the *SelfConf-Free* area proposed in [21].

The size of this CFA is determined by the Exec and Branch Thresholds used for the first pass of our sequence building algorithm.

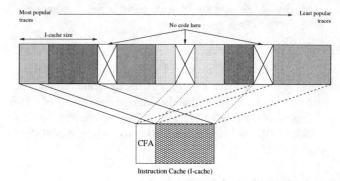

Figure 4. Sequence mapping into a direct mapped cache

When all the sequences have been mapped in the cache, we map all the remaining basic blocks in order, this time filling the entire address space. This rarely executed code is expected not to produce many conflicts with the sequences placed in the CFA.

6 Related Work

The use of profile-directed code reordering to reduce the instruction cache miss rate is not new. Hwu and Chang [8] use function inline expansion, and group into traces those basic blocks which tend to execute sequentially. Then, they map these traces in the cache so that functions which are executed close to each other are placed in the same page.

Pettis & Hansen [16] propose a reordering of the procedures in a program and the basic blocks within each procedure. Their aim is to minimize the conflicts between the most frequently used functions, placing functions which reference each other close in memory. They also reorder the basic blocks in a procedure, moving unused basic blocks to the bottom of the function code or even splitting the procedures in two, moving away the unused basic blocks. Their algorithm does not consider the target cache geometry.

Gloy *et al.* [6] extend the Pettis & Hansen algorithm at the procedure level to consider the temporal relationship between procedures in addition to the target cache information and the size of each procedure. Hashemi *et al* [7] and Kalamaitianos *et al* [11] use a cache line coloring algorithm inspired in the register coloring technique to map procedures so that the resulting number of conflicts is minimized.

Torrellas *et al* [21] propose a basic block reordering algorithm for Operating System code, running on a very conservative vector processor. They map the code in the form of sequences of basic blocks spanning several functions, and keep a Conflict Free Area for the most frequently referenced basic blocks.

Our target goes beyond an instruction cache miss rate reduction. Targeting an increase in the number of sequential instructions executed, we combine the different approaches and map out basic block traces as a unit, keeping whole sequences in the *conflict free area* instead of preserving individual basic blocks in it.

Techniques like trace scheduling [4] and superblock scheduling [9], use static branch prediction to define logical groups of basic blocks, enlarging the scope of the compiler to schedule instruction issue by moving individual instructions across basic blocks.

For more aggressive processors, the width of instructions provided to the processor becomes an important issue. Techniques like the Branch Address Cache [24], the Collapsing Buffer [2] and the Trace Cache [19, 5] approach the problem of fetching multiple, non-contiguous basic blocks each cycle. Both the Branch Address Cache and the Collapsing Buffer access non-consecutive cache lines from an interleaved i-cache each cycle and then merge the required instructions from each accessed line.

The Trace Cache does not require fetching of non-consecutive basic blocks from the i-cache. This is done by storing the dynamically constructed sequences of instructions in a special purpose *trace cache*. If a fetch request corresponds to one of the sequences stored in the trace cache, this sequence is passed to the decode unit, effectively fetching multiple basic blocks in a single cycle. On a trace cache miss, fetching proceeds from the conventional i-cache and a new sequence is created and stored in the trace cache.

Our approach targets an increase in the number of instructions provided by the instruction cache, reducing the need of the trace cache, and providing a better back-up mechanism in case of a trace cache miss.

7 Method Evaluation

As we said before, our method is based on profile information. In order to evaluate our technique we used a different set of queries for the Test and Training sets. The Test set used to obtain the simulation results consists of queries 2, 3, 4, 6, 11, 12, 13, 14, 15 and 17, executed on both the Btree and the Hash indexed databases (see Section 3). For both the Training and the Test sets, all queries were run to completion.

We compared the results of both our automatic code layout (*auto* layout) and the experience based layout (*ops* layout) with those obtained by the method proposed by Pettis & Hansen (*P&H* layout) and the work of Torrellas *et al* (*Torr* layout).

7.1 Simulation setup

We did not generate a new executable with the proposed code layouts. Instead, we generated a new address for each basic block, feeding the simulators with this faked address instead of the original PC. The code was not modified in any way, so all basic blocks have the same size for all the examined code layouts.

The fetch unit used in our simulations corresponds to the SEQ.3 fetch unit described in [19]. This fetch unit accesses two consecutive cache lines, and provides the instructions from the fetch address up to the first taken branch, or up to a maximum of three branches, or 16 instructions, whichever comes first.

We used perfect branch prediction to examine the performance limit of the examined techniques, avoiding interference due to branch and target mispredictions.

7.2 Instruction cache miss rate

Table 3 shows the miss rate for the sequential fetch unit and the different code layouts. We present results for different i-cache and CFA sizes. We also evaluated a 2-way set associative cache and the addition of a 16-line fully-associative victim cache. The numbers given are in terms of i-cache misses per instruction executed.

i-cache / CFA	Code layout					Cache	
	orig	P&H	Torr	auto	ops	2-way	victim
8/2	6.5	3.0	2.3	2.2	2.1	6.1	5.6
8/4	–	–	2.9	4.2	2.9	–	–
8/6	–	–	3.1	2.3	5.2	–	–
16/4	4.0	1.1	0.9	0.8	0.7	2.6	3.4
16/8	–	–	0.7	0.8	0.6	–	–
16/12	–	–	0.8	0.8	1.0	–	–
32/4	2.7	0.3	0.2	0.3	0.2	1.2	1.6
32/8	–	–	0.2	0.4	0.2	–	–
32/16	–	–	0.3	0.2	0.1	–	–
32/24	–	–	0.2	0.3	0.2	–	–
64/8	1.4	0.09	0.05	0.07	0.04	0.3	0.4
64/16	–	–	0.14	0.08	0.05	–	–
64/24	–	–	0.02	0.03	0.03	–	–

Table 3. Instruction cache miss rate for the different i-cache and CFA sizes examined.

Our proposed layouts obtain similar results to the *Torr* layout, and always outperform the *P&H* layout. All the code layouts obtained better results than both the 2-way associative cache and the victim cache.

From the results shown, it is clear that the most important factor regarding the miss rate reduction offered by our technique is the size of the CFA.

Intuitively, an increase in the CFA size causes both positive and negative effects. On the one hand, a larger CFA shields more routines from self-interference, and, as a result, eliminates misses in those routines. On the other hand, however, less area is left for the rest of the routines, which will suffer more conflict misses. Once the CFA size reaches a certain value, the second effect will dominate. Also, once the CFA is able to satisfy most of the references, there is little point in further increasing it, as we will be taking out cache area that may be better used to avoid conflict misses in other code.

7.3 Fetch bandwidth

We compared fetch bandwith results with those of the basic Trace Cache described in [19]. We simulated a direct mapped Trace Cache of 256 entries (16KB). All kinds of branch instructions were counted against the 3 branch limit, including unconditional branches and subroutine calls and returns. We did not stop instruction fetch on indirect jumps as was done in [5, 19].

I-cache / CFA	Code layout					Trace cache	
	orig	P&H	Torr	auto	ops	16KB	16KB+ops
Ideal	7.6	9.6	8.5–9.9	9.9	10.7	10.3	12.2
8/2	3.1	5.2	5.6	6.0	6.2	5.1	8.4
8/4	–	–	5.0	5.3	6.6	–	8.7
8/6	–	–	4.9	5.8	5.6	–	8.1
16/4	4.0	7.3	7.4	8.1	8.8	6.2	10.3
16/8	–	–	7.4	8.1	9.0	–	10.4
16/12	–	–	7.3	7.9	8.1	–	10.2
32/4	4.7	8.8	8.9	9.2	10.0	7.2	11.5
32/8	–	–	8.4	8.8	10.1	–	11.5
32/16	–	–	8.0	9.3	10.3	–	11.8
32/24	–	–	8.2	9.2	10.1	–	11.6
64/8	5.8	9.3	8.8	9.8	10.6	8.6	12.0
64/16	–	–	8.4	9.7	10.5	–	12.1
64/24	–	–	8.5	9.8	10.6	–	12.1

Table 4. Fetch bandwidth in instructions per cycle. The i-cache miss penalty is 5 cycles.

Table 4 shows the number of instructions per cycle provided by each setup.

The *Ideal* line corresponds to a perfect instruction cache. For the realistic i-cache setups, we applied a fixed miss penalty of 5 cycles. We did not count any miss penalty on a trace cache hit.

Looking at the *Ideal* fetch bandwidth provided by each technique, we observe that the *P&H* layout is very close to the *auto* reordering and the 16KB Trace Cache. The *ops* reordering has more potential bandwidth than any other technique except the combination of itself with the Trace Cache.

The method proposed by Torrellas *et al.* shows a variable behavior. The larger the CFA, the more basic blocks are included in the CFA. These basic blocks have been pulled out of their sequences to be included in the CFA, which breaks the sequential execution jumping in and out of the CFA.

Once the average number of cycles taken by each fetch request is considered, both the *auto* and the *ops* layouts become clearly better than any other technique. The Trace Cache could not remember all the executed sequences, and had to resort to sequential fetching 52% of the times, and the fetch unit could provide few instructions due to the lack of sequentiality in the original code.

Our proposed layout could use the whole memory space as a *software trace cache* to capture the most frequently executed sequences of code, and could provide more instructions per cycle using the statically stored traces. When using the *ops* layout, the fetch engine could provide more instructions per cycle, even on a Trace Cache miss, both due to the increased sequentiality of the code and to the reduced i-cache miss rate.

It is worth noting that a lower miss rate alone does not mean a higher fetch bandwidth, as can be observed comparing the results of the P&H and the Torr layouts for the larger caches. In order to improve the fetch bandwidth, both the i-cache miss rate and the sequentiality of code must be taken into account.

8 Conclusions and Future Work

Instruction fetch bandwidth is feared to be a major limiting factor to the performance of future wide-issue aggressive superscalars.

In this paper, we focus on Database applications running Decision Support workloads. We characterize the locality patterns of database kernel code and find frequently executed paths. Using this information, we propose an algorithm to lay out the basic blocks of the database kernel for improved fetch bandwith. This is achieved by both a reduction of the i-cache miss rate and an increase in the number of instructions executed between taken branches.

Our results show a miss reduction of 60-98% for realistic i-cache sizes, obtaining miss rates under 0.05% with a 64KB direct mapped cache. The proposed code layout also increases the number of instructions executed between taken branches from the 8.9 of the original code to 22.4. With this, a 16 instruction wide fetch unit could provide 10.6 instructions per cycle using our proposed code layout.

Improving only the i-cache miss rate or the potential fetch bandwidth provided is not enough. Both factors must be taken into account to provide optimal results.

A Trace Cache alone could not hold all the executed sequences, while our technique used all the memory space as a Software Trace Cache to statically store the most frequently executed traces. As a consequence, while the Trace Cache alone could only provide 8.6 inctructions per cycle, a combination of the Software-Hardware Trace Caches increased the result to 12.1.

We have shown that large first level i-caches can capture the working set of large applications like a DBMS. It is worth studying if the controlled use of code expanding techniques like function inlining and code replication can increase the potential fetch bandwidth provided by a sequential fetch unit while keeping the miss rate under control.

In the near future we plan to extend the proposed algorithm to automatize the process of selecting the thresholds and the seeds while obtaining results closer to the knowledge-based selection. Also, we will examine the effect of our technique on the IPC for a wider range of applications like OLTP workloads and the SPEC benckmark.

References

[1] L. A. Barroso, K. Gharachorloo, and E. Bugnion. Memory system characterization of commercial workloads. *Proceedings of the 16th Annual Intl. Symposium on Computer Architecture*, pages 3–14, June 1998.

[2] T. Conte, K. Menezes, P. Mills, and B. Patell. Optimization of instruction fetch mechanism for high issue rates. *Proceedings of the 22th Annual Intl. Symposium on Computer Architecture*, pages 333–344, June 1995.

[3] R. Elmasri and S. Navathe. *Fundamentals of Database Systems*. Benjamin Cummings, second edition, 1994.

[4] J. A. Fisher. Trace scheduling: A technique for global microcode compaction. *IEEE Transactions on Computers*, 30(7):478–490, July 1981.

[5] D. H. Friendly, S. J. Patel, and Y. N. Patt. Alternative fetch and issue techniques from the trace cache mechanism. *Proceedings of the 30th Anual ACM/IEEE Intl. Symposium on Microarchitecture*, Dec. 1997.

[6] N. Gloy, T. Blackwell, M. D. Smith, and B. Calder. Procedure placement using temporal ordering information. *Proceedings of the 30th Anual ACM/IEEE Intl. Symposium on Microarchitecture*, pages 303–313, Dec. 1997.

[7] A. H. Hashemi, D. R. Kaeli, and B. Calder. Efficient procedure mapping using cache line coloring. *Proc. ACM SIGPLAN'97 Conf. on Programming Languaje Design and Implementation*, pages 171–182, June 1997.

[8] W.-M. Hwu and P. P. Chang. Achieving high instruction cache performance with an optimizing compiler. *Proceedings of the 16th Annual Intl. Symposium on Computer Architecture*, pages 242–251, June 1989.

[9] W. W. Hwu, S. A. Mahlke, W. Y. Chen, P. P. Chang, N. J. Water, R. A. Bringmann, R. G. Ouellette, R. E. Hank, T. K. G. E. Haab, J. G. Hold, and D. M. Lavery. The superblock: An effective technique for vliw and superscalar compilation. *Journal on Supercomputing*, (7):9–50, 1993.

[10] T. Juan, S. Sanjeevan, and J. J. Navarro. Dynamic history-length fitting: A thrid level of adaptivity for branch prediction. *Proceedings of the 25th Annual Intl. Symposium on Computer Architecture*, pages 155–166, June 1998.

[11] J. Kalamaitianos and D. R. Kaeli. Temporal-based procedure reordering for improved instruction cache performance. *Proceedings of the 4th Intl. Conference on High Performance Computer Architecture*, Feb. 1998.

[12] K. Keeton, D. A. Patterson, Y. Q. He, R. C. Raphael, and W. E. Baker. Performance characterization of a quad pentium pro smp using oltp workloads. *Proceedings of the 25th Annual Intl. Symposium on Computer Architecture*, pages 15–26, June 1998.

[13] M. S. G. Kemnitz. The postgres next generation database management system. *Communications of the ACM*, Oct. 1991.

[14] J. L. Lo, L. A. Barroso, S. J. Eggers, K. Gharachorloo, H. M. Levy, and S. S. Parekh. An analysis of database workload performance on simultaneous multithreaded processors. *Proceedings of the 25th Annual Intl. Symposium on Computer Architecture*, pages 39–50, June 1998.

[15] A. M. Maynard, C. M. Donnelly, and B. R. Olszewski. Contrasting characteristics and cache performance of technical and multi-user commercial workloads. *Proceedings of the 6th Intl. Conference on Architectural Support for Programming Languajes and Operating Systems*, pages 145–156, Oct. 1994.

[16] K. Pettis and R. C. Hansen. Profile guided code positioning. *Proc. ACM SIGPLAN'99 Conf. on Programming Languaje Design and Implementation*, pages 16–27, June 1990.

[17] A. Ram'rez, J. L. Larriba-Pey, C. Navarro, X. Serrano, J. Torrellas, and M. Valero. Code reordering of decision support systems for optimized instruction fetch. Technical Report UPC-DAC-1998-56, Universitat Politecnica de Catalunya, Dec. 1998.

[18] P. Rangananthan, K. Gharachorloo, S. V. Adve, and L. A. Barroso. Performance of database workloads on shared-memory systems with out of order processors. *Proceedings of the 8th Intl. Conference on Architectural Support for Programming Languajes and Operating Systems*, Oct. 1998.

[19] E. Rottenberg, S. Benett, and J. E. Smith. Trace cache: a low latency aprroach to high bandwith instruction fetching. *Proceedings of the 29th Anual ACM/IEEE Intl. Symposium on Microarchitecture*, pages 24–34, Dec. 1996.

[20] A. Seznec, S. Jourdan, P. Sainrat, and P. Michaud. Multiple-block ahead branch predictors. *Proceedings of the 7th Intl. Conference on Architectural Support for Programming Languajes and Operating Systems*, Oct. 1996.

[21] J. Torrellas, C. Xia, and R. Daigle. Optimizing instruction cache performance for operating system intensive workloads. *Proceedings of the 1st Intl. Conference on High Performance Computer Architecture*, pages 360–369, Jan. 1995.

[22] T. P. P. C. (TPC). Tpc benchmark d (decision support). Standard Specification, Revision 1. 2. 3, 1993–1997.

[23] P. Trancoso, J. L. Larriba-Pey, Z. Zhang, and J. Torrellas. The memory performance of dss commercial workloads in shared-memory multiprocessors. *Proceedings of the 3rd Intl. Conference on High Performance Computer Architecture*, Feb. 1997.

[24] T. Y. Yeh, D. T. Marr, and Y. N. Patt. Increasing the instruction fetch rate via multiple branch prediction and a branch address cache. *Proceedings of the 7th Intl. Conference on Supercomputing*, pages 67–76, July 1993.

Improving Performance of Load-Store Sequences for Transaction Processing Workloads on Multiprocessors

Jim Nilsson and Fredrik Dahlgren[†]

Department of Computer Engineering
Chalmers University of Technology
SE-412 96 Göteborg, Sweden
j@ce.chalmers.se

[†] Ericsson Mobile Communications AB
Mobile Phones and Terminals
SE-221 83 Lund, Sweden
fredrik.dahlgren@ecs.ericsson.se

Abstract

On-line transaction processing exhibits poor memory behavior in high-end multiprocessor servers because of complex sharing patterns and substantial interaction between the database server and the operating system. One contributing source is a large amount of load-store sequences in the program, resulting in many read misses as well as much global invalidation traffic.

In this paper, we characterize the nature of these load-store sequences, and analyze contributing code- and data structures in the database handler, operating system, and system libraries. We explore two conceptually different approaches for detecting load-store sequences; data-centric and instruction-centric, and the goal is to load the cache block exclusively already at the load instruction so that the store instruction can perform locally. Our results were obtained using program-driven simulation of a TPC-B based workload on a four-node multiprocessor.

The results show that there is a substantial amount of load-store sequences in the database handler, the operating system, and in system libraries, and about 40% of all global writes belong to such sequences. Even though the techniques were able to reduce the execution time for the application by up to 10%, the complex behavior of the database workload reduced the effectiveness of traditional optimization techniques for migratory sharing.

1 Introduction

Several recent studies have shown that on-line transaction processing (OLTP) exhibits poor memory behavior in high-end multiprocessor servers. Barroso et al. showed in [1] that up to 90% of the total execution time of an OLTP application consists of stall time due to instruction and data cache misses. Furthermore, Ranganathan et al. pointed out the existence of migratory shared data as one possible origin of this performance bottleneck [2]. Migratory sharing [3] occurs when shared data tend to be manipulated by only one processor at a time. This manipulation can often be characterized by a load followed by a store to the same block by the same processor – a *load-store sequence*.

Several previous studies have proposed and explored techniques for detecting migratory sharing [4–6]. These techniques have been shown to reduce the amount of global

write messages substantially for scientific/engineering applications dominated by migratory sharing, but have never been applied to database applications or operating systems.

In this paper we present a detailed analysis of global load-store sequences in a transaction processing workload on a multiprocessor. We classify techniques for detecting load-store sequences into two categories; data-centric and instruction-centric, depending on whether they detect data being accessed in a load-store fashion or detect the actual load and store instructions of load-store sequences in the program. We evaluate previous techniques for detecting migratory sharing as well as some novel, instruction-centric techniques. We also made a first attempt to combine the approaches for higher coverage.

Our baseline system architecture is a sequentially consistent multiprocessor with a directory-based, write-invalidate cache coherence protocol. We have used the SimICS/sun4m program-driven simulation platform [7] to simulate the multiprocessor architecture. Our workload has been the MySQL database handler [8] executing on SparcLinux 2.0.35 and a workload based on the TPC-B benchmark [9] with 40 branches which approximately corresponds to 600 MB of database data.

We both qualitatively and quantitatively analyze the existing load-store sequences in the workload, as well as their origin in the source code of the database handler, the operating systems kernel, and the system libraries. We also quantify how effective the techniques are in reducing the memory system overhead for this application domain. The results show that there is a substantial amount of load-store sequences in the database handler, the operating system, and in system libraries, and about 40% of all global writes belong to such sequences. Even though the techniques were able to reduce the execution time for the application by up to 10%, the complex behavior of the database workload reduced the effectiveness of traditional optimization techniques for migratory sharing.

The rest of this paper is organized as follows. We begin by explaining the problem addressed in this paper as well as the load-store detection schemes in Section 2. We describe the experimental methodology in Section 3, and present our results in Section 4. In Section 5 we discuss related work before we finally conclude the paper in Section 6.

246

2 Techniques for Load-Store Sequences

This section starts in Section 2.1 by presenting how a load-store sequence, i.e. a load followed by a store to the same cache block from the same processor, interacts with the memory system in a cache-coherent multiprocessor. Thereafter, Sections 2.2 and 2.3 describe two conceptually different approaches to detect and optimize for load-store sequences. We will in the following refer to load and store as the actual load and store *instructions* in the code, while read and write refer to the actions carried out in the memory system.

2.1 Background

The sharing behavior when a cache block is accessed by load-store sequences from different processors in turn, is referred to as *migratory sharing* [3]. If it somehow could be known at the load that there is an upcoming store to the same block, the global read message could be combined with an *exclusive* request which combines the invalidation with the fetching of data. The following write to the block could then be performed locally, thereby reducing network traffic and write latency [4, 5].

While we know from a number of previous studies that blocks exhibiting migratory sharing can be handled more effectively in shared-memory multiprocessors [4–6, 10], such improvements can be even more general. All load-store sequences can potentially benefit from a mechanism that loads the block exclusively into the cache already at the initial load instruction. This include blocks that are not actively shared, so there is no apparent migratory behavior, or blocks that have not been accessed before since brought in from secondary storage, or even data that has been replaced from one cache level to the next cache level or to main memory.

Optimizing for load-store sequences and migratory data can affect performance in two major ways: as a direct decrease in write stall time, and as decreased network traffic [5]. The decrease in write stall time is most prominent in processors with a sequential memory consistency model [11], as write stall time is hidden to a larger extent in processors employing weaker consistency models [12]. Network traffic is however decreased for any type of memory consistency model.

In this paper, we target load-store sequences in a more general perspective, not just migratory sharing. There are two fundamentally different approaches for detecting load-store sequences; *data-centric techniques* that aim at detecting and tagging memory blocks that are accessed in a load-store fashion, and *instruction-centric techniques* that aim at detecting and tagging load instructions in the program that are followed by a store to the same cache block. These two approaches will be described in the following two sections, respectively.

2.2 Data-Centric Load-Store Optimization

A data-centric technique aims at detecting and tagging memory blocks that are accessed in a load-store fashion. It keeps a notion on the sequencing of read and write accesses to the memory blocks. If the sequence to a block fulfills some criteria, the memory block is tagged and subsequent read accesses to the block will render an exclusive copy of the block in the local cache. We will consider two different techniques for data-centric load-store detection; one *dynamic scheme* that tags block during the execution, and one *static scheme* that statically tag blocks prior to execution.

The original techniques for detecting migratory sharing [4, 5] were both dynamic, data-centric schemes. We will in this paper evaluate the technique proposed by Stenström et al. [5] which works as follows. In addition to the already present directory information describing the state for each memory block, the home needs to contain one bit describing if the block is migratory or not, as well as a bit-field describing which processor that last wrote to the block. Two criteria must be fulfilled in order to deem a memory block migratory: (1) the number of cached copies is exactly two, and (2) the writing processor is not the same as the previous writer. The first criterion basically limits the memory access sequences that would consider a memory block as migratory, in that it prevents a state transition when the block is shared between several processors. The second criterion prevents for example producer-consumer access sequences as being considered migratory. As it could be the case that the access behavior for a memory block changes during execution, the modified coherence protocol also has a criterion to bring a migratory block back to the normal write-invalidate state.

The static scheme that we will consider in this paper is based on a categorization of data blocks being either *exclusive* or normal. Blocks that are deemed *exclusive* will always be fetched exclusively into the local cache at each load instruction, and can never reside in two or more caches at the same time. While load-store sequences benefit from data blocks being tagged *exclusive*, tagging a block that will be simultaneously read by many processors will be devastating. Blocks that are not tagged *exclusive* are always treated according to a standard write-invalidate protocol.

2.3 Instruction-Centric Load-Store Optimization

An instruction-centric technique aims at detecting and tagging load instructions in the program that are followed by a store to the same cache block. Such loads are treated as load-exclusive instructions, and brings the requested block exclusively into the cache. With such a technique, a block is treated according to the current application behavior, and even blocks that have never been previously accessed might benefit from the technique. What complicates this approach in practice is the indeterminism of instruction flow; a load might only *sometimes* be followed by a store to the same block. First, it might be extremely difficult for a technique to find such load-store sequences. Second, only if the load is followed by a store in a majority of the cases should it be deemed load-exclusive.

The compiler-based technique targeting migratory sharing that was proposed by Skeppstedt and Stenström [6] as well as the hardware techniques proposed by Kaxiras and Goodman [10] are instruction-centric. The compiler-based technique in [6] works as follows. When it can be concluded that a particular read access in the instruction flow inevitably will be followed by a write access to the same address within some time frame, this read is tagged as *exclusive*, which means that the actual code produced for this read is a load-exclusive (if such an instruction exists in the architecture), or a prefetch-exclusive instruction followed by an ordinary load instruction. A simple situation where this detection is easy is when both the load and the store resides within the same basic block. By use of detailed datapath analysis however, a load-store pair spanning multiple basic blocks can be detected.

Furthermore, different levels of speculation are possible. In these situations, it is not always certain that the store is executed after the load. This could for example be because of a conditional branch in-between the load and the store. It is important to understand the success of speculation, since if the first load is always tagged as exclusive, unnecessary invalidations would take place if the block is actively shared between processors.

We have also explored a run-time instruction-centric technique, very similar to that in [10]. It works as follows. A small buffer keeps track of the address to the last D load instructions as well as the physical block address to their requested data. At each store instruction, the data address is matched against the data addresses of the last loads. If there is a preceding load to the same data block, the instruction address of that load is saved in a small, direct-mapped cache, the *load-exclusive directory* (LED). On each load instruction that misses in the cache, the LED is interrogated to see whether the global read miss should be combined with an ownership acquisition.

The detection mechanism depends heavily on the size D of the buffer that keeps the last load instructions. D is referred to as the *detection distance*, since the store must be issued within D loads. As we increase the detection distance, we will detect more loads as belonging to load-store sequences, but we also increase the probability of marking loads that only rarely precedes a store to the same block.

We will explore three different variations of the instruction-centric technique. In the *static* scheme, loads that are followed by a store to the same block are tagged load-exclusive during the execution, and are being tagged so until the end of execution. This is a highly speculative approach since we are bound to even tag loads that are seldom followed by a store, i.e. it is sufficient for a load to be followed by a store *once* to be tagged as exclusive. This could lead to an excessive amount of loads being wrongly tagged as exclusive with a negative impact on performance. In the *conservative* and *dynamic* schemes, a tagged load can be de-tagged if it is not followed by a store. The *conservative* scheme never re-tags loads, which means that only those loads that are always followed by a store to the same block will remain as load-exclusive instructions. The *dynamic* scheme allows loads to be tagged according to their most recent behavior.

In Section 4.3 through 4.5, respectively, we will show how the described data-centric, instruction-centric, and combined approaches perform in practice.

3 Experimental Methodology

In this section, we first describe the simulation methodology used to obtain the results in Section 3.1. The application workload is described in Section 3.2. The simulated hardware architecture is described in Section 3.3.

3.1 Simulation Methodology

For our simulations, we use the SimICS/sun4m [7] program-driven simulator. SimICS is a highly efficient execution-driven simulator of the Sparc V8 instruction set architecture. Together with a set of detailed software models of the hardware devices constituting the sun4m architecture specification from Sun Microsystems, SimICS/sun4m provides a platform on which it is possible to execute any binary file compiled for this architecture, including operating systems.

Together with SimICS/sun4m, we use a memory system simulator that model the target memory system including all latencies. Every memory access produced by the workload (application as well as operating system) is sent to the memory system simulator which handles the access according to the contents and behavior of the caches. We model processor stall according to the behavior and latencies of the memory components, so a correct interleaving of execution between the different processors can be maintained.

3.2 Workload

Our simulated workload consist of the publicly available database management system (DBMS) MySQL [8], and the also publicly available SparcLinux 2.0.35 operating system, using the posix-threads package from glibc 2.0.7. The main reason for using a public DBMS and operating system, is the availability of source code. This enables us to relate the memory access behavior to individual code and data structures in the application as well as the operating system.

MySQL is a multi-threaded client-server based DBMS designed for high performance. The workload of MySQL is based on the TPC-B OLTP benchmark [9] with 40 branches, equivalent to approximately 600 MB of database data, not including metadata and the log table. For every simulation run, the DBMS executes 400 transactions. This is equivalent to 2,000 individual queries. Although TPC-B has been replaced by TPC-C as the official benchmark for OLTP applications, it was pointed out in [1] that the memory reference behavior between the two is similar.

To clearly identify the effects of the optimization techniques, we concentrate our measurements to query processing. Consequently, we leave out processing of database initialization and shutdown, as well as the operating system boot phase.

3.3 Architecture

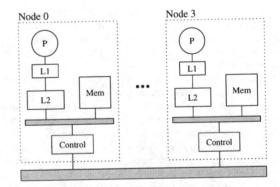

Figure 1: Multiprocessor architecture

The hardware architecture used in the experiments, depicted in Figure 1, is a cache-coherent, write-invalidate shared-memory multiprocessor with four nodes. Every node contains a processor, a two-level cache hierarchy, a memory controller, and a part of the global memory. The two levels of cache can have arbitrary configurations in terms of size, associativity, block size, and latency. Table 1 lists the cache parameters used in our experiments. The results in Section 4 are shown for a 512 kB L2 cache with a 64 byte cache block size. Similar results were obtained for other cache configurations. Physical memory pages are distributed round-robin among the nodes.

Cache parameter	Value
L1 size	64 kB
L1 associativity	2-way
L1 access time	1 cycle
L2 size	256/512/1024 kB
L2 associativity	1-way
L2 access time	20 cycles
Block size	32/128 bytes

Table 1: Cache parameters used in the experiments

Memory latency	Cycles
Memory access	40
Network traversal	40
Controller	20
Local access	100
Home access	220
Remote access	420

Table 2: Memory system latencies

The latencies of various activities are listed in Table 2. The processors are single-issue and sequentially consistent. We accurately model contention in the nodes.

4 Results

This section presents the results of our simulations. The analysis in Section 4.1 quantifies the existence of load-store sequences in the workload, and shows the potentials for gains due to load-store optimizations. In order to better understand the sources for load-store sequences and to be able to generalize the findings, Section 4.2 traces the memory reference behavior to the source code of the software system including the database handler, operating system kernel, and library code. Sections 4.3 and 4.4 present our findings of the ability of some data-centric and instruction-centric techniques, respectively, to properly handle the existing load-store sequences, as well as their impact on performance. Finally, Section 4.5 explores the potentials of a technique that combines the two approaches.

4.1 Load-Store Behavior in the Workload

The amount and characteristics of the load-store behavior present in the workload is crucial for any technique to be successful in load-exclusive fetching. In order to quantify the amount of load-store sequences in the workload, we analyzed on a per-block basis all read and write accesses during an execution on the baseline, write-invalidate cache-coherence protocol. A histogram was captured that shows both the interleaving of accesses from different processors, as well as the type (read or write) of the accesses. The histogram gave us an opportunity to identify and quantify the

sharing patterns of the workload. Of specific interest is the situation where a global write is preceded by a read to the same block and from the same processor. Between these two accesses, there are no accesses to the block from any other processor. This indicates a load-store sequence for which it could be beneficial to fetch the block exclusively at the read request. Observe that we focus entirely on those load-store sequences where the load misses in the cache, which means that the ownership acquisition of the block can be merged with the global read access.

We classified all global write requests as belonging to one of the following three categories:

Load-Store: A potential for load-exclusive fetching, since the global write is preceded by a read miss from the same processor. No other processor issued any read or write to the block in-between.

Stored-Between: At the global write, the block has been written to by another processor since it was last accessed by the same processor. This means that the writing processor does not have a copy of the block already.

Loaded-Between: At the global write, the block has been read by another processor since it was last accessed by the same processor.

As can be seen in Table 3, as much as 40% of all global write actions are due to *Load-Store* sequences. The results indicate that load-exclusive fetching of blocks seems to be a viable approach for higher performance and less coherence traffic for OLTP workloads. Interestingly, we see that the load-store sequences appear not only in the MySQL database handler, but also to a large extent in the operating system kernel and library code.

The *Stored-Between* category consists of access sequences where the processor issues a store access to a block which has been written by another node and is therefore likely to be in state Modified in a remote cache. For the application and library accesses, this type accounts for more than 60% of all accesses. By relating these accesses to the workload, we found that many of these accesses came from the clearing of buffers used for keeping temporary results in query processing. Another part comes from false sharing. In addition, some accesses was caused by process migration. A study on the behavior of a commercial database handler (Oracle 7.3.2) on the Digital Unix 4.0 operating system [1] found very little false sharing. Therefore, we expect this category of writes to be less frequent in commercial systems, and the Load-Store category to be relatively more frequent.

The *Loaded-Between* category is the case when a load and a store from one processor is interrupted by at least one read from another processor. Such loads should not trigger an ownership acquisition, since that might lead to increased read stall time by the other processors that share the block.

We also identified the amount of global write accesses belonging to migratory sharing as defined in [5] (the block is read and written in turn by different processors). The results are shown in Table 4. Overall, about 48% of all load-store sequences belong to migratory sharing. This indicates that techniques that target load-store sequences by detecting migratory sharing will be limited to less than half of the load-store sequences.

Category	Kernel	DBMS	Library	Total
Load-Store	429.19K (44%)	71.85K (31%)	45.74K (27%)	546.78K (40%)
Stored-Between	308.07K (32%)	140.32K (61%)	113.05K (66%)	561.44K (41%)
Loaded-Between	233.33K (24%)	17.48K (8%)	11.98K (7%)	262.79K (19%)

Table 3: Types of memory access sequences present in the workload.

Kernel	DBMS	Library	Total
48.4%	43.2%	54.4%	48.0%

Table 4: The fraction of global load-store sequences that have a migratory sharing access pattern

Location	1-10	11-20	21-30	31-40	41-
All	41%	7%	2%	3%	47%
Kernel	46%	7%	2%	4%	41%
DBMS	21%	11%	4%	10%	64%
Library	20%	12%	3%	0%	65%

Table 5: Distance between load and store accesses

Table 5 shows the distance in number of executed instructions between the load that misses in the cache and the subsequent store in the load-store sequences discussed above. In as many as 41%, the store is issued less than 11 instructions after the load that misses in the cache. 53% of all load-store sequences have a distance of no more than 40 executed instructions. Therefore, we expect instruction-centric techniques to be limited in their ability to find a reasonable large fraction of the loads of load-store sequences.

4.2 Sources of Load-Store Sequences

It is interesting to notice that the 650,000 global load-store sequences that appeared originated from 1,334 different load instructions. However, as few as 25 load instructions produce as many as 35% of all load-store sequences. This means that, by analyzing the most frequent contributors of load-store sequences, we will get a deeper understanding of which code constructs that contribute to load-store sequences. Therefore, we relate the obtained numbers in the previous section to data structures and code constructs in MySQL, libraries, and the operating system kernel.

Code constructs generating global load-store sequences

By exploring the code constructs that generates global load-store sequences, we found that they in almost all cases belong to one of three general groups.

Assignments — Consisting of tight read-modify-write sequences. Typical distance in instructions between the load and the store is two or three, but sometimes longer. In some cases, a variable is read at the beginning of a subroutine, used throughout the routine, and finally written back to memory with an updated value before returning to the caller.

Update of linked lists — This is a special case of assignment where the major part of the elements in a linked list are updated in a loop. This situation can only be handled by a speculative static detection of load-store sequences, unless the loop is unrolled. For a linked list of dynamically allocated data elements however, the loop upper bound is seldom known at compile-time.

Locks — Several processes repeatedly read a lock variable, waiting for it to attain some value stating that the lock is free. Before a process enters the critical section, it writes the lock variable to keep other processes from entering the critical section. To avoid a ping-pong effect where the lock variable jumps from one cache to another among the contending processor, lock variables should not be allowed to be tagged exclusive.

In the the following sections, we will further examine the individual contributions to the load-store behavior from the three workload domains; the DBMS, the libraries, and the operating system, respectively.

Load-store behavior in MySQL

In total, MySQL experienced 212,426 load-stores from 508 unique read locations, to 3,565 unique write locations, suggesting that only a small fraction of all loads in MySQL are part of a load-store sequence, but that these loads are performed frequently. 139,521 times, a global write occurred from a node that did not have a copy of the block already, i.e. the store was not preceded by a load, and these were issued from 265 unique write locations.

No single program construct or data structure in MySQL contributed with more than a few percent to the total amount of load-stores. There are, however, general areas where load-store sequences are common. One such area is operations on the *key block cache*. Analogous to the system global area (SGA) of the Oracle 7.3.2 database management system, the MySQL *key block cache* is a global data area used for frequently used database data, index tables, and metadata. Queries operate on the key block cache and when the cache is exhausted, its contents are flushed back to disk. Data in the key block cache are structured in hash tables with linked lists.

Interestingly, we found that most load-stores in MySQL are due to operations on the key block cache, specifically index scan operations such as updating of indeces and the allocation/deallocation of buffers holding temporary query results. The load-stores operating on the key block cache comes from several distinct functions, and from several locations within these functions, but the locations have in common that they are guaranteed atomicity by mutual exclusion, which is beneficial for the detection of load-store sequences.

Load-store behavior in libraries

A dominant source of load-stores in the libraries are the locking primitives in the `pthreads` library. This library contains functions for POSIX compliant thread handling and is used in Linux for multithreaded processes with lightweight threads. The locking primitives are responsible for ensuring mutual exclusion on data that is shared between threads.

Other contributors to library load-stores are memory copying (mem_cpy), which actually has a complex interaction with MySQL where MySQL does the load and the library function performs the store. We expect such situations to be hard to find for any instruction-centric load-store detection technique.

Load-store behavior in the operating system

Of the global load-stores emanating from the operating system, we found that 31.4% of them accessed the same cache block. This block held the kernel_flag spin-lock variable in the kernel system call entry point, used for mutual exclusion on kernel data structures. As of SparcLinux 2.0.35, the kernel locking mechanisms are of a simple nature, with a single lock structure for all kernel entry points. With a more fine-grained locking scheme, we expect that the contention for a single lock variable will decrease.

Furthermore, of all kernel load-store sequences, only 12 read locations were responsible for 98% of all load-stores. Of these 12 locations, 9 locations were directly involved with the kernel entry spin-lock loop, accounting for 79% of the global load-stores.

A common event in the kernel is the update of process time counters, where a single assignment accounted for 1.9% of the load-stores. Another source of kernel load-stores was register window overflow and underflow. These events involve complex transfers of register contents to and from the stack, responsible for 1.8% of all global load-stores. Various other locations in the operating system produced minor portions of the global load-store actions. We confirmed the detection of these sequences with the instruction-centric technique.

4.3 Data-Centric Load-Store Optimization

In this section, we study the ability of data-centric load-store optimization techniques to increase the performance of the database workload. We first explore the dynamic technique that detects migratory sharing according to [5]. Thereafter, we study the potentials of statically tagging data that should always be loaded exclusively.

Dynamic migratory sharing detection

In the right diagram of Figure 2, the reduction of invalidation traffic is shown for an L2 cache size of 1 MB. We see that this technique successfully reduces invalidation traffic 20%. This results in a reduction in the total number of messages of 6%, as is shown in the left diagram of Figure 2. The number of read misses was only slightly increased (right diagram of Figure 3), which shows that the technique is fairly stable and there are few read-only accesses to blocks detected as being migratory. In this diagram, *dirty exclusive* are exclusive reads to blocks that are modified in a remote cache and *clean exclusive* are exclusive reads that can be serviced directly by the memory. The technique was fairly successful in detecting migratory sharing, and 63.7% of all migratory sharing accesses (load-store sequences by alternating processors) were transformed into load-exclusive transactions.

LS-ratio:	>25%	>50%	>80%	>95%	100%
	99.8%	69.7%	36.3%	2.3%	1.8%

Table 6: The fraction of all load-store sequences that are covered when all blocks with certain *LS-ratio*s.

The resulting total execution time is shown in the left diagram of Figure 3. Each bar consists of three layers (from bottom): *busy time*, which is the number of cycles the processor is actively executing instructions, *read stall time* during which the processor is stalled waiting for cache misses to be serviced, and *write stall time* during which the processor is stalled because of global write actions. The busy time includes spin waiting for locks as well as kernel execution of the idle loop, which are components that depend on, among others, process coordination and I/O (disk) latencies. Therefore, the busy time will vary between different system configurations. The diagram shows a reduction of the total execution time of 6%. We have made the same simulations with cache sizes of 256 kB and 512 kB as well as for block sizes of 128B. The execution time reduction of some 6% seems to be consistent over this range of cache sizes and block sizes.

Static tagging of blocks

Another data-centric load-store technique is to statically tag data exclusive. To understand the potential of that approach, we measured for each block the number of (i) *processor changes*, i.e. the number of times it was accessed by a different processor than the last time it was accessed, (ii) *load-store sequences*, i.e. the number of times it was accessed by a load-store sequence between two processor changes, (iii) *initial stores*, i.e. the first access after a processor change is a store access, and (iv) *read-only sequences*, i.e. the block is only read by the processor between two processor changes.

This statistics can help us understand the feasibility of statically tagging data as being exclusive to the processor that accesses it. If a processor issues a store access to a block that resides in the home memory or in another cache, the block will be exclusively fetched into the cache. Therefore, the behavior of *initial stores* is independent of whether the block is statically tagged as exclusive.

Load-store sequences will benefit for blocks tagged exclusive, since such blocks will be loaded exclusively already at the load access. By contrast, tagging the block exclusive will be devastating if the block is often accessed by *read-only sequences*, since the block cannot be shared by different caches.

For a block to benefit from being tagged exclusive, *load-store sequences* should be more frequent than *read-only sequences*. We define the *LS-ratio* as the fraction of all *load-store sequences* and *read-only sequences* to a block that are *load-store sequences*. If the *LS-ratio* is 100%, there are no *read-only sequences* to the block. If the *LS-ratio* is 50%, the block has been accessed by as many *load-store sequences* as *read-only sequences*. For a block to benefit from being tagged as exclusive, the *LS-ratio* should be more than 50%.

If all blocks with a *LS-ratio* of 100% should be tagged exclusive, how many of all load-store sequences would be covered? Our results show that only 1.8% are to blocks

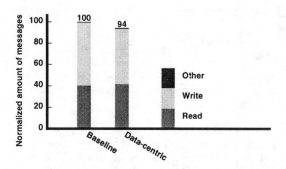
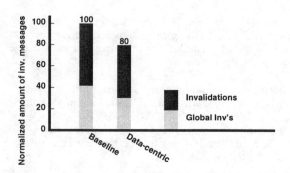

Figure 2: Total messages (left) and invalidation messages (right) for the dynamic migratory sharing detection technique

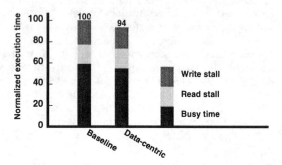
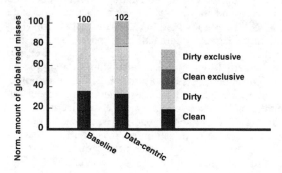

Figure 3: Execution time (left) and read miss breakdown (right) for the dynamic migratory sharing detection technique

with a *LS-ratio* of 100%. This means that if we only tag blocks that are never accessed by *read-only sequences*, we would only cover 1.8% of all load-store sequences. Table 6 shows our results in terms of coverage for other *LS-ratio*s. If we tag all blocks with a *LS-ratio* larger than 50%, we would cover 69.7% of all load-store sequences. However, since many of the tagged blocks are accessed by *read-only sequences* almost as often as *load-store sequences*, the gains from fewer global writes might be offset by a larger number of reads. Only tagging blocks with a *LS-ratio* larger than 80% might be a more conservative goal, which still covers 36.3% of all load-store sequences.

Overall, our results show that few load-store sequences are to blocks always accessed by such sequences. Tagging blocks as exclusive will be a tradeoff where a reduction of the number of global writes will also result in more read misses. Due to the overhead of actually finding and tagging blocks with a *LS-ratio* well above 50%, we assume this approach to be less feasible in practice.

4.4 Instruction-Centric Load-Store Optimization

In this section, we study the ability of instruction-centric load-store optimization techniques to increase the performance of the database workload. We explore three different schemes; *static*, *conservative*, and *dynamic*, all described in Section 2.3.

We explore three different detection distances, i.e. how close the store must follow the load for the load to be tagged as load-exclusive; within one, three, or five memory accesses. The schemes are therefore referred to as *static-X*, *conservative-X*, and *dynamic-X*, where X is either 1, 3, or 5. The results are shown in Figures 6 and 7, where *baseline* is without any optimizations. The left diagram of Figure 6 shows the number total number of messages in the network,

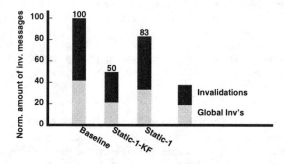

Figure 4: Invalidation messages for the instruction-centric schemes when statically tagging `kernel_flag`

while the right diagram emphasizes on the invalidation traffic. In Figure 7, the left diagram shows the execution times of the various schemes, while the right diagram shows the number of read misses.

Initially for the *static* scheme, loads that were followed by a store to the same block were tagged load-exclusive during the execution, and remained tagged so until the end of execution. This is a highly speculative approach since we are bound to even tag loads that are seldom followed by a store, i.e. it was sufficient for a load to be followed by a store *once* to be tagged as exclusive.

While the initial static technique, referred to as *static-1-KF*, was capable of reducing the amount of invalidations, as shown in Figure 4, it increased the number of read misses significantly. The number of read misses is shown in Figure 5. The high degree of speculation leads to a substantial amount of loads being wrongly tagged as exclusive with a

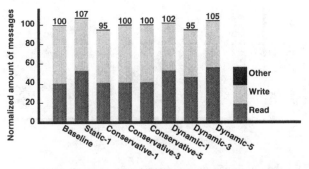

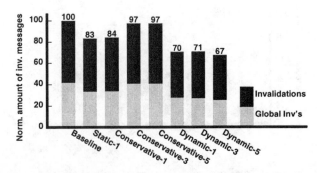

Figure 6: Total messages (left) and invalidation messages (right) for the instruction-centric techniques

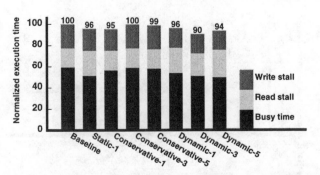

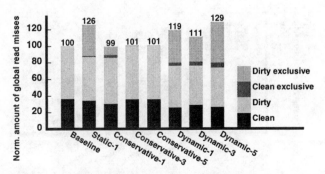

Figure 7: Execution time (left) and read miss breakdown (right) for the instruction-centric techniques

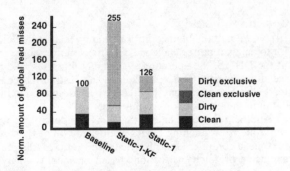

Figure 5: Read miss breakdown for the instruction-centric schemes when statically tagging kernel_flag

negative impact on performance.

Therefore, we analyzed the amount of exclusively tagged loads for the most prominent "bad" loads. A highly represented data structure in this category was the kernel entry spin-lock (kernel_flag). Since we wanted to exclude the negative impact from the kernel spin-lock, we statically tagged the loads to this variable as non-exclusive. The *static-1* in Figure 4 and 5, thus excludes tagging of the kernel spin-lock. As described above, although we see a substantial increase in invalidation messages for *static-1* as compared to *static-1-KF*, less "bad" loads are generated and we see a corresponding reduction of read misses.

In the *conservative* and *dynamic* schemes, a tagged load can be de-tagged if it is not followed by a store. The *conservative* scheme never re-tag loads, which means that only those loads that are always followed by a store to the same block will remain as load-exclusive instructions. Looking

at the results for the *conservative* scheme, *conservative-1* cuts the invalidation traffic as much as *static-1*, 16%, while the number of read misses is virtually unchanged compared to *baseline*. As a result, the total amount of network traffic compared to *baseline* is reduced by 5%.

The *dynamic* scheme allows loads to be tagged according to its most recent behavior. As a result, we see that the *dynamic-3* scheme is capable of reducing the invalidation traffic by 30%, and the total number of messages by 5%. For *dynamic-3*, it seems that the anomaly that read misses are reduced as compared to *dynamic-1* is partly due to a different interleaving of memory accesses to blocks with false sharing, and partly due to a different scheduling of transactions to processors by the operating system. Increasing the detection distance to 5 leads to further reductions of the invalidation traffic, but the much larger number of re-tags and de-tags of loads lead to a significant increase of the number of read misses that offset the reductions in write traffic.

The left diagram of Figure 7 shows the execution time breakdown of the various techniques. As can be seen, the *dynamic* scheme shows execution time reductions of up to 10%. Overall, we have seen that most of the stable gains come from a small detection distance. The difference in invalidation traffic between *conservative-1* and *dynamic-1* indicates that allowing the load and store to belong to different basic blocks that are still very close, the reduction in invalidation traffic can be nearly doubled.

It is interesting to note that, for most instructions operating on the key block cache in MySQL, we could confirm that the instruction-centric technique was successful in detecting the load-store sequences.

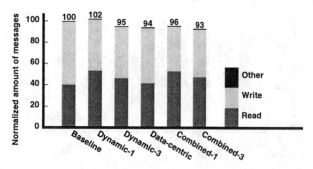 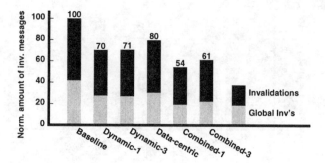

Figure 8: Total messages (left) and invalidation messages (right) for the combined data-centric and instruction-centric techniques

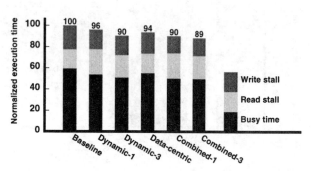 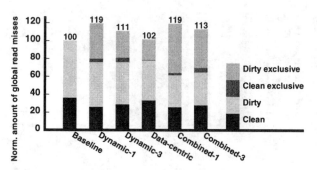

Figure 9: Execution time (left) and read miss breakdown (right) for the combined data-centric and instruction-centric techniques

4.5 Combining Data- and Instruction-Centric

Since data- and instruction-centric techniques potentially detect non-overlapping load-store sequences, we will in this section explore whether a combined technique will perform better than each of them separately. Our combined technique includes the dynamic instruction-centric scheme as well as support for the data-centric migratory sharing scheme. In order to combine the approaches, we analyzed all protocol transactions from the separate techniques that might interfere. The only modification to the data-centric scheme that we found useful was to set the *last-writer field* also at global load-exclusive requests, in addition to global write requests. The results are shown in Figures 8 and 9. *Combined-X* corresponds to the combination of the *data-centric* and the *dynamic-X* schemes.

The results show that the invalidation traffic can be reduced more heavily with the combined technique than with any of the techniques separately, while the number of read misses is hardly affected as compared to *dynamic*. Interestingly, the execution-time reductions of *combined-1* as shown in Figure 9 is additive with respect to *data-centric* and the *dynamic-1*, 10%. At larger detection distances, however, we only see a minor reduction of the execution time of *combined* as compared to *dynamic*.

5 Related Work

The work presented in this paper extends previous studies on protocols optimized for migratory sharing [4, 5] and load-store sequences [6] in several ways; (i) we make a complete characterization of the load-store behavior in an OLTP workload on both a global level and on program level,

(ii) we relate the obtained information on load-store behavior to data structures and code constructs in the source code of the DBMS, the operating system, and libraries, and (iii) we introduce the concept of data- and instruction-centric load-store optimizations. [4–6] have been described in more detail in the first sections of this paper.

Another related technique that aims at reducing the write stall time is prefetching blocks exclusively. In [13], Mowry presents a compiler algorithm that inserts non-binding read-exclusive prefetch instructions based on locality analysis. The compiler algorithm has been shown to be effective for regular, scientific/engineering applications, but it is generally difficult for the compiler to determine which references will miss in the cache. This drawback might lead to a significant instruction overhead for some applications. The compiler-based prefetching algorithm has so far not been applied to database workloads or operating systems.

For database workloads such as DSS and OLTP, several studies have gained profound knowledge on their memory behavior and performance issues [1,2,14–16]. Ranganathan et al. [2] first recognized substantial amounts of migratory sharing in OLTP. While they used traces from a commercial database server (Oracle 7.3.2), they had no potential to relate their findings to the source code and they did not include the operating system execution in their study. Their findings are important for this paper, since they show that the amount of migratory sharing in commercial database systems is in the same order as for our, open system.

Some previous studies have attacked the problem of long memory latencies in shared-memory multiprocessors for commercial applications, including relaxed memory consistency models [2], prefetching [14], out-of-order execution [2], and simultaneous multithreading [15]. While some of their techniques show tremendous potentials for execution time reductions, they are in principle orthogonal to the techniques explored in this paper. We believe that there are huge potentials for combining some of their techniques with load-exclusive fetching for even higher performance.

6 Conclusions

In this paper, we have characterized the existence of load-store sequences in a transaction processing system, and explored different techniques for detecting such load-store sequences. Our experimental methodology is based on program-driven simulation of a database handler as well as the operating system on a four-node multiprocessor system. The workload is based on the TPC-B benchmark.

Our results indicate that there is a substantial amount of load-store sequences in the database handler, the operating system, and in system libraries, and about 40% of all global writes belong to such load-store sequences. An important finding was that a majority of the load-store sequences originated from the operating system in its interaction with the database handler, which seriously limits any technique or study targeting only the DBMS software. We studied two conceptually different approaches for detecting and tagging load-store sequences exclusive; data-centric and instruction-centric.

For the data-centric technique, we evaluated two different approaches; one static and one dynamic. The dynamic data-centric technique, in essence the migratory sharing optimization proposed in [5], provided an execution time reduction in the order of 6%. As virtually all blocks accessed in load-store sequences were also accessed in a read-only fashion during parts of the execution, the static approach was limited in coverage to well below 50% of all load-store sequences. Thus, we expect performance gains from such static data-centric optimizations to be offset by the overhead to determine which blocks to tag.

We studied three different variations of an instruction-centric load-store detection scheme. Since only a minor fraction of all load-store sequences belong to the same basic block, it was important for the technique to also cover speculative load-store sequences. However, such a scheme should allow detected loads to be de-tagged, i.e. no longer being load-exclusive, in order not to offset any gain by increased read miss rates. The dynamic scheme was capable of reducing the execution time by up to 10%.

We also recognized that data- and instruction-centric detection schemes differ in which load-store sequences they successfully detect. A combination of the dynamic instruction-centric scheme and a previously proposed data-centric technique that detects migratory sharing proved to be slightly more effective.

Overall, we have shown only a limited potential for both data-centric and instruction-centric load-store optimization techniques to reduce ownership overhead for transaction processing workloads on multiprocessors as compared to scientific/engineering applications. The reasons for this are that migratory accesses only account for a fraction of all global write actions, and that the distance between loads and stores is large, imposing a high degree of speculation on instruction-centric techniques.

Acknowledgements

We are indebted to Sun Microsystems, Swedish Council for Planning and Coordination of Research (contract number 96238), Swedish National Board for Industrial and Technical Development (NUTEK) (grant number 97-09687), and Virtutech (SimICS) for being instrumental in providing us with an adequate infrastructure to carry out this research. We also thank Per Stenström and Anders Landin, for their valuable comments on this paper.

References

[1] L. A. Barroso, K. Gharachorloo, and E. Bugnion, "Memory System Characterization of Commercial Workloads," *Proc. of ISCA-25*, June 1998, pp. 3–14.

[2] P. Ranganathan, K. Gharachorloo, S. V. Adve, and L. A. Barroso, "Performance of Database Workloads on Shared-Memory Systems with Out-of-Order Processors," *Proc. of ASPLOS-8*, Oct. 1998, pp. 307–318.

[3] A. Gupta and W.-D. Weber, "Cache Invalidation Patterns in Shared-Memory Multiprocessors," *IEEE Trans. on Comp.*, vol. 41, no. 7, pp. 794–810, July 1992.

[4] A. L. Cox and R. J. Fowler, "Adaptive Cache Coherency for Detecting Migratory Shared Data," *Proc. of ISCA-20*, 1993, pp. 98–108.

[5] P. Stenström, M. Brorsson, and L. Sandberg, "An Adaptive Cache Coherence Protocol Optimized for Migratory Sharing," *Proc. of ISCA-20*, 1993, pp. 109–118.

[6] J. Skeppstedt and P. Stenström, "Using Dataflow Analysis Techniques to Reduce Ownership Overhead in Cache Coherence Protocols," *TOPLAS*, vol. 18, no. 6, pp. 659–682, November 1996.

[7] P. S. Magnusson, F. Dahlgren, H. Grahn, M. Karlsson, F. Larsson, F. Lundholm, A. Moestedt, J. Nilsson, P. Stenström, and B. Werner, "SimICS/sun4m: A Virtual Workstation," *Proc. of Usenix Annual Technical Conf.*, June 1998.

[8] Detron HB TcX AB and Monty Program KB, *MySQL v3.22 Reference Manual*, September 1998.

[9] Transaction Processing Performance Council, "TPC Benchmark B (Online Transaction Processing) Standard Specification," 1990.

[10] S. Kaxiras and J. R. Goodman, "Improving CC-NUMA Performance Using Instruction-Based Prediction," *Proc. of HPCA-5*, Jan. 1999, pp. 161–170.

[11] L. Lamport, "How to Make a Multiprocessor Computer that Correctly Executes Multiprocessor Programs," *IEEE Trans. on Comp.*, vol. C-28, no. 9, pp. 241–248, Sep. 1979.

[12] K. Gharachorloo, A. Gupta, and J. Hennessy, "Performance Evaluation of Memory Consistency Models for Shared-Memory Multiprocessors," *Proc. of ASPLOS-4*, April 1991, pp. 245–257.

[13] T. Mowry, *Tolerating Latency through Software-Controlled Prefetching*, Ph.D. thesis, Computer Systems Laboratory, Stanford University, 1994.

[14] P. Trancoso, J.-L. Larriba-Pey, Z. Zhang, and J. Torrellas, "The Memory Performance of DSS Commercial Workloads in Shared-Memory Multiprocessors," *Proc. of HPCA-3*, Feb. 1997, pp. 250–260.

[15] J. L. Lo, L. A. Barroso, S. J. Eggers, K. Gharachorloo, H. M. Levy, and S. S. Parekh, "An Analysis of Database Workload Performance on Simultaneous Multithreaded Processors," *Proc. of ISCA-25*, June 1998.

[16] M. Rosenblum, E. Bugnion, S. A. Herrod, E. Witchel, and A. Gupta, "The Impact of Architectural Trends on Operating System Performance," *Proc. of SOSP-15*, Dec. 1995, pp. 285–298.

Session C4

Network Embedding

Chair: Yuanyuan Yang
State University of New York at Stony Brook, USA

Routing and Embeddings in Cyclic Petersen Networks:
An Efficient Extension of the Petersen Graph

Chi-Hsiang Yeh and Behrooz Parhami
Department of Electrical and Computer Engineering
University of California,
Santa Barbara, CA 93106-9560, USA

Abstract

The Petersen graph is a Moore graph that has node degree 3, diameter 2, and optimal network size 10. In this paper, we present a class of interconnection networks, called cyclic Petersen networks (CPNs), which efficiently extend the Petersen graph to obtain larger networks with small diameter and node degree. We derive balanced routing algorithms and efficient embeddings for CPNs. In particular, we show that many normal mesh algorithms can be emulated on CPNs with a slowdown factor of about 1.1. We also show that complete CPNs can embed meshes, tori, meshes of trees, and folded Petersen networks with dilation 3, hypercubes and generalized hypercubes with dilation 4, and pyramids with dilation 5.

1 Introduction

The Petersen graph is a Moore graph that has 10 nodes of degree 3 and a diameter of 2, is symmetric, and is the most efficient small network in terms of node degree, diameter, and network size (see Fig. 1). Due to its unique and optimal properties, several network topologies based on the Petersen graph have been proposed and investigated in the literature [3, 4, 5, 7, 8, 9, 10, 11, 16].

In this paper, we present a class of interconnection networks called *cyclic Petersen networks (CPNs)*, which efficiently extend the Petersen graph to obtain larger networks with diameter and node degree smaller than those of a similar-size hypercube. The diameters of a 1-level CPN, a 2-level CPN, and l-level ring-CPNs, $l \geq 3$, are optimal within factors of 1, 1.25, and 1.8, respectively, given their node degrees; the "degree × diameter" costs [1] of a 1-level CPN, a 2-level CPN, and l-level CPNs, $l \geq 3$ are optimal within factors of 1, 1.25, and 1.8, respectively, for networks of any degree. We present efficient algorithms for balanced routing, efficient emulations, and constant-dilation embeddings in CPNs. In particular, we show that many normal mesh al-

Figure 1. The Petersen graph.

gorithms can be emulated on CPNs with a slowdown factor of about 1.1. Moreover, complete-CPNs can embed meshes, tori, meshes of trees, and folded Petersen networks with dilation 3, hypercubes, and generalized hypercubes with dilation 4, and pyramids with dilation 5. They can also emulate an l-D mesh under the all-port communication model with a factor of $\max(4, l+1)$ slowdown.

The remainder of this paper is organized as follows. In Section 2, we present cyclic Petersen networks and derive several basic properties and algorithms. In Section 3, we present enhanced CPNs, and derive efficient embeddings and emulation algorithms for them. In Section 4, we present clustered CPNs, which have smaller step sizes. In Section 5, we conclude the paper.

2 Basic Cyclic Petersen Networks

In this section, we define basic CPNs (also called ring-CPNs), explore some of their topological properties, and introduce the needed notation.

2.1 Definition of Basic CPNs

For convenience, for any $j_1 \geq j_2$, we let $Z_{j_1:j_2}$ denote $Z_{j_1}Z_{j_1-1}\cdots Z_{j_2}$, where Z can be any symbol, such as U, V or X.

Definition 2.1 (Ring-CPN): Let $P = (\mathcal{V}_\mathcal{P}, \mathcal{E}_\mathcal{P})$ be the Petersen graph. An l-level ring-cyclic Petersen network is defined as $(\mathcal{V}, \mathcal{E})$, where $\mathcal{V} = \{V_{l:1}|V_i \in \mathcal{V}_\mathcal{P}, i = 1, ..., l\}$ is

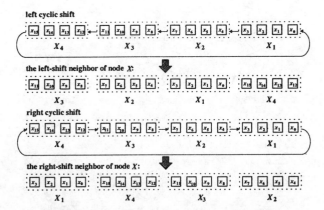

Figure 2. The derivation of shift links (neighbors) of a node $X = X_{4:1}$ in a 4-level ring-CPN. Symbols $X_i \in [0,9]$, $i = 1,2,3,4$, are represented by 4-bit binary numbers $x_{4i-1:4(i-1)}$.

the set of vertices, and $\mathcal{E} = \{(U_{l:1}, V_{l:1}) \mid U_i, V_i \in \mathcal{V}_P, i = 1,2,...,l$, satisfying $U_{l:2} = V_{l:2}$ and $(U_1, V_1) \in \mathcal{E}_P$, or $U_i = V_{(i \bmod l)+1}$, or $V_i = U_{(i \bmod l)+1}$, for $1 \le i \le l\}$ is the set of edges.

A 1-level CPN is the Petersen graph (see Fig. 1) and is called a *nucleus* of a CPN. Two nodes U and V are connected by an undirected link if and only if nodes U and V are neighbors within the same nucleus P, or the address of nodes U and V are cyclic shifts of the l-symbol addresses of one another (see Fig. 2). The former link is called a *nucleus link* and the latter is called a *left- (right-) shift link*. CPNs form a subclass of *cyclic-shift networks* (also called *cyclic networks*) [2, 17] that use the Petersen graph as the nucleus graph; cyclic-shift networks, in turn, form a subclass of *super-IP graphs* that use cyclic-shift operators as the *super-generators* [18, 20, 21].

Let $X^{(i)}$ be the address obtained from node X by performing i right cyclic shifts. That is, $X^{(0)} = X$ and $X^{(i)} = X_{i:1}X_{l:i+1}$ for $1 \le i < l$, where $X = X_{l:1}$. Note that $X^{(i)} = X^{(i \bmod l)}$. The addresses of *left- (right-) shift neighbors* of node X can be represented as $X^{(-1)}$ (or $X^{(1)}$, respectively). Let $X = X_{l:1}$ be a node in a ring-CPN, where $X_i \in \mathcal{V}_P$ and $X \ne X^{(i)}$ for $i = 1,2,...,l-1$. It can be seen that by the definition of ring-CPNs, nodes $X, X^{(1)}, X^{(2)},..., X^{(l-1)}$ form an l-node ring, connected through shift links. In general, the majority of rings formed by the shift links are of this type. However, when l is not a prime number, there will also be shorter rings with l_f nodes, where l_f divides l (see Fig. 3a). Since the addresses of shift links (neighbors) are obtained by performing cyclic shift on the address of a node, and these derived neighbors form a ring, we call such networks "ring-cyclic" Petersen networks. The rings with l nodes are called the *cyclic-shift (CS) graphs* of the ring-CPN; the rings with

l_f nodes are called the *degenerate CS graphs* of the ring-CPN.

Note that a node with the same l symbols in its address has no shift links (or, alternatively, has shift links connecting to itself) and is called a *leader*. Leaders can be used as I/O ports or be connected to other leaders via their unused ports to provide better fault tolerance or to improve the performance and reduce the diameter of ring-CPNs without increasing the node degree of the network. Varying the connectivity between leaders results in other classes of ring-CPNs.

2.2 Routing and Topological Properties

The number of nodes in a ring-CPN is increased by a factor of 10 when the level is increased by 1, and the nucleus Petersen graph has 10 nodes. Thus, the number of nodes N of an l-level ring-CPN is

$$N = 10^l. \tag{1}$$

From Eq. 1, the level of an N-node ring-CPN is

$$l = \log_{10} N. \tag{2}$$

The node degree of an l-level ring-CPN is

$$d = \begin{cases} 3 \text{ when } l = 1, \\ 4 \text{ when } l = 2, \\ 5 \text{ when } l \ge 3. \end{cases} \tag{3}$$

Suppose that a routing algorithm for the nucleus P is known. Let the addresses of nodes X and Y within the l-level ring-CPN be $X_{l:1}$ and $Y_{l:1}$, respectively, where $X_i, Y_i \in \mathcal{V}_G$. In what follows, we present a routing algorithm to route a packet from node X to node Y in an l-level ring-CPN using left- (right-) shift links and nucleus links.

Route(X,Y)

For $i = l$ downto 1 (or $i = 1$ to l)
Route the packet to node Y_i (or $Y_{(i \bmod l)+1}$)
  within the nucleus in which the packet currently resides.
If $i \ne 1$ (or $i \ne l$), send the packet
  through the left-shift link (or right-shift link).

If the routing algorithm on the nucleus P requires at most $T_R(P)$ time, the routing algorithm on an l-level ring-CPN requires time at most

$$T_R(l) = l T_R(P) + l - 1.$$

Since the diameter of the Petersen graph is 2, an optimal routing algorithm requires time at most $T_R(P) = 2$, leading to

$$T_R(l) = 3l - 1. \tag{4}$$

This leads to the diameter of an l-level ring-CPN, which is

$$3l - 1 = \frac{3}{\log_2 10} \log_2 N - 1 \approx 0.9 \log_2 N - 1.$$

The expected traffic on the network links of a ring-CPN is approximately balanced when the sources and destinations of the packets are uniformly distributed over network nodes. This can be intuitively justified by observing that the average time for an intra-nucleus routing phase is 1.5, the routing algorithm uses roughly the same number of intra-nucleus and shift routing phases, and each node has 1.5 times more nucleus links than shift links (3 versus 2). When $l = 2$ and the external arrival rate is λ, the average traffic on a network link is 0.972λ, while the traffic on a shift link is λ and the traffic on any nucleus link is smaller than λ. Therefore, the expected traffic on any network link is no more than 2.9% above the average traffic on all network links. For any $l \geq 3$ the expected traffic on a network link in an l-level ring-CPN exceeds the average traffic on all network links by no more than 6%.

2.3   Emulation of Normal Mesh Algorithms

If a mesh algorithm executes t operations (or routing steps) on the average along a dimension before executing an operation along the next consecutive dimension (cyclicly), we call it a *normal mesh algorithm with (an average of) t row operations*. Note that a node can send data to both its west and east neighbors along the same dimension at the same time. Many mesh algorithms naturally fall into this category. Many other algorithms can be easily transformed to a normal mesh algorithm without affecting the leading constant of the running time.

In what follows, we show that normal mesh algorithms can be emulated on CPNs efficiently.

Theorem 2.1 *A normal mesh algorithm for l-dimensional* $10 \times 10 \times \cdots \times 10$ *meshes with an average of t row operations can be emulated on an l-level ring-CPN with a slowdown factor of* $1 + \frac{1}{t}$.

Proof: The Petersen graph contains a 10-node linear array so transmissions along dimension-1 mesh links can be performed directly. To emulate operations along dimension a, a node X in the guest mesh is mapped onto node $X^{(a-1)}$ of the host CPN. Since operations are performed along consecutive dimensions when the dimension is changed, only one transmission along cyclic-shift links is required for the change of mapping. Note that we assume that the data held by a node for future computation can be transmitted in one unit of time, which is true for some algorithms such as sorting. If the required transmission time is increased, the overhead for emulation is simply increased accordingly. Since

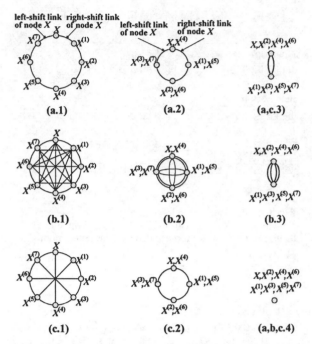

Figure 3. Various CS graphs and degenerate CS graphs containing a node X within 8-level CPNs. (a) (degenerate) CS graphs that are simple rings. (b) (degenerate) CS graphs that are complete graphs. (c) (degenerate) CS graphs that are chordal rings. (x.1) for node X with $X \neq X^{(4)}$. (x.2) for node $X = X_{8:1}$ with $X_{8:5} = X_{4:1}$ and $X \neq X^{(2)}$. (x.3) for node X with $X_{8:7} = X_{6:5} = X_{4:3} = X_{2:1}$ and $X \neq X^{(1)}$. (x.4) for node X with $X = X^{(1)}$ (i.e., $X_i = X_j$, $i, j = 1, 2, ..., 8$).

$\frac{T}{t} - 1$ additional steps are required for routing along cyclic-shift links on the average during T steps of the normal mesh algorithm the slowdown factor is $1 + \frac{1}{t}$. $\quad\square$

In many normal mesh algorithms of interest t is close to 9 so the slowdown factor is close to 1.1.

3   Enhanced Cyclic Petersen Networks

In this section we generalize the definition of basic CPNs to enhanced CPNs. We derive a variety of efficient embeddings and emulation algorithms for them and propose a scheme for routing in enhanced CPNs with balanced utilization over network links.

3.1   Definition of Enhanced CPNs

An enhanced CPN is usually obtained by adding more links to the original CS graphs (i.e., the l-node rings) of a ring-CPN. More precisely, the original CS graph formed by nodes X, $X^{(1)}$, $X^{(2)}$,..., $X^{(l-1)}$ and their shift links are replaced by another graph (or hypergraph), such as a complete graph or a chordal ring, that connects nodes $X, X^{(1)}, X^{(2)}, ..., X^{(l-1)}$; a degenerate CS graph is replaced by the degenerate version of the new CS graph. The nucleus links remain unchanged.

In what follows we formally define enhanced CPNs that use complete graphs as the CS graphs.

Definition 3.1 (Complete-CPN): Let the nucleus graph be a Petersen graph $P = (\mathcal{V}_P, \mathcal{E}_P)$. An l-level complete-cyclic Petersen network is defined as the graph complete-CPN $= (\mathcal{V}, \mathcal{E})$, where $\mathcal{V} = \{V_{l:1} | V_i \in \mathcal{V}_P, i = 1, ..., l,\}$ is the set of vertices, and $\mathcal{E} = \{(U_{l:1}, V_{l:1}) | U_i, V_i \in \mathcal{V}_P, i = 1, 2, ..., l$, satisfying $U_{l:2} = V_{l:2}$ and $(U_1, V_1) \in \mathcal{E}_P$, or $V = U^{(i)}$, for some integer $i, 1 \le i < l\}$ is the set of edges.

The directed link connecting node U to node $V = U^{(i-1)}$ is called link C^i, which corresponds to i right cyclic shifts. Link C^{-i} represent a shift link corresponding to i left cyclic shifts and $C = C^1$. The rule to construct an enhanced CPN using other CS graphs is similar (see Fig. 3 for examples using loop-based topologies [13, 14]). Note that there may be multiple links between two nodes in a degenerate CS graph. For example, node $V = 0101$ in a 4-level complete-CPN is connected to node $U = 1010$ with two links since $V = U^{(1)}$ and $V = U^{(3)}$. Several examples illustrating multiple links in degenerate CS graphs of 8-level CPNs are given in Fig. 3.

A complete-CPN has the strongest embedding and emulation capacity among all CPNs and also the highest node degree, which is equal to $\log_{10} N + 2 \approx 0.3 \log_2 N + 2$. But the degree of a complete-CPN is still a small number (e.g., $d \le 7$) for networks of practical size (e.g., $N \le 100K$).

3.2 Embeddings and Algorithms Emulation

Embeddings and emulation between hypercubic networks and for new network topologies have been an important and intensively studied research area [6, 12, 15]. In this subsection, we present efficient emulation algorithms for complete-CPNs under the all-port communication model. We also derive constant dilation embeddings and packings of trees, meshes, tori, hypercubes, meshes of trees, pyramids, generalized hypercubes, folded Petersen networks, as well as any product network in complete-CPNs.

Theorem 3.1 *Any algorithm in a $10^{l_1} \times 10^{l_2} \times \cdots \times 10^{l_m}$ mesh under the all-port communication model can be emulated on an l-level complete-CPN with a slowdown factor of at most $\max(4, l+1)$, where $\sum_{i=1}^{m} l_i = l$.*

Proof: The emulation algorithm under the all-port communication model simply performs single-dimension emulation for all dimensions at the same time with proper schedul-

Links of a complete-CPN	1 W	E	2 W	E	3 W	E	4 W	E	5 W	E
Step 1	W	E	C¹	—	—	C²	C³	—	—	C⁴
Step 2		W	C¹	C²	E	—	C³	C⁴	—	
Step 3			C⁴	E	W	C³	—	—	—	—
Step 4				C⁴	C³	W	—	—	E	
Step 5					C²	E	W	C¹		
Step 6						C²	C¹			

(a)

Links of a complete-CPN	1 W	E	2 W	E	3 W	E	4 W	E
Step 1	W	E	C¹	—	—	C²	C³	—
Step 2		W	C¹	C²	E	—	C³	
Step 3			C³	—	W	C²	—	E
Step 4				E	C²	W	C¹	
Step 5					C³	C¹		

(b)

Figure 4. Schedules for emulating meshes on complete-CPNs under the all-port communication model. Note that a certain link appears at most once in a row, and each column for dimension $j \ge 2$ consists of links C^{j-1}, W, C^{1-j} or C^{j-1}, E, C^{1-j}. (a) Emulating a 5-dimensional mesh on a 5-level complete-CPN. (b) Emulating a 4-dimensional mesh on a 4-level complete-CPN.

ing to avoid congestion. Let W (or E) represent the directed nucleus link that is connected to a node's west neighbor (or east neighbor, respectively), in the emulated l-D mesh. A packet for a dimension-j west (or east) neighbor, $2 \le j \le l$, in the emulated mesh will be sent through links C^{j-1}, W, C^{1-j} (or C^{j-1}, E, C^{1-j}, respectively). A possible schedule for emulating an l-D $10 \times 10 \times \cdots \times 10$ mesh can be obtained as follows.

We first consider the case when l is odd.

- At time 1, each node sends the packets for its dimension-1 neighbors (in the emulated mesh) through links W and E.
- At time 1, each node also sends the packets for its west neighbors of even dimension and east neighbors of odd dimension $i, i = 2, 3, 4, ..., l$, through links C^{i-1}.
- At time 2, each node sends the packets for its east neighbors of even dimension and west neighbors of odd dimension $i, i = 2, 3, 4, ..., l$, through links C^{i-1}.
- At even time $t = 2, 4, ..., l-1$, each node forwards the packets for its west neighbors of even dimension t through links W and then at the next time step, each node forwards the packets through links C^{1-t}.

- At even time $t = 2, 4, \ldots, l-1$, each node also forwards the packets for its east neighbors of odd dimension $t + 1$ through links E and then at the next time step, each node forwards the packets through links C^{-t}.

- At odd time $t = 3, 5, \ldots, l$, each node forwards the packets for its east neighbors of even dimension $t - 1$ through links E and then at the next time step, each node forwards the packets through links C^{2-t}.

- At odd time $t = 3, 5, \ldots, l$, each node forwards the packets for its west neighbors of odd dimension t through links W and then at the next time step, each node forwards the packets through links C^{1-t}.

Figure 4a shows such a schedule for emulating a 5-dimensional mesh on a 5-level complete-CPN.

In what follows we extend the previous schedule to the case when l is even and $l \geq 4$. We initially start with the schedule for an $(l + 1)$-level complete-CPN. Clearly, the transmissions corresponding to the emulation of dimension $l + 1$ in the initial schedule are not used by the l-level complete-CPN. Therefore, we can now reschedule the link E of dimension l (from time l) to time $l - 1$. We then swap the time for the rescheduled link E with that of a link E of smaller dimension. Due to the previous modifications for dimensions j, we also have to modify the schedule for some links C^{1-j} and maybe links C^{j-1}. In particular, we will move link C^{1-j} to the step after the use of link E for the emulation of dimension-l link E in the mesh. As a result, the time required for emulation under the all-port communication model is equal to $l + 1$ when $l \geq 4$, and is equal to 4 when $l = 2$ or 3. Figure 4b shows such a schedule for emulating a 4-dimensional mesh on a 4-level complete-CPN.

Since an m-D $10^{l_1} \times 10^{l_2} \times \cdots \times 10^{l_m}$ mesh is a subgraph of an l-D $10 \times 10 \times \cdots \times 10$ mesh, the results follow. $\quad\square$

An l-level folded Petersen network [11], a recently proposed competitor for the hypercube, is defined as $\underbrace{P \times P \times \cdots P}_{l}$, which is the iterative Cartesian product on the Petersen graph P. An l-level folded Petersen network is symmetric and has node degree $3l \approx 0.9 \log_2 N$, diameter $2l \approx 0.6 \log_2 N$, and average distance about $1.5l \approx 0.45 \log_2 N$, all of which are smaller than those of a similar-size hypercube. Some efficient algorithms have been developed for folded Petersen networks [5, 10, 11].

Theorem 3.2 *Any algorithm in an l-level folded Petersen network under the all-port communication model can be emulated on an l-level complete-CPN with a slowdown factor of* $\max(6, l+1)$.

Proof: The proof is similar to the proof of Theorem 3.1 and the corresponding proofs in [19, 21]. $\quad\square$

In what follows, we present constant dilation embeddings and packings of a variety of popular topologies in complete-CPNs.

Theorem 3.3 *An l-level complete-CPN can embed a $10^{l_1} \times 10^{l_2} \times \cdots \times 10^{l_m}$ mesh or an l-level folded Petersen network with load 1, expansion 1, and dilation 3, where $\sum_{i=1}^{m} l_i = l$.*

Proof: Any link of an l-level folded Petersen network can be mapped to a cyclic shift link, a nucleus link, followed by another cyclic shift link (similar to the emulation of Theorem 3.2). Since an l-level folded Petersen network contains a $10^{l_1} \times 10^{l_2} \times \cdots \times 10^{l_m}$ mesh the results follow. $\quad\square$

Theorem 3.4 *An l-level complete-CPN can pack* $\binom{l}{i}$ *copies of an*

$$\underbrace{m \times m \times \cdots m}_{i} \times \underbrace{(10-m) \times (10-m) \times \cdots (10-m)}_{l-i}$$

torus for each $i = 0, 1, 2, \ldots, l$ with load 1, expansion 1, and dilation 3, where $m = 8$ or 9. An l-level complete-CPN can pack 2^l copies of a 5-ary l-cube with load 1, expansion 1, and dilation 3.

Proof: Since a Petersen graph can pack two 5-node rings, or an 8-node and a 2-node ring, or a 9-node and a 1-node ring as subgraphs, $\binom{l}{i}$ copies of an $\underbrace{m \times m \times \cdots m}_{i} \times \underbrace{(10-m) \times (10-m) \times \cdots (10-m)}_{l-i}$ torus, $i = 0, 1, 2, \ldots, l$, form node and edge disjoint subgraphs of an l-level folded Petersen network, where $m = 5, 8,$ or 9. Therefore, the embedding results follow from Theorem 3.3 for embedding a folded Petersen network in a complete-CPN. Since these tori collectively have 10^l nodes, the expansion is equal to 1. $\quad\square$

Theorem 3.5 *An l-level complete-CPN can embed an l-dimensional radix-10 generalized hypercube, or any l-dimensional Cartesian product network with 10-node factor graphs with load 1, expansion 1, and dilation at most equal to 4.*

Proof: Since the diameter of the Petersen graph is equal to 2, any link of the above graphs can be mapped to a cyclic shift link, two links of a nucleus Petersen graph, followed by another cyclic shift link. $\quad\square$

Theorem 3.6 *An l-level complete-CPN can pack* $\binom{l}{i}$ *copies of a $(3l - 2i)$-dimensional hypercube for each $i = 0, 1, 2, \ldots, l$ with load 1, expansion 1, and dilation 4.*

Proof: Since a 10-node complete graph contains a 3-dimensional hypercube and a 1-dimensional hypercube as subgraphs, $\binom{l}{i}$ copies of a $(3l - 2i)$-dimensional hypercube for $i = 0, 1, 2, \ldots, l$, form node and edge disjoint subgraphs of a radix-10 l-dimensional generalized hypercube. The packing result follows from Theorem 3.5 for embedding a generalized hypercube in a complete-CPN. Since these hypercubes collectively have 10^l nodes, the expansion is equal to 1. $\square$

Theorem 3.7 *An l-level complete-CPN can pack a complete binary tree of height $3l - 1$ and two complete binary trees of height $3l - 4$ with load 1 and dilation 3.*

Proof: It follows from Theorem 3.3 and the fact that these three trees form node and edge disjoint subgraphs of an l-level folded Petersen network [11]. $\square$

Theorem 3.8 *An l-level complete-CPN can pack a $2^{3m-1} \times 2^{3(l-m)-1}$ mesh of trees, two $2^{3m-1} \times 2^{3(l-m)-4}$ meshes of trees, two $2^{3m-4} \times 2^{3(l-m)-1}$ meshes of trees, and four $2^{3m-4} \times 2^{3(l-m)-4}$ meshes of trees with load 1 and dilation 3.*

Proof: It follows from Theorem 3.3 and the fact that these meshes of trees form node and edge disjoint subgraphs of an l-level folded Petersen network [11]. $\square$

Lemma 3.9 *Let t_1, t_2, t_3 be the load, expansion, and dilation for embedding graph G in an l-level folded Petersen network. Then an l-level complete-CPN can embed graph G with load t_1, expansion t_2, and dilation $2t_3 + 1$.*

Proof: From Theorem 3.3, we know that a link in a folded Petersen network can be mapped to a shift link, a nucleus link, and finally another shift link in a complete-CPN. It can be seen that two connected links can be mapped to a shift link, a nucleus link, a shift link, a nucleus link, and finally another shift link, since two shift links in a CS graph of a complete-CPN (which is an l-node complete graph) can be replaced by a shift link. By induction, a path consisting of t links in a folded Petersen network can be mapped to a path consisting of $2t_3 + 1$ links in a complete-CPN. $\square$

Theorem 3.10 *An l-level complete-CPN can pack $\binom{l}{i} \cdot 2^l + \binom{l}{i} \cdot 2^{l-1}$ copies of a $2^i \times 2^i$ pyramid for all $i = 0, 1, 2, \ldots, l$ with load 1, expansion smaller than 1.25, and dilation 5.*

Proof: It follows from Lemma 3.9 and the fact that these pyramids can be packed in an l-level folded Petersen network with load 1 and dilation 2 [11]. These pyramids have $\frac{4}{5}10^l + 2^{2l-1}$ nodes collectively so the expansion is smaller than 1.25. $\square$

The embeddings presented in this subsection can be easily extended to other classes of CPNs. For example, when $l = 2$ or 3, ring-CPNs are the same as complete-CPNs, so these embedding and emulation results can be directly applied to them. When $l = 4$ or 5, the dilations for embedding and packing the previous networks (from Theorems 3.3 to 3.10) in ring-CPNs are only increased by 2 (additively), except for the embedding of pyramids, whose dilation is increased by 3 (additively). Since networks of size smaller than or equal to 100K seem to be sufficient for interconnection networks in the near future, the dilations for embedding these popular topologies in any type of CPNs are all small numbers in practice. Since many efficient algorithms have been designed for the guest graphs considered in this subsection [6, 12] and the proposed embeddings and emulation algorithms are quite efficient, we can obtain a vast variety of efficient algorithms for CPNs through embeddings and emulation.

Although enhanced CPNs using complete graphs have good performance for algorithm emulation, their node degrees will vary with the number of levels l. Therefore, it may be desirable to use loop-based networks [14] or other small networks as the CS graph (see Fig. 3bd) to obtain networks whose cost and performance fall between those of ring-CPN and complete-CPN.

3.3 Routing with Balanced Traffic

The routing algorithm presented in Subsection 2.2 can be applied to enhanced CPNs without modification as long as the new (degenerate) CS graph contains a Hamiltonian cycle. However, the traffic over network links is not balanced since the additional shift links in the CS graphs are underutilized. In this subsection, we introduce a routing scheme for enhanced cyclic Petersen networks that can uniformly utilize network links.

Assume that a nucleus Petersen graph or several nucleus Petersen graphs are placed within the same module (e.g., a chip, board, or multi-chip module (MCM)), then nucleus links become on-module links and all or most shift links become off-module links. If we can balance the traffic on shift links, then we can always find an appropriate bandwidth for on-module links so that no network link is congested. It is reasonable to make on-module links faster than this required bandwidth to further improve the performance since it is relatively cheaper to implement on-module links with higher bandwidth and the number of transmissions over nucleus links is larger than that over shift links.

Recall that the routing algorithm Route(X,Y) given in Subsection 2.2 is composed of repeated routing within a nucleus and transmission over a shift link C (or C^{-1}) for $l-1$ iterations, followed by routing within a nucleus. This algorithm works because the shift links C or C^{-1} bring each digit of the address of the source node X to the rightmost position exactly once. That is, shift links $\underbrace{CC\cdots C}_{l-1}$ bring the 2nd, 3rd, ... , l^{th} digits to the rightmost position (in that order); shift links $\underbrace{C^{-1}C^{-1}\cdots C^{-1}}_{l-1}$ bring the lth, ... , 3rd, 2nd, digits to the rightmost position. Similarly, we can find a routing algorithm for the enhanced CPN if and only if we can find a sequence of shift links that can bring each digit of the address of the source node X to the rightmost position at least once.

When l is a prime number, $l-1$ shift links C^i for any $i=1,2,\ldots,l-1$ can be used for routing. For example, when $l=5$, four shift links C^2 bring the 3th, 5th, 2nd, and finally the 4th digits to the rightmost position; four shift links C^3 bring the 4th, 2nd, 5th, and finally the 3rd digits to the rightmost position. Therefore, as long as we use shift links C^i for routing with probability $\frac{1}{l-1}$, the traffic among all the shift links of the l-level complete-CPN is exactly balanced, assuming uniformly distributed destinations. Note that the last digit brought to the rightmost position should be "corrected" to be equal to the 1st digit of the destination node Y (by routing within the nucleus to which the destination node Y belongs). If it is initially the ith digit of the source node X, then the jth digit of the source node X should be "corrected" to be equal to the $(j-i+1)^{th}$ digit of the destination node Y.

When l is not a prime number, routing with balanced utilizations is somewhat more complicated. We can see that when $l=4$, applying shift links C^2 alone cannot bring the 2nd or the 4th digits to the rightmost position, so we need a different routing algorithm. Fortunately, we can always find a combination of different classes of shift links that accomplish the job. For example, when $l=4$, we can use shift links $C^2C^1C^2$ or $C^2C^3C^2$ for routing. We can also use $l-1$ shift links C (or $C^{-1}=C^3$). If we assign probability $1/4$ to each of the above sequences for routing, it can be seen that the utilizations for these three shift links are the same; more precisely, the average number of shift links C^i that will be used for routing a packet is slightly smaller than 1 for each $i=1,2,3$. When $l=6$, we can, again, use $l-1$ shift links C^1 (or $C^{-1}=C^5$) for routing. We can also use one of the following 4 sequences

$$C^2C^2C^1C^2C^2, C^4C^4C^5C^4C^4, C^3C^1C^3C^1C^3, \text{ or } C^3C^5C^3C^5C^3$$

for routing. If we assign probability $\frac{1}{12},\frac{1}{12},\frac{1}{4},\frac{1}{4},\frac{1}{6},\frac{1}{6}$ for the above sequences to be used, the utilizations for these five shift links will be the same; more precisely, the aver-

age number of shift links C^i that will be used for a routing task is equal to 1 for each $i=1,2,\ldots,5$. Routing in complete-CPNs of higher level can be done is a similar manner. In fact, we may omit the first j iterations in algorithm Route(X,Y) when the least significant digits of the source $X_jX_{j-1}\cdots X_1$ happen to be the same as the most significant digits of the destination $Y_lY_{l-1}\cdots Y_{l-j+1}$. If we take advantage of this property, the expected traffic on the cyclic-shift links becomes slightly different. However, a set of probabilities that are slightly different from the previous ones can always be found to exactly balance the expected traffic, leading to the following theorem.

Theorem 3.11 *There exist a set of sequences of shift links and a corresponding set of probabilities for routing in a complete-CPN such that the traffic among all shift links of the complete-CPN is exactly balanced.*

When the destinations are not uniformly distributed over all network nodes, we may need to adjust the probabilities for the sequences to be used. For example, when a task in the enhanced CPN is emulating a normal mesh algorithm, the task will generate a considerable amount of traffic over shift links C and C^{-1}. Therefore, we have to use sequences that involve fewer or no shift links C or C^{-1} more frequently when performing other routing tasks, in order to balance the utilizations of shift links. This can be done in enhanced CPNs since only a subset of shift-link classes are required when routing a packet and we have several choices for the combination of shift links to be used.

The routing strategies proposed in this subsection can be easily generalized to other classes of enhanced CPNs. For example, consider $l=6$ with the CS graph of the CPN being a degree-3 chordal ring; that is, it has three shift links $C^1, C^3,$ and C^5. We can use one of the following 4 sequences $C^1C^1C^1C^1C^1, C^5C^5C^5C^5C^5, C^3C^1C^3C^1C^3,$ or $C^3C^5C^3C^5C^3$ for routing. If we assign probability $1/4$ for each of the above sequences, it can be seen that the utilizations for these three shift links are approximately the same. These techniques can also be applied to general cyclic-shift networks [17, 18].

4 Clustered CPNs – A Scalable Variant

Although CPNs have good performance and embedding capabilities, their size increases by a factor of 10 with each added level, making it difficult to closely match the network size to the need for computational power. In this subsection, we present a method for obtaining variants of CPNs with smaller step size.

A 2-level CPN is built from 10 nuclei, each of which is a Petersen graph. To obtain a smaller network, we can simply remove some of its nuclei; the resultant network is called a *2-level clustered CPN*.

Theorem 4.1 *The diameter of a 2-level clustered CPN is at most 5.*

Proof: Let $X = X_2X_1$ and $Y = Y_2Y_1$ be the addresses of the source and destination nodes. The routing algorithm Route(X, Y) for a 2-level CPN will send the packet out of nucleus X_2 to nucleus Y_2. Since nucleus Y_2 cannot be one of the removed nuclei, the algorithm Route(X, Y) is directly applicable to a clustered CPN. Therefore, the diameter of a 2-level CPN is upper bounded by 5. □

Note that the removed links of the network nodes can be reconnected to further reduce the average distance and/or diameter and to improve the fault tolerance properties. To obtain higher level CPNs with small step size, we refer the reader to [17, 18] for several possible strategies. Other variants of CPNs can be found in [16].

5 Conclusion

In this paper, we have presented cyclic Petersen networks as efficient extension of the Petersen graph for small- to large-scale parallel processing. We derived efficient embeddings and packings of meshes, tori, meshes of trees, folded Petersen networks, hypercubes, generalized hypercubes and pyramids for CPNs. We also developed algorithms for balanced routing and efficient emulations in them.

References

[1] Bhuyan, L.N. and D.P. Agrawal, "Generalized hypercube and hyperbus structures for a computer network," *IEEE Trans. Comput.*, vol. 33, no. 4, Apr. 1984, pp. 323-333.

[2] Cypher, R. and J.L.C. Sanz, "Hierarchical shuffle-exchange and de Bruijn networks," *Proc. IEEE Symp. Parallel and Distributed Processing,* 1992, pp. 491-496.

[3] Das, S.K. and A.K. Banerjee, "Hyper Petersen networks: yet another hypercube-like topology," *Proc. Symp. Frontiers of Massively Parallel Computation* 1992, pp. 270-277.

[4] Das, S.K., S.R. Öhring, and A.K. Banerjee, "Embeddings into hyper Petersen networks: yet another hypercube–like interconnection topology," *Journal of VLSI Design*, Vol. 2, no. 4, pp. 335-351, 1995.

[5] Das, S.K., D.H. Hohndel, M. Ibel, and S.R. Öhring, "Efficient communication in folded Petersen networks," *Int'l J. Foundations of Computer Science,* vol. 8, no. 2, Jun. 1997, pp. 163-185.

[6] Leighton, F.T., *Introduction to Parallel Algorithms and Architectures: Arrays, Trees, Hypercubes,* Morgan-Kaufman, San Mateo, CA, 1992.

[7] Öhring, S. and S.K. Das, "The folded Petersen network: a new communication–efficient multiprocessor topology,"

Proc. Int'l Conf. Parallel Processing 1993, Vol. I, pp. 311-314.

[8] Öhring, S., S.K. Das and D.H. Hohndel, "Scalable interconnection networks based on the Petersen graph," *Proc. Int'l Conf. Parallel and Distributed Computing Systems* 1994, pp. 581-586.

[9] Öhring, S. and S.K. Das, "Efficient communication on the folded Petersen interconnection networks," *Proc. Parallel Architectures and Languages Europe,* 1994, pp. 689-700.

[10] Öhring, S., D.H. Hohndel, and S.K. Das, "Fault tolerant communication algorithms on the folded Petersen networks based on arc-disjoint spanning trees," *Proc. Conpar 94/VAPP VI,* Vol. 854, 1994, pp. 749-760.

[11] Öhring, S. and S.K. Das, "Folded Petersen cube networks: new competitors for the hypercubes," *IEEE Trans. Parallel Distrib. Sys.,* vol. 7, no. 2, Feb. 1996, pp. 151-168.

[12] Parhami, B., *Introduction to Parallel Processing: Algorithms and Architectures*, Plenum Press, 1999.

[13] Parhami, B. and D.-M. Kwai, "Periodically regular chordal rings," *IEEE Trans. Parallel Distrib. Sys.,* vol. 10, Jun. 1999, pp. 658-672.

[14] Raghavendra, C.S., M. Gerla, and A. Avizienis, "Reliable loop topologies for large local computer networks," *IEEE Trans. Comput.,* vol. C-34, Jan. 1985, pp. 46-55.

[15] Schwabe, E.J., "Efficient embeddings and simulations for hypercubic networks," Ph.D. dissertation, Dept. Electrical Engineering and Computer Science, Massachusetts Institute of Technology, 1991.

[16] Yeh, C.-H. and B. Parhami, "Cyclic Petersen networks: efficient fixed-degree interconnection networks for large-scale multicomputer systems," *Proc. Int'l Conf. Parallel and Distributed Processing: Techniques and Applications,* 1996, pp. 549-560.

[17] Yeh, C.-H. and B. Parhami, "Cyclic networks – a family of versatile fixed-degree interconnection architectures," *Proc. Int'l Parallel Processing Symp.,* Apr. 1997, 739-743.

[18] Yeh, C.-H., "Efficient low-degree interconnection networks for parallel processing: topologies, algorithms, VLSI layouts, and fault tolerance," Ph.D. dissertation, Dept. Electrical & Computer Engineering, Univ. of California, Santa Barbara, Mar. 1998.

[19] Yeh, C.-H. and E.A. Varvarigos, "Macro-star networks: efficient low-degree alternatives to star graphs," *IEEE Trans. Parallel Distrib. Sys.,* vol. 9, no. 10, Oct. 1998, pp. 987-1003.

[20] Yeh, C.-H. and B. Parhami, "The index-permutation graph model for hierarchical interconnection networks," *Proc. Int'l Conf. Parallel Processing,* Sep. 1999, to appear.

[21] Yeh, C.-H. and B. Parhami, "A unified model for hierarchical networks based on an extension of Cayley graphs," *IEEE Trans. Parallel Distrib. Sys.,* to appear.

Contention Free Embedding of Complete Binary Trees into 3D Meshes in Half and Full-Duplexed Network Models*

Sang-Kyu Lee

Department of Computer Science
Sookmyung Women's University
Seoul, Korea

Ju-Young Lee

Department of Computer Science
Duksung Women's University
Seoul, Korea

Abstract

We consider the problem of dimension-ordered embedding of complete binary trees into 3-dimensional meshes without link contention. In this paper, the embedding problems are studied under two different network models: half-duplexed networks and full-duplexed networks.

Gibbons and Paterson [5] showed that a complete binary tree T_p could be disjointedly embedded into a full-duplexed 2-dimensional mesh of optimum size without dimension-ordered routing. Using the dimension-ordered routing, the authors showed that T_p could be embedded into a 3-dimensional mesh of optimum size with link congestion two [6].

This paper presents the dimension-ordered embedding algorithms of the complete binary trees into the wormhole routed 3-dimensional meshes without link contention achieving expansion of no larger than 1.125 of optimum in half-duplexed network model and optimum in full-duplexed network model.

Key Words: parallel processing, embedding, interconnection network

1 Introduction

In some computations on parallel and distributed systems, communications between processing elements become a bottleneck in total execution time of a parallel application. The exact matching between the communication structure of the application and the interconnection network in the system should be the best way to perform a parallel program on a parallel computer system. However, it is often a waste of time and money to redesign an algorithm and rewrite a code for each existing application every time the system is updated with a different network topologies. Some-

times, it would be better if the system supports flexible application-dependent virtual topologies. *Embedding* can give such flexibility to a system. An embedding of a guest graph $G = (V_G, E_G)$ into a host graph $H = (V_H, E_H)$ is a one-to-one function f from G to H where each node in V_G (V_H) represents a task (processor) and each edge in E_G (E_H) represents a task-to-task (processor-to-processor) communication link in a program (system, respectively). It makes possible for each parallel algorithm written in a different communication structure to simulate on the host system without any modification of the original algorithm while the communication delay caused by the different network topology of the new system is kept at minimum.

The embedding problem has been heavily studied under various settings. A summary of results on embedding problem can be found in [9]. The *dilation* of an embedding is the maximum distance (i.e., the length of a shortest path) in H between any two adjacent nodes in G. The *expansion* of an embedding is the ratio of the number of nodes in the host graph to the number of nodes in the guest graph (i.e., $|V_H|/|V_G|$). An embedding of G into H is augmented by a mapping of links in G to paths in H. The *link congestion* of such a mapping is the maximum, over all links e in H, of the number of links in G mapped to a path in H that includes e. The existence of *link contention* in an embedding means that there exists at least one edge with link congestion greater than or equal to 2.

In most of previous research of embedding, the central issue was to find embeddings with small diameters [1, 2, 3, 11] rather than small link congestion. However, when one considers wormhole routing, which is known to be insensitive to the routing distance and greatly reduce communication overhead[10], as a communication criterion, the link congestion of an embedding becomes a more important factor than the dilation of the embedding. Motivated by the application

*This work was supported by MOST grant 98-N60201A04.

to wormhole routing, we study the problem of embedding with the objective of minimizing link congestion. In this paper, we consider the problem of embedding complete binary trees into 3-dimensional meshes. A complete binary tree of depth p is denoted by T_p and the root of T_p is assumed to be at level 1; thus, T_p has $2^p - 1$ nodes. A 3-dimensional mesh with side length $l_1, \cdots, l_3$ is denoted by $M(l_1, l_2, l_3)$. In mesh interconnection network, there are more than one path between two nodes and the path selection is done by routing strategy. In the *dimension-ordered* routing for meshes, each message is routed in one dimension at a time, arriving at the proper coordinate in each dimension before proceeding to the next dimension. We call an embedding a *dimension-ordered embedding* if each edge (u, v) in the guest graph is mapped to a path in the host graph such that the path from u to v follows the dimension-ordered routing. There are several commercially available multicomputers using this strategy including Symult 2010 and MIT J-machine [12, 4].

The communication link is said to be *half-duplex* if each link can be used for both directions but only one direction at any given time. If both directions can be used on each single active link simultaneously, the communication link is called *full-duplex*. We call a system *half-duplexed (full-duplexed) network model* if each link in the system is half-duplex (full-duplex, respectively).

Gibbons and Paterson [5] showed that a complete binary tree of depth p, T_p, can be embedded into 2-dimensional meshes in the full-duplexed network model without considering the dimension-ordered routing. In [7], Lee and Choi considered the same problems on the 3-dimensional meshes with dimension-ordered routing, but their embeddings have link congestion 2 whether the network model is half-duplexed or full-duplexed. Park, Lee and Moon in [8] considered contention free embeddings on the 3-dimensional meshes with dimension-ordered routing, but their embeddings have expansion larger than 1.27 of the optimum. Considering both half-duplexed and full-duplexed network models, the dimension-ordered embedding on the 2-dimensional meshes was shown in [6].

In the following section, we present the dimension-ordered embedding algorithms of the complete binary trees into the wormhole routed 3-dimensional meshes without link contention achieving expansion of no larger than 1.125 of optimum in half-duplexed network model and optimum in full-duplexed network model. Extending the results in [6] to 3-dimensional meshes,

our embedding algorithms outperform the previous results. Conclusions are given in Section 3.

2 Embeddings

In this section, we present simple recursive algorithms for embedding complete binary trees into 3-dimensional meshes using the dimension ordered routing. We consider the embedding first in the half-duplexed network model and then in the full-duplexed network model. An address of a node i in $M(l_1, l_2, l_3)$ is denoted by (i_1, i_2, i_3) where $1 \leq i_1 \leq l_1$, $1 \leq i_2 \leq l_2$, and $1 \leq i_3 \leq l_3$.

2.1 Half-Duplexed Network Model

Theorem 1 *A complete binary tree of depth p, called T_p, can be embedded into an half-duplexed 3-dimensional mesh $M(l_1, l_2, l_3)$ with link congestion 1 using dimension-ordered routing such that*

1) $p < 9$
   (i) $M(2^k, 2^k, 2^k)$ if p is $3k$,
   (ii) $M(2^{k+1}, 2^k, 2^k)$ if p is $3k + 1$, and
   (iii) $M(2^{k+1}, 2^{k+1}, 2^k)$ if p is $3k + 2$,

2) $p \geq 9$
   (i) $M(\frac{9}{8} \cdot 2^k, 2^k, 2^k)$ if p is $3k$,
   (ii) $M(\frac{9}{8} \cdot 2^{k+1}, 2^k, 2^k)$ if p is $3k + 1$, and
   (iii) $M(\frac{9}{8} \cdot 2^{k+1}, 2^{k+1}, 2^k)$ if p is $3k + 2$,

where k is an integer.

Proof. We begin with the case (1) when $3 \leq p < 9$. Figures 3, 4, 5, and 6 in [8], respectively show possible embeddings of complete binary trees of depth 3, 4, 5, 6, 7, and 8 into $2 \times 2 \times 2$, $4 \times 2 \times 2$, $4 \times 4 \times 2$, $4 \times 4 \times 4$, $8 \times 4 \times 4$, and $8 \times 8 \times 4$ 3-dimensional meshes without link contention and clearly each is dimension-ordered embedding. This proves case (1) of Theorem 1 when $3 \leq p < 9$.

We next consider the case when $p \geq 9$ and $p = 3k$ for some integer $k \geq 3$. The embedding scheme is recursive. Let r be the root of T_p. Suppose there is an embedding, called F_p, such taht it satisfies the following properties.

($\mathcal{A}1$) Let (r_1, r_2, r_3) be the address of r. Then the node of address $(r_1, r_2, 1)$, the node of address $(l_1, r_2, 1)$, and the node of address $(l_1, l_2, 1)$ are empty.

($\mathcal{A}2$) The following links are all free:

- the dimension 3 links on the path of straight line going through r.
- the dimension 1 links on the path of straight line going through the empty node $(r_1, r_2, 1)$.
- the dimension 2 links on the path of straight line going through the empty node $(l_1, r_2, 1)$.

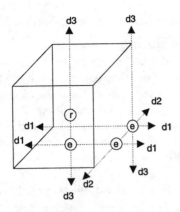

Figure 1:

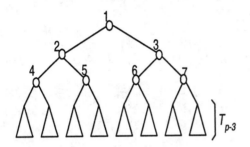

Figure 2:

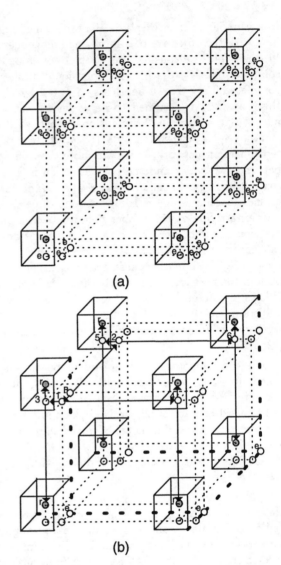

Figure 3:

- the dimension 3 links on the path of straight line going thruogh the empty node $(l_1, l_2, 1)$.

- the dimension 1 links on the path of straight line going through the empty node $(l_1, l_2, 1)$.

($\mathcal{A}$3) The link congestion is one.

($\mathcal{A}$4) F_p is a dimension ordered embedding.

Such an embedding F_p which satisfies properties $\mathcal{A}$1 - $\mathcal{A}$4 is shown in Figure 1. Dotted lines represent the free links (just those of our interest) and nodes labeled r and e represent the root and empty nodes, respectively. A complete binary tree of depth $p = 3k$ is recursively embedded using those previously constructed eight embeddings of complete binary trees of depth $p - 3$. Figure 3 illustrates the inductive step in constructing F_p from F_{p-3}. A layout of eight embeddings of F_{p-3} is shown in Figure 3 (a). Nodes labeled r and e in each submesh denote the root and empty node of T_{p-3}'s, respectively. We assume that F_{p-3} satisfies properties $\mathcal{A}$1 - $\mathcal{A}$4; thus, when laying out eight submeshes as shown in Figure 3 (a) some of free links in each submesh are connected each other to form a

line and the free links (just those of our interest) are shown in Figure 3 (a) using dotted lines.

The embedding of nodes $\{R, 1, 2, 3, 4, 5, 6\}$ at levels 1 - 3 of T_p and the set of edges $\{(R, 1), (R, 2), (1, 3), (1, 4), (2, 5), (2, 6)\}$ are embedded using the scheme shown in Figure 3 (b). Figure 3 (b) also shows the paths corresponding to the eight tree edges between nodes in $\{3, 4, 5, 6\}$ and eight roots of subtree T_{p-3}'s. It is clear to see that F_p also satisfies the properties $\mathcal{A}$1 - $\mathcal{A}$4, which ensures the construction of F_{p+3} on $M(\frac{9}{8} \cdot 2^{k+1}, 2^{k+1}, 2^{k+1})$ in the next recursive step.

As a base of the recursive construction, embedding of a complete binary tree of depth 9 into $9 \times 8 \times 8$ 3-dimensional mesh is used and it is depicted by Figure

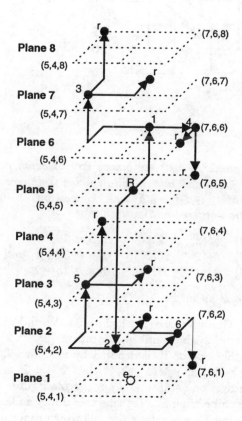

Plane 8
(5,4,8)

Plane 7
(5,4,7)

Plane 6
(5,4,6)

Plane 5
(5,4,5)

Plane 4
(5,4,4)

Plane 3
(5,4,3)

Plane 2
(5,4,2)

Plane 1
(5,4,1)

Figure 4:

4 and 5. Consider a tree in Figure 2 such that depth of tree is 9. An embedding of the top three level of tree with nodes labeled $R, 1, 2, \cdots, 6$ and 14 links among those nodes and eight subroots in subtrees of depth 6 is showed in Figure 4. $9 \times 8 \times 8$ 3-dimensional mesh is described with eight 9×8 2-dimensional meshes and each of eight subroot of T_6's embedded on each plane as shown in Figure 4. It is note that Figure 4 depicts only the center 3×3 nodes of each plane. The rest of eight subtrees of depth 6 are embedded into Plane 1 through Plane 8 in Figure 4 using one of embeddings in Figure 5(a) - (e). Embeddings in Plane 8 and Plane 4 are shown in Figure 5 (a), embeddings in Plane 7 and Plane 3 are shown in Figure 5 (b), embeddings in Plane 6 and 4 are shown in Figure 5 (c) and (e), respectively, and embeddings in Plane 5 and Plane 1 are shown in Figure 5 (d). The arrows pointing the northwest direction represent the direct connection to the right above node in the next plane through dimension 3 link. The rounded rectangles in Figure 5 (d) emphasises the free links after the embedding. Together with Figure 4 and Figure 5 they represent an embedding of T_9 into $M(9,8,8)$ and it is easy to see that it forms F_9 which satisfies $\mathcal{A}1$ - $\mathcal{A}4$. The theorem is thus proved for the case $p = 3k$.

For the cases (2) and (3) of the theorem, embeddings of F_{10} and F_{11} shown in Figure 6 (b) and (c) will be used as those bases, respectively. Since Plane 5 and Plane 1 in F_9 use the embedding in Figure 5 (d), F_9 can depict as shown in Figure 6 (a) and it ensures the existence of F_{10} and F_{11} using two and four F_9's, respectively. It is not difficult to see that both embeddings in Figure 6 (b) and (c) also satisfy the properties $\mathcal{A}1$ - $\mathcal{A}4$. This completes the proof of the theorem. ∎

The number of nodes $N(p)$ of the mesh for embedding the binary tree of depth p is $\frac{9}{8} \cdot 2^k \times 2^k \times 2^k = 9 \cdot 2^{3k-3} = 9 \cdot 2^{p-3}$ since $p = 3k$. Therefore, the expention of our embedding will be $\frac{9 \cdot 2^{p-3}}{2^p} = \frac{9}{8} = 1.125$ times the optimum.

2.2 Full-Duplexed Network Model

In this section, we consider the same embedding problem on full-duplexed network model. Let E_p be an embedding of T_p into a full-duplexed d-dimensional mesh of size 2^p nodes. An embedding $f_i(E_p)$ for $1 \leq i \leq d$ is defined to be a mirror image of E_p along the dimension i. For example, consider an embedding E_3 of T_3 into $M(2,2,2)$ shown in Figure 7 (a). Figure 7 (b - d) shows $f_1(E_3)$, $f_2(E_3)$, and $f_3(E_3)$, respectively. Observe that $f_i(f_j(E_p)) = f_j(f_i(E_p))$, and if E_p is a dimension ordered embedding, so is $f_i(E_p)$.

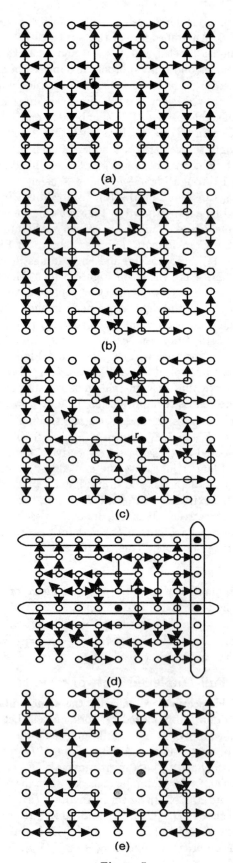

(a)

(b)

(c)

(d)

(e)

Figure 5:

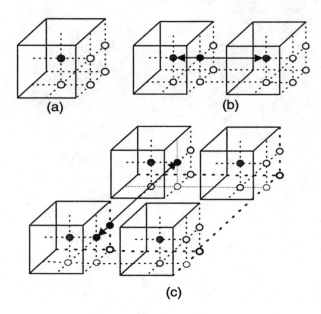

(a)

(b)

(c)

Figure 6:

Theorem 2 *A complete binary tree of depth p, T_p, can be embedded into a full-duplexed 3-dimensional mesh $M(l_1, l_2, l_3)$ with link congestion 1 using dimension-ordered routing such that*

(1) $M(2^k, 2^k, 2^k)$ *if p is $3k$,*
(2) $M(2^{k+1}, 2^k, 2^k)$ *if p is $3k+1$, and*
(3) $M(2^{k+1}, 2^{k+1}, 2^k)$ *if p is $3k+2$,*

where k is an integer.

Proof. Consider case (1) when p is $3k$. We inductively construct E_p which embeds T_p into $M(2^k, 2^k, 2^k)$, in which the root of T_p is denoted by r. Since T_p has $2^p - 1$ nodes and $M(2^k, 2^k, 2^k)$ has $2^{3k} = 2^p$ nodes, there exists one empty node in the mesh after completing embedding E_p. Let e be this empty node. Our embedding E_p will satisfy the following properties.

($\mathcal{B}1$) Let (r_1, r_2, r_3) be the address of root node r and (e_1, e_2, e_3) be the address of empty node e. Then $r_1 = e_1$ and $r_3 = e_3$.

($\mathcal{B}2$) The following links are all free:

- the dimension 1 links on the path of straight line from r to a boundary node on the right of r.
- the dimension 1 links on the path of straight line going through e.
- the dimension 2 links on the path of straight line going through r. (Note that r and e are connected by these free links.)

270

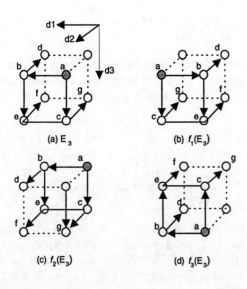

(a) E_3 (b) $f_1(E_3)$

(c) $f_2(E_3)$ (d) $f_3(E_3)$

Figure 7:

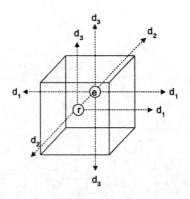

Figure 8:

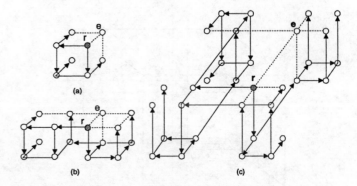

Figure 9:

- the dimension 3 links on the path of straight line from r to a boundary node above r.

- the dimension 3 links on the path of straight line going through e.

(B3) The link congestion is one.

(B4) E_p is a dimension ordered embedding.

Figure 8 dispicts such an embedding, E_p.

The base case of $k = 1$ is shown in Figure 9 (a) which clearly satisfies B1 - B4. Figure 10 illustrates the inductive step in constructing E_p from E_{p-3}. A layout of eight embeddings obtained by mirror imaging of E_{p-3} is shown in Figure 10 (a). Nodes labeled r and e in each submesh $M(2^{k-1}, 2^{k-1}, 2^{k-1})$ denote the root of T_{p-3} and the empty node, respectively. We assume that E_{p-3} satisfies properties B1 - B4; thus, when laying out eight submeshes $M(2^{k-1}, 2^{k-1}, 2^{k-1})$ as shown in Figure 10 (a), the submeshes are connected by free links. The free links (just those of our interest) are shown in Figure 10 (a) using dotted lines.

To complete the embedding E_p, the set of nodes $\{R, 1, 2, 3, 4, 5, 6\}$ at levels 1 - 3 of T_p and the set of edges $\{(R, 1), (R, 2), (1, 3), (1, 4), (2, 5), (2, 6)\}$ are embedded using the scheme shown in Figure 10 (b). Figure 10 (b) also shows the paths corresponding to the eight tree edges between nodes in $\{3, 4, 5, 6\}$ and eight roots of subtree T_{p-3}'s.

E_p also satisfies the properties B1 - B4, which ensures the construction of E_{p+3}. The theorem is thus proved for $p = 3k$.

Cases (2) and (3) of the theorem can be similarly proved using E_4 and E_5 shown in Figure 9 (b) and (c) as base case embeddings, respectively. This completes the proof of the theorem. ∎

In every embedding step, it is observed that only one node is empty in E_p. Thus, the expansion of embedding E_p is optimum.

3 Conclusions

This paper showed that a complete binary tree T_p can be embedded disjointly into a 3-dimensional mesh of size bounded by 1.125 times the optimum using the dimension-ordered routing if network model is half-duplexed. In the full-duplexed network model, we can achieve the same embedding into a mesh with optimum size.

[7] showed that a complete binary tree can be embedded into an optimal size half-duplexed 4-dimensional mesh with link congestion 1 without using the dimension-ordered routing. Considering the results in this paper and those in [7], further extensions include to consider an embedding of T_p into full-duplexed 4-dimensional mesh with dimension-ordered

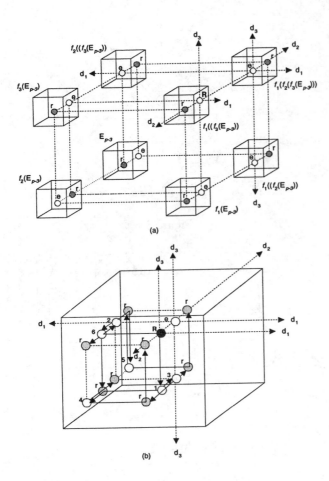

Figure 10:

routing without link contention.

Another possible extensions also include to consider developing heuristic algorithms for arbitrary binary trees using the results for complete binary trees and embeddings of other types of host and guest graphs with the objective of minimizing the link congestion which can be applicable to currently existing commercial machines.

References

[1] S. Bhatt, F. Chung, T. Leighton, and A. Rosenberg, "Optimal Simulations of Tree Machines," *Proc. 27th Annual IEEE Symp. Foundations of Computer Science*, pp. 274 - 282, October 1986.

[2] S. N. Bhatt and S. S. Cosmadakis, "The Complexity of Minimizing Wire Lengths for VLSI Layouts," *Information Processing Letters*, Vol. 25, 1987.

[3] J. E. Brandenburg and D. S. Scott, "Embeddings of Communication Trees and Grids into Hypercubes," *Technical Report*, Intel Scientific Computers, 1985.

[4] W. J. Dally, "The J-machine: System support for Actors," in *Actors: Knowledge-based Concurrent Computing* (Hewitt and Agha, eds.), MIT Press, 1989.

[5] A. Gibbons and M. Patterson, "Dense Edge-Disjoint Embedding of Binary Trees in the Mesh", *Proc. of 4th Annual ACM Symposium on Parallel Algorithms and Architecture*, pp. 257 - 263, 1992.

[6] S.-K. Lee and H.-A. Choi, "Embedding of Complete Binary Trees into Meshes with Row-Column Routing," *IEEE Trans. on Parallel and Distributed Systems*, Vol. 7, No. 5, pp. 493-497, May 1996.

[7] S.-K. Lee and H.-A. Choi, "Link-Disjoint Embedding of Complete Binary Trees In Meshes," *J. Networks*, Vol. 30, No. 4, pp. 283-292, 1997.

[8] S.-M. Park, S.-K. Lee, and B.-H. Moon, "Link-Disjoint Embedding of Complete Binary Trees Into 3D-Meshes With Dimension-Ordered Routing," *Proceedings of Parallel Processing System*, Vol 9, No. 1, pp. 85-95, Seoul, Korea, March 1998.

[9] B. Monien and H. Sudborough, "Embedding One Interconnection Network in Another," preprint, 1992.

[10] L. M. Ni and P. K. McKinley, "A Survey of Routing Techniques in Wormhole Networks," *IEEE Computers*, pp. 62 - 76, Feb. 1993

[11] A. Rosenberg, "Data Encoding and Their Costs," *Acta Informatica*, No. 9, 1978.

[12] C. L. Seitz, W. C. Ahhas, C. M. Flaig, A. J. Martin, J. Seizovic, C. S. Steele, and W. -K. Su, "The architecture ad programming of the Ametek Series 2010 multicomputer," in *Proceedings of the Third Conference on Hypercube Concurrent Computers and Applications*, Vol. I, (Pasadena, CA), pp. 33-36, Association for Computing Machinery, Jan. 1988.

Session A5

Communication Support for DSM

Chair: Mateo Valero
Universitat Politecnica de Catalunya, Spain

Coherence-Centric Logging and Recovery for Home-Based Software Distributed Shared Memory

Angkul Kongmunvattana and Nian-Feng Tzeng

Center for Advanced Computer Studies
University of Southwestern Louisiana
Lafayette, LA 70504

Abstract

The probability of failures in software distributed shared memory (SDSM) increases as the system size grows. This paper introduces a new, efficient message logging technique, called the coherence-centric logging (CCL) and recovery protocol, for home-based SDSM. Our CCL minimizes failure-free overhead by logging only data necessary for correct recovery and tolerates high disk access latency by overlapping disk accesses with coherence-induced communication existing in home-based SDSM, while our recovery reduces the recovery time by prefetching data according to the future shared memory access patterns, thus eliminating the memory miss idle penalty during the recovery process. To the best of our knowledge, this is the very first work that considers crash recovery in home-based SDSM.

We have performed experiments on a cluster of eight SUN Ultra-5 workstations, comparing our CCL against traditional message logging (ML) by modifying TreadMarks, a state-of-the-art SDSM system, to support the home-based protocol and then implementing both our CCL and the ML protocols in it. The experimental results show that our CCL protocol consistently outperforms the ML protocol: Our protocol increases the execution time negligibly, by merely 1% to 6%, during failure-free execution, while the ML protocol results in the execution time overhead of 9% to 24% due to its large log size and high disk access latency. Our recovery protocol improves the crash recovery speed by 55% to 84% when compared to re-execution, and it outperforms ML-recovery by a noticeable margin, ranging from 5% to 18% under parallel applications examined.

1. Introduction

Clusters of workstations, PCs, or SMPs represent cost-effective platforms for parallel computing. Programming on such clusters with explicit message exchange, however, is known to be difficult. Software distributed shared memory (SDSM) creates a shared memory abstraction (i.e., a coherent global address space) on top of the physically distributed processing nodes (i.e., processors) to simplify parallel programming tasks. While faster processors and higher network bandwidth continue to improve SDSM performance and scalability, the probability of system failures increases as the system size grows. This existence of vulnerability is unacceptable, especially for long-running applications and high-availability situations. Hence, a mechanism for supporting fast crash recovery in SDSM is indispensable.

Home-based SDSM [18] is one type of SDSM developed under the notion of relaxed memory consistency model [1]. While it relies on a virtual memory trap as other SDSM systems [2, 5], home-based SDSM assigns a *home* node for each shared memory page to collect updates from all writers of that page. This home node offers some advantages to SDSM as follows: (i) a read/write to a page on its home node does not cause any page fault nor requires any summary of write modifications, (ii) it takes only one round-trip message to bring a remote copy of any shared memory page up-to-date, and (iii) no garbage collection is needed. Due to these advantages, the home-based SDSM protocol has been a focus of several recent studies [7, 10, 14, 18]. Unfortunately, no prior work has ever been attempted on crash recovery in home-based SDSM. This paper is the very first one to deal with crash recovery in such SDSM.

Message logging is a popular technique for providing *home-less* SDSM with fault-tolerant capability [6, 11, 12, 13, 17]. This technique is attractive because it guarantees bounded rollback-recovery of independent checkpointing and improves the crash recovery speed of coordinated checkpointing [8]. While those earlier logging protocols work well under home-less SDSM, they cannot be applied to home-based SDSM, where each shared memory page has a home node at which updates from all writers are collected. This is because home-less SDSM maintains its coherence enforcement data differently from home-based SDSM. Specifically, home-less SDSM always keeps a summary of modifications made to each shared memory page (known as *diff*), while home-based SDSM creates diffs only for remote copies of shared memory pages and discards them after a home copy is updated.

In this paper, we propose a new, efficient logging protocol, called *coherence-centric* logging (CCL), for home-based SDSM. CCL minimizes logging overhead by overlapping disk accesses (for flushing) with coherence-induced communication in home-based SDSM, and by selecting to record only information indispensable for recovery. To assess the impacts of our CCL protocol on home-based SDSM performance, we have modified TreadMarks (a state-of-the-art home-less SDSM) to support the home-based protocol, with traditional message logging and then with our CCL incorporated in it. The experiment has been conducted on a cluster of eight Sun Ultra-5 workstations. Experimental results under four parallel applications demonstrate that our CCL protocol leads to very low failure-free overhead, ranging from 1% to 6% of the normal execution time. For fast recovery, we also introduce an efficient recovery scheme, which is specifically tailored for home-based SDSM. Our recovery scheme reads coherence enforcement data from the local disk and fetches the updates from the logged data on remote nodes (i.e., other writers) at the beginning of each time interval, reducing disk access frequency and eliminating the memory miss idle time. Because of these optimization techniques and lighter network traffic during crash recovery, our scheme shortens the recovery time substantially, ranging from 55% to 84%, when compared with re-execution.

The outline of this paper is as follows. Section 2 describes home-based SDSM [18] and its coherence enforcement protocol. Our coherence-centric logging and recovery are proposed in Section 3, along with an overview on the traditional message logging and its recovery procedure. Section 4 first states our experimental platform and the parallel applications used, and then presents the performance results of our proposed protocol. Related work is discussed in Section 5, followed by conclusion in Section 6.

2. Home-Based SDSM

Coherence-centric logging and recovery we propose aim at home-based SDSM. They take advantage of properties associated with home-based SDSM to lower failure-free overhead. In this section, we describe home-based SDSM and its coherence enforcement protocol, known as home-based lazy release consistency (HLRC), before explaining optimization steps adopted by HLRC.

2.1 Overview

SDSM simplifies parallel programming tasks by providing an illusion of shared memory image to the programmers. The implementation of SDSM often relies on virtual memory page-protection hardware to initiate coherence enforcement of a shared memory image, which spans across memories at the interconnected processors. Such hardware

support is readily available in most, if not all, commodity microprocessors. While versatile and attractive, SDSM has to minimize its coherence enforcement overhead for achieving good performance. To this end, the implementation of SDSM usually adopts a relaxed memory consistency model [1] because various optimization steps can then be applied to arrive at efficient SDSM systems.

Release consistency (RC) [1] is one of the least restrictive relaxed memory consistency models; it does not guarantee that shared memory is consistent all of the time, but rather it makes sure consistence only after synchronization operations (i.e., locks and barriers). In essence, RC ensures a synchronized program to see sequentially consistent execution through the use of two synchronization primitives: *acquire* for a process to get access to the shared variable, and *release* for a process to relinquish an acquired variable, permitting another process to acquire the variable. In a synchronized program, a process is allowed to use a shared data only after acquiring it, and the acquired data may then be accessed and modified before being released (and subsequently acquired by another process). Each process also allows to update a local copy of shared data multiple times, but all the updates have to be completed before the release is performed. Home-based SDSM employs a variant of RC implementations called home-based lazy release consistency (HLRC) [18] and also incorporates several optimization steps, as described in sequence below.

2.2 Home-Based Lazy Release Consistency

Home-based lazy release consistency (HLRC) [18] is among the efficient software implementations of RC. It assigns a home node for each shared memory page as a repository of updates from all writers, simplifying memory management of coherence enforcement mechanism. HLRC also combines the advantages of write-update and write-invalidate protocols to make a shared memory page at the home node (i.e., a home copy) up-to-date at the end of each writer time interval, and to bring other copies (i.e., remote copies) up-to-date on demands. Specifically, writers of remote copies flush updates (i.e., a summary of modifications) to its home node at the end of each time interval (i.e., via a release operation), updating its home copy. Consequently, no persistent state has to be kept in memory. All other remote copies are invalidated at the beginning of the subsequent interval (i.e., by an acquire operation), according to the write-invalidation notice piggybacked with a lock grant or barrier release message. Each remote copy is updated using only a single round-trip message to the home node, where updates from all writers are collected. Hence, HLRC minimizes memory consumption for supporting coherence enforcement via a write-update protocol and reduces coherence-induced traffic via a write-invalidate protocol, leading to good performance and scalability.

2.3 Optimization

SDSM utilizes the virtual memory trap to invoke coherence enforcement mechanisms, and therefore, coherence granularity in SDSM is of the OS page size. This coarse-grain coherence enforcement often leads to a false-sharing scenario, where several processes request to modify different portions of the same shared memory page simultaneously, resulting in a thrashing problem or ping-pong effect. A multiple-writer protocol alleviates this problem by allowing multiple writable copies of a shared memory page to coexist [5]. This is permissible under the definition of RC, and the correct execution of a program is guaranteed as long as it is data-race free. The use of a multiple-writer protocol optimizes the performance of home-based SDSM. Another optimization step taken by home-based SDSM is through diff-based write propagation [5]. It uses the summaries of modifications (i.e., diffs) for updating the home copy of a shared memory page, reducing the amount of data transfer when the write granularity is small.

3. Recoverable Home-Based SDSM

This section first gives an overview on the traditional message logging protocol and then proposes our coherence-centric logging and recovery. The proposed logging and recovery protocol takes advantage of the properties of home-based SDSM to yield low overhead. It is the first attempt to deal with fault tolerance in home-based SDSM.

3.1 Overview on Traditional Message Logging

Message logging (ML) has its root in message-passing systems [4, 8, 9, 16]. It follows the *piecewise deterministic system model* [16]: A process execution is divided into a sequence of deterministic state intervals, each of which starts at the occurrence of a nondeterministic event like a message receipt. The execution between nondeterministic events is completely deterministic. During a failure-free period, each process periodically saves its execution state in stable storage as a checkpoint, and all messages received are logged in volatile memory before being flushed to stable storage whenever the local process has to send a message to another process. Should a failure occur, the recovery process starts from the most recent checkpoint and the logged messages are replayed to reconstruct a consistent state of execution before the failure. When this traditional ML protocol is applied to home-based SDSM, it keeps in its local memory the updates (i.e., diffs) sent from writer processes, the up-to-date copy of shared memory pages delivered from their home nodes, and write-invalidation notices. These volatile logs are flushed to stable storage (i.e., a local disk) at the subsequent synchronization point. Should a failure occur, recovery starts from the most recent checkpoint and generates the execution by replaying the logged data from non-

volatile storage at each synchronization point and at each memory miss. While this logging protocol is straightforward to implement and its recovery process is easy to follow, it has high overhead due to its large log size and frequent disk accesses. To make fault-tolerant SDSM more affordable, we propose in the next subsection a new, efficient coherence-centric logging and recovery protocol for home-based SDSM.

3.2 Proposed Logging and Recovery

Our coherence-centric logging (CCL) protocol is tightly integrated into the coherence enforcement protocol employed by home-based SDSM, namely HLRC (refer to Section 2 for details). It records only information indispensable to correct recovery, minimizing the amount of logged data, and overlaps its disk accesses with coherence-induced communications already present in HLRC, reducing the adverse impacts of high disk access latency. In particular, CCL keeps in its local disk, the incoming write-invalidation notices, the records of incoming updates together with a writer process id number, and the summary of modifications (i.e., diffs) produced at the end of each time interval. Diffs are created by comparing locally a remote copy of a shared memory page with its twin (i.e., a pristine copy created before a write operation). The disk accesses (i.e., flushing operations) are performed during the release operation (i.e., right after the diffs are sent to the respective home nodes of pages), overlapping high disk access latency with inter-process communication. Hence, CCL allows HLRC to discard a diff as soon as the diff has been applied to its corresponding home copy, whereas ML needs to keep such a diff in the memory until the next synchronization point, where the disk flushing operation will be performed; additionally, when a page fault occurs at an invalid remote copy, CCL does not keep a received copy of a shared memory page that HLRC has fetched from its home node because such an up-to-date copy can be reconstructed during recovery. As a result, the total log size of CCL is only about 10% of that created by ML, as will be detailed in Section 4. This log size reduction and the disk access latency-tolerant technique save both space and time in the logging process, leading to significant failure-free overhead reduction.

To limit the amount of work that has to be repeated after a failure, checkpoints are created periodically. A checkpoint consists of all local and shared memory contents, the state of execution, and all internal data structures used by home-based SDSM. All this information is needed at the beginning of a crash recovery process to avoid restarting from the (global) initial state. The first checkpoint flushes all shared memory pages to stable storage, and then only those pages that have been modified since the last checkpoint will be included in a subsequent checkpoint, reducing the checkpoint creation overhead. While our logging protocol allows each process to create its checkpoints independently and guarantees bounded rollback-recovery, it is applicable to coordinated checkpointing as well (i.e., the logged data speed up recovery by eliminating synchronization messages and reducing memory miss idle time during the crash recovery process). The selection of checkpointing techniques, however, is beyond the scope of this paper.

Recovery

As mentioned earlier, the recovery process starts from the most recent checkpoint, followed by the execution replay of logged data. At the beginning of each time interval, the recovery process fetches the corresponding logs of updates (i.e., diffs) for its home copy from the writer process(es), as provided in the records of incoming updates. Our recovery brings a remote copy up-to-date by first requesting for an up-to-date page from its home node; if such a page is not available (i.e., a home copy has been advanced to another time interval by diffs from other writers), a remote copy has to be reconstructed by fetching both the home copy from the most recent checkpoint of its home node and logs of updates from the writer process(es), corresponding to information provided by the logged write-invalidation notices. Obviously, in the worst case, the home node must rollback to the most recent checkpoint in order to recreate its modification. While it is evident that this recovery scheme is inspired by our previous work, where an efficient approach was introduced for crash recovery in home-less SDSM [11], prefetching is more complicated in recoverable home-based SDSM than in home-less SDSM. In particular, prefetching in home-less SDSM simply relies on the diffs and write-invalidation notices maintained by a coherence enforcement protocol of home-less SDSM, whereas prefetching in home-based SDSM requires a home copy, logs of write-invalidation notices, and logs of updates to reconstruct a remote copy. Despite its higher complexity, our recovery for home-based SDSM substantially improves the crash recovery speed, ranging from 55% to 84% when compared with re-execution, under all applications examined. This reduction in recovery time results from the smaller total log size of CCL, the elimination of page faults, and lighter traffic over the network during recovery.

Example

Figure 1 shows a snapshot of coherence-centric logging and recovery in home-based SDSM. In this example, home nodes of pages x, y, and z are processes P_1, P_2, and P_3, respectively. During the failure-free execution, P_1 acquires the lock (for interval A), writes on pages x, y, and z, and then releases the lock. At the time of lock release, P_1 flushes diff of page y to P_2 and diff of page z to P_3, following the HLRC protocol. In addition, P_1 also stores those diffs in its local disk, as required by our CCL. When P_2 and P_3 receive asynchronous updates (i.e., diffs from P_1), they apply

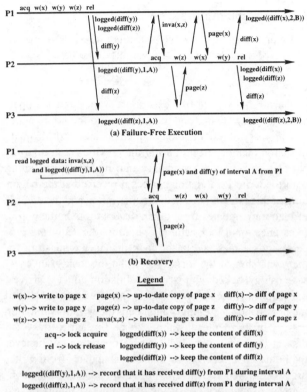

Figure 1. A Snapshot of Coherence-Centric Logging and Recovery in Action.

incoming diffs to their respective home copies and record this asynchronous update event. Later on, P_2 acquires the lock (for interval B), and invalidates its remote copies of pages x and z, according to the write-invalidation notices piggybacked with a lock grant message. When P_2 attempts to write on pages z and x, it causes virtual memory traps, which in turn fetch up-to-date copies of pages z and x from their home nodes. Accessing page y on P_2 causes no page fault because the home copy is always valid. At the time of lock release, P_2 flushes diff of page x to P_1 and diff of page z to P_3. It also stores those diffs in its local disk. When P_1 and P_3 receive asynchronous updates (i.e., diffs from P_2), they apply incoming diffs to their respective home copies and record this asynchronous update event.

Figure 1(b) assumes that P_2 crashes a certain time after the volatile logs of this interval are flushed to the local disk, but before the next checkpoint is created. After a failure is detected, the recovery process starts from the last checkpoint and replays the logged data. During this snapshot interval, the recovery process P_2 reads its local logged data and discovers that it has to update remote copies of pages x and z, and that it also receives asynchronous updates from P_1. Consequently, P_2 fetches the up-to-date copy of page z from its home node, P_3, and retrieves the up-to-date copy of page x along with a diff of page y from process P_1, following our recovery scheme.

3.3 Implementation

Figures 2 and 3 show the procedure of our logging and recovery for implementing recoverable home-based SDSM.

Lock

During the failure-free execution, a lock release operation not only creates and then flushes (to the home node) the summary of modifications, called updates or diffs, made to shared memory pages during the previous time interval, but also stores such a summary into its local disk (along with the write-invalidation notices it received at the beginning of this interval, i.e., at the lock acquire, and the records of incoming updates from other writers to its home copy). In essence, on a lock acquire operation, the acquiring process sends a message to the lock manager requesting for the ownership of the lock. When the the lock grant message (piggybacked with write-invalidation notices) arrives, the acquiring process invalidates its remote copies of shared memory pages accordingly and keeps the write-invalidation notices in its memory, waiting to be flushed to the local disk at the subsequent lock release operation. Whenever the home node receives asynchronous updates from writer processes, it records the event of such updates (not its contents) in its memory, consisting of the interval number, page id of a home copy, and the writer process id. At the lock release, a process flushes its summary of modifications to the home node(s) of corresponding pages and also stores such a summary in its local disk, along with the write-invalidation notices and the records of incoming updates.

Lock Acquire

```
if (in_recovery)
    read logs of incoming update events from its local disk;
    update home copies with logs of diffs from the writer process(es);
    read logs of write-invalidation notices from its local disk;
    reconstruct each remote copy with a home copy from its home node
        and logs of diffs from the writer process(es);
    create twin for each remote copy that will be written in the next
        time interval;
else
    send lock request to lock manager;
    wait for lock grant message (piggybacked with write-inv. notices);
    invalidate remote copies of pages according to write-inv. notices;
    keep those write-invalidation notices in memory;
endif
```

Lock Release

```
if (in_recovery)
    release the lock;
else
    create diffs and flush them to home nodes;
    flush those diffs, write-invalidation notices, and records of
        incoming updates events to local disk;
    wait for acknowledgements and then discard those diffs;
endif
```

Asynchronous Update Handler

```
apply received diffs to home copies;
send an acknowledgement back to the writer process;
records this incoming updates event in memory;
discard those diffs;
```

Figure 2. Procedure for Lock Synchronization in Coherence-Centric Logging and Recovery.

Barrier

```
if (in_recovery)
    read logs of incoming update events from its local disk;
    update home copies with logs of diffs from the writer process(es);
    read logs of write-invalidation notices from its local disk;
    reconstruct each remote copy with a home copy from its home node
        and logs of diffs from the writer process(es);
    create twin for each remote copy that will be written in the next
        time interval;
else
    if (barrier_manager)
        create diffs and flush them to home nodes;
        flush those diffs to local disk;
        wait for acknowledgements and then discard those diffs;
        wait for all other processes to check in;
        invalidate dirty remote copies of pages;
        send barrier release message piggybacked with write-inv.
            notices to all other processes;
    else
        create diffs and flush them to home nodes;
        flush those diffs to local disk;
        wait for acknowledgements and then discard those diffs;
        send check-in message to barrier manager;
        wait for barrier release message;
        invalidate dirty remote copies of pages;
    endif
endif
```

Figure 3. Procedure for Barrier Synchronization in Coherence-Centric Logging and Recovery.

When a failure is detected, the *in_recovery* flag is set. On a lock acquire, the home copy is prepared for the next time interval by updating itself with logs of diffs retrieved from the writer process(es), as recorded in the logs of incoming updates events. To get the correct remote copies of pages for the next time interval, the recovery process fetches an up-to-date copy of those pages from their respective home nodes. Remote copies that need to be updated are identified by the logs of write-invalidation notices in that time interval. If the home copy is already in a more advanced time interval (i.e., diffs from other writers have been applied to the home copy), then the recovery process has to fetch those diffs from the writer process(es) to reconstruct its remote copy to the correct time interval before proceeding beyond the lock acquire.

Barrier

During a failure free period, on arrival at a barrier, each process that has performed a write operation to shared memory page(s) creates and flushes to the respective home node(s) a summary of modifications (i.e., diff) of each remote copy. Such a process also logs those diffs into its local disk while waiting for an acknowledgement from each home node. Upon receiving asynchronous updates from a remote process, the home node applies received diffs to its home copy, sends an acknowledgement back to the writer process, records this incoming updates event, and discards the diffs. Each process also discards its local diffs after an acknowledgement has arrived, and sends a check-in message (piggybacked with the write-invalidation notice) to the barrier manager. The barrier manager waits until it received all check-in messages, before invalidates its remote copies of shared memory pages in accordance with the write-invalidation notice, and then sends back a check-out message (piggybacked with an up-to-date write-invalidation notice) to each process, allowing the recipient of a check-out message to invalidate its remote copies of shared memory pages accordingly and to proceed beyond the barrier.

When a failure is detected, the *in_recovery* flag is set. On arrival at the barrier, the home copy is prepared for the next time interval by updating itself with logs of diffs retrieved from the writer process(es), as recorded in the logs of incoming update events. To get the correct remote copies of pages for the next time interval, the recovery process fetches an up-to-date copy of those pages from their respective home nodes. The remote copies that need to be updated are identified by the logs of write-invalidation notices in that time interval. If the home copy is already in a more advanced time interval (i.e., diffs from other writers have been applied to the home copy), the recovery process has to fetch those diffs from the writer process(es) to reconstruct its remote copy to the correct time interval before proceeding beyond the barrier.

4. Performance Evaluation

In this section, we briefly describe hardware and software employed in our experiments and also present the evaluation results of our proposed protocol for recoverable home-based SDSM. We first compare the performance results of our coherence-centric logging (CCL) with those of traditional message logging (ML). Since the goal is to examine logging overhead, no checkpoint is taken in our experiments. Subsequently, we evaluate and contrast the crash recovery speeds of our recovery and ML-recovery.

4.1 Experiment Setup

Our experimental platform is a collection of eight Sun Ultra-5 workstations running Solaris version 2.6. Each workstation contains a 270 MHz UltraSPARC-IIi processor, 256 KB of external cache, and 64 MB of physical memory. These machines are connected via a fast Ethernet (of 100 Mbps) switch. We allocated 2 GB of the local disk at each workstation for virtual memory paging and left 1.2 GB of local disk space available for logged data.

Program	Data Set Size	Synchronization
3D-FFT	100 iterations on $2^7 \times 2^7 \times 2^7$ data	barriers
MG	200 iterations on $2^7 \times 2^7 \times 2^7$ grid	barriers
Shallow	5000 iterations on 25000^2	barriers
Water	120 iterations on 512 molecules	locks and barriers

Table 1. Applications' Characteristics.

We modified TreadMarks [2] to support the HLRC protocol [18], and then incorporated our proposed logging and crash recovery for quantitative evaluation. For measuring the failure-free overhead and the crash recovery speed, four

parallel applications were used in our experiments, including 3D-FFT, MG, Shallow, and Water. 3D-FFT and MG are originally from the NAS benchmark suite [3], with the former computing the 3-Dimensional Fast Fourier Transform, and the latter solving the Poisson problem on a multigrid. Shallow is a weather prediction kernel from NCAR, and Water is a molecular dynamics simulation from the SPLASH benchmark suite [15]. The data set size and the synchronization type of each application used in this experimental study are listed in Table 1.

4.2 Performance Results of Logging Protocols

Table 2 presents the failure-free overhead of different logging protocols. It lists total execution time, the mean log size, the total log size, and the number of times the volatile logs are flushed to stable storage. Since no logging exists in the home-based TreadMarks, its execution time serves as a performance baseline. Both our coherence-centric logging (CCL) and traditional message logging (ML) protocols provide home-based SDSM with crash recovery capabilities, but they involve different performance penalty amounts.

Logging Protocol	Execution Time (sec.)	Mean Log Size (KB)	Total Log Size (MB)	# of Flushes
None	363.24	-	-	-
ML	450.36	1760	359	204
CCL	385.14	221	45	204

(a) 3D-FFT

Logging Protocol	Execution Time (sec.)	Mean Log Size (KB)	Total Log Size (MB)	# of Flushes
None	300.96	-	-	-
ML	354.56	43	276	6404
CCL	307.10	4	24	6404

(b) MG

Logging Protocol	Execution Time (sec.)	Mean Log Size (KB)	Total Log Size (MB)	# of Flushes
None	744.33	-	-	-
ML	848.60	29	865	30000
CCL	765.22	2.4	71	30000

(c) Shallow

Logging Protocol	Execution Time (sec.)	Mean Log Size (KB)	Total Log Size (MB)	# of Flushes
None	139.64	-	-	-
ML	152.27	1.1	44	38842
CCL	141.60	0.05	2	38842

(d) Water

Table 2. Overhead Details under Different Logging Protocols.

From Table 2, it is apparent that our CCL consistently results in lower failure-free overhead than ML, which induces a larger mean log size and is affected significantly by high disk access latency. CCL keeps a far less amount of logged data because it stores only coherence-related information that cannot be retrieved or recreated after a failure, whereas ML simply records all incoming messages. Consequently, the total log size of our protocol is only a small

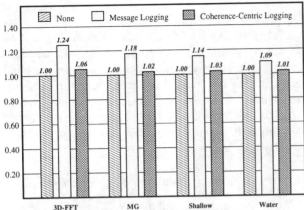

Figure 4. Impacts of Logging Protocols on Execution Time.

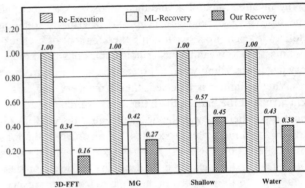

Figure 5. Impacts of Logging Protocols on Execution Time.

fraction of that of the ML protocol; namely, it is only 12.5% for 3D-FFT, 8.7% for MG, 8.2% for Shallow, and 4.5% for Water. A larger mean log size of ML also increases the disk access time during flushing operations, lengthening the critical path of program execution and hampering home-based SDSM performance. To minimize the adverse impact of disk access latency, our CCL *overlaps* flushing operations with coherence-induced communication already existing in home-based SDSM. Figure 4 depicts the impacts of different logging protocols on home-based SDSM performance using the normalized execution time. It demonstrates that our CCL protocol adds very little overhead to execution time, ranging from 1% to 6%. This low overhead results directly from a small log size and our disk access latency-tolerant technique. By contrast, ML increases the execution time by as much as 24% for 3D-FFT, 18% for MG, 14% for Shallow, and 9% for Water; it directly corresponds to the large mean log size and high disk access latency.

4.3 Performance Results of Crash Recovery

Since there is no crash recovery protocol incorporated in the original home-based TreadMarks, should a failure occur, it has to restart from the (global) initial state without any logged data for execution replay. As a result, it spends the same amount of time for re-executing the program with no time saving. This normal execution time is employed as a baseline for crash recovery performance comparison. Under our crash recovery scheme, the recovery time is shortened substantially when compared with re-execution, by as much as 84% for 3D-FFT, 73% for MG, 55% for Shallow, and 62% for Water (see Figure 5). This directly results from the avoidance of page fault via prefetching in our recovery scheme, the minimized disk access time due to a small mean log size of CCL, and lighter traffic over the networks during recovery. On the other hand, message logging recovery (ML-recovery) eliminates the need of message transmission, but suffers from memory miss idle time and high disk

access latency in reading large logged data, which lengthen the recovery time. From Figure 5, ML-recovery leads to recovery time reduction of 66% for 3D-FFT, 58% for MG, 43% for Shallow, and 57% for Water, in comparison with re-execution. Hence, our recovery scheme outperforms ML-recovery by a noticeable margin, ranging from 5% to 18% under parallel applications examined.

5. Related Work

The study of message logging for SDSM was attempted first by Richard and Singhal [13]. They considered logging and independent checkpointing protocols for sequentially consistent home-less SDSM. Their logging protocol logs the contents of all shared memory accesses and causes high overhead due to a large log size and high disk access frequency. Suri, Janssens, and Fuchs [17] reduced the overhead of that protocol by logging only the records of all shared memory accesses, instead of their contents. They also proposed a logging protocol for home-less SDSM under relaxed memory consistency models [17], realized by logging all coherence-related messages in volatile memory and flushing them to stable storage before communicating with another process. This protocol, however, suffers from communication-induced accesses to stable storage. Costa *et al.* introduced a vector clock logging protocol [6], based upon the idea of sender-based message logging protocols [9], in which the logged data are kept in volatile memory of the sender process. Unfortunately, the protocol cannot handle multiple-node failures. Park and Yeom [12] described a logging protocol known as reduced-stable logging (RSL), obtained through refining the protocol proposed in [17] by logging only the content of lock grant messages, i.e., the list of dirty pages. Their simulation results indicated that RSL utilized less disk space for the logged data than that of [17]. Recently, a superior logging protocol, dubbed lazy logging, which significantly reduces the log size and the number of accesses to stable storage, has been devised [11]. Experimental results have shown that lazy logging induces lower execution overhead than

RSL. While these earlier logging protocols work well for home-less SDSM under relaxed memory consistency models, they do not recognize the notion of home node and cannot be applied efficiently to home-based SDSM. Our new, efficient coherence-centric logging and recovery protocol is the first one to deal with logging and recovery for home-based SDSM. Its experimental results have been gathered, demonstrated, and discussed in Section 4.

6. Conclusions

We have proposed a new, efficient logging and recovery protocol for recoverable home-based SDSM implementation in this paper. The experiment outcomes reveal that our coherence-centric logging protocol incurs very low failure-free overhead, roughly 1% to 6% of the normal execution time, and that our crash recovery scheme improves crash recovery speed by 55% to 84% when compared with re-execution. This results directly from our coherence-centric logging, which keeps only information necessary for recovery to a consistent execution state, and from our disk access latency-tolerant technique, which overlaps the disk flushing operation with inter-process communication. Our proposed recovery scheme totally eliminates the memory miss idle time and obviates the need of memory invalidation by prefetching up-to-date data before they are to be accessed in a subsequent time interval, therefore giving rise to fast crash recovery. Our coherence-centric logging and recovery is readily applicable to arrive at recoverable home-based SDSM systems effectively.

Acknowledgements

This material was based upon work supported in part by the NSF under Grants CCR-9803505 and EIA-9871315.

References

[1] S. Adve and K. Gharachorloo. Shared Memory Consistency Models: A Tutorial. *Computer*, 29(12):66–76, Dec. 1996.

[2] C. Amza, A. L. Cox, S. Dwarkadas, P. Keleher, H. Lu, R. Rajamony, W. Yu, and W. Zwaenepoel. TreadMarks: Shared Memory Computing on Networks of Workstations. *Computer*, 29(2):18–28, February 1996.

[3] D. Bailey, J. Barton, T. Lasinski, and H. Simon. The NAS Parallel Benchmarks. Technical Report RNR-91-002, NASA, January 1991.

[4] A. Borg, J. Baumbach, and S. Glazer. A Message System Supporting Fault-Tolerance. In *Proc. of the 9th ACM Symp. on Operating Systems Principles*, pages 90–99, Oct. 1983.

[5] J. B. Carter, J. K. Bennett, and W. Zwaenepoel. Implementation and Performance of Munin. In *Proc. of the 13th ACM Symp. on Operating Systems Principles (SOSP'91)*, pages 152–164, October 1991.

[6] M. Costa *et al*. Lightweight Logging for Lazy Release Consistent Distributed Shared Memory. In *Proc. of the 2nd USENIX Symp. on Operating Systems Design and Implementation (OSDI)*, pages 59–73, October 1996.

[7] A. L. Cox, E. de Lara, Y. C. Hu, and W. Zwaenepoel. A Performance Comparison of Homeless and Home-Based Lazy Release Consistency Protocols in Software Shared Memory. In *Proc. of the 5th IEEE Symp. on High-Performance Computer Architecture (HPCA-5)*, pages 279–283, January 1999.

[8] E. N. Elnozahy and W. Zwaenepoel. On the Use and Implementation of Message Logging. In *Proc. of the 24th Annual Int'l Symp. on Fault-Tolerant Computing (FTCS-24)*, pages 298–307, June 1994.

[9] D. B. Johnson and W. Zwaenepoel. Sender-based Message Logging. In *Proc. of the 17th Annual Int'l Symp. on Fault-Tolerant Computing (FTCS-17)*, pages 14–19, July 1987.

[10] P. J. Keleher. Update Protocols and Iterative Scientific Applications. In *Proc. of the 12th Int'l Parallel Processing Symp. (IPPS'98)*, pages 675–681, March 1998.

[11] A. Kongmunvattana and N.-F. Tzeng. Lazy Logging and Prefetch-Based Crash Recovery in Software Distributed Shared Memory Systems. In *Proc. of the 13th Int'l Parallel Processing Symp. (IPPS'99)*, pages 399–406, April 1999.

[12] T. Park and H. Y. Yeom. An Efficient Logging Scheme for Lazy Release Consistent Distributed Shared Memory Systems. In *Proc. of the 12th Int'l Parallel Processing Symp. (IPPS'98)*, pages 670–674, March 1998.

[13] G. G. Richard III and M. Singhal. Using Logging and Asynchronous Checkpointing to Implement Recoverable Distributed Shared Memory. In *Proc. of the 12th IEEE Symp. on Reliable Distributed Systems*, pages 58–67, Oct. 1993.

[14] R. Samanta, A. Bilas, L. Iftode, and J. P. Singh. Home-Based SVM Protocols for SMP Clusters: Design and Performance. In *Proc. of the 4th IEEE Symp. on High-Performance Computer Architecture*, pages 113–124, February 1998.

[15] J. P. Singh, W.-D. Weber, and A. Gupta. SPLASH: Stanford Parallel Applications for Shared-Memory. *Computer Architecture News*, 20(1):5–44, March 1992.

[16] R. E. Strom and S. Yemini. Optimistic Recovery in Distributed Systems. *ACM Trans. on Computer Systems*, 3(3):204–226, August 1985.

[17] G. Suri, B. Janssens, and W. K. Fuchs. Reduced Overhead Logging for Rollback Recovery in Distributed Shared Memory. In *Proc. of the 25th Annual Int'l Symp. on Fault-Tolerant Computing (FTCS-25)*, pages 279–288, June 1995.

[18] Y. Zhou, L. Iftode, and K. Li. Performance Evaluation of Two Home-Based Lazy Release Consistency Protocols for Shared Virtual Memory Systems. In *Proc. of the 2nd USENIX Symp. on Operating Systems Design and Implementation (OSDI)*, pages 75–88, October 1996.

Moving Home-based Lazy Release Consistency for Shared Virtual Memory Systems

Jae Woong Chung
Central Research Institute
Samsung Heavy Industries Co., LTD.
Daeduk Science Town, Taejon, Korea
jwchung@core.kaist.ac.kr

Byeong Hag Seong, Kyu Ho Park, Daeyeon Park
Department of Electrical Engineering
Korea Advanced Institute of Science and Technology
Kusong-Dong, Yuong-Gu, Taejon, Korea
bhsung@coregate.kaist.ac.kr,
{kpark,daeyeon}@ee.kaist.ac.kr

Abstract

While Shared Virtual Memory is a cost-effective way to provide an illusion of shared memory to programmers, the performance of the system is limited by its inherent overheads. Several protocols such as Lazy Release Consistency(LRC) and Home-based LRC(HLRC) have been suggested to overcome the overheads. In this paper, we propose a new all-software protocol, Moving Home-based LRC(MHLRC). Its main contribution is to introduce a new concept, Moving Home. Using it, our protocol provides 4 efficient functionalities: a) providing migration mechanism, b) eliminating the duty of updating the home copy at the end of an interval, c) providing an adaptive home locating scheme, and d) simplifying the update procedure on a stale copy. To evaluate our protocol, we implemented a prototype of MHLRC. The experiment with 4 benchmarks showed that our protocol improved the performance of the system by on the average 10% over LRC, and by up to 96% over HLRC. From the detailed analysis, we found that the improvement mainly comes from the reduction of the coherence action overhead. Our protocol reduced the number of diff operations executed during computation up to 64%(FFT) ~ 0.4%(SOR) against LRC and 56%(FFT) ~ 0.3%(SOR) against HLRC. It also reduces the requirement for memory and network bandwidth.

1. Introduction

Distributed Shared Memory(DSM) is attractive as a solution of realizing shared memory on a large-scale system because it provides a way to scale the system rather easily. While its hardware implementations such as DASH, flash, and TYPHOON have shown their superior performance, there is a problem that they require quite an expense and a long design time. As an cost-effective alternative for it, Shared Virtual Memory(SVM) [13] was suggested. Shared Virtual Memory is one of software approaches for implementing DSM systems and requires no special hardware. To check the validity of a memory access, it uses the page protection mechanism of the operating system which is available in most of off-the-shelf products.

There are some problems to be solved in the shared virtual memory system. First, a high communication latency makes a processor stall for a long time. It is basically due to the fact that the processors in the system are usually loosely-coupled. Even though it can be alleviated with an efficiently designed network interface, an amount of communication overhead is unavoidable. Second, the coherence action overheads(such as interval processing, twin generation, diff creation and application) seriously degrade the performance of the system. Moreover, since the actions are executed in cooperation with its peer processor, the degradation is magnified. Third, it suffers a serious false sharing problem. Since it uses the page protection mechanism of the operating system to maintain the consistency of memory, its memory coherence unit is a page. In most parallel processing applications, a page is too big to be a coherence unit, and a consequential heavy false sharing is inevitable.

Some researches have been done to solve these problems. The Eager Release Consistency(ERC) protocol was first implemented at Munin [3] based on the Release Consistency(RC) memory model [7]. By adapting the RC memory model and allowing multiple writers, its coherence action overhead can be reduced. It also mitigates communication overhead by buffering modifications and propagating them at a release. The Lazy Release Consistency(LRC) [2] protocol has been proposed and implemented in TreadMarks [1]. Its main idea is to delay the propagation of modifications further to the time of an acquire. Based on the idea, it accomplishes its purpose of reducing the requirement for network bandwidth.

The Home-based Lazy Release Consistency(HLRC) protocol [4] is an all-software protocol and conceptually based on AURC. In AURC, every shared page has a *home* copy, the master copy of the page. All modifications on the page at the other nodes are automatically gathered to the home copy through the automatic update hardware. To get a reasonable performance on a common network interface such as Ethernet, HLRC creates diffs at the end of an interval and updates the home with them. As a result of introducing the home, the amount of memory consumption in each node and the number of messages needed to update a page are reduced compared to LRC.

In this paper, we propose Moving Home-based Lazy Release Consistency(MHLRC). The MHLRC protocol is an all-software page-based multiple-writer protocol. The main idea of MHLRC is that it grants *mobility* to the home; named *Moving Home*. Basically like HLRC, MHLRC uses the home copy and updates it with diffs. But unlike HLRC, a moving home can move over the system during an execution of an application.

When a home copy is requested by a non-home node, the home node checks if the given conditions are satisfied(explained in section 3). If the conditions are satisfied, a home transfer happens and the non-home node becomes a new home node. In this way, the moving home changes its location dynamically over the system depending on the memory access pattern of the application. Since only one node at a time can be a home node, if multiple nodes try to get the home copy at a time, the home transfer is allowed to only one of them. In this case, the other nodes act in the same way with the non-home nodes in HLRC; fetching the home copy and updating the home with diffs at the end of the interval. Our protocol has four strong points over the previous protocols.

- It introduces migration mechanism in addition to replication mechanism. By virtue of it, our protocol is adaptive to the various memory access patterns of applications. For some memory access patterns, it does not require any diff operation. And after the home transfer, the copy of the previous home node can be discarded freely for a better memory management.
- The update procedure to the home node at the end of an interval can be eliminated when the home transfer happens. It saves the computing power for creating and applying diffs. The network bandwidth and the memory for them are also saved.
- It provides an adaptive home locating scheme to the system. Since the remote miss handling overhead of the shared virtual memory system is serious, it is very important to decide where to locate each home. But in the previous protocols, only a static scheme is provided and it is not enough to deal with the problem. By

transferring a moving home to the node which actually accesses the page, our protocol changes the location of the moving home dynamically and adaptively.

- Our protocol inherits some of the benefits in HLRC. So a node can update its stale copy by fetching an up-to-date copy from the home node with a single roundtrip communication. It reduces communication traffics and memory consumption for the coherence actions.

The rest of the paper is organized as follows. A detailed explanation of LRC and HLRC is represented in section 2. In section 3 we explain the concept and the main idea of MHLRC. The results of the evaluation are given in section 4. We conclude this paper in section 5.

2. LRC and Home-based LRC

This section describes two important consistency protocols for Shared Virtual Memory systems: Lazy Release Consistency[2] and Home-based LRC[4].

2.1. Lazy Release Consistency

The original Lazy Release Consistency [2] is implemented in the TreadMarks system [1] which is an all-software system. It allows multiple writers and maintains the coherence of memory at a page size. Its main idea is that it does not propagate the modifications on shared pages at the time of a release, but postpones the propagation until the time of an acquire. To provide the RC memory model[7] to programmers, it uses *intervals*. So all the accesses of an execution in a processor are divided into distinct intervals. An interval begins with each special access such as a release and an acquire. By maintaining the happened-before ordering[6] between the intervals, RC can be maintained. For it, each processor has its own *vector timestamp*; the recent interval information of all processors the processor knows.

At the time of an acquire, after comparing its vector timestamp with the releasing processor's, the acquiring processor receives from the releasing processor *write notices* holding up-to-date information about shared pages and invalidates the pages indicated by them. At an actual access on the invalidated page, the processor updates the page by collecting the *diffs* which contains the previous modifications on the page. At the time of a release, the releasing processor creates diffs and write notices to record the modifications at the current interval.[1] The processor stores them in its local memory for future demands on them from

---

[1] The diff creation on a page is done using *twin*. Twin is a copy of the page made at the first modification on the page in a new interval. All the modification during the interval can be found by the comparison with it at the end of the interval.

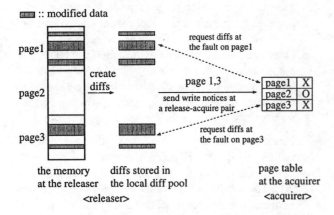

Figure 1. The coherence actions of LRC with an invalidation protocol at a release-acquire pair.

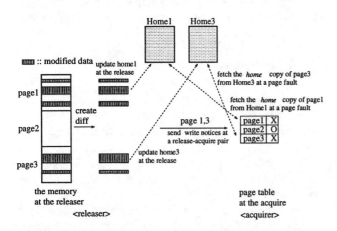

Figure 2. The coherence actions of HLRC at a release-acquire pair.

other processors. Figure 1 illustrates how the LRC protocol works at a release-acquire pair.

Since modifications on a page are propagated only to the processors which actually need to see them, LRC reduces an amount of message exchanges and the coherence action overhead. There are several week points in LRC. First, LRC still requires quite an amount of expensive diff operations for propagation of modifications on a shared page. Second, since multiple diffs should be collected to update a stale copy, its fault handling time is long. Third, LRC consumes memory substantially to store diffs, twins, and write notices. Since they can not be discarded until it is ascertained that no node needs them, the number of diffs and write notices to be stored increases quickly as time goes on. To deal with this problem, *garbage collection* mechanism is used. [1]

2.2. Home-based Lazy Release Consistency

HLRC is an all-software page-based multiple-writer protocol. Its prototype has been implemented at Princeton Univ[4]. It is conceptually based on Automatic Update Release Consistency(AURC)[5]: a software protocol with support of *automatic update hardware*(i.e. SHRIMP[8]). In AURC, every shared page has its *home* copy which is maintained up-to-date by collecting the modifications on the page at other nodes through the automatic update hardware. By fetching the home copy, a node can update its stale copy with a single roundtrip communication. The main idea of HLRC is similar to AURC so that it also uses a *home* node for each shared page. But instead of updating the home node at every write like AURC, it updates the home node with diffs only at the end of an interval.

At the time of an acquire, after comparing its vector timestamp with the releasing processor's, the acquiring processor receives write notices and invalidates the pages indicated by them. When an actual access happens on the invalidated page, the faulting node updates its stale copy by fetching the home copy from the home node. At the time of a release, the releasing processor uses diffs to update the home node. Figure 2 shows the overall operations of HLRC at a release-acquire pair.

HLRC has several advantages over LRC. First, a processor can update an invalidated page with a single roundtrip communication with the home node. Second, since all the modification on a shared page is collected and stored in the home copy, its memory requirement to store diffs and protocol data is much smaller than that of LRC. Third, there is no page fault at the home node because the home copy is always up-to-date. But there are also several weak points in HLRC. First, at the end of an interval, a non-home node has a duty to update the home copies of the pages the node has modified during the interval. The update procedure accompanies expensive diff operations. Second, the location of a home is fixed at a specific node during an execution of an application. It can cause a high remote miss ratio. Third, a programmer, not a system, has to decide which node is best to be a home node of a shared page (*home locating problem*). Moreover the performance of HLRC is quite sensitive to the locations of homes. So if a user fails to solve the problem wisely, he has to face a serious performance degradation.

3. Moving Home-based Lazy Release Consistency(MHLRC)

3.1. The basic idea and mechanism of MHLRC

We suggest a new software protocol: Moving Home-based Lazy Release Consistency(MHLRC). MHLRC is an

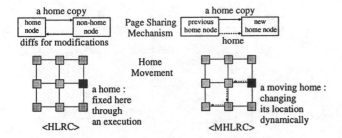

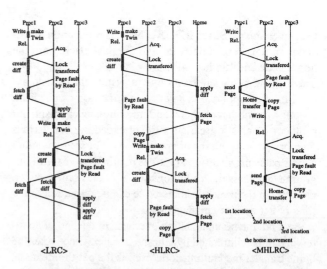

Figure 3. The characteristics of Moving Home.

Figure 4. This figure shows the difference between the protocols.

all-software page-based multiple-writer protocol. It uses *intervals* and *vector timestamps* to satisfy the requirement of RC. Its main idea is that it grants *mobility* to a home; named *Moving Home*. Similar to the *home* of HLRC, a moving home for each shared page has a home copy. When a node causes a page fault on the page, the node can update its stale copy by fetching the home copy from the moving home with a single roundtrip communication. The most distinctive characteristic of the moving home is that *it can move dynamically over nodes depending on the memory access pattern of an application*. From a close observation on HLRC, it is found that the only requirement for a node to be the home node of a page is that the node must have an up-to-date copy of the page. Since at a page fault a faulting node fetches an up-to-date copy of the page from the home node, at this moment the node becomes to have an equivalent capability to be a home node of the page.[2] Just by setting one special bit in a page transfer message, the home can be transfered to the faulting node. The characteristics of the moving home is illustrated in Figure 3. By the page fetching accompanied by the home transfer, the moving home can change its location dynamically for an execution of an application. The various advantages of this property are explained in the following section.

There are some conditions to be satisfied at the home transfer. If the conditions are not satisfied, the home transfer is not allowed. The first condition is that there has been no modification on the home copy by the home node during the current interval. By prohibiting the home transfer, the home node can avoid the coherence action overhead for the modifications at the end of the current interval. The second condition is that the page must not be a page fetched in the current interval. When a node fetches a page, it can be supposed that the node is going to use the page for quite some time. It is better to guarantee somewhat a time for the node to possess the page. When the home transfer is not allowed, the operations between the home node and a non-home node are the same with those in HLRC.

Figure 4 clearly shows the difference of MHLRC from

---

[2]In MHLRC, the home node of a page is the node in which the moving home of the page is currently located.

protocol	diff operation	page update scheme at non-home	page update scheme at home	# of roundtrip communication for page update	data structure	hardware support	migration mechanism
							X : meaningless
LRC	required	collecting diffs	X	many	complex	no	no
AURC	not used	page transfer	automatic update (cache line)	one	simple	yes	no
HLRC	required	page transfer	sending diff	one	simple	no	no
MHLRC	may not required	page transfer	sending diff if needed	one	simple	no	yes

Table 1. The difference between the protocols.

LRC and HLRC. At the first glance, it can be noticed how much our protocol simplifies the operations related to coherence actions than LRC and HLRC when the home transfer is allowed. By transferring the home itself, a lot of operations for making twins, creating diffs, and applying diffs become unnecessary. The Table 1 summarizes the main differences between the four protocols for the shared virtual memory system. Figure 5 shows the state diagram of our protocol. There are 8 states in MHLRC. The names of the states are combinations of the following characters; R(readable), W(writable), H(home), nH(non-home), M(movable), nM(immovable), T(transient state). *An event* invoking a state transition and *the action* handling the event are shown as a pair of event/action. If no action is needed, only the event is denoted.

3.2. Merits and demerits of MHLRC

MHLRC has various benefits over the previous protocols. First, page migration mechanism is provided in addition to replication mechanism. In HLRC, if a node wants to share a page, the only possible way for it is to fetch a copy of the page from the home and to update the home copy with diffs at the end of the interval. It is basically replication mechanism. But in MHLRC besides replication mechanism, a non-home node can take the page itself from the home node and can become a new home node of the page. The moving home can travel over a system through an execution of an application and that is migration mechanism. By allowing both replication and migration mechanism, our protocol obtains a great adjustment capability for various memory access patterns of applications. For some memory access patterns, *no* diff operation is required by virtue of migration mechanism. In addition to it, after the home transfer, the copy in the previous home node can be discarded freely for a better memory management.

Second, the home updating overhead at the end of an interval can be eliminated by a home transfer. Since after the home transfer the faulting node itself is the new home node, there is no need to send modifications to the previous home node at the end of the interval. The actual advantages obtained from this benefit are substantial. Expensive diff operations involved in the update procedure is eliminated. As a consequence, memory requirement for diffs and twins is reduced. The message handling overhead and the requirement for network bandwidth are also reduced because a number of message exchanges for diffs are removed. Third, our protocol solves the home locating problem nicely without support from programmers. Since a home is fixed through an execution in HLRC, the protocol can do little for the problem after the location of the home is decided by a programmer or by a runtime distributor in a system. But in MHLRC, since the moving home changes its location dynamically and automatically during the execution, programmers are relieved from the home locating problem. It also mitigates the performance degradation due to a wrong user specification on the location of the home.

Fourth, MHLRC shares some advantages of HLRC over LRC. Since the moving home is taking the role of the home in HLRC, it is natural for the moving home to inherit some advantages of the home in HLRC. One is that a non-home node can update its stale copy with a single round-trip communication. Another is that the amount of protocol data and messages required in MHLRC are much smaller than under LRC.

There is one protocol overhead in MHLRC. After a home transfer happens, the new location of the moving home should be announced to the other nodes in the system. To do so, additional message exchanges and message handling operations are required and that is *home finding overhead*. Various solutions to reduce the overhead will be explained in the following section.

3.3. Home finding overhead and the solutions for it

As said above, the home finding overhead is the overhead to find the current location of the moving home. It

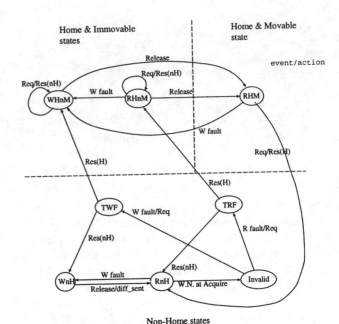

RHM : Readable & is_Home & Movable state
RHnM : Readable & is_Home & Immovable state
WHnM : Writable & is_Home & Immovable state
TWF : Transient state in Write fault
TRF : Transient state in Read fault
RnH : Readable & isn't_Home state
WnH : Writable & isn't Home state
Invalid : Invalide state

R fault : Read fault
W fault : Write fault
Req : Page Request to Home
Res(H) : Home transfer is allowed
Res(nH) : Home transfer isn't allowed
Release : perform the following release
diff_sent : a diff is sent to update Home
W.N. at Acquire :
the page is invalidated by write notice
at the acquire

Figure 5. The state diagram of the MHLRC protocol.

is basically the same problem with the page owner finding problem in the previous DSM systems [9]. There are three major schemes for the problem: broadcasting, using a home location server, or managing with linked lists. We adapted the third scheme to manage the home location information with scalability. At every home transfer, the previous home node makes a pointer to indicate the new home node. So one linked list for one moving home is generated along its migration route. With this scheme, we can manage the home location information in a distributed manner. Its weak point is that at a bad case it will take a long time for a node to trace the linked list.

Before finding techniques to shorten the tracing time, we first analyze the situation where the tracing happens. In MHLRC, a node communicates with a home node in two cases. One is at page faults, and the other is at the end of an interval. Tracing a linked list actually means forwarding a message along the linked list. In the former case, a page request message is forwarded, and it is a relatively simple problem because the size of the message is small. But in the latter case, since diffs are forwarded and they are not small, the forwarding overhead is not negligible.

To avoid the diff forwarding, we introduced an *acknowl-*

edgment directory. A moving home of a page has one acknowledgment directory for the page. At every time the home transfer is not allowed for a faulting node, the home node records the node in its acknowledgment directory. The node is removed from the acknowledgment directory when it updates the home node with diffs. When a home transfer happens, the new location of the moving home is multicasted only to the nodes recorded in the acknowledgment directory. The nodes in the acknowledgment directory can send diffs directly to the current home node because it becomes aware of the recent location of the moving home through the multicasting. Another useful technique is to flush information about the home location at the barrier. In addition to it, the locations of the moving homes can also be propagated by piggybacking them on other messages(e.g. lock transfer message, page transfer message, and so forth). With these techniques above, our protocol can substantially reduce the home finding overhead.

4. Performance Evaluation

4.1. Prototype and experimental environment

To evaluate our protocol, we have implemented a prototype of MHLRC. To lessen the difficulty of implementing it from a sketch, we used Coherent Virtual Machine(CVM) [10] as a starting point of our implementation. CVM is a software distributed shared memory system. It is written in C++ and designed typically as a platform for protocol experimentation.

Our experimental environment consists of 8 Pentium-100MHz CPU. Each node has 64MByte RAM and the operating system is LINUX. They are connected with Myrinet and 8-port Myrinet-LAN switch is used. The interface card works with 32-bit 33MHz PCI bus and has 1MByte memory for buffering. The physical cable operates at the speed of 1.28 Giga bits per second.

We evaluated our protocol with 4 benchmarks: Water-Nsquared (1000 moles), SOR (2000 × 1000 matrix), LU (1024 × 1024 matrix, 32 × 32 block), and FFT (128 × 64 × 64 matrix). Water-Nsquared, LU, and FFT are from Splash-2 [11] suite and SOR is included in CVM suite.

4.2. Speedup

We measured the execution time of each application on 1 through 8 nodes(Figure 6). From the figure, it can be clearly observed that MHLRC outperforms the others: HLRC, LRC. MHLRC works on an average 10% faster than LRC. Only for LU, the speedup line of LRC is close to MHLRC. The performance improvement of MHLRC over HLRC are from 5% to 96%. HLRC does not work as much efficiently as said in [4]. For SOR, the performance of HLRC is just

about a half of that of MHLRC. In [4], the home nodes of pages might be chosen very carefully by a programmer. In our experiment, the home nodes of pages were decided in round-robin manner for both MHLRC and HLRC. It is one of general approaches a system can do without support from the compiler or a special manipulation from a user. In Figure 6, it is shown that how efficiently and automatically MHLRC copes with the home locating problem over HLRC on the same condition. An additional enhancement was given for HLRC so that a location of a home could be changed at a barrier. HLRC worked a little better with it.

4.3. Effect of a Moving Home

To see the effect of the moving home on the performance of the system, we distinguished page faults into 4 categories and measured each one separately. In Figure 7, *data_fetch type* represents the case that a fault happens on a stale page. *Data_fetch(H) type* is only for MHLRC and account for the data fetching accompanied by the home transfer. A *valid_fault type* fault happens when the first modification on an up-to-date page is caught at non-home nodes.[3] *Home_fault type* is only in HLRC and MHLRC, and represents the faults at home nodes. Table 2 summarizes the coherence actions taken for each fault type in each protocol. Since the processing time for intervals and write notices is included in every case, it is omitted.

There are two important observations to be made in Figure 7. First, in MHLRC data_fetch type is quite small and data_fetch(H) type is large. It means that most of the page fetching are accompanied by home transfers. Since FFT, LU, and SOR exhibit a single-writer multiple-reader sharing pattern [12], the home transfer can occur frequently. Only for Water-Nsquared, data_fetch type is comparable to data_fetch(H). Since Water-Nsquared exhibits a multiple-writer multiple-reader sharing pattern, its complex sharing pattern makes frequently the situations in which the home transfer is not allowed. The large amount of data_fetch(H) type faults means that amount of elimination of the update procedure to the home node: one of the benefits in MHLRC.

Second, home_fault type increases in MHLRC. It is a favor of the adaptive home locating scheme in MHLRC. Since the moving home moves to a node which actually accesses a page, an amount of faults which are valid_fault type in LRC and HLRC are turned to home_fault type faults in MHLRC. An amount of diff operations are eliminated due to it.

To see the influence of the changes in the pattern of page faults, we measured the number of diff operations performed in each protocol. From Figure 8, it is clearly found

---

[3]In the shared virtual memory system, the first modification on a shared page during an interval is forced to cause an interrupt weather its copy of the page is up-to-date or not. It is because in the system, the only way to catch modifications of a processor on the page is to use the page protection mechanism provided by the operating system.

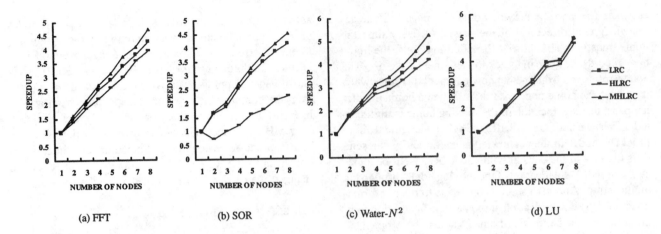

(a) FFT (b) SOR (c) Water-N^2 (d) LU

Figure 6. The speedup.

that MHLRC performs quite a smaller number of diff operations. MHLRC performs 64%(FFT) $\sim$ 0.4%(SOR) of diff operations against LRC and 56%(FFT) $\sim$ 0.3%(SOR) against HLRC. The reduction of diff operations impacts positively over all aspects of the system.

In conclusion, by changing the dominant fault type from the faults accompanied by a heavy coherence action overhead to the faults accompanied by a light coherence action overhead, MHLRC reduces the number of diff operations and overall coherence action overhead.

4.4. Memory consumption

Figure 9 shows memory requirement of each protocol. MHLRC reduces its memory consumption compared to HLRC and LRC. A protocol requiring a large amount of memory causes paging frequently, and it can seriously degrade the performance of the system. One of the benefits in MHLRC is that it reduces memory consumption and allows applications to work well in a system with a small amount of memory. Another effect of a large memory consumption is that it causes garbage collection frequently. Since in our implementation garbage collection is done at a barrier, the result of frequent garbage collection is an increment in the barrier time.

In Figure 9, HLRC uses 1.2(Water-Nsquared) $\sim$ 4.5(LU) times larger memory than MHLRC. It is mainly due to saving of memory consumption for twins. Since the update procedure to a home node is eliminated by the home transfer, the need to make twins also disappears and the memory for it is saved. LRC uses much more memory than MHLRC. The additional difference comes from memory consumption for diffs. It is one of benefits inherited from HLRC[4]. By storing all modifications from multiple writers in the master copy of a home node, both HLRC and MHLRC can save the local memory used for storing diffs. LRC uses

	at handling the fault			at the end of the corresponding interval		
	LRC	HLRC	MHLRC	LRC	HLRC	MHLRC
Home_fault type	X	None	None	X	None	None
Valid_fault type	None	None	None	a diff creation	a diff creation and sending to a home	a diff creation and sending to a home
Data_fetch (H) type	X	X	a page fetching	X	X	None
Data_fetch type	multiple diffs collecting and application	a page fetching	a page fetching	a diff creation	a diff creation and sending to a home	a diff creation and sending to a home

* The processing time for intervals and write notices isn't represented.
* X = doesn't occur

Table 2. The coherence actions of each protocol for handling a page fault.

3.8(SOR) $\sim$ 11.5(LU) times larger memory than MHLRC. The number of garbage collection executed is shown at the top of each graph.

4.5. Communication traffic

Table 3 shows the amount of communication traffic required by each protocol. The result of a comparison between LRC and MHLRC is sensitive to a sharing pattern of an application. For FFT, SOR, and LU, MHLRC and LRC generate almost the same amount of communication traffic. The result is consistent with [4]. Since these applications have a single-writer multiple-reader sharing pattern and use migratory data, a faulting node can find all diffs from the last writer with a single roundtrip communications in LRC. For Water-Nsquared, MHLRC generates more packets than LRC. It is primarily because of its multiple-writer multiple-reader sharing pattern[12]. Since it induces a lot of data transfers unaccompanied by the home transfer, the positive effect of the home transfer is diluted. As a consequence, a substantial number of packets are generated to update the master copy of the home node.

288

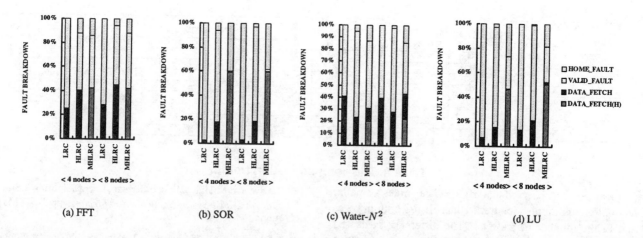

Figure 7. The analysis on the faults of each protocol.

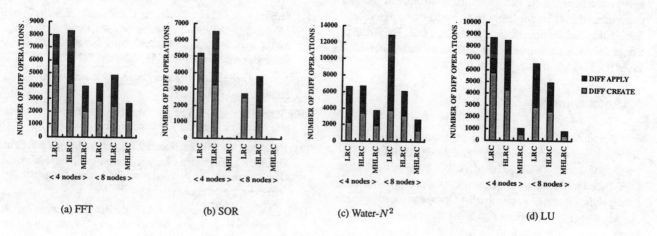

Figure 8. The number of diff creation and application.

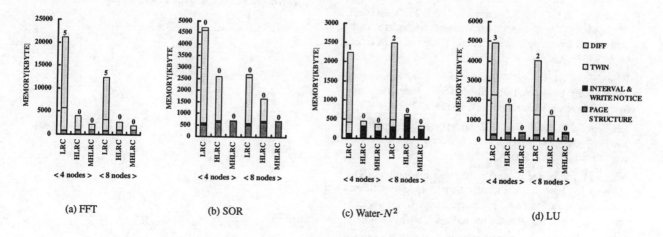

Figure 9. The memory requirement of each protocol.

APPLICATION		SEND						FORWARD					
		PACKET NUMBER			KBYTES			PACKET NUMBER			KBYTES		
		LRC	HLRC	MHLRC	LRC	HLRC	MHLRC	LRC	HLRC	MHLRC	LRC	HLRC	MHLRC
FFT	4 node	7350	13487	7470	14973.9	27561.4	15271.5	0	0	393	0	0	12.33
	8 node	4665	8158	4876	8985.5	16674	9973.3	0	0	370	0	0	11.7
SOR	4 node	1583	8801	1579	3158.5	17648.2	3166.3	0	0	5	0	0	0.1
	8 node	961	5171	959	1882.7	10363.9	1892.3	0	0	50	0	0	1.6
Water-N^2	4 node	11793	16535	13776	2702.9	6699.7	6450.1	1759	1760	2734	178.6	714.9	254.7
	8 node	12631	14976	11331	2265.3	6565.2	6783	3260	2258	4071	230.1	229.3	335.1
LU	4 node	2842	10173	2484	4953.3	6477.5	4078.2	0	0	301	0	0	9.4
	8 node	2528	6428	2136	4789	7180.1	3572.3	0	0	796	0	0	24.9

Table 3. The communication traffic.

It can be also observed that MHLRC generates a smaller amount of communication traffic than HLRC both in bytes and in the number of packets. The difference is caused by two kinds of benefits in MHLRC. One is the adaptive home locating scheme provided by MHLRC. In Table 3, especially for SOR, failing to solve the home locating problem systematically, HLRC generates a substantial number of additional packets for fetching an up-to-date page from a home node and sending diffs to the home node. By virtue of a page fetching accompanied by the home transfer, MHLRC saves packets for updating the home node.

5. Conclusion

To improve the performance of shared virtual memory systems, we proposed Moving Home-based Lazy Release Consistency(MHLRC). MHLRC is an all-software page-based multiple-writer protocol. Our protocol has four strong points over the previous all-software protocols. With the advantages, we believe that our protocol will show its excellence on larger-scale systems.

References

[1] P.Keleher, A.L.Cox, S.Dwarkadas, and W.Zwaenepoel, "TreadMarks: Distributed Shared Memory on Standard Workstations and Operating Systems", *Proc. Winter USENIX Conf.*, pp 115-132, Jan. 1994.

[2] P.Keleher, A.L.Cox, and W.Zwaenepoel, "Lazy Consistency for Software Distributed Shared Memory", *Proc. 19th Ann. Symp. Computer Architecture*, pp 13-21, May 1992.

[3] J.B.Carter, J.K.Benett, and W.Zwaenepoel, "Implementation and Performance of Munin", *Proc. 13th Symp. Operating Systems Principles*, pp 152-164, Oct. 1991.

[4] Y.Zhou, L.Iftode, and K.Li, "Performance Evaluation of Two Home-based Lazy Release Consistency Protocols for Shared Virtual Memory Systems", *Proc. 2nd Symp. Operating Systems Design and Implementation*, pp 75-88, Oct. 1996.

[5] L.Iftode, C.Dubnicki, E.W.Felten, and K.Li, "Improving Release-Consistent Shared Virtual Memory using Automatic Update", *Proc. 2nd IEEE Symp. High-Performance Computer Architecture*, Feb. 1996.

[6] S.Adve and M.Hill, "Weak ordering: A new definition", *Proc. 17th Ann. Int'l Symp. Computer Architecture*, pp 2-14, May 1990.

[7] K.Gharachorloo, D.Lenoski, J.Laudon, P.Gibbons, A.Gupta, and J.Hennessy, "Memory consistency and event ordering in scalable shared memory multiprocessors", *Proc. 17th Ann. Int'l Symp. Computer Architecture*, pp 15-26, May 1990.

[8] M.Blumrich, K.Li, R.Alpert, C.Dubnicki, E.Felten, and J.Sandberg, "A Virtual Memory mapped Network Interface for the SHRIMP Multicomputer".*Proc. 21st Ann. Int'l Symp. Computer Architecture*, pp 142-153, Apr. 1994.

[9] A.S.Tanenbaum, *Distributed Operating System*, pp 339-342, Prentice Hall 1995.

[10] P.Keleher, CVM Version 0.2 Manual, http://www.cs.umd.edu/projects/cvm.html.

[11] S.C.Woo, M.Ohara, E.Torrie, J.P.Singh, and A. Gupta, "The SPLASH-2 Programs: Characterization and Methodological Considerations", *Proc. 22nd Ann. Int'l Symp. Computer Architecture*, pp 24-36, May 1995.

[12] L.Iftode, J.P.Singh, and K.Li, "Understanding Application Performance on Shared Virtual Memory", *Proc. 23rd Ann. Int'l Symp. Computer Architecture*, May 1996.

[13] K.Li and P.Hudak, "Memory Coherence in Shared Virtual Memory Systems", *Proc. 5th Ann. ACM Symp. Principles of Distributed Computing*, pp 229-239, Aug. 1986.

Producer-Push – a Protocol Enhancement to Page-based Software Distributed Shared Memory Systems

Sven Karlsson and Mats Brorsson

Computer Systems Group, Department of Information Technology, Lund University

P.O. Box 118, SE-221 00 LUND, Sweden

email: Sven.Karlsson@it.lth.se, URL: http://www.it.lth.se

Abstract

This paper describes a technique called producer-push that enhances the performance of a page-based software distributed shared memory system. Shared data, in software DSM systems, must normally be requested from the node that produced the latest value. Producer-push utilizes the execution history to predict this communication so that the data is pushed to the consumer before it is requested. In contrast to previously proposed mechanisms to proactively send data to where it is needed, producer-push uses information about the source code location of communication to more accurately predict the needed communication.

Producer-push requires no source code modifications of the application and it effectively reduces the latency of shared memory accesses. This is confirmed by our performance evaluation which shows that the average time to wait for memory updates is reduced by 74%. Producer-push also changes the communication pattern of an application making it more suitable for modern networks. The latter is a result of a 44% reduction of the average number of messages and an enlargement of the average message size by 65%.

1. Introduction

Systems that implement a shared memory programming model on a distributed memory architecture provide a cost-effective means to create parallel computing platforms that are relatively easy to program. Such systems are generally called *software distributed shared memory*, software DSM, systems and can easily be put together from commodity components such as PCs and standard networks. Current LAN technologies are possible to use but generally deliver poor performance. However, high-bandwidth, low-latency networks such as SCI [15], have been available as off-the-shelf components for some time and it is likely that more high-performance network technologies will emerge.

Even with a standard ATM T1 network it is possible to achieve reasonable efficiency (50%-90%) for a wide range of applications on a software DSM system [16, 8]. However, given the current performance growth of microprocessor technology, it has been shown that even if the network technology keeps up with the processor performance trend, aggressive latency hiding techniques will be needed to sustain the parallel performance efficiency in the future [5, 16].

The existing standard technique to tolerate shared memory latency is to use a relaxed memory model [6]. In this paper we present a technique that complements this idea to mask and overlap some of the communication latency in shared memory applications on a software DSM system. In a shared memory parallel computing model with relaxed memory the actual transfer of data does not occur when the data is produced but is deferred to when it is needed, i.e. when a processor issues a load- or store-instruction to a data item that has previously been written by some other processor. This leads to a request-reply scheme where data is requested and the processor that has an up-to-date copy replies. As a consequence, the communication latency will directly contribute to the execution time.

We have implemented and evaluated a technique called *producer-push* that uses simple heuristics to determine when data that has been modified by one processor is needed by some other processor and to push that data to its anticipated destination before it has been requested. This communication can thus be almost completely overlapped with computation on the receiving processor. An additional advantage is that the processor that needs the data will not

The research in this paper was supported with computing resources by the Swedish council for High Performance Computing (HPDR) and Center for High Performance Computing (PDC), Royal Institute of Technology.

be required to send a request message since the data is already present in the local memory.

We have integrated the producer-push technique in TreadMarks, a state-of-the-art software DSM system [2]. The heuristics trigger producer-initiated communication automatically without modification of the application and, based on repetitive access patterns, is found to predict communication in certain parallel applications. We have performed an evaluation on seven applications from the TreadMarks distribution that we executed with and without the producer-push technique on an IBM SP2 using up to eight processing nodes. The evaluation shows that the producer-push technique indeed effectively reduces the time to request shared data. The resulting performance improvement depends on the original efficiency of the application. Our experiments show a performance improvement of 55% in one case. Producer-push also does not hurt performance for applications that do not fit into the behaviour assumed by the simple heuristics.

The performance improvement is mainly due to a reduction in the time an application spends in the communication routines. There are two reasons for this. First, the requests for memory updates can in many cases be eliminated since the updated memory is already in place; second, the interconnection network is better utilized since producer-push results in fewer and larger messages.

1.1 Contributions

The idea to transfer data before it has been requested is not new in the context of software DSM systems. The success, or lack of success, depends on the quality of the mechanism that decides what to send and when. If the mechanism decides to send more data than is actually needed, or to the wrong destinations, the performance gain is usually smaller than the performance loss because of the increased network traffic.

Keleher proposed a lazy-hybrid protocol in his Ph.D. thesis that appears similar to the protocol enhancement proposed here [11]. He later re-evaluated this protocol in the context of home-based software DSM systems [12]. The lazy-hybrid protocol is, like our technique, based on repetitive access patterns but uses more indiscriminate heuristics that lead it to send substantially more data than needed and to processors that do not use it. Seidel et al. have proposed an almost identical technique in their Affinity Entry Consistency Protocol [17].

In contrast to the techniques proposed by Keleher and Seidel, the heuristics in our producer-push technique go one step further to identify the correct time to send data proactively by means of an identification of where in the program new data is generated. This is described in detail in section 2.

Producer-push is related to producer initiated communication commonly found in message-passing applications [1]. However, it is also fundamentally different in that it does not require that explicit message passing code is inserted into the applications. Instead the software DSM system takes care of all message passing. No modification of the application's source code is needed at all.

Prefetching [4, 9] is also closely related to producer-push in that it tries to move data to its destination before it has been requested. However, while producer-push reduces the number of messages since the data is moved proactively, prefetching uses the same request-reply scheme as the normal protocol does and if the efficiency of the prefetching scheme is not very high it will send much more data over the network than needed. Producer-push eliminates many of the small request messages and thus utilizes the network better.

In short, the contributions in this paper are:
- the specification and implementation of producer-push in TreadMarks
- a thorough performance evaluation that provides valuable insight into parallel application behaviour

The performance evaluation was done on an upgraded IBM SP2 system with substantially higher performance than the experimental systems used by Keleher and Seidel.

In the rest of the paper we next describe the lazy release consistency protocol and how producer-push has a potential to increase performance. In section 3 we then describe our experimental methodology that we have used to evaluate the producer-push technique. The results are presented in section 4 and after a short discussion on potential improvements of producer-push in section 5, the paper is concluded in section 6.

2. Lazy release consistency and producer-push

2.1 The TreadMarks software DSM system

TreadMarks is a software package that provides programmers with a shared memory programming model on top of a network of workstations, NOW [2]. Although TreadMarks defines its own programming model, it has been shown that it is possible to implement a standard programming model such as OpenMP on top of TreadMarks [7, 14]. As the nodes in a NOW do not physically share memory, information about changes to the shared memory is captured through the use of the address translation mechanism in the processor which then invokes the consistency protocol. The coherence granularity is thus a virtual page. The performance penalty to maintain memory coherency in software and with such a coarse granularity is very high and therefore TreadMarks uses a relaxed memory consistency model with a multiple-writer, invalidate protocol.

In a relaxed memory model information about changes in the shared memory may be delayed to a synchronization point [6]. If all accesses to shared data in a shared memory program are protected by synchronization mechanisms, e.g. barriers or locks, we say that the program is data race free. It is thus not necessary that all processors see the same shared memory image at a given time. If a variable is protected by a lock and modified by a processor, it is only necessary to inform another processor about this update when the lock has been released and acquired by the other processor.

This memory model has been further improved in TreadMarks to reduce communication. A processor is notified about the changes to the shared memory made by other processors at the time of a lock acquire (instead of at the lock release as is normal in relaxed memory models). The actual data is of course not transferred until it is needed which is signalled by a memory access fault. This mechanism is called *lazy release consistency*, LRC. Since the implementation of producer-push is intimately related to LRC we shortly explain how LRC works with a simple example in figure 1.

In this example three processors access two variables within the same virtual page. Processor 0 first reads and writes to variable X and processor 1 reads and writes to variable Y. The processors are then synchronized with a barrier and after this, processor 2 reads and writes variable X. It should then see the value of X that was updated by processor 0 before the barrier. To achieve this, a copy of the page, called a *twin*, is created when processor 0 modifies the variable for the first time. This is done by the page fault handler that is invoked at the write access since the page is write-protected from the start of the execution.

In the code for the barrier, each processor sends a message to processor 0 to notify that it has reached the barrier. Together with this message it transmits information about which pages it has modified during the previous *interval*. This information is called a *write notice*. Processor 0 collects all write notices, including the ones that have been created by itself, and redistributes them to all processors with the same message that signals to all processors that they can proceed past the barrier.

When a processor receives the barrier release message, it continues execution after having removed all permissions to access pages for which it has received write notices. Thus, when processor 2 later accesses variable X it will experience a page fault. Processor 2 has received two write notices for this particular page since both processor 0 and 1 have modified data in the page. It will then send a message to both processor 0 and 1 and request the updated memory. In order to save time and to easier combine the changes by processors 0 and 1, these processors creates a *diff* that is an encoding of the changes made by only this processor. For this reason it uses the twin created earlier. When the diff has been created, it is sent to processor 2 that applies the changes and when all diffs have arrived it continues with its memory reference.

Lazy release protocols reduce network bandwidth requirements at the expense of increased latency caused when faulting processors have to wait for diffs to arrive. This latency is analogous to coherency miss latencies in hardware based systems. Another approach would be to let the processor broadcast all of its diffs directly when it enters a barrier. Protocols that behave like this are called eager protocols [13]. It has been shown that lazy protocols

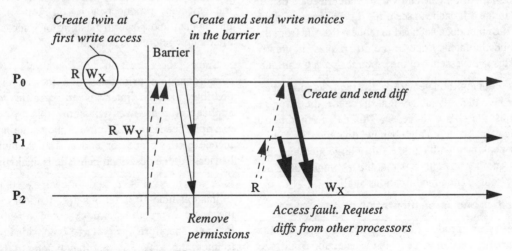

RW_X Reads and writes to address X

RW_Y Reads and writes to address Y in same page as X

Figure 1. The Lazy Release Consistency protocol in TreadMarks defers the propagation of consistency information to the latest possible moment.

outperform eager protocols since eager protocols send too much data so that even very high performance networks become saturated.

2.2 Producer-push overview

The vast majority of parallel scientific applications use some sort of iterative algorithm. It could be a system simulation by small time steps or an iterative algorithm of a numerical problem. Such an application typically performs the same calculations repetitively in each iteration and also often uses the same data. We could thus use information gathered during one iteration to predict the communication in the following iterations. Really simple applications only have one phase which is repeated over and over again. For such applications the lazy-hybrid protocol as proposed by Keleher would perform very well [11]. However, many applications consist of several phases and for these applications the simple heuristics used to send data proactively in the lazy-hybrid protocol will send too much data.

A processor can collect information on which other processors that have requested diffs during an interval, i.e., a TreadMarks interval as described earlier. The processors that have issued diff requests are called *consumers*, since they want to use data. The processor that responds to the diff requests are in this context called *producer*. From the diff requests, the producer can, when it enters a barrier or releases a lock, collect information regarding which diffs the *consumers* need in a phase of the computation. Knowing this, the producer can send these diffs directly after it has released a lock or entered a barrier the next time it comes to this phase. We call this *pushing*. The consumer stores the pushed diffs in a diff cache and when it later needs a diff, it first looks in the diff cache to see if the diff has been pushed. If so, the consumer does not need to request the diff from the producer and the latency due to the diff request is greatly reduced. This is the essence of the *producer-push* technique.

Besides reducing the latency for diff requests, producer-push also has the advantage that it cause the average network message size to increase. This can further boost performance since modern high bandwidth networks cannot reach their peak bandwidth unless fairly large messages are used [10]. Another advantage is that the technique does not require any source code modifications at all.

2.3 Heuristics and implementation

In order to make producer-push work well we need some kind of heuristic that can guide us in the selection of diffs to push, when the diffs should be pushed and which processor they should be pushed to. We describe here the heuristic that we have used and some details about the actual implementation. We first describe how we find *logical intervals* in the execution related to phases in the execution.

```
int i;
for (i=0; i<N; i++)
{
    do_computation_a();
    barrier;
    do_computation_b();
    barrier;
}
```

Figure 2. A simple example of an iterative algorithm.

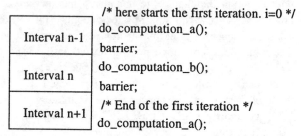

```
/* here starts the first iteration. i=0 */
do_computation_a();
barrier;
do_computation_b();
barrier;
/* End of the first iteration */
do_computation_a();
```

Figure 3. An illustration of the intervals in the simple example.

We use this information to determine when diffs are to be pushed.

Internally TreadMarks uses so called intervals to keep accurate time stamps on all diffs. The interval is a description of a small part of the application's execution time. New intervals are created at barriers and when a lock is released. A diff is associated with the specific interval when it was created. It is also the interval mechanism that drives the invalidate consistency protocol. We have implemented producer-push on top of the interval mechanism and perform pushing of selected diffs directly after a new interval is created.

Since the creation of intervals is forced by synchronization primitives like locks and barriers it is possible to bind intervals to specific regions in the application code. We will show this by using a simple example, see figure 2. Figure 3 shows the intervals created in one of the processor nodes. The example is based on barriers but the described heuristic is analogous for locks.

A new interval is created for each execution of a barrier. In this example all iterations are identical in the sense that the same instructions are executed repetitively in each interval. Therefore, interval n+1 is considered to be identical to interval n-1. We say that they belong to the same *logical interval*. In general, applications may in one loop synchronize several times and it is therefore common that a two consecutive TreadMarks intervals refer to different parts in the program. In order to bind intervals to logical intervals we assign a unique identifier to each barrier. We

Logical interval ?	Interval n-1	do_computation_a(); barrier(0);
Logical interval 0	Interval n	do_computation_b(); barrier(1);
Logical interval 1	Interval n+1	do_computation_a(); barrier(0);
Logical interval 0	Interval n+2	do_computation_b();
Logical interval 1	Interval n+3	barrier(1);

Figure 4. The simple example augmented with logical intervals.

have in our experiments done this with a label for each barrier in the source code but it could just as well be done automatically, either statically by the compiler or in run-time by TreadMarks by observing the program counter value. We have in figure 4 augmented our example with logical intervals. Note that we cannot know which logical interval is bound to interval n-1 from the example. By assigning an identifier to each barrier in an application we can during the second iteration always link a TreadMarks interval to a logical interval.

We next need to predict which diffs to send to which processor in each logical interval. The producing processor gets diff requests from a consuming processor whenever the consumer faults and it cannot find a needed diff in its diff cache. From these requests it is possible for the producer to build up sets of recently requested pages for each processor. Since the diffs are requested in a particular order it is important that this order is maintained so that diffs are sent out in the correct order.

In our implementation we maintain a linked list of page entries corresponding to pages for each logical interval and consuming processor. All lists are initially empty when the application starts. Whenever a consumer sends a request for a page diff, a page entry is inserted at the end of the list associated with the consuming processor and the current logical interval on the producer, i.e. the processor that serves the diff request.

When a processor enters a logical interval it pushes all diffs corresponding to the pages in the lists in the order that these pages occur in the list. This ensures that data that is needed early by the consumer, is pushed as early as possible. If several consuming processors have requested diffs previously in this logical interval, the producer will push diffs to all of these processors. In order not to favour any particular consumer, the producer interleaves the pushing of diffs among the consumers. In practice this means that approximately equally sized chunks of data are sent in turn

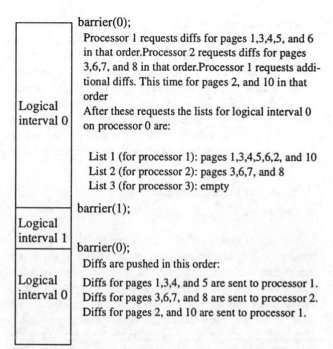

Figure 5. The simple example with producer-push actions.

to the consumers. The maximal size of these chunks depend on the network layer and is typically on the order of a few tens of kilobytes. Figure 5 shows how the lists of pages are maintained and how the pushing of data is done in the case of 4 processors. Once again our simple example is used and we show the lists maintained and the diffs pushed by processor 0. For clarity only the actions in logical interval 0 and the barrier primitives are shown.

2.4 What kind of application benefits from Producer-Push?

Some algorithms benefit more than others from producer-push. The algorithm used must first of all be iterative, i.e., several iterations in which the communication pattern is repeated. Otherwise the current heuristic will not do any predictions. Furthermore, the algorithm should be fairly regular in its data usage. It should basically use the same data-set in each iteration. Also, since producer-push reduces the time to request diffs, the number of coherency misses caused by the algorithms should be fairly high. Even though the mechanism works for lock-based algorithms, we have tuned the heuristics for barrier-based applications since iterative algorithms often use barriers as the main synchronization mechanism.

A typical application that will benefit from producer-push is eigen-value calculations where the same vector manipulations are performed on the same set of data for several iterations. An example of application that will not benefit much from producer-push is an algorithm using searches where the search pattern is irregular. Algorithms that perform different calculations in different iterations, like some heuristic-based algorithms do, will also not gain much performance from producer-push. The rule of thumb is that if an algorithm will benefit from normal prefetching, it will also benefit from producer-push. It should be noted that even with the current simple heuristic we have not noticed any negative effects on any of the applications we have run. Let us now go over to the evaluation of producer-push.

3. Experimental methodology

3.1 Experimental platform

We have integrated the producer-push algorithm in version 1.0.1 of TreadMarks. In order to evaluate the performance of producer-push we have used seven standard scientific benchmarks on an IBM SP2 with POWER2 processors running at 160MHz and an upgraded 110 Mbyte/s switch. The benchmarks were compiled with IBM's C-compiler xlc using optimization level -O. The TreadMarks library was augmented to be able to collect profiling information. The profiling adds approximately 15% overhead and thus two separate runs have been done for each application; one run without profiling to measure execution times and one with profiling to collect information on where the execution time is spent.

3.2 Applications

Seven different benchmarks from the TreadMarks 1.0.1 benchmark distribution were used in the evaluation of the relative performance benefits of producer-push. SOR is a standard stencil iterative algorithm. IS, FFT, CG and MG are originally from the NAS benchmark suite [3], and Water and Barnes-Hut are originally from the SPLASH benchmark suite [18] but rewritten to suit TreadMarks better. Like SOR, all other benchmarks also use iterative algorithms and according to the discussion at the end of the previous section, it is thus probable that their performance can be boosted by the producer-push technique. A summary of the application workloads is shown in table 1 and they are briefly described below.

Execution times are measured according to the existing timing instrumentation in the applications as they are distributed in TreadMarks. This means that only the parallel section of the program is taken into account. Our profiling measurements have been done on the same part of the execution as the timing. This means that profiling has been done on all iterations in all applications but for Barnes-Hut where profiling is done from the fifth iteration.

3.2.1 SOR and IS.
SOR iteratively applies an averaging kernel to a matrix. The algorithm is extremely regular and very little data is communicated in each time step. IS sorts a

Table 1. Applications and workloads used in the study.

Application	Workload
SOR	10 iterations, 2000*1000 matrix
IS	10 rankings, 32768 keys
FFT	6 time steps, 64*64*64 cube
CG	Kernel C
MG	Kernel B
Water	5 time steps, 512 molecules
Barnes-Hut	10 time steps, 16384 bodies

vector of integers and this algorithm is also regular in its access pattern. We can expect that producer-push will predict the communication well for both applications. However, since SOR already has a good relative speedup even without producer-push, we cannot expect a large absolute performance improvement since there is very little latency to hide.

3.2.2 FFT, CG and MG.
FFT is a PDE solver that uses a three-dimensional FFT. The solution is iterated in frequency space where each iteration consists of an inverse FFT. The CG benchmark finds an estimate of the largest eigen-value to a sparse matrix using the inverse power method. MG solves the Poisson problem in three dimensions using a finite element method. These programs all consist of simple matrix operators operating on the same data in every iteration. We thus expect that producer-push will work well on them.

3.2.3 Water.
Water is a simulation of the dynamics of several water molecules. The effect of both intra- and inter molecular forces are simulated. The version used is the so called n-squared Water where each processor is assigned a range of molecules and calculates the effect these molecules exert on all the other molecules. This means that processors will manipulate the data structures that represents the molecules assigned to other processors. Race hazards are avoided by using one lock per molecule. This means that a sizeable fraction of the execution time is spent waiting for lock acquisitions. The lock-mechanism in TreadMarks uses intervals in the same way as barriers do. A logical interval is in this case identified by the molecule for which there is a unique lock. The communication in Water is mostly regular and when a processor acquires a lock, it is often released by the same processor as the last time but as the processors are not tightly synchronized it is possible that the communication patterns change slightly from iteration to

iteration. Water also uses locks to implement global reductions which yields highly unpredictable communication. We can, however, conclude that producer-push should be able to predict at least a major part the resulting communication which in turn should reduce the diff request time.

3.2.4 Barnes-Hut. This is an N-body simulation of the motion of bodies that interact using gravitational forces. The bodies are hierarchically ordered in a tree that is rebuilt by the root node for each time step. As in Water the bodies are distributed among the processors and the effect of the forces from all bodies on each body must be evaluated. Unlike Water, however, no processor updates the body structures of another processor. The main communication is thus to and from the root node when the tree is rebuilt. Since the tree is rebuilt for each time step the set of bodies assigned to a processor changes from one time step to the next. This communication cannot be predicted but we can expect producer-push to effectively push all data corresponding to bodies that do not migrate between processors.

4. Experimental results

The main idea behind producer-push is to reduce the time to request diffs in software DSM systems. Figure 6 shows the difference in the fraction of execution time spent doing diff requests in the seven applications, without and with producer-push. As expected, the diff request is greatly reduced for all applications. The average reduction of diff request time is 74%. The reduction is smaller for Barnes-Hut. This is due to the migration of bodies between processors which the heuristics cannot predict. Thus a smaller fraction of the diffs needed by the consumer is pushed from the producer.

The reduction for Water is larger than 50%. This should normally directly correspond to a decrease in execution time of a corresponding amount but the execution time is unchanged which we can see from figure 7. This is due to the fact that the time spent waiting for a lock to be released, which in this case is the dominating latency, is increased by the same amount of time. The reason for this is that at the same time as ownership of the lock is acquired, the releasing node is also pushing data to the acquiring node which must handle the incoming data. This causes a small overhead which in this case is equal to the time gained from producer-push. It should be stated that Water is an extreme case and even so, producer-push will not decrease the performance of the application.

In figure 7 we show relative speedup with eight processors for all applications. They grey bar corresponds to executions of TreadMarks and for the white bar we have also used producer-push. The relative speedup is calculated as the execution time of an application using one processor

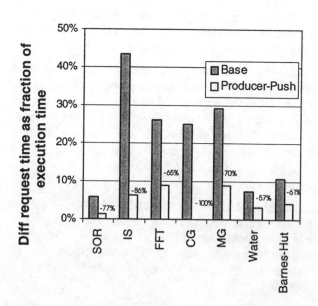

Figure 6. The fraction of execution time spent doing diff requests with and without producer-push.

divided by the execution time using eight processors. The data in figure 7 was of course obtained from executions without profiling overhead.

The numbers above the bars in figure 7 show the performance improvement we get when producer-push is used. We can see that the applications can be divided into three different groups depending on the performance improvement obtained. SOR and Water do not benefit much

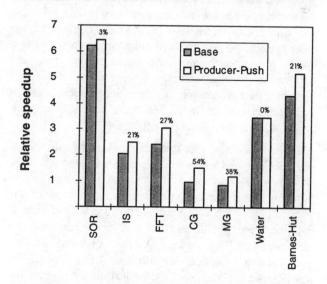

Figure 7. A comparison of the relative speedup with 8 processors, without and with producer-push. The number above the bars is the performance improvement achieved by producer-push.

from producer-push. For FFT, IS and Barnes-Hut there is a moderate performance improvement, and for CG and MG there is a relatively large performance improvement.

Although the diff request overhead is reduced for Water this has no impact on the execution time. This is, as stated earlier, due to the fact that the lock release time is increased. SOR also has a low relative speedup. In this case producer-push actually works well but the latency that can be hidden is very small. The diff request overhead is reduced by 5% to only 1% and this results in a performance improvement of about 3% on 8 nodes.

The second group of applications have all moderate relative speedups of 20-27% on 8 nodes. The applications in this group, consisting of FFT, IS and Barnes-Hut, are all affected by producer-push as one would expect. The diff request time is reduced and the overall execution time is decreased.

The last group, i.e., MG and CG, have large performance gains from using producer-push. Figure 8. shows the normalized execution time broken down into busy time, time spent in TreadMarks code and time spent in the network layers including communication time in the actual network and protocol handling time. We see in figure 8 that the execution time of these applications are totally dominated by the communication time. Note that the execution times have been normalized so that 100% corresponds to the execution time without producer-push. Roughly half of the communication time is due to diff requests and the other half is due to waiting for other processors in barriers. Producer-push effectively reduces the diff request time and thus the communication time. Since the busy time of CG and MG is so much shorter compared to the other applications, the reduced communication time has a much greater impact. Experiments show that the performance improvement of producer-push for MG is even higher for four processors. This is due to the fact that when eight processors are used, MG uses so much network bandwidth that it saturates the network.

Let us now investigate the performance of the heuristics that decides when and where to push data. Table 2 lists the efficiency, fraction late diffs and the coverage for the different applications. The *efficiency* is defined as the fraction of the pushed diffs that are found in the diff cache at the time of a page fault and thus used by the consumer. An efficiency near 100% means that almost all pushed diffs are used and that network bandwidth is not being wasted. The *late diffs* are the fraction of the pushed diffs that arrive too late to the consumer in order to be useful. This means that they arrive after the page fault has occurred. These pushed diffs waste bandwidth just as the diffs that never are requested. However, if they could have been sent earlier,

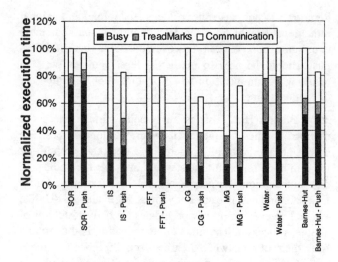

Figure 8. Normalized execution time breakdown.

they would be useful. Finally, the *coverage* is defined as the fraction of diffs requested by the consumer that were successfully pushed and used. The coverage is a metric of the ability to predict communication.

Table 2. Efficiency, late diffs and coverage of producer-push on the seven applications.

Application	Efficiency	Late diffs	Coverage
SOR	92%	2%	85%
IS	97%	0%	90%
FFT	97%	0%	72%
CG	100%	0%	100%
MG	68%	25%	75%
Water	45%	7%	64%
Barnes-Hut	98%	4%	67%

The efficiency is very high for all applications except for MG and Water. For MG the reason for the relatively low efficiency is that 25% of all pushed diffs arrive too late and not that the heuristic mispredicts the communication. However, the low efficiency for Water is a result of the inability to correctly predict the communication. As described in section 3.2, some parts of the communication in Water is hard to predict due to the fact that locks are used to implement reduction operations, and that the processors are loosely synchronized.

The coverage of producer-push varies among the applications. This is mostly because the timed regions are different in the applications. When the timing and profiling start, the only application in which the heuristic is warmed up is Barnes-Hut. Besides Water, the lowest coverage is for Barnes-Hut. This is due to the migration of bodies as described in section 3.2. The coverage of producer-push for FT, IS and SOR is a bit higher but not perfect as one would expect. The reason here is the presence of cold misses that are impossible to predict. Producer-push has an ideal coverage for CG, but at first glance not for MG. However, for MG all diffs are predicted but, as mentioned before, 25% of the pushed diffs arrive late due to network contention. In this case the consumer cannot find the late diffs in its diff cache and therefore performs a normal diff request.

One final observation is that producer-push results in a better utilization of the available network bandwidth. It has been shown that the main reason for poor performance in software DSM systems such as TreadMarks is due to communication protocol processing [16]. Therefore, each protocol improvement that reduces the number of messages will also lead to a performance improvement unless it also results in an increase of some other execution time component. Table 3 shows the number of messages and the average message sizes for the base system compared to when producer-push is used. For all applications except for Water, the actual number of bytes communicated is about the same with and without pushing. However, for the applications that perform better using producer-push, IS, FFT, CG, MG, and Barnes-Hut, the number of messages sent is only 43-64% of the number of messages without pushing. Consequently the average message size is increased for these applications.

5. Potential improvements

Even if the current implementation works well on barrier-based applications, as we saw in the previous section, there are some possible improvements to the heuristics that can be done. We will describe a few in the following passages. Although we have not implemented any of these, we feel that they can boost performance even higher.

The order in which diffs are sent to the producer to the consumer is important. MG observed a sizeable fraction late diffs and part of the reason to why these are late is because they are sent to late from the producer. The mechanism could be thus modified to send diffs earlier than is determined by the current heuristics if they are detected as late by an *adaptive-order* mechanism. It is also possible in some cases to move a page from a list in a logical interval to a list in an earlier logical interval. This is a variation of adaptive order.

If the current heuristics has determined that a diff is to be pushed in a logical interval, it will always be pushed in this interval even if it no longer will be needed by the consumer.

Table 3. Number of messages and average message sizes without and with producer-push. The numbers in parentheses show the reduction in number of messages and increase in message size respectively.

	Number of messages		Average message size (kbyte)	
	Base	Push	Base	Push
SOR	2709	2485 (92%)	2.68	2.92 (1.1x)
IS	6023	3670 (61%)	12.06	20.26 (1.7x)
FFT	11207	7072 (63%)	3.70	5.86 (1.6x)
CG	160349	83279 (52%)	0.43	0.83 (1.9x)
MG	40981	22180 (54%)	2.41	4.69 (1.9x)
Water	43812	42412 (97%)	0.41	0.50 (1.2x)
Barnes-Hut	105456	45012 (43%)	0.97	2.29 (2.4x)

In order to keep the network traffic as low as possible improvements can be done to remove pages from the producer's lists if they have not been used by the consumer. We call this extension *adaptive push-set*. We intend to investigate the effects of these improvements in our future research.

6. Conclusions

Networks of workstations provide a cost-effective way to build parallel computing environments. Software DSM systems can be utilized to make NOWs more easy to program. However, the high communication overhead in a NOW makes it necessary to reduce the implicit communication in a shared memory system as much as possible. Lazy release consistency is one such technique that reduces and hides latency in software DSM systems.

We have in this paper presented a technique called producer-push which is an extension to a lazy release consistency protocol. Producer-push boosts the performance of regular iterative applications, an important class of applications for parallel systems. Producer-push uses repetitive communication patterns to predict communication and can, for the applications used in the study, reduce stall time to wait for shared memory updates from remote processing nodes by 74% on average. The resulting performance improvement is on average 23%.

Given that the performance improvement of single-processor systems tend to improve at a faster pace than network technology that tend to have longer life-times, the relative performance of applications on software DSM systems will decrease since they will be more and more dependent on network performance. It is therefore important to be able to overlap communication and computation as much as possible and also to utilize the network as good as possible.

Although there are improvements to be made for producer-push, it is already usable to reduce remote memory access latency by overlapping communication and computation. One important side-effect is that the number of messages needed is greatly reduced and, since the amount of communication is the same, the message sizes are increased by roughly the same amount. This favours even off-the-shelf networks that have relatively long latencies but high available bandwidth.

7. References

[1] H. Abdel-Shafi et al. An evaluation of fine-grain producer-initiated communication in cache-coherent multiprocessors. In *Proceedings of the Third International Symposium on High-Performance Computer Architecture*, pages 204-215, February 1997.

[2] C. Amza, A.L. Cox, S. Dwarkadas, P. Keleher, H. Lu, R. Rajamony, W. Yu and W. Zwaenepoel. TreadMarks: Shared Memory Computing on Networks of Workstations, *IEEE Computer*, Vol. 29, no. 2, pp. 18-28, February 1996.

[3] D. Bailey, T. Harris, W. Saphir, R. Wijngaart, A. Woo, and M. Yarrow. The NAS Parallel Benchmarks 2.0, Report NAS-95-020, Nasa Ames Research Center, Moffett Field, *Ca, 94035, USA*. December, 1995.

[4] R. Bianchini, L. Kontothanassis, R. Pinto, M. De Maria, M. Abud, C. L. Amorim. Hiding Communication Latency and Coherence Overhead in Software DSMs, In *Proceedings of the 7th ACM/IEEE InternationalConference on Architectural Support for Programming Languages and Operating Systems (ASPLOS 7)*, pp. 198-209, October 1996.

[5] A. L. Cox, S. Dwarkadas, and P. Keleher. Software Versus Hardware Shared-Memory Implementations: A Case Study, In *Proceedings of the 21st International Symposium on Computer Architecture*, pp. 106-117, April 1994.

[6] K. Gharachorloo, D. E. Lenoski, J. P. Laudon, P. Gibbons, A. Gupta, and J. L. Hennessy. Memory Consistency and Event Ordering in Scalable Shared-Memory Multiprocessors. In *Proceedings of the 17th Annual International Symposium on Computer Architecture*, pp. 15-26, May 1990.

[7] J. Hård, *OdinMP – A Proposal for the Implementation of OpenMP for a Network of Workstations*, M.Sc. thesis. Department of Information Technology, Lund University, P.O. Box 118, SE-221 00 Lund, Sweden, January 1999.

[8] D. Jiang et al., Application Scaling under Shared Virtual Memory on a Cluster of SMPs, in *Proceedings of the ISC'99*, June 1999, pp. 165-174.

[9] M. Karlsson and P. Stenström, Evaluation of Dynamic Prefetching in Multiple-Writer Distributed Virtual Shared Memory Systems, In *Journal of Parallel and Distributed Computing*, vol. 43, no. 7 (July 1997), pp.79-93.

[10] S. Karlsson and M. Brorsson, A Comparative Characterization of Communication Patterns in Applications using MPI and Shared Memory on an IBM SP2, In *Proceedings of 1998 Workshop on Communication, Architecture, and Applications for Network-based Parallel Computing*, pp. 189-201, Las Vegas, January 31 - February 1, 1998

[11] P. Keleher, Lazy Release Consistency for Distributed Shared Memory, PhD Thesis, Rice University, 1994

[12] P. Keleher, Update Protocols and Iterative Scientific Applications, In *Proceedings of the International Parallel Processing Symposium*, pp. 675-681, 1998.

[13] P. Keheler, A. L. Cox and W. Zwaenepoel. Lazy Release Consistency for Software Distributed Shared Memory, *In Proc. of the 19th Annual Int'l Symp on Computer Architecture(ISCA'92)*, pp. 13-21, May 1992

[14] H. Lu, Y.C. Hu, and W. Zwaenepoel, OpenMP on Network of Workstations, In *Proceedings of Supercomputing '98*, October 1998.

[15] K. Omang and B. Parady, Scalability of SCI Workstation Clusters, a Preliminary Study, in *Proceedings of the 11th IEEE International Parallel Processing Symposium (IPPS'97)*, Geneve, April 1997, pp. 750-755.

[16] E. W. Parsons, M. Brorsson and K. C. Sevcik, Predicting the Performance of Distributed Virtual Shared Memory Applications, *IBM Systems Journal*, Volume 36, No. 4, 1997, pp. 527-549.

[17] C. B Seidel, R. Bianchini, and C. L Amorim, The Affinity Entry Consistency Protocol, In *Proceedings of the International Conference on Parallel Processing*, pp. 208-217, August 1997.

[18] J. P. Singh, W.-D. Weber, and A. Gupta. SPLASH: Stanford parallel applications for shared-memory. *Computer Architecture News*, 20(1):5-44, March 1992.

Session B5
Compiler Techniques & Analysis

Chair: Joseph Torrellas
University of Illinois at Urbana-Champaign, USA

An Incremental Methodology for Parallelizing Legacy Stencil Codes on Message-Passing Computers

N. S. Sundar [1]   S. Jayanthi   P. Sadayappan

Dept. of Computer & Information Science
The Ohio State University
Columbus, OH 43210
ns_sundar@hp.com saday@cis.ohio-state.edu

Miguel Visbal

CFD Research Branch
Air Vehicle Directorate
Air Force Research Lab
Wright Patterson Air Force Base
Dayton, OH 45433

Abstract

There is considerable interest in converting existing production sequential/vector codes into scalable portable parallel message-passing programs. However the task is very tedious and error prone. In this paper, we describe a systematic incremental *methodology that greatly eases parallelization of stencil codes, by operating in a single address space while addressing data partitioning issues and then transitioning to multiple address spaces to handle communication and synchronization issues. The approach has been successfully used in manually parallelizing a production CFD code. Since the steps in the methodology are formalized as algorithms, the approach is amenable to automation.*

Keywords: *Code parallelization, message passing, computational fluid dynamics*

1   Introduction

A great deal of effort is currently being expended in converting legacy vector codes to parallel form, especially since vector machines at the various federal high-performance computing centers are being phased out and being replaced by scalable parallel systems. The message passing model using MPI offers the potential for high performance of the converted code, and also allows portability across a wide range of computing systems. However, the task of transforming a sequential program into a message passing parallel program is tedious and error-prone. To address the twin issues of minimizing conversion effort and ensuring complete accuracy of the parallel program, we propose a systematic approach that eases manual implementation by synthesizing the parallel program through a series of intermediate steps while also ensuring accuracy by validating the output at each step. As errors can be introduced during the conversion, it is highly desirable that the approach incorporate structures and processes for tracking these errors.

This paper presents a systematic incremental approach to parallelizing a class of codes, that was motivated by a need to parallelize an application code in computational fluid dynamics. The methodology is executed in three stages. In each stage, routines are converted and tested one at a time, thus vastly simplifying parallel code development. Also, in the first two stages, the original sequential program is interleaved with partially parallelized code, which maintains the partitioned data structures corresponding to those that will eventually be used in the final parallel program. This allows a comparison of the computation of a serial routine with its parallelized counterpart at each stage of the conversion, enabling incremental testing and debugging. The first stage focuses on developing a 'blocked sequential' program, which operates in a single address space, where appropriate data arrays are partitioned and the action of n virtual processors on the partitioned arrays is simulated on a single processor. Communication among the processors is simulated by copying array elements across partitions. In the second stage, a 'replicated' program is developed, which is executed on n physical processors, each of which replicates the action of all n virtual processors. The copying of needed data across partitions is augmented with actual interprocessor communication at this stage. The final stage removes the replication and copying and then eliminates the sequential code and its data structures, leaving a purely parallel program. Thus, this approach reduces the conversion complexity by addressing data partitioning issues in the first stage and communication issues in the second.

The paper is organized as follows. Section 2 describes the steps in the parallelization methodology using simple examples. Section 3 formalizes the methodology by captur-

---

[1]Currently with Hewlett-Packard Company.

302

ing the various steps as algorithms that may be automated. Section 4 presents performance data from parallelization of a production CFD application to show that the methodology yields scalable programs. Other approaches to tackling the problem of parallelizing sequential programs are discussed in Section 5, and this approach is contrasted with them. Finally, Section 6 summarizes the work.

2 Parallelization Methodology

The parallelization methodology is organized in three stages, each altering the program one subroutine at a time.

1. **Development of a Blocked Sequential Version:** This stage generates an interleaved *blocked sequential* program in which each original routine is augmented with a corresponding 'blocked-view' routine that performs equivalent computation on partitioned arrays. In the final parallel program, each 'blocked local' array within a processor would be a 1D array of tiles, indexed by tile number; so, its precursor in the blocked sequential program would be a 2D array of tiles, indexed by tile number and processor index. The blocked sequential routines emulate the actions of the processors on the partitioned arrays by looping over the processor- and tile- dimensions of the blocked arrays. Interprocessor communication is simulated by copying array elements across tiles as needed. The routines are converted to the blocked form one at a time, with the live variables at the end of each routine compared with their blocked counterparts to validate the program after each step.

2. **Development of Replicated-MPI Version**: This stage converts the blocked sequential code to a SPMD program executed on multiple processors with MPI-based inter-processor communication. However, the simulation of virtual processors in the previous version is retained so that all computation is replicated on all processors. By redundantly replicating all computation, it is possible to verify all inter-processor communication, by comparing the values received via inter-processor communication with the locally computed values corresponding to neighboring partitions.

3. **Development of Non-Replicated-MPI Version**: All replicated computation of the previous verified version is now suppressed, so that each processor only computes its own partitions of the data arrays. The inter-processor communication from the previous version is retained. Then the original code and its arrays are eliminated to yield a fully parallel MPI program.

Converting the program to a blocked form on a routine-by-routine basis is an attractive approach that not only al-

lows incremental progress but also adapts well to team effort. The arrays computed by each sequential routine but used after its execution are compared element by element with the corresponding blocked arrays after each conversion step until the final stage eliminates the sequential code. Note that the first stage addresses data partitioning issues even while operating in a single address space; this is a unique feature of the methodology. All these features serve to greatly ease the task of parallelization.

2.1 Building a Blocked Program

Before a routine can be converted to operate on the blocked arrays, all the routines that it calls must already have been converted. This necessitates a bottom-up traversal of the call tree of the program, in which the leaf nodes are converted before the nodes that call them. The conversion of each node includes the generation not only of a blocked routine but also two others: an initialization routine which copies data values from the arrays used before definition by the original routine to the corresponding blocked arrays and a comparison routine that compares element by element each sequential array defined by the original routine and used after its execution with its blocked counterpart. Thus, the call to each sequential routine aaa is transformed into a set of 4 calls as follows.

$$\text{call aaa(xx, yy)} \implies \begin{array}{l} \text{call aaa\_init(xx, yy, xx', yy')} \\ \text{call aaa(xx, yy)} \\ \text{call aaa\_b(xx', yy')} \\ \text{call aaa\_cmp(xx, yy, xx', yy', l)} \end{array}$$

Here, aaa_init is the initialization routine, which initializes the blocked data structures (xx' and yy') using the sequential data structures (xx and yy). It also initializes the blocked common blocks. aaa_b is the blocked routine and aaa_cmp is the compare routine. aaa_cmp compares the values in the sequential and blocked sequential data structures. Since this set of routines could be invoked within a loop or at multiple points in the program, the routine aaa_cmp is given an integer argument l to identify, in the event of a discrepancy between the computations of aaa and aaa_b, the invocation of aaa_b which generated the discrepancy.

Since the call tree is traversed bottom-up, all the routines called in a given routine, say aaa, will be blocked before aaa itself is blocked. At that point, aaa can be blocked to yield aaa_b. The calls to individual initializations of the called routines are deleted and a new init routine aaa_init is written which copies only the arrays that are used within aaa before being defined. A new compare routine aaa_cmp is written and the call to aaa is then transformed into a set of 4 calls, as explained above. Eventually, the entire program will have only a single init, to initialize the blocked equivalents of the input arrays. It is desirable to retain more than a single compare call since the differences reported by them help in determining the location of errors in the blocked code.

The aim of a blocked routine is to distribute, among a set of virtual processors, the iterations of each loop that is used to index a tiled dimension of a partitioned array. In principle, this involves splitting each loop that indexes a tiled dimension of an array into two: a tiling loop that steps across the tiles in that dimension and an intra-tile loop that steps across the elements in each tile. (The loop bounds of the intra-tile loop may depend on the tile index that is varied by the tiling loop.) The tiles in the iteration space need to be assigned to processors in such a way that the processor which executes a specific iteration owns all the array elements accessed by that iteration i.e. the "owner computes" rule is followed. In other words, since the objective is to build a data parallel program, the data partitioning is used to induce a task partitioning. The issues that arise in the course of task partitioning are discussed now.

Simulation of the action of multiple processors on the partitioned arrays must be so done that it is easy to convert it into a fully parallel form. For a loop nest in the sequential program, all of whose loops are parallelizable, this is achieved by enclosing the corresponding blocked loop nest in an outer loop that steps over the range of processor indices. Subsequently, when a parallel program needs to be built from the blocked program in the last stage, the body of the processor loop can be enclosed in a conditional statement that is executed only when the loop index matches the processor identifier of the MPI program.

For a stencil code, the computation of a tile t of an array may use elements from an adjacent tile of the same array, which is not owned by the processor that owns t. Alternatively, it may use elements from a tile of another array which is adjacent to one owned by the current processor. In both these situations, it is necessary to communicate the needed elements from the processor owning the adjacent tile to the processor owning t. This can be easily incorporated into the tiling scheme by expanding each tile to include a set of *shadow elements*, which contain data copied from other processors. For example, a stencil reference of the form $temp0(i, j - 2)$ would require that each tile in the blocked local array *temp* have two shadow columns, with j values less than the lowest regular values, in which the data obtained by interprocessor communication is placed. Since the mapping scheme assigns adjacent tiles to adjacent virtual processors, this ensures that all communication is confined to neighboring virtual processors. Note that shadow elements are not "owned" by the processor which holds them.

Shadow copies in a blocked program simulate the interprocessor communication in an MPI program. A shadow copy is a loop nest that contains a set of assignment statements, each referring to a single array, with the destination being a shadow element and the source being an array element that resides on a processor adjacent to the one owning the shadow element. The replicated program replaces them with communication based on calls to the MPI library. Hence, the principal factors that reduce communication must be addressed in the placement and design of the shadow copies.

To transfer as large an amount of data as possible in each communication, it is necessary to place the shadow copies at the loop level of the lowest possible depth within its loop nest. This implies a position at the highest loop level that is common to the stencil reference that needs the shadow element and the reaching definition that defines its source. By appropriate use of loop fusion, shadow copies of several arrays can be placed in a single loop nest, which will be mapped to a single MPI communication in the final stage.

2.2 Building the MPI Program

The blocking stage yields a validated sequential program with both the original and the blocked code. This needs to be converted into a MPI program in which each processor accesses only its local data, similar to the virtual processors in the blocked code, and the shadow copies are replaced by communication across processors. These communications also serve to synchronize processors that handle the iterations of loops that carry dependences This is accomplished in the next two stages by building a replicated program which is then converted to a fully parallel program. These stages are discussed further in this subsection.

The second stage of the methodology begins by building a parallel program that essentially executes the blocked sequential program on many processors. This is done by adding a call to the MPI initialization routine MPI_INIT() at the beginning of the program and a call to the MPI termination routine MPI_Finalize at the end. Thus, all computations are completely replicated among the processors and the shadow copies are still retained. Then, each of the shadow copies is supplemented with a MPI communication. That is, following a shadow copy from source processor pe' to sink processor pe, a communication is placed in which the processor with $myid = pe'$ sends a set of array elements and the processor with $myid = pe$ receives it and updates its shadow elements. However, the shadow copies are performed for all values of the pe index while the communication-based shadow update is performed only for $pe = myid$. This is so because each processor needs to carry out the blocked routine computations for all values of pe until all interprocessor communication is in place. Another point of note is that the MPI communication is placed after the shadow copy so that it overwrites some of the shadow elements that were updated by the shadow copy. This makes it likely that errors in the communication will affect the subsequent computations and thus manifest as differences reported by the compare routines. However, it does not expose all errors.

The third stage removes the replication of computations. This is done by conditionally executing the body of each *pe* loop, except those involved in MPI communication, only for *pe* = *myid*. This renders all shadow copies invalid because the source elements of the shadow copy, which reside on a different processor, will not be computed correctly. So, all the shadow copies can be commented out. Note that conditional execution of even a single computational loop potentially renders all shadow copies invalid, so that the correctness of all the MPI communication is tested by this change. Thus, while the changes in the code are always done incrementally, testing is not incremental at this stage of the methodology. This stage results in a parallel program with purely local computations that uses interprocessor communication to update the shadow elements. However, it still retains the original sequential code and the compare routines.

The processor dimension of each blocked array is then eliminated since each processor accesses only one element in it. This can be done by a global replacement of the last subscript of all array references and the last dimension of all array declarations. Finally, all the sequential code and the compare routines are also eliminated resulting in a purely parallel program.

3 General Formulation of the Methodology

In this section, we provide more detail about the parallelization methodology, capturing the steps in the form of algorithms that may be automated.

The domain addressed by the approach is the set of non-recursive stencil programs, where each array subscript is either a constant or of the form $i \pm s$, where i is a loop variable and s is a constant. To illustrate the concepts and application of the methodology, the program fragment in Figure 1 will be used as a running example throughout this section. We name the arrays in the original program with a trailing 0 and the corresponding blocked version of the array by dropping the trailing 0. Thus a0() is an array in the original unblocked program while a() is the corresponding blocked array. It can be easily verified that this code falls in the domain of the methodology.

3.1 Data Distribution

The natural class of data distributions for stencil codes are tiled distributions, such as block, cyclic or skewed distributions. As it is difficult to automate the choice of a distribution, the user needs to choose one for each array in

```
real a0(0:M-1,0:M-1), b0(0:M-1,0:M-1)

do k = 1, NumIter
  do j = 1, M-2
    do i = 1, M-2
      a0(i,j) = b0(i-1,j) + b0(i,j-1) +
                b0(i+1,j) + b0(i,j+1)
```

Figure 1. A running example implementing an equation solver using Jacobi.

the program and map the resulting tiles to a pool of virtual processors. Since each processor follows the "owner computes" rule, the primary objective of this step is to ensure *colocation* i.e. the elements of an array that are owned by a processor p should be computable from elements of the same or other arrays that are also owned by p. In other words, for an array $a0$ that is defined using an array $b0$, some dimensions of $a0$ would need to be tiled with the same distribution and mapping as certain dimensions of $b0$, so that these dimensions are co-located. Array dimensions that cannot be distributed without ensuring co-location are replicated across the processors.

Consider a Δ-dimensional array $a0$ in which d dimensions are to be tiled to yield a blocked array a. Dimension k is split into nt_k^a tiles and is thus converted to two dimensions: a tile dimension, that steps across the tiles, and an intra-tile dimension that steps across the elements within a tile. This distribution is abstracted using a set of functions that may be implemented using table-lookup or explicit computation. Since the size of each tile in a_k (the k-th dimension of a) will not necessarily be the same, a tile size function $ts_k^a : \mathcal{N} \to \mathcal{N}$ is required which takes a tile index ti_k in a_k and returns its extent. The smallest among the tile sizes should exceed the stencil size in that dimension. The locator function $tile-elem_k^a : \mathcal{N} \to \mathcal{N}^2$ converts an index in the k-th dimension of $a0$ into a tile-element pair corresponding to that index. The tiling of the d dimensions of $a0$ generates a decomposition of $a0$ into blocks. The mapping of a block onto a unique processor is abstracted by a function $procnum^a : \mathcal{N}^d \to \mathcal{N}$, which takes a set of d tile indices that describe a block and returns the index of the processor to which that tile is mapped. The blocks within a processor are organized linearly and addressed using a *processor block number*, which is computed by a function $peblk^a : \mathcal{N}^d \to \mathcal{N}$ that takes a set of d tile indices as input arguments while the number of blocks per processor is given by $nblk^a : \mathcal{N} \to \mathcal{N}$, which takes a processor number as its argument. Block-cyclic distributions assign more than one tile from a given dimension of an array to the same processor. These tiles are also organized linearly and their count is given by the *dimension block num-*

ber, which is computed by a function $dimblk_k^a : \mathcal{N} \to \mathcal{N}$, which takes a processor number as input. These functions are so chosen that it is possible to design inverse functions $tile_k^a : \mathcal{N}^2 \times \mathcal{N}^{d-1} \to \mathcal{N}$ that calculate the tile index in a_k, given the processor number, the dimension block number and the other $d-1$ tile indices.

Consider the array $b0$ in the example of Figure 1. It has a stencil size of 1 in both its dimensions. Since the second dimension is indexed by the outermost parallelizable loop, a good choice of a data distribution is a blocking along that dimension. The blocked equivalent will be declared as $b(0 : M - 1, -1 : \frac{M}{n}, 0 : 0, 0 : n - 1)$, where n is a parameter representing the number of processors. The number of blocks of b per processor is one, as indicated by the range of the dimension before the last, which stores the processor block number. A possible choice of the needed functions can be expressed in terms of the tile index jn along the second dimension, as $ts_j^b(jn) = \frac{M}{n}$, $tile-elem_j^b(x) = (x \text{ div } \frac{M}{n}, x \text{ mod } \frac{M}{n}$ for $0 \le x \le M-1$, $procnum^b(jn) = jn$, $peblk^b(jn) = 0$, $dimblk_j^b(pe) = 1$, $nblk^b(pe) = 1$, and $tile_j^b(0, pe) = pe$, where all the free variables range from 0 through $n - 1$. It is assumed that M is a multiple of n. Note that the tile size functions return the 'normal' extent of a tile, not its extent with shadows. The first parameter of the $tile$ function is 0 because only one tile is mapped from this dimension to the processor pe and that is numbered 0. The other array in the code fragment would be declared as $a(0 : M - 1, 0 : \frac{M}{n} - 1, 0 : 0, 0 : n - 1)$ because the second dimensions of $a0$ and $b0$ must be colocated.

3.2 Building a Blocked Routine

The basic approach adopted to convert a routine to its blocked form is the same as the approach used in the example in section 2. One of the two essential points of this approach is that all blockable loops in the nest are tiled to yield a tiling loop and an intra-tile loop. The tiling loop of the innermost blockable loop runs over a set of tiles that is uniquely determined by the combination of the processor index with the tile indices of the enclosing loops. In fact, for distributions other than block-cyclic ones, that combination specifies a unique tile; but, in general, that set consists of the tiles numbered by the $dimblk_k^a(pe)$ function. The other essential feature is that, wherever possible, loop nests are enclosed by a loop that steps over the range of processors. However, iterations of a blockable loop that carries a dependence cannot be executed in parallel, i.e., its iterations must be executed in tile order rather than processor order so that enclosing such a loop in a processor loop is impermissible. Such a loop can be tiled as before and can enclose a processor loop if it does not enclose other blockable loops with loop-carried dependences (LCDs). If the innermost

blockable loop in a loop nest carries a dependence, it is not possible to have a processor loop at all, but the processor index can be calculated from the set of tile indices. These considerations motivate the need to transform loops differently based on whether or not they carry a dependence. This subsection discusses the translation of a sequential loop nest without dependences or function calls into a blocked form; algorithms to handle general loop nests are presented and discussed in [12].

Consider a loop nest L in which none of the loops has a LCD and which does not have any function calls in its body. The mechanism of converting such a loop nest is presented in Figure 2 as the algorithm *BasicConvert*. The algorithm, like the other algorithms in the methodology, is formulated in terms of converting the programming constructs involved in the loop nest, i.e, sequential, conditional and loop constructs. The main *foreach* loop that steps over the constructs invokes a routine called *GenTilingLoops* to convert blockable loops into a tiling loop and an intratile loop. For the innermost blockable loop, the tiling loop runs over the tiles specified by the *dimblk* function. Since the tile extents of the colocated dimensions of all arrays are identical, the tile index of any one of them may be used. The bounds are calculated using the algorithm *GetBounds* from the original loop bounds, which may be constants or functions of outer loop variables. Note that the value of the original loop variable is explicitly generated as it may be needed to calculate the loop bounds of an inner loop. Loops in the original loop nest that correspond to untiled dimensions are left unchanged. Each array reference within the nest is converted to refer to these intratile indices. This set of transformations creates a blocked loop nest that sequentially simulates the actions of each of the processors on each of its local blocks.

Figure 3 shows the main portion of the code generated by the methodology from the example code of 1. The outer k and the inner i loops, which are not used to index any partitioned array dimension, are left intact while the j loop is tiled.

3.3 Shadow Copies and Communication

Message startup overhead is an important factor that affects performance of parallel programs; so it is necessary to minimize the number of individual messages. The main considerations in achieving this objective are avoidance of redundant data transfers, transferring as many array elements as possible in each message and combining the transfer of the shadows of many arrays when possible. The methodology provides a well-defined framework for the user to address these performance issues. Since the shadow copies generated in the blocking stage are mechanically replaced with MPI-based communication in the second stage, these efficiency issues need to be addressed in generating the shadow copies. This subsection describes the frame-

```
algorithm BasicConvert(L)
given a loop nest, with nest number L, whose loops have loop
      variables $\{i_1, \ldots, i_n\}$, lower bounds $\{Lb_1, \ldots, Lb_n\}$
      and upper bounds $\{Ub_1, \ldots, Ub_n\}$, where each bound
      may be a constant or a function of outer loop variables.
      $tiled(L)$ is the set of blockable loops in the nest and its
      cardinality is $n_d(L)$. The control constructs forming the
      nest is given by the set $\Sigma$. None of the loops have
      loop-carried dependences or function calls. Blockable
      loops in a calling routine that enclose this nest are
      given as the possibly empty list $I_1, \ldots, I_m$.
output transformed loop nest $L_b$ in which loops that correspond
      to tiled dimensions in any array are blocked to yield new
      bounds $\{lb_1, \ldots, lb_n\}$ and $\{ub_1, \ldots, ub_n\}$.

foreach constant subscript $s$ of any array $a$ in a tiled
         dimension $a_k$ in L do
   generate the tile index in $a_k$ using $tile - elem_k^a(s)$
endfor
generate the $pe$ loop as "do pe = 0, n - 1"
foreach construct $c$ in $\Sigma$ do
   if $c$ is a loop $i_k$ then
      if $i_k$ is not blockable then
         copy it as it is
      else if $i_k$ encloses blockable loops then
         GenTilingLoops($i_k$)
      else {encloses only nonblockable loops & scalar constructs.}
         {Let $a$ be the first array reference in the body of $i_k$ to
         have a tiled dimension $a_\tau$ indexed using $i_k$. Let $a$
         have $d_a$ tiled dimensions, whose tile indices are $t_1, \ldots,$
         $t_{d_a}$.}
         generate a loop "do ndb = 0, $dimblk_\tau^a(pe) - 1$"
         generate the tile index $ti_k \longleftarrow tile_\tau^a(t_1, \ldots, t_{\tau-1},$
                  $t_{\tau+1}, \ldots, t_{d_a}, ndb, pe)$
         generate the statement $(tl_k, l_k) \longleftarrow tile - elem_\tau^a(Lb_k)$
         generate the statement $(tu_k, u_k) \longleftarrow tile - elem_\tau^a(Ub_k)$
         GenLoopBounds($a, \tau, ti_k, tl_k, tu_k, l_k, u_k; ll_k, lu_k$)
         generate processor block number for each array
                  in the body of $i_k$
         generate the loop "do $li_k = ll_k, lu_k$"
      endif
   else {$c$ is either a conditional or a statement}
      tile array references in $c$
   endif
endfor
```

Figure 2. Algorithm to parallelize a loop nest with no function calls or loop-carried dependences.

work that addresses the questions of determining the array references need shadow copies, location of the copies and generation of the copying code.

A use of an array a in the blocked program that accesses a shadow element must be preceded by a shadow copy for

```
do k = 1, NumIter
   ⋱
   do pe = 0, n - 1
      do ndb = 0, 0 !- 0 ... $dimblk_j^a(pe) - 1$
         tj = pe !- $tile_j^a(ndb, pe)$
         tl_j = 0; l_j= 1 !- $(tl_j, l_j) = tile - elem_j^a(1)$
         tu_j = n - 1
         u_j = M/n-2 !- $(tu_j, u_j) = tile - elem_j^a(M - 2)$
         ll = 0; lu = M/n - 1
         if ( tj = tl_j ) ll = l_j; if ( tj = tu_j ) lu = u_j
         nb_b = nb_a = tj !- $nb^b = nb^a = peblk^a(tj)$
         do lj = ll, lu
            do i = 1, M-2
               a(i,lj,nb_a,pe) = b(i−1,lj,nb_b,pe) + b(i+1,lj,nb_b,pe) +
                  b(i,lj−1,nb_b,pe) + b(i,lj+1,nb_b,pe)
```

Figure 3. Example: Parallelizing a loop without LCDs and function calls.

that element. Determining whether an array reference accesses a shadow element involves determining the range of elements $l_k : u_k$ accessed in each tiled dimension a_k. This range is obtained from the bounds of the loops surrounding the reference and so may involve constants or symbolic expressions involving loop variables of outer loops. If $l_k \leq 0$ or $u_k > ts_k(ti_k)$, where ti_k is the index of the tile that the reference uses, a shadow copy is needed for the shadow elements along a_k. The set of ranges $l_1 : u_1, \ldots, l_\Delta : u_\Delta$ for a reference to a Δ-dimensional array a, which includes ranges of tiled and non-tiled dimensions, is called a *reference descriptor*. The set of elements to be copied is obtained by replacing the ranges corresponding to shadow dimensions in the reference descriptor with the range of the shadow elements only, yielding a *shadow reference descriptor* (SRD). Note that, for a given shadow dimension k, the reference descriptor may have to be split into two shadow reference descriptors, one each for the increasing and the decreasing direction of k. Since many dimensions in the reference of a may require shadow copies, a single reference descriptor may yield up to $2d$ SRDs for an array with d tiled dimensions. Each SRD can be used to algorithmically generate a loop nest that copies its shadow elements. This procedure determines the smallest number of elements that need to be transferred.

Shadow copies are needed in two situations. The first situation involves a loop with a LCD in the original program whose equivalent in the blocked program indexes a tiled dimension a_k of an array a. The shadow elements of a tile of a need to be copied in each iteration of the loop in the blocked program that steps across the tiles of a_k, except possibly the first or the last. The second situation involves a definition of an array a in a loop followed by a use of a with a stencil in another loop. The algorithm for placing the shadow copy treats these two situations differently. In the case of a loop with LCD, the loop nest performing the shadow copy is placed after the loop that steps across the tiles of a_k but before the intra-tile loop. If many loops with LCDs form a part of a perfect subnest, the shadow copy is placed after all the corresponding tile loops but before any of the intra-tile loops. The loop level so chosen is guaranteed by construction not to be enclosed by a processor loop, so that the loop nest that copies the shadows will need such a loop pair of its own. This is desirable during debugging.

---

algorithm GenShadowCopy
given • a shadow reference descriptor $lb_1 : ub_1, \ldots, lb_\Delta : ub_\Delta$
   of a use reference r_a of an array a
  • the set of shadow dimensions in r_a
  • loop level λ where the shadow copy is to be placed
  • set L of loops enclosing r_a at loop levels greater than λ
  • d, the number of tiled dimensions in a
output a loop nest that copies the shadows in the given SRD.

generate a loop "do pe = 0, n - 1"
foreach non-shadow dimension a_k in r_a indexed
   by a loop i_k in L **do**
 if a_k is a tiled dimension **then**
  GenTilingLoops(i_k)
  {Let the loop variable of the tile loop be ti_k.}
  compute tile index in a_k of the source tile as "$ti_k^S \longleftarrow ti_k$"
 else
  generate the loop "do $i_k = lb_k, ub_k$"
 endif
endfor
foreach shadow dimension a_k in r_a **do**
 foreach shadow dimension $a_l \neq a_k$ **do**
  {Let i_l be the loop that indexes a_l.}
  GenTilingLoops(i_l)
  {Let the loop variable of the tile loop be ti_l.}
  compute tile index in a_l of the source tile as "$ti_l^S \longleftarrow ti_l$"
 endfor
 generate the loop "do ndb = 0, $dimblk_k^a(pe) - 1$"
 generate the tile index for a_k as "$ti_k = \text{tile}_k^a(ti_1, \ldots, ti_{k-1},$
  $ti_{k+1}, \ldots, ti_d$,ndb,pe)"
 generate a check that this tile index needs shadow copying
 generate the source tile index in a_k as $ti_k^S = ti_k - 1$ if
  $lb_k \leq ub_k \leq 0, ti_k^S = ti_k + 1$ otherwise
 generate the source processor & block as "$pe^S \longleftarrow procnum$
  $(ti_1^S, \ldots, ti_d^S); nb^S \longleftarrow peblk(ti_1^S, \ldots, ti_d^S)$"
 generate the loop "do s = lb_k, ub_k"
 generate the source point as $s^S = ts_k^a(ti_k^S) + s$ for $s \leq 0$ and
  $s^S = s - ts_k^a(ti_k^T)$ for $s > ts_k^a(ti_k^T)$
 generate "$a(i_1, \ldots, i_{k-1}, s, i_{k+1}, \ldots, i_\Delta, nb, pe) =$
  $a(i_1, \ldots, i_{k-1}, s^S, i_{k+1}, \ldots, i_\Delta, nb^S, pe^S)$"
endfor

Figure 4. Algorithm to generate code that copies the shadow elements of an array.

In the second situation, the array use that necessitates the shadow copy is compared with each of its reaching definitions that computed a source element for the needed shadow, to decide the maximum common loop level for all of them. The shadow copies are placed at this loop level after the last loop that defines its source elements. (Note that the shadow copy may be placed in this loop level anywhere after the last loop that defines its source elements and before the first loop that contains the array use. The user can exploit this flexibility to merge shadow copies in a given loop level.) It is possible that the maximum common loop level is zero i.e. there may not be a loop that spans the last reaching definition and the use. This placement guarantees that the copy for any given SRD is performed with the largest possible copy size and that there is no redundant transfer of data.

Since it is desirable to place shadow copies in a processor loop not involving computation, if the loop level chosen for the shadow copy is enclosed by a processor loop, the loop is split in two so that the reaching definitions are confined to the body of the first loop and the use falls in the second. This loop fission is always legal because the methodology never places such a processor loop around loops with LCDs.

The actual generation of the copy is done using the algorithm *GenShadowCopy*, presented in Figure 4. A processor loop is created and tile indices of the dimensions in the array a whose corresponding loops do not enclose this loop level are calculated. Since the copies will simulate a data pull from another processor, the calculated tile indices refer to the sink tile whose shadows need to be filled. As discussed earlier, there may be loops enclosing the processor loop that step across tiles in a or a colocated dimension in another array. So, the shadow copy must be performed only when the tile indices match the loop variables of those enclosing loops. This is done by generating guards suitably. Also, the extreme tiles $ti = 1$ and $ti = nt_d$ of a shadow dimension a_d may not need shadow copies; this is also ensured by generating guards that check for extreme values. Each index ti_k^S of the source tile of the shadows is then calculated from the corresponding sink tile index ti_k^T. The set of source tile indices enables the generation of code that calculates the source processor index by using the *procnum* and *peblk* functions. Blocked loops are first generated for non-shadow dimensions which do not have a corresponding loop at this loop level. For each shadow dimension, a blocked loop is generated for every *other* shadow dimension. This ensures that 'diagonal' shadow elements (i.e. those whose source tiles differ in more than one dimension from the sink tile) are properly handled.

The replication stage of the methodology augments shadow copies with interprocessor communication incrementally. The generation of the communication from the shadow copy can be formalized and is described in [12].

```
do pe = 0, n - 1
  do i = 1, M - 2
    do ndb = 1, 1
      tj = tile₂ᵃ(pe,ndb)
      if ( tj < n-1 ) then
        tjˢ = tj + 1
        peˢ = procnumᵇ(tjˢ) ; nbˢ = peblkᵇ(tjˢ)
        do s = ts₂ᵇ(tj) + 1, ts₂ᵇ(tj) + 1
          sˢ = s −ts₂ᵇ(tj)
          b(i,s,pe,nbᵇ) = b(i,sˢ,pe,nbˢ)
      endif
```

Figure 5. Example: One of the two shadow copies for the j dimension.

4 Performance Measurement

In this section we report on the application of the methodology to the development of a scalable parallel code for a CFD application in production use at Wright Laboratories called *fdl3di*. A sequential version of the code that had been tested and validated on a single processor Cray Y-MP was available. A significant constraint on the parallel programming model was placed by the data distribution needed. The implicit numerical formulation used in the code for the solution of 9 time-dependent Navier Stokes equations necessitated ADI (Alternating Direction Implicit) sweeps along each of the three physical dimensions of the problem grid. Partitioning the problem grid using a simple block distribution along any of the three dimensions would have resulted in a serialization of the ADI sweep that involved implicit coupling in that direction. Therefore a skewed block distribution as shown below had to be used, as has been done for example in [2]:

$$\to J$$

		0	1	2	3
↓		1	2	3	0
K		2	3	0	1
		3	0	1	2

The need to use a skewed block distribution of the data ruled out the use of a language like HPF for the parallelization, since it does not support such a data distribution [3]. Parallel scientific computing environments such as PETSc [1] were also not appropriate since skewed block distribution and ADI solvers are not supported. Therefore a parallelization of the sequential code using the portable MPI message-passing library was required. The sequential program consisted of around 50 routines containing around 5000 lines of source code, manipulating over 40 arrays with dimensionality ranging from one to five. Since exact match between the sequential and parallel output was one

Processors	Problem size	Time
1	$288 \times 36 \times 36$	124
2	$288 \times 72 \times 36$	128
4	$288 \times 72 \times 72$	142
8	$288 \times 144 \times 72$	158
16	$288 \times 144 \times 144$	183
32	$288 \times 288 \times 144$	217

Table 1. Execution times, in seconds, for *fdl3di* on the IBM SP2.

of the parallelization objectives, the floating point data arrays were compared for exact equality rather than equality within a tolerance factor.

The performance of the parallelized version of *fdl3di* was evaluated on an IBM SP2. The operating system for the platform was AIX 4.1 and the MPI package used was IBM's implementation of Version 1.1 of the MPI standard.

Performance data for scaled speedup are displayed in Table 1. Here the problem size is varied in proportion to the number of processors, so that the amount of computation per processor remains essentially constant. If perfect speedup were obtained, the total wallclock execution time would have remained a constant. The efficiency on 2 processors is 97% and drops to 57% on 32 processors.

5 Related Work

Considerable attention has been focused on the main tasks involved in automating parallelization, namely the determination of the best data partition that maximizes load balance and minimizes communication, locating the loops which can be parallelized and the generation and placement of communication and synchronization primitives. Surveys of tools and projects that attempt automatic parallelization of numerical codes [7] indicate that these have been handled in a wide variety of ways.

Optimal choice of a data distribution is an NP-complete problem. So, though approaches that try to automate this step may synthesize programs with good performance for regular computations with blocked or cyclic data distributions [11], far more research has to be done to make them viable in the general case. This has created interest in systems that accept directives from the user for determining the data partitioning scheme, such as High Performance FORTRAN [3]. However, as they aim at the conversion of any general sequential program, the resulting overheads reduce performance for many applications. Furthermore, in the current state-of-the-art, they handle only simple data distributions, such as blocked and cyclic distributions. These factors limit the performance of the synthesized code [5, 10]. A different way to accept user input is offered by interactive tools that work with a parallelizing compiler and aid the user in the decision-making process, such as the Interactive D-Editor [6] and Forge [4]. However, they also have limitations in dealing with legacy codes that may need complex data distributions [9]. Other researchers have attempted to overcome the performance limitations of generic approaches by focusing on specific problem domains, information about which can be used in optimizing the synthesized code. For example, the Parallelization Agent [9] focuses on regular grid-based computations that typically arise in domains such as environmental modeling.

The approach proposed in this paper avoids the problems associated with automated choice of data distributions by allowing the user to specify the data distribution scheme. While the HPF standard allows only block and cyclic distributions, this paper allows any tiled distribution, including skewed ones. Also, since it specifically focuses on stencil computation, it eliminates the overheads associated with general purpose tools. More importantly, it allows the programmer to alter the generated program manually to improve performance. This can be accomplished by altering the blocked sequential form of the program to optimize communication or computation in an incremental way and validating the changes before resynthesizing the final parallel program.

A semi-automatic approach to developing message-passing codes is implemented by CAPTools [8]. This tool allows interactive transformation of a sequential program by the user. However, a fundamental difference between that approach and the one we propose is that ours allows for *incremental* testing during the conversion process, that significantly simplifies the detection and isolation of bugs. Further, our methodology abstracts a data distribution as a collection of functions so that the generated parallel code can flexibly choose a data mapping at run-time. Thus, a code can be developed to execute either a 2D partitioning strategy (with lower number of messages transmitted) or a 3D partitioning strategy (with larger number of messages, but possibly lower volume of communication) depending on the problem size and number of processors to be deployed.

6 Conclusion

This paper has presented a systematic methodology that greatly eases accurate efficient hand parallelization of stencil codes and yet is formalized so that it is amenable to automation. The methodology achieves these goals by making changes incrementally, by validating the converted code after each step, by operating in a single address space in the initial stage and by decoupling data partitioning issues from communication issues so that conversion complexity is reduced. The ability to investigate data partitioning issues in a single address space is a unique feature of the methodology. Since it aims at a large but well-defined class of prob-

lems unlike general purpose parallelization tools, it produces efficient code. Performance data has been presented that demonstrates the efficiency of the produced code.

References

[1] S. Balay, W. D. Gropp, L. C. McInnes, and B. F. Smith. PETSc 2.0 users manual. Technical Report ANL-95/11 – Revision 2.0.22, Argonne National Laboratory, 1998.

[2] R.F. Van der Wijngaart and M. Yarrow. RANS-MP: A portable parallel Navier-Stokes solver. Technical Report NAS-97-004, NASA Ames Research Center, February 1997.

[3] High Performance FORTRAN Forum. HPF 1.0 language definition. *Scientific Programming*, 2(1-2):1–170, 1993. Also see http://www.crpc.rice.edu/HPFF/home.html.

[4] R. Friedman, J. Levesque, and G. Wagenbreth. *FORTRAN Parallelization Handbook*. Applied Parallel Research, 1995.

[5] E. Hayder, D.E. Keyes, and P. Mehrotra. A comparison of PETSC library and HPF implementations of an archetypal PDE computation. Technical Report 97-72, Institute for Computer Applications in Science and Engineering, 1997.

[6] S. Hiranandani, K. Kennedy, C.-W. Tseng, and S. Warren. The D Editor: A new interactive parallel programming tool. *Proceedings of the Supercomputing Conference*, pages 733–742, 1994.

[7] C.S. Ierotheou, M. Cross, S.P. Johnson, and P.F. Leggett. CAPTools - an interactive toolkit for mapping CFD codes onto parallel architectures. *Proceedings of the Parallel Computational Fluid Dynamics1993 Conference*, May 1993.

[8] C.S. Ierotheou, S.P.Johnson, M. Cross, and P.F. Leggett. Computer aided parallelizations tools (CAPTools) - conceptual overview and performace on the parallelization of structured mesh codes. *Parallel Computing*, 22(2):163–195, 1996.

[9] S. Mitra and S.C. Kothari. Parallelization agent: A new approach for parallelizing legacy codes. *Proceedings of the 8th SIAM Conference on Parallel Processing*, 1997. (CDROM).

[10] K.P. Roe and P. Mehrotra. Implementation of a total variation diminishing scheme for the shock tube problem in high performance FORTRAN. *Proceedings of the 8th SIAM Conference on Parallel Processing*, 1997. (CDROM).

[11] E. Su, D. Palermo, , and P. Banerjee. Automatic parallelization of regular computations for distributed memory multicomputers in the PARADIGM compiler. *Proceedings of the International Conference on Parallel Processing*, pages II:30–38, August 1993.

[12] N. S. Sundar. *Data Access Optimizations for Parallel Computers*. PhD thesis, The Ohio State University, Columbus, OH 43210, March 1998.

SvPablo: A Multi-Language Architecture-Independent Performance Analysis System

Luiz A. De Rose
laderose@us.ibm.com

Daniel A. Reed *
reed@cs.uiuc.edu

Advanced Computing Technology Center
IBM T. J. Watson Research Center
Yorktown Heights, NY 10598 USA

Department of Computer Science
University of Illinois
Urbana, Illinois 61801 USA

Abstract

In this paper we present the design of SvPablo, a language independent performance analysis and visualization system that can be easily extended to new contexts with minimal changes to the software infrastructure. At present, SvPablo supports analysis of applications written in C, Fortran 77, Fortran 90, and HPF on a variety of sequential and parallel systems. In addition to capturing application data via software instrumentation, SvPablo also exploits hardware performance counters to capture the interaction of software and hardware. Both hardware and software performance data are summarized during program execution, enabling measurement of programs that execute for hours or days on hundreds of processors. This performance data is stored in a format designed to be language transparent and portable. We demonstrate the usefulness of SvPablo for tuning application programs with a case study running on an SGI Origin 2000.

Keywords: Performance analysis and visualization; Parallel and distributed systems; Software instrumentation; Hardware monitoring; Run-time summarization; SDDF Meta-format.

Technical area: Software Tools.

This work was supported in part by the Defense Advanced Research Projects Agency under DARPA contracts DABT63-94-C0049, F30602-96-C-0161, DABT63-96-C-0027, and N66001-97-C-8532; by the National Science Foundation under grants NSF CDA 94-01124 and ASC 97-20202; and by the Department of Energy under contracts DOE B-341494, W-7405-ENG-48, and 1-B-333164.

1 Introduction

Developing applications that achieve high performance on current parallel and distributed systems requires multiple iterations of performance analysis and refinement. In each cycle, analysts first identify the key program components responsible for the bulk of the program's execution time and then modify the program to improve its performance.

The complexity of new parallel architectures further exacerbates performance analysis problems — new distributed shared memory (DSM) systems have multilevel memory hierarchies managed by distributed cache coherence protocols, all accessed by superscalar processors that speculatively execute instructions. Understanding the execution behavior of application code in such environments requires access to hardware performance counters and careful mapping of the resulting data to source code constructs.

Correlating data parallel source code with dynamic performance data from both software and hardware measurements, while still providing a portable, intuitive, and easily used interface, is a challenging task [7]. However, without such tools, the use of high-performance parallel systems will remain limited to a small cadre of application developers willing to master the arcane details of processor architecture, system software, and compilation systems.

To provide a language and architecture independent mechanism for performance analysis, we developed SvPablo (source view Pablo), a graphical environment for instrumenting application source code and browsing dynamic performance data. SvPablo

311

supports performance data capture, analysis, and presentation for applications written in a variety of languages and executing on both sequential and parallel systems. In addition, SvPablo exploits hardware support of performance counters.

During the execution of instrumented code, the SvPablo library captures data and computes performance metrics on the execution dynamics of each instrumented construct on each processor. Because only statistics, rather than detailed event traces, are maintained, the SvPablo library can capture the execution behavior of codes that execute for hours or days on hundreds of processors.

Following execution, performance data from each processor is integrated, additional statistics are computed, and the resulting metrics are correlated with application source code, creating a *performance file* that is represented via the Pablo self-describing data format (SDDF) [8, 3]. This file is the specification used by SvPablo's browser to display application source code and correlated performance metrics.

Use of the Pablo SDDF meta-format has enabled us to develop a user interface that is both portable and language independent. Moreover, because all performance metrics are defined in SDDF, the interface is also performance metric independent, allowing us to introduce new metrics or support new languages without change to the user interface code.

The remainder of this paper is organized as follows. In §2, we begin by describing the SvPablo interactive and automatic source code instrumentation system, followed in §3 by a discussion of support for hardware performance counters, and in §4, by a description of the SvPablo performance visualization interface. Following this, we describe use of SDDF to facilitate language and metric independence in §5. Building on this base, §6 demonstrates application of SvPablo to several large scientific applications. Finally, §7–§8 discuss related work and summarize our conclusions.

2   Performance Instrumentation

Interactive instrumentation provides detailed control, allowing users to specify precise points at which data should be captured, albeit at the possible expense of excessive perturbation and inhibition of compiler optimizations. In contrast, automatic instrumentation relies on the compiler or runtime system to insert probes in compiler-synthesized code. Although this reduces the probability of excessive in-

strumentation perturbation, it sacrifices user control over instrumentation points. Because each is appropriate in different circumstances, SvPablo supports both interactive and automatic instrumentation.

Currently, SvPablo supports interactive instrumentation of C, Fortran 77, and Fortran 90 and automatic instrumentation of High Performance Fortran (HPF). As described below, these choices were driven by experience with earlier generations of instrumentation systems [8, 2] and analysis of common compiler transformations on current parallel systems.

2.1   Automatic Instrumentation

To support analysis of codes written in HPF, SvPablo is integrated with the commercial HPF compiler from the Portland Group. The PGI HPF compiler emits message passing code with embedded calls to the SvPablo data capture library. This instrumentation captures data for each executable line in the original program. In addition, the compiler synthesizes instrumentation for every procedure entry and exit and for each message exchange among tasks.

Using these instrumentation points, the SvPablo data capture library automatically computes performance metrics for all procedures and source code lines. In addition, as described in §3, this library can also capture hardware performance events [6, 10] via the MIPS R10000 [6] performance counters[1].

The desire to capture performance data for data parallel code via compiler-synthesized instrumentation is based on the results of our collaboration with the Rice Fortran D project [2, 1]. The D system, a precursor to current HPF compilers, supports aggressive optimizations, including procedure inlining, loop distribution, software pipelining, and global code motion. Collectively, these optimizations result in executable code that differs markedly from the original source.

Instrumenting the data parallel source code can potentially inhibit any or all of these optimizations, dramatically reducing performance and, equally importantly, resulting in performance measurements that are not typical of normal execution. Hence, SvPablo relies on the HPF compiler to emit instrumented code.

---

[1]The hardware instrumentation interface is readily extensible to other microprocessors.

2.2 Interactive Instrumentation

In contrast to the high-level optimizations often supported by data parallel compilers, most compilers for sequential languages focus primarily on local optimizations (e.g., register reuse, common subexpression elimination, and strength reduction). Hence, SvPablo supports the interactive instrumentation of C and Fortran codes via instrumenting parsers[2], since source code instrumentation in these languages tends to have far less pernicious effects.

For each source file the user wishes to instrument, SvPablo parses the file and marks all *instrumentable constructs*. In a compromise between instrumentation detail and perturbation, SvPablo restricts these constructs to outer loops and procedure calls. This restriction draws on our earlier experience with the Pablo interactive instrumentation interface [8]. We observed that naive users tended to instrument everything, resulting in prodigious volumes of performance data, high perturbations, and little insight.

After the instrumentation is complete, the SvPablo parser generates a copy of the source code with calls to the data capture library. During execution, the SvPablo library accumulates counts and durations for all instrumented constructs. As we shall see in §4, performance metrics are shown beside each instrumentable construct. This allows users to instrument an application, examine the correlation of performance metrics and source code, and re-instrument the application using the knowledge obtained.

3 Hardware Performance Integration

Although software instrumentation can capture the interaction of compiler-synthesized code with runtime libraries and system software, understanding the effects of superscalar instruction execution and caching requires concurrent capture of both software and hardware performance metrics. This is especially true when such processors are combined to form parallel systems with hardware-managed memory hierarchies that interact with compiler-synthesized application data movement. Fortunately, new microprocessors commonly provide a set of performance

---

[2]Programs written in these languages can also be semi-automatically instrumented via command line options.

---

registers for low overhead access to hardware performance data. For example, the MIPS R10000 includes registers that count cycles, level one and level two cache misses, floating point instructions, and branch mispredictions. Similar counters exist on the SUN UltraSPARC, Intel Pentium Pro, and IBM Power2. The SvPablo instrumentation library includes a standard interface to capture hardware performance data on the SGI MIPS R10000. Within SvPablo, a user can select any desired set of hardware events by specifying an ASCII file that contains the virtual counters of interest. The interface with the hardware counters is done through the SvPablo data capture library, so the user does not need to re-compile the program to use a different set of hardware events.

During program execution, the SvPablo data capture library queries the virtual counters and records the data with extant application measurements. In addition to presenting the raw counter data, the SvPablo library also computes derived metrics for each source code line (e.g., MFLOPS and branch misprediction percentages).

After program execution, the SvPablo data capture library records its statistical analyses in a set of *summary files*, one for each executing process. A post-mortem utility program merges the summary files, computing new global statistics and correlating metrics across processors. The resulting file is then input to the analysis graphical interface.

Taken together, the application and hardware performance measurements provide a rich set of metrics for program analysis. Moreover, the SvPablo interface allows users to identify high-level bottlenecks (e.g., procedures), then explore increasing levels of detail (e.g., identifying the specific cause of poor performance at a source code line executed on one of many processors).

4 Performance Visualization

As noted at the outset, one of the design goals for SvPablo was to create an intuitive, cross-architecture, language independent performance analysis interface. Realizing such a design would allow users and performance analysts to learn a single set of software navigation skills and then apply those skills to application codes written in a variety of languages and executing on a diverse set of architectures.

Hence, the SvPablo implementation relies on a single interface for performance instrumentation and visualization. If the program was interactively instrumented, the user can refine the performance analysis by re-instrumenting the source code while visualizing performance data from earlier executions. Regardless of the instrumentation mode, one can access and load performance data from multiple prior executions, including different numbers of processors and hardware platforms. This allows one to compare executions to understand hardware and software interactions.

As an example, Figure 1 shows the SvPablo interface, together with code and performance data from an HPF program. The SvPablo interface supports a hierarchy of performance displays, ranging from color-coded routine profiles to detailed data on the behavior of a source code line on a single processor.

In the figure, the leftmost scrollbox shows the set of files comprising the HPF program, with all previously measured executions of this code shown in the scrollbox to the right. Here, the user has loaded a performance data context (i.e., a measured execution) for an eight processor SGI Origin 2000. After selecting a performance context, the list of procedures in the application code, together with two color coded metrics, is shown below the performance contexts scrollbox in the area labeled *Routines in Performance Data*. The two colored columns summarize, over all processes, the average number of calls and average cumulative time for the routines.

Clicking on a routine name loads the associated source code in the bottom pane of Figure 1, together with color-coded metrics beside each source line. By default, the SvPablo interface displays one column for each metric. However, the user can select only a subset of the metrics to appear in the color coded columns. Clicking the mouse on a colored box, either in the routine list or beside a source code line, creates a dialog box displaying the maximum value associated with the selected metric.

In addition, pop-up dialogs showing other statistics and detailed information about a particular routine or source code line, including individual processor metrics, can be obtained by clicking the mouse on the routine name or the source code line.

5 Language and Architecture Transparency

Developing a user interface that separates performance data presentation from language and architecture idiosyncrasies requires a flexible specification

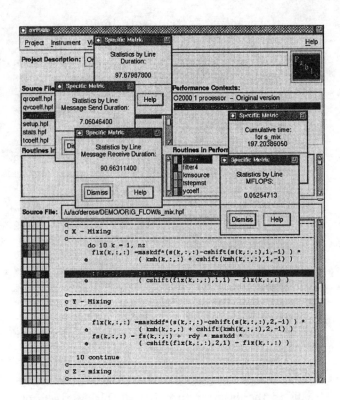

Figure 1. Baseline Performance Data (MST-FLOW HPF Code)

mechanism for both instrumentation points and performance metrics. Only with this separation can one readily add new metrics and support new languages, compilers, and architectures without requiring extensive modifications to the user interface code.

In SvPablo, the Pablo self-defining data format (SDDF) [8, 3] provides this separation. SDDF defines data streams that consist of a group of record descriptors and record instances. Much as structure declarations in the C programming language specify templates for storage allocation, SDDF descriptors define the structure for record instances. The data following the descriptors consist of a stream of descriptor tag and data record pairs. Each tag identifies the descriptor that defines the juxtaposed data. By separating the structure of data from its semantics, the Pablo SDDF library permits the construction of tools that can extract and process SDDF records and record fields with minimal knowledge of the data's deeper semantics.

The SDDF meta-format provides the generality and extensibility necessary to represent a diverse set of performance metrics and measurement points. Because this data may vary across languages or even

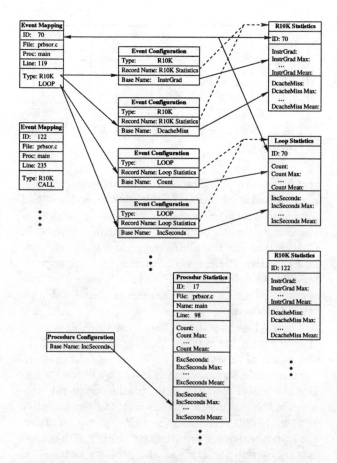

Figure 2. SvPablo SDDF Record Hierarchy

across executions of the same program (e.g., when instrumentation points are changed interactively or when a different set of hardware metrics is captured), the performance data files that define execution contexts rely on SDDF specifications that include both mandatory and optional data fields.

To isolate such language differences from the user interface, the performance metrics associated with each procedure and source line are organized as a hierarchy defined by a set of SDDF records. As Figure 2 shows, this *meta-meta-format* hierarchy contains three groups of SDDF record descriptors: *mapping*, *configuration* and *statistic*.

Mapping records define the set of statistics associated with each instrumentable construct. In turn, configuration records indicate the statistic record names and allow the SvPablo interface to extract the base names of all performance metrics before reading the statistics records, which define the actual performance metrics.

This meta-configuration is the key to SvPablo's ex-

tensibility. Tool developers can add new metrics to SvPablo simply by updating the mapping and configuration records and then generating the desired set of statistic records. Below, we describe the meta-format for both event and procedure statistics.

5.1 Event Statistics

The performance data associated with an instrumentable construct is represented by a single SDDF *Event Statistics Mapping* record and by a set of *Statistics* records, one for each associated performance metric. The mapping record defines the general information about the instrumentation point (e.g., its source code location) and specifies a group of pointers to statistics records for the actual performance metrics.

As an example, consider the mapping for event 70, shown in Figure 2. The event mapping record indicates two types of associated configuration and statistic records: "LOOP" and "R10K." The configuration records then define the base names for all statistics associated with the "LOOP" and "R10K" metrics. In turn, Figure 3 shows the SDDF statistics record descriptor for the MIPS R10000 counter data for this example. The event identifier specifies the source code location by correlating it to the parent mapping record.

Each metric (e.g., data cache misses) includes data for each process as a vector, together with standard statistics (i.e., minima, maxima, mean, and standard deviation). SvPablo uses the vector to present performance data for each process and the statistics to present data for each source code line. For each metric in the statistics record descriptor, there is an event configuration record which specifies the base name of the metric. These base names are used by SvPablo to read the corresponding performance data.

5.2 Procedure Statistics

Finally, a separate set of SDDF procedure statistics records define the performance metrics associated with all procedures. These records contain both mandatory and optional fields. The mandatory fields include procedure mapping information and two metric fields — the number of calls to the procedure and the exclusive duration of the procedure.

As illustrated in Figure 2, the mapping information is provided by the procedure statistics record and includes: a unique procedure identifier, the name

```
// "description" "Performance Statistics "
"R10K stats" {
    int "Event ID";
    // "InstrGrad" "Instructions Graduated"
    double "InstrGrad"[];
    double "InstrGrad Max";
    int "InstrGrad Max Node";
    double "InstrGrad Min";
    int "InstrGrad Min Node";
    double "InstrGrad Mean";
    double "InstrGrad Std Dev";
    // "DcacheMiss" "Data Cache Misses"
    int "DcacheMiss"[];
    int "DcacheMiss Max";
    int "DcacheMiss Max Node";
    int "DcacheMiss Min";
    int "DcacheMiss Min Node";
    double "DcacheMiss Mean";
    double "DcacheMiss Std Dev";
};;
```

Figure 3. R10000 Hardware Performance Counters Record Descriptor

of the file containing the procedure, the procedure name, and the procedure's first source code line. The SvPablo interface uses these fields to display the list of procedures and their metrics, shown in Figure 1, and the associated performance pop-up dialogs.

Finally, the remaining, optional fields define the data needed for the detailed performance metric displays. As illustrated in Figure 2, the base names of these additional metrics are specified in the procedure configuration records.

6 Application Tuning Example

The true test of any performance tool is its effectiveness when applied to poorly performing applications in a realistic context. To assess the utility of SvPablo and the possible usability penalties induced by our design's emphasis on language independence and portability, we worked with application developers from the National Center for Supercomputing Applications (NCSA). Based on this experience, we present a case study on the SGI Origin 2000 that demonstrates SvPablo's effectiveness when analyzing performance and tuning codes.

This case study explores the performance of a numerical model simulating cloud and density cur-

Stmt	Excl. Sec.	MFLOPS	Send Msg Duration	Rcv Msg Duration
loop 10	6.1		0.25	5.71
(73)	91.3	0.04	5.61	84.00
(82)	94.8	0.04	5.94	86.95

Table 1. Average Metric Values (Array "fs" in Baseline Code)

rent dynamics [4]. The code is a three-dimensional, non-hydrostatic, finite difference, convective cloud model that utilizes a quasi-compressible version of the Navier-Stokes equations. Originally written in CM Fortran for the CM5, the code was later translated to High-Performance Fortran, yielding approximately 9000 lines of HPF code. We executed two versions of the program (baseline and modified), using 8 processors.

Figure 1 shows the SvPablo interface displaying the execution behavior of the original code on eight processors of an SGI Origin. The pane `Routines in Performance Data`, which is sorted by routine duration, indicates that the main bottleneck in the program is the routine "s_mix", which had a cumulative time of 197.20 seconds. Via SvPablo, we identified the computation of "X - Mixing" and "Y - Mixing" in the routine "s_mix" as the primary bottleneck. The average metric values for the two most time consuming statements in the code and the enclosing loop, summarized in Table 1, indicate that the bottleneck was caused by communication inside the loop.

Three pertinent observations are revealed by the data shown in Figure 1:

- The compiler-synthesized communication required by the circular shift ("cshift") on the array "flx" is primary cause of the poor performance observed for this HPF statement. This is denoted by the dark color bars for the communication metric (the last two columns).

- The previous assignment also contains circular shifts and would expect compiler-synthesized communication as well. However, SvPablo shows that no communication occurred (indicated by the absence of communication metric data in the associated columns).

- SvPablo assigns communication costs to a loop, rather than to its component statements, if some loop-related communication occurs prior to execution of the loop body. For this loop, no loop-related communication should be nec-

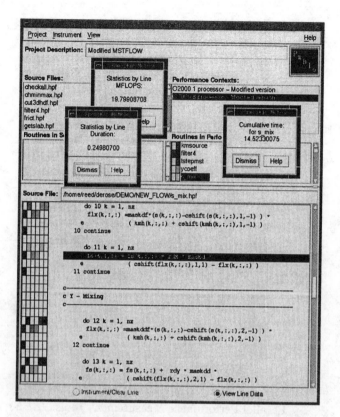

Figure 4. Performance Data (MSTFLOW HPF Modified Code)

Stmt	Excl. Sec.	MFLOPS	Send Msg Duration	Rcv Msg Duration
$\sum$ loops	10.54		0.50	9.38
(73)	0.23	16.3		
(82)	0.28	14.0		

Table 2. Average Metric Values (Array "`fs`" in Modified Code)

As expected, communication occurred between loops, reducing the subroutine's execution time by an order of magnitude, from 197.2 seconds to 14.5 seconds.

Table 2 shows the average metric values for the same two statements and for the sum of the execution times of the four loops. Clearly, the additional overhead of the loops is very small compared to the performance gained by overlapped communication. Moreover, the mean MFLOPS rate for each processor increased by four orders of magnitude.

7 Related Work

SvPablo falls into the category of tools that measure the performance of a program during run-time. These tools have been employed by several efforts described in the literature, targeting both sequential and parallel systems — far more than can be discussed here. Notable examples include Paradyn [5], developed at the University of Wisconsin, the Pablo Performance Analysis Environment [8], developed at the University of Illinois, and the Automated Instrumentation and Monitoring System (AIMS) [9], developed at NASA Ames Research Center.

Paradyn is a tool for measuring the performance of large-scale parallel programs. It performs dynamic instrumentation on long-running programs, in search of performance problems. It is distinguished from other performance measurements tools in that instrumentation and visualization are performed during run-time.

The Pablo Performance Analysis Environment consists of several components for instrumenting and tracing parallel programs and for analyzing the trace files produced by the instrumented programs. SvPablo used and extended some of these components. However, it differs from the Pablo Environment in that it performs run-time summarization instead of collecting trace data, and the data capture and presentation components are integrated into the same graphical performance browser.

essary. However, SvPablo shows that the compiler did synthesize some communication prior to the loop body.

Based on these observations, one can deduce the cause for the performance difference between the two circular shifts. Succinctly, the arrays "kmh" and "s", which must be shifted for the computation of "flx," are loop independent. Hence, the compiler can prefetch the necessary data before loop execution begins. However, the array "flx" is computed in the first statement of the loop and used in the second. Hence, the data must be circularly shifted during each loop iteration.

To improve the performance of this routine, we split the original loop, forming four loops, one for each statement inside the original loop, as shown in Figure 4. By splitting the loop, we expected the HPF compiler to begin migrating data as soon as an iteration of the previous loop is completed, overlapping computation and communication.

After splitting the original loop, we again executed the code and measured its performance with SvPablo.

A work closely related to the Pablo Environment, is AIMS, a software toolkit for performance evaluation of parallel applications on multiprocessors. AIMS accepts Fortran and C parallel programs written using two message passing libraries: MPI and PVM. It has three major software components: a source code instrumentor, a run-time performance-monitoring library, and a suite of tools that process and display execution data. SvPablo differs from AIMS in performing run-time summarization and having the instrumentation and visualization components integrated.

In general, the majority of the performance measurement tools focus on particular programming models (e.g., message passing or data parallel) or specific hardware/software platforms. In contrast, SvPablo is designed to be independent of both programming model and architecture, allowing developers to re-target the performance analysis infrastructure simply by changing SvPablo's meta-data specification of performance metrics.

8 Conclusions

In this paper, we described the design of SvPablo, a toolkit for instrumentation, data capture and analysis of sequential and parallel codes. SvPablo supports both software performance measurement and low overhead access to hardware performance counters, summarizing the performance data during program execution. Working with a group of large-scale application developers, we observed that SvPablo enabled us to rapidly identify and correct performance bottlenecks.

However, the key feature of SvPablo is its language and architecture transparency, achieved by representing performance data via a meta-meta-format presentation of events from different languages using the same graphical interface. The flexible structure of the performance file also permits the ready introduction of new metrics and support of new languages without requiring modifications to the graphical user interface.

References

[1] ADVE, V., MELLOR-CRUMMEY, J., ANDERSON, M., KENNEDY, K., WANG, J., AND REED, D. Integrating Compilation and Performance Analysis for Data-Parallel Programs. In *Proceedings of the Workshop on Debugging and Performance Tuning for Parallel Computing Systems*, M. L. Simmons, A. H. Hayes, D. A. Reed, and J. Brown, Eds. IEEE Computer Society Press, 1994.

[2] ADVE, V., MELLOR-CRUMMEY, J., WANG, J.-C., AND REED, D. Integrating Compilation and Performance Analysis for Data-Parallel Programs. In *Proceedings of Supercomputing'95* (November 1995).

[3] AYDT, R. The Pablo Self-Defining Data Format. Tech. rep., Department of Computer Science at the University of Illinois at Urbana-Champaign, April 1994.

[4] LEE, B. D., AND WILHELMSON, R. B. The Numerical Simulation of Non-Supercell Tornadogenesis. In *18th Conference on Severe Local Storms* (February 1996).

[5] MILLER, B. P., CALLAGHAN, M. D., CARGILLE, J. M., HOLLINGSWORTH, J. K., IRVIN, R. B., KARAVANIC, K. L., KUNCHITHAPADAM, K., AND NEWHALL, T. The Paradyn Parallel Performance Measurement Tools. *IEEE Computer 28*, 11 (November 1995), 37–46.

[6] MIPS TECHNOLOGIES INC. *MIPS R10000 Microprocessor User's Manual*, version 2.0 ed., October 1996.

[7] PANCAKE, C. M., SIMMONS, M. L., AND YAN, J. C. Performance Evaluation Tools for Parallel and Distributed Systems. *IEEE Computer 28*, 11 (November 1995), 16–19.

[8] REED, D. A., AYDT, R. A., NOE, R. J., ROTH, P. C., SHIELDS, K. A., SCHWARTZ, B., AND TAVERA, L. F. Scalable Performance Analysis: The Pablo Performance Analysis Environment. In *Proceedings of the Scalable Parallel Libraries Conference* (1993), A. Skjellum, Ed., IEEE Computer Society.

[9] YAN, J. C., SARUKKAI, S. R., AND MEHRA, P. Performance Measurement, Visualization and Modeling of Parallel and Distributed Programs using the AIMS Toolkit. *Software Practice & Experience 25*, 4 (April 1995), 429–461.

[10] ZAGHA, M., LARSON, B., TURNER, S., AND ITZKOWITZ, M. Performance Analysis Using the MIPS R10000 Performance Counters. In *Proceedings of Supercomputing'96* (November 1996).

Efficient Techniques for Distributed Implementation of Search-based AI Systems*

Gopal Gupta and Enrico Pontelli
Laboratory for Logic, Databases and Advanced Programming
Department of Computer Science
New Mexico State University
Las Cruces, NM 88003, USA
http://www.cs.nmsu.edu/lldap

Abstract

We study the problem of exploiting parallelism from search-based AI systems on distributed machines. We propose stack-splitting, a technique for implementing or-parallelism, which when coupled with appropriate scheduling strategies leads to: (i) reduced communication during distributed execution; and, (ii) distribution of larger grain-sized work to processors. The modified technique can also be implemented on shared memory machines and should be quite competitive with existing methods. Indeed, an implementation has been carried out on shared memory machines, and the results are reported here.

1. Introduction

Artificial Intelligence (AI) is an active field of research, that has found applications in diverse areas. The field of AI is very broad and one can find several types of AI systems: those based on neural networks, those based on tree/graph search, image recognition systems, etc. In this paper we are primarily interested in AI systems that rely on traversing a large search-space, looking for a solution that satisfies certain criteria [17, 16, 18]. We refer to such systems as search-based AI systems. Game playing programs, expert systems, constraint solving applications, and discourse analysis systems are example of such search-based AI systems. Such search-based AI systems can take a lot of time to find a solution, as the search space can be enormous. Given the compute-intensive nature of search-based AI systems, parallel execution is an obvious technique that comes to mind to speed-up the search. In fact, considerable research has been done [18, 16, 19, 17, 6] on exploiting parallelism from

search-based AI system. Two approaches have been generally been followed: (i) techniques have been developed and implemented for extracting parallelism from specific AI systems (e.g., [13, 14]), (ii) techniques have been developed and implemented for extracting parallelism from language constructs in programming languages that are typically used for coding AI applications (e.g., Prolog, or Lisp) [6, 11]. In both cases, it is the operation of searching the solution-space that is parallelized. It should also be mentioned that most work on exploiting parallelism falls under (ii). Nearly not as much work has been done on (i), for the obvious reason that (ii) represents a more general approach. Within (ii) considerable work has been done on parallelizing Prolog. In the rest of the paper, we will present our techniques and results in the context of parallel Prolog, though they can equally well be applied to specific AI systems that incorporate searching, as well as other languages that incorporate search mechanisms to facilitate programming of search-based AI applications.

Implementing search (parallel or sequential) requires that we have a representation of the search space in the computer's memory. This representation is usually a tree—called the *search tree*. Each node of this tree represents a branch point from where multiple branches emanate. These branches may lead to further nodes, which may yet split into other branches, and so on. The nodes, or branch points, are termed *choice points*, and the branches are termed *alternatives*, if we were to use Prolog's terminology [6].

The obvious way to search this tree in parallel is to have multiple processors explore the different branches of the search-tree in parallel [18, 16, 17, 19]. Given a search tree, the model of computation that is typically employed is as follows. Multiple processors traverse the search tree looking for unexplored branches. If an unexplored branch, i.e., an unexplored alternative in a choice point, is found, then the processor will select it and begin its execution. The processor will stop either if it fails, i.e., it determines that the solution cannot lie on that branch, or if it finds a solution.

*Authors are partially supported by NSF grants CCR 96-25358, INT 95-15256, CDA 97-29848, HRD 96-28450, EIA 98-10732, and CCR-9900320 and a grant from the Fullbright US-Spain Program.

In case of failure, or if the solution found is not acceptable to the user, the processor will *backtrack*, i.e., move back up in the tree, looking for other choice points with untried alternatives to explore. This process of traversing the tree in parallel is complicated by the need of guaranteeing proper synchronization between processors, e.g., to guarantee that no two processors selects the same alternative for execution.

This form of search-based parallelism is commonly termed *or-parallelism*. Efficient implementation of or-parallelism has been extensively investigated in the context of AI systems [18, 19, 17] as well as for the Prolog language [10]. In sequential implementations of search-based AI systems or Prolog, typically one branch of the tree resides on the stack of the processor at any given time. This simplifies implementation quite significantly—e.g., backtracking is reduced to a simple *pop* operation on the main stack. However, in case of parallel systems, multiple branches of the tree co-exist at the same time, making the parallel implementation complex. Efficient management of these co-existing branches is quite a difficult problem, and is referred to as the *environment management problem* [10].

Most parallel implementation of parallel AI systems and parallel Prolog systems have focused on shared-memory machines. Very few attempts have been made to realize such implementations on scalable distributed memory machines. It should be noted that the most efficient or-parallel execution models devised for shared memory machines do not scale up to distributed memory machines, highlighting the difficulty of realizing or-parallel systems on distributed machines.

In this paper we present a method for implementing or-parallelism on distributed memory machines. This method, called *stack-splitting*, reuses efficient implementation mechanisms devised for or-parallel systems on shared-memory multiprocessor to obtain scalable implementation of or-parallelism on distributed memory multiprocessors. This allows us to support or-parallelism on distributed memory architectures with reduced communication and without giving up the use of scheduling mechanisms that have been found to work well for or-parallelism. Stack-splitting has the potential to: (i) improve locality of computation, reduce communication between parallel threads, and increase memory access efficiency (e.g., improve the caching behavior). (ii) allow the use of better scheduling strategies (specifically scheduling on bottom-most choice point [1, 4]) to be realized even in distributed memory implementations of or-parallelism.

In this paper we also present results from implementing stack-splitting on top of the Muse method [1], one of the most efficient method for implementing or-parallelism on shared-memory machines.

2. Implementing Or-parallelism

A major problem in implementing or-parallelism is that multiple branches of the search tree are active simultaneously, each of which may produce a solution or may fail. Each of these branches may potentially bind a variable created earlier during the execution. In normal sequential execution, where only one branch of the search tree is active at any given time, the binding for the variable created by that branch is stored in the memory location allocated for that variable. During backtracking, this binding is removed— during the *untrailing* phase—so as to free the memory location for use by the next branch.

However, during or-parallel execution, this memory location will have to be turned into a *set of locations* shared between processors, or some other means would have to be devised to store the multiple bindings that may exist simultaneously. In addition, we should be able to efficiently distinguish the binding that is applicable to each branch, when it needs to be accessed later in that branch. This problem of maintaining multiple bindings efficiently is called the *multiple environments representation* problem. An extensive discussion can be found in [10] and a complexity-theoretic analysis of the problem is presented in [21]. Numerous solutions have been devised to solve the multiple environments representation problem, and a survey of these techniques can be found in [10].

Stack-copying [1] has been one of the most successful approaches for solving the multiple environments representation problem. It has been incorporated in the Muse or-parallel system [1]. In this approach, processors working in or-parallel maintain a *separate* but *identical* address space, i.e., they allocate their data areas starting at the same logical addresses. Whenever a processor $\mathcal{A}$ working in or-parallel becomes idle, it will start looking for unexplored alternatives generated by some other processor $\mathcal{B}$. Once a choice point p with unexplored alternatives is detected in the computation tree $\mathcal{T}_B$ generated by $\mathcal{B}$, then $\mathcal{A}$ will create a local copy of $\mathcal{T}_B$ and restart the computation by backtracking over p and executing one of its unexplored alternatives. The fact that all the the processors working on or-parallel maintain an identical logical address space reduces the creation of a local copy of $\mathcal{T}_B$ to a simple block memory copying operation (Figure 1).

However, the stack-copying operation is slightly more involved than simply copying data structures, as the choice points have to be copied to an area accessible to all processors. This is important because the set of untried alternatives is now shared between the two processors, and if this set is not accessed in a mutually exclusive way then two processors may execute the same alternative. Thus, after copying, the choice point will be transferred to a shared area. Using the terminology used by Muse, we will refer to

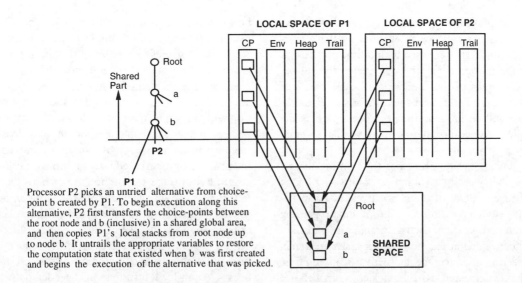

Processor P2 picks an untried alternative from choice-point b created by P1. To begin execution along this alternative, P2 first transfers the choice-points between the root node and b (inclusive) in a shared global area, and then copies P1's local stacks from root node up to node b. It untrails the appropriate variables to restore the computation state that existed when b was first created and begins the execution of the alternative that was picked.

Figure 1. Stack-copying based Or-parallelism

a choice point transferred to the shared memory area as a *shared frame*. Both the processor that copies and the processor being copied from, will replace their choice points with a pointer to the appropriate shared frame. Due to involvement of shared frames, this whole operation of obtaining work from another processor is termed *sharing* of or-parallel work. In order to reduce the number of sharing operations performed (since each sharing operation may involve a considerable amount of overhead), unexplored alternatives are always picked from the *bottom-most* choice point in the tree; during the sharing operation all the choice points between the bottom-most choice point and the top-most choice point are shared between the two processors. This means that in each sharing operation we try to maximize the amount of work shared between the two processors. Furthermore, in order to reduce the amount of information transferred during the sharing operation, copying is done *incrementally*, i.e., only the *difference* between $\mathcal{T}_A$ and $\mathcal{T}_B$ is actually copied.

3. The Stack-Splitting Model

A major reason for the success of the Muse method is that it performs *scheduling on bottom-most choice point*, as mentioned earlier. That is, an idle processor picks work (an untried alternative) from the bottom-most choice point of an or-branch. The stack segments upwards of this choice point are copied before the exploration of this alternative is begun. The copied stack segments may contain other choice points with untried alternatives. These alternatives will be tried via standard backtracking on the copied segments (of course, they may be picked by other processors looking for work as well). Thus, a significant amount of work potentially becomes available to the copying processor every time a copying operation is performed.

The shared frames in the shared memory space have to be accessed in a mutually exclusive manner, to make sure that the same alternative is not tried by two processors that have copies of the same stack-segment. This solution for building an or-parallel system based on the shared frames works fine on a shared memory multiprocessor, however, on a distributed memory machine it becomes a source of significant overhead, as the operation of accessing the shared area becomes a bottleneck. This is because sharing of information in a distributed memory machine leads to frequent exchange of messages and hence considerable overhead. Centralized data structures, such as the shared frames, are, not unexpectedly, expensive to realize in a distributed setting. Nevertheless, stack copying has been considered by most researchers as the best environment representation methodology to support or-parallelism in a distributed memory setting [5, 2]. This is because while the choice points are shared, at least all other data-structures, such as the environment, the trail, and the heap, are not. However, the fact that the choice points are shared is a major drawback for a distributed implementation of stack-copying. So the question we wish to consider is: can we avoid this sharing of choice points while doing bottom-most scheduling?

3.1. Copying with Stack Splitting

In the stack-copying technique the primary reason why a choice point has to be shared is because we want to make sure that the selection of its untried alternatives by various active processors is serialized, so that no two processors select the same alternative. The shared frame is locked while

321

the alternative is picked, to guarantee this property. However, there are other simple ways of ensuring that no alternative is simultaneously selected by multiple processors: we can *split* the untried alternatives of a choice point between the two copies of the choice point stack. We call this operation *Choice Point Stack Splitting* or simply stack-splitting. This will ensure that no two processors pick the same alternative—since no alternative is visible to more than one processor at a time.

We can envision different schemes for splitting the set of alternatives between the two choice points—e.g., each choice point receives half of the alternatives, or the partitioning can be guided by additional information regarding the unexplored computation, such as granularity and likelihood of failure. In addition, the need for a shared frame, as a critical section to protect the alternatives from multiple executions, has disappeared, as each stack copy has a choice point, though their contents differ in terms of which unexplored alternatives they contain. All the choice points can be evenly split in this way during the copying operation. The choice point stack-splitting operation is illustrated in figure 2.

3.2. Advantages of Stack-splitting

The major advantage of stack-splitting is that scheduling on bottom-most can still be used without incurring huge communication overheads. Essentially, after splitting, the different or-parallel threads become fairly independent of each other, and hence communication is minimized during execution. In particular, backtracking on a node that has been copied from a different processor does not require anymore the use of mutual exclusion. This makes the stack-splitting technique highly suitable for distributed memory machines. The possibility of parameterizing the splitting of the alternatives based on additional semantic information (granularity, non-failure, user annotations) can further reduce the likelihood of additional communications due to scheduling.

3.3. Overheads of Stack-splitting

The shared frames in the regular stack-copying technique is also a place where global information related to scheduling and work-load is kept. The shared frames provide a globally accessible description of the or-tree, and each shared frame keeps information that allows one to determine which processor is working in which part of the tree. This last piece of information is of particular importance to support the kind of scheduling typically used in stack-copying systems—work is taken from the processor that is "closer" in the computation tree, thus reducing the amount of information to be copied—since the "distance"

between the processors, and the hence the difference between their stacks, is minimized. The shared nature of the frames ensures accessibility to this information to all processors, all of whom see a consistent picture. However, because the shared frame no longer exists under the stack-splitting schema, scheduling and work-load information will have to be maintained in some other way. It could be kept in a global shared area similar to the case of shared memory machines (e.g., by building a representation of the or-tree), or distributed over multiple processors and accessed by message passing in case of non-shared memory machines. The management of scheduling in a distributed memory system will require communication between processors anyway; the use of stack-splitting allows scheduling on bottom-most and is expected to reduce the amount of scheduling-related communication needed. In particular, access to non-local information is needed only when a processor runs out of local work, and not at each backtracking step (as in the case of standard stack copying).

Thus, stack-splitting does not completely remove the need of a shared description of the computation tree. Nevertheless, the use of stack-splitting can mitigate the impact of accessing logically shared resources—e.g., stack-splitting allows scheduling on bottom-most which, in general, reduces the number of calls to the scheduler [1].

3.4. The Cost of Stack-splitting

Let us next consider the cost of the stack-splitting operation. The stack-copying operation in the stack-splitting technique is a little involved, though only slightly more than in regular (*a lá* Muse) stack-copying. In regular stack-copying, the original choice point stack is traversed and the choice points transferred to the shared area. This operation involves only those choice points that have never been shared before—if a choice point is already shared, then its copy already resides in the global shared memory-area. The update of the actual entries in the choice point stacks of the the processors takes place only after the appropriate choice points have been copied to the global shared area.

In the stack splitting technique, after the copying is done, we need to traverse both the stacks, splitting the untried alternatives in the choice points of the two stacks. In the case of shared memory implementations, this operation is expected to be considerably cheaper than transferring the choice point to the shared area. The actual splitting can be represented by a simple pair of indices that refer to the list of alternatives (which is static and shared by all the processors). In the case of distributed memory implementations, the situation is similar: since each processor maintains a local copy of the code, the splitting can be performed by communicating to the copying processor which alternatives it can execute for each choice point (e.g., described as a pair

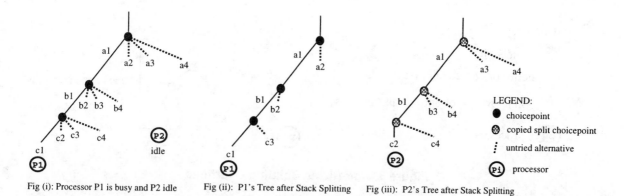

Fig (i): Processor P1 is busy and P2 idle   Fig (ii): P1's Tree after Stack Splitting   Fig (iii): P2's Tree after Stack Splitting

Figure 2. Stack-splitting based or-parallelism

of pointers to the static list of alternatives).

Thus, in both cases we expect the sharing operation to have comparable complexity; a slight delay may occur in the shared memory case, due to the need of performing a traversal of the choice point stack in both the processors. On the other hand, in stack-splitting the two traversals (one in the copying processor and one in the processor from where we are copying) can be overlapped—in the original stack copying scheme the copying processor is instead suspended until the other processor has completed the sharing operation. However, if the stack being copied is itself a copy of some other stack, then unlike regular stack-copying, we still need to traverse both the source and the target stacks and split the choice points. In such cases, the cost of the sharing operation will be slightly higher than the cost of copying in regular stack-copying.

Once a processor picks work from another processor, it will look for work again only after it finishes the exploration of this alternatives, as well as all the alternatives it acquired via stack-splitting. Incremental copying and other optimizations developed for Muse still apply to stack-splitting, though some extra work is needed. Each processor has knowledge of the parts of its stack which are shared (this information is available locally to the processor). These shared parts, if possible, should not be immediately deallocated on backtracking; otherwise, when work is picked from other processors, these shared parts will have to be copied again.

3.5. Optimizing Stack-splitting Cost

The cost incurred in splitting the untried alternatives between the copied stack and the stack from which the copy is made, can be eliminated by amortizing it over the operation of picking untried alternatives during backtracking, as shown next.

In the modified approach, no traversal and modification of the choice points is done during the copying operation.

The untried alternatives are organized as a binary tree (see Figure 3). Note that the binary alternatives can be efficiently maintained in an array, using standard techniques found in any data-structures textbook. In addition, each choice point maintains the "copying distance" from the very first original choice point as a bit string. This number is initially 0 when the computation begins. When stack-splitting takes place and a choice point whose bit string is n is copied from, then the new choice point's bit string is $n1$ (1 tagged to bit string n), while the old choice point's bit string is changed to $n0$ (0 tagged to bit string n). When a processor backtracks to a choice point, it will use its bit string to navigate in the tree of untried alternatives, and find the alternatives that it is responsible for. For example, if the bit-string of a processor is 10, then it means that all the alternatives in the left subtree of the right subtree of the binary tree are to be executed by that processor.

However, it is not very clear which of the two strategies—incurring cost of splitting at copying time vs amortizing the cost over the operation of picking untried alternatives—would be more efficient. In case of amortization, the cost of picking an alternative from a choice point is, of course, now slightly higher, as the binary tree of choice points needs to be traversed to find the right alternative.

3.6. Applicability and Effectiveness

Stack splitting essentially approximates static work distribution, as the untried alternatives are split at the time of picking work. If the choice points that are split are balanced, then we can expect good performance. Thus, we should expect to see good performance when the choice points generated by the computation that are parallelized contain a large number of alternatives. This is the case for applications which fetch data from databases and for most generate & test type of applications.

For choice points with a small number of alternatives, the stack-splitting scheme is more susceptible to problems cre-

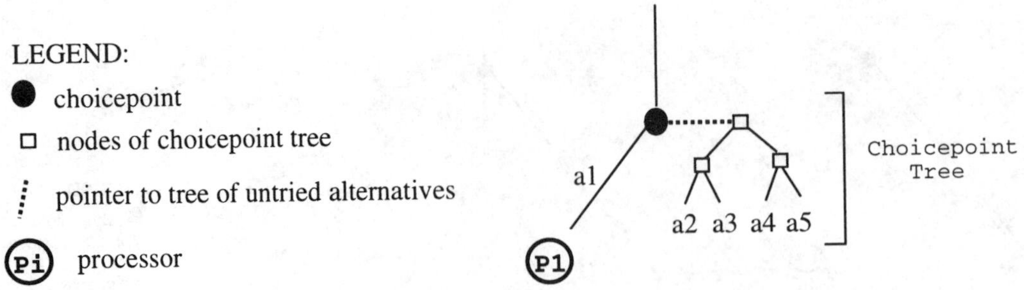

Figure 3. Amortizing Splitting Overhead

ated by the static work distribution strategy that implicitly results from it: for example, in cases where or-parallelism is extracted from choice points with only two alternatives. Such choice points arise quite frequently, since many programs generate or-parallelism from predicates like member and select:

```
member(X,[X | _]).
member(X,[_ | Y]) :-
        member(X,Y).

select(X,[X | Y],Y).
select(X,[Y | Z],[Y | R]) :-
        select(X,Z,R).
```

Both these predicates generate choice points with only two alternatives each—thus, at the time of sharing, a single alternative will be available in each choice point. The different alternatives are spread across different choice points. Stack splitting would assign all the alternatives to the copying processor, thus leaving the original processor without local work. However, the problems raised by such situations can be solved using a number of techniques discussed in [9]. Most significant of these is the technique of *vertical* splitting of the choice points. In vertical splitting each processor is given all the alternatives of alternate choice points. Thus, in this case, the alternatives are not split, rather the list of choice points available is split between the two processors [9].

3.7. Performance Evaluation

The stack-splitting technique has been implemented by modifying the Muse or-parallel system, which is itself realized on top of the SICStus Prolog (SICStus 2.1) system from the Swedish Institute of Computer Science. The first prototype of stack-splitting has been developed on shared-memory architectures. The goal of this prototype is to perform a preliminary feasibility study of the ideas discussed in this paper. Porting on distributed-memory architectures is currently in progress.

The timing results in seconds along with speedups obtained are shown in Table 1 and Table 2. All the benchmarks for which results are reported involve search. The benchmarks used are classical benchmarks used for evaluating the parallel behavior of or-parallel systems—and they have been mostly taken from the benchmarks pool of or-parallel systems Muse and Aurora.

The results reported in this paper have been obtained on: (i) A Pentium-Pro 200Mhz 4-node shared memory workstation, running Solaris 2.7 (software compiled using gcc); (ii) An 8-node Sequent shared memory system, running Dynix. The Sequent hardware is relatively old and slow with respect to current industry standards. Nevertheless it gives a good feeling for the parallel behavior of the system and it represents the largest parallel shared memory system currently available to us. Experiments on Pentium-based and Sparc-based parallel systems have provided comparable speedups.

The results presented in Table 1 illustrates the execution times and speedups observed on the Sequent system. In particular the table presents for each benchmark

- the execution times (in seconds)—the figures reported are the average execution times over a sequence of 10 runs;

- the relative speedups obtained for different number of processors;

Additionally, the table presents the results obtained using the Muse or-parallel system and the or-parallel system based on Stack Splitting. Table 2 presents the results (time in milliseconds) obtained on the Pentium-pro hardware. It can be observed that the speedups on the two systems are very similar.

All benchmarks have been executed by requiring the system to exploit parallelism only from selected promising predicates, and by declaring all other predicates sequential (i.e., non-parallelizable). We believe this situation better reflects the kind of behavior needed to guarantee adequate performance in a distributed execution (which remains the

324

Benchmark	# Processors							
	1		**3**		**5**		**7**	
	Muse	SS	Muse	SS	Muse	SS	Muse	SS
Tina	21.4	22.5	25.1 (0.85)	10.1 (2.22)	25.1 (0.85)	8.3 (2.71)	25.0 (0.85)	7.6 (2.97)
Large	131.7	144.9	118.0 (1.12)	54.3 (2.67)	120.1 (1.1)	38.8 (3.73)	118.4 (1.11)	32.3 (4.49)
Queens1	56.8	63.6	49.8 (1.14)	39.5 (1.61)	42.9 (1.32)	36.1 (1.76)	42.1 (1.35)	34.4 (1.85)
FQueens	51.3	59.0	18.8 (2.72)	24.5 (2.41)	10.8 (4.77)	13.1 (4.51)	7.5 (6.88)	9.9 (5.95)
Salt	98.8	104.7	38.7 (2.55)	36.2 (2.89)	25.1 (3.93)	23.3 (4.5)	18.6 (5.32)	18.2 (5.76)
Solitaire	22.9	24.4	8.4 (2.71)	8.7 (2.8)	5.3 (4.29)	5.6 (4.37)	4.6 (4.95)	4.1 (5.91)
Houses	37.1	41.2	13.7 (2.71)	14.5 (2.84)	8.9 (4.18)	9.3 (4.45)	6.7 (5.53)	6.9 (5.92)
constraint	67.0	69.7	25.0 (2.68)	25.7 (2.71)	15.2 (4.42)	15.5 (4.49)	10.6 (6.35)	10.8 (6.44)

Table 1. Execution Times on Sequent: Muse vs. Stack-Splitting

ultimate goal of the stack-splitting model). All the benchmarks have been executed using all-solutions queries.

As can be seen in Table 1, stack-splitting leads in general to better speed-ups. The execution time of the stack-splitting system is occasionally slightly worse than the execution times of Muse—on average the sequential stack-splitting system is 5% to 12% slower than sequential Muse. This is due to: (i) the temporary removal of some sequential optimizations from the stack-splitting system, to facilitate the development of the initial prototype; and, (ii) the presence of one additional comparison during the backtracking phase—needed to distinguish between choice points that have been split and those that have not. The first problem will be solved in the next version of the prototype. The second problem is inherent in the current representation of the alternatives in the choice points used by the SICStus system (on which the stack-splitting system has been developed). All choice points associated to the same predicate share the same list of alternatives. This complicates the implementation of stack-splitting, as the list of alternatives cannot be directly manipulated (as this may potentially affect other choice points as well). The simple alternative of duplicating the list of alternatives proved too inefficient. At present we have introduced two pointers in the choice point to maintain the segment of alternatives list of interest—and this leads to the need of discriminating between split and non-split choice points during backtracking. The adoption of a different, alternative representation in the engine could solve this problem—but requires drastic changes to the basic sequential engine and to the compiler.

In the case of *Tina* benchmark, the Muse system suffers a slowdown irrespective of the number of processors employed. This behavior is rather unusual (and at odds with the speed-ups reported for *Tina* in the literature for Muse). We conjecture it originates from the fact that we have explicitly identified all choice points as parallel or sequential. Stack-splitting is instead capable of extracting parallelism from this benchmark reaching a maximum speedup of about 3. Another interesting benchmark is *Large* which generates

a small and balanced number of relatively deep branches—an ideal situation for the splitting approach. Muse obtains marginal speed-up, while stack-splitting produces considerably better speedups. Better parallel behavior is obtained for almost all benchmarks, except *FQueens*. This benchmark generates a single choice point with a very large number of alternatives, and each alternative is small and leads quickly to success or failure. In this case stack-splitting pays the price of a slightly more expensive sharing phase. Nevertheless this is clearly not the kind of situations in which distributed execution is desired.

An implementation of the stack-splitting method is in progress on a distributed network of shared-memory multiprocessors (on a Beowulf Myrinet-based system with Pentium-2 nodes). From the analysis and discussion presented above, it is apparent that stack-splitting should perform well on distributed memory machines, primarily because of better locality and because it leads to reduced communication. A low-level performance study of our shared memory implementation of stack-splitting implementation is in progress using the SimICS Sparc multiprocessor simulator. The low level performance study of caching behavior, locality of access, etc., will give us an indication of what kind of performance to expect from a distributed implementation of stack-splitting.

Benchmark	# Processors		
	1	**2**	**3**
Tina	1215	719 (1.69)	535 (2.27)
Large	8093	4422 (1.83)	3065 (2.64)
Queens1	3520	2466 (1.43)	2207 (1.59)
Salt	6117	3274 (1.87)	2155 (2.84)
Solitaire	1364	704 (1.94)	488 (2.79)
Houses	2425	1263 (1.92)	859 (2.82)
constraint	3030	1569 (1.93)	1102 (2.75)

Table 2. Execution Times on Solaris X86

4. Conclusion and Related Work

In this paper, we presented a technique called stack-splitting for implementing or-parallelism and discussed its advantages and disadvantages. Stack-splitting is an improvement of stack-copying. Its main advantage, compared to other well-known techniques for implementing or-parallelism, is that it allows coarse-grain work to be picked up by idle processors and be executed efficiently without incurring excessive communication overhead.

Distributed implementation of AI systems has been a reasonably active area of research. There are several projects in which a specific AI system has been taken and parallelized on distributed memory multiprocessors [15, 22, 8, 12, 7, 17, 16, 18, 19]. Distributed implementation of Prolog have also been attempted [2, 5]. However, none of these systems are very effective in producing speedups over a wide range of benchmarks. Distributed implementations of Prolog have been attempted on Transputer systems (The Opera System [23] and the system of Benjumea and Troya [3]). Of these, Benjumea and Troya's system has produced quite good results. However, both the OPERA system and the Benjumea and Troya's system have been developed on now-obsolete Transputer hardware, and, additionally, both rely on a stack-copying mechanism which will produce poor performance in programs where the task-granularity is small. We hope that our distributed implementation of Prolog based on stack-splitting will be superior to these aforementioned distributed implementations. A distributed parallel implementation of Prolog based on stack-copying, with ALS Prolog system (www.als.com) as the underlying engine, is planned in the near future.

References

[1] K.A.M. Ali and R. Karlsson. The MUSE Approach to Or-parallel Prolog. In *Int'l J. of Parallel Prog.*, 19(2):129–162, 1990.

[2] L. Araujo and J.J. Ruz. A Parallel Prolog System for Distributed Memory. In *Journal of Logic Programming*, 33(1):49-79, 1997.

[3] V. Benjumea and J. M. Troya. An OR Parallel Prolog Model for Distributed Memory Systems. In *Procs. of PLILP* Springer Verlag, LNCS 714, pp. 291-301, 1993.

[4] A. Beaumont and D.H.D. Warren. Scheduling Parallel Work in Or-parallel Prolog Systems. In *Proc. International Conference on Logic Programming*. pp. 135-150. MIT Press. 1993.

[5] L. F. Castro, C. Geyer et al. DAOS: Distributed And-Or in Scalable Systems. Technical Report. Department of Computer Science, Federal University of Rio Grande del Sul, Brazil, 1998.

[6] J. C. de Kergommeaux, P. Codognet. Parallel Logic Programming Systems: A Survey. In *Computing Surveys*, 26(3): 295-336, 1994.

[7] M. Dixon and J. de Kleer. Massively parallel assumption-based truth maintenance. LNAI, Springer-Verlag. pp. 131–142. 1989.

[8] J. Gu. Parallel Algorithms and Architectures for Very Fast AI Search University of Utah, 1989

[9] G. Gupta and E. Pontelli. Stack-splitting: A Simple Technique for Implementing Or-parallelism and And-parallelism on Distributed Machines. NMSU Tech. Rep. May 1999.

[10] G. Gupta and B. Jayaraman. Analysis of Or-parallel Execution Models. *ACM Transactions On Programming Languages and Systems (ACM TOPLAS)*. Vol 15. No. 4. September 1993. pp. 659-680.

[11] D.A. Kranz, et al. Mul-T: A High-Performance Parallel Lisp. In *ACM Programming Lang. Design and Impl.*, pp. 81-90, 1989.

[12] A. Jindal, R. Overbeek, W. C. Kabat. Exploitation of parallel processing for implementing high-performance deduction systems. *Journal of Automated Reasoning*, 8(1), pp. 23–38, 1992.

[13] J. Hendler et al. Massively Parallel Support for a Case-based Planning System. In Proceedings of the Ninth IEEE Conference on AI Applications, Orlando, Florida, March 1993.

[14] H. Kitano, J. A. Hendler (eds.). *Massive Parallel Artificial Intelligence*, AAAI Press/MIT Press, Menlo Park, 1994.

[15] J.S. Kowalik. *Parallel Computation and Computers for Artificial Intelligence*. Kluwer Academic Publishers. 1987.

[16] V. Kumar, P. S. Gopalakrishnan, L. N. Kanal (eds.), *Parallel Algorithms for Machine Intelligence and Vision*. Springer-Verlag, 1990.

[17] V. Kumar and L. N. Kanal. Parallel Branch-and-Bound Formulation for AND/OR Tree Search. In *IEEE Transactions on Pattern Analysis and Machine Intelligence*. Volume 6, pp. 768–788. 1984.

[18] V. Kumar and J. N. Rao, Parallel Depth-First Search on Multiprocessors Part II: Implementation. In *International Journal of Parallel Programming*, 16(6), pp. 479-499, 1987.

[19] T-H. Lai and S. Sahni. Anomalies in Parallel Branch-and-Bound Algorithms. In *Communications of the ACM*, 27(6): 594-602, 1984.

[20] E. Lusk, D.H.D. Warren, et al. The Aurora Or-Prolog System. In *New Generation Computing*, Vol. 7, No. 2,3, pp. 243-273, 1990

[21] E. Pontelli, D. Ranjan, G. Gupta. On the Complexity of Or-parallelism. *New Generation Computing*, 1999 (to appear).

[22] N. Takahashi et al. Example-Based Machine Translation on a Massively Parallel Processor. In *Procs. of IJCAI*, 1993.

[23] O. Werner, A. C. Yamin, J. L. V. Barbosa, C. F. R. Geyer. OPERA Project: An Approach Towards Parallelism Exploitation on Logic Programming. In *Procs. of WLP*, pp. 20-23, 1994.

Session C5

Distributed Algorithms

Chair: Sandeep Gupta
Colorado State University, USA

An Efficient Quorum-Based Scheme for Managing Replicated Data in Distributed Systems

Ching-Min Lin, Ge-Ming Chiu, and Cheng-Hong Cho
Department of Electrical Engineering
National Taiwan University of Science and Technology
Taipei, Taiwan
Email: chiu@optimal.ee.ntust.edu.tw

Abstract

A new quorum-based replica control scheme for managing replicated data in distributed systems is proposed. We first introduce a concept called relaxed difference pair to establish the basics for cyclic read-write coteries. A simple and efficient model is then presented to facilitate the construction of read-write coteries. The read-write coteries generated by the model are symmetric. The proposed scheme can be applied to arbitrary number of data copies. More importantly, by introducing a parameter in the construction model, our scheme provides the flexibility of adjusting the sizes of read and write quorums. Such flexibility allows one to construct a read-write coterie that best suits the environment of the target system.

1 Introduction

A distributed system consists of a set of autonomous computers interconnected by a network. These computers communicate with each other by exchanging messages. In a distributed system, data replication technique is often used to improve availability and performance of the system. A data object is replicated and the copies are placed at different sites to facilitate system operation. The system may continue to operate even when some of the data copies are not available due to failures. However, data replication introduces the problem of maintaining consistency among different copies of a data object. From users' point of view, the system must always present the most current state of the data even under site or communication failure. In order to ensure data consistency, a system must guarantee that the effect of the operations on the replicated copies of a data object be the same as if they had been performed one at a time on a single copy of the data object, a property called *one-copy serializability* [2, 5]. For each data, we may perform read and write operations. Replica control mechanisms do not allow any two write operations or a read and a write operations to be carried out on the same data concurrently.

The simplest scheme for managing replicated data is the read-one write-all (ROWA) protocol, with which, a read operation is allowed to read any one copy, and a write operation is required to write to all the copies of the data. Data consistency is ensured since a read operation always gets the value that is updated by the most recent write operation. The *ROWA* protocol provides read operations with a high degree of availability at low cost, but it severely restricts write operations. A write operation cannot be performed after the failure of a single copy site, and the cost of write operations is high.

To remedy the drawbacks of the *ROWA* protocol, many algorithms and protocols have been proposed based on the notion of *quorums* [1, 3, 4, 7, 8, 9, 11, 12]. A quorum is a subset of the copy sites (or nodes) in the system. In the following, the terms copy sites and nodes may be used interchangeably. Each copy of a data is tagged with a *version number* which is initially set to zero and is incremented for each write operation. A set of *read quorums* and a set of *write quorums* are defined for read and write operations, respectively. A read (respectively, write) operation can proceed only if it obtains permissions from all of the copies of any read (respectively, write) quorum. For a write operation, all of the copies in the write quorum are updated. For a read operation, the copy with the highest version number in the read quorum is used. To enforce data consistency, the following properties must hold: 1. Any two write quorums must have nonempty intersection; 2. Any read quorum must have nonempty intersection with any write quorum. These properties are called *intersection* property. Note that mutual exclusion problem is closely related to the replica control problem. Several quorum-based protocols for mutual exclusion can

328

be used for ensuring data consistency by having read and write operations share the same set of quorums.

Among quorum-based protocols, the majority consensus approach [11] requires that each quorum consists of a majority of the nodes to assure the intersection property. It provides high availability. However, the quorum size is $O(N)$, where N is the number of the nodes in the system. The hierarchical quorum consensus protocol [7] uses multilevel trees to assist quorum construction. As a result, the quorum size is $O(N^{0.63})$. In order to reduce quorum sizes, several quorum-based protocols exploit logical structures that are imposed upon the nodes [1, 3, 4, 8, 12]. Among them, the grid protocol [3] logically organizes the nodes in a grid structure of rectangular shape. A read quorum consists of a node from each column, and a write quorum is composed of the union of a read quorum and all of the nodes in a column. The sizes of read and write quorums are both $O(\sqrt{N})$. However, the number of nodes is restricted so that it can form a rectangular grid. This restriction is relaxed by the protocol, called circular grid protocol for convenience, proposed in [12]. In [1] nodes are organized into a binary tree and a tree quorum protocol is presented, which reduces the quorum size to $O(\log N)$. However, it causes the nodes of the system to assume different responsibilities with respect to forming a quorum. For example, the root node of the tree is more heavily loaded than any other nodes. Recently, a geometric approach called triangular grid protocol has been proposed for mutual exclusion [4, 8]. The nodes are organized into a three-sided graph. A quorum consists of a minimal set of connected nodes that intersects all three sides of the three-sided graph. This protocol provides low quorum size ($O(\sqrt{N})$) when N forms a full regular three-sided graph. Another class of quorum-based algorithms [10, 9] are based on the combinatorial theory. Maekawa [10] applied the finite projective plane to construct quorums. Nevertheless, not all finite projective planes exist. Recently, Luk and Wong [9] proposed a quorum construction technique that is based on the idea of difference sets. It can be applied to arbitrary number of nodes and offers balanced load for the nodes. However, the algorithm depends on exhaustive search method to find good solutions.

In this paper, we propose a new quorum-based replica control scheme for managing replicated data. We first present a concept, called *relaxed difference pair*, by generalizing the notion of the relaxed difference set in [9]. A simple and efficient model based on this concept is then presented to facilitate the con-

struction of read and write quorums. The quorums generated by our model achieve the property of *symmetry* [9], that is, each node is included in the same number of quorums, and all read quorums and all write quorums have equal sizes. Our method can be applied to arbitrary number of copies. More importantly, the proposed scheme is very flexible. It allows the sizes of the read and write quorums to be adjusted to best suit the environment of the target system. For example, if the frequency of read operations is high in comparison with that of write operations, one may choose to use small-sized read quorums (with a relatively larger-sized write quorums) in order to curtail the operation cost. This last property has not been addressed in the existing schemes.

The rest of the paper is organized as follows. In Section 2 we present the basic concept of our method. A model based on the basic concept is then presented in Section 3 to facilitate the construction of the quorums. Section 4 draws the conclusion.

2 The Basic Scheme

Consider a distributed system which contains N copies of a data object. Let $U = \{0, 1, 2, ..., N-1\}$ represent the set of the copy sites. In other words, the N copy sites are indexed by numbers from 0 to $N-1$. The following definitions are required for subsequent discussion.

Definition 1 *(Coterie) A set C, which is a set of nonempty subsets of U, is called a* coterie *if and only if the following two properties hold:*

(1) *Intersection property:* $Q \cap Q' \neq \emptyset$, $\forall Q, Q' \in C$

(2) *Minimality property:* $Q \not\subset Q'$, $\forall Q, Q' \in C$

Definition 2 *(Bicoterie) Let C and D be two sets of nonempty subsets of U. The pair (C, D) is called a* bicoterie *if and only if the following two properties hold:*

(1) *Mutual intersection property:* $Q \cap Q' \neq \emptyset$, $\forall Q \in C, Q' \in D$

(2) *Minimality property:* $Q \not\subset Q'$, $\forall Q, Q' \in C$, *and* $Q \not\subset Q'$, $\forall Q, Q' \in D$

Definition 3 *(Read-Write Coterie) Let R and W be two sets of nonempty subsets of U. The ordered pair (R, W) is called a read-write coterie if and only if the following two properties hold:*

(1) (R, W) *is a bicoterie*

(2) W *is a coterie*

The sets R and W are called read coterie *and* write coterie, *respectively. Any $Q \in R$ is a read quorum and any $Q' \in W$ is a write quorum.*

Essentially, the read coterie (respectively, write co-terie) contains all the read quorums (respectively, write quorums) of the system.

The scheme we proposed is based on an extension of the notion of relaxed difference set in [9], which is, in turn, modified from the idea of cyclic difference set in combinatorial theory [6].

Definition 4 *(Group of Cyclic Sets) Let A be a subset of U. A group of cyclic sets (or GCS), $G(A)$, associated with A is a group of subsets of U, which are cyclically generated from A as follows:*

$$G(A) = \{A_i \mid i \in U,\ A_i = \{q \mid q = (a+i) \mod N, \forall a \in A\}\}.$$

A is called the generation set *of $G(A)$.*

For example, Suppose that $N = 7$ and $A = \{0, 1, 4\}$. Then we have $G(A) = \{A_0, A_1, \ldots, A_6\}$ where $A_0 = \{0, 1, 4\}$, $A_1 = \{1, 2, 5\}$, $A_2 = \{2, 3, 6\}$, $A_3 = \{3, 4, 0\}$, $A_4 = \{4, 5, 1\}$, $A_5 = \{5, 6, 2\}$, and $A_6 = \{6, 0, 3\}$. In the following treatment, we use $G(A)$ to represent the *GCS* associated with some subset A of U. Note that $G(A)$ can be generated by any element contained in it.

It has been shown [9] that $G(A)$ forms a group of cyclic quorum sets for mutual exclusion if and only if the generation set A is a relaxed difference set. That is, the intersection property, where $A_i \cap A_j \neq \emptyset$ for all $i, j \in U$, $A_i, A_j \in G(A)$, holds if and only if A is a relaxed difference set. A relaxed difference set is defined as follows:

Definition 5 *(Relaxed Difference Set)[9] A subset D of U is called a* relaxed difference set *if for every $1 \leq d \leq N-1$ there exists at least one pair (a, b), $a, b \in D$, such that $a - b \equiv d \pmod{N}$.*

The size of the cyclic quorums that are included in $G(A)$ equals the cardinality of A.

Similar to the definition of relaxed difference set, we define the relaxed difference pair to facilitate the design of read-write coteries as follows.

Definition 6 *(Relaxed Difference Pair) Let $C = \{c_0, c_1, \ldots, c_{k-1}\}$ and $D = \{d_0, d_1, \ldots, d_{l-1}\}$ be two subsets of U. The ordered pair (C,D) is called a* relaxed (N,k,l)-difference pair *if for every $d \in U$, there exists at least one pair (c_i, d_j), $c_i \in C$, $d_j \in D$, such that $c_i - d_j \equiv d \pmod{N}$.*

For example, suppose we have $N = 15$. The pair (C, D), where $C = \{0, 4, 8, 12\}$ and $D = \{0, 1, 2, 3, 7\}$, is

a relaxed (15,4,5)-difference pair since we have

$$
\begin{aligned}
0 &\equiv 0 - 0 \\
1 &\equiv 4 - 3 \\
2 &\equiv 4 - 2 \\
3 &\equiv 4 - 1 \\
4 &\equiv 4 - 0 \\
5 &\equiv 8 - 3 \\
6 &\equiv 8 - 2 \\
7 &\equiv 8 - 1 \qquad \pmod{15} \\
8 &\equiv 8 - 0 \\
9 &\equiv 12 - 3 \\
10 &\equiv 12 - 2 \\
11 &\equiv 12 - 1 \\
12 &\equiv 12 - 0 \\
13 &\equiv 0 - 2 \\
14 &\equiv 0 - 1
\end{aligned}
$$

In this example, D is a relaxed difference set but C is not. In the following, we would simply call the pair (C, D) a relaxed difference pair when no confusion arises.

Note that the notion of relaxed difference pair is a generalization of the relaxed difference set as indicated by the following theorem. The proof of the theorem is straightforward and thus is omitted.

Theorem 1 *A subset D of U is a relaxed difference set if and only if the pair (D, D) is a relaxed difference pair.*

Definition 7 *(Read-Write Pair) Let R and W be two subsets of U. The ordered pair (R, W) is called a* read-write pair *if the following conditions are satisfied:*

(1) (R, W) is a relaxed difference pair
(2) W is a relaxed difference set.

Consider the previous example where $N = 15$. The pair (C, D), where $C = \{0, 4, 8, 12\}$ and $D = \{0, 1, 2, 3, 7\}$, is a read-write pair as (C, D) is a relaxed (15,4,5)-difference pair and D is a relaxed difference set.

Lemma 1 *Let C and D be two subsets of U. The pair $(G(C), G(D))$ is a bicoterie if and only if (C, D) is a relaxed difference pair.*

Proof: First, we prove that if (C, D) is a relaxed difference pair, then $(G(C), G(D))$ is a bicoterie. Since $G(C)$ and $G(D)$ are groups of cyclic sets associated with C and D, respectively, it is obvious that the minimality property of Definition 2 holds for both $G(C)$ and $G(D)$. We now show that the mutual intersection property also exists. Let $C = \{c_0, c_1, \ldots, c_{k-1}\}$

and $D = \{d_0, d_1, \ldots, d_{l-1}\}$. We may express $G(C)$ and $G(D)$ as $G(C) = \{C_i \mid 0 \leq i \leq N - 1, C_i = \{q \mid q = (a + i) \mod N, \forall a \in C\}\}$ and $G(D) = \{D_j \mid 0 \leq j \leq N - 1, D_j = \{q \mid q = (b + i) \mod N, \forall b \in D\}\}$. We need to show that $C_i \cap D_j \neq \emptyset, \forall 0 \leq i, j \leq N - 1$. Suppose that $j \geq i$. Note that $0 \leq j - i \leq N - 1$. Let $c_{i,p}$ and $d_{j,q}$ denote the p-th element of C_i and the q-th element of D_j, respectively. Since (C, D) is a relaxed difference pair, there must exist some p and q, $0 \leq p \leq k - 1$ *and* $0 \leq q \leq l - 1$, such that $c_p - d_q \equiv j - i \pmod{N}$. By definition, we have $c_{i,p} = c_p + i \pmod{N}$ and $d_{j,q} = d_q + j \pmod{N}$. Since $c_p - d_q \equiv j - i \pmod{N}$, we have $c_{i,p} - d_{j,q} \equiv 0 \pmod{N}$, and thus $c_{i,p} = d_{j,q}$. Now consider the case of $j < i$. We have $0 < i - j \leq N - 1$, and hence $1 \leq N - (i - j) \leq N - 1$. Since (C, D) is a relaxed difference pair, there must exist some p and q, $0 \leq p \leq k - 1$ and $0 \leq q \leq l - 1$, such that $c_p - d_q \equiv N - (i - j) \pmod{N}$. By definition, we have $c_{i,p} = c_p + i \pmod{N}$ and $d_{j,q} = d_q + j \pmod{N}$. Since $c_p - d_q \equiv N - (i - j) \pmod{N}$, we have $c_{i,p} - d_{j,q} \equiv 0 \pmod{N}$, and thus $c_{i,p} = d_{j,q}$. Hence, we show that $C_i \cap D_j \neq \emptyset$.

Next, we show that the converse is also true, i.e. if $(G(C), G(D))$ is a bicoterie, then (C, D) is a relaxed difference pair. We prove it by contradiction. Assume that $(G(C), G(D))$ is a bicoterie and (C, D) is not a relaxed difference pair. Then there must exist a number $t \in U$ for which $c_i - d_j \not\equiv t \pmod{N}$, for all $0 \leq i \leq k - 1$ and $0 \leq j \leq l - 1$. Consider $C_0 = C \in G(C)$ and $D_t \in G(D)$. Since $(G(C), G(D))$ is a bicoterie, there must exist some p and q, $0 \leq p \leq k - 1$ and $0 \leq q \leq l - 1$, such that $c_p = d_{t,q}$ due to the mutual intersection property. By definition, we have $d_{t,q} = d_q + t \pmod{N}$, which then leads to $c_p = d_q + t \pmod{N}$ and thus $c_p - d_q \equiv t \pmod{N}$. However, this contradicts the previous assumption. $\square$

Theorem 2 *The ordered pair $(G(R), G(W))$ is a read-write coterie if and only if (R, W) is a read-write pair.*

Proof: First, we prove that if (R, W) is a read-write pair, then the ordered pair $(G(R), G(W))$ is a read-write coterie. In this case, we have that the set W is a relaxed difference set and the pair (R, W) is a relaxed difference pair. From Lemma 1, we know that the pair $(G(R), G(W))$ is a bicoterie. Since W is a relaxed difference set, (W, W) is a relaxed difference pair. From Lemma 1, we have that $(G(W), G(W))$ is a bicoterie, which implies that $G(W)$ is itself a coterie.

We now prove that the converse is also true. Since $(G(R), G(W))$ is a read-write coterie, it implies that

the set $G(W)$ is a coterie. This then leads to that the pair $(G(W), G(W))$ is a bicoterie. From Lemma 1, we know that the pair (W, W) is a relaxed difference pair, and thus the set W is a relaxed difference set. Note that the pair $(G(R), G(W))$ is a bicoterie by definition. Then, from Lemma 1, the pair (R, W) is a relaxed difference pair. $\square$

For example, let $N = 15$, $R = \{0, 4, 8, 12\}$ and $W = \{0, 1, 2, 3, 7\}$. Since (R, W) is a read-write pair, we can construct a read-write coterie $(G(R), G(W))$ as follows

$$
\begin{aligned}
G(R) \quad=\quad & \{\{0, 4, 8, 12\}, \{1, 5, 9, 13\}, \{2, 6, 10, 14\}, \\
& \{3, 7, 11, 0\}, \{4, 8, 12, 1\}, \{5, 9, 13, 2\}, \\
& \{6, 10, 14, 3\}, \{7, 11, 0, 4\}, \{8, 12, 1, 5\}, \\
& \{9, 13, 2, 6\}, \{10, 14, 3, 7\}, \{11, 0, 4, 8\}, \\
& \{12, 1, 5, 9\}, \{13, 2, 6, 10\}, \{14, 3, 7, 11\}\} \\
G(W) \quad=\quad & \{\{0, 1, 2, 3, 7\}, \{1, 2, 3, 4, 8\}, \{2, 3, 4, 5, \\
& 9\}, \{3, 4, 5, 6, 10\}, \{4, 5, 6, 7, 11\}, \{5, 6, \\
& 7, 8, 12\}, \{6, 7, 8, 9, 13\}, \{7, 8, 9, 10, 14\}, \\
& \{8, 9, 10, 11, 0\}, \{9, 10, 11, 12, 1\}, \{10, \\
& 11, 12, 13, 2\}, \{11, 12, 13, 14, 3\}, \{12, 13, \\
& 14, 0, 4\}, \{13, 14, 0, 1, 5\}, \{14, 0, 1, 2, 6\}\}
\end{aligned}
$$

In this example, $G(R)$ and $G(W)$ are the read coterie and write coterie, respectively.

Theorem 2 implies that we may find a cyclic read-write coterie by simply identifying a read-write pair. The sizes of the read and write quorums are thus determined by the sets of the read-write pair. Note that the size of write quorums must be large enough so that any two write quorums would have nonempty intersection. Furthermore, the sizes of the read and write quorums are interrelated as any read quorums must intersect any write quorums. The smallest possible size of the read quorums may decrease when the size of the write quorums grows. Obviously, it would be desirable that we may construct read and write quorums whose sizes are as small as possible. In many applications, striking a balance between the sizes of the read quorums and the write quorums are important. For example, if the frequency of read accesses is high relative to that of the write accesses, one may construct a read-write coterie in which the size of the read quorums is made small at the expense of increasing the size of the write quorums. The read-write pairs may be identified by exhaustive search.

3 A Model for Constructing Read-Write Coteries

Exhaustive search for read-write pairs is expensive when the system size is large. In this section, we present a practical model for constructing read-write coteries based on the basic concept for a distributed system with arbitrary number of copies. The model provides the flexibility of adapting itself to system requirement by adjusting the sizes of read and write quorums.

3.1 Read/Write Generation Sets

Consider that there are N copy sites in a distributed system. Again, these sites are represented by numbers from 0 to $N - 1$. Let m be a given integer, $1 \leq m \leq N$. Now let $l = \lceil \frac{N}{m} \rceil$ and $k = \lceil \frac{N+1}{2m} \rceil$. For a given m, a *read generation set* R_g is defined as follows: $R_g = \{r_0, r_1, r_2, ..., r_{l-1}\}$ such that $r_0 = 0$, $0 < r_{i+1} - r_i \leq m$ for all $0 \leq i \leq l - 2$, and $0 < N - r_{l-1} \leq m$. In other words, $r_i < r_{i+1}$ for all $0 \leq i \leq l - 2$ and the difference between any two (circularly) consecutive elements is no greater than m. Furthermore, we define a *write generation set* W_g as $W_g = \{0, 1, 2, ..., m-1, w_1, w_2, ..., w_{k-1}\}$ such that $m - 1 < w_1 \leq 2m - 1$, $0 < w_{i+1} - w_i \leq m$ for all $1 \leq i \leq k - 2$, and $w_{k-1} \geq \frac{N-1}{2}$. Apparently, there can be more than one read/write generation set for a given m, i.e. read and write generation sets may not necessarily be unique. In the following, we show that any pair of read and write generation sets forms a read-write pair.

Lemma 2 *For a given m, any pair of read and write generation sets (R_g, W_g) is a relaxed difference pair.*

Proof: Consider any number d, $0 \leq d \leq N - 1$.
Case 1: $d = 0$

Note that $r_0 = 0$ and $0 \in W_g$. The pair $(r_0, 0)$ gives $r_0 - 0 \equiv 0 \pmod{N}$.
Case 2: $0 < d \leq r_{l-1}$

We can always find an interval $[r_{i-1}, r_i]$, $1 \leq i \leq l - 1$, such that $r_{i-1} < d \leq r_i$. Since we have $r_i - r_{i-1} \leq m$, it must be true that $0 \leq r_i - d \leq m - 1$. Let $p = r_i - d$. p is included in W_g. Note that $r_i \in R_g$ and $p \in W_g$ gives $r_i - p \equiv d \pmod{N}$.
Case 3: $r_{l-1} < d \leq N - 1$

Note that we have $0 < N - r_{l-1} \leq m$. This leads to that $1 \leq N - d \leq m - 1$. Let $q = N - d$. q must be contained in W_g. Note that $r_0 - q \equiv d \pmod{N}$. $\square$

Lemma 3 *For a given m, consider any two write generation sets W_g and W_g', where W_g and W_g' may be identical. (W_g, W_g') is a relaxed difference pair.*

Proof: Let W_g be expressed as $W_g = \{0, 1, 2, ..., m-1, w_1, w_2, ..., w_{k-1}\}$, where $m - 1 < w_1 \leq 2m - 1$, $0 < w_{i+1} - w_i \leq m$ for all $1 \leq i \leq k - 2$, and $w_{k-1} \geq \frac{N-1}{2}$. Consider any d, $0 \leq d \leq N - 1$.
Case 1: $0 \leq d \leq m - 1$

In this case, d is included in W_g. Note that,

by definition, 0 is included in W_g'. We have $d - 0 \equiv d \pmod{N}$.
Case 2: $m - 1 < d \leq w_1$

In this case, we have $0 \leq w_1 - d < w_1 - (m-1)$. Furthermore, since $m - 1 < w_1 \leq 2m - 1$, we have $w_1 - (m-1) \leq 2m - 1 - (m-1) = m$. Hence we obtain $0 \leq w_1 - d \leq m - 1$. Let $p = w_1 - d$. By definition, p is included in W_g'. Note that $w_1 \in W_g$ and $p \in W_g'$ gives $w_1 - p \equiv d \pmod{N}$.
Case 3: $w_1 < d \leq w_{k-1}$

In this case, there must exist some t, $2 \leq t \leq k - 1$, such that $w_{t-1} < d \leq w_t$. Let $p = w_t - d$. We have $0 \leq p < w_t - w_{t-1}$. Since, by definition, we have $0 < w_t - w_{t-1} \leq m$, $0 \leq p \leq m - 1$ follows. Hence, p is included in W_g'. We then have $w_t - p \equiv d \pmod{N}$.
Case 4: $w_{k-1} < d \leq N - 1$

Let $d' = N - d$. We have $1 \leq d' < N - w_{k-1}$. By definition, we have $w_{k-1} \geq \frac{N-1}{2}$, and thus $N - w_{k-1} \leq \frac{N+1}{2}$ follows. This then leads to $1 \leq d' < \frac{N+1}{2}$. Since d' is an integer, $1 \leq d' < \frac{N+1}{2}$ implies $1 \leq d' \leq \lceil \frac{N-1}{2} \rceil$. Now let W_g' be expressed as $W_g' = \{0, 1, 2, ..., m-1, w_1', w_2', ..., w_{k'-1}'\}$, where $m - 1 < w_1' \leq 2m - 1$, $0 < w_{i+1}' - w_i' \leq m$ for all $1 \leq i \leq k' - 2$, and $w_{k'-1}' \geq \frac{N-1}{2}$. Since $w_{k'-1}'$ is an integer, $w_{k'-1}' \geq \frac{N-1}{2}$ implies $w_{k'-1}' \geq \lceil \frac{N-1}{2} \rceil$. Hence we have $1 \leq d' \leq w_{k'-1}'$. Now consider d'. By the same arguments as given in Cases 1, 2, and 3 with the roles of W_g and W_g' exchanged, we can always find p and q, $p \in W_g'$ and $q \in W_g$, such that $p - q \equiv d' \pmod{N}$. Since $d' = N - d$, this implies $q - p \equiv d \pmod{N}$. $\square$

Theorem 3 *For a given m, any pair of read and write generation sets (R_g, W_g) is a read-write pair.*

Proof: From Lemma 3, we know that the write generation set W_g is a relaxed difference set. In addition, Lemma 2 shows that (R_g, W_g) is a relaxed difference pair. Hence (R_g, W_g) is a read-write pair. $\square$

For example, let $N = 13$. Suppose $m = 3$. The following list gives some possible read generation sets of the smallest size, 5 in this case: $\{0, 3, 6, 9, 12\}$, $\{0, 3, 6, 9, 11\}$, $\{0, 3, 6, 8, 11\}$. Some possible write generation sets of the smallest size, 5 in this case, are $\{0, 1, 2, 5, 8\}$, $\{0, 1, 2, 5, 7\}$, $\{0, 1, 2, 5, 6\}$, $\{0, 1, 2, 4, 7\}$, $\{0, 1, 2, 4, 6\}$, and $\{0, 1, 2, 3, 6\}$. Any read generation set and any write generation set form a read-write pair. Now consider that $m = 4$ is used. Some smallest-sized write generation sets are $\{0, 1, 2, 3, 7\}$ and $\{0, 1, 2, 3, 6\}$. The read generation sets include $\{0, 4, 8, 12\}$, $\{0, 4, 8, 11\}$, $\{0, 4, 8, 10\}$,

$\{0, 4, 7, 11\}$, and $\{0, 4, 7, 10\}$. Note that the smallest size of the read generation sets is reduced to 4 when m is set to 4, as opposed to 5 for the case of $m = 3$, while the smallest size of the write generation sets remains the same.

3.2 Read-Write Coteries

Based on Theorem 3, one may construct a cyclic read-write coterie by identifying a read and a write generation sets for an appropriately chosen m. However, as described previously, there may be more than one read generation set for a given m. The same is true for write generation sets. In the following, we show that the union of the coteries generated from all of such read and write generation sets also forms a read-write coterie.

Theorem 4 *Suppose that, for a given m, R_1, R_2,..., and R_k are read generation sets, and W_1, W_2,..., and W_l are write generation sets. Let $Q_r = \cup_{i=1}^{k} G(R_i)$ and $Q_w = \cup_{j=1}^{l} G(W_j)$. Then (Q_r, Q_w) is a read-write coterie.*

Proof: By definition, the sizes of R_1, R_2,..., and R_k are the same. Similarly, the sizes of W_1, W_2,..., and W_l are the same. Consider any $R \in Q_r$ and any $W \in Q_w$. It must be true that R is included in $G(R_i)$ for some $1 \leq i \leq k$, i.e. $R \in G(R_i)$, and W is included in $G(W_j)$ for some $1 \leq j \leq l$, i.e. $W \in G(W_j)$. From Lemma 2, (R_i, W_j) is a relaxed difference pair. According to Lemma 1, $(G(R_i), G(W_j))$ is a bicoterie. Hence $R \cap W \neq \emptyset$, that is, the mutual intersection property holds. For any $R, R' \in Q_r$, since the sizes of R and R' are the same, $R \not\subset R'$. The same is true for Q_w. Hence the minimality property holds. Therefore, (Q_r, Q_w) is a bicoterie. Next, we will show that Q_w is a coterie. Consider any $W, W' \in Q_w$. We have that W and W' are included in $G(W_i)$ and $G(W_j)$ for some $1 \leq i, j \leq l$, respectively, i.e. $W \in G(W_i)$ and $W' \in G(W_j)$. According to Lemma 3, (W_i, W_j) is a relaxed difference pair. By Lemma 1, $(G(W_i), G(W_j))$ is a bicoterie. Obviously, it is possible that $W_i = W_j$. In this case, $G(W_i) = G(W_j)$ is a coterie. In any case, we have $W \cap W' \neq \emptyset$. In addition, $W \not\subset W'$, and so the minimality property holds. Therefore, Q_w is a coterie. Hence (Q_r, Q_w) is a read-write coterie. $\square$

Consider the previous example in which $N = 13$ and $m = 4$. We have constructed two write generation sets, $W_1 = \{0, 1, 2, 3, 7\}$ and $W_2 = \{0, 1, 2, 3, 6\}$, and five read generation sets, $R_1 = \{0, 4, 8, 12\}$, $R_2 = \{0, 4, 8, 11\}$, $R_3 = \{0, 4, 8, 10\}$, $R_4 = \{0, 4, 7, 11\}$, and $R_5 = \{0, 4, 7, 10\}$. A read-write coterie for $m = 4$ can be generated as follows: $(G(R_1) \cup G(R_2) \cup G(R_3) \cup G(R_4) \cup G(R_5), G(W_1) \cup G(W_2))$.

3.3 Properties of the Read-Write Coteries

Many quorum-based replica control protocols exploit certain logical structures in order to reduce the sizes of the read/write quorums. The logical structures often impose restriction on the number of copy sites that can be accommodated in a distributed system. Furthermore, the copy sites may assume different responsibilities according to their positions in the structures. Since our model is based on the concept of group of cyclic sets, the read-write coterie constructed using the proposed model is symmetric such that each node assumes the same responsibility in synchronizing read/write operations. In addition, our model allows a system to accommodate arbitrary number of copy sites without sacrificing the symmetric property.

For a given m, the sizes of a read quorum and a write quorum that are generated using our model described above are l and $m + k - 1$, respectively, where $l = \lceil \frac{N}{m} \rceil$ and $k = \lceil \frac{N+1}{2m} \rceil$. As m increases, the size of read quorums decreases. Note that any write quorum may also be used as a read quorum. Hence, it makes no sense to construct a read-write coterie for which the size of read quorums is larger than that of write quorums.

Theorem 5 *In our model, if the size of read quorums is no larger than that of write quorums, then we must have $m > \sqrt{\frac{N-1}{2}}$.*

Proof: In this case, we have $\lceil \frac{N}{m} \rceil \leq m + \lceil \frac{N+1}{2m} \rceil - 1$. Note that $\frac{N}{m} \leq \lceil \frac{N}{m} \rceil$. In addition, the following is always true: $\lceil \frac{N+1}{2m} \rceil < \frac{N+1}{2m} + 1$. These arguments lead to that $\frac{N}{m} < m + \frac{N+1}{2m}$. Since m is a positive integer, we may obtain $m > \sqrt{\frac{N-1}{2}}$. $\square$

Theorem 5 implies that, if m is less than or equal to $\sqrt{\frac{N-1}{2}}$, then the size of read quorums must be larger than that of write quorums using our model. The size of write quorums varies with the value of m. The following theorem governs the smallest size of write quorums that can be constructed for a given N.

Theorem 6 *In our model, the size of write quorums is the smallest when m equals $\lceil \sqrt{\frac{N+1}{2}} \rceil$.*

Proof: See Appendix A. $\square$

Since $\lceil \sqrt{\frac{N+1}{2}} \rceil$ is greater than $\sqrt{\frac{N-1}{2}}$, according to Theorem 5 and Theorem 6, we need only consider m that is greater than or equal to $\lceil \sqrt{\frac{N+1}{2}} \rceil$ in constructing a read-write coterie. In practice, one may choose a value for m that best suits the environment of the target system. For example, for many applications the frequency of read operations is high in comparison with that of write operations. In this case, a larger value of m may be used to generate a read-write coterie in which the size of read quorums is small. Note that when m equals N our model degenerates into the read-one write-all (ROWA) scheme. In addition, when $m = \left\lceil \frac{N+1}{2} \right\rceil$ our model turns out to be a modified majority consensus scheme where the size of write quorums is $\left\lceil \frac{N+1}{2} \right\rceil$ while the read quorum size is 2 for $N > 1$. This property shows the flexibility of the proposed model.

From Theorem 6 we obtain that the smallest size of a write quorum is no greater than $2\left\lceil \sqrt{\frac{N+1}{2}} \right\rceil - 1$, which is $O(\sqrt{N})$. Suppose that the number of nodes is $N = n^2$ for some n. The sizes of read and write quorums are n and $2n - 1$, respectively, for both grid and circular grid protocols. In comparison, for our model the sizes of the read and write quorums are only n and $\approx \frac{3n}{2}$, respectively, with $m = n$. Note that the triangular grid protocol also offers $O(\sqrt{N})$-sized quorums for mutual exclusion. We compute and compare the smallest sizes of write quorums for our model and the triangular grid protocol. The result shows that the sizes are identical for both methods for all numbers of copy sites (up to 10000) that exactly form full regular three-sided graphs. However, as most of the logical structure-assisted mechanisms, the triangular grid protocol may not achieve its best quorum size when N, the number of copy sites, does not correspond to any full regular three-sided graph. In contrast, our model works for arbitrary N. Moreover, the read quorum size generated by our model may be smaller than the write quorum size.

4 Conclusion

We have proposed a new quorum-based replica control scheme for managing replicated data on which read and write operations are performed. A concept called relaxed difference pair is introduced to establish the basics for cyclic read-write coteries. A simple and efficient model is then presented to facilitate the construction of read-write coteries. The read-write coteries generated by the model are symmetric. Our scheme can be applied to arbitrary number of data copies. More importantly, we have introduced a parameter m in the construction model to provide the flexibility of adjusting the sizes of read and write quorums. Such flexibility allows one to construct read-write coterie that best suits the environment of the target system.

Future research may be directed toward extending the result to related areas such as K-mutex problem [8].

Appendix A: Proof for Theorem 6

For a given m, the size of write quorums, denoted as s, is $m + \left\lceil \frac{N+1}{2m} \right\rceil - 1$. Since m is a positive integer, s can be rewritten as $s = \left\lceil \frac{N+1}{2m} + m - 1 \right\rceil$. Now let $y = \frac{N+1}{2m} + m - 1$ and consider m as a real number. Taking derivative of y with respect to m gives $\frac{dy}{dm} = -\frac{N+1}{2}m^{-2} + 1$. Setting $\frac{dy}{dm} = 0$ we obtain that $m = \sqrt{\frac{N+1}{2}}$ leads to the minimum value of y as $\frac{d^2y}{dm^2}$ is positive at such m. Note that $\frac{dy}{dm} = -\frac{N+1}{2}m^{-2} + 1$ is negative for $m < \sqrt{\frac{N+1}{2}}$ and is positive for $m > \sqrt{\frac{N+1}{2}}$. Now, consider the cases where m are positive integers only. The minimum value of y must occur at either $m = \left\lfloor \sqrt{\frac{N+1}{2}} \right\rfloor$ or $m = \left\lceil \sqrt{\frac{N+1}{2}} \right\rceil$. Obviously, $\left\lfloor \sqrt{\frac{N+1}{2}} \right\rfloor = \left\lceil \sqrt{\frac{N+1}{2}} \right\rceil$ when $\sqrt{\frac{N+1}{2}}$ is an integer. Since $\lceil y_1 \rceil \leq \lceil y_2 \rceil$ if $y_1 \leq y_2$, we obtain that the minimum value of s occur at either $m = \left\lfloor \sqrt{\frac{N+1}{2}} \right\rfloor$ or $m = \left\lceil \sqrt{\frac{N+1}{2}} \right\rceil$.

Let $m_1 = \sqrt{\frac{N+1}{2}}$. Also let $m_l = \lfloor m_1 \rfloor$ and $m_h = \lceil m_1 \rceil$. Now let s_l and s_h denote the values of s for m being equal to m_l and m_h, respectively. Henceforth, either s_l or s_h assumes the minimum value of s. In the following, we will show that s_h is no greater than s_l, i.e. $s_h \leq s_l$. Two cases are considered here:
Case 1: m_1 is an integer
    In this case we have $m_l = m_h$, and hence $s_h = s_l$.
Case 2: m_1 is not an integer
    Since m_1 is not an integer, m_h and m_l can be expressed as $m_h = m_1 + x$, where $0 < x < 1$, and $m_l = m_h - 1 = m_1 + x - 1$. Note that we have $s_l = \left\lceil \frac{m_1^2}{m_l} \right\rceil + m_l - 1$ and $s_h = \left\lceil \frac{m_1^2}{m_h} \right\rceil + m_h - 1$ as $m_1 = \sqrt{\frac{N+1}{2}}$. Considering $m_l < m_1$ we have $\left\lceil \frac{m_1^2}{m_l} \right\rceil \geq \left\lceil \frac{m_1^2}{m_1} \right\rceil = \lceil m_1 \rceil = m_h$. Two subcases are considered in the following:
Case 2.1: $\left\lceil \frac{m_1^2}{m_l} \right\rceil > m_h$
    In this case we have $s_l = \left\lceil \frac{m_1^2}{m_l} \right\rceil + m_l - 1 > m_h + m_l - 1$, which then leads to $s_l \geq m_h + m_l = 2m_h - 1$. Since $m_h > m_1$ we have $\left\lceil \frac{m_1^2}{m_h} \right\rceil \leq \left\lceil \frac{m_1^2}{m_1} \right\rceil = \lceil m_1 \rceil = m_h$. Thus we obtain $s_h = \left\lceil \frac{m_1^2}{m_h} \right\rceil + m_h - 1 \leq 2m_h - 1$. Recall that $s_l \geq 2m_h - 1$. Thus we have $s_h \leq s_l$.

Case 2.2: $\left\lceil \frac{m_1^2}{m_l} \right\rceil = m_h$

Apparently we have $\frac{m_1^2}{m_l} \leq m_h$ in this case, and thus $m_1^2 \leq m_l m_h$. This then leads to $\frac{m_1^2}{m_h} \leq m_l$. Since m_l is a positive integer, we then have $\left\lceil \frac{m_1^2}{m_h} \right\rceil \leq m_l$. Therefore, we obtain $s_h = \left\lceil \frac{m_1^2}{m_h} \right\rceil + m_h - 1 \leq m_l + m_h - 1$. Note that in this case we have $s_l = \left\lceil \frac{m_1^2}{m_l} \right\rceil + m_l - 1 = m_h + m_l - 1$. Consequently, we conclude that $s_h \leq s_l$.

The above argument then leads to that the size of write quorums is the smallest when m equals $m_h = \left\lceil \sqrt{\frac{N+1}{2}} \right\rceil$.

ACKNOWLEDGMENT

This work was supported in part by the National Science Council of the Republic of China under grant NSC-87-2213-E011-046.

References

[1] A. Agrawal and A. El Abbadi. An efficient and fault-tolerant solution for distributed mutual exclusion. *ACM Trans. on Comput. Syst.*, 9(1):1–20, February 1991.

[2] P. Bernstein and N. Goodman. The failure and recovery problem for replicated databases. In *Proc. ACM Symp. Principles of Distributed Compt.*, pages 114–122, August 1983.

[3] S. Y. Cheung, M. H. Ammar, and M. Ahamad. The grid protocol: A high performance scheme for maintaining replicated data. *IEEE Trans. Knowledge and Data Eng.*, 4(6):582–592, December 1992.

[4] C.-H. Cho and J.-T. Wang. Triangular grid protocol: An efficient scheme for replica control with uniform access quorums. In *Proc. Euro-Par '96 Parallel Processing Conf.*, pages 843–851, August 1996.

[5] G. Coulouris, J. Dollimore, and T. Kindberg. *Distributed Systems – Concepts and Design.* Addison-Wesley Ltd., 1994.

[6] Jr. M. Hall. *Combinatorial Theory.* John Wiley and Sons, 1986.

[7] A. Kumar. Hierarchical quorum consensus: A new algorithm for managing replicated data. *IEEE Trans. Computers*, 40(9):996–1004, September 1991.

[8] Y.-C. Kuo and S.-T. Huang. A geometric approach for constructing coteries and k-coteries. *IEEE Trans. Parallel and Distributed Systems*, 8(4):402–411, April 1997.

[9] W.-S. Luk and T.-T. Wong. Two new quorum based algorithms for distributed mutual exclusion. In *Proc. Int. Conf. on Distributed Computing Systems*, pages 100–106, 1997.

[10] M. Maekawa. A $\sqrt{N}$ algorithm for mutual exclusion in decentralized systems. *ACM Trans. on Comput. Syst.*, 3(2):145–159, May 1985.

[11] R. H. Thomas. A majority consensus approach to concurrency control for multiple copy databases. *ACM Trans. Database Syst.*, 4(2):180–209, June 1979.

[12] Y.-T. Wu, Y.-J. Chang, S.-M. Yuan, and H.-K. Chang. A new quorum-based replica control protocol. In *Proc. 1997 Pacific Rim Int. Symp. on Fault Tolerant Syst.*, pages 116–121, December 1997.

Local Detection of Exclusive Global Predicates

Eunjung Lee

ETRI Computer-Software Technology Laboratory,
161 Kajung-Dong, Yusong-Gu, Taejon, 305-350,Republic of Korea
ejl@etri.re.kr

Abstract

Detecting global predicates in distributed program executions is a useful tool for debugging and testing. A new form of global predicates, called exclusive global predicates, is considered in this paper to provide a natural and efficient way to describe mutual exclusion conditions. One exclusive global predicate is enough to express mutual exclusion condition for n local predicates, one for each process; the $O(n^2)$ conjunctive global predicates are required to describe the same condition.

In this paper, a local on-line detection algorithm of exclusive global predicates is presented with formal proof. This algorithm detects a violation of mutual exclusion during the execution at each local process. This algorithm uses timestamps to get dependence relations between events. The $n+2$ numbers are piggybacked to each message, and no extra communication overhead for control information is required. This allows the proposed model to be useful and efficient for testing and debugging of distributed programs compared to the previous method with conjunctive global predicates.

1. Introduction

A distributed program is one that runs on multiple processors connected by a communication network. The state of such a program is distributed across the network and no process has access to the global state at any instant. If we wish to evaluate a proposition on a shared resource of a distributed system, for example, "do any two processes access the shared variable a at the same time?" we must somehow construct a consistent global view of the states of each process. In this paper we consider "global predicates", that is, boolean-valued functions of the global state of the distributed system. Detection of a global predicate is a fundamental problem in distributed computing. This problem arises in many contexts such as designing, testing and debugging of distributed programs.

Previous work has described several types of global predicates and their detection algorithms. For a distributed system with n processes, each of which takes m steps, $O(m^n)$ distinct global states exist for the distributed system. To detect a general predicate, an algorithm must examine each global state as described in [3].

However, researchers have developed faster, more efficient global predicate detection algorithms by restricting themselves to special classes of predicates. A form of global predicates that is expressed as the conjunction of several local predicates has been a focus of research[4, 5, 12]. Especially, Hurfin et al. recently proposed a run-time detection algorithm where all the necessary information to detect predicates are piggybacked on computation messages of the application program.

Miller and Choi[10] introduced an algorithm to detect "linked predicates" in which the sequential event ordering can be specified. Our algorithm for exclusive global predicates in this paper is similar to the one for linked predicates[12, 10]. However, while a linked predicate cannot detect concurrent events, our algorithm detects prohibited concurrent events during the execution.

Our proposal of exclusive global predicates is motivated to describe mutual exclusion conditions in distributed programs. Mutual exclusion between local predicates is an important question to be tested in distributed systems. For example, let CS_i be a local predicate which is true if the local process P_i is in the critical section CS. The critical section can be one for a shared resource or an access to the common memory. Then, at most one of conditions $CS_1, CS_2, ..., CS_n$ should be true at a global state during the whole execution. An exclusive global predicate has the form $ME(CS_1, ..., CS_n)$ which is true if and only if one or zero local predicate of $CS_1, ..., CS_n$ is true. The conjunctive form of global predicates is not a good way to describe this condition: it takes either i) $O(n^2)$ predicates of the form $\neg(CS_i \wedge CS_j), i \neq j$, or ii) a disjunction of n global predicates of the form $\neg CS_1 \wedge \neg CS_2 \wedge ... \wedge \neg CS_{i-1} \wedge \neg CS_{i+1} \wedge ... \wedge \neg CS_n$, where $1 \leq i \leq n$. The same condition can be expressed by one exclusive global predicate such as $ME(CS_1, ..., CS_n)$.

In addition to the descriptive efficiency, the exclusive form of global predicates allows an efficient run-time detection algorithm. The key to making the algorithm efficient is that the exclusive global predicate is true only if less than one local predicate is true at every global state. Therefore, there is a total order sequence on the set of all states where the corresponding local predicate is true.

Detecting errors in distributed systems is more difficult than that in the sequential ones because a distributed program sometimes runs normally even though it contains errors. Errors in distributed programs might not be detected by observing the program's behavior, where detection requires the analysis of timing relations. For example, consider the example of updating a shared object in Figure 1. Even though the requests and grants seem sequentialized, the second grant to P_3 conflicts with the update in P_1(current holder of the object) since P_3 do not have the confirmation that P_1 released the resource. Testing concerned in this paper aims to detect any violation of mutual exclusion like this during the execution.

Next section will present the notation and our model of distributed systems. Section 3 discusses exclusive global predicates and their evaluation. Section 4 presents the detection algorithm with the correctness proof and Section 5 concludes this paper.

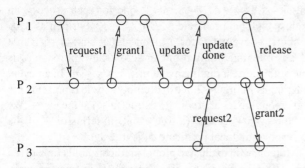

Figure 1. An example of error updates on a shared resource

2. System Model

This section presents the concepts and notation of distributed runs and events.

We assume a loosely coupled message-passing system without any logical clock. A distributed program M consists of a set of n processes denoted by $M = \{P_1, P_2, ..., P_n\}$ communicating via asynchronous messages, based on FIFO channels. We assume that no messages are lost, altered, or spuriously introduced. A

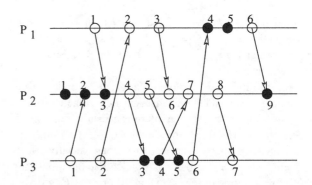

Figure 2. An event diagram of three processes

run(execution) of the system M is denoted as ρ. In this paper, we are interested in evaluating and detecting global predicates for a given run ρ.

An event $e = (P_i, m, send/receive/local)$ where $P_i \in M$ and m is a unique index of the event in the local process starting with 1. An event is a send or receive of the message, or a local event. The notation $e.p$ denotes the process P_i. Also, if e is a receive(send) event, then $e.sender(e.receiver)$ represents the corresponding send(receive) event. A run ρ is represented as a set of events taking place within it. Let $E(\rho)$ be the set of all events for a run ρ. Henceforth, E denotes $E(\rho)$.

There are two relations defined between two events a, b[2, 6, 11]. If a is a send event corresponding to the receive event b, then the relation is denoted as $a \mapsto b$. Also, $a <_{im} b$ if a, b are events in P_i and event b immediately follows a in the process. A dependence relation $\rightarrow$ is defined as a transitive closure on the relations $<_{im}$ or $\mapsto$. The event a is called a predecessor (successor) of the event b if $a \rightarrow b(b \rightarrow a)$. Two events a, b are said to be concurrent, denoted as $a \parallel b$, if $a \neq b$, $a \not\rightarrow b$ and $b \not\rightarrow a$. Also, a next event of a, denoted as $a.next$ is defined as the event b such that $a <_{im} b$, or $\top$(the final state of the execution) if a is the last event of the local process. In the same manner, a previous event of a, denoted as $a.prev$ is defined as the event b such that $b <_{im} a$, or $\bot$(an initial state of the execution) if a is the first event in the local process. Also, the corresponding sender(receiver) for a receive(send) event is denoted as $a.sender(a.receiver)$.

Figure 2 shows the event diagram of a distributed execution involving three processes. A horizontal line represents the progress of the process, a circle indicates an event(the meaning of empty and filled circles will be explained later), and a slanted arrow indicates a message transfer. Henceforth, $e_{i,j}$ denotes the j-th event in the process P_i.

The last predecessor event of b at the process P_i, denoted as $LPE(b, P_i)$, is defined as an event a in P_i such that $a \rightarrow b$ and $a.next \not\rightarrow b$. If there is no event preceding b on

P_i, then $LPE(b, P_i) = \perp$. Also, $LPE(b, b.p) = b.prev$. When the event b is happening, the process P_i should have progressed at least to $LPE(b, P_i)$ for the distributed system's consistency.

Vector time is a way to represent event dependencies in distributed systems[11]. Each event is assigned a timestamp, by which a process can infer the causality relation between events. The timestamps assigned to events obey the monotonicity property. That is, if an event a causally affects an event b, the timestamp of a is smaller than the timestamp of b. In vector time of the event e in the process P_i, $vt(e)[j]$ represents the process P_i's latest knowledge of P_j's local time, which is $LPE(e, P_j)$. If $vt(e)[j] = k$, P_i knows that the local time at P_j has progressed up to $e_{j,k}$. The entire vector $vt(e)$ constitutes P_i's view at the event occurrence of e of the logical global time; P_i uses it to timestamp the event e.

For a run ρ depicted as an event diagram such as in Figure 2, a set of global states are defined which the program may pass through during the run. A global state is an n-tuple of local states, where an i-th state of g, written as $g[i]$, is the local state of P_i. Note that an event is uniquely identified in a given run by the process where the event is taking place and by the unique index in the local process. Moreover, only states emitting events are significant for detecting global predicates. Therefore, we use the event as the equivalent term for a local state. A state represented by the event e is a local state in P_i right after e's occurrence. Therefore, a global state is an n-tuple of events, one for each process, and $g[i]$ is the last event taking place in process P_i at the moment.

A global state g is said to be *consistent* if the following condition is satisfied: for all events e, e' such that $e \rightarrow g[i]$ and e' in the process P_j for some $1 \leq i, j \leq n$, $e' \rightarrow e$ implies that $e' \rightarrow g[j]$[9]. In Figure 2, $\langle e_{1,1}, e_{2,4}, e_{3,3}\rangle$ is a consistent global state while $\langle e_{1,1}, e_{2,3}, e_{3,4}\rangle$ is not because $e_{3,4}$ depends on the send event $e_{2,4}$ while the event $e_{2,4}$ is not sent yet at $e_{2,3}$.

3. Evaluating Exclusive Global Predicates

In this section, the exclusive form of global predicates is introduced and their evaluation is visited. As mentioned in Section 1, exclusive global predicates are useful in describing mutual exclusion conditions in distributed systems. Moreover, there is a sequential property allowing an efficient evaluation algorithm.

Consider a distributed system M with n processes sharing a resource R. The shared resource is used based on mutual exclusion. At each event e of the process P_i, the process is either holding R or not at the moment. Let a local predicate ϕ_i be defined true at the event e in P_i if and only if P_i is holding R at e. Then, for a set of local ex-

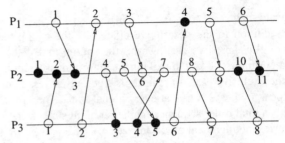

(a) An execution where ALWAYS(ME) holds

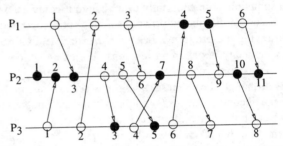

(b) An execution where ALWAYS(ME) does not hold

Figure 3. Example executions where $ALWAYS(ME)$ **is true and false.**

pressions $X = \{\phi_1, \phi_2, ..., \phi_n\}$, one for each process, an exclusive global predicate $ME(\phi_1, ..., \phi_n)$(written as ME in short) is evaluated for a given global state g such that ME is true if and only if one or zero local expression ϕ_i is true at the corresponding event $g[i]$, $1 \leq i \leq n$. In an event diagram as in Figure 2, a filled(empty) circle represents the corresponding local predicate is true(false) at the event. We say the event e is true (a true event) in terms of X if the corresponding local predicate ϕ_i is true at e.

Moreover, an exclusive global predicate holds for a given run ρ if and only if the global predicate is true for every global state in the run. This is defined as an *Always* quantifier such that $Always(ME)$ is true if and only if ME is true for every global state in the run ρ. If an exclusive global predicate is false at a global state, more than one processes are holding the shared resource at the global state, and therefore the run ρ violates the mutual exclusion.

Lemma 3.1. *Let X and ME be a set of local expressions and the exclusive global predicate on X as defined above on the system M w.r.t. a shared resource R. The run ρ contains a mutual exclusion error on using R if and only if there is a consistent global state g where ME is false.*

In Figure 3, $Always(ME)$ holds for the execution of the event diagram in (a), and false for the one in (b). Global states where ME is false in Figure 3(b) are $\langle e_{1,3}, e_{2,7}, e_{3,5}\rangle$, $\langle e_{1,4}, e_{2,7}, e_{3,6}\rangle$ and so on.

In the view of the event set E, if there is a global state evaluating the exclusive global predicate false, then two true events belong to the global state. Instead of inspecting every global state, therefore, we found conditions for two true events to be in a same global state. For a given run ρ, let $\tau \subset E$ be the set of all true events in terms of the set of local expressions X. Next lemma summerizes the condition of $Always(ME)$ w.r.t. τ. The proof is direct from the definition of ME.

__Lemma 3.2.__ *Let ρ be the execution and ME be the exclusive global predicate on the set of local predicates X as defined in Lemma 3.1. Moreover, let τ be a set of true events for the execution ρ and X. Then, ME is false on a global state g if and only if there is a pair of events $a, b \in \tau$ such that both of them belong to the global state g.*

The remained part of this section investigates the condition for two events a, b to be in a same global state. For notational convenience, we introduce two relations on a pair of events $a, b, a \neq b$: i) $a \sim b$ if two events can be in a same global state, and ii) $a \circ\!\!\rightarrow b$ if $a.next \rightarrow b$. We call the relation $\circ\!\!\rightarrow$ as the *exclusive precedence relation*.

It is clear that $a \sim b$ if $a \parallel b$, but concurrency is not a necessary condition. Note that $e_{1,1} \sim e_{3,6}$ and $e_{1,1} \rightarrow e_{3,6}$ in Figure 3. By the definition of consistent global states, $a \not\sim b$ only when there is a send event c which follows a in $a.p$ and is a predecessor of b. In other words, the event b causally depends on the send event c which has not happened yet at the state of the event a. This condition is described as $a \circ\!\!\rightarrow b$. Next lemma shows that this is the sufficient condition for two events to be $a \not\sim b$.

__Lemma 3.3.__ *Let a, b be two events in the execution ρ. Then, $a \sim b$ if and only if $a \circ\!\!\not\rightarrow b$ and $b \circ\!\!\not\rightarrow a$.*
Proof. The only if part is shown by contradiction. Assume that $a \sim b$ and $a \circ\!\!\rightarrow b$. Then, b depends on $a.next$ which has not happened at a yet, a contradiction to $a \sim b$. It is same for $a \sim b$ and $b \circ\!\!\rightarrow a$. Therefore, $a \sim b$ implies the condition $a \circ\!\!\not\rightarrow b$ and $b \circ\!\!\not\rightarrow a$. The if part is shown by counterposition. Assume that $a \not\sim b$ and $a \rightarrow b$. By the definition of consistent global states, we can assume that there is an event $c \neq a$ in $a.p$ such that $a \rightarrow c$ and $c \rightarrow b$. This is equivalent to $a \circ\!\!\rightarrow b$. The condition $a \not\sim b$ and $b \rightarrow a$ implies that $b \circ\!\!\rightarrow a$. Therefore, $a \not\sim b$ implies that $a \circ\!\!\rightarrow b$ or $b \circ\!\!\rightarrow a$. $\qquad\square$

As a result of Lemma 3.3, $a \not\sim b$ if and only if $a \circ\!\!\rightarrow b$ or $b \circ\!\!\rightarrow a$. This reflects the constraint of mutual exclusion protocol where the process should notify others when it releases a shared resource, and the new process can hold the resource only when it is sure that the resource is currently free.

Following corollary summerized several observations for $a \sim b$. These will be used in the next section to detect a violation of $Always(ME)$.

__Corollary 3.4.__ *Let a, b be two events in ρ.*

(a) if $a \sim b$ and $a \rightarrow b$, then $a = LPE(b, a.p)$,

(b) $a \circ\!\!\rightarrow b$ if and only if $a < LPE(b, a.p)$.

__Theorem 3.5.__ *Let τ be a set of true events in ρ. Also, let ME be an exclusive global predicate $ME(\phi_1, \phi_2, ..., \phi_n)$. Then $Always(ME)$ holds on a run ρ if and only if the event set τ has a total order with the relation $\circ\!\!\rightarrow$.*
Proof. i) $Always(ME)$ is true $\Leftrightarrow$ there is no global state g on which ME is false(by definition).
ii) there is no g on which ME is false $\Leftrightarrow$ there is no two events $a, b \in \tau$ such that $a \sim b$. (by Lemma 3.2)
iii) there is no two events $a, b \in \tau$ s.t. $a \sim b \Leftrightarrow$ there is a total order on τ w.r.t. $\circ\!\!\rightarrow$. (by Lemma 3.3). $\qquad\square$

In Figure 3(a), the total order sequence of τ is $e_{2,1}e_{2,2}e_{2,3}$ $e_{3,3}e_{3,4}e_{3,5}e_{1,4}e_{2,10}e_{2,11}$. The execution in Figure 3(b) does not satisfy $Always(ME)$ since $e_{2,7} \sim e_{3,5}$; they do not have the order between them either $e_{2,7} \circ\!\!\rightarrow e_{3,5}$ or $e_{3,5} \circ\!\!\rightarrow e_{2,7}$. This total ordering property provides a basis for an efficient detection algorithm introduced in the next section.

4. Local Detection Algorithm

In this section, we present a local, on-line detection algorithm of exclusive global predicates. As a result from Section 3, an exclusive global predicate is true for a given execution if and only if all true events consist a total order sequence by the exclusive precedence relation $\circ\!\!\rightarrow$. Therefore, the evaluation of an exclusive global predicate is straightforward from an event diagram (containing all information on event dependencies) as in Figure 3. However, is it possible to decide $Always(ME)$ at each local process during the execution(on line)? The local process has no access to global states during the execution.

4.1. Admissibility of an event

By the total order property on τ with the relation $\circ\!\!\rightarrow$, we can evaluate $Always(ME)$ on-line as the execution progresses.

An event is said *admissible* if no global state before this event evaluates ME as false. For a formal definition of admissibility, let $\Delta(\tau, a)$ be a subset of τ including true events preceding a such that $\Delta(\tau, a) = \{b|b \in \tau$ and $b \rightarrow a\}$ where τ is a set of true events in the execution ρ.

__Lemma 4.1.__ *An event a is admissible if there is a total order sequence on $\Delta(\tau, a)$ with $\circ\!\!\rightarrow$ relation.*
Proof. Shown by contradition. Assume that a is not admissible withe a global state g which is proceeding a. By

339

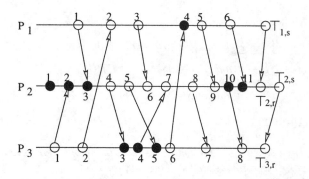

Figure 4. The event diagram of the extended execution

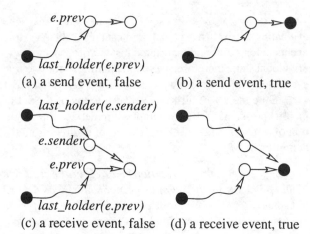

(a) a send event, false   (b) a send event, true

(c) a receive event, false   (d) a receive event, true

Figure 5. Cases for computing the last holder event

the definition of admissibility, there is two events $b, c \in \tau$ belonged to g such that $b \sim c$. This implies that there is no order between these two events with the relation $\circ\!\!\rightarrow$ by Lemma 3.3. Therefore, there is no total order on τ. □

Admissibility has several useful properties in evaluating $Always(ME)$. If a is admissible, then every predecessor b of a is admissible since $\Delta(\tau, b) \subset \Delta(\tau, a)$ if $b \rightarrow a$. This allows an on-line evaluation of admissibility at each event during the execution. Moreover, it is clear that every event e in E is admissible if and only if $Always(ME)$ is true on ρ(a subset of a total order set has a total order).

Supposed that there is one last event succeeding every other event in the execution, we can conclude that $Always(ME)$ holds for the execution if the last event is admissible. For this purpose, an extended execution ρ' is introduced which has several additional events to guarantee one last event for a given execution ρ. Each process P_i has two special events $\top_{i,r}$ and $\top_{i,s}$, where

i) $\top_{1,s}.receiver = \top_{2,r}, e_{1,m_1}.next = \top_{1,s}$,

ii) $\top_{i,r}.next = \top_{i,s}, 1 < i < n$,

iii) $\top_{i,s}.receiver = \top_{i+1,r}, 1 < i < n$,

iv) $e_{i,m_i}.next = \top_{i,r}, 1 < i \leq n$,

where e_{i,m_i} is the last event in the process P_i. With this extension, $\top_{n,r}$ is the last event succeeding every other event. Figure 4 shows the event diagram for the extended execution ρ' corresponding to Figure 3(a).

The following lemma concludes this subsection with the result on admissibility.

Lemma 4.2. *Let ρ' be the extended execution as shown above. The exclusive global predicate $Always(ME)$ is true for the execution if and only if $\top_{n,r}$ is admissible.*
Proof. The proof is straightforward from two facts: (1) if the event a is admissible, then every predecessor of a is admissible, and (2) $Always(ME)$ is true for ρ if and only if

every event in E is admissible. Since every event in E is a predecessor of $\top_{n,r}$, they are admissible. □

4.2. Deciding admissibility at a local process

In this subsection, we interested in deciding admissibility for a given event during the execution.

The last true event preceding the current event in terms of $\circ\!\!\rightarrow$ relation is called *the last holder event*. The last holder event of a is defined as $last\_holder(\rho, a) = b, a \neq b$ if for all events $c \in \Delta(\tau, a), c \circ\!\!\rightarrow b$. The last holder event is $\perp$ if there is no true events preceding a, and *undefined* if no such event b exists. The last holder event is undefined if and only if the event is not admissible.

Now, we will show that the last holder events for $e.prev$ and $e.sender$ are enough as a local knowledge at each event to decide admissibility. With the assumption that every predecessor is admissible, we can compute $last\_holder(\rho, e)$ and decide admissibility at the event e from the immediate predecessors' last holder events. At each send or local event e, if the current event is false(not contained in τ), then the current event is admissible since the set $\Delta(\tau, a)$ has not changed since the last event $e.prev$(refer Figure 5(a)). However, if the current event is in τ, then two events e and $last\_holder(e.prev)$ can be in a same global state if $last\_holder(e.prev) = LPE(e, last\_holder(e.prev).p)$(refer Figure 5(b)). On the other hand, at the receive event merging $e.prev$ and $e.sender$, we have to check several possibilities of inadmissibility of the current event. As in Figure 5(c), if the current event is not in τ, then $last\_holder(e.prev) \sim last\_holder(e.sender)$ is possible. When the current event is in τ as in Figure 5(d), $last\_holder(e.prev) \sim last\_holder(e.sender)$

340

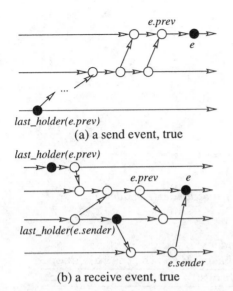

(a) a send event, true

last_holder(e.prev)

(b) a receive event, true

Figure 6. The last holder event for send and receive events

is possible as well as $last\_holder(e.prev) \sim e$ and $last\_holder(e.sender) \sim e$. Lemma 4.4 provides a formal proof for conditions on a receive event's admissibility.

Figure 6 shows two examples of inadmissible events (corresponding to (b) and (d) in Figure 5). Here, $last\_holder(e.prev) = LPE(e, last\_holder(e.prev).p)$ in Figure 6(a), and $last\_holder(e.sender) = LPE(e, last\_holder(e.sender).p)$, $last\_holder(e.prev) \parallel last\_holder(e.sender)$ in Figure 6(b). We do not have to concern events happened before $last\_holder(e.prev)$ and $last\_holder(e.sender)$.

Lemma 4.3. *Let e be a local or send event. Assume that $e.prev$ is admissible. Then, e is not admissible if and only if $e \in \tau$ and $last\_holder(e.prev) = LPE(e, P_i)$ where $last\_holder(e.prev)$ is an event in P_i.*

We omit the proof since it is clear from the discussion until now.

Lemma 4.4. *Let e be a receive event. Assume that $e.prev$ and $e.sender$ are admissible. Then, e is not admissible if and only if*

i) $last\_holder(e.prev) \parallel last\_holder(e.sender)$,

ii) $e \in \tau$ and $last\_holder(e.prev) = LPE(e, P_i)$, $last\_holder(e.prev).p = P_i$, or

iii) $e \in \tau$ and $last\_holder(e.sender) = LPE(e, P_j)$, $last\_holder(e.sender).p = P_j$.

Proof. ($\Leftarrow$) trivial.
($\Rightarrow$) Let a, b be two true events preceding e. Moreover,

$a \sim b$. We will show that two events should satisfy one of the above three conditions. First, suppose that $a \neq e, b \neq e$. Then we can assume $a \parallel b$ since a dependency, say $a \to b$, causes that b is not admissible; two events $a \sim b$ which are both preceding b. On the other hand, $a \to e.prev$ and $b \to e.sender$ by the assumption that both of $e.prev$ and $e.sender$ are admissible. Moreover, this can be extended to the fact that $a \not\to last\_holder(e.sender)$ and $b \not\to last\_holder(e.prev)$. This leads to the conclusion that $last\_holder(e.prev) \parallel last\_holder(e.sender)$.

Next, suppose $a = e, b \sim e$. Since $b \to e$, the only possibility to be $b \sim e$ is $b = LPE(e, b.p)$ by Corollary 3.4(a). Our obligation is to show that either $b = last\_holder(e.prev)$ or $b = last\_holder(e.sender)$. The event b is a predecessor of $e.prev$ or $e.sender$ or both. If $b \to e.prev$, then $b \to last\_holder(e.prev)$ by the definition of the last holder event. Assume that $b \neq last\_holder(e.prev)$. Then $b \not\to last\_holder(e.prev)$ because $e.prev$ is admissible, which means that $b \circ \to e.prev$. Then, $b \circ \to e$ since $e.prev \circ \to e$, a contradiction to the assumption that $b \sim e$. This is because of the assumption that $b \neq last\_holder(e.prev)$, therefore $b = last\_holder(e.prev)$ and $b \sim e$ as in the second condition. We can show the case of $b \to e.sender$ in the same way. As a result, if there is an event b which satisfied $b \sim e$, then the event b should be either $last\_holder(e.prev)$ or $last\_holder(e.sender)$. $\square$

Lemma 4.3 and 4.4 show that the last holder events for $e.prev$ and $e.sender$ are enough for deciding admissibility of the event e. Moreover, LPE of the event e can filter out all cases except $last\_holder(e.prev) \parallel last\_holder(e.sender)$. Next property shows a simple way to check this concurrency in terms of causal dependency.

Property 4.5. *Let e be a receive event. Assume that $last\_holder(e.prev)$ nor $last\_holder(e.sender)$ is $\perp$. Moreover, both of $e.prev$ and $e.sender$ are assumed to be admissible. Then, $last\_holder(e.prev) \circ \to last\_holder(e.sender)$ implies that $last\_holder(e.prev) \to e.sender$. Also, $last\_holder(e.sender) \circ \to last\_holder(e.prev)$ implies that $last\_holder(e.sender) \to e.prev$.*

The proof is clear since $last\_holder(e.prev) \to e.sender$ means that $last\_holder(e.prev)$ is a member of $\Delta(\tau, e.sender)$, and precedes $last\_holder(e.sender)$ by the definition of the last holder event.

4.3. Detection algorithm with vector time

Now, we present our detection algorithm of exclusive global predicates. Based on the results on admissibility, the algorithm piggybacked the last holder event information as well as the vector time for each message transmission.

341

Algorithm DETECT(e)

```
Let e be an event in process P_i
1      when e is a send event:
(1-1)    vt(e)[i] ← vt(e.prev)[i] + 1;
(1-2)    if e ∈ τ, then
(1-2.1)    let e_{j,k} ← last_holder(e.prev)
(1-2.2)    if k = vt(e)[j] then Always(ME) is false; stop.
(1-2.3)    else last_holder(e) ← e_{j,k}
(1-3)    if e ∉ τ, then last_holder(e) ← last_holder(e.prev).
(1-4)    transmit the event (e, vt(e), last_holder(e)).
2      when e is a receive event of (e.sender, vt(e.sender), last_holder(e.sender)):
(2-1)    vt(e)[i] ← vt(e.prev)[i] + 1;
(2-2)    vt(e)[j] ← max(vt(e.prev)[j], vt(e.sender)[j]), i ≠ j;
(2-3)    let e_{j,l} ← last_holder(e.prev), e_{k,m} ← last_holder(e.sender)
(2-4)    if m > vt(e.prev)[k] and l > vt(e.sender)[j], then Always(ME) is false; stop.
(2-5)    if e ∈ τ and (l = vt(e)[j] or m = vt(e)[k]), then Always(ME) is false; stop.
(2-6)    if e ∈ τ, then last_holder(e) ← e.
(2-7)    else last_holder(e) ← max(last_holder(e.prev), j(e.sender)).
3      If e is the last event T_{n,r}, then Always(ME) is true; stop.
4      else e is admissible; continue.
```

Figure 7 shows an event diagram with vector time. Vector time contains information on causal relation between events as well as the last predecessor event for each process. There are two useful properties we use in the algorithm regarding the vector time and causal dependencies.

Property 4.6. *Let $e_{j,k}$ be the k-th event of process P_j. Also, $vt(e)$ is a vector time as defined above. Then*

- $e_{j,k} = LPE(e, P_j)$ *if and only if $vt(e)[j] = k$, and*

- $e_{j,k} → e$ *if and only if $vt(e)[j] ≥ k$.*

Note that $LPE(e_{2,8}, P_1) = e_{1,3}$ where $vt(e_{2,8})[1] = 3$. Also, $LPE(e_{2,8}, P_3) = e_{3,4}$ where $vt(e_{2,8})[3] = 4$.

The algorithm DETECT runs at each processor where the local process resides, and once every event's occurrence. The algorithm stops when the first inadmissible event is found. Therefore, the algorithm runs on an event with the assumption that all predecessor events were admissible so far. When a send or receive event happens, the algorithm checks whether the event is admissible based on the results of Lemma 4.3 and 4.4. Moreover, if the algorithm reaches the last event $T_{n,r}$, then the execution finishes with the conclusion that $Always(ME)$ is true.

- (1-2.2) If $k = vt(e)[j]$, then $e_{j,k} = LPE(e, P_j)$ by Property 4.6. Therefore, e is not admissible by Lemma 4.3.

- (1-2.3) The condition in (1-2.2) filters out the inadmissible case when e is a send event. Therefore, e is admissible by Lemma 4.3, and $last\_holder(e) = e$.

- (1-3) If $e ∉ τ$, then e is admissible by Lemma 4.3 Moreover, $last\_holder(e) = last\_holder(e.prev)$.

- (2-4) The condition $m > vt(e.prev)[k]$ means that $e_{k,m} \not\to last\_holder(e.prev)$. In the same manner, the condition $l > vt(e.sender)[j]$ means that $e_{j,l} \not\to last\_holder(e.sender)$. Therefore, $e_{k,m} \parallel e_{j,l}$ by Property 4.5, and e is not admissible by Lemma 4.4, condition i).

- (2.5) If $l = vt(e)[j]$, then $e_{j,l} = LPE(e, P_j)$ by Property 4.6, and therefore $last\_holder(e.prev) \sim e$ by Lemma 4.4. Also, if $m = vt(e)[k]$, then $last\_holder(e.sender) \sim e$.

- (2.6) At this point, we have either $e_{j,l} → e.sender$ or $e_{k,m} → e.prev$ which implies that one precedes the other. Therefore we can conclude that e is admissible. The last holder event is computed as in the algorithm (2.6) and (2.7).

- (3) If the current event e is T_n, r, then the algorithm reached the final event which succeeds every other event. Therefore, the execution is true for $Always(ME)$.

This algorithm requires two more integers to be attached to each sending message to represent the last holder event(one for the process number, one for the event index). As each sending message piggybacking n more numbers to implement vector time, the overhead for the last holder

342

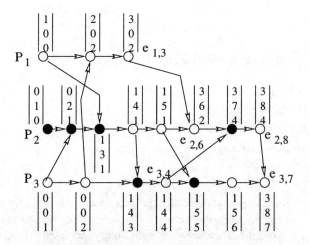

Figure 7. Vector time for the subgraph of Figure 3 with predecessors of $e_{3,7}$

event is not significant when the number of process becomes large.

5. CONCLUSION

In this paper, we presented an on-line detection algorithm of exclusive global predicates. This form of global predicates not only is natural and succinct to describe usage constraints of shared resources in distributed programs, but also has an efficient on-line algorithm to detect any violation in a given execution. The proposed algorithm runs at each process once for each event occurrence, and detects immediately whenever the global predicate is violated.

The efficient implementation of the algorithm is possible since several algorithms are known to implement timestamps. Communication overhead of our algorithm only adds the information of the last holder event, two numbers of data for each event communication, which can be piggybacked along with the vector time. Similar on-line algorithm has been proposed for linked global predicates[10, 4], which use timestamp and the marker for the next local predicate to detect. While linked predicates include timing order between local predicates which naturally implicates an online, local detection, exclusive global predicates describe simultaneous condition on the overall system without order between local predicates. Therefore, our algorithm introduced the concept of admissibility for each event to enable the detection on-line.

Moreover, the proposed algorithm can be extended to more than one shared resources without changes in the structure since each resource usage is independent to each other. We expect that the algorithm would find practical applications for testing and verification of distributed programs with many shared resources.

References

[1] H.Bal, R.Bhoedjang, R.Hofma, C. Jacobs, K. Langendoen, and T.Ruhl. Performance evaluation of the Orca shared-object system. *ACM Trans.Computer Systems*, vol.16, no.1, pp.1-40, 1998.

[2] F.Bracho, M.Droste and D.Kusker. Representation of computation in concurrent automata by dependence order. *Theoretical Computer Science*, vol.174, pp.67-96, 1997.

[3] R.Cooper and K.Marzullo, Consistent detection of global predicates. *Proc. Parallel and Distrib. Debugging*, pp. 163–173, 1991.

[4] V.Garg and B.Waldecker. Detection of string predicates in distributed programs. *IEEE Trans. Parallel and Distributed systems*, vol.7,no.12,pp.1323–1333, 1996.

[5] M.Hurfin et.al. Efficient distributed detection of conjunctions of local predicates. *IEEE Trans. Parallel and Distributed systems*, vol.24,no.8,pp.664–677, 1998.

[6] L.Lamport. Time, clocks and the ordering of events in a distributed system. *Comm. ACM*, vol.21,no.7,pp.558–565, 1976.

[7] E.J.Lee, D.H.Lee and C.S.Park. Detection algorithm of exclusive OR global predicates. *Proc. Inter. Conf. on Automated Software Engineering'98*, pp.213-216, October 1998. IEEE Press.

[8] Y.Manabe and M.Imase. Global conditions in debugging distributed programs. *J. Parallel and Distrib. Computing*, vol.15,pp.62–69, 1992.

[9] T.Masuzawa and N.Tokura. An algorithm for finding causal distributed breakpoint. *J. Parallel and Distrib. Computing*, vol.42,pp.60–66, 1997.

[10] B.Miller and J.Choi. Breakpoints and Halting in distributed programs. *Proc. Distributed Computing Systems*, pp. 316–323, 1988.

[11] M.Raynal and M.Singhal. Capturing causality in distributed systems. *IEEE Computer*, vol.29,no.2,pp.29-56,1996.

[12] S.Venkatesan and B.Dathan. Testing and debugging distributed programs using global predicates. *IEEE Trans.Software Engineering*, vol.21,no.2,pp.163-177, 1995.

An Excursion to the Zoo of Dynamic Coterie-based Replication Schemes

Oliver Theel and Thomas Strauß
Darmstadt University of Technology
Department of Computer Science
D-64283 Darmstadt, Germany
Email: theel@informatik.tu-darmstadt.de

Abstract

Dynamic replication schemes offer very high read and write operation availabilities by repeatedly modifying the configuration of the scheme as failure patterns dictate at run-time. In this paper, we describe a dynamic replication scheme framework which automatically transforms specifications of static replication schemes into their dynamic counterpart. We apply the framework to a wide variety of replication schemes, thereby obtaining novel dynamic schemes which have not been analyzed or reported in literature before. The new dynamic replication schemes are compared and an outlook on future work is given.

1 Introduction

The replication of data objects in a distributed system is a viable means for improving the system's efficiency and for increasing the data object's availability. A *replication scheme* manages the multiple replicas and offers a *single copy image* of the replicated data object to the application programmer. Furthermore, the replication scheme guarantees a certain *notion of consistency* with respect to the replicated object. *One-copy-serializability* (1SR) [1] has attracted most attention and serves as the underlying correctness criterion for almost all replication schemes. It assures that the execution of operations on a replicated data object is equivalent to the execution of the same sequence of operations on a non-replicated data object. 1SR is assumed for all replication schemes discussed or cited in this paper.

Most replication schemes assume a certain logical structure (like trees, grids, or finite projective planes) and a certain placement of replicas within this logical structure. Once structure and placement are both specified, they must remain unchanged throughout the lifespan of the replicated data object which is managed by the replication scheme. Thus, the specification (or *configuration*) does not change. The prerequisite of having an immutable configuration relieves the replication scheme from additional management overhead resulting in simpler and less costly algorithms, since, for example, "configuration version control" is not required. Allowing a configuration to change over time,

on the contrary, embodies the potential of dynamically reacting to changing network characteristics, thereby leading to replication schemes with highly increased operation availabilities. Replication schemes which have immutable configurations are called *static* schemes, whereas schemes which allow configurations to change over time are called *dynamic*.

Recently, it has been shown that operation availabilities obtained by static coterie-based replication schemes are bounded and that read/write operation availabilities directly depend on each other [2]. Nevertheless, if higher operation availabilities are crucial for the application, then dynamic replication schemes are promising candidates for solving the problem. Because of higher run-time costs and a complicated design process, only few dynamic replication schemes have been developed so far. Among them are *Dynamic Voting* [3] and the approach of Rabinovich and Lazowska [4]. Rabinovich and Lazowska have indicated that the feature of maintaining a mutable configuration can in fact be modularly added to any static replication scheme based on the concept of coteries [5]. For this purpose, they propose a scheme-specific approach and apply it to the Grid Protocol [4, 6]. Due to the requirement of exploiting scheme-specific properties – in particular the logical grid structure used by the scheme – a transformation of a static scheme into a corresponding dynamic scheme must manually be done for every replication scheme anew.

To overcome this drawback, we developed a *general* method for systematically and automatically transforming static coterie-based replication schemes into their dynamic counterparts. Our framework, called *Dynamic General Structured Voting* (dGSV) is able to model a large variety of dynamic replication schemes whose non-dynamic counterparts are explicitly or implicitly based on coteries. This includes coterie-based schemes exploiting priorities, like the Tree Quorum Protocol [7]. dGSV is an extension of *General Structured Voting* (GSV) [8], a framework which has been designed to model arbitrary *static* coterie-based replication schemes.

The remainder of the paper is organized as follows. In the next section, we present related work. In Section 3, a description of dGSV is given. In Section 4, we apply our framework to a variety of static replication schemes known from literature, among them Majority Voting [9] and Quorum Consensus [10], Hierarchical Quorum Consensus [11], the Tree Quorum Protocol [7], and the Grid Protocol [6]. Finally, Section 5 draws a conclusion and outlines future work.

2 Related Work

The underlying idea for dynamic replication schemes is the observation that the number of failures (link or site failures) mostly increase or decrease step-by-step over time. If, for instance, a static replication scheme needs the availability of at least five replicas for performing a write operation then it is possible to adjust the configuration of the replicated data object as long as five replicas are still functioning. If it is detected that only a few more replicas than minimally required are available then the replication scheme should change in such a way that it is still able to function afterwards, even when less than five replicas are available. If, at some time, the number of available replicas increases then the configuration could be changed once again, thereby re-incorporating the recovered replicas into the replication scheme. Generally, by dynamically adjusting the configuration, the dynamic replication scheme leads to increased operation availabilities, since in most failure scenarios operations on the replicated data object can still be executed at a time, when the static counterpart already had to cease operation execution. Nevertheless, care must be taken in the analysis, since one can also construct failure scenarios where the opposite holds (see [3], page 232 for an example).

The first dynamic extension of a static replication scheme was given by Jajodia and Mutchler. They extend the Majority Voting replication scheme [9] to *Dynamic Voting* [3]. In contrast to a fixed quorum threshold used by Majority Voting, Dynamic Voting allows a write operation to succeed whenever a majority of replicas which participated in the last write operation also participate in the execution of the current write operation. Information which is used to enforce this constraint is attached to every replica (for further details, see [3]).

In [4], Rabinovich and Lazowska generalize this approach for static coterie-based replication schemes in the following manner: if the replication scheme can agree at any time on the set of replicas from which a quorum must be drawn then an *a priori* defined set of rules can be used at run-time to dynamically identify the subsets of replicas for consistent operation execution. The set of replicas from which a quorum must be drawn is called an *epoch*. An epoch has a unique, never decreasing version number, called *epoch number*. A replica consists of the data, a data's version number and an epoch number. Whenever a write operation on the replicated data object is performed, a

new maximal version number as well as the maximal epoch number gets attached to the new data value. A read (write) operation can only be executed, if a valid read (write) quorum according to the rules applied to the epoch with maximal epoch number (called *actual epoch*) can be obtained. An epoch can only be changed and thereby a new epoch with a new maximal epoch number be created, when a write quorum according to the rules based on the most actual epoch can be collected. The new epoch as well as the actual replicated object's data must atomically be installed on all replicas included in the new epoch. This guarantees correctness according to 1SR (for the proof refer to [4]). A new epoch is initiated by a special operation, called *epoch checking*, which tries to contact as many replicas as possible, thereby eventually re-integrating previously unavailable or unreachable replicas. Whenever the actual epoch differs from the set of currently available replicas, an attempt is made to form a new epoch as described above. In this approach, rules together with the actual epoch present the configuration and a new configuration is obtained whenever a new epoch gets created.

3 Dynamic General Structured Voting

3.1 Basic Idea

In the approach of Rabinovich and Lazowska, the set of rules must be specified on a per-replication scheme basis. For instance when modeling the Grid Protocol [6], which logically arranges the N replicas of a data object in form of a $m \times n$ grid (if $m \cdot n > N$ then the m-th line of the grid is not complete), a rule must *a priori* be defined that states the shape of a grid to be used when $i \leq N$ replicas are available. Furthermore, it must be clear which replica resides in which position of the grid. We call a rule providing answers to both aspects a *structure rule*. Additionally, other rules must precisely state what subsets of available replicas – based on a particular grid – can be used for consistently performing read (write) operations. For the Grid Protocol, valid subsets of replicas for reading consist of at least one replica of every column of the grid (called *c-cover*), whereas for writing, a c-cover together with an entire column is required. For ease of description, we call the rule delivering subsets used for read (write) access *read (write) quorum rule*. All three rules together are referred to as *rule set*.

The aim of our approach is to define a general fixed rule set which can be used for *every* replication scheme. The core problem to be solved for our approach is to come up with a rule set which leads to a good dynamic behavior of every modeled replication scheme without exploiting replication scheme-specific knowledge. This seems to be a tough problem, since good dynamic behavior of, e.g., a Grid Protocol may be substantially different from a good dynamic behavior of a Tree Quorum Protocol [7].

3.2 Static Replication Scheme Specification

Figure 1 shows the specification of the static Tree Quorum Protocol (TQP) [7] as used by our approach. We call such a specification a *master voting structure*. The master

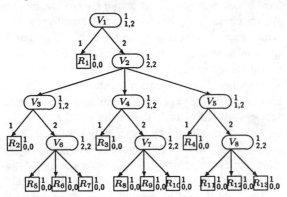

Figure 1. Master voting structure of TQP initially managing 13 replicas

voting structure is used by dGSV to derive at run-time valid *read (write) quorums sets* as well as the sequence in which these quorum sets must be used for correct operation execution. A particular read (write) quorum set is a set consisting of replicas which must *all* be contacted when consistently performing a read (write) operation. A voting structure is an acyclic connected graph with a unique root. The leaves of a voting structure represent *physical nodes* (shown as boxes), whereas inner knots represent *virtual nodes* (shown as ovals). Virtual nodes exist for grouping purposes. Nodes have an upper and two lower indices. The upper index is called a *vote*. Physical nodes, by default, host a replica. The left (right) lower index of a node is the *read (write) operation quorum*. Starting from the root, a possible *quorum set* is obtained by including as many entities of the next lower level in the quorum set as necessary for satisfying the operation quorum. A quorum is *satisfied* if the sum of the votes of the chosen entities is at least as large as the operation quorum but no entity can be removed such that the sum of votes does not drop below the quorum. Weights applied to the arcs indicate *priorities*. Priorities define which quorum sets are used *prior* to other ones. The lower the weight, the higher the priority. If no weight is given then the weight is assumed being ∞ (e.g., having minimal priority).

As shown in Figure 1, when given the master voting structure as input, 13 replicas are managed by TQP. The dGSV algorithm responsible for deriving quorum sets (called *quorum list module* (QLM)) interprets the voting structure at run-time in correspondence with the original TQP specification: a read operation first tries to read the replica located at physical node R_1. If R_1 is not available then it is tried to contact two of the three replicas located at physical nodes R_2, R_3, and R_4. Whenever it turns out that any of the chosen replicas of the former

group are not available then two out of three "spare replicas" must be contacted instead: if R_i, $i = 2, 3, 4$, is not available then it must be replaced by two replicas of $\{R_{5+3\cdot(i-2)}, R_{6+3\cdot(i-2)}, R_{7+3\cdot(i-2)}\}$. In case of a write operation, R_1 together with two of the replicas at R_2, R_3, and R_4, as well as two out of three spare replicas for every chosen replica among R_2, R_3, and R_4 must be written.

Since dGSV may detect failures of network components leading to re-configuration actions (i.e., to a new epoch), the voting structure actually used for deriving operation quorums may be different from the master voting structure. Based on the fixed, *a priori* known master voting structure and the current epoch, dGSV calculates a so-called *current voting structure*. This current voting structure includes exactly those replicas whose hosting sites are included in the actual epoch. Thus, only when the actual epoch includes all replica-hosting sites then the current voting structure is morphologically identical with the master voting structure.

In the remainder of this section, we describe how dGSV calculates the current voting structure based on a particular epoch and master voting structure.

3.3 Data Structures

It is important to note that dGSV differentiates between a physical node R_i of a (current or master) voting structure on one side and a replica together with its host on the other side, since the assignment of physical nodes to replicas may change over time. In dGSV, host and replica are synonymously addressed as S_i. Both, physical nodes R_i and sites S_i have a unique number i and all physical nodes as well as all sites can linearly be ordered according to these numbers.

Analogously to the approach of Rabinovich and Lazowska, we use the concept of epochs, i.e., all replicas managed by dGSV consist of the replicated object's data, a version number and an epoch number. Epochs are managed by dGSV as described in Section 2. The only difference is the following one: since there exist replication schemes whose replicas are of different importance for the scheme to function properly, an important but failed replica should be replaced by the most reliable replica among the still available ones. TQP, for example, heavily relies upon the availability of replica R_1 (see Figure 1). If another replica exhibits a higher availability then R_1 should be replaced by it in order to increase the availability of read and write operations offered by TQP. For this purpose, our epoch management does not just maintain a set of replicas but also maintains for every replica S_i included in the epoch an *availability indicator* $\wp_i \in (0, 1]$. The lower $\wp_i$, the higher the expectation that replica S_i will fail in the future.

As already mentioned, the replication scheme in dGSV is specified solely by means of a master voting structure. All physical nodes of the master voting structure initially have a replica assigned to it (how this assignment is done, will be shown below). All sites with replica S_i (also called *replica servers*) know the master voting structure and own an implementation of dGSV which includes the rule set, a copy of the epoch, and epoch management.

3.4 Initialization

Initially, we assume that all replicas are mutually consistent, i.e., they have a unique value and their version number as well as epoch number are both 1. Additionally, every replica server stores the epoch belonging to epoch number 1. This initial epoch consists of all sites hosting replicas and their availability indicators (i.e., $\{(S_i, \wp_i) \mid i = 1, \ldots, 13\}$ in the TQP example). The availability indicators are always set by the replica server which is in charge of coordinating an epoch checking operation. They are set according to some dynamically observed statistics by this particular site. "Good" estimations of site availabilities are important for the run-time behavior of many dynamic replication schemes. Due to the generality of the problem, we do not discuss possible solutions in the scope of this paper.

3.5 Read Operation

Whenever a client submits a read operation request to an arbitrary replica server then the server acts as *coordinator* for the operation execution and applies the structure rule on the locally stored epoch (which may not be actual). This results in the construction of a so-called *current voting structure*. This current voting structure is now used to derive a list of possible read quorum sets. Read quorum sets in this list are sorted with respect to decreasing priorities as specified by the voting structure. Consequently, "*Apply QLM on the current voting structure for obtaining read quorum sets*" represents the read quorum rule of our rule set. Next, the read quorum set at the head of the list is extracted. Subsequently, all replica servers included in this read quorum set are ask to read-lock their replica and to return the replica's value together with the version number, the epoch number, and the epoch to the coordinator. Whenever the coordinator receives a higher epoch number than the locally stored one, it atomically overwrites its local epoch and local epoch number with the more recent values, informs all currently participating replica servers to abort, and restarts the read operation by applying the structure rule on the newly updated local epoch. If the coordinator does not receive a higher epoch number than the locally stored one and if all contacted replica servers respond then an actual replica has the highest version number among all contacted replicas. In this case, all replica servers are ask to unlock their replicas and the coordinator finally returns the data of an actual replica to the client. If a single participant does not properly answer or was unable to read-lock its replica then the coordinator informs all participants to unlock their replicas and restarts the algorithm by using the new head element of

the read quorum list. If this list is empty at that time then the read operation finally fails.

3.6 Write Operation

The write operation is performed analogously to the read operation as described above. The only differences are 1) write-locks must be acquired instead of read-locks, 2) the write quorum rule "*Apply QLM on the current voting structure for obtaining write quorum sets*" must be used instead of the read quorum rule, and 3) whenever a write quorum set could be found whose members all cooperate with the coordinator then the coordinator performs an atomic commit protocol [1] together with all participants in order to install the object's new data and a new version number at all participating replica servers.

Clearly, there are ample optimizations possible to the manner read and write operations are performed. Nevertheless, the description above suffices for demonstrating read and write operation functionality as necessary for understanding dGSV.

3.7 Rule Set

The specification of the structure rule is all that is left to entirely specify the rule set. Based on the actual epoch and a master voting structure, the structure rule must identify a unique current voting structure. This current voting structure includes all replicas which are present in the epoch and which are also included in the master voting structure. In particular, three major issues must be addressed. First, an assignment of replicas to physical nodes must be given. Second, unused physical and virtual nodes must be deleted from the current voting structure, and third, operation quorums must be adjusted. These three issues are addressed by the following three steps.

Step 1 (Replica Assignment) Calculate an *importance indicator* for every node (physical or virtual) of the master voting structure according to the algorithm and execution sequence as given by the algorithm in Figure 2. The importance indicator is a natural number. The lower the importance indicator the higher is the importance of the node. Generally, importance indicators calculated as described by the algorithm comply with the following rules (some restrictions apply).

(A1) The importance of every node is higher than the importance of any of its sons.

(A2) The importance of a node is higher than (equal to) the importance of a brother, if the priority of the arc connecting the node with its father is higher than (equal to) the priority of the arc connecting the brother with the same father.[1]

---
[1] Due to the acyclic nature of a voting structure, nodes can have multiple

347

```
SetImportanceIndicator(ii ∈ N₀, v ∈ node)
{
  ii := ii + 1;
  /* note that ii is a global variable */
  if (max < ii) /* remember max ii */
    max := ii;
  iiᵥ := ii; /* set ii of node v */
  N := succ(v); /* all successors of v */
  while (N̄ != ∅)
  {
    M := {w | w ∈ N, <weight(v,w) is min>};
    lmax := max;
    for all (w ∈ M)
      SetImportanceIndicator(lmax, w);
    N := N \ M;
  }
}
max := 0;
SetImportanceIndicator(max, <root node>);
```

Figure 2. Algorithm for calculating importance indicators

(A3) If priorities are defined for read and write operations then the priority as used in rule (A2) is the sum of both priorities. Note, that a priority of ∞ is regarded as being not defined.

Using the actual epoch, sort the replicas included in this epoch according to their availability indicators in decreasing order. If multiple replicas exhibit identical availability indicators then they are additionally sorted in increasing order within this subsequence with respect to their unique number. Analogously, the same sorting procedure is applied to the physical nodes of the master voting structure with respect to their importance. Subsequently, for all elements of the replica list, assign the i-th element of the replica list to the i-th element of the physical nodes list.

This procedure leads to a deterministic assignment of replicas to physical nodes based on a particular epoch such that the most important replicas of a certain replication scheme are represented by replicas whose hosting sites are regarded as being most available. At this point, it is possible to have a class of physical nodes with identical importance indicators of which only a subclass actually has replicas assigned to its members. In order to preserve the characteristics of the original replication scheme as much as possible, reassignments of physical nodes and replicas within this class are considered according to the following criterion.

Let C_{rr} be the number of physical nodes in the class and let C_{vr} be the number of all fathers of these physical nodes. C_{rr}^{new} is the number of physical nodes having a replica assigned to them and C_{vr}^{new} is the number of fathers of physical nodes with replica. Note that only C_{vr}^{new} is unknown. In order to achieve our aim, we calculate C_{vr}^{new} by preserving in the current voting structure as long and as closely as possible the ratio between the mean number of physical nodes per father and the number of direct fathers as given by the

master voting structure (see Formula (1)).

$$\frac{(C_{rr}^{new}/C_{vr}^{new})}{C_{vr}^{new}} = \frac{(C_{rr}^{old}/C_{vr}^{old})}{C_{vr}^{old}} \tag{1}$$

Based on C_{vr}^{new}, we assign – within the particular class – physical nodes to replicas such that only $round(C_{vr}^{new}) := \lfloor C_{vr}^{new} + 0.\overline{5} \rfloor$ fathers have sons with assigned replicas.

Step 2 (Restructuring) The current voting structure constructed so far is re-organized according to the following rules. A physical node is called *unused* if after Step 1 no replica has been assigned to it.

(D1) An unused physical node is deleted.[2]
(D2) A virtual node without sons is deleted.
(D3) A virtual node with only a single son having a unique father is replaced by the son. The son keeps his quorum but inherits from the father the vote and the arcs which lead from the grandfathers to the father.

Step 3 (Quorum Adjustment) In order to increase the availability of read and write operations after a certain replica has failed and/or has been excluded from the epoch, any quorum which could use the votes of this replica can now be reduced by exactly those votes since they are not available any longer. The primary goal while recalculating the quorums is to preserve the characteristics of the master voting structure (and therefore the characteristics of the modeled replication scheme) as closely as possible: if the read (write) quorum Q_{read}^{old} (Q_{write}^{old}) of a father was, for instance, 60% of the sum of votes V^{old} of all sons prior to the failure of a son then the recalculated new read (write) quorum Q_{read}^{new} (Q_{write}^{new}) should be as close as possible to 60% of the votes V^{new} of all still available sons. This is enforced by Formulae (2) – (5).

$$Q_{write}^{new'} := Q_{write}^{old} \cdot V^{new}/V^{old} \tag{2}$$

$$Q_{read}^{new'} := Q_{read}^{old} \cdot V^{new}/V^{old} \tag{3}$$

$$Q_{write}^{new} := \lceil Q_{write}^{new'} \rceil \tag{4}$$

$$Q_{read}^{new} := \lceil Q_{read}^{new'} - (Q_{write}^{new} - Q_{write}^{new'}) \rceil \tag{5}$$

This re-calculation concludes Step 3. The voting structure constructed by applying Steps 1–3 on the master voting structure leads to a unique current voting structure for any possible actual epoch.

After having described dGSV, we apply in the following section the framework to a variety of replication schemes.

4 The Zoo

The aim of this section is two-fold. First, we would like to apply dGSV on various static replication schemes

---

"fathers." We adopt the "brother," "son," "father" etc. terminology even for acyclic graphs, since it allows a simple description.

[2]"deleting a node" means removing the node, its vote, quorums, and all arcs leading to it from any father.

thereby obtaining their dynamic counterpart. We chose the Quorum Consensus Strategy, the Grid Protocol, Hierarchical Quorum Consensus and the Tree Quorum Protocol. For the former two protocols, dynamic variants have already been reported in literature. For the latter two protocols this is not the case. In particular, the dynamic variant of the Tree Quorum Protocol requires the full potential of dGSV since for correct behavior, the Tree Quorum Protocol must exploit priorities defined among the various read and write quorum sets. Second, we would like to compare the operation availabilities of the static vs. the dynamic replication schemes under certain conditions. This provides for a first feeling whether dynamic schemes perform superior in terms of operations availabilities. An analysis in terms of operation costs has not been done yet. It is subject of our future research.

In a first attempt, we tried to perform the availability anayses based on Markov chains. Due to state space explosion – except for the Quorum Consensus Strategy – this turned out to be far too complex. We therefore chose to evaluate the protocols' behavior through discrete event simulation. The underlying assumptions for these simulations are stated below.

- site failures are independent of each other

- link failures do not occur

- the network is fully connected

- new epochs are formed whenever possible

- the *mean time to repair* MTTR is set to 1.201 [days]. This value is considered being typical for the Internet [12].

- the probability p that a site is available (e.g., up) is varied in the interval $(0, 1)$

- the up-time of any site is exponentially distributed with a *mean time to failure* MTTF $= (p/(1 - p)) \cdot$ MTTR

- the down-time of any site is exponentially distributed with a *mean time to repair* MTTR $= 1.201$

Although dGSV also tolerates link failures, such a failure type is excluded for the scope of the analysis. This is common praxis for the analysis of replication schemes since doing so tremendously simplifies the calculations. Consequently, one has to bear in mind that by excluding link failures theoretically from occuring, all stated operation availabilities represent upper bounds.

For every presented replication scheme, a brief outline of how to perform read and write operations is given. If existing, the logical structure used by the scheme to group replicas is shown. We state the master voting structure which models the static scheme as used by the dGSV framework for obtaining the dynamic counterpart and give the importance indicators belonging to the master voting structure.

Finally, read and write availabilities of the static vs. the dynamic scheme is given. Although not explicitly presented, the *mean time to failure* (MTTF) of read and write operations can be obtained by using the following formula: MTTF $= (A_{op}/(1 - A_{op})) \cdot$ MTTR, with A_{op} being an operation availability and MTTR $= 1.201$ days.

4.1 Dynamic Quorum Consensus Strategy

The Quorum Consensus Strategy (QCS) [10] was presented by Gifford in 1979 as an extension to the Majority Voting Strategy (MCS) of Thomas [9]. MCS requires a true majority $\lceil (n + 1)/2 \rceil$ of n replicas to co-operate for either a read or a write operation. QCS, on the contrary, assigns possibly different *weights* or *votes* to the replicas and requires a *quorum* (or *threshold*) of weights to be collected prior to executing a read or a write operation. Quorums for read and write operations can be different, as long as the sum of both quorums is larger than the sum of all weights assigned to replicas. Additionally, a write quorum must hold a true majority of all weights. By assigning different weights to different replicas, more reliable replicas can be given a higher responsibility for the accessibility of the replicated data object and through different operational quorums, instances of QCS can be designed which minimize costs with respect to a given workload. A dynamic version of QCS is known and has been presented in [13]. In the following, we present a special case of dynamic QCS, namely dynamic MCS. The modeling of an arbitrary instance of dynamic QCS is straightforward.

The master voting structure which models a static MCS having 9 replicas is shown in Figure 3. Figure 4 shows the

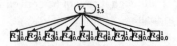

Figure 3. Master voting structure of MCS

assignment of importance indicators to the physical and virtual nodes of the master voting structure. Since all physical

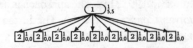

Figure 4. Importance indicators of the MCS master voting structure

nodes have the same importance indicator of 2, all replicas (which are exclusively assigned to physical nodes) are of equal importance. This is in correspondence with the MCS specification which does not favor particular replicas.

Note that static MCS must cease read and write operation execution after the failure of five replicas. The dynamic variant can still provide consistent access to the replicated data object as long as even a single replica is available, although providing only reduced operation availability. If, in the extreme, only a single replica forms the current voting structure (i.e., after eight replicas have failed), the scheme behaves as if the data object is not replicated. This observation, in fact, holds for all dynamic schemes modeled by dGSV.

Figure 5 shows the read and write availabilities of static vs. dynamic MCS when the site availability p for each site is varied between 0 and 1. The graphs of the read and write

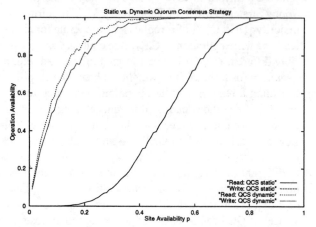

Figure 5. Simulation results of static vs. dynamic MCS

availabilities of static MCS are identical so that they appear as a single continuous line in the figure. It can be observed that the operation availabilities of dynamic MCS are always higher than the corresponding operations of the static counterpart. This observation holds in particular in the interval $0.8 \leq p < 1$ although it cannot be derived from the given figure due to scaling.

4.2 Dynamic Hierarchical Quorum Consensus Strategy

A replication scheme which hierarchically layers groups of replicas on top of each other was presented – among others – by Kumar in 1991 [11]. The approach is called *Hierarchical Quorum Consensus* (HQC). The instance presented here assumes nine replicas arranged as three groups having three replicas each. Consistent read (write) access is possible as long as a majority of replicas within a majority of groups can be contacted. In the example, replicas assigned to physical replicas R_1, R_2, R_4, and R_5, for instance, form a valid quorum set for either operation. Figure 6 gives the logical arrangement of the replicas. In Figure 7, the master voting structure of HQC as used by dGSV is given. Figure 8 shows the assignment of importance indicators to the physical and virtual nodes of the master voting structure. The three groups of replicas are all of importance 2, indicating that no group is favored against any other group. Replicas

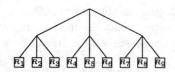

Figure 6. Logical arrangement of nine replicas within HQC

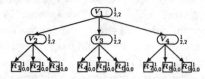

Figure 7. Master voting structure of HQC

within each group are also of equal importance. This corresponds to the fact that an arbitrary majority of replicas within a particular group can be chosen.

The operation availabilities of static vs. dynamic HQC are given in Figure 9. Since the graphs of the read and write operation of the static HQC are identical, they form a single continuous line in the figure. It can be seen that the read availability of dynamic HQC is greatly increased wrt. the read availability of static HQC. Nevertheless, the write availability of dynamic HQC shows that the particular instance of HQC is not always a suitable dynamic replication scheme if write operation availabilities are required to be very high. This is due to the small group size of three: when the group size is reduced to two or fewer replicas then requiring a majority of replicas within a write operation means requiring all replicas of the group. This leads to the bad write availability characteristic of a read-one/write-all replication scheme [1]. If all replicas of a group are required for writing then accessing a single replica for reading suffices, leading to a high read availability as observed for dynamic HQC.

4.3 Dynamic Tree Quorum Protocol

The *Tree Quorum Protocol* (TQP) [7] assumes a tree-like arrangement of replicas. Figure 10 shows an instance of TQP having 13 replicas. A read operation is performed by accessing replica R_1. If this fails then two out of three replicas of the next lower layer are contacted. For any failed replica of the second level an arbitrary majority of its sons of the next lower level must be used instead. R_2, R_8, and R_9 is an example of a valid read quorum set if R_1 and R_3 have both failed. For a write operation, replica R_1 together

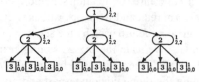

Figure 8. Importance indicators of the HQC master voting structure

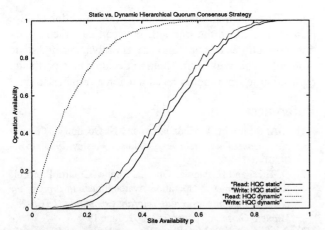

Figure 9. Simulation results of static vs. dynamic HQC

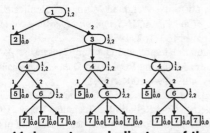

Figure 10. Logical structure of TQP managing 13 replicas

with two sons as well as two grandsons of each contacted son must be modified, e.g., R_1, R_2, R_3, R_6, R_7, R_8, and R_9. TQP owns – in contrast to MCS, QCS, HQC, and the Grid Protocol – the *graceful degradation* property, meaning that quorum set sizes increase as more failures occur. The master voting structure of TQP as used by dGSV has already been given by Figure 1 of Section 3.2. Figure 11 gives TQP's master voting structure with assigned importance indicators. It can be observed that some replicas are

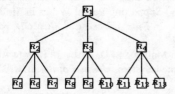

Figure 11. Importance indicators of the TQP master voting structure

more important than others. For example, the replica residing at the physical node R_1 having an importance indicator of 2 is most important. It represents the replica at the root of the logical structure given in Figure 10. Through the dGSV mechanism, it is guaranteed that the replica with highest observed availability is assigned to this physical node.

Figure 12 gives the operation availabilities of static vs. dynamic TQP. Analogously to dynamic HQC, dynamic TQP offers a high read availability at the expense of a very

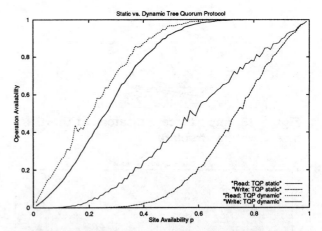

Figure 12. Simulation results of static vs. dynamic TQP

low write availability. Once again, it can be observed that the operation availabilities of the dynamic variant are always higher than the corresponding operation availability of the static protocol.

4.4 Dynamic Grid Protocol

Finally, we present a dynamic version of the Grid Protocol (GP) [6]. GP arranges replicas as a logical grid. An example of a grid with nine replicas is given in Figure 13. For read access, at least one replica per column must be

Figure 13. Logical structure of GP managing nine replicas

contacted. Such a set of replicas is referred to as a *c-cover*. R_1, R_6, and R_9, for example, constitute a c-cover. For write access, a c-cover together with an entire column of replicas must be updated. For example, R_1, R_6, R_7, R_8, and R_9 form a valid write quorum set. The master voting structure modeling GP with nine replicas is given by Figure 14. Its importance indicator assignment is shown in Figure 15.

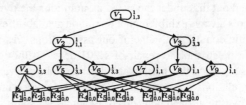

Figure 14. Master voting structure of GP

The result of the availability analysis is shown in Figure 16. Here, it can be observed that the operation availabilities of the dynamic GP are greatly improved: generally, the operation availabilities of dynamic GP are much higher than those of the corresponding static operation.

351

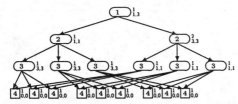

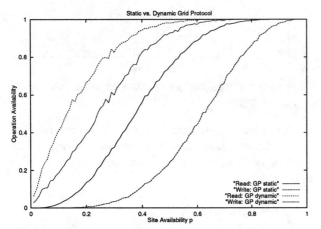

Figure 15. Importance indicators of the GP master voting structure

Figure 16. Simulation results of static vs. dynamic GP

5 Conclusion and Future Work

In this paper, we presented a framework called *Dynamic General Structured Voting* which automatically interprets the specification of a static replication scheme in such a way that it exhibits the behavior of its dynamic counterpart. This general transformation is done without the exploitation of any scheme-specific knowledge, and thus without human intervention.

We performed simulations with various replication schemes, including Quorum Consensus, Hierarchical Quorum Consensus, the Tree Quorum Protocol, and the Grid Protocol. They all confirm the suitability of our approach. In particular, we examined the operation availabilities obtained via simulation of the static vs. the dynamic protocols. It turned out that under the stated assumptions the dynamic protocols always exhibit higher operation availabilities than the static counterpart. One of our assumptions was to assume a mean time to repair of 1.201 days. Although we always assumed this particular value due to its relevance in the simulations presented in this paper, we conjecture that the above-mentioned behavior of dynamic vs. static protocols holds for many other values of MTTR and for more relaxed assumptions.

We have recently completed the implementation of a CORBA-based prototype of GSV for transparent access of replicated WWW documents through off-the-shelf WWW browsers [14, 15]. In a further step, we plan to substi-tute GSV by dGSV within this prototype. Additionally, we plan to investigate the trade-off between increased operation availabilities and operation costs of dynamic and static protocols. This will further help to decide which particular replication scheme should be adopted in a certain setting.

References

[1] P. A. Bernstein, V. Hadzilacos, and N. Goodman. *Concurrency Control and Recovery*. Addison Wesley, 1985. ISBN 0-201-10715-5.

[2] O. Theel and H. Pagnia. Optimal Replica Control Protocols Exhibit Symmetric Operation Availabilities. In *Proc. of the 28th Intern. Symp. on Fault-Tolerant Computing (FTCS-28), Munich, Germany*, pages 252–261, June 1998.

[3] S. Jajodia and D. Mutchler. Dynamic Voting. In *Proc. of the ACM SIGMOD*, pages 227–238, 1987.

[4] M. Rabinovich and E. D. Lazowska. Improving Fault Tolerance and Supporting Partial Writes in Structured Coterie Protocols. In *Proc. of the ACM SIGMOD*, pages 226–235, July 1992.

[5] H. Garcia-Molina and D. Barbara. How to Assign Votes in a Distributed System. *Journal of the ACM*, 32(4):841–860, 1985.

[6] S. Y. Cheung, M. Ahamad, and M. H. Ammar. The Grid Protocol: A High Performance Scheme for Maintaining Replicated Data. In *Proc. of the 6th Intern. Conf. on Data Engineering*, pages 438–445, February 1990.

[7] D. Agrawal and A. El Abbadi. The Tree Quorum Protocol: An Efficient Approach for Managing Replicated Data. In *Proc. of the 16th VLDB Conference*, pages 243–254, 1990.

[8] O. Theel. General Structured Voting: A Flexible Framework for Modelling Cooperations. In *Proc. of the 13th Intern. Conf. on Distr. Computing Systems, Pittsburgh, PA*, pages 227–236. IEEE, May 1993.

[9] R. H. Thomas. A Majority Consensus Approach to Concurrency Control for Multiple Copy Databases. *ACM ToDS*, 4(2):180–207, 1979.

[10] D. K. Gifford. Weighted Voting for Replicated Data. In *Proc. of the 7th ACM Symp. on Operating Systems Principles*, pages 150–162, 1979.

[11] A. Kumar. Hierarchical Quorum Consensus: A New Algorithm for Managing Replicated Data. *IEEE Trans. on Computers*, 40(9):996–1004, 1991.

[12] D. D. Long, A. Miur, and R. Golding. A Longitudinal Survey of Internet Host Reliability. Technical Report UCSC-CRL-95-16, Dept. of Computer Science, University of California, Santa Cruz, CA 95064, March 1995.

[13] S. Jajodia and D. Mutchler. Dynamic Voting Algorithms for Maintaining the Consistency of a Database. *ACM ToDS*, 15(2):230–280, June 1990.

[14] H. Pagnia, O. Theel, and J. Iwik. Replicated Documents for the World-wide Web. In *Proc. of Euromedia, Leicester, UK*, pages 57–64, January 1998.

[15] S. Löhr. Design and Implementation of a CORBA-based Framework for Data Replication (in German). Master's Thesis DA-BS-1998-02, Institute for System Architecture, Dept. of Computer Science, Darmstadt University of Technology, Darmstadt, Germany, October 1998.

Session A6

Multimedia Systems

Chair: Wu-Chi Feng
Ohio State University, USA

Parallel Media Processors for the Billion-Transistor Era

Jason Fritts, Zhao Wu, and Wayne Wolf

Dept. of Electrical Engineering, Princeton University, Princeton, NJ 08544

{jefritts, zhaowu, wolf}@ee.princeton.edu

Abstract

This paper describes the challenges presented by single-chip parallel media processors (PMPs). These machines integrate multiple parallel function units, instruction execution, and memory hierarchies on a single chip. The combination of programmability and high performance on data parallelism is necessary to meet the demands of next-generation multimedia applications. Many research issues must be solved to realize the full potential of programmable media processors. This paper provides both a survey of research trends and issues in architecture and compiler design for programmable media processors, and an exploration of the potential performance of media processors over the next decade.

Keywords: media processor, PMP, billion transistors, parallel architecture, cluster scheduling, data partitioning

1. Introduction

This paper explores the parallel processing challenges presented by single-chip media processors. Advances in VLSI technology will make possible chips with one billion transistors within a decade [1]. There are many multi-media applications that are quite capable of absorbing this increase in available computational power. With access to a billion transistors, architectures will become feasible that will make many of these applications possible. But advances in VLSI technology will not result in advanced parallel media processors unless a variety of other research issues in architecture and compiler design are also addressed.

Current multimedia applications manipulate media such as images, video sequences, and audio channels. Many new applications, such as video libraries, MPEG-4, and MPEG-7, require a great deal of video processing using advanced algorithms [2]. To permit these new methods, multimedia is moving away from simple channel and frame-based representations towards an object-based representation of multimedia. These objects describe real-world objects, each with its own audio, visual, and graphical characteristics specifying its spatial and temporal behavior. This representation enables higher compression rates, more freedom for interactive media, and content-based processing.

The new freedom and flexibility of the object-oriented representation introduces much greater processing demands and irregularity than seen in the first generation of multimedia. This is especially true for video and computer graphics, the most data intensive media. Adequate support for the next generation of media processing will require the flexibility and computing power of high-level language (HLL) programmable media processors.

Support for the first generation of multimedia was predominantly in the form of either application-specific hardware or multimedia extensions to general-purpose processors [3]. Both methods provide support for multimedia at low cost, but neither provides both the flexibility and performance necessary for future multimedia applications. Application-specific hardware provides excellent performance, but has limited flexibility and is unable to support evolving and future applications. General-purpose processors with multimedia extensions provide the flexibility, but are designed primarily for general-purpose applications and cannot adequately support the distinctive multimedia workloads, which are characterized by large amounts of streaming data, high computation rates, and extensive data parallelism. For the next generation of multimedia, unique processors for multimedia, *parallel media processors (PMPs)*, will prove the best alternative as they can offer both the performance and flexibility through specialized high-speed, highly parallel architectures that are programmable using high-level languages.

Some programmable media processors have started to appear in the marketplace with DSP (digital signal processing) and VLIW (very long instruction word) architectures [3], but these early processors achieve only a fraction of their potential performance. They do not have the frequency or parallelism for high throughput and offer only limited programmability through special libraries or programming paradigms. The increasing frequencies and numbers of transistors over the next decade will help solve these problems, but the question remains on how to utilize these resources most effectively.

354

To achieve their full potential, media processors will undergo some significant changes in the coming decade. There are three primary differences that are expected between existing and future media processors:

- much more on-chip memory
- wider processors with more functional units
- more regular architectures (less dedicated hardware)

Large, aggressive on-chip memory hierarchies are necessary to accommodate the high data rates and minimize penalties from large external memory latencies. Much wider processors are required to provide the parallelism necessary for meeting the throughput demands of many multimedia applications. More regular architectures are needed both for greater flexibility over a wide range of applications, as well as better high-level language programmability. These are considerable differences and much research in architecture and compiler design is required to realize the potential of future media processors.

This paper continues with an examination of the potential of future PMPs and a survey of the current trends and research issues being explored towards achieving that potential. Section 2 will examine some architecture issues including the competing factors of high parallelism and high frequency and the open issues regarding memory hierarchy design. Section 3 will explore the compiler issues including extraction of data parallelism and parallel compilation problems such as cluster scheduling and data partitioning. Section 4 will perform experiments to investigate the potential performance of PMPs over the next decade and illustrate the limited capabilities of current compilers with respect to multimedia. Section 5 closes with the conclusions.

2. Architecture issues

Proceeding into the next century, technology is approaching the billion-transistor era. What does this imply for next-generation media processors? While it is certainly possible to put more functional units on chip, using the extra silicon estate for memory will likely prove more productive. First, functional units are small, consuming only a minor portion of the entire chip area, even for processor widths of 16 to 32 issue slots. Secondly, many multimedia applications, particularly video and graphics, tend to access memory frequently and intensively. For many video applications, it was found that memory is the bottleneck of the entire system [4]. As the performance gap between processors and memories continues to widen, its impact on media processors will become significant. Consequently, it is expected that the increasing numbers of transistors will likely be devoted primarily to larger on-chip memory hierarchies.

In the remainder of this section, the design issues surrounding the processor core and memory hierarchy will

be explored. Also presented is the design of a datapath expected to resemble those for future media processors. This design shall be used for experiments in Section 4 that estimate the potential performance of future PMPs.

2.1. Datapath

A variety of architecture alternatives exist for parallel media processors. Many researchers have been speculating on various architectures that will become feasible with billion-transistor chips. Included in some of the proposals are wide superscalar designs, trace processors, single-chip multiprocessors, simultaneous multi-threading, and array processors [5]. It is difficult to say whether these architecture models will be desirable for media processing, but there have been additional proposals specifically for media processing, including vector IRAM [5], simultaneous multi-threading [6], and array processors [7]. While the question of architecture style for future PMPs certainly remains an open issue, one truth exists for any design: media processors will need to achieve high degrees of processing throughput to meet the intense computation and data rates found in many multimedia applications.

High parallelism and high frequency will both be necessary for achieving the processing throughput required in many multimedia applications. The data parallelism inherent in most multimedia can enable significant parallelism, but even with this parallelism, a high frequency processor is still necessary for meeting the demands. One example of the computational requirements on PMPs is given by the MPEG-2 encoder, which can require in excess of one billion operations to compress only a few frames of 720x480 resolution video. This means many billions of operations per second to achieve real-time MPEG-2 encoding. MPEG-4 encoding will exacerbate this situation, as it must also perform segmentation of video frames into objects.

Unfortunately, high parallelism and high frequency are counter-productive goals. Very high frequency processors are quite feasible with low issue widths, but as parallelism increases, the demands on the register file, memory, and datapath grow significantly, often exponentially. Each additional issue slot added to a processor adds 3-4 ports to the register file, potentially a memory port, one or more bypass paths, and extra function units and wires that increase area and loading. Consequently, increased parallelism results in decreased frequency for conventional architectures. To achieve both high parallelism and high frequency, more distributed architectures are required.

An effective way to increase the parallelism with much less impact on frequency is through a clustered architecture. A clustered architecture divides the architecture into disjoint groups of issue slots. Each group has 2 to 4 issue slots, its own register file and possibly its

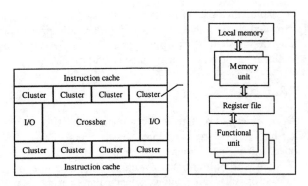

Figure 1. Clustered architecture

own local memory or cache. This distributed design allows high frequency by limiting the register ports, memory ports, bypass paths, and area within each cluster. The clusters are all connected by an interconnect network, which passes results between clusters as required. Any number of clusters may be used to achieve the desired parallelism, with the primary impact on frequency coming from the increased demands on the interconnect network, the memory hierarchy, and the control logic. In essence, a clustered architecture is a group of processors that share a common control stream and are tightly connected by a low-latency interconnect.

An example of an aggressive clustered architecture we have proposed for media processing is a 32-issue cluster architecture that is divided into 8 clusters of 4 issue slots per cluster, as shown in Figure 1. These clusters are homogeneous clusters, each offering 4 ALUs, 2 memory ports, 1 multiplier, and 1 shifter. Full bypassing is provided among all issue slots within the cluster. Local storage consists of a register file with 128 registers and 32 KB of local memory in each cluster. Results from other clusters can be easily obtained using a single-cycle 32x32 crossbar network that fully connects all issue slots between clusters. Architecture simulations indicate frequencies of up to 650 MHz using 0.25 μm technology [8]. This architecture design will be used for the performance experiments of future PMPs in Section 4.

2.2. Memory hierarchy

The memory hierarchy of a HLL programmable media processor is an ill-defined area. Whereas general-purpose processors use caches, typical DSPs often use local memory with some form of prefetching, such as DMA or stream buffers. Our initial studies on video application traces [9] have shown good performance with hybrid memory architectures that combine a stream buffer with cache. However, these studies are based on trace-driven simulations that assume perfect branch prediction and memory disambiguation.

Previous research in multimedia memory hierarchies includes a study performed by Zucker, et al. [10] at Stanford. Using the JPEG and MPEG multimedia applications, the study examined three prefetching techniques for streaming data: stream buffer, stride prediction table, and a hybrid of the two called a *stream cache*. Compared to a cache system without any prefetching, all the techniques were effective at eliminating many of the cache misses, though the effectiveness of each varied according to the size of the cache used. For small caches, the stream buffer and stream cache were more effective, while the stride prediction table performed best for large caches sizes.

In addition to providing support for streaming memory, the large data rates can place significant burdens on external memory, so the external memory bandwidth often becomes a bottleneck. To meet the necessary data rates, either memory hierarchies must be designed to reduce the external memory traffic, or scheduling methods will be required to restructure the program for improved data locality [7][11].

Aside from the issue of the type of memory hierarchy to use, there is an added complication of supporting numerous memory accesses each cycle. Large multi-ported memories are not feasible at high frequencies, so highly banked or distributed memories are required instead. This may even entail separate local memory for each cluster, with memory coherency handled by the compiler and/or higher levels of the memory hierarchy. One study provided an interesting alternative by combining a clustered architecture with a stream buffer-like prefetching structure called a *stream register file* [12]. This architecture and memory hierarchy enable a high-frequency clustered architecture coupled with the benefits of prefetching support. However, their scheme also requires a special programming paradigm, which is undesirable for generic HLL programmability.

The memory hierarchy for PMPs is poorly understood. It is unknown whether cache, memory with prefetching, cache with prefetching, or even some other novel memory structure will prove most suitable for multimedia. Furthermore, the problems of reducing external memory bandwidth and supporting numerous memory accesses per cycle are also areas open areas. Considerable research remains in the area of memory hierarchy design for media processors, with the only definitive facts being that:

- PMPs require aggressive memory hierarchies to support the large amounts of data, and
- the increasing availability of transistors on chip over the next decade will allow interesting multi-level memory hierarchy alternatives.

Many research issues regarding the media processor datapath and memory hierarchy have been presented that define key areas for realizing efficient media processor designs. These are far from the only areas of research, however. Many additional questions exist, such as whether smaller datapath sizes (less than 32 bits) would enable faster video signal processing since video signals usually operate predominantly on 8-bit and 16-bit data types. Also, the question of supporting mixed-signal multimedia is an issue. For example, video and images use small integer data types whereas graphics more commonly uses single-precision floating point. These and many other issues require further study.

3. Compiler issues

The design of HLL programmable media processors requires an aggressive optimizing compiler and a high frequency parallel architecture that complement each other to meet the intense demands of future multimedia. The high degrees of parallelism and large volumes of streaming data within multimedia applications have been well studied, but much research remains towards the design of media processors that are both programmable and can support these computation and data intensive applications. The architecture and compiler designs must be balanced so that the compiler can take full advantage of all architectural resources.

The compiler is a critical component in any HLL programmable processor. This is no less true for PMPs. The high degrees of data parallelism offer optimistic opportunities for achieving high levels of throughput, but they also offer additional problems for the compiler to tackle. These problems can be broken down into two primary categories: a) extraction of the data parallelism, and b) scheduling for highly parallel architectures.

3.1. Extracting data parallelism

The foremost problem with a compiler for PMPs is extracting the parallelism from the applications. Numerous studies have shown the existence of considerable parallelism in multimedia applications [13][14]. Taking advantage of this parallelism, significant speedups have been achieved in many implementations, including application-specific hardware [3], a software approach for multiprocessors [15], and several proposed designs for media processors [7][12][16]. However, it has not yet been shown how compilers can successfully extract similar levels of parallelism.

The problem lies in the level of granularity of the parallelism available in multimedia applications. The compilers of today are good at finding instruction level parallelism (ILP), but the data parallelism in multimedia applications is of a coarser granularity than ILP, so current compilers are unable to effectively exploit it. While multimedia applications typically have considerable data parallelism, they usually have no more ILP than general-

purpose applications, as found in a recent compiler-directed workload evaluation [17]. Successful extraction of the data parallelism by compilers will be crucial for the success of PMPs.

Data parallelism is the parallelism that exists between data elements that have little or no processing dependency between them. It may exist between any data elements, but most commonly occurs between data elements that are not in close proximity to each other in either the spatial or temporal domains. The independence of such data allows computations on them to occur in parallel.

While two data elements with independent processing may be relatively close together in the spatial or temporal domains, the computations on these elements are typically several hundreds or thousands of operations apart in sequential program order. This presents a problem for compilers, which are most effective at finding the instruction level parallelism within scheduling windows comprised of a limited number of sequential operations. The size of these instruction sequences is usually no more than a hundred instructions, which is much smaller than the range of operations for most data-parallel elements. Consequently, current compilers are unable to extract any significant degrees of parallelism from multimedia applications.

An example of this is the 2-D discrete cosine transform (DCT) algorithm, which is a critical kernel for both JPEG image compression and MPEG video compression. This algorithm takes an 8x8 block of an image or video frame and turns the 2-D spatial information into the corresponding 2-D frequency domain. A straightforward implementation of this algorithm encompasses a four-level nested loop where the two outer loops process the 64 elements of an 8x8 block. The two inner loops perform the processing on a single element. It can be seen that the statement '$y[k][l] = y[k][l] + x[i][j] * c[i][k] * c[j][l]$' creates a loop carried dependence in the two inner loops. However, there is no such dependence in the outer loops. Each iteration in the two outer loops is independent of all other iterations, so the 64 iterations of the two outer loops can be run in parallel. Additionally, the DCT is independent over all separate 8x8 blocks in each image or video frame, allowing for even greater degrees of parallelism. The compiler, however, has difficulty seeing the parallelism. There are nine operations in the inner loop, so an iteration of the two inner loops over a single element has at least 9*64 = 576 operations. This minimum distance between two data-parallel elements is much greater than typical scheduling window sizes in compilers, so a compiler is unlikely to find the data parallelism.

The issue of finding data parallelism in multimedia applications is closely related to the issues of automatic parallelization in multiprocessors. Significant research has been performed in parallelizing compilers for taking ad-

```
for (k = 0; k < 8; k++)
   for (l = 0; l < 8; l++)
   {

   y[k][l] = 0.0;

   for (i = 0; i < 8; i++)
      for (j = 0; j < 8; j++)
         y[k][l] = y[k][l] + x[i][j] * c[i][k] * c[j][l];
   }
```

Figure 2. Straightforward implementation of the 2-D DCT Algorithm

vantage of loop-level parallelism at various loop levels in program code [18][19]. However, these methods were initially designed for large-scale parallel machines that provide coarser granularities of parallelism, and will need to be adapted to the finer granularities of parallelism in single-chip parallel media processors.

3.2. Compiling to highly parallel architectures

As mentioned earlier, highly parallel architectures require a distributed design to provide the high frequencies necessary for multimedia. For single-chip media processors, it is expected that the distributed architectures will be tightly coupled like the clustered architecture proposed earlier. This tight coupling enables clusters to communicate data and results to each other with a minimal latency of only one or two cycles.

Compiler scheduling is complicated by clustered architectures because operation results are not uniformly available to the entire processor at the same time. Instead, each result is available first on the cluster that performed the operation and must be copied to other clusters via an inter-cluster *copy* operation as needed. Other clusters needing this result must incur additional latency while *copy* operations transfer the result over the interconnect network. To keep the additional latencies from impacting execution time, it is desirable to schedule critical dependent operations on a single cluster and minimize the communication between clusters.

A number of studies have been performed in the area of scheduling for clustered architectures. Two such works include list scheduling of acyclic dependency graphs [20], and modulo scheduling of cyclic dependency graphs [21]. These studies have produced good methods for scheduling operations over multiple clusters and scheduling the necessary *copy* operations, while minimizing the impact of inter-cluster communication on overall performance. Typically the performance degradation using a clustered architecture is no more than 20-30% compared to a non-clustered architecture of the same issue width.

There is a benefit to scheduling to a clustered architecture for media processing versus general-purpose processing, in that a compiler for media processing will be able to exploit data parallelism. Whereas instruction level parallelism defines parallelism only at the level of individual operations, data parallelism defines parallelism at the level of a group of operations. By definition, data parallelism requires that the processing between data elements be relatively independent, which indicates the groups of operations processing separate data elements are also relatively independent. The relative independence of each group corresponds well with the independence of each cluster, so each group can be scheduled onto a separate cluster. The independence of separate groups eliminates most inter-cluster communication, so there is negligible degradation in overall performance. Using data parallelism, a PMP compiler can perform cluster scheduling with little impact on the performance, and still maintain exceptional parallelism.

A second problem that exists in compiling to a clustered architecture is the need for data partitioning. As discussed in Section 2.2, supporting numerous memory accesses per cycle will likely require either a highly banked or distributed memory structure. However, it is expected that a highly banked memory will only work for up to 4 (or at most 8) parallel memory accesses, because with any more parallel memory accesses the additional logic for control and bank conflict checking will be prohibitive at high frequencies. Consequently, the use of separate local memory structures in each cluster is more likely for a 32-issue processor with 16 parallel memory accesses, as proposed in Section 2.1. Effective scheduling to clusters with separate memories requires intelligent partitioning of data among the clusters to minimize the communication overhead.

An ideal example of data partitioning is the DCT algorithm examined earlier. Recall from Figure 2 that the algorithm uses 4 levels of loops to compute the DCT over a single 8x8 block. The two outer loops (indices k and l) have independent iterations, while the two inner loops (indices i and j) have dependent iterations. Also, the processing of separate 8x8 blocks is independent as well. The data parallelism in this example therefore exists at three different levels:

a) single iteration of the l loop,
b) single iteration of the k loop (all 8 iterations of the l loop), or
c) a single 8x8 block (all 8 iterations of the k loop)

In each case, data in the c, x, and y arrays is either read or written, but different amounts of these arrays are required depending upon the level of data parallelism. The appropriate data elements required from each array for the different data parallelism levels are shown in Figure 3.

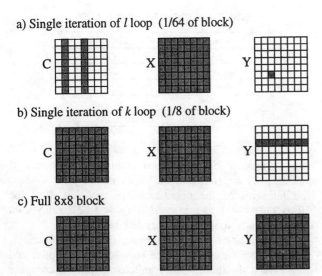

a) Single iteration of *l* loop (1/64 of block)

C   X   Y

b) Single iteration of *k* loop (1/8 of block)

C   X   Y

c) Full 8x8 block

C   X   Y

Figure 3. Data required for DCT algorithm according to level of data parallelism

From the figure, it can be seen that alternatives a) and b), where the data parallelism size is less than a full 8x8 block, require a much finer granularity of data. This is particularly evident in the *y* array. Another important distinction of the *y* array is that it is a data array to which data is being written, not simply read. Finer levels of granularity are easier to accommodate when the data is only being read as it can be shared among multiple clusters without violating memory coherency. Data sets that may be written cannot be shared without potentially violating memory coherency. In the case of the DCT, the entire *y* array cannot be easily shared among the clusters. Using alternative a) or b), it may instead be necessary for one cluster to act as a 'collector', a cluster that alone has write privileges to the *y* array, which collects the *y* results from other clusters and stores them into the *y* array.

The problem of data partitioning by the compiler is a complicated issue that still requires much research. The DCT is a relatively trivial example. For algorithms with more irregular data access, the problem can become very convoluted. Also, many tradeoffs exist between the level of data parallelism and the granularity of the data set. While coarser granularities of data are typically desirable, larger levels of data parallelism may not always be the most efficient. Furthermore, coarser granularities of data may also lead to extensive read sharing that might consume much more local memory than another level data parallelism might require. Examples are tables or arrays of constants such as the *c* array in the DCT. MPEG-2 in particular has numerous large look-up tables for variable bit rate coding which would take up considerable space if a copy was required in each cluster's local memory.

Media processors are gradually moving to wider architectures, presenting new problems for compilers to tackle. Foremost among these is extraction of data parallelism, since effective support of multimedia requires high parallelism as well as high frequency to achieve the necessary throughput. Once the data parallelism is found, there are also issues to resolve for compiling to highly parallel architectures, including cluster scheduling and data partitioning. Again, these are not the only outstanding problems. Other problems such as the role of the compiler in handling streaming data are still open issues, but the problem of finding parallelism in multimedia applications is crucial to the success of programmable media processors.

4. Experiments

This section describes the results of experiments that track the potential performance of parallel media processors over the next decade. The first experiment compares the performance of a trace-driven simulator and a compiler to show the considerable difference between the currently achievable parallelism and the potential parallelism. To bridge this gap and fully realize the potential parallelism, compilers will need to exploit the data parallelism available in multimedia applications, as discussed in section 3. To determine where the data parallelism resides in multimedia applications, a second experiment examines the granularities of parallelism using trace-driven simulation over different-sized scheduling windows. This experiment demonstrates the level of granularity of data parallelism that a compiler must be able to extract. A final experiment tracks the expected progress of PMPs as transistor densities and processor frequencies continue to improve over the next decade.

4.1. Trace-driven simulation vs. compilation

There are many ways to evaluate an architecture, trace-driven simulation and compilation being the two most popular methods. In trace-driven simulation, a program is instrumented and then run on a processor to generate a program trace, which contains all the operations used during the execution of the program. To simulate an architecture, the simulator takes in the trace and attempts to schedule the operations to achieve the greatest parallelism. Meanwhile the simulator performs a variety of experiments such as cache and pipeline simulation. The procedure on an SGI workstation is depicted in Figure 4. Details of the trace-driven simulation method can be found in our previous work [14]. The second method of evaluation is compilation. The basic idea is to compile the program for the target architecture and then simulate execution of the assembly code.

Both approaches have pros and cons. While trace-driven simulation is fast and relatively easy to implement,

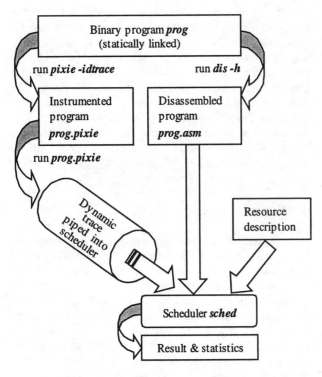

Figure 4. Flow chart of trace-driven simulation on SGI workstations

it has some difficulties dealing with issues like branch prediction and memory disambiguation. This is because the input trace only contains instruction and data addresses. When data is accessed its address is immediately available in the trace, but in reality that address may not be disambiguated from other accesses, which could limit the actual parallelism. On the other hand, despite providing precise results in terms of parallelism measurement, a good retargetable compiler is very sophisticated and hard to develop. Moreover, it takes considerably more time to compile and simulate real applications. Generally speaking, trace-driven simulation may over-estimate the parallelism (due to lack of information about branch prediction and address disambiguation), whereas a compiler usually under-estimates the parallelism (due to lack of optimality in the compiler).

For multimedia applications, the difference in the performance of these two methods is considerable. To illustrate this disparity, three applications, H.263, MPEG-2, and MPEG-4, are simulated using both the trace-driven simulator and the IMPACT compiler [22]. Both methods targeted the same media processor architecture, the 32-issue 8-cluster architecture described in Section 2.2. The IMPACT compiler optimized the code with aggressive ILP optimizations, but was only able to target a 32-issue unclustered architecture, as it does not currently support cluster scheduling.

Table 1. Operation latencies

Operation	Latency
ALU	1
Memory	2
Shift	1
Multiply	7
Divide	34

The target media processor architecture has 4 ALUs, 2 memory units, 1 multiplier, and 1 shifter per cluster. It contains 128 registers and 32 KB of memory per cluster. The latencies of the operations are modeled after the Alpha 21264 [23], as presented in Table 1. Floating-point is not currently supported in this architecture.

The results of this experiment, shown in Figure 5, display a significant difference between the compiler and trace-driven simulator. The parallelism from the compiler varies from 1.5 to 2.6 instructions per cycle, indicating that no data parallelism, only ILP, is being exploited. The trace-driven simulator indicates much greater parallelism, though we do not believe these results over-estimate the available parallelism. It is expected that with improved compiler technology, particularly with compiler algorithms that can take advantage of the data parallelism exhibited by multimedia, media processors can operate at parallelism levels close to the potential shown by the trace-driven studies.

4.2. Level of data parallelism

To determine the potential performance obtainable by a compiler from data parallelism, an experiment was performed with the trace-driven simulator, examining the parallelism available in the application traces using different scheduling window sizes. As indicated in Section 3.1, the level of granularity of data parallelism in multimedia applications is on the order of many hundreds

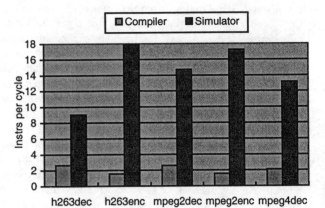

Figure 5. Average instruction issue rate for various resources in an MPEG-2 encoder

or thousands of operations. By varying the scheduling window size, it is possible to determine the amount of parallelism available in different-sized section of the program trace. Comparing the parallelism available in different-sized scheduling windows will illustrate the different granularities of parallelism in the application.

The experiment was performed using the MPEG-2 encoder and decoder application traces, varying the scheduling window size from 16 to one billion operations. The results are shown in Figure 6. At the smaller scheduling window sizes, only instruction level parallelism is available, so the parallelism from ILP is 8 for the encoder, and 1 for the decoder. Once the instruction scheduling window size increases above 4k operations, data parallelism begins to become available, and the parallelism increases to 14 for both the encoder and decoder. Consequently, for the MPEG-2 application, the results indicate the minimum level of data parallelism is on the order of 4k+ operations, and that significant data parallelism occurs at scheduling window sizes of around 64-256k operations.

While the observed granularity of data parallelism in these applications seems somewhat large, the true granularity of the data parallelism is actually a bit smaller than this experiment indicates. The trace-driven simulator is unable to define the actual level of data parallelism, because it schedules the operations in the trace exactly as they occur and does not perform any optimizations on the code, as a compiler would. Many parallelizable loops may not be run in parallel because of the loop-carried dependences from loop induction variables. Therefore, the trace-driven simulator is not able to model the actual level of data parallelism. The effect on the results in Figure 6 would be to shift the slope at 4-64k operations a bit to the left. The actual minimum level of data parallelism will likely be on the order of 1-4k operations.

4.3. Increasing numbers of on-chip transistors

Having realized the importance of memory systems, many CPU designers are putting much more on-chip memory in their microprocessors (e.g. the Intel mobile Pentium II has 256 KB second-level cache integrated on the same processor die). With the increasing silicon resources during the next decade, it is expected that media processors will use the majority of the additional real estate for larger on-chip memory hierarchies. More on-chip memory will allow higher datapath-to-memory bandwidths and lower average latencies for memory accesses.

As mentioned earlier, choosing the appropriate memory structures and devising innovative memory architectures for application-specific systems are subjects of active research. For purposes of this experiment, we will only consider on-chip cache memories, as this is the most widely used and thoroughly studied memory model. Evaluations of other memory types require corresponding changes in the compilers and simulators, which are not addressed in this paper due to space limitations. Comparisons of different memory architectures and their impact on multimedia applications can be found in the literature [4][10].

In all cache simulations, a block size of 64 bytes and two-way set associativity are used, as this configuration outperforms others cache configurations of similar area [9]. The datapath model is that presented in Section 2.1, i.e. 8 clusters, each containing 128 registers, 4 ALUs, 2 memory units, 1 multiplier and 1 shifter.

In the deep sub-micron era, interconnect wires also play an essential role in addition to transistors, so we use area instead of transistor count as a metric. The area measurements are based on Dutta's work [8]. Using a 0.25μm CMOS technology, Dutta designed parameterizable versions of some key modules, including

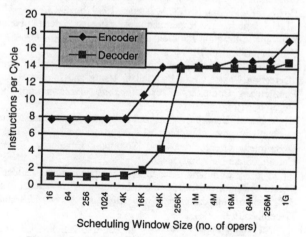

Figure 6. Instructions per cycle of MPEG-2 coding for different scheduling window sizes

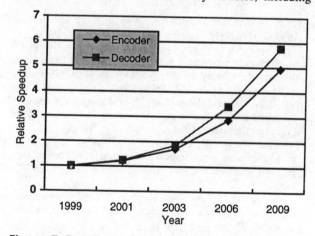

Figure 7. Relative speedup of MPEG-2 coding for increasing on-chip cache over next decade

memory. The simulation results, taking into account clock rate increase according to the *National Semiconductor Technology Roadmap* [1], are shown in Figure 6. As can be seen, the curves are slightly better than linear. As chip area (number of transistors) and speed increase, so does performance. We assume that a 32 KB on-chip cache is used in 1999 and the size doubles every two or three years, and finally reaches 1024 KB after ten years. Notice that this only considers a single-die, so the actual performance could be even higher with more aggressive techniques such as a multi-chip module (MCM).

5. Conclusions

Advances in VLSI technology are making possible single-chip parallel media processors (PMPs). These processors offer significant challenges in parallel processing: architectures must be able to operate at high frequencies with high degrees of parallelism while making efficient use of memory hierarchies; compilers must be able to take advantage of the large amounts of data parallelism available in multimedia and perform efficient scheduling onto a clustered architecture. Parallel media processors will be early examples of single-chip parallel processors and will offer significant research opportunities. Such chips will enable continued growth and many new advances in the multimedia computing industry.

6. Acknowledgements

This work was funded by the New Jersey Center for Multimedia Research and by the National Science Foundation.

7. Bibliography

[1] "*The National Technology Roadmap for Semiconductors*", 1997 Edition, Semiconductor Industry Association, 1997.

[2] Wayne Wolf, Yiqing Liang, Michael Kozuch, Heather Yu, Michael Phillips, Marcel Weekes, and Andrew Debruyne, "A digital video library on the World Wide Web," *Proceedings, ACM Multimedia '96*, ACM Press, 1996.

[3] Zhao Wu and Wayne Wolf, "Parallel Architectures for Programmable Video Signal Processing," Technical Report, Princeton University, 1998.

[4] Zhao Wu and Wayne Wolf, "Design study of shared memory in VLIW video signal processors", *Proc. IEEE Int'l Conf. on Parallel Architectures and Compilation Techniques*, pp. 52-59, Oct. 1998.

[5] C. Kozyrakis and D. Patterson, "A New Direction for Computer Architecture Research," *IEEE Computer*, November 1998, vol. 31, no. 11, pp. 24-32.

[6] M. Berekovic, P. Pirsch, and J. Kneip, "An Algorithm-Hardware-System Approach to VLIW Multimedia Processors,"

[7] Y. K. Chen and S. Y. Kung, "Multimedia Signal Processors: An Architectural Platform with Algorithmic Compilation," *Journal of VLSI Signal Processing Systems for Signal, Image, and Video Technology*, vol. 20, pp. 181-204, 1998.

[8] Santanu Dutta, "VLSI issues and architectural tradeoffs in advanced video signal processors", Ph.D. Thesis, Princeton University, Nov. 1996.

[9] Zhao Wu and Wayne Wolf, "Study of cache system in video signal processors", *Proc. IEEE Workshop on Signal Processing Systems*, pp. 23-32, Oct. 1998.

[10] D. Zucker, M. Flynn, and R. Lee, "A comparison of hardware prefetching techniques for multimedia benchmarks", *Technical Report CSL-TR-95-683*, Stanford Univ. Dec. 1995.

[11] C. Kulkarni, K. Danckaert, F. Catthoor, and M. Gupta, "Interaction Between Data Parallel Compilation and Data Transfer and Storage Cost for Multimedia Applications," IBM Research Report, February 1999.

[12] Scott Rixner, William J. Dally, Ujval J. Kapasi, Brucek Khailany, Abelardo Lopez-Lagunas, Peter R. Mattson, and John D. Owens, "Media Processors Using Streams," *SPIE Photonics West: Media Processors '99*, San Jose, California, January 28-29, 1999, pp. 122-134.

[13] Heng Liao and Andrew Wolfe, "Avaliable Parallelism in Video Applications," *Proceedings of the 30th Annual International Symposium on Microarchitecture*, December 1997.

[14] Zhao Wu and Wayne Wolf, "Trace-driven studies of VLIW video signal processors", *Proc. 10th ACM Symp. on Parallel Algorithms and Architectures*, pp. 289-297, June 1998.

[15] Angelos Bilas, Jason Fritts, and Jaswinder P. Singh, "Real-Time Parallel MPEG-2 Decoding in Software," *11th International Parallel Processing Symposium*, Geneva, Switzerland, April 1997.

[16] A. Wolfe, J. Fritts, S. Dutta, and E. S. T. Fernandes, "Datapath Design for a VLIW Video Signal Processor," *3rd International Symposium on High-Performance Computer Architecture*, San Antonio, Texas, Feb. 1997, pp. 24-35.

[17] Jason Fritts, Wayne Wolf, and Bede Liu, "Understanding multimedia application characteristics for designing programmable media processors," *SPIE Photonics West, Media Processors '99*, San Jose, CA, January 1999, pp. 2-13.

[18] U. Banerjee, R. Eigenmann, A. Nicolau, and D. Padua, "Automatic Program Parallelization," *Proceedings of the IEEE*, February 1993, vol. 81, no. 2, pp. 211-243.

[19] M. Hall, S. Amarasinghe, B. Murphy, S. Liao, and M. Lam, "Detecting Coarse-Grain Parallelism Using and Interprocedural Parallelizing Compiler," *Proceedings of Supercomputing '95*, December 1995.

[20] Sanjeev Banerjia, "Instruction scheduling and fetch mechanisms for clustered VLIW processors," PhD thesis, Department of Electrical and Computer Engineering, North Carolina State University, 1998.

[21] Erik Nystrom and Alexandre E. Eichenberger, "Effective Cluster Assignment for Modulo Scheduling," *Proceedings of the 31st Annual International Symposium on Microarchitecture*, December 1998.

[22] IMPACT compiler group: http://www.crhc.uiuc.edu/Impact

[23] L. Gwennap, "Digital 21264 sets new standard," *Microprocessor Report*, 10(14), October 1996.

Adaptive Disk Scheduling Algorithms for Video Servers *

Wonjun Lee and Jaideep Srivastava

Department of Computer Science & Engineering
University of Minnesota at Minneapolis
Minneapolis, MN 55455
{WJLEE|SRIVASTA}@CS.UMN.EDU

Won-Ho Lee

Department of Electronic Engineering
Korea University
Seoul, Korea
LWH@DALI.KOREA.AC.KR

Abstract

Soft-real time applications, such as continuous media (CM) systems, have an important property, namely, they allow for graceful adaptation of the application Quality-of-Service (QoS), and therefore are able to have acceptable performance with reduced resource utilization. This can be used by the admission control process to decide if an application can be admitted, even if the resource is congested. In this paper, we present a Soft-QoS framework for Continuous Media servers, which provides a dynamic and adaptive admission control and scheduling algorithm. Using our policy, we could increase the number of simultaneously running clients that could be supported and could ensure a good response ratio and better resource utilization under heavy traffic requirements. The observations and findings from the model are validated with simulation studies.

Keywords: Admission Control and Scheduling, Quality of Service, Video Server, Continuous Media

1 Introduction

1.1 Motivation

The goal of conventional disk scheduling policies is to reduce the cost of seek operations and to achieve a high throughput, while providing fair access to every process that seeks its services. In contrast, the goal of disk scheduling for continuous media (CM) is to meet the deadlines of the periodic I/O requests generated by the stream manager to meet rate requirements. An additional goal is to minimize buffer requirements. In order to ensure continuous and stringent real-time constraints of video delivery in CM servers [4, 13], several factors such as disk bandwidth, buffer capacity, network bandwidth, etc., should be considered carefully and should be handled efficiently. The reservations of these resource factors are required for supporting an acceptable level of display quality and for providing on-time delivery constraints. In particular, disk bandwidth constraint may be the most important factor, given that the I/O bandwidth reserved for each stream on disk depends on latency overhead time, transfer time, defined cycle length, and contention of multiple streams. Hence, we should be able to guarantee that the request of each stream can be fairly supported with good disk utilization and server cost-performance. A video stream being viewed requires timely delivery of data, but it is able to tolerate some loss of the data for small amounts of time. Thus, an acceptable method of degrading service quality is simply to reduce the requested resources of CM applications. The idea of achieving higher utilization by introducing *soft-QoS* is not novel in the networking field. There are several references [2, 11] that study soft-QoS provision in

---

*This work is supported by Army Research Lab number DA/DAKF11-98-9-0359 to the University of Minnesota.

broadband networks for video traffic and its impact on network utilization. The problem here is dual (i.e., admission control and disk I/O bandwidth management in CM server systems) to that of network call admission control and dynamic bandwidth management.

To handle these issues in CM server systems, we propose a dynamic and adaptive admission control strategy which achieves better performance than the conventional greedy admission control strategies generally used for CM servers. It recognizes that CM (e.g., video) applications can tolerate certain variations on QoS parameters. It develops an algorithm for sharing processing resources at the server to share available resources effectively among contending streams. The proposed algorithm provisions are for *reclamation* (i.e., scheduler-initiated negotiation) to reallocate resources among streams to improve overall the QoS.

1.2 Research Contributions

According to the evaluation of a human's perception on video and audio [20], up to 23% of aggregate video loss and 21% of aggregate audio loss are tolerable. The acceptable values for consecutive loss of both video and audio are approximately 2 Logical Data Units (LDU). Up to about 20% of video and 7% of audio rate variations are tolerable. Henceforth, using this fact, we could *restrict and steal* some resources of running streams, and give them to the other new input requests, based on the logged information and the status of remaining resources given by our admission control algorithm, without causing any perceptible changes for users. It is a reasonable requirement for the CM server to guarantee the given QoS parameters. When the load of CM server is low, it is possible to meet this requirement. But when the number of concurrent CM streams increases in the CM server, it becomes difficult to guarantee all the QoS parameters. Given certain resources, we want to support as many CM streams whose QoS parameters are all acceptable as possible. Furthermore, as more and more clients require CM streams, the QoS of CM server will degrade. It is a good choice

to make it degrade gracefully. To guarantee that each client is served with some reasonable quality, admission control is also necessary.

In this paper, we present a dynamic/adaptive admission control strategy for providing a fair scheduling and better performance for video streaming. It efficiently services multiple clients simultaneously and satisfies the real-time requirement for continuous delivery of video streaming at specified bandwidths in distributed environments. This new stream scheduler provides a proficient admission control functionality which can optimize disk utilization with a good response ratio for the requests of clients; in particular, under heavy loaded traffic environments. It still presents similar levels of stream qualities (how well the requested rate is attained in CM servers) compared to the basic greedy admission control algorithm. We will present the comparison of the simulation result on the behavior of conventional greedy admission control mechanisms with that of our admission control and scheduling algorithm.

The rest of this paper is organized as follows. In Section 2, we briefly describe an assumed CM server architecture and the admission control constraints (I/O bandwidth requirement and buffer constraint). The detailed description of our admission control and scheduling algorithm is presented in Section 3. Section 4 gives the quantitative results of experimental evaluations, and describes experimental designs and parameters. Section 5 describes the related work, and finally concluding remarks and on-going work appear in Section 6.

2 Architecture of CM Server

The CM server system is a typical *client/server* application. It is based on several file systems: for example, the *Presto File System (PFS)* [10] and the *Unix file system (UFS)*. The core part of the *CM server* involves the *network manager*, the *QoS manager*, *I/O managers*, and *proxy servers*. These sub-modules in the CM server are threads running in a single process More details of the architecture of CM server system where the admission decision is made, can be found in [7, 9]. The admission control for input CM streams is managed by the *QoS Manager*, which is composed of the *Admission Controller* and the *QoS Handler*. The Admission Controller provides two constraint tests: (1) I/O bandwidth test; and (2) available buffer test. Each request (stream) arrives with some *rate* value (e.g., playing-back rate : i.e., frames per second) and the Admission Controller determines whether to admit it or not. The QoS Handler takes care of data rate handling according to a rate input parameter provided by the client's request. In case the playing time gets delayed due to some kind of system overhead, this module will drop some frames properly so as to keep the data rate.

2.1 Basic Conditions of Admission Control

Every time either (1) a new client's request arrives; (2) a rate control operation (such as *Set_Rate, Pause, Resume,* and *Fast_Forward*) is received; (3) the playing of a running stream is over; or (4) when the resources in the reserves are not used for some time, the following constraint must be checked for admission control requirement.

$$\left(t_s + \sum_{i=1}^{n+1} \lceil \frac{T_{svc} \cdot r_i}{b} \rceil \cdot t_r \right) + \sum_{i=1}^{n+1} \frac{T_{svc} \cdot r_i}{R} \leq T_{svc} \quad (1)$$

i.e., latency overhead time(= seek time + rotational latency) + transfer time ≤ cycle length

where, t_s: seek time (msec); T_{svc}: cycle length (msec); r_i: consumption rate (Byte/msec); b: disk block size (Byte); t_r: rotation time (msec); and R: transfer rate (Byte/msec).

The first element (t_s) explains that the maximum disk seek latency overhead in a cycle. The second component shows the sum of each rotational latency incurred for retrieving each disk block (for each request r_i) in a given cycle length (T_{svc}). The last component describes the time to transfer r_i during a cycle. Finally, the overall time for disk access time in a given cycle length must be done in the service cycle length (T_{svc}).

Since we only consider the I/O bandwidth constraint in this paper, we do not present the details of the constraint of buffer requirement here.

3 Adaptive Disk Scheduling

Most of the existing admission control approaches are purely greedy strategy in the sense that a new application (video stream) can be accepted only if the server could give the client all the requested resources [1, 18]. These approaches are too conservative and admit too few streams, thereby under-utilizing the server resources. Although probabilistic methods exist to amortize the cost of this failure, this is undesirable in general [12].

We propose an enhanced admission control algorithm ($\mathcal{RAC}$: *Reserve-based Admission Control Algorithm*) in that it is capable of readjusting resources according to the amount of remaining resources. The key idea here is to assign a portion of the resources as the reserves, and when the applications start to dip into the reserves, another strategy is invoked. In heavy loaded traffic (when a fairly large number of client requests want services; for example, the total disk bandwidth utilization gets over 70%), if the remaining available resources become smaller than some value (**threshold:** $T_{reserve}$), we assign only some portion of the requested resources to the new requests according to the **done_ratio** and *available resources*. For the degraded streams to adapt based on the availability of resource, **resource-negotiation** is required. *Resource-negotiation (reclamation)* occurs under these circumstances: (1) when a running request returns the resources back to the system; (2) when *set_rate* video functions, such as *Fast_Forward*, are received, or (3) after some period elapses without any further resources being used. Table 1 describes the attributes used in the algorithms.

3.1 $\mathcal{RAC}$ Algorithm

The key advantage of the basic greedy strategy is that it is simple. However, due to the other shortcomings of basic greedy admission control

Attributes	Descriptions
s_i	stream i
q_i	initially requested resource of s_i
v_i	currently serviced resource of s_i := $q_i \star d_i$
$\mathcal{RS}$	set of all the running streams : $\bigcup_i s_i$, where $\{s_i \mid F_{min,i} < d_i \leq 1.0\}$
$\mathcal{DS}$	set of degraded streams : $\mathcal{RS} - \bigcup_i s_i$, where $\{s_i \mid d_i = 1.0\}$
s_{min}	stream j of which d_j is smallest in $\mathcal{DS}$: $s_{min} = \{s_j \mid \forall_{s_j,s_k \in \mathcal{DS}} d_j \leq d_k\}$
m	number of streams in $\mathcal{RS}$
$done\_ratio$	ratio of serviced resource to requested resource for a stream
$remaining\_ratio$	ratio of resource yet serviced to requested resource for a stream: (= $1.0 - done\_ratio$)
$remaining\_rate_i$	amount of resource which is yet serviced in stream i : (= $q_i - v_i$)
sum_rem_ratio	total sum of remaining_ratio of degraded streams : $\sum_k e_k$, where $s_k \in \mathcal{DS}$
MIN_FRACT	minimum amount of resource to be assigned for a stream
$MIN\_RESERVE$	minimum amount of reserve which must be at least maintained in $\mathcal{DRA}$ mode
d_i	done_ratio of s_i
e_i	remaining_ratio of s_i : (= $1.0 - d_i$)
$F_{min,i}$	MIN_FRACT of s_i
T_{total}	total available resources initially given
$T_{reserve}$	amount of resources assigned to the reserve
T_{free_res}	available resources in Reserve
$T_{free\_non\_res}$	available resources outside Reserve
T_{alloc}	allocated resources to the requesting stream
T_{avail}	available resources to assign: (= $T_{total} - T_{used}$)
T_{used}	total resources currently used : $\sum_i v_i$, where $s_i \in \mathcal{RS}$
$\Psi(T_{free\_res})$	heuristic function for reserve assignment in *Admission Test* : e.g. $\frac{T_{free\_res}}{k}$, where $k = k_1^{(T_{used}-T_{reserve}) \cdot k_2}$
$\Phi(T_{free\_res})$	heuristic function for reserve assignment on *Close of streams* : e.g. $\frac{T_{free\_res}}{k}$, where $k = k_3 \cdot (T_{used} - T_{reserve}) + 1$
$congestBit$	bit flag to indicate congested state : $\begin{cases} 1 & \text{if } T_{used} > T_{total} - T_{reserve} \\ 0 & \text{otherwise} \end{cases}$
$\mathcal{SU}(t)$	total system utilization defined by $\sum_k d_k$, where $\forall_k s_k \in \mathcal{RS}$ at time t
$\mathcal{QT}(t)$	total video quality defined by $\mathcal{SU}(t)/m$ at time t

Table 1: Attributes Used in Algorithm

algorithms, we should be able to think of another strategy to allow more streams to run concurrently in the continuous media servers by degrading the requested quality of newly arriving streams and by adapting the returned resources to these streams. Given the average seek time (t_s), cycle length (T_{svc}), disk block size (b), rotation time (t_r), and disk transfer rate (R), the consumption rate of each client request (q_i) is a variable in the I/O bandwidth constraint equation (Eq. 1). We initialize the total available rate (T_{avail}) with $T_{svc}(= T_{total})$, and set $T_{reserve}$ (the **threshold** value for criteria to check *congested_bit*). Initially the *congested_bit* is 0 (not congested). The resource (here I/O bandwidth) is **congested** if the resource usage (T_{used}) is more than (T_{svc} - $T_{reserve}$). We can set the $T_{reserve}$ amount of resources for admitting more requests at a reduced quality. Here, $T_{usage} + T_{avail} = T_{svc}$. That is, the *congested_bit* is set (= 1) only when T_{avail} becomes smaller than $T_{reserve}$; otherwise, the basic I/O bandwidth constraint is just applied (i.e., the new request is admitted without being degraded). Under the *congested_bit* being set, we restrict the amount of assignment of resources to the new request because there is no sufficient resource remaining any longer). We explain the details in the following:

1. On adding the request q_i, if the resource remains uncongested, then admit it with no degradation.
   $$T_{alloc} = q_i.$$

2. Let the current usage be T_{used}; then, adding the application q_i will increase the usage to ($T_{new} = T_{used} + q_i$). If ($T_{new} \geq T_{svc} - T_{reserve}$); then, adding q_i will make the resource congested. When the resource gets congested, we have to dip into the resources.
   $$T_{free\_res} = \max(0, T_{svc} - T_{reserve} - T_{used}).$$
   This is the unused resource outside the reserves.
   Let T_{avail} be the amount of resources in the reserves.
   $$T_{free\_res} = \min(T_{reserve}, (T_{svc} - T_{used})).$$
   The new application is allocated, and then
   $$T_{alloc} = T_{free\_res} + \min(\ (q_i - T_{free\_res}), \Psi(T_{free\_res})).$$
   That is, we allocate the resources that are outside the reserves and, in addition, we give a maximum $\Psi(T_{free\_res})$ of the resources in the reserves. $\Psi(.)$ is a function of T_{free_res} and returns an appropriate amount of resources according to T_{free_res}.

3. If $\Psi(T_{free\_res})$ is too small (in this case, we had better not support the new request because display quality may be too poor), we simply reject the request.

4. If the running stream (s_k) is over, then the resource v_i is reclaimed. We return the resource occupied by the stream and adjust (if required) the resource allocation of streams not being fully serviced. Here the unused resource is allocated to applications such that the least serviced streams could get the returned resource first.

5. **Negotiation (Reclamation) algorithm**: we have implemented two heuristic-based methods ($\mathcal{DRA}$ and $\mathcal{RWR}$) and tested their performance.

6. *Dynamic Reserve Adaptation ($\mathcal{DRA}$)*: this is invoked only if there are applications that need resources and do not have them. On departure of streams, $\mathcal{DRA}$ returns the assigned resources to the leaving streams (q_i) back to the available resource pool and re-calculates the new T_{avail} using the total available resource (i.e. old $T_{avail} + q_i$). Among the requests that are not fully serviced yet, we select a request (s_{min}) from the queue ($\mathcal{DS}$), whose *done_ratio* is the smallest first, and assign the proper resource to the request. The **maximum** $\Phi(T_{free\_res})$**-rule** applies here.
   Assign $T_{alloc} = \min (\Phi(T_{free\_res})$, remaining_rate$_{min}$) to the selected request (s_{min}).
   The loop continues until there is no more available resource to assign or T_{alloc} is too small to assign.

7. *Reclamation within Returned Reserve ($\mathcal{RWR}$)*: this is a similar method to the Dynamic Reserve Adaptation method, but the difference is that it redistributes the only resources returned from the leaving streams (v_i). In $\mathcal{DRA}$, we used T_{avail} (instead of v_i) for reclamation. The T_{alloc} per stream is calculated according to the ratio of *remaining_ratio* to *sum_remaining_ratio*.
$$T_{alloc} = T_{avail} * (remaining\_ratio_k / sum\_remaining\_ratio)$$
The key idea here is not to touch the reserves, but to utilize the only returned resource due to the departure of streams. We will validate the better performance of this policy compared to that of $\mathcal{DRA}$.

8. When the resources in the reserves are not used for a long time, some of it is reclaimed. For every k period, if there is no request to the reserve, then we release some amount of the reserve to be reclaimed. This is kind of a *reserve adaptation* method.

We present the algorithm (*Reserve-based Admission Control and Scheduling Algorithm* ($\mathcal{RAC}$)) here.

Algorithm 1 $\mathcal{RAC}$ ($T_{reserve}$, event E_i)

```
        ▷ Reserves-based Admission Control
        ▷ E_i = {(START, q_i), (CLOSE, v_i)}
 1  switch EVENT of
 2    case "START" :
 3      if (! congested) then
            ▷ Admit the application with no degradation
 4        T_alloc ← q_i;
 5        T_used ← T_used + q_i;
 6      else /* congested */
 7        if ( Ψ(T_free_res) > MIN_FRACT ) then
              ▷ Admit at a lower quality
 8          T_alloc ← min( Ψ(T_free_res), q_i ) /* ∈ (0, q_i) */
 9          T_used ← T_used + T_alloc;
10          degraded = 1;
11        else
              ▷ too small to admit
12          Reject s_i;
13    case "CLOSE" :
          ▷ with parameters of appl_inst_ID
14      if (degraded)
            ▷ add back resource v_i to our count
15        T_used = T_used − v_i;
16      switch MODE of
17        case "DRA" :
              ▷ resource v_i + T_avail is reclaimed to distribute
                it to the degraded application instances
18          T_avail ← T_total − T_used;
19          while (1) do
20            s_min ← Select a request of which done_ratio
                is the smallest;
21            if (Φ(T_free_res) > MIN_RESERVE) then
22              T_alloc = min (Φ(T_free_res), remain-
                  ing_rate_min);
23              T_used ← T_used - T_alloc;
24          end while
25        case "RWR" :
              ▷ resource v_i is reclaimed to distribute it to
                the degraded application instances
26          T_avail = v_i;
27          sum_remaining_ratio = Σ_k remaining_ratio_k ;
28          for (each degraded application k) do
29            T_alloc = T_avail *
                  (remaining_ratio_k / sum_remaining_ratio);
30            T_used ← T_used − T_alloc;
31          end for
32      end switch
33  end switch
```

4   Experimental Evaluation

We performed extensive simulation to validate our admission control and scheduling algorithm. In this section, we present the performance results obtained from simulations under the various load conditions. For results presented in this section, we simulated an environment: i.e., a Sun Ultra Sparcstation with a Seagate Barracuda 4GB disk (ST34371N). The details of the simulation parameters can be found in [8].

4.1 Experiment Design

We simulate the situation where the applications with soft-QoS requirements arrive at the system in an arbitrary order. The applications also come with a play-out rate (which maps into an amount of required resource), depending on the user profile and the data content, which is a value of the data rate parameters. The applications arrive based on a Poisson process with an average inter-arrival rate (λ). The duration of the applications is described using a Gaussian process with the mean (μ_d) and the standard deviation (σ_d) of the distribution. The admission control and scheduling algorithm is tried on each one of the application traffic traces. We measure the following: (1) *Accumulated number of admitted streams over time*; (2) *Total system utilization*; (3) *Total quality*; and (4) *Admission ratio*. For our simulation, we made various application load traffic sequences and different application load conditions, and chose the following two distributions: *Heavy traffic* is generated by setting $\lambda = 0.333$, $\mu_d = 90$, and $\sigma_d = 3.5$. *Medium traffic* is generated by having $\lambda = 0.125$, $\mu_d = 60$, and $\sigma_d = 3.5$. The values on the x-axis are normalized. Under the heavy traffic, the resource demands arrive more frequently than under the medium traffic.

4.2 Experiment 1: Number of Admitted Streams

The major advantage of the $\mathcal{RAC}$ is its guaranteeing more numbers of streams to be admitted and to run simultaneously with a tolerable degradation of quality. As shown in Figure 1, under traffic loads that demand more than the available resources, the accumulated occurrences of admission decreases (rejection increases), both in the basic method and in our strategy. The heavier the traffic is, the better performance the $\mathcal{RAC}$ algorithm achieves compared to the basic greedy algorithm (as shown in Figure 1(a)). In another point of view, the $\mathcal{RWR}$ algorithm achieves a 200 ~ 300% increase in the number of streams that can be serviced simultaneously by the server. In case of the $\mathcal{DRA}$ algorithm, it also achieves about a 100% increase. In other words,

our $\mathcal{RAC}$ algorithm (both $\mathcal{RWR}$ and $\mathcal{DRA}$) noticeably reduces the rejection ratio compared to the basic greedy method.

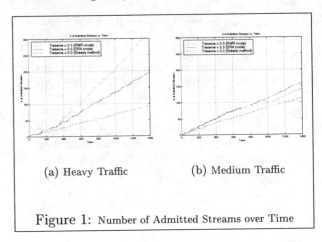

(a) Heavy Traffic   (b) Medium Traffic

Figure 1: Number of Admitted Streams over Time

4.3 Experiment 2: System Utilization and Total Quality

In this section, we mainly focus on visualizing the effect of the $\mathcal{RAC}$ algorithm with respect to total system utilization and display quality. Figure 2 plots the total system utilization that is achieved by the sum of each application's *done_ratio*. It is observed that the total system utilization achieved by $\mathcal{RWR}$ is much higher during most of the period. Hence, the $\mathcal{RWR}$ algorithm is able to utilize the system resources more efficiently than the greedy algorithm.

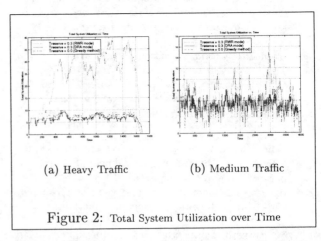

(a) Heavy Traffic   (b) Medium Traffic

Figure 2: Total System Utilization over Time

To investigate the display quality of the $\mathcal{RAC}$ algorithm, we plot another curve. Figure 3 illustrates the total quality which is quantified by dividing the sum of each application's done_ratio by the number of current running streams. It is observed that the total quality achieved by the $\mathcal{RWR}$ algorithm is almost the same as that achieved by the greedy algorithm. In contrast, the performance of $\mathcal{DRA}$ algorithm in total quality is kind of low most of the time. This arises due to the fact that the $\mathcal{DRA}$ algorithm holds off the reserves for future streams, which arrive soon before some of the current running streams depart. Under medium traffic, though the performance of $\mathcal{DRA}$ gets better, it is still too low.

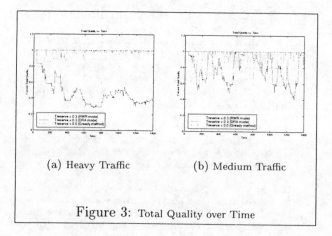

(a) Heavy Traffic   (b) Medium Traffic

Figure 3: Total Quality over Time

4.4 Experiment 3: Admission Ratio

Under the heavy load, $\mathcal{RWR}$ achieves the best admission ratio (a $150 \sim 250\%$ increase), and $\mathcal{DRA}$ achieves the next (about 100% increase). Under the medium load, the increase rates of the two $\mathcal{RAC}$ methods are decreased compared to under the heavy load. Unlike the heavy load, the $\mathcal{DRA}$ method achieves even better performance than $\mathcal{RWR}$. This is because when the traffic load is not too heavy, $\mathcal{DRA}$ is able to utilize the resources more efficiently by taking off some resources from the reserves. The probability of reserves running out under medium/light loads is smaller than that under the heavy load. However, we can observe that the $\mathcal{RAC}$ (both $\mathcal{RWR}$ and $\mathcal{DRA}$) strategy noticeably increases the admission ratio compared to the greedy method. Degradation makes the applications use a lower (but fully reasonable due to the properties of CM) amount of resources; therefore, more ap-

plications can be supported on the resource.

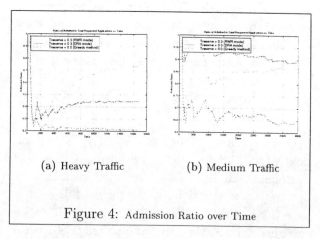

(a) Heavy Traffic   (b) Medium Traffic

Figure 4: Admission Ratio over Time

5 Related Work

Several techniques for the admission controlling of continuous media have been proposed in the literature. Ensuring continuous retrieval of each strand requires that the service time not exceed the minimum of playback durations of the blocks retrieved for each strand during a round, which is a typical greedy admission control strategy [5, 19]. Usually the simple admission control decisions are based on the **worst case** scenario. The worst case policy is based on the observation that multimedia traffic is characterized by its bursty nature; therefore, if sufficient resources are not available for the worst case scenario, then the applications may fail [16]. Similar admission control based on the worst case analysis of the application stream has been formulated by other researchers [14, 15, 3].

To improve the resource utilization, predictive (observation-based) admission control algorithms for clients have been suggested [17]. It simply uses the average amount of time spent in retrieving a media block instead of the worst-case assumptions Vin et al. [18] described a statistical admission control algorithm in which new clients are admitted for service as long as the statistical estimation of the aggregate data rate requirement, rather than the corresponding peak data rate requirement, can be met by the server, They improve the utilization of server resources by exploiting the variation in the disk access times of media blocks, as well as by exploiting the variation in playback rate requirement by variable rate compression techniques. Statistically they are safe but in the worst case it may cause applications to fail because of resource congestion.

6 Concluding Remarks

We presented an integrated adaptive admission control and scheduling algorithm for CM server systems. We have also presented results of a simulation evaluation of our algorithm and a greedy algorithm with respect to several metrics designed to measure the admission ratio, total quality, and system utilization. It was observed that under heavy traffic, our algorithm achieves much better performance than the greedy algorithm. Using our scheme, we could expect that more streams could be running with an acceptable range of data quality in a given system resource. Our ongoing [6] and future work include extending the QoS metrics considered in our algorithm to multi-dimensional ones (e.g., frame size, buffer requirement, compression quality factor, scalability, network bandwidth, etc.).

References

[1] F. T. Ernst W. Biersack. Statistical Admission Control in Video Servers with Constant Data Length Retrieval of VBR Streams. In *Third International Conference on Multimedia Modeling*, Toulouse, France, Nov 1996.

[2] J. W. G. de Veciana, G. Kesidis. Resource Management in Wide-Area ATM Networks Using Effective Bandwidths. *IEEE Journal on Selected Areas in Communication*, 13(6):1081–1090, Aug 1995.

[3] D. Gemmell and S. Christodoulakis. Principles of Delay Sensitive Multimedia Data Storage and Retrieval. *ACM Trans. Information Systems*, 10(1):51–90, 1992.

[4] R. Haskin and F. Schmuck. The Tiger Shark File System. In *COMPCON 96*, 1996.

[5] S. W. Lau and J. C. S. Lui. A Novel Video-On-Demand Storage Architecture for Supporting Constant Frame Rate with Variable Bit Rate Retrieval. In *5th International Workshop on Network and Operating Systems Support for Digital Audio and Video*, Durham, N.H. , 1995.

[6] W. Lee and B. Sabata. Admission Control and QoS Negotiations for Soft-Real Time Applications. In *Proceedings of the IEEE International Conference on Multimedia Computing and Systems (ICMCS'99)*, Florence, Italy, June 1999.

[7] W. Lee and J. Srivastava. CORBA Evaluation of Video Streaming wrt QoS Provisioning. In *Proceedings of the Workshop on Multimedia Networking held in conjunction with the 17th IEEE Symposium on Reliable Distributed Systems (SRDS '98)*, West Lafayette, Indiana, October 1998.

[8] W. Lee and J. Srivastava. Dynamic/Adaptive Algorithms for Admission Control and Scheduling of Video Servers. *Submitted for publication in IEEE Transactions on Computers*, 1999.

[9] W. Lee, D. Su, and J. Srivastava. QoS-based Evaluation of File Systems and Distributed System Services for Continuous Media Provisioning. *To appear in Information and Software Technology, Elsevier Science*, 1999.

[10] W. Lee, D. Su, J. Srivastava, D. Kenchammana-hosekote, and D. Wijesekera. Experimental Evaluation of PFS Continuous Media File System. In *6th ACM Int'l Conf. on Information and Knowledge Management (CIKM '97)*, November 1997.

[11] D. M. Grossglauser. Measurement-Based Call Admission Control: Algorithms and Analysis. In *IEEE INFCOM'97*, April 1997.

[12] D. Makaroff, G. Neufeld, and N. Hutchinson. An Evaluation of VBR Disk Admission Algorithms for Continuous media File Servers. In *Proceedings of the ACM Multimedia Conference*, Seattle, Wa, Dec 1997.

[13] C. Martin, P. S. Narayanan, B. Ozden, R. Rastogi, and A. Silberschatz. The Fellini Multimedia Storage Server. In S. M. Chung, editor, *Multimedia Information Sotrage and Management*. Kluwer Academic Publishers, 1996.

[14] P. V. Rangan and H. M. Vin. Designing a Multiuser HDTV Storage Server. *IEEE Journal on Seleted Areas in Communications*, 11(1):153–164, January 1993.

[15] A. Reddy and J. Wyllie. I/O Issues in a Multimedia System. *Computer*, 27(3):69–74, 1994.

[16] S. K. T. S.V.Raghavan. *Networked Multimedia Systems: Concepts, Architecture, and Design*. Prentice Hall, 1998.

[17] H. M. Vin, A. Goyal, , P. Goyal, and A. Goyal. An Observation-Based Approach for Designing Multimedia Servers. In *Proceedings of the IEEE International Conference on Multimedia Computing and Systems*, Boston, MA, May 1994.

[18] H. M. Vin, P. Goyal, A. Goyal, and A. Goyal. A Statistical Admission Control Algorithm for Multimedia Servers. In *Proceedings of ACM Multimedia '94)*, San Francisco, October 1994.

[19] H. M. Vin and P. V. Rangan. Admission Control Algorithms for Multimedia On-Demand Servers. In *3rd International Workshop on Network and Operating Systems Support for Digital Audio and Video*, 1992.

[20] D. Wijesekera and J. Srivastava. Experimental Evaluation of Loss Perception in Continuous Media. *to appear in ACM Springer Multimedia Systems Journal*, 1999.

Solving Temporal Constraint Networks with Qualitative Reasoning and Fuzzy Rules

Timothy K. Shih and Anthony Y. Chang
Department of Computer Science and Information Engineering
Tamkang University
Tamsui,Taiwan
R.O.C.
email: tshih@cs.tku.edu.tw
g5190315@tkgis.tku.edu.tw
fax: Intl. (02) 620 9749

Abstract

Constraint satisfaction techniques play an important role in current computer science. Many difficult problems involving search from areas such as machine vision, scheduling, graph algorithms, machine design, and manufacturing can be considered to be the cases of the constraint satisfaction problem. In this paper, we construct a Infinite Temporal Interval Group for temporal constraint propagation. This interval algebra is also extended for spatial constraint reasoning. We develop an O(n)-time algorithm for propagation temporal constraint between two time events. For solving point/interval algebra networks, we develop an $O(n^2)$-time algorithm for finding all pairs of feasible relations, where n is the number of points or intervals. A set of algorithms is proposed to manage spatio-temporal knowledge.

1 Introduction

Relations among temporal intervals can be used to model time dependent objects. The extension of temporal relation results in many researches related to the spatio-temporal modeling of symbolic objects.

We use the qualitative representation to composite the spatio-temporal relations, since humans are not very good at determining exact object lengths, volumes, etc., whereas they can easily perform context-dependent comparisons. For example, given the relations between objects X and Y, and between objects Y and Z, we want to know the relation between X and Z. If specify "X is left_below to Y" and "Y is left_close to Z", we can derived the relations implies "X is left_below to Z".

The importance of knowledge underlying temporal interval relations was found in many disciplines. As pointed out in [1], researchers of artificial intelligence, linguistics, and information science use temporal intervals as a time model for knowledge analysis. This research contribution has been used in many temporal modeling of multimedia systems including ours [2, 10, 11]. However, the work [1] only states temporal interval relations. No spatial relation was discussed. We found that these relations can be generalized for spatial modeling.

Many researchers propose temporal/spatial modeling of object representations. The authors also defined spatial events in terms of these n-ary relations. Temporal events were then specified in terms of these spatial events. However, there was no discussion of the conflict situation among relations. Based on Allen's temporal interval relations, a set of directional and topological spatial relations was addressed in [7]. The authors also provided a set of spatial inference rules for automatic deduction. A methodology for spatial and temporal object composition was proposed in [8]. A set of n-ary temporal relations with their temporal constraints were discussed in [9], which is an early result of the work addressed in [3]. The temporal model of reverse play and partial interval evaluation for midpoint suspension and resumption were also discussed. Algorithms for accessing objects in a database were presented. However, no discussion of

371

the conflict situation among relations was found. Efficient indexing schemes based on the R-tree spatial data structure were proposed in [12]. The mechanism handles 1-D and 2-D objects, as well as 3-D objects, which treat a time line as the third axis. The discussion in [4] identified various temporal interaction forms and discussed their temporal dependencies.

The use of spatio-temporal relations can serve as a reasonable semantic tool for the underlying representation of objects in many applications. Composite objects can have arbitrary timing relationships. In this paper, we extend the interval relations by means of a complete analysis of all temporal relation domains and constraint reasoning. These domains are also extended for spatial computation.

2 Reasoning with Composed Endpoint Relations

Timeline representations assume that whenever something happens a time can be assigned to it. Fundamental to this capability is the idea of a timestamp, which associates temporal domain values with events or objects being described. Timeline representations are the mainstay of time-oriented databases, which are useful in applications where times can be assigned to every event.

While quantitative timeline approaches are useful in which exact data is available, they have some drawbacks. Due to the very nature of quantitative approach, when a value is not known exactly, it has to be either ignored or assigned a range of possible values. Humans are not very good at determine exact values, whereas they can easily perform content-dependent comparisons. For some tasks, all that matters is a qualitative metric such as the ordering of events in time. For such reasoning it is enough to answer which event comes first.

The value of a quantitative variable specifies only one element in the set of possible values. If the set is the entire real number timeline, a value represents a specific time point. On the other hand, the value of a qualitative variable can represent an element as well as a set of elements.

Qualitative calculus is calculus of intervals instead of real numbers. To deal with qualitative representation, we subdivide the real number in timeline into three intervals: $[-\infty, 0]$, $[0, 0]$ and $[0, +\infty]$. We denote these three intervals by $\{<\}$, $\{=\}$ and $\{>\}$ for representing relation between two points. The notation R1 and R2 denotes the point relations over three points A, B, and C which A R1 B and B R2 C. The meaning of some qualitative operators are defined

as follows. Note that some values are uncertain and denoted by T.

Table 1: Addition: R1 + R2

R1 \ R2	<	=	>
<	<	<	T
=	<	=	>
>	T	>	>

3 The Infinite Temporal Interval Group

Based on qualitative point relations, we use an encoding method to generalize and prove the 13 interval exclusion relations. Suppose A_s and A_e are the starting and ending points of the line segment A. And, B_s and B_e are those of B. We define a binary relation, $\diamond$, (either <, =, or > for "A is before B", "A is the same as B", or "A is after B") of two points. The 13 *interval relations* introduced by Allen make the binary relations hold in the first part of the following table:

Table 2: Starting and Ending Point Relations

As$\diamond$Bs	As$\diamond$Be	Ae$\diamond$Bs	Ae$\diamond$Be	ID	Interval Relations
<	<	<	<	1	{ < }
>	>	>	>	2	{ > }
>	<	>	<	3	{ d }
<	<	>	>	4	{ di }
<	<	>	<	5	{ o }
>	<	>	>	6	{ oi }
<	<	=	<	7	{ m }
>	=	>	>	8	{ mi }
=	<	>	<	9	{ s }
=	<	>	>	10	{ si }
>	<	>	=	11	{ f }
<	<	>	=	12	{ fi }
=	<	>	=	13	{ e }
=	=	>	>	14	{los}
<	<	=	=	15	{loe}
=	<	=	<	16	{ols}
>	=	>	=	17	{ole}
=	=	=	=	18	{oo}

The second part of the table has five special cases for *point-interval relations*. For instance, we use *A 10s B* to represent A is a line and B is a point (i.e., the starting and the ending points are located at the same position), where A and B meets at the starting point of A (see figure 1). These five special cases were not considered in [1]. The situations of points of two line segments could have unto $3^4 = 81$ rows in the above table. However, except for the 18 cases illustrated in Figure 1, others are conflict situations (i.e., it is physically impossible for the situation to occur). For example, a relation ($As < Bs$, $As < Be$, $Ae > Bs$, $Ae < Be$) has conflict between four point relations.

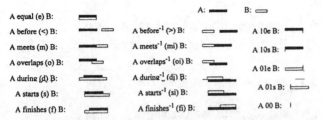

Figure 1: Extended Interval Relations (Interval and point-interval Relations)

Based on Allen's work, compositions of three or more relations are computed using algorithms based on set operations, such as set union and intersection. These set operations are expensive. We argue that, an extension of *Table13* [1], named *Table29*[14], can be calculated. The compositions of three or more relations can be obtained directly from our table. Based on the *Table29*, we found many properties of spatio-temporal relations and proved the temporal relation composition is a algebraic *group*[14].

4   Temporal Constraint Network

Based on *Table29*, we propose a set of algorithms, using a directed graph, for fast temporal relation compositions. These algorithms can be used to compute the binary relation between an arbitrary pair of intervals. User edge conflicts are eliminated and derived edges and cycles without conflict are added. This conflict elimination is achieved by invoking the *EliminateConflict* algorithm. Suppose G is a graph of the reduce relation domain, and GV and GE are the vertex set and edge set of G, respectively. The algorithm computes derived edges based on user edges.

Algorithm : *ComputeRD1*
Input : $G = (GV, GE)$
Output: $K_n = (K_nV, K_nE)$
Preconditions : true
Postconditions : $GV = K_nV \wedge GE \setminus UE \cup UE' \subseteq K_nE$
Steps :
1 : $G = EliminateConflicts (G)$
2 : $K_n = G \wedge pl = 2$
3 :   repeat until $| K_nE | = | K_nV | * (| K_nV | -1) / 2$
    3.1 : for each $e = (a, b)$ $\wedge$ $e \notin K_nE$ $\wedge$ $a \in K_nV$ $\wedge$ $b \in K_nV \bullet$
    there is a path of user edges from a to b, with path length $= pl$
    3.2 : suppose $((n_1, n_2), (n_2, n_3),..., (n_{k-1}, n_k))$

is a path with $a = n$ $\wedge$ $b = n$ $\wedge$ $k = pl + 1$
3.3 : set $e.rs = Table29 ((a, n_{k-1}).rs, (n_{k-1}, b).rs)$
3.4 : $K_nE = K_nE \cup \{ e \}$
3.5 : $pl = pl + 1$

The first algorithm, *ComputeRD1*, starts from taking each path of user edges of length 2, and computes a derived edge from that path. The insertion of edge $e = (a, b)$ results a cycle, but no conflict. The reasonable set of edge e (i.e., $e.rs$) is computed from two edges, (a, n_{k-1}) and (n_{k-1}, b), which are user edges or derived edges. Since we increase the path length, pl, of the path of user edges one by one. The derived edge (a, n_{k-1}) must have been computed in a previous interaction. The algorithm repeats until all edges are added to the complete graph K_n.

Algorithm : *EliminateConflicts*
Input : $G = (GV, GE)$
Output : $G' = (G'V, G'E)$
Preconditions : G contains only user edges $\wedge G' = G$
Postconditions : $G' = G$, but the reasonable sets of edges in G' may be changed.
Steps :
1.   for each $P = ((n_1, n_2), (n_2, n_3),..., (n_{k-1}, n_k))$ in G'
    with $n_1 = n_k$ $\wedge$ $k > 3$
    1.1 : for each i, $1 \leq i \leq k-2$
        1.1.1 : set $(n_i, n_{i+2}).rs = Table29 ((n_i, n_{i+1}).rs, (n_{i+1}, n_{i+2}).rs)$
    1.2 : $rs = Table29 ((n_k, n_{k-2}).rs, (n_{k-2}, n_{k-1}).rs)$
    1.3 : if $(n_k, n_{k-1}).r \notin rs$ then
        1.3.1 : ask user to choose a $r' \in rs$
        1.3.2 : set $(n_k, n_{k-1}).r = r'$

Considering the five user edges, the algorithm computes derived edges until the last edge is added to K_n :

User edges :
  (A, B) = { < } = [1]
  (B, C) = { m } = [7]
  (C, D) = { d } = [3]
  (C, E) = { s } = [9]
  (F, D) = { < } = [1]

Derivation based on user edges:

1. Path Length = 2
  $(A, C) = (A, B) \circ (B, C) = [1] \circ [7] = [1] = \{ < \}$
  $(B, D) = (B, C) \circ (C, D) = [7] \circ [3] = [16] = \{o, d, s \}$
  $(C, F) = (C, D) \circ (D, F) = [3] \circ [1]^{-1} = [3] \circ [2] = \{ > \}$
  $(D, E) = (D, C) \circ (C, E) = [4] \circ [9] = [14] = \{o, di, fi \}$
  $(B, E) = (B, C) \circ (C, E) = [7] \circ [9] = [7] = \{ m \}$

2. Path Length = 3
  $(A, E) = (A, B) \circ (B, C) \circ (C, E) = (A, C) \circ (C, E)$
  $= [1] \circ [9] = [1] = \{ < \}$
  $(A, D) = (A, B) \circ (B, C) \circ (C, D) = (A, C) \circ (C, D)$

$$= [1] \mathbin{\mathbf{o}} [3] = [22] = \{ <, o, m, d, s \}$$
$$(B, F) = (B, C) \mathbin{\mathbf{o}} (C, D) \mathbin{\mathbf{o}} (D, F) = (B, D) \mathbin{\mathbf{o}} (D, F)$$
$$= [16] \quad \mathbin{\mathbf{o}} [1]^{-1} = [23] = \{ >, oi, mi, di, si \}$$
$$(E, F) = (E, C) \mathbin{\mathbf{o}} (C, D) \mathbin{\mathbf{o}} (D, F) = (E, D) \mathbin{\mathbf{o}} (D, F)$$
$$= [14]^{-1} \mathbin{\mathbf{o}} [2] = [15] \mathbin{\mathbf{o}} [2] = [2] = \{ > \}$$

3. Path Length = 4
$$(A, F) = (A, B) \mathbin{\mathbf{o}} (B, C) \mathbin{\mathbf{o}} (C, D) \mathbin{\mathbf{o}} (D, F)$$
$$= ((A, B) \mathbin{\mathbf{o}} (B, C)) \mathbin{\mathbf{o}} ((C, D) \mathbin{\mathbf{o}} (D, F))$$
$$= (A, C) \mathbin{\mathbf{o}} (C, F) = [1] \mathbin{\mathbf{o}} [2] = [29]$$
$$= \{ <, >, d, di, o, oi, m, mi, f, fi, s, si, e \}$$

The restricted relation domain is a tree. The reason for using a tree is to avoid cycles which may introduce conflicts. A distributed system and a multimedia presentation contains a number of objects. When a new object is added to the presentation, an user edge and a node representing the new object is added. A number of derived edges are also inserted. Adding a new node to the complete graph K_n requires adding n new edges, where n is the number of nodes, to complete K_{n+1}. Since a complete graph is strongly connected, there exists an edge between each pair of nodes. When a new user edge is added, we can compute other derived edges from checking the composed relations between an existing edge and this new user edge. Algorithm *AddUERD* adds an user edge $l = (a, b)$ to a complete graph K_n :

Algorithm : *AddUERD*
Input : $l = (a, b)$, $K_n = (K_nV, K_nE)$
Output : $K_{n+1} = (K_{n+1}V, K_{n+1}E)$
Preconditions : $l \notin K_nE \;\land\; a \in K_nV \;\land\; b \notin K_nV$
Postconditions : $|K_{n+1}V| = |K_nV| + 1 \;\land$
$\qquad\qquad\qquad |K_{n+1}E| = |K_nE| + n$
Steps :
  1: $K_{n+1}E = K_nE \cup \{ l \}$
  2: for each $e = (c, b) \;\land\; c \neq a \;\land\; c \in K_nV$
   2.1: $e.rs = \cap \; \forall \, d \in K_nV, (c, d) \in K_nE, (d, b) \in K_nE$
     $(Table29((c, d).rs, (d, b).rs))$
   2.2: $K_{n+1}E = K_{n+1}E \cup \{e\}$
  3: $K_{n+1}V = K_nV \cup \{ b \}$

Considering an example as follow, if we add an user edges toaccording to the complete graph K_6 , the derived edges are computed :

Adding an user edge:
  Add $(G, E) = \{ f \} = [11]$

Derived edges :

Derive $(E, G) = (G, E)^{-1} = [11]^{-1} = [12] = \{ fi \}$
Derive $(A, G) = (A, E) \mathbin{\mathbf{o}} (E, G) = [1] \mathbin{\mathbf{o}} [12]$
$\qquad\qquad = [1] = \{ < \}$
Derive $(B, G) = (B, E) \mathbin{\mathbf{o}} (E, G) = [7] \mathbin{\mathbf{o}} [12]$
$\qquad\qquad = [1] = \{ < \}$

Derive $(C, G) = (C, E) \mathbin{\mathbf{o}} (E, G) = [9] \mathbin{\mathbf{o}} [12] = [18]$
$\qquad\qquad = \{ <, o, m \}$
Derive $(D, G) = (D, E) \mathbin{\mathbf{o}} (E, G) = [14] \mathbin{\mathbf{o}} [12]$
$\qquad\qquad = [24] = \{ <, o, m, di, fi \}$
Derive $(F, G) = (F, E) \mathbin{\mathbf{o}} (E, G) = (E, F)^{-1} \mathbin{\mathbf{o}} (E, G)$
$\qquad\qquad = [1] \mathbin{\mathbf{o}} [12] = [1] = \{ < \}$

5 Temporal Neighborhoods and Qualitative Theory of Fuzzy Sets

5.1 Qualitative Temporal Fuzzy Sets

Consider The following example:
There exists interval or instant events X and Y and Z, if " X before Y " and " Y before Z ", then plainly event X has to be before Z. The composition may result in a multiple derivation. For example, if "X before Y " and "Y during Z " , the composed relation for X and Z could be "before", "overlaps", "meets", "during", or "starts".

The example shows that intervals can be used to express inexact knowledge in interval-based event models, and introduce a different issue: temporal uncertainty. Uncertainty processing is a fact of life. With unfuzzified foundations, we can apply both fuzzy and traditional mathematics to real world problems simultaneously, and find consistent solutions.

In general, a set of qualitative equations cannot be solved to obtain a unique solution. The qualitative propagation is inherently ambiguous, as indicated by the many uncertain relations in the qualitative operators. This ambiguity leads to a very large number of possible courses of behavior being predicted as the size of the system becomes large. This means to reduce the ambiguity is to use more quantitative information. To improve qualitative calculus we use qualitative temporal fuzzy set for reasoning.

There are more than one membership functions for a given temporal fuzzy set. Let the membership space T be the unit interval [0,1]. Let F be a membership function.

F: Temporal Relations $\rightarrow$ T = [0,1]

The subset where membership function F taking value α will be given a geometric term, α-level-curve when α is not explicitly given:

$[\alpha] = \{ \; x\colon F(x) = \alpha \; \} = \alpha$-level-curve

There are two special α-level-curves: 1-level-curve and 0-level-curve.

Let 2ε be a smallest time unit atom. A sub-interval in [0, 1] is said to be an ε-neighborhood, if the length of the sub-interval is 2ε (ε is the radius, 2ε is the diameter). A mapping

H: [0, 1] $\rightarrow$ [0, 1]

Is called an ε-homeomorphism.

The temporal neighborhood will be discussed in next section.

5.2 Relational-Distance Computing

In this section we discuss some of the properties that need to be satisfied by spatial similarity functions. Relations are similar to each other in certain degree. For example, "during" and "starts" are similar since the only difference is the starting points of the two intervals are different. However, "before" and the inverse of "meets" are not quite the same.

A *relational-distance* of two relations belong to two different temporal relations occurs if those two temporal relations hold different relations.

Definition 5.1: A *point relation distance* (PRD) defined with respect to a point relation r of index n have n incompatible differences from r. The following table gives a definition of point relation distance:

Table 3: Point Relation Distance (PRD)

PRD	>	=	<
>	0	1	2
=	1	0	1
<	2	1	0

Definition 5.2: An *interval relation distance* (IRD) defined with respect to a interval relation r of index n have n incompatible differences from r. Let R and R' are two interval relations. The encoding point relation of R is $R_{As \cdot Bs}$, $R_{As \cdot Be}$, $R_{Ae \cdot Bs}$, $R_{Ae \cdot Be}$, and the encoding point relation of R' is $R'_{As \cdot Bs}$, $R'_{As \cdot Be}$, $R'_{Ae \cdot Bs}$, $R'_{Ae \cdot Be}$. We have a *IRD* formula:

$$IRD (R, R') = PRD (R_{As \cdot Bs}, R'_{As \cdot Bs}) +$$
$$PRD (R_{As \cdot Be}, R'_{As \cdot Be}) +$$
$$PRD (R_{Ae \cdot Bs}, R'_{Ae \cdot Bs}) +$$
$$PRD (R_{Ae \cdot Be}, R'_{Ae \cdot Be})$$

Table 4: Interval Relation Distance (IRD)

IRD	<	>	d	di	o	oi	m	mi	s	si	f	fi	e
<	0	8	4	4	2	6	1	7	3	5	5	3	4
>	8	0	4	4	6	2	7	1	5	3	3	5	4
d	4	4	0	4	2	2	3	3	1	3	1	3	2
di	4	4	4	0	2	2	3	3	3	1	3	1	2
o	2	6	2	2	0	4	1	5	1	3	3	1	2
oi	6	2	2	2	4	0	5	1	3	1	1	3	2
m	1	7	3	3	1	5	0	6	2	4	4	2	3
mi	7	1	3	3	5	1	6	0	4	2	2	4	3
s	3	5	1	3	1	3	2	4	0	2	2	2	1
si	5	3	3	1	3	1	4	2	2	0	2	2	1
f	5	3	1	3	3	1	4	2	2	2	0	2	1
fi	3	5	3	1	1	3	2	4	2	2	2	0	1

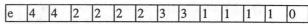

e	4	4	2	2	2	2	3	3	1	1	1	1	0

6 Qualitative Representation of Spatial Knowledge

6.1 Spatial Relation Representation

To analyze a generalized model of spatio-temporal relations, we consider the following situations. Conclusively, the generalized model of temporal/spatial relations include four cases:

- two points on a line
- two points on a plan
- two line segments on a line
- two line segments on a plan
- two 2-D objects on a plan
- two 3-D object project onto x-y, z-x and y-z plans

For an arbitrary pair of points, A and B, located on a 1-dimensional line, there are three *point relations*: $A < B$, $A = B$, or $A > B$, for A is before B, A is at the same position as B, and A is after B, respectively. If these two points are located on a 2-dimensional plan, there exists nine (i.e., 3 * 3) cases. The X and the Y coordinates of these two points on the plan are independent. The possible relations between these two points on a plan can be denoted as A (<, <) B, A (<, =) B, A (<, >) B, A (=, <) B, A (=, =) B, A (=, >) B, A (>, <) B, A (>, =) B, and A (>, >) B, where the first element in the pair representing a point relation denotes the order on the X coordinate while the second is for the Y coordinate.

Considering two line segments on a 2-dimensional plan, according to the above table and since the position of these two line segments are independent at the X and the Y coordinates, there exists $13^2 = 169$ possible relations between these two line segments on a plan. These relations, similar to those of two points on a plan, are denotes by pairs as: (< , <), (< , >), (< , d), (< , di), ..., (00 , 01e), and (00 , 00). We use these 169 binary relations to model spatial point-interval relations of two lines on a plan.

Relations of n-D objects can be used in object representation and recognition. A object in 3-D space can be projected onto y-x, z-x, and y-z planes. The projections correspond to surfaces generated from 3D objects. Similarly, a 2-D object is projected to x and y axes. If we look at two objects in the n-dimensional space, we can project the positional relation between these two objects from n directions to n 1-D space. The projections of 2-D object are x-interval and y-interval, but not the point. Thus, an n-dimensional relation can be formularized by a conjunction of n 1-D interval relations. A conjunction of two 1-D relations, which denotes a 2-D relation, has 13^2 variations, i.e. $\{(<, <), (<, >), (<, d),..., (=, fi), (=, =)\}$ where the first element in the pair representing a interval relation denotes the order on the X coordinate while the second is for the Y coordinate. Similarly, there are 13^3 3-D relations.

The first two cases are trivial and they do not efficiently express intervals. The third case can represent the relations of two temporal intervals. The fourth case is the semantic tool that we rely on to develops shape matching. The fifth and sixth cases can be used for symbolic subsequence matching.

6.2 Spatial Reasoning

In this section, we introduce a mechanism to extend the spatial reasoning of objects to an n-dimensional space.

Let rs denote a set of 1-D temporal interval relations(i.e., $rs \in 29Relset$). The relation composition table discussed in Section 3 can be refined (e.q., make each relation as an atomic set of that relation) to a function maps from the Cartesian product of two rs to a rs. Assuming that f^1 is the mapping function interpreting Allen's table, we can compute f^2, the relation composition function of 2-D objects, and f^3, the one for 3-D objects, from f^1. There are 13 relations for 1-D objects. A conjunction of two 1-D relations, which denotes a 2-D relation, has 13^2 variations. Similarly, there are 13^3 3-D relations. Fortunately, 4-D relations are not quite applicable and the memory space required for 2-D and 3-D relation tables is manageable by nowadays computers.

Since a 2-D relation is conjunction of two 1-D relations, we use the notation, $rs_1 \times rs_2$, to denote a 2-D relation set where rs_1 and rs_2 are two 1-D relation sets. Thus f^2 is a mapping from Cartesian product of two (rs o rs) to an (rs o rs). Similarly f^3 is obtained. The following are signatures of these functions:

$$f^1 = 29RelSet \times 29RelSet \rightarrow 29RelSet$$
$$f^2 = 29RelSet \times 29RelSet \times 29RelSet \times 29RelSet \rightarrow$$
$$29RelSet \times 29RelSet$$
$$f^3 = 29RelSet \times 29RelSet \times 29RelSet \times 29RelSet \times$$
$$29RelSet \times 29RelSet \rightarrow 29RelSet \times 29RelSet \times$$
$$29RelSet$$

where $29RelSet \times 29RelSet \in \{ \{<\} \times \{<\}, \{<\} \times \{>\}, ... , \{=\} \times \{=\} \}$
$29RelSet \times 29RelSet \times 29RelSet \in \{ \{<\}\times\{<\}\times\{<\}, \{<\}\times\{<\}\times\{>\},..., \{=\}\times\{=\}\times\{=\}\}$

Functions f^2 and f^3 are computed according to the following formulas :

$$\forall i_1 \times j_1, i_2 \times j_2 \in P (29RelSet \times 29RelSet)$$

$$f^2 (i_1 \times j_1, i_2 \times j_2) = \prod f^1 (i_1, i_2) \times f^1 (j_1, j_2)$$
$$\forall i_1 \times j_1 \times k_1, i_2 \times j_2 \times k_2 \in P (29RelSet \times 29RelSet \times 29RelSet)$$
$$f^3 (i_1 \times j_1 \times k_1, i_2 \times j_2 \times k_2) = \prod f^1 (i_1, i_2) \times f^1 (j_1, j_2) \times f^1 (k_1, k_2)$$
where $\prod A \times B = \{ a \times b \mid \forall a \in A, b \in B \}$
$\prod A \times B \times C = \{ a \times b \times c \mid \forall a \in A, b \in B, c \in C \}$

The functions are implemented as table mappings. Table generated by the above formula are stored in memory to reduce run-time computation load. These tables are used in the algorithm discussed in Section 4, depending on which dimension of objects the algorithm is computing.

Example 6.1: Considering the five user spatial relations exist between objects. The reasoning algorithm discussed in Section 4 computes derived spatial relation edges until the last edge is added to K_n :

User edges:

$(A, B) = \{ (<, m) \} = ([1], [7])$
$(B, C) = \{ (oi, s) \} = ([6], [9])$
$(C, D) = \{ (f, m) \} = ([11], [7])$
$(B, E) = \{ (fi, di) \} = ([12], [4])$

Derivation based on user edges:

1. Path Length = 2
$(A, C) = (A, B) \text{ o } (B, C) = ([1], [7]) \text{ o } ([6], [9])$
$= ([1] \text{ o } [6], [7] \text{ o } [9]) = ([2], [7]) = \{ (>, m) \}$
$(B, D) = (B, C) \text{ o } (C, D) = ([6], [9]) \text{ o } ([11], [7])$
$= ([6] \text{ o } [11], [9] \text{ o } [7]) = ([6], [1]) = \{ (oi, <) \}$
$(A, E) = (A, B) \text{ o } (B, E) = ([1], [7]) \text{ o } ([12], [4])$
$= ([1] \text{ o } [12], [7] \text{ o } [4]) = ([1], [1]) = \{ (<, <) \}$
$(C, E) = (C, B) \text{ o } (B, E) = (B, C)^{-1} \text{ o } (B, E)$
$= ([5], [10]) \text{ o } ([12], [4]) = ([5] \text{ o } [12], [10] \text{ o } [4])$
$= ([18], [4]) = \{ (<, di), (o, di), (m, di) \}$

2. Path Length = 3
$(A, D) = (A, B) \text{ o } (B, C) \text{ o } (C, D) = (A, C) \text{ o } (C, D)$
$= ([2], [7]) \text{ o } ([11], [7]) = ([2] \text{ o } [11], [7] \text{ o } [7])$
$= ([2], [1]) = \{ (>, <) \}$

7 Distributed Multimedia Application

7.1 Content-Based Image Retrieval from WWW

7.1.1 Shape Matching
If we consider two line segments on the plan, based on the relative positions of two lines, it is feasible to construct a mechanism to compare the similarity between two polygons since polygons are made of line segments. Therefore, an evaluation mechanism is

necessary to compute *relation similarity*.

In a multimedia resource database that we built [11], pictures are bitmapped images associated with *shape representation polygons* (SRPs). An image processing mechanism is used to compute the shapes of objects in a picture. The outcome is then adjusted by a database administrator. Each picture has a set of SRPs. It is this SRP sets that we based on to compute polygon similarity between a *query polygon* (QP) and those in the SRP sets.

7.1.2 Similarity on Consecutive Edges

Suppose the query polygon has n sides and a candidate shape representation polygon has m sides, where n and m are not necessarily equal. We have

Definition 7.1: Let

$SRP = \{(a_1\ S_1\ a_2), (a_2\ S_2\ a_3), ..., (a_{m-1}\ S_{m-1}\ a_m),$ and $(a_m\ S_m\ a_1)\}$

be a relational description with shape representation polygon SRS,

where a_i, $1 \leq i \leq n$, are the n sides of the query polygon, and $S_i \in$ *324REL*, $1 \leq i \leq n$, are relations of two line segments project on a plan. ∎

In the same way, we have

Definition 7.2: Let

$QP = \{(b_1\ Q_1\ b_2), (b_2\ Q_2\ b_3), ..., (b_{m-1}\ Q_{m-1}\ b_m),$ and $(b_m\ Q_m\ b_1)\}$

be a relational description with query polygon QP,

where b_i, $1 \leq i \leq n$, are the n sides of the query polygon, and $Q_i \in$ *324REL*, $1 \leq i \leq n$, are relations of two line segments project on a plan. ∎

Moreover, each spatial relation $r_i = (r_{ix},\ r_{iy}) \in$ *324REL* holds for line segments A and B. Assume that A_s, A_e, B_s, and B_e are the starting and ending points of the two line segments on a plan, we want to define a *length ratio function*, $LR(\ r_{ix})$ and $LR(\ r_{iy})$:

$LR(\ r_{ix}) = (A_{e.x} - A_{s.\ x})\ /\ (\ max(A_{e.x}, B_{e.x}) - min(A_{s.x}, B_{s.x}))$

$LR(\ r_{iy}) = (A_{e.y} - A_{s.y})\ /\ (\ max(A_{e.y}, B_{e.y}) - min(A_{s.y}, B_{s.y}))$

where $A_{s.x}$ and $A_{s.y}$ are the X and the Y coordinates of the starting point of line segment A (other notations are prepresented in a similar manner).

Let function $sim(r_i, r_j)$ be a similarity function, which takes as input two relations, r_i, and r_j, and returns a similarity:

$r_i = r_j \Rightarrow sim(r_i, r_j) = (LR(r_{ix})+LR(r_{iy})) - (LR(r_{jx})+LR(r_{jy})) \lor$

$r_i \neq r_j \Rightarrow sim(r_i, r_j) = EPIRD324(r_i, r_j)$ * $(LR(r_{ix})+LR(r_{iy})) - (LR(r_{jx})+LR(r_{jy}))$

The similarity function, $sim(r_i, r_j)$, estimates the similarity between two project line segments on a plan based on distance similarity index and the length ratio function.

Based on the similarity function, we construct the polygon similarity function. Polygons are represented as sets of line segments (polygon sides).

The polygon similarity function, *psim(QP, SRP)*, takes as input the query polygon and the candidate shape representation polygons, and returns an integer:

$psim(QP, SRP) = \sum_{i=1}^{m} sim(QP_{r.i}, SRP_{r.i})$

Given the coordinates of pointts, it is easy to compute the relations of two consecutive sides of a polygon. Therefore, the sets of $QP_{r.i}$s and $SRP_{r.i}$s are computed.

7.2 Multimedia Presentations

The multimedia presentations of several media objects requires simultaneous and sequential presentation. In [10], we use interval temporal logic to represent the schedule of a multimedia presentation. Using our proposed Temporal Interval Group and algorithms in this paper, inference rules can be generalized to generate a better presentation. The generation of presentation schedule includes the following steps:

• compute temporal relations among presentation resources. Possible conflicts are eliminated by asking the user to give a correct relation.

• use a partial order set to denote the topological order of presentation objects.

• generate a relative time table for presentation objects from the partial order set.

• allocate multimedia devices for each resources. Hardware limitations are considered.

The mechanism proposed in this paper can also be used in generating multimedia presentation layouts. As long as the spatial relations of objects are decided, the algorithm can compute the location of each presentation resource in a window. However, parameters to spatial relations need to be added to precisely specify relative screen coordinates.

7.3 Multimedia Synchronization Specification

Multimedia resources are not used along usually. Instead, they have some degree of associations. For instance, a motion picture resource is synchronized with a MIDI song as its background music. In addition, an explanation of human voice is overlapped or embraced with the song. These three resources are linked by *association links*. We are planning on extending association links to deal with temporal relations. In the interval-based synchronization specification, the presentation duration of an object is regarded as interval. Two time intervals may be synchronized in 13 different modes, and the Temporal Interval Group can handle these interval relations.

8 Conclusions

The main contributions of this paper is in building the algebra system of spatio-temporal interval relations and the set of enhanced mechanism for spatio-temporal relation composition. These algorithms deal with an arbitrary number of objects in an arbitrary n-dimensional space. We propose many properties of temporal interval relations and prove the correctness of these properties. We also argue that, many interesting researches in multimedia applications can benefit from using the Infinite/Finite Temporal Interval Group and our algorithms.

The proposed algorithms are used in the implementation of a spatio-temporal relation computation program. This program is used in a system to detect conflicts and generate presentation schedule and layout from user specifications. Temporal and spatial knowledge are managed by Finite Temporal Interval Group. The system is able to help the user to keep away from conflicts of synchronization specification.

We have developed a multimedia resource database for intelligent multimedia presentation. We use spatio-temporal interval relations allowing the users to specify polygons represents the shapes of candidate objects in still image. Thus the content-based picture retrieval is possible.

The algorithm proposed in this paper can be used in other computer applications for maintaining temporal knowledge. We hope that, with our analysis and algorithms, the knowledge underlying temporal intervals can be used in many computer applications, especially in managing multimedia spatio-temporal knowledge and representing distributed multimedia objects and knowledge.

References

[1] James F. Allen , " Maintaining Knowledge about Temporal Intervals " ,Communications of the ACM , Vol. 26 , No. 11 , 1983.

[2] Chi-Ming Chung, Timothy K. Shih, Jiung-Yao Huang, Ying-Hong Wang, and Tsu-Feng Kuo, " An Object-Oriented Approach and System for Intelligent Multimedia Presentation Designs , " in proceeding of the International Conference on Multimedia Computing and Systems (ICMCS '95) , Washington DC, U.S.A. May 15-18,1995, pp 278-281.

[3] Young Francis Day, et. al. ," Spatio-Temporal Modeling of Video Data for On-Line Object-Oriented Query Processing ," in proceedings of the International Conference on Multimedia Computing and Systems, Washington DC,U.S.A., May 15-18 ,1995 , pp 98-105 .

[4] Thomas Wahl, et. al., "TIEMPO: Temporal Modeling and Authoring of Interactive Multimedia " in proceedings of the international conference on multimedia computing and systems, Washington DC, U.S.A., May 15-18, 1995, pp 274-277.

[5] Venkat N. Gudivada, and Vijay V. Raghavan, "Content-Based Image Retrieval Systems," IEEE Computer, September 1995, pp 18 -- 22.

[6] Cherif Keramane and Andrzej Duda, " Interval Expressions -a Function Model for Interactive Dynamic Multimedia Presentations," in proceedings of the 1996 International Conference on Multimedia Computing and Systems , Hiroshima, Japan, June 17-23, 1996 , pp 119-133.

[7] John Z. Li, M. TamerOzsu, and Duane Szafron, " Spatial Reasoning Rules in Multimedia Management Systems,"in proceedings of the 1996 Multimedia Modeling International Conference (MMM'96), Toulouse, France, November 12-5,1996, pp 119-133.

[8] Thomas D. C. Little and Arif Ghafoor, " Spatio-Temporal Composition of Distributed Multimedia Objects for Value-Added Networks," IEEE Computer, October 1991, pp 42-50.

[9] Thomas D. C. Little and Arif Ghafoor " Interval Based Conceptual Models for Time-Dependent Multimedia Data," IEEE transactions on knowledge and data engineering , Vol. 5, No. 4,1993, pp 551-563.

[10] Timothy K. Shih, Steven K. C. Lo, Szu-Jan Fu, and Julian B. Chang, " Using Interval Temporal Logic and Inference Rules for the Automatic Generation of Multimedia Presentations," in Proceedings of the IEEE International Conference on Multimedia Computing and Systems, Hiroshima, Japan, June 17-23, 1996, pp. 425-428.

[11] Timothy K. Shih, Chin-Hwa Kuo, Huan-Chao Keh, Chao T. Fang-Tsou, and Kuan-Shen An, " An Object-Oriented Database for Intelligent Multimedia Presentations," in proceedings of the 1996 IEEE International Conference on Systems, Man and Cybernetics, Beijing, China, October 14-17, 1996.

[12] Yannis Theodoridis, Michael Vazirgiannis, and Timos Sellis, " Spatial Temporal Indexing for Large Multimedia Applications," in proceedings of the 1996 International Conference on Multimedia Computing and Systems, Hiroshima, Japan, June 17-23, 1996, pp 441-448.

[13] Michael Vazirgiannis, Yannis Theodoridis, and Timos Sellis " Spatio-Temporal Composition in Multimedia Applications," in proceedings of the International Workshop on Multimedia Software Development, March 25-26, Berlin, Germany, 1996, pp 120-127.

[14] Timothy K. Shih and Anthony Y. Chang, "The Algebra of Spatio-Temporal Intervals," in Proceedings of the 12th International Conference on Information Networking, Japan, January 21-23, 1998.

Session B6

Adaptive Communication & Groupware Systems

Chair: Ken-Ichi Okada
Keio University, Japan

Object-Based Ordered Delivery of Messages in Object-Based Systems

Tomoya Enokido, Hiroaki Higaki, and Makoto Takizawa
Department of Computers and Systems Engineering
Tokyo Denki University
e-mail {eno, hig, taki}@takilab.k.dendai.ac.jp

Abstract

Distributed applications are realized by cooperation of multiple objects. A state of an object depends on in what order the objects exchange request and response messages. In this paper, we newly define an object-based precedent relation of messages based on a conflicting relation among requests. Here, only the messages to be ordered in the object-based system are ordered and the others are not ordered. We discuss a protocol which supports the object-based ordered delivery of request and response messages. Here, an object vector is newly proposed to order messages.

1. Introduction

Distributed applications are realized by a *group* of multiple application objects. Many papers [3,11] discuss how to support a group of the objects with the causally ordered (CO) and totally ordered (TO) delivery of messages at the network level in presence of message loss and stop faults of the objects. Cheriton *et al.* [4] point out that it is meaningless at the application level to causally order all the messages transmitted in the network. Only messages required by the applications have to be causally delivered in order to reduce the overhead. Ravindran *et al.* [12] discuss how to support the ordered delivery of messages based on the message precedence explicitly specified by the application. Agrawal *et al.* [9] define *significant* requests which change the state of the object. Raynal *et al.* [1] discuss a group protocol for replicas of files where write–write semantics of messages are considered. The authors [6] discuss a group protocol for replicas where a group is composed of transactions issuing read and write requests to the replicas.

An object is an encapsulation of data and methods. On receipt of a *request message* with a method *op*, an object *o* performs *op* and sends

back a *response message* with the result of *op*. Here, *op* may further invoke other methods, i.e. *nested invocation*. States of the objects depend on in what order conflicting methods are performed. If a pair of methods exchanged by the methods conflict in an object, the messages have to be received in the computation order of the methods. Thus, the *object-based ordered (OBO) relation* among request and response messages is defined based on the conflicting relation. In this paper, we present an *Object-based Group (OG) protocol* which supports the *OBO delivery* of messages where only messages to be ordered at the application level are delivered to the application objects in the significant order. Takizawa *et al.* [13] show a protocol for a group of objects, which uses the real time clock. However, it is not easy to synchronize real time clocks in distributed objects. We newly propose an *object vector* to order messages, which is independent of the group membership.

In section 2, we discuss the object-based precedence among messages. In section 3, the OG protocol is discussed. In section 4, we present an evaluation of the OG protocol.

2. Object-Based Ordered Delivery

2.1. Object-based systems

A *group* G is a collection of objects $o_1, \ldots, o_n$ ($n \geq 1$) which are cooperating by exchanging request and response messages in a network. We assume that the network is less reliable and is asynchronous, i.e. messages sent by an object are delivered to the destinations with message loss, not in the sending order, and the delay time among objects is not bounded.

Let $op(s)$ denote a state obtained by applying a method *op* to a state *s* of an object o_i. A pair of methods op_1 and op_2 of o_i are *compatible* iff $op_1(op_2(s)) = op_2(op_1(s))$ for every state *s* of o_i. op_1 and op_2 *conflict* iff they are not compatible. The *conflicting relation* among the methods is specified when o_i is defined. The conflicting relation is assumed to be symmetric but not transitive. A pair of request messages m_1 of a method op_1 and m_2 of op_2 *conflict* iff op_1 and op_2 conflict. Suppose op_1 is issued to o_i. If op_1 is compatible with every method being performed on o_i, op_1 is started to be performed. Otherwise, op_1 has to wait until op_2 completes.

Each time an object o_i receives a request message of a method op, a thread is created for op. The thread is referred to as an *instance* of op in o_i, which is denoted by op^i. Only if all the events performed in op complete successfully, i.e. *commit*, op commits. Otherwise, *op aborts. op* may further invoke methods of other objects. Thus, the invocation is *nested*.

2.2. Significant precedence

A method instance op_1^i *precedes* op_2^i ($op_1^i \Rightarrow_i op_2^i$) in an object o_i iff op_2^i is started after op_1^i completes. op_1^i *precedes* op_2^j ($op_1^i \Rightarrow op_2^j$) iff $op_1^i \Rightarrow_i op_2^j$ for $j = i$, op_1^i invokes op_2^j, or $op_1^i \Rightarrow op_3^k \Rightarrow op_2^j$ for some instance op_3^k. op_1^i and op_2^j are *concurrent* ($op_1^i \| op_2^j$) iff neither $op_1^i \Rightarrow op_2^j$ nor $op_2^j \Rightarrow op_1^i$.

A message m_1 *causally precedes* another message m_2 if the sending event of m_1 precedes the sending event of m_2 [3,8]. In the totally ordered delivery, messages not causally ordered are delivered to the common destinations in the same order in addition to the causal delivery. Suppose an object o_i sends a message m_1 to objects o_j and o_k, and o_j sends m_2 to o_k after receiving m_1. Since m_1 causally precedes m_2, the object o_k has to receive m_1 before m_2. For example, if m_1 is a question and m_2 is the answer for m_1, m_1 has to be received before m_2. However, independent questions m_1 and m_2 can be received in any order. We define a *significantly precedent relation "→"* among messages m_1 and m_2, where *"$m_1 \to m_2$"* is meaningful for applications in the object-based system. There are the following cases for a pair of messages m_1 and m_2 which an object o_i sends and receives:

S. An object o_i sends m_2 after m_1 [Figure 1].

S1. m_1 and m_2 are sent by op_1^i.

S2. m_1 is sent by op_1^i and m_2 is sent by op_2^i:

   S2.1. op_1^i precedes op_2^i ($op_1^i \Rightarrow op_2^i$).

   S2.2. op_1^i and op_2^i are concurrent ($op_1^i \| op_2^i$).

R. o_i sends m_2 after receiving m_1 [Figure 2].

R1. m_1 and m_2 are received and sent by op_1^i.

R2. m_1 is received by op_1^i and m_2 is sent by op_2^i:

   R2.1. $op_1^i \Rightarrow op_2^i$. **R2.2.** $op_1^i \| op_2^i$.

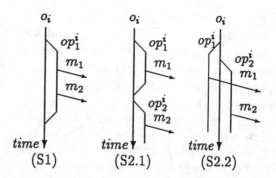

Figure 1: Send-send precedence.

In the case S [Figure 1], an object o_i sends a message m_1 before m_2. In S1, m_1 *significantly precedes* m_2 ($m_1 \to m_2$) since m_1 and m_2 are sent by the same instance op_1^i. In S2, m_1 and m_2 are sent by different instances op_1^i and op_2^i in o_i. In S2.1, op_1^i precedes op_2^i ($op_1^i \Rightarrow op_2^i$). Unless op_1^i and op_2^i conflict, there is no relation between op_1^i and op_2^i, i.e. neither $m_1 \to m_2$ nor $m_2 \to m_1$. Here, m_1 and m_2 are *significantly concurrent* ($m_1 \| m_2$). If op_1^i and op_2^i conflict, the output data carried by m_1 and m_2 depend on a computation order of op_1^i and op_2^i. Thus, if op_1^i and op_2^i conflict, the messages sent by op_1^i have to be delivered before the messages sent by op_2^i, i.e. $m_1 \to m_2$. In S2.2, $op_1^i \| op_2^i$. Since op_1^i and op_2^i are not related, $m_1 \| m_2$.

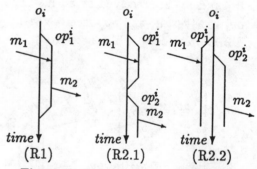

Figure 2: Receive-send precedence.

In the case R [Figure 2], the object o_i sends a message m_2 after receiving m_1. In R1, $m_1 \to m_2$ since the same instance op_1^i receives m_1 and sends m_2. m_1 is received and m_2 is sent by op_1^i. Here, m_1 is the request of op_1^i or a response of a method invoked by op_1^i. m_2 is the response of op_1^i or a request of a method invoked by op_1^i. For example, suppose m_1 is a response of op_2^j invoked by op_1^i and m_2 is a request of op_3^k. The output of op_2 may be the input of op_3^k. In R2, m_1 is received by op_1^i and m_2 is sent by op_2^i ($\neq op_1^i$). In R2.1, $op_1^i \Rightarrow op_2^i$. If op_1^i and op_2^i conflict, $m_1 \to m_2$. Unless $m_1 \| m_2$. In R2.2, $op_1^i \| op_2^i$ and $m_1 \| m_2$.

[**Definition**] A message m_1 *significantly precedes* another message m_2 ($m_1 \to m_2$) iff one of the following three conditions holds:

1. An object o_i sends m_1 before m_2 and
   a. the same instance sends m_1 and m_2, or
   b. an instance sending m_1 conflicts with another one sending m_2 in o_i.

2. o_i receives m_1 before sending m_2 and
   a. m_1 and m_2 are received and sent by the same instance, or
   b. an instance receiving m_1 conflicts with another one sending m_2.

3. $m_1 \to m_3 \to m_2$ for some message m_3. □

[**Theorem 1**] A message m_1 causally precedes m_2 if $m_1 \to m_2$. □

A message m_1 is significantly preceded by only messages related with m_1. m_1 does not necessarily significantly precede m_2 even if m_1 causally precedes m_2.

2.3. Object-based ordered delivery

We discuss how to deliver messages received. Suppose an object o_i receives a pair of messages m_1 and m_2. There are the following cases on what instances in o_i receive m_1 and m_2:

T. o_i receives m_2 before m_1 [Figure 3].

T1. m_1 and m_2 are received by an instance op_1^i.

T2. op_1^i receives m_1 and op_2^i receives m_2.

   T2.1. $op_1^i \Rightarrow op_2^i$.   **T2.2.** $op_1^i \| op_2^i$.

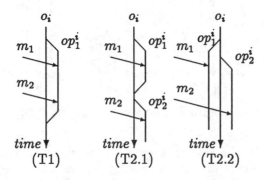

$$(T1) \qquad (T2.1) \qquad (T2.2)$$

Figure 3: Receive-receive precedence.

In T1, the message m_1 has to be delivered to the object o_i before m_2 if m_1 significantly precedes m_2 ($m_1 \to m_2$). In T2, m_1 and m_2 are received by different instances op_1^i and op_2^i. In T2.1, first suppose op_1^i and op_2^i conflict. If m_1 or m_2 is a request, m_1 has to be delivered before m_2 since $m_1 \to m_2$. Suppose m_1 and m_2 are responses. Unless m_1 is delivered before m_2, op_1^i waits for m_1 and op_2^i is not performed since op_1^i does not complete. That is, deadlock among op_1^i and op_2^i occurs. Furthermore, suppose m_3 is sent to op_1^i, m_4 is sent to op_2^i, and $m_4 \to m_3$. Even if op_1^i precedes op_2^i ($op_1^i \Rightarrow op_2^i$) and m_1 is delivered before m_2, deadlock occurs because $m_4 \to m_3$. Thus, messages destined to different instances cannot be delivered to o_i in the order "$\to$" unless at least one of the messages is a request. Next, suppose op_1^i and op_2^i do not conflict. The messages m_1 and m_2 can be delivered in any order even if $m_1 \to m_2$ or $m_2 \to m_1$. If $op_1^i \| op_2^i$ in T2.2, m_1 and m_2 can be independently delivered to op_1^i and op_2^i.

Suppose an object o_h sends a message m_1 to o_i and o_j, and another o_k sends m_2 to o_i, o_j, and o_h. o_i and o_j are common destinations of m_1 and m_2. There are the following cases on the types of the messages m_1 and m_2:

C. Multiple objects receive messages m_1 and m_2.

C1. m_1 and m_2 are request messages.

C2. One of m_1 and m_2 is a request message and the other is a response one.

C3. m_1 and m_2 are response messages.

In C1, suppose m_1 and m_2 are requests of methods op_1 and op_2, respectively, and op_1 conflicts with op_2 in not only o_i but also o_j. If $m_1 \| m_2$, o_i and o_j may deliver m_1 and m_2 in different orders. However, the state of o_i obtained by performing op_1 and op_2 may be inconsistent with o_j because op_1 and op_2 conflict in o_i and o_j. Therefore, a pair of requests m_1 and m_2 have to be delivered in every pair o_i and o_j of common destination objects in the same order if m_1 and m_2 conflict in o_i and o_j. In C2 and C3, m_1 and m_2 can be delivered in any order.

[**Object-based ordered (OBO) delivery**] A message m_1 is delivered before another message m_2 in a common destination object o_i of m_1 and m_2, i.e. m_1 *object-based precedes* (*OB-precedes*) m_2 ($m_1 \preceq m_2$) if the following condition holds :

1. if m_1 significantly precedes m_2 ($m_1 \to m_2$),
   1.1 an instance receives both m_1 and m_2, or
   1.2 m_1 and m_2 are received by different instances op_1^i and op_2^i, op_1^i and op_2^i conflict in o_i, and one of m_1 and m_2 is a request.

2. if $m_1 \| m_2$, m_1 and m_2 are conflicting requests and m_1 is delivered before m_2 in every other

382

common destination of m_1 and m_2. □

A message m_1 is referred to as *significant* $m_1 \preceq m_2$ or $m_2 \preceq m_1$ for some message m_2.

[**Theorem 2**] No communication deadlock occurs if every message is delivered by the OBO delivery. □

[**Theorem 3**] $m_1 \preceq m_2$ if $m_1 \rightarrow m_2$. m_1 totally precedes m_2 if $m_1 \preceq m_2$. □

In the OBO delivery, only messages to be ordered in the object-based system are ordered. On the other hand, every message transmitted in the network is ordered in the CO and TO delivery.

3. Object-Based Group Protocol

3.1. Object vector

The *vector clock* [10] $V = \langle V_1, \ldots, V_n \rangle$ is widely used to causally order messages [3]. Each object o_i manipulates a vector clock $V_i = \langle V_{i1}, \ldots, V_{in} \rangle$ $(i = 1, \ldots, n)$. Each element V_{ij} is initially 0. o_i increments V_{ii} by one each time o_i sends a message m. The message m carries the vector clock $m.V(=V_i)$. On receipt of a message m', o_i updates V_i as $V_{ij} := max(V_{ij}, m'.V_j)$ for $j = 1, \ldots, n$ and $j \neq i$. m_1 causally precedes m_2 iff $m_1.V < m_2.V$.

It is critical to discuss which instances send messages for ordering only the messages significant in the applications. The OB-precedent relation "$\preceq$" is defined for messages exchanged by the instances invoked in a nested manner while the causality is defined for messages exchanged by objects. Hence, a group is considered to be composed of instances, not objects. If the vector clock composed of instances is used, the group has to be frequently synchronized [3, 4, 8–10, 13] each time an instance is initiated and terminated. The vector clock can be used to causally order messages sent by objects but not by instances. Hence, we newly propose an *object vector* to order only the significant messages in "$\preceq$" which is independent of what instances are being performed.

The object vector V is a tuple $\langle V_1, \ldots, V_n \rangle$ where each element V_i shows an identifier of a method which has been most recently performed. First, we discuss an instance identifier $id(op_t^i)$. o_i manipulates a variable oid, whose value is initially 0, showing the linear clock [8] as follows:

- $oid := oid + 1$ if an instance is initiated in o_i.
- On receipt of a message from an instance op_u^j, $oid := max(oid, oid(op_u^j))$.

When op_t^i is initiated in the object o_i, an identifier $id(op_t^i)$ is a concatenation of the value of oid and the object number $ono(o_i)$ of o_i. Here, let $oid(op_t^i)$ show oid of $id(op_t^i)$. $id(op_t^i) > id(op_u^j)$ if

1) $oid(op_t^i) > oid(op_u^j)$ or 2) $oid(op_t^i) = oid(op_u^j)$ and $ono(o_i) > ono(o_j)$. It is clear that the following properties hold:

I1. If op_t^i is initiated after op_u^i in an object o_i, $id(op_t^i) > id(op_u^i)$.

I2. If o_i receives a request from op_u^j and initiates op_t^i, $id(op_t^i) > id(op_u^j)$.

Each event e in the instance op_t^i is given an event number $no(e)$. The event number is incremented by one each time op_t^i sends a message. The object o_i manipulates a variable no_i to give the event number to each event e, i.e. $no(e) := no_i$ in o_i as follows:

- Initially, $no_i := 0$.
- $no_i := no_i + 1$ if e is a sending event.

Each event e in op_t^i is given a *global event number* $tno(e)$ as the concatenation of $id(op_t^i)$ and $no(e)$.

An object o_i manipulates a vector $V^i = \langle V_1^i, \ldots, V_n^i \rangle$. Each time an instance op_t^i is initiated in o_i, op_t^i is $V_t^i = \langle V_{t1}^i, \ldots, V_{tn}^i \rangle$ where $V_{tj}^i := V_j^i$ for $j = 1, \ldots, n$. Each element V_t^i is manipulated for op_t^i as follows:

- When op_t^i sends a message m, $no_i := no_i + 1$ and $V_{ti}^i := \langle id(op_t^i), no_i \rangle$. m carries the vector V_t^i as $m.V$ where $m.V_j := V_{tj}^i$ $(j = 1, \ldots, n)$.
- When op_t^i receives a message m from o_j, $V_{tj}^i := max(V_{tj}^i, m.V_j)$ $(j = 1, \ldots, n)$.
- When op_t^i commits, $V_j^i := max(V_j^i, V_{tj}^i)$ $(j = 1, \ldots, n)$.
- When op_t^i aborts, V^i is not changed.

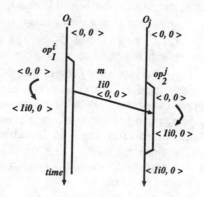

Figure 4: Object vector.

Initially, the object vectors V^i and V^j are $\langle 0, 0 \rangle$ in Figure 4. An instance op_1^i is initiated in o_i

where $V_1^i = V^i = \langle 0, 0 \rangle$. The identifier $id(op_1^i)$ is "$1i$". op_1^i sends a message m to another instance op_2^j. The message m carries the vector $V_1^i(= \langle 0, 0 \rangle)$ to o_j. Here, suppose m is a request message of a method op_2. After sending m, V_1^i is changed to $\langle 1i0, 0 \rangle$ where "$1i0$" is the global event number of the sending event of m. On receipt of m, op_2^j is initiated where $id(op_2^j) = 2j$. Here, V_2^j is $\langle 1i0, 0 \rangle$. If op_2^j commits, the vector V^j of o_j is changed to $\langle 1i0, 0 \rangle$.

3.2. Message transmission and receipt

A message m includes the following fields:

$m.src$: sender object of m.

$m.dst$: set of destination objects.

$m.typ \in \{request, response, commit, abort\}$

$m.op$: method.　　$m.dat$: data.

$m.tno = \langle m.id, m.no \rangle$: global event number.

$m.V = \langle V_1, \ldots, V_n \rangle$: object vector.

$m.SQ = \langle sq_1, \ldots, sq_n \rangle$: sequence numbers.

If m is a request message, $m.tno$ is a global event number of the sending event of m. $m.id$ shows the identifier of the instance which sends m and $m.no$ indicates the event number in the instance. If m is a response of a request m', $m.tno = m'.tno$ and $m.op = m'.op$.

An object o_i manipulates variables $sq_1, \ldots, sq_n$ to detect a message gap, i.e. messages lost or unexpectedly delayed. Each time o_i sends a message to another object o_j, sq_j is incremented by one. Then, o_i sends a message m to every destination in $m.dst$. o_j manipulates variables $rsq_1, \ldots, rsq_n$. rsq_i shows a sequence number of a message which o_j expects to receive next from o_i. On receipt of m from o_i, there is no gap, i.e. o_j receives every message which o_i sends to o_j before m if $m.sq_j = rsq_i$. If $m.sq_j > rsq_i$, there is a gap message m' where $m.sq_j > m'.sq_j \geq rsq_i$. That is, o_j has not yet received m' which o_i sends to o_j. o_j correctly receives m if o_j receives every message m' where $m'.sq_j < m.sq_j$ and $m'.src = m.src(= o_i)$. That is, o_j receives every message which o_i sends to o_j before m. If o_i does not receive a gap message m in some time units after the gap is detected, o_j requires o_i to send m again. The object o_j enqueues m in a receipt queue RQ_j even if a gap is detected on receipt of m.

When an instance op_t^i in an object o_i invokes a method op, o_i constructs a message m as follows:

$m.src := o_i$;

$m.dst :=$ set of destination objects;

$m.typ := request$;　　$m.op := op$;

$m.tno = \langle m.id, m.no \rangle := \langle id(op_t^i), no_i \rangle$;

$m.V_j := V_{tj}^i$ for $j = 1, \ldots, n$;

$sq_h := sq_h + 1$ for every object $o_h \in m.dst$;

$m.sq_j := sq_j$ for $j = 1, \ldots, n$;

3.3. Message ordering

Let us consider three objects o_i, o_j, and o_k [Figure 5]. An instance op_1^i in o_i sends a message m_1 to o_j and o_k. An instance op_2^i is interleaved with op_1^i in o_i, i.e. op_1^i and op_2^i are concurrent $(op_1^i \| op_2^i)$. op_2^i sends m_3 to o_k. An instance op_3^j sends m_2 to o_k after receiving m_1. Here, m_1 significantly precedes m_2 $(m_1 \rightarrow m_2)$. o_k has to receive m_1 before m_2. However, m_1 and m_3 are significantly concurrent $(m_1 \| m_3)$ since $op_1^i \| op_2^i$. Similarly $m_2 \| m_3$. However, since op_3^j is initiated after receiving m_1 from op_1^i and $op_1^i \| op_2^i$, $m_1.V = m_3.V$. Hence, $m_2.V > m_3.V$. Although o_k can receive m_2 and m_3 in any order since $m_2 \| m_3$, "m_2 precedes m_3" because $m_2.V > m_3.V$. In order to resolve this problem, an additional receipt vector $RV = \langle RV_1, \ldots, RV_n \rangle$ is given to each message m received from o_i. $m.RV$ shows RV given to m. $m.RV$ is the same as $m.V$ except that $m.RV_i$ shows the global event number of the sending event of m in o_i which sends m. $m.RV$ is manipulated as follows :

- $m.RV_i := m.tno$.

- $m.RV_h := m.V_h$ for $h = 1, \ldots, n$ $(h \neq i)$.

In Figure 5, $id(op_1^i) < id(op_2^i)$ because op_2^i is invoked after op_1^i. Hence, $m_1.RV < m_3.RV$ as shown in Table 1. op_1^i sends m_1 to o_j and o_k where $m.tno = 1i0$ and $m.V = \langle 0, 0, 0 \rangle$. On receipt of m_1, o_j enqueues m_1 into a receipt queue RQ_j. Here, o_j gives RV to m_1, i.e. $m_1.RV = \langle 1i0, 0, 0 \rangle$ while $m_1.V$ is still $\langle 0, 0, 0 \rangle$. Table 1 shows values of tno, V, and RV of the messages. $m_1.V < m_2.V$ and $m_1.RV < m_2.RV$. On the other hand, $m_2.V > m_3.V$ but $m_2.RV$ and $m_3.RV$ are not comparable. Following this example, a pair of messages m_1 and m_2 are ordered by the following rule.

[Ordering rule] A message m_1 precedes another m_2 $(m_1 \Rightarrow m_2)$ if the following condition holds:

1. if $m_1.V < m_2.V$ and $m_1.RV < m_2.RV$, $m_1.op = m_2.op$ or $m_1.op$ conflicts with $m_2.op$,

2. otherwise, m_1 and m_2 are requests, $m_1.op$ conflicts with $m_2.op$, and $m_1.tno < m_2.tno$. □

In Figure 5, op_1^i sends a request m_1 to o_j and o_k where op_3^j and op_4^k are initiated. Then, op_3^j sends a request m_2 to o_k. Here, $m_1.V < m_2.V$ and $m_1.RV < m_2.RV$. Suppose op_4^k conflicts with op_5^k. $m_1 \Rightarrow m_2$ since $m_1.op$ and $m_2.op$ conflict.

Table 1: Object vectors.

m	$m.tno$	$m.V$	$m.RV$
m_1	$1i0$	$\langle 0,0,0 \rangle$	$\langle 1i0,0,0 \rangle$
m_2	$2j0$	$\langle 1i0,0,0 \rangle$	$\langle 1i0,2j0,0 \rangle$
m_3	$2i0$	$\langle 0,0,0 \rangle$	$\langle 2i0,0,0 \rangle$

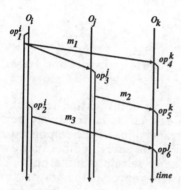

Figure 5: Receipt vector.

Next, suppose that m_2 is a data message and op_4^k receives m_2 after op_4^k is initiated by m_1. Here, $m_1 \Rightarrow m_2$ since $m_1.op = m_2.op = op_4^k$. On the other hand, $m_1.V = m_3.V$ but $m_1.RV < m_3.RV$. Accordingly, we check if $m_1.op$ and $m_3.op$ conflict. Since op_1^i and op_2^i are compatible, m_1 and m_3 are not ordered in the precedent relation "$\Rightarrow$". It is clear that $m_1 \Rightarrow m_2$ if $m_1 \preceq m_2$.

[Theorem 4] If a message m_1 OB-precedes another m_2 ($m_1 \prec m_2$), $m_1 \Rightarrow m_2$. □

"$m_1 \Rightarrow m_2$" is assumed to hold if instances op_1^i and op_2^i are serially performed in Figure 1. In S2.1, if op_2^i conflicts with op_1^i, data carried by m_1 and m_2 depend on the computation order of op_1^i and op_2^i. Hence, "$m_1 \Rightarrow m_2$" has to hold. However, m_1 and m_2 are independent if op_1^i and op_2^i are compatible. Hence, there is no need "$m_1 \Rightarrow m_2$" holds. In the OG protocol, "$m_1 \Rightarrow m_2$" even if op_2^i is compatible with op_1^i. Further mechanisms are required not to order m_1 and m_2. For example, each request m sent by an object o_i carries information on what requests conflicting with m precede m. There is a trade off between the complexity and overhead of additional mechanisms and the reduction of delay time of messages obtained by reducing the number of significant messages. Thus, if "$m_1 \Rightarrow m_2$" only for a pair of conflicting requests m_1 and m_2 in S2.1, "$m_1 \prec m_2$ iff $m_1 \Rightarrow m_2$" holds.

3.4. Message delivery

The messages in a receipt queue RQ_i are ordered in the precedent order $\Rightarrow$.

[Stable message] Let m be a message which an object o_i sends to another one o_j and is stored in the receipt queue RQ_j. The message m is *stable* in o_j iff one of the following conditions holds:

1. There exists such a message m_1 in RQ_j that $m_1.sq_j = m.sq_j + 1$ and m_1 is sent by o_i.

2. o_j receives at least one message m_1 from every object, where $m \Rightarrow m_1$. □

The top message m in RQ_j can be delivered if m is stable because every message preceding m in $\Rightarrow$ is surely delivered.

[Ready message] A message m in a receipt queue RQ_j is *ready* if no method instance conflicting with $m.op$ is being performed in o_j. □

The messages in RQ_j are delivered by the following procedure.

[Delivery procedure] If the top message m in RQ_j is stable and ready, m is delivered. □

[Theorem 5] The OG protocol delivers m_1 before m_2 if $m_1 \preceq m_2$. □

If an object o_i sends no message to another one o_j, messages in RQ_j cannot be stable. In order to resolve this problem, o_i sends every object o_j a message without data if o_i had sent no message to o_j for some predetermined δ time units. δ is proportional to delay time between o_i and o_j. o_j considers that o_j loses a message from o_i if o_j receives no message from o_i for δ or o_j detects a message gap. o_i also considers that o_j loses a message m unless o_i receives a receipt confirmation of m from o_j in 2δ after o_i sends m to o_j. Here, o_i resends m.

4. Implementation and Evaluation

4.1. Implementation

An OG protocol module is implemented as a process of Solaris 2.6 in the Sun workstation. Each object o_i has one OG protocol module OGM_i ($i = 1, \ldots, n$). OGM_i exchanges messages with other OG modules. OGM_i delivers messages to o_i in the object-based order "$\preceq$" by using the ordering rule. OGM_i is realized by two threads, Rec for receiving messages and Snd for sending messages [Figure 6]. Rec and Snd share the variables showing the sequence numbers sq, rsq, the object vector V, the event number no, and the instance identifier id in the shared memory. The Snd thread takes messages from o_i and sends the messages to the destinations. The Rec thread receives messages from other objects, orders them according to the ordering rule, and delivers them to o_i. OGM_i delivers messages in the delivery queue DQ_i in o_i according to the ordering rule. The size of the OG module is 2KB.

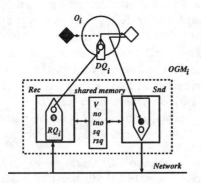

Figure 6: Implementation of OG protocol.

Each object o_i is realized by one process. o_i takes the top message in the delivery queue DQ_i. On taking a request op_t from DQ_i, o_i is locked in a mode $\mu(op_t)$. If methods conflicting with op_t are neither being performed in o_i nor blocked, o_i is locked in the mode $\mu(op_t)$. If o_i could be locked, a thread for op_t is created. Otherwise, op_t is blocked in a block queue of o_i. Unless an object could be locked by a transaction in a fixed time, the transaction aborts in order to avoid the deadlock.

4.2. Evaluation

In the evaluation, three objects o_1, o_2, and o_3 are implemented in Sun Enterprise 450 with 2 CPUs (300MHz) and 512MB memory. Each of o_1 and o_2 supports 8 types of methods and o_3 supports 9 types of methods. Some of the methods invoke other methods. Figure 7 indicates tree structures named *invocation tree* showing invocations of methods. Here, op_t^i shows a method op_t supported by o_i. In this paper, we assume that the methods in the same invocation tree are compatible with each other while every pair of methods in different trees conflict. Each transaction is initiated on τ[msec] after the first one is initiated. τ is a random number generated among 0 to 9,999. Each transaction randomly selects one method out of 25 methods supported by o_1, o_2, and o_3. For example, one transaction selects op_0^3 of o_3 which invokes totally ten methods and another transaction selects op_7^2 which totally invokes two methods op_7^3 and op_8^3.

The response time and the queue length of the receipt queue RQ_i in each object o_i is measured for the OG protocol and the message-based group

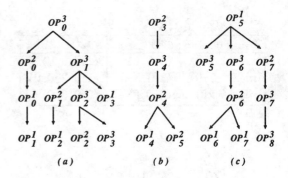

Figure 7: Invocation trees.

protocol. For the invocation trees shown in Figure 7, the evaluation is iteratively performed until the average value of the response time and the queue length are saturated because each transaction randomly selects one method. The average time for performing all the transactions is measured. Figure 8 shows that the OG protocol is about 50% faster than the message-based protocol because fewer number of messages are required to be waited in the receipt queue in the OG protocol than the message-based one.

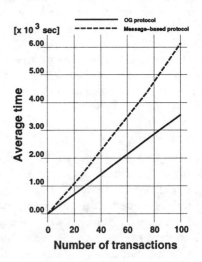

Figure 8: Average time.

In addition, we measure the length of the receipt queue RQ_i of each object o_i. Figure 9 shows the average queue length of three objects for number of transactions. The queue length in the OG protocol is 25-30% shorter than the message-based protocol because messages can be delivered without waiting for messages insignificant for the application. The computation overhead of the OG protocol module is almost the same as the

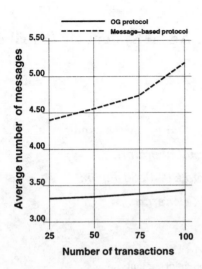

Figure 9: Average queue length.

message-based protocol.

5. Concluding Remarks

In this paper, we have discussed how to support the object-based ordered (OBO) delivery of messages. While all messages transmitted in a network are causally or totally ordered in most group protocols, only messages to be causally ordered at the application level are ordered to reduce the delay time. Based on the conflicting relation among methods, we have defined the object-based (OB) precedent relation among request and response messages. We have discussed the object vector to order messages in the object-based systems. The size of the object vector depends on the number of objects, not the number of instances. We have shown how the OG protocol reduces the response time of transactions.

References

[1] Ahamad, M., Raynal, M., and Thia-Kime, G., "An Adaptive Protocol for Implementing Causally Consistent Distributed Services," *Proc. of IEEE ICDCS-18*, 1998, pp.86–93.

[2] Bernstein, P. A., Hadzilacos, V., Goodman, N., "Concurrency Control and Recovery in Database Systems," *Addison-Wesley*, 1987.

[3] Birman, K., Schiper, A., and Stephenson, P., "Lightweight Causal and Atomic Group Multicast," *ACM Trans. on Computer Systems*, Vol.9, No.3, 1991, pp.272-314.

[4] Cheriton, D. R. and Skeen, D., "Understanding the Limitations of Causally and Totally Ordered Communication," *Proc. of ACM SIGOPS'93*, 1993, pp.44–57.

[5] Enokido, T., Tachikawa, T., and Takizawa, M., "Transaction-Based Causally Ordered Protocol for Distributed Replicated Objects," *Proc. of IEEE ICPADS'97*, 1997, pp.210–215.

[6] Enokido, T., Higaki, H., and Takizawa, M., "Group Protocol for Distributed Replicated Objects," *Proc. of ICPP'98*, 1998, pp.570–577.

[7] Enokido, T., Higaki, H., and Takizawa, M., "Protocol for Group of Objects," *Proc. of DEXA'98*, 1998, pp.470–479.

[8] Lamport, L., "Time, Clocks, and the Ordering of Events in a Distributed System," *CACM*, Vol.21, No.7, 1978, pp.558–565.

[9] Leong, H. V. and Agrawal, D., "Using Message Semantics to Reduce Rollback in Optimistic Message Logging Recovery Schemes," *Proc. of IEEE ICDCS-14*, 1994, pp.227–234.

[10] Mattern, F., "Virtual Time and Global States of Distributed Systems," *Parallel and Distributed Algorithms* (Cosnard, M. and Quinton, P. eds.), *North-Holland*, 1989, pp.215–226.

[11] Nakamura, A. and Takizawa, M., "Causally Ordering Broadcast Protocol," *Proc. of IEEE ICDCS-14*, 1994, pp.48–55.

[12] Ravindran, K. and Shah, K., "Causal Broadcasting and Consistency of Distributed Shared Data," *Proc. of IEEE ICDCS-14*, 1994, pp.40-47.

[13] Tachikawa, T., Higaki, H., and Takizawa, M., "Significantly Ordered Delivery of Messages in Group Communication," *Computer Communications Journal*, Vol. 20, No.9, 1997, pp. 724–731.

[14] Tachikawa, T., Higaki, H., and Takizawa, M., "Group Communication Protocol for Realtime Applications," *Proc. of IEEE ICDCS-18*, 1998, pp.40–47.

[15] Tanaka, K., Higaki, H., and Takizawa, M., "Object-Based Checkpoints in Distributed Systems," *Journal of Computer Systems Science and Engineering*, Vol. 13, No.3, 1998, pp.125–131.

Adaptive QoS Management Using Layered Multi-Agent System for Distributed Multimedia Applications

Masakatsu Kosuga, Tatsuya Yamazaki, Nagao Ogino, Jun Matsuda

ATR Adaptive Communications Research Laboratories.

2-2 Hikaridai, Seika-cho, Soraku-gun, Kyoto 619-0288 Japan.

{kosuga, yamazaki, ogino, matsuda}@acr.atr.co.jp

Abstruct

Owing to advances in terminal performance and network speed, communication-intensive distributed multimedia applications have grown. Hence the development of end-to-end quality of service (QoS) management mechanisms is increasingly demanded for the applications. Since user's QoS requirements change and available resources for network and terminal fluctuate occasionally, adaptability is required for QoS management mechanisms. In this paper, we propose a multi-agent-based, decentralized, adaptive QoS management framework that is suitable to a distributed multimedia environment. In this framework, the QoS management task is divided into subtasks, and the agents that take charge of the subtasks are designed. The adaptability is realized using collaborative QoS adaptation among the agents. A layered structure of multi-agent system is introduced to segregate long-term QoS adaptation from short-term QoS adaptation. Experimental and simulation results show the validity of layered QoS management using Application Agent (AA) and Stream Agent (SA).

1. Introduction

Through the past decade, multimedia communications and mobile computing have expanded widely because of development of new communication technologies and progress in computer performance. Hence, a user can avail him/herself of a multimedia service under various situations such as using the video-conferencing application on a desktop computer or accessing a video-on-demand or news-on-demand server from a portable handheld terminal outside the office. In such situations, the system performance, including network and terminal, changes dynamically as well as user's requirements. Consequently, it is important to guarantee quality of service (QoS) for communication-intensive distributed multimedia applications, in particular for continuous media such as video and audio, according to the various operational environments.

A number of studies on QoS support has been done in individual architectural layers so far [1]. Recent research has focused on end-to-end QoS management, including terminals and network [1]-[3]. Difficulties in end-to-end QoS management lie in coordinating multiple QoS management mechanisms in an individual architectural layer. To address this problem, one possible approach is the multi-agent system (MAS) [7]. Here, the term "agent" means an entity that is capable of acting in its environment to satisfy its goals [4]. Each agent autonomously behaves according to what it perceives, while cooperating with other agents if necessary. This characteristic contributes to the distributed implementation and parallel processing of end-to-end QoS management and to the realization of flexible end-to-end QoS management.

This paper presents an adaptive QoS management mechanism on the basis of layered MAS. In the proposed mechanism, the QoS management task is divided into six subtasks and these subtasks are managed by the corresponding agents: Personal Agent (PA), Application Agent (AA), Stream Agent (SA), Terminal Resource Agent (TRA), Network Resource Agent (NRA), and Network Agent (NA). We will describe how the agents cooperate in the proposed mechanism, and in particular, we will focus on a layered QoS adaptation by AAs and SAs. Puliafito et al. [2] proposed an agent-based framework for QoS management, using a server-client model. Fischer et al. [3] also presented an application-oriented QoS agent for multimedia applications that included multicasting for teleconferencing or educational applications. In contrast to these studies, our work segregates the QoS adaptation task and manages subtasks with the layered multi-agents. Namely, in our approach, the AAs work in the flow establishment phase for long-term QoS adaptation, and the SAs work in the QoS maintenance phase for short-term QoS adaptation.

The rest of the paper is organized as follows. Section 2

describes the QoS modeling we studied. In Section 3, we propose a multi-agent-based adaptive QoS management mechanism, and in Section 4, we describe the QoS management tasks of the AA and the SA. Section 5 shows the experimental and simulation results that verify the proposed QoS management mechanism. Finally, Section 6 gives the conclusions of this manuscript.

2. QoS modeling

Fig. 1 shows the system model we developed. Each terminal has multiply distributed multimedia applications running, and each application serves single or multiple media stream(s) transmitting to other terminals through the network. This paper will focus on point-to-point streams to make the discussion simple. The model can be extended to point-to-multipoint (multicast) streams. The user interface provides the user an access point to the terminal, and the network interface transfers the network resource information between the terminal and the network. The terminal and network resources and the user's requirements change depending on the time, place, and situation. Terminal resources include the CPU, memories, and residual battery power. Network resources include bandwidths and buffers of the network nodes.

The layered QoS model shown in Fig. 2 is defined. At the user level, QoS is defined as the User QoS, which is sometimes expressed abstractly in order to help novice users specify stream QoS without any *a priori* knowledge on QoS. In the application layer, the Application QoS is provided for each media stream by each application. This Application QoS is specified by the application-level parameters. For example, for video media, parameters include the frame rate, frame size, quantization factor, and, in some cases, the delay. The Network QoS is also defined on the terminal. The Network QoS is the QoS required by

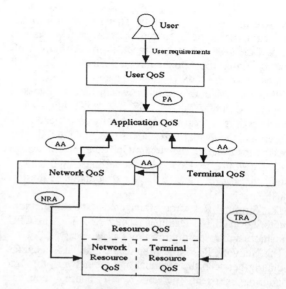

Figure 2. QoS levels

the network for each media stream and is defined by network-level parameters such as throughput, delay, jitter, and loss rate. The Resource QoS is defined as the resources to be allocated for the media stream and is separated into the Terminal Resource QoS and the Network Resource QoS. The Terminal Resource QoS includes CPU utilization and memory size. and the Network Resource QoS includes bandwidth and node buffer size. The Terminal QoS, such as the program thread scheduling period, can be defined in some cases as correspondence to the Network QoS, but it is identified with the Terminal Resource QoS in this paper. Thus, QoS can be specified at each level, and there is a relationship between QoS levels. QoS mapping is the process that translates the QoS parameters from level to level.

3. Adaptive QoS Management and Agents

In this section, the QoS management task for the system model described in the previous section is divided into subtasks. Then, the agents that take charge of the subtasks are introduced.

3.1. Task division

We divide the adaptive QoS task into six subtasks: User Interaction, Flow Establishment, QoS Maintenance, Terminal Resource Management, Network Resource Management, and Network Control.

The User Interaction subtask mediates between the user and the application. Its main purpose is to help the user specify QoS, for instance, by illustration. QoS mapping from the User QoS to the Application QoS is also included here.

The Flow Establishment subtask at the beginning of the applications establishes flows to transfer the media streams concerned. In this subtask, the QoS negotiation among multiple applications allocates resources to

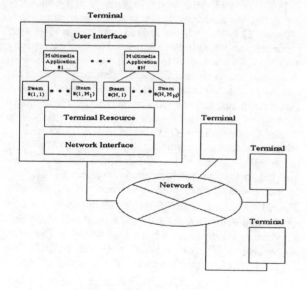

Figure 1. System model

maximize the users' total utility. Then, as a result of the QoS negotiation, the resource reservation requests are issued, if the system has such mechanisms. Also, the QoS mapping among the Application QoS, Network QoS, and Terminal Resource QoS is included here.

While the object of the Flow Establishment subtask is the global optimization of QoS, the QoS Maintenance subtask works to adjust QoS locally and reactively according to the available resources being monitored. This subtask tries to retain the stream QoS determined through the QoS negotiation. However, if it becomes impossible to sustain the stream QoS, a QoS renegotiation request is issued.

The Terminal Resource Management subtask includes monitoring available terminal resource use such as CPU or memory and reserving resources as necessary.

The Network Resource Management subtask includes mediating between the terminal and the network through monitoring existent network performance such as bandwidth and delay and reserving resources as necessary.

The Network Control subtask is designed to manage and control the streams in the network. The management depends on the network configuration, protocols, and so on.

3.2. Adaptive QoS management by MAS

We apply the MAS to execute the above-mentioned subtasks of QoS management adaptively and cooperatively. Fig. 3 shows the agent model for the adaptive QoS management. Each agent performs a separate subtask: Personal Agent (PA) does User Interaction; Application Agent (AA) does Flow Establishment; Stream Agent (SA) does QoS Maintenance; Terminal Resource Agent (TRA) does Terminal Resource Management; Network Resource Agent (NRA) does Network Resource Management; and Network Agent (NA) does Network Control. A typical QoS management flow is as follows.

[STEP 1] When a new multimedia application is invoked by the utilization demand from the user, an AA is created attached to the application. QoS requirements for the application from the user are translated by the PA and passed to the AA.

[STEP 2] Next the Flow Establishment subtask is carried out. The AA determines the stream QoS using QoS negotiation or renegotiation, which consists of an intra-terminal phase and an inter-terminal phase. The intra-terminal QoS (re)negotiation is performed first among all of the AAs on the terminal, and then the inter-terminal QoS (re)negotiation is performed between the terminals. Once the stream QoS is determined, the AA passes the stream QoS to the SA and requests the TRA or the NRA reserve the terminal or network resource if they can. To converse with TRA or NRA, the AA translates the QoS parameters using QoS mapping.

[STEP 3] After the new stream flows are established, the QoS Maintenance subtask is carried out. In this subtask, each SA adjusts the stream QoS, which it directs, reactively and autonomously. During the QoS Maintenance subtask, the TRA and the NRA monitor the terminal and network resources. If the SA can no longer guarantee the stream QoS because of, for example, a decrease in the available resources, it issues a QoS renegotiation request.

4. QoS Management by AA and SA

In this section, we describe in detail QoS negotiation among AAs and QoS adaptation among SAs.

4.1. Preparation

First, we will describe the system model concretely and define the notations. In the model, a user can specify a stream QoS through the ranged application-level QoS parameters and the utility parameter. The user can specify multiple QoS candidates for stream s at the beginning of an application to prevent frequent interaction between the user and the application. Therefore, when stream s has N QoS candidates, and one QoS candidate $Q_n(s)$ is regulated by a set of L application-level QoS parameters, the n-th stream QoS candidate $Q_n(s)$ is defined as $Q_n(s) = (q_n(1, min), q_n(1, max), q_n(2, min), q_n(2, max),..., q_n(L, min), q_n(L, max))$, where $n = 1,..., N$. $q_n(l, min)$ and $q_n(l, max)$ are the maximum and minimum values of the l-th application-level QoS parameter specified by the user. The utility parameter $u(Q_n(s))$,(1, 100) is given for each QoS candidate stream s, and represents the user's satisfaction when stream s has a QoS of $Q_n(s)$. The larger the value of $u_n(Q(s))$ is, the higher the user's satisfaction. An example of stream QoS candidates is shown in Fig. 4.

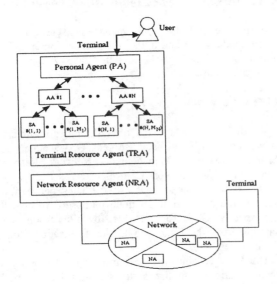

Figure 3. Layered multi-agent model

390

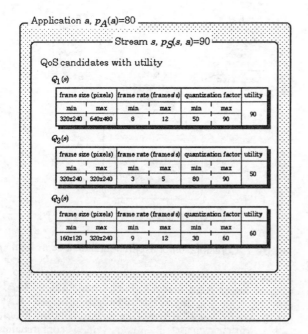

Figure 4. Example of QoS candidates

Three priority parameters, ranging from 1 to 100, are also provided by the user. The magnitude of the priority parameters proportionally indicates the priority. The first priority parameter is application priority $p_A(a)$, which represents the rank of application a among all applications in the terminal. The second priority parameter is stream priority $p_s(s, a)$, which represents the rank of stream among all streams managed by application a. The third priority parameter is QoS parameter priority $p_Q(q, s)$, which represents the rank of QoS parameter q among all QoS parameters that regulate stream s.

4.2. Intra-terminal QoS negotiation using AA

In the intra-terminal phase, the AAs negotiate to allocate resources to maximize a users' total utility. The procedure of the QoS negotiation is as follows.

When a new application is invoked in the terminal, an AA is created and attached to it. The AA then sends a QoS negotiation request message to all AA as concerned on the terminal. The AA who sends the request message is called the master agent. AAs who receive the request message are called the slave agents. If a slave agent can participate in the negotiation, it returns its own multiple sets of the stream QoS and utility parameter to the master agent. Assuming that each stream s involved in the negotiation possesses N QoS and utility parameters, $u_1(Q_1(s)), u_2(Q_2(s)), ..., u_N(Q_N(s))$, the master agent selects a set of QoS for the streams so that the total utility U defined in (1) is maximized under the resource constraint conditions in (2).

$$U = \sum_s w(s) \log u_n(Q_n(s)) \quad n \in (1,2,...,N) \quad (1)$$

$$\sum_s r_m(Q_n(s)) \le R_m \quad m = 1,2,...,M \quad (2)$$

In (1), the summation is operated for all streams involved in the negotiation, and $w(s)$ is the weight of stream s related to the priority of s. In this paper $w(s)=p_s(s, a)p_A(a)$. In (2), M is the number of the resources concerned with the QoS negotiation, and $r_m(Q_n(s))$ is the amount of the m-th resource required by processing of stream s with QoS $Q_n(s)$. R_m indicates the maximum availability of the m-th resource. In this paper, the maximum value of the ranged QoS is used for evaluation of (2).

4.3. Inter-terminal QoS negotiation through AA

After the intra-terminal QoS negotiation, the AAs begin inter-terminal QoS negotiation to resolve QoS conflicts between the stream sender and the receiver. As an example of inter-terminal QoS negotiation, Fig. 5 shows the p-p QoS negotiation protocol. The p-p QoS negotiation is conducted when the stream QoS determined by the receiver exceeds the QoS determined by the sender or when the available resources decrease to the extent that the stream QoS between the sender and receiver can be no longer maintained. In Fig. 5, the utility functions exchanged between the sender and the receiver define the relationship between QoS and the utility for respective sites. Also, the concept of fairness in the cooperative game theory[6] instantiates the pre-determined criteria for calculating the negotiated QoS, though this requires that utility functions be convex.

4.4. QoS adaptation by SA

As the QoS Maintenance subtask, the SAs adjust the ranged QoS parameters. The SA uses stream priority to order QoS adjustment, and a priority threshold parameter is shared among the SAs as a common datum. The QoS adaptation procedure shown in Fig. 6 is as follows.

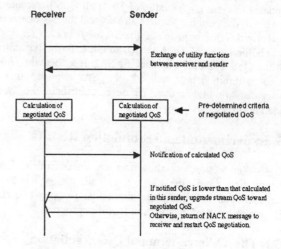

Figure 5. Inter-terminal QoS Negotiation Protocol

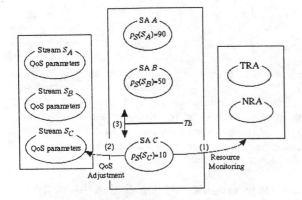

(1) An SA monitors the resources.
(2) By comparing its own stream priority with the threshold parameter Th, the SA decides whether to execute the QoS adjustment or not.
(3) If the conditions of the QoS adjustment execution are satisfied, the SA updates the threshold parameter, even though it cannot change the QoS parameters because all parameters are already set to the boundary values.

Figure 6. QoS adaptation mechanism by SA

An SA monitors resources periodically with the support of the TRA or the NRA. If the SA recognizes a shortage or surplus of resources, it refers to Th. By comparing its own stream priority $p_s(s)$ with Th, it decides whether to execute QoS adjustment or not. Although the behavior of the SA for the QoS adaptation differs between the resource shortage and the resource surplus cases, we describe only the case of resource shortage here. However, the QoS adaptation mechanism in a resource surplus case can be obtained by substituting "increase (increasing)" for "decrease (decreasing)," "decrease (decreasing)" for "increase (increasing)," "high" for "low," and "<" for ">" in the following resource shortage case.

In the case of a resource shortage, when $p_s(s) < Th$, the SA starts the QoS adaptation. Otherwise it only waits until the next resource monitoring. In the QoS adjustment process, the SA decreases the QoS parameter stepwise by the increasing order of the QoS parameter priorities. The adjustment steps of the QoS parameters are determined empirically. After the QoS adjustment process, the SA updates (increases) the value of Th. If all QoS parameters are set to the boundary values already and the SA does not perform the QoS adjustment, the SA only updates Th.

The updating of Th is needed to alleviate the partiality of the QoS adaptation by specific SAs. If a constant Th is used without being updated, the SAs whose stream priorities are higher than Th never contribute the QoS adaptation.

5. Experimental and Simulation Results

In this section, we show the AA intra-terminal QoS negotiation and the SA QoS adaptation through experimental and computer simulation results. The AA inter-terminal QoS negotiation is still in progress.

5.1. The AA intra-terminal QoS negotiation

Fig. 7 shows the configuration of the experimental

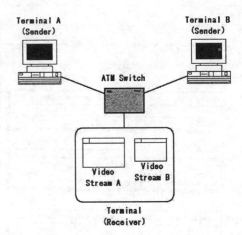

Figure 7. Configuration of experimental testbed system

testbed system, where two senders are connected to a receiver via an ATM network. Each terminal is a PC-AT machine with 266 MHz Intel Pentium processor II, a 64MB memory, a CCD camera, an image capturing board, and a JPEG CODEC board. A video conferencing application is used that is designed on the basis of the proposed QoS management framework. In it, the receiver simultaneously presents two video streams, s_A and s_B, captured by the senders in real-time fashion. The videos are encoded in Motion-JPEG format by the senders and decoded by the receiver. The video stream QoS is defined by the coding parameters, that is, the frame rate, frame size, and quantization factor, and each QoS of the two videos is specified by the receiver. In the experiment, it is assumed that enough stream bandwidth is always provided by the ATM network and that the sender CPU power is sufficiently capable of video encoding and transmission, so that the resource to be considered is the receiver's CPU power.

We verify through a typical experimental result that the intra-terminal QoS negotiation performs well. Table 1 presents two sets of QoS parameters (maximum value) and the accompanied utility for each stream. The stream priorities for s_A and s_B are 100 and 50, respectively, and the application priority is the same for both streams because they belong to the same application. The CPU utilization is the resource QoS, which was calculated using the QoS mapping from the application QoS. According to (1) and (2) with $R_1 = R_{receiverCPU} = 90$, the combination of QoS that maximizes the total utility is $Q_1(s_A)$ and $Q_2(s_B)$. Moreover, when the user demands a QoS renegotiation by changing the utility values (QoS requirements) as in Table 2, $Q_2(s_A)$ and $Q_1(s_B)$ are selected as the best QoS combination. Thus, the system can adapt to select the most appropriate QoS parameters for the streams according to the user QoS requirements and the available resources.

In this experiment, only two QoS parameter sets for each stream were considered. Nevertheless, in other experiments, it has been verified that the adaptive QoS mechanism works well for up to five QoS parameter sets

Table 1. QoS parameters and utility (initial values)

	Frame size	Frame rate	Quantization factor	CPU utilization(%)	Utility
$Q_1(S_A)$	320 x 240	5	100	71	100
$Q_2(S_A)$	160 x 120	7	60	17.85	30
$Q_1(S_B)$	320 x 240	2	100	28.4	100
$Q_2(S_B)$	160 x 120	2	100	7.15	50

Table 2. QoS parameters and utility
(after user's QoS requirement change)

	Frame size	Frame rate	Quantization factor	CPU utilization(%)	Utility
$Q_1(S_A)$	320 x 240	5	100	71	20
$Q_2(S_A)$	160 x 120	7	60	17.85	100
$Q_1(S_B)$	320 x 240	2	100	28.4	100
$Q_2(S_B)$	160 x 120	2	100	7.15	50

Table 3. Stream QoS parameters

	Maximum value	Minimum value
Frame size	320 x 240	160 x 120
Frame reate	5	3
Quantization factor	80	50

for each stream.

5.2. QoS adaptation by SA

The QoS adaptation mechanism by the SAs was verified by a number of computer simulations. A representative result is presented to show how the mechanism works.

In simulations, three streams A, B, C are managed by an application and have the same ranged QoS parameters, as in Table 3, but have different stream priorities: 90, 50, 10, as shown in Fig. 6. It is assumed that $p_0(quantization\_factor, s) < p_0(frame\_rate, s) < p_0(frame\_size, s)$, where $s = A, B, C$ and CPU utilization is the only resource QoS considered. Here, $R(s)$ represents the resource QoS used by stream s and the status of $R_{min}^{avail} < \sum_s R(s) < R_{max}^{avail}$ is defined as *the stable status*, and the opposite, as *the unstable status*. $R_{min}^{avail} = R_{min}^0 - \Delta R$ and $R_{max}^{avail} = R_{max}^0 - \Delta R$ are the minimum and maximum values of the available resources, where R_{min}^0 and R_{max}^0 are the initial minimum and maximum availabilities of the resource, and ΔR is the incremental load of the resources. Usually R_{max}^0 equals R_m in (2), and ΔR is the resource consumed by the applications on the terminal that have no QoS management mechanism. R_{min}^0 is determined

empirically.

Initially, it is assumed that all of the streams have the maximum QoS parameters and the resource allocation is in the stable status with $\Delta R = 0$. Then, we provide a positive value of ΔR so that the resource allocation moves to the unstable status (a resource shortage). The SAs start the QoS adaptation until resource allocation becomes stable again. We have evaluated the SA behaviors on two indices of measurement: convergence time and priority cost. The convergence time is the period from the start of the unstable status until a return to the stable status. A shorter convergence time is preferred. The priority cost is the accumulated stream priority that belongs to a SA that has tried the QoS adjustment. Since the QoS adjustment should be executed by a SA with lower stream priority, a smaller priority cost is preferred. In the simulations, the update of Th is performed by increasing or decreasing the constant value (ΔTh), and the QoS adjustment is performed by changing the QoS parameter from the maximum (minimum) to the minimum (maximum) value in one step.

Fig. 8 and Fig. 9 present the convergence time and the priority cost for $\Delta R = 10, 30, 60$ and $\Delta Th = 10, 20, 30, 40$. For a larger ΔTh, the higher stream priority tends to engage the QoS adjustment. The simulation results for the Sequential and Parallel cases are also presented in Fig. 8 and Fig. 9 for comparison. In the Sequential case, the SA adjusts the QoS sequentially using the exact order of the stream priority. In the Parallel case, the SA adjusts the QoS parallelly regardless of the stream priority. In both cases, the threshold no longer has any meaning. The simulation results reveal that the convergence time tends to be long and the priority cost remains low when ΔTh is small (for instance, $\Delta Th = 10$), and convergence time shortens and priority cost increases when ΔTh becomes large (for instance, $\Delta Th = 40$)[†]. This shows that the SAs successfully and autonomously perform the QoS adaptation simply by referring to the common threshold parameter and updating it, and that ΔTh can be used as a control parameter for SA behavior.

6. Concluding Remarks

We have presented a multi-agent-based, end-to-end QoS management mechanism for distributed multimedia applications. The adaptability to various user's QoS requirements as well as to various networks and terminal performances is accomplished through a division of QoS management tasks and cooperation among agents. The AA and SA are introduced to perform long-term and short-term QoS adaptations, respectively. The AA needs to be deliberative to determine optimal resource allocation from a long-term viewpoint using intra-terminal and inter-terminal QoS negotiations. In contrast, the SA needs to be

---

[†] For $\Delta R = 60$ in Fig. 9, the priority cost constant, because $\Delta R = 60$ is regarded as a very heavy load and all SAs had to contribute to the QoS adjustment equally regardless of ΔTh.

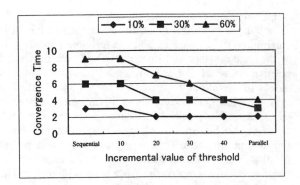

Figure 8. Simulation results (convergence time).

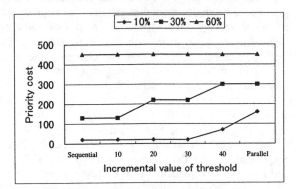

Figure 9. Simulation results (priority cost).

able to react quickly since it has to instantly adjust the stream QoS under its management according to the available resources.

The AA has been implemented in a laboratory testbed, and it was confirmed that the resources could be allocated appropriately using the AA intra-terminal QoS negotiation. In addition, we have tested a number of computer simulations of QoS adaptation using the SA. We have found that the SA adjusts its stream QoS autonomously using the common priority threshold parameter and that SA behavior correlates to the quantity of the threshold update.

Though we have utilized Motion JPEG stream in our experimental testbed, our framework can also handle a variable bit rate (VBR) stream such as an MPEG-2 coded video. In this case, effective management of QoS using the structure of MPEG stream is needed.

In regard to network resources, allocating bandwidth to the VBR stream at peak rate results in low network utilization. The introduction of traffic smoothing [8] to each Group of Picture (GoP) makes network utilization more efficient, while it causes additional buffer delay. This trade-off should be taken into consideration in QoS mapping and QoS adaptation.

In regard to terminal resources, dropping frames on a terminal in response to temporary load increase can reduce CPU utilization. While each frame can drop individually in JPEG stream, units of GoP must generally drop in MPEG stream because the inter-frame encoding is used in MPEG scheme. That is, a group of frame (e.g. 15 frames in a maximum case) drops at a time. Therefore, a fine-grained dropping is needed by reducing the number of frames in a GoP composition. However, GoP consisting of a few frames increases bandwidth. Thus, QoS negotiation needs consider this trade-off between the fine-grained QoS management and bandwidth increase.

We are now working on merging the mechanism of the SA into the testbed. The whole framework proposed in this paper will be implemented soon.

Acknowledgment

The authors would like to thank Dr. Bokuji Komiyama, president of ATR Adaptive Communications Research Laboratories, for his guidance and support.

Reference

[1] C. Aurrecoechea, A. T. Campbell and L. Hauw, "A Survey of QoS Architectures," ACM/Springer Verlag Multimedia Systems Journal, Special Issue on QoS Architecture, Vol.6, No.3, May 1998.

[2] A. Puliafito, O. Tomarchio and H. de Meer, "An agent-based framework for QoS management," in Proc. of WCSS'97, Singapore, pp.392-396, Sept. 1997.

[3] S. Fischer, A. Hafid, G. V. Bochmann and H. de Meer, "Cooperative QoS Management for Multimedia Applications," in Proc. of the IEEE Int. Conf. on Multimedia Computing and Systems (ICMCS'97), Ottawa, Canada, pp.303-310, Jun. 1997.

[4] E. H. Durfee, "Blissful Ignorance: Knowing Just Enough to Coordinate Well," in Proc. of ICMAS-95, pp.406-413.

[5] N. Nishio and H. Tokuda, "Simplified Method for Session Coordination Using Multi-level QOS Specification and Translation," in Building QoS into Distributed Systems, ed. A. Campbell and K. Nahrstedt, Chapman Hall, Tokyo, 1997.

[6] X. Cao, "Preference function and bargaining solutions," in Proc. of the 21th IEEE Conf. on Decision and Control, WA6-10:15, pp. 164-171, 1982.

[7] C. Zhang and D. Lukose eds., "Multi-Agent Systems Methodologies and Applications (Lecture Notes in Artificial Intelligence 1286)," Springer-Verlag, Tokyo, 1997.

[8] K. Joseph, D. Reininger, "Source Traffic Smoothing and ATM Network Interfaces for VBR MPEG Video Encoders", Proceedings of IEEE ICC'95, pp1761-1767, June 1995.

Development and Application of a Distance Learning Support System Using Personal Computers via the Internet

Takashi Yoshino[1], Jun Munemori[2], Takaya Yuizono[1],

Yoji Nagasawa[1], Shiro Ito[1] and Kazutomo Yunokuchi[1]

[1]*Faculty of Engineering, Kagoshima University,*

1-21-40 Korimoto Kagoshima 890-0065, Japan

[2]*Center for Information Science, Wakayama University,*

930 Sakaedani Wakayama 640-8510, Japan

yoshino@be.kagoshima-u.ac.jp, munemori@sys.wakayama-u.ac.jp

Abstract

A distance learning support system using the Internet for communication, which can support 40 personal computers, has been developed. The system supports audio and video communication channels. During Q&A sessions, the teacher and one student can communicate with each other through audio and video equipment. The system is also equipped with two shared cursors (one for the teacher, the other for the students) and the Blackboard system and Note system for students. The system has been tested on three different kinds of classes (a lecture on human interface engineering, an exercise on applied mathematics II, and a lecture on high frequency engineering). The results of distance learning experiments suggested: (1) After applying the system to actual classes, we found that the system required the additional functions of a randomly controlled remote-control camera, card materials transfer, and an interlocking marker. (2) We found that student participants in distance learning felt as if they were in the same building as the teacher. Students wanted to take more distance learning classes, about six times out of 15 times on average. (3) There were seldom questions during school hours. We must improve the Q&A function to increase the number of questions from students.

1. Introduction

The Internet has come into wide use recently and high performance personal computers (PCs) have appeared. We have applied this computer technology to the field of education and developed a distance learning system. Distance learning support systems have been much studied and developed [1]-[4] in Japan. There is almost no example to apply multiple real classes. One of our goals has been to build an effective distance learning support system for Japanese people. Thus, we have created a relatively inexpensive distance learning support system that is capable of using up to 40 PCs for 40 students.

In this system, a teacher can lecture students from a remote site via the Internet. The PC on the teacher site continually displays the situation of the classroom using a remote control camera. The PCs at the students' site (the classroom) display the teacher from the waist up. During Q&A sessions, the teacher and one student can communicate through audio and video equipment. The students' PCs also display teaching materials as they are presented and controlled by the teacher.

2. Distance learning support system

2.1 Design policy

Multimedia environment of our classroom consists of the following:

- 40 computers, 15-inch monitors, CCD cameras, and microphones.

- A projector, a screen and two speakers.

- Each computer is connected to Ethernet in the classroom, and the network of the classroom is connected to the Internet.

Before developing above system, the following items were requested:

- The capacity for 40 students per class.

Because 40 students are a unit to take lessons in most of Japanese university.

- Distance learning classes communicated via the Internet.

Because teachers in the provinces take a business trip frequently. They want to teach at the place where they are staying.

- Q&A sessions between a teacher and one student.

Seldom students ask a teacher question during school hours in Japanese university. We should develop functions for Q&A to increase the number of questions.

- The ability of the teacher to observe the situation of the classroom from a distant location.

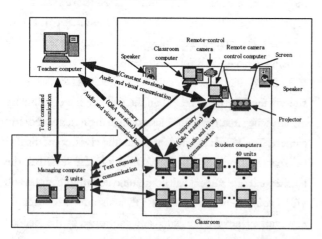

Figure 1. Configuration of distance learning support system. Managing and students computers are in the same building. The fine lines are a text command communication (several-ten bytes). The bold lines are a audio and visual communication (several frame per second).

Teachers will be difficult to teach efficiently, if they can't catch the students' reaction.

- The contents on the teacher's monitor are displayed on each student's monitor, as well as two shared cursors.

Because WYSIWIS is necessary for distance learning.

- Two shared cursors (one for the teacher, the other for the students).

A teacher's shared cursor is used for directing his explain point and a student's shared cursor is used for directing his question point.

-The card type screen for teacher (the Blackboard system) and student (the Note System).

Because the card system is popular to Japanese students.

Based on the above specifications and requests, we had developed the system.

2.2 Hardware configuration

An overall view of the distance learning support system is indicated in Figure 1. The following are the specifications for the individual pieces of equipment:

(1) The Teacher and student computer

The hardware equipment for the teacher and students consists of the Power Macintosh 8100/100AV (Apple Computer) with a 15-inch monitor, CCD camera (QCAM Connectix), and a microphone (Plain Talk Microphone, Apple Computer).

(2) The managing computer

The managing computer is a so-called reflector, which implements synchronous operations on both the teacher and student sides. The managing computer used here is the same ability as the student computer. Since a public network (the Internet) is used for long-distance communication, the managing computer was introduced to reduce the amount of extra-classroom communication, and to decrease the load of the teacher's computer. Two computers are used due to the limited number (31 computers) of linked computers in QuickTime Conferencing (Apple Computer)[5] which we use the basic function for communication.

Table 1. A list of supported functions.

Supporting functions	Explanations
1. Audio and video switching button	Names of students that are input upon registering to the class are shown. The name list can also be used as seating list.
2. Remote-control camera operating pointer	It enables a teacher to view specific spots in the classroom using a mouse pointer. It controls panning, angle of elevation and zoom.
3. Remote-control camera random operating function	Randomly centers on a student every 10 seconds and shows them on the monitor.
4. Teacher's shared cursor	Teacher's cursor is shown on the students' monitor as it is moved.
5. Student's shared cursor	A student's cursor is displayed on monitors of both the teacher and a student during Q&A session.
6. Interlocking card turning function	It allows the display, on the students' monitor, of a page of text, as the teacher moves from one page to the next.
7. Question button	As a student pushes the button, his or her name on the "Audio and video switching button" on a teacher's monitor is highlighted.
8. Card material transmission system	It enables the transmission of the teacher's material in card form to all students. Adding and correcting of the material can also be done. Furthermore, it enables students' questions and comments to be transmitted to all participants using the Blackboard system during Q&A session.
9. Interlocking card creation function / Interlocking card deletion function	As a teacher creates/deletes a card in the blackboard system, a card is created/deleted in the blackboard system on the students' side.
10. Interlocking marker function	A teacher can write a shared color marking to a teaching material using this function. This color markers are easy to move or correct or delete, because this function is drawn on another layer of teaching materials.
11. A teacher and one student directly Q&A session	During Q&A sessions, a teacher and one student can communicate directly using audio and video equipment.

2.3 Software configuration

The software for this system consists of the Blackboard system, Note system, audio and video switching system, and NetGear[6] and MediaCore which are intercomputer multimedia communications software. All software was made by ourselves. The Blackboard and Note system, based on our card-type database software called Wadaman [6], have been developed and enhanced with additional functions. Table 1 indicates all the supporting functions of the system. NetGear is the software for text command communication, while MediaCore is used for audio and video communication.

(1) The Blackboard system

The Blackboard system is displayed on the monitors of the teacher and all students, and allows the teacher to show the materials to students. Normally, only the teacher can control the system. This system is based on the card-type database Wadaman. The Blackboard system corresponds to the conventional blackboard which a teacher write on contents of teaching. The same contents are displayed on all computer monitors. Distance learning support functions of the Blackboard system are: two shared cursors, interlocking card turning, a card materials transfer, interlocking card making, interlocking card removal, and an interlocking marker function. Also, the Blackboard system for the students comes with a question button.

(2) The Note system

This is a system for students to use as in note taking. Its interface is almost the same as the Blackboard system. Students cannot control the Blackboard system, but they can freely use the Note system. The Note system uses exactly the same materials as the Blackboard system. During a lecture, the student can display the same material from the Blackboard system, and directly write into the Note system. Also, it is possible for students to display other page of teaching materials.

2.4 Intercomputer multimedia communications

This system uses NetGear and MediaCore for intercomputer communications. Both are communication applications that use QuickTime Conferencing. Since TCP/IP is used for the text command communication, and UDP/IP for the audio and video communication, this system can be used from anywhere as long as Internet connection is possible. With this system, NetGear is used for the text command communication, and MediaCore for audio and video communication.

The Internet, the communication channel for this system, has the problem of not being able to guarantee sufficient bandwidth. Therefore, we used two computers for audio and video connections at most times, and three during Q&A sessions. As for the text command communication that controls teaching material synchronism, the system distributes text commands to individual computers via the managing computer to reduce the amount of online communication.

(1) Text command communication

The configuration of the text command communication is indicated by the fine line in Figure 1. Text command communication is achieved through the managing computer, and is sent and received between the teacher computer and all of the student computers. Because of this communication form, it is possible to send commands with a capacity of several-ten bytes per communication between computers. The communication form is used for the following purposes: to control the Blackboard system and the shared cursor synchronously; to control the data of Q&A sessions, to switch audio communications, and to control the remote-control camera.

(2) Audio and video communication

The configuration of the audio and video communication is indicated by the bold line in Figure 1. Due to the large data amount of the audio and video communication, the limitations on the network, and the computer processing capabilities, the teacher and student computers cannot be connected all the time. Thus, after examining the necessary audio and video elements, we decided that the teacher computer and classroom computer should be connected constantly. Three computers would be connected in Q&A sessions. As a result, one-on-one communication between the teacher and any student is possible.

2.5 Interface

(1) Interface of the teacher computer

The image on the teacher computer monitor during distance learning classes is indicated in Figure 2: the upper part of the teacher's body, the view of the classroom by the remote-control camera, the Blackboard system, and the audio and video switching window. During Q&A sessions with the student, his or her image window is displayed as well.

(2) Interface of the student computer

The image on the student computer monitor is shown in Figure 3: the student, the Blackboard system, and the Note

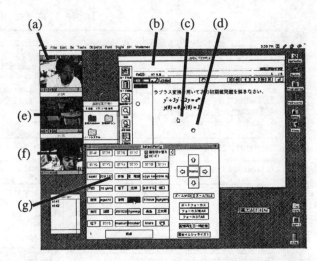

Figure 2. An example of a screen on a teacher side.
(a) teacher's video; (b) Blackboard system; (c) teacher's shared cursor; (d) student's shared cursor; (e) classroom video; (f) student's video (only Q&A sessions); (g) audio and video switching window.

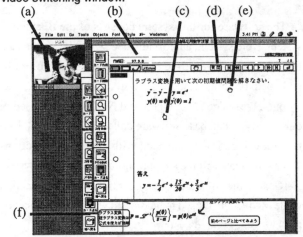

Figure 3. An example of a screen on a student side.
(a) student's video; (b) Blackboard system; (c) teacher's shared cursor; (d) question button; (e) student's shared cursor; (f) Note system.

system. During Q&A sessions with the teacher, the teacher's image window is displayed as well.

(3) The screen in the classroom

The Blackboard system, the image of the classroom, and the image of the teacher is displayed on the classroom screen.

3. Application to actual classes

The distance learning support system has been evaluated

and improved by applying it to three actual classes. The functions discussed in Chapter 2 are the results of a number of additions and modifications based on the class findings. The following are the functions developed based on the findings from actual classes.

3.1 Application to human interface engineering

(1) Content of the class

The distance learning class on human interface engineering was conducted on July 11, 1997. This class was conducted between a teacher of Osaka University and twelve graduate students in the classroom, which is located on the second floor of the Information Engineering Department at Kagoshima University. The geographical distance between the two universities was approximately 900 km. In the class, the teacher discussed groupware-related topics as a preliminary explanation of the summer intensive seminars. Each student listened to the teacher while reading the materials on the Blackboard system, which were displayed on the student computer monitor.

(2) Improvements after the class

After the experiment, the teacher pointed out that there was little time to operate the remote-control camera, and that a function to correct card materials was needed. It was very difficult to conduct a lecture while frequently trying to adjust the remote-control camera. However, if the teacher did not move the camera, he would be looking at the same image all the time, thus making it difficult to grasp the atmosphere of the classroom. A randomly controlled camera which is to observe students in different places was requested.

The reason that the transfer function of the card materials was necessary is because teachers sometimes make errors when preparing the materials.

3.2 Application to the exercise of applied mathematics II

(1) Content of the class

The class on the exercise of applied mathematics II was conducted on September 11, 1997. The class was carried out between a Kagoshima University teacher in the sixth-floor Teachers Room at Department of Electrical and Electronics Engineering and 32 sophomores of the same department in another building. The geographical distance between the two buildings was approximately 150 m. In the class, the teacher discussed topics related to the Laplace transforms as a summary of previous classes.

One student noticed a mistake in one of the exercises, and informed it to the teacher using the question button. The teacher redistributed the exercises using the card materials transfer function, then instructed the students to answer the corrected exercise.

(2) Improvements after the experiment

Some students expressed a desire to see the card materials in color, especially in red and blue for emphasis. Thus, we decided to develop a color expression.

3.3. Application to high frequency engineering

(1) Content of the class

The first and second classes on high frequency engineering were conducted on December 2 and December 9, 1997 respectively. The participants were five juniors and three juniors of the department for the first and second classes respectively. Since both the teacher and students stayed in the same room, it was not a distance learning class though the distance learning support system was used. In a distance learning class there is a delay in voice transmission, of approximately one second, due to compression or expansion processing of the data. On the other hand, the shared cursor also moves with a delay about 1.4 seconds, thus making little difference in time between the voice of the teacher and cursor movements. However, when the teacher and students are in the same room, the delay in the shared cursor movements seems more conspicuous. Thus, the teacher moved to computer located to the right and behind a student, and used it as the teacher computer. Then, the teacher conducted the class directly addressing the student, while checking the student's monitor in front and to his left, in accordance with the movement of the shared cursor.

(2) Improvements after the experiment

In the first class, the teacher used the marker function, trying to indicate specific areas in the diagrams of the card materials. There was already a shared cursor for the purpose of pointing at certain locations in the material, but a shared cursor could not cover a certain area. Since the marker function was available for only the Note system, we incorporated an interlocking marker function into the Blackboard system.

4. Evaluations and comments

4.1 Evaluation based on questionnaire surveys

After the classes, questionnaire surveys on a scale of 1 to 5 were conducted with the students. The survey results are shown in Figure 4. Surveys with students who had taken conventional class were also conducted.

(1) Understanding the content of the class

The students who were in the class using the distance learning support system said that they understood the class content almost as well as in a conventional class. It is believed that the voice and Blackboard system helped in understanding the content of the class. The results showed that the voice through the distance learning communication device was as good as the voice in direct speaking. In fact, the Blackboard system actually received better estimations than the conventional blackboard. The students evaluated highly the shared cursor and the materials in front of their eyes. It was easy to understand what the teacher was trying to say.

(2) Delays in communication and processing

The general impression was that students were not bothered much by the delay in communication. As for the clarity of the teacher's voice, with the exception of some "howling" and interruptions, the voice was clear enough to be understood in the class. Video channels were mostly two to three frames per second.

(3) Comments on the classes

The distance learning class on human interface engineering was conducted with between Osaka University and Kagoshima University, and that on the exercise of applied mathematics II was done between different buildings on the Kagoshima University campus. In spite of the distances, the students in both cases felt as if the teachers were in the same building. When we asked "given the chance, would you like to take this kind of distance learning class again?", they indicated a relatively positive trend. When we asked "how

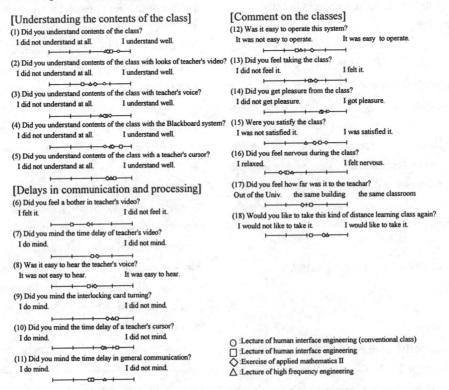

Figure 4. Results of questionnaire surveys.

many times out of 15 lectures would you like to take distance learning classes?", the average was about 6 times. We found from those comments that although they did not wish to have all classes on a distance learning, the students thought that they could take a distance learning class approximately 40 % of 15 lectures.

There were only two questions in three different classes. Question button and student's shared cursor were used only two times. Japanese students seldom ask teacher questions during school hours from the first. Most students ask a teacher questions after classes. Take into considering above facts, the frequency of questions was very small, we must improve the system to ask a question easily.

4.2 Comparisons with the existing system

There are many examples of collaboration systems available today. Most of Internet based educational systems are video teleconferencing systems, and net-based virtual auditorium or lecture room systems.

We compare our system with several other commercial and research activities briefly: Microsoft NetMeeting [7], TANGO [8], Habanero [9], Centra [10], Placeware [11], KMi Stadium [12] and the system of Zaslavsky and Baker [13]. Microsoft NetMeeting supports for the basic collaborative tools (audio-video conferencing, chat rooms and whiteboard).

TANGO, Habanero, Centra, Placeware and KMi Stadium are Web-based collaboratory packages. TANGO and Habanero are written in Java and their application can be shared via exchange of API calls between the core and the application. Centra, Placeware and KMi Stadium allow many simultaneous participants system. Their systems make available as a reusable resource. Centra supports up to 250 simultaneous user per events. Centra includes multi-way audio conferencing, yes/no responses and feedback, live application sharing, whiteboard, just-in-time content updates, text chat, and spontaneous polling. Placeware supports up to 1000 people at the same time. The features of Placeware are almost the same as those of Centra. KMi Stadium is a Java-implemented system, allowing thousands of simultaneous participants even over 28.8kbps dial-up modems. The features of KMi Stadium also look like those of Centra. Unlike Centra and Placeware, KMi Stadium can run live 'streaming video' on higher-bandwidth clients.

The system of Zaslavsky and Baker resembles our system about an arrangement of an instructor and students, and the form of lectures. In their system, an instructor was at a distance site and students were in the lab. The demo computer in the lab was connected to an LCD panel and a projector. Audio was transmitted through speakers connected to the demo computer. Real-time video images were captured with video cameras of the instructor's and demo computers. The

Table 2. Comparison of our system and Zaslavsky and Baker system [13].

	Specifications and functions	Our system		Zaslavsky and Baker system [13]	
		Existence	Specifications	Existence	Specifications
Hardware	Teacher and each student computer	O	PC	O	PC and WS
	Network	O	Internet	O	Internet
	Each student camera	O		X	
	Classroom remote-control camera	O		X	
Software function	Teaching materials displayed on all the members	O	Card-base system, made from our lab.	O	Whiteboard in NetMeeting.
	The right of write-in to teaching materials	O	A teacher is always available. Students are available only at Q & A sessions.	O	Always possible.
	Note system/Lecture notes	O		O	Web-based lecture notes.
	Question method	O	Students ask questions using a question button for each student's computer, and then audio and video one-on-one communication is available.	O	Students ask questions using the chat window and whiteboard, semi-anonymously identified only by computer number.
	Shared cursor	O	Two cursors (one for the teacher, the other for the students)	O	One cursor for each member on a whiteboard
	Interlocking marker function	O	This function often used by a teacher to emphasize important lecture concepts.	X	
	Remote-control camera operating pointer	O		X	
	Remote-control camera randomly operating function	O		X	
	Seating arrangement table with a virtual classroom	O		X	
	Application sharing	X		O	By NetMeeting
	Chat function	X		O	By NetMeeting
	E-mail function	X		O	
Others	The number of students which participated at applications		from 3 to 32		from 8 to 14

pictures of both the instructor and the students were superimposed on Web-based lecture notes. Students could join the meeting between the instructor and TA from their client computers in the lab. They could gain access to shared textual and drawing windows (a shared whiteboard). Moreover their system has both Web-based lecture notes and frequent email.

Comparisons between our system and the system devised by Zaslavsky and Baker are shown in Table 2. Unlike their system, our system has a remote control camera for observing a classroom, a remote-control camera random operating function, one-on-one communication using audio and video for the students directly Q&A sessions and interlocking marker function. Additionally, in Zaslavsky and Baker system, TA has an essential role, for example, she controlled the organization of program windows in the demo computer. In our system, although TA has an important role, it is not indispensable. A teacher can operate our system all alone.

5. Conclusion

A distance learning support system has been developed, with which a teacher at a distant site can lecture students in a classroom, using personal computers. The following results were learned by applying the system to three different classes

(1) The distance learning support system was equipped with the following; the Blackboard system, the Note system, the shared cursor for the teacher and students, the remote-control camera pointer, the seating arrangement, interlocking card turning, and the Question button. After applying the system to actual classes, we learned that the additional functions of a randomly controlled remote-control camera, card materials transfer, and an interlocking marker were needed.

(2) We found that the student participants in distance learning felt as if they were in the same building as the teacher. The students expressed the desire to take further distance learning classes, six times out of 15 times on average.

(3) Our system gained public favor generally, but the limitation of our system is not to break the fewness of questions.

We are going to develop the function, named a shared

temporarily drawing function [14], for enhanced interaction of a teacher and students. We are planning to further evaluate the cases in which the same students continue to take distance learning classes.

Acknowledgement

For help with this paper we would like to Professor Norio Shiratori.

References

[1] Y. Takemoto et. al.: "Construction and Examination of Operational Environment by Lectures in a Distributed Education System", *Trans. of IPSJ*, Vol.36, No.9, pp. 2215-2227 (1995).

[2] T. Dasai et. al.: "Support for Collaborative Distance Learning by Multi-agent Functions", *Trans. of IPSJ*, Vol.39, No.2, pp.199-210(1998).

[3] K. Maeda et. al.: "Multimedia Communication Environment for Distance Learning", *Trans. of IEICE*, Vol.J80-B-I, No.6, pp. 348-354(1997).

[4] K. Maeda, R. Aibara, K. Kawamoto, M. Terauchi and S.Otsuki, An environment for Multimedia Communication Literacy, *Proc. of ED-MEDIA/ED-TELECOM 97*, pp. 653-658 (1997).

[5] Y. Inoue et. al.: "A Development of Remote Teaching Support System", *Technical report of IPSJ*, GW-21-24, pp.139-144 (1997).

[6] J. Munemori et. al.: "Remote Seminar Support System and Its Application and Estimation to a Seminar via Internet", *Trans. of IPSJ*, Vol.39, No.2, pp. 447-457 (1998).

[7] Microsoft NetMeeting Web Site : http://www.microsoft.com/netmeeting/

[8] TANGO Web Site : http://trurl.npac.syr.edu/tango/

[9] Habanero Web Site : http://havefun.ncsa.uiuc.edu/habanero/

[10] Centra Web Site : http://www.centra.com/

[11] Placeware Web Site : http://www.placeware.com/

[12] KMi Stadium Web Site : http://kmi.open.ac.uk/stadium/

[13] Ilya Zaslavsky and Kathleen Baker, "The experimental Web-based interactive environment in distance teaching of GIS and Geographic Data Handling", *Proc. of the 1998 ACSM Annual Convention and Exhibition*, Baltimore, MD, Vol. 2, pp. 437-446 (1998).

[14] T. Yoshino, J. Munemori, T. Yuizono, N. Kamiman, Y. Nagasawa, K. Yunokuchi and S. Ito, "Improvement of Distance Learning Supported System SEGODON and its Continuous Application to Classes", *DICOMO'99 Multimedia, Distributed, Cooperative and Mobile*, IPSJ Symposium Series Vol.99 (1999), pp.565-570.

Session C6

Job Scheduling

Chair: Wei Zhao
Texas A&M University, USA

Multi-Capacity Bin Packing Algorithms
with Applications to Job Scheduling under Multiple Constraints *

William Leinberger, George Karypis, Vipin Kumar
Department of Computer Science and Engineering, University of Minnesota
(leinberg, karypis, kumar) @ cs.umn.edu

Abstract

Multi-capacity bin-packing is a generalization of the classical one-dimensional bin-packing problem in which the bin capacity and the item sizes are represented by d-dimensional vectors. Previous work in d-capacity bin-packing algorithms analyzed variants of single capacity bin-packing, extended to deal with the d capacities. These extended algorithms are oblivious to the additional capacity information, however, and do not scale well with increasing d. We provide new packing algorithms which use the additional capacity information to provide better packing and show how these algorithms might lead to better multi-resource allocation and scheduling solutions.

1. Introduction

Multi-capacity bin-packing is a generalization of the classical one-dimensional bin-packing problem in which the bin capacity and the item sizes are represented by d-dimensional vectors [3]. Past research in multi-capacity bin-packing has focused on extending the single capacity bin-packing to deal with the multiple capacities, and on providing performance bounds on these simple algorithms. In general, these naive algorithms did not use the additional capacity information to guide them so do not scale well with increasing capacity counts. Our contribution is to provide multi-capacity *aware* bin-packing algorithms which make use of the information in the additional capacities to guide item selection in the packing process. Simulation results show that the multi-capacity aware algorithms provide

*This work was supported by NASA NCC2-5268, by NSF CCR-9423082, by Army Research Office contract DA/DAAG55-98-1-0441, DA/DAAH04-95-1-0244, and by Army High Performance Computing Research Center cooperative agreement number DAAH04-95-2-0003/contract number DAAH04-95-C-0008. Access to computing facilities was provided by AHPCRC and Minnesota Supercomputer Institute. Related papers are available via WWW at URL: http://www.cs.umn.edu/~karypis

a consistent performance improvement over the previous naive algorithms. Further simulation results shows that the multi-capacity aware algorithms can produce a better packing from a short input list, which supports their use in online job scheduling in the presence of multiple constraints.

The remainder of this document is outlined below. Section 2 provides a summary of past research in multi-capacity bin-packing algorithms and discusses some of the limitations of these algorithms. Our new multi-capacity aware bin-packing algorithms are presented in Section 3, with experimental results and conclusions provided in Section 4.

2. Related research

A variety of past research has dealt with single and d-capacity bin-packing problem formulations and their connection to the generalized scheduling problem [1], [2], [3], [5]. A brief summary of this work is provided below.

The classical single capacity bin-packing problem may be stated as follows. We are given a positive bin capacity C and a set (or list) of scalar items $L = \{x_1, x_2, \ldots, x_i, \ldots, x_n\}$ with each item x_i having an size $s(x_i)$ satisfying $0 \leq s(x_i) \leq C$. What is the smallest m such that there is a partition $L = B_1 \bigcup B_2 \bigcup \ldots \bigcup B_m$ satisfying $\sum_{x_i \in B_j} s(x_i) \leq C, 1 \leq j \leq m$? B_i is interpreted as the contents of a bin of capacity C and the goal is to pack the items of L into as few bins as possible.

The single capacity bin-packing problem formulation has been generalized to support d-capacities as follows [9], [7]. The capacity of a container is represented by a d-capacity vector, $\vec{C} = (C_1, C_2, \ldots, C_j, \ldots, C_d)$, where $C_j, 0 \leq C_j$, represents the kth component capacity. An item is also represented by a d-capacity vector, $\vec{X}_i = (X_{i1}, X_{i2}, \ldots, X_{ij}, \ldots, X_{id})$, where $X_{ij}, 0 \leq X_{ij} \leq C_j$, denotes the jth component requirement of the ith item. Trivially, $\sum_{j=1}^{d} C_j > 0$ and $\sum_{j=1}^{d} X_{ij} > 0 \, \forall \, 1 \leq i < n$. An item $\vec{X}_i$ can be *packed* (or fit) into a bin $\vec{B}_k$, if $\vec{B}_k + \vec{X}_i \leq \vec{C}$, or $B_{kj} + X_{ij} \leq C_j \, \forall \, 1 \leq j \leq d$. The items are obtained from an initial list L, and the total number of items to be packed is denoted by n. Again, the goal is to partition the list L into as few bins $\vec{B}_k$ as possible.

The approach to solving the d-capacity bin-packing problem has mainly been to extend the single capacity bin-packing algorithms to deal with the d-capacity items and bins. The Next-Fit (NF) algorithm takes the next d-capacity item $\vec{X}_i$ and attempts to place it in the current bin $\vec{B}_k$. If it does not fit (ie, if $X_{ij} + B_{kj} > C_j$ for some j) then a new bin, $\vec{B}_{k+1}$, is started. Note that no bin $\vec{B}_l, 1 \leq l < k$ is considered as a candidate for item $\vec{X}_i$. The First-Fit (FF) algorithm removes this restriction by allowing the next item $\vec{X}_i$ to be placed into any of the k currently non-empty bins. If $\vec{X}_i$ will not fit into any of the current k bins, then a new bin $\vec{B}_{k+1}$ is created and accepts the item. The Best-Fit adds a further bin selection heuristic to the First-Fit algorithm. Best-Fit places the next item into the bin in which it leaves the least total empty space. Other variations of these simple algorithms have also been extended to support the d-capacity formulation.

Orthogonal to the item-to-bin placement rules described above is the method for pre-processing the item list before packing. For the single capacity bin-packing problem, sorting the scalar item list in non-increasing order with respect to the item weights generally improves the performance of the packing. First-Fit Decreasing (FFD) first sorts the list L in non-increasing order and the applies the First-Fit packing algorithm. Next-Fit and Best-Fit may be extended in a similar manner. Sorting in the d-capacity formulation has also been explored with similar success as in the single capacity case. In the d-capacity formulation, however, the items are sorted based on a *scalar* representation of the d components. A simple extension to the single capacity case is to sort the items based on the sum of their d components (Maximum Sum). Other methods include sorting on the maximum component, sum of squares of components, product of components, etc.. The goal is to somehow capture the relative *size* of each d-capacity item.

The performance bounds for d-capacity bin-packing have also been studied [4]. If A is an algorithm and $A(L)$ gives the number of bins used by that algorithm on the item list L, then define $R_A \equiv A(L)/OPT(L)$ as the *performance ratio* of algorithm A, where $OPT(L)$ gives the optimal number of bins for the given list. It has been shown that $R_A \leq d + 1$ for any *reasonable* algorithm. Reasonable implies that no two bins may be combined into a single bin. Note that the Next-Fit algorithm is not reasonable whereas the First-Fit and Best-Fit are reasonable. While this bound may seem a bit dismal, simulation studies have shown that the simple algorithms described above perform fairly well over a wide range of input.

3. The windowed multi-capacity aware bin-packing algorithms

The d-capacity First-Fit (FF) bin-packing algorithm presented in Section 2 looks at each item $\vec{X}_i$ in the list L in order and attempts to place the item in any of the currently existing bins $\vec{B}_1 \ldots \vec{B}_k$. If the item will not fit in any of the existing bins, a new bin $\vec{B}_{k+1}$ is created and the item is placed there. An alternate algorithm which achieves an identical packing to FF is as follows. Initially, bin $\vec{B}_1$ is created and the first item in the list L, $\vec{X}_1$, is placed into this bin. Next, the list L is *scanned* from beginning to end searching for the next element $\vec{X}_i$ which will fit into bin $\vec{B}_1$. Place each successive $\vec{X}_i$ which fits into bin $\vec{B}_1$. When no element is found which will fit, then bin $\vec{B}_2$ is created. Place the first of the remaining elements of L into $\vec{B}_2$. The process is repeated until the list L is empty. The primary difference is that each bin is filled completely before moving on to the next bin.

The list scanning process provides the basic algorithm structure for our new multi-capacity aware bin-packing algorithms. The key differences between the new algorithms and the FF algorithm is the criteria used to select the next item to be packed into the current bin. Recall that FF requires only that the item fits into the current bin, essentially ignoring the current component weights of the item and the current component capacities of the bins. As a result, a single capacity in a bin may fill up much sooner than the other capacities, resulting in a lower overall utilization. This suggests that an improvement may be made selecting items to pack into a bin based on the current relative weights or *rankings* of its d capacities. For example, if B_{kj} currently has the lowest available capacity, then search for an item $\vec{X}_i$ which fits into $\vec{B}_k$ but which also has X_{ij} as its *smallest* component weight. This reduces the pressure on B_{kj}, which may allow additional items to be added to bin $\vec{B}_k$. This multi-capacity aware approach is the basis for our new algorithms. The multi-capacity aware algorithms will use heuristics to select items which attempt to correct a *capacity imbalance* in the current bin. A capacity imbalance is defined as the condition $B_{ki} < B_{kj}, 1 \leq i, j \leq d$ in the current bin $\vec{B}_k$. Essentially, at least one capacity is fuller than the other capacities. The general notion is that if the capacities are all kept balanced, then more items will likely fit into the bin. A simple heuristic algorithm follows from this notion.

Consider a bin capacity vector in which B_{kj} is the component which is currently filled to a lower capacity than all other components. A *lowest-capacity aware* packing algorithm searches the list L looking for an item which fits in bin $\vec{B}_k$ *and* in which X_{ij} is the largest resource requirement in $\vec{X}_i$. Adding item $\vec{X}_i$ to bin $\vec{B}_k$ heuristically lessens the capacity imbalance at component B_{kj}. The lowest-capacity aware packing algorithm can be generalized to the case where the algorithm looks at the $w, 0 \leq w \leq d - 1$, lowest capacities and searches for an item which has the same w corresponding largest component requirements. The parameter w is a *window* into the current bin state. This is the general *windowed multi-capacity bin-packing heuristic*. Similar heuristics have been successfully applied to the multi-constraint graph partitioning problem [6]. Two variants of this general heuristic applicable to the d-capacity bin-packing problem are presented below.

Permutation Pack. Permutation Pack (PP) attempts to find items in which the largest w components are *exactly ordered* with respect to the ordering of the corresponding smallest elements in the current bin. For example, consider the case where $d = 5$ and the capacities of the current bin $\vec{B}_k$ are ordered as follows:

$$B_{k1} \leq B_{k3} \leq B_{k4} \leq B_{k2} \leq B_{k5}$$

The limiting case is when $w = d - 1$. In this instance, the algorithm would first search the list L for an item in which the components were ranked as follows:

$$X_{i1} \geq X_{i3} \geq X_{i4} \geq X_{i2} \geq X_{i5}$$

which is exactly opposite the current bin state. Adding $\vec{X}_i$ to $\vec{B}_k$ has the effect of increasing the capacity levels of the smaller components $(B_{k1}, B_{k3} \ldots)$ *more* than it increases the capacity levels of the larger components $(B_{k2}, B_{k5}, \ldots)$. If no items were found with this relative ranking between their components, then the algorithm searches the list again, relaxing the orderings of the smallest components first, and working up to the largest components. For example, the next two item rankings that would be searched for are:

$$X_{i1} \geq X_{i3} \geq X_{i4} \geq X_{i5} \geq X_{i2}$$

$$X_{i1} \geq X_{i3} \geq X_{i2} \geq X_{i4} \geq X_{i5}$$

... and finally,

$$X_{i5} \geq X_{i2} \geq X_{i4} \geq X_{i3} \geq X_{i1}$$

In the limiting case, the input list is essentially partitioned into $d!$ logical sublists. The algorithm searches each logical sublist in an attempt to find an item which fits into the current bin. If no item is found in the current logical sublist, then the sublist with the next best ranking match is searched, and so on, until all lists have been searched. When all lists are exhausted, a new bin is created and the algorithm repeats. The drawback is that the search has a time complexity of $O(d!)$. A simple relaxation to this heuristic is to consider only w of the d components of the bin. In this case, the input list is partitioned into $d!/(d - w)!$ sublists.

Each sublist contains the items with a common permutation of the largest w elements in the current bin state. Continuing the previous example, if $w = 2$, then the first list to be searched would contain items which have a ranking of the following form:

$$X_{i1} \geq X_{i3} \geq X_{i4}, X_{i2}, X_{i5}$$

The logic behind this relaxation is that the contribution to adjusting the capacity imbalance is dominated by the highest relative item components and decreases with the smaller components. Therefore, ignoring the relative rankings of the smaller components induces a low penalty. The algorithm time complexity is reduced by $O(d - w)!$. The simulation results provided in Section 4 show that substantial performance gains are achieved for even small values of $w \leq 2$, making this a tractable option.

Choose Pack. The Choose Pack (CP) algorithm is a further relaxation of the PP algorithm. CP also attempts to match the w smallest bin capacities with items in which the corresponding w components are the largest. The key difference is that CP does not enforce an ordering between these w components. As an example, consider the case where $w = 2$ and the same bin state exists as in the previous example. CP would search for an item in which

$$X_{i1}, X_{i3} \geq X_{i4}, X_{i2}, X_{i5}$$

but would not enforce any particular ordering between X_{i1} and X_{i3}. This heuristic partitions the input list into $d!/w!(d - w)!$ logical sublists thus reducing the time complexity by $w!$ over PP.

An example is provided in Tables 1 and 2 which further illustrates the differences between the FF, PP, and CP algorithms. Table 1 provides an item list for $d = 5$. Associated with each item is an *item rank* which indicates the relative rank of a component with respect to the other components in the same item. Item components are ranked according to the *maximum* so the largest component is ranked 0, the second largest is ranked 1, etc.. Table 2 shows the items selected by the FF, PP, and CP algorithms in packing the first bin, given $w = 2$. All algorithms initially select the first item, $\vec{X}_1$. The *bin rank* is analogous to the item rank in that it ranks the relative sizes of each component capacity. However, the bin rank uses a minimum ranking so the smallest component is ranked 0, the next smallest is ranked 1, and so forth. For each algorithm, Table 2 shows the item selection sequence, the resultant cumulative bin capacities, and the resultant bin ranking. The bin ranking is used by the PP and CP algorithms to filter the input list while searching for the next item. The FF algorithm ignores the current bin ranking.

After the selection of item $\vec{X}_1$, the FF algorithm searches the list for the next item which will fit. It finds that item $\vec{X}_2$

Table 1. Example item input list with item rankings; $d = 5$.

Item#	Capacities					Item Rank (Max)				
	X_{i1}	X_{i2}	X_{i3}	X_{i4}	X_{i5}	r_1	r_2	r_3	r_4	r_5
1	0.1	0.3	0.2	0.5	0.4	4	2	3	0	1
2	0.4	0.1	0.1	0.2	0.5	1	3	4	2	0
3	0.1	0.3	0.2	0.1	0.4	3	1	2	4	0
4	0.4	0.1	0.6	0.2	0.3	1	4	0	3	2
5	0.5	0.1	0.3	0.2	0.3	0	4	1	3	2
6	0.5	0.3	0.2	0.1	0.1	0	1	2	3	4
7	0.1	0.5	0.3	0.1	0.2	3	0	1	4	2
8	0.4	0.1	0.2	0.1	0.1	0	2	1	3	4
9	0.3	0.1	0.1	0.2	0.1	0	2	3	1	4
10	0.1	0.2	0.3	0.5	0.4	4	3	2	0	1

Table 2. Example item selection for FF, PP($w = 2$) and CP($w = 2$); $d = 5$.

Algo.	Item#	Item Capacities					Cum. Bin Capacities					Bin Rank (Min)				
		X_{i1}	X_{i2}	X_{i3}	X_{i4}	X_{i5}	B_{k1}	B_{k2}	B_{k3}	B_{k4}	B_{k5}	r_1	r_2	r_3	r_4	r_5
FF	1	0.1	0.3	0.2	0.5	0.4	0.1	0.3	0.2	0.5	0.4	0	2	1	4	3
	2	0.4	0.1	0.1	0.2	0.5	0.5	0.4	0.3	0.7	0.9	2	1	0	3	4
	6	0.5	0.3	0.2	0.1	0.1	1.0	0.7	0.5	0.8	1.0	3	1	0	2	4
	Total Bin Weight = 4.00															
PP	1	0.1	0.3	0.2	0.5	0.4	0.1	0.3	0.2	0.5	0.4	0	*	1	*	*
	5	0.5	0.1	0.3	0.2	0.3	0.6	0.4	0.5	0.7	0.7	*	0	1	*	*
	7	0.1	0.5	0.3	0.1	0.2	0.7	0.9	0.8	0.8	0.9	0	*	1	*	*
	9	0.3	0.1	0.1	0.2	0.1	1.0	1.0	0.9	1.0	1.0	1	*	0	*	*
	Total Bin Weight = 4.90															
CP	1	0.1	0.3	0.2	0.5	0.4	0.1	0.3	0.2	0.5	0.4	0	*	0	*	*
	4	0.4	0.1	0.6	0.2	0.3	0.5	0.4	0.8	0.7	0.7	0	0	*	*	*
	6	0.5	0.3	0.2	0.1	0.1	1.0	0.7	1.0	0.8	0.8	*	0	*	0	*
	Total Bin Weight = 4.30															

fits and selects it next. The next item, $\vec{X}_3$ will not fit as the capacity B_{k5} would be exceeded. Therefore, $\vec{X}_3$ is skipped as is $\vec{X}_4$ and $\vec{X}_5$. Item $\vec{X}_6$ fits into the bin and completely exhausts B_{k1} and B_{k5} so the algorithm creates a new bin and and selects item $\vec{X}_3$ as the first item.

The PP algorithm revises the bin rank as each item is selected and uses it to guide the selection of the next item. After the selection of item $\vec{X}_1$, the bin rank is $(0, *, 1, *, *)$ indicating that the smallest capacity is B_{k1} and the next smallest capacity is B_{k3}. The $*$'s represent don't cares to the PP algorithm (remember that only the w largest component capacities are of interest). PP then attempts to find an item in which the X_{i1} is the largest component and X_{i3} is the next largest. This item will have a ranking identical to the current bin ranking, due to the fact that item ranks are based on the maximum and bin ranks are based on the minimum components. Therefore, PP skips all items in the input list which are not ranked the same as the bin ranking for the first w components. Item $\vec{X}_5$ matches the bin ranking and fits into the bin so it is selected next. After the addition of item $\vec{X}_5$, the new bin ranking is $(*, 0, 1, *, *)$. Item $\vec{X}_7$ is the first item in the list which matches this ranking and

fits within the space remaining in the bin, so it is selected next. This results in a bin ranking of $(0, *, 1, *, *)$. Item $\vec{X}_8$ matches this ranking but does not fit in the bin as it would exceed capacity B_{k1}. No other item which matches this bin ranking will fit either so PP searches for items which match the next best bin ranking of $(0, *, *, 1, *)$. Item $\vec{X}_9$ matches this ranking and fits, so it is selected and results in filling all capacities in $\vec{B}_k$ except B_{k3}, so PP creates a new bin and continues by selecting item $\vec{X}_2$ as the first item.

The CP algorithm works much the same way as the PP algorithm except that the w smallest bin items are all ranked equally. When comparing a bin rank to an item rank, the w largest item components are all treated equally as well. After the selection of item $\vec{X}_1$, CP searches for an item in which X_{i1} and X_{i3}. To reiterate, the ordering between X_{i1} and X_{i3} is not considered. Therefore, CP selects item $\vec{X}_4$ and adds it to the bin. Note that this item was skipped by PP because it did not have the exact ordering of $X_{i1} \leq X_{i3}$. However, since CP has relaxed this requirement, $\vec{X}_3$ is an acceptable item candidate. Next, CP selects item $\vec{X}_6$ which succeeds in filling bin capacities B_{k1} and B_{k3}. CP creates a new bin and selects item $\vec{X}_2$ as the first item.

Note that other multi-capacity aware heuristics may be employed which essentially look at the *relative state or ordering* of the individual bin capacities and search for items which exhibit compatible relative state which could be used to correct a capacity load imbalance. We are currently exploring other such algorithms.

4. Experimental results

The following subsections present simulation results for the Permutation Pack (PP) and Choose Pack (CP) bin-packing algorithms. The simulation results showed that the performance of both PP and CP decreases with large w and large average item size $\overline{X}$ so an adaptive packing algorithm, Adaptive Pack (AP) was designed which adjusts w as the average item size of the remaining items in the list changes. Finally, results are presented for the case where the item list L is *short* but constantly renewed. The scenario represents a constrained case of on-line job scheduling in the presence of multiple resource requirements.

The performance measure of interest is the number of bins required to pack all the items in the list. Note that $PP(w = 0)$ and $CP(w = 0)$ are identical to the FF algorithm where w is the number (or window) of capacity components used to guide the packing process. Recall that $w = 0$ implies that the only criteria for selection is that the item fits in the bin. A $w = a; a \geq 1$ implies that the largest a capacity requirements of the bin and item are compared and evaluated as the selection criteria. The results are reported as normalized to the First-Fit (FF) algorithm. The FF algorithm was used as a baseline for two reasons. First, the PP and CP algorithms are derivatives of the FF algorithm. Second, the simulated performance of the FF on our synthetic data set was comparable to Best Fit and Next Fit. In the following discussion, FF refers to PP or CP with $w = 0$ and PP and CP imply that $w \geq 1$.

Both the PP and CP algorithms were tested with d, the capacity count, ranging from 1 to 32 and w, the capacity window, ranging from 0 to 4. Results are reported for $d = 8$ and the full range of w tested. The results for the other test cases had similar characteristics as those provided below so are omitted here for the sake of brevity.

The input list of $n = 32768$ items is generated as follows. For item $\vec{X}_k\ 1 \leq k \leq n$, the lth capacity component, $X_{kl}\ 1 \leq l \leq d$, was drawn from the lth independent random number generator. The d independent random number generators each followed an exponential distribution with a mean of $\overline{X}$. The mean weight, $\overline{X}$, was varied from 0.05 to 0.35 which provides substantial range of test input cases for the packing algorithms. The most profound effect of the average weight is the resultant average number of items which can be packed into a bin. At the low end of 0.05, the packing algorithms pack between 15 and 25 items per bin, with an average of approximately $1.0/(\overline{X})$, or 20. As the average weight increases, the average number of items packed drops due to the items being larger but also due to there being fewer *small* items to fill in the gaps in the bins. At an average weight of 0.35, only 2 or 3 items can be packed into a bin on the average no matter which packing algorithm is used. Above this average weight, we found the results to be approximately the same with all the algorithms so they are omitted here for the sake of brevity.

4.1. Performance of the PP and CP algorithms on unsorted lists

The PP and CP algorithms were implemented and simulated on the synthetic test cases as described above. Figure 1 (a) shows the results for the PP algorithm with similar results provided for CP in Figure 2 (a). These Figures plot the bin requirement for the PP and CP algorithms, respectively, normalized to the FF algorithm versus the average capacity weight, $\overline{X}$. The data represents the ratio of the FF bin requirement to the PP or CP bin requirement. Therefore, a value greater than 1.0 represents a performance *gain*.

Consider the results for the PP algorithm shown in Figure 1 (a). For the case where $w \geq 1$ and the average weight $\overline{X}$ is low, the PP algorithm provides approximately a 10% improvement over the classical FF algorithm. The performance difference diminishes as the average weight $\overline{X}$ grows, due to granularity issues. The larger component weights result in a less efficient packing of any single capacity in a bin, and is independent of d. Basically there are not enough *small* items to pair with the many *large* items. As w increases above 1 the additional performance gains also diminish. This is due to three different effects. First, the influence of the largest weight is most important in achieving a balanced capacity state. As w increases, the impact to the capacity balancing by the lesser weighted components is also smaller. The second reason for the diminishing performance at higher w is a reflection of the static and finite population of the input list. Essentially, there are a fixed and limited number of *small* items in the input list. An item, $\vec{X}_k$ is considered small if the individual components are generally much smaller than the average item weight, $\overline{X}$. Small items are valuable for filling in the cracks of a bin which has already has several items. Initially, there is a large sample of items to select from, and PP has a lot of success in packing the first few bins. In doing so, however, PP essentially *depletes* the input list of small items. Simulations have shown that as PP progresses, the average item size in the input list increases more rapidly than with FF. Additionally, as the bin number grows, the average number of items packed into a bin decreases more rapidly than with FF. The overall result is that, for large w, the performance gains from intelligent item selection are offset by the performance losses due to

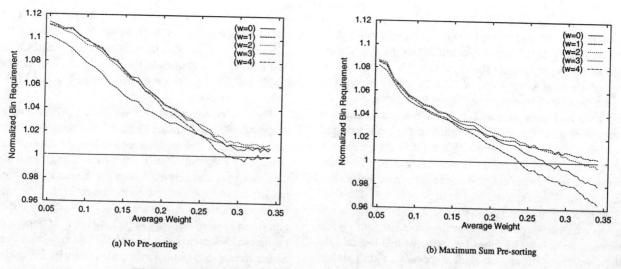

(a) No Pre-sorting

(b) Maximum Sum Pre-sorting

Figure 1. Performance gains for Permutation Pack (d=8).

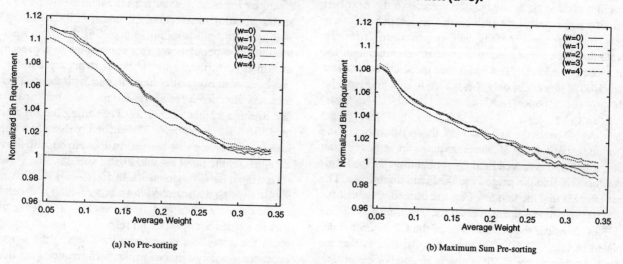

(a) No Pre-sorting

(b) Maximum Sum Pre-sorting

Figure 2. Performance gains for Choose Pack (d=8).

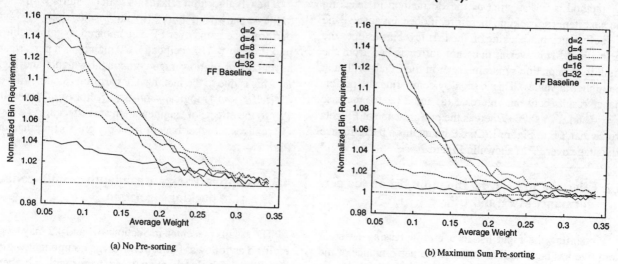

(a) No Pre-sorting

(b) Maximum Sum Pre-sorting

Figure 3. Performance gains for Adaptive Pack.

depleting the supply of small items early in the packing process. In fact, for large average weights, FF performs slightly *better* than PP as this effect is amplified by the larger average item sizes initially in the input list. This is evident in Figure 1 (a) for $w = 4$ and $\overline{X} > 0.25$. This situation is exacerbated by pre-sorting the input item list and will be explored further in Section 4.2. Note that this situation is primarily due to the finite population of the input list used for bin-packing experiments. When PP is applied to job scheduling, the input stream is constantly re-newed so the impact of small item depletion does not become a global issue. This will be explored further in Section 4.4. The third reason for a diminished performance with increasing w has to do with the way PP splits up the input list into logical sublists. Recall that PP filters the input list into logical sublists, searching for an item with a specific ranking among its component weights. If it does not find an item with this specific ranking, it then adjusts its search to the next best ranking and repeats its search on that logical sublist. As w gets larger, the number of logical lists grows as $d!/(d-w!)$. Note that each list represents a specific permutation of the w capacity rankings. The windowed multi-capacity aware heuristic is successful only if it is able to find an item with the proper component rankings among the $d!/(d-w)!$ lists. For this to be true, $d!/(d-w)!$ must be small with respect to n. As PP packs the first few bins, this relationship is true (for our experiments). However, as items are removed from the input list, n is reduced and the probability that the PP algorithm will find the properly ranked item diminishes. The net effect is that the first few bins are packed very well but the *average* improvement over all the bins is less.

Now consider the performance of the CP algorithm depicted in Figure 2 (a). The first thing to note is that the general performance of CP is nearly as good or better than PP even though it uses a relaxed selection method. The CP method is not as strict as the PP method in selecting the next item for packing, therefore, it does not achieve the high efficiency bin-packing on the first few bins as does the PP method. However, it does not suffer as bad from the small item depletion syndrome seen in the PP algorithm at the higher w values. This is seen by comparing the performance results between Figures 1 (a) and 2 (a) for the case $w = 4$ and $\overline{X} > 0.25$. Whereas the performance of PP gets worse than FF in Figure 1 (a), CP maintains a performance advantage over FF as shown in Figure 2 (a).

4.2. Effects of pre-sorting the input list on the performance of PP and CP

Pre-sorting the input list in a non-increasing order of item size has been used to improve the performance of the single capacity bin-packing algorithms. Our simulations show that this general trend continues for the d-capacity

aware algorithms. For this experiment, the input list was sorted using a maximum sum method to assign a scalar key $(\vec{X}_i(key) = \sum_{j=1}^{d} X_{ij})$ to an item. The PP and CP algorithms were then applied to the sorted list. The results for the PP and CP algorithms are depicted in Figures 1 (b) and 2 (b) respectively.

The results depicted for PP in Figure 1 (b) show approximately an 8% performance gain at low average component weights for $w \geq 1$ as compared to the FF applied to the same pre-sorted list. Note that this performance gain is less than the approximately 10% seen for the case when the input list is unsorted as depicted in Figure 1 (a). The reasons for this diminished return are twofold. First, since the PP algorithm is *more selective* in picking the next item to pack into a bin, it searches deeper into the list to find an item to adjust the capacity imbalance. Alternatively, FF finds the next item which fits. Since the list is pre-sorted, the item found by PP is *no greater than* the item found by FF. After the initial item selection, PP tends to fill the current bin with smaller items resulting in depleting the small items in the finite list population. This contributes to a overall diminished performance as the larger items are left for the last bins, with no smaller items to pair with them. This effect was also noted for PP on the unsorted list for $w = 4$ and average weight $\overline{X} > 0.25$. Pre-sorting the list merely amplifies this phenomena. The second reason for a diminished performance with increasing w has to do with the way PP splits up the input list into logical sublists. The globally sorted input list is fragmented into $d!/(d-w!)$ locally sorted sublists which are searched in an order which is dependent on the capacity ranking of the current bin. The net result is that as w increases (with with respect to constant input list size), the *actual search order* of the items in the input list becomes globally random so the performance gain due to pre-sorting is nullified.

The CP algorithm relaxes its search criteria with respect to PP. As shown in Figure 2 (b), this results in slightly higher performance gains over FF as compared to gains achieved by PP for $w > 1$. Specifically, CP maintains a performance advantage at high average component weights and higher w. This is due to the fact that CP partitions its input list into $d!/(w!(d-w!))$ logical sublists (a factor of $w!$ fewer than PP) so the effects of fragmentation are reduced. As a result, CP realizes a higher benefit from the pre-sorting than does PP.

4.3. Adaptive Pack: An adaptive multi-capacity aware packing algorithm

The results presented in Sections 4.1 and 4.2 may be generalized as follows. For lower average component weights, the PP and CP algorithms perform better with a higher w. At higher average weights, they perform better with a lower

w. This is a reflection of the ability of the PP and CP algorithms to aggressively pack the first few bins with the smaller items in the finite population list, leaving the larger grained items for packing last. The high packing efficiency on the first bins is offset by the lower efficiency on the later bins. In view of these results, an *adaptive* packing algorithm could be devised which modifies the window, w, based on the probability of finding smaller items among those remaining in the input list. As this probability gets higher, a more aggressive w (larger) could be used to pack the abundant smaller items into bins to a higher capacity. Conversely, as the probability gets lower, a less aggressive w (smaller) could be used to pack the larger items greedily as done by FF. Adaptive Pack (AP) adjusts w based on the average component weight of the items remaining in the input list after each bin is packed. The performance results for AP are shown in Figures 3 (a) and (b) for unsorted and pre-sorted input lists for a range of capacity counts $2 \leq d \leq 32$.

In general, the AP performs as good or better than the PP and CP algorithms over the range of input simulated. Specifically, the degradation seen in the PP and CP algorithms at high average weights, $\overline{X}$, and high windows, w, is avoided by the AP algorithm. Also, the performance gains for each d value are as good or better than the PP or CP algorithms using any single w value. This may be seen by comparing the data for $d = 8$ in Figures 3 (a) and (b) with the data in Figures 1 (a) and (b). In Figure 3 (a), for $d = 8$ and $\overline{X} = 0.15$, the performance gain of AP over FF is approximately 8% while for the same case in Figure 1 (a), the gain is approximately 7%. A similar comparison between Figures 3 (b) and 1 (b) shows that AP maintains the performance seen by PP($w = 4$).

4.4. A first step towards job scheduling under multiple constraints

Bin-packing is an abstraction of a restricted batch processing scenario in which all the jobs arrive before processing begins and all jobs have the same execution time. Basically, each bin corresponds to a scheduling epoch on the system resources, and the scheduling algorithm must pack jobs onto the system in an order such that it all jobs are scheduled using the fewest epochs. Define A_i as the arrival time and T_i as the expected execution time of job i. In the batch processing scenario, $A_i = 0$, and $T_i = T$ for some constant T. The results of Sections 4.1 and 4.2 suggest that the windowed multi-capacity aware bin-packing algorithms may be used as the basis for a scheduling algorithm.

The next level of complexity is to remove the restriction on A_i to allow the continuous arrival of new jobs. Now the performance of the scheduling algorithm depends on the packing efficiency of only the *first* bin or epoch from a much *smaller* item list or job queue. The PP and CP

algorithms work even better under this dynamic item list population scenario. In the static input list scenario, the PP and CP are able to pack a lot of smaller items into the first few bins. However, this depleted the supply of small items on the earlier bins resulting in a less efficient packing of the remaining items due to their large granularity. In the dynamic item list scenario, each bin is packed from essentially a new list as items are replaced as soon as items are packed. Also, since the PP and CP algorithms select the first element of the input list before initiating capacity balancing, the waiting time of any item is bounded by the number of items ahead of it in the queue. Figure 4 shows the performance of the PP algorithm on first-bin packing efficiency for $d = 8$. In this simulation, the number of items in the item list is initialized to 4 times the expected number of items which would optimally fit into a bin. Specifically, $n = 4.0 * \lceil 1.0 / \overline{X} \rceil$. Note that this n is much smaller than the n used for the bin-packing experiments. This reflect the smaller size of job wait queues expected to be seen by the scheduler. The simulation loops between packing an empty bin and replacing the items drawn from the list. In this manner, the *number* of items that a packing algorithm starts with is always the same. The d-capacity items are generated as in previous simulations. As shown in Figure 4, for small average weights $\overline{X}$ and $w > 0$, the PP algorithm achieves a 13% to 15% performance gain over the FF algorithm. Compare this performance gain to the 11% gain seen by the AP algorithm in Figure 3 (a). The multi-capacity aware algorithms can pack any *single* bin much better than the naive FF algorithm, when starting from the same input list. For higher w and $\overline{X}$, maintains its performance gain over FF. The results for other d were simulated and showed similar trends. In general, the packing efficiency of the PP algorithm increases with increasing w. The diminished increases in performance for higher w, while positive and finite, are due primarily to the lower impact of considering the smaller item components when performing capacity balancing. Additionally, for higher w, the probability of finding an item which best matches the current bin capacity imbalance is decreased due to the relatively small population from which to choose ($n \ll !d/(d-w)!$). Recall that the search performed by PP($w = i$) is a refinement of the search used by PP($w = j$) for $i > j$. If PP($w = i$) cannot find the exact item it is looking for, then it should heuristically find the item that PP($w = j$) would have found. Therefore, increasing w should heuristically do no worse than for lower w at the cost of higher time complexity. Essentially, when $(d!/(d - w)! \gg n)$, PP($w = i$) collapses to PP($w = j$).

The relaxed selection criteria used by the CP method results in little performance gains for $w > 1$ so those results are omitted from the graph for the sake of clarity. However, the CP algorithm still has a much lower time complexity for higher w than does the PP algorithm, so a trade is available.

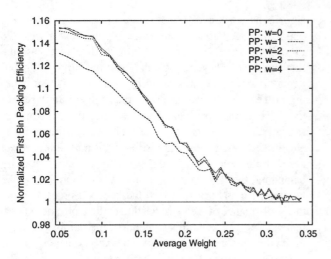

Figure 4. Performance gains in first-bin packing efficiency for PP (d=8; no pre-sorting).

The final level of complexity in bridging the gap from bin-packing to job scheduling is to allow each item to have a different execution time. This is the subject of our current work in progress [8].

4.5. Summary of experimental results

The experimental results for the PP and CP algorithms are summarized below.

1. The windowed multi-capacity aware bin-packing algorithms, PP and CP, provide a consistent performance increase over the classical FF algorithm for items with smaller average weights and comparable performance for items with higher average weights in an unsorted list. Furthermore, a large percentage of the performance gains are achieved by a small window $w \leq 2$ which relieves the time complexity pressure.

2. Pre-sorting the input list provides performance gains for all the tested bin-packing algorithms but the gains are less for the multi-capacity aware algorithms using high window values on lists with high average component weights due to list fragmentation and small item depletion.

3. An adaptive algorithm, AP, was devised which maximizes the performance gains by adapting the capacity window according to the average weight of the items remaining in the input list. AP performs as good or better than the PP and CP algorithms and does not suffer from the same degradation seen by PP and CP at high average component weights.

4. The first-bin packing efficiency of the PP algorithms provides substantial performance over the FF algorithm which provides a proof-of-concept that the windowed multi-capacity aware heuristic may be applied to the generalized online multi-constraint job scheduling problem.

As a final note, the simulation results presented here are in some respect an artifact of the synthetic input data. Specifically, the *relationship* between the d components in a given item was uncorrelated as they were drawn from *independent* random number streams. In the job scheduling scenario, the relationships between the the resource requirements of a job may be quite correlated. If the requirements are proportional, (e.g. large memory implies large CPU requirements), then the dimension of the packing problem is effectively reduced from a 2-capacity to a 1-capacity. The performance gain seen by multi-capacity aware algorithms would be smaller. with respect to the naive packing algorithms. If the requirements are *inversely related*, (e.g. Large memory requirement with small CPU requirements), then the performance gains seen by the multi-capacity aware algorithms should be substantial. Job scheduling workload characterization with multiple resource requirements is also a subject of our current work in progress.

References

[1] J. E. G. Coffman, M. R. Garey, and D. S. Johnson. An application of bin-packing to multiprocessor scheduling. *SIAM J. Comput.*, 7(1):1–17, Feb. 1978.

[2] J. E. G. Coffman, M. R. Garey, and D. S. Johnson. Dynamic bin packing. *SIAM J. Comput.*, 12(2):226–258, May 1983.

[3] J. E. G. Coffman, M. R. Garey, and D. S. Johnson. Approximation algorithms for bin-packing - an updated survey. In G. Ausiello, M. Lucertini, and P. Serafini, editors, *Algorithm Design for Computer System Design*, pages 49–99. Springer-Verlag, New York, 1984.

[4] M. R. Garey and R. L. Graham. Bounds for multiprocessor scheduling with resource constraints. *SIAM J. Comput.*, 4(2):187–201, June 1975.

[5] M. R. Garey, R. L. Graham, D. S. Johnson, and A. C.-C. Yao. Resource constrained scheduling as generalized bin packing. *Journal of Combinatorial Theory*, pages 257–298, 1976.

[6] G. Karypis and V. Kumar. Multilevel algorithms for multi-constraint graph partitioning. Technical Report 98-019, University of Minnesota, Department of Computer Science, Army HPC Research Center, 1998.

[7] L. T. Kou and G. Markowsky. Multidimensional bin packing algorithms. *IBM J. Res. Dev.*, 21(5):443–448, Sept. 1977.

[8] W. Leinberger, G. Karypis, and V. Kumar. Job scheduling in the presence of multiple resource requirements. In *To appear in Supercomputing '99*, 1999.

[9] K. Maruyama, S. K. Chang, and D. T. Tang. A general packing algorithm for multidimensional resource requirements. *Intl. J. of Comput. and Inf. Sci.*, 6(2):131–149, May 1976.

SLC: Symbolic Scheduling for Executing Parameterized Task Graphs on Multiprocessors

Michel Cosnard
LORIA INRIA Lorraine
615, rue du Jardin Botanique
54602 Villers les Nancy, France
Michel.Cosnard@loria.fr

Emmanuel Jeannot
LIP ENS-Lyon
46, allée d'Italie
69364 Lyon, France
ejeannot@ens-lyon.fr

Tao Yang
CS Dept. UCSB
Engr Building I
Santa Barbara, CA 93106, USA
tyang@cs.ucsb.edu

Abstract

Task graph scheduling has been found effective in performance prediction and optimization of parallel applications. A number of static scheduling algorithms have been proposed for task graph execution on distributed memory machines. Such an approach cannot be adapted to changes in values of program parameters and the number of processors and also it cannot handle large task graphs. In this paper, we model parallel computation using parameterized task graphs which represent coarse-grain parallelism independent of the problem size. We present a scheduling algorithm for a parameterized task graph which first derives symbolic linear clusters and then assigns task clusters to processors. The runtime system executes clusters on each processor in a multi-threaded fashion. We evaluate our method using various compute-intensive kernels that can be found in scientific applications.

1. Introduction

Directed acyclic task graphs (DAGs) have been used in modeling parallel applications and performing performance prediction and optimization [1, 3, 7, 11, 12, 21]. There are a number of algorithms which have been proposed to perform static task graph mapping on distributed memory machines [8, 14, 15, 19, 20, 21, 23, 25]. Because a task graph is obtained statically and the number of processors must be given in advance before scheduling, these methods present two major drawbacks:

- Static scheduling is not adaptive. Each time the problem parameter values change or the number of available processors, a scheduling solution has to be recomputed.

- Static scheduling is not scalable. For large problem sizes, the corresponding task graph may contain a large number of tasks and dependence edges, and a static scheduler might fail due to memory constraint.

The previous work in parallelizing compilers [2, 10, 17] has studied the compact parallelism representation based on fine-grain level dependence analysis and their model normally deals with DOALL parallelism. Our goal is to extend these results for exploiting coarse grain DAG parallelism in a symbolic manner, in order to overcome the two drawbacks mentioned above. In this paper we use a parameterized task graph (PTG) [5, 16] to model computation. A PTG can be considered as a DAG, and is augmented by a set of parameters. Thus such a graph is symbolic and its size does not vary if program parameters change. This paper focuses on symbolic scheduling of parameterized task graphs on distributed memory machines.

Our algorithm, called SLC (Symbolic Linear Clustering), first performs symbolic clustering and assigns tasks from the same cluster to the same processor in order to reduce inter-task communication while still preserving available parallelism. Then it assigns symbolic clusters evenly to processors. Since each processor may own several symbolic task clusters, our runtime scheme executes clusters on each processor using a multithreaded and message-driven fashion to overlap computation with communication.

Section 2 describes definitions of parameterized task graphs. Section 3 gives an overview of our approach. Section 4 presents our symbolic clustering method. Section 5 discusses how clusters can be numbered explicitly so that symbolic clusters can be mapped to physically processors. Section 6 presents simulation and experimental results. Section 7 concludes the paper.

2. Definitions and Notations

Parameterized Task Graphs. A parameterized task graph (PTG) is a compact model for parallel computation [5]. It contains a set of symbolic tasks and each sym-

```
param n
assert n >= 3
real a(n, n+1)
real s
for k = 1 to n-1 do
  task                         /*T1(k)*/
    s= 1 / a(k,k)
    for l = k + 1 to n do
      a(l,k) = a(l,k) * s
    endfor
  endtask
    for j = k + 1 to n+1 do
      task                     /*T2(k,j)*/
        for i= k + 1 to n do
          a(i,j) = a(i,j) -
                   a(k,j) * a(i,k)
        endfor
      endtask
    endfor
endfor
```

Figure 1. Gaussian Elimination

bolic task is represented by a name and an iteration vector. A PTG also contains a set of communication rules that describe data items transfered among tasks. Since each task can contain a set of instructions executed sequentially, this model mainly is targeted at coarse-grain parallelism.

There are types of communication rules which are either emission or reception rules to model how tasks send or receive data. Reception and emission rules are dual forms of each other. Reception rules describe a set of parents that a task depends on. Emission rules describe a set of children that a task needs to send data. An emission rule R (a reception rule) has the form:

$$R : Ta(\vec{u}) \longrightarrow Tb(\vec{v}) : D(\vec{y})|P$$

where $\vec{u}$ and $\vec{v}$ are the iteration vectors of tasks Ta and Tb. Rule R means that if predicate P is true, task $Ta(\vec{u})$ sends data $D(\vec{y})$ to task $Tb(\vec{v})$. Vector $\vec{y}$ describes which part of the data D is sent to task Tb. P is a polyhedron which describes valid values of vectors $\vec{u}$, $\vec{v}$ and $\vec{y}$.

The number of components in $\vec{y}$ depends on the dimension of data variable D. For example, it is 0 if D is a scalar, and 1 if D is a 1D vector. We assume that the variables $\vec{y}$ do not appear in the predicates describing the variables of $\vec{u}$ and $\vec{v}$. Hence, the data part of a rule can be removed easily without getting *holes* in the polyhedron.

Derivation of a parameterized task graph. We have used the PlusPyr software tool [16] in order to construct a PTG from a sequential program. PlusPyr is able to derive a parameterized task graph for a sequential program if a user also provides an annotation to describe how this program is partitioned into tasks. Figure 1 illustrates an

annotated program for Gaussian Elimination without pivoting. It contains two generic tasks $T1(k)$ and $T2(k,j)$. Key words "task" and "endtask" specify the beginning and end of a task and "param" specifies symbolic parameters used in this program, which could vary based on the actual problem size. Figure 5 illustrates an instantiated Gaussian Elimination task graph (along with a linear clustering as we will explain later) when program parameter n is 6.

The current implementation of PlusPyr supports dependence analysis and communication synthesis among tasks if the input program has static control and only deals with matrix vector or scalar computation. The techniques for dependence analysis and communication summarization are based on the work done by Feautrier and others on integer parametric programming (see [9, 22] for an introduction and [5, 6] for more details).

For the input GE program shown in Figure 1, the emission rules of the corresponding parameterized task graph, computed by our tool PlusPyr, are shown in Figure 2. For example, the third emission rule indicates that for any k and j such that $1 \le k \le n-2$ and $k+2 \le j \le n+1$, task $T2(k,j)$ sends part of column j to task $T2(k+1,j)$.

---

1. $T1(k) \longrightarrow T2(k,j) : A(i,k)|1 \le k \le n-1, k+1 \le j \le n+1, k+1 \le i \le n$

2. $T2(k,j) \longrightarrow T1(k+1) : A(i,k+1)|1 \le k \le n-2, j = k+1, k+1 \le i \le n$

3. $T2(k,j) \longrightarrow T2(k+1,j) : A(i,j)|1 \le k \le n-2, k+2 \le j \le n+1, k+1 \le i \le n$

Figure 2. Emission rules for the Gaussian Elimination

Bijective Emission Rules. Our symbolic clustering algorithm identifies a type of rules called *bijection rules* to cluster and we present its definition as follows. Given an emission rule of format $R : Ta(\vec{u}) \longrightarrow Tb(\vec{v}) : D(\vec{y})|P$, this rule is **bijective** if for each instance of iteration vector $\vec{u}$, there exists exactly one corresponding instance of iteration vector $\vec{v}$. For example, in Figure 2, the first emission rule is not bijective because this rule describes a dependence from task $T1(k)$ to many of its children $T2(k, k+1), T2(k, k+2) \cdots$. The second and third rules are bijective.

We further discuss how to judge if an emission rule is bijective. We assume that a task contains nested loops and its iteration vector is an affine function of program parameters and loop indices. Let $\vec{i}$ be the vector composed of all the problem parameters and loop indices in the lexicographic order. Thus we can express vectors $\vec{u}$ and $\vec{v}$ as:

$$\vec{u} = D_1\vec{\imath} + \vec{k_1} \quad \text{and} \quad \vec{v} = D_2\vec{\imath} + \vec{k_2}.$$

where $\vec{k_1}$ and $\vec{k_2}$ are constant integer vectors. $D1$ and $D2$ are constant integer matrices. Notice that if there are equalities in P, we should substitute variables to remove some variables before constructing D_1 and D_2.

To find if this rule is bijective, we find E_1 and $\vec{w_1}$ such that $\vec{\imath} = E_1(\vec{u} - \vec{k_1}) + \vec{w_1}$. There could exist many E_1 and $\vec{w_1}$ that satisfy this equation. We impose a condition that $\vec{w_1}$ is composed of the indices that do not appear in $\vec{u}$. Formally, $w_{1_j} = \delta_j i_j$, where the w_{1_j} (resp. i_j) is j^{th} element of $\vec{w_1}$ (resp. $\vec{\imath}$); $\delta_j = 0$ if i_j appears in $\vec{u}$, and $\delta_j = 1$ if i_j does not appear in $\vec{u}$.

Then we have: $\vec{v} = D_2E_1(\vec{u} - \vec{k_1}) + D_2\vec{w_1} + \vec{k_2}$. Similarly we can build E_2 and $\vec{w_2}$ such that: $\vec{u} = D_1E_2(\vec{v} - \vec{k_2}) + D_1\vec{w_2} + \vec{k_1}$.

The above rule is bijective if and only if $D_2\vec{w_1}$ and $D_1\vec{w_2}$ are both constant. This condition ensures that for each instance of $\vec{u}$ there is only one instance of $\vec{v}$ and for each instance of $\vec{v}$ there is only one instance of $\vec{u}$.

In Figure 2, the fact that the first rule is not bijective can be verified as follows. Since $\vec{u} = (k)$, $\vec{v} = \begin{pmatrix} k \\ j \end{pmatrix}$, and the vector of the program parameters and all the loops indices is $\vec{\imath} = (n\ k\ l\ j\ i)^T$, $D_1 = (0, 1, 0, 0, 0)$ and

$$D_2 = \begin{pmatrix} 0 & 1 & 0 & 0 & 0 \\ 0 & 0 & 0 & 1 & 0 \end{pmatrix}.$$

We deduce that: $E_1 = (0\ 1\ 0\ 0\ 0)^T$ and $\vec{w_1} = (n\ 0\ l\ j\ i)^T$ so that $\vec{\imath} = E_1\vec{u} + \vec{w_1}$. Then, $D_2\vec{w_1} = \begin{pmatrix} 0 \\ j \end{pmatrix}$, which is not a constant.

On the other hand, the second emission rule in Figure 2 is bijective. In this case, $\vec{u} = \begin{pmatrix} k \\ j \end{pmatrix}$ and $\vec{v} = (k + 1)$. According to the predicate $j = k + 1$, we substitute all the occurrences of j by $k+1$. Hence we have: $\vec{u} = \begin{pmatrix} k \\ k+1 \end{pmatrix}$.

Thus, $D_1 = \begin{pmatrix} 0 & 1 & 0 & 0 & 0 \\ 0 & 1 & 0 & 0 & 0 \end{pmatrix}$ and $D_2 = (0\ 1\ 0\ 0\ 0)$. We deduce that: $\vec{w_1} = \vec{w_2} = (n\ 0\ l\ j\ i)^T$. Therefore, both $D_2\vec{w_1}$ and $D_1\vec{w_2}$ are constant.

3. Overview of the SLC Method

The optimization goal of our symbolic clustering algorithm is the same as that of static scheduling algorithms [21, 25]: eliminate unnecessary communication and preserve data locality, map symbolic clusters to processors evenly to achieve load balance, and execute clusters within each processor using the multithreading technique to overlap computation with communication. The mapping and scheduling process is symbolic in the sense that the change in the problem size and the number of processors does not affect the solution derived by our algorithm.

The main steps involved in our method for scheduling and executing a parameterized task graph are summarized as follows:

1. Given a PTG, we first simplify this graph by merging rules, when possible, in order to reduce the number of rules. Then we extract and sort all bijective rules in the PTG. Then, we perform a linear clustering on these bijection rules, The clustering process is discussed in details in Section 4. The important aspect of this process is that merged clusters are always linear whatever parameter values are, namely, no independent task are placed in the same cluster. In this way, parallelism is preserved while unnecessary communication is eliminated.

   Clustering is conducted by assigning two end tasks of a dependence edge to the same cluster (so communication between these two tasks is considered zero). This process is called *edge zeroing*. Since each emission rule represents a set of dependence edges, we will call this process as "rule zeroing".

2. Given a linear cluster of a PTG, the second step of SLC is to provide the identification of each cluster, which is a mapping function from a task ID to a cluster number. For example, mapping function $\kappa(T1, (3, 7))$ is the cluster ID of task $T1(3, 7)$. This procedure is trivial if clustering is not done symbolically. In our setting, this mapping function allows us to map a cluster symbolically to a physical processor.

3. The third step is to derive the mapping and packaging of data items used during execution. This is done using communication rules. When a rule is not zeroed this means that data will be sent from a processor to another. Rules with cluster mapping describe which kind of data (scalar, vector, matrix,...) should be sent. We use these informations for generating message packaging code.

4. The last part is the execution of symbolic clusters assigned to each processor. At runtime, symbolic clusters are mapped to the given number of processors (p) evenly using a cyclic (cluster ID mod p) or block mapping formula (cluster ID /p).

   Task execution is asynchronous and is driven by message communication. Each processor maintains a ready queue and if all data items needed for a task are available locally, this task becomes ready. For each processor, we maintain t active threads and each of them can pick up a ready task for execution. The advantage of having multiple threads is that the system can take advantages of SMP nodes if applicable. After a task completes its execution, data items are sent following the emission rules related to this task.

There is an important issue on how to initiate execution. At the beginning of execution, each processor needs to find starting tasks (i.e. tasks without parents) and put them on its ready task queue. This is done by computing all valid instances of each task assigned to this processor, called $valid(Ta)$. Then this processor computes all the instances of Ta that need to receive data following the reception rules (call it $recv(Ta)$). The difference $valid(Ta) - recv(Ta)$ is a polyhedron that describes all starting task instances of Ta assigned to this processor.

In the next two sections, we will discuss in details how tasks can be clustered and mapped symbolically.

4. Symbolic Linear Clustering

In this step, we allocate tasks to an unbounded number of virtual processors and in the literature this is often call clustering. All the tasks assigned to the same cluster will be executed on the same physical processor.

A cluster is said **linear** if all its task form a path in the instantiated task graph of a PTG for given program parameters. The motivation for linear clustering is based on a study by Yang and Gerasoulis [13]. They have proven that a linear clustering provides good performance on an unbounded number of processors for coarse grain graphs. If g is the granularity a task graph G, PT_{lc} is the parallel time of any linear clustering, and PT_{opt} is the parallel time of an optimal clustering applied to G, then $PT_{lc} \leq (1 + 1/g)PT_{opt}$. Thus as long as g is not too small, linear clustering produces a schedule competitive to the optimum when there are a sufficient number of processors.

Our clustering algorithm contains two parts: 1) merge rules together if possible to reduce the searching space for clustering. 2) find bijective clusters and cluster those rules linearly.

Rule merging. Before clustering the given PTG, we merge a few emission rules if possible. Two emission rules are mergable if each rule describes the same set of dependence edges and their data items communicated can be combined. For example, let us consider the two following rules:

$$R1 : T1(k) \longrightarrow T2(k+1) : A(k)|1 \leq k \leq n$$

and

$$R2 : T1(k) \longrightarrow T2(k+1) : A(i)|1 \leq k \leq n, k+1 \leq i \leq n.$$

Figure 3. The rule clustering algorithm.

$R1$ and $R2$ describe the same set of edges. We see that rule $R1$ sends element $A(k)$ and rule $R2$ sends elements of vector A from $k + 1$ to n. Hence, these two rules can be merged in a rule R that sends elements of vector A from k to n:

$$R : T1(k) \longrightarrow T2(k+1) : A(i)|1 \leq k \leq n, k \leq i \leq n.$$

Merging of rules is important because it reduces the number of rules. In that way, the clustering algorithm discussed below can spend less time in searching and zeroing bijective rules.

Rule zeroing. We give a formal definition of rule zeroing as follows. Given a rule with form $Ta(\vec{u}) \longrightarrow Tb(\vec{v}) : D(\vec{y})|P$, it is *zeroed* if and only if $\kappa(Ta, \vec{u}) = \kappa(Tb, \vec{v})$ for all the valid instances of $\vec{u}$ and $\vec{v}$ in P. The zeroing algorithm is summarized in Figure 3.

The zeroing algorithm extracts all bijection rules, using the method described in Section 2. Then it sorts all bijective emission rules. The sorting is done such that rules implying more communication are to be zeroed first. The rule ordering is done by taking into consideration the dimension of data communicated (i.e. a scalar, a row or a column, a matrix block). Once bijective emission rules are sorted by a decreasing dimension of data communication, *transitive* rules (as defined below) are placed at the end of this sorted list.

An emission rule R is called *transitive* if it sends data from task $T1$ to $T3$ and there exist two rules $R1$ and $R2$ such that $R1$ sends data from $T1$ to $T2$ and $R2$ sends data from $T2$ to $T3$ (see Figure 4). As shown in

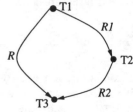

Figure 4. R: a Transitive Rule

---

next section, it appears that a clustering decision based on R may be in conflict with that for $R1$ and $R2$. But the clustering decisions for $R2$ and $R1$ do not conflict with each other.

Since our goal is to zero as many rules as possible, we rank the zeroing proiority of rules $R1$ and $R2$ higher than that for rule R and thus we place transitive rules at the end of the sorted rule list.

During the zeroing loop shown in Figure 3, the algorithm checks if zeroing a selected rule is not in conflict with a rule already zeroed. Two rules are in conflict if, once zeroed, the produced clustering is not linear. If the rule is not in conflict with any other zeroed rules then the algorithm adds this newly-zeroed rule to the set of zeroed rules. The algorithm repeats this process until all rules have been examined once in the sorted order. We have decribded a method in [4] on how to determine if two rules are in conflict.

We can prove the following theorem to show the correctness of our rule zeroing algorithm.

Theorem 1 *If bijective emission rules of a PTG are zeroed using the SLC zeroing algorithm, then the result of clustering is linear.*

Sketch of proof: When a bijective rule is zeroed, exactly one edge for each instance of the rule is zeroed in the instantiated task graph.

Since SLC ensures that there are no conflict in zeroing multiple bijective rules. Therefore, zeroing those rules produces a clustering with no independent task instances assigned to the same cluster. ∎

5   Cluster Identification

The previous algorithm zeros a number of rules and as a result it zeros a number of edges in the instantiated task graph for a given set of program parameter values. However, there is no cluster ID given for each cluster. We need such an ID number explicitly so we can assign clusters evenly to physical processors using a symbolic mapping function. In static scheduling research [21, 25], producing such a number is easy since clusters can be explicitly numbered.

Given a set of zeroed rules, we show how to explicitly build a symbolic function $\kappa(Ta, \vec{u})$ such that for any generic task Ta and any valid instance $\vec{u}$, this function gives a cluster number for this task instance. We call this procedure as *cluster identification* or *cluster numbering*.

Notice that all the tasks in the same cluster will have the same cluster number and tasks from different clusters should not have the same cluster number. More formally, let us consider a zeroed rule:

$$R1 : Ta(\vec{u}) \longrightarrow Tb(\vec{v})|P_1$$

Under constrain P_1, we must have:

$$\kappa(Ta, \vec{u}) = \kappa(Tb, \vec{v}). \tag{1}$$

We briefly discuss our method using an example as follows. The basis of our method is the same as the one used by Feautrier in [10] for automatic distribution. We assume that our clustering function is affine with respect to program parameters and the iteration vector. Thus we let

$$\kappa(Ta, \vec{u}) = \vec{\alpha_a}\vec{u} + \beta_a + \vec{\gamma_a}\vec{p}$$

where $\vec{\alpha_a}$ and γ_a are vectors of unknowns which have to be found, β_a is a constant and $\vec{p}$ is the vector of the program parameters. We also have

$$\kappa(Tb, \vec{v}) = \vec{\alpha_b}\vec{u} + \beta_b + \vec{\gamma_b}\vec{p}.$$

Then solving Equation 1 leads to $\vec{\alpha_a}\vec{u} + \beta_a + \vec{\gamma_a}\vec{p} = \vec{\alpha_b}\vec{v} + \beta_b + \vec{\gamma_b}\vec{p}$.

For example, let us look at the second rule in Figure 2: $T2(k, j) \longrightarrow T1(k + 1) : A(i, k + 1)|1 \leq k \leq n - 2, j = k + 1, k + 1 \leq i \leq n$. By zeroing this rule, we have $\kappa(T2, (k, j)) = \alpha_{2,1}k + \alpha_{2,2}j + \beta_2 + \gamma_{2,1}n$ and $\kappa(T1, (k + 1)) = \alpha_{1,1}(k + 1) + \beta_1 + \gamma_{1,1}n$. This leads to

$$\begin{cases} \alpha_{2,1}k + \alpha_{2,2}j + \beta_2 + \gamma_{2,1}n = \alpha_{1,1}(k + 1) + \beta_1 + \gamma_{1,1}n \\ j = k + 1 \end{cases} \tag{2}$$

Equation 2 is satisfied with $\alpha_{2,1} + \alpha_{2,2} = \alpha_{1,1}$, $\beta_2 + \alpha_{2,2} = \beta_1 + \alpha_{1,1}$ and $\gamma_{2,1} = \gamma_{1,1}$.

For emission Rule 3 in Figure 2: ($T2(k, j) \longrightarrow T2(k + 1, j) : \{A(i, j)|1 \leq k \leq n - 2, k + 2 \leq j \leq n + 1, k + 1 \leq i \leq n\}$), we have:

$$\alpha_{2,1}k + \alpha_{2,2}j + \beta_2 + \gamma_{2,1}n = \alpha_{2,1}(k+1) + \alpha_{2,2}j + \beta_2 + \gamma_{2,1}n. \tag{3}$$

Equation 3 is satisfied with $\alpha_{2,1} = 0$.

The above analysis for the second and third rules of Figure 2 leads to the following linear system:

$$\begin{cases} \alpha_{2,1} + \alpha_{2,2} - \alpha_{1,1} = 0 \\ \beta_2 + \alpha_{2,2} - \beta_1 - \alpha_{1,1} = 0 \\ \gamma_{2,1} = \gamma_{1,1}\alpha_{2,1} = 0 \end{cases} \tag{4}$$

System 4 has many solutions. In particular,

$$\begin{cases} \alpha_{2,2} = \alpha_{1,1} = 1 \\ \beta_1 = \beta_2 = \alpha_{2,1} = \gamma_{1,1} = \gamma_{2,1} = 0 \end{cases} \tag{5}$$

Thus, one explicit clustering function κ for the Gaussian Elimination PTG is:

$$\kappa(T2, (k, j)) = j$$

and

$$\kappa(T1, (k)) = k.$$

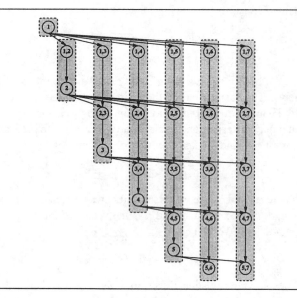

Figure 5. A clustering for an instantiated Gaussian Elimination graph with $n = 6$.

This clustering is depicted in Figure 5.

The above example looks simple; however there is a complication we need to handle. The mapping derivation from two rules for the same task may lead to a restrictive condition on the $\vec{\alpha}$ vector value in computing the cluster affine function of this task. For instance, given the following two zeroed rules :

$$R1 : T1(k,j) \longrightarrow T1(k+1,j)|1 \le k \le n, 1 \le j \le k$$

$$R2 : T1(k,j) \longrightarrow T1(k,j+1)|1 \le k \le n, k+1 \le j \le n.$$

Zeroing rule R1 leads to $\alpha_{1,1} = 0$ but zeroing rule R2 leads to $\alpha_{1,2} = 0$. We do not want the $\vec{\alpha}$ solution vector to be zero for all the tasks because this solution maps all task instances into one cluster, which yields no parallelism. In the above case, we know that zeroing these two rules are not in conflict in terms of the linear clustering constraint. To fix this problem, we can use the two mapping functions for task $T1$ with two disjoint polyhedra:

$$\kappa(T1, (k,j)) = \begin{cases} j & \text{if } 1 \le k \le n, 1 \le j \le k \\ k & \text{otherwise.} \end{cases}$$

In general, we have proposed a technique called graph splitting which uses multiple mapping functions for each selected task if the derived solution is $\vec{\alpha} = \vec{0}$ for all tasks. Given a zeroing of a PTG, we construct a dependence graph G only based on all zeroed bijective rules. We compute the cluster mapping function for each task based on zeroing results. If for all the tasks Ta the mapping solution is $\vec{\alpha} = 0$,

we identify the rules that cause setting, we split the G into a few sub-PTGs by dividing the polyhedra domain of Ta into disjoint parts based on these rules. For the above example, the restriction is caused by two rules among the instances of the same task. Then we apply the cluster numbering procedure recursively to each subgraph. The obtained solution for task T_a is no longer an affine function but a *piecewise affine function*. Notice if a task has multiple out-going edges in G, those rules can also potentially impose a restrictive condition on cluster numbering and we can also split based on these rules. Figure 6 illustrates splitting of a task $T2$ based on the rules "$T2 \rightarrow T3$" and "$T2 \rightarrow T4$". Notice that all rules in G are bijective, thus subgraphs $G1$ and $G2$ deal with disjoint sets of all task instances. For example, task instances of $T2$ are divided into two parts, one in $G1$ and another in $G2$. Then task instances of $T1$ are also divided in two parts accordingly due to bijection and rule "$T1 \rightarrow T5$" will only need to appear in $G2$.

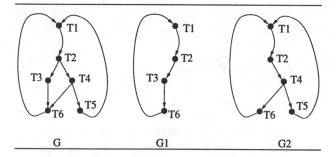

Figure 6. Spliting of Graph G into G_1 and G_2 at node $T2$ (note that G_2 may be partitioned again at node $T4$)

6. Simulation and Experimental Results

We have implemented the SLC for compile-time symbolic scheduling of a PTG, which automatically finds the clustering function κ for each task. We have also implemented part of runtime support for executing a PTG using the SLC schedule, which allows us to conduct experiments in assessing performance of an SLC symbolic schedule.

The benchmarks used in this paper are several compute-intensive kernels in scientific applications: Gaussian elimination, Cholesky factorization, Givens algorithm, Jordan diagonalization, and matrix multiplication. The advantage of our algorithm is that it requires small memory space in clustering and produces symbolic solutions independent of problem sizes and the number of processors used. In this section, we mainly assess if the scheduling performance of our algorithm is still competitive to a static algorithm while retaining symbolic processing advantages.

Graph	n	Sequential time	No. clusters DSC	Sched. length DSC	No. clusters SLC	Sched. length SLC	R
Gauss	100	1009800	92	364532	102	402572	0.91
Gauss	200	8039600	196	994960	202	1033735	0.96
Gauss	400	64159200	402	2979410	402	2990280	0.98
Jordan	100	1509950	92	495149	101	779170	0.64
Jordan	200	12039900	199	1325682	201	1978317	0.67
Jordan	400	96159800	395	3895200	401	5645048	0.69
Givens	100	3720750	114	896350	101	913707	0.98
Givens	200	39214956	371	2654398	201	2539794	1.05
Givens	400	257418656	1269	6964054	401	7845122	0.89
Cholesky	100	510150	93	241918	101	312250	0.77
Cholesky	200	4040300	212	521662	201	687350	0.76

Table 1. Comparison between SLC and DSC on an unbounded number of processors (relatively slow machine/coarse grain tasks)

A performance comparison of SLC and DSC. Table 1 and Table 2 compare performance of SLC with the DSC static clustering algorithm [25] for parameter size of 100, 200 and 400 (matrix dimension). We have not been able to perform tests for larger matrix sizes because task graphs become too large (over 1 million tasks/edges) and DSC cannot schedule them in our machine. The difference between Table 1 and Table 2 is that in Table 2, the edge cost has been reduced, simulating a fast parallel machine and thus increasing the task granularity. The result of matrix multiplication is not shown because SLC and DSC always find the optimal clustering, which yields no difference. The last column of these two tables is the ratio R of the DSC schedule length over the SLC schedule length. If R is greater than 1, it means that SLC outperforms DSC. The results show that despite that DSC computes a clustering suitable to each graph, R is never lower than 0.64. For coarser graphs R is never lower than 0.83. It appears that SLC outperforms DSC for some graph instances. These results indicate that the SLC algorithm delivers a symbolic scheduling solution with performance highly competitive to the DSC static solution in terms of scheduling quality.

We also have simulated the execution of clusters on a bounded number of processors (from 2 to 64). We have used the PYRROS scheduling tool [24] to merge clusters and simulate execution of tasks. The results are shown in Figure 7. In that case R is between 0.75 and 1.4, thus the scheduling quality of SLC is also good on a bounded number of processors.

Gaussian elimination on IBM SP2. For Gaussian elimination code, we have developed a preliminary version of multithreaded code to execute symbolically mapped clusters using a multithreading package called *PM2* [18]. We

have run it on an IBM SP2 with 15 RS6000 processors (the 16-th processor was out of order at the time of the experiments). Figure 8 shows the speedup of the Gaussian elimination code with various matrix sizes. We have a speedup of 11.74 for 15 processors when the matrix size is 4000. The result shows that our Gaussian elimination code scales well.

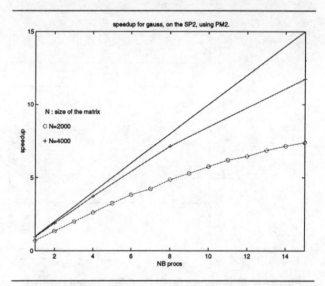

Figure 7. Speedups of the Gaussian Elimination on IBM SP2.

7. Conclusions

In this paper we have presented the SLC algorithm which symbolically schedules parameterized task graphs and can

Graph	n	Sequential time	No. clusters DSC	Sched. length DSC	No. clusters SLC	Sched. length SLC	R
Gauss	100	1009800	101	25093	102	30001	0.84
Gauss	200	8039600	201	100193	202	120001	0.83
Gauss	400	64159200	401	400393	402	480001	0.83
Jordan	100	1509950	101	40002	101	40202	0.99
Jordan	200	12039900	201	160002	201	160402	1.00
Jordan	400	96159800	401	640002	401	640802	1.00
Givens	100	3720750	98	166393	101	175906	0.95
Givens	200	39214956	318	671163	201	755580	0.89
Givens	400	257418656	496	2668550	401	2844880	0.94
Cholesky	100	510150	100	32156	101	30100	1.07
Cholesky	200	4040300	239	121759	201	120200	1.01

Table 2. Comparison between SLC and DSC on an unbounded number of processors (relatively fast machine/fine-grain tasks)

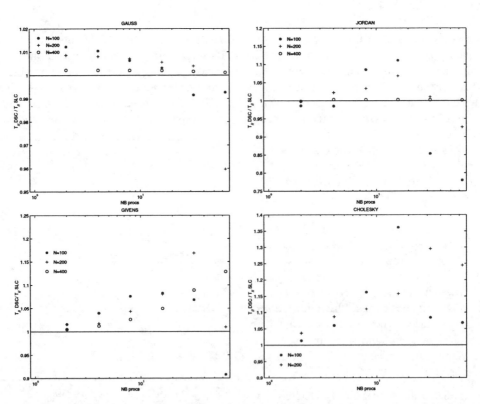

Figure 8. Makespan ratio DSC/SLC for a bounded number of processors (using PYRROS cyclic cluster merging). Cluster execution within each processor is done using the PYRROS RCP* algorithm.

perform optimization used in static scheduling, independent of program parameter values and the number of processors.

Our contribution is twofold. First, we have shown how to find a linear clustering for a PTG. Second, we have modified and augmented the Feautrier's algorithm with graph splitting for deriving an explicit clustering function in order to allocate clusters onto the processors. We have demonstrated that symbolically scheduled tasks can be executed efficiently on multiprocessors and can deliver good performance for several compute-intensive kernel benchmarks.

Our experimental results indicate that SLC finds symbolic schedules with performance highly competitive to static scheduling algorithms such as DSC.

Currently we are developing a code generator that transforms an annotated sequential program into parallel code using the SLC algorithm and evaluate our method in a wider range of benchmarks.

Acknowledgement. This work is supported in part by the European Community Eurêka EuroTOPS Project, the NSF/CNRS grant 139812, and NSF grant INT-95113361/CCR-9702640.

References

[1] Vikram S. Adve and Mary K. Vernon. A Deterministic Model for Parallel Program Performance Evaluation. (Submited for publication).

[2] J. M. Anderson and M. S. Lam. Global Optimizations for Parallelism and Locality on Scalable Parallel Machines. In *ACM SIGPLAN'93 Conference on Programming Language Design and Implementation*, June 1993.

[3] F. T. Chong, S. D. Sharma, E. A. Brewer, and J. Saltz. Multiprocessor Runtime Support for Fine-Grained Irregular DAGs. In Rajiv K. Kalia and Priya Vashishta, editors, *Toward Teraflop Computing and New Grand Challenge" Applications.*, New York, 1995. Nova Science Publishers.

[4] M. Cosnard, E. Jeannot, and T. Yang. Symbolic Partitionning and Scheduling of Parameterized Task Graphs. Technical Report RR1998-41, Laboratoire de l'Informatique du Parallélisme, Ecole Normale Supérieure de Lyon, France, September 1998. (www.ens-lyon.fr/LIP/publis.us.html).

[5] M. Cosnard and M. Loi. Automatic Task Graph Generation Techniques. *Parallel Processing Letters*, 5(4):527–538, 1995.

[6] M. Cosnard and M. Loi. A Simple Algorithm for the Generation of Efficient Loop Structures. *Internationnal Journal of Parallel Programming*, 24(3):265–289, June 1996.

[7] E. Deelman, A. Dube, A. Hoisie, Y. Luo, R. Oliver, D. Sunderam-Stukel, H. Wasserman, V.S. Adve, R. Bagrodia, J.C. Browne, E. Houstis, O. Lubeck, J. Rice, P. Teller, and M.K. Vernon. POEMS: End-to-End Performance Design of Large Parallel Adaptive Computational Systems. In *Proceedings of the First International Workshop on Software and Performance*, Santa Fe, USA, October 1998.

[8] H. El-Rewini, T.G. Lewis, and H.H. Ali. *Task Scheduling in Parallel and Distributed Systems*. Prentice Hall, 1994.

[9] P. Feautrier. Dataflow analysis of array and scalar references. *Internationnal Journal of Parallel Programming*, 20(1):23–53, 1991.

[10] P. Feautrier. Toward Automatic Distribution. *Parallel Processing Letters*, 4(3):233–244, 1994.

[11] C. Fu and T. Yang. Sparse LU Factorization with Partial Pivoting on Distributed Memory Machines. In *Proceedings of ACM/IEEE Supercomputing'96*, Pittsburgh, November 1996.

[12] A. Gerasoulis, J. Jiao, and T. Yang. Scheduling of Structured and Unstructured Computation . In D. Hsu, A. Rosenberg, and D. Sotteau, editors, *Interconnections Networks and Mappings and Scheduling Parallel Computation* , pages 139–172. American Math. Society, 1995.

[13] A. Gerasoulis and T. Yang. On the Granularity and Clustering of Direct Acyclic Task Graphs. *IEEE Transactions on Parallel and Distributed Systems*, 4(6):686–701, June 1993.

[14] Y.-K. Kwok and I. Ahmad. Dynamic Critical-Path Scheduling: An Effective Technique for Allocating Task Graphs to Multiprocessors. *IEEE Transactions on Parallel and Distributed Systems*, 7(5):506–521, May 1996.

[15] J.-C. Liou and M. A. Palis. A New Heuristic for Scheduling Parallel Programs on Multiprocessor. In *Proceedings of IEEE Intl. Conf. on Parallel Architectures and Compilation Techniques (PACT'98)*, pages 358–365, Paris, October 1998.

[16] M. Loi. *Construction et exécution de graphe de tâches acycliques à gros grain*. PhD thesis, Ecole Normale Supérieure de Lyon, France, 1996.

[17] C. Mongenet. Affine Dependence Classification for Communications Minimization. *IJPP*, 25(6), dec 1997.

[18] R. Namyst and J.-F. Méhaut. PM2: Parallel Multithreaded Machine. A computing environment for distributed architectures. In *Parallel Computing (ParCo'95)*, pages 279–285. Elsevier Science Publishers, September 1995.

[19] M.A. Palis, J-C. Liou, and D.S.L. Wei. Task Clustering and Scheduling for Distributed Memory Parallel Architectures. *IEEE Transactions on Parallel and Distributed Systems*, 7(1):46–55, January 1996.

[20] C.H. Papadimitriou and M. Yannakakis. Toward an Architecture Independent Analysis of Parallel Algorithms. *SIAM Journal on Computing*, 19(2):322–328, 1990.

[21] V. Sarkar. *Partitionning and Scheduling Parallel Program for Execution on Multiprocessors*. MIT Press, Cambridge MA, 1989.

[22] A. Schrijver. *Theory of linear and integer programming*. John Wiley & sons, 1986.

[23] M. Wu and D. Gajsky. Hypertool a programming aid for message-passing systems. *IEEE Transactions on Parallel and Distributed Systems*, 1(3):330–343, 1990.

[24] T. Yang and A. Gerasoulis. Pyrros: Static Task Scheduling and Code Generation for Message Passing Multiprocessor. In *Supercomputing'92*, pages 428–437, Washington D.C., July 1992. ACM.

[25] T. Yang and A. Gerasoulis. DSC Scheduling Parallel Tasks on an Unbounded Number of Processors. *IEEE Transactions on Parallel and Distributed Systems*, 5(9):951–967, September 1994.

Algorithms for a Job-Scheduling Problem within a Parallel Digital Library

Norbert Sensen *
Department of Mathematics and Computer Science
University of Paderborn, Germany
sensen@uni-paderborn.de

Abstract

In this paper we examine a new scheduling problem that shows up in the construction of a parallel digital library. This library performs a large amount of operations on a huge amount of stored data items. As each single operation is sequential, the data items and the sequential operation have to "meet" on one processor. Thus, a scheduling and dynamic mapping problem has to be solved to optimize the overall throughput of the server system.

We present a theoretical model of this new scheduling problem and analyze heuristics for it. These heuristics use greedy strategies and local search principles; their performance is valued comparing the results with a lower bound which bases on a lp-relaxation. We have done a large amount of experiments due to get knowledge of the behavior of the heuristics.

Keywords: *Parallel digital library, scheduling, data remapping, NP completeness, complexity, heuristics, local search, greedy algorithm*

1 Introduction

Digital library servers become more and more important for the provision of structured and unstructured information. Based on the advance in storage technology, digital libraries store huge amounts of data and provide efficient access to this data. Searching for a given pattern is one of the most important operations performed by a digital library. Since these servers cannot only store structured documents such as tables and ASCII texts, search operations become much more difficult if they are performed on picture libraries, or formated texts, e. g. postscripts. This type of search operation requires huge amounts of processing power. Since digital libraries are often connected to a public network, which allows access of a large number of

*This work is partly supported by the MWF Project "Die Virtuelle Wissensfabrik", German Science Foundation (DFG) Project SFB-376

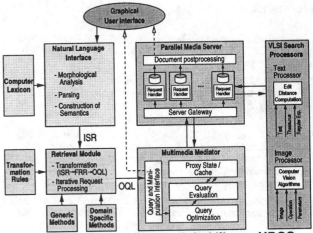

Figure 1. Structure of the digital library HPQS

users in parallel, the demand for computational power becomes even more important. Thus, parallel computing systems can be a right design alternative for high performance digital libraries.

We are involved in the construction of the HPQS, a digital library that supports the whole process of querying from a natural language interface to intelligent information mining. The system is described in [8] and its structure is presented in Figure 1. As a sample application of the digital library a meteorological scenario is used. So a huge amount of data such as satellite images have to be managed. Allowing an efficient access to the data a parallel server is used, the Parallel Media Server. This parallel server has two tasks, on the one hand it has to manage the access to the data and on the other hand it has to perform methods, e. g. image processing algorithms, on the data.

Since each of these methods has to be worked sequentially on one processor, a set of such methods can be processed by the system simultaneously allowing us the utilization of the parallel computing power. So the parallel server offers an interface allowing clients, i. e. the Multimedia Mediator inside the HPQS, to initiate the processing of a set of sequential methods. Each of these methods needs a different set of data for its execution. The parallel server

422

has to assign each job of this set of jobs to one processor such that the finishing time of the whole set of jobs will be as early as possible.

In this paper we present an exploration of this scheduling problem. One of the main characteristic feature of the problem is the requirement of specific objects for each job. A good schedule has to consider these object dependencies of the jobs, i. e. jobs which need the same objects for their execution should be assigned to the same processor. The complexity of the problem is presented and algorithms approximately solving the problem are examined. These algorithms base on greedy heuristics and local search strategies.

Our work is related to work previously done in the area of scheduling as well as in the area of parallel server design. In [9] and [16] complexity results of a couple of scheduling problems are given. In [5] a survey and classification of different scheduling problems is given. The scheduling problem we are looking at is related to the well known scheduling on unrelated parallel machines. Horowitz and Sahni presents different heuristics for it in [6], local search algorithms are presented in [4] and [1], approximation results regarding it are presented in [17], [14], and [10]. In [12] exact algorithms are presented.

Recently, there is a lot of work done to develop efficient parallel servers which have to handle masses of data and have to execute jobs. In [2] a scalable WWW-Server is presented, in [11] and [15] distributed Multimedia servers a presented. In [13] a general purpose server is presented which allows efficient requests of huge amounts of data and arbitrary functions can be used for manipulating the data on the parallel system. In [3] a digital library (DLITE) is presented which incorporates data delivery and user task execution.

The structure of this paper is as follows: In the next section we describe the theoretical model that forms a basis for this paper. Section 3 presents the complexity of the scheduling problem and the NP-completeness is proven. In section 4 greedy algorithms that solve the scheduling problem are presented and in section 5 some simple local search strategies are examined.

2 The Scheduling Model

In this section we give a precise definition of the scheduling problem. Corresponding to the realization of the Parallel Media Server inside the HPQS we use the following assumptions modeling the scheduling problem:

- The parallel server is implemented on a shared nothing system. Every processor has a local disk which can be accessed by this processor only. The processors have to use an arbitrary message passing system for communication. In the HPQS system MPI is used.

- Every object is stored exactly once in the system. So each object can be accessed directly by only one processor. This allows a good utilization of the available disk space.

- Due to the scheduling problem a set of jobs is given. Every job has to be executed sequentially and non-preemptively. Every job needs a set of objects for its execution. These objects have to be available at the processor which executes the job. To get an efficient job processing, temporary copies of objects are used.

- Due to process the jobs assigned to each processor the processor firstly has to get a temporary copy of all required objects which are not stored on the local disk. Secondly, the processor has to execute the jobs.

- In order to simplify the scheduling problem the execution time of every job is equal. Additionally the time to copy each object is equal. Both assumptions are realistic since in the HPQS system all jobs of one set of jobs correspond to the same method (but use different objects) and nearly all objects are satellite images of similar size.

Since for the scheduling only the ratio of the execution and copy time is important, we assume a unit copy time of one in the model. The execution time, which is part of the input of a problem instance, should be given relative to this. Assuming a copy time of one, we loose the possibility of a copy time of zero. But this is no problem, because if the copy time is zero, it is simple to compute an optimal schedule by distributing the jobs equally on the processors.

- The goal of the scheduling is to minimize the makespan, i. e. the finishing time of the last processor should be as early as possible. Since the results of the jobs are delivered at the time when all jobs are finished, a minimal makespan leads to a minimal response time of the parallel server.

So we are dealing with a scheduling problem which has a set J of n jobs. Each of these jobs has to be assigned to one processor of a set P of m processors. Furthermore a set O of objects exists. Each object $o \in O$ resides at the processor $v(o) \in P$. Each job $j \in J$ needs a set $w(j) \subseteq O$, $|w(j)| = k$, of k objects for its execution. So every object, which is needed by a job which is assigned at a processor where this object does not reside, has to be copied to this processor. This copying needs time 1 for every object.

The problem is to compute a schedule with a minimal makespan. Every processor requires time t for each job which is assigned to it and time 1 for each object which has to be copied from another processor. Altogether we get the following definition of the ODScheduling problem (Object Depending Scheduling):

Definition 1 (ODScheduling)

Input:

$J, |J| = n$	*set of n jobs*
$P, |P| = m$	*set of m processors*
O	*set of objects*
$v : O \to P$	*place for each object*
$w : J \to O^k$	*k objects for each job*
t	*running time of every job*

Output:

Schedule $s : J \to P$ such that the makespan T_s is minimized with $T_s := \max_{p \in P} T_{s,p}$ and

$$T_{s,p} := t \cdot |\{j \in J | s(j) = p\}|$$
$$+ |\{o \in O | \; v(o) \neq p \; \wedge$$
$$\exists j \in J : s(j) = p \; \wedge o \in w(j)\}|$$

3 Complexity of the Scheduling Problem

In this section the complexity of the ODScheduling problem is presented. Here we use a decision version of the problem (Is there a schedule with makespan M?). We expose that the decision version of the problem is NP-complete even if it is restricted to two processors and two objects needed by each job. We can show that this restricted problem is NP-complete by reducing the following problem onto it:

Definition 2 (BCBS)

Input:

A bipartite Graph $G = (V, E)$ and a $K \in \mathbb{N}$

Output:

Are there two subsets $V_1, V_2 \subseteq V$ such that $|V_1| = |V_2| = K$ and $u \in V_1, v \in V_2$ implies that $\{u, v\} \in E$?

This BCBS problem is NP-complete, see [7].

Theorem 1 *BCBS $\leq_p$ ODScheduling holds even with $k = 2$ and $m = 2$.*

Proof: In the following we assume that $V = V_a \cup V_b$ with $|V_a| = |V_b| \wedge V_a \cap V_b = \emptyset$. If this is not true, we can expand V_a or V_b respectively with nodes of degree zero without changing the solution of the BCBS problem. First we describe how we construct an ODScheduling problem from an arbitrary BCBS problem: We use the following parameters for the ODScheduling problem: $m = 2$, $k = 2$, and $t = 0$. For each node $v \in V$ we use one object, so $O = V$. We place the objects on the two processors corresponding to bipartite structure of G: $v(o) = 1 \iff o \in V_a$. Finally, for each pair $u \in V_1$ and $v \in V_2$ with $\{u, v\} \notin E$ we use one job $j \in J$ which needs the two objects u and v: $w(j) = \{u, v\}$.

Now we can show: $(G, K) \in BCBS \iff$ the constructed ODScheduling problem has a schedule s with makespan $M = \frac{|V|}{2} - K$.

Assume that $(G, K) \in BCBS$; then there are two subsets V_1 and V_2 fulfilling the condition of the BCBS problem. Then there is a schedule s by which only these objects have to be copied, which corresponds to nodes which are not in V_1 or V_2. This is true due to the construction of the jobs. This schedule s has a makespan $\frac{|V|}{2} - K$ since the only costs can arise from the copying of objects and each processor has to copy $\frac{|V|}{2} - K$ objects at most.

Assume that there is a schedule s with makespan $\frac{|V|}{2} - K$. This means that both processors have to copy $\frac{|V|}{2} - K$ objects at most. Now we can choose V_1 and V_2 such that they contain only those objects which are not copied by one of the processors. So both sets have at least K elements and due to the construction of the jobs depending on the edges of the graphs, V_1 and V_2 is a complete bipartite subgraph. ∎

Corollary 1 *The decision version of the ODScheduling problem is NP-complete even when it is restricted to two processors and each job needs two objects.*

4 Greedy Heuristics

In this section we present some heuristical algorithms solving the ODScheduling problem. Since the problem has to be solved online in the sense that the time for solving the problem is part of the response time, the scheduling algorithms have to be fastly computable and have to deliver good results. So it is clear that we should not try to solve the scheduling problem optimally.

4.1 Algorithms

4.1.1 Algorithmic Frame

All heuristical algorithms that we have investigated use the same greedy approach: The set of jobs is worked one after the other and for each job we select one processor the job is assigned to. This algorithmic frame is presented in Algorithm 1.

Algorithm 1 Algorithmic Frame for all heuristics

1: J := set of Jobs;
2: s := ∅;
3: **while** $J \neq \emptyset$ **do**
4:     choose $j \in J$; $J := J \setminus \{j\}$;
5:     choose $p \in P$; $s := s \cup (j, p)$;
6: **end while**
7: return s;

So we have to specify for each heuristic, which job j is worked next (line 4) and on which processor p this job j is scheduled (line 5). We use the following greedy approach for the selection of a processor for a job j in all of our algorithm: Assuming that there is a schedule s of a subset of jobs which are scheduled already. Then we take a processor p such that $\tilde{T}_{s,p,j}$ with $\tilde{T}_{s,p,j} := T_{s,p} + u_{s,p,j}$ being minimal for the job j. The value $T_{s,p}$ is the time on processor p according to s and $u_{s,p,j}$ is the additional time needed on processor p if the job j is assigned to it basing on the previously scheduled jobs according to s:

$$u_{s,p,j} := t + |\{o \in w(j) \mid v(o) \neq p \land \\ \forall j : s(j) \neq p \lor o \notin w(j)\}|$$

If there are several processors with the same $\tilde{T}_{s,p,j}$ we take a random one of these.

4.1.2 Different Strategies

We get different heuristics by using different strategies for the selection of the next job. We have examined the following principles:

Random Order: The first and simplest strategy is using a random order of the jobs.

Minimal New Time: Take the job with the smallest value of $\min_p \tilde{T}_{s,p,j}$ as the next one. So we obtain that this good $\min_p \tilde{T}_{s,p,j}$ is indeed realized by the schedule.

Minimal Number: Take the job with the minimal number of different optimal processors regarding $\tilde{T}_{s,p,j}$. So this job can use its best processor and since other jobs have a greater number of good processors there are still some good processors left for them.

Minimal Time and Number: Take the job with the smallest $\min_p \tilde{T}_{s,p,j}$. If two jobs have the same time, use the one with the smallest number of different optimal processors. So we have combined both strategies that have been mentioned before.

Minimal Additional Time: Take the job with the smallest $u_{s,p,j}$ concerning the processor which fulfills the $\min_p \tilde{T}_{s,p,j}$ minimization. So the biggest amount of unused processor time remains after this assignment. As secondary criterion we use the value $\min_p \tilde{T}_{s,p,j}$ and as third criterion the number of optimal processors is used again.

The selection of the processor has to be done correspondingly.

Further we have looked for some other principles, e.g. using the job with the biggest $\min_p \tilde{T}_{s,p,j}$ first. But all these other ideas had no advantage compared to the ones listed above.

4.2 The Representation of the Problem as a Linear Program

In order to get an idea of the solution quality of a schedule, we have computed a lower bound on the optimal makespan. Thus, we express the ODScheduling problem as an integer linear programming problem. Ignoring the integer constraints we get the LP-Relaxation. The value of an optimal solution of the LP-Relaxation is a lower bound on the makespan of the optimal schedule. The LP representation is built from a given ODScheduling problem using the following scheme:

For each job $j \in J$ we use m 0-1 variables with the meaning $x_{j,p} = 1 \Leftrightarrow$ job j is scheduled to processor p. A 0-1 variable is a variable which has only two permitted values: zero and one. A second set of 0-1 variables is used for the representation of a copy process of an object: $y_{o,p} = 1 \Leftrightarrow$ object o has to be copied to processor p. Finally, we need one variable M representing the makespan of the schedule. So altogether we use $m(n + |O|)$ 0-1 variables and one non-integer variable.

Since we have to achieve an unambiguous job processor assignment, we have to enforce that each job is assigned to exactly one processor, so we use the constraints $\forall j \in J : \sum_p x_{j,p} = 1$. Additionally, we have to achieve that all necessary objects are copied, so the constraints $\forall j \in J, p \in P : \sum_{o \in w_p(j)} y_{o,p} \geq x_{j,p} \cdot |w_p(j)|$ are used with $w_p(j) := \{o \in w(j) \mid v(o) \neq p\}$. Finally, m constraints are needed in order to achieve that every processor needs at most time $M : \forall p \in P : t \sum_j x_{j,p} + \sum_o y_{o,p} \leq M$.

Altogether we need $n + mn + m$ constraints. Since the goal is to minimize the makespan all variables have a cost of zero except the variable M, which has a cost of one; and the LP should be minimized.

5 Local Search Algorithms

A second kind of algorithms we have examined are simple local search algorithms. Since the time for solving the scheduling problem is part of the total response time of a request, it is crucial for the algorithms to have a good running time. So tricky local search algorithms as simulated annealing, tabu search, or genetic algorithms are no good choice for our problem since their running time is to large. So we have concentrated our investigations on simpler hillclimbing algorithms. The procedure of these algorithms is fairly simple and the general frame is presented in Algorithm 2.

Applying this algorithmic frame to the ODScheduling problem some points have to be clarified: Which schedules are in the neighborhood of a schedule s. When is a schedule s better than a schedule s'. How can we generate initial solutions and how often should the procedure be repeated.

Algorithm 2 Algorithmic frame for a local search algorithm
```
1:  N := number of repetitions;
2:  s̃ := ∅;
3:  for i = 1 to N do
4:      s := initial solution;
5:      while there is a neighbor of s with better quality do
6:          s := one arbitrary neighbor of s with better quality;
7:      end while
8:      if s is better than s̃ then
9:          s̃ := s;
10:     end if
11: end for
12: return s̃;
```

Neighborhood: Given a schedule s we use two kinds of modifications on s generating a neighbor schedule s'. Firstly, we allow the change of an assignment of exactly one job. So for each job assignments to every processor are done leading to different neighbor schedules. Secondly, we permit the exchange of the assignment of two jobs. So we get neighbor schedules while swapping the processor assignments for each pair of jobs.

So every schedule s has at most $nm + n^2$ neighbor schedules. Since the size of the neighborhood determines the performance of the algorithm, we have tried to use only the first described kind of neighborhood. In this case each schedule has nm neighbors so the algorithm is much faster, but we have seen that the quality of the solutions is clearly worse.

Quality of a schedule: Usually the value which should be optimized is used as the quality of a solution. But minimizing the makespan in a scheduling problem often leads to schedules which have a number of processors all of which are fulfilling the makespan of the schedule. Due to the neighborhood of a schedule at most two processors could have a better time in the neighbor schedule so using the makespan of the schedule as quality would result very often in local optima.

We have used the following criterion determining if a schedule s is better than a schedule s': Firstly, s is better if it has a smaller makespan. Secondly, s is better if it has the same makespan but has a smaller number of processors which reach this makespan. Thirdly, s is better if it has the same makespan, and the same number of processors which reach this makespan, and the sum of the times of all processors is less.

Initial solution: Since the initial solution is the only non-deterministic step in our implementation of Algorithm 2, it should be different every time it is calculated. We have tried two different strategies: Firstly, we compute

Makespan	46	47	48	49	50	51
Random	0.002	3.013	42.052	47.539	7.248	0.146
BestFit	0.301	39.595	55.294	4.789	0.021	0.000

Figure 2. Probability distribution (in %) of the achieved makespan depending on the used initial solution regarding one specific problem

an initial schedule by assigning each job to a random processor. In the following this strategy is called 'Random'.

Secondly, we compute an initial schedule by assigning each job to a random processor of the set of processors where this job has most of its objects. In the following this strategy is called 'BestFit'. This second strategy delivers initial schedules of better quality but has a more restricted range. In the following we will show the results comparing both strategies.

Number of repetitions: There is no general solution for this problem. The number of repetitions is a trade-off between the running time of the algorithm and the solution quality. So we have made some experiments the results of which can be used as a foundation of a good choice.

A good choice for the number of repetitions can be done basing on the quality distribution of the solutions of one pass of the local search algorithm. Figure 2 presents the probabilities of the achieved quality in one pass concerning one specific ODScheduling problem. We have taken a randomly generated problem with the parameters of $n = 100$, $m = 8$, $k = 2$, $t = 3$, and each object is needed by three jobs; these parameters corresponds to typical requests in the HPQS. We have determined the presented values doing 100.000 passes of the local search algorithms. It is worth noticing that we have computed the probabilities regarding some other specific problems also. The distribution of the solutions quality has been of the same type.

Using these values we can compute the expected makespan depending on the number of repetitions. Figure 3 presents this expected makespan depending on the number of repetitions. Since the running time of the local search algorithm has to be added to the makespan of the scheduling problem resulting to the total response time of a request inside the parallel server, this total time is also presented in Figure 3. In fact, this total time is the one which should be minimized.

Conclusion on the Local Search Algorithms

Evaluating the results of Figure 2 and 3 we come to the following observations:

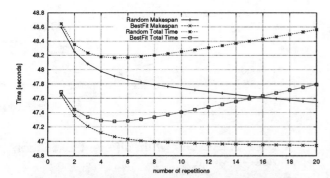

Figure 3. Expected makespan and total running time depending on the number of repetitions and the used initial solution basing on the probabilities of Figure 2

- It is clearly better to use the BestFit strategy for computing the initial solution.

- The solution quality of the local search algorithms can be arbitrarily good if you permit an arbitrarily large number of repetitions.

- Good choices of the number of repetitions depends on the execution and copy time of the ODScheduling problem. If they are big, a large number of repetitions should be used since the resulting improvement of the makespan dominates the increasing running time of the algorithms. On the other hand if the times are small, a small number of repetitions should be used.

- For typical parameters of scheduling problems inside the HPQS a repetition number of five seems to be a good choice.

6 Experimental Results

We have done a large amount of experiments studying which algorithm is the best one and which one should be used in which case. We have compared the described heuristics of section 4 and the local search algorithm of the last section. Within the local search algorithm we have used the Best Fit initial solution since it gives better makespans and running time compared with a random initial solution. In the experiments we have used five repetitions of the local search procedure since as we have seen in the last section the choice is a good trade off between a good solution value and running time of the algorithm.

We present some results comparing the algorithms and the lp-relaxation with the optimal makespan. We have computed the optimal makespan using a simple branch & bound algorithm. Due to the NP-completeness of the ODScheduling problem it is clear that this branch & bound algorithm

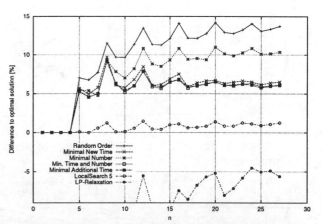

Figure 4. Error of the heuristics depending on a different number of jobs

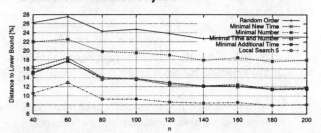

Figure 5. Results with different number of jobs

has exponential worst case running time. So we can compute this optimal solution for small problem instances only.

Figure 4 presents the results of the different heuristics compared with the optimal makespan depending on a different number of jobs. We have used random problem instances with $m = 4$, $k = 2$, $t = 3$, and each object is used by three jobs (i. e. $\forall o \in O : |\{j \in J : o \in w(j)\}| = 3$). The displayed values are averaged over 1000 randomly generated problems.

Furthermore, we have compared the different algorithms using realistically sized problem instances. Doing this we have generated random problems with the parameters $n = 100$, $m = 8$, $k = 2$, $t = 3$, and each object is used by exactly three jobs. In Figures 5 – 9 the results are presented. In every figure one of the parameters is changed so the dependency of the quality of the heuristics on this parameter is presented. In every figure the error of the heuristics compared to the lower bound is presented. All shown results are averaged over 10 randomly generated problems.

Conclusions drawn from the Experiments

Looking at the results of the experiments presented in Figures 4 – 9 we come to the following conclusions:

- The Random Order heuristic is clearly worse than the

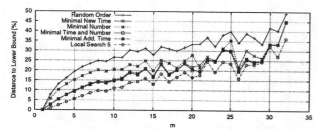

Figure 6. Results with different number of processors

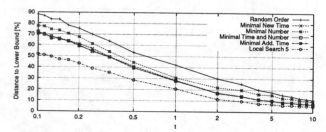

Figure 8. Results with different execution times

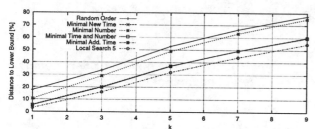

Figure 7. Results with different number of objects needed by each job

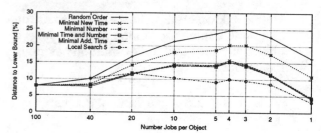

Figure 9. Results with different degree of disjointness

other heuristics. It is worth making an additional effort to compute a more intelligent order of the jobs.

- Using the Minimal Number strategy results in an improvement compared with the Random Order. As can be seen in Figure 6 the strategy is particularly good if the number of processors is large.

- All other heuristics are comparably good and better than Random Order and Minimal Number. Especially the use of the Minimal Number strategy as a secondary criterion leads to good solutions independently from the number of processors.

- Generally, the local search algorithm provides clearly better solutions than the heuristics. But as can be seen in Figure 9 the local search is worse if there is a low degree of disjointness.

- The quality of the solutions is slightly better for a large number of jobs as can be seen in Figure 5.

- The larger the parameters m, k and $\frac{1}{t}$ are, the worse are the solutions of the heuristics as can be seen in Figures 6 – 8.

  Though we expect that the error of the lp-relaxation we have used as lower bound increases with these named parameters also. So in fact it is not clear what the main reason for the decreasing quality is.

- The ODScheduling problem is most complicated for an average degree of disjointness. With a high degree of disjointness we mean that the set of objects which are needed by the different jobs are nearly disjoint. A

minimum degree of disjointness means that all jobs needs the same set of objects.

So if this disjointness is minimal this means that all jobs need the same objects and a very good schedule is simply computed by copying all objects to all processors and distributing the jobs equally on the processors. On the other hand if this disjointness is maximal this means that there is no object which is needed by more than one job. Then there is a very low dependency of the different jobs and they can be scheduled relatively independently. This fact is clarified in Figure 9.

So altogether the local search algorithm provides the best quality of solution. But since the problem has to be solved online the running time of the algorithms has to be taken in consideration. From this point of view it is clear that the 'Random Order' heuristic is the fastest one since it needs $\Theta(mn)$ steps. All other greedy heuristics need $\Theta(mn^2)$ steps. Finally, the local search algorithm is the slowest one. In fact, no polynomial bound on the number of steps can be shown for it. These theoretic considerations are engaged by the practical running times of the different algorithms. Figure 10 presents these running times. The times corresponds to the computations we have done while computing the results presented in Figure 5, which were made on a Sun Ultra 1 Model 140. Notice that the time axis is scaled logarithmically.

So the selection of an algorithm for solving the ODScheduling problem should depend on the order of magnitude of the expected makespan. If the makespan is very small, even the 'Random Order' heuristic could be the right choice. If the makespan is large and a better solution would

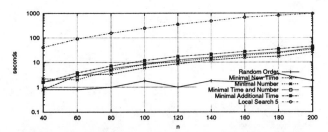

Figure 10. Average running times of the different algorithms

result in a big time advantage, the local search algorithm should be used.

7 Conclusion

We presented a new scheduling problem which arises in the construction of a parallel server as a part of a digital library. We expect that this problem arises in other applications also, which will make its discussion even more valuable. We have shown the general np-hardness of the problem and investigated simple heuristics. It concludes that simple greedy algorithms have low running times but compute bad makespans. Local search algorithms compute much better makespans but have much worse running times. So in our practice the greedy algorithms are used.

For further research it would be very interesting to investigate other algorithms which have low running times and compute good makespans. We will try to design such algorithms as well as derive lower bound results such as "There is no linear time algorithm with error at most 2, unless P=NP".

References

[1] Anderson, Glass, and Potts. Machine scheduling. In E. Aarts and J. K. Lenstra, editors, *Local Search in Combinatorial Optimization, Wiley, 1997.* 1997.

[2] D. Andresen, T. Yang, and O. H. Ibarra. Toward a scalable distributed WWW server on workstation clusters. *Journal of Parallel and Distributed Computing*, 42(1):91–100, Apr. 1997.

[3] S. B. Cousins, A. Paepcke, T. Winograd, E. A. Bier, and K. Pier. The digital library integrated task environment (DLITE). In R. B. Allen and E. Rasmussen, editors, *Proceedings of the 2nd ACM International Conference on Digital Libraries*, pages 142–151, New York, July 23–26 1997. ACM Press.

[4] C. Glass, C. Potts, and P. Shade. Unrelated parallel machine scheduling using local search. *Math. Comput. Modelling*, 20(2):41–52, 1994.

[5] R. L. Graham, E. L. Lawler, J. K. Lenstra, and A. H. G. R. Kan. Optimization and approximation in deterministic sequencing and scheduling: A survey. *Ann. Discrete Mathematics*, 5:287–326, 1979.

[6] E. Horowitz and S. Sahni. Exact and approximate algorithms for scheduling nonidentical processors. *Journal of the ACM*, 23(2):317–327, Apr. 1976.

[7] D. S. Johnson. The NP-completeness column: An ongoing guide: Announcements, updates, and greatest hits. *Journal of Algorithms*, 8(3):438–448, Sept. 1987.

[8] A. Knoll, C. Altenschmidt, J. Biskup, H.-M. Blüthgen, I. Glöckner, S. Hartrumpf, H. Helbig, C. Henning, Y. K. R. Lüling, B. Monien, T. Noll, and N. Sensen. An integrated approach to semantic evaluation and content-based retrieval of multimedia documents. *Lecture Notes in Computer Science*, 1513:409–??, 1998.

[9] E. Lawler, J. Lenstra, A. Kan, and D. Shmoys. Sequencing and scheduling: Algorithms and complexity. In S. Graves, A. Kan, and P. Zipkin, editors, *Handbooks in Operations Research and Management Science*. Elsevier Science Publishers, 1993.

[10] J. K. Lenstra, D. B. Shmoys, and E. Tardos. Approximation algorithms for scheduling unrelated parallel machines. *Mathematical Programming*, 46:259–271, 1990.

[11] R. Lüling, F. Cortes, and N. Sensen. Parallel interactive media server systems. *Lecture Notes in Computer Science*, 1521:149–??, 1998.

[12] Martello, Soumis, and Toth. Exact and approximation algorithms for makespan minimization on unrelated parallel machines. *DAMATH: Discrete Applied Mathematics and Combinatorial Operations Research and Computer Science*, 75, 1997.

[13] W. O'Connell, I. T. Ieong, D. Schrader, C. Watson, G. Au, A. Biliris, S. Choo, P. Colin, G. Linderman, E. Panagos, J. Wang, and T. Walters. Prospector: A content-based multimedia server for massively parallel architectures. In H. V. Jagadish and I. S. Mumick, editors, *Proceedings of the 1996 ACM SIGMOD International Conference on Management of Data*, pages 68–78, Montreal, Quebec, Canada, 4–6 June 1996.

[14] C. N. Potts. Analysis of a linear programming heuristic for scheduling unrelated parallel machines. *Discrete Applied Mathematics*, pages 155–164, 1985.

[15] V. Rottmann, P. Berenbrink, and R. Lüling. Simple distributed scheduling policy for parallel interactive continuous media servers. *Parallel Computing*, 23(12):1757–1776, Dec. 1997.

[16] V. Tanaev, V. Gordon, and Y. Shafransky. *Scheduling Theory. Single-Stage Systems.* Kluwer Academic Publishers, 1994.

[17] S. van de Velde. Duality-based algorithms for scheduling unrelated parallel machines. *ORSA Journal on Computing*, 5(2):192–205, 1993.

Keynote Address
Digital Revolution at the Crossroads

Prof. Yutaka Matsushita
Keio University, Japan

Session A7

Collective Communication

Chair: Loren Schwiebert
Wayne State University, USA

A Bandwidth-Efficient Implementation of Mesh with Multiple Broadcasting

Jong Hyuk Choi
LG Electronics
Seoul 137-724, Korea
choix@lge.co.kr

Bong Wan Kim, Kyu Ho Park
CORE Lab., E.E. KAIST
Taejon 305-701, Korea
{bwkim,kpark}@core.kaist.ac.kr

Kwang-Il Park
LG Semicon
Seoul 135-738, Korea
kipark@lgsemicon.co.kr

Abstract

This paper presents a mesh with virtual buses as the bandwidth-efficient implementation of the mesh with multiple broadcasting on which many computational problems can be solved with reduced time complexity. The new system provides a low latency and high bandwidth communication mechanism without the disadvantage of the dual network approach: the possible bandwidth waste. The virtual buses are built using those communication links of the base point-to-point mesh network only upon request. Even if bus requests are not made, the full network bandwidth is harnessed by the point-to-point communication. On the contrary, the bandwidth assigned to the conventional real buses will be wasted when there is little bus request.

This paper introduces a wormhole router design equipped with the virtual bus functions, describes the connections among these routers, and presents various virtual bus transactions. We prove the effectiveness of the virtual bus by showing that a representative semigroup computation can be solved very efficiently on it: a vector maxima finding is accelerated by 2.66 times in the experiment. We also explore the network characteristics by the distribution-driven simulation of the system. These evaluations convinced us that the mesh with virtual buses is a promising approach to low latency and high bandwidth communication which has applications in many parallel computations such as in parallel simulations, computer graphics, real time systems, and many others.

1. Introduction

The mesh of processing nodes is one of the most attractive models of parallel computation in practice as well as in theory. Its simple intuitive structure enables easy development of parallel algorithms. It scales up without requiring additional communication ports in each node and without long communication links between distant nodes. The large diameter and average distance, however, make it not suit-able for problems having many non local communications.

One of the solutions to this long distance problem is enhancing the mesh with buses [2, 3, 5, 15, 16]. The bus is a common access medium to which some or all of the processing nodes of the mesh are attached. Through the bus, those nodes on the mesh that are not neighbors can communicate directly and a source node can communicate with multiple destination nodes simultaneously.

The mesh with a global bus is the mesh augmented with a single bus that connects all processing nodes on the mesh. Many algorithms can benefit from the addition of the single global bus: their time complexity can be reduced considerably. They include semigroup computations [1, 5, 18], sorting [18], matrix multiplication [1], and many others. As an example, the maximum finding algorithm is one of the semigroup computations. On the $N^{1/2} \times N^{1/2}$ mesh system, its time complexity is $O(N^{1/3})$ with the addition of the single global bus, while $O(N^{1/2})$ otherwise.

In the mesh with row and column buses, there is one bus on each row and one bus on each column. Because every row or column bus has its own access control, multiple independent bus transactions can coexist at the same time. Further, the length of the row or the column bus increases at a much less rate ($O(N^{1/2})$) than that of the global bus ($O(N)$). Many algorithms of semigroup computations [3, 6, 11], sorting [10, 11], selection [11], searching [3], computational geometry [4], and dynamic programming [20] can benefit from the introduction of the row and the column buses. For example again, the maximum finding algorithm can be solved in $O(N^{1/8})$ time on the mesh with row and column buses.

The realization of the mesh with buses is exemplified in [15]. Although this dual network approach provides very low latency and collective communication facility, it has its intrinsic bandwidth waste problem: one of the two networks may be underutilized, while the other may be saturated. In the extreme, it may happen that one of them is not utilized at all. For example, an algorithm having only local communications may not utilize the buses. At the other end, an algorithm having only collective communications may not utilize the mesh network.

To make an even utilization of the two networks, programmers should balance the loads on the mesh and the buses, or the compiler should detect the type of communications and distribute them to the mesh and the buses equally. This is quite a burden to programmers or to compiler writers. Moreover, the load balance may not always be possible, especially in dynamic algorithms.

This paper presents a new method of implementing the mesh with multiple broadcasting, called the *mesh with virtual buses*. The virtual buses are dynamically built on those communication links of the mesh network. Ongoing messages on the mesh are frozen intact at the bypassed message buffers of the network routers. The virtual bus data is transmitted using the wave pipelining [14] technique to increase the bandwidth. After the bus data transmission, the frozen messages continue to proceed toward their destinations. We can equip the mesh networks with the virtual bus functionality by modifying the conventional wormhole or cut-through router architectures and their connections.

Because the virtual bus does not require additional physical bus data wires, the wiring complexity of the virtual buses is significantly lower than that of the conventional real buses. The mesh with virtual buses provides the low latency communication and the collective communication facility, as does the mesh with real buses, but in a bandwidth-efficient manner. If there is no request to the bus, the whole network is used as a point-to-point mesh. During the bus transaction, the whole bandwidth of the corresponding channels is assigned to the bus. The mesh with virtual buses can adapt itself to any communication patterns over the mesh and the buses without a bandwidth waste.

The virtual bus concept was first introduced in [9]. This paper gives more detailed descriptions and performance analyses. We introduce the virtual bus concept in Section 2. Then, in Section 3, we present a modified router architecture for virtual bus functions and its intra and inter router datapaths. Section 4, then, illustrates different virtual bus transactions and their protocols. Section 5 shows the effectiveness of the mesh with virtual buses. First, we take the above-mentioned maximum finding workloads as examples to show the effects of the increased bandwidth utilization. Then, we analyze the performance characteristics through a distribution-driven simulation of the mesh with virtual buses. Section 6 concludes the paper. In the following discussions, we refer to both rows and columns as *lines*.

2. Mesh with Virtual Buses: A Logical View

In this section, we introduce the virtual bus concept and illustrate the virtual bus transaction on a single line. The virtual bus is established by bypassing the existing datapaths inside the network router. Figure 1 shows the conceptual

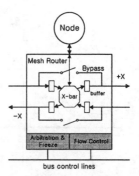

Figure 1. Virtual Bus Concept.

view of the router architecture with the virtual bus facility. A single virtual bus can be built on each row or each column. Here, only the row channels (+X and -X) are shown for the simplicity of description. Upon a bus setup request, the arbitration logic is responsible for the exclusive access to the virtual bus. Only one of the requesters is granted the virtual bus access. All other routers on the virtual bus make a detour connection inside the router bypassing their message buffers: routers on the right side of the requester build virtual buses of +X direction; routers on the left side of the requester build virtual buses of -X direction. The virtual bus transaction always has higher priority than the base mesh network communication. Ongoing mesh messages are frozen intact at the message buffers during the bus data transfer. After the requester detects that all other routers on the bus are ready to start the virtual bus data transfer, it begins driving data towards both ends of the row along +X and -X directions. The data transmission is under control of an end-to-end flow control between the requester and destination(s). The wave pipelining [14] is used for high bandwidth communication. The actual bypass paths inside the routers are much shorter than those shown in Figure 1. We will present the actual architecture in detail later in the next section.

Figure 2 shows snapshots of two virtual bus transactions. A source node S1 tries to send a unicast message to D1 while at the same time, another source S2 tries to send a multicast message to destinations D1, D2, D3, and D4. Figure 2 (a) shows the situation that S1 wins the arbitration of the middle row virtual bus. Since the source and destination nodes are not on the same line, two orthogonal virtual buses are built. Figure 2 (b) shows the situation that S2 wins the arbitration of the middle row virtual bus. For a multicast on different lines, we build a multicast tree of the minimum cardinality (the number of participating buses) rooted at the source. S2 drives the root - the middle row - virtual bus first. Then, the routers S2 and D2 act as bus bridges, forwarding the root virtual bus data to the two column virtual buses.

Ongoing mesh messages interfering with the virtual bus-

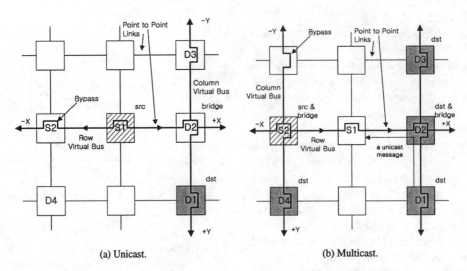

(a) Unicast. (b) Multicast.

Figure 2. Virtual Bus Transactions on Top of the Mesh.

es are stopped at the routers' message buffers. Those that do not interfere with the virtual buses can proceed irrespective of the virtual buses. For example, a mesh message from D1 to S1 of Figure 2 (b) can progress concurrently with the virtual bus transaction, because it propagates in the reverse directions to the virtual buses.

The virtual bus transaction has two main differences from the conventional bus transaction: 1) the virtual bus data are transmitted not through the common access media but through a series of switches and links; 2) the virtual bus arbitration requires the freeze process. In other respects, the virtual bus operates in the same way as the conventional bus.

A single line virtual bus transaction of +X direction on the middle row of Figure 2 consists of the following steps. Those involving multiple virtual buses and multicast transactions will be presented in Section 4.

1. When the virtual bus is idle, the network routers deliver conventional mesh messages.

2. Two sources, S1 and S2, try to acquire the same virtual bus by driving their IDs inside their row on the bus arbitration lines at exactly the same time.

3. We opt a distributed arbitration mechanism [19]. S1 and S2 compare their own IDs with the ID present on the arbitration bus which eventually has the combined (logical wired-OR) value of the IDs of requesters. If the ID of S2 is higher than that of S1 the combined arbitration bus will contain the ID of S2. After a combining period, S2 finds itself the winner of the arbitration. As a result, S2 starts its virtual bus transaction, whereas S1 retreats its virtual bus request, which will be retried after S2's transaction. Figure 3 (a) shows the virtual bus arbitration of this step and the message freeze process of the next step.

4. All but the requester router establish the bypass paths in a bounded amount of time. The ongoing mesh network data are frozen at the message buffers inside the routers. The requester first transmits a bit vector as a destination list on the line. The destination routers also set up the port datapaths to node computers. All routers on the line assert the bus grant after setting up all the required datapaths. The bus grant signal is the wired-AND combined signal, which becomes asserted after all the routers assert it.

5. The virtual bus data is being transmitted to the destination, D2. The requester starts transmitting data after sensing the combined bus grant. The data is synchronized to the receiver's clock domain using a skew tolerant synchronization method [8]. Using byteports and bitports, this method detects the amount of skew the message header has experienced during transit, by which it synchronizes the rest of the message. As shown in Figure 3 (b), the source and destination are connected directly through the virtual bus connection without intervening buffers. The requester sends data to the destination through an end-to-end flow control mechanism between them.

6. After the virtual bus data transmission ends, the requester deasserts the request signal. Other routers, after sensing the deassertion, release the bypass paths and restore the mesh datapaths to their previous status.

7. The frozen mesh network data continue to proceed to their destinations.

8. Other requests for the virtual bus, including the retreated one from S1, compete for the bus access.

436

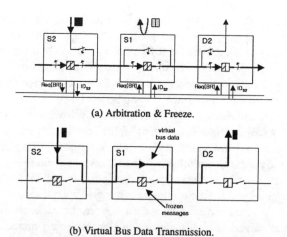

(a) Arbitration & Freeze.

(b) Virtual Bus Data Transmission.

Figure 3. Abstract Virtual Bus Operations.

3. Network Router with Virtual Bus Functions

The detailed design of the wormhole router equipped with the virtual bus function is shown in Figure 4. The virtual bus datapaths added to the wormhole router are depicted in dotted lines. Although the virtual bus is designed for the 2D mesh network in this paper, it can also be implemented in higher dimension meshes in the same way. The router for the 2D mesh network has 10 channels according to their orientation (+X, -X, +Y, -Y, and Node) and their direction (In and Out). There exist flit (flow control digit) buffers at each of these channels.

For the virtual bus connection, we prepare a detour path for each channel, bypassing the flit buffers of the channel. As shown in Figure 4, the bypass datapath is physically short. It consists of a multiplexer and buffer-bypassing wires. During the virtual bus data transmission, the flit buffers of the corresponding channels are isolated while retaining the buffer data in them, and the status of the crossbar switch is stored in special registers associated with the channels. When the row virtual bus of +X direction is built, the +Xin and the +Xout channels are directly connected by the crossbar switch. In the same way, the column virtual bus of -Y direction is built through the straight crossbar connection of -Yin and -Yout channels. After the virtual bus transaction terminates, the multiplexer connects the flit buffers back to the channel, and the original crossbar connections are restored from the saved status in the registers.

What is important in the virtual bus setup phase is that all the mesh messages interfering with the virtual bus must be saved intact in the network buffers. In the freeze process, ongoing flits must neither be missing nor be duplicated. We assume an asynchronous router which sends data between its neighbors using a Req - Ack handshaking. When a router has a flit to send, it places the flit on the corresponding channel and toggles the Req signal. In response

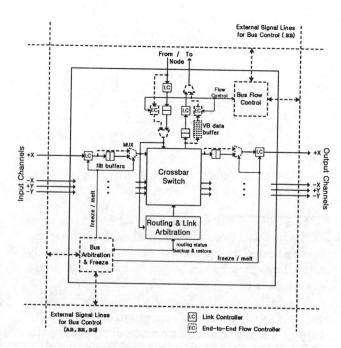

Figure 4. Architecture of Virtual Bus Router.

to this, the receiving router toggles the Ack signal after the received flit is latched into its input buffer. This signalling is illustrated in Figure 5 for +X direction. The virtual bus signals are also shown in the figure. BR and BG are the virtual bus request and grant signals, respectively. BB is the bus busy signal for the end-to-end flow control. AB is the arbitration bus for a row or a column virtual bus.

When the router detects the virtual bus setup by sensing the BR and AB, different situations can arise with respect to the mesh router messages: 1) If Req and Ack are in the same logic level, the last flit has been successfully transmitted and the new flit is not yet in transit. In this case, we can safely disconnect the flit buffers at both the sending and the receiving routers from the datapaths. 2) If they are not equal, the sender has placed a new flit which is not yet delivered to the receiver: 2-1) If there are free slots in the receiver buffer, then the receiver accepts the flit and toggles the Ack. After observing the Ack toggled, the sender discards the flit. 2-2) If the receiver buffer is full, then the receiver does not accept the data and does not toggle the Ack. When the sender cannot sense the Ack toggling within a specified amount of time, it backs off the request by toggling the Req back, preserving the data in its buffer.

At the node input channel of the router, a relatively deep buffer may be required for the end-to-end flow control of the virtual bus data. Another option is to move this buffer to the network interface inside each node. The BB line controls the data transmission. When the fill level of the buffer is below a certain low watermark, the requester begins transmission.

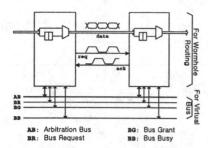

AB: Arbitration Bus   BG: Bus Grant
BR: Bus Request   BB: Bus Busy

Figure 5. Router and Virtual Bus Signals.

If it goes higher than the high watermark, the BB is asserted and the requester stops the transmission. Both the spaces above and below the high and low watermarks, respectively, must be larger than the round-trip delay between the farthest nodes in the network.

When multiple virtual buses are involved in a transaction, there should exist at least one pair of orthogonal virtual buses. The router at the intersection of two virtual buses becomes the bus bridge which forwards one bus data to the other and relays bus control signals between them. If the row (column) virtual bus is established first, then the bridge router sets up the column (row) virtual bus. The bridge router connects the two virtual buses by joining them through the crossbar switch inside the router.

We need a multiple access control mechanism for an exclusive access of the bus by a node at a given time. For high speed bus setup, we choose a distributed self selection arbitration scheme such as that of the IEEE Futurebus [19]. When a router wants to grab the virtual bus, it asserts the BR with its ID on the AB. The AB lines will have a combined (logical wired-OR) value of the IDs of multiple requesters. A router wins the virtual bus if the combined AB value is the same as its ID. By changing routers' ID after each bus transaction, we can implement a variable priority arbitration.

The AB requires $\log N^{1/2}$ bits, since it carries a router's ID within a line of the $N^{1/2} \times N^{1/2}$ mesh. A 16×16 mesh, for example, requires four bit AB, thus requiring seven physical bus bits (including BR, BG, and BB) per each line. These physical bus lines for bus control are also required in the mesh with real buses. To reduce the number of physical bus lines further, we can compromise the bus setup speed by choosing low cost mechanisms, such as the collision detection scheme and the daisy chain arbitration.

As we can see in Figure 4, the logic and datapath overhead of the virtual bus is negligible. Because the bypass paths are geographically short and the multiplexer can be made very fast with the current generation VLSI technology, the latency of the base mesh network is minimally affected. The virtual bus follows the repeater delay model [12] which exhibits similar latency characteristics to those of the real bus delay model [12]. For the virtual

bus transmission, we can benefit from the wave pipelining technique [14] to increase the effective bandwidth. This becomes possible because the virtual bus datapaths are purely combinational. As a result, the virtual bus transaction has a high bandwidth as well as a low latency. At the same time, the virtual bus has much fewer physical bus lines which are for control signals only. The reduced physical bus wires enable easier implementation of higher speed network. These are the advantages of the virtual bus system in addition to the beforementioned bandwidth savings from using the same set of data wires both for the point-to-point mesh operations and for the multiaccess bus grid operations.

With the virtual bus, we do not require expensive bus transceivers of high speed and of high power any more. It is less costly to design the virtual bus system than to design the real buses, because there is little need to adjust bus signal impedance and to minimize signal flight time, branch stubs, device spacing, and power consumption of long multi-drop wires which has multi-access nature.

For the high speed data transmission over the virtual bus, it is very important to limit the skew among data bit lines. Because the virtual bus connection is a series of logic gates and their connections, only a small amount of skew of the individual routers and off-chip wires adds up to a considerable amount of end-to-end skew that could slow down the data transmission speed by much. In fact, the speed of the wave pipelining depends mainly on the amount of skew between signal lines. It requires lots of painstaking tasks to bound the skew within a very small range. The skew compensation logic [8] mentioned in the previous section is utilized to mitigate this requirement. With this logic at each router, quite a large amount of skew can be tolerated, thereby enabling the high speed operation of the wave pipelined data transmission on the virtual bus with reduced design time, efforts, and cost.

4. Virtual Bus Transactions

We implement three types of virtual bus transactions: unicast, multicast, and broadcast. The unicast transaction provides very fast communication between distant nodes. In the multicast transaction, a source node can send data to multiple destinations. The broadcast is a special case of the multicast in which a source node delivers data over the entire system. The simple unicast transaction on a single line was already explained in Section 2. In this section we will focus on more sophisticated virtual bus transactions.

4.1. Single Line Transactions

Figure 6 shows the virtual bus message formats for different transactions. The Figure 6 (a) shows the header structure for single line bus transactions. The headers are

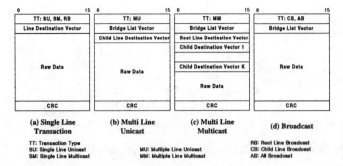

TT: SU, SM, RB	TT: MU	TT: MM	TT: CB, AB
Line Destination Vector	Bridge List Vector	Bridge List Vector	Bridge List Vector
	Child Line Destination Vector	Root Line Destination Vector	
		Child Destination Vector 1	
Raw Data	Raw Data	Child Destination Vector K	Raw Data
		Raw Data	
CRC	CRC	CRC	CRC
(a) Single Line Transaction	**(b) Multi Line Unicast**	**(c) Multi Line Multicast**	**(d) Broadcast**

TT: Transaction Type
SU: Single Line Unicast
SM: Single Line Multicast
MU: Multiple Line Unicast
MM: Multiple Line Multicast
RB: Root Line Broadcast
CB: Child Line Broadcast
AB: All Broadcast

Figure 6. Virtual Bus Message Formats.

broadcast to all routers on the line before the raw data transmission begins. For single line unicast, only one bit of the line destination vector is set, while for the single line multicast, multiple destination vector bits are set. For broadcast on a single root line, all bits of the vector are set to one. Every destination on the line identifies oneself as the destination after examining this bit vector. The combined (logical wired-AND) BG signal, asserted by all routers of the line after receiving the vector, will trigger the bus transaction.

4.2. Multiple Line Unicast: Bus Bridges

When the source and the destination nodes reside neither on the same row nor on the same column, two virtual buses orthogonal to each other are required for a unicast transaction. We let the requester try to set up the row virtual bus first. After the requester is granted the exclusive access to the row, it sends a bridge list vector each bit of which pinpoints whether the corresponding router on the row should act as the bus bridge. For the unicast, there is only one bridge router which is on the same column as the destination. The selected bus bridge on the row, then, try to set up the column virtual bus by asserting BR of that column bus. In case that the requester fails to grab the row virtual bus, it tries to acquire the column virtual bus first. If the requester fails to grab both virtual buses, the transaction will be retried as soon as one of them becomes available.

Figure 6 (b) shows the message header for a multiple line unicast. After driving the bridge list vector, the requester emits the child line destination vector. The bridge relays the vector to the child line, by which the unicast destination can be identified. The routers on the child line assert the BG signal as in the single line transactions. After the bridge observes the child line BG signal asserted, it asserts the root BG signal which, in turn, will initiate data transmission.

During the data transmission, the bridge router forwards data present on the root virtual bus to the child virtual bus. Once the destination message buffer becomes full, the bridge relays the BB back from the child line to the root.

4.3. Multiple Line Multicast and Broadcast

For general multicast and broadcast, a multicast tree of virtual buses are built. A simple tree construction algorithm is sufficient for a single multicast on a grid of buses. Let the number of row and column virtual buses on which the source and destinations are located be R and C, respectively. If R is no less than C, the requester selects the row virtual bus as the root. Otherwise, the requester selects the column bus as the root. The virtual buses orthogonal to the root constitute the child buses. In this way, we can construct a multicast tree with minimum cardinality.

The header structure for the multiple line multicast is shown in Figure 6 (c). Here, we also assume that the requester builds the row virtual bus first. After the requester drives the bridge list vector for the root, it delivers the row destination vector. This vector is required because there may be non-bridge destinations on the root. Then, the requester starts driving as many child destination vectors as there are bridges. Each bridge forwards the corresponding child destination vector to its child virtual bus. The routers on the established virtual buses, and, in turn, the bridges assert the BG to initiate the requester to start the transaction.

For multicast and broadcast, the destination routers direct the incoming bus data to the local node computer as well as to the next router. The requester sends a sequence of data to multiple destinations through the wave pipelining. During the transmission, when a destination router has its message buffer filled beyond the high watermark, it asserts the wired-OR BB signal. The requester stops data transmission until the BB signal is deasserted. Other destinations as well will wait for the resumption of the data transmission.

Figure 6 (d) shows the header format for the all broadcast (AB) and the child line broadcast (CB) transactions. For child line broadcast, messages will be broadcast to child line(s) orthogonal to the root bus. The all broadcast has its bridge list vector all bits of which are set to one. The messages will be broadcast over the entire system.

If the destination lines of two virtual bus transactions overlap, there is a chance of deadlock. We employ a timeout mechanism to avoid the deadlock. If the bridges fail to acquire their destination lines within a specified amount of time, the corresponding virtual bus transaction will be aborted and retried from the start. We have employed an exponential back-off strategy similar to one devised for the Ethernet. An improved mechanism is to break one virtual bus transaction into row and column transactions after some retries. The requester now communicates with those bridges and destinations only on the root bus. After the root transaction terminates, every bridge will try to start the single line bus transaction separately. A sufficient amount of buffering will be required at each bridge for this improvement. Otherwise, the system software should be invoked to

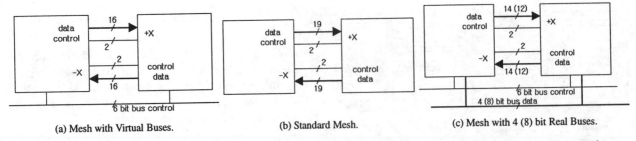

(a) Mesh with Virtual Buses.   (b) Standard Mesh.   (c) Mesh with 4 (8) bit Real Buses.

Figure 7. Bit Assignments in Different Bus Systems (Total 42 Bits between Adjacent Routers).

forward data between buses.

5. Performance Evaluation

We conducted two experiments to show the effectiveness of the virtual bus: one with a real workload of finding maximum; the other with the distribution-driven workload. Prior to the performance analysis, we first describe the experimental environment and the target system parameters.

5.1. Experimental Frame

We used the MultiSim++ [13] network simulator on top of the CSIM [17] simulation environment. The 8×8 and 16×16 2D mesh networks with deterministic wormhole routing are considered. We compare the performance of the standard mesh, the mesh with conventional real buses, and finally, the mesh with virtual buses proposed in this paper.

For fair comparison, we assign the same bisection bandwidth to all the networks under evaluation. The channel data bandwidth between two virtual bus routers is set to 16 bits per direction as shown in Figure 7 (a). Including two such channels, four handshaking control signals, and six bus control signal lines, total 42 bits are connecting two neighboring routers in the 8×8 mesh. Under the same bisection bandwidth condition, the conventional routers for the standard mesh (Figure 7 (b)) can provide two 19 bit unidirectional channels. Figure 7 (c) shows the bandwidth assignments for the meshes with real buses. Two 14 bit unidirectional channels are provided when we assign 4 bits to each row bus and to each column bus. If we assign 8 bits to each bus, 12 bits will be given to each unidirectional channel. We did not evaluate wider buses, since, in general, the buses are to be less frequently used than the point-to-point networks.

The bus arbitration time is set to 120nsec for both types of buses. The virtual bus setup requires additional 100nsec delay for the flit freeze and the initial end-to-end data propagation. We consider the wormhole router having 20nsec flit transition time between neighbors. We study the virtual buses of three different speeds in the evaluation. The slowest one (No-Wave) does not rely on the wave pipelining.

The source router injects data to the virtual bus every 20ns, the same speed as the wormhole router flit transmission. After the initial end-to-end data propagation delay, destinations will receive one flit every 20ns. The fastest one (4-Wave) issues four successive data to the virtual bus during the 20nsec by the virtue of the wave pipelining. The middle one (2-Wave) employs the wave pipelining whose injection rate is two. Duato et al. [7] has shown that the data injection speed of the wave switching network could be reduced to as low as 1.17nsec for the wormhole router operating at about 100MHz. On the other hand, we study two different operating speeds of real buses: 50MHz as a typical speed and 100MHz as a fast speed requiring high hardware cost.

5.2. Finding Maximum on Mesh with Virtual Buses

First, we evaluate the performance of the mesh with virtual buses for a representative semigroup computation: finding maximum of N data values. In the standard mesh, there exists $O(N^{1/2})$ time algorithm [2].

For the mesh with row and column buses, there exists $O(N^{1/8})$ time algorithm [6] which is described in full detail in [2]. Only the single line bus transactions are used in this algorithm. The communication is organized to be contention free: there is no contention among mesh messages and among bus messages; there is no interference between these two, either.

Figure 8 shows how much the different types of buses improve the performance of the maximum finding algorithm. The leftmost bar in each group is the execution time on the standard mesh. The rightmost bar is that on the mesh with virtual buses. The middle two bars are those on the mesh with conventional buses. The left one of them is the result with 4 bit wide real buses, and the right one with 8 bit wide real buses. The real bus operating speed is set to 50MHz, and the wave pipelining degree of the virtual bus is set to two. The communication setup and receive overhead is set to 3.62μsec.

To study the effect of bandwidth, we apply the maximum finding algorithm to a vector of data sets. Different groups in Figure 8 have different vector sizes. The first group of the four bars is the execution time of the scalar maximum

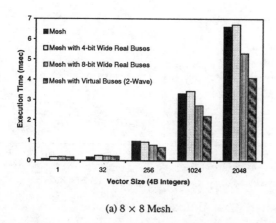 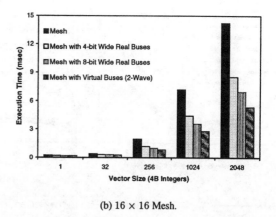

| (a) 8 × 8 Mesh. | (b) 16 × 16 Mesh. |

Figure 8. Performance of Maximum Finding Workloads.

finding out of a single set of N data. The next four groups are the execution times of finding 32, 256, 1024, and 2048 maxima, respectively.

For small data sets of size less than 256 maxima, the 8 × 8 mesh is not big enough to benefit from the reduced time complexity of the improved algorithm. The standard mesh performs the best. As the size of data sets increases, the communication time increases. The execution time is proportional both to the number of steps and to the time each step takes. The communication time constitutes the main portion of the step. Therefore, as data set grows, the effect of the improved time complexity arises. 2048 maxima can be found on the mesh with virtual buses 62% faster than on the standard mesh. The 4 bit real buses augmenting the mesh, however, do not accelerate the program execution because of the low bandwidth. The 8 bit buses do accelerate the program, by about 25%. If we had widened the real bus more, the program execution might have been sped up a bit further. In this case, however, less bandwidth will be assigned to the point-to-point mesh network, which will lead to a significant decrease in the aggregate bandwidth of the entire system and to a possible waste of the bandwidth assigned to buses.

In the 16 × 16 mesh, we can see the prominent effect of the reduced time complexity. The mesh with real buses performs better than the standard mesh for all cases. Thanks to the efficient use of bandwidth, the mesh with virtual buses outperforms the mesh with real buses by much. The addition of 4 bit wide real buses accelerates the 2048 maxima finding by about 67%. With the 8 bit wide buses, the program execution speed is almost doubled. The virtual buses, on the other hand, make the maxima finding 2.66 times faster than the original execution on the standard mesh.

Further, because there is no statically assigned data bus lines in the virtual bus system, the bandwidth is utilized very

efficiently. If the program does not use the buses at all, the virtual bus system does not allocate data bandwidth to bus communications unlike the real bus system. As a result, there is little bandwidth waste for a wide range of applications. This bandwidth saving makes the mesh with virtual buses have much higher aggregate bandwidth than the mesh with real buses. When we look into the scalar maximum case further, we can find that the virtual bus performs as well as the real bus also for the small message size, despite the extra bus setup delay.

5.3. A Distribution-Driven Evaluation

We have also analyzed the performance characteristics of the virtual bus system by conducting a distribution-driven simulation for the mixed unicast and broadcast communication workloads. Unicast messages are delivered through the point-to-point mesh network, while broadcast messages through the buses. We have obtained both the unicast and the broadcast latency characteristics of the mesh with buses for a range of message generation intervals of exponential distributions. The messages are assumed to be immediately consumed upon arrival at their destinations. The message size is fixed for all evaluations: the unicast and the broadcast messages are 512 bytes and 64 bytes in length, respectively.

Figure 9 shows the characteristics of the unicast messages for different volumes of broadcast traffic. The real buses are assumed to be 4 bits in width and assumed to operate at 50MHz.

The two dotted lines of Figure 9 (a) show the unicast latencies when there is no broadcast communications at all. Due to the unused bandwidth assigned to the real buses, the average communication time of the mesh with real buses is higher than that of the mesh with virtual buses at all points.

The solid lines of Figure 9 (a) show the unicast latencies

441

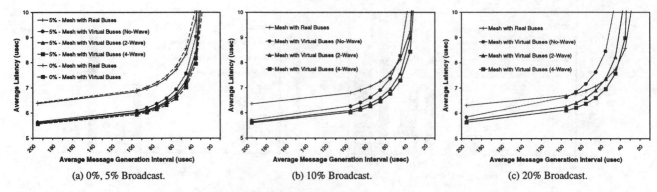

Figure 9. Performance Characteristics: Unicast Latency.

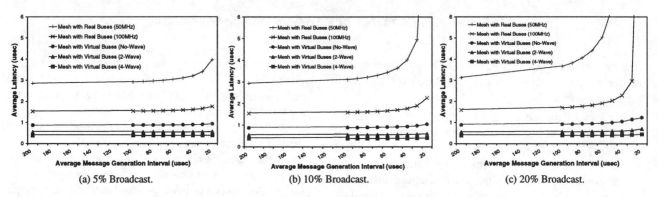

Figure 10. Performance Characteristics: Broadcast Latency.

when 5% of the communication is broadcast. In the mesh with virtual buses, the broadcast transaction interferes with the unicast transactions by stopping them for a while. Thus, the unicast latencies are different for different bus operation speeds. The faster the broadcast is, the lower the unicast latency is. The longer broadcast transaction slows down the unicast transaction more, by stopping them for a longer period. For 5% broadcast, the meshes with virtual buses of all speeds outperform the mesh with real buses.

Figure 9 (b) and (c) show the unicast latencies for 10% and 20% broadcasts, respectively. Still, all three meshes with virtual buses provide lower unicast latency than the mesh with real buses for long average message generation intervals. As the messages are generated frequently, the unicast messages in the virtual bus system are frequently overridden by the virtual bus transactions. For 10% broadcast, we can find that the unicast communication of the slowest virtual bus system is saturated faster than that of the real bus system. Even for 20% broadcast, however, the mesh with the fast virtual buses still performs better than the mesh with real buses. It provides lower latencies than the real bus system and becomes saturated at about the same time.

In the above analyses, we assumed a fully concurrent operation of the mesh messages and the real bus transactions. In the real system, however, there may well be a serializa-

tion at the network interface inside the node. Even the real bus transaction would slow down the unicast messages in such a configuration. Thus, the above analyses are somewhat distorted for the mesh with real buses.

Figure 10 shows the dramatic improvements in the broadcast bandwidth. The big difference in average latency comes from the big difference in widths of the real and virtual buses. The real bus is 4 bits wide, whereas, on the virtual bus, 16 bit datapath is dynamically established on demand. For all three broadcast conditions, the virtual buses are not saturated even under high message generation rates. On the other hand, 50MHz real buses become saturated from 10% broadcast and 100MHz buses from 20% under frequent message generation. The uncontended speed of the fastest virtual bus is almost 10 times faster than that of the 50MHz real bus.

From the above distribution-driven analyses, we are convinced that the virtual bus provides the mesh with the high speed communication both for unicast and broadcast much better than does the conventional real buses.

6. Conclusions

This paper presented the virtual bus as an effective secondary network to the mesh connected computers. A line of modified routers can establish the virtual bus only when there is a bus request. Therefore, we can provide the bus functionality to each row and each column of the mesh without the actual real data bus lines and costly bus driving circuits. The virtual bus system is superior to the real bus system in three respects: 1) better bandwidth utilization, 2) the low latency communication with higher bandwidth, and 3) the ease of implementation.

We took the maximum finding algorithm as an example computation which can benefit from the addition of buses. With the mesh with virtual buses, the vector maxima algorithm is accelerated much better than with the mesh with real buses, because of the improved bandwidth and its utilization. The scalar maximum can be found in a short time as well, because of the low latency. With virtual buses, the vector maxima finding of 2048 data is sped up by a factor of 2.66.

We also conducted a distribution-driven network performance evaluation, which convinced us of the effectiveness of the virtual bus again: it provides lower latency and higher bandwidth both for the unicast through the mesh and for the broadcast through the buses, than the real buses augmenting the mesh can do. For the evaluated configuration, the virtual buses provide the broadcast which is 10 times as fast as the real buses can.

The implementation of the virtual buses is less complex and less costly than the addition of real buses to the mesh. The real bus of the same operating speed as the virtual bus requires expensive transceivers and a high design cost. The virtual buses can be implemented at a lower cost, because all data channels of the virtual bus are point-to-point.

Acknowledgements

This work has been supported by HPC-COSE project of MOST (Ministry of Science and Technology), Korea.

References

[1] A. Aggarwal. Optimal bounds for finding maximum on array of processors with k global buses. *ACM Trans. on Computer Systems*, 4(1):62–64, Jan. 1986.

[2] S. G. Akl. *Parallel Computation: Models and Methods*. Prentice-Hall, 1997.

[3] D. Bhagavathi, S. Olariu, W. Shen, and L. Wilson. A unifying look at semigroup computations on meshes with multiple broadcasting. *Parallel Processing Letters*, 4(1):73–82, 1994.

[4] D. Bhagavathi, J. L. Schwing, W. Shen, L. Wilson, and J. Zhang. Convexity problems on meshes with multiple broadcasting. *Journal of Parallel and Distributed Computing*, 27:142–156, 1995.

[5] S. H. Bokhari. Finding maximum on an array processor with a global bus. *IEEE Trans. Comput.*, C-33(2):133–139, Feb. 1984.

[6] Y. C. Chen, W. T. Chen, G. H. Chen, and J. P. Sheu. Designing efficient parallel algorithms on mesh-connected computers with multiple broadcasting. *IEEE Trans. on Parallel and Distributed Systems*, 1:241–245, 1990.

[7] J. Duato, P. López, F. Silla, and S. Yalamanchili. A high performance router architecture for interconnection network. In *Proc. of the 1996 Int'l Conf. on Parallel Processing (ICPP'96)*, pages I–61–I–68, 1996.

[8] B. W. Kim, H. J. Choi, K.-I. Park, J. H. Choi, and K. H. Park. A skew tolerant wave pipelined router on FPGA. In *Proc. of Hot Interconnects 7, to appear*, Aug. 1999.

[9] B. W. Kim, J. H. Choi, K. I. Park, and K. H. Park. A wormhole router with embedded broadcasting virtual bus for mesh computers. *submitted to Parallel Processing Letters*.

[10] C. S. R. Krishnan and C. S. R. Murthy. A faster algorithm for sorting on mesh-connected computers with multiple broadcasting using fewer processors. *Int'l Journal of Computer Mathematics*, 48:15–20, 1993.

[11] R. Lin, S. Olariu, J. L. Schwing, and J. Zhang. Simulating enhanced meshes with applications. *Parallel Processing Letters*, 3(1):59–70, 1993.

[12] Y.-W. Lu, J. B. Burr, and A. M. Peterson. Permutation on the mesh with reconfigurable bus: Algorithms and practical considerations. In *Proc. of the 7th Int'l Parallel Processing Symp. (IPPS'93)*, pages 298–308, 1993.

[13] P. K. McKinley and C. Trefftz. MultiSim: A simulation tool for the study of large-scale multiprocessors. In *Proc. Int'l Workshop on Modeling, Analysis, and Simulation of Computer and Telecommunication Networks (MASCOTS) '93*, pages 57–62, Jan. 1993.

[14] K. J. Nowka. *High-Performance CMOS Design Using Wave Pipelining*. PhD thesis, Stanford University, 1995.

[15] D. Parkinson, D. J. Hunt, and K. S. MacQueen. The AMT DAP 500. In *Proc. of the 33rd IEEE Int'l Computer Conf. (COMPCON Spring'88)*, pages 196–199, 1988.

[16] V. K. Prasanna Kumar and C. S. Raghavendra. Array processor with multiple broadcasting. *Journal of Parallel and Distributed Computing*, 4(2):173–190, Apr. 1987.

[17] H. D. Schwetman. CSIM: A C-based, process-oriented simulation language. In *Proc. 1986 Winter Simulation Conference*, pages 387 – 396, 1986.

[18] Q. F. Stout. Mesh-connected computers with broadcasting. *IEEE Trans. Comput.*, C-32(9):826–830, Sept. 1983.

[19] D. M. Taub. Improved control acquisition scheme for the IEEE 896 Futurebus. *IEEE Micro*, 7(3):52–62, June 1987.

[20] D. R. Ulm and J. W. Baker. Solving a two-dimensional k-napsack problem on a mesh with multiple buses. In *Proc. of the 1995 Int'l Conf. on Parallel Processing (ICPP'95)*, pages III.168–III.171, 1995.

Configurable Complete Exchanges in 2D Torus-Connected Networks*

Young-Joo Suh

Dept. of Computer Science and Engineering
Pohang University of Science and Technology
San 31, Hyoja-Dong
Pohang 790-784, Korea
yjsuh@postech.edu

Kang G. Shin

Real-Time Computing Laboratory
Department of EECS
The University of Michigan
Ann Arbor, MI 48109-2122
kgshin@eecs.umich.edu

Syungog An

Dept. of Computer Engineering
Paichai University
439-6 Doma-2-Dong
Taejeon 302-735, Korea
sungohk@mail.paichai.ac.kr

Abstract

Complete exchange communications are found necessary in many important parallel algorithms. This paper presents algorithms for complete exchange for 2D torus-connected multiprocessors. The proposed algorithms are unique in that they are configurable while trading the time for message startups against larger message sizes. At one extreme, the algorithm minimizes the number of message startups at the expense of increased message-transmission time. At the other extreme, the message-transmission time is reduced at the expense of increased number of message startups. The algorithms are structured such that intermediate solutions are feasible, i.e., the number of message startups can be increased slightly and the message-transmission time is correspondingly reduced. The ability to configure these algorithms makes the proposed algorithms distinct from others and leads to efficient portable implementation of complete exchange algorithms.

1. Introduction

In distributed memory multicomputer systems, it is often required that each processor communicates its data with all other processors. The *all-to-all personalized* or *complete exchange* is one of the most demanding communication patterns in parallel computing. In this communication pattern, every processor communicates a block of distinct data to every other processor in the system [2,3,5,6]. Many scientific applications require the all-to-all personalized exchange communication pattern.

Several studies by Bokhari and Berryman [1], Sunder *et al.* [16] and Tseng *et al.* [19] have produced algorithms using message combining in $2^d \times 2^d$ meshes or tori. These algorithms incur an $O(2^d)$ execution time due to message start-ups and $O(2^{3d})$ time due to message transmissions. Recently, Suh and Yalamanchili [13] proposed algorithms using message combining in $2^d \times 2^d$ and $2^d \times 2^d \times 2^d$ tori having time complexities of $O(d)$ due to message start-ups and $O(2^{3d})$ (in 2D) or $O(2^{4d})$ (in 3D) time due to message transmissions.

This paper presents a set of configurable algorithms for complete exchange for two-dimensional torus-connected networks. The salient feature of the proposed algorithms is that they can be tuned to trade the overheads of message initiation or start-ups against message-transmission time. At one extreme, the algorithm minimizes the number of

message start-ups at the expense of increased message-transmission time. At the other extreme, the message-transmission time is significantly reduced at the expense of increased number of message start-ups. The algorithm is structured to yield intermediate solutions, i.e., the number of message start-ups can be slightly increased and the message-transmission time reduced accordingly. The ability to configure these algorithms allows us to match the algorithm characteristics with machine characteristics based on message-initiation overhead and link speeds, to minimize overall execution time. In effect the algorithms can be configured to strike a balance between direct and message-combining approaches on a specific architecture for a given problem size.

2. Performance Model and Parameters

Our target architecture is a torus-connected, wormhole-switched multiprocessor. Each message is partitioned into a number of *flits*. We assume that each processor has N distinct m-flit message blocks. We also assume that the channel is one flit wide and each processor has one pair of injection/consumption buffers for the internal processor-router channel (i.e., one-port architecture). All links are full duplex channels.

We will focus on the two dominant components of message latency: start-up time (t_s) and message-transmission time (t_c). In our model, a step is the basic unit of contention-free communication, i.e., in one-time step, a set of nodes can communicate via disjoint network paths. The duration of a step is determined by the message size and, for large messages, is insensitive to the distance between communicating nodes. The number of steps corresponds to the number of message start-ups. A phase is a sequence of multiple steps.

3. Two Algorithms

We now summarize two algorithms (T1 and T2) proposed in [13]. They are message-combining algorithms with a bottom-up approach. The communication proceeds as a number of phases and, within each phase, the algorithms differ in the number of steps. The two algorithms are combined to construct a set of configurable algorithms for 2D tori in Section 4.

3.1 Algorithm T1

Special Node Groups

For a $2^d \times 2^d$ torus, in exchange phase i, $1 \le i \le d$, the communication steps are performed within a $2^i \times 2^i$ sub-

---

* This research was supported in part by Pohang University of Science and Technology, Korea, 1998.

mesh or torus. In a $2^p \times 2^p$ submesh, $2 \le p \le d-1$, we identify two special sets of nodes. The first special group (SG) of nodes in phase p ($SG_p(1)$) is defined as the set of nodes along the two main diagonals. The second SG ($SG_p(2)$) is the set of nodes along the main diagonals of the four quadrants *excluding* the elements already in the first SG. If each node is labeled $P(x, y)$, $0 \le x, y \le 2^d - 1$, we can formally define the two groups, $SG_p(1)$ and $SG_p(2)$, as follows.

$P(x, y) \in SG_p(1)$

iff $(y = x) mod 2^p$ OR $(x + y = 2^p - 1) mod 2^p$.

$P(x, y) \in SG_p(2)$

iff $(y = x - 2^{p-1}) mod 2^p$ OR $(x + y = 2^{p-1} - 1) mod 2^p$.

An important property of SGs is that the nodes in the first SG are partitioned into two SGs in the next phase. That is, $SG_j(1) \equiv SG_{j+1}(1) \cup SG_{j+1}(2)$, where $2 \le j \le d-2$.

Communication Pattern:

For a $2^d \times 2^d$ torus, the algorithm consists of d exchange phases. Each exchange phase consists of exactly two steps for a total of $2d$ steps. If $d \ge 4$, there is an additional send phase.

In phase 1, message exchanges are performed on each 2×2 submesh. In this phase, all nodes in the submesh belong to the first SG. In step 1 (step 2) of phase 1, each node sends a block of message to a node whose address is complemented in the least significant bit of the X-coordinate (Y-coordinate). This is represented as follows.

Phase 1 Step 1:

$$P(x_{d-1} \ldots x_0, y_{d-1} \ldots y_0) \to P(x_{d-1} \ldots x_1 \overline{x_0}, y_{d-1} \ldots y_0) .$$

Phase 1 Step 2:

$$P(x_{d-1} \ldots x_0, y_{d-1} \ldots y_0) \to P(x_{d-1} \ldots x_0, y_{d-1} \ldots y_1 \overline{y_0}) .$$

Starting with phase 2 until phase $d-1$, each node in the first SG sends blocks horizontally, while each node in the second SG sends blocks vertically in the first step. In the second step of a phase, each node in the SGs changes dimensions and sends blocks along the new dimension. The message transmissions in two steps of phase p, $2 \le p \le d-1$, are summarized as follows.

Phase p Step 1:

If ($iam \in SG_p(1)$)

$$P(x_{d-1} \ldots x_0, y_{d-1} \ldots y_0) \to P(x_{d-1} \ldots x_p \overline{x_{p-1}} \ldots \overline{x_0}, y_{d-1} \ldots y_0) .$$

If ($iam \in SG_p(2)$)

$$P(x_{d-1} \ldots x_0, y_{d-1} \ldots y_0) \to P(x_{d-1} \ldots x_0, y_{d-1} \ldots y_p \overline{y_{p-1}} \ldots \overline{y_0}) .$$

Phase p Step 2:

If ($iam \in SG_p(1)$)

$$P(x_{d-1} \ldots x_0, y_{d-1} \ldots y_0) \to P(x_{d-1} \ldots x_0, y_{d-1} \ldots y_p \overline{y_{p-1}} \ldots \overline{y_0}) .$$

If ($iam \in SG_p(2)$)

$$P(x_{d-1} \ldots x_0, y_{d-1} \ldots y_0) \to P(x_{d-1} \ldots x_p \overline{x_{p-1}} \ldots \overline{x_0}, y_{d-1} \ldots y_0) .$$

where *iam* indicates an arbitrary node $P(x_{d-1} \ldots x_0, y_{d-1} \ldots y_0)$

In phase d, the nodes in SGs in phase $d-1$ are also active. The following operations are performed in phase d.

Phase d Step 1:

If ($iam \in SG_{d-1}(1)$)

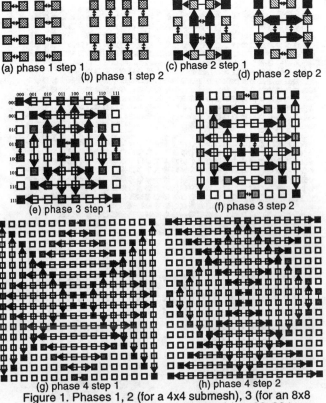

(a) phase 1 step 1
(b) phase 1 step 2
(c) phase 2 step 1
(d) phase 2 step 2
(e) phase 3 step 1
(f) phase 3 step 2
(g) phase 4 step 1
(h) phase 4 step 2

Figure 1. Phases 1, 2 (for a 4x4 submesh), 3 (for an 8x8 submesh), and 4 (for a 16x16 submesh) in a 32x32 torus.

$$P(x_{d-1} \ldots x_0, y_{d-1} \ldots y_0) \to P(\overline{x_{d-1}} \ldots \overline{x_0}, y_{d-1} \ldots y_0) .$$

If ($iam \in SG_{d-1}(2)$)

$$P(x_{d-1} \ldots x_0, y_{d-1} \ldots y_0) \to P(x_{d-1} \ldots x_0, \overline{y_{d-1}} \ldots \overline{y_0}) .$$

Phase d Step 2:

If ($iam \in SG_{d-1}(1)$)

$$P(x_{d-1} \ldots x_0, y_{d-1} \ldots y_0) \to P(x_{d-1} \ldots x_0, \overline{y_{d-1}} \ldots \overline{y_0}) .$$

If ($iam \in SG_{d-1}(2)$)

$$P(x_{d-1} \ldots x_0, y_{d-1} \ldots y_0) \to P(\overline{x_{d-1}} \ldots \overline{x_0}, y_{d-1} \ldots y_0) .$$

If $d \ge 4$, there is an additional send phase consisting of $d-3$ steps. After phase d, each node in $SG_{d-1}(1)$ or $SG_{d-1}(2)$, i.e., each node in $SG_{d-2}(1)$, has all blocks from every other node, each node in $SG_{d-2}(2)$ has blocks from $2^{2(d-1)}$ nodes, each node in $SG_{d-3}(2)$ has blocks from $2^{2(d-2)}$ nodes, and so on. In step s of the send phase, $1 \le s \le d-3$, the following operation is performed.

Send phase Step s:

If ($iam \in SG_{d-s-1}(1)$)

$$P(x_{d-1} \ldots x_0, y_{d-1} \ldots y_0) \to P(x_{d-1} \ldots x_{d-s-2} \overline{x_{d-s-3}} \ldots \overline{x_0}, y_{d-1} \ldots y_0)$$

Examples:

Consider a 32×32 torus. The steps in phases 1 and 2 are shown in Figures 1(a)-(d) for one 4×4 submesh (the remaining submeshes are identical). In phase 3 (or 4), message exchange operations are performed within each 8×8 (or 16×16) submesh as illustrated in Figures 1(e) and (f)

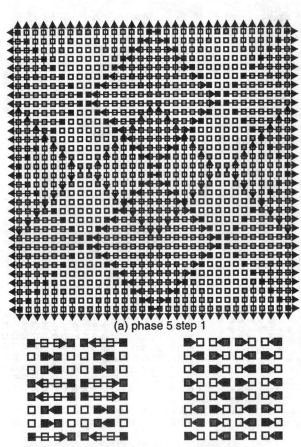

(a) phase 5 step 1

(b) send phase step 1   (c) send phase step 2

Figure 2. Phase 5 step 1 and two steps in the send phase (for an 8x8 submesh) in a 32x32 torus.

(or Figures 1 (g) and (h)). After phase 4, the nodes in $SG_4(1)$ or $SG_4(2)$ have blocks from all nodes in the quadrant in which those are located. Figure 2(a) shows the first step in phase 5. As shown in the figure, only the active nodes in phase 4 (marked nodes in Figure 2(a), i.e., nodes in $SG_4(1)$ or $SG_4(2)$) participate in exchanging messages. In the next step, the active nodes change dimensions and exchange messages. Now, each node in $SG_4(1)$ or $SG_4(2)$ (i.e., $SG_3(1)$) has all blocks from all nodes in the torus. Starting with phase 3, we note that for subsequently larger size submeshes, all processors are not active, i.e., some processors are not members of either SG. The solution is to require one additional phase referred to as a send phase after d exchange phases. In two steps in the send phase, the blocks for non-active nodes are sent as shown in Figures 2(b) and (c), where only one 8×8 submesh is shown (the remaining submeshes are identical).

Complexity Analysis:

The number of steps is $2d$ steps if $d < 4$ and $3d - 3$ steps if $d \geq 4$. If $d < 4$, 2^{2d-1} blocks are exchanged in each step. Since there are $2d$ steps, the total message transmission time is $(d \cdot 2^{2d})mt_c$. If $d \geq 4$, the number of exchanged blocks per step is not always identical. The total message transmission time is $\{9 \cdot 2^{3d-4} + (d^2 - 5d + 3)2^{2d-1}\}mt_c$.

3.2 Algorithm T2

Algorithm T1 focused on minimizing the number of phases (i.e., message start-ups). Algorithm T2 requires more communication steps, but it is simpler and has lower transmission times. The primary distinguishing feature of T2 is that it doesn't have any send phase.

In T1, each exchange phase comprises exactly two steps. For larger size submeshes, not all processors can participate, hence needing a send phase. In T2, each phase is extended to ensure participation of all processors within a phase by identifying additional node groups that are active in the additional steps in a phase.

Node Groups:

Groups of nodes (Gs) are defined for Algorithm T2, where the Gs are defined for phases 2 to $d - 1$. The Gs in phase $d - 1$ are also used in phase d. Until phase 2, the Gs in T2 are the same as the SGs in T1. In phase p, $3 \leq p \leq d - 1$, there are 2^{p-1} Gs as follows:

$P(x, y) \in G_p(1)$

iff $(y = x)mod2^p$ OR $(x + y = 2^p - 1)mod2^p$.

$P(x, y) \in G_p(2)$

iff $(y = x - 2^{p-1})mod2^p$ OR $(x + y = 2^{p-1} - 1)mod2^p$.

$P(x, y) \in G_p(2k + 1)$

iff {{ $(y = x - 2k)mod2^p$ OR $(x + y = 2^p - 2k - 1)mod2^p$ }

AND $(y)mod2 = 0$ } OR {{ $(y = x - 2^p + 2k)mod2^p$ OR $(x + y = 2k - 1)mod2^p$ } AND $(y)mod2 = 1$ }.

$P(x, y) \in G_p(2k + 2)$

iff {{ $(y = x - 2k)mod2^p$ OR $(x + y = 2^p - 2k - 1)mod2^p$ }

AND $(y)mod2 = 1$ } OR {{ $(y = x - 2^p + 2k)mod2^p$ OR $(x + y = 2k - 1)mod2^p$ } AND $(y)mod2 = 0$ }.

where $1 \leq k \leq 2^{p-2} - 1$. Note that the first two Gs in each phase are the same as the two SGs in T1.

Communication Pattern:

For $d < 4$, T2 is identical to T1. For $d \geq 4$, Algorithm T2 consists of d exchange phases but no send phase. The following two steps are performed in phase 1.

Phase 1 Step 1:

$$P(x_{d-1}\cdots x_0, y_{d-1}\cdots y_0) \to P(x_{d-1}\cdots x_1\overline{x_0}, y_{d-1}\cdots y_0)$$.

Phase 1 Step 2:

$$P(x_{d-1}\cdots x_0, y_{d-1}\cdots y_0) \to P(x_{d-1}\cdots x_0, y_{d-1}\cdots y_1\overline{y_0})$$

From phase 2, there are 2^{p-1} steps in phase p, where $2 \leq p \leq d - 1$. In step $2i - 1$ or $2i$, $1 \leq i \leq 2^{p-2}$, of phase p, the following operations are performed.

Phase p Step $2i$-1:

If $(iam \in G_p(2i - 1))$

$$P(x_{d-1}\cdots x_0, y_{d-1}\cdots y_0) \to P(x_{d-1}\cdots x_p\overline{x_{p-1}}\cdots\overline{x_0}, y_{d-1}\cdots y_0)$$

If $(iam \in G_p(2i))$

$$P(x_{d-1}\cdots x_0, y_{d-1}\cdots y_0) \to P(x_{d-1}\cdots x_0, y_{d-1}\cdots y_p\overline{y_{p-1}}\cdots\overline{y_0})$$

Phase p Step $2i$:

If $(iam \in G_p(2i - 1))$

446

$$P(x_{d-1}...x_0, y_{d-1}...y_0) \rightarrow P(x_{d-1}...x_0, y_{d-1}...y_p\overline{y_{p-1}...y_0})$$

If $(iam \in G_p(2i))$

$$P(x_{d-1}...x_0, y_{d-1}...y_0) \rightarrow P(x_{d-1}...x_p\overline{x_{p-1}...x_0}, y_{d-1}...y_0)$$

In phase d, there are 2^{d-2} steps, which is the same as those in phase $d-1$. In step $2i-1$ or $2i$, where $1 \leq i \leq 2^{d-3}$, the following operations are performed.

Phase d Step $2i$-1:

If $(iam \in G_p(2i-1))$

$$P(x_{d-1}...x_0, y_{d-1}...y_0) \rightarrow P(\overline{x_{d-1}...x_0}, y_{d-1}...y_0)$$

If $(iam \in G_p(2i))$

$$P(x_{d-1}...x_0, y_{d-1}...y_0) \rightarrow P(x_{d-1}...x_0, \overline{y_{d-1}...y_0})$$

Phase d Step $2i$:

If $(iam \in G_{d-1}(2i-1))$

$$P(x_{d-1}...x_0, y_{d-1}...y_0) \rightarrow P(x_{d-1}...x_0, \overline{y_{d-1}...y_0})$$

If $(iam \in G_{d-1}(2i))$

$$P(x_{d-1}...x_0, y_{d-1}...y_0) \rightarrow P(\overline{x_{d-1}...x_0}, y_{d-1}...y_0)$$

Examples:

Consider the following example. For a 16×16 torus, phases 1 and 2 are identical to T1. In phase 3, there are four steps. The first two steps in phase 3 are identical to T1 shown in Figures 1 (e) and (f). Steps 3 and 4 in phase 3 are shown in Figures 3 (a) and (b). In T1, nodes in $G_3(1)$ and $G_3(2)$ exchange blocks while nodes in $G_3(3)$ and $G_3(4)$ do not participate in message exchange operations in phase 3 and eventually receive data during the send phase. The key modification here is to add two more steps to phase 3 and enable these nodes in $G_3(3)$ and $G_3(4)$ to acquire blocks. This was prevented in the first two steps of phase 3 due to link contention in T1. In phase 4, there are also four steps. The first two steps in phase 4 are identical to T1 shown in Figure 3 (c), where only step 1 is shown. In step 2, active nodes in step 1 change dimensions and exchange blocks. Step 3 in phase 4 is shown in Figure 3 (d) and, in step 4, active nodes in the step change dimensions and exchange blocks. After the 4 steps in the phase 4, all processors have all blocks from all processors.

Complexity Analysis:

For a $2^d \times 2^d$ torus, two steps are required in phase 1. From phase 2 until phase $d-1$, there are 2^{p-1} steps in phase p, where $2 \leq p \leq d-1$. In phase d, there are 2^{d-2} steps. Thus, the total number of steps is $3 \cdot 2^{d-2}$. In each step, the number of exchanged blocks is 2^{2d-1}. So, the total number of exchanged blocks is $3 \cdot 2^{3(d-1)}$. Total message start-up time is $(3 \cdot 2^{d-2})t_s$ and total message transmission time is $(3 \cdot 2^{3(d-1)})mt_c$.

4. Configurable Algorithms

In the previous section, we described two bottom-up algorithms: T1 and T2. Algorithm T1 focused on minimizing the message start-up cost while T2 focused on minimizing the message-transmission cost. An interesting feature of these algorithms is that they can produce a range

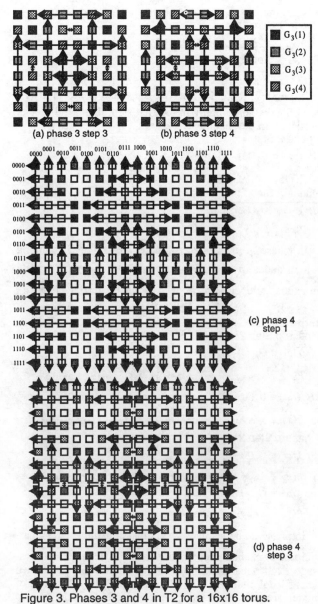

(a) phase 3 step 3   (b) phase 3 step 4

$G_3(1)$
$G_3(2)$
$G_3(3)$
$G_3(4)$

(c) phase 4 step 1

(d) phase 4 step 3

Figure 3. Phases 3 and 4 in T2 for a 16x16 torus.

of implementations by trading off message start-up time for message-transmission time. Within an exchange phase, a small number of additional steps may be added at the expense of a smaller send phase. Such tradeoffs can be made to balance message size against the cost of message start-ups. These algorithms improve the start-up time for T2 at the expense of message-transmission time, or vice versa. We now propose such configurable algorithms, called T1.x, where $x = 1, ..., d-4$. First, we propose algorithm T1.1, and then general algorithms T1.x are proposed.

4.1 Algorithm T1.1

Communication Pattern:

In a $2^d \times 2^d$ torus, the algorithm T1.1 consists of d exchange phases followed by one send phase. In phase 1, there are two steps and the communication pattern in phase

1 is the same as the those in algorithms T1 and T2:

Phase 1 Step 1:

$$P(x_{d-1}...x_0, y_{d-1}...y_0) \rightarrow P(x_{d-1}...x_1\overline{x_0}, y_{d-1}...y_0)$$

Phase 1 Step 2:

$$P(x_{d-1}...x_0, y_{d-1}...y_0) \rightarrow P(x_{d-1}...x_0, y_{d-1}...y_1\overline{y_0})$$

In phase 2, there are also two steps and nodes in $G_2(1)$ send blocks horizontally in the first step, then send blocks vertically in the second step:

Phase 2 Step 1:

If $(iam \in G_2(1))$

$$P(x_{d-1}...x_0, y_{d-1}...y_0) \rightarrow P(x_{d-1}...\overline{x_1}x_0, y_{d-1}...y_0)$$

Phase 2 Step 2:

If $(iam \in G_2(1))$

$$P(x_{d-1}...x_0, y_{d-1}...y_0) \rightarrow P(x_{d-1}...x_0, y_{d-1}...\overline{y_1}y_0)$$

In phase p, $3 \leq p \leq d-1$, there are 2^{p-1} Gs, among which nodes in 2^{p-2} Gs that constitute $G_2(1)$ participate in exchange operations in 2^{p-2} steps. In step $2i-1$ or $2i$, $1 \leq i \leq 2^{p-3}$, of phase p, the following operations are performed.

Phase p Step $2i$-1:

If $(iam \in G_p(4i-3))$

$$P(x_{d-1}...x_0, y_{d-1}...y_0) \rightarrow P(x_{d-1}...x_p\overline{x_{p-1}...x_0}, y_{d-1}...y_0)$$

If $(iam \in G_p(4i-2))$

$$P(x_{d-1}...x_0, y_{d-1}...y_0) \rightarrow P(x_{d-1}...x_0, y_{d-1}...y_p\overline{y_{p-1}...y_0})$$

Phase p Step $2i$:

If $(iam \in G_p(4i-3))$

$$P(x_{d-1}...x_0, y_{d-1}...y_0) \rightarrow P(x_{d-1}...x_0, y_{d-1}...y_p\overline{y_{p-1}...y_0})$$

If $(iam \in G_p(4i-2))$

$$P(x_{d-1}...x_0, y_{d-1}...y_0) \rightarrow P(x_{d-1}...x_p\overline{x_{p-1}...x_0}, y_{d-1}...y_0)$$

In phase d, nodes in 2^{d-3} Gs that constitute $G_2(1)$ participate in exchange operations in 2^{d-3} steps, where message exchanges among one half of nodes are performed using local channels while those among the other half of nodes are performed using wrap-around channels. In step $2i-1$ or $2i$, $1 \leq i \leq 2^{d-4}$, of phase d, the following operations are performed.

Phase d Step $2i$-1:

If $(iam \in G_p(4i-3))$

$$P(x_{d-1}...x_0, y_{d-1}...y_0) \rightarrow P(\overline{x_{d-1}...x_0}, y_{d-1}...y_0)$$

If $(iam \in G_p(4i-2))$

$$P(x_{d-1}...x_0, y_{d-1}...y_0) \rightarrow P(x_{d-1}...x_0, \overline{y_{d-1}...y_0})$$

Phase d Step $2i$:

If $(iam \in G_p(4i-3))$

$$P(x_{d-1}...x_0, y_{d-1}...y_0) \rightarrow P(x_{d-1}...x_0, \overline{y_{d-1}...y_0})$$

If $(iam \in G_p(4i-2))$

$$P(x_{d-1}...x_0, y_{d-1}...y_0) \rightarrow P(\overline{x_{d-1}...x_0}, y_{d-1}...y_0)$$

After phase d, each node in $G_2(1)$ has all blocks from all other nodes, destined for itself and a neighboring node.

In one step in the send phase, each node in $G_2(2)$ receives blocks destined for itself from a node in $G_2(1)$ as follows.

Send Phase Step 1:

If $(iam \in G_2(1))$

$$P(x_{d-1}...x_0, y_{d-1}...y_0) \rightarrow P(x_{d-1}...x_1\overline{x_0}, y_{d-1}...y_0)$$

Example:

Consider an example for a 32×32 torus. The communication patterns until phase 3 are the same as those of T1 shown in Figures 1 (a)-(f). The communication operations in phase 4 are illustrated in Figure 4. Due to channel contention, nodes in $G_2(1)$ cannot exchange blocks in two steps. So, in the first two steps, nodes in $G_4(1)$ and $G_4(2)$ (i.e., nodes in $G_3(1)$) exchange blocks, then nodes in $G_4(5)$ and nodes in $G_4(6)$ (i.e., nodes in $G_3(2)$) exchange blocks in the next two steps. Figure 5 shows the communication patterns in phase 5. In the first two steps of phase 5, nodes in $G_4(1)$ and $G_4(2)$ exchange blocks, then nodes in $G_4(5)$ and nodes in $G_4(6)$ exchange blocks in the next two steps. Now, each node in $G_2(1)$ possesses all blocks from all nodes in the 32×32 torus destined for itself and a neighbor node with which it exchanged blocks in step 1 of phase 1. Thus, in a single step in the send phase, the blocks destined for the neighbor node are transmitted as shown in Figure 2(c).

Complexity Analysis:

For a $2^d \times 2^d$ torus, there are two steps per phase in phases 1 and 2. In phase p, $3 \leq p \leq d-1$, there are 2^{p-2} steps. In phase d, there are 2^{d-3} steps and there is one step in the send phase. Thus, the total number of steps is $3 \cdot 2^{d-3} + 3$. In the first step of phase 1, 2^{2d-1} blocks are transmitted. In each step of the remaining $3 \cdot 2^{d-3} + 2$ steps, the number of transmitted blocks is 2^{2d}. Thus, the total number of transmitted blocks is $3 \cdot 2^{3d-3} + 5 \cdot 2^{2d-1}$.

4.2 Algorithm T1.x

Communication Pattern:

Algorithm T1.x is defined for a $2^d \times 2^d$ torus, where $d \geq x+4$. In a $2^d \times 2^d$ torus, T1.x consists of d exchange phases followed by one send phase which consists of x steps. Until phase $x+1$, there are two steps per phase and communication patterns are very similar to those in Algorithm T1. After phase $x+1$, nodes in $G_{x+1}(1)$ have all blocks from nodes in a $2^{x+1} \times 2^{x+1}$ submesh. From phase $x+2$, nodes in $G_{x+1}(1)$ cannot exchange blocks in two steps due to channel contention. In phase p, $x+2 \leq p \leq d-1$, there are 2^{p-1} Gs, among which nodes in 2^{p-2} Gs that constitute $G_{x+1}(1)$ participate in exchange operations in 2^{p-2} steps. In phase d, there are 2^{d-3} steps. In x steps of the send phase, each node not in $G_{x+1}(1)$ receives blocks destined for itself from a node in $G_{x+1}(1)$.

448

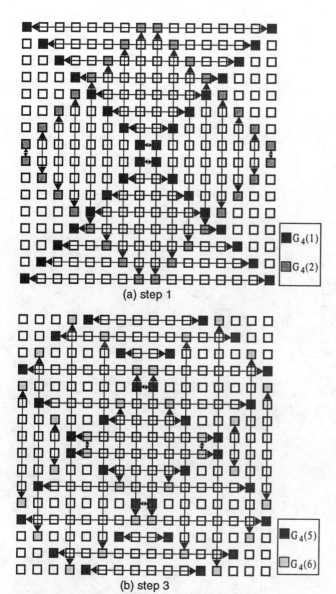

(a) step 1

(b) step 3

Figure 4. Phase 4 (in each 16x16 submesh) in algorithm T1.1 for a 32x32 torus.

Complexity Analysis:

For a $2^d \times 2^d$ torus, $d \geq x + 4$, there are two steps per phase until phase $x + 1$. In phase p, $x + 2 \leq p \leq d - 1$, there are 2^{p-2} steps. In phase d, there are 2^{d-3} steps and there are x steps in the send phase. Thus, the total number of steps is $(3 \cdot 2^{d-3} + 3x + 2) - 2^x$. In the first $2x - 1$ steps, 2^{2d+x-2} blocks are transmitted in each step. In the remaining $(3 \cdot 2^{d-3} + 3) - 2^x$ steps in exchange phases, 2^{2d+x-1} blocks are transmitted in each step. In step s of the send phase, where $1 \leq s \leq x$, 2^{2d+x-s} blocks are transmitted. Thus, the total number of transmitted blocks is $3 \cdot 2^{3d+x-4} + (2x+3)2^{2d+x-2}$.

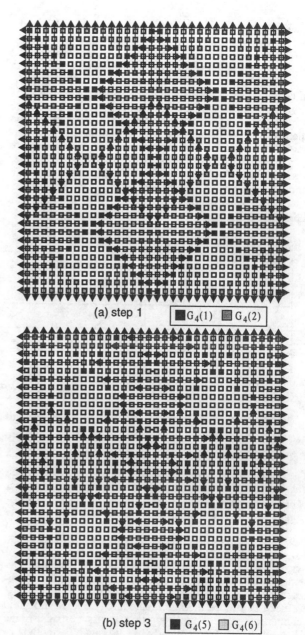

(a) step 1

(b) step 3

Figure 5. Phase 5 in algorithm T1.1 for a 32x32 torus.

5. Performance Evaluation

We have presented a set of configurable complete exchange algorithms for 2D tori, which operate in a bottom-up fashion proceeding from contiguous 2×2 submeshes to higher-order submeshes.

In Algorithm T1, exchanges continue in larger and larger submeshes, until some of the processors in each quadrant have blocks from all of the processors. Getting to this point requires a relatively few steps since all processors in each quadrant need not have the blocks from all processors. At this point a send phase can be initiated. The basic idea of Algorithm T1 is that the number of steps required for some processors to acquire all the blocks is relatively small. The additional number of steps in the send phase also grows

449

slowly. The small number of steps, in turn, reduces the total start-up time. T1 focused on minimizing start-up cost at some expense of message-transmission cost, whereas T2 focused on minimizing message-transmission cost with an increased start-up cost. Existing algorithm [19] has identical characteristic as T2 and thus the performance of T2 is very similar to that of the algorithm [19]. When software overhead of message initiation is high, T1 is preferred, and when message-transmission time is dominant, T2 is preferred. The variants between the two are possible where the time for message start-ups can be traded against larger message sizes. This is useful in configuring the algorithm for different message-passing machines based on message-initiation overhead and link speeds. A set of configurable algorithms of T1.x has been developed for this purpose.

Table 1: Performance summary of algorithms.

	Range of d	Start-up Time	Message Transmission Time
T1	$d < 4$	$(2d)t_s$	$(d \cdot 2^{2d})m \cdot t_c$
	$d \geq 4$	$(3d-3)t_s$	$\{9 \cdot 2^{3d-4} + (d^2 - 5d + 3)2^{2d-1}\}m \cdot t_c$
T2	$d < 4$	$(2d)t_s$	$(d \cdot 2^{2d})m \cdot t_c$
	$d \geq 4$	$(3 \cdot 2^{d-2})t_s$	$(3 \cdot 2^{3d-3})m \cdot t_c$
T1.x	$d \geq x+4$	$\{3 \cdot 2^{d-3} + 3x + 2 - 2^x\}t_s$	$\{3 \cdot 2^{3d+x-4} + (2x+3)2^{2d+x-2}\}mt_c$

The time complexities of T1, T2, and T1.x are summarized in Table 1. For $2^d \times 2^d$ tori, message start-up costs are $O(2^d)$ for T2 while they are $O(d)$ for T1. Algorithms T1.x also show $O(2^d)$ start-up cost and $O(2^{3d})$ message-transmission cost. But, they have start-up costs that are higher than T1 but lower than T2. In addition, message-transmission costs are lower than T1 and higher than T2.

Ideally, we would like to evaluate the performance of these algorithms on commercial parallel supercomputers. However, evaluation of their scalability across a range of system sizes is hampered by the unavailability of large systems, and by the lack of control over the shape of sub-meshes allocated in commercial sizeable machines. What we need is a more flexible methodology that would yield reliable estimates of execution time across a broader range of system sizes. Consequently, we use analytic models of execution time that are based on real values of parameters measured on commercial machines. Where relevant, the values of parameters were measured as a function of problem size. In order to derive the interconnection network parameters, roundtrip test messages of known (large) size were transmitted between pairs of processors. The measured times were averaged over the number of messages. Given this parameterized model, with values of t_c and t_s, it is now possible to study the performance of different algorithms over a wide range of systems and problem sizes without requiring access to the machine configurations of these sizes. While not as realistic as time measured on real implementations, the model is detailed enough to provide insight into the performance over a range of system parameters.

Figures 6 and 7 illustrate the completion times of T1, T2, and T1.x for different network sizes as a function of block

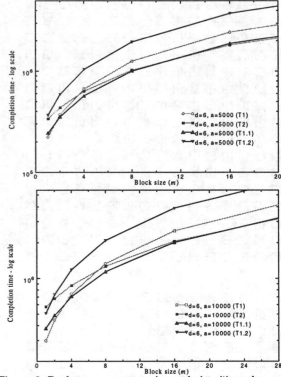

Figure 6. Performance comparison of algorithms for a $2^6 \times 2^6$ torus.

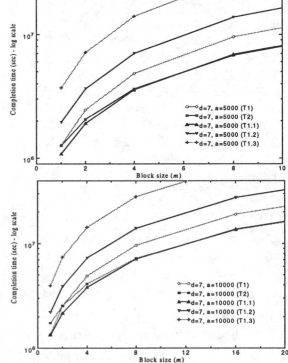

Figure 7. Performance comparison of algorithms for a $2^7 \times 2^7$ torus.

size, while considering only the two dominant terms: start-up cost and message-transmission cost. In this analysis, the comparison is parameterized with the normalized ratio of t_s to t_c, a, assuming that t_c has a value of one time unit. According to our measurements of the start-up costs and message transmission costs in commercial multicomputers such as Intel Paragon or Cray T3D, we found that the normalized ratio a is between 2500 to 10000. So, we evaluate the performance of the proposed algorithms for two values of a in this range, 5000 and 10000. Note that, since existing algorithms and the proposed algorithm T2 yield almost the same performance [13], we compare the performance of T1, T2, and T1.x.

Figure 6 shows the completion times of T1, T2, T1.1, and T1.2 in a 64×64 torus as functions of block size and the ratio a. The completion time plot indicates that when the block size is small, T1 is shown to have the best performance while T2 or T1.2 shows the worst performance. As the block size increases, T1.1 exhibits the best performance, while T1 becomes worse. When the block size further increases, T2 exhibits the best performance. Note that the cross-over points both between T1 and T1.1, and T1.1 and T2 appear in large block sizes as the ratio a increases. It indicates that as start-up cost is a more dominant factor, T1 provides the best performance until larger block sizes, while T2 shows the best performance for larger block sizes. Between ranges of the two points of block sizes, T1.1 shows the best performance. In this network, T1.2 does not show good performance. Figure 7 shows the completion times of T1, T2, T1.1, T1.2, and T1.3 in a 128×128 torus as functions of block size and the ratio a. The general characteristics of these plots are very similar to those in Figure 6. But, the cross-over points appear in smaller block sizes, indicating that, as the network size increases, T1 becomes a less powerful algorithm while T2 becomes more efficient. In this network, T1.2 and T1.3 do not show good performance.

From the above performance figures, we can observe some important facts: i) in a given network, T1, T1.1, T2 show the best performance when block sizes are relatively small, medium, and large, respectively, ii) in a given network, T1 shows better performance when the start-up cost is dominant, iii) for a given performance parameters, T2 shows better performance in larger networks and larger block size.

6. Conclusion

In this paper, we presented a set of configurable algorithms for complete exchange for two-dimensional torus-connected networks. They can be tuned to trade message-initiation or start-ups overhead against message-transmission time. The ability to configure these algorithms allows us to match the algorithm characteristics with machine characteristics based on message-initiation overhead and link speeds, in order to minimize overall execution time. Our performance evaluation results have shown T1, T1.1, T2 to perform best when block sizes are relatively small, medium, and large, respectively in a given network.

References

[1] S. H. Bokhari and H. Berryman, Complete Exchange on a Circuit Switched Mesh, *Scalable High Performance Computing Conference*, pages 300-306, 1992.

[2] S. H. Bokhari, Multiphase Complete Exchange on Paragon, SP2, and CS-2, *IEEE Parallel & Distributed Technology*, pages 45-59, Fall 1996.

[3] J. Bruck, C. T. Ho, S. Kipnis, and D. Weathersby, Efficient Algorithms for All-to-All Communications in Multi-Port Message-Passing Systems, *Symposium on Parallel Algorithms and Architectures*, pages 298-309, 1994.

[4] W. J. Dally, "Performance Analysis of *k*-ary *n*-cube Interconnection Networks," *IEEE Trans. on Computer*, vol. 39, no. 6, pp. 775-785, June 1992.

[5] S. Hinrichs, C. Kosak, D. R. O'Hallaron, T. M. Sticker, and R. Take, An Architecture for Optimal All-to-All Personalized Communication, *Symposium on Parallel Algorithms and Architectures*, pages 310-319, 1994.

[6] S. L. Johnsson and C. T. Ho, Optimum Broadcasting and Personalized Communication in Hypercubes, *IEEE Trans. on Computers*, vol. 38, no. 9, pages 1249-1268, Sep. 1989.

[7] P. K. McKinley, Y.-J. Tsai, and D. F. Robinson, "Collective Communication Trees in Wormhole-Routed Massively Parallel Computers," Technical Report MSU-CPS-95-6, Michigan State University, March 1995.

[8] P. K. McKinley and Y.-J. Tsai and D. Robinson, "Collective Communication in Wormhole-routed Massively Parallel Computers," IEEE Computer, pages 39--50, December 1995.

[9] L. M. Ni and P. K. McKinley, "A Survey of Wormhole Routing Techniques in Direct Networks," *IEEE Computer*, vol. 26, pp. 62-76, February 1993.

[10] D. K. Panda, "Issues in Designing Efficient and Practical Algorithms for Collective Communication on Wormhole-Routed Systems," Technical Report TR-25, Dept. of Computer and Information Science, Ohio State University.

[11] D. S. Scott, Efficient All-to-All Communication Patterns in Hypercube and Mesh Topologies, *Proceedings of 6th Conference. Distributed Memory Concurrent Computers*, pages 398-403, 1991.

[12] Y. J. Suh and S. Yalamanchili, "Algorithms for All-to-All Personalized Exchange in 2D and 3D Tori," Proceedings of the 10th International Parallel Processing Symposium, pages 808-814, April 1996.

[13] Y. J. Suh and S. Yalamanchili, "All-to-All Communication with Minimum Start-Up Costs in 2D/3D Tori and Meshes," IEEE Transactions on Parallel and Distributed Systems, Vol. 9, No. 5, May 1998.

[14] Y. J. Suh and K. G. Shin, "Efficient All-to-All Personalized Exchange in Multidimensional Torus Networks," Proceedings of the 27th International Conference on Parallel Processing, August 1998.

[15] Y. J. Suh, K. G. Shin, and S. Yalamanchili, "Complete Exchange in General Multidimensional Mesh Networks," Proceedings of the 10th International Conference on Parallel and Distributed Computing Systems, 1997.

[16] N. S. Sundar, D. N. Jayasimha, D. K. Panda, and P. Sadayappan, Complete Exchange in 2D Meshes, *Scalable High Performance Computing Conference*, pages 406-413, 1994.

[17] R. Thakur and A. Choudhary, All-to-All Communication on Meshes with Wormhole Routing, *Proceedings of 8th International Parallel Processing Symposium*, pages 561-565, Apr., 1994.

[18] Y.-C. Tseng and S. Gupta, All-to-All Personalized Communication in a Wormhole-Routed Torus, *Proceedings of International Conference on Parallel Processing*, volume 1, pages 76-79, 1995

[19] Y.-C. Tseng, S. Gupta, and D. Panda, An Efficient Scheme for Complete Exchange in 2D Tori, *Proceedings of International Parallel Processing Symposium*, pages 532-536, 1995.

[20] Message Passing Interface Forum, "MPI: A Message-Passing Interface Standard," Technical Report CS-93-214, University of Tennessee, April 1994.

[21] Cray T3D, *System Architecture Overview*, 1994.

Session B7

Network Monitoring & Analysis

Chair: Timothy K. Shih
Tamkang University, Taiwan

New Delay Analysis in High Speed Networks

Chengzhi Li   Riccardo Bettati   Wei Zhao

Department of Computer Science
Texas A & M University
College Station, TX 77843-3112
Phone 409 - 845 - 5098
Email: {chengzhi,bettati,zhao}@cs.tamu.edu

Abstract

The implementation of bounded-delay services over integrated services networks relies admission control mechanisms that in turn use end-to-end delay computation algorithms. For guaranteed-rate scheduling algorithms, such as fair queueing, delay computation based on Cruz's service curve model performs very well. Many currently deployed networks, be they packet-switched or ATM based, rely on non-guaranteed-rate disciplines, most prominently FIFO and static-priority disciplines. We show that for this class of disciplines the service curve model performs poorly. We propose the Integrated Approach as alternative to the service curve model to cluster servers for delay computation purposes, and show in a series of evaluations that this new approach outperforms approaches based on the service curve model as well as other currently used approaches.

1. Introduction

A major challenge in the design of high-speed integrated services networks is the implementation of a *bounded-delay* service, that is, a communication service with deterministically bounded delays for all packets in a connection. In such a network, the number of connections with a bounded-delay service requirement that can be supported is mostly determined by (i) traffic characterizations used to describe the traffic of connections, (ii) the packet scheduling disciplines at each server or switch in the network, and (iii) the accuracy of the delay analysis used for connection admission control tests.

In order to guarantee that all the connections can meet their deadline requirements, an effective and efficient method to derive the upper bound for the end-to-end delay experienced by connection's traffic is needed. By a delay analysis method being *effective*, we mean that the method is able to produce delay bounds that are relatively tight. A method that overestimates the delay bounds reduces the

utilization of the network. By *efficient*, we mean that the method is simple and fast in order to be used as part of on-line connection admission control. During the past decade, a number of service scheduling disciplines that aim to provide per-connection performance guarantees have been proposed in the context of high speed packet switching networks, such as Fair Queueing, Virtual Clock, Self Clocked Fair Queueing, Stop and Go Queueing, Earliest Deadline First, Static-Priority Scheduling, Rate Controlled Service Discipline, and SCED Scheduling. Along with these service scheduling disciplines, various delay analysis techniques have been devised to evaluate upper bounds for end-to-end delays experienced by connections in a network.

We can group these delay analysis techniques into two classes, depending on whether they decompose the network into isolated servers that are analyzed separately, or whether they integrate individual servers in the network into larger superservers. We distinguish therefore *decomposition-based* from *service-curve based* methods. A brief description of these methods is presented as following.

1.1 Decomposition-Based Methods

The basic idea for any decomposition-based method is to partition the network into isolated servers, and base the end-to-end delay analysis on the local delay analysis on the isolated servers. First, the local traffic is characterized on a per-connection basis at each server inside the network. The traffic is dependent on the source traffic for the connection and on the delay experienced by the traffic at previous servers. Next, the local delay bounds are independently computed. Finally, the upper bound for the end-to-end delay of the connection is computed as the sum of the local delay bounds at the individual servers on the path of the connection. The fundamental approach was proposed in [8, 9] and has been widely adopted in various forms.

Decomposition-based methods are very simple to use

and are suitable for networks with arbitrary topology. On the other hand, they often overestimate the end-to-end delay suffered by the connection's traffic and so reduce the network resource utilization. This is because this approach assumes that a packet suffers the worst-case delay at every server along its path. This assumption is conservative; while a packet may suffer the worst case delay at one server, it may not incur the worst case delay at a successive server. It follows that some real time connections may be rejected by a decomposition-based admission control algorithm even though the network can guarantee their QoS requirements.

1.2 Service-Curve Based Methods

The basic idea in service-curve based methods is to find a representation of a sequence of servers on the path of the connection as a single server. Successive servers are therefore integrated and dependencies between delays on successive servers can be taken into account. Servers are represented by their *service curve* $s_{i,k}(t)$, which defines the minimum amount of service (in bits transferred) that a server k can give to a particular connection i during time interval $[0, t]$ [10, 5].

Cruz [10] describes how the service curve can be used to effectively evaluate the end-to-end delay suffered by a connection. Suppose that Connection i passes through m servers and the k-th server offers the connection a service curve $s_{i,k}(t)$. Furthermore, suppose that the amount of traffic entering the network on Connection i during time interval $[0, t]$ is bounded by $F_i(t)$. Then the end-to-end delay of Connection i is bounded by

$$D_i = \max_{t \geq 0}\{S_i^{-1}(t) - F_i^{-1}(t)\}, \tag{1}$$

where $S_i(t)$ is called as *network service curve* of Connection i and is defined as

$$S_i(t) = \min\{\sum_{k=1}^{m} s_{i,k}(t_k) \parallel t_k \geq 0, \sum_{k=1}^{m} t_k = t\}. \tag{2}$$

Service curves can be used in two ways for delay computation, depending on whether scheduling algorithms are derived from pre-defined service curves, or whether service curves are derived from pre-defined scheduling algorithms.

Allocated Service Curve Method First, service curves are assigned to every connection at each server. Then, the end-to-end delay bound is derived based on the source traffic characterization and *network service curve*, which can be computed from the service curves of all servers on the path of the connection. The scheduling disciplines on the servers can be *synthesized* in a separate step from the service curves that were assigned earlier. See [10, 32] for some examples.

Theoretically this method fully utilizes the network resource and can be applied to networks with arbitrary topology. However, the scheduling discipline synthesized from the service curves always relies on a dynamic priority assignment. Therefore, the scheduling overhead is not negligible, and will impair utilization of the network resource.

Induced Service Curve Method As opposed to the allocated service curve method, here servers are assigned scheduling disciplines first. Then, service curves are derived for each server based on the local server scheduling discipline. Next, the network service curve is derived based on these service curves. Finally, the end-to-end delay bound is derived based on the source traffic characterization and the network service curve [29].

Once the service curve is known for the scheduling disciplines in the system, delay analysis is straightforward. Unfortunately, except for guaranteed-rate scheduling algorithms [18], deriving service curves is very difficult, if not impossible. This is indeed the case for static-priority (SP) schedulers, simple earliest-deadline-first (EDF) schedulers, and first-in-first-out (FIFO) schedulers. In this paper we will derive an approximation for the service curve of a FIFO server and use it to compare the performance of a service-curve based approach with the integrated approach presented in this paper.

1.3 Integrating Servers

As noted above, both general approaches to end-to-end computation do not work well for non-guaranteed-rate scheduling disciplines. Decomposition-based approaches over-estimate end-to-end delays for all disciplines by not taking into consideration self-regulating effects as traffic traverses the network on common paths. Service-curve based approaches work fine for guaranteed-rate disciplines, but fail for other disciplines. Indeed, we will illustrate later with an example of a chain of FIFO servers (Section 4) that service-curve based approaches can perform substantially worse than decomposition based ones.

In this paper we propose an *integrated* approach to analyze networks of non-guaranteed-rate servers. The general approach is to determine an accurate integrated service description for a collection of servers. Similar to the network service curve described earlier, that allows for a computation of output traffic descriptors for connections leaving the collection of servers under consideration. End-to-end delays can then be computed by partitioning the network into collections of servers, and then applying a decomposition-based method collections of servers instead of individual servers, thus greatly reducing the amount of over-estimation occurring in the delay computation.

We will describe the new delay analysis method in Section 2 on for a simple subnetwork containing two servers. While the approach itself is generic for a large class of service disciplines, we will focus our attention to systems with FIFO servers. In Section 3 we will apply the results of Section 2 to define an algorithm for end-to-end delay computation. We provide a detailed evaluation of the new algorithm by comparing it with a decomposition-based and a service-curve based algorithm. Section 5 concludes the paper.

2 Integrated Delay Analysis for a Subsystem with Two Multiplexors

In this section, we study a subsystem with two multiplexors, the topology for this subsystem is illustrated in Figure 1. An integrated method for the delay analysis in this system is presented. Although the approach is generic in nature, we will assume that the multiplexors are use a FIFO scheduling policy.

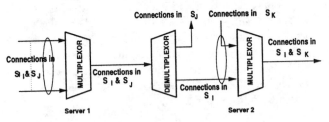

Figure 1. A Subsystem with two Multiplexors.

To evaluate the worst-case delay suffered by traffic, the description for network traffic is needed. We give the following definitions and notations for this purpose.

Definition 1 *The traffic arrival function $f_{i,j}(t)$ of Connection i at Server j is defined as the amount of data arriving at Server j from Connection i during the time interval $[0,t)$.*

Definition 2 *We call function $b_{i,j}(I)$ the traffic constraint function of $f_{i,j}(t)$ if for any $t > 0$ and $I > 0$*

$$f_{i,j}(t+I) - f_{i,j}(t) \leq b_{i,j}(I). \qquad (3)$$

Similarly, we define the amount of traffic leaving the server as follows:

Definition 3 *The amount of traffic leaving the Server j during the interval $[0,t)$ is denoted by $W_j(t)$. We call $W_j(t)$ the output traffic function at Server j.*

Referring to the two-server subsystem depicted in Figure 1, we use S_{12} to denote the set of all connections that traverse both Server 1 and Server 2. We use S_1 to denote the set of all connections that traverse Server 1 only and

then leave the subsystem. We use S_2 to denote the set of all connections that join the subsystem after Server 1 and traverse Server 2 only.

Throughout this paper, we will assume that the traffic of every connection is controlled at the source by a token bucket, that is, for $i \in S_{12} \cup S_1, j = 1$ or $i \in S_2, j = 2$

$$b_{i,j}(I) = \min\{I, \alpha_i + \rho_i * I\}. \qquad (4)$$

2.1 Main Results

The delay at a server can be determined once the output traffic at that server is known. The following lemma, which was first presented in [1], addresses this.

Lemma 1 *For a single FIFO server j, if the aggregated arrival traffic function $G_j(t)$ is known, its output traffic function $W_j(t)$ can be written as*

$$W_j(t) = \min_{0 \leq s \leq t}\{t - s + G_j(s)\}, \qquad (5)$$

where

$$G_j(t) = \sum_{k \in S_j} f_{k,j}(t), \qquad (6)$$

where S_j is the set of connections that traverse Server j.

Once we know the output traffic of a server, we also know the arrival time for the data leaving at any particular point in time. The following lemma gives the relationship between the output traffic and the data arrival time.

Lemma 2 *During the time interval $[0,t)$, if the total amount of data leaving Server j is $W_j(t)$, the time $H_j(t)$ when the $W_j(t)$-th bit arrives at Server j is given as*

$$H_j(t) = G_j^{-1}(W_j(t)). \qquad (7)$$

Note: $H_j(t) \leq t$.

Proof: The lemma follows from the definition of function $G_i(t)$. Q.E.D

Similarly, we can formulate when the arriving data will leave the server, as the following lemma shows.

Lemma 3 *If the total amount of data arriving at Server j during the time interval $[0,t)$ is $G_j(t)$, then the $G_j(t)$-th bit leaves Server j at time $W_j^{-1}(G_j(t))$.*

Proof: The lemma follows from the definition of function $W_j(t)$. Q.E.D

We can now apply these results to accurately determine the end-to-end delay suffered by traffic as it traversed the two-server subsystem depicted in Figure 1.

Lemma 4 *The end-to-end delays of connections in S_{12} (that is, traversing both Server 1 and Server 2) are bounded by*

$$d_{S_{12}} = \max_{t \geq 0}\{W_2^{-1}(G_2(t)) - G_1^{-1}(W_1(t))\}. \qquad (8)$$

Proof: During the time interval $[0, t)$, the total amount of traffic arriving at Server 2 is $G_2(t)$. According to Lemma 3, the $G_2(t)$-th bit leaves Server 2 at time $W_2^{-1}(G_2(t))$. Furthermore, these $G_2(t)$ contains $W_1(t)$ bits coming from Server 1. According to Lemma 2, the $W_1(t)$-th bit arrives at Server 1 at time $G_1^{-1}(W_1(t))$. Therefore, the delay suffered at time t by connections traversing both servers is given as $W_2^{-1}(G_2(t)) - G_1^{-1}(W_1(t))$. So we have

$$d_{S_{12}} = \max_{t \geq 0}\{W_2^{-1}(G_2(t)) - G_1^{-1}(W_1(t))\}, \quad (9)$$

Q.E.D

Unfortunately, Equation (8) is only of theoretical value. This is because it requires the knowledge of internal network traffic (in form of $G_2(t)$). Since the only information we assume are the traffic constraint functions at the sources, and the traffic is not reshaped internally, the internal network traffic is difficult, if not impossible, to describe. In order to provide a useful integrated method for delay analysis in this subsystem, we need to deeply analyze Equation (8).

The following central theorem in this paper provides an estimation for $d_{S_{12}}$ in Lemma 4 To streamline the presentation of the theorem, we define the following auxiliary notations:

- $\bar{G}_1(t) = \sum_{i \in S_{12} \cup S_1} b_{i,1}(t)$.

- $\bar{W}_1(t) = \min_{0 \leq s \leq t}\{t - s + \bar{G}_1(s)\}$.

- $\bar{H}_1(t) = \bar{G}_1^{-1}(\bar{W}_1(t))$.

- $F_{12}(t) = \sum_{i \in S_{12}} b_{i,1}(t)$.

- $F_2(t) = \sum_{i \in S_2} b_{i,2}(t)$.

Theorem 1 *The delay suffered by Connections in S_{12} is bounded by*

$$d_{S_{12}} \leq \max_{0 \leq s \leq B_1}\{\max_{B_1 + B_2 \geq T \geq s}\{s + \\ \min\{T - s, F_{12}(T - \bar{H}_1(s))\} + F_2(T - s) \\ - \min\{T, \bar{G}_1^{-1}(T)\}\}\},$$

where B_1 and B_2 are the length of maximum busy periods on Server 1 and Server 2, respectively.

Proof: See [25]. Q.E.D

We note that, according to Theorem 1, the end-to-end delay $d_{S_{12}}$ of connections traversing both servers can be computed using only bounding functions for the traffic entering the subsystem. This eliminates the problems described earlier with Equation (8) and provides a practical method to analyze end-to-end delays, as we proceed to describe below.

3 New Delay Analysis Algorithm

A common method to analyze the end-to-end delays suffered by connections in networks, with or without traffic regulation at intermediate nodes, consists of two steps. In a first step, a single-server analysis technique is developed to estimated the local worst case delay and characterize the output traffic, provided characterizations of all input traffic of the server. In a second step, starting from characterizations of all source traffic, local delay analysis is successively performed on each server along the path of the connection. As described earlier, the main disadvantage of this method is that the delay dependencies in successive servers without traffic regulation on a connection's path is ignored. So the obtained end-to-end delay bounds are very loose and the bursts are overestimated.

3.1 A New algorithm

Algorithm *Integrated:*

Step 1: Partition the network into subnetworks, each of them consists at most of two servers..

Step 2: Chose the appropriate order for all subnetworks such that each input traffic of $(i + 1)$-th subnetwork can be estimated by all input traffic of subsystems with order less than $(i + 1)$-th.

Step 3: Traverse in the subnetworks in the topological ordering, performing the following steps for each subnetwork:

    Step 3.1: Compute the delay bounds suffered by connections in the subnetwork.

    Step 3.2: Estimate the output traffic of the subnetwork.

Step 4: Compute the end-to-end delays for each connection by summing up all local delays suffered at every subnetwork along its path.

Figure 2. Algorithm *Integrated*.

Equation (10) can be used as the basis for improved end-to-end analysis methods, which better take into account delay dependencies. Algorithm *Integrated*, described in Figure 2, computes end-to-end delays in a cycle-free network with FIFO servers. It first partitions the network into subnetworks of one or two servers each (Step 1). It then identifies a topological ordering of subnetworks (Step 2). Next, it computes the local delays (Step 3.1) and the output traffic (Step 3.2) at each subnetwork. Finally, it determines the end-to-end delays by summing up the previously computed local delays (Step 4).

4 Evaluation

In a suite of simulation experiments we compared the proposed new method for end-to-end delay analysis with that of two commonly used methods ([8, 9]), which we call Algorithm *Decomposed* and Algorithm *Service Function*. These methods were originally proposed by Cruz and adopted in various forms by many others. We compare their performance on a network with FIFO servers arranged in a feedforward topology. These experiments show that our new method generally computes tighter bounds on end-to-end delays than the other approaches.

4.1 Experiments

We evaluate the performance of the new approach by comparing Algorithm *Integrated* to the delay computation methods described by Cruz in [8, 9], which we call Algorithm *Cruz*. In this section, we first define the performance metric and then describe the system configuration considered. The performance results will be presented and discussed in the next section.

Topology and Traffic Descriptions. In our evaluation, we consider a simple tandem network with n 3×3 switches, which are connected in a chain. An example of such a

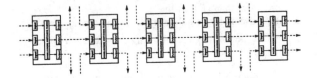

Figure 3. A Tandem Network.

tandem network with 5 switches is illustrated in Figure 3. There are $2n + 1$ connections in this network. Connection 0 is the longest; it enters the network at the middle input port of the first switch and exits the network from the middle output port of the n-th switch. For $k = 0$ to $n - 1$, the $(2k + 1)$-th session enters the network by the upper input port of the k-th switch and exits the network from the upper output port of the $(k + 1)$-th switch, the $(2k + 1)$-th session enters the network by the lower input port of the k-th switch and exits the network from the upper lower output port of the $(k+2)$-th switch. The middle output port of each switch, excepted the first one, carries four connections, including Connection 0. In order to simplify the evaluation, we assume that every source traffic is controlled by a token bucket with a unit bucket size ($\alpha = 1$) and the token arrival rate $\rho = \frac{U}{4}$, where U is the work load of the network. While an increase of the traffic burstiness (larger value for α) increases the overall end-to-end delays, our experiments indicate that it does not affect the relative performance of

the approaches evaluated in these experiments. In particular, increasing the traffic burstiness has no effect on the relative improvement $R_{X,Y}$ (defined below) for any pairing of methods.

Performance Metric. We quantify the performance of algorithms using two measures. One is the *end-to-end delay* $D_0^G(U)$ estimated by Algorithm X for the end-to-end delay suffered by the connection which travels the longest path in the network (Connection 0 in our case) under the work load U. The other is called the *relative improvement* $R_{X,Y}(U)$, which is used to compare two algorithms and is expressed as

$$R_{X,Y}(U) = \frac{D_0^X(U) - D_0^Y(U)}{D_0^X(U)}. \tag{10}$$

4.2 Delay Computation

In [25] we summarize the formulas used for the delay calculation in the decomposition based and service-curve based approach as described in [8, 9, 10, 5, 32]. We use these formulas to derive closed forms for the worst-case delay for Connection 0 in the topology used in these experiments. We call the resulting delay computation algorithms Algorithm *Decomposed* for the decomposed approach and Algorithm *Service Curve* for the service-curve based approach.

Algorithm *Decomposed*   We derive the worst-case end-to-end delay of Connection 0 by adding the local delays on the servers along its path. For this, we let E_k be the local delay suffered by traffic of Connection) at Server k. In [25], we derive the following equations for E_k:

$$E_1 = \frac{2\alpha}{1 - \rho}; \quad E_2 = \alpha \frac{3 - \rho + 4\rho^2}{(1 - \rho)^2}$$

$$E_k = 3\alpha + \rho E_{k-1} + 3\rho \frac{\alpha + \rho \sum_{i=1}^{k-1} E_i}{1 - \rho}, k \geq 3$$

The end-to-end delay D_0^D for Connection 0 using Algorithm *Decomposed* is then obtained by adding the local delays:

$$D_0^D = \sum_{k=1}^{n} E_k$$

Algorithm *Service Curve*   The delay calculation in this approach is based on the definition for the service curve given in [10]. As we compare the performance of the various approaches for a network with pre-defined servers (FIFO servers in this case), synthesizing scheduling algorithms from pre-defined service curves is not viable. We must use an induced service curve approach, where we derive the service curve from the scheduling policy used in the server. The performance of such a method, however, greatly depends on how tight service curves can be defined for a given service discipline. In [25] we derive an *upper bound* on the service curve for a FIFO server, which in turn give raise to a lower bound for the end-to-end delay D_0^{SC} for Connection 0 with the service curve method. As we derive in [25], the worst case delay D_0^{SC} is lower-bounded by the following expression:

$$D_0 \geq \frac{2\alpha}{1 - 2\rho} + \frac{\alpha(3 - 2\rho)}{(1 - \rho)(1 - 3\rho)} + \frac{(n - 2)\alpha(3 - \rho)}{(1 - \rho)(1 - 3\rho)}.$$

It is important to emphasize at this point that the following comparisons are between *upper bounds* on end-to-end delays for both Algorithm *Integrated* and Algorithm *Decomposed*, and *lower bounds* for Algorithm *Service Curve*. The results for the performance of Algorithm *Service Curve*, both in terms of end-to-end delays and in terms of relative performance, must therefore be considered as optimistic.

4.3 Numerical Results and Observations

The results of our experiments comparing the performance of the three approaches are depicted in Figures 4, 5, and 6. Figure 4 compares the service-curve based approach to the decomposition-based approach and illustrates how the former is not well suited (as was to be expected) for analyzing non-guaranteed-rate service disciplines (i.e. FIFO scheduling). As the network load increases, the inadequacy of modeling a FIFO server with a service curve becomes evident. For larger systems, this gets partly offset by the compounding effects of summing conservative local delay bounds in the decomposition-based approach.

From Figure 5 we see that Algorithm *Integrated* always outperforms Algorithm *Decomposed*. Furthermore, for loads up to 80%, the performance improvement increases with growing network size. This is expected as Algorithm *Integrated* takes delay dependence within server pairs into account.

While the performance improvement of Algorithm *Integrated* over Algorithm *Service Curve* can be inferred by transitivity, we show a comparison in Figure 6 for illustrative purposes. The results of this experiment show that the performance gains are significant, except for large systems under high load.

5 Conclusion

In this paper, we have proposed a new method for deriving end-to-end delay bounds for connections in tandem

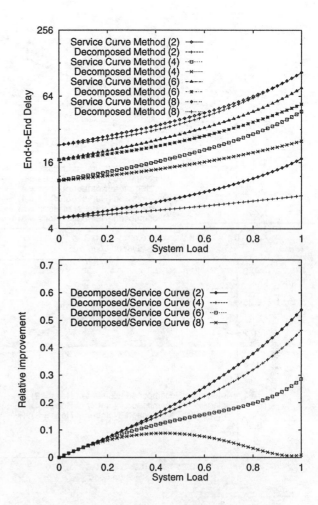

Figure 4. Comparison between Decomposed Method and Service Curve Method.

network, which uses a FIFO scheduling discipline. Our new method takes into account delay dependencies in successive servers along the path of a connection, which is in general very difficult for delay analysis, and achieves better performance than the method provided in [8, 9]. This can be observed through the extensive simulation experiments provided in previous section.

When servers do not have traffic regulation mechanisms (as is the fact with all work conserving servers), circular dependencies among connections introduce feedback effects on local delays, which in turn show up as non-linearities in the local delay calculations. For this reason, the analysis method described in this paper is limited to sets of connections that do not generate cycles in the network. Based on our previous work on decomposition-based analysis with feedback effects of networks with both FIFO and static-priority servers ([23]), we currently working on extending the approach proposed in this paper to general networks.

Although the integrated approach for analyzing pairs of

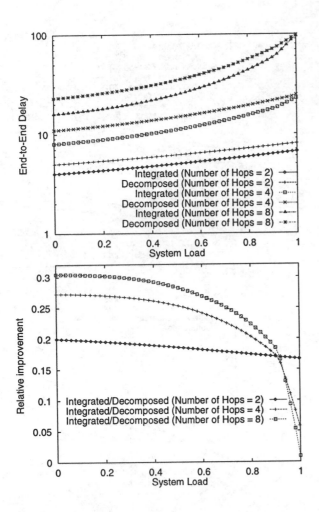

Figure 5. Comparison between Integrated Method and Decomposed Method.

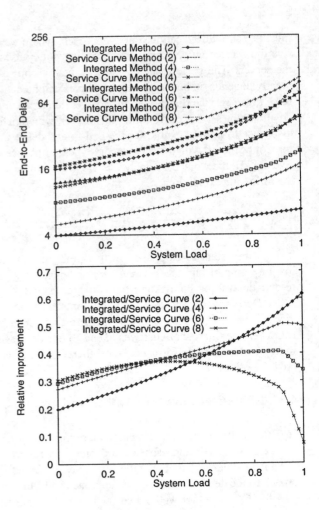

Figure 6. Comparison between Integrated Method and Service Curve Method.

servers presented in this paper is generic in principle, we derived the closed form delay formulas for the FIFO service discipline (in Theorem 1). We are currently extending the applicability of this approach to the static-priority discipline by deriving the appropriate closed form solutions of the delay formulas.

Acknowledgment

This work was partially sponsored by the Air Force Office of Scientific Research, Air Force Material Command, USAF, under grant number F49620-96-1-1076, by the Defense Advanced Research Projects Agency (DARPA) through the Honeywell Technology Center under contract number B09333438, and by Texas Higher Education Coordinating Board under its Advanced Technology Program with grant number 999903-204. The U.S. Government is authorized to reproduce and distribute reprints for governmental purposes notwithstanding any copyright notation thereon. The views and conclusions contained herein are those of the authors and should not be interpreted as necessarily representing the official policies or endorsements, either expressed or implied, of the Air Force Office of Scientific Research, Honeywell, DARPA, the U.S. Government, Texas State Government , Texas Higher Education Coordinating Board, or Texas A&M University.

References

[1] R. Agrawal and R. Rajan. Performance bounds for guaranteed and adaptive services. In *IBM research report RC 20469(91385)*, 1996.

[2] C. M. Aras, J. Kurose, D. S. Reeves, and H. Schulzrinne. Real-time communication in packet-switched networks. In *Proceedings of IEEE*, vol. 82, no. 1, 1994.

[3] A. Banerjea and S. Keshav. Queueing delays in rate controlled ATM networks. *Proceedings of Inforcom'93*, 1993.

[4] J. Bennett and H. Zhang. WF^2Q: worst-case fair weighted fair queueing. *Proc. of IEEE INFOCOM'96*, 1996.

[5] J.-Y. Le Boudec. Application of network calculus to guaranteed service networks. *Accepted for Trans. on Information Theory*, 1997.

[6] J.-Y. Le Boudec, G. D. Veciana and J. Walrand. QoS in ATM: Theory and Practice. *Inforcom'98*, 1998.

[7] D. D. Clark, S. Shenker, and L. Zhang. Supporting real-time applications in an integrated services packet network: Architecture and mechanism. In *Proceedings of ACM SIGCOMM'92*, pages 14–26, Aug. 1992.

[8] R. L. Cruz. A calculus for network delay. *IEEE Transactions on Information Theory*, 37(1):114–131, Jan. 1991.

[9] R. L. Cruz. A calculus for network delay, part II: Network analysis. *IEEE Transactions on Information Theory*, 37(1):132–141, Jan. 1991.

[10] R. L. Cruz. Quality of service guarantees in virtual circuit switched networks. *IEEE Journal on Selected Areas in Communications*, vol. 13, no. 6, 1995.

[11] A. Dailianas and A. Bovopoulis. Real-time admission control algorithms with delay and loss guarantees in ATM networks. In *Proceedings of INFOCOM'94*, pages 1065–1072, 1994.

[12] A. Demers, S. Keshav, and S. Shenker. Analysis and simulation of a fair queueing algorithm. In *Proceedings of ACM SIGCOMM'89*, pages 1–12, Sept. 1989.

[13] D. Ferrari. Client Requirements for real-time communication services. *IEEE Communication Magazine*, vol. 28, no. 11, 1990.

[14] N. R. Figueira and J. Pasquale. An upper bound on delay for the virtual clock service discipline. *IEEE/ACM Trans. Networking*, vol. 3, no. 4, 1995.

[15] V. Firoiu, J. Kurose, and D. Towsley. Efficient admission control for EDF schedulers. *Proceedings of Inforcom'97*, 1997.

[16] L. Georgiadis, R. Guérin, V. Peris, and K. Sivarajan. Efficient network QoS provisioning based on per node traffic shaping. *IEEE ACM Transactions on Networking*, 4(4):482–501, Aug. 1996.

[17] S. J. Golestani. Network delay analysis of a class of fair queueing algorithms. *IEEE J. on Selected Areas in Communications*, vol. 13, no. 6, 1995.

[18] P. Goyal, S. S. Lam, and H. Vin. Determining end-to-end delay bounds in heterogeneous networks. In *5th Int. Workshop on network and Op. Sys. support for Digital Audio and Video*, 1995.

[19] E. W. Knightly. On the accuracy of admission control tests. *Proceedings of ICNP'97*, 1997.

[20] E. W. Knightly. Enforceable quality of service guarantees for bursty traffic systems. *Proceedings of the IEEE Infocom'97*, 1997.

[21] K. Lee. Performance bounds in communication networks with variable-rate links. *Proceedings of SigComm'95*, 1995.

[22] C. Li, A. Raha, and W. Zhao. Stability in ATM networks. In *Proceedings of the IEEE Infocom'97*, 1997.

[23] C. Li, R. Bettati, and W. Zhao. Static priority scheduling for ATM networks. *Proceedings of the 18th IEEE Real-Time Systems Symposium*, 1997.

[24] C. Li, R. Bettati and W. Zhao. Response time analysis for distributed real-time systems with bursty job arrivals. *Proceedings of IEEE ICPP*, 1998.

[25] C. Li, R. Bettati and W. Zhao. New delay analysis in high speed networks. *Technical Report, Department of Computer Science, Texas A&M University*, 1999.

[26] J. Liebeherr, D.E. Wrege, and D. Ferrari. *"Exact admission control in networks with bounded delay services."*, to appear in *IEEE/ACM Transactions on Networking*.

[27] S. Low. Traffic management of ATM networks: service provisioning, routing, and traffic shaping. Ph.D Dissertation. UC Berkeley, 1992.

[28] R. Nagarajan, J. Kurose, and D. Towsley. Local allocation of end-to-end quality of service measures in high speed networks. In *IFIP Int. Workshop on Modeling of ATM Networks*, 1993.

[29] J. K. Ng, S. Song, C. Li, and W. Zhao. A new method for integrated end-to-end delay analysis in ATM networks. *Accepted by Journal of Communications and Networks*.

[30] A. K. J. Parekh and R. G. Gallager. A generalized processor sharing approach to flow control in integrated services networks: the single-node case. In *IEEE/ACM Trans. Networking*, vol. 1, no. 3, 1993.

[31] A. K. J. Parekh and R. G. Gallager. A generalized processor sharing approach to flow control in integrated services networks: the multiple-node case. In *IEEE/ACM Trans. Networking*, vol. 2, no. 2, 1994.

[32] H. Sariowan and R. L. Cruz. Scheduling for quality of service guarantees via service curves. *Proceedings of ICCCN'1995*, 1995.

[33] H. Sariowan. A service-curve approach to performance guarantees in integrated-service networks. Ph. D. Dissertation. University of California, San Diego, 1996.

[34] D. Stiliadis and A. Varma. Latency-rate server: a general model for analysis of traffic scheduling algorithms. *Proceedings of the IEEE Inforcom'96*, 1996.

[35] D. E. Wrege, E. W. Knightly, H. Zhang, and J. Liebeherr. Deterministic delay bounds for vbr video in packet-switching networks: Fundamental limits and practical tradeoffs. *IEEE/ACM Trans. on Networking*, 4(3), 1996.

[36] H. Zhang. Service disciplines for guaranteed performance service in packet switching networks. In *Proc. IEEE*, 1995.

[37] Q. Zheng and K. G. Shin. On the ability of establishing real-time channels in point-to-point packet-switched networks. *IEEE Trans. on Communications*, vol. 42, no. 2, 1994.

461

Network Congestion Monitoring and Detection using the IMI infrastructure

Takeo Saitoh, Glenn Mansfield, Norio Shiratori
Graduate School of Information Sciences
Tohoku University
2-1-1 Katahira, Aoba, Sendai 980-8577, Japan
E-mail: {saito,glenn,norio}@shiratori.riec.tohoku.ac.jp

Abstract

IMI provides a scalable and flexible measurement infrastructure. It essentially uses RMON-type passive monitoring and on demand, active probes. It is built on the SNMP framework so all interactions are through MIB-variables; security and access control is in place. Detecting congestion is a challenge and diagnosing it is an even greater challenge. In this work we have experimented with techniques of detecting congestion in the network using the distributed infrastructure of IMI. As a symptom of congestion, retransmission packets in the network traffic are detected, counted and analysed. The related information from various IMId's (IMI-daemons) are collated and used in conjunction with configuration information to detect and then locate a congestion bottleneck.

Keywords

TCP retransmission, Congestion detection, Distributed Network management, Internet, Traffic analysis

1 Introduction

There has been an explosive expansion in the Internet. Users, applications, speed and bandwidth all have seen tremendous growth. Along with this growth comes the requirement to understand and monitor the traffic pattern for better operation and management. This is a challenging problem.

There have been efforts to study, experiment, and understand the Internet dynamics. Van Paxson carried out a study of the Internet routing dynamics [1]. NetSpec [2] has used emulated traffic sources to measure the performance of the Internet. The National Internet Measurement Infrastructure (NIMI) [3] is being promoted as another project based on international cooperation. NetraMet [4] looks at details of network traffic for accounting purposes. The Shared Passive Network Perormance Discovery (SPAND) [5] system envisages modified clients and servers that will carry out passive measurements and forward the results to a *Performance Server*.

Van Paxsons study essentially relied on homegrown mechanisms for information access. NetSpec carries out active measurements using distributed applications but the issues of security and access control are not well addressed moreover the control protocols are proprietary. NIMI essentially uses active measurements and has the security and access control mechanisms essential for distributed applications, it does not use any standard management protocol for access. NeTraMet provides a nice mechanism for monitoring local traffic, though for accounting purposes only, and offers SNMP as an access mechanism thereby offering security and access control. The information content is limited and is non-distributed.

2 IMI - The Internet Measurement Infrastructure Architecture

2.1 Requirements of an Internet Measurement Infrastructure (IMI).

Any framework that targets to monitor and understand Internet dynamics will need to have the following characteristics:

(1) Distribution: The framework will necessarily have to be distributed from the scalability point of view. It will be practically impossible to monitor the Internet in a centralized fashion.

(2) Standard Access Protocol: A standard access protocol will need to be used to overcome the heterogeneity that characterises the Internet.

(3) Access Control: An appropriate access control mechanism will need to be in place to decide who can access what information.

(4) Information Content: Appropriate information will need to be gathered at the data collection nodes. The information content is in general closely related to the measurement mechanisms employed. Measurement mechanisms can generally be classified as active probe or passive probe mechanisms.

462

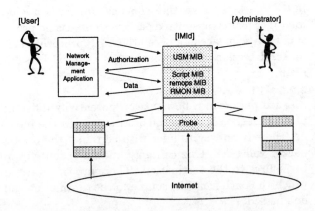

Figure 1. The IMI architecture

TraceRouteEntry ::= SEQUENCE	{
traceRouteOwnerIndex	SnmpAdminString,
traceRouteHostAddress	HostAddress,
traceRouteByPassRouteTable	TruthValue,
traceRoutePacketSize	Integer32,
traceRouteTimeOut	Integer32,
traceRouteProbesPerHop	Integer32,
traceRoutePort	Integer32,
traceRouteMaxTtl	Integer32,
traceRouteTos	Integer32,
traceRouteSourceAddress	HostAddress,
traceRouteInterfaceName	OCTET STRING,
traceRouteMiscOptions	Utf8String,
traceRouteMaxFailures	Integer32,
traceRouteOperStatus	OperationStatus,
traceRouteCurHopCount	Integer32,
traceRouteCurProbeCount	Integer32,
traceRouteRowStatus	RowStatus
}	

Table 1. DISMAN-TRACEROUTE-MIB

It may be noted that there is a cost associated with active measurements, traffic is generated, and the target characteristics are distorted to a certain extent.

Passive measurements generate no traffic, and provide more detailed information about the network. E.g. an analysis of the ICMP destination unreachable packets will provide an indication of the problematic network sites and routes. But on the other hand, passive traffic analysis generally does not provide indications about the route the packets traverse or the latency of the underlying network.

2.2 Architecture

We have built on the pioneering effort of the trailblazers. The IMI architecture essentially uses RMON[6]-type passive monitoring, and uses active probes on demand (Fig.1). The architecture envisages the existence of several IMId's (IMI-daemons) which are configured to collect and distribute information as required by their clients. The infrastructure is built on the SNMP framework so all interactions are through MIB-variables; security and access control is in place. SNMP is the access protocol.

To provide a really scalable and flexible measurement infrastructure it needs to be

(1) customisable: users can configure existing measurement tools and can setup new tools.

(2) distributed: the IMId's need to be managed in a distributed fashion. Management authority and functions will need to be delegated from remote administrators to local administrators and/or agents.

(3) secure: security and privacy needs to be maintained, access-control needs to be put in place. This calls for authentication mechanisms in a

distributed environment

IMId's respond to requests from users and other IMId's. A request maybe for

(a) installation of a new measurement tool

(b) customisation of an existing measurement tool

(c) results of a measurement exercise.

2.3 Measurement tools

The primary remote measurement tools are realised by implementing the remote operations MIB[7] defined by the ietf-disman-wg viz. the **Ping MIB** the **traceroute MIB** (Tbl.1) and the **Lookup MIB**

A remote operation is initiated by performing an SNMP set request on the ⟨remote operation⟩ **RowStatus** object. Where, ⟨remote operation⟩ is one of **ping**, **traceroute** and **traceroute**. The first index element, ⟨remote operation⟩ **OwnerIndex**, enables the use of SNMPv3 VACM [8] security model features. For more general purpose tools the disman-scriptMIB [9] is used.

2.4 Security

The IMI architecture is designed to enable multiple groups to use the measurement facilities. This requires a secure mechanism for delegating authority and enforcing access control. The SNMPv3 security framework is used for this purpose. The Userbased Security Model [10] of SNMPv3 has a MIB which is defined for remote configuration of the security parameters of an SNMP entity.

3 Distributed monitoring and diagnosis

3.1 Congestion monitoring and Diagnosis

IMI provides a powerful framework for distributed monitoring and diagnosis. In this section we use the example of network congestion to show how IMI can be effectively deployed to monitor congestion and to locate the bottleneck. Congestion has probably been around as a problem from the day traffic of any form started. Detecting congestion is a challenge and diagnosing it is an even greater challenge.

One approach would be to talk to all the routers in the network and obtain the counts on discards and/or retransmissions to detect signs of congestion. Over the Internet this would be a formidable task. And even if that was done we would still not have the complete picture as, we would not know the exact contents of the discarded/retransmitted packets and we would not know exactly when the congestion occurred (unless we are polling at very short intervals which is impractical). We will also not have any clue regarding which flow(s) are possibly causing the congestion. We would not know what the flows are - from which source to which destination and originating from which application.

One clue to congestion is the retransmission. A retransmission generally occurs when the sender does not receive an acknowledgment within a reasonable period of time. The sender assumes that the packet is lost in transmission and retransmits. Packets are lost in transmission when they are silently dropped by routers. When the buffers of the routers are (nearly) full this phenomenon occurs. And a router's buffer gets full when there are more transit packets arriving than leaving. This is indeed a symptom of congestion. So we may scan the traffic for retransmissions. And when we find a retransmitted packet we examine the source and destination. and thereby know that the congestion is probably occuring between the source and the destination. At this stage we have detected the presence of congestion and know that it is occurring on the route from source to the destination.

3.2 The IMId Probe and its functions

3.2.1 Network Flows

For both the TCP and the UDP suite of protocols we define a flow as a train of packets with the same { *source IP address, source PORT number, destination IP address, destination PORT number*}. We call this tuple the **flow-identifier**. In this sense the flow starts when a packet with a new flow-identifier is found. And the flow logically terminates when the flow-identifier is discarded from the local list of flow-identifiers. This happens when the list overflows. The flow-identifier of the least recently active flow is discarded.

TCP packets carry a **sequence number** in the TCP header to identify the portion of the stream that is carried in the packet. For a TCP flow this sequence number is unique and it is duplicated only in retransmitted packets. Thus the sequence number is a good identifier for retransmitted packets. There is no provision for a sequence number in the UDP protocol. This makes detection of retransmission of UDP packets difficult.

3.2.2 Flow route

Each packet in a flow takes a potentially different path from the source to the destination. In the Internet there is no way to infer with certainty the path a packet will take. One can only guess the route from the source to the destination. There are two ways in which the path from the source to the destination can be guessed

(1) Use the traceroute utility to find the route that packets traverse while travelling from source to destination. An approximation of this route would be the concatenation of the routes from the source to the probe and from the probe to the destination. traceroute gives the route followed by the packets at that point of time and it may be very different at a different point of time for the same source destination pair.

(2) Refer to network MAP databases [11] and compute the routes taken based on network configuration information. Or, Examine the policy information available in the policy databases and compute the routes based on the policy [12]. These information sources indicate the routes that "should" have been followed. However there is not always a direct relation between the policy defined in the routing registry and the actual network operation. Thus the likelyhood of a mismatch is always there. Also the information in the Routing registry may be outdated and inaccurate. We have used the information provided in the CHAIN project [13] to obtain network configuration related information.

3.2.3 IMId Probe Operation

The IMId probe offers features similar to RMON agents and TCP-dump based systems. It allows the setting of filters, based on which packets may be gathered and/or counted. It generates the Source-Destination traffic matrix which can further be refined to give application-wise or port-wise traffic.

In addition the probe also offers some more powerful features like retransmission detection. The retransmission detection works by storing the sequence numbers of each flow in a table. The size of the table for each flow is decided depending on available buffer and the estimated timeout for that flow. The sequence number of each packet is compared against the sequence

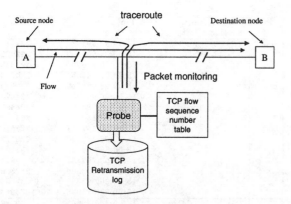

Figure 2. Probe

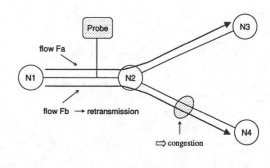

Figure 3. Same source flows

numbers in the list if the sequence number does not exist then it is a fresh packet and is added to the list if it exists then it is a retransmission - the retransmitted packet details are stored in the retransmission log table (Fig.2).

3.3 Route analysis

We use the retransmission information gathered by the probe and the network configuration information to locate the point of congestion. To locate the congestion bottleneck we use network configuration information in conjunction with the retransmission information. We assume that the traffic in the network is not controlled - i.e. all flows are treated equally.

The routes of the various flows that are passing through the point of observation are compared. For example, say there are flows $\{F_{r1}, F_{r2}, F_{r3}, ...\}$ in which congestion is being detected and, flows $\{F_{n1}, F_{n2}, F_{n3}, ...\}$ in which no congestion is detected during some time window at the IMId probe P. By overlapping the routes of the retransmission-less flows and the the routes of the retransmission-full flows the potentially problematic segments, along which there is congestion, are obtained.

The analysis technique is explained in Fig.3. We focus on two flows F_a, F_b. F_a is from N1 to N3 and F_b is from N1 to N4. N2 is a network on the path common to both flows F_a and F_b. The IMId Probe P is located between N1 and N2. Now, if there are no retransmissions detected by P for F_a while, there are retransmissions detected for F_b we can infer that there is a problem in the network segment between N2 and N4.

3.4 Route based Distributed congestion analysis

But we still do not know where the bottleneck is. Here we can use the distributed infrastructure in con-

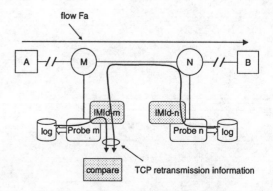

Figure 4. Distributed analysis

junction with knowledge about network configuration and advanced time synchronizing mechanisms to talk to monitors in other parts of the network along the path from A to B, to find out if congestion is being detected there too.

In Fig.4 the probe in network M detects TCP retransmissions in flow F_a. **IMId-m** then uses the following algorithm to locate the bottleneck along the path of F_a.

(1) Find the source A and destination B of F_a

(2) Locate other **IMId-ms**, if any, between A and B.

(3) If there are other **IMIds** along the path of A and B then fetch their retransmission logs.

(4-1) If the same retransmission is detected by the other **IMIds** viz. **IMId-m** and **IMId-n** then there is no bottleneck between **IMId-m** and **IMId-n**.

(4-2) if retransmissions detected at **IMId-m** are not detected at **IMId-n** then the bottleneck is likely to be between **IMId-m** and **IMId-n**.

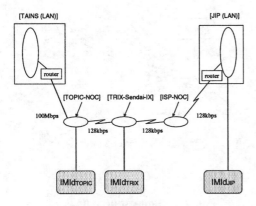

Figure 5. The Experimental network

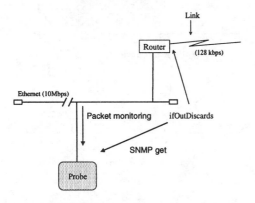

Figure 6. The information collected at the probes

flow	srcIP.srcPort dstIP.dstPort	Time	Seq No.
1	130.34.11.88.3698	14:59:58.691534	221514
	192.47.180.26.119	15:00:05.630542	222026
		15:00:05.890581	222538
		15:00:05.891054	223050
		15:00:06.083740	223562
		15:00:06.084213	224074
		15:00:06.084686	224586
		15:00:06.182423	225098
		15:00:06.182917	225610
		15:00:06.183176	226122
		15:00:06.252356	236362
		15:00:06.252827	236874
		15:00:06.253300	237386
		15:00:06.253620	237898
		15:00:07.077995	1081874348
2	202.11.109.34.80	14:59:46.646967	2288
	175.64.79.62212	14:59:54.673744	8761
3	202.11.109.34.80	15:00:00.626695	10221
	210.175.64.79.62212	15:00:00.650615	11681
		15:00:01.780261	13141
		15:00:01.804198	14601
		15:00:02.329136	16061
		15:00:02.353028	17521
		15:00:02.910898	18981
		15:00:06.219607	16061
4	130.34.247.138.119	15:00:16.197789	339
	210.134.33.2.3544	15:00:17.698016	360
		15:00:44.698127	1074
		15:01:00.698516	1620
5	210.156.48.93.1191	15:00:18.007851	2188049
	202.226.192.36.80	15:00:25.961268	2189231
		15:00:27.260736	2194044
		15:00:27.458487	2194044

Table 2. TCP retransmissions detected at TOPIC Probe (from TOPIC to TRIX)

4 Case Study Results and Analysis

To experiment with the distributed monitoring and diagnosis algorithms described in the earlier section we used the network shown in Fig.5. TAINS [14] is Tohoku University's operational campus network and TOPIC [15] is the regional academic and research network of the Tohoku district. It presently connects 92 sites. TRIX [16] is the regional internet exchange for academic and commercial providers and has 7 members at present.

Three **IMId**s are deployed: $IMId_{TOPIC}$, at the connection point of TOPIC and TRIX, $IMId_{TRIX}$, on the TRIX segment and $IMId_{JIP}$, at the connection point of TRIX and JIP (a participant of TRIX). As is shown in Fig.6, the **IMId**s gather information on TCP-retransmissions, and the queue discard statistics of the relevant routers.

In the following we carry out our diagnosis based on the data collected on 28th January 1999.

4.1 Traffic Information

As an example of the data collected at the probes we show the data collected at $IMId_{TOPIC}$. In Fig.7(a) the output queue discard statistics,

IF-MIB:ifOutDiscards, of the router connecting TOPIC-NOC and TRIX is shown. At 14:59:51 there was a burst 6 of discards. During that period the traffic from TOPIC to TRIX as measured by $IMId_{TOPIC}$ is shown in Fig.7(b). The bandwidth of the connectivity between TOPIC and TRIX is 128 kbps. It is evident that the traffic has exceeded the link capacity.

The TCP-retransmissions detected around the same period as that when the discards were detected are shown in Fig.7(c). In Tbl.2 the flow-wise retransmissions are tabulated. By comparing Fig.7(b) and Fig.7(c) we can see the close correspondence between the occurance of retransmissions and the instances of traffic exceeding the link-capacity.

4.2 Detection of bottleneck

4.2.1 Route Analysis

As an example of using the **IMId** information in conjunction with configuration information to diagnose congestion we use the data from the $IMId_{TRIX}$.

Tbl.3 shows the retransmissions in the flows which originated from TAINS (130.34.0.0/16) during a 60 second interval starting at 09:07 hours. There were 15 flows and two $\{srcIP, dstIP\}$ pairs $HP_1 = \{130.34.148.202, 202.226.196.6\}$ and $HP_2 =$

466

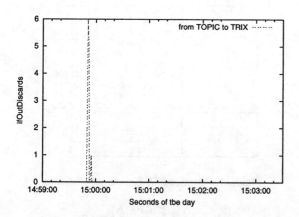

(a) The discards on congested link

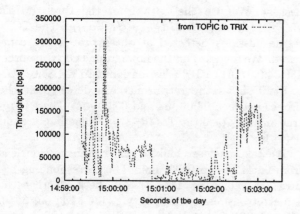

(b) The Traffic on the congested link

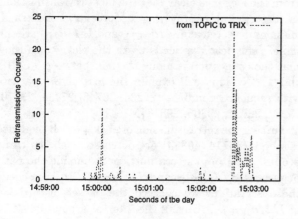

(c) The detected TCP-retransmissions

Figure 7. Traffic Information

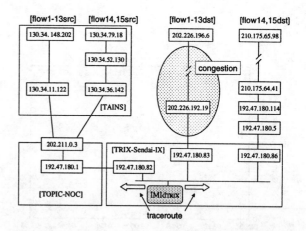

Figure 8. traceroute results at TRIX-Sendai-IX Probe

$\{130.34.79.18, 210.175.65.98\}$. By comparing the number of retransmissions with the number of packets in the flow we can see that there is a congestion somewhere along the path of HP_1 while the path of HP_2 is relatively congestion-free.

In Fig.8 we show the results of traceroute from the $IMId_{TRIX}$ to the corresponding hosts (source and destination of each flow). It can be observed that all the flows have a common segment $\{202.211.0.3, 192.47.180.1, 192.47.180.82\}$. It is clear that there is no congestion in this segment. From network configuration information one can find out that TAINS and TOPIC are connected by a highspeed link (FDDI,100Mbps), and that in TRIX the routers $\{192.47.180.82, 192.47.180.83, 192.47.180.86\}$ are connected to the same Ethernet segment.

From the above information one can infer that during the period under investigation there was congestion somewhere along the path $\{192.47.180.83,$

flow	srcIP.srcPort,dstIP.dstPort	Pakets	Count
1	130.34.148.202.80,202.226.196.6.61984	8	3
2	130.34.148.202.80,202.226.196.6.61985	4	1
3	130.34.148.202.80,202.226.196.6.61986	4	1
4	130.34.148.202.80,202.226.196.6.61987	8	3
5	130.34.148.202.80,202.226.196.6.61988	6	2
6	130.34.148.202.80,202.226.196.6.61989	61	32
7	130.34.148.202.80,202.226.196.6.61990	10	5
8	130.34.148.202.80,202.226.196.6.61991	10	5
9	130.34.148.202.80,202.226.196.6.61993	10	4
10	130.34.148.202.80,202.226.196.6.61994	5	2
11	130.34.148.202.80,202.226.196.6.61995	6	2
12	130.34.148.202.80,202.226.196.6.61996	6	2
13	130.34.148.202.80,202.226.196.6.61997	6	2
14	130.34.79.18.80.210,175.65.98.61091	10	2
15	130.34.79.18.80.210,175.65.98.61092	390	1

Table 3. TCP retransmissions detected at TRIX-Sendai-IX Probe (09:07am)

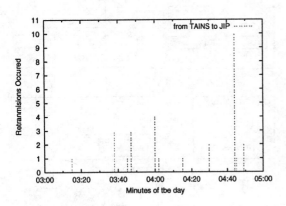

(a) Probe at $IMId_{TOPIC}$

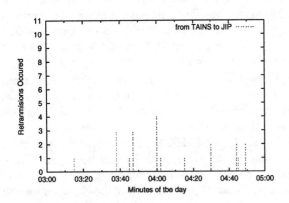

(b) Probe at $IMId_{TRIX}$

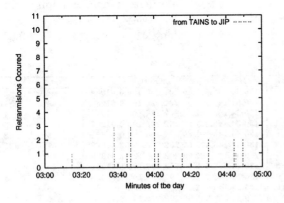

(c) Probe at $IMId_{JIP}$

Figure 9. TCP retransmission from TOPIC to JIP

Probe	Time	Seq No.
$IMId_{TOPIC}$	04:44:39.762047	26234
	04:44:41.116711	26746
	04:44:41.284935	27258
	04:44:41.285409	27770
	04:44:41.454008	28282
	04:44:41.454479	28794
	04:44:41.489285	29306
	04:44:41.489483	29818
	04:44:42.470431	46714
	04:44:42.963293	46853
$IMId_{TRIX}$	04:44:42.569888	46714
	04:44:42.982538	46853
$IMId_{JIP}$	04:44:42.680361	46714
	04:44:43.000114	46853

Table 4. Detected TCP retransmissions

202.226.192.19, ... ,202.226.196.6}.

4.2.2 Route based Distributed analysis

In the following we show how the distributed framework of IMI helps in detecting congestion bottlenecks. We use the data from the three IMId's viz. $IMId_{TOPIC}$, $IMId_{TRIX}$, $IMId_{JIP}$. The TCP-retransmissions detected at these probes are compared. We focussed on the flows from TOPIC (source: 130.34.0.0/16) to JIP (destination: 210.134.33.0/24).

Fig.9 shows the retransmissions detected at the probes between 03:00 hrs and 05:00 hrs. There is retransmission peak at $IMId_{TOPIC}$ sometime around 04:44 hrs.

We take a closer look at the retransmission logs from 04:44 hrs to 04:46 hrs. The corresponding figures are shown in Tbl.4. We check whether the same retransmission in a flow: {130.34.11.66, 3640, 210.134.33.1, 25} is detected at the probes. The *sameness* of a retransmission is verified by the checking the TCP-sequence number of the retransmitted packet. From the logs it is clear that the most retransmissions are detected at $IMId_{TOPIC}$. Moreover, the retransmissions detected at $IMId_{TRIX}$ and $IMId_{JIP}$ are the same. This leads us leads us to the clear conclusion that the congestion is along the link between TOPIC and TRIX. This will explain the loss of the packets with sequence numbers {26234, 26746, 27258, 27770, 28282, 28794, 29306, 29818}.

Further the retransmission of packets with sequence numbers {46714, 46853} are detected at all the three probes. This points to a bottleneck outside the path between $IMId_{TOPIC}$ and $IMId_{JIP}$. To crosscheck the observations we checked the packet discard log of $IMId_{TOPIC}$. During the interval around 04:44:37 there were 21 packets discarded. This corroborates the conclusion.

5 Open issues

IMI essentially works by looking at the packet contents. This gives rise to several issues related to security and privacy. Moreover when IPSec [17] and/or IPv6 gets widely deployed further considerations will be required.

We haven't looked into the problem of detecting lost UDP packets. This is an open issue at present.

If and when ECN(Explicit Congestion Notification) [18] gets widely deployed, this information can be used and serviced by the IMId.

To find the path between the source and destination of a flow we have used traceroute from the IMId probe and concatenated the results. This does not always give the correct path. Morover the routes dynamically change on the Internet. The Internet Routing Registry [12] may be used as to find out what the path *should* be according to policy considerations.

6 Conclusion

We have introduced IMI, a framework for the Internet Measurement Infrastructure. IMI offers a powerful and scalable architecture for Internet and Intranet measurement and management. IMI uses the passive measurement technique of monitoring packets and flows. We have established the power and flexibility of IMI. We have described mechanisms for detecting and locating congestion in the network using information from an IMId.

We have carried out a case study on a Metropolitan Area Network (MAN). By using the retransmission information from IMI we have achieved near 100% accuracy in detecting congestion in the Metropolitan Area Network (MAN). We have also shown how the distributed infrastructure of IMI can be used in diagnosing and localising bottlenecks. We are presently deploying the IMI infrastructure on a small scale centered around the Tohoku Regional Internet eXchange (TRIX).

We intend exploring means of monitoring and controlling the impact of audio/video flows on the network by monitoring UDP flows. Plans are afoot to experimentally deploy IMI on the national GigaBit backbone network[19].

References

[1] V.Paxson, "Measurements and Analysis of End-to-End Internet Dynamics," Ph.D. Thesis, LBNL-40319, UCB//CSD-97-945, Apr.1997.

[2] R,Jonkman, "NetSpec:Philosophy, Design and Implementation," http://www.ittc.ukans.edu/Projects/AAI/products/netspec/roel.ps, 1994.

[3] A.Adams, J.Mahdavi, M.Mathis, V.Paxson, "Creating a ScalableArchitecture for Internet Measurement," Proc.INET'98, Geneva, Jul.1998.

[4] N.Brownlee, "Traffic Flow Measurement: Experiences with NeTraMet," RFC2123, Mar.1997.

[5] Srinivasan Seshan, Mark Stemm, Randy H. Katx, "SPAND: Shared Passive Network Performancs Discovery," http://www.cs.berkeley.edu:80/~ss/papers/usits97/html/photo.html

[6] S. Waldbusser, "Remote Network Monitoring Management Information Base Version 2 using SMIv2," RFC2021, Jan.1997.

[7] Kenneth White, "Definitions of Managed Objects for Remote Ping, Traceroute, and Lookup Operations Using SMIv2," draft-ietf-disman-repos-mib-05.txt, Jun.1999.

[8] B. Wijnen, R. Presuhn, K. McCloghrie, "View-based Access Control Model (VACM) for the Simple Network Management Protocol (SNMP)," RFC2575, Apr.1999.

[9] D. Levi, J. Schoenwaelder, "Definitions of Managed Objects for the Delegation of Management Scripts," RFC2592, May.1999.

[10] U. Blumenthal, B. Wijnen, "User-based Security Model (USM) for version 3 of the Simple Network Management Protocol (SNMPv3)," RFC2574, Apr.1999.

[11] Glenn Mansfield et.al , "Techniques for Automated Network Map Generation Using SNMP," Infocom96, March 26-28, 1996, San Francisco, USA.

[12] C. Alaettinoglu, T. Bates, E. Gerich, D. Karrenberg, D. Meyer, M. Terpstra, and C. Villamizar, "Routing policy specification language (rpsl)," RFC 2280, Jan.1998.

[13] "Charting the Internet:CHAIN", http://www.cysols.com/IPAMaps/

[14] "TAINS," http://www.tohoku.ac.jp/TAINS/

[15] "TOPIC," http://www.topic.ad.jp/

[16] "TRIX," http://www.tia.ad.jp/trix/

[17] S. Kent, R. Atkinson, "Security Architecture for the Internet Protocol," RFC2401, Nov.1998.

[18] K. Ramakrishnan, S. Floyd "A Proposal to add Explicit Congestion Notification (ECN) to IP," RFC2481, Jan.1999.

[19] "JGN," http://www.tao.go.jp/JGN/

Session C7

Agent-Based Computing

Chair: Tetsuo Kinoshita
Tohoku University, Japan

Mobile-Agents for Distributed Market Computing

Shinji Tanaka, Hirofumi Yamaki,and Toru Ishida
Department of Social Informatics, Kyoto University
Kyoto, 606-8501, JAPAN
{stanaka,yamaki,ishida}@kuis.kyoto-u.ac.jp

Abstract

This paper discusses the implementation using mobile agent and the performance of the market computing to allocate network quality of service most efficiently, based on users' preference. Though the protection of users' private preference and the efficient calculation are both important, these two requirements often contradict each other.

By implementing QoS Market, a market-based network resource allocation system, using mobile agents, the communication time between agents and an auctioneer, which is the largest overhead in market computing, is reduced dramatically whthout leeking users' privacy information. The result of experiments show a mobile agent approach is more efficient then others, and the overhead of one market computing cycle in this system is about 450msec, which means that the system achieves sufficient efficiency.

1. Introduction

In usual networks such as the Internet, a number of users share the network resource, which causes the users' demands frequently conflict. In such an environment, the importance of a communication link varies according to the application and its usage, but network control policy of "best-effort" type, such as CSMA/CD, fails to consider such an aspect. What we need here is a resource allocation policy that reflects users private preference and allocates limited network resource efficiently.

We have already proposed an approach which is based on a competitive price mechanism explained by *general equilibrium theory* [10]. In our model, the preference of users and the characteristics of application programs are represented by *consumer* and *producer* agents respectively. Each agent updates their bids based on the price of goods, which is determined by the pricing mechanism of the market to balance demand and supply. A Pareto optimal resource allocation is obtained as the result of the interaction [2].

Our challenge here is to calculate such an efficient resource allocation in a practical length of time without leaking users' private information about preference for applications. A market-based algorithm generally consists of a large number of iterations to derive an equilibrium that balances the demand and the supply of goods, which results in a slow response to the given environment. The situation of the network used by a number of people, however, changes dynamically according to the change in the usage of application programs. This dynamics allows the allocation system only a few seconds of delay at the most.

In previous research [9], we applied the market-based mechanism into FreeWalk [5], a multimedia desktop meeting environment with shared virtual 3D space (Figure. 6), and controled the transmission of pictures. In this experiment, the whole allocation system is implemented in a single process in order to suppress the number of messages exchanged via network and achieved a practical quality of allocation in real-time. This approach, however, makes the users' private preference in its nature, leak to the auctioneer, which is a part of the market mechanism that modifies the price according to the demand.

To resolve this problem, this paper proposes an approach to implement a group of agents as a mobile agent that dynamically changes its place to an appropriate position. By moving agents to the server where the interaction among agents is performed, the users' privacy is preserved while keeping the smallest delay of the allocation.

We have implemented a market-based network resource allocation system with mobile agents on Windows NT, and validated the above scenario by performing several experiments.

2. Market-Based Resource Allocation

In this section, we present the general idea of market-based network resource allocation and the algorithm of the market calculation.

2.1. QoS Market Model

Our approach to achieve efficient resource allocation by merging various preferences of individual users is to introduce a market mechanism. Below, we describe the framework of our market-based application QoS control as the basis of the implementation issues discussed in this paper.

The two basic ideas to construct a market model for QoS control are as follows.

1. Users evaluate application QoS, which is the quality of service provided by network application programs, rather than the raw network resource, such as bandwidth, that they use.

2. We distinguish the "current" and the "future" networks, so that inactive users can obtain the incentive to transfer their rights to use current network resources to other active users, in exchange for the rights to use future network resources.

Figure 1 shows the market model for application QoS allocation. The rectangles in the figure represent the goods exchanged in the market. There are two types of goods, bandwidth and QoS, and each of them is divided into current and future goods. CBW and FBW stand for current and future bandwidth respectively, which are both shared by all the users.

The QoS of the communication from user j to user i is represented by q_{ij}, and $FQoS_i$ stands for the QoS that is received by user i in the future. The future QoS is assumed to be a single good for simplifying the model.

The circles in the figure are agents. Those on the left are *consumer* agents each of which represents the preference of each user, and those on the right are *producer* agents, each of which represents the conversion from bandwidth into application QoS performed by application programs.

The specifics of this model, such as the modeling of user preference and application performance, and the evaluation of resource allocation by simulation have been reported in our previous work [10].

2.2. Algorithm for Computing Equilibrium

In this market-model, there are two types of elements: agents and auctioneers. Figure 2 shows messages exchanged in the market. The underlying model of network usage is single-cast communication with network resource reservation mechanism, such as an intranet with RSVP [1] support.

A consumer agent represents user's preference, which is modeled as a utility function that takes a bunch of goods consumed as its input and returns a higher value for more

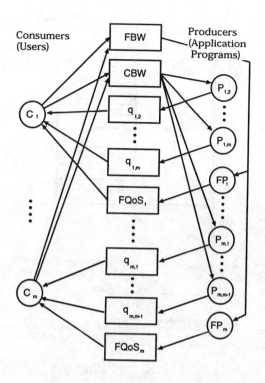

Figure 1. QoS Market Model

preferred bunch. There is a one-to-one correspondence between a user and a consumer agent. The user informs his/her preference on application QoS to the corresponding consumer agent(preference message), which reflects it in the utility function, typically by changing coefficients in the formula. Each consumer acts to acquire a bunch of goods that maximizes the value of the utility function (we call this value as just "utility," hereafter), by changing the bid for the goods in its interest.

A producer agent represents the characteristic of a network application program, which transforms raw network resource into a service to be consumed by the user. Thus, there is a one-to-one correspondence between a producer agent and a service that is provided by an application program. Note that multiple services can be provided by a single program and that a single service can consist from multiple type of network resources. There is no one-to-one correspondence between a program and a producer agent, nor between a producer agent and any single type of network resources. The transformation from network resources to an application service is modeled as a production function, which takes the set of network resources as its input and output the corresponding service. When a service starts or finishes, a user provides or erases the agent which is corresponded the service(service message). Each producer selects its production level so as to maximize its profit,

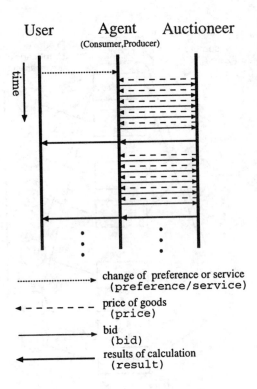

User   Agent   Auctioneer
(Consumer,Producer)

..............▸ change of preference or service
             (preference/service)

◂ — — — — — price of goods
             (price)

————————▸ bid
             (bid)

◂———————— results of calculation
             (result)

Figure 2. Message Exchange

which is defined as the difference between the income obtained by selling the services and the cost to purchase the network resources.

An auctioneer exists for each good. It adjusts the price of a good based on the bid from consumers and producers, so as to balance supply and demand of the corresponding good. The adjusted price is then sent to the agents and used by them to change their bid.

The market calculation in this model is performed as follows (Figure 3).

1. The auctioneer reports price of goods to agents(price message)(l.3).

2. Each agent calculates supply or demand of goods based on price information, to maximize their utility or profit(l.4). They then report them to the auctioneer(bid message).

3. The auctioneer aggregates the supply and the demand of goods reported by agents(l.5), and raises (lowers) the price if the demand is over (under) the supply(ll.6–13).

4. If the difference between the supply and the demand is under the threshold, which is decided by users, the calculation terminates and the price exactly reflects the final allocation of network resources(l.15). If not, the auctioneer and the agents repeat from 1.

```
1: repeat
2:   begin
3:     Actioneer reports price to agents;
4:     Agent calculates supply or demand;
5:     Auctioneer aggregates supply and demand;
6:     if(supply over demand) then
7:       begin
8:         Auctioneer raises price;
9:       end
10:    if(supply under demand) then
11:      begin
12:        Auctioneer lowers price;
13:      end
14:   end
15: until(|supply - demand| > threshold);
16:
17: Agent calculates its share of bandwidth;
18: Agent reports it to QoS Client;
```

Figure 3. Market Calculation

5. When the calculation terminates, each producer agent calculates its share of network resources based on the final price, and reports it to QoS Client to control the communication of the corresponding application program (resource message), which uses the network resources and provides services to users(l.17,18).

The allocation has to be recalculated to adapt to the dynamically changing environment, and thus the above process ("calculation cycle" or just "cycle" hereafter) is repeated on every recalculation. If the overhead of computing equilibrium is large, resource allocation cannot follow the change of environment, not to mention that market computing itself occupies a considerable size of resource both in the network and computers. Therefore, the overhead of market computing should be as small as possible.

The resource message, which is used for auctioneers to report resource allocation to users, is transmitted whenever the auctioneers finish calculation. The preference message is used for users to report changes of their preference to agents, while the service message is used for network applications to report the changes in the services they provide to agents. The service message is transmitted whenever the behavior of application programs changes as well as the start of a new process. The number of above messages exchanged in the market computing is comparatively small compared to the messages defined below.

The price message is used for the auctioneers to report the price of goods to agents, and the bid message is used for agents to report the supply and the demand for goods. Both of them are transmitted whenever price of goods are changed, thus the number of these messages exchanged is largest among other messages (typically, 10 to 100 times the number of agents in a calculation cycle). To minimize the overhead of market calculation, reducing the number of these two types of message is effective.

3. Implementation

In the rest of this paper, we present the underlying implementation issues, and discuss the implementation with mobile agents to our market-based network resource control system.

3.1. Mobile Agent Approach

In our market-based approach, agents send the auctioneers their bids, which are derived from the preference or the usage of network application program by users. Since users are distributed over network, there are typically two possible approaches to implement the agents.

The first one is to implement each agent in the host of the corresponding user, which is called *distributed implementation with static agents*(Figure 4(a), messages in the figure are the same as figure 2) here. In this case, since the calculation for generating bids can be performed simultaneously in their hosts, processors in the network are utilized effectively. On the other hand, as described in the previous section, all the bid and the price messages transmitted between agents and the auctioneers are performed as network communications, which causes large overhead in market computing.

We formulate this overhead as follows. Assume that the number of clients is n_c, and the number of calculation cycles necessary for market to reach an equilibrium is n_r. If the time to send and receive price information of goods is T_{price}^d, the time that agents calculate the most suitable supply and demand of goods is T_{agent}, the time to transmit supply and demand of goods is T_{bid}^d, the time for the auctioneers to adjust price of goods is $T_{auctioneer}$, and the time to transmit the results of calculation to users is T_{result}, then the time of one calculation cycle T_{static} is given as follows.

$$
T_{static} = n_r(T_{price}^d + T_{agent} \\
+ T_{bid}^d + T_{auctioneer}) + T_{result} \quad (1)
$$

The second approach is to implement all the utility functions in the host where the auctioneers reside. This is called *centralized implementation*(Figure 4(b)). In this case, the utilization of computation resource is worse than the first approach, while the communication cost is minimized.

Assuming the time to send and receive price information of goods is T_{price}^c and the time to transmit supply and

demand of goods is T_{bid}^c, then the time of one calculation cycle $T_{centralized}$ is given as follows.

$$
T_{centralized} = n_r(T_{price}^c + n_c T_{agent} \\
+ T_{bid}^c + T_{auctioneer}) + T_{result} \quad (2)
$$

The difference of one market calculation of equilibrium time between the case of distributed implementation (with static agents) and the case of centralized implementation is given as follows.

$$
T_{static} - T_{centralized} = n_r(T_{price}^d + T_{bid}^d \\
- T_{price}^c - T_{bid}^c - (n_c - 1)T_{agent}) \quad (3)
$$

The balance between the time to transmit the bid and the price messages, and the time to derive bids based on the maximization problems of the agents determine which approach is suitable. In current network environment, it is obvious that the former surpasses the latter. This fact makes the distributed implementation far more costly than the centralized implementation.

In the centralized implementation, utility and production functions are defined statically in the same process as the auctioneers ("market server" hereafter). Users report their preference on applications by sending coefficients to be set in the functions to the auctioneers. Although this approach is relatively simple, the available utility function cannot be changed, which prevents the users from setting various types of preference, thus the system designer has to know all the types of user preference.

Since the privacy problem is serious in the centralized implementation, we examine the following two approaches by extending the distributed implementation with static agents.

1. Remote agent approach (Figure 4(c)) : Agents are implemented in the market server, but utility functions and production functions can be changed dynamically. Users send the expressions of utility and production functions to the market server. The expressions are interpreted by the remote agents.

2. Mobile agent approach (Figure 4(d)) : A group of agents is implemented as a mobile agent which keeps utility functions and production functions inside, and moves to auctioneer. Users send their preference on applications to their own agents.

The first approach provides more flexibility than the centralized implementation. However, this approach uncovers the users' private preference, which is not preferable in the context of the market-based approaches, where minimal

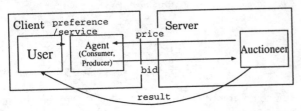

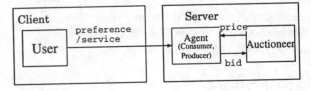

(b) Centralized Implementation

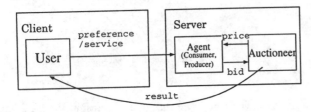

(d) Mobile Agent Approach

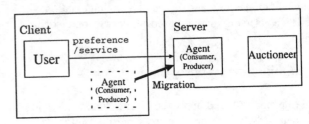

Figure 4. Implementation Model

information is sufficient to achieve the optimality of the whole system.

The second approach conforms both of above requirements, flexibility and privacy. It can implement dynamic change of user preference and network usage by nature, and security issue in mobile agent systems has been discussed extensively in the preceding work [7].

A mobile agent is a process object that can travel from one place to another in the middle of its execution preserving its context, and continue to run in the new place. A mobile agent can interact with the place it visits or with other mobile agents. Some of such environments provide a bidirectional authentication mechanism, where the servers authenticate the agents to protect themselves against malicious agents while the agents authenticate the servers.

These features enables our market-based allocation mechanism to achieve the efficiency and the flexibility of market calculation resolving the security issue that the users' preference must be kept private.

3.2. QoS Market

The system called QoS Market that we implement adopts mobile agents to solve the problem of computing equilibrium shown in the previous subsection.

Below, we explain the configuration of QoS Market, and the message interactions performed in it.

Figure 5 shows the configuration and the message flow of the system. The messages in the figure are the same as figure 2. The system consists of three types of processes : QoS Client, Mobile Agent, and Auctioneer. The arrows

indicate the interaction among them, including the move of agents and the flow of information, such as bids, price and resource allocation. Their functionality is as follows.

1. QoS Client

   A QoS Client locates at each user's local computer, provides user interface to obtain preference from its user. A QoS Client tells the user's preference and the usage of network application to the corresponding Mobile Agents. It also receives the result of market computing, i.e., the allocation of network resource, and controls the transmission of data performed by the network application programs.

2. Mobile Agent

   A Mobile Agent includes a consumer agent that represents its user's preference, and producer agents that represent application programs, and participates in market calculation generating bids based on current price information. The move of a Mobile Agent to the market server is done only once when its user starts QoS Client. The update of utility or production functions is done by receiving parameters from the corresponding QoS Client. A Mobile Agent informs the current resource allocation at the end of every calculation cycle.

3. Auctioneer

   Auctioneers reside in the market server, and perform the adjustment of the price of goods. In our current system, they are implemented as a single thread that

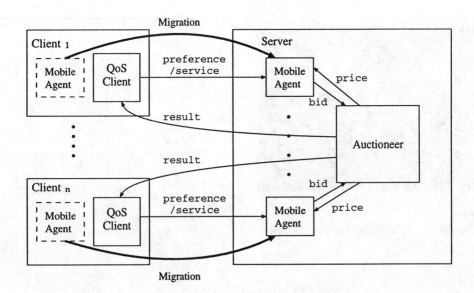

Figure 5. System Configuration

handles all the goods. The thread judges the convergence of the resource allocation, and tells the end of a cycle to all Mobile Agents.

All these components have been implemented on Windows NT, and, except for the move of mobile agents, the network communication are performed using Microsoft's Distributed COM(DCOM) technology, which extends the Component Object Model (COM) to support communication among objects on different computers

Even though many mobile agent systems are being developed, such as Aglets, Odyssey, and Voyager [4, 3, 6], most of them are based on Java, Tcl or other interpreters, thus are not suitable for our application where the overhead in computation is critical. We decided to implement a subset of a mobile agent system with the minimal set of functionality, using Microsoft's ActiveX technology, a Component Object Model optimized for a network, on WindowsNT. A group of agents is implemented as an ActiveX component, which are downloaded from the client processes to the market server and run as a part of it.

At first, a mobile agent exists as a DLL file, a Dynamic Link Library, at each client. When a user logs in the QoS Market, the user sends the information about his/her mobile agent to the market server. Then the market server downloads the DLL of mobile agent. The market server links the DLL dynamically, and initializes the mobile agent. After this, the mobile agent communicates the QoS Client, and receives the information about the preference of the user and applications, then provides a consumer and producers. In market calculation, the communication between the mar-

ket server and the mobile agent is executed by the market server's calling a function of the mobile agent.

Because the mobile agent by ActiveX is written in native code, to know users' utility function, which is privacy, we have to analyze the code by reverse engineering, or presume from the answers of the mobile agent to various questions. These usually require a great deal of time, and we think this mobile agent is secure enough.

Since the component of ActiveX moves without context, we do not assert that this is an ideal mobile agent system. Actually, this made our design of the agent interactions a little tricky, and we think this is a temporary, but practical enough for evaluating the feasibility of the mobile agent approach. We plan to adopt other mobile agent systems with more run-time efficiency in the future.

4. Experiment

Here, we examine the performance of QoS Market in order to verify the mobile agent approach to the market-based network resource allocation.

4.1. Settings

To estimate the system performance, we make two experiments as follows.

1. The evaluation environment consists of two PCs with Windows NT 4.0. The market server is running at Host B. They are connected by 10Mbps Ethernet, and the

Figure 6. FreeWalk: A Multimedia Conferencing Tool

Table 1. The Times for Each Stage of the Calculation

	Static Agent Approach(ms)	Mobile Agent Approach(ms)
T_{moving}	0	700
T_{price}	86	0
T_{agent}	0.64	0.64
T_{bid}	86	0
$T_{auctioneer}$	0.2	0.2
T_{result}	82.75	82.75
Estimated Total Time of Market Computing	3419.8	95.8

data have been recorded at Host A without the market server.

Two applications on Host A communicate Host B, so there are two communication from Host A to Host B. Thus there are five goods, which are CBW, FBW, q_{AB1}, which represents the one of the commnunication from Host A to Host B, q_{AB2}, and FQoS.

To estimate the system performance, we measured the time for the calculation and the communication performed in each stage of a market calculation cycle. This is to estimate the difference between the mobile agent approach and the static agent approach.

2. Evaluation environment consists of three PCs with Windows NT 4.0. The FreeWalk, a multimedia conferencing tool, is running at each host, and the market server is running at one of them. They are connected by 10Mbps Ethernet, and the data have been recorded at the two hosts without the market server.

In this environment, only one user change his/her preference, while the preference of the other two users is kept unchanged. Since there are three users in the 3D meeting space, two network services are provided to each user. The user inputs his/her preference on these services as a ratio of their importance.

The user inputs twenty times a random ratio of importance of one service every three seconds. A ratio of importance of another service is set the rest ratio.

To estimate the system performance, we measured the deviation in the resource allocation, which is caused by the delay of market computing. When the user changes his/her preference, there is always a certain amount of delay before the new resource allocation that reflects the change is derived. During this period, network communication is performed using the old allocation, which causes the data to be transmitted more/less than ideal amount in each connection and to cause loss in the user's utility.

4.2. Results

Table 1 shows the time for each stage of the calculation. The T_{price}, which is the time to transmit price from an Auctioneer to a QoS Client via network, is as large as 0.86msec. On the other hand, in the mobile agent approach, there is almost no overhead because it can be done as an inter-process communication inside the same host. The time consumed by the calculation in an agent and an auctioneer, T_{agent} and $T_{auctioneer}$ respectively, are the same in both implementations. The time to send the allocation result to QoS Market via network, T_{result}, is 82.75msec in both implementation.

Mobile agent approach requires the time to move agents in the network other than those shown in Table1, and the T_{moving}, which is the mean time for a mobile agent to move from the QoS Client to the market server is about 700msec. This, however, does not have much impact in the efficiency, since the move is performed only once in the lifetime of the agent and does not occur in each of the calculation cycle.

The total time of a market calculation cycle is then estimated by applying these results to the equation 1 and 2 in Section 3.1. Assuming $n_r = 20$, the time of one cycle in the static agent approach is

$$T_{static} = 20(83 + 0.64 + 83 + 0.2) + 83 = 3419.8(ms),$$

while that in the mobile agent approach is

$$T_{mobile} = 20(0 + 0.64 + 0 + 0.2) + 83 = 95.8(ms).$$

478

From this result, we conclude that there is a large difference in the efficiency of market calculation between static / mobile agent approaches.

According to the result of the second experiment, the average overhead is suppressed 457.8msec, which means that the system achieves practically sufficient efficiency.

We believe superiority of the mobile agent approach to the static agent approach will not be changed in several years. Since the size of each message is small enough compared to the total bandwidth, the delay in the transmission of the messages are caused almost exclusively by the network latency. Thus, the performance will not be improved much even if the network technology advances, because such progress is usually in bandwidth rather than in latency.

5. Conclusion

The protection of users' private preference and the efficient calculation are both important in the market computing to allocate network quality of service most efficiently, based on users' preference. In this paper, we discussed the implementation of the market-based application QoS control system, which derives optimal resource allocation based on users' preference, from the viewpoint of efficiency, flexibility and privacy. To achieve these objectives, we proposed an approach based on mobile agent technology, and implemented the QoS Market system to validate the discussion.

From the experimental results, we conclude as follows/

1. The mobile agent approach achieves far more efficient calculation than the static agent approach, preserving the merits in flexibility and privacy.

2. Our implementation succeeds in responding to the change of user preference fast enough, with the delay of approximately 450ms, and causes minimal communication overheads.

In this paper, we assumed an intranet of average size. Future research will cover a large-scale intranet, where the performance must be further improved because the delay by networks becomes more serious in the process of resource allocation.

References

[1] R. Braden, L. Zhang, B. Berson, S. Herzog, and S. Jamin, "Resource ReSerVation Protocol (RSVP) – Version 1 Functional Specification," *Internet Request for Comments*, RFC2205, 1997.

[2] S. H. Clearwater (Ed.), *Market-Based Control: A Paradigm for Distributed Resource Allocation*, World Scientific, 1996.

[3] General Magic Odyssey WWW Page, http://www.genmagic.com/agents/odyssey.html, 1996.

[4] D. B. Lange, D. T. Chang, "IBM Aglets Workbench – Programming Mobile Agents in Java," IBM Corporation White Paper, Sept. 1996.

[5] H. Nakanishi, C. Yoshida, T. Nishimura, and T. Ishida, "FreeWalk: Supporting Casual Meeting in a Network," *Proc. of CSCW'96*, pp. 308 – 314, 1996.

[6] Object space, Inc., "ObjectSpace Voyager Technical Overview," http://www.objectspace.com/Voyager, 1997.

[7] T. Sander, C. F. Tschudin, "Protecting Mobile Agents Against Malicious Hosts," Givanni Vigna (Ed.), *Mobile Agents and Security*, LNCS 1419, Springer, 1998.

[8] M. P. Wellman, "A Market-Oriented Programming Environment and Its Application to Distributed Multicommodity Flow Problems," *Journal of Artificial Intelligence Research*, Vol. 1, pp. 1–22, 1993.

[9] H. Yamaki, Y. Yamauchi and T. Ishida "Implementation Issues on Market-Based QoS Control," *ICMAS-98*, pp. 357 – 364, 1998.

[10] H. Yamaki, M. P. Wellman and T. Ishida "A Market-Based Approach for Allocating QoS to Multimedia Applications," *ICMAS-96*, pp. 385 – 392, 1996.

Coordinated flows in a formal Multi-Agent System based on a Modal Algebra

Panos A. Patsouris
(*panos@cs.wits.ac.za*)
Department of Computer Science, University of the Witwatersrand
Johannesburg, S. Africa

Abstract

We develop a formal multi-agent system based on a modal algebra enabling us to preserve the essential characteristics of its autonomous software agents (autonomy, mobility, etc.), as well as to explore the formal properties and management of the cooperations (non-hierarchical or flat structures) and coordinations (hierarchical structures) among those simple agents, that can be constructed through the operations of the model. We show the potential of these operations that allow us to construct different cooperations and coordinations based on the same set of autonomous agents (as alternative solutions with respect to the same given problem), while, in parallel we provide the means in order to explicitly specify different types of coordinated flows of information specified and governed by these structures. We illustrate all the above via a number of algorithms referring to the development of a simple (in structure) data mining system. We simply selected an adequate application area with no purpose to compare data mining methods and techniques. The various algorithmic solutions we suggest, unveil the resilience of the alternative design approaches aiming at improving issues like decentralization of services, as well as enhancing performance through concurrent organization by thus exploiting the different possibilities of the model.

Keywords

Autonomous agent, Multi-agent system, Modal algebra, Concurrency, Cooperation, Coordination, Coordinated flow.

1. Introduction

Modelling services and/or actions (further called under the general term *services*) in environments like the Web requires the consistent combination of different modelling and design paradigms. Amongst them we consider formal modelling theories and techniques that represent in an appropriate and manageable way the structure of the environment itself, as well as the services that apply on it. Focusing on models for services we may say that their structural and dynamic principles must lead to develop systems that provide structural soundness (at the level of construction of hierarchical and non-hierarchical (flat) structures), and dynamic resilience at the level of reusability of their various components for both structural and functional purposes. In this paper we develop a formal multi-agent system based on a ***modal algebra*** by properly extending our previous work [18]. A modal algebra's essential "kernel" consists of its reduct [19] (a reduct of an algebra is an algebra itself having the same carrier, while its operations constitute a subset of the operations' set of the initial algebra) called ***mode***. A mode is *idempotent* and *entropic* (see in section 2). A modal has an additional binary operation aiming (in our system) at modelling concurrent organization of simple or composite services. Moreover, every operation of the mode distributes over this binary operation. We then explore its formal static and dynamic properties and its potential in representing and managing different types of services. In turn, we will not deal with the environment's structure (it is assumed to be given). Central to this multi-agent system are the notions of **(i)** an autonomous software agent, which can be understood as a software unit (the candidate model for this software unit is an "object" in the standard sense from the object-oriented field [11]), **(ii)** a set of flow capabilities that allow various ways of exchanging information among agents, i.e. *(1)* sending or receiving data/methods, *(2)* migrating active

480

agents (threads of execution) to resume their execution elsewhere or *(3)* accessing proxies of agents residing in remote sites. The flow capabilities presuppose the existence of the appropriate infrastructure. The above two building blocks will be used for the development of **(iii)** a multi-agent system that supports complex and dynamically evolving services, i.e. the development of a multi-agent environment including *(a)* autonomous agents, *(b)* simple and composite cooperations (flat structures), and *(c)* coordinations (hierarchical structures). The plexus between cooperations and coordinations constitutes the framework of the various flow capabilities. We use the term coordination as a structural feature of our model. We thus assume that there is a distinction between the process of coordination and its underlying structure in this paper focusing here to the latter. Moreover, in this system we will concentrate in different coordinated flows that can be explicitly defined by the modellers/users in the course of the coordination structures we suggest. Further, we will illustrate them through the development of a simple data mining system and its various algorithmic implementations. Security is considered as a pair of (precondition, postcondition) along the information flows at each algorithmic step. However, further reference on security aspects is out of the scope of this work. The notion of a coordinated flow requires a brief overview of coordination as a generic problem in hierarchical systems. Firstly it was in [14] where a formal theory in hierarchical systems was founded by Mesarovic et al. Within this context the notions of *coordinability* and *coordination* have been established. The requirement to place coordination in a more practical perspective, led groups of scientists in the University of Warsaw, as well as in the University of Minnesota, to study and expose their experiences in various engineering and other problems by using different formal techniques [8]. Concurrently, a more managerial approach on coordination was developed in [13], and further refined in [5] as a framework for managing the interdependencies in a software system consisting of software components where a clear distinction between their functionality as opposed to their interconnection dependencies was considered. Recently, in [1] the authors consider the architectural connectors in software systems as explicit semantic entities defined as protocols where the components participating in every

connection are specified according to their roles (how they interact), while in this sense a connector is represented as an interaction protocol. Moreover, a general framework for hierarchical structures in object-oriented databases was developed in [17] where the links between the different objects are special attributes encapsulated in the adequate objects being dynamically updateable by the object-oriented database management system. This facility on the structural links allows for reusability and dynamic flexibility contributing to the dynamic schema evolution of an object-oriented database. Additionally, for more than one decade, successful coordination models have been developing aiming at supporting concurrent and/or distributed computation and their study has been providing approaches resulting to different models like Linda [9] using a multiset of tuples as its dataspace, Gamma [4] using a reaction condition as its primitive mechanism for coordination, and LO [2] where every agent has its own multiset of resources and output from an agent is broadcasted to all other active agents. Moreover, in IWIM [3], the semantic distinction between computation and communication modules promises to provide (through the latter ones) a pure set of coordination primitives by overcoming the message passing paradigm's drawbacks. Additionally, the emergence of different families of agents (software, intelligent, etc.) has also led to study various coordination techniques on autonomous and/or multi-agent environments [6, 7, 15, 16, 20], and therefore, to suggest how these agents should interrelate and which are the prerequisites of their structure and behavior. This paper is organized as follows: in section 2 we develop the theoretical framework of our model by providing the mode algebra **L**, the modal algebra **M**, their formal properties and functional perspectives. *The above algebras are identical in structure and formal properties as in [19].* We only provide here the specific semantics of the operations that are pertinent to the nature of our model and its entities, while we additionally introduce the notion of a coordinated flow. In section 3, we develop a simple data mining system consisting of autonomous agents interconnected to form a multi-agent system under the operations of **M**. We then explore different ways of implementation of this system. Finally, we conclude in section 4.

2. A modal algebra for modelling a multi-agent system

In this section we will develop the theoretical framework by defining a mode (a universal algebra idempotent and entropic) and a modal algebra (an extension of a mode by a binary operation over which all the operations of the mode distribute). The modal theory has been developed in the works of Romanowska and Smith in [19]. We will include the formal issues of our previous work in [18] aiming at making this paper as self-contained as possible.

2.1. The mode algebra L

Consider a set A (called throughout alphabet) of finitely many autonomous agents. The elements of A will further be written as $\alpha_i^f(s_k), i = 1,2,...,f = 1,2,...$, where the subscript distinguishes the agents, the superscript distinguishes different instantiations of identical agents, and s_k signifies the site in which the agent is currently residing (if no site name is used then it is meant to be the default site of the agent's initial construction, while if the special name "*next*" is used for the site, it refers to the next site to be accessed in the environment where the agents apply). A universal algebra of words L with respect to the alphabet A and the set of operations W in the sense of [10, 12] is denoted by $L = <L, W>$. The carrier L includes the words with respect to A, and W, which are defined inductively as follows: (1) every element of A is a word, (2) for n words $\ell_1,...,\ell_n$ and every n-ary operation $\rho \in W$ we have that the expression $\rho(\ell_1,...,\ell_n)$ is a word, and (3) all the words are constructed only according to (1) and (2). Such a universal algebra is called a *mode* if it is *idempotent* and *entropic*. Idempotent means that every singleton of A constitutes a subalgebra of **L**, while entropic means that every operation in W is a homomorphism. The notion of entropicity, that means "inner turning" is used extensively in the development of the modal theory in [19]. The above properties offer an easy descriptive interpretation: the notion of idempotency expresses the "autonomy" of the agents, i.e. every agent can operate as an autonomous entity and each operation in W does not affect its structure and functionality, while the notion of entropicity ensures that there is sufficient semantic resilience (both at the level of mobility, as well as at the level of composition

for constructing equivalent interaction patterns amongst agents) in order to enable the multi-agent system to function by selecting different alternatives. Whenever the operation defines a hierarchical structure between autonomous agents then we use a special name for it, which appears as a subscript of the operation. The result is then a hierarchical structure with the agents' internal structure included in curly brackets. For cooperation (flat) structures we assume that the default name of the hierarchy is $\varnothing$, i.e. the null hierarchy which generally is not used as a subscript. The empty hierarchy is then denoted by $H\{\}, H \neq \varnothing$, while the simultaneous empty and null hierarchy is by definition $\varnothing\{\}$. The operations in W are unary and binary. They are defined below through the use of the abstract symbols "#" representing any unary operation, and "*" representing any binary operation. We distinguish between the agent that takes the initiative by using square brackets as the first argument of every operation and the agent(s) that will be involved in the cooperation/coordination process according to the semantics of the operation symbol. In the unary operations we obviously have only one agent in square brackets. **(I)** $\#_H : L \to L$, for every $\alpha_i^f(s_k) \in L$, we have $\#_H([\alpha_i^f(s_k)]) = H\{\alpha_i^f(s_k)\}$, **(II)** $*_{H_2}^{H_1} : L \times L \to L$, for every $\alpha_i^f(s_k), \alpha_j^g(s_m) \in L$, we have $*_{H_2}^{H_1}([\alpha_i(s_i)], \alpha_j(s_j)) \equiv H_1\{\alpha_i(s_i)\} * H_2\{\alpha_j(s_j)\}$, is the name of the hierarchical structure, i.e. the agent $\alpha_i^f(s_k)$ takes the initiative to ask from the agent $\alpha_j^g(s_m)$ the service that is specified by the operation symbol "*". For all operations every inadequate selection of arguments either from the agents' or from the hierarchies' point of view will result (if not otherwise specified) to the null hierarchy $\varnothing\{\}$. The agent that takes the initiative will be further called the *motivator*, while the agent that must respond to the action (or service) is called *fellow*. The involved hierarchies define possible flows between the motivator and the fellow through their structures. Omission of a subscript and/or superscript in an operation implies that we refer, by default, to the null hierarchy. The detailed definitions of the operations are:

2.1.1. Unary operations

(I-1) "$-_H$": The motivator takes the initiative to delete the structure that is specified by the hierarchy's

name, i.e. $(-_H([\alpha_i^f(s_k)]) = \varnothing\{\}$. In case that the motivator does not form part of the hierarchy H, the operation gives as result the intact hierarchy.

2.1.2. Binary operations

(II-1) "$\rightarrow$": The motivator takes the initiative to send information to the fellow, i.e.

$$([\alpha_i(s_i)] \rightarrow \alpha_j(s_j)) = \varnothing\{[\alpha_i(s_i)] \rightarrow \alpha_j(s_j)\}$$

(II-2) "$\leftarrow$": The motivator takes the initiative to ask information from the fellow, i.e.

$$([\alpha_i(s_i)] \leftarrow \alpha_j(s_j)) = \varnothing\{[\alpha_i(s_i)] \leftarrow \alpha_j(s_j)\}$$

(II-3) "$\Rightarrow$": The motivator takes the initiative to migrate to the fellow's site, i.e.

$$([\alpha_i(s_i)] \Rightarrow \alpha_j(s_j)) = \varnothing\{[\alpha_i(s_i)] \Rightarrow \alpha_j(s_j)\}$$

(II-4) "$\Leftarrow$": The motivator takes the initiative to ask the fellow to migrate to the motivator's site, i.e. $([\alpha_i(s_i)] \Leftarrow \alpha_j(s_j)) = \varnothing\{\alpha_i(s_i) \Leftarrow \alpha_j(s_i)\}$

(II-5) "$\lrcorner$": The motivator asks for a proxy from the fellow, i.e.

$$([\alpha_i(s_i)]\lrcorner\alpha_j(s_j)) = \varnothing\{\alpha_i(s_i)\lrcorner\alpha_j(s_j)\}$$

(II-6) "$\|$": The motivator takes the initiative to propagate itself, i.e. to create an exact copy which is going to reside in the same site, i.e.

$$([\alpha_i^f(s_k)] \| \alpha_i^g()) = \varnothing\{\alpha_i^f(s_k) \| \alpha_i^g(s_k)\}.$$

Note that two agents where the second has been created by the first by propagation are considered two distinct entities, although they are identical in their structure and they may eventually reside in the same site. The cooperations in this section can also be used taking into account hierarchies as parameters by preserving the algebraic properties.

2.1.3. Binary operations forming coordinations (hierarchical structures)

The following two operations differ from the previous six operations in the sense that they establish hierarchical structures between autonomous agents and consider them under a global name referring to that type of structure. The structural rules (and/or constraints) for the type of hierarchies we will use within the scope of this work are developed in [17] are as follows: **(a)** The operations construct two level hierarchies. At the higher level there is only one agent called representative (REP), while at the lower level there may exist more than one agent. These agents are called components (CO(s)). The communication and therefore the transmission of

information can be bidirectional (REP to CO) and (CO to REP) depending on the specific characterization of the links between every REP and a CO. **(b)** One REP can coordinate more than one COs all of them being in the same hierarchy although this may require (for the proper construction) multiple applications of the hierarchical operations. If in a two level hierarchy there exist more than one CO then these are meant to co-exist in a concurrent way. This adds one more structural constraint below and it will also be shown later in the examples of the operations. Inversely, if two COs have the same REP then they must belong to the same t-l-h. **(c)** The COs in a two level hierarchy are not allowed to be interrelated hierarchically, while their communication is indirect within the hierarchy and always realized through their REP, i.e. (CO1 to CO2) means (CO1 to REP) and (REP to CO2). **(d)** Every REP can be simultaneously a CO for another hierarchy and vice versa, provided that, the rules **a, b,** and **c** hold.

In detail, the binary operations for constructing coordinations are: **(II-6)** "$\otimes_H$": The motivator takes the initiative to establish a coordination structure (two level hierarchy) with the fellow. The fellow will be the representative (REP), while the motivator will participate as the (CO) component:

$$(\alpha_i(s_i) \otimes_H [\alpha_j(s_j)]) = H\{\alpha_j(s_j) \otimes \alpha_i(s_i)\}$$

(II-7) "$\otimes^H$": The motivator takes the initiative to establish a coordination structure (two level hierarchy) with the fellow. The fellow will be the component (CO) while the motivator will be the representative (REP).

$$([\alpha_i(s_i)] \otimes^H \alpha_j(s_j)) = H\{\alpha_i(s_i) \otimes \alpha_j(s_j)\}$$

Important Note: In the case where both superscript and subscript are non-null and mutually unequal, as well as both agents coincide, then we have the case of the vertical composition of existing hierarchies provided that the common agent is both a CO for the subscript's hierarchy, and a REP for the superscript's hierarchy. Otherwise, the hierarchies are non-composable and the result is by default the superscript hierarchy.

Formal properties of the operations of the mode L: We need to stress that the operations are non-commutative, non-associative. However, they are idempotent and entropic. Further, any binary operation between cooperations having as arguments cooperations (and not simply autonomous agents) works according to the following example:

$$[\alpha_i^f(s_k) \rightarrow \alpha_j^g(s_l)] \Rightarrow \alpha_m^h(s_n) \equiv ([\alpha_i^f(s_k)] \rightarrow [\alpha_j^g(s_m)]) \Rightarrow \alpha_m^h(s_n)$$

i.e. the motivator results in assigning the initiative to all the autonomous agents that form part of it.

2.2. The modal algebra M

We will now define the Modal algebra $M = \langle L, W, + \rangle$, where the reduct $\langle L, W \rangle$ of the algebra M is the mode L as defined in 2.1, and every operation in W distributes over the binary operation "+". The operation "+" means concurrent construction of the agent-words, i.e. concurrent organization of the cooperations. In the case where superscript and subscript appear above, we refer to concurrent organization that involves the hierarchies under consideration. *Formal properties of the operation "+"*: The operation "+" is also idempotent, as well as commutative and associative. Every operation of W distributes (both from left and right) over "+".

3. A simple data mining system

We consider a simple system called *"dataminer"*. Its components "surf" a network (whose configuration is already known together with its accessibility rules) and access a distributed (object-oriented) database residing in the network's sites in order to retrieve information that fit a list of keywords. This information is then processed and stored in a personal (object-oriented) database. The system is developed using algorithms whose steps consist of cooperations and/or coordinations formed by the autonomous agents coming out from the analysis phase. We will use the symbol ";" to denote sequence of steps and the expression *while(more){}* for repetition both in italics for readability purposes. Instead, we will not consider error-handling and conditional expressions assuming that both are managed by the steps internally. Additionally we will introduce high-level security units as pre- and post-conditions with no further details.

3.1. Dataminer's analysis

The dataminer consists of a number of application and security primitives modelled as autonomous agents. These (application primitives) are the following agents: (i) retriever (RT), (ii) semantic-analyzer (SA), (iii) redundancy-minimizer or refiner (RF), We also consider that there has to be (iv) the dataminer (DM) itself., while the personal (object-oriented) database can also be modelled as an agent (PDB). The security primitives are (i) encrypt (ENC) and (ii) decrypt (DEC). They do not constitute autonomous agents. Instead they are used as preconditions and postconditions along the flows of the various cooperations. With no loss of generality, we assume that the distributed (object-oriented) database constituting the repository from which we apply the data mining process can also be considered as an autonomous agent (DDB).

3.2. Dataminer's coordinations

Different alternatives appear for constructing the multi-agent system. These depend mainly on issues that take into account decentralization and performance criteria. Moreover the propagation capabilities of the model allows to dynamically construct new cooperations/coordinations and direct them to the sites of the network. This contributes to the decentralization of the services in combination with their concurrent organization in order to improve performance. We will provide here two design approaches (not necessarily the best ones) and their respective coordinations in order to develop certain algorithms for every approach each encompassing different capabilities as direct consequences of the model. In the algorithms the cooperations will appear as algorithmic steps, while the coordinations play the role that is analogous to the declaration section of most programming languages. There is also possibility to apply concurrent structures at every step. In figure 1 below, we illustrate the coordinations that correspond to the design approaches we adopt. Note, once more, that the default site "()" expresses the site where the cooperation currently resides. In this sense any sequence of the type $X() \Rightarrow X(next); X() \rightharpoonup Y()$; means that X migrates from its current site to the next site of the environment. Then X being residing in the new site asks for a proxy of Y (from its own current site) to become available.

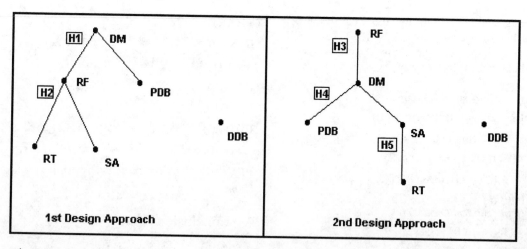

1st Design Approach   **2nd Design Approach**

Figure 1. In the 1st design approach we have the following coordinations: $([DM()] \otimes^{H1} (RF() + PDB(s_1)) = H1\{DM() \otimes (RF() + PDB()\}$, $([RF()] \otimes^{H2} (RT() + SA()) = H2\{RF() \otimes (RT() + SA()\}$ Note that the vertical composition of the coordinations denoted by $\otimes_{H2}^{H1} ([RF()], RF())$, is used to specify coordinated flows. In the 2nd design we have the coordinations:

$([RF()] \otimes^{H3} DM()] = H3\{RF() \otimes DM()\}$ $([DM()] \otimes^{H4} (PDB(s_1) + SA()) = (H4\{DM() \otimes (PDB(s_1) + SA())\}$, and

$([SA() \otimes^{H5} R()] = H5\{SA() \otimes RT()\}$. Note also that the overall vertical composition of the coordinations H3, H4, and H5 is also used to specify coordinated flows.

An algorithm for the 1st design approach is:

start

/* coordinations' declarations*/

$([DM()] \otimes^{H_1} (RF() + PDB(s_1)) =$
$H_1\{DM() \otimes (RF() + PDB()\}$;

$([RF()] \otimes^{H_2} (RT() + SA()) =$
$H_2\{RF() \otimes (RT() + SA()\}$;

while (more) {

$H_2\{\}()^{ENC(H_2\{\})} \Rightarrow^{DEC(H_2\{\})} H_2\{\}(next)$;

$RT()^{DEC(\text{data-set})} \leftarrow^{ENC(\text{data-set})} DDB()$;

$H_2(RT())^{ENC(\text{data-set})} \rightarrow^{DEC(\text{data-set})} SA()$;

$H_2(SA())^{ENC(\text{data-set})} \rightarrow^{DEC(\text{data-set})} RF()$;

$DM()^{DEC(\text{data-set})} \leftarrow^{ENC(\text{data-set})} PDB()$;

$H_1(DM())^{ENC(\text{data-set})} \rightarrow^{DEC(\text{data-set})} RF()$;

$H_1(RF())^{ENC(\text{data-set})} \rightarrow^{DEC(\text{data-set})} DM()$;

$DM()^{ENC(\text{data-set})} \rightarrow^{DEC(\text{data-set})} PDB()$;

}end

A second algorithm of the 1st design approach, that aims at improving performance, is to propagate the coordination $H_2\{\}$ and send it concurrently to all the adjacent nodes of the network for information retrieval. The algorithm is:

start

/* coordinations' declarations*/

$([DM()] \otimes^{H_1} (RF() + PDB(s_1)) =$
$H_1\{DM() \otimes (RF() + PDB()\}$;

$([RF()] \otimes^{H_2} (RT() + SA()) =$
$H_2\{RF() \otimes (RT() + SA()\}$;

while (more) {
while (more adjacent nodes) {

$H_2\{\} \parallel (H_2^1\{\} + \dots + H_2^n\{\})$;

$H_2^1\{\}()^{ENC(H_2^1\{\})} \Rightarrow^{DEC(H_2^1\{\})} H_2^1\{\}(next) +$

$\dots + H_2^n\{\}()^{ENC(H_2^n\{\})} \Rightarrow^{DEC(H_2^n\{\})} H_2^n\{\}(next)$;

$RT()^{DEC(\text{data-set})} \leftarrow^{ENC(\text{data-set})} DDB() + \dots$

$+ RT()^{DEC(\text{data-set})} \leftarrow^{ENC(\text{data-set})} DDB()$;

$H_2^1(RT())^{ENC(\text{data-set})} \rightarrow^{DEC(\text{data-set})} SA() + \dots$

$+ H_2^n(RT())^{ENC(\text{data-set})} \rightarrow^{DEC(\text{data-set})} SA()$;

$H_2^1(SA())^{ENC(\text{data-set})} \rightarrow^{DEC(\text{data-set})} RF() + \dots$

$+ H_2^n(SA())^{ENC(\text{data-set})} \rightarrow^{DEC(\text{data-set})} RF()$;

$DM()^{DEC(\text{data-set})} \leftarrow^{ENC(\text{data-set})} PDB()$;

$H_1(DM())^{ENC(\text{data-set})} \rightarrow^{DEC(\text{data-set})} RF() + \dots$

$+ H_1(DM())^{ENC(\text{data-set})} \rightarrow^{DEC(\text{data-set})} RF()$;

$H_1(RF())^{ENC(\text{data-set})} \rightarrow^{DEC(\text{data-set})} DM()$;

$DM()^{ENC(\text{data-set})} \rightarrow^{DEC(\text{data-set})} PDB()$;

}}end

The suggested algorithm for the 2nd design approach propagates and sends RT() to all adjacent nodes. Thus the retrieval process is carried out in a concurrent way.

start

/* coordinations' declarations*/

$([RF()] \otimes^{H_3} DM()] = H_3\{RF() \otimes DM()\}$;

$([DM()] \otimes^{H_4} (PDB(s_1) + SA()) =$

$H_4\{DM() \otimes (PDB(s_1) + SA())\}$;

$([SA() \otimes^{H_5} RT()] = H_5\{SA() \otimes RT()\}$;

while (more) {

while (more adjacent nodes) {

$RT() \| (RT^1() + ... + RT^n())$;

$RT^1()^{ENC(RT^1())} \Rightarrow^{DEC(RT^1())} RT^1(next) +$

$... + RT^n()^{ENC(RT^n())} \Rightarrow^{DEC(RT^n())} RT^n(next)$;

$RT^1()^{DEC(data-set-1)} \leftarrow^{ENC(data-set-1)} DDB() +$

$... + RT^n()^{DEC(data-set-n)} \leftarrow^{ENC(data-set-n)} DDB()$;

$H_5(RT^1())^{ENC(data-set-1)} \rightarrow^{DEC(data-set-1)} SA() + ...$

$+ H_5(RT^n()^{ENC(data-set-n)} \rightarrow^{DEC(data-set-n)} SA()$;

$H_5(SA())^{ENC(data-sets)} \rightarrow$

$\rightarrow^{DEC(data-sets)} DM() + H_4(PDB()) \rightarrow DM()$;

$H_3(DM())\rightarrow RF())$;

$H_3(DM())^{ENC(data-sets)} \rightarrow^{DEC(data-sets)} PDB()$;

}}end

Yet another algorithm for the 2nd design approach propagates and sends the composite coordination $H_4 \otimes H_5$ to all the adjacent nodes by thus decentralizing the retrieving and semantic analysis processes to run on the nodes themselves, and the DMs' activities.

start

/* coordinations' declarations*/

$([RF()] \otimes^{H_3} DM()] = H_3\{RF() \otimes DM()\}$;

$([DM()] \otimes^{H_4} (PDB(s_1) + SA()) =$

$H_4\{DM() \otimes (PDB(s_1) + SA())\}$;

$([SA() \otimes^{H_5} RT()] = H_5\{SA() \otimes RT()\}$;

while (more) {

while (more adjacent nodes) {

$H_4 \otimes H_5\{\} \| (H_4 \otimes H_5^1\{\} + ... + H_4 \otimes H_5^n\{\})$;

$H_4 \otimes H_5^1\{\}() \Rightarrow H_4 \otimes H_5^1\{\}(next) + ...$

$+ H_4 \otimes H_5^n\{\}() \Rightarrow H_4 \otimes H_5^n\{\}(next)$;

$RT^1()^{DEC(data-set-1)} \leftarrow^{ENC(data-set-1)} DDB() + ...$

$+ RT^n()^{DEC(data-set-n)} \leftarrow^{ENC(data-set-n)} DDB()$;

$H_5^1(RT())^{ENC(data-set-1)} \rightarrow^{DEC(data-set-1)} SA() + ...$

$+ H_5^n(RT())^{ENC(data-set-n)} \rightarrow^{DEC(data-set-n)} SA()$;

$H_5^1(SA())^{ENC(data-sets)} \rightarrow^{DEC(data-sets)} DM() +$

$... + H_4^1(DM())^{DEC(data)} \leftarrow^{ENC(data)} PDB()$;

$H_5^n(SA())^{ENC(data-sets)} \rightarrow^{DEC(data-sets)} DM() +$

$H_4^n(DM())^{DEC(data)} \leftarrow^{ENC(data)} PDB()$;

$H_4^1(DM())^{ENC(data-set-1)} \rightarrow^{DEC(data-set-1)} RF()) +$

$... + H_4^n(DM())^{ENC(data-set-n)} \rightarrow^{DEC(data-set-n)} RF()$;

$RF()^{ENC(ref.-data-set)} \rightarrow^{DEC(ref.-data-set)} PDB()$;

}}end

4. Conclusions

In this paper a formal multi-agent system was developed based on a modal algebra **M**. Alternative ways of composing the same set of simple (autonomous) agents in forming cooperations (flat structures) and coordinations (hierarchical structures) was shown to be one of the strong points of this approach, as well as the dynamic management through the operations of **M** (different capabilities in defining coordinated flows) that provide a flexible framework for resolving problems in distributed and/or mobile environments. Algorithmic examples were given for a simple data mining system illustrating the potential of our approach and the flexibility in exploring more than one solution for a given problem.

References

[1] Allen R., Garlan R., *A Formal Basis for Architectural Connection*, ACM Transactions in Software Engineering, Vol. 6, No. 3, pp213-249, 1997.

[2] Andreoli J.M., Ciancarini P., Pareschi R., *Interaction Abstract Machines*, in Research directions in Concurrent Object-Oriented Programming, MIT Press, 1993.

[3] Arbab F. et al, *Reusable Coordinator Modules for Massively Concurrent Applications*, Software Practice and Experience, Vol. 28, No. 7, pp703-735, 1998.

[4] Banatre J., Metayer D.L., *Programming by Multiset Transformation*, Communications of the ACM, Vol. 36, No 1, pp98-111, 1993.

[5] Dellarocas C., *A Coordination Perspective on Software System Design*, in Proc. of the 9th International Conference on Software Engineering and Knowledge Engineering (SEKE97), pp569-578, 1997.

[6] Durfee E.H., Montgomery T.A., *Coordination as Distributed Search in a Hierarchical Behavior Space*, IEEE Transactions on Systems, Man, and Cybernetics, Vol. 21, No. 6, pp-1363-1378, 1991.

[7] Ferguson I.A., *Integrated Control and Coordinated Behavior: a Case for Agent Models*, IEEE Computer, pp203-218, 1995.

[8] Findeisen W., et al, *Control and Coordination in Hierarchical Systems*, Wiley IIASA International Series on Applied Systems Analysis, No. 9, John Wiley & Sons, 1980.

[9] Gelertner D., *Generative Communication in Linda*, ACM Transactions on Prog. Languages and Systems, Vol. 7, No. 1, pp80-112, 1985.

[10] Gratzer G., *Universal Algebra*, D. Van Nostrand Company, Inc., 1968.

[11] Henderson-Sellers B., Edwards J., *Book Two of Object-Oriented Knowledge: The Working Object*, Prentice Hall Object-Oriented Series, 1994.

[12] Kurosh A. G., *General Algebra*, Chelsea Publishing Company, 1963.

[13] Malone T.W., Crowston K, *The Interdisciplinary Study of Coordination*, ACM Computing Surveys, Vol. 26, No. 1, 1994.

[14] Mesarovic M.D., Macko D., Takahara Y., *Theory of Hierarchical, Multilevel Systems*, Academic Press New York and London, 1970.

[15] Murthy V.K., *Transactional Programming for Distributed Agent Systems*, IEEE Computer, pp64-71, 1996.

[16] Okada R., Lee E-S, Shiratori N., *Agent-based Approach for Information Gathering on Highly Distributed and Heterogeneous Environment*, Proc. of the International Conference on Parallel and Distributed Systems (ICPADS 96), pp80-87, 1996.

[17] Patsouris P.A., *Two-level-hierarchies of Objects: A Unit of Reference for Distributed Object-Oriented Databases*, Proc. of the International Conference on Parallel and Distributed Systems (ICPADS 96), Tokyo, 3-6 June, pp466-471, 1996.

[18] Patsouris P.A., *Algebraic Modelling of an Ad Hoc Network for Mobile Computing*, Proc. of the 19th ICPP '98 Workshops: "Wireless Networks and Mobile Computing", pp141-123, 1998.

[19] Romanowska A.B., Smith J.D.H, *Modal Theory, An Algebraic Approach to Order, Geometry, and Convexity*, R&E Research and Exposition in Mathematics, Heldermann Verlag Berlin, 1983.

[20] Zlotkin G., Rosenschein J.S., *Cooperation and Conflict Resolution via Negotiation among Autonomous Agents in Noncooperative Domains*, IEEE Transactions on Systems, Man, and Cybernetics, Vol. 21, No. 6, pp1317-1324, 1991.

Session A8

Mobile Computing

Chair: Sajal Das
University of North Texas, USA

Mobility Tolerant Maintenance of Multi-cast Tree in Mobile Multi-hop Radio Networks

Sandeep K. S. Gupta and Pradip K. Srimani

Department of Computer Science

Colorado State University

Ft. Collins, CO 80523

Abstract

When the nodes in a mobile ad hoc network move, existing links often no longer exist and/or new links are created. Any communication protocol designed for such multi-hop ad hoc networks must be able to tolerate such change in network topology that can occur anywhere in the network. Another characteristics of such networks is that bandwidth is a comparatively precious resource and needs to be conserved. Our purpose in the present paper is to explore the possibilities of applying the relatively new paradigm of self-stabilization in distributed fault tolerant algorithm design to tackle the problem of topology change in mobile networks. Self-stabilizing distributed algorithms converge to a global legitimate state in presence of any number of intermittent faults and still use only local knowledge for actions at each node. Our objective is to view the topology change as a change in the node adjacency information at one or more nodes and utilize the tools of self-stabilization to converge to a stable global state in the new network graph. We illustrate the concept by designing a new efficient distributed algorithm for multi-cast in a mobile network that can accommodate any change in the network topology due to node mobility.

1 Introduction

Mobile ad hoc networks are being increasingly used for military operations, law enforcement, rescue missions, virtual class rooms, and local area networks. A mobile multi-hop network consists of n identical mobile hosts (nodes) with unique ids $1, \ldots, n$. These mobile hosts communicate among each other via a packet radio network. When a node transmits (broadcasts) a message, the nodes in the *coverage area* of the sender can simultaneously receive the message. A node i is called a *neighbor* of node j in the network if node j is in the *coverage area* of node i. This relationship is time varying since the nodes can and do move. At any given time a

node i can correctly receive a message from one of its neighbors, say j, iff j is the only neighbor of i transmitting at that time. A multiple access protocol is used by a nodes to get contention-free access to the wireless channel. Since, a limited communication bandwidth is shared between several neighboring nodes the available communication bandwidth between any two neighboring nodes depends upon number of nodes in the vicinity and their communication activity. Further, since nodes are battery-powered they can go to sleep in order to conserve battery power. Hence, in mobile ad hoc network i) old links fail and new links are formed over time due to node movement ii) nodes can be unreachable since they may go to sleep iii) the bandwidth available on a (logical) link between two neighboring nodes varies with time, and iv) the topology may get disconnected.

Multi-cast is an important group communication primitive; it involves sending a message to an arbitrary subset of nodes in the network. It is useful in a large number of applications in a distributed system, where a set of nodes need be informed of a specific event. Multi-cast protocols for distributed systems with a static network have been widely studied. Multi-cast protocols are evaluated in terms of bandwidth consumed in the entire process. A multi-cast message can be send to each member of the multi-cast group separately; this wastes bandwidth since the message may be repeatedly sent over the same communication link. Conceptually, this wastage can be avoided by constructing a minimal cost tree spanning only the members of the multi-cast group in the entire network graph and then forwarding the message from the root of the tree (source of the message) along the tree edges. Unfortunately, the problem of computing the minimal cost multi-cast tree spanning an arbitrary number of nodes (members of the multi-cast group) in a given weighted graph is NP-complete [1]; hence, people have concentrated on designing heuristic algorithms for designing near optimal multi-cast trees for given multi-cast groups and analyzing their performance. All these studies are made under the assumption that the underlying network topology does not change.

Recently, several protocols for delivering multi-cast messages in mobile networks have been developed [2, 3]. These works are also based on the assumption that the node mobility does not alter the network topology, i.e., mobile hosts can directly communicate to the fixed mobile switching stations, which are connected by fixed wired network. Multi-hop radio or the so called ad-hoc [4, 5, 6] networks present another dimension of complexity in the sense that node movements do change the network topology and any protocol for multi-cast or broadcast must provide mechanism to ensure delivery of messages to the recipients even when the topology changes during the process. The constraint of bandwidth conservation becomes even more stringent especially when multiple multi-cast groups are present in the system. Several routing mechanisms for unicast messages in ad-hoc networks have been developed [7, 8]. Chlamtac and Kutten [4] describe a tree based broadcasting in multi-hop radio networks. A general framework for developing reliable group communication primitives is given in [9]. The "best effort" multi-cast algorithm in [10] algorithm does not guarantee reliability in the sense that messages may be lost if the topology changes during multi-casting of a message. This method is suitable when the rate of topology change is low. Pagani and Rossi have presented a reliable broadcast algorithm in [6] which is also based on underlying multi-cluster multi-hop packet network [5, 11].

Our purpose in the present paper is to propose a new distributed algorithm to maintain the multi-cast tree in a given radio network for a given multi-cast group; our algorithm is fault tolerant (reliable) in the sense that the algorithm automatically can detect occasional link failures and/or new link creations in the network (due to mobility of the hosts) and can readjust the multi-cast tree. Our approach is to use the relatively new paradigm for distributed fault tolerance, e.g., *self-stabilization* to design the fault tolerant multi-cast tree computation algorithm and thereby to investigate the appropriateness of this paradigm (and thus to use the various algorithms therein) to solve the problems associated with mobile networks (dynamic topology or graph).

2 Mobility Tolerance and Self-Stabilization

2.1 Self-stabilizing Distributed Systems

Self-stabilization is a relatively new way of looking at system fault tolerance, especially it provides a "built-in-safeguard" against "transient failures" that might corrupt the data in a distributed system. The objective of

self-stabilization is (as opposed to mask faults; the common approach to design the fault tolerant systems is to mask the effects of the fault) to recover from failure in a reasonable time and without intervention by any external agency. One of the goals of a distributed system is that the system should function correctly in spite of intermittent faults. In other words, the global state of the system should ideally remain in the legitimate state. Often, due to node failures or other perturbations, the global state of a distributed system is in some illegitimate state, and is desirable that it reaches the legitimate state without the interference of an external agency. Systems that reach a legitimate state starting from any illegitimate state in a finite number of steps are called self-stabilizing systems [12, 13]. Recently there has been a spurt of research in designing self-stabilizing distributed graph algorithms for many applications; a good survey of self-stabilizing algorithms can be found in [14].

2.2 Mobility Tolerant Multi-cast Tree

In our context of computing a multi-cast tree in a network with dynamic topology, we see that each node maintains an adjacency set (set of the nodes adjacent to it). In absence of any mobility, these adjacency sets are constant. When any node moves sufficiently enough to change the network topology, the adjacency set of at least one node has changed. Note that it is neither possible nor necessary that each node of the system will be aware of this change. In this paper, we assume that the graph is edge-weighted, i.e., each edge is assigned a *unique* nonzero positive weight. In a mobile network when a new link comes up, we assume that the system can determine the edge weight (depending on available bandwidth, .. etc.). This assumption of uniqueness of the edge weights is for convenience of description only; if the edge weights are not unique, lexicographic information can be easily added to make them unique [15]. The proposed algorithm constructs the multi-cast tree in three logical stages. First, it computes the minimal spanning tree (MST) of the new topology; second, it establishes the unique path from each node to the root node (the source node for the multi-cast message) by establishing a predecessor pointer for each node in the tree; third, it determines for each node if the node needs to further propagate the multi-cast message down the tree based on the multi-cast group membership of its successors in the tree. The following features of the algorithm are to be noted: (1) the multi-cast tree maintained by the algorithm is not the minimal multi-cast tree; it simply prunes the MST of the topology to include the necessary nodes to propagate the message all group members; (2) whenever there is a topology change due to mobility of the nodes, the algorithm is automatically kicked in (without the need of intervention by any external agency) to construct the new minimal spanning tree of the graph and the subsequent pruning operations. It takes finite amount of time for the system to stabilize to the new tree, nodes may further move during that time, but the mobility rates are low enough to allow the system to stabilize before the next move; (3) the entire process is distributed in nature; no central coordination is necessary.

3 Assumptions for the System Model

We make the following assumptions about the system.

- A data link layer protocol at each node i maintains the identities of its neighbors in some list $neighbors(i)$. This data link protocol also resolves any contention for the shared medium by supporting logical links between neighbors and ensures that a message sent over a correct (or functioning) logical link is correctly received by the node at the other end of that link. The link layer protocol informs the upper layer of any creation/deletion of logical links using the *neighbor discovery protocol* described below.

- Each node periodically (at intervals of t_b) broadcasts a *beacon* message. This forms the basis of *neighbor discovery protocol*. When a node i receives the beacon signal from a node j which is not in its neighbors list $neighbors(i)$, it adds j to its neighbors list (data structure $neighbors_i$ at node i), thus establishing link (i,j). For each link (i,j), node i maintains a timer t_{ij} for each of its neighbors j. If node i does not receive a beacon signal from neighbor j in time t_b, it assumes that link (i,j) is no longer available and removes j from its neighbor set. Upon receiving a beacon signal from neighbor j, node i resets its appropriate timer.

- When a node j sends a beacon message to any of its neighbors, say node i, it includes some additional information in the message that are used by node i to compute the cost of the link (i,j) as well as other information regarding the state of the node j, as used in the algorithm.

- The links between two adjacent nodes are always bidirectional.

- The topology of the ad-hoc network is modeled by a (undirected) graph $G = (V, E)$, where V is the set of nodes and E is the set of links between neighboring nodes[1]. Since the nodes are mobile, the network topology changes with time. We assume that no node leaves the system and no new node joins the system; we also assume that transient link failures are handled by the link layer protocol by using timeouts, retransmission, and per hop acknowledgment. Thus, the network graph has always the same node set but different edge sets.

4 Fault Tolerant Multi-cast Tree Protocol

4.1 The General Approach

Our protocol for fault tolerant maintenance of the multi-cast tree for a given source node (we call it root node r) and its multi-cast group consists of 3 logical steps: (1) construction of the minimal spanning tree (MST) of the mobile network graph in presence of topology change due to node mobility; (2) once the MST stabilizes for the new topology, rooting the MST with respect to the given source node of the multi-cast message (establishing unique parent pointer for each node in the MST); (3) pruning from the MST the nodes that are not needed to send the message to the multi-cast group members.

(1) MST of the Network in Presence of Topology Change

Our purpose is to design a *distributed* algorithm to construct the MST of a given weighted graph; the requirement is that when the topology changes, the algorithm will be automatically kicked in and the system will recompute the new MST of the changed topology. As stated earlier, whenever there is a change in topology of the network, at least node will be aware of that fact in the sense that the set of neighbor nodes for that node will change. We use similar concepts as developed in the self-stabilizing MST construction in a symmetric graph [16]. The minimal spanning tree (MST) of the graph is defined to be a spanning tree of the graph such that the sum of the weights of the edges in the tree is less than or equal to that for all possible spanning trees of the graph.

Remark 1 *If the weights $\{w_{ij}\}$ of a graph are unique (distinct), the graph has a unique MST [17].*

To design a mobility tolerant algorithm for the MST of a graph, we introduce a new characterization of any path in a given graph.

Definition 1 *α-cost of any path from node i to j is defined to be the maximum of the weights of the edges belonging to the path. $Mcost_{ij}$ is defined as the minimum*

---

[1]Note that all links are bidirectional.

cost among the α-cost of all possible paths between the nodes i and j.

Remark 2 *We call the path, along which $Mcost_{ij}$ is defined, to be the minimum-α path between nodes i and j; this should not be confused with the traditional shortest path between nodes i and j. The shortest path is defined to be the path of minimum length where the length of a path is the sum of the weights of the edges on the path. Most significant difference between the two metrics, α-cost and length, of a path, assuming nonzero positive edge weights, is that when a path is augmented by an additional edge, length must increase while α-cost may remain constant.*

Remark 3 *Consider a graph G with unique edge weights. An edge (i, j) is in the unique MST if and only if $Mcost_{ij} = w_{ij}$ [15]. for details of the proof, see [15].*

We use Remark 1 and Remark 3 to develop our algorithm for MST construction. First, we can safely assume the edge weights to be unique; this is no restriction since if not, we can easily add lexicographic information to make them unique [15]. Second, if a distributed algorithm can compute the α_{ij} values for all nodes, we can add an additional data structure $Tree\_Neighbors_i$ at each node i that keeps track of the MST edges incident on node i, i.e., $Tree\_Neighbors_i = \{k|\ the\ edge\ e_{ik} \in MST\}$. Computing α_{ij} values for all nodes is not similar to the all pairs shortest path problem since the metric α-cost does not have the desirable properties of the metric length (see Remark 2); in order for the algorithm to stabilize, we need to have additional data structures $Mcost_i$ at each node to keep track of the minimal α-cost paths from node i to every other node in the graph. The details of the pseudo-code of the algorithm and the different events are described in the next section.

(2) Rooting the MST at the Multi-cast Source r

Once the MST has stabilized, we need to root the MST at the multi-cast source node r. When the MST has stabilized, each node i knows its neighbors in the MST (the data structure $Tree\_Neighbors_i$ keeps track of that information). In order to root the MST at r, we use two variables $Level_i$ and $Parent_i$ at each node i. The node r knows it is the source node and hence it unilaterally sets its $Level_r$ at 0 and makes its $Parent_r$ Null to indicate that it is the root node. Every other node i looks at all of its neighbors in the MST and sets its $Level_r$ value at one plus the minimum of the Level values of its tree neighbors and accordingly sets its parent pointer $Parent_i$.

(3) Pruning the MST to Build the Multi-cast Tree

The multi-cast source node r needs to send the message to the members of the arbitrary multi-cast group.

Each node in the network knows whether it is a member of the multi-cast group (IS_Member_i is true). In the rooted MST, each node i can determine if it is a leaf node in the MST (size of the $Tree\_Neighbors_i$ is 1) and if node i does not belong to the multi-cast group, it sets its $Flag_i$ variable to 0; otherwise 1. Any other node i (i is not a leaf node in the MST) will look at all its successors in the MST and will set its $Flag_i$ to 1 iff at least one of its successors either has a Flag of 1 or is a member of the multi-cast group or node i is a member of the the multi-cast group. When this process stabilizes, each node i, when it receives the multi-cast message from its parent in the tree, knows that it needs to forward the message to its successors if $Flag_i$ is 1. Note that the nodes with $Flag_i$ value 1 constitute the multi-cast tree (although not all the nodes in the multi-cast tree are necessarily members of the multi-cast group).

4.2 Description of the Algorithm

Each node i executes in an event driven mode – it executes the main procedure. There are 2 different types of messages in the system as described in subsequent subsections; the actions initiated by the nodes in response to different events are also described as the set of events.

4.2.1 Data Structures

We assume there are n nodes (mobile hosts) in the system; the nodes are numbered 1 through n. There is one designated node r which is to be the root of the multi-cast tree (source of the multi-cast message). MAX is a large positive constant greater than the sum of the edge weights in the graph. Each node i in the system maintains the following local data structures:

- $neighbors_i$: A set of node identifiers denoting the immediate neighbors of node i.

- Is_member_i: A Boolean variable; the value Is_member_i is true if node i is a member of the given multi-cast group otherwise it is false.

- $W_i[\ ]$: An array of positive real numbers. The value $W_i[j]$ is the edge weight of the link (i, j) where $j \in neighbors_i$.

- $Mcost_i[1 : n]$: An array of positive real numbers; $Mcost_i[j]$ is the current estimate of the minimum α-cost path from node i to j. Initially, $Mcost_i[i] = 0$ and $Mcost_i[j] = MAX$ for all $j \neq i$.

- $mcost_{ij}[1 : n]$ ($j \in neighbors_i$): A set of n-tuples; for each $j \in neighbors_i$, $mcost_{ij}$ is a copy of the array $Mcost_j[1 : n]$ as stored at node i.

- $Hops_i[1 : n]$: An array of positive integers; $Hops_i[j]$ is the number of hops in the minimum α-cost path between node i and j as currently known to node i. $Hops_i[j] = n$ for any j indicates that node i currently does not know of any path between i and j. Initially, $Hops_i[i] = 0$ and $Mcost_i[j] = n$ for all $j \neq i$.

- $hops_{ij}[1 : n]$ ($j \in neighbors_i$): set of n-tuples; for each $j \in neighbors_i$, $hops_{ij}$ is the local copy of $Hops_j[1 : n]$ as stored at node i.

- $Tree\_Neighbors_i$: A set of node identifiers denoting the neighbors of node i are also its neighbors in the MST.

- $Parent_i$: A node identifier; $Parent_i = k$ if node k is the parent of node i in the multi-cast tree with node r as the root node), otherwise $Parent_i = NULL$. Initially, $Parent_i = NULL$.

- $Children_i$: A set of node ids; $Children_i$ is the set of node i in the multi-cast tree.

- $Level_i$: A positive integer that denotes the level of node i in the multi-cast tree rooted at node r (the core node of the multi-cast tree.

- $level_i[1..j]$: An array to keep a local copy at node i the values of $Levl_j$ for each node $j \in neighbors_i$.

- $Flag_i$: A boolean flag which is true when the node i needs to forward a multi-cast message down to its children in the multi-cast tree.

- $flag_i[1..j]$: An array to keep a local copy at node i the values of $Flag_i$ for each node $j \in neighbors_i$.

- MH_Set_i: A set of triplets of the form (k, m, h). An element (k, m, h), where $m = Mcost_i[k]$ and $h = Hops_i[k]$ is included in set MH_Set_i if either $Mcost_i[k]$ or $Hops_i[k]$ changed since node i broadcasted the last BEACON message. In case node i has a new neighbor since it last BEACON message, it includes $(k, Mcost_i[k], Hops_i[k])$, $1 \leq k \leq n$, in the $MHset_i$. Node i includes the MH_Set in its BEACON messages. After sending out a BEACON message it sets the $MH\_Set_i = \emptyset$.

4.2.2 Message Types

- **BEACON** (i, MH_SET, LEVEL, FLAG, MEM-BER) — is the beacon message from node i; MH_SET is a set of triplets (k, m, h) where $1 \leq$

$k \leq n$, $m = Mcost_i[k]$ and $h = Hops_i[k]$; $LEVEL = Level_i$; $FLAG = Flag_i$; and $MEMBER = Is\_Member_i$.

- **MULTICAST** (m) — indicates that the sender wants to propagate the message m down the multi-cast tree.

4.2.3 System Primitives

The following primitives are used in the pseudo code given in the next subsection. They are used to simplify the presentation of the algorithm and their functions are described below.

- **set_timer** $(timer, t)$: sets the timer $timer$ for time t. If the timer expires without being reset, the event "$timer$ expired" is generated.

- **compute_link_weight** (i, j): computes the weight of link (i, j) based on factors such as the contention a node is experience in communicating with it neighbors, signal-to-noise ratio etc.

- **Add** $(mh\_set, (k, m, h))$: adds the triplet (k, m, h) to the set mh_set. Add() ensures that (k, m, h) is the only triplet in the set with the first component as k. Hence, before adding (k, m, h) to mh_set, Add() deletes any triplet with the first component as k from mh_set.

4.2.4 Events

Node i wants to Multi-cast a Message: When a node wants to multi-cast message m it sends a MULTICAST(i, m) to the core node r of the multi-cast group.

Node i receives MULTICAST message: When a node receives a MULTICAST(j, m) messages it broadcasts it to nodes in $Children_i$ if the value of $Flag_i$ is true.

Beacon timer expired: When the beacon timer expires node i broadcasts BEACON$(i, MH\_Set_i, Level_i, Flag_i)$ to its neighbors and sets $MH\_Set_i = \emptyset$.

Node i receives a BEACON message: When a node receives a beacon message BEACON$(j, MH\_SET, LEVEL, FLAG)$ from another node j it invokes procedure process_beacon_msgs(). If this is a message from a node whose id is not currently in $neighbors_i$ then this indicated that a new node has moved to the vicinity of node i. The procedure $Link\_Established$ is invoked to update the $neighbors_i$ set. Node i then sets the expiration timer for link (i, j) and computes the weight $W_i[j]$ of link (i, j). Then it updates $mcost_{ij}[k]$ and

$hops_{ij}[k]$ using (k, m, h) in the MH_SET and recomputes $Mcost_i[k]$ and $Hops_i[k]$ using the procedure compute_mhcost().

After processing all the triplets in the MH_SET, node i determines its new level in the multi-cast tree rooted at node r and the its parent in this rooted tree. Node i computes its level to be one plus the minimum level of all its tree neighbors. Further, the parent node of i is the node which has the minimum level among its tree neighbors. Once node i has determined its parent node $Parent_i$ in the rooted multi-cast tree, it determines its children set $Children_i$. Lastly it computes the new value of $Flag_i$ by OR-ing the $flag_{ij}$ values of all its neighbors and its Is_Member_i value.

New link to node j established: When node i comes to know the existence of a new link to node j, it invokes the procedure Link_Established. This procedure adds id of node j to $Neighbors_i$ set and adds triplets $(k, Mcost_i[k], Hops_i[k])$ for all $1 \le k \le n$ so that node j can learn about the $Mcost_i[]$ and $Hops_i[]$ from the node i's next BEACON message.

Failure of link to node j: In case the timer for link (i, j) expires, node i assumes that link to node j has been lost. In this event node i invokes procedure Link_Failed(). This procedure removes the id of node j from $Negihbor_i$, $Tree\_Neighbors_i$, and $Childern_i$ sets. Further, if node j was its parent node in the multi-cast tree, it sets $Parent_i = NULL$. Node i recomputes $Mcost_i[k]$ for each node k in the system and determines its current neighbors in the MST, $Tree\_Neighbors_i$.

5 Correctness of the Algorithm

The correctness of the proposed algorithm follows from the correctness of the underlying three processes: stabilization of the MST reconstruction process when there is any change in the topology (due to failure of an existing link or creation of a new link caused by mobility of the nodes: (2) once the MST is stabilized, convergence or stabilization of the process of rooting the MST at the multi-cast source node; (3) stabilization of the process of properly setting of the $Flag_i$ variable at each node i to indicate if the multi-cast message needs to be further propagated down to the successors of node i.

Stabilization of the MST construction process directly follows from the correctness proof of the algorithm described in [16]. It is to be noted that the data structures at each node as well as the actions taken by each node in [16] and in the current algorithm are identical; the only exception is that the algorithm in [16] operates in a shared memory paradigm while the proposed algorithm works in a distributed message passing paradigm in the sense that each node first collects the

information about the local states of its neighbors (by making local copies at the node) and then takes necessary action to change its own local state. We should also note that it has been shown in [16] that the algorithm converges to the new MST after any transient failure (change of topology in our case here) in finite amount of time; no analysis was presented in [16] regarding time needed to stabilize after each change. In the present context, we claim that the system will converge to a new MST after each topology change in finite time; but, we also need to evaluate the average time needed for the system to do that in order the algorithm to be useful in real life application. We present some preliminary experimental results (via simulation) to show that the algorithm does indeed converges very fast, taking almost linear (in number of nodes in the system) time to converge.

The correctness of the process of rooting the MST at the multi-cast source node (once the MST is stabilized) involves essentially maintaining a *Level* pointer at each node indicating the level of the node on the tree as well as maintaing a parent pointer at each node to denote to its predecessor in the tree. Note that the multi-cast source node r knows that it is the source node and it unilaterally sets its predecessor to be Null and its $Level_r$ to be zero. Every other node checks the *Level* variables of all of its neighbors in the MST and sets its own *Level* variable to one plus the minimum of its neighbors as well as sets its predecessor to its neighbor (in the MST) with the minimum *Level* value. The rule at each node is then

$$i \ne r \land L(\mathcal{S}(i)) \ne n-1 \land \{L(i) \ne L(\mathcal{S}(i))+1 \lor P(i) \notin \mathcal{S}(i)$$

$$\Rightarrow L(i) = L(\mathcal{S}(i)) + 1; P(i) = k, k \in \mathcal{S}(i)$$

where n is the number of nodes in the graph, $N(i)$ is the set of the neighbors of node i, $L(i)$ is the level of node i and $P(i)$ is the predecessor pointer of node i, pointing to one of the nodes in N(i); the set $\mathcal{S}(i)$ defined as $\mathcal{S}(i) = \{j : j = N(i) \land L(j) = min_{k \in N(i)}\{L(k)\}\}$ contains neighboring nodes of i with minimum level.

In order to show the convergence of this process after the MST algorithm has stabilized, we observe the following lemmas; details can be found in [18].

Lemma 1 *In any illegitimate state there exists at least one privileged node, i.e., in an illegitimate state some action is always guaranteed.*

Note that the level of a node can assume values in the range 0 to $n - 1$ and hence total number of possible distinct state vectors or system states is finite, e.g., n^{n-1} (root node has a constant level). Our approach in proving that the algorithm brings back the stable state in finite number of moves is to show that the system, starting from any arbitrary illegitimate state can never return to the same state. Whenever a node i is privileged and takes action (i.e., is active), it does so because of the presence of a node j, one of its neighbors with $L(i) \neq L(j) + 1$, and $j \in \mathcal{S}(i)$. The node j is called the *forcing* node for node i for that move where node i changes its level from $L(i)$ to $L(j) + 1$. Note that any node in $\mathcal{S}(i)$ can be viewed as the forcing node for node i when node i is active. Note that each move is characterized by an active node and a forcing node.

Lemma 2 *Regardless of the initial state and regardless of the order in which the nodes are selected to take actions, the system is guaranteed to reach the legitimate state after a finite number of moves.*

Proof : Since the total number of states is finite, it is sufficient to show that starting from any arbitrary state the system cannot come back to the same state. We prove this by contradiction. Assume that i-th and j-th states are identical, $i \neq j$ (i-th state is the state reached by the system after i moves starting from the initial illegitimate state). Assume that at the i-th state node A (possibly along with other nodes) is active (i.e., makes the $(i + 1)$st move); A can either decrease or increase its own level. We consider two cases separately.

Case A: Suppose node A decreases its level from $L(A)$ to $L(A) - k$, where $k \geq 1$. Then there must exist a forcing node B, a neighbor of A and B has a level $L(A) - k - 1$ in state i (action by node A depends on state3 of B in state i even if B is active concurrently with A). We now use method of induction. The induction hypothesis is: if there exists a forcing node X with level p, then there must exist another forcing node Y with level $p - 1$ or less. Since X is a forcing node, there is a node Z, neighbor of X, which changes its level to $p + 1$; call this m-th move, $i < m < j$ (m must be distinct from i and j since actions taken in a move must depend on current states only). We need to consider two different cases:

Case I: The node X was active, i.e., made a move between i-th and the m-th moves. Hence, node X didn't have a level p in the i-th state and it has acquired the level p because of the move and consequently there must exist a forcing node Y

Case II The node X was not active, i.e., didn't make any move between the i-th and the m-th states. That is, node X has a constant level p from i-th to the m-th states. We need to consider the node Z that changes its level to $p + 1$ in m-th move. There are 3 possible subcases: **(a)** Z has a level $\leq p$ in i-th state. Then Z must go back to its original level by j-th state and consequently there must be a forcing node Y with level $p - 1$ or less. **(b)** Z had a level $p + 1$ in i-th state. Since Z is active for the m-th move, Z must have changed its level in between i-th and m-th moves. Since X, a neighbor of Z, has a constant

level from i-th to the m-th states, Z must have decreased its level and hence there is a forcing node Y with level $p - 1$ or less. **(c)** Z has a level $p + \mu$, $\mu > 1$, in i-th state. Then after m-th move Z must be active again to get back to the level of $p + \mu$ by j-th state. Since X is a neighbor of Z and X has a constant level of p between i-th and m-th states, X must have increased its level before the final move by Z. Again X must also come back to level p by j-th state and hence there must be a forcing node Y with level $p - 1$.

Thus, if the i-th and the j-th states are the same, existence of a forcing node with level p implies the existence of another forcing node with level $p - 1$ or less. Since in the i-th state, there exists a forcing node with level $L(A) - k - 1$, then there must exist another forcing node with level $L(A) - k - 2$ or less and proceeding similarly by induction, there must exist a forcing node with level less than zero, which is a contradiction.

Case B: Similarly, if in the i-th state the level of A increases, say from $L(a)$ to $L(a) + k$, the argument is almost the same. After the level of A is increased, A must return to its own level $L(a)$ by j-th state. This would then require a forcing node with level $L(a) - 1$. Now again we can follow the previous induction argument and arrive at a contradiction.

Thus, the system is always brought back to a stable state starting from any arbitrary state in finite number of moves. □

The correctness of the process of setting of the $Flag_i$ variable at each node i in the MST directly follows from the correctness of the self-stabilizing algorithm of [19]. Note that once the MST is stabilized and the MST has been rooted at the source node r (each node knows its unique predecessor in the tree), each node can determine if it is a leaf node in the tree. As soon as a node determines that it is a leaf node, it can unilaterally decide its $Flag_i$ variable based on the fact if the node i is a member of the multi-cast group or not. Every other node looks at the $Flag$ variables of its immediate successors in the tree and sets its own $Flag$ variable if at least one of its successors has its $Flag$ True. Thus, the process is essentially a bottom up one anchored at the leaf nodes of the tree; the rest of the argument for convergence is identical to those in [19].

6   Conclusion

Our objective in the present paper has been to demonstrate the applicability of the tools of self-stabilization (a relatively new paradigm to design fault tolerant distributed algorithms) to solve the problems associated with dynamic topology change in a mobile multi-hop radio network due to mobility of the host nodes. We have developed a new distributed algorithm for multi-casting a message form a given source node in a mobile network; our algorithms maintains the multi-cast tree in the presence of dynamic topology change of the network. The unique features of the algorithms are: (1) it is distributed in nature; no central coordination is necessary to recompute the underlying minimal spanning tree (MST) of the network; (2) the network nodes take local actions based on local knowledge (the states of its immediate neighbors only); (3) in presence of a topology change, the algorithm is automatically kicked in, i.e., at least one node is always aware of the topology change (due to the change of its node adjacency information). We have designed the multi-cast tree based on the MST of the network graph by pruning the nodes properly using the multi-cast group membership. On one hand, we do not get the minimal multi-cast tree for a given multi-cast group; then again computing the minimal multi-cast spanning tree is computationally intractable [1]. On the positive side, although the algorithm has been developed in the paper based on one multi-cast group, it can be extended in a straightforward way to handle multiple multi-cast groups and each multi-cast group will generate different multi-cast trees, but each of them will use the same underlying minimal spanning tree (thus the reconfiguration due to topology change would be minimal). It'd be interesting to conduct elaborate experiments to come to a better understanding of the cost of the algorithm in terms of time to converge as well as to explore to arrive at a theoretical upper and/or lower bound. It'd also be interesting to explore applicability of self-stabilization to solve other problems related to mobile networks.

References

[1] R. M. Karp. Reducibility among combinatorial problems. In *Complexity of Computer Computations*. Plenum Press, New York, 1972.

[2] A. Acharya and B. R. Badrinath. A framework for delivering multicast messages in networks with mobile hosts. *ACM/Baltzer Journal of Mobile Networks and Applications*, 1:199–219, 1996.

[3] K. Chao and K. P. Birman. A group communication approach for mobile communication. In *Proc. Mobile Computing Workshop*, Santa Cruz, CA, December 1994.

[4] I. Chlamtac and S. Kutten. Tree based broadcasting in multihop radio networks. *IEEE Transactions on Computers*, C-36(10), October 1987.

[5] M. Gerla and J. T. C. Tsai. Multicluster, mobile, multimedia radio network. *ACM Journal on Wireless Networks*, 1(3):255–265, 1995.

[6] E. Pagani and G. P. Rossi. Reliable broadcast in mobile multihop packet networks. In *Proceedings of MOBICOM 97*, pages 34–42, Budapest, Hungary, 1997.

[7] D. B. Johnson. Routing in adhoc networks of mobile hosts. In *Proceedings of Workshop on Mobile Computing and Applications*, 1994.

[8] C. Perkins and P. Bhagwat. Routing over multihop wireless network of mobile computers. In T. Imielinski and H. F. Korth, editors, *Mobile Computing*, pages 182–205. Kluwer Academic Publisher, 1996.

[9] V. Hadzilacos and S. Toueg. Fault tolerant broadcasts and related problems. In S. Mullender, editor, *Distributed Systems*. Addison-Wesley, New York, 1993.

[10] C. C. Chiang and M. Gerla. Routing and multicast in multihop, mobile wireless networks. In *Proceedings of ICUPC '97*, October 1997.

[11] A. Ephremides, J. E. Wieselthier, and J. D. Baker. A design concept for reliable mobile radio networks with frequency hopping signaling. *Proceedings of IEEE*, 1(1):56–73, 1987.

[12] E. W. Dijkstra. Self-stabilizing systems in spite of distributed control. *Communications of the ACM*, 17(11):643–644, November 1974.

[13] E. W. Dijkstra. A belated proof of self-stabilization. *Distributed Computing*, 1(1):5–6, 1986.

[14] M. Schneider. Self-stabilization. *ACM Computing Surveys*, 25(1):45–67, March 1993.

[15] B. M. Maggs and S. A. Plotkin. Minimum-cost spanning tree as a path finding problem. *Information Processing Letters*, 26:291–293, January 1988.

[16] G. Antonoiu and P. K. Srimani. A self-stabilizing distributed algorithm for minimal spanning tree problem in a symmetric graph. *Computers Mathematics and Applications*, 35(10):15–23, October 1998.

[17] E. Horowitz and S. Sahni. *Fundamentals of Computer Algorithms*. Computer Science Press, 1984.

[18] S. Sur and P. K. Srimani. A self-stabilizing algorithm for coloring bipartite graphs. *Information Sciences*, 69:219–227, 1992. Information Sciences.

[19] G. Antonoiu and P. K. Srimani. A self-stabilizing leader election algorithm for tree graphs. *Journal of Parallel and Distributed Computing*, 34:227–232, 1996.

Maintenance of Ambiences for Mobile Systems

Toshihiko Ando, Kaoru Takahashi, Yasushi Kato
Sendai National College of Technology
1, Kitahara, Kami-ayashi, Aoba-ku,
Sendai 989-3124, Japan
{tando,kato}@info.sendai-ct.ac.jp,
kaoru@cc.sendai-ct.ac.jp

Norio Shiratori
Research Institute of Electrical
Communication, Tohoku University
2-1-1, Katahira, Aoba-ku,
Sendai 980-8577, Japan
norio@shiratori.riec.tohoku.ac.jp

Abstract

We propose a formal method to maintain mobile systems placed on fluidal ambiences using a process calculus in this paper. Behavior of physically movable entities of mobile systems, e.g. mobile telephone systems and intelligent transport systems (ITSs), may be affected by their surrounding. We have focused on effects of ambiences to behavior of mobile systems and have introduced the notion of a field into a concurrent calculus. πF, an extension of π-calculus, formalizes processes constrained by ambiences. Based on πF, our maintenance method indicates us how an ambience should be recovered when it is damaged.

1. Introduction

Recently, mobile phones and mobile terminals have been widespread in some years[1, 2]. Connecting to computer networks using these communication tools, people can easily obtain necessary information anytime and anywhere. In addition to these, research and development of *intelligent transport systems* (ITSs) have been advanced in this decade[3]. The targets of an ITS development are advances in navigation systems, electronic toll collection systems (ETCs), assistance for safe driving (included automated highway systems (AHSs)), optimization of traffic management, etc. It is hoped that an ITS may decrease numbers of traffic accidents and traffic jams in a city. Development of an ITS needs a car-car and car-road communication technology which must make it possible to identify each other among fast moving cars and static roads, and to transfer signals among them. Development and standardization of protocols used in an ITS are recent research problems. ITSs will be realized in some years. These mobile systems will widely change our life styles near future.

Formal description of such mobile systems have been proposed by many researchers, i.e. process calculi, finite state machines, Petri nets, chemical abstract machines, etc. In these formalizations, process calculi are useful tools. Especially, π-calculus[4, 5] is one of the most powerful tools used to describe dynamical linking between processes, which is the most important feature of a mobile system.

However, π-calculus is not always useful to describe real mobile systems. For instance, π-calculus is inconvenient to describe cellular systems employed in mobile phone systems. The radio powers of mobile phones are too weak to connect with far base stations in a cellular system, so that connections of mobile phones are restricted to the nearest base stations. For example, there are following cases. Geographical obstacles, e.g. buildings, may disturb communications. In an ITS, An accident of a car may damage a road and may obstruct not only traffic flows but car-car communications. It is difficult to express such local constraints of communications because communications between π-processes are global. To make up for locality, various extensions of π-calculus have been tried.

In the context of describing locality, Sangiorgi proposed a method using located processes [6]. Amadio et al. focused detection of failures and mobility of processes using optional functions [7, 8]. Recently, Amadio has applied such a mobile calculus to IPv6 [9]. From the point of view of communication restriction, distances among processes are introduced in the works of Isobe et al. [10] and Cleaveland et al.[11]. Besides them, Fournet et al. have proposed join-calculus to express mobile agents. Their calculus has π-calculus like syntax and chemical abstract machine style semantics [12].

We have regarded an ambience surrounding a mobile system as local constraints of communications among entities included in the system. To formalize an ambience, the notion of a *field* has been introduced, and π-calculus has extended with this notion. In this extension, πF [13], process descriptions are separated from local constraints, i.e. a field. Such separation gives two advantages to πF; (1) descriptions of a system can be simple. (2) explicit description of

498

an ambience of a system can make effects of the ambience to behaviors of the system clear. Located processes, called labors, may differently behave according to fields because two processes can achieve a connection between them for some field but not for others. Thus, πF specifications can indicate which local conditions may obstruct behaviors of a mobile system.

In this paper, a maintenance method of a mobile system using πF is proposed. A mobile system may be broken down by damage of an ambience surrounding this system. Focusing on *connectivity*, we show how to modify such an damaged ambience to recover connections among entities. Mobile systems such as mobile phone systems have been going to be indispensable for our lives today, so that it is necessary to manage these systems stably. Importance of a maintenance method may increase hereafter.

The rest of this paper consists of the following. A brief explanation of πF is shown in Section 2. Next, the notion of connectivity between processes is introduced in Section 3. Based on this notion, we show a repairing method for an injured field, and propose, furthermore, a maintenance method for a dynamically varying ambient in Sections 4. fFinally, we will conclude this paper in Section 5.

2. πF : an extension of π-calculus with a field

We show πF, an extension of π-calculus, in this Section. In πF, each πF process is accompanied with a parameter called a *location*. A process with a location is called a *labor*. Main difference of πF from the the standard π-calculus is that process communication is restricted according to locations. A set of location forms a *field* that is expressed as a finite directed graph and reflects effects of an ambient of a target system.

2.1. Syntax of πF

At first, the definitions of a field and the movement of processes are shown as follows.

Definition 1 *Field*

A field $\mathcal{F}$ is defined as $\mathcal{F} = \langle Loc, RL \rangle$, where Loc is a set of locations (places at which processes can be located) and $RL \subseteq Loc \times Loc$ is a binary relation such that a communication between a sending process at l and a receiving process at m is possible if $(l, m) \in RL$. If $(l, m) \in RL$, then (l, m) is called a road *from l to m, or simply a* road.

Next, we define constraints on movement of processes. Hereafter, $\mathcal{P}roc$ is the set of all process identifiers (abbreviated to PID). PIDs mean initial process names from which current processes are reduced by the reduction rules in Definition 5.

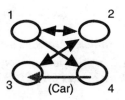

Figure 1. An example of an ambient:$\mathcal{A}_1$

Definition 2 *Movement*

Let $P \in \mathcal{P}roc$, $l \in Loc$, $A \subset Loc - \{l\}$ and $A \neq \emptyset$. $(P, l, A) \in MV$ expresses that a process with the PID P may move from the location l to some location $m \in A$. We call it a 'move' and the set of all moves '$\mathcal{M}ovs$'. Constraints on movement of processes are represented by $MV \subset \mathcal{M}ovs$ and we call MV a 'movement'.

Definition 3 *Ambient*

We call the pair $\mathcal{A} = \langle \mathcal{F}, MV \rangle$ of a field $\mathcal{F}$ and a movement MV an 'ambient'.

We use a term '*ambient*' to express what affects *local* behaviors of mobile systems instead of 'environment' or 'ambience'. For example, Fig. 1 is corresponding to the following ambient $\mathcal{A}_1 = \langle \mathcal{F}_1, MV_1 \rangle$.

$$
\begin{aligned}
\mathcal{F}_1 &= \langle Loc_1, RL_1 \rangle \\
Loc_1 &= \{1, 2, 3, 4\} \\
RL_1 &= \{(1, 4), (1, 2), (2, 1), (2, 3), (3, 2)\}. \\
MV_1 &= \{(Car, 4, \{3\})\}.
\end{aligned}
\tag{1}
$$

In this figure, an arrow represents a communicating direction. For example, the arrow '1' to '4' expresses that a sending process at '1' can communicate with a receiving process at '4', but not vice versa. Moreover, the above MV_1 represents that a process with the PID Car can move from '4' to '3' on this field.

Syntax of πF is shown in Definition 4. In this paper, let $L, M, \cdots$ range over the set $\mathcal{LAB}$ of all labors, $P, Q, \cdots$ the set $\mathcal{P}roc$ of all PIDs, $a, b, \cdots$ the set Ch of all channel name constants, $f, \cdots$ the set $\mathcal{NF}$ of all name functions, $l, m, \cdots$ the set $\mathcal{L}oc$ of all locations, and $\tilde{b}, \tilde{c}, \cdots$ the set of all channel name vectors.

Definition 4 *Syntax of πF*

Name functions, names, actions, processes and Labors are defined as follows.

name functions :	$\underline{f} \quad : \quad Ch^n \to Ch^m; \underline{f}(\tilde{b}) = \tilde{c}$
names	: $\mathbf{a} ::= a \mid \underline{f}(\tilde{b})$
actions	: $\alpha ::= \mathbf{a}(\tilde{b}) \mid \bar{\mathbf{a}}[\tilde{b}]$
processes	: $P ::= 0 \mid \alpha.P \mid P + Q \mid P|Q \mid \nu\tilde{c}P \mid D(\tilde{b})$
labors	: $L ::= \{P\}l \mid L|M \mid \nu\tilde{c}L$

Note that $\underline{f}$ gives an m-name vector $\tilde{c}$ ($\#\tilde{c} = m$) for an n-name vector $\tilde{b}$ ($\#\tilde{b} = n$). In the definition of names, name functions are restricted to ones like $\#\underline{f}(\tilde{b}) = 1$.

In the above definition, a name function returns a name constant vector for a given name vector, e.g. $\underline{name\_and\_ID}(Smith) = \langle Joe, 385\rangle$, similar to channel names. Actions occur through channels, and processes receive ($a(\tilde{b})$) / send ($\overline{a}[\tilde{b}]$) messages (channel names). The definitions of processes represent inaction, action prefix, sum, parallel composition, restriction of a name and constant application respectively. In the definitions of labors, $\{P\}l$ represents that the process P is at the location 'l'. The rest of the definitions of labors are corresponding to parallel composition and restriction of a name. If $\tilde{b}$ is empty, then brackets [ ] and ( ) will be omitted. D is defined as $D(\tilde{c}) \overset{\text{def}}{=} P$, where $\tilde{c}$ is formal parameters. $D\langle\tilde{b}\rangle$ means that $\tilde{c}$ is replaced with actual parameters $\tilde{b}$ in D. For example, when $D(x, y)$ is defined as $x(u).\mathbf{0} + \overline{y}[a].\mathbf{0}$, $D\langle b, c\rangle$ is obtained as $b(u).\mathbf{0} + \overline{c}[a].\mathbf{0}$ by replacing x and y with b and c respectively. The operator $\nu\tilde{c}P$ and $\nu\tilde{c}L$ bind all occurrences of names $\tilde{c}$ in P and L respectively. Congruence relations on processes are the same as the relations of the standard π-calculus[13].

For example, let three processes be given on the ambient $\mathcal{A}_1$ of Fig. 1 as follows.

$$Center \overset{\text{def}}{=} \overline{call}[id].\,\mathbf{0}\ +\ warning.\,\mathbf{0},$$

$$Base \overset{\text{def}}{=} call(x).\,\overline{x}.\,\mathbf{0}\ +\ \overline{warning}.\,\mathbf{0}, \qquad (2)$$

$$Car \overset{\text{def}}{=} id.\,\mathbf{0} + warning.\,\mathbf{0}.$$

Then, the following Sys_1 is a labor.

$$Sys_1 \overset{\text{def}}{=} \{\,Center\,\}1 \mid \{\,Base\,\}2 \mid \{\,Car\,\}4 \qquad (3)$$

2.2. Reduction Rules of πF

Descriptions of labors shown in the previous subsection is reduced by the following reduction rules. There exist some differences of them from the standard π-calculus. Reductions according to these reduction rules are called *located reductions*.

Definition 5 *Reduction rules*

Let an ambient $\langle\langle\mathcal{L}oc, RL\rangle, MV\rangle$ be given. Reduction rules of labors are the followings.
COMM:

$$\frac{\#\tilde{b} = \#\tilde{c},\ (l, l_\lambda) \in RL\ for\ \lambda \in \Lambda,\ \Delta(\neq \emptyset) \subseteq \Lambda}{\{\cdots + \overline{a}[\tilde{b}].P\}l \mid \displaystyle\prod_{\lambda\in\Lambda}\{\cdots + a(\tilde{c}).Q_\lambda(\tilde{u})\}l_\lambda}$$

$$\xrightarrow{a@(\{l\}\cup\{l_\lambda|\lambda\in\Delta\})}$$

$$\{P\}l \mid \displaystyle\prod_{\lambda\in\Delta}\{Q_\lambda(\tilde{b})\}l_\lambda \mid \displaystyle\prod_{\lambda'\in\Lambda-\Delta}\{\cdots + a(\tilde{c}).Q_{\lambda'}(\tilde{u})\}l_{\lambda'}$$

MOVE: $\quad\dfrac{(P, l, A) \in MV, m \in A}{\{P\}l \xrightarrow{\tau} \{P\}m}$

PAR: $\quad\dfrac{L \xrightarrow{\zeta} L'}{L|M \xrightarrow{\zeta} L'|M}$

STRUCT: $\quad\dfrac{M \equiv L,\ L \xrightarrow{\zeta} L',\ L' \equiv M'}{M \xrightarrow{\zeta} M'}$

RES1: $\quad\dfrac{L \xrightarrow{a@Pls} L',\ x \neq a}{\nu x L \xrightarrow{a@Pls} \nu x L'}$

RES2: $\quad\dfrac{L \xrightarrow{a@Pls} L',\ x = a}{\nu x L \xrightarrow{\tau} \nu x L'}$

$L \xrightarrow{a@Pls} L'$ represents that L is reduced to L' by the occurrence of the action through the channel a, and processes at locations listed in Pls are related to this reduction. In $COMM$, $\prod_{\lambda\in\Lambda} L_\lambda = L_{\lambda_1}|L_{\lambda_2}|\cdots$ ($\lambda_1, \lambda_2, \ldots \in \Lambda$). Λ is a possible process index set. In this case, the arities (the number of names) of both $\tilde{b}$ and $\tilde{c}$ must be the same. τ represents an unobservable communication or an unobservable action. ζ is $a@Pls$ or τ.

Note that we will treat reductions of πF processes themselves in the following Sections. πF processes (labors without locations) are almost similarly reduced by these rules except for COMM. The communication rule for πF processes is COMM without its premise on locations.

In the definition, COMM and MOVE are the main difference of πF from the standard π-calculus. $COMM$ allows broadcast or multicast transmission. Cases $\Delta = \Lambda$ and $\Delta \subset \Lambda$ correspond to broadcast and multicast respectively. The case that Δ is a singleton corresponds to one-to-one transmission. Movement of processes is represented by $MOVE$. Observation of communications is emphasized in these reduction rules, so that hidden communications ($RES2$) and movement of processes ($MOVE$) are regarded as internal actions and represented by τ.

An example of reduction of a labor is shown as follows. The labor shown in Eq. (3) is reduced by these reduction rules. There exist some reductions from the initial state Eq. (3) as follows.

1. Communications occur through the channels *call* and *id*:

$$\{Center\}1 \mid \{Base\}2 \mid \{Car\}4$$

$\xrightarrow{call@\{1,2\}}\quad \{0\}1 \mid \{\overline{id}.\,0\}2 \mid \{Car\}4 \qquad$ (COMM)

$\xrightarrow{\tau}\quad \{0\}1 \mid \{\overline{id}.\,0\}2 \mid \{Car\}3 \qquad$ (MOVE)

$\xrightarrow{id@\{2,3\}}\quad \{0\}1 \mid \{0\}2 \mid \{0\}3 \qquad$ (COMM)

Process $Base$ receives the name $call$ through the channel $call$, and then the new sending port id appears on $Base$. So, moving from '4' to '3', Car can communicate with $Base$ through the channel id.

2. A communication occurs through the channel $warning$:

$$\xrightarrow{\tau} \begin{array}{l} \{Center\}1 \mid \{Base\}2 \mid \{Car\}4 \\ \{Center\}1 \mid \{Base\}2 \mid \{Car\}3 \\ \hspace{3cm} \text{(MOVE)} \end{array}$$

$$\xrightarrow{warning@\{2,3\}} \{Center\}1 \mid \{0\}2 \mid \{0\}3 \quad \text{(COMM)}$$

Moving from '4' to '3', Car can communicate with $Base$ through the channel $warning$.

3. Broadcast occurs through the channel $warning$.

$$\xrightarrow{\tau} \begin{array}{l} \{Center\}1 \mid \{Base\}2 \mid \{Car\}4 \\ \{Center\}1 \mid \{Base\}2 \mid \{Car\}3 \\ \hspace{3cm} \text{(MOVE)} \end{array}$$

$$\xrightarrow{warning@\{1,2,3\}} \{0\}1 \mid \{0\}2 \mid \{0\}3 \quad \text{(COMM)}$$

When Car is at '3', $Base$ can simultaneously communicate with $Center$ and Car through $warning$.

As shown in the above example, all reduction sequences form a tree, called a *reduction tree*, whose root is the initial state Eq. (3). In most cases, trees become large because of including movement of processes.

3. Connectivity of processes

Suppose a situation that a new building is constructed near one base station of a mobile phone system. People using mobile phones may be obstructed to call someone by this building. How will this situation be restored? There may be several ways to restore it; by reconstructing the building, by constructing a new base station, etc., which some of them are easy and others are difficult. We have to select one of them.

Thus, a system may not normally run according to its ambient, even if this system itself can run normally. So, an appropriate maintenance method is necessary for a mobile system with an evolving ambient. To find such a maintenance method, we focus on *connectivity* of processes. Connectivity means an ability to send a message from one process to a corresponding process. Ideally, it is better to take the bisimulations mentioned in [5] than connectivity in a sense that the behavior of new system can be equivalent to the previous system. However, bisimulations are too strong to find out such another system. Thus, we employ connectivity more tractable than the preceding bisimulations.

3.1. Connectivity

At first, to define connectivity of πF-processes, two operations, *ping* and *marking*, and *transition* are introduced. Ping operation is that a connection seeking message is emitted from the first marking process to other processes. Then, connectable processes with the first processes are marked with this message by marking operation. Transitions are almost the same as ones used to verify bisimulation relations in other mobile calculi (see e.g. [8]). However, we focus on the result of reduction sequences to verify connections, so that labels for reductions are omitted in this paper.

The following definition is for the operation *ping*. Ping marks processes connectable with the first marking process using an additional message. Note that we use the following notations to define connectivity. In this definition, let a πF-process $Procs \stackrel{\text{def}}{=} \prod_{k=1}^{n} P_k$, a labor $Sys \stackrel{\text{def}}{=} \prod_{k=1}^{n} L_k$, where $L_k = \{P_k\}l_k$ for $1 \le k \le n$, and let an ambient $\mathcal{A} = \langle\langle Loc, RL \rangle, MV \rangle$ be given.

Definition 6 *Ping*

Select a process P_i which has the form $\overline{a}[\tilde{b}].Q_i$. For Procs,

$$Ping(Procs, P_i) = \nu m (\prod_{k=1}^{i-1} P_k \mid m \triangleright P_i \mid \prod_{k=i+1}^{n} P_k),$$

and for Sys,

$$Ping(Sys, P_i) = \nu m (\prod_{k=1}^{i-1} L_k \mid \{m \triangleright P_i\}l_i \mid \prod_{k=i+1}^{n} L_k),$$

where m is a marking name *to check connections with the first marking process P_i. The definition of the above* marking operator $\triangleright$ *is as follows;*

$$m \triangleright P = \begin{cases} \mathbf{0}_m & \text{if } P = \mathbf{0} \\ \overline{a}[\tilde{b}, m].(m \triangleright Q) & \text{if } P = \overline{a}[\tilde{b}].Q \\ a(\tilde{b}).(m \triangleright Q) & \text{if } P = a(\tilde{b}).Q \\ (m \triangleright Q) \mid (m \triangleright R) & \text{if } P = Q \mid R \\ (m \triangleright Q) + (m \triangleright R) & \text{if } P = Q + R \\ \nu\tilde{b}(m \triangleright Q) & \text{if } P = \nu\tilde{b}Q \end{cases}$$

'$m \triangleright P$' means that the process P is marked by the marking message m. Once a process is marked, the process will send the marking message to other processes ($m \triangleright (\overline{a}[\tilde{b}].Q) = \overline{a}[\tilde{b}, m].(m \triangleright Q)$) until the process terminates ($\mathbf{0}_m$). The marked process can receive messages from non-marked processes ($m \triangleright (a(\tilde{b}).Q) = a(\tilde{b}).(m \triangleright Q)$).

Next, a *marking rule $MARK$* is added to the reduction rules to express that a marking message is passed by communications.

Definition 7 *Marking rule: $MARK$*

The marking rule $MARK$ is defined as follows.

$$\cfrac{\sharp\tilde{c} = \sharp\tilde{v}}{\begin{array}{l}\{\overline{a}[\tilde{c}, m].\,P + P'\}l \mid \{\sum_i a(\tilde{v}).\,Q_i + Q'\}l' \\[4pt] \longrightarrow \{\overline{a}[\tilde{c}, m].\,P + P'\}l \mid \{\sum_i a(\tilde{v}, x).\,(x \rhd Q_i + Q')\}l'.\end{array}}$$

$MARK$ makes processes waiting an input action ready to receive the marking message if the channel name of the input action is the same as that of an output action of a marked process. Note that the arrow '$\longrightarrow$' is used instead of $\rightarrow$ to discriminate marking from other reductions.

Connectivity means that marking messages from the first marking process can reach a corresponding process by the operation *ping*. To define connectivity, we introduce *transitions*, which are reductions attracted to only single process in some sense and express its possible behaviors.

Definition 8 *Transitions*

Let α be an action, $\tilde{b}$ a name vector, and P, P', Q and Q' πF-processes. Transitions are defined as follows.

$$\alpha.\,P \succ P \qquad \cfrac{P \succ P'}{P + Q \succ P'}$$

$$\cfrac{P \succ P',\; Q \succ Q'}{P \mid Q \succ P' \mid Q'} \qquad \cfrac{P \succ P'}{\nu b P \succ \nu b P'}$$

Note that binding or bounded variables appeared in a process can be replaced with other channel names.

For example, the above three processes $Center$, $Base$ and Car (Eq. 2) may be transited as follows.

$$\begin{array}{rcl} Center &=& \overline{call}[id].0 + warning.0 \succ 0 \\ Base &=& call(x).\overline{x}.0 + \overline{warning}.0 \succ \overline{x}.0 \succ 0 \\ Car &=& id.0 + warning.0 \succ 0 \end{array}$$

$Base$ is transited to $\overline{x}.0$ by the action $call(x)$, it, furthermore, is transited to 0 by the action $\overline{x}$. x is a name variable and can be replaced with other names.

Now, we can define connectivity of πF-processes using the above operations.

Definition 9 *Connectivity of πF-processes*

Let a πF-process, $Procs = \prod_{k=1}^{n} P_k$, and a labor, $Sys = \prod_{k=1}^{n} L_k$, be given, where $L_k = \{P_k\}l_k$ for $1 \le k \le n$. Sys is a labor on an ambient $\langle \mathcal{F}, MV \rangle$. We say that P_i is connectable to P_j on $\langle \mathcal{F}, MV \rangle$, written P_i con P_j on $\langle \mathcal{F}, MV \rangle$, if the following is satisfied;

$$\begin{array}{l} Ping(Sys, P_i)((\rightarrow)^* \longrightarrow)^* \\ \nu m(\prod_{1 \le k \le n, k \ne j} \{Q_k\}l'_k \mid \{m \rhd P'_j\}l'_j) \end{array} \qquad (4)$$

In this definition, P_j $(\succ)^*$ P'_j, and l'_j is a location movable from l_j for P_j. On the other hand, omitting any local conditions, we just say P_i con P_j if the following is satisfied;

$$\begin{array}{l} Ping(Procs, P_i)((\rightarrow)^* \longrightarrow)^* \\ \nu m(\prod_{1 \le k \le n, k \ne j} Q_k \mid (m \rhd P'_j)). \end{array} \qquad (5)$$

Now, we show an example of connectivity of πF-processes using the processes of Eq. (2). We consider connectivity of $Center$ to Car in this case. At first, connectivity of $Center$ to Car without an ambient can be checked as follows using ping and marking. In the case of these processes, transitions are already shown in the above. Let $MobPhone$ be the process consisting of $Center$, $Base$ and Car without an ambient. Connectivity of $Center$ to Car is shown as follows in this case.

$$\begin{array}{cl} & Ping(MobPhone, Center) \\ = & \nu m((m \rhd Center) \mid Base \mid Car) \\ = & \nu m((\overline{call}[id, m].0_m + warning.0) \mid Base \mid Car) \\ = & \nu m((\overline{call}[id, m].0_m + warning.0) \\ & \quad \mid (call(x).\overline{x}.0 + \overline{warning}.0) \mid Car) \\ \longrightarrow & \nu m((\overline{call}[id, m].0_m + warning.0) \\ & \quad \mid (call(x, y).(y \rhd (\overline{x}.0)) + \overline{warning}.0) \mid Car) \\ \longrightarrow & \nu m(0_m \mid m \rhd (\overline{id}.0) \mid Car) \\ = & \nu m(0_m \mid \overline{id}[m].0_m \mid Car) \\ = & \nu m(0_m \mid \overline{id}[m].0_m \mid (id.0 + warning.0)) \\ \longrightarrow & \nu m(0_m \mid \overline{id}[m].0_m \mid (id(z).0_m + warning.0)) \\ \longrightarrow & \nu m(0_m \mid 0_m \mid 0_m) \end{array}$$

Thus, Car may stop with a message m from $Center$, so that $Center$ is connectable to Car in the case of no restrictions.

In the case of the ambient $\mathcal{A}_1$ (Eq. 1), '$Center$ **con** Car on $\mathcal{A}_1$' can be shown similarly to $Center$ **con** Car.

However, $Center$ is not connectable to Car on the ambient $\mathcal{A}_2 = \langle \mathcal{F}_2, MV_2 \rangle$, where

$$\begin{array}{rcl} \mathcal{F}_2 &=& \langle Loc_2, RL_2 \rangle \\ Loc_2 &=& \{1, 2, 3, 4\} \\ RL_2 &=& \{(1, 2), (1, 4)\}. \\ MV_2 &=& \{(Car, 4, \{3\})\}. \end{array} \qquad (6)$$

Let $Sys_2 = \{Center\}1 \mid \{Base\}2 \mid \{Car\}4$ on $\mathcal{A}_2$. In fact, Car is not marked by m in this case.

$$\begin{array}{cl} & Ping(Sys_2, Center) \\ = & \nu m(\{m \rhd Center\}1 \mid \{Base\}2 \mid \{Car\}4) \\ = & \nu m(\{\overline{call}[id, m].0_m + warning.0\}1 \\ & \quad \mid \{call(x).\overline{x}.0 + \overline{warning}.0\}2 \mid \{Car\}4) \\ \longrightarrow & \nu m(\{\overline{call}[id, m].0_m + warning.0\}1 \\ & \quad \mid \{call(x, y).y \rhd (\overline{x}.0) + \overline{warning}.0\}2 \mid \{Car\}4) \\ \longrightarrow & \nu m(\{0_m\}1 \mid \{m \rhd (\overline{id}.0)\}2 \mid \{Car\}4) \\ \longrightarrow & \nu m(\{0_m\}1 \mid \{m \rhd (\overline{id}.0)\}2 \mid \{Car\}3) \end{array}$$

As having seen in the above, Car is not marked with m, which means that Car can not receive a message from $Center$ in this case.

3.2. Connecting sequences of πF-processes

Connections of πF-processes consist of sequences of direct communications of adjoining processes. Namely, checking each communication of adjoining processes implies verifying connectivity of target processes. So, we focus on a condition for communication of adjoining processes.

At first, the following relation is introduced to describe a communication between two adjoining πF-processes.

Definition 10 *Adjoining communication*

Let P_1, $P_2 \in \mathcal{P}roc$. Now, let $Q_1 \succ Q_1'$ be some transitions of P_1, i.e. $P_1 (\succ)^* Q_1 \succ Q_1'$. Similarly, let $Q_2 \succ Q_2'$ be some transitions of P_2. Then, we write $P_1 \succeq P_2$ if

$$(m \rhd Q_1)|Q_2(\rightarrow)^* \longrightarrow (m \rhd Q_1')|(m \rhd Q_2').$$

$P_i \succeq P_j$ means that P_i will directly communicate with P_j after some transitions of both. For the above example, $Center \succeq Base \succeq Car$.

Def. 9 of connectivity is given from the context of simulations. Using adjoining communications, the definition of connectivity for πF-processes can be rewritten as follows.

Proposition 1 *Let $Procs = \prod_{k=1}^n P_k$. If the following condition*

$$\exists (P_{k_1}, P_{k_2}, \cdots, P_{k_p}) \\ \bullet (P_i = P_{k_1} \succeq P_{k_2} \succeq \cdots \succeq P_{k_p} = P_j). \quad (7)$$

*is satisfied for πF-processes P_i and P_j, then P_i **con** P_j.*

The proof of this proposition is shown in Appendix A. Proposition 1 is a formalization of a natural property such as connections of πF-processes consist of communication sequences of adjoining processes. This concept of adjoining communications is a basis of our method.

Hereafter, our important results about connectivity of πF-processes accompanied with an ambient is shown. Generally, even if a connection of processes without constraints is possible, such a connection is not always possible according to the ambient of the system. To prove our results, the notations of *distance* and *reachability* are defined. Distance between locations is defined in the context of road sequences with the minimum length between locations. And, reachability of a process is defined in the context that which locations this process can move to by iteration of $COMM$.

Definition 11 *Distance between locations*

Let Loc and RL be a location set and a road set respectively. We call $\langle (l, l_1), (l_1, l_2), \cdots, (l_{n-1}, l') \rangle \in RL^+$ a 'road sequence' from the location l to the location l', and write $\langle l, l_1, \cdots, l_{n-1}, l' \rangle$. A distance $d(l \rightarrow l')$ from l to l' is defined as follows:

$$d(l \rightarrow l') = \begin{cases} \min\{n|\langle l, l_1, \cdots, l_{n-1}, l' \rangle \in RL^+\} \\ \infty \quad \text{if no road sequences from } l \text{ to } l'. \end{cases}$$

Furthermore, for A, $B \subset Loc$, the distance $d(A \rightarrow B)$ from A to B is defined as follows:

$$d(A \rightarrow B) = \min\{d(l \rightarrow l')|l \in A, l' \in B\}.$$

These distances are defined from the context of the number of roads between two locations, and these mean a kind of difficulty of communication between πF-processes at those locations. Note that $d(l \rightarrow l') \neq d(l' \rightarrow l)$ because a field is a finite directed graph. For the previous field $\mathcal{F}_1$, $d(1 \rightarrow 3) = 2$ in spite of $d(3 \rightarrow 1) = \infty$.

The next, *reachability* is defined. $Reach(P, l)$ is an area to which P is reachable from the location l by applying $MOVE$ repeatedly.

Definition 12 *Reachability*

For πF-processes P and locations l and l', we say that P is reachable from l to l', written $P : l \hookrightarrow l'$, if $\exists A \subset Loc$ $\bullet (P, l, A) \in MV$, $l' \in A$. Furthermore, the reachable area, $Reach(P, l)$, of P from l is defined as follows:

$$Reach(P, l) = \{l'|P : l(\hookrightarrow)^* l'\}.$$

To clarify connection of πF-process on an ambient, the concept of adjoining communications is extended to labors.

Definition 13 *Adjoining communication of labors*

Adjoining communication of labors for a given field is defined as follows. Let an ambient $\langle \mathcal{F} = \langle Loc, RL \rangle, MV \rangle$ be given. Let P_1, P_2 be πF-processes such as $P_1 \succeq P_2$ and l_1, l_2 be locations. Here, let there exist transitions, $Q_1 \succ R_1$, of P_1 and transitions, $Q_2 \succ R_2$, of P_2. And, let there exist $l_{k_1} \in Reach(P_1, l_1)$ and $l_{k_2} \in Reach(P_2, l_2)$. We write $\{P_1\}l_1 \succeq \{P_2\}l_2$ on $\langle \mathcal{F}, MV \rangle$, if

$$\{m_i \rhd Q_1\}l_{k_1} \mid \{Q_2\}l_{k_2} \\ (\rightarrow)^* \longrightarrow \{m_i \rhd R_1\}l_{k_1} \mid \{m_i \rhd R_2\}l_{k_2}.$$

Next lemma shows that an adjoining communication of labors results to the distance between reachable areas. Note that we use the index '0' to indicate the initial locations of corresponding processes such that $l_{1,0}$ is the initial locations of P_1 hereafter.

Lemma 2 *If $P_1 \succeq P_2$ and $\{P_1\}l_{1,0} \succeq \{P_2\}l_{2,0}$ on $\langle \mathcal{F}, MV \rangle$, then*

$$d(Reach(P_1, l_{1,0}) \rightarrow Reach(P_2, l_{2,0})) = 1$$

The proof of this lemma is shown in Appendix B.

Finally, we show a main result of this Section, which is a basis of our method.

Theorem 3 *Let $Procs = \prod_{k=1}^n P_k$, $Sys = \prod_{k=1}^n \{P_k\}l_{k,0}$ on $\langle \mathcal{F}, MV \rangle$. If $\{P_i\}l_{i,0}$ **con** $\{P_j\}l_{j,0}$ on $\langle \mathcal{F}, MV \rangle$, then there exist processes $P_{k_1}, \cdots, P_{k_p}$ such that $P_i = P_{k_1} \succeq P_{k_2} \succeq \cdots \succeq P_{k_p} = P_j$, and*

$$1 \leq \forall q < p \bullet REACH(P_{k_q}, l_{k_q,0}, P_{k_{q+1}}, l_{k_{q+1},0})$$

is satisfied, where $REACH(P_{k_q}, l_{k_q,0}, P_{k_{q+1}}, l_{k_{q+1},0})$ is

$$d(Reach(P_{k_q}, l_{k_q,0}) \rightarrow Reach(P_{k_{q+1}}, l_{k_{q+1},0})) = 1 \quad (8)$$

(Proof) It is clear from Lemma 2.

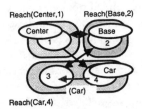

(a) The reachable area for $\mathcal{A}_1$.

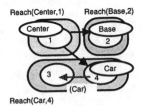

(b) The reachable area for $\mathcal{A}_2$

Figure 2. The reachable areas of *Center, Base* **and** *Car*

Theorem 3 means that connectivity of πF-processes on an ambient results to distances among reachable areas corresponding to them. If connectivity of πF-processes is satisfied, it is sufficient to verify whether the above condition Eq. (8) (abbreviated $REACH$) is satisfied or not.

An overview of Theorem 3 is explained using examples in Sec. 3.1. In these examples, *Center* is connectable to *Base* on $\langle \mathcal{F}_1, MV_1 \rangle$ but not on $\langle \mathcal{F}_2, MV_2 \rangle$. This fact can be explained from the view of reachable areas of processes. The reachable areas of *Center*, *Base* and *Car* for $\langle \mathcal{F}_1, MV_1 \rangle$ is shown in Fig. 2 (a). In this case, *Center* $\succeq$ *Base* $\succeq$ *Car*, and *Center* **con** *Base*.

In general, an equation $d(A \rightarrow B) = 1$ corresponds to the existence of direct roads from A to B. For the field $\mathcal{F}_1$, there exists a road, $(1, 2)$, from $Reach(Center, 1)$ to $Reach(Base, 2)$, and there also exists a road, $(2, 3)$, from $Reach(Base, 2)$ to $Reach(Car, 4)$. So,

$$d(Reach(Center, 1) \rightarrow Reach(Base, 2)) = 1$$
$$d(Reach(Base, 2) \rightarrow Reach(Car, 4)) = 1$$

Thus, $\{Center\}1$ **con** $\{Car\}4$ on $\langle \mathcal{F}_1, MV_1 \rangle$. On the other hand, the case of $\langle \mathcal{F}_2, MV_2 \rangle$ is shown in Fig. 2 (b). Processes *Center*, *Base* and *Car* satisfy the same conditions as the case $\langle \mathcal{F}_1, MV_1 \rangle$. However, there are no roads from $Reach(Base, 2)$ to $Reach(Car, 4)$, i.e.

$$d(Reach(Base, 2) \rightarrow Reach(Car, 4)) = \infty. \quad (9)$$

Therefore, *Center* is not connectable to *Car* on $\langle \mathcal{F}_2, MV_2 \rangle$.

4. Modification of an ambient for maintenance of connectivity

In this section, we show a method to maintain connectivity of πF-processes for defective fields simply. Our approach was planned from the fact that maintenance of ambients is effective and important for mobile systems. For example, communications using mobile phone systems are not always available even if phones themselves run normally. Most of obstacles of communications are decays of a radio wave by buildings. For such a case, communications may be recovered by adjustment of positions of base stations or construction of new stations. Our method is the formalization of such a recovering in the context of πF.

The method shown in this section is based on the discussion in Sec. 3. As mentioned above, communications of πF-processes are restricted by an ambient. Theorem 3 says that the condition $REACH$ Eq. (8) must be satisfied to allow connections of πF-processes for each adjoining process pair. This means that defects of connections are due to failure of $REACH$. So, a field is modified to hold $REACH$ in our approach.

4.1. A policy for modifications of fields

There are some approaches to recover connections of communication processes. If processes losing connections would be moved to other locations at which communications are possible, then these connections may be recovered. New communication routes may recover them. Thus, in order to recover connections of πF-processes using only a few modifications of fields, we take the following policies.
[Modification policy]

Let the current ambient be $\langle \mathcal{F} = \langle Loc, RL \rangle, MV \rangle$. We will modify them to $NewLoc$, $NewRL$ and $NewMV$ according to the following policy.

(I) Modify only MV.
   It is for the case that communications can be recovered by extension of process movements.

$$NewLoc = Loc, NewRL = RL, NewMV \supset MV$$

(II) Modify only RL.
   It is for the case that communications can not be recovered by (I).

$$NewLoc = Loc, NewRL \supset RL, NewMV \supset MV$$

(III) Increase locations.
   It is for the case that communications can not be recovered by (I) or (II).

$$NewLoc \supset Loc, NewRL \supset RL, NewMV \supset MV$$

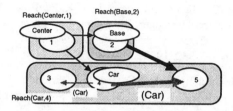

Figure 3. The result of modification for the defective ambient $\mathcal{A}_2$.

The policy that we take is due to the fact that it is easier to recover communications by treating process movement than by making new communication routes.

4.2. An example

We show an simple example of an defective ambient modification using the previous ambient $\mathcal{A}_2$. In this case, Eq. (9) obstructs $Center$ **con** Car on $\mathcal{A}_2$. Eq. (9) reflects the situation that a kind of building disturbs the communication between the base station and the car. To satisfy Theorem 3, $\mathcal{A}_2$ can be modified according to the policy (III). Omitting the detail, the result of modification is shown in Fig. 3. In this modification, new location '5' is accompanied with new road $(2,5)$ and new movement $(Car, 4, \{3,5\})$ to satisfy $REACH(Base,2,Car,4) = 1$. This modification may correspond to the situation that the car becomes movable to the area where it is possible to receive signals from the base station in real life.

An ambient corresponds to lower layers of a communication protocol in a broad sense. The physical layer includes not only communication media but roads, buildings, a climate and a topography surrounding the system. Accordingly, modification of an ambient may be implemented by various ways in real life, e.g. by connecting cables, by making a (real) road or constructing a building. Such an implementation is according to the system and its environment.

5 Conclusion

We have considered stability of mobile systems from the point of view of their ambients and have proposed a maintenance method of these ambients in this paper. In our formalization, mobility of processes is separated from communications among processes. Doing this, process descriptions can be simple, and causes of restriction of communications can be explicit. Clarity of causes of such restrictions are effective to maintenance systems.

Explicit treatments of physical distribution of processes on a heterogeneous computer network have also been shown by De Nicola, et al. [16] and Cardelli and Gordon [17]. De Nicola et.al have also introduced environments, called KLAIM nets, of processes and have proposed a language for interaction and mobility of agents. Cardelli and Gordon have emphasized in-out features of processes. While they have focused on mobility of mobile agents in a network, we have focused on mobility of *physical* processes, e.g. cars. It is not easy to include locality of such processes to their process descriptions, so that we make explicit structures of locations on which processes are placed. Directed graphs may be not suitable to express these structures because the same environment may differently affect processes according to properties of these processes. We think that it is necessary to separate mobility from restrictions of communications despite of such a situation.

Our method is simulation oriented in a sense that maintenance of complex system ambients can not be established without a computational support system. We plan to implement a support environment on a computer network based on our maintenance method. In general, it is not necessary to repair all connections to preserve connectivity between particular processes. So, it may be sufficient to partially automatize this maintenance method. We think that people must finally decide how they repair when accidents occur. So, people may select one of prescriptions indicated by this support environment. Monitoring conditions about locations, e.g. a town or a road, of a mobile system using distributed sensors, location information can be available to maintain this mobile system based on our formalization. Development of this support system on a distributed environment is a future work. Furthermore, we are going to formalize limitation by competition among processes on a restricted resources. Finite channels available to each base station in mobile telephone systems and finite packets through a communication trunk are applications of it.

References

[1] J. Padgett, C. Gunther and T. Hattori, "Overview of Wireless Personal Communications", *IEEE Communication Magazine*, vol.33, pp.28–41, 1995.

[2] M. Shafi, A. Hashimoto, M. Umehira, S. Ogose and T. Murase, "Wireless Communications in the Twenty-First Century: A Perspective", *Proceedings of the IEEE*, Vol.85, No.10, pp.1622-1638, 1997.

[3] Japanese Ministry of Construction ITS homepage, http://www.moc.go.jp/road/ITS/index.html.

[4] R. Milner, "The poliadic π-calculus: a tutorial", *Technical Report* ECS – LFCS – 91 – 180, Labo. for Foun-

dations of Comp. Sci., Dept. Comp.Sci., Univ. Edinburgh, UK, 1991.

[5] R. Milner, J. Parrow and D. Walker, "A calculus of mobile processes, Part I and II", *Journal of Information and Computation*, vol.100, pp. 1–77, September, 1992.

[6] D. Sangiorgi, "Locality and non-interleaving semantics in calculi for mobile processes", *Technical Report ECS-LFCS-94-282*, Laboratory for Foundations of Computer Science, Department of Computer Science, University of Edinburgh, UK, 1994.

[7] R.M. Amadio, and S. Prasad, "Localities and failures", *Proceedings FST-TCS'94, LNCS 880*, pp. 205–216. Springer-Verlag, 1994.

[8] R.M. Amadio, "An asynchronous model of locality, failure, and process mobility", *Rappoit Interne LIM*, February 1997, and *INRIA Research Report 3109*, 1997.

[9] R.M. Amadio and S. Prasad, "Modeling IP Mobility", *Proceedings CONCUR'98, LNCS 1466*, pp. 301–, Springer-Verlag, 1998.

[10] Y. Isobe, Y.Yutaka and K. Ohmaki, "Approximative Analysis by process algebra with graded spatial actions", *Proceedings AMAST'96, LNCS 1101*, pp.336-350, Springer-Verlag, 1996.

[11] R. Cleaveland, G. Lüttgen and V. Natarajan, "A Process Algebra with Distributed Priorities", *Proceedings CONCUR'96, LNCS 1119*, pp.34–49, Springer-Verlag, 1996.

[12] C. Fournet and G. Gonthier, J. Lévy, L. Maranget and D. Rémy, "A Calculus of Mobile Agents", *Proceedings CONCUR'96, LNCS 1119*, pp.406–421, Springer-Verlag, 1996.

[13] T. Ando, K. Takahashi and Y. Kato, "On a Concurrency calculus for design of mobile telecommunication systems", *Proceedings FORTE(X)/PSTV(XVII)'97*, pp.535-546, 1997.

[14] R.M. Amadio, I. Castellani and D. Sangiorgi. "On Bisimulations for the Asynchronous π-calculus", *Proceedings CONCUR'96, LNCS 1119*, pp.147–162, Springer-Verlag, 1996.

[15] M. Boreale, "On the Expressiveness of Internal Mobility in Name-Passing Calculi", *Proceedings CONCUR'96, LNCS 1119*, pp.163–178, Springer-Verlag, 1996.

[16] R. De Nicola, G.F. Ferrari and R. Pugliese, "KLAIM: A Kernel Language for Agents Interaction and Mobility," *IEEE Trans. Software Engineering*, Vol.24, No.5, pp.315-330, 1998.

[17] L.Cardelli and A.D. Gordon, "Mobile Ambients", *Proceedings FoSSaCS'98, LNCS 1378*, pp.140-145, Springer-Verlag, 1998.

A. The proof of Proposition 1

We prove Proposition 1. To prove this proposition, we prove that Eqs. (5) and (7) are equivalent to each other.

(5) $\Rightarrow$ (7): From the definitions of $MARK$ and $COMM$, there exist $P_{k_{p-1}}, R_{k_{p-1}}, P'_{k-p-1}$ and R_{k_p} such as

$$P_{k_{p-1}}(\succ)^* R_{k_{p-1}} \succ P'_{k-p-1}, P_j = P_{k_p}(\succ)^* R_{k_p} \succ P'_{k_p},$$
$$(m \triangleright R_{k_{p-1}})|R_{k_p} (\to)^* \longrightarrow (m \triangleright P'_{k_{p-1}})|(m \triangleright P'_{k_p}).$$

Namely, $P_{k_{p-1}} \succeq P_{k_p}$. Furthermore, for the above $R_{k_{p-1}}$, there exist $P_{k_{p-2}}, S_{k_{p-2}}, R_{k_{p-2}}$ and $S_{k_{p-1}}$ such as

$$P_{k_{p-2}}(\succ)^* S_{k_{p-2}} \succ R_{k_{p-2}}, P_{k_{p-1}}(\succ)^* S_{k_{p-1}} \succ R_{k_{p-1}},$$
$$(m \triangleright S_{k_{p-2}})|S_{k_{p-1}} (\to)^* \longrightarrow (m \triangleright R_{k_{p-2}})|(m \triangleright R_{k_{p-1}}).$$

Thus, $P_{k_{p-2}} \succeq P_{k_{p-1}} \succeq P_{k_p}$. Similarly, there exist $P_{k_1}, \cdots, P_{k_{p-3}}$ such as

$$P_i = P_{k_1} \succeq P_{k_2} \succeq \cdots \succeq P_{k_{p-2}}.$$

Therefore, (7) is satisfied.

(7) $\Rightarrow$ (5): $P_{k_{p-1}} \succeq P_{k_p}$ implies that there exist $R_{k_{p-1}}$, $P'_{k_{p-1}}, R_{k_p}$ and P'_{k_p} such as

$$P_{k_{p-1}}(\succ)^* R_{k_{p-1}} \succ P'_{k_{p-1}}, P_j = P_{k_p}(\succ)^* R_{k_p} \succ P'_{k_p}$$
$$(m \triangleright R_{k_{p-1}})|R_{k_p} (\to)^* \longrightarrow (m \triangleright P'_{k_{p-1}})|(m \triangleright P'_{k_p}).$$

Thus,

$$Ping(Procs, P_i)((\to)^* \longrightarrow)^* \prod_{1 \le k \ge, k \ne j} Q_k|(m \triangleright P'_j)$$

Therefore, Eq. (5) is satisfied. (Q.E.D.)

B. The proof of Lemma 2

We prove Lemma 2 here. If $\{P_1\}l_{1,0} \succeq \{P_2\}l_{2,0}$ on $\langle \mathcal{F}, MV \rangle$, then

$P_1(\succ)^* \exists Q_1 \succ \exists R_1, P_2(\succ)^* \exists Q_2 \succ \exists R_2,$
$\exists l_1 \in Reach(P_1, l_{1,0}), \exists l_2 \in Reach(P_2, l_{2,0})$
$\bullet \{m \triangleright Q_1\}l_1|\{Q_2\}l_2 \longrightarrow \{m \triangleright R_1\}l_1|\{m \triangleright R_2\}l_2.$

This means $(l_1, l_2) \in RL$. Thus, $d(l_1 \to l_2) = 1$. Therefore,

$$d(Reach(P_1, l_{1,0}) \to Reach(P_2, l_{2,0})) = 1$$

(Q.E.D)

Session B8

Networking Protocols

Chair: Teruo Higashino
Osaka University, Japan

An Efficient Fault-Tolerant Multicast Routing Protocol

with Core-Based Tree Techniques

Weijia Jia[+]   Wei Zhao[*]
[+]Department of Computer Science
City University of Hong Kong
Kowloon, Hong Kong
Email: {wjia, gxu}@cs.cityu.edu.hk

Dong Xuan[*] Gaochao Xu[+]
[*]Department of Computer Science
Texas A & M University
College Station, TX77843-3112
Email: {zhao, dxuan}@cs.tamu.edu

Abstract

In this paper, we study an efficient fault-tolerant CBT multicast routing protocol. With our strategy, when a faulty component is detected, some pre-defined backup path(s) is (are) used to bypass the faulty component and enable the multicast communication to continue. Our protocol only requires that routers near the faulty component be reconfigured, thus reducing the runtime overhead without compromising much of the performance. Our performance evaluation shows that our new protocol performs nearly as well as the best possible global method while utilizing much less runtime overhead and implementation cost.

1. Introduction

Reliable multicast communication is critical for the success of many applications such as video/audio-broadcasting, resource discovery, server location, etc. Recently, these applications have become increasingly popular due to the availability of the Internet.

In general, there are two approaches for multicast routing protocols over the Internet: source-based-tree routing and shared-tree routing. Many protocols have been developed including *Distance-Vector Multicast Routing Protocol* (DVMRP)[WPD88], *Multicast Extensions to Open Shortest-Path First* (MOSPF) [M94b], Protocol Independent Multicast (PIM) [DEFJLW96], and Core Based Tree Multicast (CBT) [BFC93] etc.

A problem associated with *source-based-tree* routing is that a router has to keep the pair information (source, group) and it is a ONE tree per source. In reality the Internet is a complex, heterogeneous environment, which potentially has to support many thousands of active groups, each of which may be sparsely distributed, this technique clearly does not scale.

Shared tree based multicast routing is more scalable than source-based-tree routing. For example, in comparison with the source-based-tree approach, a shared tree architecture associated with the CBT method offers an improvement in scalability by a factor of the number of active sources. Because of its scalability and simplicity, core-based tree multicast protocols have been widely used in many multicast systems.

However, the core-based-tree method may have a reliability problem. Without any enhancement, a single point of failure on the tree will partition the tree and hence make it difficult, if not impossible, to fulfill the requirement of multicasting [B97]. While various solutions have been proposed to address the problem, they usually require relatively large tree reformation when faults occur [BFC93 and B97]. A global strategy of this type can be costly and complicated.

In this paper, we aim at enhancing the CBT protocol with fault-tolerant capability and improving its performance in terms of packet delay and resource consumption. Our approach can be briefly summarized as follows:

1) A localized configuration methodology is used. When a faulty component in the network is detected, some pre-defined backup path(s) is (are) used to bypass the faulty component and thus enable the multicast communication to continue. Backup paths can be identified off-line. At runtime, our protocol will only require that routers on the backup path(s) be reconfigured. In this way, we are able to reduce the runtime overhead of the protocol without compromising a significant amount of the performance.

2) Traditional CBT method routes a multicast packet from its source towards the core of the shared tree. In many situations, this could create traffic congestion (near the core). We propose to route a multicast packet from its source to the nearest node on the tree. This eliminates potential congestion problem and improves the network performance such as packet delay and resource consumption.

3) Faults in the network occur randomly at runtime. In a faulty situation, several routers may detect the fault and initiate reconfiguration processes. A protocol should be *consistent* in the sense that no matter how faults occur and are detected, routers co-operate and restore the network in an agreeable and operational state. In our protocol, the functionality of routers during the fault management process is clearly specified in accordance with the status information available to the router. As a result, while routers act asynchronously in a distributed environment, the consistency requirement is met.

We evaluate the performance of our new fault-tolerant multicast protocol. Performance data in terms of packet delay and resource consumption are collected. They indicate that in normal (i.e., non-faulty) situations, our protocol outperforms the traditional core-based tree protocol due to the fact that our protocol is capable of eliminating potential traffic congestion. In the case when

508

faults do occur, our protocol performs very closely to the best global reconfiguration method that provides the theoretical performance bound.

2. Models and Notations

The network we consider consists of a number of nodes (e.g., routers and hosts). Nodes are connected by physical (dual directional) links along which packets can be transmitted. Each link has an attribute called *delay*. A network is modeled as a graph $N(V, E)$ where V is a finite set of vertices in N, representing nodes in the network concerned; E is a finite set of edges, representing the links between nodes.

A node (say R) is *next hop* from another node (say R') if R can receive a packet directly from R' without going through any other router. The key data structure which a router uses for routing is *routing table*. An entry in a routing table usually consists of fields for destination address, next hop, distance, etc. For an incoming packet, the router locates an entry in a routing table such that the destination address of the packet matches the destination address of the entry. In a router, once the next hop of a packet is determined, the packet will be transported to a proper output interface where the packet will be transmitted into the associated output link, which, in turn, connects to the next hop.

Obviously, if the network status is changed (e.g., some link fails, some router joins, etc), the routing tables of routers in the network may need to be updated. We say that a router is *reconfigured* if its routing table is updated (in accordance to some protocol).

Routers in the network cooperatively decide a path for a packet and transmit the packet along the path. Formally, P(X, Y) denotes a *path* from X to Y where X and Y are nodes. Sometimes, we would like to list explicitly the sequence of nodes in a path. We use terms "route" and "path" interchangeably. $d(P(X, Y))$ denotes the *total distance* of links on path P(X, Y). It is usually defined by a numeric sum of the individual link distances.

A *shortest path* from X to Y is usually denoted as $SP(X, Y)$. That is, among all the path between X and Y, $d(P(X, Y)) \geq d(SP(X, Y))$.

In this paper, we assume that for given X and Y, the shortest path between them is unique. This assumption simplifies our analysis but can be easily removed.

A packet is specified by addresses of its source and destination. The source of a packet is usually a host. The destination for a multicast packet is denoted as G that represents a group of designated recipient hosts. That is, a packet with multicast address G should be sent to all the hosts in the recipient group.

At runtime, network components (e.g., links and routers) can fail. We assume that the faulty state of a component can be detected by (some of) its neighboring routers. This can be achieved by a "keep-alive" mechanism operating between adjacent (directly linked) routers. A keep-alive mechanism may be implemented by means of ICMP echo request/reply messages [D91].

3. Fault-Tolerant Multicast Protocol

3.1. Overview

As stated earlier, our strategy is to enhance the existing CBT protocol so that it will have fault tolerance capability and at the same time its effectiveness and efficiency are improved. Design and implementation of such a protocol is, nevertheless, a challenging task. There are three primary objectives:

1) Network performance. One of the protocol objectives is to optimize various network performance metrics such as the message delay, resource usage, etc.
2) Runtime overhead. To make the protocol fault-tolerant, fault management function may be invoked at runtime. Thus, the overhead of this function should be minimized in order for the network to provide the best possible services to the payload applications.
3) Consistency. The protocol should ensure that no matter how a fault occurs and is detected, routers co-operate and restore the network in an agreeable and operational state. The consistency issue will be addressed in Section 3.4.

While all these objectives are important, they may conflict with each other. For example, reducing the runtime overhead may compromise the network performance. In our design of the protocol, we take a balanced approach: we seek near-optimal performance and at the same time we take measures to reduce runtime overhead and to guarantee consistency.

Our fault-tolerant multicast routing protocol can be divided into two parts:

1) Packet Transmission Sub-Protocol that is responsible for delivering multicast packets;
2) Fault Management Sub-Protocol that will detect faults, reconfigure the network, and hence provide necessary infrastructure for the packet transmission sub-protocol to achieve its mission.

3.2. Packet Transmission Sub-Protocol

Many protocols have been proposed and analyzed for transmitting multicast packets. Proposed in [BFC93], the Core-Based Tree Protocol (CBT) is a multicast routing protocol that builds a single delivery tree per group that is shared by all of the group's sources and receivers. An advantage of the shared-tree approach is that it typically offers more favorable scaling characteristics than all other multicast algorithms [M94a, M94b, WPD88]. Because of this, we choose CBT as our baseline protocol and intend to enhance it with fault-tolerance capability and improve its efficiency and effectiveness.

Step 1. Selecting a core for a given multicast group;
Step 2. For each member in the multicast group, locating the shortest path from the member to the core;
Step 3. Merging the shortest paths identified in Step 2.

At runtime, when a source generates a multicast packet the packet is first transmitted from the source to (somewhere of) the tree. Once on the tree, the packet is dispatched to all the branches of the tree and delivered to all the receivers.

An interesting problem is what path to use for transmitting a packet from its source to the tree. In [BFC93], it is recommended that the shortest path from the source to the core of the tree should be used. We call it the "SP-To-Core" method. This method is simple, but it may cause traffic congestion on the links close to the core because the traffic from different sources is concentrated there.

To improve network performance, we propose a new method: For an off-tree router, we first find the shortest paths from the router to all the nodes on the multicast tree. Then, we select the path that is the shortest among these shortest paths and use it to route a multicast packet from this router to the tree. Because our method uses the shortest of the shortest paths to the tree, we call it "SSP-to-Tree".

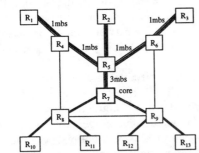

Link on CBT ▬▬ Link taken by off tree multicast traffic ─── Other Link

R_1, R_2, and R_3 are source routers, each transmits 1 MBS multicast traffic. As a result, the bandwidth usage on link from R_5 to R_7 is 3MBS, significantly higher than others.

Figure 3-1. A Traffic Flow with SP-To-Core Method

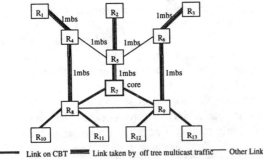

Link on CBT ▬▬ Link taken by off tree multicast traffic ─── Other Link

R_1, R_2, and R_9 are source routers, each transmits 1 MBS multicast traffic. Due to the SSP-To-Tree method, the bandwidth usage on links is better balanced.

Figure 3-2. Traffic Flow with SSP-To-Tree Method

Our method may appear to be more complex. But it merely will take more off-line time to collect locations of nodes and compute the shortest paths. Once the route is determined, the runtime overhead is the same as the SP-to-Core method.

Nevertheless, our new method may eliminate the potential problem of traffic congestion. Figures 3-1 and 3-2 show the traffic flow in a network with these two methods. It is clear that with SSP-To-Tree method, the bandwidth usage is better balanced and the traffic congestion is removed.

3.3. Fault Management Sub-Protocol

Recall that Fault Management Sub-Protocol (FMSP) is responsible for detecting faults and reconfiguring the network once faults are detected. Thus, it provides necessary infrastructure for the Packet Transmission Sub-Protocol to deliver multicast packets. In this sub-section, we will focus on the technique for handling single fault that occurs on the Core-Based Tree.

3.3.1. General Approaches

Consider that at runtime a component (link or router) on the Core-Based Tree becomes faulty. To continue multicast communication, alternative routes for the multicast packets, that used to be transmitted through the faulty component, must be utilized. Two approaches can be taken. With a *global* approach, the faulty status will be informed to all the routers in the network. Consequently, based on the faulty status the core-base tree may be rebuilt and (potentially all) the routers may be reconfigured. Note that all these operations have to be performed on-line. Thus, while this may help to achieve theoretically optimal performance, the runtime overhead (including the notification of the faulty state and reconfiguration of routers) may be too large to make this approach practical.

We take a *local* approach. Rather than rebuilding the core-base tree and reconfiguring all the routers, we will use pre-defined backup paths to bypass the faulty component. We then just reconfigure the routers that are on the involved backup paths. All the packets that were supposed to be transmitted over the faulty link will be routed via the backup path(s).

Obviously, our local approach is simple, and involves very small runtime overhead in comparison with the global approach. The performance evaluation in Section 4 will show that our local reconfiguration approach performs closely to the best possible global approach in most cases. The fault management sub-protocol involves the following tasks:

1) Initialization. The task here is to select backup paths.

2) Fault detection. Assume that each router is continuously monitoring the status of upstream link and router and hence is able to determine if they are in a faulty state.

3) Backup path invocation. Once detecting a fault of upstream link, the router should start notifying this state information to all the routers on its backup path so that they are ready to be used.

4) Router configuration. After all the routers on a backup path confirm their readiness, they will be configured in order to let traffic re-route via the backup path.

Before we describe each of the above tasks in detail, we will first discuss the methods used for router configuration. As we will see, these reconfiguration methods have impact on the functions of other tasks.

3.3.2. Configuration Methods

We consider two methods to configure the routers on a backup path. They differ in overhead and potential performance. The first method is the *virtual repair* method. With this method, no routing table is to be changed on the invoked backup path. Instead, a pre-programmed agent will be installed at the two end routers. The agent will encapsulate a multicast packet, which was supposed to be transmitted via the faulty component. The encapsulated packet will be source-routed (via. the backup path) to the other end of the backup path. The agent at the other end of the backup path, once receiving the encapsulated packet, will de-encapsulate it and transmit along the normal path(s) where the packet should be dispatched. Thus, the topology of the tree is virtually unchanged, except that the faulty component is bypassed.

The second method is called the *real repair* method. With this method, all the routing tables on the backup path will be changed to reflect the new topology of the tree. Packets are routed according to new routing table.

Figure 3-3 shows an example of using these two methods. In Figure 3-3 (a) shows a portion of the network with the original core-based tree. Assume that there is a fault on the link between R_4 and R_6. Let the backup path that is used to reconnect the disjoint tree be $<R_6, R_5, R_3>$. Figure 3-3 (b) shows the situation after virtual repair. In this case, the agent on R_3 will encapsulate the multicast packets and source-route encapsulated packets to R_6 via R_5. Vice versa for the packets from R_6 to R_3. However, R_3 still has to send multicast packets to R_5. Hence, the load between R_3 and R_5 is doubled because the tree is virtually repaired. The situation will improve when the real repair method is used as shown in Figure 3-3 (c). In this case, R_5 and R_6 will be reconfigured to recognize that while R_5 continues to be a son of R_3, R_6 is now a new son of R_5. Hence, the packets between R_3 and R_5 will not be transmitted twice.

Clearly, the virtual repair method is simple and can quickly restore a path. But, it may utilize extra bandwidth

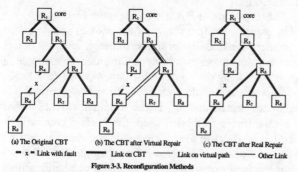

(a) The Original CBT   (b) The CBT after Virtual Repair   (c) The CBT after Real Repair
━ x ━ Link with fault   ━━ Link on CBT   ━━ Link on virtual path   ━━ Other Link
Figure 3-3. Reconfiguration Methods

and cause longer delay because the routers on the path are not configured to take the advantage of the new topology. On the other hand, the real repair method may produce better performance (in terms of packet delay, for example). But this method is complicated and takes more runtime overhead during the reconfiguration process. backup path they can use. We discuss this topic next.

3.3.3. Selection of Backup Paths
3.3.3.1. Backup Paths with the Virtual Repair Method

For the sake of simplicity, we will first consider the situation where fault only occurs on the core-based tree and there is at most one fault at a time.

First, we need to introduce some notations. For any two routers (R and R') on the core-base tree, R is a *son* of R' and R' is the *father* of R if there is a link between R and R' and R' is (in terms of distance) closer to the core than R. R" is the *grandfather* of R if R" is the father of R' and R' is the father of R. Note that the core router has neither father nor grandfather. The sons of the core router have father (which is the core), but have no grandfather. All other routers have both father and grandfather.

One of the sons of the core is selected to be the *backup-core* that will become core if the core fails. How to select the backup-core is irrelevant to the function of the fault management. In practice it may be selected from network administrative point of view, as suggested in selecting the

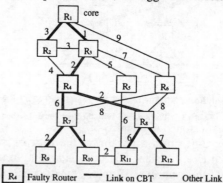

Figure 3-4. Backup Path with the Virtual Repair Method

core [BFC93].

With this method, every router on the tree, except the core, *owns* a pre-defined *backup path*. For a router that has grandfather (i.e., the one that is not a son of the core), its backup path is a path that connects itself to its grandfather. A constraint on the backup path of a router is that the path does not contain the father of the owner. In Figure 3-4, for example, $<R_7, R_4, R_2, R_3>$ cannot be the backup path of R_7 because it contains R_4 which is the father of R_7. But $<R_7, R_{10}, R_{11}, R_5, R_3>$ can be the backup path of R_7.

For a router that has no grandfather, its backup path is a path that connects this router to the backup-core. In Figure 3-4, if the backup core is R_3, then the backup path of R_2 could be $<R_2, R_3>$. For the backup-core router, its backup path is a path that connects itself to the core, but bypasses the link between itself and the core. In Figure 3-4, if the backup-core is R_3, then the backup path of R_3 could be $<R_3, R_2, R_1>$.

We assume that for each router on the tree (except the core), at least one backup path exists. It easy to verify that if a non-core router has no backup path, then the network is not single fault tolerable. For a router, if multiple backup paths exist, we select the one with the shortest distance.

The routers on a backup path can be divided into three kinds, namely owner, terminator, and on-path routers, depending on their function in the fault management. The first router on the backup path is the *owner* of backup path. The router at the other end of a backup path is called *terminator*. Other routers on the backup path excluding the owner and terminator routers are called *on-path routers*.

3.3.3.2. Backup Paths with the Real Repair Method

As discussed above, with the virtual repair method the shortest path from a router to its grandfather is used as its backup path. One would think that we could define the backup path in the same way for the real repair method. Unfortunately, this idea does not work as shown by the

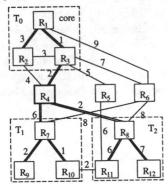

$\boxed{R_4}$ Faulty Router ▬▬▬ Link on CBT ▬▬▬ Other Link T_0, T_1, T_2: Sub-trees

Figure 3-5. Backup Path With the Real Repair Method

examples illustrated in Figure 3-5.

Figure 3-5 shows a portion of the network with the core-based tree. Assume that there is a faulty router, R_4. Because of this, sub-trees T_1 and T_2 are disconnected from the original core-based tree. In Figure 3-5, let the shortest path from R_7 to its grandfather (R_3) be $<R_7, R_{10}, R_{11}, R_5, R_3>$ and the shortest path from R_8 to its grandfather be $<R_8, R_6, R_3>$. It is easy to see in Figure 3-5 that if these two shortest paths were used as backup paths, a loop $<R_3, R_5, R_{11}, R_8, R_6, R_3>$ would occur. The example show that if the backup path of a router transverses another partitioned sub-tree, a loop may occur. Thus, the selection of backup path with the real repair method is not a trivial task. Before stating our selection method, we need to establish some properties of the core-based tree.

Assume that there is a faulty router, R, on the core-based tree. Because of this, the core-based tree is split into m+1 sub-trees, namely $T_0, T_1, \ldots, T_m$ where T_0 is the sub-tree that contains the core, and T_i (i = 1, ..., m) is the sub-tree whose root is a son of the faulty router. Let the routers on T_i be indexed $R_{i,j}$. In particular, $R_{i,0}$ is the root of T_i.

Let P_i be the shortest path from $R_{i,0}$ to the father of R. Define relation $\Rightarrow$ as follows: $T_i \Rightarrow T_j$ if and only if:
1) P_i contains a router (say, $R_{j,k}$) that belongs to T_j and
2) for any other $R_{j',k'}$ that is on $T_{j'}$ and is contained in P_i, $R_{j,k}$ is closer to $R_{i,0}$ than $R_{j',k'}$ is.

In this case, we say T_i relates itself to T_j, i.e. $T_i \Rightarrow T_j$ if T_j is the first sub-tree which transverses, except T_i itself.

For this relation, we have the following results.

Lemma 3-1. The relation $\Rightarrow$ has the following properties:
Property A. The relation $\Rightarrow$ is not cyclic. That is, there is no subset of sub-trees (say, $T_{k1}, T_{k2}, \ldots, T_{kh}$) such that $T_{k1} \Rightarrow T_{k2} \Rightarrow T_{k3} \Rightarrow \ldots \Rightarrow T_{kh} \Rightarrow T_{k1}$.
Property B. Sub-tree T_0 does not relate itself to any other sub-tree T_i (i = 1, 2, ..., m).
Property C. Every other sub-tree T_i (i > 0) uniquely relates itself to some other sub-tree. That is, there is an unique T_j (j ≠ i) such that $T_i \Rightarrow T_j$.

With this lemma, we can get the following theorem:
Theorem 3-1. For every sub-tree T_i (i > 0), either
$$T_i \Rightarrow T_0 \qquad (3\text{-}1)$$
or there is a unique non-empty sequence of sub-trees $<T_{i1}, T_{i2}, \ldots, T_{ik}>$ such that
$$T_i \Rightarrow T_{i1} \Rightarrow T_{i2} \Rightarrow T_{i3} \Rightarrow \ldots \Rightarrow T_{ik} \Rightarrow T_0. \qquad (3\text{-}2)$$
Proof. If $T_i \Rightarrow T_0$, then the theorem is proved. Assume (3-1) is not true. By Property C, T_i has to relate itself to some sub-tree, say (T_{i1}). That is, $T_i \Rightarrow T_{i1}$. If $T_{i1} = T_0$, we are done. Otherwise, T_{i1} has to relate to another sub-tree, say (T_{i2}). So $T_i \Rightarrow T_{i1} \Rightarrow T_{i2}$. We can keep doing this until we reach T_{ih} that does not relate to any other sub-tree. The termination of this process is guaranteed because $\Rightarrow$ is not cyclic and there are finite number of sub-trees. Now, T_{ih} must be T_0. Otherwise we violate Property C. The sequence $<T_{i1}, T_{i2}, \ldots, T_{ih-1}>$ satisfies (3-2). Again by Property C, this sequence has to be unique.

By Theorem 3-1, we have the following algorithm to select backup paths with the real repair method.
1) If Let P be the shortest path from $R_{i,0}$ to its grandfather.
2) If $T_i \Rightarrow T_0$ then trim the tail part of P such that it terminates when it first reaches a router on T_0. Else if $T_i \Rightarrow T_{i1} \Rightarrow T_{i2} \Rightarrow T_{i3} \Rightarrow \ldots \Rightarrow T_{ik} \Rightarrow T_0$, then trim the tail part of P such that it terminates when it first reaches a router on T_{i1}.
3) The remaining of P is the backup path for $R_{i,0}$.

Once again, the first router of the backup path is called the owner, the last one is the terminator, and the others between them are on-path routers. Consider the example in Figure 3-5. Using the above algorithm, we will select $<R_7, R_{10}, R_{11}>$ as the backup path of R_7. R_7 is the owner, R_{10} is an on-path router, and R_{11} is the terminator. Note that if the virtual repair method is used, the backup path will be much longer because over there we do not trim the path.

It is obvious that Theorem 3-1 guarantees that for every son of the faulty router R, a backup path can be identified with the above procedure. Trimming is necessary to avoid the loops as shown in Figure 3-5.

3.3.4. Backup Path Invocation

Backup path invocation is the key part of fault management algorithm. For the sake of completeness, Figure 3-6 shows the entire fault Management algorithms which are executed by different kinds of routers. These algorithms are executed in the routers concurrently with other tasks the routers have. In case a router plays multiple roles, these algorithms will be executed simultaneously in

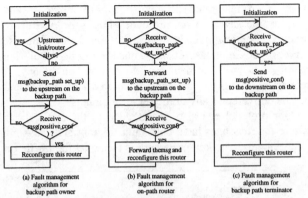

(a) Fault management algorithm for backup path owner

(b) Fault management algorithm for on-path router

(c) Fault management algorithm for backup path terminator

Figure 3-6. Fault Management Algorithms

the router.

It is clear from the above discussion that only the routers on a backup path need to be re-configured in order to repair a fault that occurs on the tree. This will result in very small runtime overhead and can be scaled to large networks. This is the advantage of our local configuration approach.

3.4. Discussion

Our fault tolerant multicast protocol has the following properties

1) In a normal situation (e.g., without any fault), our protocol operates as a CBT protocol.

2) After the backup path is established, a tree is formed. It consists of the backup path and all the links and routers on the original tree except the faulty link or router.

3) For the newly formed tree, if the original core is not fault, it will still be the core for the new tree. Otherwise, the core of the new tree will be the backup-core.

Nevertheless, the above properties imply that while the routers act asynchronously, our fault management sub-protocol guarantees to bring the system into an agreeable and operational state after a fault is detected. Thus, the consistency requirement is met.

We would also like to argue that in addition to the consistency requirement, our other design objectives (stated in Section 3.1) are also well satisfied. Our local approach obviously reduces the runtime overhead without compromising much of the performance. Our SSP-To-Tree method used in the packet transmission sub-protocol eliminates the problem of potential traffic congestion and will improve the delay performance. In Section 4, we will show performance data that will quantitatively justify the above claims.

Finally, we would like to say that our protocol can be easily extended to deal with the case of multiple faults that will not only impact paths on the CBT but also off-tree ones. Due to the space limitation, we can not discuss the extension in detail. The interested readers can refer our paper [XXJZ99].

4. Performance Evaluation
4.1. Simulation Model

In this section, we will report performance results of the new protocol introduced in this paper. To obtain the performance data, we use a discrete event simulation model to simulate data communication networks. The simulation program is written in C programming language and runs in a SUN SPARC work station 20. The network simulated is the ARPA network [PG97]. During the simulation, the multicast packets are randomly generated as a Poisson process. Faults are also randomly generated with X being the average life-time of a fault and Y being the average inter-arrival time of faults. Thus, we have

$$Pf = Prob(\text{The system is in a faulty state}) = X/Y \quad (4\text{-}1)$$

That is, Pf is the probability that the system is in a faulty state. We will measure the network performance as function of Pf. We are interested in the following metrics:

1) *Average end-to-end delay* (or *average delay* in short): The end-to-end delay of a packet is the sum of the delays at all the routers through which the packet passes.

2) *Network resource usage*: This is defined as the total number of hops that (copies of) a multicast packet travel in order to reach all the members in the multicast group.

Four systems are simulated:

1) SPP-To-Tree/V.R. In this system, our newly proposed fault-tolerant multicast communication protocol is simulated. For the router configuration method, the virtual repair method (V.R.) is used.

2) SPP-To-Tree/R.R. This system is the same as SPP-To-V.R. except that the real repair method (R.R.) is used.

3) SPP-To-Tree/N.F. In this system, our newly proposed fault-tolerant multicast communication protocol is simulated. But no fault is generated.

4) SP-To-Core/N.F. In this system, the original CBT protocol is used. No fault is generated in the simulation.

We are interested in SP-To-Core/N.F. because it uses the original CBT protocol. We take it as a baseline system. All the performance measures of SPP-To-Tree/V.R., SPP-To-Tree/R.R., and SPP-To-Tree/N.F. will be normalized by the corresponding data of SP-To-Core/N.F. Thus, the data we reported will be relative ones, relative to SP-To-Core/N.F.

4.2. Performance Observations

The results of the average delay metric are shown in Figure 4-1, while the results of network resource usage metric are shown in Figure 4-2. In Figure 4-2, the performance curve of SSP-to-Tree/N.F is virtually covered by that of SSP-to-Tree/R.R, and is not easily visible. From these data, we can make the following observations:

1) As expected, the SSP-to-Tree/N.F system achieves better performance than the SP-to-Core/N.F. For example, in Figure 4-1, the average of relative delay of SSP-To-Tree/N.F is 0.899. That is, on average the delay of SSP-To-Tree is only 89.9% of that by SP-To-Core. Similarly, in Figure 4-2, the network resource usage of SSP-To-Tree/N.F is 0.928, meaning the delay of SSP-To-Tree is, on average, 92.8% of SP-To-Core/N.F.

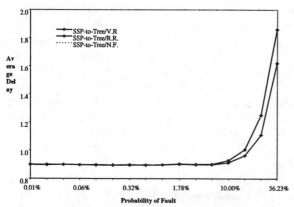

Figure 4-1. Average Delay Relative to SP-to-Core/N.F

2) In the case of low probability of fault (say, Pf < 10%), both SSP-to-Tree/V.R and SSP-to-Tree/R.R perform almost identical to SSP-to-Tree/N.F. As we mentioned earlier, SSP-To-Tree/N.F. provides a lower bound that any (global) fault management algorithm can achieve. Hence, we claim that when the fault probability is not too high, our Fault Management Sub-Protocol with a localized approach performs almost identically as the best possible global one can. Meanwhile, our localized approach would involve with low runtime overhead.

3) when the probability of fault becomes very large (i.e., greater than 10%), the performance of both the SSP-To-Tree/V.R and SSP-To-Tree/R.R is clearly impacted. The greater the Pf value, the worse the end-to-end delay and resource usage are. Specifically, the delay performance increases much more rapidly than the network resource usage as Pf increases. This is because as more faults occur, less functional links and routers are available. Hence, some functional links and routers may become congested. We note that 10% fault probability is really high and is unlikely to happen in reality.

4) The system that uses the real repair method (SSP-To-Tree/R.R.) always performs better than that with the virtual repair method (SSP-To-Tree/V.R.). This coincides with our intuition because the real repair method explicitly takes into account the new topology after a fault occurs. and hence better utilizes the system resources.

5. Final Remarks

We have proposed and analyzed a new fault-tolerant multicast communication protocol. Our protocol consists of two sub-protocols: the Packet Transmission Sub-Protocol and Fault Management Sub-Protocol. The Packet Transmission Sub-Protocol uses an improved version of the original CBT protocol. While maintaining the same level of scalability, our improved CBT protocol has much better performance because of the SSP-To-Tree technology. For the Fault Management Sub-Protocol, we take a localized approach that has a relatively low runtime overhead. Our performance evaluation indicates that it performs very closely to the possible theoretical bound.

Several extensions to our work are possible. We may apply the technology we developed for the fault-tolerant

CBT protocol to anycast messages, and consequently develop an integrated protocol for both multicast and anycast messages. This protocol should be useful in practice. For example, in a group of replicated database servers, the multicast packets must be sent to all the members in order to maintain information consistency. A request of clients can be taken as an anycast message and can be delivered to any of the server members.

Our protocol can also be extended to the applications where the messages have both fault-tolerant and real-time requirements. The key issue here is to model the traffic on

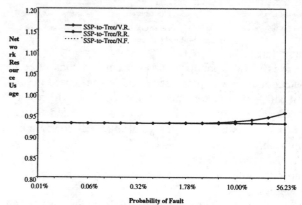

Figure 4-2. Network Resource Usage relative to SP-to-Core/N.F

the shared multicast tree so that a delay bound can be derived [MZ94, XJZ98].

Appendices

A-1. Proof of Lemma 4-1

Proof. By definition of T_0, Property B is evident. Because of the uniqueness of the shortest path, Property C is also obvious. Here, we focus on the proof of Property A using contradiction.

Assume Property A is not true. That is, there is a sequence of sub-tree $<T_{k1}, T_{k2}, ..., T_{k(n-1)}, T_{kn}, T_{k(n+1)} ...T_{kh}>$ such that $T_{k1} \Rightarrow T_{k2} \Rightarrow ... \Rightarrow T_{k(n-1)} \Rightarrow T_{kn} ... \Rightarrow T_{kh} \Rightarrow T_{k1}$. See Figure A-1. Note that T_0 is the sub-tree that contains the core.

For a sub-tree (say, $T_{kn}, 1 \leq n \leq h$) in the subset, let $R_{kn,0}$ be the root, P_{kn} be the shortest path from $R_{kn,0}$ to the father of the faulty router (In figure A-1, $R_{0,1}$ is the father of R_f). Because $T_{kn} \Rightarrow T_{k(n+1)}$[1], P_{kn} transverses $T_{k(n+1)}$. Assume that $R_{k(n+1),1}$ is the first router in $T_{k(n+1)}$ encountered by P_{kn}. Similarly, we assume that

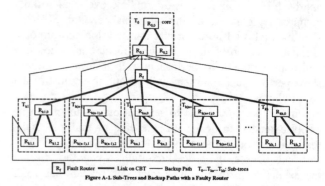

Figure A-1. Sub-Trees and Backup Paths with a Faulty Router

---

[1] For the convenience of discussion, (n+1) presents an addition operation with mod n. That is, (n+1) = n+1 if n < h;

$R_{kn,1}$ is the first router in T_{kn} encountered by the shortest path from $R_{k(n-1),0}$ to $R_{0,1}$.

Denote $SP_f(X, Y)$ to be the shortest path from X to Y conditioned on that a fault (R_f) has occurred. Recall that $SP(X, Y)$ represent the shortest path from X to Y in the normal case (where there is no fault). Obviously, $SP_f(X, Y)$ varies depending on the location of the fault. Nevertheless, $SP_f(X, Y)$ will be different from $SP(X, Y)$ if $SP(X, Y)$ involves with the faulty component.

Since the P_{kn} is the shortest path from $R_{kn,0}$ to $R_{0,1}$ when R_f is faulty, it is then denoted as $SP_f(R_{kn,0}, R_{0,1})$. Similarly, $SP_f(R_{kn,0}, R_{k(n+1),1})$ denotes the portion of P_{kn} from $R_{kn,0}$ to $R_{k(n+1),1}$, and $SP_f(R_{k(n+1),1}, R_{0,1})$ the portion of P_{kn} from $R_{k(n+1),1}$ to $R_{0,1}$.

Using the above notations related path P_{kn} and sub-tree T_{kn} where $1 \le n \le h$, we can derive some inequalities. Because $d(SP(R_{kn},1, R_f)$ is the shortest path from $R_{kn,1}$ to R_f under normal situation and

$$d(SP(R_{kn,1}, R_f)) = d(SP(R_{kn,1}, R_{kn,0})) + d(SP(R_{kn,0}, R_f)) \quad (A-1)$$

we have:

$$d(SP(R_{kn,1}, R_{kn,0})) + d(SP(R_{kn,0}, R_f)) <$$
$$d(SP_f(R_{kn,1}, R_{k(n-1),0})) + d(SP(R_{k(n-1),0}, R_f)). \quad (A-2)$$

Furthermore, because when R_f is faulty

$$d(P_{kn}) = d(SP_f(R_{kn,0}, R_{0,1})) =$$
$$d(SP_f(R_{kn,0}, R_{k(n+1),1})) + d(SP_f(R_{k(n+1),1}, R_{0,1})) \quad (A-3)$$

we have

$$d(SP_f(R_{kn,0}, R_{k(n+1),1})) + d(SP_f(R_{k(n+1),1}, R_{0,1})) <$$
$$d(SP(R_{kn,0}, R_{kn,1})) + d(SP_f(R_{kn,1}, R_{0,1})). \quad (A-4)$$

Summing up both sides of (A-2) and (A-4), we have:

$$d(SP(R_{kn,1}, R_{kn,0})) + d(SP(R_{kn,0}, R_f)) + d(SP_f(R_{kn,0}, R_{k(n+1),1})) +$$
$$d(SP_f(R_{k(n+1),1}, R_{0,1})) < d(SP_f(R_{kn,1}, R_{k(n-1),0})) + d(SP(R_{k(n-1),0}, R_f))$$
$$+ d(SP(R_{kn,0}, R_{kn,1})) + d(SP_f(R_{kn,1}, R_{0,1})) \quad (A-5)$$

Further, if we sum up (A-5) both sides for n from 1 to h, we have

$$LHS < RHS \quad (A-6)$$

where

$$LHS = \sum_{n=1}^{h} d(SP(R_{kn,1}, R_{kn,0})) + \sum_{n=1}^{h} d(SP(R_{kn,0}, R_f)) \quad (A-7)$$
$$+ [\sum_{n=1}^{h-1} d(SP_f(R_{kn,0}, R_{k(n+1),1})) + d(SP_f(R_{kh,0}, R_{k1,1}))]$$
$$+ [\sum_{n=1}^{h-1} d(SP_f(R_{k(n+1)}, R_{0,1})) + d(SP_f(R_{k1}, R_{0,1}))]$$

$$RHS = [\sum_{n=2}^{h} d(SP_f(R_{kn,1}, R_{k(n-1),0})) + d(SP_f(R_{k1,1}, R_{kh,0}))]$$
$$+ [\sum_{n=2}^{h} d(SP(R_{k(n-1),0}, R_f)) + d(SP(R_{kh,0}, R_f))]$$
$$+ \sum_{n=1}^{h} d(SP(R_{kn,0}, R_{kn,1})) + \sum_{n=1}^{h} d(SP_f(R_{kn}, R_{0,1})) \quad (A-8)$$

Since we assume that the links are dual directional, for any routers X and Y, we have $d(SP(X, Y)) = d(SP(Y, X))$ and $d(SP_f(X, Y)) = d(SP_f(Y, X))$. Because of this, (A-8) can be reorganized as follows:

$$RHS = [\sum_{n=2}^{h} d(SP_f(R_{k(n-1),0}, R_{kn,1})) + d(SP_f(R_{kh,0}, R_{k1,1}))]$$
$$+ [\sum_{n=2}^{h} d(SP(R_{k(n-1),0}, R_f)) + d(SP(R_{kh,0}, R_f))]$$
$$+ \sum_{n=1}^{h} d(SP(R_{kn,1}, R_{kn,0})) + \sum_{n=1}^{h} d(SP_f(R_{kn}, R_{0,1})) \quad (A-9)$$

Exchanging some items in (A-9), we have

$$RHS = [\sum_{n=1}^{h-1} d(SP_f(R_{kn,0}, R_{k(n+1),1})) + d(SP_f(R_{kh,0}, R_{k1,1})] + \sum_{n=1}^{h} d(SP(R_{k(n-1),0}, R_f))$$
$$+ [\sum_{n=1}^{h} d(SP(R_{kn,1}, R_{kn,0})] + [\sum_{n=1}^{h-1} d(SP_f(R_{k(n+1)}, R_{0,1})) + d(SP_f(R_{k1}, R_{0,1})]$$
$$= \sum_{n=1}^{h} d(SP(R_{k(n-1),0}, R_f)) + [\sum_{n=1}^{h} d(SP(R_{kn,1}, R_{kn,0}))$$
$$+ [\sum_{n=1}^{h-1} d(SP_f(R_{kn,0}, R_{k(n+1),1})) + d(SP_f(R_{kh,0}, R_{k1,1})]$$
$$+ [\sum_{n=1}^{h-1} d(SP_f(R_{k(n+1)}, R_{0,1})) + d(SP_f(R_{k1}, R_{0,1})]$$
$$= LHS \quad (A-10)$$

where LHS is given in (A-7). This contradicts to (A-6).

Acknowledgement

This work was partially sponsored by the Air Force Office of Scientific Research, Air Force Material Command, USAF, under grant (F49620-96-1-1076), by City University of Hong Kong under grant 7000765, and by Cery HK with grant 9040352. The U.S. Government is authorized to reproduce and distribute reprints for governmental purposes not withstanding any copyright notation thereon. The views and conclusions contained herein are those of the authors and should not be interpreted as necessarily representing the official polices or endorsements, either express or implied, of the Air Force Office of Scientific Research, the U.S Government, Texas A&M University, City University of Hong Kong or Cerg Hong Kong.

References

[BFC93] A. J. Ballardie, P. F. Francis and J. Crowcroft, Core based trees, *Proc. ACM SIGCOM*, San Francisco, 1993, pp.85-95.
[B97] A. Ballardie. Core Based Trees (CBT & CBT version 2) Multicast Routing Architecture. Sept. 1997, RFC2201&RFC2189.
[D91] S. Deering. ICMP Router Discovery Messages. RFC 1257, Sept., 1991.
[DEFJLW96] S. Deering, D. L. Estrin, D. Farinacci, Van Jacobson, C. Liu, and L. Wei. The PIM Architecture for Wide-Area Multicast Routing, *IEEE/ACM Transactions on Networking*, Vol. 4, No. 2, April 1996, pp. 153-162.
[MZ94] N. Malcolm and Wei Zhao, Hard Real-Time Communication in Multiple-Access Networks, Journal of Real-Time Systems, Vol. 8, No. 1, Jan. 1994, pp 35-77.
[M94a] J. Moy. OSPF Version 2. *RFC1583*, Mar. 1994.
[M94b] J. Moy. Multicast Extensions to OSPF. *RFC 1584*, Mar. 1994.
[PG97] M. Parsa and J.J. Garcia-Luna-Aceves. A protocol for Scalable Loop-Free Multicast Routing, IEEE JSAC, Vol 15, No.3, April 1997.
[WPD88] D. Waitzman, C. Partridge, and S. Deering, Distance Vector Multicast Routing Protocol, RFC 1075, 1988.
[XJZ98] D. Xuan, W. Jia, and W. Zhao, Routing Algorithms for Anycast Messages, *Proc. International Conference on Parallel Processing* , 1998, pp.122-130.
[XXJZ99] Gaochao Xu, Dong Xuan, Weijia Jia and Wei Zhao, An Efficient Fault-Tolerant Multicast Routing Protocol with Core-Based Tree Techniques, Tech Report, CS/TAMU, Feb. 1999.

For the convenience otherwise (n+1) = 1. Similarly, (n-1) = n −1 if n > 1; otherwise (n-1) = h.

Caching Neighborhood Protocol: a Foundation for Building Dynamic Web Caching Hierarchies with Proxy Servers

Cho-Yu Chiang   Ming T. Liu   Mervin E. Muller
Department of Computer and Information Science
The Ohio State University
Email: {chiang, liu, muller-m}@cis.ohio-state.edu

Abstract

In this paper, we propose a Caching Neighborhood Protocol (CNP) that describes an infrastructure upon which proxy servers can build dynamic Web caching hierarchies. Such a scheme decreases the response times for the requests by increasing the availability of documents without compromising the currency of the rendered documents. Some qualitative reasonings and studies on the request accessing traces collected by a proxy server at NLANR [16] are presented to justify CNP. A five-day trace analysis shows that the top 20% Web sites (in terms of frequency of accesses) provide 93% of the most frequently accessed top 20% documents and such top 20% documents account for 94% of the documents that have been accessed more than once. Hence, an important observation is that caching the most popular documents provided by the most popular Web sites would be a very effective approach for Web caching.

1. Introduction

Web caching [14] has been generally recognized as an effective approach that employs the intermediate servers to act as proxies [4,12] for the Web servers. The proxies, denoted by *proxy servers* in this paper, maintain individual cache storages for documents that have been downloaded in the past and provide the cached documents if they are requested afterwards. The Web servers, denoted by *origin servers* to reflect their identities in providing the original copies of the documents, process the requests and return appropriate responses. The responses can be cached by the proxy servers and returned to the requesting users.

The conventional caching hierarchy schemes, such as *Harvest* [2], *Squid* [19], and their variants [21] based on *Internet Cache Protocol* (*ICP*) [7] or Cache Digest [22], are the forerunners. Such caching hierarchy schemes are considered "static" in the sense that they lack flexibility in the communication paths among proxy servers. All unresolved requests follow the same path in the caching hierarchy before being forwarded to the origin servers. In contrast, we propose a *dynamic* caching hierarchy scheme, *Caching Neighborhood Protocol* (*CNP*), by incorporating ideas from [8,10,11,15,20] along with making observations

from the proxy traces. This new approach is considered *dynamic* because the set of proxy servers that collaboratively handle the requests may change for every single request and thus the request handling paths may vary.

CNP introduces the idea of *Caching Representatives*, which essentially are partially replicate servers [13] and devoted to distributing loads for frequently accessed origin servers. The goals of proposing *CNP* are to deal with the cache coherency problem [3,6,9] as well as reduce the network traffic and response times for the document requests. Some insights were obtained from examining the traces of the request accessing logs collected by a proxy server at NLANR [16], which identified some characteristics of collective user accessing patterns that were transformed into the foundation for *CNP*.

The remainder of the paper is organized as follows. Section 2 introduces the fundamentals of the caching neighborhood approach. Section 3 describes *CNP* in detail. Section 4 provides analysis based on the traces of the request accessing logs and argues why the static caching hierarchy schemes are inferior to the proposed dynamic scheme. Lastly, Section 5 discusses the potential advantages of using *CNP* as the Web caching infrastructure.

2. Fundamentals

2.1 Caching neighborhood

The notion of the *caching neighborhood* unveils the fundamentals of our scheme upon which the dynamic caching hierarchies can be built. Basically, a *caching neighborhood* is a logical relationship that (i) consists of an origin server and a variable number of proxy servers acting as *Caching Representatives* (*C-Reps*) for the origin server; (ii) defines an information disseminating partnership such that the data objects provided by the origin server can be distributed by any *C-Rep* in the neighborhood with authority. By authority, we mean that any document fetched by a *C-Rep* can be regarded as being retrieved directly from the origin server the *C-Rep* represents. Note that the concept of the caching neighborhood does not impose any constraint on the physical proximity among an origin server

516

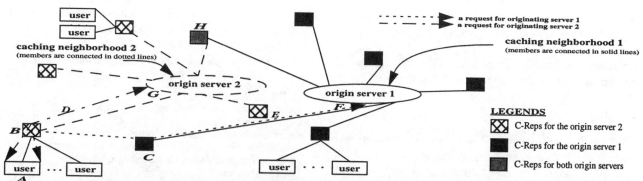

Figure 1. An illustrative scenario consisting of two caching neighborhoods

and its *C-Reps*. Each origin server builds its own neighborhood with exclusively proxy servers functioning as *C-Reps*. A *C-Rep* would assume the responsibility of resolving a document request if the request it receives is for an origin server that it represents.

Fig. 1 is used to introduce the basic concept of the caching neighborhood. There are two origin servers denoted by *F* and *G* in the figure. Each origin server holds its own caching neighborhood marked by either solid connecting lines or dotted connecting lines. The lines can be regarded as specifying HTTP persistent connections [17] among the origin servers and their *C-Reps*. On the other hand, a line connecting a user and a proxy server only indicates that the proxy server handles all the requests for the user and the connection does not have to be HTTP persistent. The following properties for the caching neighborhoods are illustrated in Fig. 1.

1. The members of each caching neighborhood, except the origin server being represented, are all proxy servers.

2. A proxy server may represent multiple origin servers. For example, the proxy server *H* represents both origin servers in the figure. Therefore, caching neighborhoods can overlap each other.

3. The sizes of the caching neighborhoods may vary -- in terms of both the number of *C-Reps* and the geographical coverage.

4. Requests destined for different origin servers travel through different caching neighborhoods. Since the data inquiry paths are established dynamically with different *C-Reps*, the caching hierarchies thus built are dynamic.

The criteria for fulfilling a request using the caching neighborhood scheme is that every single request has to be processed by at least one member of the caching neighborhood, either a *C-Rep* or the origin server. Therefore, a request from the user *A* to the origin server *F* providing the needed document may follow the path *user -> client-side proxy server -> C-Rep -> origin server*, which corresponds to *A->B->C->F* in the figure. This scenario describes the case in which there is never a cache hit along the path. Another example is to access a document on the other origin server *G* from the same user *A*. The request may take

the route *A->B->G* if the cache misses at the proxy server *B*, otherwise *B* just returns the document to *A*.

2.2 Proxy servers as C-Reps

A proxy server can choose to be either *client-side* or *non client-side*, both of which can function as *C-Reps* for the origin servers. If a proxy server opts to be non client-side, it only accepts requests from other proxy servers and dedicates itself to representing multiple origin servers. On the other hand, a client-side proxy server needs to handle the requests for the users who register with it.

The role of a proxy server can be viewed from the following perspectives.

From the perspective of the users, the operations of the proxy servers are invisible. The only user involvement is registering with a client-side proxy server, which becomes the user's entry point to the Web. All the requests from this user will be delivered to and processed by this proxy server. The selection of the client-side proxy server might be based on a predetermined precedence of a group of proxy servers set up by the network administration staff or decided at the discretion of the users. A proxy server in the vicinity of an user's network environment may be a natural choice. However, any proxy server in the Internet can be appointed as the client-side proxy server provided that the access to the server is permitted. The idea is that the users are allowed to look for the best Web community to join so as to receive the best quality of service.

We can also view the proxy servers from the persepective of their operations. Each client-side proxy server internally has a table for consulting the request forwarding destination provided that a request is not satisfied. Under such circumstances, the proxy server needs to "figure out" in addition to the origin server, who else are the candidates that the request can be forwarded to. The decision hinges on the criteria for selecting among the candidates. One possible such criterion is the estimated response times. In addition to relying on the prior experience in communicating with these candidates, the proxy servers can establish virtual communication links with nearby proxy servers to

517

regularly exchange the request forwarding information. As a result, information items such as representing status, how and when such information was acquired, and various information relating to the response times can be used to determine where to forward the unfulfilled requests.

2.3 Origin servers

The major tasks for an origin server to maintain its own caching neighborhood are listed as follows.

1. An origin server needs to maintain the number of *C-Reps* and the load distribution in the caching neighborhood. An origin server may invite proxy servers to join its neighborhood to distribute its load and it may drop a *C-Rep* off the list at its own discretion.

2. An origin server assists a newly-recruited *C-Rep* by providing a certain percentage of the most frequently accessed documents to set up the cache for the *C-Rep* and reduce the likely initial high demand for the *C-Rep*.

3. An origin server has to regularly communicate with its *C-Reps*. The purpose is to collect information such as the number of requests for the documents that have been serviced by the *C-Reps* since the last communication and allow the origin server to regularly update the frequently accessed data objects already disseminated to the *C-Reps*. These goals can be accomplished by employing techniques such as logging and piggybacking.

3. Caching Neighborhood Protocol (CNP)

We will focus on the major functions of *CNP* in this section and the detail can be found in [23]. Basically *CNP* can be divided into two major components: HTTP request fulfillment and caching neighborhood maintenance. The former dictates how proxy servers and origin servers behave as they handle the incoming requests, while the latter stresses how a caching neighborhood is maintained and why the *C-Reps* can oftentimes respond to the requests with the cached information without verifying the consistency with the origin server in the neighborhood.

3.1 HTTP request fulfillment

This section focuses on the behaviors of the request handling duties that the origin servers and their *C-Reps* assume. The following assumptions are used in the ensuing discussion.

- Only *Get* and *Get-IMS* requests are considered.
- The *timestamp* of a cached document refers to the "last modified time" of the document.
- The *last-known unchanged time* of a cached document on a *C-Rep* refers to the latest time the *C-Rep* receives a confirmation message from the response to a Get-IMS request for the origin server.

Since handling the requests is a complicated procedure for the proxy servers, we divide it into two pieces. The protocol segment described below specifies the behaviors of a proxy server when it assumes the responsibility of a *C-Rep*.

For the proxy servers:
```
// after receiving a request for a document  (part 1: C-Rep's behaviors)
if the proxy server is a C-Rep {
  if the proxy server has the requested document in its cache {
   if the timestamp of the cached entry still satisfies the X tolerance conherency
       requirement currently adopted by this caching neighborhood {
     if it is a Get request
      return the document to the requesting party;
     else {
       if the timestamp in the request is older than that of the cached document
         return the cached document
       else
         return the code 304, indicating "not modified."
    }
   }
   else { // the entry violates the coherency requirement
    send Get-IMS request to the Orig-Svr and wait for reply;
    if timeout and no reply yet {
      return the message "cannot connect to the origin server" to the requesting party;
    }
    else { // get the reply from the Orig-Svr
      return the document to the requesting party;
      update the last-known unchanged time of the cached entry and save the reply if
      needed;
    }
   }
  }
  else { // not having the requested document
   send a Get request to the Orig-Svr and wait for reply;
   if timeout and no reply yet {
     return the message "cannot connect to the origin server" to the requesting party;
   }
   else { // receive the reply from the Orig-Svr
     if the original request is in the Get-IMS format and there is no change to the doc-
     ument {
       return an appropriate HTTP message to indicate no change on the requested
       document;
     }
     else { // the original request is in the Get format
       return the document to the requesting party;
     }
     save a copy of the document in the local cache and perform some logging, if
     instructed by the Orig-Svr;
   }
  }
} // the end of part 1
```

Figure 2. Request processings by the C-Reps

The *X tolerance coherency requirement* is a coherency-efficiency tradeoff adjustment utility that defines the coherency level among copies of the documents stored on an origin server and its *C-Reps*. The initial, X, is a variable which can be set by an origin server to adjust the relative currency of the documents rendered by the members of the caching neighborhood. The value of X can be viewed as a degree of distributing the load of an origin server to its *C-*

Reps, which could be any time duration ranging from zero second, ten minutes, two hours, five days to *MAX*, the maximum time duration an origin server considers appropriate. One of the extreme case is *zero second tolerance*, or *zero tolerance*, which indicates that every single request has to be processed by the origin server. The other extreme is setting the value of X to *MAX*. It implies that the *C-Reps* can always reply to the requests on behalf of the origin server without confirming the currency of the cached documents. Intuitively, the larger the value of X is, the less the number of requests an origin server receives. Therefore, if a server's demand is high, the origin server might want to increase the value of X to decrease the number of messages from its *C-Reps*. In case the origin server's demand is low or it intends to stress the importance of the coherency among copies of the documents, the value of X can be decreased accordingly. The actual effect of setting the value of X depends on many factors such as the average and the variance of the document update frequency as well as the fluctuation of a server's demand. Hence, fine-tuning the value of X requires more studies.

The piece of the protocol specified in Fig. 3 focuses on the behaviors of the client-side proxy servers. Even the proxy server may have the requested document, due to not being a *C-Rep*, this proxy server needs to make a Get-IMS request to a caching neighborhood member instead of returning the document directly to the requesting user. It speaks for the philosophy of *CNP* in emphasizing the importance of document coherency.

After viewing the protocols given in Fig. 2 and Fig. 3, we can see that for the components pertaining to the HTTP request fulfillment, the origin servers only needs to do loggings so that they can remember what documents have been downloaded by their *C-Reps*. On the other hand, the proxy servers play a crucial role in this component. The *C-Reps* partially replicate the content of the origin server and work on an autonomous and cooperative basis.

3.2 Caching neighborhood maintenance

The origin server plays a prominent role in the effort of maintaining the caching neighborhood information. The primary task is to keep the content of the cached documents on the *C-Reps* coherent with the corresponding documents on the origin server. Besides, the requests for becoming a *C-Rep* and the requests for the dismissal of the representing responsibility are also administrative jobs for the origin servers.

The procedure for updating caching entries on the *C-Reps* deserves more treatment. The origin servers do not deliver all the updated documents to the *C-Reps*. Only the transmission of the most popular documents are initiated by the origin server. Such an approach ensures that for the documents in high demand, even if they are cached, can be

```
// after receiving a request for a document (part 2, continue from the end of part 1)
else { // the proxy server is not a C-Rep
  if the requesting party is a proxy server
    return the message "no longer a C-Rep";
  else { // requesting party is an end-user
    check up the request forwarding table to decide the forwarding destination among
      the Orig-Svr and C-Reps;
    if the proxy server has a local copy of the requested document {
      if the request is in the Get-IMS format
        set the time to be the newer one between timestamp of the request and times-
          tamp of the local copy;
      else // the method is Get
        set the time to be the timestamp of the locally cached entry;
      use time to make a Get-IMS request;
      send the request to the forwarding destination and wait for reply; -------- (A)
      if timeout and no reply yet
        if the forwarding destination is Orig-Svr
          return the locally cached entry along with a possibly stale indication to the
            requesting party;
        else { // forwarding destination is not Orig-Svr
          set forwarding destination to Orig-Svr;
          update the routing information of the C-Rep to reflect the timeout situation.
          go back to step (A) in the above;
        }
      else { // receive the reply
        if the reply is a document { // The document the CSP has is outdated
          return the document to the requesting party;
          save it in local cache storage if space permitted;
        }
        else // The reply is a 304 code
          if the original request is in the Get-IMS format {
            if the timestamp in the request is older than that of the cached document
              return the locally cached document;
            else // The document WC has isn't outdated
              relay the 304 code to the requesting party;
            else // The original request is in the Get format
              return the cached document;
          update the routing information of the forwarding destination;
        }
    }
    else { // if the proxy server does not have a copy of the requested document
      forward the request to the forwarding destination and wait for reply; -------- (B)
      if timeout and no reply yet
        if the forwarding destination is Orig-Svr
          return the message "cannot connect to the origin server";
        else { // forwarding destination is not Orig-Svr
          set forwarding destination to Orig-Svr;
          update the local routing information of the C-Rep.
          go back to step (B) in the above;
        }
      else { // receive the reply
        if the reply is a requested document {
          return the document to the requesting party;
          update the local routing information of the forwarding destination if necessary;
        }
        else
          relay the 304 code to the requesting party;
          save it in the local cache storage if space permitted;
      }
    }
  }
}
```

Figure 3. Request processings by the non C-Reps

coherent with the original copies and delivered as current by the *C-Reps* irrespective of what *X tolerance coherency requirement* is used. To reduce the processing and transmission times of those update information, the origin servers take active roles in invalidating the documents cached by its *C-Reps*. The invalidation messages can be coded in a compact format and piggybacked with the response to reduce the transmission time and traffic. As a result, we can see that the *X tolerance coherency requirement* only specifies the baseline of the required coherency level and the actual coherency level for the rendered documents could be much higher, depending on the frequency of transmitting the update information.

The correlation of adjusting such update frequency and the *X tolerance coherency requirement* can be observed as follows. Suppose an origin server adopts *one-minute tolerance coherency requirement*. Because the *C-Reps* have to resort to the origin server regardless of having the document or not, the request is guaranteed to be fulfilled with the current document but at the expense of generating more network traffic and prolonging the request response time. Therefore, the frequency of updating the currency information for the cached entries should be low. On the other hand, if the origin server opts to use the *MAX tolerance coherency requirement*, the updating frequency needs to be high to ensure that the *C-Reps* oftentimes render the current documents.

Note that dropping a *C-Rep* from a caching neighborhood should be handled discreetly. By recording the number of bytes of maintainence information an origin server delivers to the *C-Reps* and the number of bytes of data handled by the *C-Reps* without contacting the origin server, an origin server can make a decision based on the ratio of the two kinds of transmitted bytes. If the amount of neighborhood maintenance information far exceeds the amount of information handled by the *C-Reps*, the origin server needs to drop such *C-Reps* since otherwise it defeats the purpose of distributing the load of the origin server. Some criteria needs to be identified to aid such decision.

If the origin servers can detect the changes to the documents at the time of modification, its *C-Reps* would receive accurate and complete update information regularly and thus the coherency level can be maintained close to the strong cache coherency. On the contrary, if the origin servers are incapable of detecting what documents have been updated since the previous delivery of the caching neighborhood update information, the origin servers can only deliver the document update information based on the recent requests that have been handled. Whenever the demand for an origin server is low, The server can perform a partial or complete walkthrough on its file system to acquire the update information for all the documents that it had instructed its C-Reps to cache.

4. Analysis

Our observations on the traces of user requests collected by a proxy server at NLANR [16] during the period 01/12/99 - 01/16/99 are presented. In total there are 5,427,907 accesses made to 1,797,264 distinct documents spreaded over 112,955 Web sites. The collected statistics indicate that *CNP* is a promising approach for the Web caching.

The foundation of our argument relies upon the assumption that in the caching neighborhood approach, proxy servers would obtain the document request frequency for their own Web community and represent a handful of Web sites that attract the most accesses. Nevertheless, we would like to argue that establishing caching neighborhoods for a small percentage of Web sites is sufficient to benefit the Internet users. Derived from the trace study, we made the following claims.

Claim 1. A low percentage of the Web sites account for a high percentage of the total requests.

Claim 2. The most popular x% of the documents (in terms of the frequency of accesses) cover y% of the total accesses and the rest (100-y)% of the accesses are mostly for the rarely accessed documents.

Claim 3. The most popular documents are mostly located at the popular Web sites.

The first claim implies that caching only the popular Web sites is a good idea. As will be seen in Fig. 8, more than 90% of the total accesses accounted for by only 20% Web sites being accessed. In the second claim, if the value of y is large while the value of x is small, it indicates that caching mostly popular documents will help make the Web caching succeed. The myth is clarified in Fig. 6 where we see that 20% of the documents accounted for about 60% of the total accesses while the rest 40% of the accesses was covered by 80% of the documents. The encouraging news is, as observed in Figure 5, at least 33% of the total accesses were made to the documents that had been accessed only once! To summarize, the first claim indicates that Web caching should focus on the popular Web sites and the second claim indicates that caching would be most effective if only the most popular documents are cached. In practice, finding out popular sites can be easily achieved by collecting statistics, but how to identify if a document is popular and better be cached in the first place?

Fortunately, the third claim answers the above question. Basically it says that caching documents retrieved from the popular Web sites is a great idea. It is quite amazing to find that the most popular 20% Web sites provide over 90% of the most popular 20% documents (see Fig. 9). By simple math, we can see that the most popular 20% Web sites are responsible for 90% * 60% = 54% of the total accesses with requests for the most popular 20% documents. There-

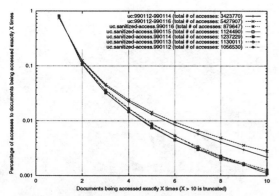

Figure 4. Document accessing distribution

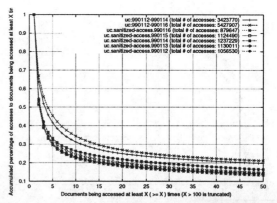

Figure 5. Accumulated document accessing distribution

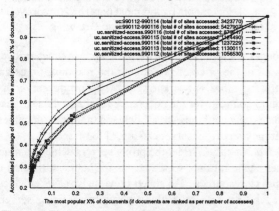

Figure 6. The most popular X% of the documents and the accumulated accessing percentage

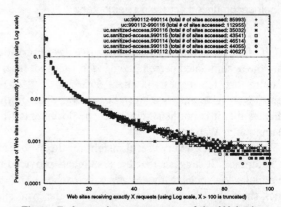

Figure 7. Accessing percentage of the Web sites

fore, the remaining 90% - 54% = 36% of the total accesses directed to the most popular 20% sites hardly benefit Web caching. It suggests that not every single document provided by the popular Web sites deserves to be cached. This fact is taken into account by *CNP* since a Web server can easily identify the popularity of the documents it provides by keeping their access counts and instruct the *C-Reps* not to cache the documents that were not frequently accessed.

For each figure shown in this section, we supply statistics on the accesses collected in single days as well as accumulated accesses collected over multiple days because *(i)* we want to examine if the statistics vary dramatically for a fixed proxy server on different days and *(ii)* we have not performed extensive study on the update frequency for the Web documents and it is hard to arbitrarily decide the length of trace evaluation period.

Fig. 4 displays the document access distribution. We can see that a high percentage (around 75% in multiple days' trace and 80% in a single day's trace) of documents are only accessed once. The drop in percentage of such accesses from 80% to 75% is not surprising because the rarely accessed documents have a better chance of getting hit again in a longer period of time. As we look into the accesses accumulated over five and three consecutive day periods we find the document access distribution for the

both are very similar. Hence, we speculate that the situation does not change a lot if we extend the observation period on the traces. The evidence in Fig. 4 strongly suggests that a good percentage of documents do not deserve to be cached and caching such documents is just wasting time and storage space.

The curves in Fig. 5 indicates that the accumulated percentage of the accesses to documents that have been accessed at least twice is about 54% in a single day's trace, and climbing to around 66% in a five day trace. It also indicates that at least 34% of accesses in the five day trace are made to documents receiving only one hit.

The curves appear in Fig. 6 directly justify the truth of the Claim 2. The curve grows exponentially as the value of X is small, which indicates that for the Web caching to be effective, those top documents are "can't misses". Another important information revealed by this figure is that only the most popular 25% documents were hit at least twice and the most popular 20% of the documents account for about 63% of the total accesses. Therefore, the top 20% documents cover 94% of the documents that have been accessed more than once. This result turns out to have a profound effect in designing Web caching strategies.

Fig. 7 points out that a considerable percentage of Web sites receive very few requests, even as we prolong the

521

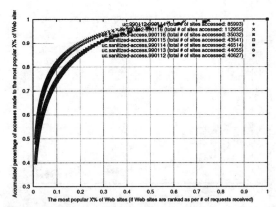

Figure 8. The most popular X% of the Web sites and their accumulated accessing percentage

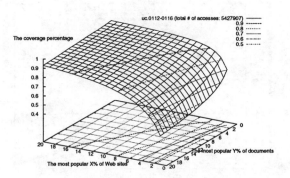

Figure 9. Coverage percentage of the most popular 20% of documents by the most popular 20% of Web sites for accesses accumulated in 5 days

length of the observation period. For a five day observation span, the accumulated percentage of Web sites that receive no more than ten requests is about 65% and 25% of the Web sites receive only one hit in that period. This further indicates that it is not beneficial to cache documents from the unpopular Web sites.

Fig. 8 identifies a very useful insight for the Web caching solutions. It suggests that the documents provided by the popular Web sites really deserve to be cached. The statistics show that the most popular 20% of the Web sites account for almost 90% of the total accesses and the most popular 30% of the Web sites receive about 93% of the total accesses. That's a huge factor in designing caching strategies.

Claim 3 is vindicated by what is shown in Fig. 9. In the five day trace, the most popular 20% Web sites account for almost 90% of the total accesses. More than 40% of the most popular 20% documents are supplied by the most popular 1% Web sites, 90% of the most popular 20% documents are supplied by the most poular 15% Web sites, and about 93% of the most popular 20% documents are supplied by the most popular 20% Web sites. The concentration of document accesses on a small percentage of sites is so overwhelming that it again indicates the direction of caching mainly the most popular Web sites is rather promising.

5. Discussion

In this section, we would like to discuss the advantages of the *CNP* approach. Recall that the major motivations for proposing *CNP* is to handle the cache coherency problem and reduce the response times and the amount of network traffic.

Advantage 1: CNP provides an effective solution for the cache coherence problem. With the introduction of the X tolerance coherency requirement, the coherency problem is no longer compromised for shorter response times or over-stressed at the price of prolonging the response times and generating more network traffic. The origin server has absolute control over the coherency level and thus strikes a balance between the server demand and the document coherency an origin server can afford to offer.

Advantage 2: CNP let the proxy servers achieve a much higher cache hit rate, which stands for better utilization of the proxy resources. As stated previously, *CNP* enhances the cache hit rate by making partially replicate servers, incarnated as *C-Reps*, bring the most frequently accessed documents to the Web communities. Because the *C-Reps* avoid caching the unpopular documents with instructions from the origin servers, the potential cache hit rate could be even higher than expected.

Arguable advantage 1: Assuming that CNP is widely adopted and many proxy servers have participated as *C-Reps* for the most frequently accessed server. Very likely *CNP* can reduce the response times, if compared to *Squid*. There are two major components contributing to the response time -- turnaround time and proxy processing time. The intuition is that *CNP* is capable of reducing the turnaround time by spreading out the *C-Reps* all over the places. Chances are the needed documents are moved much "closer" to the end users and thus the turnaround time should decrease. The argument that claims *CNP* can also reduce proxy processing time is as follows.

a. Redundant hierarchies in the static caching hierarchy schemes are removed, so are the inquiry timeouts. *CNP*'s hierarchy structure is simple and only has two layers -- *client-side* proxy servers and *C-Reps*.

b. The potential hit rate for requests received by the proxy servers, if using *CNP*, is much higher than using Squid.

c. CNP enforces a persistent HTTP connection for each *C-Rep* connecting to its origin server. The HTTP connection setup time overhead is saved.

d. Since the origin servers have distributed the loads to their C-Reps, they would have more capacity to handle the requests that mostly come from its *C-Reps*. Furthermore, a possible enhancement technique could be applied to *CNP* in which the origin servers give higher processing priority to the requests coming from the *C-Reps* than from the others.

Arguable advantage 2: CNP likely will generate lesser amount of network traffic, if compared to Squid. The basis for such a claim has credibility mainly because the potential hit rate for the requests received by the proxy servers, if using *CNP*, is higher than using either *ICP* or *Cache Digest*. Therefore, smaller number of requests need to get to the origin server for services. However, in *CNP*, the origin servers need to deliver the update information regularly to the *C-Reps*. The validity of this arguable advantage hinges on the degree of load distribution that is achieved by the *C-Reps*. If the degree is high, i.e., the *C-Reps* handle a considerable amount of requests on behalf of the origin server and are much "closer" to the client-side proxy server in terms of the hop distance, the amount of traffic caused by the deliveries of the caching neighborhood update information can be easily offset. The actual tradeoff requires more studies.

6. Summary

In this paper, the possibility of employing dynamic Web caching hierarchies for using a distributed infrastructure was discussed. First, we introduced the notion of the caching neighborhood in which origin servers and proxy servers form cooperative partnerships to distribute information. Then we use concrete examples to show how the caching neighborhood concept can be applied to establishing the dynamic caching hierarchies. Some insightful statistics derived from the trace of a Web proxy server access logs were presented, which in many ways justify *CNP*. We also discuss how *CNP* compare favorably against Squid using qualitative reasoning.

7. Acknowledgement

We would like to thank NLANR for collecting and providing the traces of the Web proxy access logs.

References

[1] W. R. Stevens. "TCP/IP illustrated, volume 1" Addison Wesley, 1994

[2] A. Chankhunthod, P. B. Danzig, C. Neerdals, M. F. Schwartz and K. J. Worrell. "A Hierarchical Internet Object Cache" in Proceedings of the USENIX Technical Conference, San Diego, CA, January 1996 (http://catarina.usc.edu/danzig/cache/cache.html)

[3] A. Dingle and T. Partl "Web Cache Coherence" Computer Network and ISDN Systems, 28(1996), pp. 907-920

[4] A. Luotonen, K. Altis "World-Wide Web Proxies" Computer Networks and ISDN Systems 27(1994) pp. 147-154

[5] T. Berners-Lee, R. Calliau, A. Luotonen, H. Nielsen, and A. Secret. "The World-Wide Web". Communications of the ACM, 37(8), pp.76-82, 1994

[6] C. Liu and P. Cao. "Maintaining Strong Cache Consistency in the World-Wide Web" in Proceedings International Conference on Distributed Computing Systems, 1997

[7] D. Wessels and K. Claffy. Internet cache protocol (ICP), version 2. (http://ds.internic.net/rfc/rfc2186.txt, 1998.

[8] J. Gwertzman and M. Seltzer. "The case for geographical push caching" in Proceedings of the 1995 Workshop on Hot Operating Systems, 1995 (http://www.eecs.harvard.edu/~vino/web/hotos.ps)

[9] J. Gwertzman and M. Seltzer. "World Wide Web Cache Consistency" in Proceedings of the 1996 USENIX Technical Conference, San Diego, January 1996.

[10] K. J. Worrell. "Invalidation in Large Scale Network object Caches" Master Thesis, Dept. of Computer Science, 1994.

[11] L. Zhang, S. Floyd, and V. Jacobson. "Adaptive Web caching" in the 2nd Web Caching Workshop, Boulder, Colorado, June 1997. (http://ircache.nlanr.net/Cache/Workshop97/Papers/Floyd/floyd.ps)

[12] M. Abrams, C. R. Standridge, G. Abdulla, S. Williams and E.A. Fox. "Caching proxies: Limitations and potentials", Proc. Fourth Intl. World Wide Web Conference., Dec. 1995, Boston, MA

[13] M. Baentsch, L. Baum, G. Molter, S. Rothkugel and P. Sturm. "Enhancing the Web's infrastructure: from Caching to Replication" IEEE Computing, pp. 18-27, March-April, 1997

[14] M. Baentsch, L. Baum, G. Molter, S. Rothkugel and P. Sturm. "World Wide Web Caching: The application-level view of the Internet", IEEE Communications Magazine, June 1997

[15] M. Nabeshima. "The Japan Cache Project: An Experiment on Domain Cache" in Proceedings of the 6th International World Wide Web Conference, 1997.

[16] National Lab of Applied Network Research, Sanitized access log, Jan. 1999. (ftp://ircache.nlanr.net/Traces/)

[17] R. Fielding, J. Gettys, J. C. Mogul, H. Frystyk and T. Berners-Lee. "Hypertext Transfer Protocol - HTTP/1.1 "

[18] Steven Glassman. "A caching Relay for the World Wide Web" in Proceedings of the 1st International Conference on the WWW, 1994.

[19] Squid Internet Object Cache (http://squid.nlanr.net/Squid/)

[20] V. N. Padmanabhan and J. C. Mogul. "Using Predictive prefetching to improve World-Wide Web Latency" ACM Computer Communication Review, pp.22-36, v.27, n3, July 1996.

[21] L. Fan, p. Cao, J. Almeida and A. Z. Broder. "Summary Cache: A scalable wide-area cache sharing protocol" in Proceedings of the ACM SIGCOMM'98, October, 1998.

[22] A. Rousskov and D. Wessels. "Cache Digest" Computer Network and ISDN Systems, Vol. 30, No 22-23, Nov. 1998.

[23] C. -Y. Chiang, M. T. Liu, and M. E. Muller, "Caching Neighborhood Protocol: A Foundation for Building Dynamic Caching Hierarchy Schemes with WWW Proxy Servers," Technical Report, OSU-CISRC-3/99-TR08. (http://www.cis.ohio-state.edu/~chiang/cnp/icpp-99.submission.ps)

Performance Study of Token-passing Protocol for Traffic Multiplicity in Optical Networks

S. Selvakennedy
TMPRC, Physics Dept.,
University Malaya,
50603 Kuala Lumpur, Malaysia.
skennedy@rndtm.net.my

A. K. Ramani
Institute of Computer Science,
Devi Ahilya University, Khandwa Road,
Indore 452001 INDIA.
ramaniak@hotmail.com

Abstract

This paper extended a mathematical technique to model the behaviour of token-passing protocol in a star-coupled wavelength-division multiplexing (WDM) optical network for traffic multiplicity, based on a semi-Markov process. This analytical model is able to predict the results accurately. It is found that the proposed static priority scheme performs reasonably well in relatively stable and predictable network load. The performance of lower priority traffic can be improved by employing bigger buffer space.

1. Introduction

Wavelength multiplexing eases the speed mismatch between optics and electronics by partitioning the enormous optical bandwidth into multiple channels so that each channel operates at the data-rate limited by the interface electronics. A multiple access environment can be achieved through a variety of optical channel topologies [1]. A star-coupled network has an optical power budget advantage over optical bus-based systems such that a larger system size can be supported. Two different approaches have been proposed for WDM-based networks: multihop and single-hop networks. The multihop network assumes the employment of the fixed-tuned or slowly tuneable component. The key advantage is that each node only needs to access a small number of channels in which high concurrency and scalability can be achieved [2]-[4]. On the other hand, the promise of a direct connection among nodes provided by single-hop network seems to make it particularly more attractive in the local environment [5], [6].

Media access control (MAC) protocol governs the access arbitration of the nodes. It may be classified as random, deterministic or node polling. From the node polling class, token passing (TP) is a common scheme. The MAC protocols may also be classified into three categories based upon the way the channels are allocated [6]. They are *random access* protocol, *scheduling based slot assignment* protocol and *pre-transmission coordination* protocol. Based upon the requirements, each protocol requires a distinctive configuration of transceivers. Ganz *et al.* [7] considered a system with N nodes and W ($1 \leq W \leq N$) wavelengths. Here, each node is assumed to have one tuneable transmitter, a fixed receiver and also a tuneable receiver. This protocol is in the random access category. Time division multiple access (TDMA) is an example of the scheduling based slot assignment protocol [7]. For a TDMA scheme, a similar transceiver configuration as the previous class, is needed. However, the tuneable receiver is not necessary, as no feedback from the channel is required at the end of each transmission due to its collisionless nature. In [8], the authors proposed a protocol that belongs to the pre-transmission coordination category. Each node is equipped with a fixed transmitter and receiver pair for accessing the channels; one fixed tuned transmitter to a unique data channel and one tuneable receiver capable of tuning over all of the data channels. The TP protocol requires one tuneable transmitter and an arrayed receiver at each node, enabling spatial disjointedness in data reception.

The TP protocol on an optical fibre medium with many channels using WDM has been presented in [9]. The scheme uses a separate reservation channel to carry the token, while the remaining channels (the data channels) carry only data and acknowledgement packets. In a system with small number of channels (< 5) and under high load, the bandwidth utilisation is degraded due to the inability of the reservation channel to transmit data. This limitation is overcame in [10], where a multichannel piggybacked TP protocol suitable for use with the WDM optical fibre LAN has been proposed. Both data and the token are given access to all the channels. This results in higher bandwidth utilisation at high traffic loads.

Networks normally carry a variety of data, with mixed specifications and constraints. The data type, called as real-time data, imposes specific delay requirements, either due to urgency (as in network control data), or due to reconstruction constraints (as in digitised voice). When deciding on the access priority for the various traffic classes, it may be predetermined statically anticipating determinable behaviour. This is termed as static priority scheme. This paper uses a mathematical technique to model the behaviour of the TP protocol in a star-coupled single-hop WDM network, based on a semi-Markov process (SMP). This approximate modelling approach achieves a significant reduction in state space complexity over embedded Markov chains. The protocol is studied for traffic multiplicity with different traffic natures. The model is validated through discrete-event simulation.

2. System description

The system of interest in this study, depicted in Fig. 1, is a star-coupled WDM network that has M number of nodes connected via C number of WDM channels. Each node has a tuneable transmitter and an arrayed receiver. The transmitter at each node is assumed to be tuneable to any wavelength in the pool. A demultiplexer is used to separate the wavelengths to individual detectors of the receiver. This enables each node to send or receive messages using any channel.

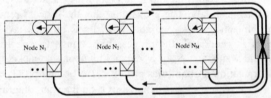

Figure 1. Star-coupled configuration with tuneable transmitters and arrayed receivers

In the multichannel TP protocol, each channel may be used to transmit data, token and acknowledgement packets. The protocol operates as follows: if two or more channels are available to the node when it transmits, then data and the token packets are sent on separate channels. If, however, a second channel is not available for the token, the data packet may be transmitted on the same channel and piggybacked behind the token. Thus, at higher traffic loads, token and data packets are shared over all channels with TP MAC protocol, so increasing bandwidth utilisation. When the transmission is completed, the channel is released. In this scheme, the token is being used to grant access to the media. To implement TP on a physical star topology, the token is passed in a logical sequence over all the nodes using a 'round robin' strategy. Each node has access to the network once in every token rotation time (TRT).

The above protocol needs modifications, to make it adaptable for real-time applications. This calls for assigning the priorities to the different traffic types. Any request for packet transmission generated into the system can have its own priority level depending upon the attributes. Typically a request can be categorised as real-time and non real-time indicating the different traffic types. According to the proposed priority scheme, real-time packets would be given priority for transmission over non real-time packets at any network condition. Each node is assumed to have 2 buffers of capacity one packet, to enable buffering the two packet types. Whenever the token is received, the request from the buffer holding real-time packet is transmitted first. The non real-time request will only be transmitted if there is no real-time request pending in its buffer.

The transmitter (Tx) changes states most often in a node. Thus, the model will only consider the state transitions of the Tx. The Tx in a network may be in any of the five states: i) *idle* - Tx is idle as long as there is no packet generated at a node; ii) *transmit* - Tx transmits the packet and the token; iii) *full-wait* - while transmitting a packet, if another request is generated, Tx goes into full-wait state, i.e. Tx waits for the token which has just left the node (a full TRT); iv) *residual-wait* - if a request is generated in the idle state, Tx waits for the residual time needed for the token to arrive at the node; and v) *monitor* - when the token reaches a node and finds all the channels busy, Tx monitors for a free channel to enable transmission.

3. System operation assumptions

The behaviour of a node in a WDM star network operation is characterised by the following assumptions:

i. The behaviour of the nodes can be modelled as stochastic processes.

ii. The period at each state is normalised to a slot time. The slot time is defined as the transmission time of a packet and acknowledgement.

iii. The nodes may generate a packet at any slot. The arrival process is *Poisson* with rate λ packets per second per node. Only one packet can arrive at each node per slot. Each Tx has two buffers to store real-time and non real-time packets, respectively, and each buffer has a capacity of holding at most one packet.

iv. The Tx initially will be in idle state. At the end of the idle period, it will generate a request for packet transmission.

v. The Tx will be in the residual-wait after generating a packet. Packets originating from the same node are independent of each other.

vi. When the token arrives at the node, it checks the buffer with real-time packets, and if a channel is available, it schedules the packet for transmission, which lasts for one slot. If this buffer is empty, non real-time request is considered. If no channel is free, the token monitors for a free channel. The monitoring period is one slot.

vii. When the token leaves a node and a packet is pending in any of the buffers or another packet is generated, the Tx waits for a full TRT (i.e. full-wait time) before next transmission.

viii. The waiting period of Tx, which will be an integer number of slots, is characterised by a random variable W, which is dependent upon token cycle time (T) and time between the packet arrival and the first access of the node by the token, (T_R).

4. Model development

A SMP is a stochastic process that can be in any of k states 1,2,...k [11]. Each time it enters state i ($1 \leq i \leq k$), it remains there for a random amount of time (the sojourn time) having mean τ_i, and then makes a transition into state j ($1 \leq j \leq k$) with probability p[i,j]. As a special case, a discrete time Markov chain is a SMP with a deterministic sojourn time of value one. If the SMP has an irreducible embedded Markov chain, then the steady-state probability of being in state i, denoted by P_i, can be expressed as follows:

$$P_i = \frac{\tau_i V_i}{\sum_{j=1}^{k}(\tau_j V_j)}, \tag{1}$$

where V_i is the limiting probability of state i in the embedded Markov chain. The rate of leaving state i, η_i, is defined as the reciprocal of the average time elapsed between two consecutive departures from state i. The rate can be obtained using the following equation:

$$\eta_i = \frac{P_i}{\tau_i} = \frac{V_i}{\sum_{j=1}^{k}(\tau_j V_j)}. \tag{2}$$

Since the average sojourn time in any one of the states of the SMP that appears, is at least one slot, the η_i falls in the range [0,1], and it is possible to view η_i as the probability of leaving state i at the beginning of a slot.

The SMP model to approximate the behaviour of the system in study is depicted in Fig. 2. The states of the SMP denote the different states of the Tx, and they can be partitioned into five disjoint subsets, namely idle, residual-wait, monitor, transmit and full-wait. Fig. 2(a) shows the transitions from the idle and residual-wait states, Fig. 2(b) depicts the transitions out of the monitor states, Fig. 2(c) from the transmit states and finally, Fig. 2(d) from the full-wait states.

It is convenient to introduce some terms that will be used in formulating the transition probabilities These terms are: BUSY and Y(k). The term BUSY is defined as the probability that a node finds a particular channel busy at the beginning of a slot. In other words, one of the other (M-1) nodes is accessing that channel and is not at the point of releasing it. Hence, BUSY is the probability that one of (M-1) nodes is using the channel and the particular node is not at the point of releasing the channel. By definition, the probability that a node is using a channel is $P_6+P_7+...+P_{11}$. Thus, the probability that it is using and will not leave one of the

transmit states (S_6, S_7,..., S_{11}) in the next slot is ($P_6+P_7+...+P_{11}$)-($\eta_6+\eta_7+...+\eta_{11}$). Therefore, BUSY can be expressed as:

$$BUSY = \frac{(M-1)}{C}\sum_{i=6}^{11}(P_i - \eta_i), \tag{3}$$

where P_i is the probability that a node is using a channel (transmit state) and η_i probability of leaving state i at the beginning of a slot ($6 \leq i \leq 11$). The term Y(k) is the probability that there are k free channels. The probability that k out of C channels are free is:

$$Y(k) = {}^{C}C_k.BUSY^{C-k}.(1-BUSY)^k \tag{4}$$

The probability of a transition from state S_i to state S_j is denoted as p[i,j]. The average sojourn time of S_i ($0 \leq i \leq 14$) is denoted as τ_i. In the state diagram, the parameter ρ represents the probability of a real-time request is generated at a node. In Fig. 2, state S_0 represents the idle state of Tx, with sojourn time τ_0 of one slot. A packet may be generated in any slot while the process is in state S_0. If a packet is not generated in a slot during in this state, Tx remains idle and is represented by the self-loop on state S_0. The probability of generating a real-time and a non real-time packet are ρ and (1-ρ), respectively. The probability that the process remains idle with no packet generated in a slot is p[0,0] = $e^{-\lambda}$. If a packet is generated, the process may transit to one of the residual-wait states S_1 or S_2 depending upon the packet type. The transition probabilities p[0,1] = (1-$e^{-\lambda}$)ρ and p[0,2] = (1-$e^{-\lambda}$)(1-ρ), with (1-$e^{-\lambda}$) is denoted as β on the state diagram in Fig. 2.

In residual-wait state, the SMP waits for the token to arrive. On its arrival, from the residual-wait state, if there is no free channel available, the process will transit to any of the monitor states (S_3, S_4, S_5) (Fig. 2(a)). The sojourn time of the residual-wait states is denoted as τr. The probability of generating m packets (m $\leq \tau r$) of ρ priority factor in the residual-wait time is given by pr(m,ρ) = ${}^{\tau r}C_m(\beta\rho)^m(1-\beta\rho)^{\tau r-m}$. From state S_1, if no other packet is generated, the process transits to state S_3, with transition probability of P[1,3] = Y(0)*pr(0,1-ρ). If a non real-time packet is generated, the process transits to state S_5 with the probability of P[1,5] = Y(0)*{1-pr(0,1-ρ)}. Similarly, transition probabilities from residual-state S_2 to state S_4 and S_5 are derived.

States S_i, $6 \leq i \leq 11$, represent the transmit states of Tx. If there is a free channel, the transition from the residual-wait states S_1 and S_2 will be to one of the transmit states. Considering state S_1, if no packet is generated the process will transit to the transmit state S_6. If a real-time packet is generated, the process moves to state S_8. If a non real-time packet is generated, the process transits to state S_9.

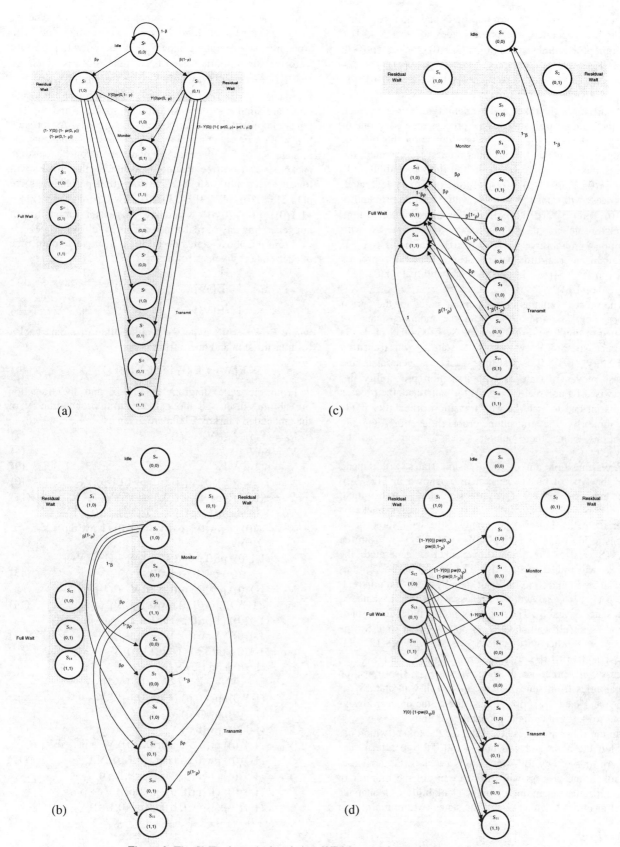

Figure 2. The SMP of a typical node in a WDM network, employing static scheme

Otherwise, if one or more real-time and non real-time packets are generated, the process goes to state S_{11}. The transition probabilities are $p[1,6] = \{1-Y(0)\}*pr(0,\rho)*pr(0,1-\rho)$, $p[1,8] = \{1-Y(0)\}*\{1-pr(0,\rho)\}*pr(0,1-\rho)$, $p[1,9] = \{1-Y(0)\}*pr(0,\rho)*\{1-pr(0,1-\rho)\}$ and $p[1,11] = \{1-Y(0)\}*\{1-pr(0,\rho)\}*\{1-pr(0,1-\rho)\}$.

On arrival of the token and availability of a free channel, from the residual-wait state S_2, the process may go to one of the transmit states S_7, S_9-S_{11} depending upon the type of packet being generated. If no other request is generated, the process moves to state S_7, with transition probability $\{1-Y(0)\}*pr(0,\rho)*pr(0,1-\rho)$. If a real-time packet is generated, the process will transit to state S_9, with transition probability $\{1-Y(0)\}*pr(1,\rho)*pr(0,1-\rho)$. If one or more non real-time packets are generated, the process transits to state S_{10} with transition probability $\{1-Y(0)\}*pr(0,\rho)*\{1-pr(0,1-\rho)\}$. If more than one real-time packets are generated, the process moves to state S_{11}, with transition probability $\{1-Y(0)\}*\{1-[pr(0,\rho)+pr(1,\rho)]\}$.

The process remains in the monitor states for the period of one slot. The transitions from the monitor states are depicted in Fig. 2(b). From the state S_3, if no other packet is generated, the process will transit to state S_6 with transition probability $(1-\beta)$. If a real-time packet is generated, the process moves to state S_8 with transition probability $\beta\rho$. Otherwise, if a non real-time packet is generated, the process transits instead to state S_9 with transition probability $\beta*(1-\rho)$. Similarly, the transition probabilities for outgoing transitions from other monitor states S_4 and S_5 can be derived.

Any transition out of the transmit states will depend upon the type of packet generated, as shown in Fig. 2(c). After the active packet in any transmit state is transmitted, the process will go into full-wait state, if another packet is generated or the buffer is not empty. Otherwise, the process returns to idle state S_0 with $p[6,0] = p[7,0] = 1-\beta$. From the states S_6 and S_7, if a real-time packet is generated, the process will transit to state S_{12}. The transition probabilities from states S_6 and S_7 to full-wait state S_9 is $\beta\rho$. If a non real-time packet is generated, the process will transit to state S_{13} from states S_6 and S_7. The transition probabilities from states S_6 and S_7 to full-wait state S_{13} is $\beta(1-\rho)$. From state S_8, the process will either go to state S_{12} or S_{14} with $p[8,12] = 1-\beta(1-\rho)$ and $p[8,14] = \beta(1-\rho)$. From state S_9 and S_{10}, the process will either go to state S_{13} or S_{14}. The transition probabilities from states S_9 and S_{10} to full-wait state S_{13} is $(1-\beta\rho)$ and state S_{14} is $\beta\rho$. From state S_{11}, the process always moves to state S_{14} with the probability of unity.

In the full-wait states, Tx waits for the token, which has just left the node and will take a full TRT to return. The sojourn time of any full-wait state is τw slots. On arrival of the token, the process will transit to any of the monitor or transmit states depending upon the availability of a channel. The transitions to either one of the states (within monitor or

transmit group), will occur depending upon the type of packet being generated, while in its sojourn time slots. The probability of generating m packets ($m \leq \tau$w) with ρ priority factor in the sojourn time of τw time slots is given by $pw(m,\rho) = {}^{\tau w}C_m(\beta\rho)^m(1-\beta\rho)^{\tau w-m}$. The transitions from full-wait states S_{12} and S_{13} (Fig. 2(d)) to monitor and transmit states are similar to the residual-wait states S_1 and S_2. The transition probabilities can be derived similarly. As for state S_{14}, when a free channel is available, the transitions may be to state S_{10} or S_{11}, depending upon generation of real-time packet type. If no free channel is available, the process will transit to monitor state S_5. The transition probabilities are $p[14,5] = Y(0)$, $p[14,9] = \{1-Y(0)\}*pw(0,\rho)$ and $p[14,11] = \{1-Y(0)\}*\{1-pw(0,\rho)\}$, where $pw(0,\rho)$ is the probability of not generating any of real-time packets in full-wait time.

From the above states description, average sojourn time of each state is given as follows:

$$\tau_i = \begin{cases} 1 & i = 0, 3-11 \\ E\{W\}/2 & i = 1, 2 \\ E\{W\} & i = 12-14 \end{cases} \quad (5)$$

where $E\{W\}$ is the expected waiting time of a data packet for transmission and taken from [10]:

$$E\{W\} = E\{T_R\} / (1-\lambda.E\{T\}) \quad (6)$$

From the state diagram in Fig. 2 and the transition probabilities discussed above, the limiting probabilities V_i of the embedded Markov Chain are given as:

$$V_0 = (1-\beta)(V_0 + V_6 + V_7) \quad (7)$$

$$V_1 = \beta\rho V_0 \quad (8)$$

$$V_2 = \beta(1-\rho)V_0 \quad (9)$$

$$V_3 = Y(0).pr(0,1-\rho).V_1 + Y(0).pw(0,1-\rho).V_{12} \quad (10)$$

$$V_4 = Y(0).pr(0,\rho).V_2 + Y(0).pw(0,\rho).V_{13} \quad (11)$$

$$V_5 = Y(0).(1-pr(0,1-\rho)).V_1 + Y(0).(1-pr(0,\rho)).V_2 + Y(0).(1-pw(0,1-\rho)).V_{12} + Y(0).(1-pw(0,\rho)).V_{13} + Y(0).V_{14} \quad (12)$$

$$V_6 = (1-Y(0)).pr(0,\rho).pr(0,1-\rho).V_1 + (1-\beta).V_3 + (1-Y(0)).pw(0,\rho).pw(0,1-\rho).V_{12} \quad (13)$$

$$V_7 = (1-Y(0)).pr(0,\rho).pr(0,1-\rho).V_2 + (1-\beta).V_4 + (1-Y(0)).pw(0,\rho).pw(0,1-\rho).V_{13} \quad (14)$$

$$V_8 = (1-Y(0)).(1-pr(0,\rho)).pr(0,1-\rho).V_1 + \beta\rho.V_3 + (1-Y(0)).(1-pw(0,\rho)).pw(0,1-\rho).V_{12} \quad (15)$$

$$V_9 = (1-Y(0)).pr(0,\rho).(1-pr(0,1-\rho)).V_1 + (1-Y(0)).pr(1,\rho).V_2 + \beta(1-\rho).V_3 + \beta\rho.V_4 + (1-\beta\rho).V_5 + (1-Y(0)).pw(0,\rho).(1-pw(0,1-\rho)).V_{12} + (1-Y(0)).pw(1,\rho).V_{13} + (1-Y(0)).pw(0,\rho).V_{14} \quad (16)$$

$$V_{10} = (1-Y(0)).pr(0,\rho).(1-pr(0,1-\rho)).V_2 + \beta(1-\rho).V_4 + (1-Y(0)).pw(0,\rho).(1-pw(0,1-\rho)).V_{13} \quad (17)$$

$$V_{11} = (1-Y(0)).(1-pr(0,\rho)).(1-pr(0,1-\rho)).V_1 + (1-Y(0)).(1-(pr(0,\rho)+pr(1,\rho))).V_2 + \beta\rho.V_5 + (1-Y(0)).(1-pw(0,\rho)).(1-pw(0,1-\rho)).V_{12} +$$

$$(1-Y(0)).(1-(pw(0,1-\rho)+pw(1,\rho))).V_{13} +$$
$$(1-Y(0)).(1-pw(0,\rho)).V_{14} \quad\quad (18)$$
$$V_{12} = \beta\rho.(V_6 + V_7) + (1-\beta(1-\rho)).V_8 \quad\quad (19)$$
$$V_{13} = \beta(1-\rho).(V_6 + V_7) + (1-\beta\rho).(V_9 + V_{10}) \quad\quad (20)$$
$$V_{14} = \beta(1-\rho).V_8 + \beta\rho.(V_9 + V_{10}) + V_{11} \quad\quad (21)$$

The SMP steady-state probabilities can be derived by substituting the limiting probabilities of the embedded Markov chain into the following equation:

$$P_i = \frac{V_i \tau_i}{\sum_{j=0}^{14}(V_j \tau_j)} . \quad\quad (22)$$

The P_i's are then used to derive the performance measures of the model. The derivations of these measures are not given due to space limitations.

5. Results and discussions

A number of input parameters characterising the system in study are considered. The sizes of data, acknowledgement and token packets are 5000, 20 and 50 bits long, respectively. The propagation delay is assumed as 10µs (2 km-diameter ring), and the tuning latency of the transmitter is fixed at 2µs. Each channel transmission rate is taken as 100 Mbps. The results are obtained for system size of 100 nodes and 2 channels, and $\rho = 0.5$, with each node having two buffers of capacity one packet. The performance measures plots of real-time traffic are shown in Fig. 3. The results from the SMP model are represented by continuous lines and the simulation results by dots. The average delays (Fig. 3(a)) show a match within 10% deviation for any load level. The metrics blocking probability (Fig. 3(b)) and throughput (Fig. 3(c)) show a match within 5% deviations. Thus, the SMP model for static priority scheme is able to predict the results accurately, and used further for the system's investigations.

To study the impact of number of WDM channels in the network, analysis is carried for 100 nodes and with different number of channels, $C \in \{2, 5, 10, 20\}$. Results are obtained for real-time and non real-time traffic, as shown in Figs. 4 and 5. In Fig. 4, it can be noticed that when $C = 2$, average delays experienced by both traffic types are the highest. When packet generation rate (i.e. mean arrival rate), λ is about 300 pkts/sec, delay increased exponentially in both cases. This arrival rate is about 75% of mean transmission rate. When $C = 5$, the delay experienced exponential increment, again after about 75% mean transmission rate. Thus, it shows that the network employing this scheme has lower delays at up to about 75% of the network capacity. Also, when the number of channels is increased beyond 10, no further improvement is seen in the delays.

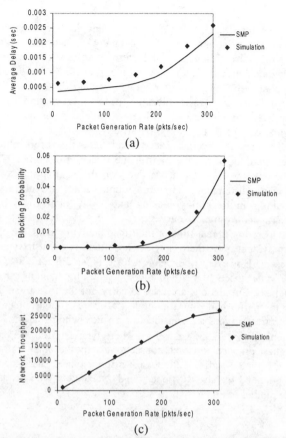

(a)

(b)

(c)

Figure 3. Performance metrics of real-time traffic against packet generation rate for M = 100 nodes and C = 2 channels: (a) average delay, (b) blocking probability and (c) network throughput

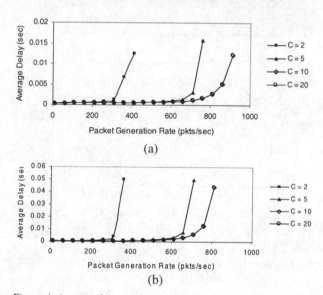

(a)

(b)

Figure 4. Average delay against packet generation rate for M = 100 nodes and C ∈ {2, 5, 10, 20} channels: (a) real-time traffic and (b) non real-time traffic

The plots for blocking probability obtained for the same network configuration are shown in Fig. 5. It can be seen that they also follow similar pattern of results, as average delay. When C = 2 or 5, blocking probability increased exponentially only for arrival rates beyond 75% of mean transmission rate. The blocking probability continuously improves for the system with 10 channels. After that, no further change is seen for both traffic types.

The results average delay and blocking probability presented above can be used for the selection of number of channels in the system, needed for the optimisation of network throughput. The maximum packet arrival rate, resulting in tolerable blocking and delay limits, can be ascertained from these curves.

Operating in real-time or multimedia environment, which is prevalent now, there may be more than two traffic types present. However, when more traffic types are introduced, the state space of SMP model becomes too complex for analysis. Simulations are used to carry out the investigation on the performance in a multiple traffic types environment. Four traffic types are considered for study with equal traffic intensity ($\rho_i = 0.25$, $1 \leq i \leq 4$), where type-1 traffic has the highest priority, followed consecutively by the other traffic types (type-4 traffic is the lowest priority type). The system is assumed to have 100 nodes and 2 channels. The results are plotted in Fig. 6.

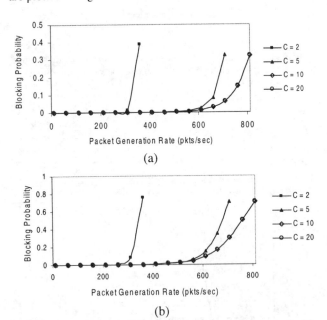

(a)

(b)

Figure 5. Blocking probability against packet generation rate for M = 100 nodes and C ∈ {2, 5, 10, 20} channels: (a) real-time traffic and (b) non real-time traffic

In Fig. 6, the plots for average delay and blocking probability for the different traffic types are shown. When operating at lower mean packet arrival rates, the performance of each traffic type is almost similar. This performance level is maintained up to more than 50% of the system mean transmission rate. However, the weakness of the static priority assignment becomes evident at higher loads. It can be seen that type-1 traffic enjoys the highest performance level. It experiences both the lowest delays and packet losses. However, type-4 traffic experiences the worst service in both measures. Normally, the lower priority traffic is loss sensitive, and may tolerate longer delays. Thus to improve its performance in terms of blocking probability, critical analysis on the buffer capacity is necessary.

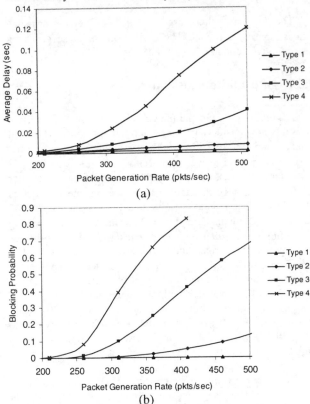

Figure 6. Performance metrics against packet generation rate for 4 traffic types for M = 100 nodes and C = 2 channels: (a) average delay and (b) blocking probability

To see the impact of transmitter's buffer size, further simulations are carried out. Packets of each traffic type are queued separately in its own buffer, which is of the same size for all types. The results of type-2 traffic are presented here as similar pattern of results is obtained for the different traffic types. In Fig. 7(a), plots of average delay for various buffer sizes are shown. It can be noted that by increasing the buffer capacity, the delay is not affected significantly. However, the blocking probability improved with the increment of buffer size, as shown in Fig. 7(b). When the buffer capacity is increased beyond 10, blocking probability is almost zero for the various load levels. Thus, these results can be used for the selection of appropriate buffer resource, depending upon the traffic type's access priority.

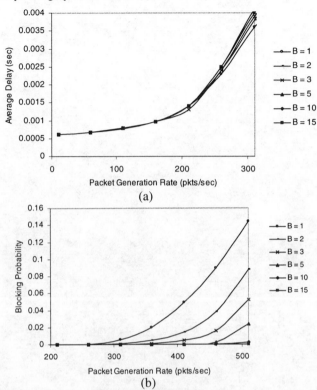

(a)

(b)

Figure 7. Performance comparison of type-2 traffic for M = 100 nodes, C = 2 channels and B ∈ {1, 2, 3, 5, 10, 15}: (a) average delay and (b) blocking probability

From these results (Figs. 6-7), it can be seen that this scheme is extendable to multiple traffic, when higher delays are acceptable for some traffic types. The static priority scheme performs reasonably well in relatively stable and predictable network load. However, the system performance degrades when operating at higher or unpredictable loads. The scheme is able to guarantee the provision of an acceptable performance level for each traffic type by having larger buffers at the nodes. The investigations are beneficial in planning the capacity of network resources like, channels and buffers, to optimise the performance. This is useful in static scheduling cases of real-time systems.

6. Conclusions

In this paper, due to traffic multiplicity in the present networks, a priority scheme is proposed for the token-passing protocol, to cater various traffic types in WDM all-optical networks. A semi-Markov process is developed to study the system performance. From the comparison of the model's results with simulations, it is found that the results are within acceptable limits. The investigations of the static priority scheme has led to a conclusion that for two traffic types in optical network, the higher priority traffic has better delay characteristics and packet loss performance. However, the packet loss performance of loss sensitive traffic can be improved by employing larger buffer resource. It is concluded that the model's quantitative results can be used for hard real-time system scheduling, where knowledge of priority is a priori. The investigations benefit the planning of capacity of all-optical network resources like, channels and buffers, for optimised performance.

7. References

[1] M. Fine and F. A. Tabogi, "Demand assignment multiple access schemes in broadcast bus local area network", *IEEE Trans. on Computers*, vol. c-33, pp. 1130-1159, Dec. 1984.

[2] B. Mukherjee, "Architectures and protocols for WDM-based local lightwave networks – Part II: Multihop systems", *IEEE Network*, vol. 6 no. 4, July 1992.

[3] C. A. Brackett, A. S. Acampora, J. Swietzer, G. Tangonan, M. T. Smith, W. Lennon, K-C. Wang and R. H. Hobbs, "A scalable multiwavelength multihop optical network: A proposal for research on all-optical network", *IEEE/OSA J. Lightwave Tech.*, vol. 11 no. 5/6, May/June 1993.

[4] A. Ganz and B. Li, "Implementation schemes of multihop lightwave networks", *IEEE/OSA J. Lightwave Tech.*, vol. 11 no. 5/6, May/June 1993.

[5] K. M. Sivalingam, "High-speed communication protocols for all-optical wavelength division multiplexed computer networks", *Ph.D. Dissertation*, State Univ. of NY, US, 1994.

[6] B. Li, "Bandwidth management for high speed LANs using wavelength division multiplexing", *Comp. Comm.*, vol. 18 no. 8, pp. 572-581, Aug. 1995.

[7] A. Ganz and Z. Koren, "Performance and design evaluation of WDM stars", *IEEE J. Lightwave Tech.*, vol. 11 no. 2, 1993.

[8] R. Chipalkatti, Z. Zhang and A. S. Acampora, "High-speed communication protocols for optical using WDM star networks", *Infocom'92*, Florence, Italy, May 1992.

[9] J. M. Senior, S. D. Cusworth, and A. Ryley, "Wavelength Division Multiplexing in optical fibre", in *LANs' Europ. Comput. Commun. Conf.: Networks `87* (London, UK), pp. 231-244, June 1987.

[10] A. Ryley, S. D. Cusworth and J. M. Senior, "Piggybacked token-passing access protocol for multichannel optical fibre LANs", *Computer Communications*, vol. 12 no. 4, pp. 213-222, August 1989.

[11] H. Humoud, "A study in memory interference models," *Ph.D. Dissertation*, The University of Michigan, April 1985.

Session C8

Resource Management

Chair: Yoshitaka Shibata
Iwate Prefecture University, Japan

FLB: Fast Load Balancing for Distributed-Memory Machines *

Andrei Rădulescu   Arjan J.C. van Gemund
Faculty of Information Technology and Systems
Delft University of Technology
P.O.Box 5031, 2600 GA Delft, The Netherlands
{*A.Radulescu,A.J.C.vanGemund*} @*its.tudelft.nl*

Abstract

This paper describes a novel compile-time list-based task scheduling algorithm for distributed-memory systems, called Fast Load Balancing (FLB). Compared to other typical list scheduling heuristics, FLB drastically reduces scheduling time complexity to $O(V(\log(W) + \log(P)) + E)$, where V and E are the number of tasks and edges in the task graph, respectively, W is the task graph width and P is the number of processors. It is proven that FLB is essentially equivalent to the existing ETF scheduling algorithm of $O(W(E + V)P)$ time complexity. Experiments also show that FLB performs equally to other one-step algorithms of much higher cost, such as MCP. Moreover, FLB consistently outperforms multi-step algorithms such as DSC-LLB that also have higher cost.

1 Introduction

Scheduling heuristics exist for both bounded and un-bounded number of processors. Although attractive from a cost perspective, scheduling for an unbounded number of processors is rarely of practical use, because the required number of processors is not usually available. Hence, their application is typically found within the multi-step scheduling method for a bounded number of processors [8, 9].

Alternatively, scheduling for a bounded number of processors can be performed in a single step. Using this one-step approach, the results are usually better, but at a higher cost. Scheduling for a bounded number of processors can be done either using duplication (e.g., DSH [4], BTDH [2] or CPFD [1]) or without duplication (e.g., MCP [11], ETF [3], DLS [10] or FCP [7]). Duplicating tasks results in better scheduling performance but significantly increases scheduling cost. Non-duplicating task heuristics have a lower complexity and still obtain good schedules. However, when compiling large programs for large systems, the complexity of current approaches is still prohibitive.

This paper presents a new compile-time task scheduling algorithm, called Fast Load Balancing (FLB). We prove that given a partial schedule, FLB schedules at each iteration the

*This research is part of the Automap project granted by the Netherlands Computer Science Foundation (SION) with financial support from the Netherlands Organization for Scientific Research (NWO) under grant number SION-2519/612-33-005.

ready task that starts the earliest. The main idea is to keep the processors busy, in this respect being close to a load balancing scheme (hence the acronym). The same criterion is also used by ETF, however at a much higher complexity of $O(W(E + V)P)$ compared to FLB's $O(V(\log(W) + \log(P)) + E)$ complexity, where V and E are the number of tasks and edges in the task graph, respectively, W is the task graph width, and P is the number of processors. Experiments also show that FLB performs equally to existing one-step scheduling algorithms of much higher complexity such as MCP. Moreover, FLB consistently outperforms multi-step algorithms like DSC-LLB which also have higher cost.

The paper is organized as follows: The next section specifies the scheduling problem and introduces some definitions used in the paper. Section 3 briefly reviews some of the well-known scheduling algorithms for bounded number of processors on which we base our comparisons. In Section 4, the FLB algorithm is presented. Section 5 illustrates the functionality of the algorithm through an execution trace. Section 6 describes its performance. Section 7 concludes the paper.

2 Preliminaries

A parallel program can be modeled by a directed acyclic graph $\mathcal{G} = (\mathcal{V}, \mathcal{E})$, where $\mathcal{V}$ is a set of V nodes and $\mathcal{E}$ is a set of E edges. A node in the DAG represents a task, containing instructions that execute sequentially without preemption. Each task $t \in \mathcal{V}$ has a weight $comp(t)$ associated with it, which represents the *computation cost* of executing the task. The edges correspond to task dependencies (communication messages or precedence constraints). Each edge (t, t') has a weight $comm(t, t')$ associated with it, which represents the *communication cost* to satisfy the dependence. The *communication to computation ratio* (CCR) of a parallel program is defined as the ratio between its average communication cost and its average computation cost. If two tasks are scheduled to the same processor, the communication cost between them is assumed to be zero. The task graph *width* (W) is defined as maximum number of tasks that are not connected through a path.

A task with no input edges is called an *entry* task, while a task with no output edges is called an *exit* task. A task is said to be *ready* if all its parents have finished their execution. Note that at any given time the number of ready tasks never exceeds W. A task can start its execution only after all its messages have been received.

As a distributed system we assume a set $\mathcal{P}$ of P processors connected in homogeneous clique topology. Inter-processor communication is performed without contention.

Once scheduled, a task t is associated with a processor $PROC(t)$, a *start time* $ST(t)$ and a *finish time* $FT(t)$. If the task is not scheduled, these three values are not defined.

The *processor ready time* of a given processor $p \in \mathcal{P}$ on a partial schedule is defined as the finish time of the last task scheduled on the given processor, according to $PRT(p) = \max_{t \in \mathcal{V}, PROC(t)=p} FT(t)$.

The *enabling processor* of a ready task t, $EP(t)$ is the processor from which the last message arrives. The *last message arrival time* of a ready task t is defined as $LMT(t) = \max_{(t',t) \in \mathcal{E}} \{FT(t') + comm(t',t)\}$. When task t is tentatively scheduled to a processor p, the messages sent by t's predecessors that are already scheduled to p are assumed to take 0 communication time. Therefore, the *effective message arrival time* will be $EMT(t,p) = \max_{(t',t) \in \mathcal{E}, PROC(t') \neq p} \{FT(t') + comm(t',t)\}$. The estimated start time when scheduling a ready task t to a processor p is defined as $EST(t,p) = \max\{EMT(t,p), PRT(p)\}$.

Given a partial schedule and a ready task t is said to be of *type EP* if its last message arrival time is greater than the ready time of its enabling processor: $LMT(t) \geq PRT(EP(t))$. and of *type non-EP* otherwise. Thus, for EP type tasks start the earliest on their enabling processor. A processor is called *active* if there are EP type tasks for which it is the enabling processor and *passive* otherwise.

The objective of the scheduling problem is to find a scheduling of the tasks in $\mathcal{V}$ on the processors in $\mathcal{P}$ such that the parallel completion time (schedule length) is minimized. The parallel completion time is defined as $T_{par} = \max_{p \in \mathcal{P}} PRT(p)$.

3 Related Work

In this section, three existing scheduling algorithms and their characteristics are described, namely the one-step scheduling algorithms MCP [11] and ETF [3], and the multi-step method DSC-LLB [8, 12].

3.1 MCP

MCP (Modified Critical Path) is a list scheduling algorithm in which task priorities are based on the *latest possible start time* of the tasks. The latest possible start time is computed as difference between the critical path of the graph and the longest path from the current task to any exit task. A path length is the sum of the execution times and the communication costs of the tasks and edges belonging to the path. A task with the smallest latest possible start time has the highest priority. Ties are broken considering the priorities of the task's descendents. The tasks are selected in the order of their priorities and scheduled on the processor that can execute it the earliest. The time complexity of MCP is $O(V^2(\log(V) + P))$.

MCP is relatively fast compared with other one-step scheduling algorithms. Furthermore, its scheduling performance is shown to be superior compared to most of the other algorithms for bounded number of processors [5, 8]. MCP can be modified to run faster by choosing a random tie breaking

scheme at a negligible loss of performance. In this case, the time complexity is reduced to $O(V \log(V) + (E + V)P)$.

3.2 ETF

ETF (Earliest Task First) is a one-step scheduling algorithm in which at each iteration, the ready task that can start the earliest is scheduled. The earliest starting task is determined by tentatively scheduling all the ready tasks to all processors. The task with the minimum starting time is selected and scheduled to the corresponding processor on which it starts the earliest. The time complexity of ETF is $O(W(E+V)P)$.

ETF has a high complexity because at each iteration, it is required to compute the start times of each task for every processor scheduling. The main idea behind ETF is to keep the processors busy, in this respect being close to a load balancing scheme. Its scheduling performance is shown to be comparable with MCP's performance [5].

3.3 DSC-LLB

DSC-LLB is a multi-step scheduling algorithm composed of DSC (Dominant Sequence Clustering) and LLB (List-Based Load Balancing). The first step, using DSC, is intended to minimize communication by grouping the highly communicating tasks together in clusters. The second step, using LLB, maps the clusters to the existing processors and orders the tasks within the clusters.

In the DSC algorithm, task priorities are dynamically computed based on the sum of their *top level* and *bottom level*. The top level and bottom level are the sum of the computation and communication costs along the longest path from the given task to an entry task and an exit task, respectively. Again, the communication costs are assumed to be zero between two tasks mapped to the same processor. While the bottom level is statically computed at the beginning, the top level is computed incrementally during the scheduling process. The tasks are scheduled in the order of their priorities, where the largest sum of top and bottom levels takes priority. The destination processor is either the processor from which the last message arrives, or a new processor depending on which the given task can start earlier. The time complexity of DSC is $O((E+V)\log V)$.

In the LLB algorithm, a task is mapped to a processor if there is at least another task from the same cluster scheduled on that processor and not mapped otherwise. LLB is a load balancing scheme. First, the destination processor is selected as the processor that becomes idle the earliest. Second, the task to be scheduled is selected. There are two candidates: (a) a task already mapped to the selected processor having the least bottom level, or (b) an unmapped task with the least bottom level. The one starting the earliest is scheduled. The time complexity of LLB is $O((C \log(C) + V)$, where C is the number of clusters obtained in the clustering step.

DSC-LLB is a low-cost algorithm. Not surprisingly, compared to a higher cost scheduling algorithm as MCP, it has worse scheduling performance. However, the DSC-LLB output performance is still shown to be within 40% of the MCP output performance, while outperforming other known multi-step scheduling algorithms [8].

4 The FLB Algorithm

As mentioned earlier, list scheduling algorithms generally perform better compared to other scheduling algorithms for a bounded number of processors, such as multi-step methods [8]. Recently, a list scheduling algorithm, called FCP, has been proposed [7] whose time complexity is significantly reduced without sacrificing performance. For FCP, it has been proven that given a partial schedule and an arbitrary ready task, only *two* processors need to be considered to find the minimum start time of the given task. However, given the partial schedule and the set of ready tasks, the selected task need not always be the preferred one (i.e., the ready task that can actually start the earliest). In the FLB heuristic proposed in this paper, we improve this task selection by scheduling the ready task that can start the earliest. We prove that only two cases need to be considered to indeed select the preferred task and its corresponding processor. The scheduling process is therefore improved, while the low time complexity is maintained.

Note that FLB uses the same task selection criterion as in ETF. In contrast to ETF however, the preferred task is identified in $O(\log P)$ instead of $O(WP)$. Although essentially similar, there is a small difference in the task selection scheme. Throughout the scheduling process it may happen that several ready tasks can start at the same earliest time. ETF an FLB have different criteria to break this tie, and as a consequence in some cases they may still select a different task-processor pair to be scheduled.

Priority-based scheduling algorithms have three parts: (a) task priorities computation, (b) sorting tasks according to their priorities and (c) task scheduling. Computing task priorities takes at least $O(E + V)$ time, since the whole task graph has to be traversed. Sorting tasks takes $O(V \log W)$ time. The variety of scheduling approaches refers to the last part (c).

For most list scheduling algorithms, the task scheduling part takes $O((E + V)P)$ time complexity caused by the fact that all processors are considered to find the processor on which the current task can start the earliest. ETF [3] uses an even more elaborate approach. At each iteration, it schedules the ready task that can start the earliest to the processor on which this earliest start time is achieved. However, the complexity is $O(W)$ higher ($O(W(E + V)P)$), caused by the fact that at each iteration all the tasks need to be considered in the selection process. In [7] has been proven that processor selection in list scheduling algorithms can be performed at a considerable lower time complexity of $O(V \log (P) + E)$. In this paper we go one step further and prove that even the stronger task selection criterion used in the ETF scheduling algorithm can also be achieved at the same cost of $O(V \log (P) + E)$.

4.1 Algorithm Description

In FLB, at each iteration of the algorithm, the ready task that can start the earliest is scheduled to the processor on which that start time is achieved. To select the earliest starting task, pairs of a ready task and the processor on which it starts the earliest need to be considered.

In order to obtain the earliest start time of a given ready task on a partial schedule, the given task must be scheduled either (a) to the processor from which the last message is sent from

or (b) to the processor becoming idle the earliest (as proven in [7]). An informal explanation is that if the processor the last message is sent from is idle before that message is received, then the start time of the task can be improved by scheduling the task on that processor. If that processor is busy at the time the last message arrives, then the task cannot start earlier than the last message arrival time which ever processor is selected. Consequently, the task will start the earliest on the processor becoming idle the earliest. It follows that an EP type task starts the earliest on its enabling processor and a non-EP type task start the earliest on the processor becoming idle the earliest.

Given a partial schedule, there are only two pairs task-processor that can achieve the minimum start time for a task: (a) the EP type task t with the minimum estimated start time $EST(t, EP(t))$ on its enabling processor, and (b) the non-EP type task t' with the minimum last message arrival time $LMT(t')$ on the processor becoming idle the earliest. The first case minimizes the earliest start time of the EP type tasks, while the second case minimizes the earliest start time of the non-EP type tasks. If in both cases the same earliest start time is obtained, the non-EP type task is preferred, because the communication caused by the messages sent from the task's predecessors are already overlapped with the previous computation. Considering the two cases discussed above guarantees that the ready task with the earliest start time will be identified. A formal proof is given in the appendix.

For each processor, there are two sorted lists storing the EP type tasks for which the given processor is the enabling processor. The tasks in the first list (EMT_EP_task_l) are decreasingly sorted by the effective message arrival time on their enabling processor ($EMT(t, EP(t))$). The tasks in the second list (LMT_EP_task_l) are decreasingly sorted by their last message arrival time ($LMT(t)$). The non-EP type tasks are also stored in a list (nonEP_task_l), decreasingly sorted by $LMT(t)$. For all three task lists, ties are broken by selecting the task with the longest path to any exit tasks.

There is a list of active processors (active_proc_l), decreasingly sorted by the minimum $EST(t)$ of the EP type tasks enabled by them. The minimum $EST(t)$ of the EP type tasks enabled by a processor is computed in $O(1)$ as the maximum between EMT of the first task in the processor's EMT_EP_task_l and the processor's PRT. A second global processor list (all_proc_l) stores all processors, decreasingly sorted by the PRT.

The FLB algorithm is formalized below.

```
FLB ()
BEGIN
   FORALL t ∈ V DO
      IF t is an entry task THEN
         SetEMT (t, 0)
         SetLMT (t, 0)
         Enqueue (nonEP_task_l, t, 0)
      END IF
   END FORALL
   FORALL p ← 0 TO P-1 DO
      Enqueue (all_proc_l, p, 0)
      END IF
   END FORALL
   WHILE NOT all tasks scheduled DO
      (t,p) ← ScheduleTask();
      UpdateTaskLists (t, p)
      UpdateProcLists (t, p)
      UpdateReadyTasks (t, p)
   END WHILE
END
```

At the beginning, the set of ready tasks consists of the entry tasks. None of them satisfies the EP type condition. Consequently, they are stored in the non-EP type task list. Moreover, as there are no EP type tasks, there is no active processor and the active processor list is empty. All the processors have the ready time 0, so all of them have the same priority, 0, in the global processor list.

The scheduling loop is repeated as long as there exist unscheduled tasks. At each iteration, one task is scheduled using `ScheduleTask`. After each task scheduling, the task lists, the processor lists and the ready task set must be updated, according to the new conditions following the last scheduling step.

The four procedures FLB is based on `Schedule-Task`, `UpdateTaskLists`, `UpdateProcLists` and `UpdateReadyTasks` are described below.

```
ScheduleTask ()
BEGIN
  p1 ← Head (active_proc_l)
  IF p1 ≠ NULL THEN
    t1 ← Head (EMT_EP_task_l[p1])
  END IF
  p2 ← Head (all_proc_l)
  t2 ← Head (nonEP_task_l)

  IF (p1 ≠ NULL) ∧ (EST(t1,p1) < EST(t2,p2)) THEN
    Schedule task t1 on processor p1
    Dequeue (active_proc_l)
    Dequeue (EMT_EP_task_l[p1])
    RemoveItem (LMT_EP_task_l[p1], t1)
    RETURN (t1, p1)
  ELSE
    Schedule task t2 on processor p2
    Dequeue (all_proc_l)
    Dequeue (nonEP_task_l)
    RETURN (t2,p2)
  END IF
END
```

The `ScheduleTask` procedure selects two task-processor pairs for the scheduling step. The first pair consists of the EP type task with the minimum EMT time and its enabling processor. The second pair is the non-EP task with the minimum LMT and processor becoming idle the earliest. The pair which achieves the minimum start time is selected and the selected task is scheduled to the selected processor. Scheduling a task also implies assigning to it its corresponding processor, start time and finish time. The `Dequeue` and `RemoveItem` procedures are used to remove the heads and the elements from the sorted lists, respectively.

```
UpdateTaskLists (t,p)
BEGIN
  WHILE true DO
    t ← Head (LMT_EP_task_l[p])
    IF t = NULL THEN
      BREAK
    END IF
    IF LMT(t) ≥ PRT(p) THEN
      BREAK
    Dequeue (LMT_EP_task_l[p])
    RemoveItem (EMT_EP_task_l[p], t)
    Enqueue (nonEP_task_l, t, LMT(t))
  END WHILE
END
```

After scheduling a task to a processor, the processor's ready time changes. Consequently, some of the EP type tasks enabled by that processor may no longer satisfy the condition to be of EP type. `UpdateTaskLists` moves the tasks that no longer satisfy the EP type condition to the non EP type task list. The tasks are tested in the order of their LMT. Finally, if there are no more EP type tasks enabled by the given processor, the processor is removed from the active processor list.

```
UpdateProcLists (t,p)
BEGIN
  t ← Head (EMT_EP_task_l[p])
  IF t = NULL THEN
    RemoveItem (active_proc_l,p)
  ELSE
    prio ← EST(t,p)
    BalanceList (active_proc_l, p, prio)
  END IF
END
```

`UpdateProcLists` updates the active processor list. If there is no EP type task enabled by the given processor, the processor must be removed from the active processor list. If there are still EP type tasks enabled by the given processor they may not be the same and as a consequence the processor priority in the active processor list could be modified. Therefore, the processor priority and the active processor list must be updated. Also, the global processor list must be updated because the current processor has changed the time it becomes idle.

```
UpdateReadyTasks (t,p)
BEGIN
  FORALL t' ∈ Succ(t) DO
    IF Ready(t') THEN
      p' ← GetEnablingProc (t')
      ComputeLMT (t')
      ComputeEMT (t',p')
      IF LMT(t') < PRT(p') THEN
        Enqueue (nonEP_task_l, t', LMT(t'))
      ELSE
        IF Head(EMT_EP_task_l[p']) = NULL THEN
          prio ← EST(t',p')
          Enqueue (active_proc_l, p', prio)
        ELSE
          t'' ← Head(EMT_EP_task_l[p'])
          IF EMT(t',p') < EMT(t'',p') THEN
            prio ← maxEMT(t'),PRT(p')
            BalanceList (active_proc_l, p, prio)
          END IF
        END IF
        Enqueue (EMT_EP_task_l[p'],t',EMT(t',p'))
        Enqueue (LMT_EP_task_l[p'],t',LMT(t'))
      END IF
    END IF
  END FORALL
END
```

`UpdateReadyTasks` adds the tasks that become ready due to the current task scheduling to one of the ready task lists, depending if it is of type EP or not. Moreover, if the task is of type EP, its enabling processor may become active and it must be added to the active processor list. Also, if the processor is already active and its priority changes, the active processor list must be updated.

4.2 Complexity Analysis

The complexity of the FLB algorithm is as follows. To compute task priorities throughout the algorithm, all the tasks and dependencies must be considered once. Consequently, the total complexity of computing task priorities takes $O(E + V)$ time.

Scheduling a task involves a comparison between two tentative task scheduling operations. The decision is taken based

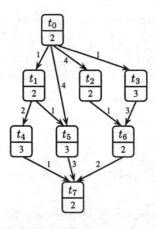

Figure 1. Example task graph

EP tasks		non-EP	Scheduling
on p_0	on p_1	tasks	$t \to p,$
$t[EMT(t,p), BL/LMT(t)]$		$t[LMT(t)]$	$[ST(t) - FT(t)]$
—	—	$t_0[0]$	$t_0 \to p_0, [0 - 2]$
$t_3[2,12/3]$	—	—	
$t_1[2,11/3]$	—	—	
$t_2[2,9/6]$	—	—	$t_3 \to p_0, [2 - 5]$
$t_2[2,9/6]$	—	$t_1[3]$	$t_1 \to p_1, [3 - 5]$
$t_2[2,9/6]$	$t_4[5,6/7]$	—	
$t_5[6,8/6]$	—	—	$t_2 \to p_0, [5 - 7]$
$t_6[7,6/8]$	$t_4[5,6/7]$	$t_5[6]$	$t_4 \to p_1, [5 - 8]$
$t_6[7,6/8]$	—	$t_5[6]$	$t_5 \to p_0, [7 - 10]$
—	—	$t_6[8]$	$t_6 \to p_1, [8 - 10]$
$t_7[12,2/13]$	—	—	$t_7 \to p_0, [12 - 14]$

Table 1. Execution trace of the FLB algorithm.

on the two estimated start times of the tasks tentatively scheduled. Computing the estimated start times takes $O(1)$ time, since the estimated start times are computed as the maximum of the task effective message arrival time on that processor on the one hand and the processor ready time on the other hand. These values are already computed at the time the decision is made. Since there are V tasks, the resulting task scheduling complexity is $O(V)$.

Task lists operations are adding and removing tasks from sorted lists. Every task is added and removed at most once from the two lists of EP type tasks and once from the non-EP type task list. Since there are at most W ready tasks at any moment in time, a list operation takes $O(\log W)$ time. As there are V tasks, the total complexity of maintaining task lists is $O(V \log W)$.

At each scheduling iteration, the global processor list changes, because the processor ready time changes for the destination processor of the scheduling. As a consequence, an operation $O(\log P)$ time complexity must be performed, which implies a total complexity for maintaining the global processor list of $O(V \log P)$.

After becoming idle or being scheduled, a task may change the active or passive status of a processor or its priority in the active processor list. As a consequence, a total complexity of $O(V \log P)$ is required to maintain the active processor list.

Finally, the cost of finding ready tasks takes $O(E+V)$ time, since all the tasks and edges must be scanned throughout the algorithm.

In conclusion, the total time complexity of the FLB algorithm is $O(V(\log(W) + \log(P)) + E)$.

5 Execution Trace

In this section, we illustrate the steps of the FLB algorithm by scheduling the task graph in Fig. 1 on two processors. The execution trace of the FLB algorithm is presented in Table 1. The first two columns in the table list the EP type tasks enabled by p_0 and p_1, respectively, as they are sorted in the corresponding lists. The task's EMT and bottom level are included to illustrate their sorting order, as well as their LMT to motivate their EP type. The third column in the table lists the non-

EP type tasks sorted by LMT. Finally, the last column shows the scheduling at the current iteration, including the task's start time and finish time.

At the beginning, there is only one ready task, namely t_0. It is of non-EP type as it has no enabling processor. Task t_0 is scheduled on one randomly selected processor p_0, as all the processors have zero workload.

After scheduling t_0, three tasks become ready, namely t_1, t_2 and t_3. As there are no non-EP type tasks, the active processor accommodating the earliest starting EP type task is selected, in this case being the only active processor p_0. The EP type task with the higher priority is selected. Since the EMT is the same for all three tasks, the tie breaking mechanism stipulates that the task with the higher bottom level t_3 be selected and scheduled.

After scheduling t_3, t_1 becomes non-EP type, because $PRT(p_0)$ becomes larger than $LMT(t_1)$. The other ready task t_2 still satisfies the EP type condition. The two task-processor pairs to be compared for the next scheduling iteration are now t_2-p_0 and t_1-p_1. Processor p_1 is selected for the latter, because it is the processor becoming idle the earliest. Thus, t_1-p_1 is selected since $EST(t_1) = 3$ is lower than $EST(t_2) = 5$.

Two other tasks become idle: t_4 and t_5, both of type EP, enabled by p_1 and p_0, respectively. There are no non-EP tasks, so the first starting EP type task t_2 is selected and scheduled to its enabling processor p_0.

Task t_5 becomes non-EP type and is moved to the non-EP type task list. Task t_6 becomes ready and of EP type, so it is stored to the EP task list of its enabling processor p_0. The first starting EP type task is t_4 which starts on p_1 at 5. The non-EP task with the lowest LMT, t_5, starts on the processor becoming idle the earliest, p_0, at 6. Consequently, t_4 is scheduled on p_1 at 5.

At the next iteration both EP type and non-EP type tasks, namely t_6 and t_5, respectively, start at the same time: 7. The non-EP type task is preferred and scheduled on p_0.

In each of the next two iterations, no choice need be made as there is only one task to be scheduled. First t_6 is scheduled on p_1 at 8, then t_7 is scheduled on $p0$ at 12.

538

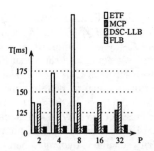

Figure 2. Scheduling algorithm costs

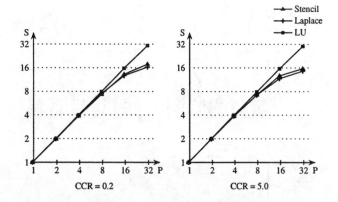

Figure 3. FLB speedup

6 Performance Results

The FLB algorithm is compared with three algorithms, namely MCP, ETF, and DSC-LLB. The three algorithms are well-known, use different scheduling schemes, and were shown to obtain competitive results [5, 8, 11]. We selected the lower-cost version of MCP, in which if there are more tasks with the same priority, the task to be scheduled is chosen randomly.

We consider task graphs representing various types of parallel algorithms. The selected problems are *LU decomposition* ("LU"), *Laplace equation solver* ("Laplace") and a *stencil algorithm* ("Stencil"). For each of these problems, we adjusted the problem size to obtain task graphs of about $V = 2000$ nodes. For each problem, we varied the task graph granularities, by varying the communication to computation ratio (CCR). The values used for CCR were 0.2 and 5.0. For each problem and each CCR value, we generated 5 graphs with random execution times and communication delays (i.i.d., uniform distribution with unit coefficient of variation). A larger set of problems and granularities has been used to measure the FLB's performance in [6].

6.1 Running Times

Our main objective is to reduce task scheduling cost (i.e., running time), while maintaining performance. In Fig. 2 the average running time of the algorithms is shown in CPU seconds as measured on a Pentium Pro/233MHz PC with 64Mb RAM running Linux 2.0.32. ETF is the most costly among the compared algorithms. Its running time increases from 185 ms for $P = 2$ up to 2.6 s for $P = 32$. MCP also increases its running times with the number of processors, but its cost is significantly lower. For $P = 2$, it runs for 41 ms, while for $P = 32$, the running time is 139 ms. DSC-LLB does not vary significantly with P, as its most costly step, clustering, is independent of the number of processors. The DSC-LLB running times vary around 180 ms.

FCP achieves the lowest running time, varying from 33 ms for $P = 2$ to 41 ms for $P = 32$. FLB running time is at the same level compared to FCP. It increases from 38 ms for $P = 2$ up to 49 ms for $P = 32$. The FLB's actual running times are comparable to FCP's running times, despite the fact that the FLB's complexity of $O(V(\log(W) + \log(P)) + E)$ is higher compared to FCP's complexity of $O(V \log(P) + E)$. This is due to the fact that usually, the width of the task graph has reasonable low values.

6.2 Scheduling Performance

In Fig. 3 we show the FLB speedup for the considered problems. For all the problems, FLB obtains significant speedup. There are two classes of problems: (a) Stencil and FFT which achieve linear speedup and (b) LU and Laplace for which there less speedup is obtained for large number of processors. Stencil and FFT are more regular. Therefore more parallelism can be exploited and better speedup is obtained. For LU and Laplace, there are a large number of join operations. As a consequence, there is not much parallelism available and the speedup is lower.

To compare the FLB algorithm with the other algorithms, we use the *normalized schedule lengths* (NSL), which is defined as the ratio between the schedule length of the given algorithm and the schedule length of MCP.

In Fig. 4 we show the average normalized schedule lengths for the selected algorithms and problems. For each of the considered CCR values a set of NSL values is presented.

MCP and ETF consistently yield relatively good schedules. Depending on the problem and granularity, either one or the other performs better. The differences become larger for fine-grained problems, which are more sensitive to scheduling decisions. For LU, MCP schedules are up to 23% better, while for Laplace, ETF schedules are up to 5% better. For coarse-grain problems, the results are comparable.

DSC-LLB is a multi-step method intended to obtain acceptable results while aiming for minimum complexity. Its scheduling performance is not much worse compared to MCP and ETF. Typically, the schedule lengths are no more than 20% longer than the MCP and ETF's schedule lengths. Although in some cases the difference can be higher (up to 42%) there are also cases in which DSC-LLB performs better (up to 10%) compared to a list scheduling algorithm.

FCP has both low-cost and good performance. FCP obtains comparable performance with MCP, because it uses the same scheduling criteria as MCP, but in a more efficient manner. Compared to ETF, the overall performance is also comparable. However the differences between FCP and ETF (up to 18%) are higher compared to the differences between FCP and MCP (5%). Finally, compared to DSC-LLB, FCP obtains consistently better performance.

FLB has both low-cost and good performance. FLB obtains

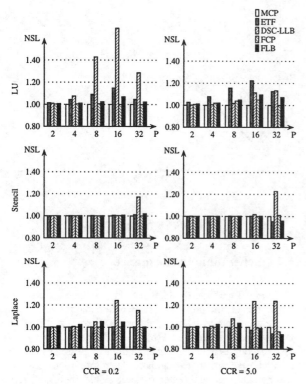

Figure 4. Scheduling algorithm performance

an overall comparable performance with ETF, MCP and FCP, and consistently outperform DSC-LLB. Compared to ETF, FLB performs better in most of the cases, up to 12%, despite they have the same task selection criterion. As explained earlier, this is due to the fact that ETF an FLB have different criteria to break ties. ETF uses statically computed task priorities. FLB uses message arrival times as task priorities and if the tie persists, the task bottom level. If there are more tasks starting at the same earliest time, the task with the highest priority is chosen. As the priorities are different, FLB and ETF may select a different task-processor pair to be scheduled. FLB performs better because its priority scheme is dynamic, therefore being more accurate.

Compared with MCP, FLB performs better or worse if ETF performs better or worse, respectively. FLB performs better than MCP for communication-intensive problems that have a regular structure (e.g., Stencil or Laplace). For LU, which involves many successive forks and joins, the relative performance of FLB compared to MCP is lower. The reason is that FLB, like ETF, does not consider future communication and computation when taking a scheduling decision, which in this case yields worse schedules. Finally, compared to DSC-LLB, FLB performs consistently better.

7 Conclusion

In this paper, a new scheduling algorithm, called Fast Load Balancing (FLB), is presented which is intended as a compile-time scheduling algorithm for distributed-memory systems. We prove that FLB uses the same criterion for task selection and scheduling as ETF, which is to schedule at each iteration the task starting the earliest. However, FLB's time complexity of $O(V(\log(W) + \log(P)) + E)$ is drastically lower compared to ETF's $O(W(E + V)P)$ complexity.

Experimental results indeed show that FLB obtains a comparable performance with ETF as well as MCP. Compared to ETF, FLB performs equal or better in most of the cases, up to 12% due to differences in the particular heuristic used to break ties with respect to ready tasks that can start at the same earliest time. FLB's tie breaking heuristic performs better because its priority scheme is dynamic, therefore being more accurate. Compared with MCP, FLB performs better or worse if ETF performs better or worse, respectively. Again, note that MCP's cost is much higher compared to FLB's cost. Furthermore, FLB has consistently better performance compared to DSC-LLB, which has a higher cost compared to FLB's cost.

References

[1] I. Ahmad and Y.-K. Kwok. A new approach to scheduling parallel programs using task duplication. In *Proc. ICPP*, pages 47–51, Aug. 1994.

[2] Y. C. Chung and S. Ranka. Application and performance analysis of a compile-time optimization approach for list scheduling algorithms on distributed-memory multiprocessors. In *Proc. Supercomputing*, pages 512–521, Nov. 1992.

[3] J.-J. Hwang, Y.-C. Chow, F. D. Anger, and C.-Y. Lee. Scheduling precedence graphs in systems with interprocessor communication times. *SIAM J. on Computing*, 18:244–257, Apr. 1989.

[4] B. Kruatrachue and T. G. Lewis. Grain size determination for parallel processing. *IEEE Software*, pages 23–32, Jan. 1988.

[5] Y.-K. Kwok and I. Ahmad. Benchmarking the task graph scheduling algorithms. In *Proc. IPPS/SPDP*, pages 531–537, Mar. 1998.

[6] A. Rădulescu and A. J. C. van Gemund. FLB: Fast load balancing for distributed-memory machines. TR 1-68340-44(1999)03, Delft Univ. of Technology, Feb. 1999.

[7] A. Rădulescu and A. J. C. van Gemund. On the complexity of list scheduling algorithms for distributed-memory systems. In *Proc. ICS*, pages 68–75, June 1999.

[8] A. Rădulescu, A. J. C. van Gemund, and H.-X. Lin. LLB: A fast and effective scheduling algorithm for distributed-memory systems. In *Proc. IPPS/SPDP*, pages 525–530, Apr. 1999.

[9] V. Sarkar. *Partitioning and Scheduling Parallel Programs for Execution on Multiprocessors*. PhD thesis, MIT, 1989.

[10] G. C. Sih and E. A. Lee. A compile-time scheduling heuristic for interconection-constrained heterogeneous processor architectures. *IEEE Trans. on Parallel and Distributed Systems*, 4(2):175–187, Feb. 1993.

[11] M.-Y. Wu and D. D. Gajski. Hypertool: A programming aid for message-passing systems. *IEEE Trans. on Parallel and Distributed Systems*, 1(7):330–343, July 1990.

[12] T. Yang and A. Gerasoulis. DSC: Scheduling parallel tasks on an unbounded number of processors. *IEEE Trans. on Parallel and Distributed Systems*, 5(9):951–967, Dec. 1994.

A   Task Selection

In this appendix we prove that given a partial schedule and a set of ready tasks, the selection of a task starting the earliest is restricted to comparing only two cases. The two choices are either (a) the EP type task with the minimum estimated start time on its enabling processor, or (b) the non-EP task with the minimum last message arrival time on the processor becoming idle the earliest. The first choice clearly minimizes the EP type tasks' EST. The second choice is proven to minimize the non-EP type tasks' EST. Consequently, selecting from these two tasks the one starting the earliest guarantees that the earliest starting task is chosen.

The next lemma states that a non-EP type task cannot start earlier than its LMT. To prove this, two cases have to be considered. First, the start time on the task's enabling processor, which is greater than the processor ready time, cannot be greater than LMT due to the definition of the non-EP type task. Second, if the task is scheduled on any other processor than the enabling processor, the task's EMT will be equal to its LMT. Consequently, the task will start at LMT the earliest.

Lemma 1 *Let $t \in V$ be a non-EP type task. Then*

$$\forall p \in \mathcal{P}, \quad LMT(t) \leq EST(t,p)$$

Proof
Let (t', t) be the dependence corresponding to $EP(t)$. By definition of LMT it holds

$$LMT(t) = FT(t') + comm(t', t) \tag{1}$$

By definition of EMT it follows that

$$\forall p \neq EP(t), \quad FT(t') + comm(t', t) \leq EMT(t,p) \leq LMT(t) \tag{2}$$

From (1) and (2) it follows that

$$\forall p \neq EP(t), \quad EMT(t,p) = LMT(t) \leq EST(t,p) \tag{3}$$

By definition of a non-EP type task it follows that for $p = EP(t)$

$$LMT(t) < PRT(EP(t)) \leq EST(t, EP(t)) \tag{4}$$

From (3) and (4) it follows that

$$\forall p \in \mathcal{P}, \quad LMT(t) \leq EST(t,p) \tag{5}$$

$\square$

We use the lemma to show that the start time of a non-EP type task t on a processor p is the maximum of $LMT(t)$ and $PRT(p)$. $LMT(t)$ can be used instead of $EMT(t,p)$, because LMT is always the greater of the two and as the previous lemma states, $LMT(t)$ is always less than the task start time for a non-EP type task.

Corollary 2 *Let $t \in V$ be a non-EP type task. Then*

$$\forall p \in \mathcal{P}, \quad EST(t,p) = \max\{LMT(t), PRT(p)\}$$

Proof
Combining Lemma 1 and TST definition we can state that

$$\forall p \in \mathcal{P}, \quad EST(t,p) = \max\{LMT(t), EMT(t,p), PRT(p)\} \tag{6}$$

From the definitions of LMT and EMT it follows that the EMT term can be removed as stated by

$$\forall p \in \mathcal{P}, \quad EST(t,p) = \max\{LMT(t), PRT(p)\} \tag{7}$$

$\square$

The following theorem proves that the two task-processor pairs considered by the FLB algorithm are sufficient to find the earliest starting ready task. The first pair, consisting of the EP type task with the minimum $EST(t, EP(t))$ on its enabling processor, minimizes the start time of the EP type tasks. The second pair consists of the non-EP type task with the minimum $LMT(t)$ on the processor becoming idle the earliest. Corollary 2 proves that the start time for the non-EP tasks has two independent components, namely $LMT(t)$ and $PRT(p)$ which are both minimized by the way the task and processor are selected. As a consequence, the task-processor pair that determines the earliest start time can be found using only the two cases mentioned above.

Theorem 3 *Let $t \in V$ be a ready task and $p \in P$ a processor such that*

$$EST(t,p) = \min_{t_x \in \mathcal{V}, p_x \in \mathcal{P}} EST(t_x, p_x)$$

Then t and p are either (a) the EP type task t_1 with the minimum estimated start time ($EST(t_1, EP(t_1))$) on its enabling processor p_1, or (b) the non-EP type task t_2 with the minimum last message arrival time ($LMT(t_2)$) on the processor becoming idle the earliest.

Proof
(a) t_1 is the earliest starting EP type task, simply by its selection criterion.
(b) t_2 is the non-EP task with the lowest LMT and p_2 is the processor with lowest PRT. From Corollary 2 it follows that t_2 is the earliest starting non-EP type task if scheduled on p_2.

From (a) and (b) it follows that the task-processor pair that determines the earliest start time can be found using only the two cases mentioned above.

$\square$

Load Balancing in Counter-Rotated SONET Rings *

Peng-Jun Wan
Department of compputer Science
Illinois Institute of Technology
Chicago, IL 60616
Email: wan@cs.iit.edu

Yuanyuan Yang[†]
Department of ECE
SUNY at Stony Brook
Stony Brook, NY 11794
Email: yang@ece.sunysb.edu

Abstract

Load-balanced routing in SONET rings has attracted much attention recently. Most prior works model the SONET rings as undirected rings and the traffic as undirected chords. While this model fits well to the traditional telephony applications, it is inefficient for the explosive Internet traffic and multimedia data communications, which exhibit unidirectional and asymmetric nature. For these applications, it is proper to model the SONET rings as a pair of counter-rotated rings and the traffic as directed chords. In this paper, we first explore general flow properties in counter-rotated rings, and then introduce flow rounding and unsplitting techniques. Afterwards an optimal integral routing algorithm is provided. Finally, we show the NP-completeness of optimal unsplit routing, and present several polynomial-time approximation algorithms.

Keywords: *SONET, counter-rotated rings, routing, load balancing, approximation algorithms.*

1. Introduction

With the explosion of the Internet traffic and multimedia data communication, Synchronous Optical Network (SONET) has been adopted by many network service providers as a faster, more efficient, and less expensive transport technology [1]. While the fiber itself offers virtually unlimited bandwidth, the add-drop multiplexers (ADMs) determine the actual bandwidth available along any fiber link of the SONET ring [8]. With the rapid growth of the data traffic in recent years and the exhaust of the fiber links in the plant, load-balanced routing becomes an important problem in the planning of the SONET rings.

The optical transmission in the fibers is unidirectional in nature because of the unidirectional operation of optical amplifiers. Accordingly, a SONET ring usually consists of two working counter-rotated fiber rings carrying the traffic in opposite directions, with additional transmission capacity provided for fault protection [4]. In the past, the dominant traffic carried was mainly the voice traffic which are both full-duplex (i.e., bidirectional) and symmetric (i.e., the traffic rates in the two directions are the same). In such an environment, the SONET rings can be modeled simply as undirected rings and traffic as undirected chords. The data traffic, on the other hand, has a different nature from the voice traffic in the sense that it is in nature either simplex (i.e. unidirectional) or asymmetrical. To reduce the capacity requirement and improve the utilization of fiber links, it is more proper to model the underlying network as a pair of counter-rotated rings, and each traffic demand as a directed chord. For example, in Figure 1, we show a request i in such a ring, where s_i and t_i are the source and target of the request respectively and d_i is the demand of the request. The demand can be viewed as a directed chord from s_i to t_i. In the actual routing, a portion of the demand d_i, x_i, can be routed in clockwise direction, and the other portion, $d_i - x_i$, can be routed in counterclockwise direction. This paper focuses on the load balancing problem in routing multiple requests in such ring networks to achieve minimum link load.

---

*This research is partially supported by the U.S. National Science Foundation under Grant No. OSR-9350540 and the U.S. Army Research Office under Grant No. DAAH04-96-1-0234.

[†] Contact author

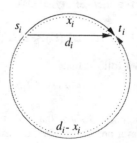

Figure 1. Request i in a SONET ring.

Various restrictions might be imposed on the routings in practice. An *unsplit routing* is the one in which each demand must be carried either entirely clockwise, or entirely counterclockwise. A *split routing*, on the other hand, allows the splitting of a demand into two portions to be carried in two directions. A demand, if allowed to be split, can be split in different ways. A *fractional routing* allows a demand to be split into two arbitrary portions to be carried in two directions. An *integral routing* only allows a demand to be split into two integral arbitrary portions to be carried in two directions. *Semi-integral routing* is a fractional routing with the additional constraint that the total demands routed in both directions are integers. It is a generalization of the concept of the flush routing defined in [10], and serves as a bridge between the fractional routing and the integral routing. In real implementations, the integral routing and the unsplit routing are more practical and common.

The load-balanced routing in undirected rings has been well studied recently in [2, 5, 7, 8, 9]. They heavily reply upon many structural and flow properties such as the *cut condition* given by the well-known Okamura-Seymour theorem [6]. While some of them hold in both type of rings, many others such as the cut condition are specific to undirected rings. Therefore, new techniques and approaches are needed to develop optimal routings in counter-rotated rings. Furthermore, we observe that some approaches used in undirected rings, such as the one used in [5], can be significantly improved and such improvements are reflected in our solutions to the counter-rotated rings. A recent work [10] gives a polynomial-time optimal load-balancing unsplit routing in counter-rotated rings when all requests have unit traffic demands. However, this algorithm cannot be generalized to optimal unsplit routing under the arbitrary traffic which is NP-complete. Also its generalization to the integral routing under arbitrary traffic leads to only a pseudo-polynomial time algorithm, which is not acceptable.

The remaining of this paper proceeds as follows. Section 2 describes the terminologies and notations. Section 3 explores basic flow properties in counter-rotated rings, which lead to an algorithm for optimal semi-integral routing. Section 4 introduces the concept of parallel routing and an unsplitting technique which are very useful in the design of optimal integral routing and optimal unsplit routing. Section 5 presents a rounding technique which transforms any optimal parallel semi-integral routing into an optimal integral routing. Section 6 shows the NP-completeness of optimal unsplit routing and provides several polynomial-time approximation algorithms. Finally, Section 7 concludes this paper.

2. Terminologies and Notations

We assume that a SONET ring consists of n nodes labeled clockwise by 0 through $n-1$. All arithmetic involving nodes is performed implicitly using modulo n operations. For nodes s and t, the half-closed arc $\{s, s+1, \cdots, t-1\}$ is denoted by $[s, t)$, and the closed arc $\{s, s+1, \cdots, t\}$ is denoted by $[s, t]$. The readers should be able to tell whether an interval is an arc or a normal interval of real numbers in the context.

The traffic in the ring consists of m unidirectional requests. The requests are numbered clockwise (starting from node 0) by their sources. The requests sharing the same source are numbered clockwise (starting from the source) by their targets. Furthermore, the requests sharing the same source and target are numbered arbitrarily. As we will see later, such numbering plays an important role in describing the structural and flow properties. The source, target and the demand of the request i are denoted by s_i, t_i and d_i, respectively. The demand represents the number of time slots required, and therefore is always an integer. For presentational convenience, we use d to denote the m-dimensional vector $(d_1, d_2, \cdots, d_m)$. A (*feasible*) routing in which the portion of the demand of request i to be routed clockwise is x_i is represented by an m-dimensional vector $x = (x_1, x_2, \cdots, x_m)$, where $0 \leq x_i \leq d_i$. For each vector $x = (x_1, x_2, \cdots, x_m)$, we use $\|x\|$ to denote $\sum_{i=1}^{m} x_i$. Therefore $\|d\|$ is the total demand of all requests in the ring, and for each routing x, $\|x\|$ is the total demand routed clockwise by x.

Let x be any routing. The loads of the link $k \to k+1$ and link $k+1 \to k$ induced by x are

$$\ell_k^+(x) = \sum_{i:k\in[s_i,t_i)} x_i, \ell_k^-(x) = \sum_{i:k\notin[s_i,t_i)} (d_i - x_i)$$

respectively. The clockwise and counterclockwise ring loads of x are

$$\ell^+(x) = \max_{0\leq k\leq n-1} \ell_k^+(x), \ell^-(x) = \max_{0\leq k\leq n-1} \ell_k^-(x)$$

respectively. Finally, the ring load of the routing x is

$$\ell(x) = \max\left\{\ell^+(x), \ell^-(x)\right\}.$$

The optimal fractional, semi-integral, integral and unsplit ring load are denoted by L_F^*, L_{SI}^*, L_I^* and L_U^* respectively. Obviously, $L_F^* \leq L_{SI}^* \leq \lceil L_{SI}^* \rceil \leq L_I^* \leq L_U^*$. Tighter relationships among them will be derived later in this paper.

Among all these optimal routing problems, only optimal fractional routing problem is obviously solvable in polynomial time by solving a linear program. For each $\alpha \in [0, \|d\|]$, define

$$L(\alpha) = \min_{\sum_{i=1}^{m} x_i=\alpha, x_i\in[0,d_i], 1\leq i\leq m} \ell(x). \qquad (1)$$

Then $L(\alpha)$ can also be obtained in polynomial time by solving a linear program. Notice that

$$L^*_{SI} = \min_{\alpha \in \{0,1,\cdots,\|d\|\}} L(\alpha).$$

This might suggest one algorithm for the optimal semi-integral routing as follows: for each $\alpha = 0,1,\cdots,\|d\|$, find a routing x with $\|x\| = \alpha$ and $\ell(x) = L(\alpha)$, and then take the best one. However, the time-complexity of such an algorithm is $\Omega(\|d\|)$. Noticing that $\|d\|$ could be as exponentially large as n or m, the algorithm is thus pseudo-polynomial and is not acceptable.

3. Basic Structural and Flow Properties

In this section, we will explore several elegant properties of the function L defined in Equation (1) in the last section. To begin with, we first observe the convexity of the function L.

Lemma 1 *The function L is convex over the interval $[0,\|d\|]$.*

Proof. $\forall\, 0 \leq \alpha_1 < \alpha_2 \leq \|d\|$, and $\forall \lambda \in (0,1)$, we want to prove

$$L(\lambda\alpha_1 + (1-\lambda)\alpha_2) \leq \lambda L(\alpha_1) + (1-\lambda)L(\alpha_2).$$

Let x be any routing with $\|x\| = \alpha_1$ and $\ell(x) = L(\alpha_1)$. Let y be any routing with $\|y\| = \alpha_2$ and $\ell(y) = L(\alpha_2)$. Let $z = \lambda x + (1-\lambda)y$. Then z is a feasible routing and $L(\lambda\alpha_1 + (1-\lambda)\alpha_2) \leq \ell(z)$ as $\|z\| = \lambda\alpha_1 + (1-\lambda)\alpha_2$. For $0 \leq k \leq n-1$,

$$\ell^+_k(z) = \lambda\ell^+_k(x) + (1-\lambda)\ell^+_k(y)$$
$$\leq \lambda L(\alpha_1) + (1-\lambda)L(\alpha_2)$$
$$\ell^-_k(z) = \lambda\ell^-_k(x) + (1-\lambda)\ell^-_k(y)$$
$$\leq \lambda L(\alpha_1) + (1-\lambda)L(\alpha_2).$$

Therefore, $\ell(z) \leq \lambda L(\alpha_1) + (1-\lambda)L(\alpha_2)$ and thus the lemma follows. ♠

Lemma 1 provides a simple way to find optimal semi-integral routing. Let α^* be the total demand routed clockwise by any optimal fractional routing. Then Lemma 1 implies that the function L is non-increasing over the interval $[0,\alpha^*]$ and non-decreasing over the interval $[\alpha^*,\|d\|]$. This follows that $L^*_{SI} = \min\{L(\lfloor\alpha^*\rfloor), L(\lceil\alpha^*\rceil)\}$, and it can be obtained as follows:

1. Find an optimal fractional routing x. If $\|x\|$ is an integer, return x.

2. Find a semi-integral routing y with $\|y\| = \lfloor\|x\|\rfloor$ and $\ell(y) = L(\|y\|)$.

3. Find a semi-integral routing z with $\|z\| = \lceil\|x\|\rceil$ and $\ell(z) = L(\|z\|)$.

4. If $\ell(y) \leq \ell(z)$, return y otherwise return z.

The following theorem summarizes the above discussions.

Theorem 2 *The optimal semi-integral routing problem can be solved in polynomial time; furthermore, $L^*_{SI} = \min\{L(\lfloor\alpha^*\rfloor), L(\lceil\alpha^*\rceil)\}$, where α^* is the total demand routed clockwise by any optimal fractional routing.*

Intuitively, if the total demand routed clockwise by a routing is very small, then the clockwise ring load would be smaller than the counterclockwise ring load. When the total demand routed clockwise by a routing becomes very large, then the counterclockwise ring load would be smaller than the clockwise ring load. Such intuition is verified by the following lemma.

Lemma 3 *Let α^* be the total demand routed clockwise by any optimal fractional routing and x be any routing. Then $\ell(x) = \ell^-(x)$ if $\|x\| \leq \alpha^*$, and $\ell(x) = \ell^+(x)$ otherwise.*

Proof. We prove the lemma by contradiction. We first prove the first part. Assume that $\|x\| \leq \alpha^*$ and $\ell^-(x) < \ell^+(x) = L(\|x\|)$. Then $\exists\, 0 < \epsilon \leq 1$, such that $\forall 1 - \epsilon \leq \lambda \leq 1$, $\ell^-(\lambda x) \leq \ell^+(\lambda x)$. For any $0 < \delta \leq \epsilon\|x\|$, $\left(1 - \frac{\delta}{\|x\|}\right)x$ is a feasible routing. As $\left\|\left(1 - \frac{\delta}{\|x\|}\right)x\right\| = \|x\| - \delta$ and $1 - \epsilon \leq 1 - \frac{\delta}{\|x\|} \leq 1$,

$$L(\|x\| - \delta)$$
$$\leq \ell\left(\left(1 - \frac{\delta}{\|x\|}\right)x\right) = \ell^+\left(\left(1 - \frac{\delta}{\|x\|}\right)x\right)$$
$$= \left(1 - \frac{\delta}{\|x\|}\right)\ell^+(x) = \left(1 - \frac{\delta}{\|x\|}\right)L(\|x\|)$$
$$< L(\|x\|).$$

This contradicts to that the function L is non-increasing over the interval $[0,\alpha^*]$, which is implied by the concavity of L.

Now we prove the second part. Assume that $\|x\| \geq \alpha^*$ and $\ell^+(x) < \ell^-(x) = L(\|x\|)$. Then $\exists\, 0 < \epsilon \leq 1$, such that $\forall\, 0 \leq \lambda \leq \epsilon$, $\ell^+(x + \lambda(d - x)) \leq \ell^-(x + \lambda(d - x))$. For any $0 < \delta \leq \epsilon(\|d\| - \|x\|)$, $x + \frac{\delta}{\|d\| - \|x\|}(d - x)$ is a feasible routing. As $\left\|x + \frac{\delta}{\|d\| - \|x\|}(d - x)\right\| = \|x\| + \delta$ and

$$0 < \frac{\delta}{\|d\| - \|x\|} \le \epsilon,$$

$$L(\|x\| + \delta) \le \ell\left(x + \frac{\delta}{\|d\| - \|x\|}(d - x)\right)$$

$$= \ell^-\left(x + \frac{\delta}{\|d\| - \|x\|}(d - x)\right)$$

$$= \left(1 - \frac{\delta}{\|d\| - \|x\|}\right)\ell^-(x)$$

$$= \left(1 - \frac{\delta}{\|d\| - \|x\|}\right)L(\|x\|) < L(\|x\|).$$

This contradicts to that the function L is non-decreasing over the interval $[\alpha^*, \|d\|]$. ♠

Now we are ready to show that the function L is Lipschitz continuous, i.e., there is an $\epsilon > 0$ such that for any $0 \le \alpha, \beta \le \|d\|$, $|L(\alpha) - L(\beta)| \le \epsilon|\alpha - \beta|$.

Lemma 4 *Let α^* be the total demand routed clockwise by any optimal fractional routing. The following statements are true.*

1. *If $\alpha \le \alpha^*$, then for any $0 \le \delta \le \alpha$, $L(\alpha) \le L(\alpha - \delta) \le L(\alpha) + \delta$.*

2. *If $\alpha \ge \alpha^*$, then for any $0 \le \delta \le \|d\| - \alpha$, $L(\alpha) \le L(\alpha + \delta) \le L(\alpha) + \delta$.*

3. *For any α and δ with $0 \le \alpha \le \alpha + \delta \le \|d\|$, $|L(\alpha + \delta) - L(\alpha)| \le \delta$.*

Proof. Let x be any routing with $\|x\| = \alpha$ and $\ell(x) = L(\alpha)$.

(1). The first inequality follows from that the function L is non-increasing over the interval $[0, \alpha^*]$. In the next we prove the second inequality. For any $0 \le \delta \le \alpha$, $\left(1 - \frac{\delta}{\|x\|}\right)x$ is a feasible routing and $\left\|\left(1 - \frac{\delta}{\|x\|}\right)x\right\| = \alpha - \delta$. Thus from Lemma 3,

$$L(\alpha - \delta) \le \ell\left(\left(1 - \frac{\delta}{\|x\|}\right)x\right)$$

$$= \ell^-\left(\left(1 - \frac{\delta}{\|x\|}\right)x\right)$$

$$= \max_{0 \le k \le n-1}\ell_k^-\left(\left(1 - \frac{\delta}{\|x\|}\right)x\right)$$

$$= \max_{0 \le k \le n-1}\left(\ell_k^-(x) + \frac{\delta}{\|x\|}\sum_{i:k\notin[s_i,t_i)}x_i\right)$$

$$\le \max_{0 \le k \le n-1}\left(\ell_k^-(x) + \delta\right) = \ell^-(x) + \delta$$

$$= \ell(x) + \delta = L(\alpha) + \delta.$$

(2). The first inequality follows from that the function L is non-decreasing over the interval $[\alpha^*, \|d\|]$. For any $0 < \delta \le \|d\| - \alpha$, $x + \frac{\delta}{\|d\| - \|x\|}(d - x)$ is a feasible routing and $\left\|x + \frac{\delta}{\|d\| - \|x\|}(d - x)\right\| = \alpha + \delta$. Thus from Lemma 3,

$$L(\alpha + \delta) \le \ell\left(x + \frac{\delta}{\|d\| - \|x\|}(d - x)\right)$$

$$= \ell^+\left(x + \frac{\delta}{\|d\| - \|x\|}(d - x)\right)$$

$$= \max_{0 \le k \le n-1}\ell_k^+\left(x + \frac{\delta}{\|d\| - \|x\|}(d - x)\right)$$

$$= \max_{0 \le k \le n-1}\left(\ell_k^+(x) + \frac{\delta}{\|d\| - \|x\|}\sum_{i:k\in[s_i,t_i)}(d_i - x_i)\right)$$

$$\le \max_{0 \le k \le n-1}\left(\ell_k^+(x) + \delta\right) = \ell^+(x) + \delta$$

$$= \ell(x) + \delta = L(\alpha) + \delta.$$

(3). If $0 \le \alpha \le \alpha + \delta \le \alpha^*$ or $\alpha^* \le \alpha \le \alpha + \delta \le \|d\|$, the inequality follows from (1) and (2) respectively. If $0 \le \alpha \le \alpha^* \le \alpha + \delta \le \|d\|$, we have

$$|L(\alpha + \delta) - L(\alpha)|$$
$$\le |L(\alpha^*) - L(\alpha)| + |L(\alpha + \delta) - L(\alpha^*)|$$
$$\le (\alpha^* - \alpha) + (\alpha + \delta - \alpha^*) = \delta$$

where the last inequality also follows from (1) and (2). ♠

Based on the above lemma, we can bound the difference between the optimal semi-integral ring load and the optimal fractional ring load.

Corollary 5 $L_F^* \le L_{SI}^* \le L_F^* + \frac{1}{2}$.

Proof. The first inequality is obvious. We next prove the second inequality. From Lemma 4,

$$L(\lfloor\alpha^*\rfloor) \le L(\alpha^*) + \alpha^* - \lfloor\alpha^*\rfloor = L_F^* + \alpha^* - \lfloor\alpha^*\rfloor,$$
$$L(\lceil\alpha^*\rceil) \le L(\alpha^*) + \lceil\alpha^*\rceil - \alpha^* = L_F^* + \lceil\alpha^*\rceil - \alpha^*.$$

Thus from Theorem 2,

$$L_{SI}^* = \min\{L(\lfloor\alpha^*\rfloor), L(\lceil\alpha^*\rceil)\}$$
$$\le L_F^* + \min\{\alpha^* - \lfloor\alpha^*\rfloor, \lceil\alpha^*\rceil - \alpha^*\}$$
$$\le L_F^* + \frac{1}{2}. \quad ♠$$

4. Parallel Routing

In this section, we introduce the concept of parallel routing and unsplit technique. Two requests i and j are said to

545

be *parallel* if either $[s_i, t_i] \subseteq [s_j, t_j]$ or $[s_j, t_j] \subseteq [s_i, t_i]$; otherwise, they are said to be *crossing*. Figure 2 illustrates four possible scenarios of parallel pairs of requests. Regarding a link also as a directed chord, a request is parallel to a link just when the request can be routed through that link. Thus any link partitions the requests into two groups: those which are parallel to it, and those which are parallel to its reverse.

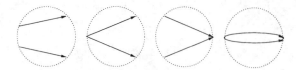

Figure 2. Parallel pairs of requests.

A routing is said to be *parallel* if no two parallel requests are both split. In any parallel routing, any two split requests must be crossing, and therefore cannot share a source. This implies that the number of split requests is at most the ring size n. Moreover, the targets of any two split requests split must follow the same clockwise order of their sources as shown in Figure 3. Thus we have the following lemma.

Figure 3. The targets of requests split by any parallel routing follow the same clockwise order of their sources.

Lemma 6 *Any parallel routing splits at most n requests where n is the ring size. Moreover, the targets of those split requests follow the same clockwise order of their sources.*

Now we describe how to obtain a parallel routing from any given routing by unsplitting some requests without increasing the ring load. he following lemma generalizes the transforming technique in [10].

Lemma 7 *Any routing x can be transformed to a parallel routing y in polynomial time satisfying that $\|y\| = \|x\|$ and every link load is either not increased.*

Proof. Suppose that requests i and j are a pair of parallel requests that are both split by x. Without loss of generality, we assume that $[s_i, t_i] \subseteq [s_j, t_j]$, as shown in Figure 4(a).

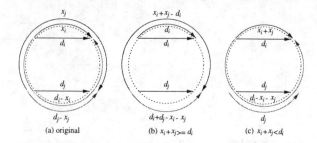

Figure 4. Unsplit one request in a parallel pair.

If $x_i + x_j > d_i$, then define a new routing y by setting

$$y_i = d_i,$$
$$y_j = x_i + x_j - d_i,$$
$$y_k = x_k, \forall k \neq i, j$$

as illustrated in Figure 4(b). If $x_i + x_j \leq d_i$, we define a new routing y by setting

$$y_i = x_i + x_j,$$
$$y_j = 0,$$
$$y_k = x_k, \forall k \neq i, j$$

as illustrated in Figure 4(c). In both cases, one of two requests is no longer split, every link load is either maintained or reduced, and the total demand routed clockwise remains unchanged. This procedure can be performed repeatedly until no two parallel requests are both split. Since each time we reduce by one (or two) the total number of split demands, at most m such procedures will produce the desired routing. ♠

By applying the unsplitting technique in Lemma 7 to any optimal fractional routing, we can get an optimal fractional routing which is also parallel, referred to as an *optimal parallel fractional routing*. Similarly, By applying the same unsplitting technique to any optimal semi-integral routing, we get an optimal semi-integral routing which is also parallel, referred to as an *optimal parallel semi-integral routing*.

5. Integral Routing

In this section, we first describe how to round parallel semi-integral routing to an integral routing. The following lemma generalizes the rounding techniques used in [8] [10].

Lemma 8 *Any parallel semi-integral routing x can be rounded in polynomial time into an integral routing y satisfying that $\|y\| = \|x\|$ and the increase of every link load is less than one.*

Proof. From Lemma 6, the number of requests split by x is at most the ring size n. In particular, the number of fractionally split requests is at most n. Let $\{f_1, f_2, \cdots, f_q\}$ be the set of fractionally split requests with $f_1 < f_2 < \cdots < f_q$ where $q \leq n$. We define an integral routing y by rounding fractionally split requests of x as follows. For each request $i \notin \{f_1, f_2, \cdots, f_q\}$, set $y_i = x_i$. We then define integers $y_{f_1}, y_{f_2}, \cdots, y_{f_q}$ sequentially by ensuring every partial sum

$$\sum_{j=1}^{i} (y_{f_j} - x_{f_j}) \in [-\frac{1}{2}, \frac{1}{2})$$

for all $1 \leq i \leq q$. Since x is semi-integral and y is integral, the sum $\sum_{i=1}^{m}(y_i - x_i) = \sum_{i=1}^{m} y_i - \sum_{i=1}^{m} x_i$ is an integer. Thus

$$\sum_{i=1}^{m}(y_i - x_i) = \sum_{j=1}^{q}(y_{f_j} - x_{f_j}) \in [-\frac{1}{2}, \frac{1}{2})$$

implies

$$\sum_{i=1}^{m}(y_i - x_i) = \sum_{j=1}^{q}(y_{f_j} - x_{f_j}) = 0$$

i.e., $\|y\| = \|x\|$.

Now we the second part of the lemma. By Lemma 6, the sources and targets of requests $\{f_1, f_2, \cdots, f_q\}$ are positioned in the ring in the same clockwise order. Thus for any $0 \leq k \leq n - 1$, there is an interval $[a_k, b_k] \subseteq \{1, \cdots, q\}$, interpreted if necessary "around the corner" modulo q, such that

- the set $\{f_j : j \in [a_k, b_k]\}$ contains exactly the indices of those fractionally split requests which are parallel to the link $k \to k+1$;

- the set $\{f_j : j \notin [a_k, b_k]\}$ contains exactly the indices of those fractionally split requests which are parallel to the link $k+1 \to k$.

Therefore the load increment of the clockwise link $k \to k+1$ is

$$\ell_k^+(y) - \ell_k^+(x) = \sum_{j \in [a_k, b_k]} (y_{f_j} - x_{f_j}).$$

If $a_k \leq b_k$,

$$\ell_k^+(y) - \ell_k^+(x) = \sum_{j \in [a_k, b_k]} (y_{f_j} - x_{f_j})$$

$$= \sum_{j=1}^{b_k}(y_{f_j} - x_{f_j}) - \sum_{j=1}^{a_k-1}(y_{f_j} - x_{f_j})$$

$$< \frac{1}{2} - \left(-\frac{1}{2}\right) = 1.$$

If $a_k > b_k$,

$$\ell_k^+(y) - \ell_k^+(x) = \sum_{j \in [a_k, b_k]} (y_{f_j} - x_{f_j})$$

$$= \sum_{j=1}^{q}(y_{f_j} - x_{f_j}) + \sum_{j=1}^{b_k}(y_{f_j} - x_{f_j}) - \sum_{j=1}^{a_k-1}(y_{f_j} - x_{f_j})$$

$$= \sum_{j=1}^{b_k}(y_{f_j} - x_{f_j}) - \sum_{j=1}^{a_k-1}(y_{f_j} - x_{f_j})$$

$$< \frac{1}{2} - \left(-\frac{1}{2}\right) = 1$$

as well. A symmetric argument for the counterclockwise links shows that link load increment is also less than one. ♠

Let x be any optimal parallel semi-integral routing. If it is integral, $L_I^* = L_{SI}^* = \lceil L_{SI}^* \rceil$; otherwise, we apply the rounding technique in Lemma 8 to x and let y be the resulting integral routing. Then $\ell(y) < \ell(x) + 1 = L_{SI}^* + 1$, which implies that $\ell(y) \leq \lceil L_{SI}^* \rceil$. As $\ell(y) \geq L_I^* \geq \lceil L_{SI}^* \rceil$, y is and optimal integral routing and $L_I^* = \lceil L_{SI}^* \rceil$. Therefore, we have the following theorem.

Theorem 9 *The optimal integral routing problem can be solved in polynomial time. Furthermore, $\lceil L_F^* \rceil \leq \lceil L_{SI}^* \rceil = L_I^* \leq \lceil L_F^* + \frac{1}{2} \rceil$; in particular if L_{SI}^* is an integer, $L_I^* = L_{SI}^*$.*

6. Unsplit Routing

Unlike the optimal integral routing which can be solved in polynomial time, the optimal unsplit routing is NP-complete. Therefore, we shift our attention to polynomial-time approximation algorithms. In this section, we first show the NP-completeness of the optimal unsplit routing. We then present several polynomial-time approximation algorithms from simple to complex.

Lemma 10 *The optimal unsplit routing problem is NP-complete even with following patterns of requests:*

1. All requests share the same source;

2. *Any pair of requests is crossing;*

3. *Any pair of requests is parallel but shares no source nor target.*

Proof. A simple reduction is available from the PARTITION problem [3], in which positive integers $d_1, d_2, \cdots, d_m$ are given and the question is whether one can divide them into two groups of equal sum.

(1). Set $n = m + 1$ and construct the m requests as follows: all these m requests have the node 0 as their source, the target of the request i is node i, and the demand of request i is d_i (see Figure 5(a)). Then any request routed clockwise must pass through the link $0 \to 1$, and any request routed counterclockwise must pass through the link $0 \to m$. Therefore for any routing x, $\ell^+(x) = \|x\|$ and $\ell^-(x) = \sum_{i=1}^{m} d_i - \|x\|$. This implies that the optimal unsplit ring load is at least $\sum_{i=1}^{m} d_i/2$, and the ring load is optimal if and only if the set of integers $d_1, d_2, \cdots, d_m$ can be divided into two groups of equal sum.

(2). Set $n = 2m$ and construct the m requests as follows: the request i is from node $i-1$ to node $m+i-1$ with demand d_i (see Figure 5(b)). Then any request routed clockwise must pass through the link $m - 1 \to m$, and any request routed counterclockwise must pass through the link $0 \to 2m - 1$. Therefore for any routing x, $\ell^+(x) = \|x\|$ and $\ell^-(x) = \sum_{i=1}^{m} d_i - \|x\|$. This implies that the optimal unsplit ring load is at least $\sum_{i=1}^{m} d_i/2$, and the ring load is optimal if and only if the set of integers $d_1, d_2, \cdots, d_m$ can be divided into two groups of equal sum.

(3). Set $n = 2m$ and construct the m requests as follows: the request i is from node $i - 1$ to node $2m - i$ with demand d_i (see Figure 5(c)). Then any request routed clockwise must pass through the link $m - 1 \to m$, and any request routed counterclockwise must pass through the link $0 \to 2m - 1$. Therefore for any routing x, $\ell^+(x) = \|x\|$ and $\ell^-(x) = \sum_{i=1}^{m} d_i - \|x\|$. This implies that the optimal unsplit ring load is at least $\sum_{i=1}^{m} d_i/2$, and the ring load is optimal if and only if the set of integers $d_1, d_2, \cdots, d_m$ can be divided into two groups of equal sum. ♠

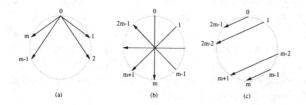

(a)   (b)   (c)

Figure 5. Reductions from the PARTITION problem.

In the next we will present several polynomial-time approximation algorithms for unsplit routing.

6.1. Edge-Avoidance Routing

For any $0 \le i \le n - 1$, the $(i, i + 1)$-*avoidance routing* routes each request along the unique path which avoids the link $i \to i + 1$ and the link $i + 1 \to i$. An alternative interpretation is to cut these two links turning the counter-rotated ring into two unidirectional chains, on which each request has a unique path. Despite the simplicity of the edge-avoidance routing, the next theorem states that the ring load of any edge-avoidance routing is within twice the optimal unsplit ring load.

Theorem 11 *Edge-avoidance routing is a 2-approximation.*

Proof. Let x be any optimal unsplit routing and i be any node. Then the reversing of all requests routed through the link $i \to i + 1$ in x induces a load of no more than L_U^* on any other counterclockwise link. Similarly, the reversing of all requests routed through the link $i + 1 \to i$ in x also induces a load of no more than L_U^* on any other clockwise link. Therefore, the ring load of the $(i, i + 1)$-avoidance routing is at most $2L_U^*$. ♠

6.2. Short-Way Routing

A request is said to be routed in the short (or long) way if it is routed along the shorter (or longer) of the two paths connecting the request. If the two paths connecting the request have the same length, one of them is chose arbitrarily as the short way, and the other as the long way. The *short-way routing* is a routing in which each request is routed short way. The next theorem states that the ring load of any short-way routing is within twice the optimal unsplit ring load.

Theorem 12 *Short-way routing is a 2-approximation.*

Proof. Let x be any optimal unsplit routing and y be any short-way routing. We first assume that $\ell(y) = \ell_k^+(y)$ for some $0 \le k \le n - 1$. Let S be the set of requests whose routes pass through the link $k \to k + 1$ in y. Then $\ell(y) = \sum_{i \in S} d_i$. Let S' be the set of requests in S which are also routed through the link $k \to k + 1$ in x. Then $\ell_k^+(x) \ge \sum_{i \in S'} d_i$. But on the other hand, all requests in $S - S'$ must be routed through the link $\lfloor \frac{n}{2} \rfloor + k + 1 \to \lfloor \frac{n}{2} \rfloor + k$. This implies that $\ell_{\lfloor \frac{n}{2} \rfloor + k}^-(x) \ge \sum_{i \in S - S'} d_i = \ell(y) - \sum_{i \in S'} d_i$.

Therefore

$$L_U^* = \ell(x) \geq \max\left\{\ell_k^+(x), \ell_{\lfloor\frac{n}{2}\rfloor+k}^-(x)\right\}$$

$$\geq \max\left\{\sum_{i\in S'} d_i, \ell(y) - \sum_{i\in S'} d_i\right\} \geq \ell(y)/2.$$

Similarly, we can prove that $L_U^* \geq \ell(y)/2$ if $\ell(y) = \ell_k^-(y)$ for some $0 \leq k \leq n-1$. ♠

6.3. $(1+\epsilon)$-Approximation Algorithm

In this subsection, we will show that for any fixed $\varepsilon > 0$, we can find in polynomial time an unsplit routing whose ring load is within $(1+\varepsilon)$ times the optimum. The approximation algorithm uses a rounding technique which obtains a suboptimal unsplit routing from a parallel optimal fractional routing.

Lemma 13 *Any parallel routing x can be rounded in polynomial time into an unsplit routing y satisfying that $\ell(y) - \ell(x) < 3d_{\max}/2$ where $d_{\max} = \max\{d_i \mid 0 < x_i < d_i\}$, i.e., the maximum of the demands of split requests by x.*

Proof. The proof given here is similar to that in Lemma 8 with minor modifications. Let $\{f_1, f_2, \cdots, f_q\}$ be the set of split requests with $f_1 < f_2 < \cdots < f_q$ where $q \leq n$. Define an unsplit routing y by unsplitting the requests split by x as follows. For all request $i \notin \{f_1, f_2, \cdots, f_q\}$, set $y_i = x_i$. Then define $y_{f_1}, y_{f_2}, \cdots, y_{f_q}$ sequentially by ensuring every partial sum $\sum_{j=1}^i (y_{f_j} - x_{f_j}) \in [-\frac{d_{\max}}{2}, \frac{d_{\max}}{2})$ for all $1 \leq i \leq q$. The we can prove $\ell(y) - \ell(x) < 3d_{\max}/2$ in a similar way we did in the proof of Lemma 8. The detail is omit here. ♠

By applying the transform described in Lemma 13 to an optimal parallel fractional routing, we get an unsplit routing whose does not exceed L_F^* by $3/2$ times the maximum demand. In addition, Lemma 13 implies that if a routing x with $\ell(x) \leq L_U^*$ splits no request with demand more than $2\varepsilon L_U^*/3$ and $\ell(x) \leq L_U^*$, then it can be transformed in polynomial time to an unsplit routing with load no more than $(1+\varepsilon)L_U^*$. In the next we will study how to find such an routing x in polynomial time. Let L^* denote the ring load of any short-way routing. A request is said to be *light* if its demand is at most $\varepsilon L^*/3$ ($\leq 2\varepsilon L_U^*/3$), and *heavy* otherwise. The next lemma bounds the total number of heavy requests.

Lemma 14 *There are less than $6n/\varepsilon$ heavy requests.*

Proof. The proof uses the classical double counting technique. For any $0 \leq i \neq j \leq n-1$, the pair of links $i \to i+1$ and $j+1 \to j$ are called a *cut*. A request is said to be *across*

a cut if each of its two paths of the request passes through one link in the cut. Obviously, the total demand of all requests across any cut can not exceed $2L_F^*$. Let h be the number of heavy requests. Since every request participates in at least $n-1$ cuts and each heavy request has demand at least $\varepsilon L^*/3$,

$$(n-1)\frac{\varepsilon L^*}{3}h < n(n-1)\cdot 2L_F^*.$$

The left hand side gives a (loose) lower bound on the total contribution to the requests across all possible cuts, while the right hand side specifies an upper bound on the aggregated demand across all possible cuts. As $L_F^* \leq L^*$, $h < 6n/\varepsilon$. ♠

The next lemma bounds the total number of heavy requests that could be routed in the long way in any optimal unsplit routing.

Lemma 15 *In any optimal unsplit routing, less than $12/\varepsilon$ heavy requests are routed in the long way.*

Proof. Suppose to the contrary that at least $12/\varepsilon$ heavy requests were routed in the long way in some optimal unsplit routing x. As a request that is routed the long way must traverse at least $\lceil n/2 \rceil$ links, the total load induced by those heavy requests routed in the long way is more than $\lceil n/2 \rceil \cdot \frac{\varepsilon L^*}{3} \cdot \frac{12}{\varepsilon} \geq 2nL^*$. By pigeonhole principle, some link must have load more than $\frac{2nL^*}{2n} = L^* \geq L_U^*$, which contradicts the optimality of x. ♠

Let Π denote the collection of all sets consisting of less than $12/\varepsilon$ heavy requests in an unsplit routing. From Lemma 14 and the well-known inequality $\binom{n}{k} \leq \left(\frac{en}{k}\right)^k$,

$$|\Pi| < \sum_{i=0}^{12/\varepsilon} \binom{6n/\varepsilon}{i} \leq \frac{12}{\varepsilon}\left(\frac{e\cdot 6n/\varepsilon}{12/\varepsilon}\right)^{12/\varepsilon}$$

$$\leq \frac{12}{\varepsilon}\left(\frac{en}{2}\right)^{12/\varepsilon}.$$

This means that the size of Π is a polynomial function of n.

For any set $S \in \Pi$, let Γ_S denote the set of all feasible (possibly fractional) routings, in which all requests in S are routed in the long way, the remaining heavy requests are routed in the short way. From Lemma 15,

$$\min_{S\in\Pi}\min_{x\in\Gamma_S}\ell(x) \leq L_U^*.$$

As the size of Π is a polynomial function of n and for each $S \in \Pi$ a routing in Γ_S with ring load $\min_{x\in\Gamma_S}\ell(x)$ can be obtained by solving a linear program in polynomial time, we can find a set $S \in \Pi$ and a routing $x \in \Gamma_S$ which has ring load

$$\ell(x) = \min_{S\in\Pi}\min_{z\in\Gamma_S}\ell(z).$$

Notice that $l(x) \leq L_U^*$ and any light request has demand at most $2\varepsilon L_U^*/3$. Thus, once x is obtained, we can transform x in polynomial time into an unsplit routing y with $\ell(y) < (1 + \varepsilon)L_U^*$. Therefore we have the following result.

Theorem 16 *For any $\varepsilon > 0$, we can find an unsplit routing whose ring load is within $(1 + \varepsilon)$ of the optimal unsplit ring load.*

A remark that should be made here is that our $(1 + \varepsilon)$-approximation algorithm is different from the $(1 + \varepsilon)$-approximation algorithm given in [5] for the optimal unsplit routing problem in undirected rings. The first difference is that the algorithm in [5] first assumes that the optimal unsplit load is known and later use some standard techniques to bypass such clairvoyance assumption. Our algorithm does not make such an assumption at all and therefore is simpler. Secondly, the algorithm in [5] transforms each fractional routing into an unsplit routing and then picks the best unsplit routing. We observe that it is unnecessary. In fact we can first choose the best fractional routing and then transform *only* the best fractional routing into an unsplit routing just *once*. The resulting routing is still an $(1 + \varepsilon)$-approximation, but the time-complexity is reduced by a factor of $\Theta(n^3/\log n)$.

7. Conclusions

In this paper, we have studied several variants of load balancing in counter-rotated directed SONET rings. The optimal fractional routing can be obtained by solving a linear program. The optimal semi-integral routing can be obtained by solving at most three linear programs. The optimal integral routing can be obtained by rounding any optimal parallel semi-integral routing. The optimal unsplit routing is NP-complete. Both the edge-avoidance routing and the short-way routing are 2-approximations. Finally, a polynomial-time approximation algorithm is presented for any fixed $\varepsilon > 0$ to find an unsplit routing whose ring load is within $(1 + \varepsilon)$ times the optimum.

References

[1] D. Clark. Heavy Traffic Drives Networks to IP over SONET. IEEE Computer, Dec. 1998: 17-20.

[2] S. Cosares and I. Saniee. An Optimization Problem Related to Balancing Loads on SONET Rings. Telecommunications Systems, 3:165-181, 1994.

[3] M. R. Garey and D. S. Johnson. Computers and Intractability: A Guide to the Theory of NP-Completeness. W.H. Freeman and Co., San Francisco, CA, 1979.

[4] I. Haque, W. Kremer, and K. Raychauduri, Self-Healing Rings in a synchrnous envioronemnt, SONET/SDH: a sourcebook of synchronous networking, Eds. C.A. Siller and M. Shafi, IEEE Press, New York, pp. 131-139, 1996.

[5] S. Khanna. A Polynomial-Time Approximation Scheme for the SONET Ring Loading Problem, Bell Laboratories Tech. J., Vol. 2, No. 2, Spring 1997.

[6] H. Okamura and P. Seymour, Multicommodity Flows in Planar Graphs, Journal of Combinatorial Theory, Series B 31, pp. 75-81, 1981.

[7] I. Saniee, Optimal Routing in Self-Healing Communications Networks, International Transactions in Operations Research, 3, pp. 187-195, 1996.

[8] A. Schrijver, P.D. Seymour, and P. Winkler. The Ring Loading Problem, SIAM J. Disc. Math., Vol. 11, No. 1, pp. 1-14, February 1998.

[9] R. Vachani, A. Shulman, P. Kubat, J. Ward, Multicommodity Flows in Ring Networks, INFORMS Journal on Computing, 8, pp. 235-242, 1996.

[10] P. Wilfong, P. Winkler, Ring Routing and Wavelength Translation, Proceedings of the Ninth Annual ACM-SIAM Symposium on Discrete Algorithms, pp. 333-341, 1998.

Link Contention-Constrained Scheduling and Mapping of Tasks and Messages to a Network of Heterogeneous Processors

YU-KWONG KWOK[1] AND ISHFAQ AHMAD[2]

[1]Department of Electrical and Electronic Engineering
The University of Hong Kong, Pokfulam Road, Hong Kong

[2]Department of Computer Science
The Hong Kong University of Science and Technology, Clear Water Bay, Hong Kong

Email: *ykwok@eee.hku.hk, iahmad@cs.ust.hk*

Abstract[†]—In this paper, we consider the problem of scheduling and mapping precedence-constrained tasks to a network of heterogeneous processors. In such systems, processors are usually physically distributed, implying that the communication cost is considerably higher than in tightly coupled multiprocessors. Therefore, scheduling and mapping algorithms for such systems must schedule the tasks as well as the communication traffic by treating both the processors and communication links as important resources. We propose an algorithm that achieves these objectives and adapts its tasks scheduling and mapping decisions according to the given network topology. Just like tasks, messages are also scheduled and mapped to suitable links during the minimization of the finish times of tasks. Heterogeneity of processors is exploited by scheduling critical tasks to the fastest processors. Our extensive experimental study has demonstrated that the proposed algorithm is efficient, robust, and yields consistent performance over a wide range of scheduling parameters.

Keywords: algorithms, parallel processing, heterogeneous systems, scheduling, link contention, task graphs.

1 Introduction

One of the major goals of using a heterogeneous system is to minimize the completion time of a parallel application by exploiting the heterogeneous processing requirements within the application [5]. To achieve this goal, a judicious scheme is needed to properly schedule and allocate the tasks of the application to the most suitable processors. In this study, we are interested in the static scheduling of precedence-constrained tasks to a network of heterogeneous processors. Static scheduling is normally done at compile-time with available information about the structure of the parallel application in terms of its task execution times, task dependencies, communication, and synchronization [4], [9]. The goal of static scheduling is to allocate a set of tasks to a set of processors such that the overall completion time of the application, called the *schedule length*, is minimized while the precedence constraints among the tasks are preserved. Since this scheduling problem is NP-complete [4], [6], it is commonly tackled by using heuristics [7]. While each heuristic may perform well under different circumstances, there are three important criteria that must be considered for evaluating a heuristic: (1) Does the heuristic make realistic assumptions about the application and architecture of the system? (2) Is it problem-specific or can it work under a wide range of parameters without compromising the solution quality? (3) Does the complexity of the heuristic permit it to be practically used for compile-time scheduling?

The first criterion relates to the assumptions made by the scheduling algorithm about the program tasks and architecture models. Indeed, to simplify the design of the scheduling method, earlier approaches usually rely on simplifying assumptions such as assuming all tasks to have equal execution times, or ignoring the communication delays among tasks altogether [4], [9]. With the emergence of a wide variety of architectures in recent years, the architectural attributes such as system topology, message routing strategy, overlapped communication and computation, and processors heterogeneity, must also be taken into account by a scheduling algorithm. The second criterion dictates that the scheduling algorithm should generate good solutions for a variety of applications and target systems. A scheduling algorithm tailored for one particular application and architecture may not generate efficient solutions on another architecture [8]. The third criterion which is related to the execution time of the heuristic itself is an important consideration for effectively using it for compile-time scheduling of large-scale applications [1].

We are interested in scheduling algorithms that both schedule tasks and messages on arbitrary networks consisting of heterogeneous processors and communication links. Scheduling tasks while considering link contention for a heterogeneous system is a relatively less explored research topic and very few

---

† This research was supported by the Hong Kong Research Grants Council under contract number HKUST619/94E and a grant from the HKU CRCG.

algorithms for this problem have been designed. One well-known algorithm is the *dynamic level scheduling* (DLS) algorithm [11], which employs a dynamic list scheduling approach. In this paper, we propose a new algorithm, the primary objective of which is to generate efficient solutions while simultaneously handles arbitrary communication and execution costs in the parallel application, schedules tasks and messages by considering link contention as well as processors heterogeneity, and adapts to arbitrary network topology. The algorithm has a practicable complexity and is suitable for regular and irregular parallel program structures.

In a traditional algorithm, the tasks are first arranged as a list using some priority measure and then each task is scheduled one after another to a processor which allows the earliest finish time [2], [4], [8], [9], [10], [11]. To find such a processor in a heterogeneous target system where message scheduling has to be handled, a routing table is also needed, as in the DLS, for determining the most suitable route for messages in order to minimize the data ready time of each task. The problem with using a routing table is two-fold: (i) the routing table has to be pre-determined, usually using shortest-path algorithm, for the input target topology; (ii) during the scheduling process, the routing table, which has to be frequently updated, may not give optimized routes. Checking such routing information for every candidate processors inevitably results in high time complexity. Furthermore, the routing information is usually maintained for only a few common network topologies which may not be useful for an arbitrary network.

The proposed algorithm is different from traditional scheduling schemes in several aspects. First, in the algorithm, the tasks are not fixed in one single list throughout the entire scheduling process as in the traditional approach. Initially, the tasks are all scheduled to a single processor—effectively the parallel program is serialized. Then, each task is considered in turn for possible migration to the neighbor processors. The objective of this process is to improve the finish times of tasks because a task migrates only if it can "bubble up". If a task is selected for migration, the communication messages from its predecessors (some of which may remain in the original processor while others may have also migrated) are scheduled to the communication link between the new processor and the original processor. After all the tasks in the original processor are considered, the first phase of scheduling completes. In the second phase, the same process is repeated on one of the neighbor processor. Thus, a task migrated from the original processor to a neighbor processor may have an

opportunity to migrate again to a processor one more hop away from the original processor. This incremental scheduling by migration process is repeated for all the processors in a breadth-first fashion. The advantage of this incremental approach is that no pre-specified routing table is needed because the algorithm adapts its scheduling decisions to each input topology, which may be arbitrary. More importantly, the incremental scheduling of tasks and messages can lead to optimized routes.

The remainder of this paper is organized as follows. In the next section, we provide a formal problem statement, followed by a detailed description and explanation of the proposed algorithm. An illustrative example is used throughout to explicate the features of the algorithm. Section 3 presents the experimental results. The last section concludes the paper.

2 The Proposed Algorithm

In this section, we first formally define the scheduling problem and the model used. We then outline our proposed algorithm, called *Bubble Scheduling and Allocation* (BSA). A small example is used for illustrating the algorithm's characteristics.

2.1 The Scheduling and Mapping Model

A parallel program is composed of n tasks $\{T_1, T_2, ..., T_n\}$ in which there is a partial order: $T_i < T_j$ implies that T_j cannot start execution until T_i finishes due to the data dependency between them. Thus, a parallel program can be represented by a directed acyclic *task graph* [2]. Parallelism exists among independent tasks—T_i and T_j are said to be independent if neither $T_i < T_j$ nor $T_j < T_i$. Each task T_i is associated with a nominal execution cost τ_i which is the execution time required by T_i on a reference machine in the heterogeneous system. Similarly, a nominal communication cost c_{ij} is associated with the message M_{ij} from T_i to T_j. Assume there are e messages where $(n-1) \le e < n^2$ so that the task graph is a connected graph.

To model heterogeneity of the target system which consists of m processors $\{P_1, P_2, ..., P_m\}$, *heterogeneity factors* are used. For example, if a task T_i is scheduled to a processor P_x, then its actual execution cost is given by $h_{ix}\tau_i$ where h_{ix} is the heterogeneity factor which is determined by measuring the difference in processing capabilities (e.g., speed) of processor P_x and the reference machine with respect to task T_i. Similarly, if a message M_{ij} is scheduled to the communication link L_{xy} between processors P_x and P_y, its actual communication cost is given by $h'_{ijxy}c_{ij}$. An example parallel program graph is shown in Figure 1.

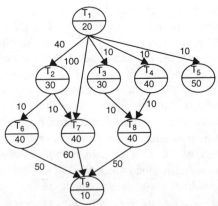

Figure 1: A parallel program task graph.

The start time and finish time of a message M_{ij} from T_i to T_j on a communication link L_{xy} are denoted by $MST(M_{ij}, L_{xy})$ and $MFT(M_{ij}, L_{xy})$, respectively. Thus, we have $MFT(M_{ij}, L_{xy}) = MST(M_{ij}, L_{xy}) + h'_{ijxy}c_{ij}$. The start time of a task T_i on processor P_x is denoted by $ST(T_i, P_x)$ which critically depends on the task's *data ready time* (DRT). The DRT of a task is defined as the latest arrival time of messages from its predecessors. The finish time of a task T_i is given by $FT(T_i, P_x) = ST(T_i, P_x) + h_{ix}\tau_i$. The objective of scheduling is to minimize the maximum FT, which is called the *schedule length* (SL).

2.2 Serialization

The serialization process, which determines the order of subsequent tasks migration, is a crucial step of the algorithm. A parallel program can be serialized using many different methods because there are many total orders which do not violate the original partial order. In the BSA algorithm, the serialization process is centered around a *critical path* of the parallel program.

DEFINITION 1: A critical path (CP) is defined as the set of tasks and messages forming a path with the largest sum of execution costs and communication costs.

In the case that there are multiple CPs, we select the one with a larger sum of execution costs and ties are broken randomly. The CP is a crucial structure of a parallel program because it is the longest execution path and thus, timely scheduling of its tasks can potentially lead to a shorter schedule length. However, to preserve the precedence constraints among tasks, we cannot arrange all the CP tasks first. Instead, in the serialization process, we have to first consider a CP task's predecessors, which need not be CP tasks themselves. Such predecessors are called *in-branch* (IB) tasks. The remaining tasks, which are neither CP tasks nor IB tasks, are called *out-branch* (OB) tasks. This partitioning of the tasks induces a serial order of the parallel program, in which CP tasks are arranged to occupy the earliest

possible positions, with IB tasks inserted among them, and OB tasks are appended at the end.

To determine whether a task is a CP task, we can use two attributes: *t-level* (top level) and *b-level* (bottom level). The *b-level* of a task is the length of the longest path beginning with the task. The *t-level* of a task is the length of the longest path reaching the task. Thus, all tasks on the CP have the same value of (*t-level* + *b-level*), which is equal to the length of the CP. Based on this observation, we can easily partition the parallel program into CP, IB, and OB tasks by in $O(e)$ time because the *t-level* and *b-level* of all tasks can be computed by using depth-first search. A task with a larger *b-level* implies that it is followed by a longer chain of tasks, and thus, is given a higher priority. The serialization process can be performed by an $O(e)$ time algorithm outlined below.

SERIALIZATION:

Input: a program task graph with n tasks $\{T_1, T_2, ..., T_n\}$

Output: a serial order of the tasks

1. compute the *t-level* and *b-level* of each task by using depth-first search;
2. identify the CP; if there are multiple CPs, select the one with the largest sum of execution cost and ties are broken randomly;
3. put the CP task which does not have any predecessor to the first position of the serial order;
4. $i \leftarrow 2$; $T_x \leftarrow$ the next CP task
5. while not all the CP tasks are included do
6.   if T_x has all its predecessors in the serial order then
7.   put T_x at position i and increment i;
8.   else let T_y be the predecessor of T_x which is not in the serial order and has the largest *b-level* (ties are broken by choosing the predecessor with a smaller *t-level*);
9.   if T_y has all its predecessors in the serial order then put T_y at position i and increment i; otherwise, recursively include all the ancestors of T_y in the serial order such that the tasks with a larger *b-level* are included first;
10.   repeat the above step until all the predecessors of T_x are in the serial order;
11.   put T_x at position i and increment i;
12. $T_x \leftarrow$ the next CP task;
13. append all the OB tasks to the serial order in descending order of *b-level*;

For example, consider the parallel program graph shown earlier in Figure 1. Based on the nominal execution and communication costs, the *t-levels* and *b-levels* of the tasks can be computed and the tasks $\{T_1, T_7, T_9\}$ form the CP. Since T_1 is the first CP task, it is placed in the first position in the serial order. The second task is T_2 because it is another unexamined predecessor of the next CP task T_7. After T_2 is appended to the serial order, all predecessors of T_7 have been considered and, therefore, it can also be added. Now, the last CP task, T_9 is considered. It cannot be appended to the serial order because some of its predecessors (i.e., the IB tasks) have not been examined yet. Since both T_6 and T_8 have the same value of *b-level* and T_8 has a smaller *t-level*, T_8 is considered first. However, both predecessors of T_8 have not been examined. Thus, its two predecessors, T_3 and T_4 are appended to the list first. Next, T_8 is appended followed by T_6. The only OB task, T_5, is the last task in the serial order. The final serialized list is: $\{T_1, T_2, T_7, T_4, T_3, T_8, T_6, T_9, T_5\}$.

In the serialization process, the tasks are all scheduled to a single processor, called the *pivot* processor, which is selected as follows. The first processor in the heterogeneous system is considered and the corresponding heterogeneity factor is multiplied to the nominal execution cost of each task. Based on the set of actual execution costs, the CP is constructed. This process is repeated for other processors and eventually the processor that gives the shortest CP length based on actual execution costs is selected as the first pivot processor. To illustrate, consider the actual execution costs of the tasks on the four processor heterogeneous system as shown in Table 1. Given the actual execution costs, the CPs with respect to P_1, P_2, P_3, and P_4 are $\{T_1, T_7, T_9\}$, $\{T_1, T_2, T_6, T_9\}$, $\{T_1, T_2, T_7, T_9\}$, and $\{T_1, T_2, T_6, T_9\}$, respectively. The CP lengths are 240, 226, 235, and 260, respectively. Thus, the first pivot processor is P_2 because the CP is shortest with respect to this processor. The serial order is $\{T_1, T_2, T_6, T_7, T_3, T_4, T_8, T_9, T_5\}$, which is different from that determined earlier using nominal execution costs.

Table 1: The task execution cost of each task on a four heterogeneous processors.

task	P_1	P_2	P_3	P_4
T_1	39	7	2	6
T_2	21	50	57	56
T_3	15	28	39	6
T_4	54	14	16	55
T_5	45	42	97	12
T_6	15	20	57	78
T_7	33	43	51	60
T_8	51	18	47	74
T_9	8	16	15	20

2.3 Tasks Migration

After the parallel program is serialized to the first pivot processor, tasks have to be considered for possible migration to the neighbor processors in order to improve their finish times (bubble up). To determine whether a migration is beneficial, we have to compute the finish time of the task on a neighbor processor. To compute the start time, we need to know the DRT of the task, which in turn depends on the scheduling of messages. We outline below an algorithm for computing the finish time of a message on a communication link between two processors. Using a procedure called *ComputeMFT*, we can determine the finish times of every incoming messages of the task on a neighbor processor. The maximum finish time is then the DRT of the task. The corresponding predecessor which sends this latest message is called the *very important predecessor* (VIP) of the task.

After the DRT of the task on a neighbor processor is computed, the potential finish time of the task can also be determined. Then, using another procedure called *ComputeFT*, we can determine whether a task can improve its finish time through migrating to a neighbor processor of the pivot processor. If the finish time does improve, the task is rescheduled to the neighbor processor and its incoming and outgoing messages are also rearranged. If the finish time does not improve, then a task will also migrate if its VIP is scheduled to that neighbor processor. The rationale behind this heuristic decision is that if a task and its VIP are scheduled to the same processor, the successors of the task may subsequently improve their finish times also. This process is repeated for all the remaining tasks on the pivot. Then a neighbor processor is chosen to be a new pivot. Thus, each processor in the heterogeneous system in turn will be assigned as the pivot in a breadth-first manner. Throughout the entire bubbling up process, messages are automatically routed in the migration process of tasks from the pivot processor to other processors. There is no need to use a routing table. If the routing of messages has to be static (as in some commonly used networks, such as a hypercube that uses the E-cube routing method), we can just put a constraint on the destinations a task can migrate to. Moreover, the routes taken by such messages are optimized routes in that, at every step, a task migrates if its finish time is not increased.

Using the techniques discussed above, the BSA algorithm can be formalized below. In the following, the procedure *BuildProcessorList* constructs a list of processors in a breadth-first order from the first pivot processor.

BSA ALGORITHM:

Input: a parallel program graph with n tasks $\{T_1, T_2, ..., T_n\}$ and a heterogeneous system with m processors $\{P_1, P_2, ..., P_m\}$

Output: a program schedule

1. initial *Pivot* ← the processor that gives the shortest CP length;
2. *Serialization(Pivot)*;
3. *BuildProcessorList(Pivot)*;
4. while *ProcessorList* is not empty do
5.   *Pivot* ← remove the first processor from *ProcessorList*;
6.   for each T_i on *Pivot* do
7.   if $FT(T_i, Pivot) > DRT(T_i, Pivot)$ or VIP of T_i is not scheduled to *Pivot* then
8.   for each neighbor processor P_y of *Pivot*, compute $DRT(T_i, P_y)$ and $FT(T_i, P_y)$;
9.   if there is a neighbor processor P_y' such that $FT(T_i, P_y') < FT(T_i, Pivot)$ then
10.   make T_i migrate from *Pivot* to P_y';
11.   else if $FT(T_i, P_y') = FT(T_i, P_y')$ and VIP of T_i is scheduled to P_y' then
12.   make T_i migrate from *Pivot* to P_y';

The time complexity of the BSA algorithm is derived as follows. The procedure *BuildProcessorList* takes $O(m^2)$ time while *Serialization* takes $O(n^2)$ time. Thus, the dominant step is the while-loop, which takes $O(e)$ time to compute the *FT* and *DRT* values of the task on each neighbor processor. If migration is done, it also takes $O(e)$ time. Since there are $O(n)$ tasks on the *Pivot* and $O(m)$ neighbor processor, each iteration of the while loop takes $O(men)$ time. Thus, the BSA algorithm takes $O(m^2en)$ time.

2.4 An Example

To illustrate the novel characteristics of the BSA algorithm, let us consider applying it to schedule the parallel program graph shown in Figure 1 to a four-processor heterogeneous ring system with the actual execution costs depicted in Table 1. For simplicity, we assume that the communication links are homogeneous; that is, $h'_{ijxy} = 1$ for all messages M_{ij} and links L_{xy}. Initially, the tasks are injected by the procedure *Serialization* to the first pivot processor P_2 in the order: $T_1, T_2, T_6, T_7, T_3, T_4, T_8, T_9, T_5$, as we have shown in Section 2.2. Note that the actual execution costs on P_2 are quite different from the nominal execution costs. Then, tasks are considered for possible migration. In the first phase, T_1, being the first CP task, does not migrate because its migration is not beneficial. Also, T_2 and T_6 do not migrate because their finish times cannot be improved by migration. However, T_3 and T_4 migrate to P_1 and P_3, respectively as their finish times are

improved. Note that the reduction of T_3's finish time is contributed not only by the "bubbling up" process but also by the heterogeneity of the processors—the execution cost of T_3 on P_2 is 28 while on P_1 is only 15. Similarly, T_7 also migrates to P_1 since it can also be "bubbled up" and its execution cost is reduced. After two more migrations from the first pivot processor P_2, the first phase is completed; the intermediate schedule at this point is shown in Figure 2(a). In the second phase, the pivot processor is P_1. Only T_3 migrates while the other tasks cannot improve their finish times. No more migration can be performed after this stage and the final schedule is shown in Figure 2(b). The schedule length is only 138 which is considerably smaller than that can be achievable on homogeneous processors.

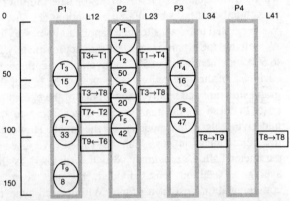

(a) Intermediate schedule after T8 and T9 migrate to neighbor processors (schedule length = 147, total communication costs = 200)

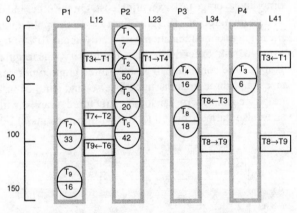

(b) final schedule after T3 migrates from P1 to P4 (schedule length = 138, total communication costs = 200)

Figure 2: Schedules generated by the BSA algorithm.

3 Performance Results

In this section, we present the experimental performance of the BSA algorithm and also compare it with a previous algorithm, called the *dynamic level scheduling* (DLS) algorithm, which was also designed for heterogeneous systems. The DLS algorithm is also a greedy algorithm in that it chooses a task for scheduling if its potential start time is the earliest and it has the largest *b-level*.

In our experiments, we applied the two algorithms to two suites of task graphs using a Sun Ultrasparc workstation. The first suite consisted of regular graphs representing a number of parallel applications including the mean value analysis [1], Gaussian elimination [3], Laplace equation solver [1], LU-decomposition [3], containing regular patterns of tasks and communication messages. Since these applications operate on matrices, the number of tasks (and messages) in their task graphs depends on the matrix dimension N. Each application has its own equation in terms of N for determining the exact number of tasks but all of the equations are $O(N^2)$. We generated ten graphs for each application by varying N such that the graph size varies from approximately 50 to 500 with increments of 50. The average execution cost each task of the applications is about 150. Note that the graph structure and relative magnitudes of the execution costs in these applications are fixed according to the underlying algorithm modeled by the graph. However, the communication costs can be varied. We used a parameter called *granularity*, which is defined as the average execution cost divided by the average communication cost in a graph. Within each type of graph, we used three granularities: 0.1, 1.0, and 10.0. Thus, in a fine-grained (i.e., granularity = 0.1) application, the average communication cost is about ten times the average task execution cost. On the other hand, in a coarse-grained (i.e., granularity = 10.0) application, the average communication cost is only about 10% of the average task execution cost. In summary, the regular graphs suite contained 90 graphs (three graph types, ten sizes, and three granularities). The second suite of task graphs consisted of randomly structured graphs with sizes also varied from 50 to 500 with increments of 50.

The execution cost of each task was randomly selected from a uniform distribution with range [100, 200]. Again, three granularities (0.1, 1.0, and 10.0) were selected for each graph size. Unless otherwise state, the heterogeneity factors (i.e., h_{ix} and h'_{ijxy}) were selected randomly from a uniform distribution with range [1, 50]. Thus, the nominal execution and communication costs in each graph represented the costs of the fastest processor.

To investigate the effect of processor network topology (i.e., processor connectivity), we used four different topologies in the experiments: 16-processor ring, 16-processor hypercube, 16-processor fully-connected network, and 16-processor randomly structured topology. The random topology was generated such that the degree of each processor ranged from two to eight.

In our first experiment, we compared the schedule lengths produced by the BSA algorithm with those by the DLS algorithm. For the regular graphs, it turned out that each algorithm generated similar performance for the three types of applications and thus, we computed the average schedule lengths across different applications. To examine the effect of graph size, we also computed the average schedule lengths across the three granularities. These average schedule lengths for the four topologies are shown in Figure 3. From the plots, we make a number of observations:

- the BSA algorithm consistently outperformed the DLS algorithm;
- the improvement was about 20% and increased slightly with graph size;
- the improvement was slightly larger for lower processor connectivity (e.g., a ring); and
- both algorithms gave shorter schedule lengths for higher processor connectivity (e.g., a clique).

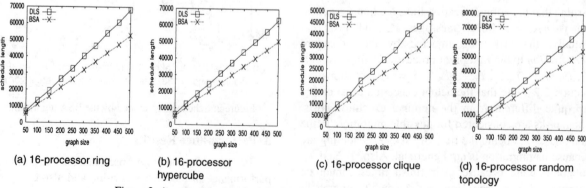

(a) 16-processor ring (b) 16-processor hypercube (c) 16-processor clique (d) 16-processor random topology

Figure 3: Average schedule lengths for the regular graphs with different graph sizes using four different network topologies.

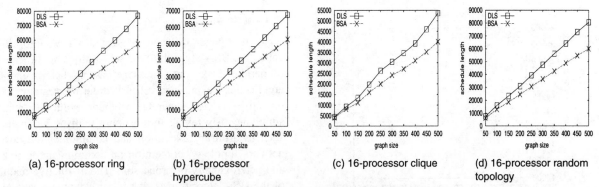

(a) 16-processor ring   (b) 16-processor hypercube   (c) 16-processor clique   (d) 16-processor random topology

Figure 4: Average schedule lengths for the random graphs with different graph sizes using four different network topologies.

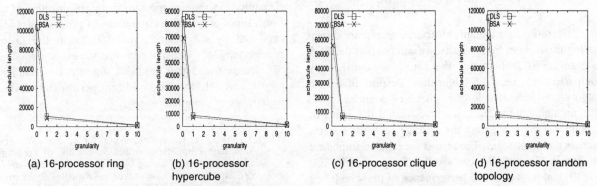

(a) 16-processor ring   (b) 16-processor hypercube   (c) 16-processor clique   (d) 16-processor random topology

Figure 5: Average schedule lengths for the regular graphs with different granularities using four different network topologies.

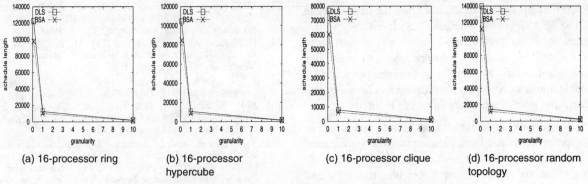

(a) 16-processor ring   (b) 16-processor hypercube   (c) 16-processor clique   (d) 16-processor random topology

Figure 6: Average schedule lengths for the random graphs with different granularities using four different network topologies.

These observations can be explained as follows. First, notice that the DLS algorithm selects a task for scheduling if its start time is the earliest. This greedy decision is made without regard to the scheduling of subsequent tasks and hence, such a decision may be too "local" in that the communication links are not properly utilized leading to inefficient scheduling of communication messages of subsequent tasks. Indeed, when we looked into the schedules produced by the DLS algorithm more closely, we found that there were many cases in which a task could not be scheduled to a better

time slot due to the inefficient scheduling of messages of previous tasks. The adverse effect of inefficient scheduling of messages and tasks was also more profound for increasing graph size and decreasing processor connectivity. In this aspect, the BSA algorithm has a better design because the messages are incrementally scheduled to suitable slots such that the finish times of tasks can be improved. When the connectivity was high, both algorithms generated shorter schedules because the message scheduling was easier to handle.

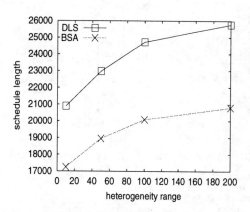

Figure 7: Effect of heterogeneity.

The results for randomly structured graphs are shown in Figure 4. From these results, we can see that the BSA algorithm is robust in that it also consistently outperformed the DLS algorithm, despite that both algorithms generated longer schedules compared with the regular graphs. Next, we investigated the effect of granularity by computing the average schedule lengths across the graph sizes. The results for regular graphs are shown in Figure 5. We can see that the granularity had significant impact on the performance of the scheduling algorithms. First, the schedule lengths increased sharply with decreasing granularity. At a low granularity (e.g., 0.1), the message scheduling was a dominant factor in determining the schedule length. Thus, the improvement of the BSA algorithm over the DLS algorithm was also larger for lower granularity. Finally, it is interesting to note that the effect of network topology was less significant from a granularity perspective. Similar conclusions can be drawn from the results for randomly structured graphs, which are shown in Figure 6.

We also investigated the effect of heterogeneity. For this purpose, we used ten different randomly structured task graphs with 500-task each (the granularity was 1.0). We chose the 16-processor hypercube topology and varied the range of heterogeneity as follows: [1, 10], [1, 50], [1, 100], and [1, 200]. Thus, a large range implies that there are more slow processors in the system. Again we computed the average schedule lengths, which are shown in Figure 7. As can be seen, both algorithms generated longer schedules as the heterogeneity range increased. However, the rate of increase in schedule lengths generated by the BSA algorithm was lower than that of the DLS algorithm. This indicates that the BSA algorithm is more adaptive to a highly heterogeneous system. We also measured the running times of both algorithms, which were about the same because the two algorithms are of comparable time complexity.

4 Conclusions

In this paper we have presented a new algorithm, called the BSA algorithm, for scheduling and allocation of parallel tasks onto message-passing heterogeneous architectures using a novel task ordering strategy. The objective is to generate efficient solutions while simultaneously taking into account realistic parameters such as arbitrary execution and communication costs, network topology, contention on communication links, and heterogeneity of processors. The distinctive feature of the BSA algorithm is that it can adapt its tasks and messages scheduling decisions according to the given network topology. Messages are incrementally scheduled to suitable links during the optimization of the finish times of tasks. Heterogeneity of processors is also exploited by scheduling critical tasks to the fastest processors. Our extensive performance evaluation study has demonstrated that the BSA algorithm is efficient, robust, and able to give consistent performance over a wide range of parameters.

References

[1] I. Ahmad, Y.-K. Kwok, M.-Y. Wu, and W. Shu, "Automatic Parallelization and Scheduling of Programs on Multiprocessors Using CASCH," *Proceedings of the 1997 International Conference on Parallel Processing*, pp. 288-291, Aug. 1997.

[2] M. Cosnard and M. Loi, "Automatic Task Graphs Generation Techniques," *Parallel Processing Letters*, vol. 5, no. 4, pp. 527-538, Dec. 1995.

[3] M. Cosnard, M. Marrakchi, Y. Robert, and D. Trystam, "Parallel Gaussian Elimination on An MIMD Computer," *Parallel Computing*, vol. 6, pp. 275-296, 1988.

[4] H. El-Rewini, T.G. Lewis, and H.H. Ali, *Task Scheduling in Parallel and Distributed Systems*, Englewood Cliffs, New Jersey: Prentice Hall, 1994.

[5] R.F. Freund and H.J. Siegel, "Heterogeneous Processing," *Computer*, pp. 13-17, June 1993.

[6] M.R. Garey and D.S. Johnson, *Computers and Intractability: A Guide to the Theory of NP-Completeness*, W.H. Freeman and Company, 1979.

[7] Y.-K. Kwok and I. Ahmad, "Dynamic Critical Path Scheduling: An Effective Technique for Allocating Tasks Graphs to Multiprocessors," *IEEE Transactions on Parallel and Distributed Systems*, vol. 7, no. 5, pp. 506-521, May 1996.

[8] —, "Benchmarking the Task Graph Scheduling Algorithms," *Proceedings of the 12th International Parallel Processing Symposium*, pp. 531-537, Mar. 1998.

[9] —, "Static Scheduling Algorithms for Allocating Directed Task Graphs to Multiprocessors," *ACM Computing Surveys*, accepted for publication and to appear.

[10] M.A. Palis, J.-C. Lien, and D.S.L. Wei, "Task Clustering and Scheduling for Distributed Memory Parallel Architectures," *IEEE Transactions on Parallel and Distributed Systems*, vol. 7, no. 1, pp. 46-55, Jan. 1996.

[11] G.C. Sih and E.A. Lee, "A Compile-Time Scheduling Heuristic for Interconnection-Constrained Heterogeneous Processor Architectures," *IEEE Transactions on Parallel and Distributed Systems*, vol. 4, no. 2, pp. 75-87, Feb. 1993.

Author Index

IEEE
COMPUTER
SOCIETY

IEEE Computer Society Publications

The world-renowned IEEE Computer Society publishes, promotes, and distributes a wide variety of authoritative computer science and engineering texts. These books are available from most retail outlets. Visit the Online Catalog, *http://computer.org*, for a list of products.

IEEE Computer Society Proceedings

The IEEE Computer Society also produces and actively promotes the proceedings of more than 141 acclaimed international conferences each year in multimedia formats that include hard and softcover books, CD-ROMs, videos, and on-line publications.

For information on the IEEE Computer Society proceedings, send e-mail to cs.books@computer.org or write to Proceedings, IEEE Computer Society, P.O. Box 3014, 10662 Los Vaqueros Circle, Los Alamitos, CA 90720-1314. Telephone +1 714-821-8380. FAX +1 714-761-1784.

Additional information regarding the Computer Society, conferences and proceedings, CD-ROMs, videos, and books can also be accessed from our web site at *http://computer.org/cspress*

1/29/99